Microsoft 365 Excel
The Only App That Matters

Excel Worksheet, Power Query, Power Pivot, Power BI
Calculations, Analytics, Modeling, Data Analysis, and Dashboard Reporting for the New Era of Dynamic Data-Driven Decision Making and Insight!

The Definitive Guide to Building Excel Solutions with the Excel Worksheet, Power Query, Power Pivot, and Power BI Desktop Using Worksheet Formulas, DAX Formulas, M Code Formulas, and Standard PivotTables

by
Mike "excelisfun" Girvin

Holy Macro! Books
PO Box 541731
Merritt Island, FL 32953

T0076523

Microsoft 365 Excel: The Only App That Matters

Authors: Mike Girvin

Layout: Bronkella Publishing

Copyediting: Kitty Wilson

Cover Design: Shannon Travise

Indexing: Cheryl Lenser

Published by: Holy Macro! Books, PO Box 541731, Merritt Island FL 32953, USA

Distributed by: Independent Publishers Group, Chicago, IL

First Printing: July 2022

ISBN: 978-1-61547-070-9 Print, 978-1-61547-156-0 e-Book

Library of Congress Control Number: 2022934005

Dedications

Dedicated to:

My family: Hien Luong "Mama" Girvin, Isaac "Iceman" Girvin, and Dennis "Big D" Ho

My lifelong Oakland friends Dean Washington and Kenny Noline for always inspiring me to be rad

My cool bosses at Highline College, Emily Lardner, Raegan Copeland, and Shawna Freeman, and my awesome Highline Excel teammate, Mary Kiando

About the Author

Mike Girvin has been a Microsoft Excel MVP since 2013, a Highline College business instructor since 2002, and the creator and mastermind of the excelisfun YouTube channel since 2008. The excelisfun channel has been the internet leader in bringing free Excel education to the world since 2008, with more than 3,500 Excel videos and 100 playlists of Excel video topics, including 10 free Excel YouTube courses covering topics such as Excel basics, advanced Excel, data analysis, analytics, statistics, math, and much more. Mike has also authored a number of Excel books and DVDs and has won numerous awards for teaching Excel. Before joining academia in 2002, Mike (nicknamed "Gel") ran the boomerang manufacturing company Gel Boomerangs, in Oakland, California, from 1984 to 2002 and won numerous boomerang design and competition awards. It was while Mike was running Gel Boomerangs in the 1990s that Steve Kavanaugh showed him Excel for the first time. From that point forward, the power and fun of Excel was inescapable, and Mike has gone on to be an Excel teacher for the world. Currently, when Mike is not creating Excel solutions, you can find him racing and parking BMX bikes with fellow rad old guys.

Acknowledgements

My number-one Excel guy in the world is Bill "MrExcel" Jelen. He is the first Excel guy to make Excel videos, and he has inspired me and many other Excel people to make and share videos. MrExcel also started the MrExcel Message Board, where I learned many of my advanced Excel skills. In addition, MrExcel has written more than 60 Excel books! I also want to thank the smartest Power Query guy I know, Bill "Power Query Poet" Szysz. He has kindly and graciously helped me to learn Power Query and M code. In addition, without Marco Russo and Alberto Ferrari's DAX books and live classes, I could not have learned DAX. Still further, without the editing superhero skills of Kitty Wilson, I never could have created this book. With so many great edits, it is really Superhero Kitty who wrote this book! Thanks to Cheryl Lenser for creating a rad index and Tricia Bronkella for layout. Finally, I want to thank the more than 750,000 subscribers to my excelisfun YouTube channel because in the comments below every one of the videos that I post, I get to learn new things about making efficient Excel solutions and having fun doing it!

Contents at a Glance

Table of Contents

Introduction

There has never been a book like this in Excel history. This book covers worksheet formulas, standard PivotTables, array formulas, Power Query, M code formulas, Power Pivot, DAX formulas, Power BI Desktop, Power BI Online, worksheet model theory, data analysis theory, rules for visualizing data, dashboarding, financial cash analysis, simple linear regression, and even some history of Excel, data analysis, finance, and math. Microsoft 365 Excel (and the free download Power BI Desktop) really does offer all this and more.

> **Note:** The official name of the app discussed throughout this book is Microsoft 365 Excel, but I often call it Excel 365 for short.

This is a crazy book. It is too much. It is for the hard core who want to know it all: the hows and the whys! But this book is also for anyone who uses Excel to create solutions to make working life easier.

Excel has expanded its capabilities outward to a new level with the addition of:

- Dynamic spilled array formulas that make all worksheet formulas array formulas
- Power BI and Power Pivot DAX formulas that can handle big data and perform magic calculations, iterating over tables within tables at any grain
- Power Query M code formulas that behave more like SQL than Excel formulas and can transform data with such ease that no other tool inside or outside Excel and Power BI can compete
- Power BI Desktop and its interactive and sharable visualizations (Yes, I consider this free download part of Excel.)

Microsoft 365 Excel is amazing and powerful. It can make calculations and data analysis much easier than any other version of Excel in history.

The first 16 chapters of this book (about 400 pages) are all about using worksheet formulas to build worksheet models. Chapter 17 (about 100 pages) is all about standard PivotTables, Excel charts, visualizing data, dashboarding, and other data analysis features. Chapter 18 (about 150 pages) includes a full description of data analysis theory and terminology, as well as an introduction to data modeling, reporting, and dashboarding with three main tools: worksheets and standard PivotTables, PowerPivot with Power Query and DAX formulas, and Power BI Desktop and Power BI Online with Power Query and DAX formulas. Chapter 19 (about 200 pages) covers big data, complex data modeling projects, and advanced DAX and M code formulas. Chapter 20 takes a brief look at recorded macros. Chapter 21 covers financial cash flow worksheet functions and the basics of financial model building. Chapter 22 looks at building simple linear regression models.

This book includes some detail that exists in no other book. For example:

- Chapter 12 includes 25 examples of the different types of worksheet formulas you can create. This chapter also lists all the types of formula input that are possible.
- Chapter 13 includes 38 examples of the different type of logical tests and formulas available in Excel. This is particularly important in a book of everything because many of the formulas people build in Excel models do not add or count columns of values; rather, many formulas are based on logical tests that add, count, filter, or do other calculations based on conditions and criteria. Chapter 13 even includes a big table that shows every possible D function and its IFS aggregate function (SUMIFS, COUNTIFS, etc.) equivalent.
- Chapter 14 includes examples of 27 different types of lookup formulas.
- Chapter 15 includes 45 examples of different array formulas. It also includes long lists of the different structures and syntactical elements that can be used in array formulas.
- Chapter 17 describes many of the standard PivotTable scenarios that people use and includes a section on the fundamentals of visualizing data.
- Chapter 18 describes the fundamentals of data analysis and business intelligence and provides comprehensive information on Power Query, Power Pivot, Power BI Desktop, Power BI Online, DAX formulas, and M code formulas. This chapter also includes a table that compares worksheet formulas, standard PivotTables, DAX, and M code.

- Chapter 19 teaches you how to work with big data and complex data analysis projects. This chapter covers advanced topics related to building DAX formulas and M code formulas.
- Chapter 21 teaches you all fundamentals of financial cash flow analysis.

At the end of each chapter, you will find practice problems that you can work through to test what you have learned in each chapter. These problems help make this book a perfect textbook for Excel, analytics, and data analysis classes.

You can read this book straight through or use it as a reference. However, I recommend that you start by reading the whole thing, so you get the story I tell from beginning Excel to the upper levels of Excel. Doing so will help you get the most from the book. Then you can use the book as a reference. You are likely to come back to some of the chapters—like Chapter 14 for lookup formulas, Chapter 15 for array formulas, and Chapter 18 for a comprehensive intro to all the power tools—again and again.

Excel 365 is an app that provides more than ever before in Excel history. You can use this single app to make calculations, build models, and perform data analysis. Never has so much been possible with just one app. This is why I say Excel 365 is the only app that matters!

> **Note:** The title of this book was inspired by the 1977 promotional posters hung on telephone poles as part of the world tour of the punk rock band The Clash. The posters read "Come and see The Only Band That Matters!" along with the show date, time, and location. I saw The Clash that year at the Berkeley Community Center in Berkeley, California. You are going to have a rocking good time with this cutting-edge book, learning how to harness the power of the only app that matters to create effective and efficient solutions!

Who This Book Is For

This book is for almost everyone. If you are interested in reading a story that intertwines worksheet formulas, DAX formulas, M code formulas, standard PivotTables, Power BI, Power Pivot, worksheet modeling, data modeling, dashboarding, and data analysis all into one tale of Excel awesomeness, this book is for you. If you want to be the best in Excel, this book is for you. If you are a business student, this book is a 100% *must* book for you as it will help you become a hired, promoted, and respected Excel model builder in the working world. If you want a reference book with a lot of useful Excel stuff, this book is for you. If you are a teacher who wants to teach the true power of Excel to make calculations, build models, and perform data analysis, this book is perfect for you! And of course, if you are an Excel person who just wants to have fun with worksheet and data analysis models, this is the book for you!

PC Versus Mac Excel

The differences between Mac Excel and Windows PC–based Excel go way back. I fell in love with Excel in the 1990s, using a Mac computer. Even back then, there were fundamental differences. For example, the average function on a Mac was named AVE, and the average function on a Windows computer was AVERAGE. When I got my first accounting job, I was told to switch to a Windows-based computer. That was smart advice. Even in the 1990s, job security meant learning Excel on a Windows PC–based computer. Three decades later, the gap between PC and Mac has widened: Important tools like Power Pivot, Power BI, and the full version of Power Query are not available on the Mac. As a result, this book teaches you to use Microsoft Excel 365 on a Windows PC.

Following Along with Excel Files

Before you read any further, you should download the Excel and data analysis files used throughout this book. That way, you can follow along as you read. Go to https://excelisfun.net/files/TheOnlyAppMatterBook.zip to download the zipped folder, which also contains some practice problems with solutions for selected chapters so that you can practice what you learn in the book and become an Excel master.

After you download the file and unzip it, you should see the structure shown in Figure I.1. Throughout the book, you will open and save files to this system of folders.

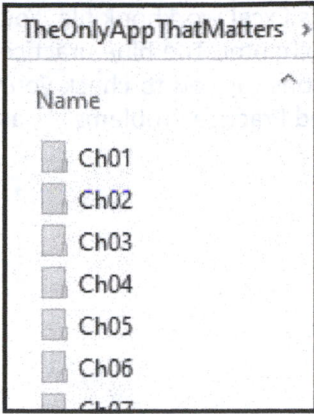

Figure I.1 *This system of folders contains all the files for the book.*

I've color-coded the Excel files so you can easily tell what's what:

- **Blue:** The blue worksheets are for you to work on as you follow along with the examples in the book and the practice problems.

- **Red:** The red worksheets contain finished examples that you can use to check your work when you are finished with the blue worksheets. Figure I.2 shows an example. Notice that the name of each red sheet contains the text *an*, which stands for *answer*.

- **Yellow:** The yellow worksheets (not pictured) are informational only.

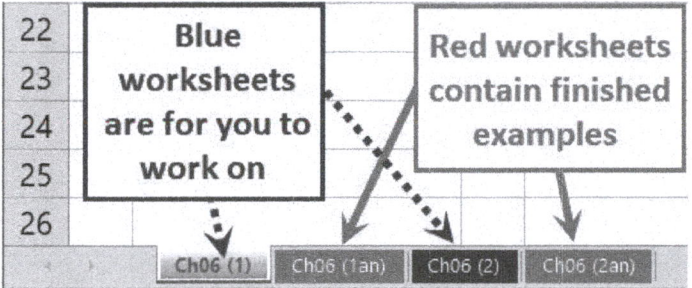

Figure I.2 *Blue worksheets allow you to follow along and practice, and red ones provide solutions for you to check your work.*

For Chapters 18, 19, and 20, the Excel files contain so many elements that I've provided extra files. A file with the word "Start" in it is the one you should use to follow along and practice, and the file with the word "Finished" in it is the one that provides the solutions.

I've also used color-coding within worksheets (see in Figure I.3):

- Column headers have a dark blue fill.
- Cells containing raw data, like text and numbers, have no fill color.
- Cells containing formulas have a green fill.
- Formula input labels have a red fill.

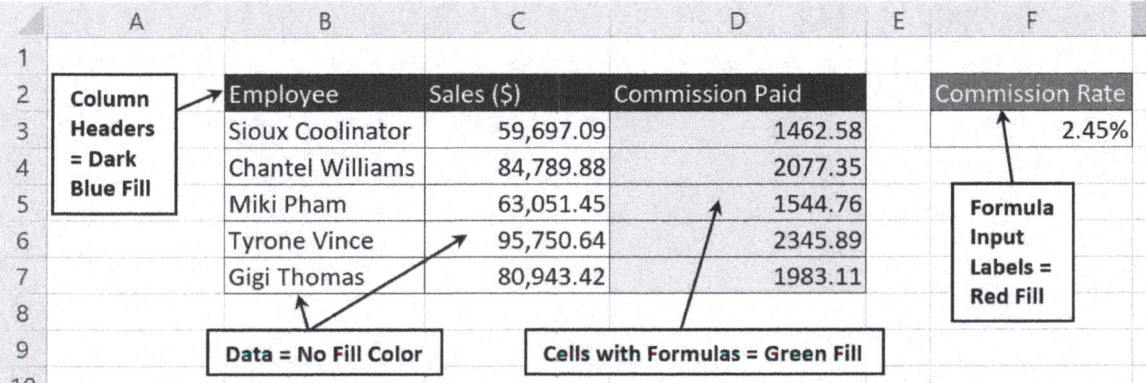

Figure I.3 *Color formatting for column headers, raw data, formulas, and formula input labels.*

Starting in Chapter 8, you will find extra worksheets at the end of each chapter's Excel workbook file. You can use these worksheets as homework, to practice what you've learned in the chapter. The blue practice worksheets are for you to work with, and the red answer sheets contain solutions for you to check your work. The blue and red practice sheets are always listed after a blank sheet named Practice Problems >>, as shown in Figure I.4.

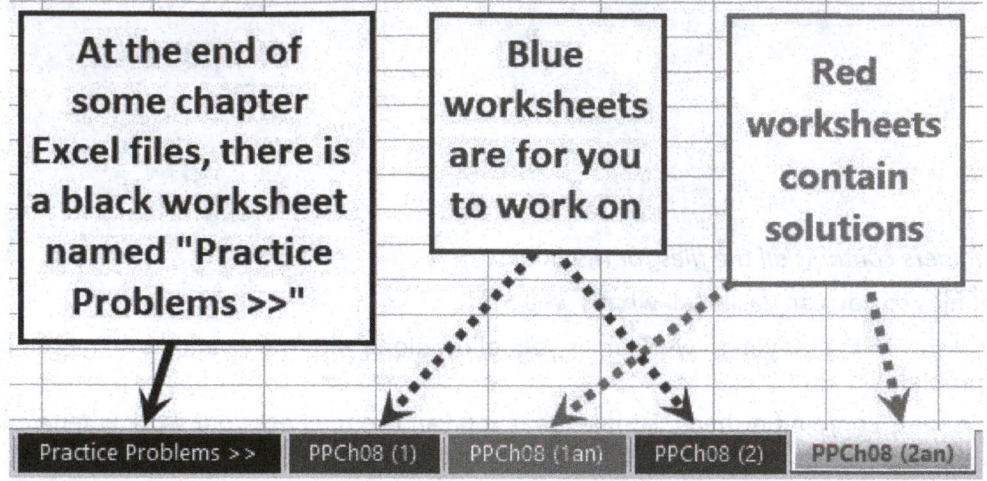

Figure I.4 *Some chapters include extra practice problems as well as solutions.*

Chapter 1: Why Excel 365?

This chapter compares Excel 365 to older versions and showcases the major improvements that Excel 365 offers over past versions. In doing so, it provides an overview of the benefits of Excel 365. The details of the features and techniques introduced in this chapter are covered later in the book. If you are just learning Excel, you might want to skip this chapter for now or read it with the understanding that it describes many tools and features without first teaching you the fundamentals of Excel. (You will learn those fundamentals in subsequent chapters.)

> **Note:** To follow along with the examples in this chapter, you can use the file named Ch01-Excel365-WhyExcel365.xlsx. If you haven't yet downloaded the files that accompany this book, see the Introduction for details on how to do so.

Excel 365 is a huge improvement over earlier versions for many reasons, including these:

- The worksheet formula calculation engine makes creating formulas easier than ever before.
- Array formulas no longer require the special keystroke Ctrl+Shift+Enter.
- New array functions like FILTER and UNIQUE make complicated formula tasks simple.
- New functions like XLOOKUP and LET are available.
- Power Query allows you to import and transform data with different structures, from different sources, and from small and large datasets alike. The M code formula language is built specifically as a data transformational formula language.
- You can use the Power Pivot or Power BI Data Model and DAX formulas to store and make efficient calculations on big data.
- You can use Power BI Desktop to create interactive and shareable reports, visualizations, and dashboards.

The following sections discuss these improvements in detail.

The Worksheet Formula Calculation Engine

In Excel 365, the worksheet formula calculation engine that works behind the scenes to calculate the answers for worksheet formulas has fundamentally changed. The engine now enables you to more quickly and easily create formulas. In all versions of Excel before Excel 365, when you create a formula, you enter it into a cell and then copy the formula to other cells. Figure 1.1 shows an example of that type of "old-school" formula. The formula in this case calculates the commission paid to each employee. This formula uses a relative cell reference and an absolute cell reference inside the ROUND function. Figure 1.2 shows the result you get after copying the formula down the column. With this older method, which involves using single cell references (in this case, C3 and $F$3), different types of cell references (relative and absolute) have to be considered, and the formula must be manually copied down the column.

A	B	C	D	E	F
1					
2	Employee	Sales ($)	Commission Paid		Commission Rate
3	Sioux Coolinator	59,697.09	=ROUND(C3*$F$3,2)		2.45%
4	Chantel Williams	84,789.88			
5	Miki Pham	63,051.45			
6	Tyrone Vince	95,750.64			
7	Gigi Thomas	80,943.42			

Figure 1.1 *Old-school Excel worksheet formulas require relative and absolute cell references.*

A	B	C	D	E	F
1					
2	Employee	Sales ($)	Commission Paid		Commission Rate
3	Sioux Coolinator	59,697.09	1462.58		2.45%
4	Chantel Williams	84,789.88	2077.35		
5	Miki Pham	63,051.45	1544.76		
6	Tyrone Vince	95,750.64	2345.89		
7	Gigi Thomas	80,943.42	=ROUND(C7*$F$3,2)		

Figure 1.2 *Old-school Excel worksheet formulas require a manual copy action.*

Figure 1.3 shows a "new-school" Excel 365 formula that uses the whole column of sales values (C3:C7) and the cell reference F3 inside the ROUND function. When the formula is entered, as shown in Figure 1.4, the formula automatically spills down the column and delivers all the correct commission amounts. Because the range C3:C7 is used in the formula, the formula is forced to deliver an array of answers, one for each cell in the range C3:C7. This type of formula is called a *spilled array formula* because the answers automatically spill down the column. Using this new method takes significantly less effort than using the old-school approach.

	A	B	C	D	E	F
1						
2		Employee	Sales ($)	Commission Paid		Commission Rate
3		Sioux Coolinator	59,697.09	=ROUND(C3:C7*F3,2)		2.45%
4		Chantel Williams	84,789.88			
5		Miki Pham	63,051.45			
6		Tyrone Vince	95,750.64			
7		Gigi Thomas	80,943.42			

Figure 1.3 Excel 365 worksheet formulas often do not require that you use relative and absolute cell references.

	A	B	C	D	E	F
1						
2		Employee	Sales ($)	Commission Paid		Commission Rate
3		Sioux Coolinator	59,697.09	1462.58		2.45%
4		Chantel Williams	84,789.88	2077.35		
5		Miki Pham	63,051.45	1544.76		
6		Tyrone Vince	95,750.64	2345.89		
7		Gigi Thomas	80,943.42	1983.11		

Figure 1.4 Excel 365 worksheet formulas can automatically spill down a column, without any manual copying.

With Excel 365, you do not have to decide about using relative or absolute cell references, and you do not have to copy a formula down a column. The calculation task requires significantly fewer steps and less effort. However, because people have been making Excel formula solutions in the old-school way for 40 years, Excel users have to make the conceptual jump and remember to select all the cells that are needed in a formula rather than select one cell at a time. Throughout this book you will see many spectacular examples of the efficiency of spilled array formulas.

Array Formulas

In versions of Excel prior to Excel 365, when you want to create an array formula, you have to enter the formula with a special keystroke to signal to Excel that the formula is an array formula. With Microsoft 365 Excel, you no longer have to do this. As shown in Figure 1.5, in older versions of Excel, if you want to use the TRANSPOSE array function, you have to highlight the correct number of cells, create the formula, and then use the keystrokes Ctrl+Shift+Enter to get the formula to calculate correctly. With Excel 365, all you have to do is create the formula in the top cell, and the results automatically spill to the cells below; you don't need to use any special keystrokes.

	A	B	C	D	E	F
1						
2		Names:	Sioux	Gigi	Chantel	
3						
4		Names:		Names:		Formula with Excel 365, in cell: D5:
5		Sioux		Sioux		=TRANSPOSE(C2:E2)
6		Gigi		Gigi		
7		Chantel		Chantel		
8						
9		Formula before Excel 365, in range B5:B7:				
10		{=TRANSPOSE(C2:E2)}				

Figure 1.5 *Array formulas can be entered without Ctrl+Shift+Enter.*

New Array Functions: UNIQUE and FILTER

Excel 365 has numerous new built-in array functions that deliver arrays of results (that is, multiple answers) and replace complicated formulas that are otherwise used to solve certain tasks. New Excel 365 array functions, like FILTER and UNIQUE, will amaze long-time Excel users with their elegant simplicity. For newer Excel users, these functions make it easy to quickly solve tasks that once required advanced knowledge. The new array functions make it possible, for example, to create a unique list (the UNIQUE function) and look up an item to retrieve multiple records (the FILTER function).

The UNIQUE Function

Figure 1.6 shows a complex formula that is required in older versions of Excel to create a unique list of values. Figure 1.7 shows how to use the UNIQUE function to extract a unique list of values from a column in a *much* simpler way. In my second book, *Ctrl+Shift+Enter: Mastering Excel Array Formulas*, published in 2012, I had to spend chapters building up and describing the logic of a formula like the one in Figure 1.6. In Excel 365, such formulas are not necessary!

	A	B	C	D	E	F	G	H	I	J	K
1											
2		**Product**		**Unique List**							
3		Carlota		=IF(ROWS(D$3:D3)>SUM(IF(FREQUENCY(IF($B$3:					Result		**Unique List**
4		Carlota		$B$9<>"",MATCH($B$3:$B$9,$B$3:$B$9,0)),ROW(							Carlota
5		Quad		$B$3:$B$9)-ROW($B$2)),1)),"",INDEX($B$3:$B$9,					> > >		Quad
6		Carlota		SMALL(IF(FREQUENCY(IF($B$3:$B$9<>"",MATCH($B$3:							Yanaki
7		Yanaki		$B$9,$B$3:$B$9,0)),ROW($B$3:$B$9)-ROW($B$2)),							
8		Carlota		ROW($B$3:$B$9)-ROW($B$2)),ROWS(D$3:D3))))							
9		Quad									

Figure 1.6 *In earlier versions of Excel, formulas for extracting unique lists of values are very difficult.*

	A	B	C	D	E	F	G	H
1								
2		**Product**		**Unique List**				**Unique List**
3		Carlota		=UNIQUE(B3:B9)		Result		Carlota
4		Carlota		Quad				Quad
5		Quad		Yanaki		> > >		Yanaki
6		Carlota						
7		Yanaki						
8		Carlota						
9		Quad						

Figure 1.7 *The Excel 365 UNIQUE function easily extracts a unique list of values.*

The FILTER Function

The FILTER function is another new Excel 365 function that greatly simplifies formula calculations, models, and analysis. This new Excel 365 function allows you to easily look up an item and returns multiple records, spilled down the column. Figure 1.8 shows the formula required to look up all the records for the Quad product in versions of Excel prior to Excel 365. This type of complex formula to look up a single item and return multiple records has been very common throughout Excel history. But as you can see in Figure 1.9, it will be banished to the history books by the FILTER function.

	A	B	C	D	E	F	G	H	I	J
1										
2		Product	Sales Rep	Sales ($)		Lookup:	Quad			
3		Carlota	Sioux	93.55						
4		Carlota	Chantel	220.00		Product	Sales ($)			
5		Quad	Miki	146.47		=IF(ROWS(F$5:F5)>COUNTIFS($B$3:$B$9,$G$2),"",				
6		Carlota	Tyrone	94.02		INDEX(C$3:C$9,SMALL(IF($B$3:$B$9=$G$2,ROW(C$3:				
7		Yanaki	Gigi	57.88		C$9)-ROW(C$2)),ROWS(F$5:F5))))				
8		Carlota	Chantel	132.30		IF(logical_test, [value_if_true], [value_if_false])				
9		Quad	Tyrone	199.44		Result	v v v			
10						Product	Sales ($)			
11						Miki	146.47			
12						Tyrone	199.44			

Figure 1.8 *Looking up the records for Quad in versions of Excel prior to Excel 365 requires a complex formula.*

	A	B	C	D	E	F	G	H	I	J
1										
2		Product	Sales Rep	Sales ($)		Lookup:	Quad			
3		Carlota	Sioux	93.55						
4		Carlota	Chantel	220.00		Product	Sales ($)			
5		Quad	Miki	146.47		=FILTER(C3:D9,B3:B9=G2)				
6		Carlota	Tyrone	94.02		Tyrone	199.44			
7		Yanaki	Gigi	57.88						
8		Carlota	Chantel	132.30		Result	v v v			
9		Quad	Tyrone	199.44		Product	Sales ($)			
10						Miki	146.47			
11						Tyrone	199.44			

Figure 1.9 *Looking up the records for Quad with the Excel 365 FILTER function is a breeze.*

Throughout this book, you will see many more examples of how the new array functions in Excel 365 can dramatically reduce formula complexity and increase your speed at building formula solutions.

The New XLOOKUP and LET Functions

There are many new functions in Excel 365, but two in particular stand out:

- XLOOKUP is a new lookup function that addresses many of the problems with the older lookup function VLOOKUP.
- LET is a new function that allows you to define variables that help formulas calculate more quickly, make complex formulas easier to understand, and condense a multistep formula into a single cell.

The XLOOKUP Function

The VLOOKUP function is one of the most widely used functions in Excel history. Figure 1.10 shows a classic VLOOKUP formula that looks up a product name and returns the price for each product. In this formula, VLOOKUP uses the lookup table in H3:I5 to match the product name in the first column of the lookup table (H3:H5) and return the price from the second column of the lookup table (I3:I5). VLOOKUP knows to return the price because there is a 2 in the function's third argument, which tells VLOOKUP to get the value from the second column in the lookup table.

	A	B	C	D	E F	G	H	I
1								
2		**Units**	**Product**	**Price?**		**Product ID**	**Product**	**Price**
3		60	Quad	$43		Q102	Quad	$43
4		132	Carlota	$26		C210	Carlota	$26
5		72	Quad	$43		S311	Sunshine	$19
6		24	Sunshine	$19				
7		96	Sunshine	$19				
8		60	Carlota	$26				
9		72	Carlota	$26				
10		96	Quad	=VLOOKUP(C10,$H$3:$I$5,2,0)				

Figure 1.10 *A classic VLOOKUP formula can be used to look up the price of a product.*

One of the problems with this classic VLOOKUP formula is that if you insert a new column into the lookup table—such as the new column for cost in Figure 1.11—the formula no longer returns the correct price. Because this VLOOKUP formula uses the number 2 to indicate that the second column in the lookup table contains the price, now the formula mistakenly returns cost rather than price. In the first row for the Quad product, rather than returning the correct price, $43, the formula returns the incorrect price $22.

	A	B	C	D	E F	G	H	I	J
1			**Incorrect**						
2		**Units**	**Product**	**Price?**		**Product ID**	**Product**	**Cost**	**Price**
3		60	Quad	$22		Q102	Quad	$22	$43
4		132	Carlota	$14		C210	Carlota	$14	$26
5		72	Quad	$22		S311	Sunshine	$9	$19
6		24	Sunshine	$9					
7		96	Sunshine	$9					
8		60	Carlota	$14					
9		72	Carlota	$14			**Cost is now**		
10		96	Quad	=VLOOKUP(C10,$H$3:$J$5,2,0)			**2nd column**		

Figure 1.11 *If you add a new Cost column, the VLOOKUP formula does not work correctly to retrieve the price for the product.*

There is a workaround to this VLOOKUP problem in older versions of Excel, but it is not as easy as the solution provided by the new Excel 365 function XLOOKUP. As shown in Figure 1.12, XLOOKUP solves the problem of having to specify the column number of the items you want to return by using separate ranges for the products to match (with the second argument, *lookup_array*) and the values to retrieve (with the third argument, *return_array*). With two separate ranges in XLOOKUP, it doesn't matter if you add new columns to the lookup table; the formula will always work.

	A	B	C	D	E F	G	H	I	J
1									
2		**Units**	**Product**	**Price?**					
3		60	Quad	=XLOOKUP(C3:C10,H6:H8,J6:J8)					
4		132	Carlota	$26					
5		72	Quad	$43		**Product ID**	**Product**	**Cost**	**Price**
6		24	Sunshine	$19		Q102	Quad	$22	$43
7		96	Sunshine	$19		C210	Carlota	$14	$26
8		60	Carlota	$26		S311	Sunshine	$9	$19
9		72	Carlota	$26					
10		96	Quad	$43					

Figure 1.12 *When new columns are added to the lookup table, XLOOKUP instantly updates to show the correct answer.*

Another notorious problem plagues the VLOOKUP function: You have to give it a lookup table, and you can only match items from the first column of the lookup table. This means that if you ever have to look up an item to the left of the first column, VLOOKUP cannot do it without a crazy formula workaround. This problem, commonly referred to as the VLOOKUP "lookup left" curse, can easily be solved by using the XLOOKUP function. Because XLOOKUP uses a separate range for matched values (*lookup_array*) and values to retrieve (*return_array*), as shown in Figure 1.13, XLOOKUP can find a match in the Product column (on the right) and retrieve a value from the Product ID column (on the left).

	A	B	C	D	E	F	G	H	I	J
1										
2		Units	Product	Product ID						
3		60	Quad	=XLOOKUP(C3:C10,H6:H8,G6:G8)						
4		132	Carlota	C210						
5		72	Quad	Q102			Product ID	Product	Cost	Price
6		24	Sunshine	S311			Q102	Quad	$22	$43
7		96	Sunshine	S311			C210	Carlota	$14	$26
8		60	Carlota	C210			S311	Sunshine	$9	$19
9		72	Carlota	C210						
10		96	Quad	Q102						

Figure 1.13 *"Lookup left" is simple for the new XLOOKUP function.*

There are other lookup situations that VLOOKUP cannot perform but that XLOOKUP can. For example, XLOOKUP can look up cell references, sort a lookup table in descending order (which is helpful when performing lookups for taxes or grades), and look up the last item when there are duplicates. You will see examples of the use of XLOOKUP in Chapter 14.

The LET Function

A second noteworthy new Excel 365 function is the LET function, which allows you to define a variable inside a formula. LET exists only in Excel 365 and Excel 2021, and there is no comparable worksheet option in any other version of Excel. Although it is not common to use LET when creating basic Excel solutions, when advanced solutions with complex formulas are required, the LET function comes to the rescue by allowing variables to be defined in a formula. There are several benefits to defining variables:

- Formulas with repeating elements calculate more quickly.
- Complex formulas are easier to read.
- Formulas that span multiple columns can be condensed into a single cell.

Figure 1.14 shows an example of a LET formula that defines three variables and then delivers a sorted frequency distribution. This example shows how the LET function replaces a very complex set of formulas that span multiple columns and condenses them into a single cell. This frequency distribution report has three benefits: It requires you to manage only one cell, it replaces complex formulas, and it instantly updates and sorts correctly when the source data changes.

	A	B	C	D	E
1					
2		Survey Results:		Frequency Distribution:	
3					
4		Rank Soft Drink by Category		Rank Soft Drink by Category	Count
5		Superior		=LET(	
6		Superior		u,UNIQUE(B5:B44),	
7		Poor		c,COUNTIFS(B5:B44,u),	
8		Good		r,CHOOSE({1,2},u,c),	
9		Great		SORT(r,2,-1))	
10		Good			
11		Superior		Result	v v v
12		Good			
13		Good		Rank Soft Drink by Category	Count
14		Great		Superior	11
15		Poor		Great	10
16		Great		Good	8
17		Okay		Okay	7
18		Okay		Poor	4

Figure 1.14 *The LET function allows you to define variables inside a formula.*

Power Query and the M Code Formula Language

Many people argue that the PivotTable is the single greatest tool in Excel. And, indeed, it is the number-one tool in the world for creating summary reports and dashboards based on data. But the main problem with PivotTables has always been that the data required to use a PivotTable must be in the form of a proper dataset table. Much of the data that is used in Excel is not in this format, and it can be difficult to simultaneously import data, transform it into the correct format, and then load it to a PivotTable or an Excel worksheet. For decades, importing and converting all the sss data sources into a single table has been mostly a manual process. Sometimes VBA code can be used to automate the process, but that is almost always difficult as well. Power Query changes the game.

Power Query is the greatest Excel invention since the PivotTable. With this single tool, you can use Excel to connect to almost any data source; connect simultaneously to multiple data sources; clean and transform data into the required structure; and load data to a worksheet, directly to a PivotTable, or, if required, to the Data Model. Then, if one or more of the data sources changes, you can simply click the refresh button, and everything updates, including any summary reports or dashboards. For people who have had to deal with data and reporting, there is no other tool quite like Power Query.

> **Note:** Technically, Power Query is a feature in Excel 2016 and 2019. In Excel 365, it has been improved and streamlined to make importing, cleaning, and transforming data for analysis much easier than in earlier versions.

To briefly illustrate the power of Power Query, let's look at an example involving a single Excel file. Figure 1.15 shows an Excel workbook file with daily sales on sheets named T(1), T(2), and T(3). If the goal is to make a single summary PivotTable report based on all the tables, in Excel versions that do not have Power Query, you would have to combine the tables manually or by using VBA code and then create the report.

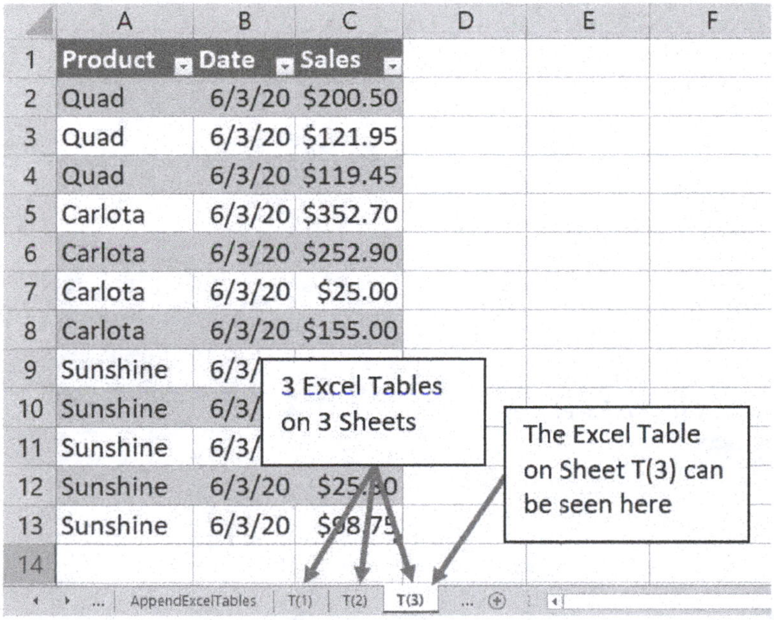

Figure 1.15 *Without Power Query, combining these three tables, which exist on different sheets, would be a manual process.*

By using the Power Query function Excel.CurrentWorkbook(), shown in Figure 1.16, you can combine all the Excel Tables in the current Excel workbook file into a single table that you can use to create a summary PivotTable report (see Figure 1.17).

> **Note:** A *Power Query function* is also known as an *M code function*.

fx = Excel.CurrentWorkbook()

Figure 1.16 *The M code function shown here can grab all the Excel Tables from the current Excel workbook.*

	A	B	C	D	E
1					
2		Summary Report from Tables on Sheets T(1), T(2), T(3)			
3					
4		Product	Sales ($)		
5		Carlota	1,715		
6		Quad	2,655		
7		Sunshine	2,407		
8		Grand Total	6,777		

Figure 1.17 *With Power Query, it is easy to create summary reports from data that exists in multiple locations.*

The Excel.CurrentWorkbook() function is very efficient. If new Excel Tables are created in the Excel file where this function is used, a simple refresh adds the new data to the summary PivotTable. Figures 1.18 shows a new Excel Table that is added to the Excel file, and Figure 1.19 shows the updated report.

	A	B	C
1	Product	Date	Sales
2	Quad	6/4/20	$282.75
3	Sunshine	6/4/20	$263.14
4	Quad	6/4/20	$79.27
5	Carlota	6/4/20	$267.31
6	Carlota	6/4/20	$101.38
7	Carlota	6/4/20	$138.02
8	Carlota	6/4/20	$309.88
9	Sunshine	6/4/	
10	Quad	6/4/	
11	Quad	6/4/	
12	Sunshine	6/4/20	$146.13
13	Carlota	6/4/20	$105.49

4 Excel Tables on 4 Sheets

New T(4) Excel Table added

AppendExcelTables   T(1)   T(2)   T(3)   T(4)

Figure 1.18 *A new Excel Table with data is added to the Excel file.*

Refresh

	A	B	C	D	E
1					
2		Summary Report from Tables on Sheets:			
3				T(1), T(2), T(3), T(4)	
4		Product	Sales ($)		
5		Carlota	2,637		
6		Quad	3,332		
7		Sunshine	2,992		
8		Grand Total	8,961		

Figure 1.19 *Clicking the Refresh button causes the Excel.CurrentWorkbook() function to include the new data in the report.*

This example illustrates the power of Power Query to import from multiple data sources, transform the data into the correct form, and load it into a finished PivotTable report. However, you are not limited to just data coming from an Excel worksheet. You can also use Power Query to get data from a database and bring it into Excel. If you have text files or Excel files or Access files, or if you have data in all three types of files and you need it combined into one table with a summary report or dashboard, you can use Power Query to easily do that. Power Query can also connect to websites, online data sources, Microsoft Azure, Power BI, and many more sources.

As an example of Power Query's vast ability to do feats that seem impossible, Figure 1.20 shows a scenario that you will encounter later in this book that involves getting data from seven different Excel CSV files, a database, and an Excel Table. Figure 1.21 shows the four final tables that Power Query helps you create, and Figure 1.22 shows the final dashboard Power Query creates to display the data. If any of the source data changes, or if a new table of data is required, you simply click the Refresh button in the final dashboard, and everything updates. Isn't this breathtakingly awesome?

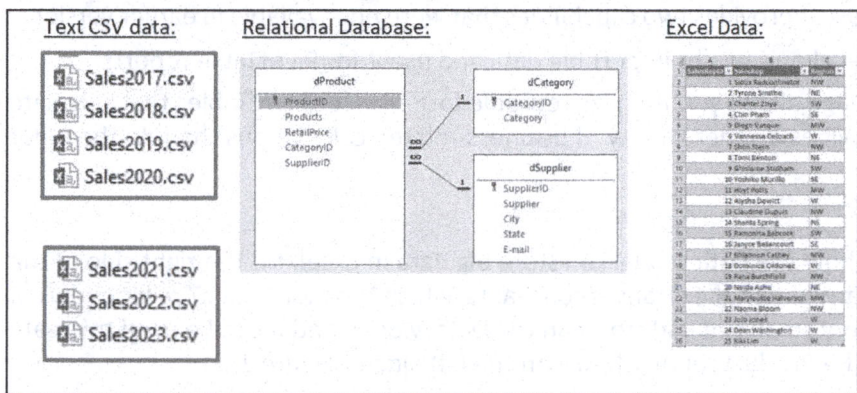

Figure 1.20 *A lot of data is needed for analysis in this case: seven different Excel CSV files, a database, and an Excel Table.*

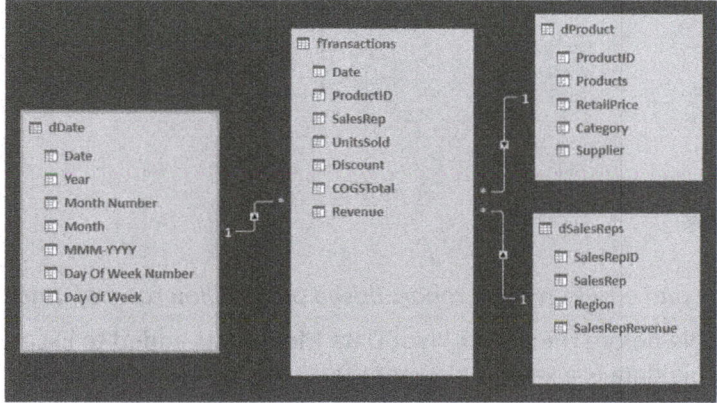

Figure 1.21 *Power Query transforms the data from various sources into the four tables needed for the dashboard.*

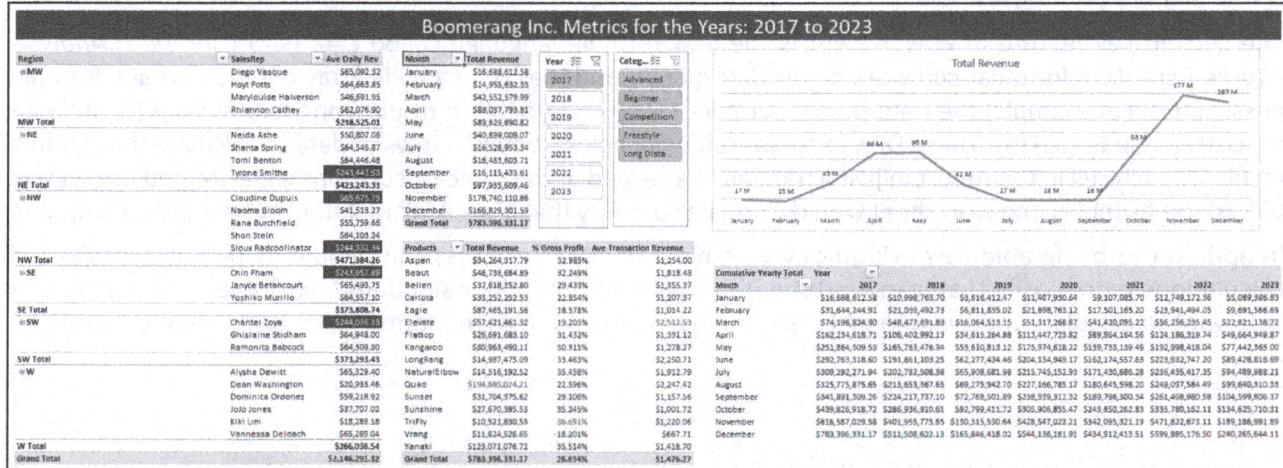

Figure 1.22 *Without Power Query to gather and transform the data, creating dashboards like this is very difficult.*

Excel 365 Power Query gives users exceptional capabilities in terms of importing, transforming, and loading data, and it makes data analysis simple. Throughout this book, you will see many more examples of how Power Query can connect to almost any data source and then clean, transform, and load the data and enable you to update your analysis with a simple click of the Refresh button. You will also see that Power Query can be used to create some efficient and useful worksheet solutions that do not involve importing data from an external source. In addition, you will learn about the Power BI app, which provides functionality very similar to that of Power Query.

Power Pivot, the Data Model, and DAX Formulas

Another amazing improvement in Excel 365 is Power Pivot. Although Power Pivot was available in a few older versions of Excel, Microsoft charged extra money for it. Excel 365 has Power Pivot included by default, for no additional fee.

Power Pivot is a game changer because it provides two capabilities that were not available in earlier versions:

- **Data Model:** The Data Model allows you to import big data and use it for PivotTable reports.
- **DAX:** The DAX formula language allows you to make reusable formulas for PivotTables that calculate quickly on big data. DAX provides a wider variety of business-related calculations than do the older Excel standard PivotTables.

The Data Model

Figure 1.23 provides an example of how the Data Model can store big data in Excel. On the right side of the figure, the Queries & Connections pane shows the fTransactions table, which has more than 7 million rows of data. This data is compressed to a very small size and stored in the Data Model, and it can be used to create Data Model PivotTable reports like the Product report shown on the left side of Figure 1.23.

	A	B	C
1	Product	Net Sales ($)	Cost of Goods Sold ($)
2	Alpine	87,505,275	5,133,646
3	Aspen	104,688,960	6,147,893
4	Bellen	216,208,221	12,741,047
5	Carlota	191,558,396	11,286,062
6	Darnell Tri Fly	34,556,881	2,049,208
7	Fun Fly	279,717,911	16,466,229
8	Sunshine	95,776,408	5,649,720
9	Grand Total	1,010,012,052	59,473,805
10			

Queries & Connections

Queries | Connections

2 queries

AppendExcelTables
44 rows loaded.

fTransactions
7,742,561 rows loaded.

7 million rows loaded to Data Model

Figure 1.23 *With the Data Model, you can quickly and easily create a report based on 7 million rows of data.*

Creating reports based on big data was not possible before the Power Pivot Data Model was added to Excel. In this data-driven age, effortlessly dealing with big data is a key requirement for many projects and makes the Data Model a beneficial new feature in Excel 365.

The DAX Language

The second key feature in Power Pivot is the new formula language called *DAX* (short for *Data Analysis eXpressions*). DAX formulas can work on big data quickly, and they offer a wide array of functions and formula possibilities. For example, the Data Model in Figure 1.23 uses two DAX formulas: one for net sales ($) and one for cost of goods sold ($). These DAX formulas can work across 7 million rows of data to calculate the formula result for each cell in the report in just a fraction of a second. If the same calculations were created using Excel worksheet formulas, the worksheet would calculate so slowly that it would completely freeze up the computer.

In addition to being able to work quickly with big data, DAX formulas can handle many business-related calculations more easily than can worksheet formulas and the older standard PivotTables. For example, if you want to calculate the average daily sales for each product in each month, using DAX formulas would be much easier than using worksheet formulas or a standard PivotTable. Figure 1.24 shows how to make this calculation by using worksheet formulas with an intermediate formula table (columns F, G, H) and the final report (columns J, K, L). It requires a total of six different formulas. In addition, this report does not show any subtotals or a grand total, and if you included subtotals and a grand total, you would have to create three additional formulas.

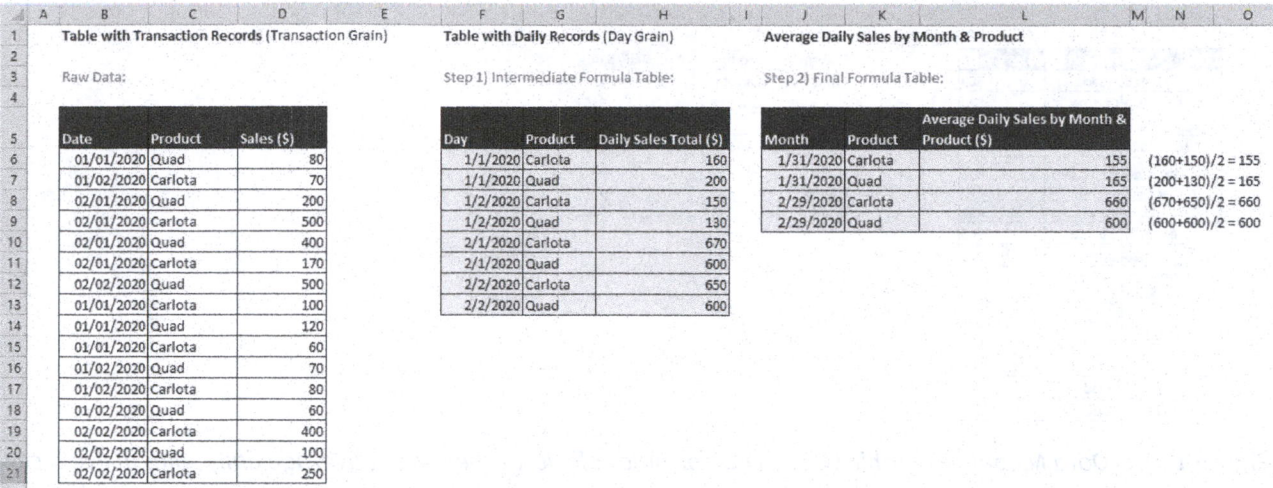

Figure 1.24 *Formulas to calculate the average daily sales for each product in each month are complicated.*

Another limitation to a formula report like this is that the formulas are bound to the conditions—in this case, month and product—and cannot be changed without significantly editing the formulas. Figure 1.25 shows a second attempt at creating a report of average daily sales for each product in each month; this attempt uses a combination of worksheet formulas and a standard PivotTable. In this solution, the subtotals would not calculate the correct amount! So you can see that worksheet formulas require a lot of effort and are bound to the conditions initially placed in the formulas, and a standard PivotTable does not always give the correct results. DAX formulas used in a Data Model PivotTable solve all these problems easily.

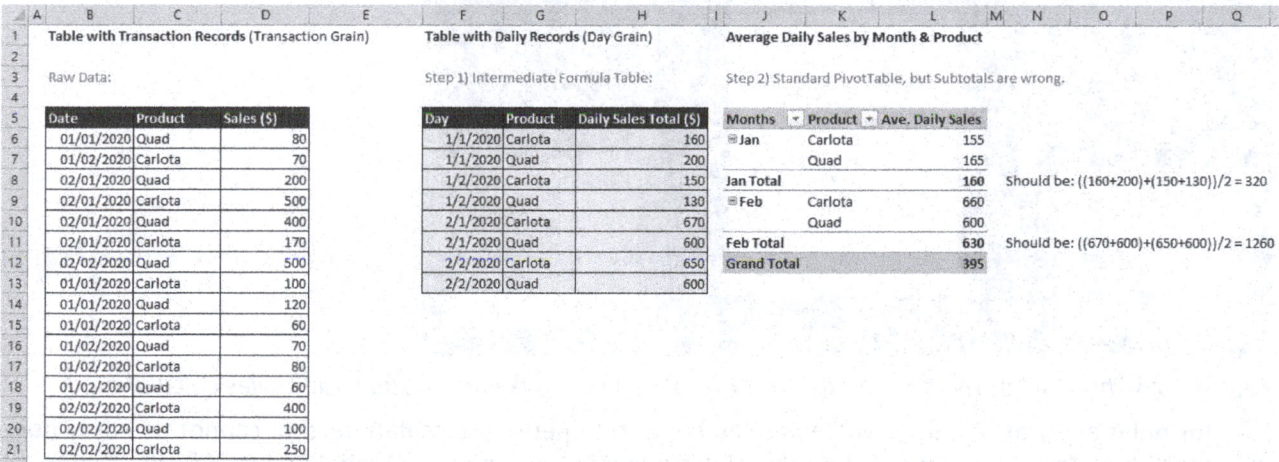

Figure 1.25 *A standard PivotTable requires intermediate formula steps, and subtotals do not calculate correctly.*

Figure 1.26 shows a Data Model PivotTable with a DAX formula that correctly calculates the average daily sales in three different ways: as product by month (in the Rows area), by month (as a subtotal), and as daily averages in the Grand Total cell.

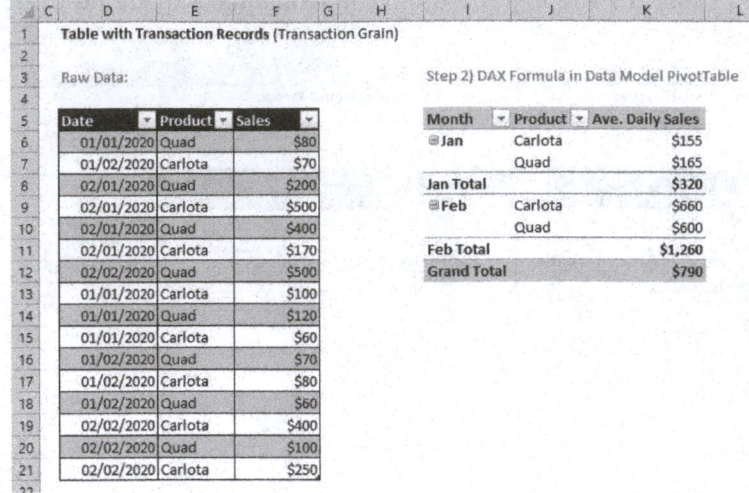

Figure 1.26 *A Data Model PivotTable with a DAX formula calculates the correct average daily sales in every cell.*

Figure 1.27 shows the DAX formula used in the Data Model PivotTable in Figure 1.26. This DAX formula is significantly less complicated to create and is much more versatile than the previous two solutions.

Ave. Daily Sales:=AVERAGEX(VALUES(dDate[Date]),[Total Sales])

Figure 1.27 *This DAX formula (called a DAX measure) is simple compared to worksheet formulas.*

To get the DAX formula to work correctly, however, you need to take the extra step of creating a data model with related tables, like the one shown in Figure 1.28. This extra step is well worth the effort when a big data report is required, though.

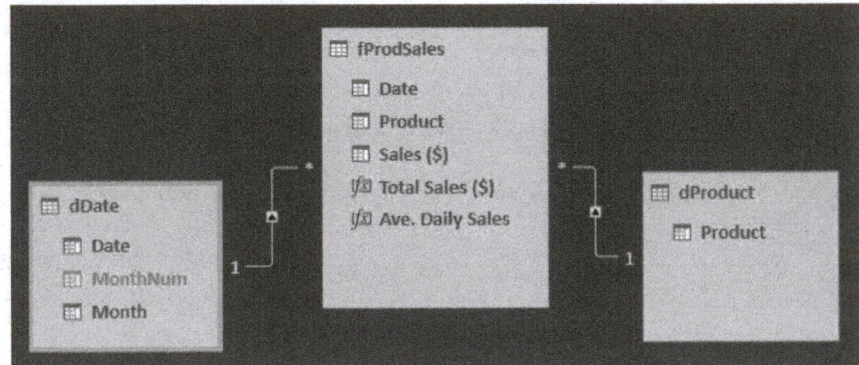

Figure 1.28 *This is what the data model looks like when you make an average daily sales calculation.*

DAX formulas and Data Model PivotTables can be used to perform calculations that cannot be easily done with worksheet formulas and standard PivotTables. In addition, the Data Model and DAX formulas provide great versatility. For example, Figure 1.29 shows an example of the same DAX formula as before for average daily sales, but now the new column Sales Rep is added to the Rows area of the Data Model PivotTable, and all the calculations are correct! Worksheet formulas cannot accommodate the addition of new conditions to a report, but a Data Model PivotTable and DAX formula can easily accomplish such changes.

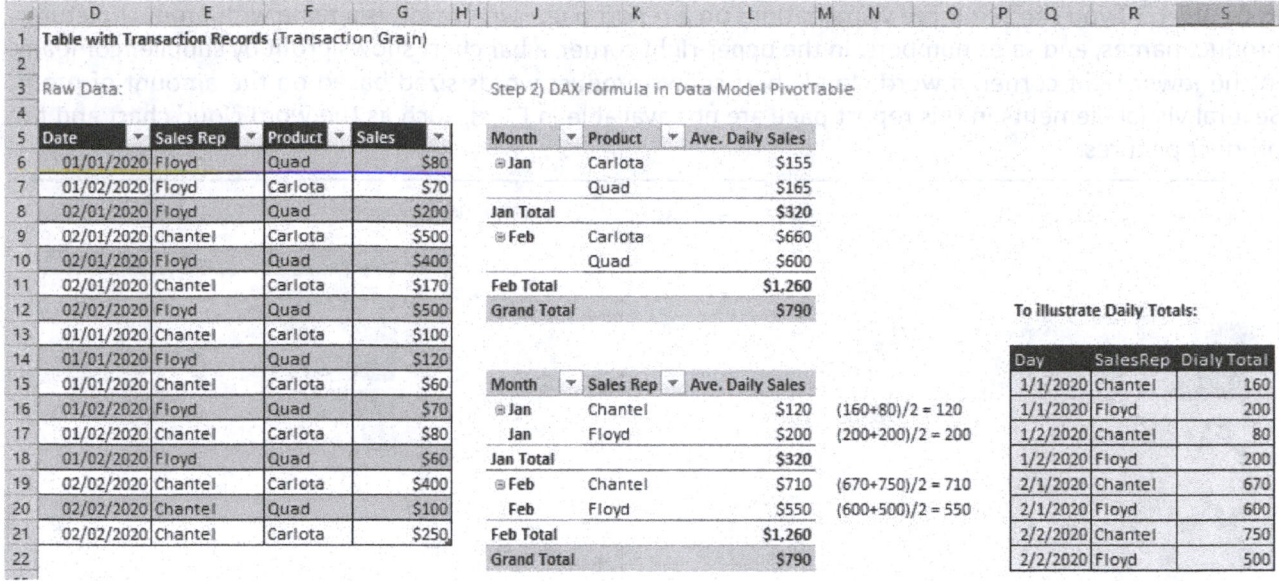

Figure 1.29 *DAX can do tasks that are nearly impossible with standard PivotTables and worksheet formulas.*

The Excel 365 Data Model can hold more than 100 million rows of data, and there are more than 200 DAX functions. Excel 365 Power Pivot, the Data Model, and DAX formulas greatly enhance your ability to make any sort of summary report or dashboard that might be required.

Power BI Desktop for Creating Visualizations and Reports

Power BI Desktop is a separate tool that is not integrated into Excel 365. Even though it is a separate tool, it is worth learning about Power BI Desktop because it interacts seamlessly with Excel as if it were a tool inside Excel 365. In addition, the Power Query and Data Model tools in Excel are almost identical to tools in Power BI. This means that many of the skills that you learn in Excel 365 are directly applicable in Power BI Desktop. Power BI Desktop offers a number of benefits over Excel alone:

- It gives you a wider variety of visualizations.
- The visualizations and reports are interactive.
- Once you create reports and visualizations, you can share them online.

In Figure 1.30 you can see three visualizations on a report page. On the left is a table with product pictures, product names, and sales numbers. In the upper-right corner, a bar chart shows profit by supplier company. In the lower-right corner, a word cloud chart shows product words sized based on the amount of profit. Several visual elements in this report page are not available in Excel, such as the word cloud chart and the product pictures.

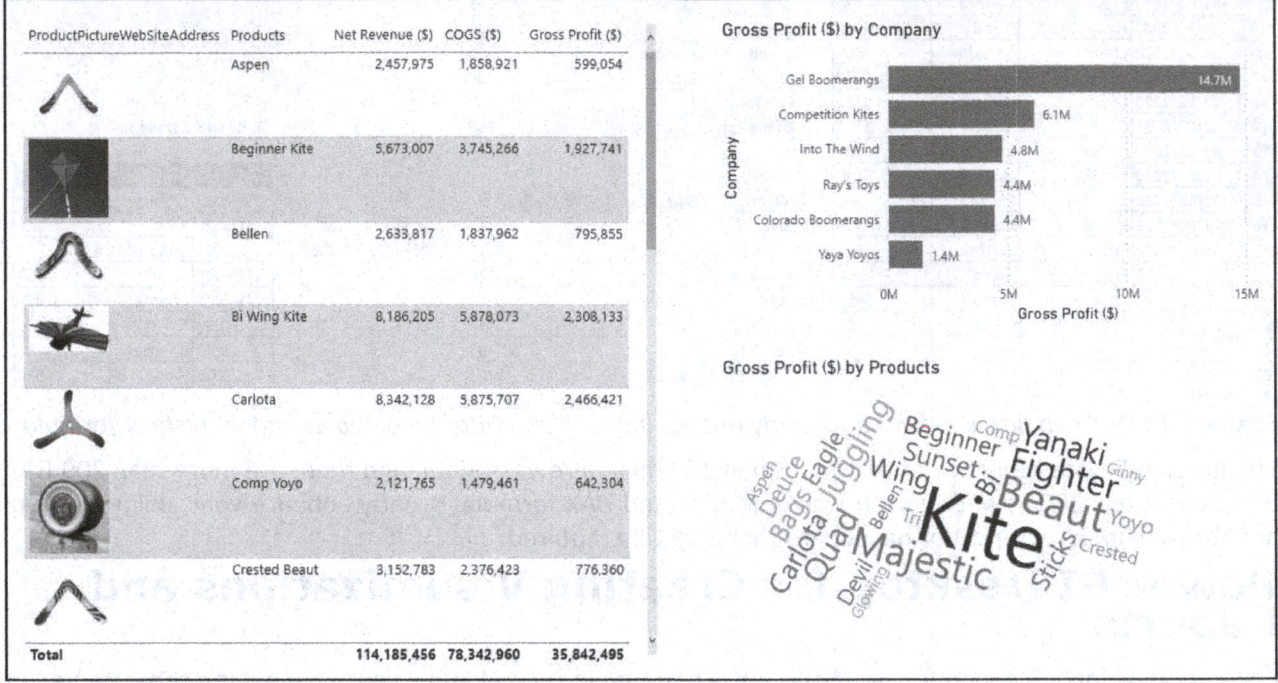

Figure 1.30 *This Power BI Desktop report includes three visualizations.*

The most amazing Power BI feature is illustrated in Figure 1.31: When you click on the word Kite in the word cloud chart, the other visuals on the page instantly filter to show the kite products and supplier companies that sell kites. This is an example of the interactive Power BI visuals that make drill-down analysis as easy as a single click. Such report and visualization interaction is not available in Excel.

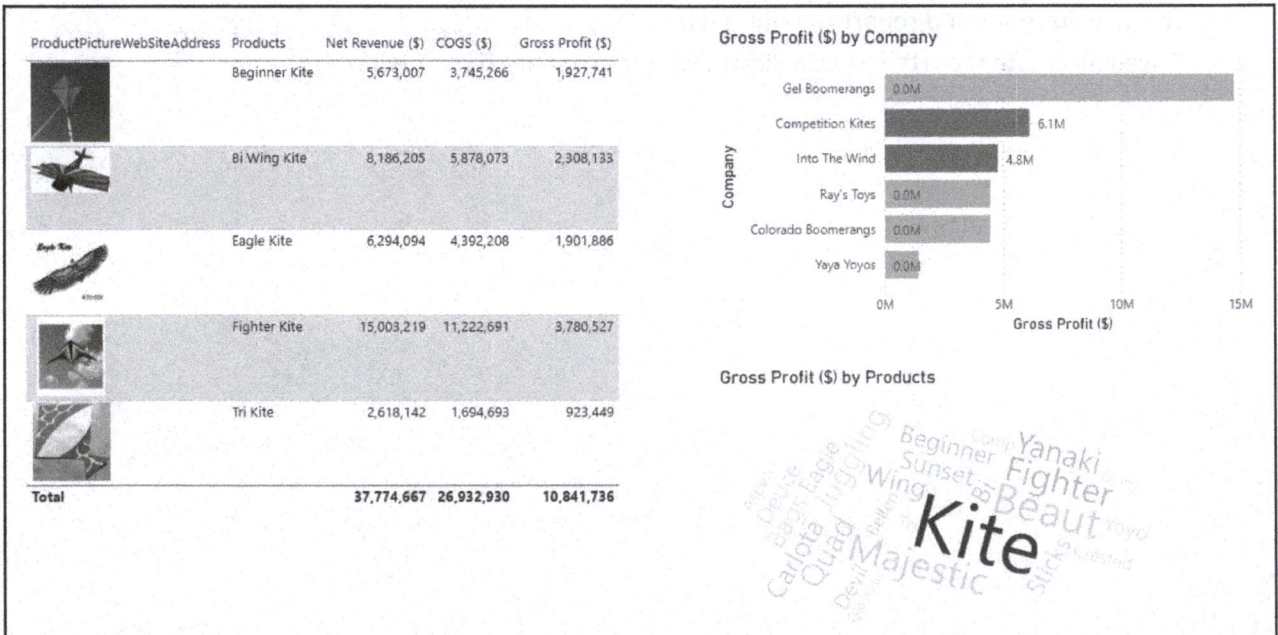

Figure 1.31 *With Power BI Desktop, clicking on the word Kite in the word cloud chart filters the other visualizations.*

With Power BI, changing the filtering is as easy as clicking on a different element. For example, Figure 1.32 shows that if you click on the Gel Boomerangs bar in the bar chart, the word cloud chart shows Majestic Beaut as the largest word, which gives an instant visual cue that the Majestic Beaut product had the greatest amount of profit. As you can see, with Power BI Desktop visualizations, you get interactive and insightful information with a single click.

Figure 1.32 *Power BI Desktop brings real interactive power to analysis.*

There are two Power BI tools: Power BI Desktop and Power BI Online. Power BI Desktop allows you to import data and build reports and visualizations. This is the tool that you will learn about in this book. You will also briefly publish and share reports to the Power BI Online website.

Key Concepts in Chapter 1

- Excel's new **worksheet formula calculation engine** and many new Microsoft 365 functions radically transform how you create worksheet formula solutions. In particular, spilled array formulas significantly reduce the time it takes to make and update formula solutions.

- **Power Query** allows you to import and transform data with different structures, from different sources, and from small and large datasets alike. The M code formula language is built specifically as a data transformational formula language.

- You can use the **Power Pivot Power BI Data Model** and **DAX formulas** to store and make efficient calculations on big data.

- You can use **Power BI Desktop** to create interactive and shareable reports, visualizations, and dashboards.

Chapter 2: Why the Spreadsheet Was Invented

Note: To follow along with the examples in this chapter, you can use the file named Ch02-Excel365-WhySpreadsheetInvented.xlsx.

Figure 2.1 *VisiCalc, the first spreadsheet tool, was invented by Dan Bricklin (left) and Bob Frankston.*

Excel was not the first spreadsheet program. VisiCalc holds that distinction. It was invented in 1979 by Dan Bricklin and Bob Frankston in 1979, pictured in Figure 2.1.

Dan Bricklin was the one who had the original idea for the spreadsheet. His epiphany for creating the spreadsheet, or "visual calculator," came out of his frustration with having to type many inputs into his handheld calculator to get an answer—and then having to retype all the inputs when one of them changed. Figure 2.2 shows Bricklin's idea of a visual calculator, where the goal is to add all the expenses, subtract them from revenue, calculate the tax expense, and then make the final calculation for net income. To make this calculation on a handheld calculator, you would type the following:

Net Income = (4500 – (500 + 150 + 200 + 150 + 1500)) * (1 – 10.00%) = 1800

	A	B	C	D	E	F
1						
2		Income Statement for Period ($)				
3		Expenses				
4		Rent	500			
5		Utilities	150			
6		Insurance	200			
7		Auto	150			
8		Wages	1,500			
9		Total Expenses	2,500	=SUM(C4:C8)		
10		Total Revenue	4,500			Tax Rate
11		Income Before Tax	2,000	=C10-C9		10.00%
12		Tax Expense	200	=C11*F11		
13		Net Income	1,800	=C11-C12		
14						
		Ch02 (1)	⊕			

Figure 2.2 *Dan Bricklin's visual calculator idea makes understanding and updating calculations dramatically easier.*

The beauty of Bricklin's idea is that everything is visual: You can see the numbers, the labels that indicate what each number represents, the formulas, the tax rate, and the final result. But the real power of this setup is that if some of the numbers change, the calculations can be updated much more easily. For example, if the auto expense changes to $200 and the tax rate changes to 12.00%, with a visual calculator (initially VisiCalc and now Excel), you just change the two calculation inputs, and everything else updates instantly, as shown in Figure 2.3. If you were using a handheld calculator, you would have to once again type in all the inputs, like this:

Net Income = (4500 – (500 + 150 + 200 + 200 + 1500)) * (1 – 12.00%) = 1716

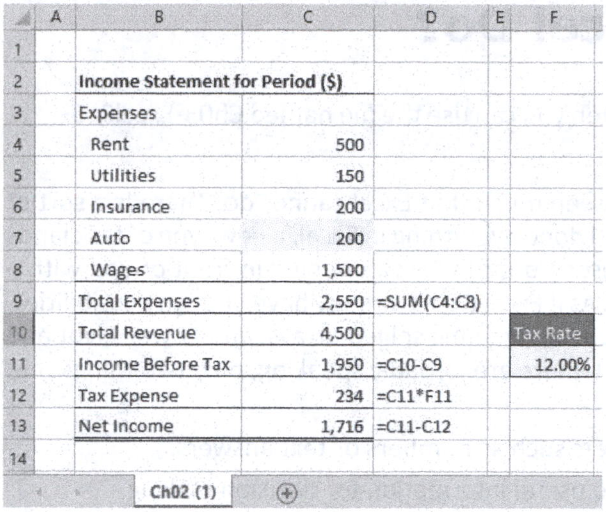

	A	B	C	D	E	F
1						
2		Income Statement for Period ($)				
3		Expenses				
4		Rent	500			
5		Utilities	150			
6		Insurance	200			
7		Auto	200			
8		Wages	1,500			
9		Total Expenses	2,550	=SUM(C4:C8)		
10		Total Revenue	4,500			Tax Rate
11		Income Before Tax	1,950	=C10-C9		12.00%
12		Tax Expense	234	=C11*F11		
13		Net Income	1,716	=C11-C12		
14						

Ch02 (1)   ⊕

Figure 2.3 *When you change a formula input, everything updates instantly.*

In addition to handling calculations for you, a visual calculator gives you an even greater benefit: It gives you repeatability. Once you create a solution, you can use it again in the next period and the one after that by simply changing the inputs—and everything will update!

Just as Bricklin and Frankston envisioned with VisiCalc in 1979, today we use Excel to more easily understand and update calculations. However, Excel now makes more than just calculations easy: It allows you to perform data analysis quickly and easily, as you will see throughout the rest of this book.

> **Note:** In Microsoft 365 Excel, there are currently more than 450 built-in functions. The 1979 VisiCalc spreadsheet manual lists 21 functions: @SUM, @NA, @ERROR, @MAX, @MIN, @AVERAGE, @COUNT, @NPV, @LOOKUP, @ABS, @INT, @EXP, @LOG10, @LN, @PI, @SIN, @COS, @TAN, @ASIN, @ACOS, and @ATAN.
>
> Why the @ symbol? In early spreadsheets, instead of using an equal symbol in front of a function name, you used the @ symbol. Just for fun, the next time you try to use the SUM function, rather than starting with an equal sign, try to start the formula with an @ symbol. When you complete the formula and press Enter, the formula will work correctly. Excel converts the @ symbol to an equal sign for you. It allows you to use @ as a silent nod to the spreadsheet's history.

Key Concepts in Chapter 2

- The first spreadsheet program, **VisiCalc**, was created in 1979.
- The fundamentals of Excel today are based on Dan Bricklin's original ideas of **placing formula inputs in cells** and **building formulas based on those cells** so that when you change a formula input, the whole spreadsheet solution updates.

Chapter 3: What Does Excel Do?

Note: To follow along with the examples in this chapter, you can use the file named Ch03-Excel365-WhatExcelDoes.xlsx.

In my 25 years using Excel to solve problems, I have not seen much that Excel cannot do. There is a sort of infinite beauty to it. Just when you think you have seen and done everything in Excel, a new type of task lands on your desk, and there it is waiting: yet another unforeseen door in Excel, opening in front of you with a new and bright panorama of unmasked Excel possibilities. As if Excel didn't already have enough possibilities, Microsoft keeps adding new levels of utility, like Power Query, dynamic spilled arrays, and Power Pivot and Power BI. Despite the seemingly infinite potential of Excel, there are, broadly speaking, only two things that Excel does:

- **Make calculations:** Excel can calculate final answers such as numbers or text answers.
- **Perform data analysis:** Excel can convert data into useful information for decision making.

Before Excel, calculations required tools such as paper and calculators. Now you can make calculations in Excel with a variety of tools, such as worksheet formulas, PivotTables, and DAX formulas. Before Excel, it was hard to perform data analysis, and paper, calculators, and rulers (to draw the straight edge of a column chart) were required. Now you can perform data analysis with Excel tools like PivotTables, PivotCharts, and Power Query.

There are other things besides calculations and data analysis that some people do in Excel. For instance, I wrote a 110-page accounting book in Excel (*Windsport Inc. Accounting Practice Set*), and Tatsuo Horiuchi paints pictures in Excel. But these are fringe uses, and almost every task you will do in Excel is either a calculation or data analysis—or a combination of calculation and data analysis. Of course, within these two categories, there is a lot that you can do!

Figure 3.1 illustrates a simple calculation task. In cell E3, there is a formula to extract the name of the employee from the Employee, ID column. In cell F3, there is a formula to calculate the commission paid. Both of these are examples of calculations, but whereas the formula in E3 yields text answers, the formula in F3 yields numeric answers.

	A	B	C	D	E	F
1						
2		Employee, ID	Sales ($)		First Name	Commission Paid
3		Chantel Williams, 05-7939-309	84,789.88		Chantel	2077.35
4		Miki Pham, 03-7736-583	63,051.45		Miki	1544.76
5		Floyd Tyson, 04-9005-751	95,750.64		Floyd	2345.89
6		Abdi Mohamed, 06-3443-518	80,943.42		Abdi	1983.11
7						
8			Commission Rate		Formula in cell E3:	Formula in cell F3:
9			2.45%		=LEFT(B3:B6,SEARCH(" ",B3:B6)-1)	=ROUND(C3:C6*C9,2)

Figure 3.1 *You can do calculations in Excel such as extracting a first name or calculating the commission paid.*

Figure 3.2 illustrates a simple data analysis task. The Survey Data column contains raw data from a survey. To the right of the column of data are a PivotTable report and a column chart that yield useful information: the survey results. In these results, you can see that the majority of responses were "No."

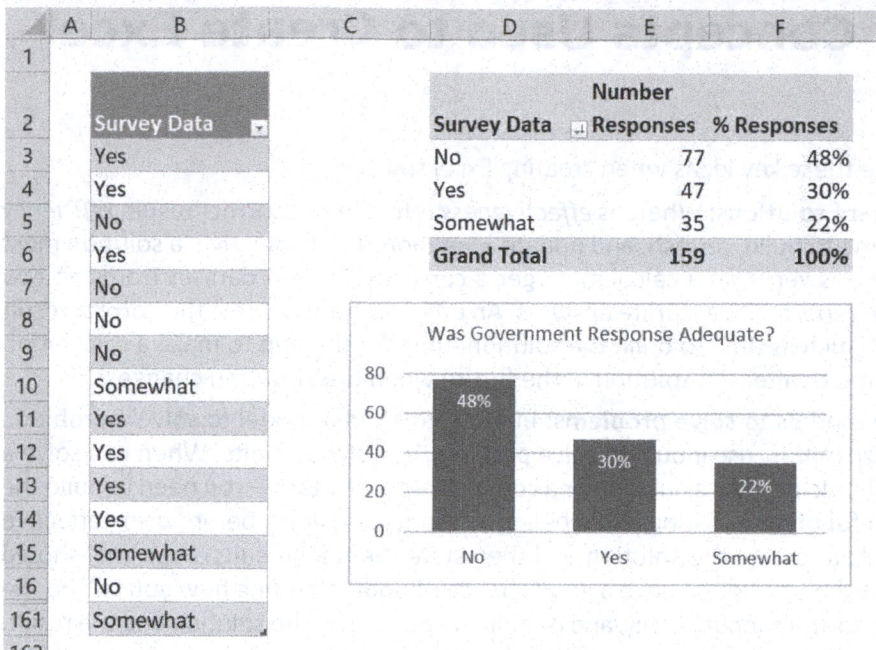

Figure 3.2 *You can create data analysis solutions in Excel such as creating survey results.*

Key Concepts in Chapter 3

- Broadly speaking, Excel performs two tasks: making calculations and performing data analysis.
- **Making calculations** involves calculating some final answer, such as a number, text, date, time, or logical value.
- **Data analysis** involves converting raw data into useful information for decision making.

Chapter 4: Key Concepts Used to Create Excel Solutions

Throughout this book, you will use these key ideas when creating Excel solutions:

- **Create effective and efficient solutions:** Whereas *effectiveness* refers to the correct result, *efficiency* refers to minimizing the time to build, refresh, and update a solution. To be effective, a solution must be able to get the correct answer from a calculation, get a correctly formed dataset from the raw data, or get an appropriate report with accurate answers. An efficient solution gets the correct result with the fewest resources (such as time to build the solution, time for the app to make a calculation or refresh the data, and time to alter the solution in the future when the situation changes).

- **Build easy-to-understand models to solve problems:** In order to build a model to solve a problem, you need to clearly organize inputs, use inputs to solve problem, and state results. When you solve a problem—whether it is a simple payroll calculation or a complex reporting task—you need to build the solution in a clear and careful manner, listing and labeling all inputs and goals before using effective and efficient Excel methods to create the solution and then state the final results. Your goal should be for anyone who looks at the solution to have a good chance of understanding how you solved the problem, be able to change formula inputs easily, and be able to understand the solution and the result.

- **Answer questions with data:** Answering questions with data means that you answer questions by using evidence created from the data. You need to be careful in how you gather and prepare the data before creating and presenting the data analysis results in the form of final useful information for answering the questions. Answering questions with data yields effective and efficient Excel data analysis solutions.

- **Investigate to make discoveries:** Investigating to make discoveries means playing around with the inputs for models and trying different conditions and criteria for the data analysis results until you see something new, see an unexpected pattern, or gain insight. This is often called what-if analysis or experimenting with data.

Key Concepts in Chapter 4

- The solutions that you build with Excel need to be **effective** and **efficient**.

- When you **build models to solve problems**, you list goals and labeled formula inputs, organize for ease of understanding, allow for easy updates, and state the final results.

- When you **answer questions with data**, you need to be careful with the preparation and presentation of the data and useful information.

- When you **investigate to make discoveries**, you either change the inputs or models or change the conditions and criteria in the data analysis results.

Chapter 5: The Structure of Excel Files and Worksheets

Note: To follow along with the examples in this chapter, you can use the file named Ch05-Excel365-StructureOfExcel.xlsx.

The Two-Way Grid: Cells, Worksheets, and Workbooks

Before you can get started learning about the amazing tools and features in Excel, you have to understand how an Excel file is set up. In particular, you need to understand the structure of Excel's two-way grid and its various elements. Excel is said to have *a two-way grid* because data, formulas, and other elements can be copied in only two directions: vertically (numbers) and horizontally (letters). Figure 5.1 illustrates the following important elements of an Excel file:

1. **Column** = Lettered

2. **Row** = Numbered

3. **Cell** = Intersection of column and row

4. **Worksheet** = Sheet = All the cells

5. **Sheet tab** = Name of the worksheet

6. **Workbook** = Excel file = Contains all worksheets

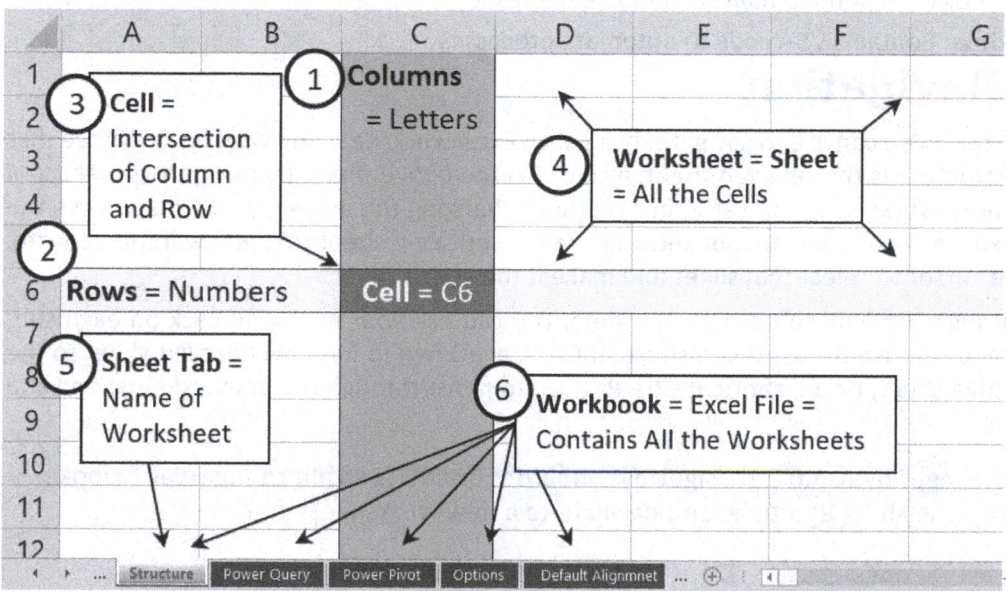

Figure 5.1 *Excel's two-way grid is made up of columns, rows, and cells.*

The magnificent two-way grid is the foundation for everything in Excel. It can hold many useful values, such as number data, text data, formulas, charts, PivotTables, and much more. The two-way grid features columns, represented by letters (for example, column C), and rows, represented by numbers (for example, row 6). A cell occurs at the intersection of a column and a row and is denoted by the column letter and then the row number (for example, C6). Almost everything in Excel involves columns and rows, whether it is a single cell (for example, C6), a range of cells (for example, C6:C8), or a spilled array of values across columns and rows (for example, C6:E12).

When you refer to a cell in a formula, a chart, a PivotTable, or another Excel feature, this is called a *cell reference*. When you refer to a group of cells like the cells C6, C7, C8, and C9, the notation C6:C9 is used to refer to the *range of cells* (also called just a *range*). The term *worksheet* is used to refer to all the cells together. You will often hear the terms *spreadsheet* and *sheet* used as synonyms for *worksheet*.

There are a lot of cells in any given worksheet. An Excel worksheet has 16,384 columns and 1,048,576 rows, for a total of 17,179,869,184 cells. However, you can never use all 17 billion cells because that much data in an

Excel worksheet grid would significantly slow down the computer—and possibly stop it all together. You can use all the columns and just some of the rows, or you can use all the rows and just some of the columns, but you can't use all of them at the same time. However, as you will learn later in this book, when you are working with big data, rather than store it in the worksheet, you can store it in the Data Model, which is much more efficient.

The name of a worksheet is found in the *sheet tab*. In Figure 5.1, notice the name of each sheet on its sheet tab. Sheets begin with default names like Sheet1, Sheet2 and so on, but you should always give your sheets logical names that help you and others understand the purpose of each sheet. You can rename a sheet by double-clicking its sheet tab, typing a new name, and pressing Enter. Just as cell references are used every-where in Excel solutions, *sheet references* are also used everywhere. Cell references and sheet references help you understand where a particular feature, such as a formula, is pointing to get its input.

Finally, the term *workbook* refers to an entire Excel file, which is made up of one or more worksheets. For exam-ple, the workbook file that you are using for this chapter is named Ch05-Excel365-StructureOfExcel.xlsx, and it contains multiple worksheets. In addition, a workbook file can contain other objects, such as behind-the-scenes queries made with Power Query, a data model made with Power Pivot, or VBA code made with the VBA Editor.

There are other behind-the-scenes locations where you can work and store solutions, including the following, which you will learn about throughout this book:

- **Power Query window:** Allows you to create and edit queries
- **PivotTable cache:** Contains the data in a standard PivotTable
- **Power Pivot window:** Allows you to create and edit a data model
- **Data Model columnar database:** Contains the data in a Data Model PivotTable
- **Name Manager:** Contains defined names and table names
- **VBA Editor window:** Contains VBA code to automate processes

Worksheet Navigation

Figure 5.2 illustrates the tools you can use to navigate through an Excel worksheet and workbook. Notice that the worksheet named Structure is the selected sheet, also called the *active sheet*. By using the *sheet scroll arrows*, you can show more worksheets, one at a time, without changing the active sheet. You can use the sheet scroll arrows to expose sheets that are not showing. When you see a sheet that you want to activate, you can use your mouse cursor to select that sheet and make it the active sheet.

If you want to move through the worksheets one at a time, you can use your mouse to click on each sub-sequent worksheet, or you can use the keyboard shortcut Ctrl+PageDown to jump to the next sheet to the right and make it the active sheet, or the shortcut Ctrl+PageUp to move through the active sheets, one at a time, in the left direction.

> **Note:** Using the Ctrl+PageDown and Ctrl+PageUp keyboard shortcuts is an alternative way to look through a workbook, one sheet at a time, and navigate to a new worksheet.

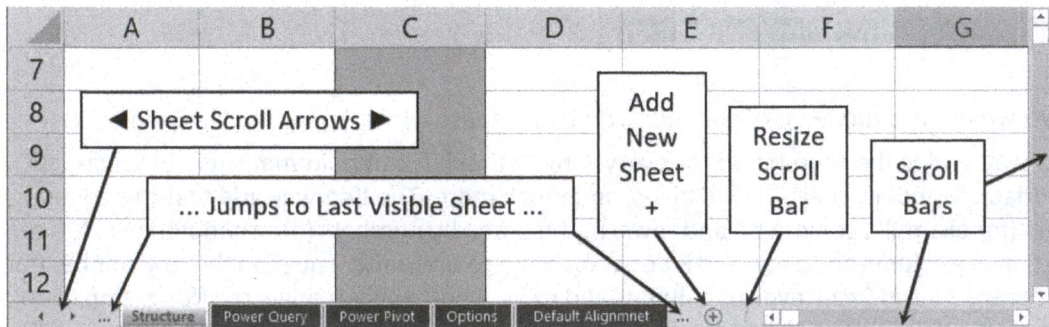

Figure 5.2 *Worksheet navigation features.*

In Figure 5.2, notice the three dots buttons. By clicking the three dots button on the bottom right of the screen, you can jump to the last visible sheet on the right; by clicking the one on the bottom left, you can jump to the first visible sheet on the left. For example, in Figure 5.2, if you click the three dots button on the right, you will jump to the last visible sheet on the right, named Default Alignment.

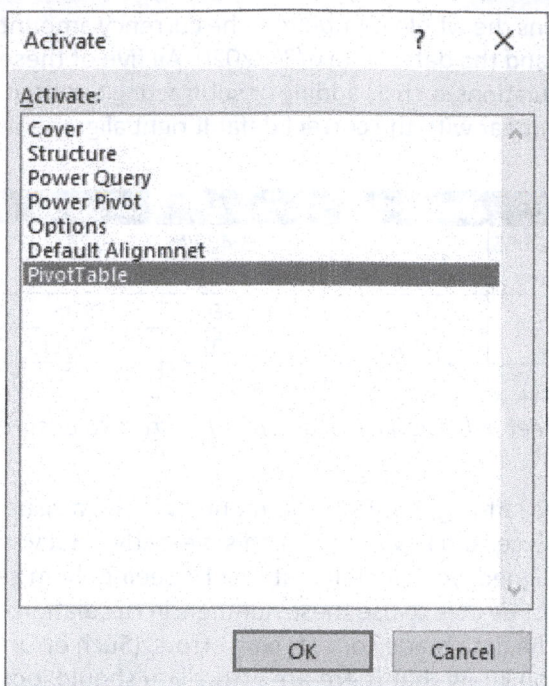

If you want to move around within the active sheet, you can use the *scroll bars*. By using the scroll bars, you can move the view of columns and rows within the active sheet. The key to moving through the columns and rows in a worksheet without getting lost is to look at the row numbers or column letters to see where you are in the worksheet. For example, in Figure 5.2, it looks like cell A7 is the first cell in this worksheet, but this is because the view is scrolled down, and the first six rows are temporarily concealed. If you get lost in a worksheet and need to jump back to cell A1, you can use the keyboard shortcut Ctrl+Home. If you need to jump to the last cell that you used in the worksheet, you can use the keyboard shortcut Ctrl+End. You can also see in Figure 5.2 that there are buttons to add a new sheet and to resize the scroll bars.

When you have many worksheets in a workbook, the fastest way to jump to a different worksheet (including to a worksheet that is not in the current view) is to right-click the sheet scroll arrows to open the Activate dialog box. As shown in Figure 5.3, the Activate dialog box lists all the worksheets in the workbook. When you select a worksheet in this list (such as the one named PivotTable) and click OK, Excel takes you to that sheet. Figure 5.4 shows the PivotTable worksheet as the active sheet.

Figure 5.3 *Right-clicking the scroll arrows opens the Activate dialog box, which lists all worksheets in the workbook.*

▲	A	B	C	D	E	F	G
1							
2		Product ▾	Sales ▾		Product ▾	Sum of Sales	
3		Quad	5		Carlota	$78.00	
4		Carlota	10		Quad	$60.00	
5		Quad	15		Sunshine	$30.00	
6		Sunshine	12		Grand Total	$168.00	
7		Carlota	6				
8		Quad	15				
9		Carlota	40				
10		Quad	25				
11		Sunshine	18				
12		Carlota	22				
13							

◄ ► ... | Power Query | Power Pivot | Options | Default Alignmnet | PivotTable | ... ⊕ | ◄

Figure 5.4 *When you select a sheet in the Activate dialog box and click OK, Excel takes you to that sheet.*

Should you use the Activate dialog box or the sheet scroll arrows and the mouse to go to another worksheet? It depends on how many worksheets you have. When there are many worksheets, it is usually faster to use the Activate dialog box. If there are not many worksheets, it is probably faster to just use sheet scroll arrows and the mouse.

Excel Data and Default Alignment in Cells

The table in Figure 5.5 shows the different types of data you can have in an Excel worksheet. In addition, it shows the default alignment for each type of data. Knowing the default alignment for different data types helps you track down errors in data entry and ensure that your calculations will be accurate. For example, in

Figure 5.5, you can see that the row with number values contains the whole number 43, the currency amount $14.95, the decimal number 69.129, the time value 3:42 PM, and the date value 6/25/2020. All five of these are considered numbers in Excel because you can do math calculations such as adding or subtracting on them. Numbers in Excel appear right-aligned. If a number does not appear with the correct default right alignment, the calculations made on it will probably be incorrect.

Type of Data	Default Alignment	Example 1	Example 2	Example 3	Example 4	Example 5
Number Values:	Right	43	$14.95	69.129	3:42 PM	6/25/2020
Text Values:	Left	Excel	Power Query	69.1.29	3:42PM	25/6/2020
Logical Values:	CENTER ALL CAPS	TRUE	FALSE	TRUE	FALSE	TRUE
Formula Errors:	CENTER ALL CAPS	#DIV/0!	#N/A	#N/A	#DIV/0!	#SPILL!
Empty Cells:						

Figure 5.5 *Knowing the default alignment for data in a worksheet helps you track down data errors to ensure that your formulas can calculate correctly.*

In the row containing text values, you can see that all values are left-aligned. This alignment gives you a visual cue that Excel thinks that these are text values. For the words Excel and Power Query, this is exactly what you want. But because 69.1.29, 3:42PM, and 25/6/2020 are left-aligned, you can tell that Excel is seeing them as text numbers rather than as a numeric data types, so you will not be able to use these numbers in calculations. In the case of these three text numbers, the person entering the data made some typing errors. (Such errors are very common.) Luckily, the default left alignment helps you know that there are errors you should look for and fix. By removing the extra period between the 1 and the 2 in 69.1.29, you get the correct number, 69.129; by adding a space between the 2 and the P in 3:42PM, you will create the correct time value, 3:42 PM; and in 25/6/2020, by putting the month, 6, before the day, 25, you will get the correct date value, 6/25/2020.

> **Note:** The format of date values depends on the regional settings in the Control Panel. I'm assuming that you have your regional settings set to English (United States), but if your regional settings were set to France, then Excel would see 25/6/2020 as a number (because it would be in the European date format, with the day first), and 6/25/2020 would be text (because the month value can go up to 12 only).

For numeric and text data, you *could* manually change the alignment to show something different than the default alignment, but then you would lose an important visual cue about the type of data that is in a cell. When you are creating effective and efficient solutions in Excel, it is a good idea to avoid changing the default alignment in an Excel worksheet unless you have a final solution that needs a presentation that requires an alignment different than the default. (You'll learn more about presentation Example 19 in Chapter 17.)

The third type of data that you can see in Figure 5.5 is logical values, also called Boolean values. This type of value is important when you're determining something like whether an employee passed the sales hurdle to get a bonus. There are only two possibilities with logical values: TRUE or FALSE. By default, logical values are centered and shown in all capital letters.

Finally, Figure 5.5 also shows formula error values, which are always centered and all capital letters by default, and empty cells, which are not really values but will cause trouble for some solutions, and so you need to be on the lookout for them. (You will learn more about formula error values in Chapter 12.)

The Excel Command Environment

Excel's Ribbon tabs, Quick Access Toolbar, and other areas allow you to enact a command such as to insert a PivotTable or add some formatting. Figure 5.6 shows the full Excel command environment, with the following elements labeled:

- **Name box:** Shows the selected part of the worksheet (in this case, cell B2).
- **Quick Access Toolbar (QAT):** Allows you to add your favorite commands for easy access.
- **Home Ribbon tab:** Contains common commands like Wrap Text and Conditional Formatting.
- **Groups of commands:** Include related commands within the Ribbon tab.
- **Status bar:** Contains a few commands and shows quick calculations for selected cells.

- **Login name:** Shows who is logged in and can connect to important data analysis online features such as Power BI Online.

- **Minimize:** Reduces the Excel workbook to an icon on the taskbar without closing the file, which enables you to move between the current Excel file and other files.

- **Restore:** Maximizes or restores the workbook file down to the last window size that was used. When it is restored down, and not maximized to the full computer window size, you can resize the window by pointing to the edge of the window and readjusting the size.

- **Close:** Closes the workbook file.

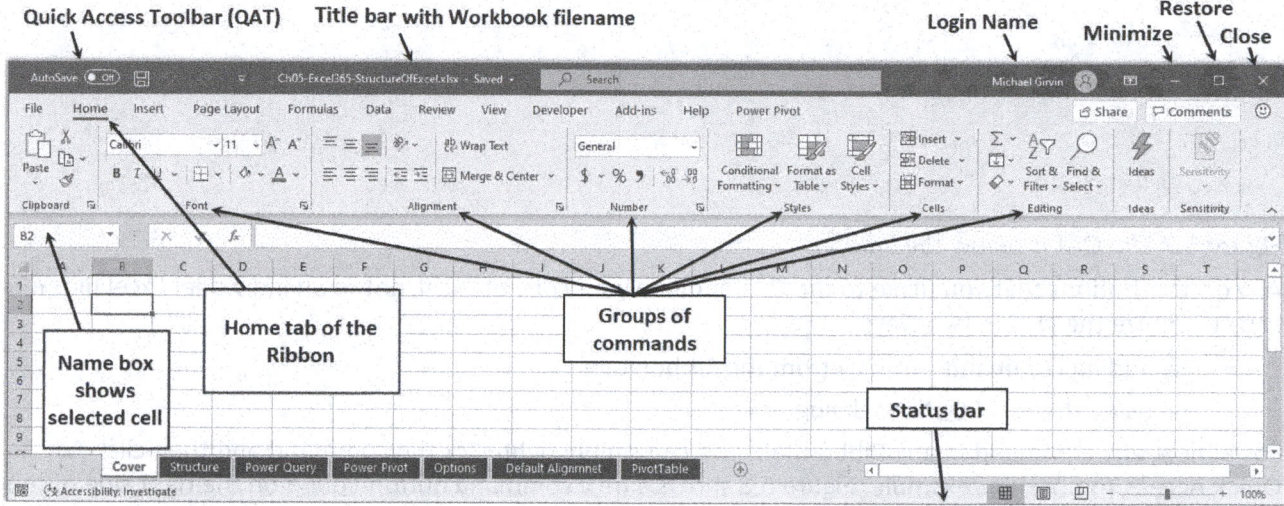

Figure 5.6 *The Excel command environment.*

The Ribbon holds all the tabs and all the commands on each tab. In Figure 5.6, the Home tab of the Ribbon is selected, and you can choose from the different commands. To the right of the Home tab are other tabs, such as Insert, Page Layout, Formulas, Data, Review, Developer, Add-ins, Help, and Power Pivot. (Your tabs may be different. Later in the book, you will see how to add the different tabs.) Throughout this book, you will work with all of these tabs.

The sizes of the buttons on the Ribbon change depending on the width of the window. When you reduce the size of a window, the buttons also shrink and become smaller. When this happens, you can hover your mouse over a button until you see a screentip pop up with a description of the command.

> **Note:** You should try looking at an Excel window at various sizes to familiarize yourself with how the buttons change in size depending on the width of the window.

The Quick Access Toolbar

The most unused element in Figure 5.6 is the default Quick Access Toolbar, which is typically called the QAT. The default QAT is almost useless because its buttons are not as handy as keyboard shortcuts. Here is a list of the default features in the QAT and the keyboard shortcut for each of them:

Command	Description	Keyboard Shortcut
Save	Saves changes in a file	Ctrl+S
Undo	Undoes the change you just made	Ctrl+Z
Redo	Undoes the undo you just did	Ctrl+Y

Although the *default* QAT is not very useful, the QAT is a wonderful tool that you can customize to create a personal toolbar that is tailored to your work habits. The QAT is always visible, no matter what Ribbon tab you are working with. This means your favorite commands are always in view.

To customize the QAT, you must first move it from its default position above the Ribbon to below the Ribbon. To do this, you need to right-click the QAT and select Show Quick Access Toolbar Below the Ribbon. Figure 5.7 shows the QAT positioned below the Ribbon.

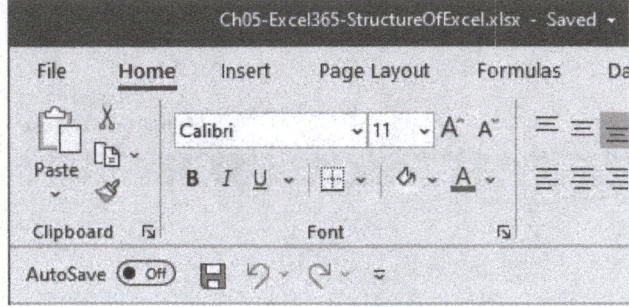

Figure 5.7 *The QAT is below the Ribbon.*

Any customizations that you make to the QAT apply to your copy of Excel, not to an individual Excel file. You can customize the QAT in two ways:

- By adding commands directly from the Ribbon tabs
- By using the Excel Options dialog box

For almost any command in any Ribbon tab, you can simply right-click the command and then click Add to Quick Access Toolbar. For example, Figure 5.8 shows a new command button added on the right side of the QAT. This is the command for a new blank query in the Power Query window. (In Project 4 in Chapter 19, you will learn why this is a great command.) I added this command to the QAT because I use it a lot and because it takes five steps to get to it using the Ribbon tab method: click the Data Ribbon tab, go to the Get & Transform group, click the Get Data dropdown, click From Other Sources, and then finally right-click Blank Query and then click Add to Quick Access Toolbar. By adding this command to the QAT, I have created a much faster way of getting to it.

Figure 5.8 *You can add command buttons directly from the Ribbon tabs to your QAT.*

To open the Excel Options dialog box so that you can add, remove, or reorder the commands on the QAT, you need to right-click the QAT and then click the Customize Quick Access Toolbar option. Figure 5.9 shows the Excel Options dialog box, opened to the Quick Access Toolbar tab. The first thing you must do to use this tab of the dialog box is to select the All Commands option under Choose Commands From so that you can see a list of every possible command that exists in Excel.

Note: There are commands in this list that are not available anywhere else in the Ribbon tabs. The *only* way to access some commands is by adding them to the QAT.

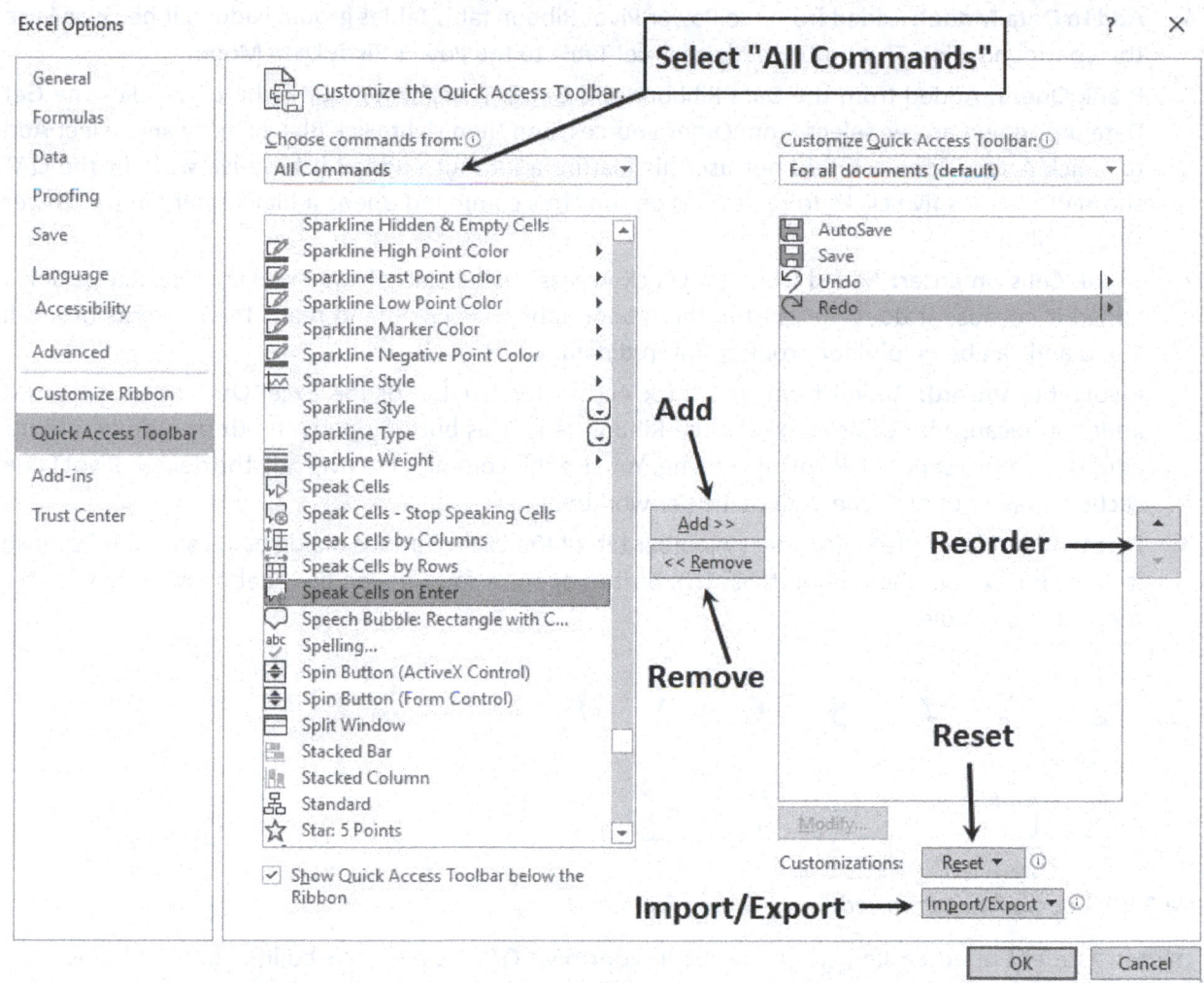

Figure 5.9 *You can remove, add, and reorder buttons in the QAT to create a personalized toolbar.*

A number of types of QAT customizations are possible. For example, you can:

- **Remove commands:** To remove a command from the QAT, select the command from the list on the right (for example, the Redo command in Figure 5.9) and then click the << Remove button.

- **Add commands:** To add a command to the QAT, select the command from the list on the left (for example, the Speak Cells on Enter command in Figure 5.9) and then click the Add >> button.

- **Reorder commands:** To reorder the commands in the QAT, select a command from the list on the right and then click the appropriate reorder button.

- **Reset the QAT:** You can reset the QAT to the original default state.

- **Import/export the QAT:** If you like your QAT and want to move it to a different computer, you can export it and save it as an Excel Customizations.exportedUI file. Then you can import it into a different computer.

When you customize your QAT, you should add commands and buttons that suit your personal taste. Figure 5.10 shows the QAT that I currently use. These are commands that I use a lot based on my personal work habits. They are, from left to right:

1. **Increase Decimal:** Added from the Home Ribbon tab's Number group. I added it because I use this command all the time. This button increases the number of decimal places displayed for numbers.

2. **Decrease Decimal:** Added from the Home Ribbon tab's Number group. I added it because I use this command all the time. This button decreases the number of decimal places displayed for numbers.

3. **Queries & Connections:** Added from the Data Ribbon tab's Queries & Connections group. I added it because I use this command a lot. This button opens the Queries & Connections pane so you can see the queries that have been created in the workbook.

4. **Add to Data Model:** Added from the Power Pivot Ribbon tab's Tables group. I added it because I use this command a lot. This button adds an Excel Table to the Power Pivot Data Model.

5. **Blank Query:** Added from the Data Ribbon tab's Get & Transform group (where you click the Get Data dropdown arrow, select From Other Sources, and then right-click Blank Query and select Add to Quick Access Toolbar). I do not use this feature a lot, but I added it because without the QAT shortcut, it takes five clicks to get to this option. This command opens a blank query in the Power Query editor.

6. **Speak Cells on Enter:** Added from the Quick Access Toolbar tab of the Excel Options dialog box. I added it because it does not exist in the Ribbon tabs. This command reads the contents of a cell aloud and can be helpful for proofing entered data.

7. **PivotTable Wizard:** Added from the Quick Access Toolbar tab of the Excel Options dialog box. I added it because it does not exist in the Ribbon tabs. This button opens the three-step wizard for adding data to a separate PivotTable cache. You use this command to override the default PivotTable cache behavior of only one data cache per workbook.

8. **Form:** Added from the Quick Access Toolbar tab of the Excel Options dialog box. I added it because it does not exist in the Ribbon tabs. This button opens a form dialog box that allows you to enter records into a table.

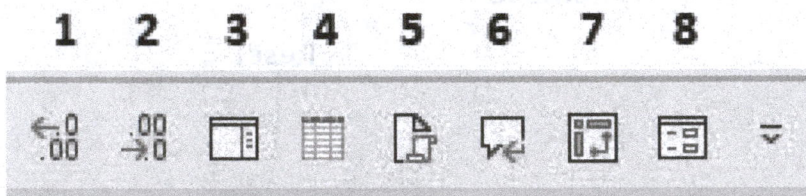

Figure 5.10 *A personal customized Quick Access Toolbar.*

> **Note:** As mentioned earlier, when you build your own QAT, you should build it to match your preferences. Customizing the QAT is a key to working efficiently in Excel because it gives you access to commands no matter what Ribbon tab you are working on, and it gives you fast access to commands that may otherwise be difficult to access.

> **Note:** Throughout this book, I let you know when the most efficient way to use a command is to click a QAT button. If you want to follow along with everything in this book, exactly as you see it, you should build your custom QAT to match the one shown in Figure 5.10.

The File Menu and Backstage View

In Figure 5.11, you can see that the File menu is to the left of the Home tab on the Ribbon. However, the File menu does not open a tab but instead opens the Backstage view, which is shown in Figures 5.12 and 5.13.

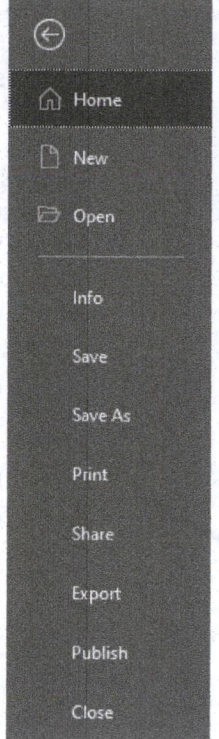

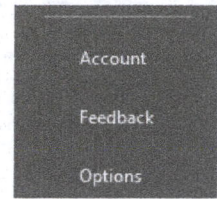

Figure 5.11 *The File menu is to the left of the Home tab.*

Figure 5.12 *The top part of the Backstage view.*

Figure 5.13 *The bottom part of the Backstage view.*

Most of the Backstage view options can be more efficiently accomplished with keyboard shortcuts. However, these Backstage view options are helpful:

- **Info:** Gives you information about the currently open Excel file, such as when it was created and when it was last modified.
- **Publish:** Allows you to publish workbooks to Power BI Online.
- **Account:** Gives you information about and allows you to make changes to your Microsoft 365 account.
- **Options:** Allows you to set default options. You saw an example of the Excel Options dialog in Figure 5.9, and you will use that dialog many more times throughout the book.

For the rest of the commands in the Backstage view, you are likely to use keyboard shortcuts:

Command	Description	Keyboard Shortcut
New	Creates a new Excel workbook file	Ctrl+N
Open	Opens an existing file	Ctrl+O
Save	Saves changes in a file	Ctrl+S
Save As	Creates a new file with a new name, location, and file extension	F12
Print	Shows a print preview and print options	Ctrl+P
Close	Closes the current Excel workbook	Alt+F4

You are not likely to use the Share and Export options in Backstage view because using Save As (discussed in the next section) is a more universal method to accomplish both options.

File Management

Next, we need to talk about file management, which is almost universally left out of Excel books and classes, even though it is of paramount importance. There are two specific topics we need to address:

- Save versus Save As
- Naming conventions

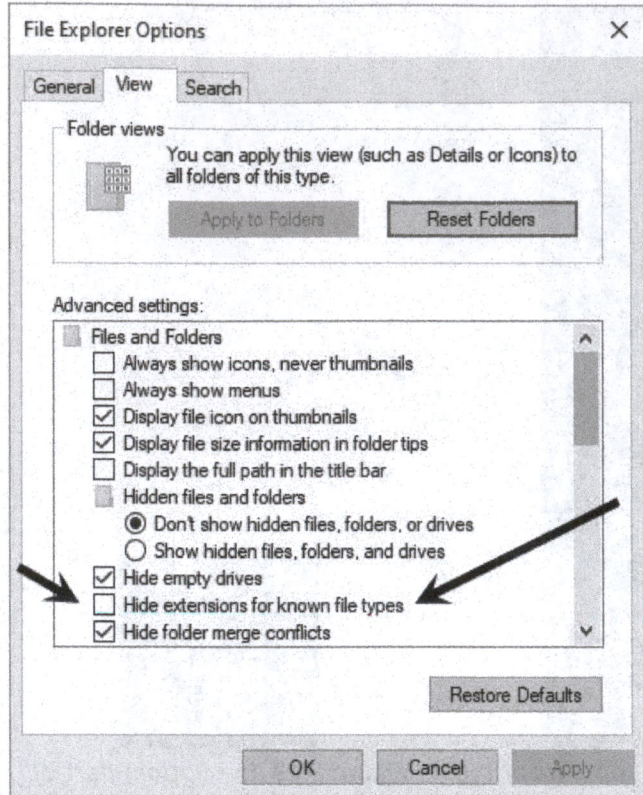

Figure 5.14 *When you uncheck Hide Extensions for Known File Types, File Explorer shows file extensions such as .xlsx and .pdf.*

Before you can proceed with these topics, you need to change a default setting for the file and folder options on your computer so you can view *Save As types*, also known as *file types* or *file extensions*. When using Excel, file extensions are important because they help you quickly determine what sort of file type you are dealing with, such as Excel default files, Excel files that contains VBA code, Excel files that contain text, and PDF or website files created directly from within Excel. To change the default setting for file types, you need to follow these steps:

1. Click the Start button.
2. Type **Control Panel**.
3. Click the option for Control Panel.
4. Click the option File Explorer Options (or, on some systems, Folder Options). The File Explorer Options dialog box appears.
5. Click the View tab.
6. Uncheck the option Hide Extensions for Known File Types (see Figure 5.14).
7. Click OK.

Once your computer is showing file extensions, you are ready to look at the difference between Save and Save As.

Many people don't know there's a difference between Save and Save As, but there is. Basically, Save saves the latest changes to a file, using the same filename and location, whereas Save As allows you to preserve the original file and create a new copy of it with at least one of the following file attributes changed: filename, file location, or file extension. There are more differences, and we'll get to them shortly. For now, you need to know the keyboard shortcuts for Save and Save As:

Keyboard Shortcut	Command	Description
Ctrl+S	Save	Saves changes in the current file
F12	Save As	Creates and saves a new file with a new name and, possibly, location and file extension

Note: Use the keyboard shortcuts rather than the Backstage view to invoke Save or Save As because they are faster and require fewer mouse clicks.

What happens when you use Ctrl+S to invoke the Save command on a file depends on whether the file has already been saved:

*   If the file has already been saved to a location, Excel saves any changes you have made since the last time you saved it and overwrites the existing file. You should use the Save command often so you don't lose work when the computer unexpectedly crashes, which seems to happen a lot with Microsoft products.
*   If the file has never been saved before, Excel opens the Save This File dialog box, which is new in Microsoft 365 and is shown in Figure 5.15. This dialog box does basically the same thing as the Save As dialog box, but it takes more clicks and offers fewer options. So, when you want to save a file that has never been saved before, rather than using Ctrl+S, you are better off pressing F12 to directly open the Save As dialog box.

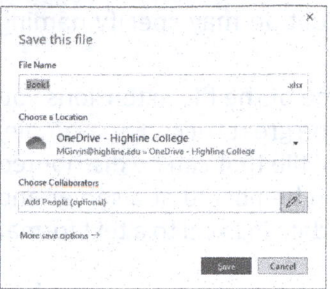

Figure 5.15 *The Save This File dialog box isn't as efficient as the Save As dialog box, shown in Figure 5.16.*

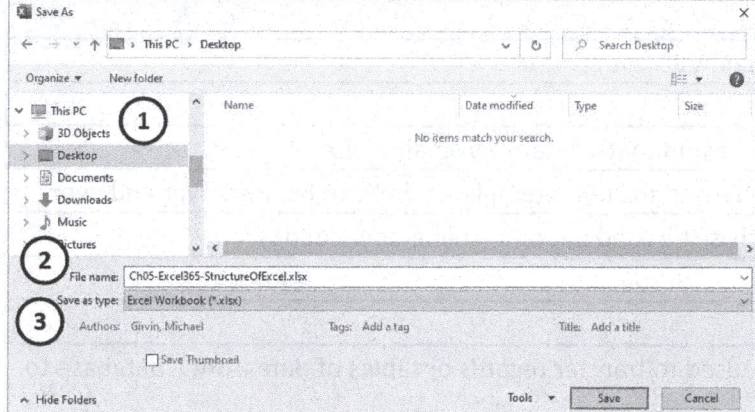

Figure 5.16 *The Save As dialog box allows you to change the file location, filename, and file extension.*

When you press F12 to invoke the Save As command, Excel opens the Save As dialog box and allows you to immediately save the new file and change the three parameters highlighted in Figure 5.16:

1. The location of the file, or file path

2. The filename

3. The type of file and the file extension

You typically use the Save As dialog box in two situations:

- When you have never saved the file before, you press the F12 key to open the Save As dialog box to then define the file location, filename, and file extension.

- When you have a previously saved file open, you can use Save As to convert this file to a new type of file with either a different location, different filename, or different file type. For example, say that you have created an Excel file, and you need to create a second version of it in PDF format. To do this, you simply press the F12 key and change the file extension (in the Save As Type textbox) to the PDF option. When you click the Save button in the Save As dialog box, the finished Excel file remains as a separate file in its original location, and a second file—a new PDF file—is created. There are other reasons you might want to use F12 to create a second file, such as to create a second backup file with a new name, create a second file in a new location, or create a second file that allows VBA code. You will see examples of all these uses throughout this book.

The Save As options give you some important benefits:

- **File location:** You do *not* want to be like most computer users in the world and save everything to My Documents. Every time you save a file for the first time, it's a good idea to save it to a logical location, in a folder with a sensible name. When you do this, you can more easily find and use files. In addition, the full file path (for example, something like C:\Users\mgirvin\Desktop\TheOnlyAppThatMatters\ Chapter05\ Ch05-Excel365-StructureOfExcel.xlsx) is important in some data analysis projects where a file serves as a data source.

- **Filename:** You do *not* want to ever use a default name like Book.xlsx. You should instead give a file a name that makes it obvious what the purpose of the file is. For example, the filename for the Excel file associated with Chapter 5 in this book is Ch05-Excel365-StructureOfExcel.xlsx. A filename like this clearly communicates that the file goes with Chapter 5, the version is Excel 365, and the topic is the structure of Excel. Adding numbers like 01, 02, 03, and so on can be helpful for files in a series.

Following a naming convention is important. Your employer or job situation may specify naming conventions, or you may be able to invent your own.

- **File type:** A file type is associated with a file extension. Table 5.1 lists some of the file extensions you are likely to encounter. With Save As, you can use file extensions to do some great tricks. For example, you can choose the .pdf extension to convert an Excel budget file to a PDF file that can be distributed to colleagues, choose .htm to convert an Excel schedule to a file that can be posted at a server and become part of a website, or choose the .txt or .csv extensions to convert data in Excel to a text format that can be used by almost any data system in the world.

Table 5.1 Useful File Extensions for Converting an Excel File into a Different Type of File

File Extension	Description
.xlsx	Excel file that does not contain VBA code
.xlsm	Excel file allows VBA code
.xlsb	Excel file that allows VBA code and that is relatively small in size
.xlst	Excel template file extension, used to create templates that can be used over and over
.xls	Excel 1997 file format, which is still used by some online downloads
.pdf	PDF file
.htm	Website file
.txt	Tab-delimited text data file, used to transfer records or tables of data from a database to Excel
.csv	Comma-delimited text data file, used to transfer records or tables of data from a database to Excel

To see an example of the power of Save As and file management, let's look at the steps to convert an Excel report to a report in PDF format:

1. In the Excel file Ch05-Excel365-StructureOfExcel.xlsx, click on the sheet named Power Pivot.
2. Press the F12 key to open the Save As dialog box.
3. On the left side of the Save As dialog box, in the file location area, select Desktop.
4. To create a new folder on the Desktop, press the keyboard shortcut Ctrl+Shift+N. As shown in Figure 5.17, a folder is created and ready to be named.

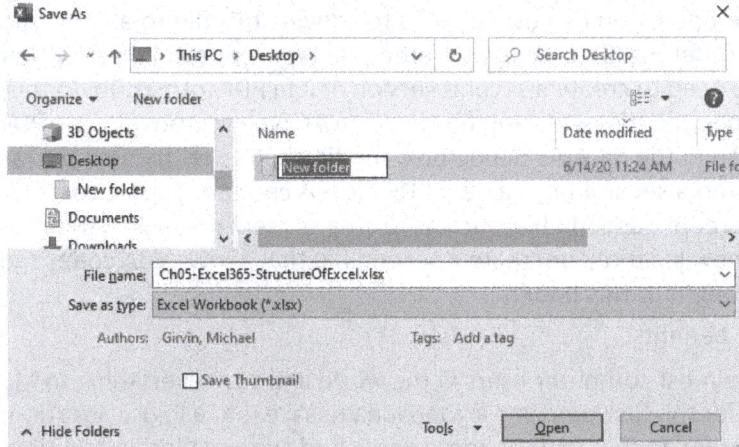

Figure 5.17 *You can create a new folder when you're using the Save As dialog box by using the keyboard shortcut Ctrl+Shift+N.*

5. Type the new name **Oakland Street Potholes Reports** in place of the highlighted text New Folder. (The reports you will save to this folder deal with unresolved potholes in the city of Oakland.)
6. Press Enter to save the folder name.
7. Press Enter a second time to open the folder.

8.   In the File Name textbox, as shown in Figure 5.18, type the name **Top 10 Number Potholes by Street**.

9.   From the Save As Type dropdown, select PDF (*.pdf).

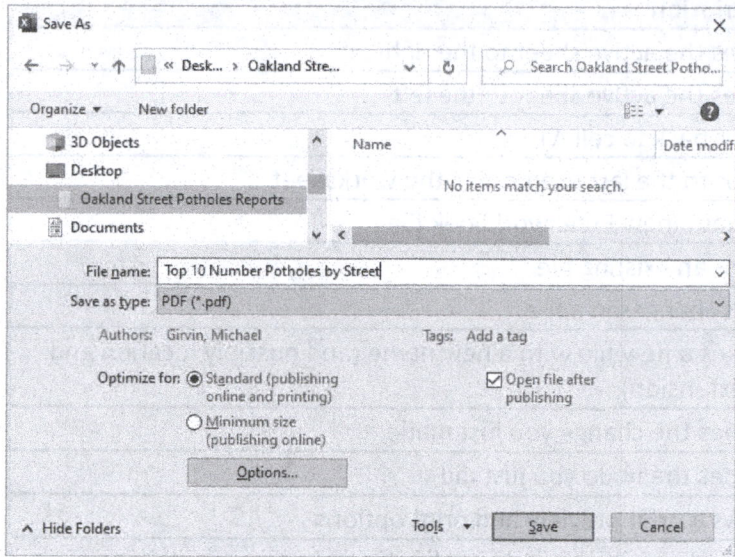

Figure 5.18 *Save As helps you manage files efficiently.*

10. Click OK. The Excel file remains in the original location, and the new PDF report is created in the correct location. Figure 5.19 shows the final PDF file.

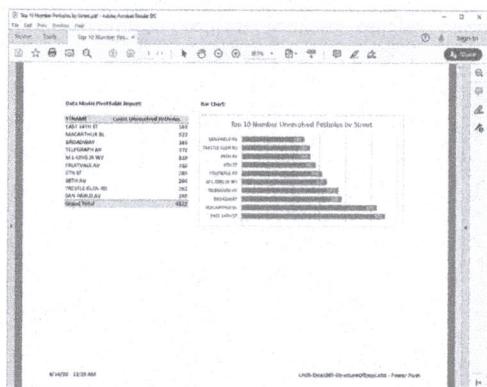

Figure 5.19 *This report, in PDF format, was created from within an Excel workbook file by using the F12 Save As command.*

Key Concepts in Chapter 5

- The Excel two-way grid is made up of **columns**, **rows**, and **cells**.

- All the cells make up a **worksheet**.

- All the worksheets and some other objects make up a **workbook** file.

- **Default alignment in cells** is key to understanding what type of data you have in a worksheet and helps you track down errors. By default, number values (including dates and times) are right-aligned. By default, text values are left-aligned. Logical vales and error values are centered and in all uppercase. Although empty cells are not values, you must be aware of them because they can cause problems in some datasets. When creating effective and efficient solutions in Excel, never change the default alignment in an Excel worksheet unless you have a final solution that needs a presentation that requires an alignment different than the default.

- The Excel command environment is made up of the **Ribbon tabs**, the customizable **QAT**, and the **Backstage view**.

- **File management** is an often-overlooked but important skill when creating solutions in Excel.

Keyboard Shortcuts Learned in Chapter 5

Keyboard Shortcut	Command	Description
Ctrl+PageDown		Moves the active sheet to the right
Ctrl+PageUp		Moves the active sheet to the left
Ctrl+Home		Jumps back to cell A1
Ctrl+End		Jumps to the last used cell in the worksheet
Ctrl+N	New	Creates a new Excel workbook file
Ctrl+O	Open	Opens an existing file
Ctrl+S	Save	Saves changes in a file
F12	Save As	Creates a new file with a new name (and possibly location and file extension)
Ctrl+Z	Undo	Undoes the change you just made
Ctrl+Y	Redo	Undoes the undo you just did
Ctrl+P	Print	Shows a print preview and print options
Alt+F4	Close	Closes the current Excel workbook
Ctrl+Shift+N		Creates a new folder in a file environment such as a Save As dialog box or Windows Explorer

Chapter 6: Keyboard Keys and Shortcuts

Note: To follow along with the examples in this chapter, you can use the file named Ch06-Excel365-Keyboards.xlsx.

If you want to create Excel solutions efficiently, the keyboard matters. On a computer without a number pad or function keys, it often takes longer to complete a task. If you are stuck with a laptop that has limited keys, you can still use Ribbon methods, right-click methods, and alternative keyboard shortcuts, but completing tasks can take longer than if you have access to all the keyboard options. When I get stuck working for extended periods on my laptop with limited keys, I plug in a standard keyboard so I can work more efficiently.

The standard keyboard, shown in Figure 6.1, has several areas that help you work more efficiently:

- The number pad helps you enter number data and some formulas more quickly.
- The navigation pad helps you navigate around in Excel with greater speed.
- The Right-click key and the Windows keys are sometimes useful for quick keyboard shortcuts.
- The function keys, or F keys, help you quickly invoke commands such as Save As.

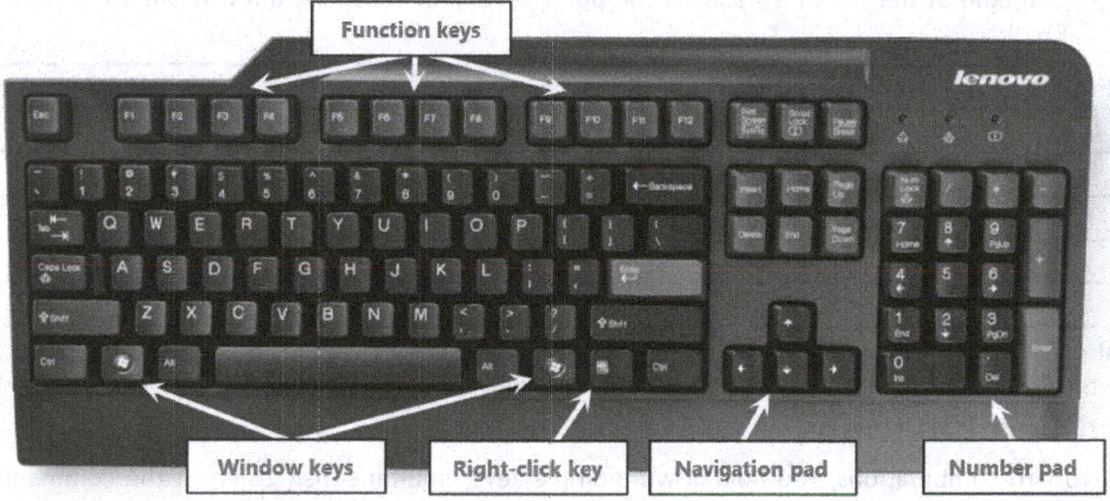

Figure 6.1 *A standard keyboard can help you create Excel solutions more quickly.*

Unfortunately, on some computers and laptops, you must us the Fn or Fx key to access the function keys (see Figure 6.2). With such keyboards, to invoke the Save As command, you must press Fn+F12 or Fx+F12. Because there are many useful function key keyboard shortcuts in Excel, it is wise to either change the default settings for this type of keyboard or avoid this type of keyboard altogether.

Fx key or Fn key must be used to access function keys

Figure 6.2 *Annoyingly, some keyboards require that you use the Fx or Fn button to access F keys.*

Keyboard Shortcuts

Keyboard shortcuts are very important in Excel. The fastest way to invoke many commands is by using keyboard shortcuts rather than by using the Ribbon or right-clicking. Using the scroll bar or your mouse to scroll down 500 rows to highlight your sales numbers for the SUM function could take a minute or more. Instead, you can use the keyboard shortcut Ctrl+Shift+DownArrow to make the same selection in less than a second. Keyboard shortcuts are important because they are fast—and because they are fast, you should use them as often as possible!

You will learn many keyboard shortcuts throughout the book, and you will see that they fall into three main categories:

- Function (or F) keys
- Keyboard combinations
- Alt (or succession) keyboard shortcuts

The following sections look more closely at these three categories.

Function (or F) Keys

The function keys appear at the top of a standard computer keyboard. These are a few of the most useful function keys in Excel:

Keyboard Shortcut	Description
F12	Saves as
F2	Puts a cell in edit mode
F4	Toggles between the different types of cell references in a formula
F7	Runs a spell check
F9	Evaluates formula elements

As you have already seen in this book, F keys can save you a lot of unneeded clicks. In addition to using the F12 key to invoke the Save As dialog box, you can use F7 to run a spell check (on text in a formula, for example).

Keyboard Combinations

With some keyboard combinations, you hold down multiple keys simultaneously to enact the command. These are a few of the most useful keyboard combinations in Excel:

Keyboard Shortcut	Description
Ctrl+C	Copies the selection
Ctrl+V	Pastes the selection
Ctrl+X	Cuts the selection
Ctrl+Shift+Arrow	Selects everything in the direction the arrow is pointing, stopping before the first empty cell
Alt+=	Inserts the SUM function into the cell
Fx+F12	Invokes Save As on a keyboard that requires the use of the Fx function key
Ctrl+Backspace	Jumps back to the active cell

Some keyboard shortcuts—such as those for copy, paste, cut, and undo—are faster than Ribbon and right-clicking methods, and they also work in a larger variety of areas. For example, in some textboxes, right-click and Ribbon methods do not work for the copy and paste commands, but the Ctrl+C and Ctrl+V work quickly and easily.

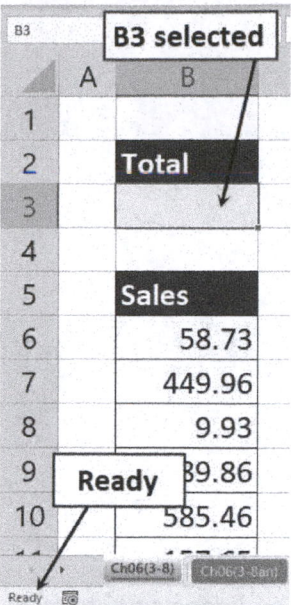

Figure 6.3 *Ready in the status bar indicates that Excel is ready for you to create a formula or enter data.*

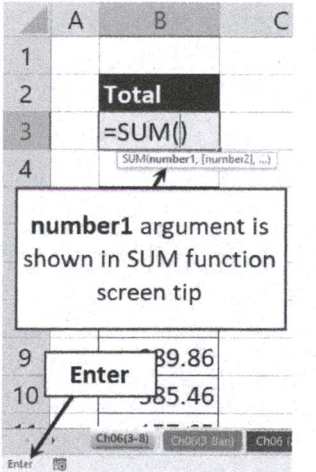

Figure 6.4 *Alt+= invokes the SUM function. Enter mode indicates that you can use arrow keys to select a range.*

As an example of the power of the keyboard combinations, let's look at an example of how to create an Excel formula to add a column of numbers using the SUM function:

1. Open the file Ch06-Excel365-Keyboards.xlsx.

2. As shown in Figure 6.3, select cell B3 on the worksheet named Ch06(3-8). When you select the cell, the status bar in the lower-left corner of the screen shows the word Ready. This is the mode of the cell and indicates that Excel is ready for you to enter a formula.

> **Note:** The *mode of a cell* is listed in the lower-left corner of the status bar. The four modes the status bar lists tell you what you can do with a formula. Ready indicates that the cell is selected and ready for you to enter text, a number, or a formula. Enter indicates that you can use arrow keys or the mouse to select a range or the keyboard to enter a formula. Point indicates that that you are using your arrow keys or mouse to select a range. Edit indicates that that the arrow keys will move the insertion point cursor from left to right in the formula. If you want to toggle between the modes, you can press the F2 key.

3. With cell B3 selected, use the keyboard shortcut Alt+= to invoke the SUM function. As shown in Figure 6.4, Excel enters the equal sign (required as the first character in the cell for any formula), the SUM function, and opening and closing parentheses. The cursor is flashing inside the parentheses, indicating that Excel is waiting for you to enter a range of cells. The SUM function screentip shows the boldfaced word **number1**, which is an argument (that is, an input area) in the function that expects numbers. In the lower-left corner of the status bar, the word Enter appears, indicating that you can enter a range of cells into the formula with either the arrow keys and keyboard shortcuts or the mouse and keyboard. The rule of thumb is that you should use your arrow keys and keyboard shortcuts if the cells that you want are close to the active cell (in this case, the cell that contains your formula); otherwise, you can use your mouse. Because in this case the sales numbers are close to the formula, you should use your arrow keys and keyboard shortcuts.

4. To select a range of cells, tap the DownArrow key three times to point to cell B6 (see Figure 6.5). Notice that the lower-left corner of the status bar says Point, which means you are selecting cells for your formula. Also notice that the selected cell, B6, has a dotted line (known as "dancing ants") moving around the outside edge of the cell. The dancing ants indicate that you are in Point mode and have the freedom to move the selected cell in any direction by using your arrow keys. This is important because if you go too far in one direction with your arrow keys, as long as the dancing ants are still moving and the status bar reads Point, you can just use arrow keys to get back to the correct location.

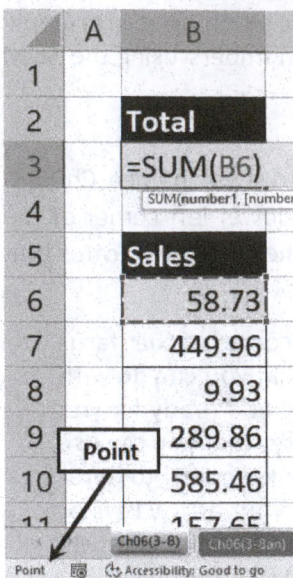

Figure 6.5 *When you are selecting cells for a formula, the status bar says Ready, and dancing ants move around the selected cell.*

5.   To select the whole range below cell B6 (499 rows in this case), use the keyboard shortcut Ctrl+Shift+DownArrow to nearly instantly highlight the range of cells (see Figure 6.6).

> **Note:** When you press Ctrl+Shift+DownArrow, Excel keeps selecting cells until it bumps into an empty cell, and it stops the selection process one cell before the empty cell.

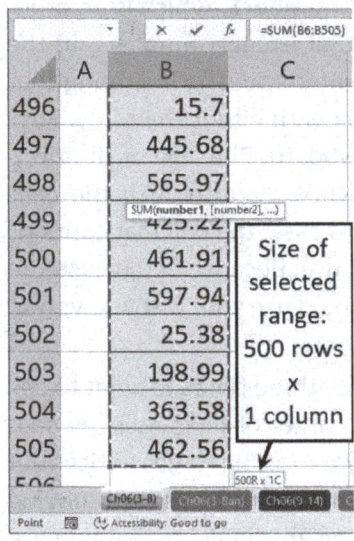

Figure 6.6 *Ctrl+Shift+DownArrow selects the full range lightning fast!*

6.   To jump back to the active cell that contains your formula, use the keyboard shortcut Ctrl+Backspace (see Figure 6.7).

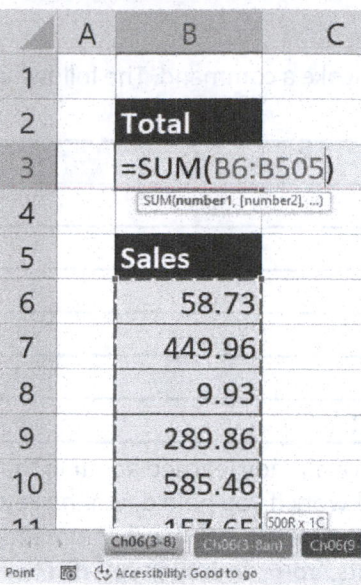

Figure 6.7 *Ctrl+Backspace jumps back to the active cell, which in this case is the cell containing the formula.*

7. With the cursor still in the active cell, B3, press Enter to enter the formula, calculate the result, and select cell B4 (see Figure 6.8).

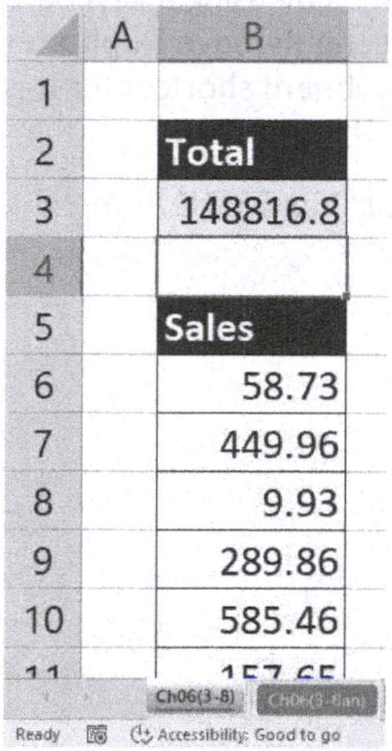

Figure 6.8 *When you use the Enter key with a formula, the formula is entered into the active cell, the formula calculates the result, and the cell below the cell containing the formula is selected.*

Here is an even faster way to accomplish the SUM function task you just completed:

1. Press Alt+=.

2. Press DownArrow three times.

3. Press Ctrl+Shift+DownArrow.

4. Press Shift+Enter.

The difference here is that, at the end, rather than use Ctrl+Backspace and then Enter (two clicks), you use Shift+Enter (one click), which puts the formula into the active cell and moves the cursor up one cell, to cell B2.

> **Note:** If you want to look at your formula in edit mode before officially entering it, you should use the two-step method Ctrl+Backspace and then Enter. Otherwise, you can use Shift+Enter, which is the fastest way to get from deep down in a worksheet and then put the formula in the active cell and jump up one cell.

Throughout this book, you will see many more amazing keyboard shortcuts that will save you a lot of time.

Alt (or Succession) Keyboard Shortcuts

With Alt (or succession) keyboard shortcuts, you tap each key in succession to invoke a command. The following are some Alt shortcuts that are commonly used in Excel:

Keyboard Shortcut	Description
Alt, N, V, T	Opens the Create PivotTable dialog box
Alt, P, S, P	Opens the Page Setup dialog box
Alt, A, M	Removes duplicates
Alt, A, D, M	Opens the Data Model
Right-click, B, V	Converts an Excel Table to a range
Alt, *number*	Invokes a particular command on the QAT

The Alt keyboard shortcuts are different from the keyboard combinations you've already learned about in that you must press each key, one after the other. These keyboard shortcuts will not work if you hold down the keys simultaneously, as you do with keyboard combinations. Alt keyboard shortcuts are essential. Most commands in Excel do not have keyboard combinations, but with Alt keyboard shortcuts, you can either self-discover what the keyboard sequence is by simply tapping the Alt key, or you can invent your own keyboard shortcuts by adding the commands to the QAT.

Let's look at the self-discovery process for Alt keyboard shortcuts. In the worksheet shown in Figure 6.9, the range D5:D13 is already selected. Say that your goal is to remove the duplicate names by using a keyboard shortcut. However, there is not a keyboard combination for this. If you know that the Remove Duplicates command is in the Data Ribbon tab, you can use the Alt key to teach yourself the keyboard shortcut for this feature. To see how this works, select the worksheet named Ch06(9-14) and follow these steps:

> **Note:** Before you try this, notice in Figure 6.9 that screentips do not appear anywhere in the ribbon at this point.

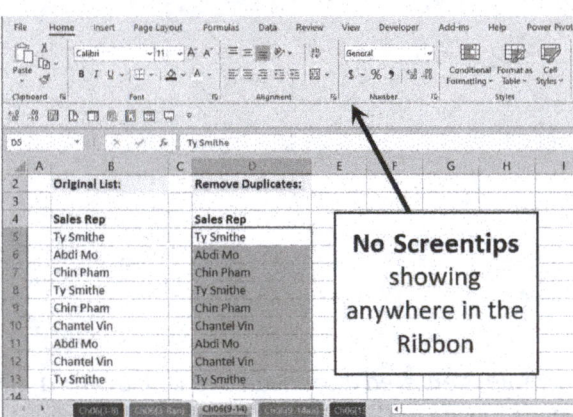

Figure 6.9 *Before you press the Alt key, the Ribbon shows no screentips anywhere.*

1. Press the Alt key and quickly let go. (Do not hold down the Alt key.) As you can see in Figure 6.10, black screentips show up all over the place. These screentips offer you a path to get to any of the ribbons and to enact commands that have been added to the QAT. In this case, you need to move to the Data Ribbon tab, so you look for the screentip for that tab and see that it is the letter A.

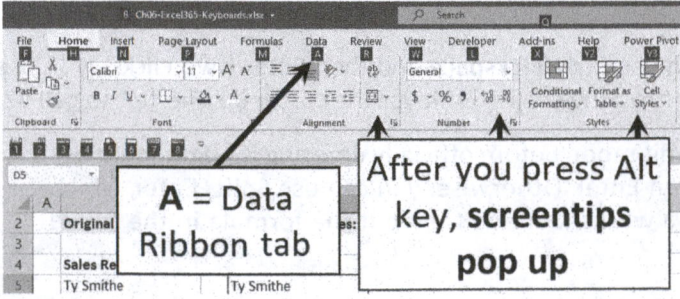

Figure 6.10 Press Alt to show the Alt keyboard screentips.

2. Press (and quickly release) the A key on the keyboard to jump to the Data Ribbon tab and to open up the screentips for the commands on this tab. As you can see in Figure 6.11, the letter M represents the Remove Duplicates feature.

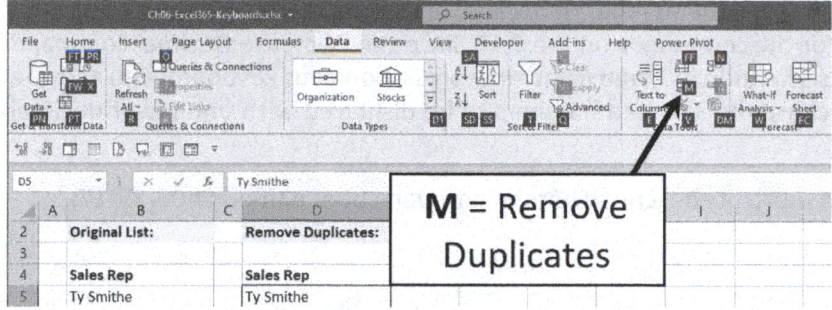

Figure 6.11 *When you arrive at the Data Ribbon tab, new screentips pop up for this tab's commands.*

3. Press (and quickly release) the M key on the keyboard to open the Remove Duplicates dialog box (see Figure 6.12).

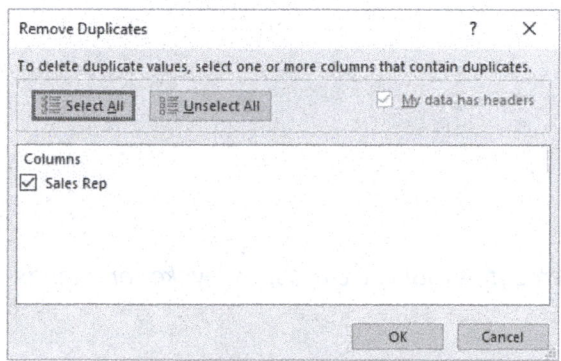

Figure 6.12 *Remove Duplicates dialog box.*

4. Verify that the column selected in the Remove Duplicates dialog box is the column that you want to use and click OK. Figures 6.13 and 6.14 show the results.

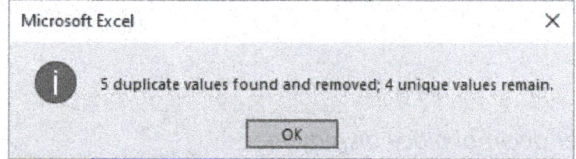

Figure 6.13 *This message appears to let you know how many duplicates were removed and how many unique values remain.*

Figure 6.14 *All that remains is a unique list of names.*

You can see from this example that you can figure out the keyboard shortcut for almost any command in the Ribbon tabs—and you should take advantage of this feature. You don't need or want to fill up your head with keyboard shortcuts for all the commands. Instead, learn and use the Alt keyboard shortcuts for the commands that you use often. If you use the Page Setup dialog box every day, for example, then take the time to learn the Alt keyboard shortcut to open that dialog box, and you will be able to complete your tasks more quickly.

For operations you do more infrequently, you can save the brain space for something else and rely on the self-discovery option Microsoft has so helpfully given you.

The Alt keyboard shortcuts work efficiently with a customized QAT. For example, as shown in Figure 6.15, if you highlight sales numbers that need to have the number of decimal places decreased, you can press (and release) the Alt key to see screentips for the commands on the QAT. Since the Decrease Decimal command is in the second position on the QAT, its screentip is 2, and if you now press 2 on your keyboard, you activate the Decrease Decimal command and cause the selected numbers to be displayed with one fewer decimal place showing (see Figure 6.16).

Note: You can try the Alt keyboard shortcuts described here on the worksheet named Ch06(15-17).

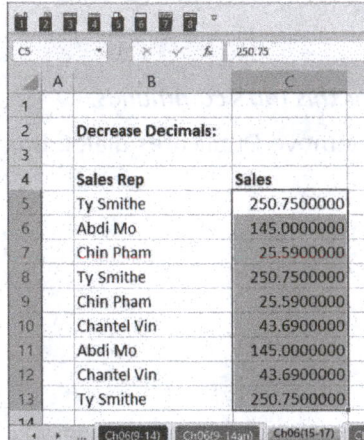

Figure 6.15 *When you press the Alt key, the QAT lists numeric screentips that you can use to invoke commands.*

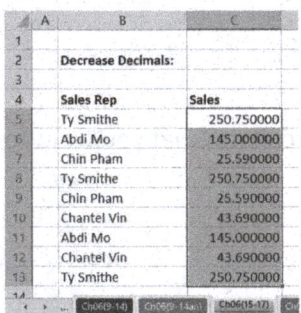

Figure 6.16 *Alt, 2 shows the selected numbers with one fewer decimal place displayed.*

Another great feature of the Alt keyboard shortcuts is that you can really easily repeat a command. For example, with the sales numbers selected, you can hold the Alt key down and then tap the 2 key four times in a row to show four fewer decimal places. Figure 6.17 shows the result of pressing Alt, 2, 2, 2, 2.

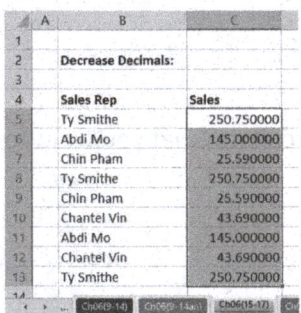

Figure 6.17 *Alt, 2, 2, 2, 2 shows the selected numbers with four fewer decimal places displayed.*

Key Concepts in Chapter 6

- **Keyboard shortcuts** help you work quickly and efficiently.
- The **function (or F) keys** are at the top of a standard computer keyboard.

- With a **keyboard combination (typically containing Ctrl+*key*)**, you must hold down the keys simultaneously to enact the command.
- The **Alt (or succession) keyboard shortcuts** require that you press (and release) each key in succession to invoke a command. Microsoft allows you to self-discover the keyboard shortcuts by simply pressing and releasing Alt.
- The **mode of a cell** is listed in the lower-left corner of the status bar. The four modes it lists—Ready, Enter, Point, and Edit—tell you what you can do with a formula.
- A moving dotted outline around a selected cell, referred to as **dancing ants**, indicates that you are free to edit and redirect the range if it is not correct.

Keyboard Shortcuts Learned in Chapter 6

Keyboard Shortcut	Description
F12	Saves as
F2	Puts a cell in edit mode
F4	Toggles between the different types of cell references in a formula
F7	Runs a spell check
F9	Evaluates formula elements
Ctrl+C	Copies the selection
Ctrl+V	Pastes the selection
Ctrl+X	Cuts the selection
Ctrl+Shift+Arrow	Selects everything in the direction the arrow is pointing, stopping before the first empty cell
Alt+=	Inserts the SUM function into the cell
Fx+F12	Invokes Save As on a keyboard that requires the use of the Fx function key
Ctrl+Backspace	Jumps back to the active cell
Shift+Enter	Puts content into the active cell and moves the selected cell up one row
Alt, N, V, T	Opens the Create PivotTable dialog box
Alt, N, V	Opens the Create PivotTable dialog box if you do not have a Power BI account or you are not logged in
Alt, P, S, P	Opens the Page Setup dialog box
Alt, A, M	Removes duplicates
Alt, A, D, M	Opens the Data Model
Right-click, B, V	Converts an Excel Table to a range
Alt, *number*	Invokes a particular command on the QAT

Chapter 7: Worksheet Efficiency Tricks

This chapter presents four sets of efficiency tricks that you will be using throughout this book:

- Using worksheet mouse cursors
- Entering content into cells with five different keyboard shortcuts
- Selecting a range of cells
- Jumping around in a worksheet

Using Worksheet Mouse Cursors

These are the mouse cursors you are most likely to see in worksheets:

Cursor	Cursor Name	Description
⊕	Selection cursor	Allows you to select a cell or range of cells in a worksheet or formula
Test 1	Move cursor	Allows you to move a cell or range of cells in a worksheet
Test 1	Fill handle	Allows you to increment data or copy cell contents such as text or formulas
✛	Crosshairs (angry rabbit) cursor	Allows you to grab the fill handle to increment data or copy cell contents
B ✛ C / Student Sioux Coolinator	Change column width cursor	Allows you to change the width of a column
✛	Change row height cursor	Allows you to change the height of a row
➡	Select row cursor	Allows you to select an entire row
⬇	Select column cursor	Allows you to select an entire column
↖	Select cursor	Allows you to select a command button or another object
I	I-beam cursor	Allows you to click in a cell that is in edit mode
S	Insertion point cursor	Shows the position where you can type when the cell is in edit mode

Note: Wondering how the crosshairs cursor got the nickname *angry rabbit cursor*? It is a play on the English word *crosshairs*: A "cross hare" is an *angry rabbit*.

Entering Content into Cells with Five Different Keyboard Shortcuts

How do you put cell content—whether a number, text, or a formula—into a cell? It depends on what your next task will be after you enter the cell content. These five keys and keyboard shortcuts are invaluable for putting content in a cell:

Key or Keyboard Shortcut	Description	When to Use It
Ctrl+Enter	Puts content into the active cell and keeps the active cell selected	When your goal is to put the content into the active cell and immediately do something to the active cell, like copy or format it
Enter	Puts the content into the active cell and moves the selected cell down one row	When your goal is to put the content into the active cell and immediately do something in the cell below, like enter more content
Shift+Enter	Puts the content into the active cell and moves the selected cell up one row	When your goal is to put the content into the active cell and move the selected cell up one row, such as when you need to enter a formula but the worksheet screen does not show the active cell
Tab	Puts the content into the active cell and moves the selected cell to the right by one column	When your goal is to put the content into the active cell and immediately do something in the cell to the right, like enter more content
Shift+Tab	Puts the content into active cell and moves the selected cell to the left by one column	When your goal is to put the content into the active cell and immediately do something in the cell to the left, like enter more content

Selecting a Range of Cells

When selecting a range of cells with no cell content, you use the mouse to click and drag the selection cursor. However, if the range of cells you want to select has cell content, then these three selection methods are faster than clicking and dragging with the selection cursor:

Keyboard Shortcut	Description	When to Use It
Ctrl+Shift+Arrow	Selects a range of cell content in the direction of the arrow and stops right before the first empty cell.	When you want to quickly highlight a column or row of cell content. If there is no content when you invoke this shortcut, the cursor jumps all the way to the edge of the worksheet.
Ctrl+* (on the number pad) or Ctrl+Shift+8 (using standard keys)	Selects the current region, which means everything in all directions from the active cell, to right before the first complete row or column of empty cells.	When you want to instantly select a whole table.
Shift+Arrow	Highlights one cell at a time in the direction of the arrow, incrementing slowly on each click of the arrow. The trick is to hold the Shift key and then tap the arrow key once for each cell that you want to select.	When you have a small selection to make within a larger block of cells.

Jumping Around in a Worksheet

If you need to instantly jump somewhere else in a worksheet, here are five fast ways to do so:

Keyboard Shortcut	Description	When to Use It
Ctrl+Home	Jumps the active cell to cell A1	When you want to jump to the very top of the worksheet
Ctrl+End	Jumps the active cell to the last cell used in the entire worksheet	When you want to jump to the very bottom of the work area
Ctrl+Arrow	Jumps the active cell to the last cell that contains content, in the direction of the arrow, up to right before the first empty cell	When you want to jump to the last bit of data in a row or a column
Ctrl+. (period)	Jumps the active cell to the next of the four corners in a selected range	When you want to navigate the four corners of a large table
Ctrl+Backspace	Jumps the screen back to the active cell, whether the active cell is in edit mode or the cell is just selected	When the active cell is offscreen but you need to instantly jump back to the active cell

Key Concepts in Chapter 7

- A number of **worksheet cursors** can bring great efficiency to your Excel tasks.
- There are five different ways to **enter content into a cell**. The method to use depends on the task you want to perform next.
- You can quickly **select cells** containing data by using keyboard shortcuts such as Ctrl+Shift+Arrow.
- The keyboard shortcuts for **jumping to other parts of a worksheet** help you navigate a worksheet quickly.

Chapter 8: Worksheet Formulas, Formatting, and Setup to Solve Problems

> **Note:** To follow along with the examples in this chapter, you can use the file named Ch08-Excel365-WorksheetSolution.xlsx.

Excel can make solving problems easy if you go about creating a solution in a smart way. For example, you might use Excel to do a math calculation, calculate grades for a set of students, chart the results of a survey, or make a sophisticated data model for reporting. The following guidelines will help you intelligently create solutions in Excel:

- List your goals for the project.
- Enter all the project inputs into the cells and label the inputs with informative names.
- If you have a table of data, make sure the dataset is in the proper structure.
- Create effective and efficient Excel solutions.
- Check your work.
- Document your work.
- Present results clearly.
- Use formatting and/or page setup to present your solution.

In this chapter, you will learn the basics of setting up problems in a worksheet and solving them by using worksheet formulas. As you do, you will see examples of how to follow these guidelines.

Creating a Sample Worksheet

Figure 8.1 shows a sample worksheet that presents a problem that is similar to the many problems you will see throughout this book. You can see that the requirements are as follows:

- You need to calculate the total test score and % grade for each student and sort the % grades from biggest to smallest.
- Because new data will be sent later, the solution must be able to accommodate new data.
- You need to create a PDF file from your solution.

In this chapter, you will create this project, starting with listing the goals that need to be accomplished. The list of goals will give you and any other users a clear direction and allow users to discern the intent of this Excel problem. that you can solve by using these guidelines.

Please calculate the total test scores for each student and their percentage grade.					
New student names and test scores will be sent later.					
Also, please send PDF file with results, sorted biggest to smallest by % grade.					
Sioux Coolinator	Test 1 = 75.4	Test 2 = 95.2	Test 3 = 85.0	Test 4 = 73.7	Test 5 = 97.0
Chantel Williams	Test 1 = 83.0	Test 2 = 92.0	Test 3 = 96.7	Test 4 = 89.8	Test 5 = 93.7
Miki Yu	Test 1 = 77.0	Test 2 = 68.6	Test 3 = 81.4	Test 4 = 69.9	Test 5 = 75.0
Tyrone Zion	Test 1 = 96.3	Test 2 = 81.2	Test 3 = 93.3	Test 4 = 86.0	Test 5 = 98.5

Figure 8.1 *Goals: Calculate total scores, ensure that the solution accommodates new data, and create a PDF file.*

> **Note:** A bonus of creating this project is that it will give you practice working in Excel and creating a worksheet!

To begin creating a solution in Excel, follow these steps:

1. Open the file named Ch08-Excel365-WorksheetSolution.xlsx.
2. Click on the worksheet named Ch08 (1). As you can see in Figure 8.2, when you select the worksheet, cell A1 is selected and is the active cell; you know this because A and 1 are both green, and there's

a green border around the cell. Using your mouse, hover over cell B2 until you see the selection cursor, as also shown in Figure 8.2.

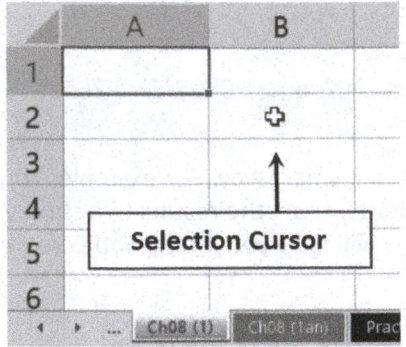

Figure 8.2 *The selection cursor is hovering over cell B2.*

3.   With the selection cursor, click cell B2 to make cell B2 the active cell (see Figure 8.3).

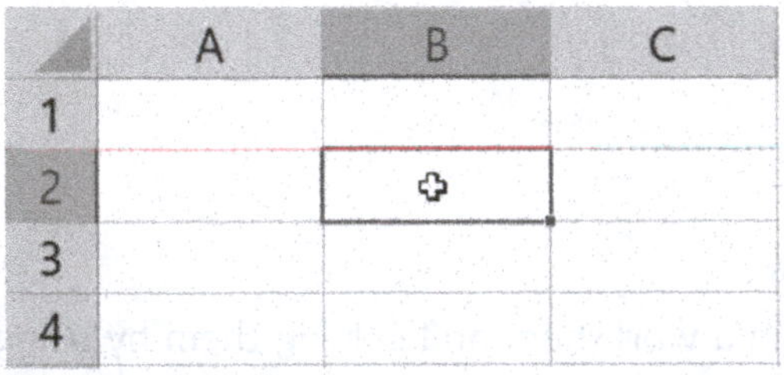

Figure 8.3 *Using the selection cursor, you can select cell B2.*

4.   Type the text **Goals of Project:** in the selected cell B2. As soon as you start typing in the cell, the insertion point cursor starts flashing at the end of the text, as shown in Figure 8.4.

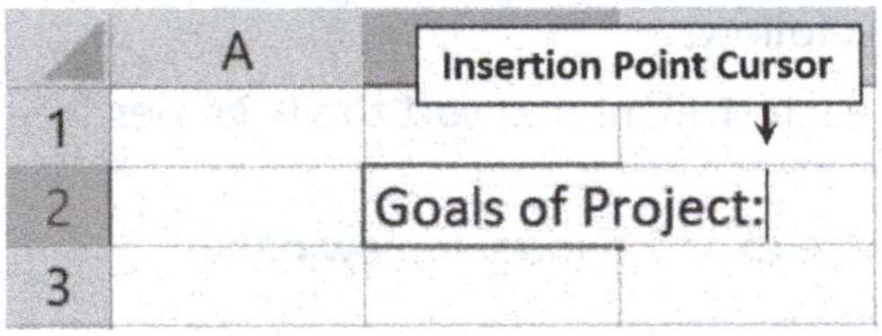

Figure 8.4 *When you start typing in a cell, the insertion point cursor flashes at the end of the text.*

> **Note:** In this case, you will immediately add boldface to the text **Goals of Project:** that you've entered in cell B2. To save a click, you can press Ctrl+Enter rather than just Enter to enter the cell content. Ctrl+Enter puts the content into the active cell and keeps the cell selected. If you use just press the Enter key (as most Excel users in the world do), you will have to then click back on cell B2 to add the bold formatting. Even though using Ctrl+Enter in this case only saves one click, over your lifetime in Excel, it will save you a profound amount of time.

5.   Press Ctrl+Enter. Figure 8.5 shows that the text is entered in cell B2, and cell B2 is selected.

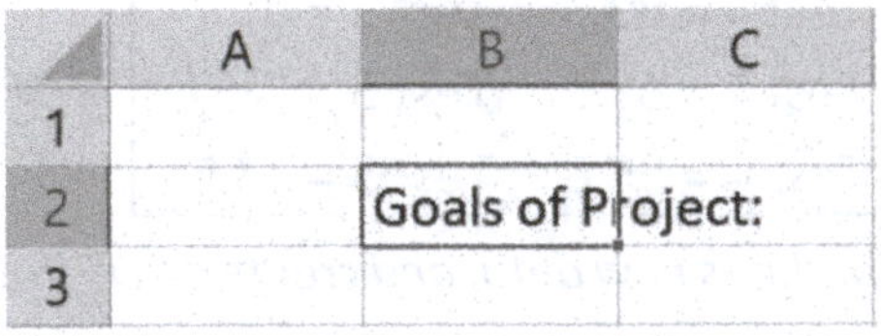

Figure 8.5 *Press Ctrl+Enter to put the text into the active cell and keep the cell selected.*

6.   Either use the Home tab of the Excel Ribbon, as shown in Figure 8.6, to click the Bold button to apply bold style format or use the (much faster) keyboard shortcut for bold font: Ctrl+B.

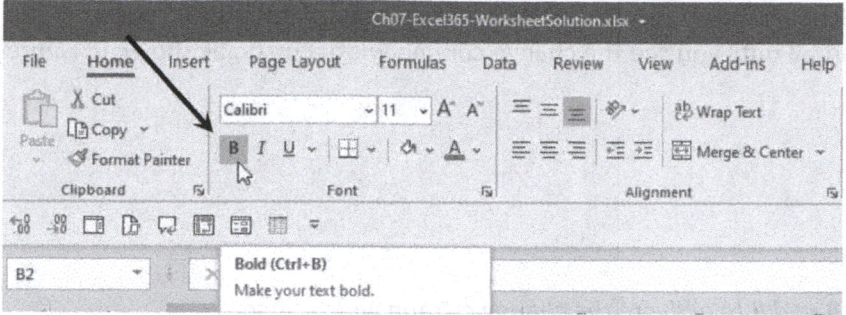

Figure 8.6 *Style formatting options are available in the Font and Alignment groups in the Home tab of the Ribbon.*

Figure 8.7 shows the result.

Note: Why do you need to add the style format bold to the label for the list of goals? The bold visually emphasizes the label at the top of the three lines of text to inform anyone who looks at this worksheet that the text represents the goals. This is a small and seemingly unimportant detail, but if you are consistent about details such as this when you build solutions, your results will be more effective and efficient.

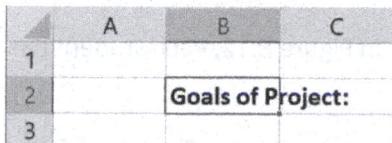

Figure 8.7 *Ctrl+B adds bold font.*

7. Because your next task is to enter your goals for the project in a vertical column, press Enter to move to cell B3 (see Figure 8.8).

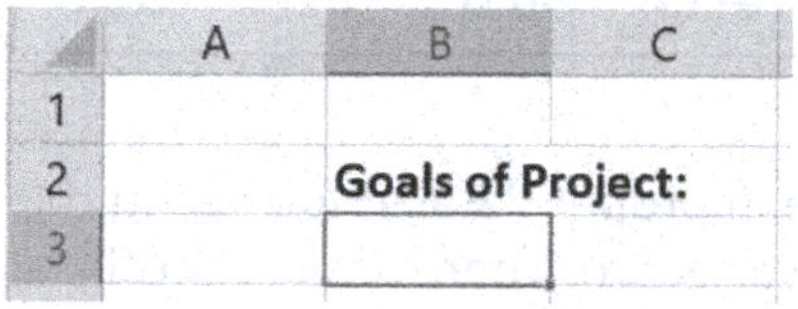

	A	B	C
1			
2		Goals of Project:	
3			

Figure 8.8 *Press Enter to move the selected cell down so you can enter content into cell B3.*

8. In cell B3, type the goal **Calculate total test score and % grade for each student. Sort the % grades from biggest to smallest.** Press Enter to enter the text in cell B3 and to move to cell B4.

9. In cell B4, type the goal **Because new data will be sent later, the solution must be able to accommodate new data.** Press Enter to enter the text in cell B4 and move to cell B5.

10. In cell B5, type the goal **Need to create a PDF file from our solution.** Press Enter to enter the text in cell B5 and to move to cell B6.

Figure 8.9 shows these goals entered in the worksheet.

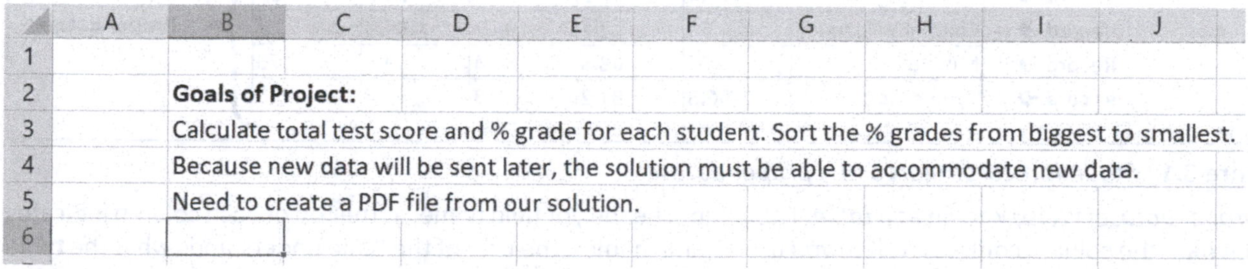

	A	B	C	D	E	F	G	H	I	J
1										
2		Goals of Project:								
3		Calculate total test score and % grade for each student. Sort the % grades from biggest to smallest.								
4		Because new data will be sent later, the solution must be able to accommodate new data.								
5		Need to create a PDF file from our solution.								
6										

Figure 8.9 *These are the goals of the project.*

Note: Any time you enter data vertically into a column, it is better to use the Enter key than the DownArrow key to enter content in a cell. Although the DownArrow key *could* work to move down when entering data, the arrow keys have unique behavior when you're entering formulas, so you want to try to not use them when entering cell content. You don't want to get into a habit that might cause problems in some situations.

11. To change the width of column A, move your cursor to the right side of column A, hovering the cursor between columns A and B until you see the change column width cursor, as shown in Figure 8.10.

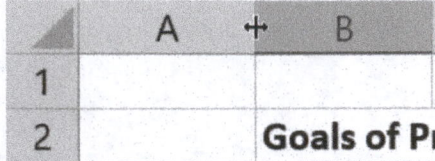

Figure 8.10 *Hover between columns A and B to activate the change column width cursor.*

12. Click and drag to change the column width, as shown in Figure 8.11.

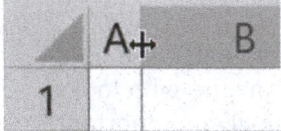

Figure 8.11 *Click and drag with the change column width cursor to resize the column.*

Using the Proper Dataset Format

Next, you need to enter the student data into the worksheet. As you can see in Figure 8.12, each student has five test scores. However, this data is not in the proper dataset format.

Sioux Coolinator:	Test 1 = 75.4	Test 2 = 95.2	Test 3 = 85.0	Test 4 = 73.7	Test 5 = 97.0
Chantel Williams:	Test 1 = 83.0	Test 2 = 92.0	Test 3 = 96.7	Test 4 = 89.8	Test 5 = 93.7
Miki Yu:	Test 1 = 77.0	Test 2 = 68.6	Test 3 = 81.4	Test 4 = 69.9	Test 5 = 75.0
Tyrone Zion:	Test 1 = 96.3	Test 2 = 81.2	Test 3 = 93.3	Test 4 = 86.0	Test 5 = 83.8

Figure 8.12 *The raw data is not in the proper dataset format.*

If you are planning to do data analysis on records of data, the data must be in proper dataset format. In this example, each student has a set of test scores, and those scores constitute a record. There are a few official rules for creating a proper dataset:

- Field names must appear in the first row.
- Records must appear in subsequent rows.
- The dataset must be surrounded by empty cells (or worksheet row headers [numbers] or column headers [letters]).

Figure 8.13 shows the student records stored in proper dataset format.

	Student	Test 1	Test 2	Test 3	Test 4	Test 5	
Field names in first row →	Student	Test 1	Test 2	Test 3	Test 4	Test 5	
Record →	Sioux Coolinator	75.4	95.2	85	73.7	97	
Record →	Chantel Williams	83	92	96.7	89.8	93.7	Proper dataset
Record →	Miki Yu	77	68.6	81.4	69.9	75	
Record →	Tyrone Zion	96.3	81.2	93.3	86	83.8	

Figure 8.13 *Student records stored in a proper dataset.*

A *proper dataset* is also known as a *table*. The column header, or field name, at the top of each column indicates what data the column contains. When you use column names, the user of the table understands what the table contains. In this dataset, for example, it is clear that student names are listed in the column named Student, the scores on Test 1 are listed in the column named Test 1, and so on. There is also an implied data type for each column, so that text values go in the Student column, and number values go in the remaining columns.

Each row in a proper dataset is called a *record*. In the student data table, each row contains a record showing a student's test scores.

Proper datasets you are important for stored data for three reasons:

- They help you avoid repetition. For example, in this example, each test field name is listed only once.
- They enable you to easily make calculations, perform data analysis, and create formulas. For example, in this example, you can easily add the scores and calculate the % grade.
- Many of the tools and features in Excel (such as PivotTables, filtering, Power Query, and Power Pivot) require proper datasets.

To create the proper dataset within the sample worksheet, follow these steps:

1. To begin entering field names, select cell B7 and type the text **Student** (see Figure 8.14). Then press Tab to enter the text and select cell C7.

   Note: Because your next task is to enter text into cell C7 (which is the cell to the right of B7), you press the Tab key rather than the Enter key to put the content into the cell.

	A	B	C	D
6				
7		Student		

Figure 8.14 *Type* **Student** *in cell B7 and then press Tab.*

2. With cell C7 selected, type the text **Test 1**, as shown in Figure 8.15. Press Ctrl+Enter to enter the text into the active cell and keep the cell selected.

   Note: In this case, you use Ctrl+Enter because your next task is to copy the contents of cell C7.

	A	B	C	D
6				
7		Student	Test 1	

Figure 8.15 *Type* **Test 1** *into cell C7 and then press Ctrl+Enter.*

Figure 8.16 shows that cell C7 is selected, and the text has been entered.

	A	B	C	D
6				
7		Student	Test 1	

Figure 8.16 *The cell remains selected after you enter the text because you pressed Ctrl+Enter.*

3. Take a closer look at the selected cell, cell C7, and notice that there is small green box in the lower-right corner (see Figure 8.17). This small green box, called the *fill handle*, allows you to use your *crosshairs cursor*, also known as the *angry rabbit cursor*, to quickly copy the contents of cells and to increment alphanumeric values (that is, text values that contain numbers). In this case, you need to increment the alphanumeric value Test 1 so that you get Test 2, Test 3, and so on.

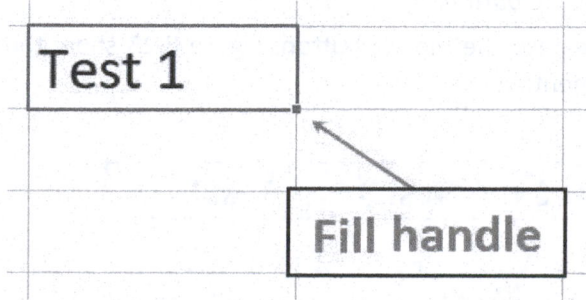

Figure 8.17 *The fill handle can do many magical things!*

4.   To increment the value Test 1, hover your cursor over the fill handle until the cursor changes to the angry rabbit cursor, as shown in Figure 8.18.

6		
7	Student	Test 1
8		

Figure 8.18 *The angry rabbit cursor allows you to grab the fill handle and increment the alphanumeric value.*

Note: In this case, you do not want to use the move cursor, shown in Figure 8.19, because it would move the cell instead of incrementing it. You also do not want to use the selection cursor, shown in Figure 8.20, because it would select the cell instead of incrementing it.

6		
7	Student	Test 1
8		

Figure 8.19 *Be careful not to accidentally use the move cursor.*

6		
7	Student	Test 1
8		

Figure 8.20 *Be careful not to accidentally use the selection cursor.*

5.   With the angry rabbit cursor, click on the fill handle to grab it and then click and drag to the right, as shown in Figures 8.21 and 8.22.

6			
7	Student	Test 1	
8			Test 2

Figure 8.21 *When you use the angry rabbit cursor, the screentip shows how far you have incremented.*

6					
7	Student	Test 1			
8				Test 5	

Figure 8.22 *When the screentip reads Test 5, release the mouse button.*

6.   Watch the screentip, and when it reads Test 5, release the mouse button. Figure 8.23 show the happy result of this efficient mouse trick for incrementing.

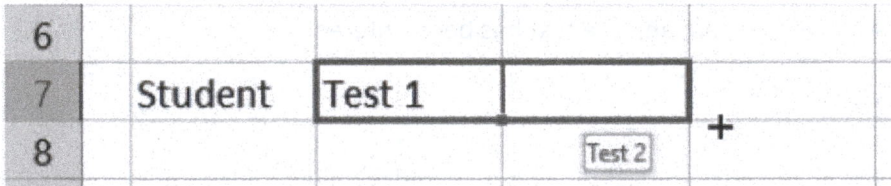

6						
7	Student	Test 1	Test 2	Test 3	Test 4	Test 5
8						

Figure 8.23 *Using the angry rabbit cursor and the fill handle is much faster than typing in all the column heads.*

Note: Any time you want to increment alphanumeric values, such as week, quiz, or group numbers, you can use the angry rabbit cursor to quickly create the values. You will see many more magical efficiency tricks that this angry rabbit cursor can perform throughout this book.

7. Go to the vertical scroll bar on the right side of the worksheet and click the down scroll arrow five times so that the first row showing is row 6 (see Figure 8.24).

8. As shown in Figure 8.24, type the text **Total Scores** in cell H7 and type the student names into the range B8:B11.

	A	B	C	D	E	F	G	H
6								
7		Student	Test 1	Test 2	Test 3	Test 4	Test 5	Total Scores
8		Sioux Coolinator						
9		Chantel Williams						
10		Miki Yu						
11		Tyrone Zion						
12								

Figure 8.24 *Type the label* **Total Scores** *and the student names.*

9. With the change column width cursor, change the width of columns B and H so they more comfortably hold their text (see Figure 8.25).

	A	B	C	D	E	F	G	H
6								
7		Student	Test 1	Test 2	Test 3	Test 4	Test 5	Total Scores
8		Sioux Coolinator						
9		Chantel Williams						
10		Miki Yu						
11		Tyrone Zion						

Figure 8.25 *Adjust the widths of columns B and H.*

10. Select cell H7 and press Ctrl+* on the number pad or Ctrl+Shift+8 on the standard keyboard to select the entire table (see Figure 8.26). Either keyboard shortcut works here as long as you have a cell with content inside the table selected. The command moves in all directions until it finds completely empty rows and columns, and then it knows to stop selecting.

Note: If you start with cell H10 in this example, the shortcuts will not work because although the selected cell is in the table, there is no data from the table directly surrounding cell H10.

	A	B	C	D	E	F	G	H
6								
7		Student	Test 1	Test 2	Test 3	Test 4	Test 5	Total Scores
8		Sioux Coolinator						
9		Chantel Williams						
10		Miki Yu						
11		Tyrone Zion						

Figure 8.26 *The keyboard shortcut to select the entire table is Ctrl+* on the number pad or Ctrl+Shift+8 on the standard keyboard.*

11. Now that the table is selected, in the Home tab of the Ribbon, in the Font group, you can click the Borders dropdown arrow and then click on All Borders, as shown in Figure 8.27. Figure 8.28 shows the result.

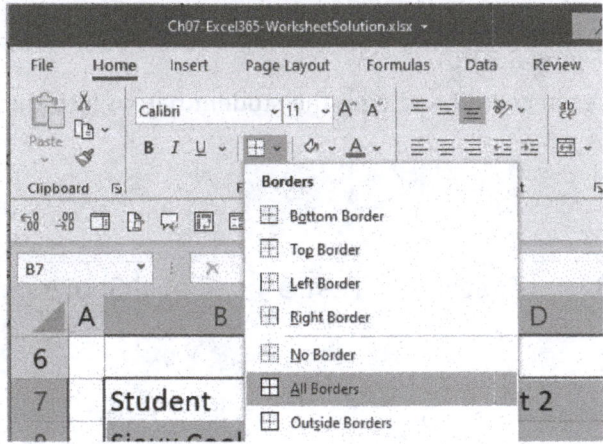

Figure 8.27 *The All Borders command adds black borders around each cell.*

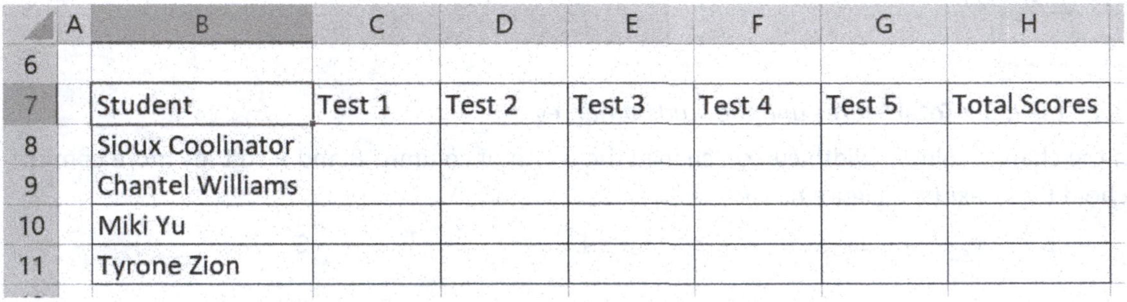

	A	B	C	D	E	F	G	H
6								
7	Student		Test 1	Test 2	Test 3	Test 4	Test 5	Total Scores
8	Sioux Coolinator							
9	Chantel Williams							
10	Miki Yu							
11	Tyrone Zion							

Figure 8.28 *You can add black borders to emphasize that the table is one object.*

Adding Style Formatting

Style formatting consists of cell formatting commands such as bold font, cell borders, cell fill color, and font color, as well as other types of formatting. When you add formatting to a worksheet solution, you want to do so in a way that helps add clarity in communicating how you solved the problem and the results.

Three important concepts can help you to create formatting that communicates effectively:

- Make sure the value difference between the fill color and font color is big enough that the viewer can read the worksheet and the printed results easily. For example, dark blue fill color and white font is easy to read, but red fill color and black font color is not easy to read.

- Add bold font to important elements, like field names. If you like the minimalist spreadsheet look, you do not have to use fill color and font color, but emphasizing important elements with bold helps them stand out.

- Be consistent: Pick a formatting style and stick with it. Consistency makes your Excel solutions easier for users to understand.

For the proper dataset in the student test scores example, you want to make sure that anyone looking at the table can differentiate between field names, raw data, and cells containing formulas. In this example, you will use the following formats for the various elements of the proper dataset:

- **Field names:** Dark blue fill color, white font color, and bold font
- **Records containing raw data:** No fill color, font color, or alignment
- **Cells containing formulas:** Light green fill color

One easy way to add formatting in Excel is to use the mini toolbar, which pops up when you right-click a cell or range of cells in a worksheet. The mini toolbar, shown in Figure 8.29, includes common formatting commands.

Mini Toolbar
Calibri
11
Cut

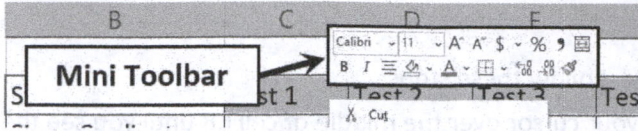

Figure 8.29 *Right-click a cell or range of cells to open the mini toolbar.*

To use the mini toolbar to add formatting to the field names for the student score table in the sample worksheet, follow these steps:

1. Click in cell B7 and then press Ctrl+Shift+RightArrow to select all the filed names. This keyboard shortcut selects all the cells with content in the direction of the arrow (in this case, right) and stops directly before the first empty cell (see Figure 8.30).

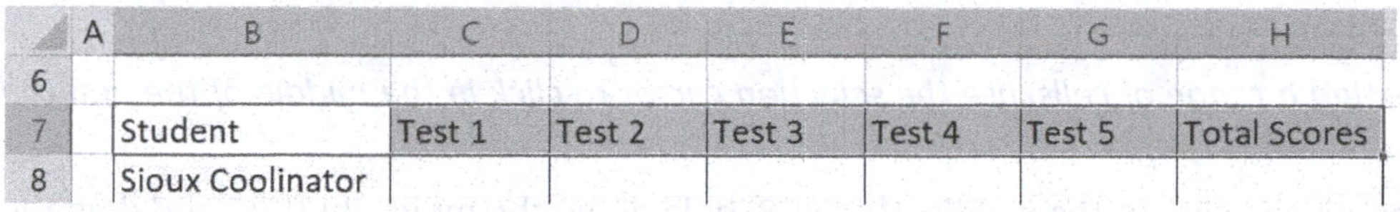

A
B
C
D
E
F
G
H
6
7
Student
Test 1
Test 2
Test 3
Test 4
Test 5
Total Scores
8
Sioux Coolinator

Figure 8.30 *Use the Ctrl+Shift+RightArrow keyboard shortcut to select all the field names.*

2. Right-click anywhere in the selected range to open the mini toolbar.
3. Using the Fill Color dropdown arrow, select Dark Blue, as shown in Figure 8.31.

Calibri
11
Theme Colors
Standard Colors
Recent Colors
Dark Blue

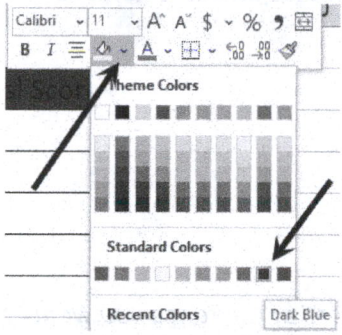

Figure 8.31 *By selecting a fill color, you can fill a selected cell with color.*

4. Using the Font Color dropdown arrow, select White, as shown in Figure 8.32.

Calibri
11
Test 1
Automatic
Theme Colors
White, Background 1

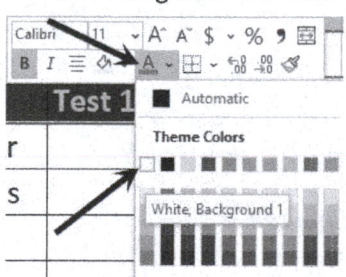

Figure 8.32 *The Font Color dropdown allows you to add color to selected characters.*

5. Press Ctrl+B to add bold to the selected range.

   Figure 8.33 shows the formatted field names.

A
B
C
D
E
F
G
H
6
7
Student
Test 1
Test 2
Test 3
Test 4
Test 5
Total Scores
8
Sioux Coolinator
9
Chantel Williams

Figure 8.33 *Formatted field names.*

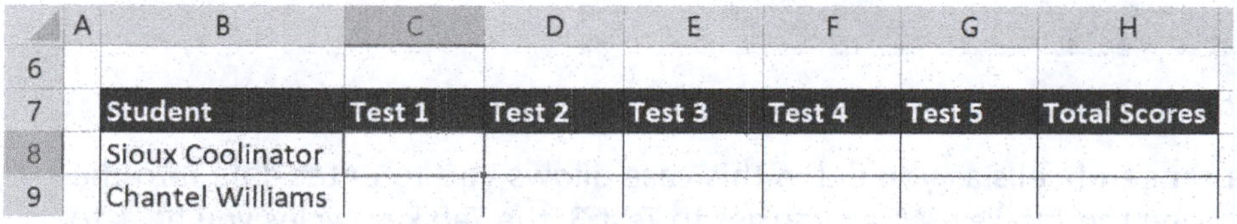

Entering the Data

Next, you need to enter the test score data in the table. Follow these steps:

1. To select the range C8:G11, begin by hovering your cursor over the middle of cell C8 until you see the selection cursor, as shown in Figure 8.34.

	A	B	C	D	E	F	G	H
6								
7		Student	Test 1	Test 2	Test 3	Test 4	Test 5	Total Scores
8		Sioux Coolinator	⊕					
9		Chantel Williams						
10		Miki Yu						
11		Tyrone Zion						

Figure 8.34 *To begin selecting a range of cells, use the selection cursor to click in the middle of the first cell in the range.*

2. With the selection cursor, click in the middle of cell C8, hold down the mouse button, and drag the mouse toward cell G11. Figures 8.34 to 8.37 show the path made by the slow glide of the mouse as you select from cell C8 to cell G11.

Note: The key to selecting a range with your mouse is to hold down the mouse button and make sure you can see the selection cursor throughout the whole movement.

	A	B	C	D	E	F	G	H
6								
7		Student	Test 1	Test 2	Test 3	Test 4	Test 5	Total Scores
8		Sioux Coolinator						
9		Chantel Williams		⊕				
10		Miki Yu						
11		Tyrone Zion						

Figure 8.35 *Holding down the mouse button, drag your mouse toward the last cell of the range you want to select.*

	A	B	C	D	E	F	G	H
6								
7		Student	Test 1	Test 2	Test 3	Test 4	Test 5	Total Scores
8		Sioux Coolinator						
9		Chantel Williams						
10		Miki Yu				⊕		
11		Tyrone Zion						

Figure 8.36 *As you drag your mouse, the selection cursor leads the way to the final cell.*

	A	B	C	D	E	F	G	H
6								
7		Student	Test 1	Test 2	Test 3	Test 4	Test 5	Total Scores
8		Sioux Coolinator						
9		Chantel Williams						
10		Miki Yu						
11		Tyrone Zion					⊕	

Figure 8.37 *When you reach the last cell, let go of the mouse. The range C8:G11 is now selected.*

Note: Pre-highlighting a range of cells as you did in this case allows you to enter data into the row for each student by using the Tab key. When you get to Test 5, the Tab key cycles you back to Test 1 for the next student, in the row below. If you need to go backward—that is, from right to left—you can use the keyboard shortcut Shift+Tab. Also, because you began the selection process in cell C8, that cell is the active cell (the non-shaded cell in the upper-left corner), and you can begin there, entering the Test 1 score for the first student.

3. To enter the test scores for the first student, Sioux Coolinator, in the active cell, type **75.4**, as shown in Figure 8.38. Then press the Tab key to enter this value into cell C8 and move to cell D8.

	A	B	C	D	E	F	G
6							
7		Student	Test 1	Test 2	Test 3	Test 4	Test 5
8		Sioux Coolinator	75.4				
9		Chantel Williams					
10		Miki Yu					
11		Tyrone Zion					

Figure 8.38 *Type a test score and then press the Tab key to enter the content and move to the right.*

4. Type the test score **95.2** and press Tab, as shown in Figure 8.39.

	A	B	C	D	E	F	G
6							
7		Student	Test 1	Test 2	Test 3	Test 4	Test 5
8		Sioux Coolinator	75.4	95.2			
9		Chantel Williams					
10		Miki Yu					
11		Tyrone Zion					

Figure 8.39 *Type another test score and press Tab.*

5. Using Figure 8.40 as a guide, type the remaining scores for Sioux Coolinator, using the Tab key to enter each score. When you get to Test 5, press the Tab key to move from cell G8 to cell C9.

	A	B	C	D	E	F	G
6							
7		Student	Test 1	Test 2	Test 3	Test 4	Test 5
8		Sioux Coolinator	75.4	95.2	85	73.7	97
9		Chantel Williams					
10		Miki Yu					
11		Tyrone Zion					

Figure 8.40 *When you reach the last column in the selected range, Tab moves you to the next row.*

Figure 8.41 shows that when you use the Tab key, after entering the Test 5 score for Sioux Coolinator, the active cell moves to the first score for the next student.

	A	B	C	D	E	F	G
6							
7		Student	Test 1	Test 2	Test 3	Test 4	Test 5
8		Sioux Coolinator	75.4	95.2	85	73.7	97
9		Chantel Williams					
10		Miki Yu					
11		Tyrone Zion					

Figure 8.41 *After pressing Tab to enter the score for Test 5, you are ready to enter data for the next student.*

6. Using Figure 8.42 as a guide, type the remaining test scores in the selected range. Press Tab to move forward and Shift+Tab to move backward. When you are done entering scores, select cell H8.

	A	B	C	D	E	F	G	H
6								
7		Student	Test 1	Test 2	Test 3	Test 4	Test 5	Total Scores
8		Sioux Coolinator	75.4	95.2	85	73.7	97	
9		Chantel Williams	83	92	96.7	89.8	93.7	
10		Miki Yu	77	68.6	81.4	69.9	75	
11		Tyrone Zion	96.3	81.2	93.3	86	83.8	

Figure 8.42 *After you enter all the student test scores, click in cell H8.*

Using Worksheet Formulas, Functions, Cell References, and Aggregate Operations

Now that you have created the goals and the table in the worksheet, the next task is to sum the scores for each student. To do this, you need to create a worksheet formula that adds many numbers quickly and that updates if any of the scores change.

A worksheet formula starts with an equal sign as the first character in the cell and can contain various formula elements, such as cell references, worksheet functions, and math operators, and it has a direct connection to the cell references—and therefore to the source data—so that when the source data changes, the formula result updates instantly. Worksheet formulas can deliver number results, text results, and other types of results. A worksheet formula can include a variety of elements. Before you begin creating formulas, you need to understand the following important terms and concepts:

- **Equal signs:** Every worksheet formula starts with an equal sign. An equal sign as the first character in a cell signals to Excel that you are making a worksheet formula.

- **Worksheet functions:** Built-in function like SUM, AVERAGE, and PMT are programmed to make defined calculations based on the formula inputs entered into the function's arguments. There are more than 450 built-in Excel worksheet functions. The worksheet function SUM, which you will use next, is programmed to add numbers and perform an aggregate operation to deliver a single answer.

- **Parentheses:** All worksheet functions require open and close parentheses. They indicate the start and end areas where you put the formula inputs into the function arguments.

- **Ranges:** The terms *range*, *range of cells*, *range reference*, and *cell reference* are all synonyms for two or more cells separated by a colon. For the range C8:G8, C8 is the start cell, and G8 is the end cell. All the cells between the start cell and the end cell are included in the range.

- **Cell references:** When cell references are used in worksheet formulas, the formulas instantly update when source data changes. Cell references are unique to worksheet formulas and do not exist with other Excel features, such as PivotTables and Power Query.

- **Aggregate operations:** An aggregate calculation is a calculation that takes many items in a dataset and delivers a single result that represents the underlying data, such as a sum to get the total or an arithmetic mean to get the average. The single result represents the entire dataset.

- **Array operations:** An array operation (which you will learn about later in this chapter), unlike an aggregate operation, takes many items from a dataset and delivers an array of results.

In the formula you will be creating shortly, you will be using the math operator for division. Excel provides a number of other math operators for Excel worksheets (see Table 8.1).

Table 8.1 Excel Math Operators for Use in Worksheet Formulas

Operator	Description	Operator	Description
+	Addition	/	Division
-	Subtraction or negation	^	Power, or raising to an exponent
*	Multiplication	( )	Parentheses, for grouping

To sum the scores for each student in the sample worksheet, you need a formula that adds numbers quickly and updates if any of the scores change. You need to enter this formula into cell H8 and then copy it down the column. Follow these steps:

1. Select cell H8. Then use the keyboard shortcut Alt+= (equal sign) to add the SUM function. In Figure 8.43, you can see that the keyboard shortcut Alt+= automatically creates the formula and inserts all the correct formula elements: an equal sign at the beginning of the formula, the SUM function, open and close parentheses, and the range of cells, C8:G8. In Figure 8.43, the screentip below the function lists the function name, SUM, and the open and close parentheses, which surround the function arguments. The screentip indicates that *function arguments*, such as *number1*, are required inputs for the function to make a calculation. As you can see, Excel inserts the range C8:G8 into the SUM function as argument *number1*.

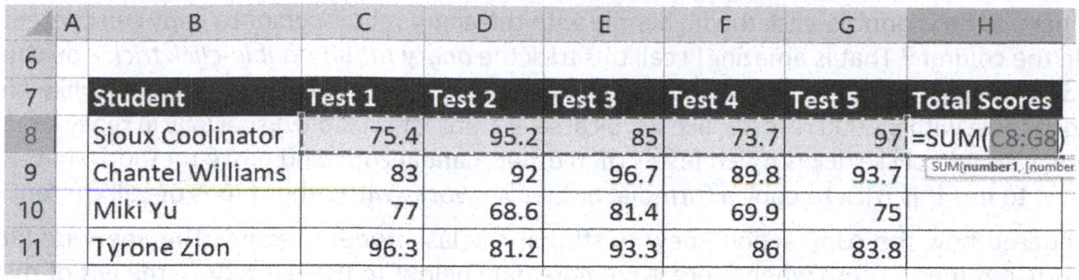

	A	B	C	D	E	F	G	H
6								
7		Student	Test 1	Test 2	Test 3	Test 4	Test 5	Total Scores
8		Sioux Coolinator	75.4	95.2	85	73.7	97	=SUM(C8:G8)
9		Chantel Williams	83	92	96.7	89.8	93.7	SUM(number1, [number
10		Miki Yu	77	68.6	81.4	69.9	75	
11		Tyrone Zion	96.3	81.2	93.3	86	83.8	

Figure 8.43 *Alt+= adds the SUM function and grabs the correct cell range (that is, C8:G8).*

Note: When you use the keyboard shortcut for the SUM function, be sure to verify that the SUM function gets the correct range of cells. If it does not select the correct range, you can use the selection cursor to redirect the selection to the correct range. In this case, because the formula is directly next to the set of numbers you want to add, the function gets the correct cells.

2. To enter the SUM formula into cell H8 and keep the cell selected, press Ctrl+Enter. Figure 8.44 show the number result. Notice that the cell shows the aggregate operation result 426.3, and the *formula bar* shows the final formula =SUM(C8:G8) for the selected cell.

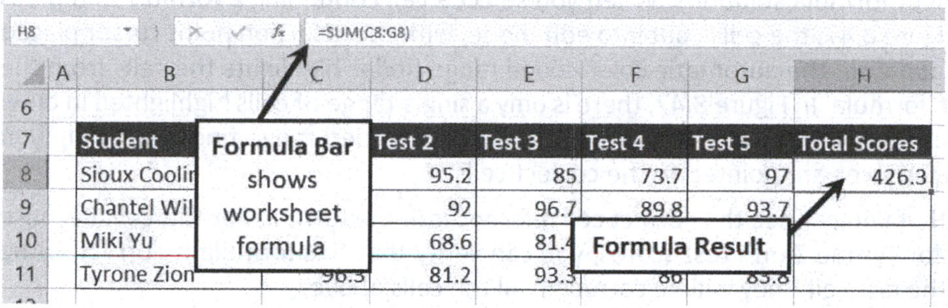

H8		×	✓	*fx*	=SUM(C8:G8)			
	A	B	C	D	E	F	G	H
6								
7		Student	Test 2	Test 2	Test 3	Test 4	Test 5	Total Scores
8		Sioux Coolir		95.2	85	73.7	97	426.3
9		Chantel Wil		92	96.7	89.8	93.7	
10		Miki Yu		68.6	81.4			
11		Tyrone Zion	96.3	81.2	93.3	86	83.8	

Formula Bar shows worksheet formula — **Formula Result**

Figure 8.44 *The formula bar shows the formula, and the cell that contains the formula shows the result.*

3. To copy the formula down to new rows in the column, use the angry rabbit cursor to double-click the fill handle, as shown in Figure 8.45. Figure 8.46 shows the result of copying the formula down the column.

Note: You could also copy the cell contents by clicking and grabbing the fill handle with the angry rabbit cursor and manually pulling the copy action down the column, but that method would take longer.

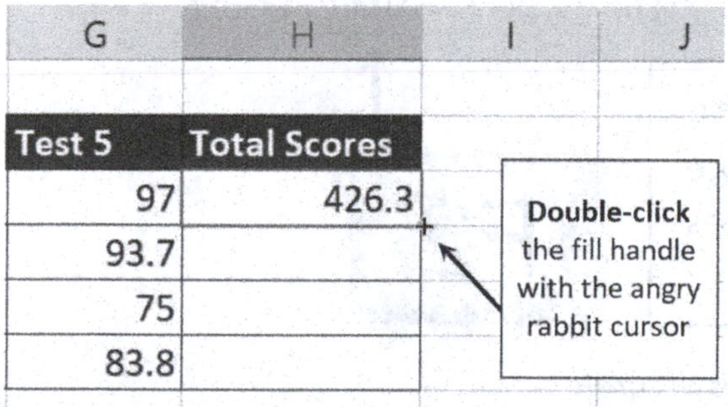

G	H	I	J
Test 5	Total Scores		
97	426.3		
93.7			
75			
83.8			

Double-click the fill handle with the angry rabbit cursor

Figure 8.45 *Double-clicking with the angry rabbit cursor copies the formula down to the rows below.*

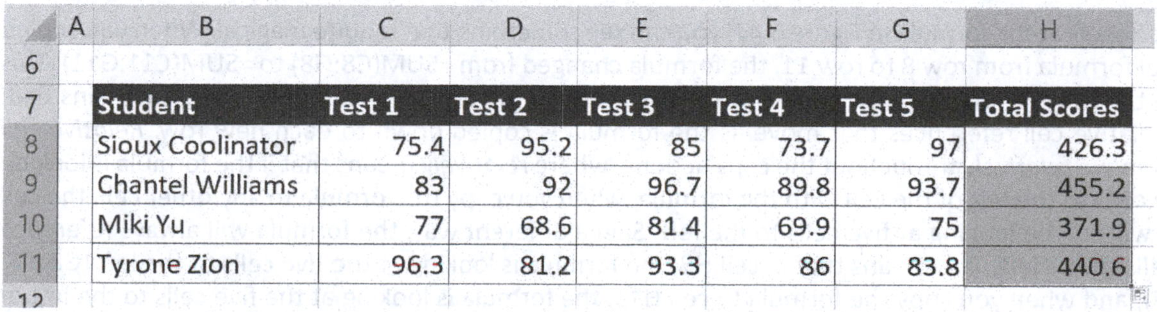

	A	B	C	D	E	F	G	H
6								
7		Student	Test 1	Test 2	Test 3	Test 4	Test 5	Total Scores
8		Sioux Coolinator	75.4	95.2	85	73.7	97	426.3
9		Chantel Williams	83	92	96.7	89.8	93.7	455.2
10		Miki Yu	77	68.6	81.4	69.9	75	371.9
11		Tyrone Zion	96.3	81.2	93.3	86	83.8	440.6
12								

Figure 8.46 *The angry rabbit double-click trick copies the formula down to the last record in the table.*

Wait, what? All you have to do is double-click the fill handle with the angry rabbit cursor to copy cell content down to new rows in the column? That is amazing! I call this trick the *angry rabbit double-click trick*. You can begin to see how handy it is with this 4-row table; imagine using this trick in a table with 360 rows, like an amortization table, or a table with 35,000 records, like a typical sales transaction table. Especially in really large tables, the angry rabbit double-click trick is much faster than other manual copy and paste methods. In this example, you saw how to use this trick to copy a formula, but it also works with other types of cell content.

You might have wondered how the copy action knew to stop at the last student record. The angry rabbit double-click trick is programmed to stop when there is no more data below, to the right, or to the left of the column containing the copy action. (In the preceding steps, you had data to the left, and so the copy action stopped at the last bit of data to the left.) If there is data in all three places—below, right, and left—then when you double-click to copy the cell content down, Excel only copies over the data that exists below. If there is data to the left and to the right—but none below—Excel copies down and stops in the row with the most data. Again, the preceding example only had data to the left, and so Excel stopped the copy action when it hit the last bit of data on the left.

Checking Your Work and Verifying Your Formulas

Checking your work and verifying that formulas include the correct cell references is one of the most important steps in building Excel worksheet formula solutions. When you select a cell containing a formula and press the F2 key, as you can see in Figure 8.47, the cell is put into edit mode, with the insertion point cursor placed at the end of the formula. In addition, the automatic color-coded range finder highlights the cells from the worksheet that are used in the formula. In Figure 8.47, there is only a single range of cells highlighted in blue. But later, when you create formulas with more formula inputs, the color-coded range finder will help you easily verify that all the cell references are pointed to the correct cells.

In Figure 8.47, you can verify that you can see the correct cell references in the formula for this cell. Because C11:G11 is the correct range for Tyrone Zion's test scores, you can verify that this formula is correct. If the cell references are correct in the last cell, they will be correct in all the cells above.

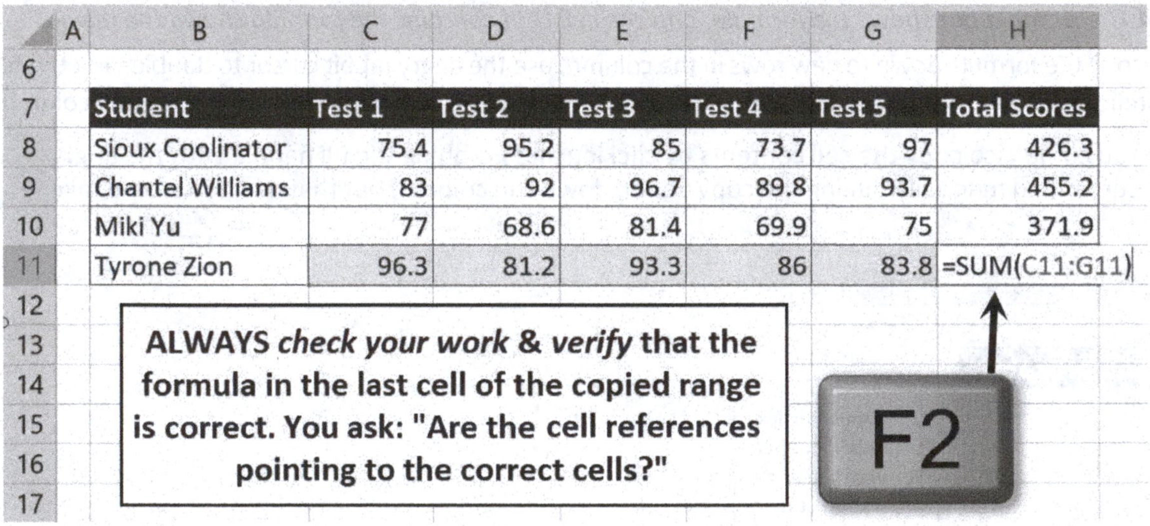

	A	B	C	D	E	F	G	H
6								
7		Student	Test 1	Test 2	Test 3	Test 4	Test 5	Total Scores
8		Sioux Coolinator	75.4	95.2	85	73.7	97	426.3
9		Chantel Williams	83	92	96.7	89.8	93.7	455.2
10		Miki Yu	77	68.6	81.4	69.9	75	371.9
11		Tyrone Zion	96.3	81.2	93.3	86	83.8	=SUM(C11:G11)
12								
13								
14								
15								
16								
17								

ALWAYS *check your work & verify* that the formula in the last cell of the copied range is correct. You ask: "Are the cell references pointing to the correct cells?"

F2

Figure 8.47 *Press F2 in the last cell to verify that the formula is accurate.*

Using Relative Cell References

If you look closely at the formula in Figure 8.47, you can see something that is quite magical. When you copied the original formula from row 8 to row 11, the formula changed from =SUM(C8:G8) to =SUM(C11:G11). This is because the cell references in row 8, C8:G8, are not locked onto row 8 as absolute cell references; instead, they are relative cell references that move as the formula is copied down to each new row. *Relative cell references* move *relatively* throughout the copy action—where *relatively* means that if the formula is looking at the five cells to the left of the cell with the formula, when you copy the formula to any other cell, the cell reference will still be looking at five cells to the left. Said a different way, the formula will always reference the five cells to the left. This means that in cell H8, the formula is looking at the five cells to the left (G8, F8, E8, D8, C8), and when you copy the formula to cell H11, the formula is looking at the five cells to the left of that (G11, F11, E11, D11, C11). The inventors of the spreadsheet, Bricklin and Frankston (refer to Chapter 2), were pretty clever to come up with the idea of using relative cell references to create a lot of calculations quickly and easily.

With your formulas created, now you need to add green fill color to the cells containing the formulas to clearly signal to the user of the worksheet that the cells contain formulas. This way, someone who needs to change the raw data test scores won't accidentally click in a green cell and delete a formula. Follow these steps to add green fill to the cells with the formulas:

1. Use your selection cursor to select the cells H3:H6, then right-click to open the mini toolbar, click the Fill Color dropdown arrow, and click on More Colors, as shown in Figure 8.48.

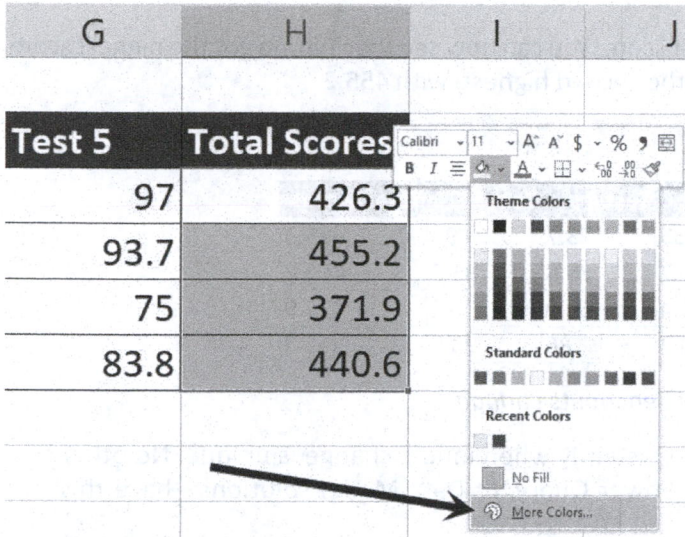

Figure 8.48 *From the Fill Color dropdown, select More Colors.*

2. In the Colors dialog box that appears, select the Standard tab and then select a light green color (see Figure 8.49). (You can pick a different color that you like, but if you do, stick with it and be consistent in terms of when and how you use the color.)

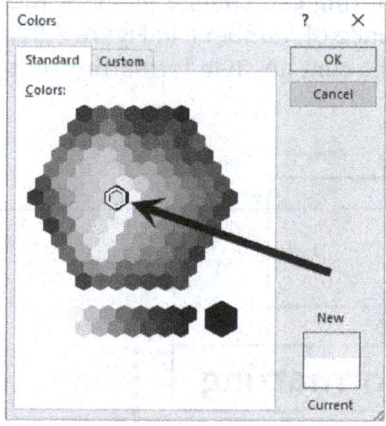

Figure 8.49 *Select the standard light green color.*

3. Click OK in the Colors dialog box. Figure 8.50 shows that the actual test scores are still in cells with no fill color, and number results from formulas are now in cells that have green fill color.

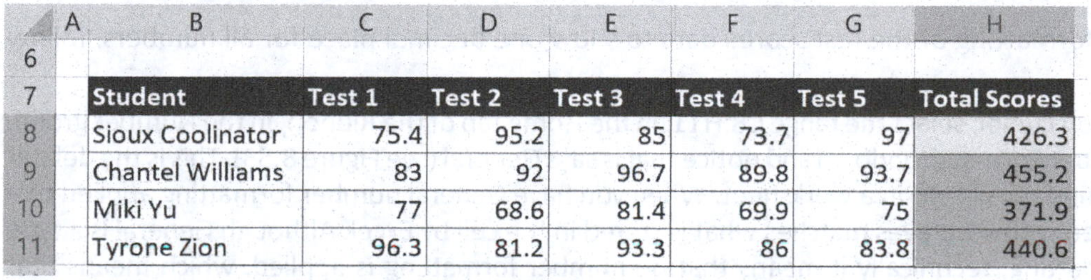

	A	B	C	D	E	F	G	H
6								
7		Student	Test 1	Test 2	Test 3	Test 4	Test 5	Total Scores
8		Sioux Coolinator	75.4	95.2	85	73.7	97	426.3
9		Chantel Williams	83	92	96.7	89.8	93.7	455.2
10		Miki Yu	77	68.6	81.4	69.9	75	371.9
11		Tyrone Zion	96.3	81.2	93.3	86	83.8	440.6

Figure 8.50 *The green fill color signals that a cell contains a formula.*

Note: When you select a range in a worksheet, the active cell (the one that you can put in edit mode and work with) appears in a lighter color than the rest of the range. So in Figure 8.50, H8 is the active cell, and that's why it's a lighter green than the other cells in column H.

As an example of the power of Excel worksheet formulas, say that it turns out that Tyrone Zion's Test 5 score was actually 98.5, not 83.8. You can easy update his total by following these steps:

1. Select cell G11. Do *not* press the Delete key.

2. Type **98.5**.

3. Press Enter.

Figure 8.51 shows the result of changing Tyron's test score. You can now see that Tyrone got the highest score in the class, with a total of 455.3, and Chantel got the second highest, with 455.2.

	A	B	C	D	E	F	G	H
6								
7		Student	Test 1	Test 2	Test 3	Test 4	Test 5	Total Scores
8		Sioux Coolinator	75.4	95.2	85	73.7	97	426.3
9		Chantel Williams	83	92	96.7	89.8	93.7	455.2
10		Miki Yu	77	68.6	81.4	69.9	75	371.9
11		Tyrone Zion	96.3	81.2	93.3	86	98.5	455.3

Figure 8.51 *Worksheet formulas instantly update when inputs change.*

Note: The Excel worksheet's ability to update instantly when inputs change is unique. No other Excel tools—including standard PivotTables, Power Query, or Data Model solutions—have this ability

Adding Number Formatting

Next, you need to add some number formatting to display all the numbers consistently—in this case, with a single decimal place showing. This type of visual consistency in numbers helps make a solution easier to read.

Number formatting is different from style formatting. Whereas style formatting can change many of the aspects of formatting for cells, number formatting only changes the appearance of numbers. In Figure 8.52, you can see that in the Home tab of the Ribbon, there are three groups that contain style formatting, but there is only one group for number formatting.

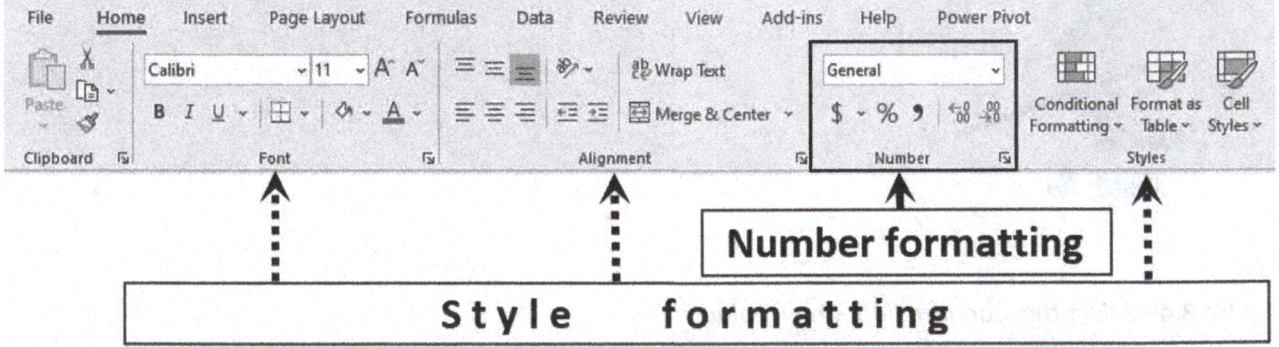

Figure 8.52 *Some of the important commands for number formatting are in the Number group in the Home tab of the Ribbon.*

To change the number formatting of the test scores data to show one decimal place for all numbers, follow these steps:

1. With the selection cursor, select the range C8:H11. In the Home tab of the Ribbon, in the Number group, look at the Number Format dropdown and notice that is says General (see Figure 8.53). This is the default number formatting on all cells in a worksheet. When you have General number formatting applied to a cell, what you see with your eyes matches what is stored in the cell by Excel. Although General is a type of number formatting, technically it means that no number formatting is applied, which means that

what you see is what is stored in the cell. Later, you will see how helpful General number formatting can be when you need to remove all number formatting to more easily detect errors or mistakes.

Default number format is **General**, which means no number formatting is applied
Increase Decimal
General
Student Test 1 Test 2 Test 3 Test 4 Test 5 Total Scores
Sioux Coolinator 75.4 95.2 85 73.7 97 426.3
Chantel Williams 83 92 96.7 89.8 93.7 455.2
Miki Yu 77 68.6 81.4 69.9 75 371.9
Tyrone Zion 96.3 81.2 93.3 86 98.5 455.3

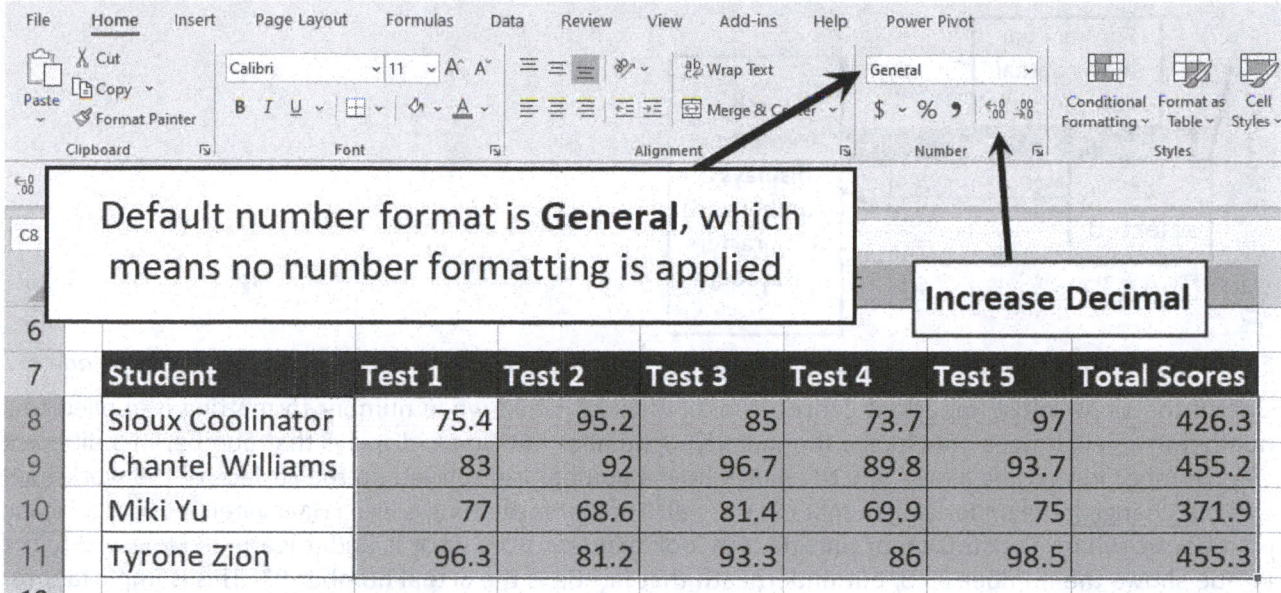

Figure 8.53 *The Number Format dropdown in the Number group tells you what number formatting is applied to the selected cells.*

2. To display an additional decimal place, you can click the Increase Decimal button in the Number group in the Home tab of the Ribbon, or if your QAT is set up as showed back in Chapter 5, you can use the keyboard shortcut Alt, 1. Figure 8.54 shows the result. You can see that the General number format is no longer applied; instead, a number format called Number is applied.

Number number format
Number
Student Test 1 Test 2 Test 3 Test 4 Test 5 Total Scores
Sioux Coolinator 75.40 95.20 85.00 73.70 97.00 426.30
Chantel Williams 83.00 92.00 96.70 89.80 93.70 455.20
Miki Yu 77.00 68.60 81.40 69.90 75.00 371.90
Tyrone Zion 96.30 81.20 93.30 86.00 98.50 455.30

Figure 8.54 *You have now displayed the numbers with two decimal places.*

3. When you clicked the Increase Decimal button, Excel recognized that some of the numbers had a single place decimal showing, and as a result, Excel added another decimal place to that existing single decimal place to show two decimal places for all numbers. This is not what you want. To fix it, click the Decrease Decimal button in the Number group in the Home tab of the Ribbon or use the keyboard shortcut Alt, 2. Figure 8.55 shows the result.

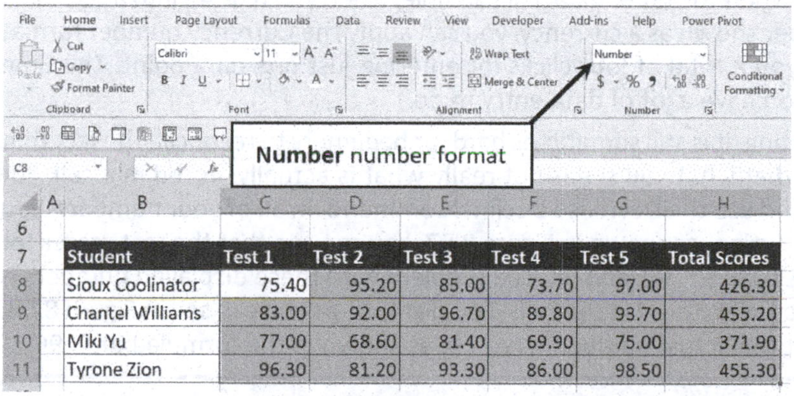

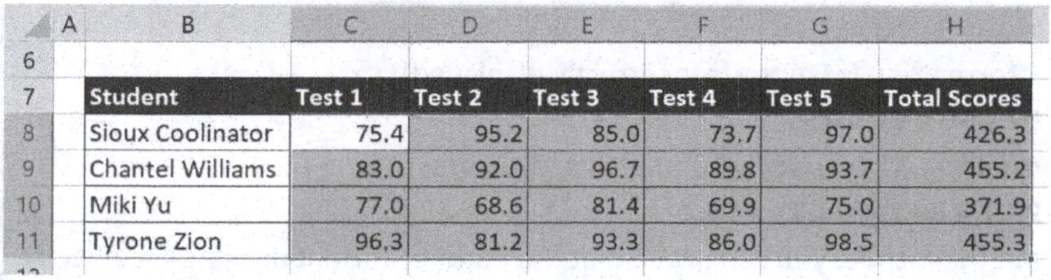

Student Test 1 Test 2 Test 3 Test 4 Test 5 Total Scores
Sioux Coolinator 75.4 95.2 85.0 73.7 97.0 426.3
Chantel Williams 83.0 92.0 96.7 89.8 93.7 455.2
Miki Yu 77.0 68.6 81.4 69.9 75.0 371.9
Tyrone Zion 96.3 81.2 93.3 86.0 98.5 455.3

Figure 8.55 *You have now displayed the numbers with one decimal place.*

4.   Click in cell C9 and look at the difference between what is displayed on the surface of the worksheet (in cell C9) and what Excel is storing in the cell, as shown in the formula bar (see Figure 8.56).

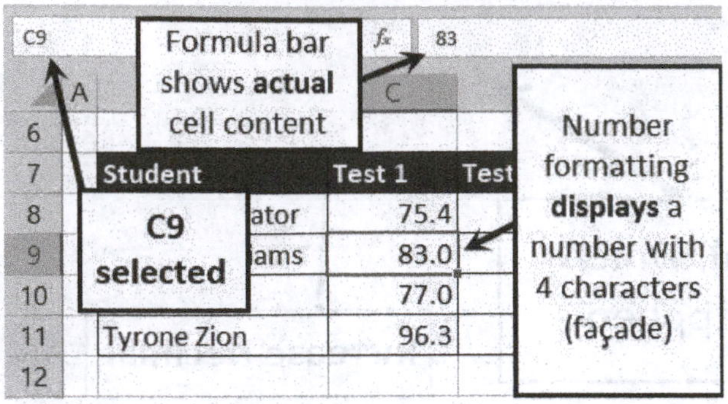

Figure 8.56 *Number formatting does not change the underlying number; it just displays it with a façade.*

One of the single most important concepts in all of Excel is that when number formatting is applied to a number in a cell, it does *not* change the underlying number but simply displays that number in a different way. Number formatting allows you to change how a number is displayed on the surface of the worksheet without changing the underlying number in the cell. Number formatting is like a Halloween mask or a façade on a house, where the surface, or outside, can look different from what is underneath. In Figure 8.56, the façade shows the number 83.0, but underneath that façade is the actual number 83. This is important for several reasons:

- Number formatting can help reduce file size because Excel can store fewer numbers; for example, in Figure 8.56, Excel has to store only the two characters 8 and 3 rather than the four characters 8, 3, ., and 0. This matters a lot when you get big tables of numbers.

- As you will learn later in this book, making calculations on dates and times is dramatically easier with number formatting applied.

- Number formatting can save time when you enter data. For example, when you type 43 into a cell—just two clicks—if you need the number shown as a currency, you can apply the Currency number format to show it as $43.00; this saves you a total of four clicks for entering just one data point. The time savings can really add up when you have a lot of data entry to do.

Despite all the benefits of number formatting, it is still sometimes hard for beginners to reconcile the fact that with numbers, there is always a chance that what you see is not really what is actually stored in a cell. For example, if you were to make a mistake and use the Decrease Decimal command on all of your numbers, you would accidentally create a misleading solution, as shown in Figure 8.57. You can see that the test scores for Chantel now appear to be the numbers 83, 92, 97, 90, and 94. The problem with these displayed numbers is that they appear different from what is actually stored in the cells. For example, as you can see in Figure 8.58, the displayed number in cell E9 is 97, but the actual number in cell E9, as shown in the formula bar, is 96.7.

	A	B	C	D	E	F	G	H	I	J
6										
7		Student	Test 1	Test 2	Test 3	Test 4	Test 5	Total Scores		
8		Sioux Coolinator	75	95	85	74	97	426		
9		Chantel Williams	83	92	97	90	94	455		
10		Miki Yu	77	69	81	70	75	372		
11		Tyrone Zion	96	81	93	86	99	455		
12										
13		What we see because of number formatting (results are incorrectly displayed):								
14		**Chantel Williams: 83 + 92 + 97 + 90 + 94 = 455**								
15		Formula do NOT see number formatting. They work on underlying numbers:								
16		**Chantel Williams: 83 + 92 + 96.7 + 89.8 + 93.7 = 455.2**								
17		If you add up what you "see" from the façade, you can prove that the number format displays incorrectly.								
18		**Chantel Williams: 83 + 92 + 97 + 90 + 94 = 456**								

Figure 8.57 *Using number formatting to display the scores with no decimal places is unclear and inaccurate.*

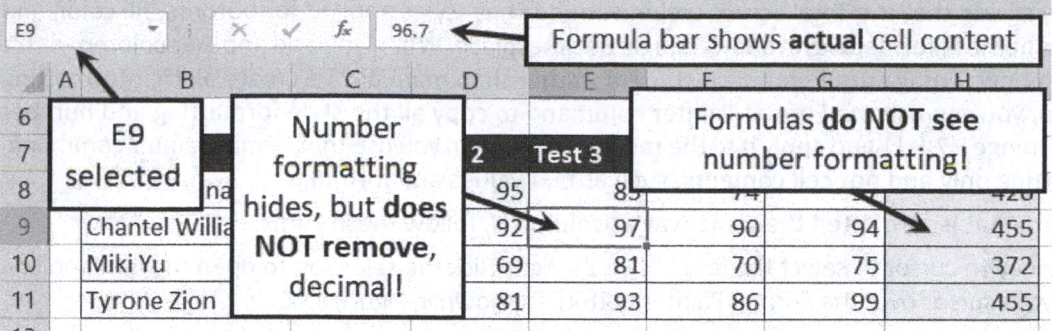

Figure 8.58 *Number formatting is a façade that formulas cannot see. Formulas act on the underlying numbers.*

Using number formatting to display the scores with no decimals places is very misleading because *formulas do not see number formatting*. The SUM function in cell H9 does not see the numbers 83, 92, 97, 90, and 94; it can only see the underlying numbers 83 + 92 + 96.7 + 89.8 + 93.7 = 455.2. The SUM function correctly calculates 455.2, and then with the reduced decimal display, it shows 455. You can prove that this is misleading by making this calculation: 83 + 92 + 97 + 90 + 94 = 456. The total for Chantel is *not* 456, even though the whole numbers that are displayed on the worksheet make it look this way. This means that if you left the Excel solution with zero decimal places showing, the viewer of the solution would be confused by the visually inaccurate results. Since your goal is to always create solutions that are accurate and clear, in this case, you should leave all the numbers with a single decimal place showing, as shown in Figure 8.59.

	A	B	C	D	E	F	G	H
6								
7		Student	Test 1	Test 2	Test 3	Test 4	Test 5	Total Scores
8		Sioux Coolinator	75.4	95.2	85.0	73.7	97.0	426.3
9		Chantel Williams	83.0	92.0	96.7	89.8	93.7	455.2
10		Miki Yu	77.0	68.6	81.4	69.9	75.0	371.9
11		Tyrone Zion	96.3	81.2	93.3	86.0	98.5	455.3

Figure 8.59 *Always apply the correct number formatting to help communicate the correct results.*

But what if you really want to change the underlying numbers and round the numbers to the ones position? No problem. You can use the Excel worksheet function ROUND, which you will learn about in Chapter 10. However, *you will not get accurate results if you try to round numbers by using number formatting*! One of the questions most commonly asked in online Excel help forms for the past 25 years has been "Why are my totals wrong when I round numbers that have number formatting applied?"

> **Note:** To keep it clear in your head that you don't use number formatting to round numbers, always think of it this way: "I change the decimals with number formatting to *display* the number differently."

Reviewing what you just learned about number formatting and formulas in Figures 8.53 through 8.59 and then assimilating the concepts is mandatory if you are going to become an Excel master who can consistently build accurate, clear, and useful results. As you move forward in this book, keep in mind the following facts about number formatting:

- Number formatting changes the display of numbers without changing the underlying numbers.
- Number formatting provides benefits such as smaller file size, facilitates date and time calculations, and speeds up data entry.
- Formulas do *not* see number formatting and make calculations on the underlying numbers.

Using the Format Painter

Next, you need to add a new column to your table and calculate the percentage grade for each student. In the process, you will learn a great style formatting trick—how to insert rows into a worksheet—and learn about absolute cell references.

In Figure 8.60, you can see that the Total Scores column already has styles applied for borders, fill color, and font color, as well as number formatting to show a single decimal place. When you add another column to this table to calculate the percentage grade for each student, rather than manually re-create all that formatting for the new column, you can use the Format Painter command to copy all the style formatting and number formatting from the range H7:H11 and apply it to the range I7:I11. When you use the Format Painter command, Excel copies formatting only and not cell contents, such as text values and formulas.

To add a new column that is formatted the same way as column H, follow these steps:

1.   Use your selection cursor to select the range H7:H11, right-click the selection to open the mini toolbar, and hover your cursor over the Format Painter button, as shown in Figure 8.60.

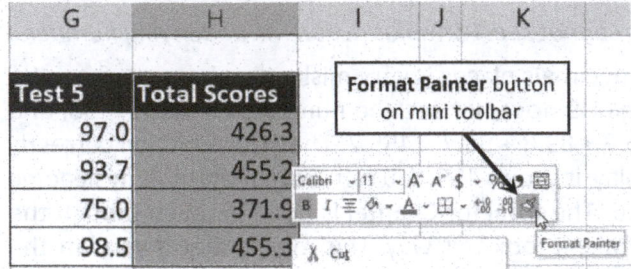

Figure 8.60 *The Format Painter command copies formatting only.*

2.   Click the Format Painter button once to load the cursor with the formatting applied to the selected range. In Figure 8.61, you can see that the cursor indicates that the cursor is loaded with formatting. When you see this, the next click that you make will apply the formatting and convert the cursor back to a selection cursor.

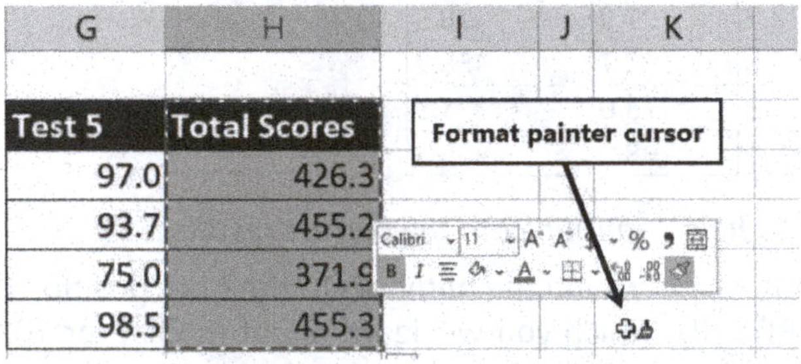

Figure 8.61 *Your cursor is loaded with copied formatting.*

3.   Carefully hover over cell I7 with the format painter cursor, as shown in Figure 8.62.

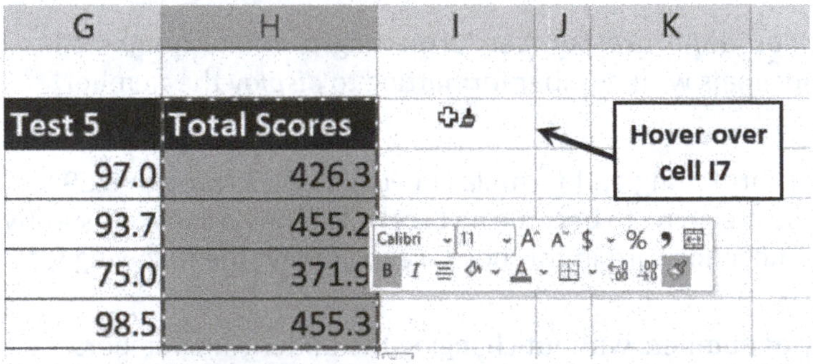

Figure 8.62 *Carefully hover over the cell in the top of the range where you want the formatting to spill.*

4.   Click on cell I7 to apply all the formatting to the full range I7:I11. Figure 8.63 shows the correct application of the formatting and shows that the format painter cursor reverts to a selection cursor.

Note: If you click on the wrong cell, the formatting is copied to the wrong range. If this happens, you need to undo the action with the keyboard shortcut Ctrl+Z and try again.

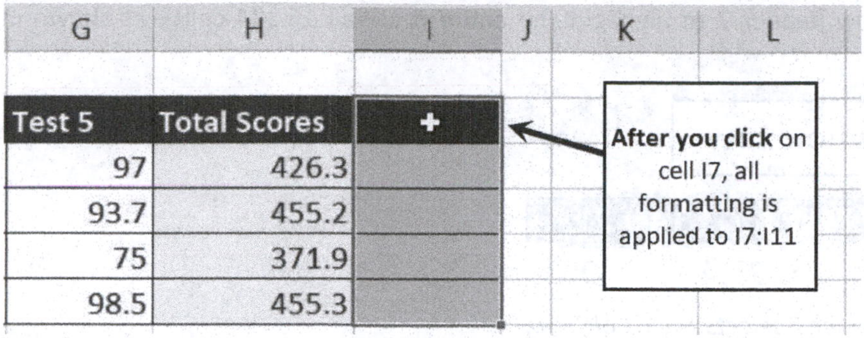

G	H	I	J	K	L
Test 5	**Total Scores**	**+**			
97	426.3				
93.7	455.2				
75	371.9				
98.5	455.3				

After you click on cell I7, all formatting is applied to I7:I11

Figure 8.63 *When you click, the formatting is applied, and the cursor reverts to a selection cursor.*

5. Select cell I7, type the label **% Grade**, and press Enter.

In this example, you clicked the Format Painter button one time to load the cursor with a single application of the copied formatting. Then, when you clicked with the cursor, you applied the formatting and turned off the Format Painter command. If you need to use the format painter cursor to apply copied formatting more than one time, you can double-click the Format Painter button. When you do this, each time you click on a cell with your cursor, the formatting is applied. To stop applying the formatting, you need to turn off the command by clicking the Format Painter button again or pressing the Esc key.

Inserting Rows into a Worksheet

Before you can calculate the percentage grade for each student, you need to know the total possible points available. You can easily find this number by adding to your worksheet a section that lists each test and the maximum possible points. However, it would be nice if you could put the maximum scores above the student score table. Unfortunately, as you can see in Figure 8.64, there is not enough room above the table. It is common for plans to change midstream like this. Luckily, Excel is programmed to easily allow you to make structural changes such as inserting new rows. In addition, when you insert the rows and everything is pushed down, all of your formulas will update perfectly!

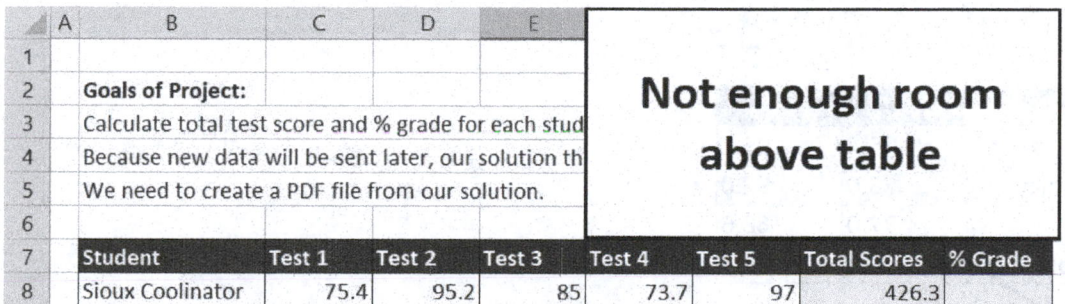

Figure 8.64 *There is not enough room above the table to display the total points possible for each test.*

To insert new rows above your table, follow these steps:

1. To insert three completely new rows and push the top of the table down from row 7 to row 10, hover your cursor over the worksheet row header 7 until you see the select row cursor, as shown in Figure 8.65.

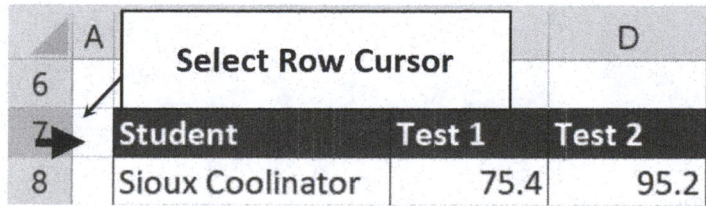

Figure 8.65 *The black horizontal arrow is the select row cursor.*

2. Click on the worksheet row header 7 to highlight the entire row—all 16,384 cells—as shown in Figure 8.66.

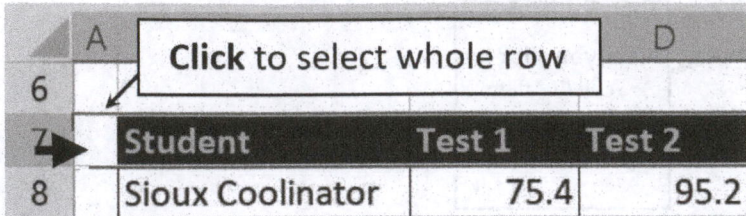

	A		D
6			
7	Student	Test 1	Test 2
8	Sioux Coolinator	75.4	95.2

Figure 8.66 *Clicking on the row header 7 selects the whole row.*

3. Carefully click the worksheet row header and drag down to row 9, as shown in Figure 8.67. When you click and drag, the cursor changes to a selection cursor.

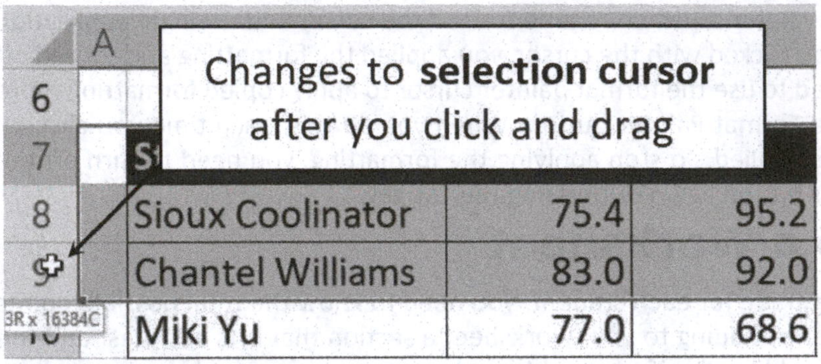

	A		
6			
7	S		
8	Sioux Coolinator	75.4	95.2
9	Chantel Williams	83.0	92.0
3R x 16384C 10	Miki Yu	77.0	68.6

Changes to **selection cursor** after you click and drag

Figure 8.67 *All cells in rows 7 to 9 are selected.*

4. Right-click the three selected rows and then click Insert (see Figure 8.68). Because you are right-clicking the worksheet row headers (not the cells), when you use the Insert command, Excel properly inserts rows. Figure 8.69 shows the newly inserted rows and your table, which now starts in row 10.

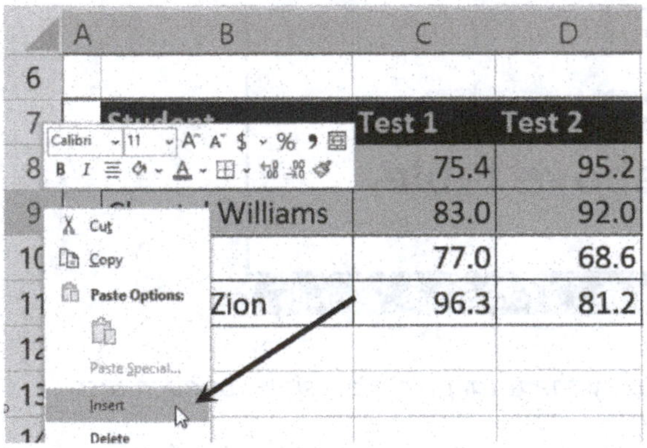

	A	B	C	D
6				
7	Student		Test 1	Test 2
8			75.4	95.2
9	Williams		83.0	92.0
10			77.0	68.6
11	Zion		96.3	81.2
12				
13				
14				

(Context menu: Calibri 11 A A $ % ; B I ≡ ◇ A ⊞; X Cut; Copy; Paste Options; Paste Special...; Insert; Delete)

Figure 8.68 *Right-click the selected rows and then click Insert.*

	A	B	C	D	E
6					
7					
8					
9					
10	Student	Test 1	Test 2	Test 3	
11	Sioux Coolinator	75.4	95.2	85	
12	Chantel Williams	83	92	96.7	
13	Miki Yu	77	68.6	81.4	

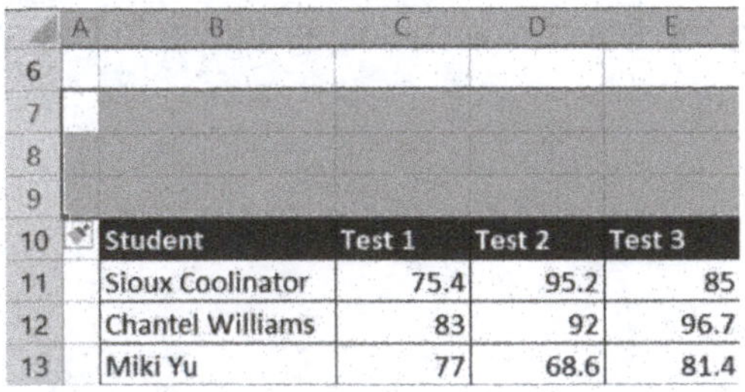

Figure 8.69 *Three rows are inserted above the table.*

Note: If you see the dialog box shown in Figure 8.70, you mistakenly right-clicked the cells rather than the worksheet row headers.

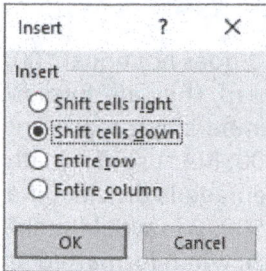

Figure 8.70 *You do not want to see this. If you see this, it means you right-clicked the cells rather than the row headers.*

5. Using Figure 8.71 as a guide, enter the text, numbers, formatting, and formula to properly total the maximum possible points for all five tests. Hint: Use the angry rabbit double-click trick to copy Test 1 from cell C7 to cell H7 and to copy the number 100 from cell C8 to cell H8. Remember to use Alt+= to enter the SUM function.

	A	B	C	D	E	F	G	H	I
6									
7			Test 1	Test 2	Test 3	Test 4	Test 5	Total Possible	
8			100	100	100	100	100	=SUM(C8:G8)	
9								SUM(number1, [number2], ...)	
10		Student	Test 1	Test 2	Test 3	Test 4	Test 5	Total Scores	% Grade
11		Sioux Coolinator	75.4	95.2	85	73.7	97	426.3	

Figure 8.71 *Above the student score table, you create a total of all the points possible.*

Calculating Percentages

As shown in Figure 8.72, now you have the total maximum possible points for all five tests. A student who gets 100 points on all five tests earns 500 points, which is 100% correct. But what does 100% mean? 100% means the student got all points possible out of 500; in other words, the student got 500 out of 500. The math operation that is used when you calculate a percentage is division. For a student who earns 500 points out of 500, the math calculation is 500/500 = 1. However, often in business, science, and other endeavors, a perfect score is not shown as the number 1 but as a percentage: 100%.

Note: In Excel, the operator used in worksheet formulas for division is the forward slash. A full list of math operators is shown later in this chapter.

	A	B	C	D	E	F	G	H	I	J	K
6											
7			Test 1	Test 2	Test 3	Test 4	Test 5	Total Possible			
8			100	100	100	100	100	500			
9											
10		Student	Test 1	Test 2	Test 3	Test 4	Test 5	Total Scores	% Grade		
11		Sioux Coolinator	75.4	95.2	85	73.7	97	426.3			◄ 426.3/500
12		Chantel Williams	83	92	96.7	89.8	93.7	455.2			◄ 455.2/500
13		Miki Yu	77	68.6	81.4	69.9	75	371.9			◄ 371.9/500
14		Tyrone Zion	96.3	81.2	93.3	86	98.5	455.3			◄ 455.3/500

Figure 8.72 *Calculating % grade requires that you compare each student's earned score to the total possible score.*

The process of formatting the number 1 as a percentage involves two steps, as shown in Figure 8.73:

1. Slide the decimal two positions to the right.
2. Add a percent symbol.

Format as Percent	
Step 1:	**Step 2:**
Slide decimal point 2 positions to right.	Add % Symbol.
1.00 10.0 100. ▶ ▶	100%

Figure 8.73 *Formatting a number as a percentage.*

Division and then Format.
$\dfrac{\text{Numerator}}{\text{Denominator}} = \dfrac{455.2}{500} = 0.9104 \blacktriangleright 91.04\%$

Figure 8.74 *Dividing the numerator by the denominator.*

Because the actual perfect score of 1 does not equal 100, percentages are not numbers; instead, they are formatted symbolic representations of numbers that represent how many parts there are out of 100. Because the math operation used to calculate a percentage is division, if a student earned 400 points out of 500, you would make the calculation 400/500 = 0.8, which, when formatted as a percentage, is 80%. You would then know that for every 100 points possible, this student earned 80 points, or 80 parts out of 100.

As another example to help you understand percentages, if the tax rate at a store is 6%, this means that for every 100 pennies ($1.00), the customer must pay 6 pennies ($0.06), or 6 parts out of 100. As yet another example, if a business has a profit margin of 9%, this means that for every 100 pennies of sales that the company earns, 9 pennies is kept as profit, or 9 parts out of 100.

As you can see in Figure 8.72 in column K, to determine a percentage grade for each student, you need to compare the points each student earned to the total points possible. In the numerator (the top part of a fraction), you use the student's earned points, and in the denominator (the bottom part of a fraction), you use the total points possible. For the student Chantel Williams, for example, the calculation is 455.2/500 = 0.9104, which translates to the percentage 91.04%, as shown in Figure 8.74.

Understanding Absolute Cell References

You need to be careful about how you build Excel formulas to calculate percentages. If you look at Figure 8.72, you can see that in this case, the formula will have to use the student's score from each row (which is a relative cell reference) as the numerator. In the denominator, you have to get the formula to lock onto cell H8, which contains 500, in every row as you copy the formula down. To do this, you need to understand absolute cell references.

Figure 8.75 shows the four formulas that you need to calculate the % grade for each student. However, if you create the first formula for the student Sioux in cell I11 using the formula =H11/H8 and then copy it down to the next row, because the two cell references are relative cell references, the formula would become =H12/H9. But as you can see in Figure 8.76, the formula =H12/H9 is not correct because the denominator is not cell H8. This is because the relative cell reference, H8, moved to become cell H9, which is an empty cell! You need to lock the cell reference H8 to make it an absolute cell reference.

	A	B	C	D	E	F	G	H	I	J	K
6											
7			Test 1	Test 2	Test 3	Test 4	Test 5	Total Possible			4 formulas
8			100	100	100	100	100	500			
9											
10		Student	Test 1	Test 2	Test 3	Test 4	Test 5	Total Scores	% Grade		
11		Sioux Coolinator	75.4	95.2	85	73.7	97	426.3			◀ =H11/H8
12		Chantel Williams	83	92	96.7	89.8	93.7	455.2			◀ =H12/H8
13		Miki Yu	77	68.6	81.4	69.9	75	371.9			◀ =H13/H8
14		Tyrone Zion	96.3	81.2	93.3	86	98.5	455.3			◀ =H14/H8

Figure 8.75 *The four formulas that you need use relative cell references in the numerator and cell H8 in the denominator.*

	A	B	C	D	E	F	G	H	I	J	K
6											
7			Test 1	Test 2	Test 3	Test 4	Test 5	Total Possible			
8			100	100	100	100	100	500			
9											
10		Student	Test 1	Test 2	Test 3	Test 4	Test 5	Total Scores	% Grade		
11		Sioux Coolinator	75.4	95.2	85	73.7	97	426.3	0.8526	◄ =H11/H8	
12		Chantel Williams	83	92	96.7	89.8	93.7	455.2	=H12/H9	◄ =H12/H9	
13		Miki Yu	77	68.6	81.4	69.9	75	371.9			
14		Tyrone Zion	96.3	81.2	93.3	86	98.5	455.3			

Figure 8.76 *If you copy the formula to a new row without locking the formula to H8, the formula is not correct.*

An *absolute cell reference* is a reference that is locked and will not move in a copy action. As you will see in just a moment, the way to lock a cell reference is to press F4 to convert the cell reference H8 to $H$8. In this case, the $ signs do not have anything to do with money; instead, they stop the column reference H and the row reference 8 from moving throughout the copy action.

To create the % grade formula and use an absolute cell reference, follow these steps:

1. Click in cell I11 and type an equal sign, as shown in Figure 8.77.

	F	G	H	I	J	K
	Test 4	Test 5	Total Possible			
100	100	100	500			
	Test 4	Test 5	Total Scores	% Grade		
85	73.7	97	426.3	=		
6.7	89.8	93.7	455.2			

Figure 8.77 *Start your formula with an equal sign.*

To quickly insert the relative cell reference into your formula, press the LeftArrow key (see Figure 8.78).

	F	G	H	I	J	K
	Test 4	Test 5	Total Possible			
100	100	100	500			
	Test 4	Test 5	Total Scores	% Grade		
85	73.7	97	426.3	=H11		
6.7	89.8	93.7	455.2			
1.4	69.9	75	3			
3.3	86	98.5	4			

Figure 8.78 *Press the LeftArrow key to insert cell H11 into the formula.*

2.   Type the division operator, as shown in Figure 8.79.

	F	G	H	I	J	K
	Test 4	Test 5	Total Possible			
LOO	100	100	500			
	Test 4	Test 5	Total Scores	% Grade		
85	73.7	97	426.3	=H11/		
6.7	89.8	93.7	455.2			

Figure 8.79 *Type the division operator.*

3.   Hover the mouse selection cursor over cell H8, as shown in Figure 8.80.

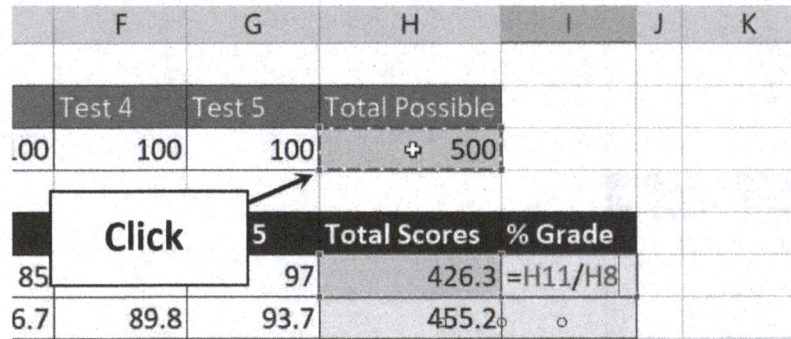

Figure 8.80 *Hover the mouse selection cursor over cell H8.*

4.   Click on cell H8 to put the cell reference into your formula, as shown in Figure 8.81. You can use your mouse to put the cell reference in the formula because the cell you want is not close to the formula.

Note: Choosing between the arrow keys and the mouse to put a cell reference into a formula is a matter of preference and personal keyboard speed. I typically find using an arrow key to put a cell reference into a formula faster than using the mouse. You could have easily entered the H8 cell reference by pressing LeftArrow once and then UpArrow four times.

	F	G	H	I	J	K
	Test 4	Test 5	Total Possible			
LOO	100	100	✥ 500			
	Click	5	Total Scores	% Grade		
85		97	426.3	=H11/H8		
6.7	89.8	93.7	455.2			

Figure 8.81 *To insert H8 into the formula, click with the mouse.*

5.   With the insertion point cursor touching cell H8, press the F4 key to make the reference an absolute cell reference, as shown in Figure 8.82.

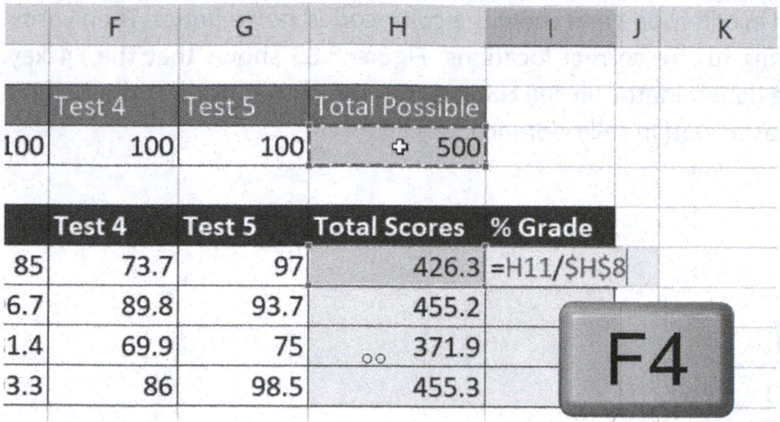

	F	G	H	I	J	K
	Test 4	Test 5	Total Possible			
100	100	100	⊕ 500			

	Test 4	Test 5	Total Scores	% Grade		
85	73.7	97	426.3	=H11/$H$8		
6.7	89.8	93.7	455.2			
1.4	69.9	75	371.9			
3.3	86	98.5	455.3			

F4

Figure 8.82 *The $ signs stop the column reference H and the row reference 8 from moving throughout the copy action.*

6.   Because the goal is to enter the formula and immediately copy the formula, use the keyboard short-cut Ctrl+Enter, as shown in Figure 8.83. Figure 8.84 shows the number result 0.8526.

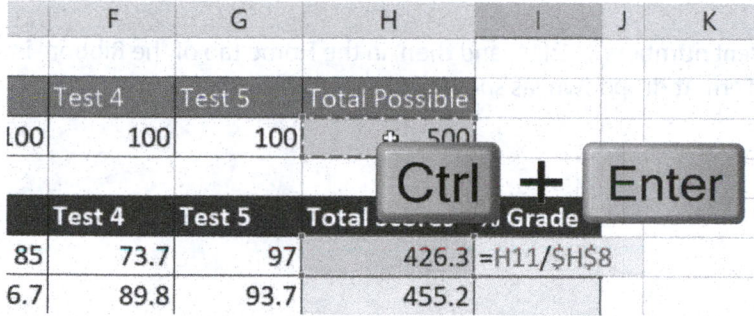

	F	G	H	I	J	K
	Test 4	Test 5	Total Possible			
100	100	100	⊕ 500			

Ctrl + Enter

	Test 4	Test 5	Total	Grade		
85	73.7	97	426.3	=H11/$H$8		
6.7	89.8	93.7	455.2			

Figure 8.83 *Ctrl+Enter puts your formula in cell I11 and keeps the cell selected.*

7.   With the angry rabbit cursor, double-click the fill handle to copy the formula to the rows below, as shown in Figure 8.84.

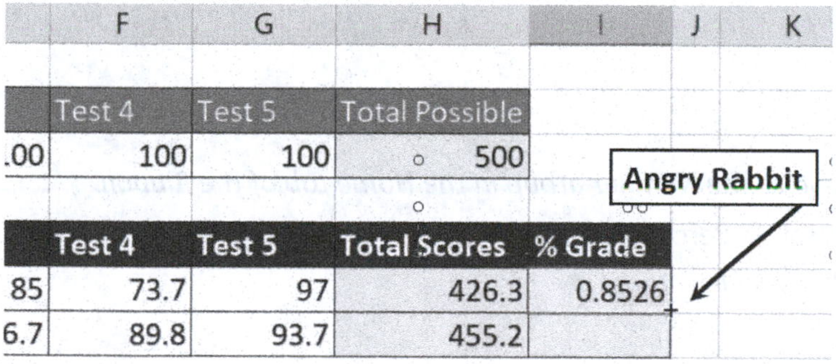

	F	G	H	I	J	K
	Test 4	Test 5	Total Possible			
.00	100	100	○ 500			

Angry Rabbit

	Test 4	Test 5	Total Scores	% Grade		
85	73.7	97	426.3	0.8526		
6.7	89.8	93.7	455.2			

Figure 8.84 *Double-click the fill handle with the angry rabbit cursor to copy the formula down the column.*

8. Press the F2 key to put the last cell in edit mode and show the color-coded range finder. Then verify that the cell references are pointing to the correct locations. Figure 8.85 shows that the F4 key and the $ signs worked to lock the denominator on cell H8 and that the numerator has the correct earned points for the last student as a relative cell reference.

	F	G	H	I	J	K
	Test 4	Test 5	Total Possible			
LOO	100	100	500			
	Test 4	Test 5	Total Scores	% Grade		
85	73.7	97	426.3			
6.7	89.8	93.7	455.2	**F2**		
1.4	69.9	75	371.9			
3.3	86	98.5	455.3	=H14/$H$8		

Figure 8.85 *Use the F2 key on the last cell to verify that the cell references are pointing to the correct location.*

Finally, you need to apply the Percentage number format to display the decimals as percentages. To do this, follow these steps:

1. Select the range with the decimal student numbers, I11:I14, and then, in the Home tab of the Ribbon, in the Number group, click the Number Format dropdown, as shown in Figure 8.86.

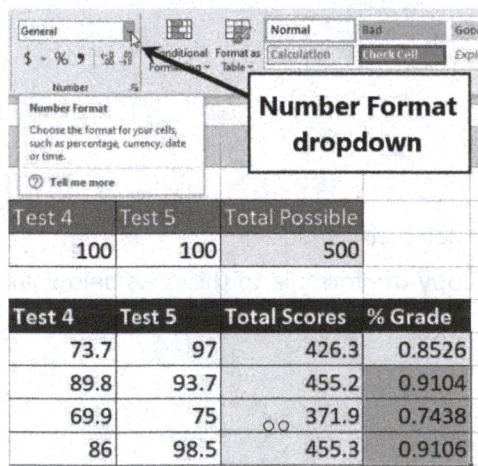

Figure 8.86 *Select the range I11:I14 and then go to the Number group in the Home tab of the Ribbon.*

2. From the Number Format dropdown, select Percentage to apply a percentage number format with two decimal places showing (see Figure 8.87).

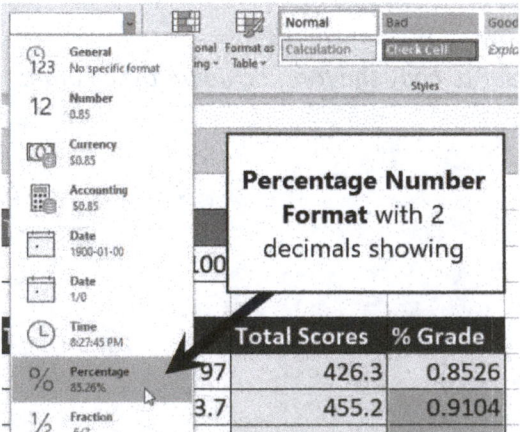

Figure 8.87 *The Percentage format from the Number Format dropdown displays a percentage with two decimal places.*

Figure 8.88 shows the final percentage grades for the students.

	Test 1	Test 2	Test 3	Test 4	Test 5	Total Possible
	100	100	100	100	100	500

Student	Test 1	Test 2	Test 3	Test 4	Test 5	Total Scores	% Grade
Sioux Coolinator	75.4	95.2	85	73.7	97	426.3	85.26%
Chantel Williams	83	92	96.7	89.8	93.7	455.2	91.04%
Miki Yu	77	68.6	81.4	69.9	75	371.9	74.38%
Tyrone Zion	96.3	81.2	93.3	86	98.5	455.3	91.06%

Figure 8.88 *The final percentage grades.*

Documenting Your Work

Once you have created a table of student scores with formulas and formatting, you need to add documentation so that someone looking at the worksheet can see at a glance what formulas were used in the worksheet.

When you create an Excel solution, it is helpful to document how you created the solution by listing goals, placing inputs in the cells, labeling the inputs, showing formulas that you used, and presenting results clearly. Documentation allows you and other users of the solution to have a clear understanding of the problem, how you solved it, and the results.

Documenting an Excel solution can take many forms, but regardless of the form, it is crucial to include these elements of clear documentation:

- List goals.
- Place inputs in cells.
- Label inputs with informative labels.
- Use the FORMULATEXT function to show the formulas on the face of the worksheet.
- Present results clearly.

In the example you have been working through in this chapter, you have already listed your goals and labeled the formula inputs. Now you're ready to learn about the FORMULATEXT worksheet function.

To document a worksheet, you can use the FORMULATEXT function to show the formulas used for the calculations on the face of the worksheet. The FORMULATEXT function is programed to take a formula from a cell, but rather than show the formula result, it shows the formula itself. Documenting the formulas you use in an Excel solution is not always necessary, and you will not do it for all the solutions that you build, but it does add clarity about how a solution was built for anyone who looks at the solution. If you want others to be clear about how you built your solution, then documenting the formulas used is greatly beneficial.

The FORMULATEXT function has one argument: *reference*. However, unlike the SUM function you used earlier, the FORMULATEXT function is not an aggregate function. This means that if you put one cell reference into the *reference* argument, FORMULATEXT delivers one answer. However, if you put a range of cells into the *reference* argument, FORMULATEXT does not aggregate to yield one answer but instead delivers an array of answers—which is exactly what you want in this case.

To document your worksheet by using the FORMULATEXT function, follow these steps:

1. In cell K11, enter the label shown in Figure 8.89, add bold to it, and adjust the column width as needed.

Student	Test 1	Test 2	Test 3	Test 4	Test 5	Total Scores	% Grade		Formulas used for Total Scores:
Sioux Coolinator	75.4	95.2	85	73.7	97	426.3	85.26%		
Chantel Williams	83	92	96.7	89.8	93.7	455.2	91.04%		
Miki Yu	77	68.6	81.4	69.9	75	371.9	74.38%		
Tyrone Zion	96.3	81.2	93.3	86	98.5	455.3	91.06%		

Figure 8.89 *You will document the formulas used off to the side of your project.*

2. With cell K11 selected, type **=form**, as shown in Figure 8.90. Notice that the dropdown list of functions shows the FORMULATEXT function highlighted in blue. (If the function you want is not already highlighted in blue, select it.) Notice also that the screentip gives you a description of what the function does: "Returns a formula as a string." *String* is the term used to describe text values—and that is what you would like in this case. Rather than have a formula that works as a formula to calculate an answer, you want to show the formula as a text value so that you can show the formula.

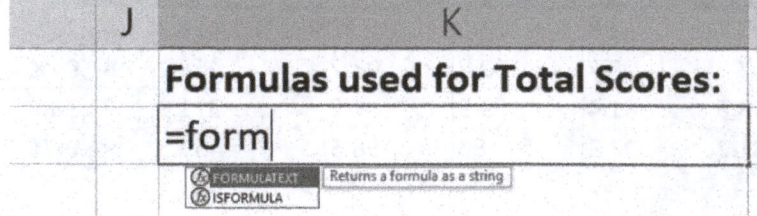

Figure 8.90 *When you type an equal sign and the first few letters, you see a list of functions to choose from.*

3. Press the Tab key to enter the function into the cell. In Figure 8.91, you can see that the function argument is *reference*.

> **Note:** By pressing the Tab key as soon as you see the correct function highlighted in blue, you can save many clicks in typing out a formula.

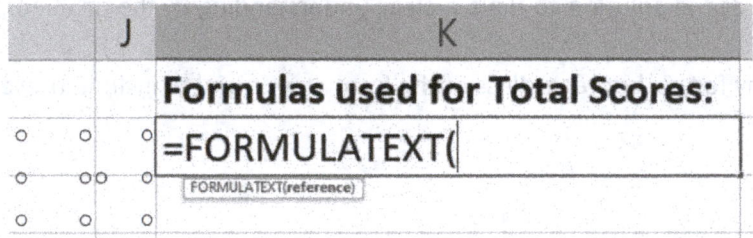

Figure 8.91 *The reference argument accepts a single cell reference or a range of cells.*

4. As shown in Figure 8.92, for the *reference* argument, select the full range of cells H11:H14 from the table.

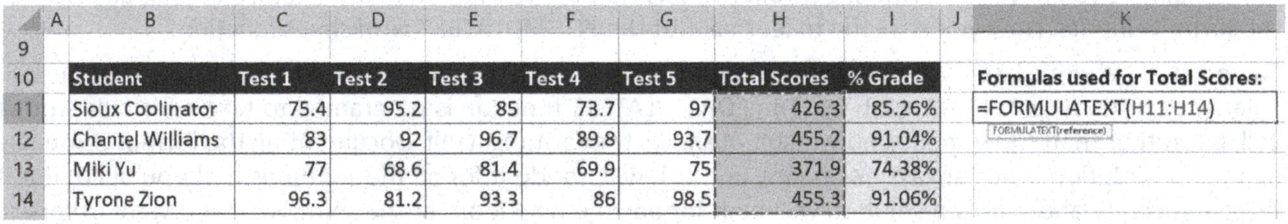

Student	Test 1	Test 2	Test 3	Test 4	Test 5	Total Scores	% Grade		Formulas used for Total Scores:
Sioux Coolinator	75.4	95.2	85	73.7	97	426.3	85.26%		=FORMULATEXT(H11:H14)
Chantel Williams	83	92	96.7	89.8	93.7	455.2	91.04%		FORMULATEXT(reference)
Miki Yu	77	68.6	81.4	69.9	75	371.9	74.38%		
Tyrone Zion	96.3	81.2	93.3	86	98.5	455.3	91.06%		

Figure 8.92 *When you enter multiple cells into the reference argument, FORMULATEXT delivers multiple answers.*

5. To enter the formula, press Ctrl+Enter. Excel puts the formula in cell K11, keeps cell K11 selected, and spills the text results down the column. Figure 8.93 shows the results.

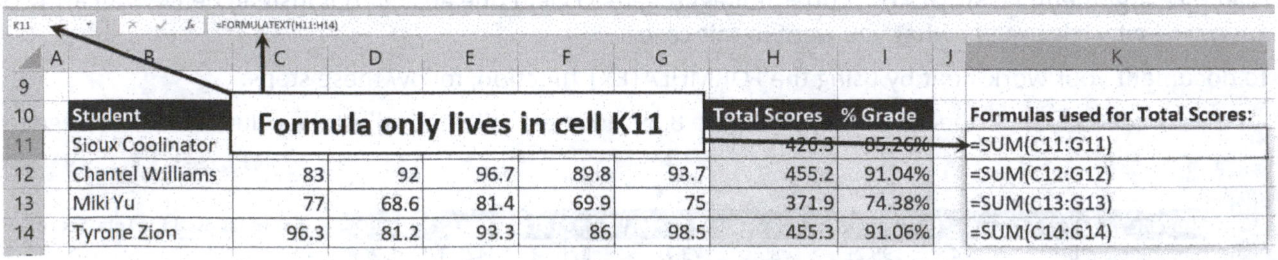

K11 · × ✓ *fx* =FORMULATEXT(H11:H14)

Student						Total Scores	% Grade		Formulas used for Total Scores:
Sioux Coolinator						426.3	85.26%		=SUM(C11:G11)
Chantel Williams	83	92	96.7	89.8	93.7	455.2	91.04%		=SUM(C12:G12)
Miki Yu	77	68.6	81.4	69.9	75	371.9	74.38%		=SUM(C13:G13)
Tyrone Zion	96.3	81.2	93.3	86	98.5	455.3	91.06%		=SUM(C14:G14)

Formula only lives in cell K11

Figure 8.93 *Cell K11 contains the formulas. The remaining results are spilled into the cells below.*

Spilling Dynamic Array Formulas and Array Operations

What you just did is amazing! With only one formula, you created four results. This ability to enter a single formula and have the results spill to other cells exists only in Microsoft 365 Excel and Excel 2021. It is not possible in any other version of Excel. This ability comes from the redesigned Excel worksheet formula calculation engine. In versions of Excel prior to Microsoft 365 Excel, if you try to do have the results spill to other cells, you get an error. With the new worksheet formula calculation engine, you have a choice between either putting a single cell reference or a range of cells into non-aggregate functions like FORMULATEXT:

- If you choose to put a single cell reference into FORMULATEXT, you enter the formula, get one answer, and then manually copy the formula down the column.
- If you choose to put a range of cells into FORMULATEXT, you enter the formula and then are done. You don't have to copy the formula down the column.

A big advantage of having the results spill to other cells is that when you have to edit the formula, you only have to edit one cell rather than all four cells. In Figures 8.93, you can see that when cell K11 is selected, the formula in the formula bar is shown in a black font and is not grayed out. This means you can edit the formula. In all the other spilled cells, the formula in the formula bar is grayed out, as shown in Figure 8.94. This means that you do not use these cells to edit the formula. If you click in one of these cells, you see nothing in the cell! However, the good news is that if you use one of the cells from the spilled range as a cell reference in a formula, the cell reference picks up the value perfectly.

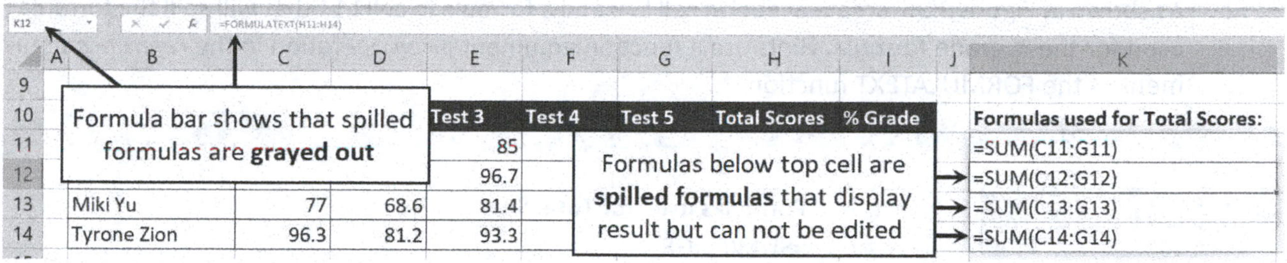

Figure 8.94 *Cells below cell K11 display results.*

Any time you put a range of values, rather than a single value, into a function argument for a non-aggregate function, as with the *reference* argument to FORMULATEXT, you are making a function argument array operation. An *array operation* is a calculation that operates on an array of values rather than on a single value and that delivers an array of answers. If the array of answers is the final result for an Excel formula, the results are spilled into the cells. An array operation is sort of the opposite of an aggregate operation because, whereas an array operation takes multiple inputs and delivers an array of answers, an aggregate operation takes an array of inputs and delivers a single answer.

Figure 8.95 shows the final result of the spilled array for the total score formulas and illustrates two advantages of using spilled arrays:

- You simply create the formula and enter it, and there is no need to manually copy the formula.
- When you edit the formula later, you only have to do it in one cell rather than in all four.

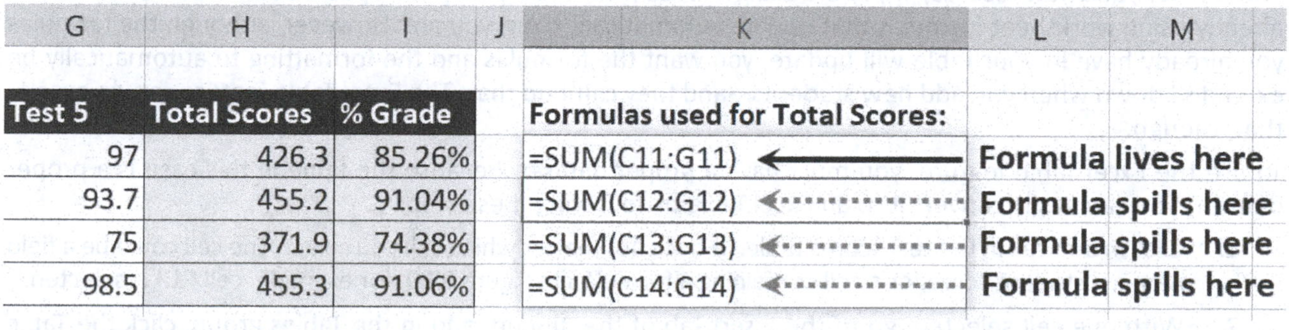

Test 5	Total Scores	% Grade	Formulas used for Total Scores:		
97	426.3	85.26%	=SUM(C11:G11)	←	Formula lives here
93.7	455.2	91.04%	=SUM(C12:G12)	◄········	Formula spills here
75	371.9	74.38%	=SUM(C13:G13)	◄········	Formula spills here
98.5	455.3	91.06%	=SUM(C14:G14)	◄········	Formula spills here

Figure 8.95 *When you edit the formula later, you only have to edit one cell!*

To finish your formula documentation, follow these steps:

1. As shown in Figure 8.96, create a label in cell K7 and the formula in K8. Notice that in this case, you use FORMULATEXT with a single cell reference.

G	H	I	J	K
Test 5	Total Possible			Formulas used for Total Scores:
100	500			=FORMULATEXT(H8)
				FORMULATEXT(reference)

Figure 8.96 *Here you use FORMULATEXT with a single cell reference.*

Figure 8.97 shows that when you enter the FORMULATEXT function with a single cell reference, Excel delivers a single answer.

G	H	I	J	K
Test 5	Total Possible			Formulas used for Total Scores:
100	500			=SUM(C8:G8)

Figure 8.97 *When you use FORMULATEXT with a single cell reference, you get a single answer.*

2. As shown in Figure 8.98, create a label in cell L10 and a formula in cell L11 that will spill the formulas used for the % grade formula. Hint: Use a function argument array operation in the *reference* argument of the FORMULATEXT function.

G	H	I	J	K	L
Test 5	Total Possible			Formulas used for Total Scores:	
100	500			=SUM(C8:G8)	
Test 5	Total Scores	% Grade		Formulas used for Total Scores:	Formulas used for % Grade:
97	426.3	85.26%		=SUM(C11:G11)	=H11/$H$8
93.7	455.2	91.04%		=SUM(C12:G12)	=H12/$H$8
75	371.9	74.38%		=SUM(C13:G13)	=H13/$H$8
98.5	455.3	91.06%		=SUM(C14:G14)	=H14/$H$8

Figure 8.98 *You finish your documentation by creating formula documentation for the % grade formula.*

Using the Excel Table Feature

The next task in this project is to convert the proper dataset table to an official Excel Table by using the Excel Table feature. The advantage of using the Excel Table feature is that if you need to add new students to the table (that is, add new records), if you are using an Excel Table, everything will update automatically. Aren't you already using worksheet formulas that update automatically? Yes, you are. However, although the formulas you already have in your table will update, you want the formulas and the formatting to automatically be extended down when you add new students—and they can't do that. The Excel Table feature can do exactly that, though.

To use the Excel Table feature, you must have a proper dataset. Because the table in this case is a proper dataset, you can easily convert it to an Excel Table by following these steps:

1. Click in one cell in the test scores table. (It does not matter which cell you select. The cell could be a field name, a student score, or a cell containing a formula.) In Figure 8.99, for example, cell F13 is selected.

2. With one cell selected, go to the Insert tab of the Ribbon, and in the Tables group, click the Table button. Alternatively, use the much faster keyboard shortcut Ctrl+T. The Create Table dialog box appears.

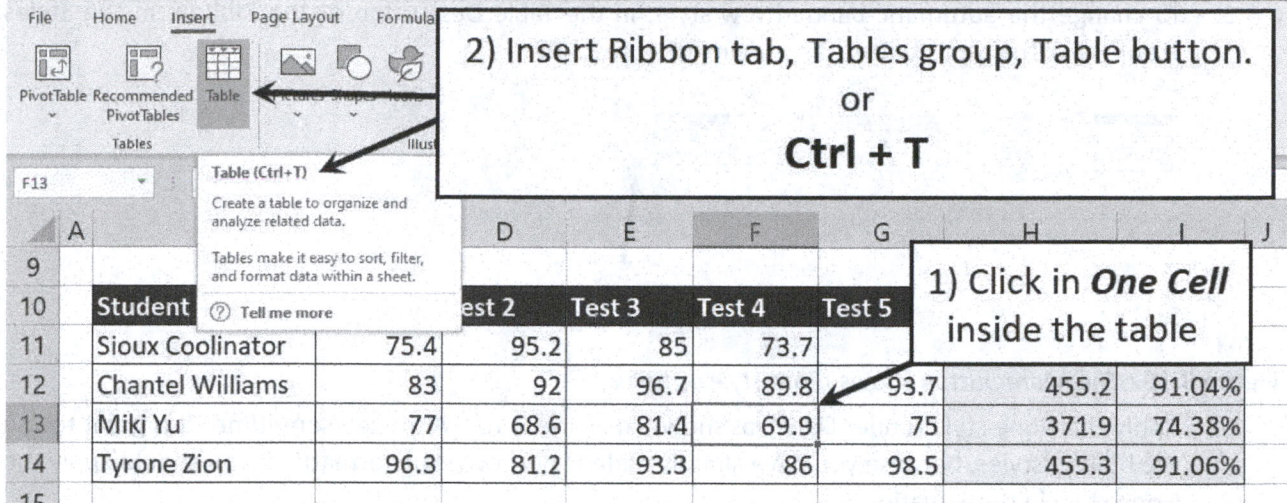

Figure 8.99 *Ctrl+T is the keyboard shortcut to convert a proper dataset to an Excel Table using the Excel Table feature.*

3. In the Create Table dialog box, make sure My Table Has Headers is checked, as shown in Figure 8.100. (*Header* is a synonym for *field name*.) Click the OK button. Excel creates an Excel Table from your proper dataset.

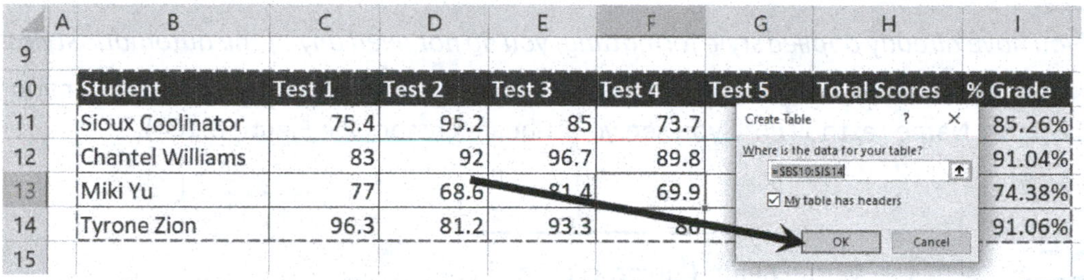

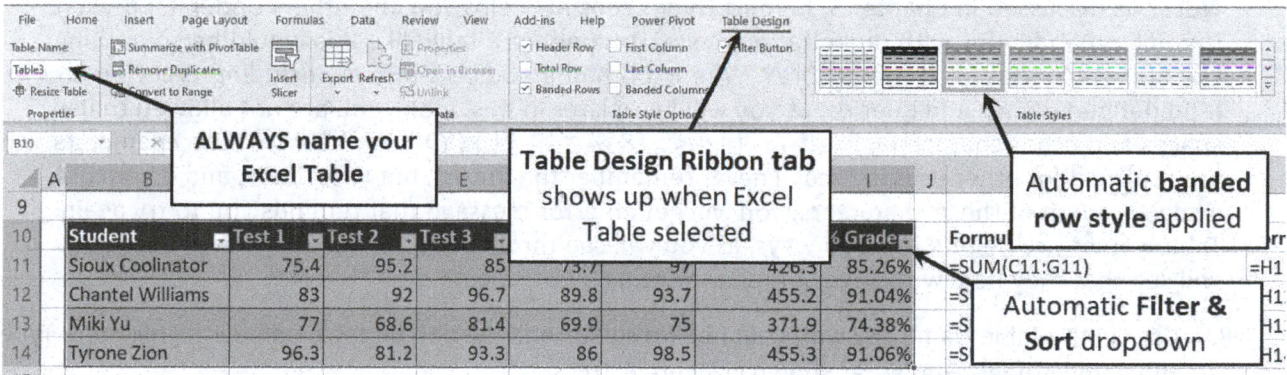

Figure 8.100 *In the Create Table dialog box, make sure My Table Has Headers is checked.*

4. Select any part of your new Excel Table, and the Table Design tab of the Ribbon appears. (This is a context-sensitive ribbon that appears only when you have all or part of an Excel Table selected.) Figure 8.101 shows the important elements in the Table Design tab of the Ribbon.

Figure 8.101 *When any part of an Excel Table is selected, the context-sensitive Table Design tab of the Ribbon pops up.*

5. To change the automatic banded row style, in the Table Design tab of the Ribbon, in the Styles group, click the More button, as shown in Figure 8.102.

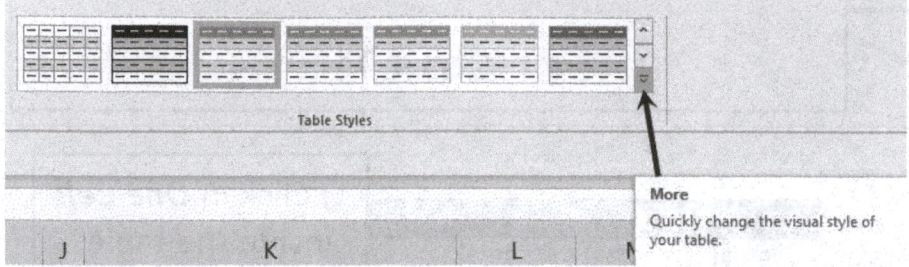

Figure 8.102 *The More button shows more style options.*

6. Apply the None style (under Light), as shown in Figure 8.103. Although sometimes it is great to use the built-in styles, because you have already added your own style formatting, you should apply the None style in this situation.

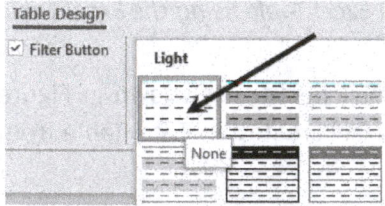

Figure 8.103 *Because you have already applied style formatting, you do not need any of the automatic styles.*

7. To name your table, in the Table Design tab of the Ribbon, go to the Properties group and hover your mouse over the Table Name textbox until you see your I-beam cursor (see Figure 8.104).

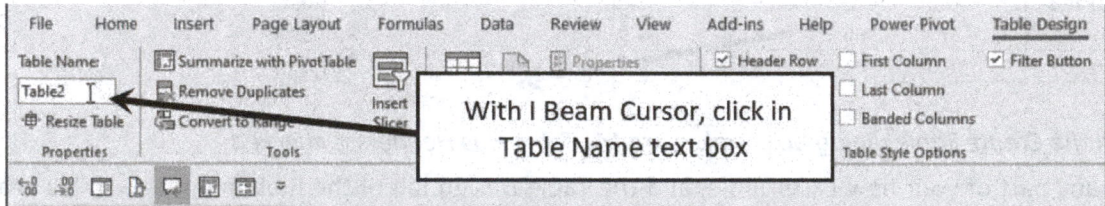

Figure 8.104 *Use your I-beam cursor to click in the Table Name textbox.*

> **Note:** As discussed in Chapter 5, naming things sensibly helps you and others understand what is going on and helps with organization. A smart name for a table like this would be something like StudentGrades or StudentScores. When you name objects in Excel, including Excel Tables (and defined names and queries, as you will learn later in this book), you are not allowed to use spaces and other characters, like * /+- ( ) ^ < >+& % ~ ` |] [} { @ " ; : , ' $ # !. These characters are reserved for other uses in Excel. I never remember the full list, but Excel does, and if type use a space or one of these characters, you will get an error message that reminds you to try again. Table names are helpful in many ways, as you will see throughout the book. In this chapter, you will see that they help with page setup for printing a PDF document.

8. Click in the Table Name box with your I-beam cursor, and the default table name is highlighted. Type the name StudentGrades, as shown in Figure 8.105.

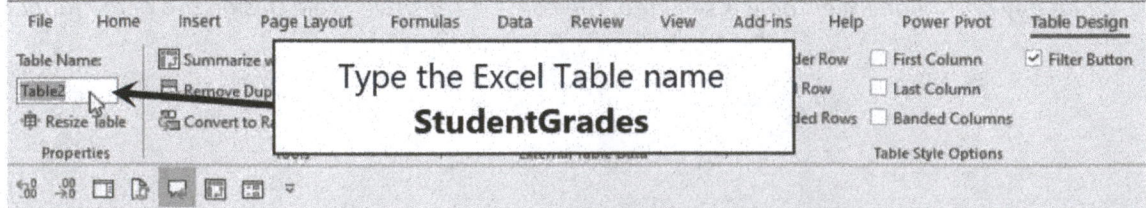

Figure 8.105 *Spaces and characters like * /+- ( ) ^ < >+& % ~ ` |] [} { @ " ; : , ' $ # ! are not allowed in table names.*

9. As you type the table name, the insertion point cursor remains at the end of the name, as shown in Figure 8.106.

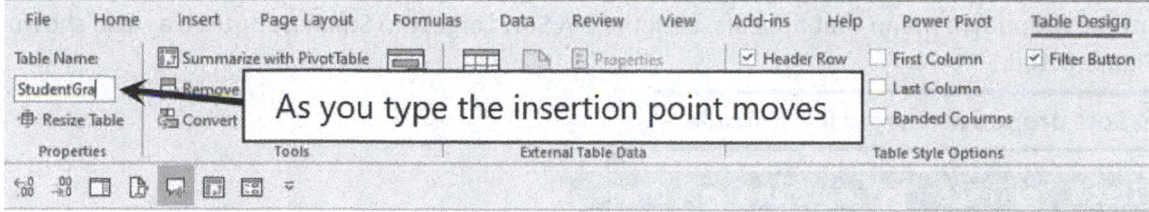

Figure 8.106 *Type a name.*

10. When you are done typing, press Enter. If the name is longer than the textbox, you see only as much of the beginning of the name as will fit in the textbox. For example, in Figure 8.107, the last letter in the name StudentGrades is not shown.

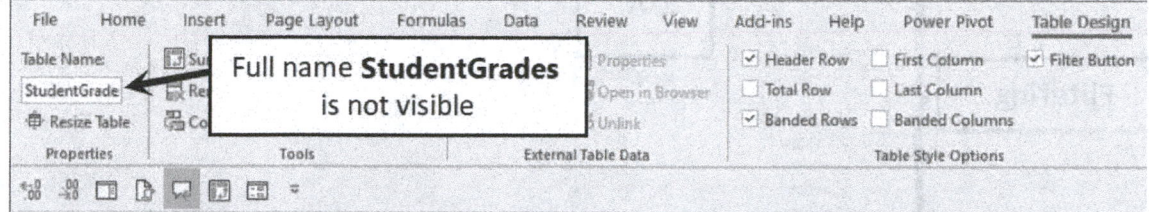

Figure 8.107 *When you press Enter, the Excel Table is officially named.*

Note: Dynamic spilled array formulas do not work inside Excel Tables. In your Excel Table, in the % grade column, you created a formula where you used a relative cell reference and an absolute cell reference. The formula used in cell I11 was =H11/$H$8. If you had created the solution without using the Excel Table feature, you could have used a single spilled array formula in cell I11—for example, =H11:H14/H8—which would not have required the copy action or the locking action. But in an Excel Table, spilled array formulas are not allowed. You get an error if you try to create a spilled array formula in a column in an Excel Table: "The formula you typed could return multiple items, which is not supported in Excel Tables." I am not sure why Microsoft programmed them this way, but it is something that you have to deal with. If you want to see an example of this error, you can open the Excel downloadable file for this chapter and go to the worksheet named Ch08(1an). We will talk more about spilled array formulas and Excel Tables throughout the rest of the book.

Sorting and Filtering

One of the many advantages of using Excel Tables is that you can sort and filter a table easily by using the Sort & Filter dropdown arrow at the top of each column:

- **Sort:** To sort means to organize the records in a table from smallest to biggest (A-Z, or ascending) or biggest to smallest (Z-A, or descending), based on a specified column.

- **Filter:** To filter means to show only certain records, based on a condition from a column. For example, you might want to show only student records where the % grade was bigger than 90%.

Because one of the original goals given to you in this chapter's example is to create a PDF file with the student records sorted from biggest to smallest, based on the % grade column, you can just use the Sort & Filter dropdown arrow at the top of the % Grade column to sort the records Z-A (largest to smallest). Sometimes new Excel users worry that if they sort the % Grade column, Excel might sort that % Grade column only (and not the rest of the columns) and destroy the integrity of the student records in the table. This is not the case with the Sort & Filter feature. When you sort a column in a proper dataset, that column determines the sort for the entire table, and Excel sorts each row or record based on the value in the % Grade column. For example, when you sort the % Grade column Z-A, the student records are sorted perfectly so that the student with the biggest % grade will have their full record appear at the top, and the remaining records are sorted correctly, from biggest to smallest based on % grade.

To sort your table, follow these steps:

1. Click the Sort & Filter dropdown arrow at the top of the % Grade column, as shown in Figure 8.108.
2. From the dropdown menu that appears, click the Z-A Sort Largest to Smallest option, as also shown in Figure 8.108.

1) Filter & Sort dropdown arrow for % Grade
Test 3
Test 4
Test 5
Total Scores
% Grade
Sorting
Sort Smallest to Largest
Sort Largest to Smallest
Sort by Color
Sheet View
2) Click Z-A
Clear Filter From "% Gr
Filter by Color
Number Filters
Filtering
Search
(Select All)
74.38%
85.26%
91.04%
91.06%

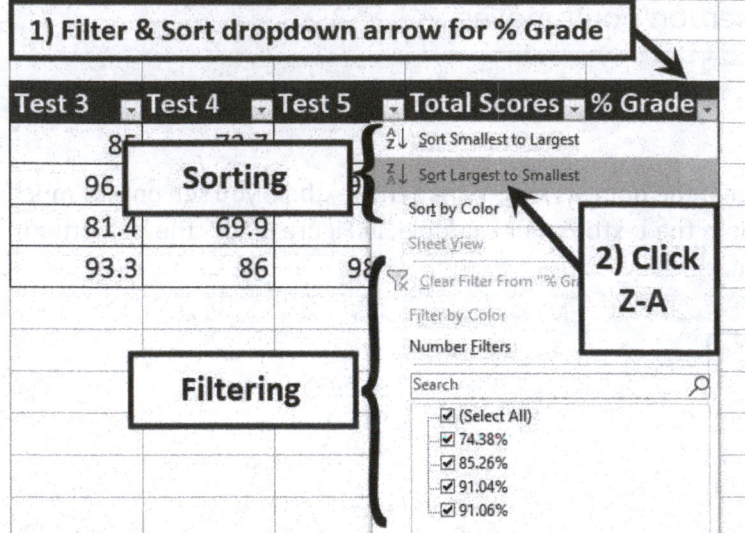

Figure 8.108 *Sort the % Grade column using the Z-A Sort Largest to Smallest option.*

3. Click outside the table in cell L11, as shown in Figure 8.109.

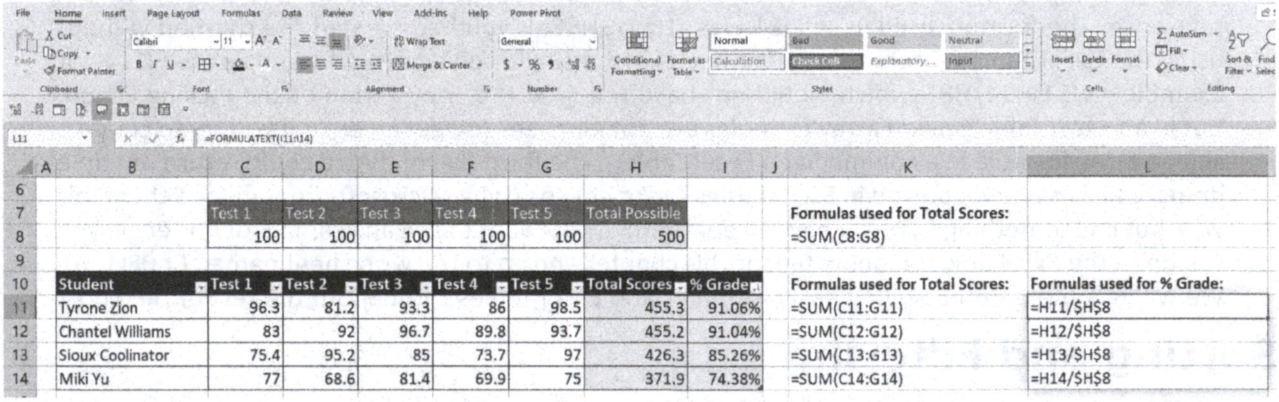

=FORMULATEXT(L11:I14)
Test 1 | Test 2 | Test 3 | Test 4 | Test 5 | Total Possible
100 | 100 | 100 | 100 | 100 | 500
Formulas used for Total Scores:
=SUM(C8:G8)
Student | Test 1 | Test 2 | Test 3 | Test 4 | Test 5 | Total Scores | % Grade
Tyrone Zion | 96.3 | 81.2 | 93.3 | 86 | 98.5 | 455.3 | 91.06%
Chantel Williams | 83 | 92 | 96.7 | 89.8 | 93.7 | 455.2 | 91.04%
Sioux Coolinator | 75.4 | 95.2 | 85 | 73.7 | 97 | 426.3 | 85.26%
Miki Yu | 77 | 68.6 | 81.4 | 69.9 | 75 | 371.9 | 74.38%
Formulas used for Total Scores:
=SUM(C11:G11)
=SUM(C12:G12)
=SUM(C13:G13)
=SUM(C14:G14)
Formulas used for % Grade:
=H11/$H$8
=H12/$H$8
=H13/$H$8
=H14/$H$8

Figure 8.109 *The table is now sorted from highest % grade to lowest.*

In Figure 8.109, you can see that Tyrone Zion's full record appears at the top of the table because his % grade is the largest. You can also see in Figure 8.109 that because a cell outside the Excel Table is selected, the Table Design tab of the Ribbon is no longer in view. Context-sensitive Ribbon tabs such as Table Design appear only when the corresponding object is selected.

Setting Up a Page for Printing

If your goal is to print out the information you now have as a PDF file, you probably do not want the goals and documented formulas to be part of the final printout. You can indicate which parts of an Excel page to print by using the Page Setup dialog box. Most computer users in the world (including myself) have made the mistake of clicking the Print button in Excel before first using the Page Setup dialog box. When you do this, you might end up with partial tables and the wrong elements printed out across multiple pages. By using the Page Setup dialog box, you can fine-tune the setup of your Excel file and print only the parts that are needed, eliminating waste and helping the audience see the important information. (On the first day of my accounting job at Broderick Consulting back in 1999, I amazed my boss by giving her printouts that showed only the information needed.)

To set up your grade report for printing, follow these steps:

1. To see what you do *not* want, press Ctrl+P. As shown in Figure 8.110, if you printed now, you would end up with two pages printed, including the goals and documented formula—which you do not want.

2. To close the print preview, press the Esc key.

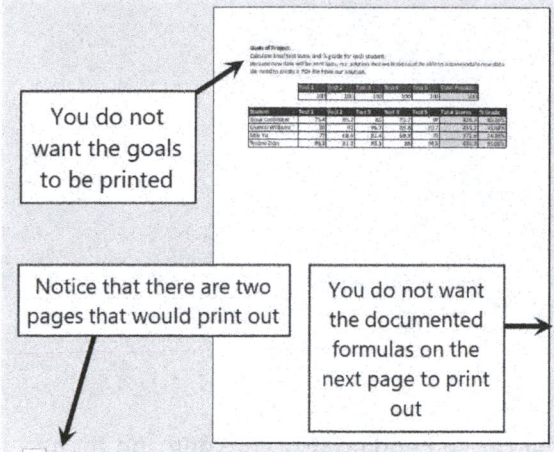

Figure 8.110 *Ctrl+P opens the print preview, where you can see that there are elements that you do not want to print.*

3. Look at Figure 8.111, which shows how you want the page to print. Notice that you need to print a scoring area, print in landscape view (because the table is wider than it is tall), and print a helpful footer.

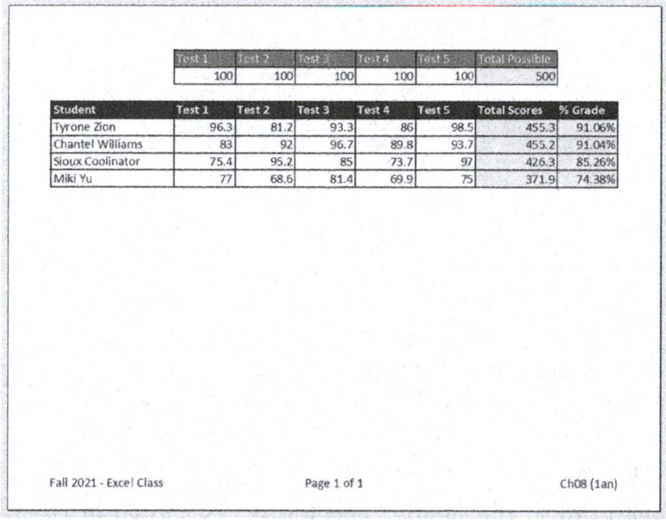

	Test 1	Test 2	Test 3	Test 4	Test 5	Total Possible	
	100	100	100	100	100	500	

Student	Test 1	Test 2	Test 3	Test 4	Test 5	Total Scores	% Grade
Tyrone Zion	96.3	81.2	93.3	86	98.5	455.3	91.06%
Chantel Williams	83	92	96.7	89.8	93.7	455.2	91.04%
Sioux Coolinator	75.4	95.2	85	73.7	97	426.3	85.26%
Miki Yu	77	68.6	81.4	69.9	75	371.9	74.38%

Fall 2021 - Excel Class   Page 1 of 1   Ch08 (1an)

Figure 8.111 *This is what the printout will look like after you correctly set up the page for printing.*

4. To open up the Page Setup dialog box to set your printing parameters, go to the Page Layout tab of the Ribbon, and then, in the Page Setup group, click the Page Setup dialog launcher, as shown in Figure 8.112. Alternatively, use the keyboard shortcut Alt, P, S, P.

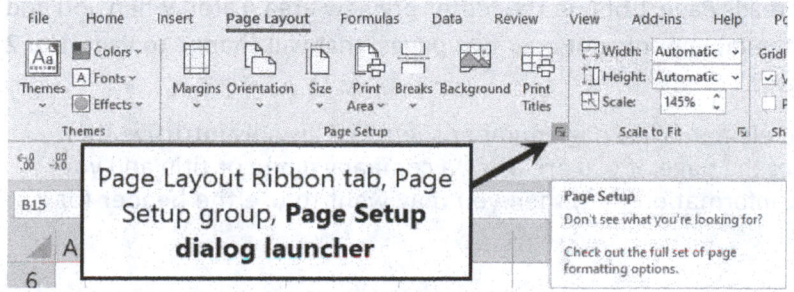

Figure 8.112 *To open the Page Setup dialog box with a keyboard, use the keyboard shortcut Alt, P, S, P.*

5. As shown in Figure 8.113, on the Page tab in the Page Setup dialog box, choose Landscape orientation. In the Adjust To textbox in the Scaling section, scroll up or down until you hit the right size.

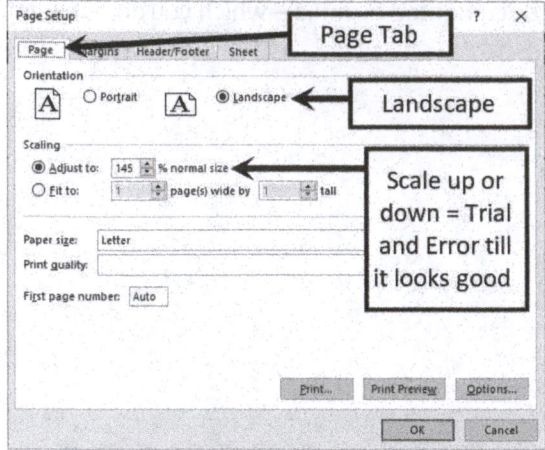

Figure 8.113 *The Page tab in the Page Setup dialog box.*

Note: I rarely get the scaling setting just right on the first try, so I end up first guessing and then closing dialog box and pressing Ctrl+P to see how it looks. Then I go back and forth a few times until it is just right. In this case, I ended up using 145% of normal size.

6. Click on the Margin tab of the Page Setup dialog box and set your margins—which are the distance from the edge of the page to your table—as shown in Figure 8.114. Under Center on Page, select the Horizontally checkbox.

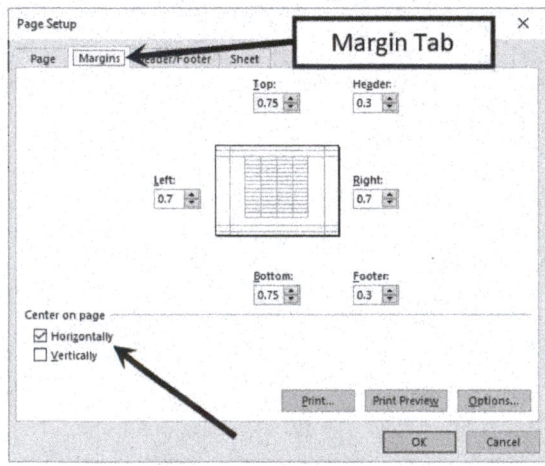

Figure 8.114 *The Margins tab in the Page Setup dialog box.*

7. In the Header/Foot tab, determine what will print in the header and footer, as shown in Figure 8.115. You can see that there are preview areas for the header and footer that appear blank before you apply anything. There are also two dropdowns—one for the header and one for the footer—with useful built-in options. In this case, select Page 1 of ? from the Footer dropdown. This option will dynamically show the correct individual and total page numbers, no matter how many pages there are. Currently, your footer reads Page 1 of 1 in the footer preview area. Later, when you add more students to the table, and the table prints out over two pages, that will change to Page 1 of 2 on page 1 and Page 2 of 2 on page 2.

Note: I usually create footers so that elements like page number seem less visually intrusive than if they are in the header, at the top of the page. If you are using a company name or title and you want the viewer to be hit with that information first, then you may want to use the header for that information.

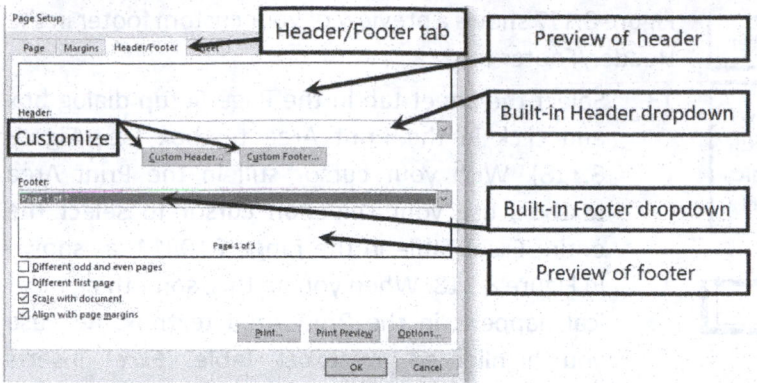

Figure 8.115 *Header/Foot tab in the Page Setup dialog box.*

8.   Click the Custom Footer button to open the Footer dialog box.

9.   As you can see in Figure 8.116, the Footer dialog box shows three sections of the footer: left, center, and right. The Center Section box is already filled out from the automatic footer than you created in the previous step. Above the three sections are buttons you can use to insert dynamic code for things like date, time, page number, sheet tab name, and even pictures. For example, the code that was automatically placed in the center section reads Page &[Page] of &[Pages]. &[Page] is the code that dynamically inserts the correct individual page number, and &[Pages] inserts the total page count. The rest of the text in the center section is just static text. Together, this code gives you Page 1 of 2, Page 2 of 2, and so on.

10.   Click in the Left Section box in the Footer dialog box and type **Fall 2021 - Excel Class**, which is the class name for the scores in the student score table (see Figure 8.116).

11.   Click in the Right Section box in the Footer dialog box and click on the Sheet Name button, which is the third button from the right. As shown in Figure 8.116, Excel inserts dynamic code that will always list the sheet name in the footer, no matter how many times you change it.

12.   Click the OK button in the Footer dialog box to close it and jump back to the Page Setup dialog box.

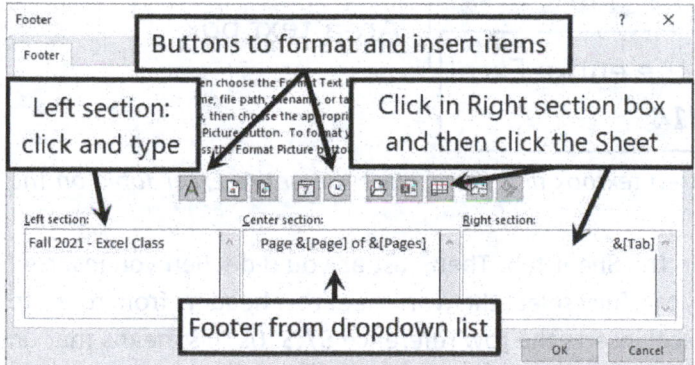

Figure 8.116 *The 10 buttons in the middle provide real power to you in building dynamic footers and headers.*

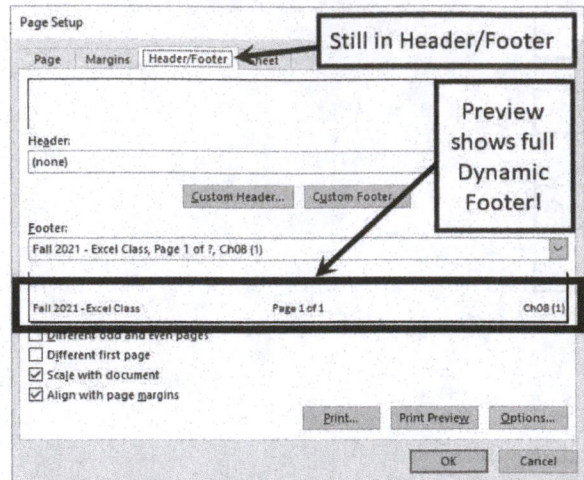

Figure 8.117 *This footer is dynamic and will update based on the number of pages and the worksheet name.*

Figure 8.117 shows a preview of your custom footer in the Header/Footer tab.

13.   Select the Sheet tab in the Page Setup dialog box and click in the Print Area textbox (see Figure 8.118). With your cursor still in the Print Area textbox, use your selection cursor to select the entire Excel Table in the range B10:I14, as shown in Figure 8.118. When you do this, something magical happens in the Print Area textbox: Because you highlighted an Excel Table, Excel inserts code that represents the whole table. This code, StudentGrades[#All], means "always retrieve the whole table, even when new records are added or taken away." This is a huge advantage because later, when you add more student records, this code will pick up all the new records as part of the expanded table, and your print job will include the new data.

Note: As you will learn in Chapter 12, there is a special name for code associated with an Excel Table: *table formula nomenclature.*

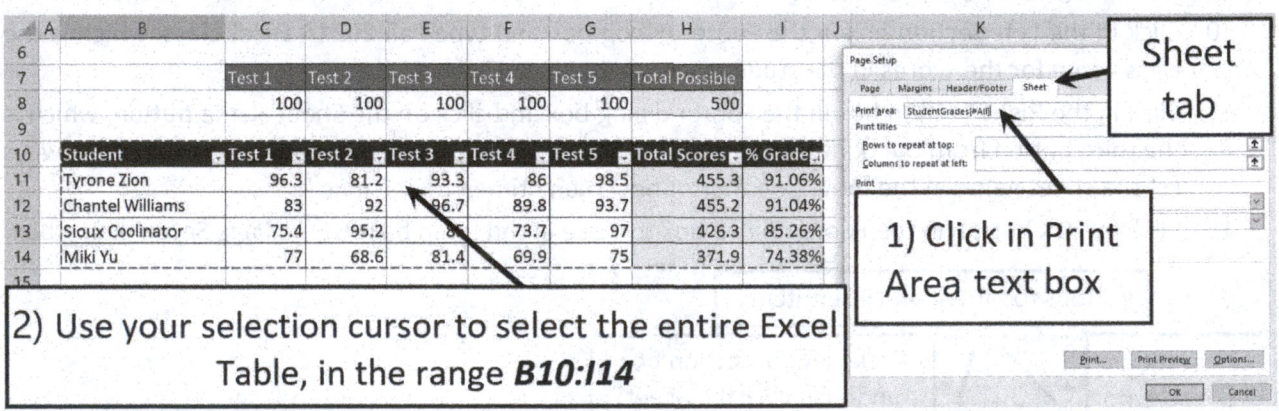

Figure 8.118 *In the Sheet tab, click in the Print Area textbox and then select the entire Excel Table on the worksheet.*

14.   Click the Rows to Repeat at Top textbox in the Sheet tab. Then, just as you did when you inserted rows into the worksheet a few pages back, carefully select the worksheet row headers from row 7 to row 10. As you can see in Figure 8.119, Excel inserts the row reference $7:$10. This means that on every page that you print out, the field names and maximum possible points table will be repeated; this is exactly what you want. If you did not repeat the field names, then the numbers would be hard to interpret.

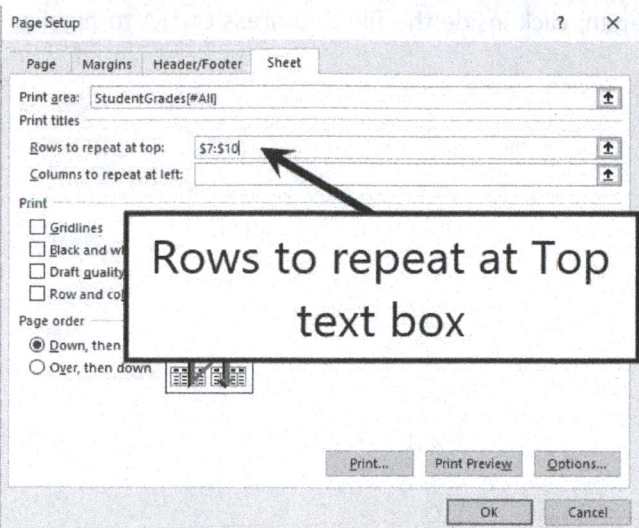

Figure 8.119 *In the Rows to Repeat at Top textbox, select rows 7 to 10.*

15. To complete the page setup, click the OK button in the Page Setup dialog box.

16. To check your work, press Ctrl+P and compare your print preview to Figure 8.111. You can use the Esc key to close the print preview without printing.

Adding New Data to a Dynamic Solution by Using a Text File

So far in this chapter, you have completed a lot of steps. Thanks to all the steps you've carefully taken, the real magic can happen now. When you add new student data, everything should update perfectly.

At the beginning of this project, you had to manually enter data by typing student names and stores. Now you can enter new data from a text file that is specifically structured to hold records (or rows) of data: Ch08NewScoreData.txt.

> **Note:** As discussed in Chapter 5, there are numerous file extensions, such as .xlsx, .pdf, and more. The file extension .txt is the file type of the source data file you are about to use. Although you will learn much more about text files with the extension .txt, for now all you need to know is that this file type is very convenient for holding records of data. In fact, all you have to do is open the file, copy the data, and paste it into Excel, and all the student records will be in perfect record form for your table.

To add new data to your Excel Table, follow these steps:

1. Open the file named Ch08NewScoreData.txt (see Figure 8.120).

> **Note:** The Ch08NewScoreData.txt file is in the same folder as the Excel file for this chapter: TheOnlyAppMatterBook\Ch08.

Figure 8.120 *Text files are perfect for holding records of data.*

2.   As shown in Figure 8.121, with the text file open, click inside the file and press Ctrl+A to highlight all records.

3.   Press Ctrl+C to copy all the student records.

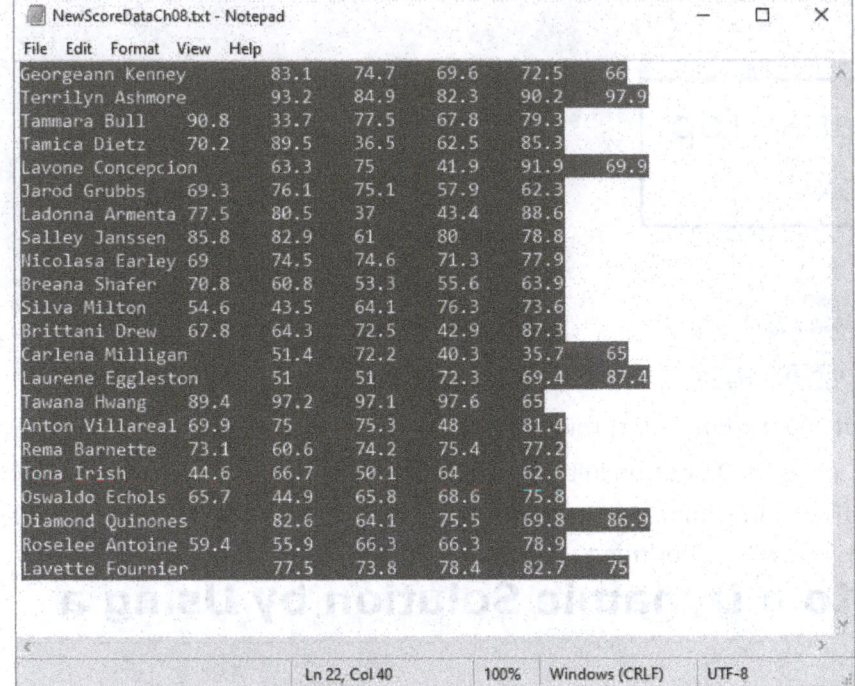

Figure 8.121 *Open the text file named NewScoreDataCh08.txt and then copy all the records.*

4.   Back in your Excel file, on the sheet named Ch08(1), click in cell B15, which is (very importantly) the first cell directly below the first column in the Excel Table. Figure 8.122 shows cell B15 selected.

5.   With cell B15 still selected, press Ctrl+V to paste all the new records below the table.

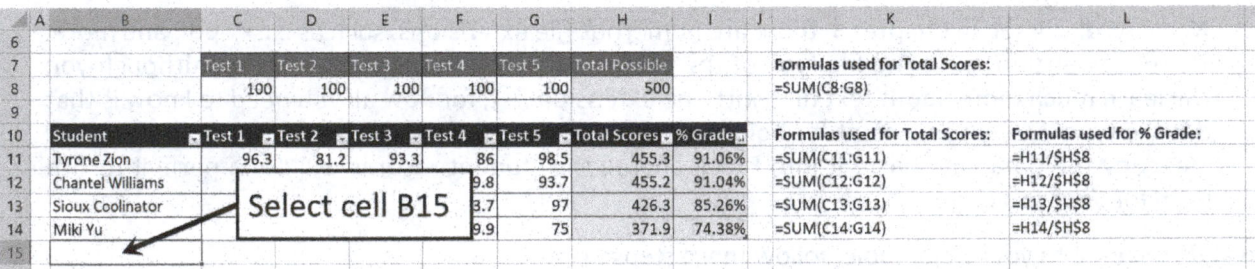

Figure 8.122 *Select the first cell directly below the first column in the Excel Table.*

6.   Sort the % Grade column Z-A. Figure 8.123 shows that everything in the table automatically updates.

	Student	Test 1	Test 2	Test 3	Test 4	Test 5	Total Scores	% Grade	Formulas used for Total Scores:	Formulas used for % Grade:
7		Test 1	Test 2	Test 3	Test 4	Test 5	Total Possible		Formulas used for Total Scores:	
8		100	100	100	100	100	500		=SUM(C8:G8)	
9										
10	Student	Test 1	Test 2	Test 3	Test 4	Test 5	Total Scores	% Grade	Formulas used for Total Scores:	Formulas used for % Grade:
11	Tyrone Zion	96.3	81.2	93.3	86	98.5	455.3	91.06%	=SUM(C11:G11)	=H11/$H$8
12	Chantel Williams	83	92	96.7	89.8	93.7	455.2	91.04%	=SUM(C12:G12)	=H12/$H$8
13	Terrilyn Ashmore	93.2	84.9	82.3	90.2	97.9	449	89.70%	=SUM(C13:G13)	=H13/$H$8
14	Tawana Hwang	89.4	97.2	97.1	97.6	65	446.3	89.26%	=SUM(C14:G14)	=H14/$H$8
15	Sioux Coolinator	75.4	95.2	85	73.7	97	426.3	85.26%	=SUM(C15:G15)	=H15/$H$8
16	Salley Janssen	86	83	61	80	79	389	77.70%	=SUM(C16:G16)	=H16/$H$8
17	Lavette Fournier	77.5	73.8	78.4	82.7	75	387.4	77.48%	=SUM(C17:G17)	=H17/$H$8
18	Diamond Quinones	82.6	64.1	75.5	69.8	86.9	378.9	75.78%	=SUM(C18:G18)	=H18/$H$8
19	Miki Yu	77	68.6	81.4	69.9	75	371.9	74.38%	=SUM(C19:G19)	=H19/$H$8
20	Nicolasa Earley	69	75	75	71	78	367	73.46%	=SUM(C20:G20)	=H20/$H$8
21	Georgeann Kenney	83.1	74.7	69.6	72.5	66	365.9	73.18%	=SUM(C21:G21)	=H21/$H$8
22	Rema Barnette	73.1	60.6	74.2	75.4	77.2	360.5	72.10%	=SUM(C22:G22)	=H22/$H$8
23	Anton Villareal	69.9	75	75.3	48	81.4	349.6	69.92%	=SUM(C23:G23)	=H23/$H$8
24	Tammara Bull	90.8	33.7	77.5	67.8	79.3	349	69.82%	=SUM(C24:G24)	=H24/$H$8

Figure 8.123 *Paste the records using Ctrl+V. All records become part of table, and all documenting formulas update.*

7. Use Ctrl+P to open print preview, and as shown in Figures 8.124 and 8.125, everything is updated there as well.

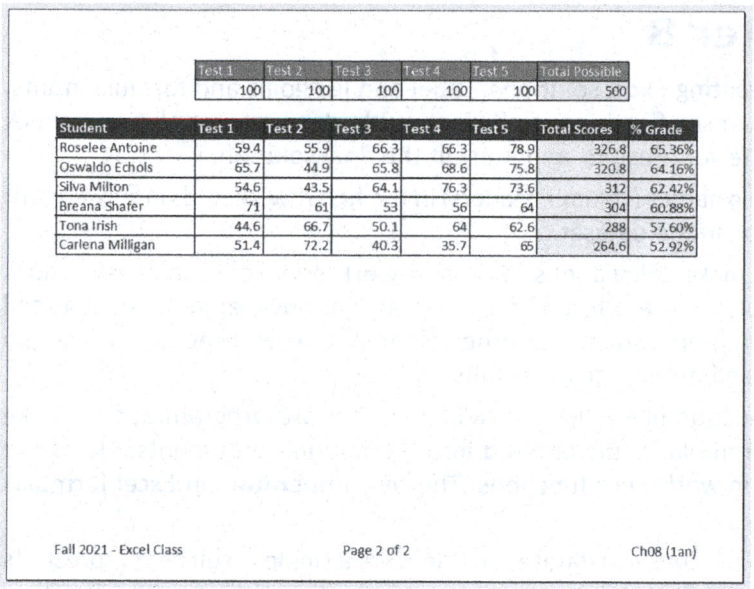

	Test 1	Test 2	Test 3	Test 4	Test 5	Total Possible	
	100	100	100	100	100	500	
Student	**Test 1**	**Test 2**	**Test 3**	**Test 4**	**Test 5**	**Total Scores**	**% Grade**
Tyrone Zion	96.3	81.2	93.3	86	98.5	455.3	91.06%
Chantel Williams	83	92	96.7	89.8	93.7	455.2	91.04%
Terrilyn Ashmore	93.2	84.9	82.3	90.2	97.9	449	89.70%
Tawana Hwang	89.4	97.2	97.1	97.6	65	446.3	89.26%
Sioux Coolinator	75.4	95.2	85	73.7	97	426.3	85.26%
Salley Janssen	86	83	61	80	79	389	77.70%
Lavette Fournier	77.5	73.8	78.4	82.7	75	387.4	77.48%
Diamond Quinones	82.6	64.1	75.5	69.8	86.9	378.9	75.78%
Miki Yu	77	68.6	81.4	69.9	75	371.9	74.38%
Nicolasa Earley	69	75	75	71	78	367	73.46%
Georgeann Kenney	83.1	74.7	69.6	72.5	66	365.9	73.18%
Rema Barnette	73.1	60.6	74.2	75.4	77.2	360.5	72.10%
Anton Villareal	69.9	75	75.3	48	81.4	349.6	69.92%
Tammara Bull	90.8	33.7	77.5	67.8	79.3	349	69.82%
Tamica Dietz	70.2	89.5	36.5	62.5	85.3	344	68.80%
Lavone Concepcion	63.3	75	41.9	91.9	69.9	342	68.40%
Jarod Grubbs	69.3	76.1	75.1	57.9	62.3	340.7	68.14%
Brittani Drew	68	64	73	43	87	335	66.96%
Laurene Eggleston	51	51	72.3	69.4	87.4	331.1	66.22%
Ladonna Armenta	78	81	37	43	89	327	65.40%

Fall 2021 - Excel Class   Page 1 of 2   Ch08 (1an)

Figure 8.124 *After you add new data, your printout updates.*

	Test 1	Test 2	Test 3	Test 4	Test 5	Total Possible	
	100	100	100	100	100	500	
Student	**Test 1**	**Test 2**	**Test 3**	**Test 4**	**Test 5**	**Total Scores**	**% Grade**
Roselee Antoine	59.4	55.9	66.3	66.3	78.9	326.8	65.36%
Oswaldo Echols	65.7	44.9	65.8	68.6	75.8	320.8	64.16%
Silva Milton	54.6	43.5	64.1	76.3	73.6	312	62.42%
Breana Shafer	71	61	53	56	64	304	60.88%
Tona Irish	44.6	66.7	50.1	64	62.6	288	57.60%
Carlena Milligan	51.4	72.2	40.3	35.7	65	264.6	52.92%

Fall 2021 - Excel Class   Page 2 of 2   Ch08 (1an)

Figure 8.125 *When you add new data, a second page appears in your printout.*

8. To close the print preview without printing, press the Esc key.

Now wait a second! How does your solution know to update so perfectly? Here is how:

- Because you used the Excel Table feature, the table is programed to automatically expand as soon as you enter records in the first row below the table, bringing down the formatting and formulas to all new student records. If your table does not expand, you must change this default setting by selecting the following: File, Options, Proofing, AutoCorrect Options button, AutoFormat as You Type tab, Include New Rows and Columns in Table.

- Because you used the Excel Table feature, as soon as the new rows below the table are added, the formulas in the Total Scores and % Grade columns automatically copy down.

- Because the spilled array documentation formulas point to a full column in the Excel Table, they also spill all the way down to incorporate the new formulas.

- Because the Page Setup dialog box Print Area textbox points to the full Excel Table, the print job knows to expand to include all the new student records.

The bottom line is that anything in Excel that points to an Excel Table will automatically update when the table object expands. Excel has not always had Excel Tables, and without Excel Tables, it is very difficult to make fully dynamic solutions like this. As you work through this book and prepare for your Excel future, you should try to use Excel Tables as much as possible so that your solutions will be filled with the same kind of dynamic updatable magic you just learned about.

Converting a Solution to a PDF File

Now that you have completed the rest of your project, you can create a PDF file, using the file management skills you learned back in Chapter 5. In that chapter, you learned that with the Save As feature (which you activate by pressing the F12 key), you can create a new PDF file from an Excel file. To create the PDF file, follow these steps:

1. Select the sheet named Ch08(1).

2. Press the F12 key to activate the Save As command.

3. In the Save As dialog box, change the location to the folder where you are saving files for Chapter 8, change the filename to Student Grade Table, and change the file type to PDF(*.pdf).

4. In the Save As dialog box, click the OK button.

Now you have two files: the Excel file and the PDF file.

As you have completed this project, you have seen how powerful Excel can be. It allows you to build Excel solutions to solve problems in a dynamic way. You now have real power to complete tasks effectively and efficiently.

Key Concepts in Chapter 8

-   Keep in mind these **guidelines for creating Excel solutions**: Label and list goals and formula inputs, use proper datasets to store raw data, use effective and efficient methods to create solutions, check your work, document your work, state your results, and present the final solution.

-   A **proper dataset** is a table that has field names (column headers) in the first row, records in subsequent rows, and empty cells all the way around the dataset.

-   **Worksheet formulas** enable you to make calculations in cells. A worksheet formula always starts with an equal sign as the first character in the cell, and it can contain various elements, such as cell references, worksheet functions, math operators, and other elements. A worksheet formula can deliver number results, text results, and other types of results.

-   **Worksheet functions** are built-in function like SUM and AVERAGE that are programmed to make defined calculations based on the formula inputs entered into a function's arguments. There are more than 450 different Excel built-in worksheet functions. The **math operators** in Excel formulas are -, +, ?, *, ^, and ( ).

-   An **aggregate operation** takes multiple values in a dataset and delivers a single result that represents the underlying data, such as a sum to get the total or an arithmetic mean to get the average. In either case, the single number represents the entire dataset.

-   An **array operation** takes multiple inputs and delivers multiple outputs as a result. If the multiple outputs are the final result for an Excel formula, the results are spilled into the cells and are called dynamic spilled arrays.

-   When **cell references** are used in worksheet formulas, the formulas instantly update when source data changes. Cell references are unique to worksheet formulas and do not exist with other Excel features such as PivotTables and Power Query. Cell references can be relative or absolute.

-   **Relative cell references** move relatively throughout the copy action—where *relatively* means that if the formula is looking at the five cells to the left of the cell with the formula, when you copy the formula to any other cell, the cell reference will still be looking at five cells to the left. The formula will always point to cell references a given distance away from the formula and move as the formula is copied.

-   An **absolute cell reference** is a reference that is locked and will not move throughout the copy action. To lock a cell reference, you can press F4 to convert, for example, the cell reference H8 to $H$8. In this case, the $ signs do not have anything to do with money; instead, they stop the column reference H and the row reference 8 from moving throughout the copy action.

- The **angry rabbit double-click trick** allows you to quickly copy cell content down a column and is programmed to stop when there is no more data below, to the right, or to the left of the column with the copy action.

- **Checking your work** and **verifying** that formulas have the correct cell references is one of the most important steps in building Excel worksheet formula solutions. You can use the F2 key in the last cell of the copied range to invoke the color-coded range finder to help verify that all the cell references are pointed to the correct cells.

- **Style formatting** consists of cell formatting commands such as **bold font**, **cell borders**, **cell fill color**, **font color**, and other types of formatting. You can add formatting to a worksheet solution to add clarity and communicate a message.

- **Number formatting** allows you to change how a number is displayed on the surface of the worksheet without changing the underlying number in the cell; however, number formatting is a façade, and formulas do not see number formatting but act on the underlying number. Number formatting has many advantages, such as reducing file size, making date and time calculations possible, and saving time when doing data entry.

- When you have **General number formatting** applied to a cell, what you see with your eyes matches what is stored by Excel in the cell. Although General is a type of number formatting, technically it means that no number formatting is applied so that there is a difference between what you see on the surface of the cell and the underlying number that Excel stores in the cell.

- The **Format Painter command** copies cell formatting only and not cell content, such as text values and formulas.

- When you **insert rows or columns**, Excel moves existing solutions to accommodate the new rows or columns.

- **Percentages** are not numbers but instead are formatted symbolic representations of numbers that indicate how many parts there are out of a 100. The math operation used to calculate a percentage is division. For example, 400/500 = 0.8, which translates to 80%.

- When you create an Excel solution, it is helpful to **document how you created the solution** by listing goals, placing inputs in the cells, labeling the inputs, showing formulas that you used, and presenting results clearly. This allows you and other users of the solution to have a clear understanding of what the problem is, how you solved it, and what the results are.

- When you make an array operation that delivers multiple answers as part of the final result for an Excel formula, the results are spilled into the cells. For these **dynamic spilled arrays**, the formula lives in the top cell only, and the remaining spilled cells are displayed as values. To edit a spilled array formula, you use the top cell.

- You can use the **Excel Table feature** on proper date sets to convert tables into Excel Tables. Excel Tables automatically update when new records or columns are added. Excel Tables have automatic formatting, filtering, and sorting for ease of use. The number-one advantage of using Excel Tables is that anything that points to an Excel Table, like formulas and other features, can update when new data is added to the Excel Table.

- In Excel, you can name Excel Tables, cells, ranges of cells, and queries. **Names of Excel objects** cannot contain spaces and other characters, like * /+- ( ) ^ < >+& % ~ ` |] [} { @ " ; : , ' $ # !. These characters are reserved for other uses in Excel.

- To **sort** means to organize the records in the table from smallest to biggest (A-Z, or ascending) or biggest to smallest (Z-A, or descending) based on a specified column. When you sort based on a column, the records in the table remain intact. To **filter** means to show only certain records, based on a condition from a column. For example, you might want to show only student records where the % grade was bigger than 90%. With filtering, the records that do not match the condition are hidden. You can turn sorting and filtering on and off by using the Sort & Filter dropdown arrow at the top of each column in an Excel Table or manually from the Data tab of the Ribbon.

- You can use the **Page Setup dialog box** to determine how a worksheet looks when you print it or convert it to a PDF file. To open the Page Setup dialog box, you can use the keyboard shortcut Alt, P, S, P.

- **Text files** that use the file extension .txt are structured to hold records or tables of data.

Keyboard Shortcuts Learned in Chapter 8

Keyboard Shortcut	Description
Esc	Turns off the Format Painter command, closes the Print Preview and Options dialog boxes, and closes many other windows and dialog boxes
F4	When the insertion point is touching a cell reference in a formula, makes the cell reference absolute, or locked, by adding one $ sign to the column reference and another $ sign to the row reference
Ctrl+P	Opens the Print Preview and Options dialog boxes
Alt, P, S, P	Opens the Page Setup dialog box
Ctrl+A	Highlights everything inside a text file
Ctrl+C	Copies the selection
Ctrl+V	Pastes the selection

Practice Problems for Chapter 8

Practice Problem 1

In the Excel file for this chapter (Ch08-Excel365-WorksheetSolution.xlsx), go to the worksheet named PPCh08(1), which contains the data table for this practice problem.

Figure 8.126 shows a table with four boomerang products that the company Fun Fly Boomerangs sells to customers at boomerangs.com. Figure 8.127 shows sales records for Fun Fly Boomerangs. Your goal is to calculate the sales for each record in the sales table, sort the records to show records with the oldest date at the top (A-Z), create a PDF file, and allow for new data to be added later.

Boomerang Products	Picture	Price	Flight Range	Manufacturer
Quad		$43.00	20 meters	Gel Boomerangs
Carlota		$19.95	22 meters	Gel Boomerangs
Aspen		$22.95	25 meters	Colorado Boomerangs
Yanaki		$24.95	30 meters	Colorado Boomerangs

Figure 8.126 *Boomerangs sold by the Fun Fly Boomerangs company.*

	A	B	C	D	E	F
1						
2		Date	Product	Price	UnitsSold	
3		01/20/2021	Yanaki	24.95	12	
4		01/20/2021	Yanaki	24.95	4	
5		01/28/2021	Quad	43	4	
6		01/09/2021	Carlota	19.95	1	
7		01/20/2021	Carlota	19.95	96	
8		01/07/2021	Quad	43	3	
9		01/12/2021	Yanaki	24.95	84	
10		01/17/2021	Yanaki	24.95	4	
11		01/27/2021	Yanaki	24.95	24	
12		01/13/2021	Aspen	22.95	4	
13		01/28/2021	Yanaki	24.95	4	
14		01/18/2021	Quad	43	60	
15		01/31/2021	Yanaki	24.95	84	
16		01/25/2021	Quad	43	60	
17		01/15/2021	Carlota	19.95	4	
18		01/01/2021	Yanaki	24.95	1	
19						

Figure 8.127 *Records of sales made at boomerangs.com.*

Here are the steps you should complete:

1. Insert rows above the table and list your goals.
2. Add style and number formatting to the proper dataset.
3. Create a new column named Sales that calculates the sales for each record by multiplying price by units sold.
4. Document the formulas.
5. Convert the proper dataset to an Excel Table and name it.
6. Set up the table for printing. Use common sense when preparing the table for printing. Consider the following ideas: Portrait is good here because it is taller than it is wide. Maybe you want the company name in the footer. Rows to Repeat at Top should be set to just a single row with field names.
7. Open the file Ch08-PP01-NewSalesRecords.txt and copy and paste the records below your Excel Table.
8. Sort the date field A-Z.
9. Create a PDF file.

When you are done with this problem, you can check your work against the answer sheet named PPCh08(1an).

Practice Problem 2

In your Excel file for this chapter (Ch08-Excel365-WorksheetSolution.xlsx), go to the worksheet named PPCh08(2).

Figure 8.128 shows the data you need to enter into a proper dataset and the instructions for the two formula columns you need to create.

Jamal Harwood's gross pay = $1,097.00
Porsha Bentley's gross pay = $1,100.00
Amberly Ng's gross pay = $905.00
Treasa Lange's gross pay = $1,110.00
Twanda Polk's gross pay = $786.00
Maria Phelan's gross pay = $838.00

To calculate the deduction for each employee, multiply gross pay by 7.00%.
To calculate the net pay for each employee, subtract the deduction amount from the gross pay amount.

Figure 8.128 *The goal is to enter the data into a proper dataset and make the calculations.*

Here are the steps you should complete:

1. Enter data into a proper dataset.
2. Create helpful names for the fields (for example, Employee, Gross Pay, Deduction, Net Pay).
3. Enter the tax rate into a cell and label it.
4. Create a formula for deduction.
5. Create a formula for net pay.
6. Document the formulas. Because you have two columns of formulas, side-by-side, when you enter the range of cells into the FORMULATEXT function *reference* argument, you can highlight all cells in both columns. This allows the formula to spill all the formulas across the rows and columns.
7. Convert the data to an Excel Table and name it well.
8. Set up the table for printing.
9. Sort the records alphabetically.

When you are done with this problem, you can check your work against the answer sheet named PPCh08(2an).

Practice Problem 3

In your Excel file for this chapter (Ch08-Excel365-WorksheetSolution.xlsx), go to the worksheet named PPCh08(3).

In your own words, see if you can answer these conceptual questions:

1. What are the requirements for a proper dataset?
2. Describe what a worksheet formula is and describe its benefits.
3. What guidelines should you follow for solving problems in Excel?
4. What is the purpose of using the F2 key on the last cell in a column of formulas?
5. Compare and contrast an aggregate operation and an array operation.
6. What is the difference between a relative cell reference and an absolute cell reference?
7. What are the default alignments for the different types of data in an Excel worksheet, and why are they important?
8. What is number formatting, and how does it work?
9. What are the advantages of using the Excel Table feature on a proper dataset?

When you are done with this problem, you can check your work against the answer sheet named PPCh08(3an).

Chapter 9: A Golden Rule for Building Excel Models

> **Note:** To follow along with the examples in this chapter, you can use the file named Ch09-Excel365-GoldenRule.xlsx.

I created a Golden Rule for building Excel models and have used it in my classes and videos for almost two decades. The good news is that it is based on topics that you have already read about in this book:

- **Dan Bricklin's original "visual calculator" idea (refer to Chapter 2):** You should place formula inputs in cells and build formulas based on those cells so that when you change a formula's input, the whole spreadsheet solution updates.
- **"Build easy-to-understand models to solve problems" (refer to Chapter 4):** When you build models to solve problems, you should list your goals and labeled formula inputs, organize for ease of understanding and updating, and state your final results.
- **Guidelines for building Excel solutions (refer to Chapter 8):** You need to list your goals for a solution and label formula inputs with informative names.

The condensed version of my Golden Rule for building Excel models is **"If an Excel solution input can change, put it into a cell, label it, and refer to it with a cell reference."** This is the version of the Golden Rule that you can keep at the top of your mind as you build Excel solutions.

These are the details of my Golden Rule:

- If an Excel solution input (for example, a sales number, a commission rate, or a product name) can change, put it in a cell, label it, and refer to it using a cell reference.
- Do not directly type inputs into Excel formulas or textboxes. Hard-coding a number into a formula is dangerous. For example, coding =C3*0.03, where 0.03 is a 3% commission rate, makes it hard to track down and change the commission rate.
- If a formula input will not change (for example, 24 hours in a day, 12 months in a year, or 1 to represent 100%), you can hard-code it into a formula. For example, you could use the formula =C4/12, where 12 represents 12 months in a year.
- If you cannot decide or are not sure whether the input will change, be safe and just put it in a cell, label it, and refer to it with a cell reference.
- Always label your inputs with informative labels that clearly indicate what the input represents. By being clear and properly documenting an Excel spreadsheet solution, you ensure that anyone looking at the solution understands what is going on.
- Inputs are mostly used in formulas, but inputs can also be put into textboxes and dialog boxes for features such as conditional formatting, data validation, charts, PivotTables, Power Query, and Power Pivot.

How Violating the Golden Rule Can Get You into Trouble

Before we look at the benefits of following my Golden Rule, let's look at how violating the rule can get you into trouble. In Figure 9.1, you can see a formula for cell E3 in the formula bar. This formula multiplies Timmy's sales by the commission rate. In this case, the commission rate is 0.03, which means Timmy earns 3%, or $0.03 for every $1.00 of sales. As you can see in the figure, Timmy's total earned commission on $16,983 in sales is $509.49. Although this amount is correct, the formula is inefficient and dangerous. The formula shows a commission rate that is hard-coded into a formula, but in the real world, commission rates often change.

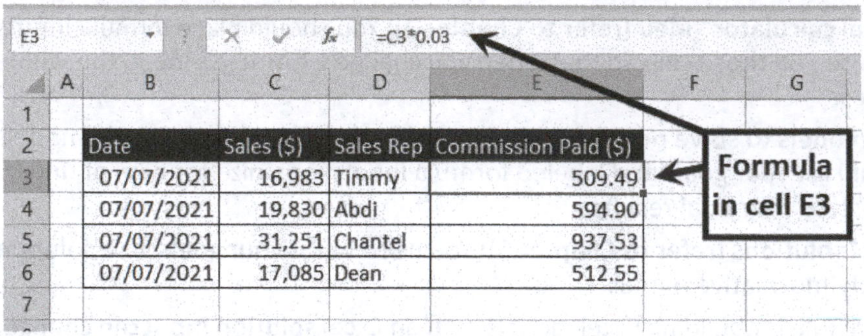

E3	▼	:	×	✓	fx	=C3*0.03	

	A	B	C	D	E	F	G
1							
2		Date	Sales ($)	Sales Rep	Commission Paid ($)		
3		07/07/2021	16,983	Timmy	509.49		
4		07/07/2021	19,830	Abdi	594.90		
5		07/07/2021	31,251	Chantel	937.53		
6		07/07/2021	17,085	Dean	512.55		
7							

Formula in cell E3

Figure 9.1 *Do not hard-code numbers into formulas if they can change.*

If you hard-code the 0.03 value into the formula, three main problems will appear when you come back to this solution later (see Figure 9.2):

- **Inputs that are hard to track down and find:** By just looking at the solution, you or another user cannot easily see how the solution was built. It may also be difficult to find the cells containing the hard-coded values.

- **Inputs that are hard to change:** Input values may be buried and hidden in formulas, which makes it is harder to edit and change the formula input than if the input were in a labeled cell.

- **Lack of informative labels:** When you finally do find the buried formula input, the input may not have an informative label, which makes it hard to know exactly what the input means.

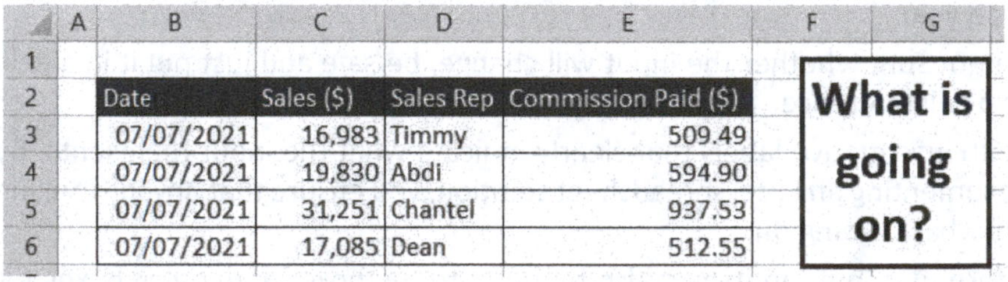

	A	B	C	D	E	F	G
1							
2		Date	Sales ($)	Sales Rep	Commission Paid ($)		
3		07/07/2021	16,983	Timmy	509.49		
4		07/07/2021	19,830	Abdi	594.90		
5		07/07/2021	31,251	Chantel	937.53		
6		07/07/2021	17,085	Dean	512.55		

What is going on?

Figure 9.2 *When you come back later, it is unclear how the commission paid was calculated or how to change it.*

Figure 9.3 shows another inefficient way to attempt a solution to this problem. Although the formula input is in a cell, there is no label, and it is unclear what the 0.03 represents. In addition, the input sits directly next to the proper dataset, which violates our rules for proper datasets in Excel.

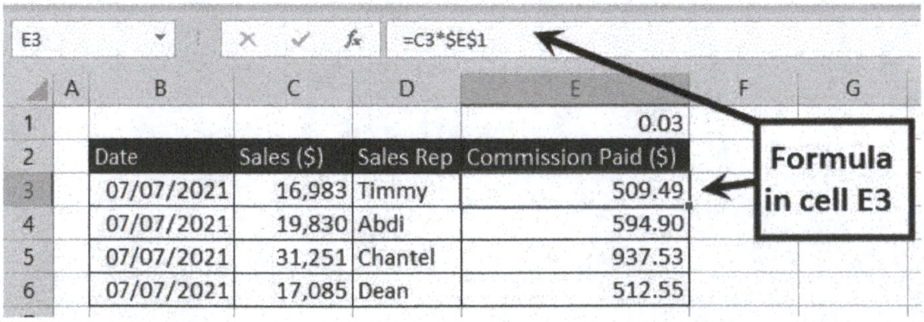

E3	▼	:	×	✓	fx	=C3*$E$1	

	A	B	C	D	E	F	G
1					0.03		
2		Date	Sales ($)	Sales Rep	Commission Paid ($)		
3		07/07/2021	16,983	Timmy	509.49		
4		07/07/2021	19,830	Abdi	594.90		
5		07/07/2021	31,251	Chantel	937.53		
6		07/07/2021	17,085	Dean	512.55		

Formula in cell E3

Figure 9.3 *Do not place formula inputs directly next to a proper dataset. Always label your inputs.*

In Figure 9.4, my Golden Rule is followed almost perfectly, except that there is no informative label, so it is unclear why 0.03 is floating in cell E2.

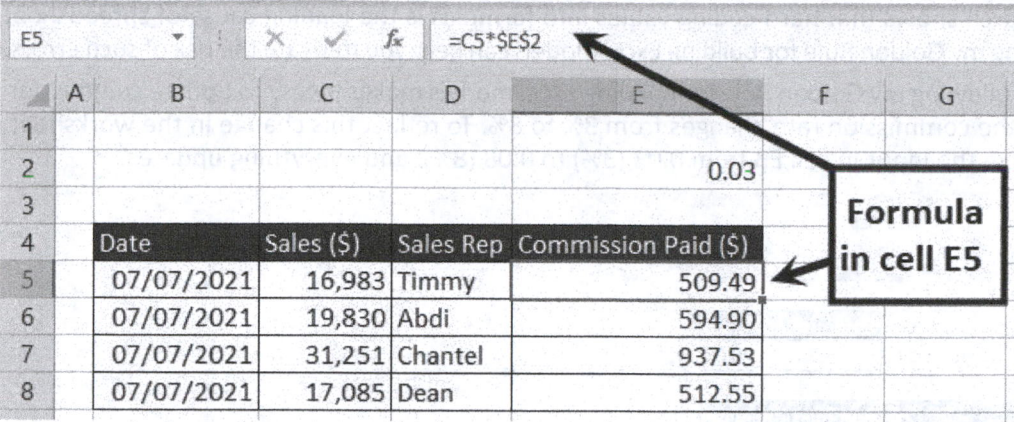

Figure 9.4 *The formula input is not labeled.*

Figure 9.5 shows a solution with all parts of my Golden Rule faithfully followed.

	A	B	C	D	E	F	G
1							
2					Commission Rate:		
3					0.03		
4							
5		Date	Sales ($)	Sales Rep	Commission Paid ($)		
6		07/07/2021	16,983	Timmy	509.49		
7		07/07/2021	19,830	Abdi	594.90		
8		07/07/2021	31,251	Chantel	937.53		
9		07/07/2021	17,085	Dean	512.55		

E6 = C6*$E$3   Formula in cell E6

Figure 9.5 *Following my Golden Rule by allowing changeable input in a cell and labeling input for the cell reference used in the formula.*

Why all the fuss about being clear with putting inputs in cells and labeling? Many people truly think they can hard-code formula inputs and later remember them. It is just not true. In my two decades of consulting and teaching, I have seen many inefficient spreadsheets hindered by hard-coded values and filled with errors. Beyond my personal experience, empirical research on spreadsheet errors shows that the number-one cause of spreadsheet errors throughout spreadsheet history is Excel users hard-coding formula inputs into formulas. However, you do not need to worry about such errors if you just follow my Golden Rule for building Excel models.

> **Note:** A few research projects have addressed spreadsheet errors. Here is one great article that summarizes this grave errors that plague many spreadsheets around the world: http://www.strategy-at-risk.com/2009/03/03/the-risk-of-spreadsheet-errors/.

Benefits of Following the Golden Rule

As illustrated in the examples you just looked at, following my Golden Rule offers several important benefits:

- It is easy to find the inputs when they are listed on the face of the worksheet. When you list the inputs with labels, you make the solution transparent.
- The label for an input indicates exactly what the input represents.
- It is easy to change the inputs when they are listed on the face of the worksheet.
- It is easy to understand how the Excel solution is constructed if the inputs are visible on the face of the worksheet. When you follow my Golden Rule for building Excel models, you document your Excel solution so that it is easy for others and your future self to understand.

- Empirical research shows that hard-coding values into formulas is the leading cause of spreadsheet errors. Following my Golden Rule for building Excel models can help you mitigate the risk of such errors.

Figure 9.6 shows how following my Golden Rule for building Excel models makes it easy to update commission calculations. Say that the commission rate changes from 3% to 8%. To reflect this change in the worksheet, you only need to change the input in cell E3 from 0.03 (3%) to 0.08 (8%), and everything updates.

E6	▼ : × ✓ fx	=C6*$E$3			
	A	B	C	D	E	F

	A	B	C	D	E	F
1						
2					Commission Rate:	
3					0.08	
4						
5		Date	Sales	Sales Rep	Commission Paid	
6		07/07/2021	16,983	Timmy	1,358.64	
7		07/07/2021	19,830	Abdi	1,586.40	
8		07/07/2021	31,251	Chantel	2,500.08	
9		07/07/2021	17,085	Dean	1,366.80	
10						

Figure 9.6 *My Golden Rule makes an Excel model easy to understand and to update.*

For a simple solution like this commission example, if you are the only one who will use it, and if you understand the formulas, then it may not be necessary to document the formulas in the worksheet. You can label just the input, as shown in Figure 9.6. However, if you need people to understand how a full solution or model is built, you might want to also document the formulas in the solution, as shown in Figure 9.7.

E6	▼ : × ✓ fx	=C6*$E$3				

	A	B	C	D	E	F	G
1							
2					Commission Rate:		
3					0.08		
4							
5		Date	Sales	Sales Rep	Commission Paid		Commission Paid Formulas:
6		07/07/2021	16,983	Timmy	1,358.64		=C6*$E$3
7		07/07/2021	19,830	Abdi	1,586.40		=C7*$E$3
8		07/07/2021	31,251	Chantel	2,500.08		=C8*$E$3
9		07/07/2021	17,085	Dean	1,366.80		=C9*$E$3
10							

Figure 9.7 *This example follows my Golden Rule, the rules for proper datasets, and the rules for documenting formulas in a solution.*

To get a better idea of how to use my Golden Rule for building Excel models, walk through the following examples.

Example 1: Commission Pay Worksheet Formula

To practice using my Golden Rule for building Excel models, solve this problem:

- Your monthly base pay is $5,000.
- You also get a commission of 5% of your sales for the month added to your base pay. The result is your total gross pay.
- Your sales for the month are $45,000.
- What is your total gross pay for the month?
- Hint: Gross pay = Base pay + Commission pay = $5,000 + ($45,000 * 5%).
- A commission of 5% means that for every $1 of sales you make, you get paid $0.05.

Knowing whether these numbers will change requires that you know something about the payroll department. You can assume that all three numbers have the potential to change—even the base salary. Solve this problem using my Golden Rule for building Excel models.

To complete this example, follow these steps:

1. In the workbook file for this chapter, go to the sheet named Ch09(8-13) and enter the goals and formula inputs shown in Figure 9.8.

	A	B	C	D	E	F
1						
2		**Goals:**				
3		What is your total gross pay for the month?				
4		Hint: gross pay = base pay + commission pay = $5,000 + $45,000 * 5%.				
5						
6		Monthly Sales =	45000			
7		Monthly Base Pay =	5000			
8		Commission Rate on Sales =	0.05			

Figure 9.8 *Enter goals and labeled formula inputs.*

2. Select cell C8 and then, from the Number Format dropdown in the Number group on the Home tab of the Ribbon, select Percentage to display a percentage with two decimal places.

3. Because the two numbers in the range C6:C7 represent dollar amounts, select the cells and then, from the Number Format dropdown in the Number group on the Home tab of the Ribbon, select Currency to display the amounts with two decimal places, as shown in Figure 9.9.

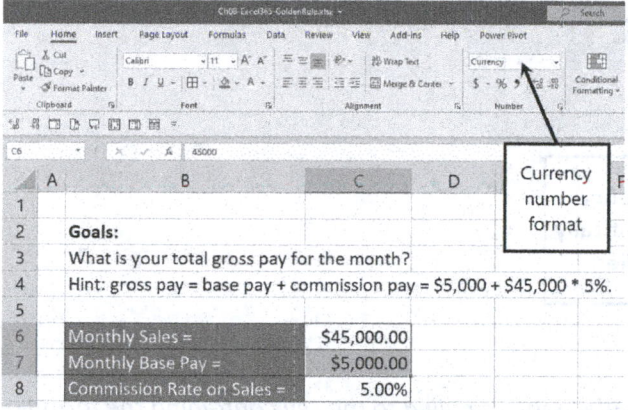

Figure 9.9 *By using the Currency number format, you saved 10 total clicks!*

4. Enter the labels and formatting for the formulas as shown in Figure 9.10. Then select cell C9 and look at the Number Format dropdown in the Number group on the Home tab of the Ribbon and notice that it says General. General is the default on all cells before you add number formatting. This is important because when you create your formula in a moment, the cell references in the formula will pull the Currency number format from the formula input cell to the cell containing the formula.

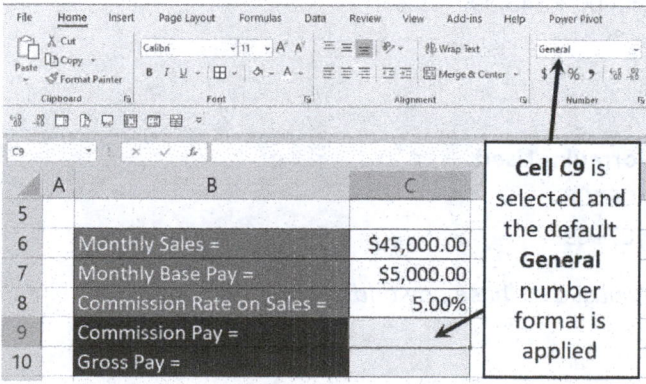

Figure 9.10 *The General number format is applied to all cells before you add number formatting.*

5. Create the formula to multiply monthly sales by commission rate, as shown in Figure 9.11.

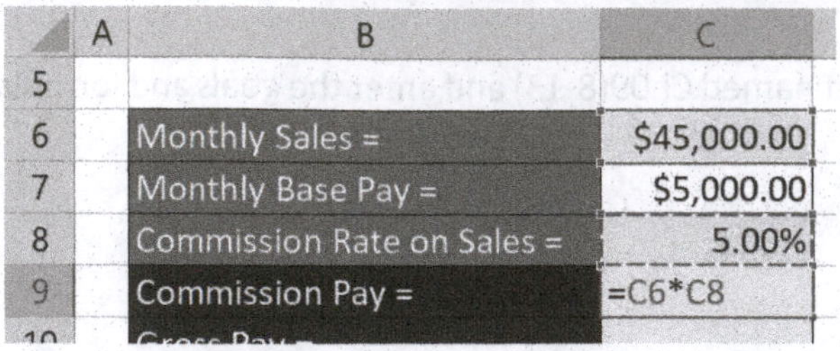

	A	B	C
5			
6		Monthly Sales =	$45,000.00
7		Monthly Base Pay =	$5,000.00
8		Commission Rate on Sales =	5.00%
9		Commission Pay =	=C6*C8
10		Gross Pay	

Figure 9.11 *Because the formula input cells are close to each other, you can use your arrow keys to quickly create the formula.*

6. Press Ctrl+Enter to put the formula in the cell and keep the cell selected. Figure 9.12 shows that cell C9, the cell containing the formula, automatically received the Currency number format when you entered your formula. The number formatting came from the formula input cells, and even though the two cells you used in your formula had two different types of number formatting, because one of them had a money format, Excel assumed that the money format was also required for the cell containing the formula. Most of the time, this is exactly what you want. If it is not what you want, then you must change it. However, Microsoft designed it this way with the intention of trying to make it easier when you have formulas with money, which is very common.

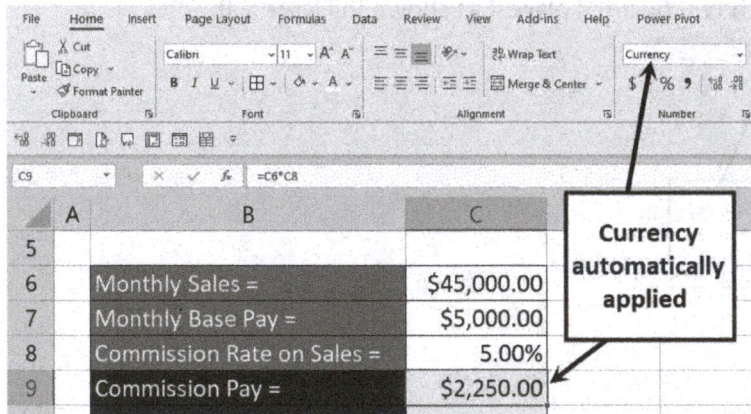

Currency automatically applied

Figure 9.12 *The Currency number format from the formula inputs is pulled to the cell containing the formula.*

7. Create the formula for gross pay and your documentation formulas, as shown in Figure 9.13.

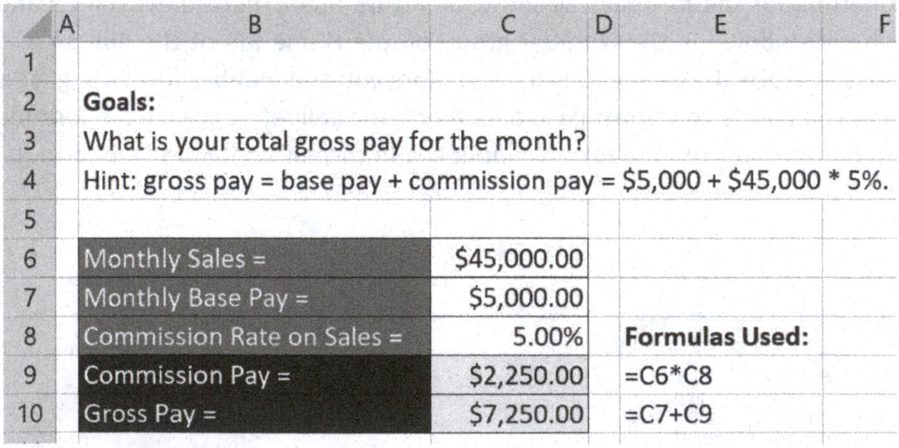

	A	B	C	D	E	F
1						
2		**Goals:**				
3		What is your total gross pay for the month?				
4		Hint: gross pay = base pay + commission pay = $5,000 + $45,000 * 5%.				
5						
6		Monthly Sales =	$45,000.00			
7		Monthly Base Pay =	$5,000.00			
8		Commission Rate on Sales =	5.00%	**Formulas Used:**		
9		Commission Pay =	$2,250.00	=C6*C8		
10		Gross Pay =	$7,250.00	=C7+C9		

Figure 9.13 *The final solution for calculating gross pay based on base pay and commission pay.*

Example 2: Monthly Expense Formula with Hard-Coded Formula Input

Your goal in this example is to divide the annual insurance expense by 12 to get the monthly insurance expense (see Figure 9.14). The question is: Do you need to put the formula input 12 into a cell and label it? The answer is no because the input in this case—12, for months in a year—is a number that does not change.

	A	B	C
1			
2		**Goal**: Calculate Monthly Insurance Expense.	
3			
4		Annual Insurance Expense =	$12,500.00
5		Monthly Expense =	

Figure 9.14 *Are there enough formula inputs and labels in the cells?*

To follow complete this example, follow these steps:

1. Click on the worksheet named Ch09(14-15).
2. Create the formula shown in Figure 9.15.

	A	B	C	D	E
1					
2		**Goal**: Calculate Monthly Insurance Expense.			
3					
4		Annual Insurance Expense =	$12,500.00		Monthly Expense Formula:
5		Monthly Expense =	$1,041.67		=C4/12

Figure 9.15 *Because the number of months in a year will not change, this is an example of a formula input that you can hard-code into a formula.*

Example 3: COUNTIFS Worksheet Function to Count with a Condition

To see that inputs are not always numbers but are sometimes text values, let's look at another example of following my Golden Rule for building Excel models.

The goal of this example is to count how many Quad products there are in the range B9:B16 (see Figure 9.16). Just using your eyes on this small dataset, you can easily count three Quad values. But you do not always want to leave it up to your eyes, especially when you have a lot of data. Luckily, there is a built-in Excel worksheet function that counts specified items: COUNTIFS. The COUNTIFS function does not count all the items; instead, it counts only items that you specify. The COUNTIFS function is only available in Excel worksheets and not in any of the other tools that you will study in this book (for example, Power Query's M Code and the Data Model's DAX formula language).

To complete this example, follow these steps:

1. Click on the sheet Ch09(16-39).
2. Select cell C6 and type **=COUNTIFS(** (see Figure 9.16).

3. For the *criteria_range1* argument to the COUNTIFS function, select the range B9:B16. This range contains all the items to potentially count. Figure 9.16 shows the result.

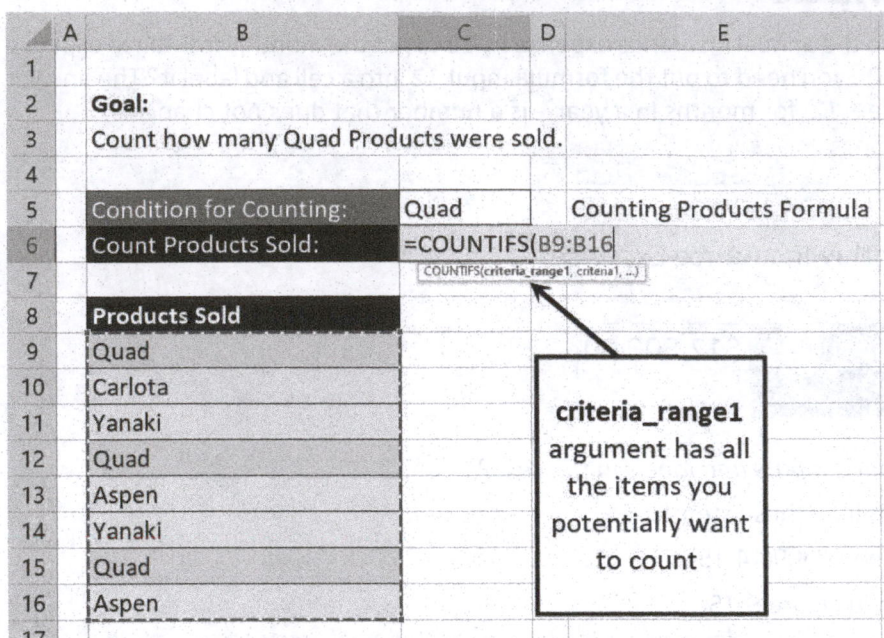

Figure 9.16 *Enter the cell range B9:B16 into the criteria_range1 argument.*

4. Type a comma to get to the *criteria1* argument in the COUNTIFS function (see Figure 9.17).

5. As shown in Figure 9.17, select cell C5 to put the Quad condition into the *criteria1* argument. When you put the cell reference C5 into the *criteria1* argument, COUNTIFS knows to count only Quads. (Did you notice that here you are following my Golden Rule for building Excel models by entering a text formula input into your formula?)

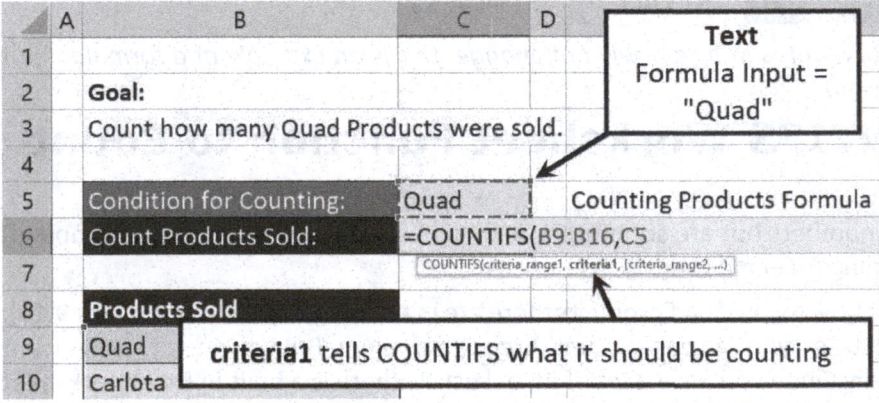

Figure 9.17 *Give COUNTIFS the condition Quad so it will count only the cells that contain the product Quad.*

6. As shown in Figure 9.18, when you type a close parenthesis for the COUNTIFS function and then press Enter to enter the formula, you see the result 3 because there are three Quad products in the column of product names.

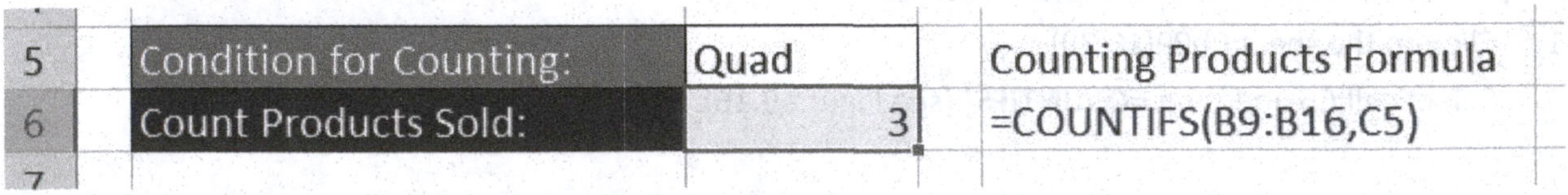

5	Condition for Counting:	Quad	Counting Products Formula
6	Count Products Sold:	3	=COUNTIFS(B9:B16,C5)
7			

Figure 9.18 *COUNTIFS delivers a count of 3.*

7. As shown in Figure 9.19, when you change the text formula input from Quad to Aspen, the formula instantly updates to report a count of 2.

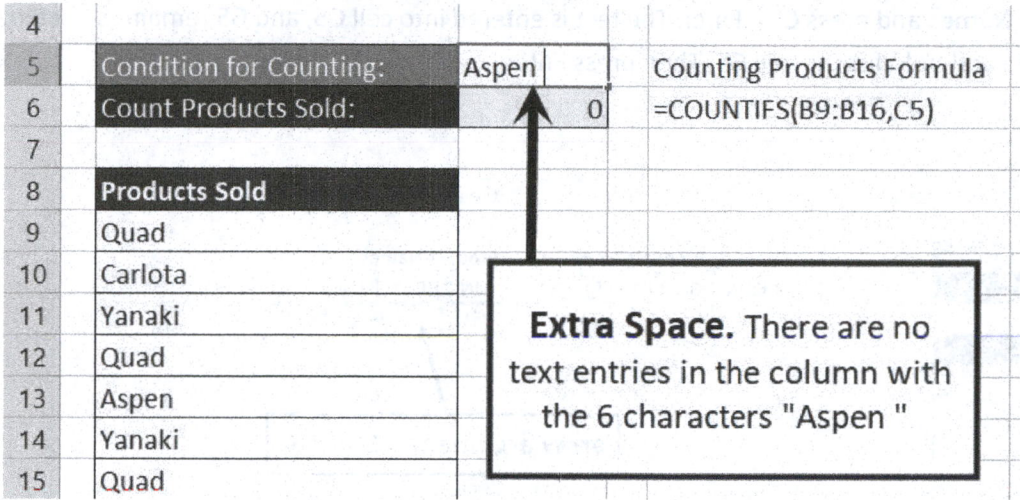

| 5 | Condition for Counting: | Aspen | Counting Products Formula |
| 6 | Count Products Sold: | 2 | =COUNTIFS(B9:B16,C5) |

Figure 9.19 *If you change the text formula input, the count updates.*

8. If you misspell the product name or accidentally type an extra space, COUNTIFS properly delivers a count of 0, as shown in Figure 9.20. In Excel, spaces are characters, so Aspen with no trailing space is five characters and is different from Aspen with a trailing space, which is six characters.

4			
5	Condition for Counting:	Aspen	Counting Products Formula
6	Count Products Sold:	0	=COUNTIFS(B9:B16,C5)
7			
8	**Products Sold**		
9	Quad		
10	Carlota		
11	Yanaki		
12	Quad		
13	Aspen		
14	Yanaki		
15	Quad		

Extra Space. There are no text entries in the column with the 6 characters "Aspen "

Figure 9.20 *If you spell the name wrong or type an extra space, COUNTIFS properly reports a count of 0.*

In this COUNTIFS function example, you counted with one condition. In Chapter 13, you will see how to use COUNTIFS to count with two or more conditions. In this example, you also saw that formula inputs are not always numbers. Many times you have text values as formula inputs. Remember that =COUNTIFS(B9:B16,"Quad") violates my Golden Rule for building Excel models—so don't use it!

Example 4: UNIQUE Array Function and Data Validation List

As shown in Figure 9.20, if you type into cell C5 a value that is not in the Products Sold column, you get a count of 0. If you had a way of preventing misspellings or extra spaces in cell C5, your solution would be more effective and robust. Excel does, in fact, provide such a way: You can use a feature called Data Validation and the UNIQUE array function. This example examines this method of applying my Golden Rule for building Excel models.

In this example, you need to prevent users from entering invalid product names into cell C5. As shown in Figure 9.21, for cell C5, you need to prevent a user from entering a product name that is not a valid name from the column. To do this, you first need a valid list of product names. For this you can use the UNIQUE array worksheet function, which can look through a column and deliver a unique list of values (that is, a list without any duplicates). Then you can use the unique list of values to validate what goes into cell C5.

Note: At this point in the book, you will use the UNIQUE array function and its first argument, *array*, to create a unique list. Later in the book, you will learn about the other available arguments.

To complete this example, go to the worksheet Ch09(16-39) and follow these steps:

1. Select cell G4, type **Create unique list:**, and press Enter twice.

2. Type **Product Names** and press Ctrl+Enter. The text is entered into cell G5, and G5 remains selected.

3. Press Ctrl+B to add bold font to cell G5. Then press Enter.

	A	B	C	D	E	F	G	H
1								
2		Goal:						
3		Count how many Quad Products were sold.					Create unique list:	
4								
5		Condition for Counting:	Quad		**Counting Products Formula:**		**Product Names**	
6		Count Products Sold:	3		=COUNTIFS(B9:B16,C5)		=UNIQUE(B9:B16)	
7							UNIQUE(array, [by_col], [exactly_once])	
8		**Products Sold**						
9		Quad						
10		Carlota						
11		Yanaki						
12		Quad						
13		Aspen						
14		Yanaki						
15		Quad						
16		Aspen						

array argument = B9:B16

Figure 9.21 *By entering a range of cells into the UNIQUE array function, you are following my Golden Rule for building Excel models.*

4. In cell G6, create the formula **=UNIQUE(B9:B16)**, as shown in Figure 9.21. Then press Ctrl+Enter to enter the formula and keep cell G6 selected. In Figure 9.22, the formula bar shows that the formula lives in cell G6, and you can see that the unique list of text values spilled into the cells below. Here you have followed my Golden Rule for building Excel models because you have entered a range of cells into UNIQUE, and if anything changes, the formula will update.

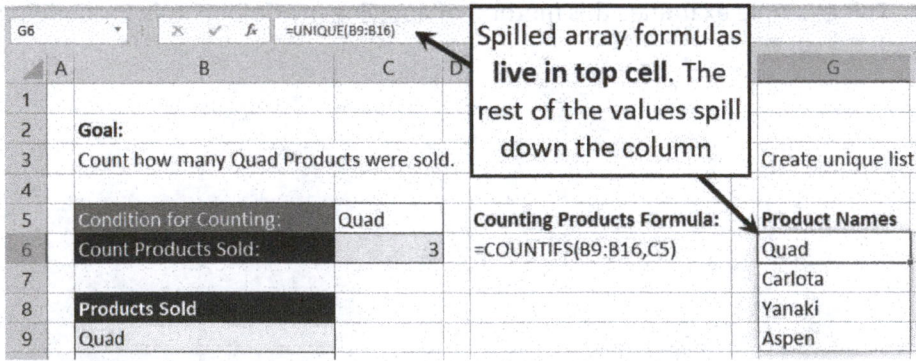

Spilled array formulas **live in top cell**. The rest of the values spill down the column

Figure 9.22 *The UNIQUE function spills a unique list of product names.*

To continue this example, you need to know about spilling dynamic array functions, you need to know how to add a data validation list to a worksheet, and you need to know how to refer to a spilled array in a formula. The following sections walk through how to do all this.

Spilling Dynamic Array Functions

In Figure 9.22, you can see that because the worksheet formula delivered more than one value, the values spilled into the cells. In Chapter 8, you saw a formula that spilled values into the cells when you used the FORMULATEXT function. But in Chapter 8, sometimes you entered a single cell into the FORMULATEXT function to deliver a single answer, and other times you entered a range of cells to deliver an array of answers. The UNIQUE array function you just used is different because it is an array function.

An *array function* is a worksheet function that is programed to deliver a spilled array of values from the cell that contains the array function formula. The full name for array functions, *dynamic spilled array functions*, refers to the fact that they spill the values from the formula cell and automatically update in a dynamic way. For example, with the UNIQUE array function, if the function spills four answers and later a new value is added to increase the number of unique values to five, the UNIQUE array function automatically updates and spills five values. Throughout the book, you will learn more about other dynamic spilled array functions, including SORT, FREQUENCY, and FILTER.

The Data Validation List Feature

Now that you have a list of valid product names, you can use the Data Validation List feature to add a dropdown list to cell C5 that will allow a user to select from a valid list of names. *Data validation* refers to ensuring that the data that goes into a cell is a valid value and in the proper format. If you use the Data Validation feature on a cell and someone then enters an invalid value in that cell, Excel prevents the user from entering that value and shows an error message about it. This is exactly what you need for cell C5.

To complete this example, follow these steps:

1. Select cell C5, click on the Data tab of the Ribbon, and then click the Data Validation button in the Data Tools group (see Figure 9.23).

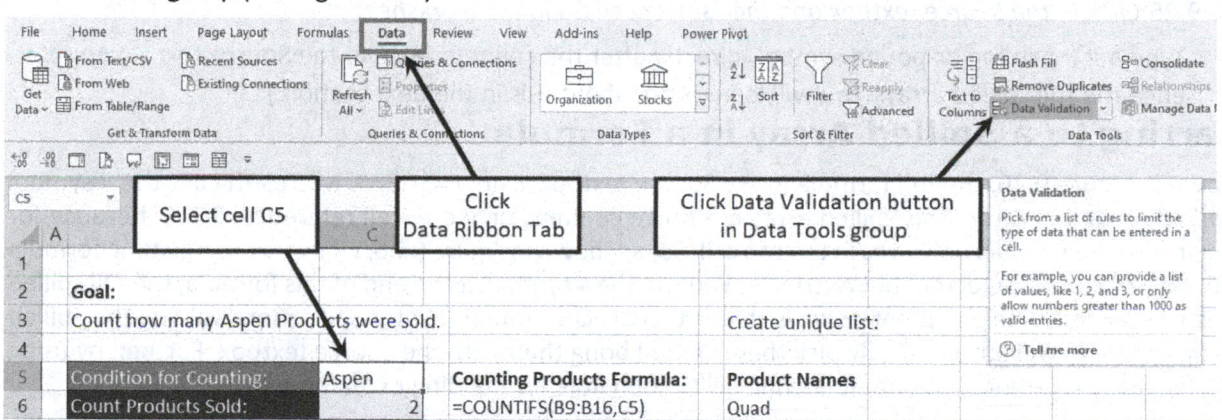

Figure 9.23 *Select cell C5 and click the Data Validation button.*

2. As shown in Figure 9.24, in the Data Validation dialog box, click on the Settings tab and then select List from the Allow dropdown.

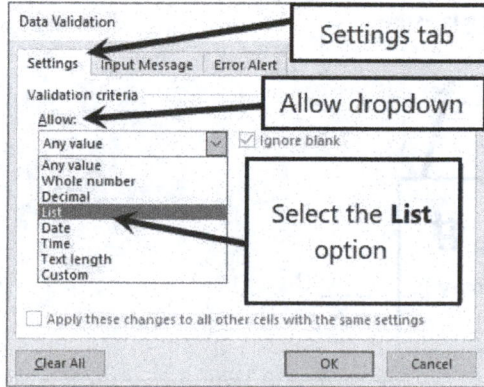

Figure 9.24 *From the Allow dropdown, select List.*

Note: As you can see in Figure 9.24, the Allow dropdown includes a number of options for validating data. When you set data validation, if you want to include an input message, use the Input Message tab; if you want to create an error message, use the Error Alert tab.

3.   As shown in Figure 9.25, click in the Source textbox, and then, with that textbox still selected, click in the worksheet on cell G6 to insert a cell reference to G6 into the Source textbox. By default, the cell reference is locked so that if you ever copy the cell to somewhere else, the same data validation list appears because the cell is locked. Also, notice that the dancing ants are surrounding cell G6 only.

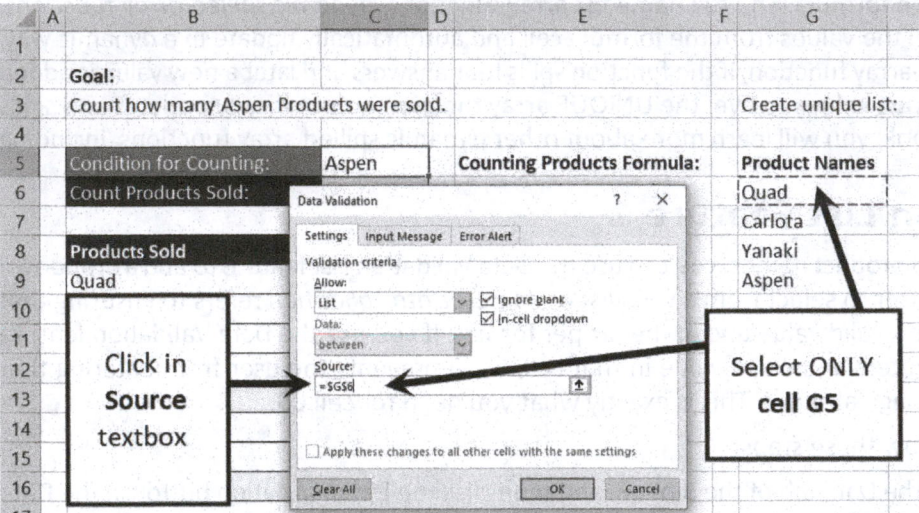

Figure 9.25 *Click in the Source textbox and then select cell G6 in the worksheet.*

4.   Type a # (hash tag or pound symbol) directly after the cell reference in the Source textbox to reference the full spilled array. (You will learn more about this in the next section.)

Referring to a Spilled Array in a Formula

As shown in Figure 9.26, the full formula in the Source textbox is now =$G$6#. Microsoft calls the # symbol the *spilled range operator*. This spilled array reference contains only one cell reference, $G$6, because for spilled arrays, the formula only lives in the top cell. So, as shown in Figure 9.26, when you use just the formula =$G$6, only one cell is selected. But as soon as you use the # symbol at the end of this formula, the full spilled array is referenced. And the great news is that if the UNIQUE function later spills more values, the spilled range operator (#) will automatically pick them up and bring them into the Source textbox. Further, by using the spilled array reference, you are following my Golden Rule for building Excel models.

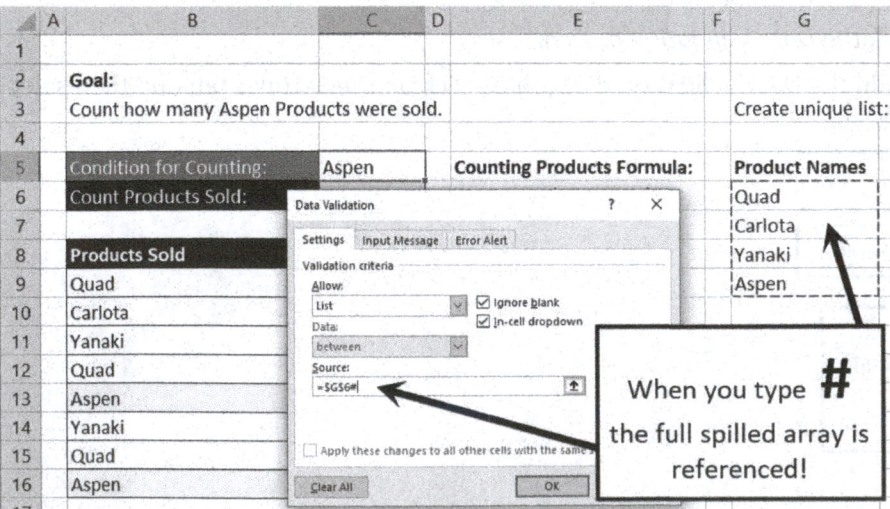

Figure 9.26 *The Source textbox in the Data Validation dialog box dynamically picks up new values when the spilled array changes.*

To see for yourself how to put references into a dialog box's textbox, follow these steps:

1. Click the OK button in the Data Validation dialog box to enter the validation into cell C5. As you can see in Figure 9.27, there is a dropdown arrow in cell C5 that contains a list of product names. If you try to type a name that is not in the dropdown list, you get an error message.

> **Note:** It is important to understand that there is one way to override data validation: If you copy a cell from a different part of the worksheet with text that is not one of the items in the data validation dropdown list and then select cell C5 and paste your selection, Excel removes the data validation dropdown list and pastes your copied value and cell formatting. You want to avoid doing that!

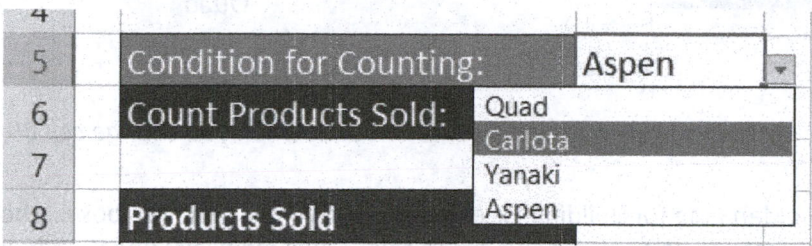

Figure 9.27 *The data validation dropdown list shows the items from the UNIQUE function spilled array.*

2. In Figure 9.27, notice that the unique list of product names is not sorted alphabetically. To sort this list, select cell G6 (the cell that contains the UNIQUE list formula) and press the F2 key to put the cell into edit mode. Then, as shown in Figure 9.28, edit the formula so that the UNIQUE function sits inside the *array* argument of the SORT array function. When you do this, Excel sorts the values alphabetically, A-Z. As you will see later in the book, additional arguments are also available.

▲	A	B	C	D	E	F	G	H
1								
2		Goal:						
3		Count how many Quad Products were sold.					Create unique list:	
4								
5		Condition for Counting:	Quad		Counting Products Formula:		Product Names	
6		Count Products Sold:	3		=COUNTIFS(B9:B16,C5)		=SORT(UNIQUE(B9:B16))	

Put the UNIQUE array function inside the **array argument** of the SORT array function

SORT(array, [sort_index], [sort_order], [by_col])
Yanaki
Aspen

Figure 9.28 *The array functions SORT and UNIQUE are often used together to create a unique sorted list.*

3. Press Enter and then check the data validation dropdown list in cell C5. You should see the same sorted order shown in Figure 9.29.

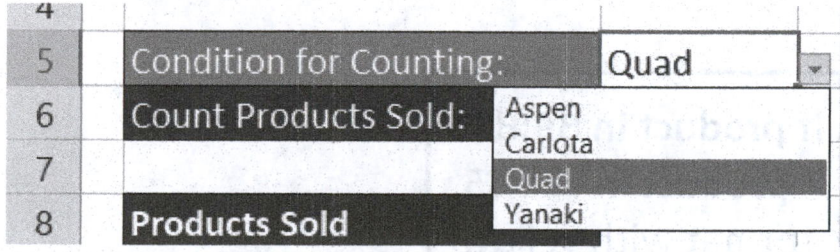

Figure 9.29 *The dropdown validation list is sorted.*

4. Click in cell B9 and type the new product name **Sunshine**. Then press Enter. Figure 9.30 shows the result.

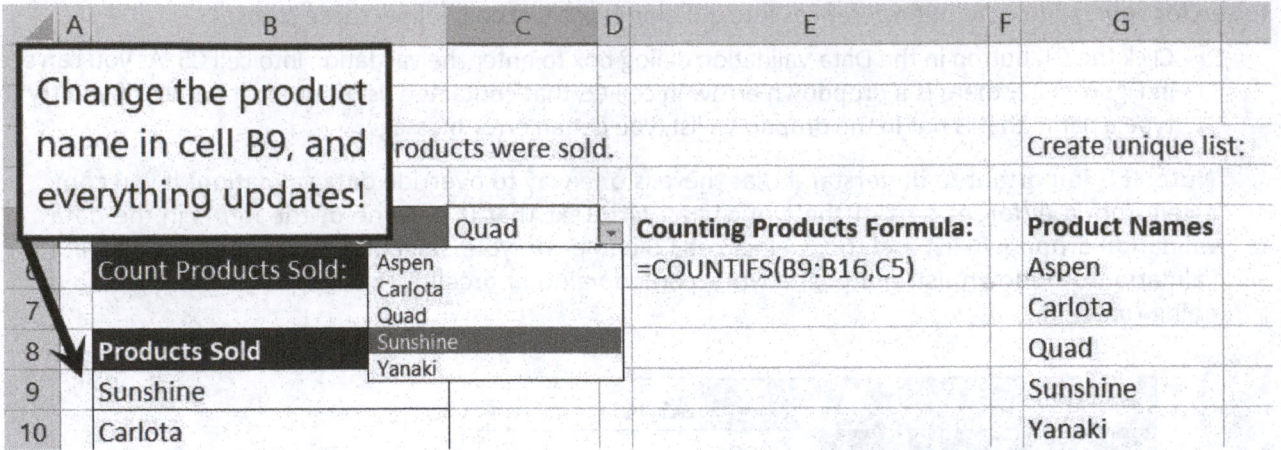

Figure 9.30 *Because you have followed my Golden Rule for building Excel models, when you change cell B9, everything updates.*

If you are careful to always follow my Golden Rule for building Excel models in formulas and textboxes, the spilled array formula in cell G6 and the data valuation dropdown list in cell C5 will magically update when data is changed—as shown in Figure 9.30.

Example 5: Conditional Formatting

This last example of the beauty and magic of my Golden Rule for building Excel models involves using Excel's Conditional Formatting feature. With *conditional formatting*, the formatting for a cell is conditioned on a logical test. Conditional formatting helps to visualize data and highlight items of interest.

For example, say that in the example shown in Figure 9.31, your goal is to apply a yellow fill color to any cell where the product name is equal to Quad so that you can visually see how many items in the list are Quad. Cells B12 and B15 contain Quad, and as a result, they have the yellow fill color formatting applied. Then, as shown in Figure 9.32, when you change the value in cell C5 to Aspen, the conditional formatting changes to show yellow fill color in cells B13 and B16, which now contain Aspen. When you use conditional formatting, you must create a logical test. The logical test is this case is: "Is any cell value in the range B9:B16 equal to the value in cell C5?" For any logical test question, you can only get one of two answers: TRUE or FALSE. Figure 9.31 shows that cells B12 and B15 evaluate to TRUE, and so the formatting is applied to them. Cells B9, B10, B11, B13, B15, and B16 all evaluate to FALSE, and so the formatting is not applied to them.

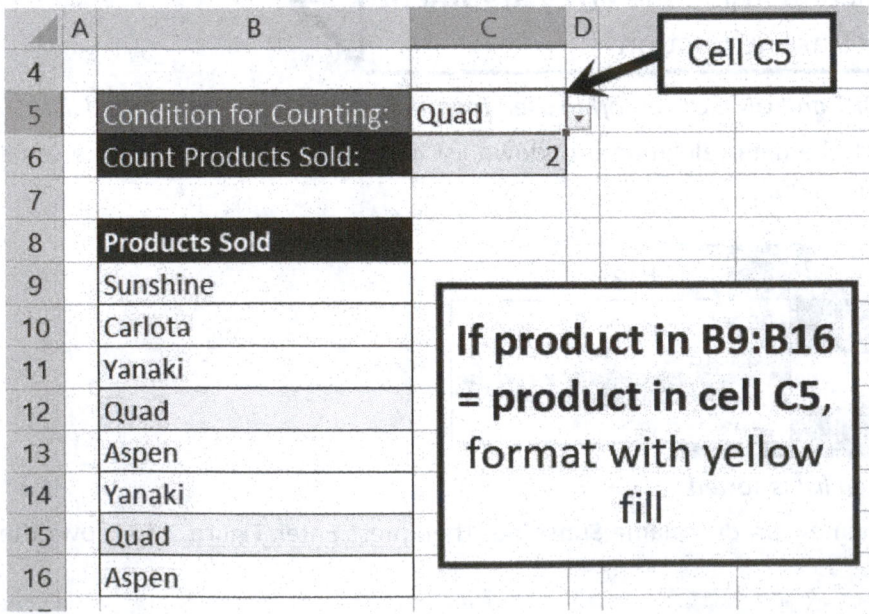

Figure 9.31 *Cell C5 contains Quad, so conditional formatting is applied to cells B12 and B15.*

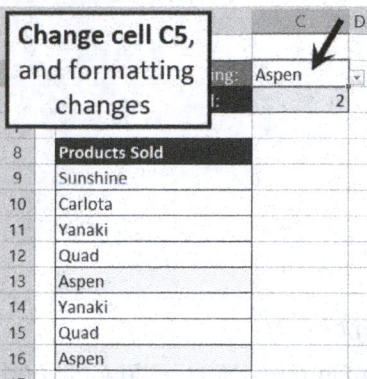

Figure 9.32 *Cell C5 contains Aspen, so conditional formatting is applied to cells B13 and B16.*

To apply conditional formatting to the range B9:B16, follow these steps:

1. As shown in Figure 9.33, starting in cell B9, select the range B9:B16. In the Home tab of the Ribbon, go to the Style group and click the Conditional Formatting dropdown arrow. Then hover over Highlight Cells Rules and click the Equal To option.

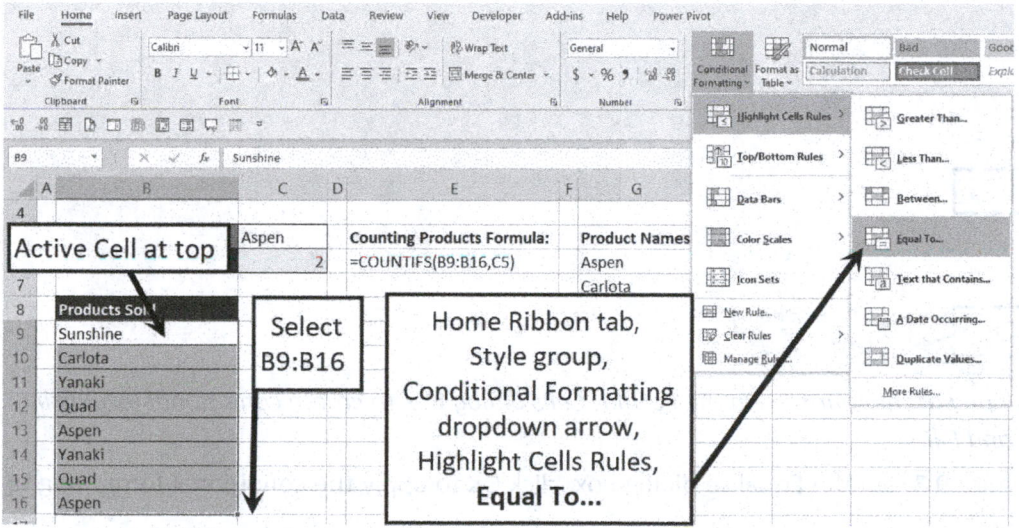

Figure 9.34 *Select B9:B16 and then choose the Equal To option under Conditional Formatting.*

2. As shown in Figure 9.34, in the Equal To dialog box, click in the Format Cells That Are EQUAL TO textbox and then, with your selection cursor, click cell C5 in the worksheet. By default, Excel enters an absolute cell reference in the textbox—which is what you want in this case.

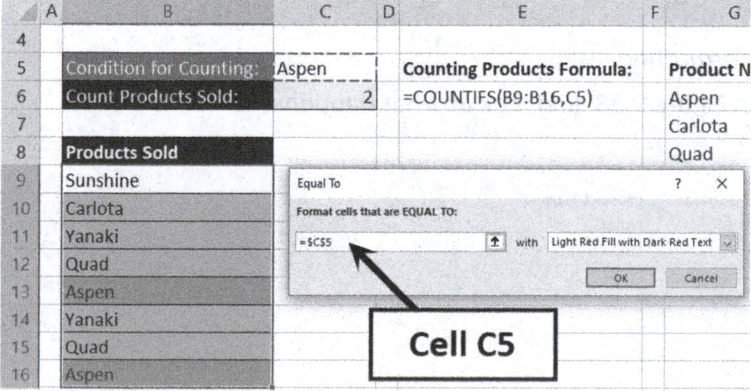

Figure 9.34 *Cell C5 now determines the formatting for the range B9:B16.*

3. As shown in Figure 9.35, from the With dropdown, click Custom Format.

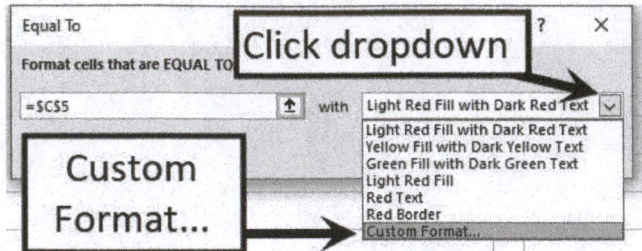

Figure 9.35 *Choose the Custom Format option to open the Format Cells dialog box.*

4. As shown in Figure 9.36, in the Format Cells dialog box, click on the Fill tab, select yellow fill, and click OK.

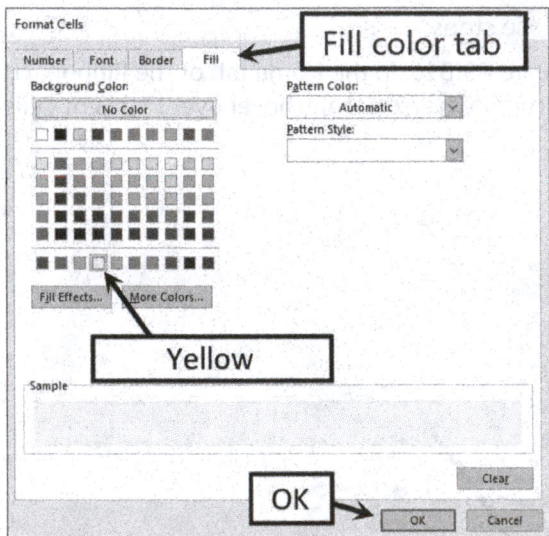

Figure 9.36 *You can use any of the four tabs in the Format Cells dialog box to create conditional formatting: Number, Font, Border, and Fill.*

5. As shown in Figure 9.37, in the Equal To dialog box, click OK to apply the conditional formatting to the cells.

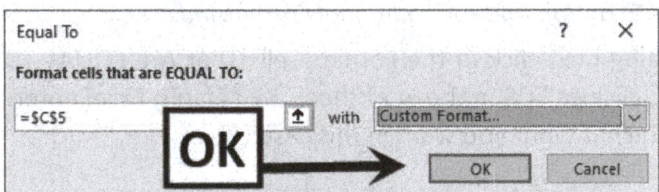

Figure 9.37 *Click OK to apply the conditional formatting.*

6. Enter **Sunshine** in cell C5, as shown in Figure 9.38, and look at what happens.

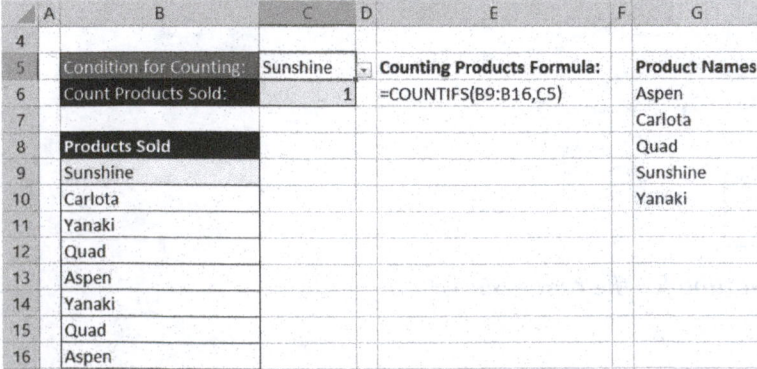

	A	B	C	D	E	F	G
4							
5		Condition for Counting:	Sunshine		Counting Products Formula:		Product Names
6		Count Products Sold:	1		=COUNTIFS(B9:B16,C5)		Aspen
7							Carlota
8		Products Sold					Quad
9		Sunshine					Sunshine
10		Carlota					Yanaki
11		Yanaki					
12		Quad					
13		Aspen					
14		Yanaki					
15		Quad					
16		Aspen					

Figure 9.38 *Cell C5 controls the formatting. When you change the contents of cell C5 to Sunshine, only cell B9 gets the formatting.*

7. Using Figure 9.39 as a guide, insert enough rows to accommodate your updated list of goals, type the new goals, and then document the sorted unique list formula.

	A	B	C	D	E	F	G	H	I	J
1										
2		**Goals:**								
3		1) Count the number of products sold.								
4		2) Create a sorted unique list.								
5		3) Add data validation dropdown List to cell C8, based on Spilled Array in cell G9.								
6		4) Add Conditional Formatting to range B12:B19, based on the value in cell C8.								
7										
8		Condition for Counting:	Quad			**Counting Products Formula:**		**Product Names**	**Unique List Formula:**	
9		Count Products Sold:	2			=COUNTIFS(B12:B19,C8)		Aspen	=SORT(UNIQUE(B12:B19))	
10								Carlota		
11		**Products Sold**						Quad		
12		Sunshine						Sunshine		
13		Carlota						Yanaki		
14		Yanaki								
15		Quad								
16		Aspen								
17		Yanaki								
18		Quad								
19		Aspen								

Figure 9.39 *This solution uses my Golden Rule for building Excel models in formulas and dialog boxes.*

Using my Golden Rule for building Excel models, you created four elements in this example:

- A count of Quad products sold in cell C9
- A sorted unique list in cell G9
- A data validation dropdown list in cell C8, based on the spilled array in cell G9
- Conditional formatting on the range B13:B19, based on the value in cell C8

By faithfully following my Golden Rule for building Excel models, you created a solution that will update when any part changes—including when you insert rows to accommodate an updated list of goals and force all the formulas and dialog box entries to update. When you insert rows and push cells and formulas down, you perform a *move operation*. When you move cells with formulas or cells that are being used in a dialog box, they are programmed to update. Excel is just pure magic!

What-If Analysis and Excel Models

Two Excel topics that are closely related to my Golden Rule for building Excel models are what-if analysis and Excel models.

What-If Analysis

With what-if analysis, you answer a particular "What if...?" question. When you follow my Golden Rule for building Excel models, it is easy to answer what-if questions because you can simply change a formula input and discover the answer. For example, say that you want to find the answer to this question: How much is my gross pay if my monthly sales are $60,000? Looking at Figure 9.40, you can quickly see that the answer is $8,000.

	A	B	C	D	E	F
1						
2	**Goals:**					
3	What is your total gross pay for the month?					
4	Hint: gross pay = base pay + commission pay = $5,000 + $60,000 * 5%.					
5						
6	Monthly Sales =		$60,000.00			
7	Monthly Base Pay =		$5,000.00			
8	Commission Rate on Sales =		5.00%		**Formulas Used:**	
9	Commission Pay =		$3,000.00		=C6*C8	
10	Gross Pay =		$8,000.00		=C7+C9	

Figure 9.40 *My Golden Rule for building Excel models makes what-if analysis and Excel model building easy.*

What-if analysis can be done on small models like the one in Figure 9.40, and it can also be used with much bigger models, as you will see later in this book.

Excel Models

An *Excel model* is an Excel solution that you build in a worksheet and use to solve a problem, perform data analysis, or do what-if analysis that can be used more than one time. An Excel model always starts with assumptions (formula inputs) or raw data. When building Excel models, you should always follow my Golden Rule for building Excel models and the rules for proper datasets.

An Excel model can be a simple gross pay model, like the one shown in Figure 9.40. It can also be a complex data model like the one shown back in Figure 1.20. Or it can be a financial cash flow model or a statistical regression model, both of which you will see later in this book.

Key Concepts in Chapter 9

- According to my **Golden Rule for building Excel models**, if an Excel solution input can change, put it into a cell, label it, and refer to it with a cell reference. This rule provides a number of benefits, including making it easy to find, understand, and change inputs; making it easy to understand how the Excel solution is constructed; and mitigating the risks related to hard-coding values into formulas.

- The **COUNTIFS function** is a counting function that does not count all the items in a range of cells but that counts only the ones that you specify based on conditions. The COUNTIFS function can count with one or more conditions in an AND logical test (where all conditions must be true in order for it to be counted).

- **Dynamic spilled array functions** are worksheet functions that are programmed to deliver an array of spilled values from the cell that contains the array function formula. These functions automatically update in a dynamic way when the source data changes. Examples of array functions are UNIQUE, SORT, FREQUENCY, and FILTER.

- The **Data Validation List** feature lets you add a dropdown list to a cell to allow a user to select from a valid list of names. The feature shows an error message if the user types something that is not in the validation list.

- **Conditional formatting** allows you to build a logical test that applies particular formatting only when the test evaluates to TRUE.

- When you follow my Golden Rule for building Excel models, it is easy to do **what-if analysis** because you can simply change a formula input to find the answer to your what-if question.

- An **Excel model** is an Excel solution that you build to solve a problem, perform data analysis, or do what-if analysis that can be used more than one time. Examples of Excel models include a simple payroll calculation, a financial cash flow model, or a complex data model.

- When you use a cell reference in a formula, Excel can **pull the number formatting from the formula input cell** and apply it to the cell containing the formula.
- With a **move operation**, when you move cells with formulas or cells that are being used in a dialog box, they are programmed to update. For example, when you insert new rows, all the formulas and dialog boxes update perfectly. This makes structural change easy.

Keyboard Shortcuts Learned in Chapter 9

Keyboard Shortcut	Description
Alt, D, L	Opens the Data Validation dialog box
Alt, H, L, N	Opens the Conditional Formatting dialog box

Practice Problems for Chapter 9

Practice Problem 1

In your Excel file for this chapter (Ch09-Excel365-GoldenRule.xlsx), go to the worksheet named PPCh09(1) and create the solution for this practice problem.

Figure 9.41 shows data for this practice problem as well as instructions. Be sure to follow my Golden Rule for building Excel models and the rule for proper datasets. There is more than one way to efficiently solve this problem.

Chantell Williams

   Test 1 = 93, Test 2 = 91, Test 3 = 75

Maria Fox

   Test 1 = 93, Test 2 = 61, Test 3 = 92

Sioux Noline

   Test 1 = 70, Test 2 = 83, Test 3 = 98

Dean Watts

   Test 1 = 80, Test 2 = 78, Test 3 = 99

Total the student test scores, and then give each student extra credit of 25 Points. Use the Excel Table feature for your proper data set.

Figure 9.41 *Solve this problem following my Golden Rule for building Excel models and rules from proper datasets.*

When you are done with this problem, you can check your work against the answer sheet named PPCh09(1an), which shows two examples of ways to solve this problem.

Practice Problem 2

In your Excel file for this chapter (Ch09-Excel365-GoldenRule.xlsx), go to the worksheet named PPCh09(2) and create the solution for this practice problem.

For this problem, you need to consider the following data and goal:

- You have been asked to calculate the cost of goods sold (COGS) for the Aspen product.
- The formula for calculating COGS is COGS = (Begin Units – End Units) * Cost Each.
- Begin Units is the number of units on the store shelf at the start of the month.
- End Units is the number of units on the store shelf at the end of the month.
- Cost Each is how much the company paid for each Aspen product.
- If Begin Units = 114, End Units = 45, and Cost Each = $10, what is COGS?

There is more than one way to efficiently solve this problem.

When you are done with this problem, you can check your work against the answer sheet named PPCh09(2an), which shows two examples of ways to solve this problem.

Practice Problem 3

In your Excel file for this chapter (Ch09-Excel365-GoldenRule.xlsx), go to the worksheet named PPCh09(3) and create the solution for this practice problem. Figure 9.42 shows the goals for this problem, as listed on the worksheet PPCh09(3). Figure 9.43 shows the proper dataset provided on the worksheet PPCh09 (3).

> **Goals:**
>
> In the below data set, each row or record represents a sales transaction for a product.
>
> Goal is to create a solution that will count how many of a specified product were sold
>   and to add conditional formatting to the Product field for that product.
>
> From the Product field create a sorted unique list in cell K13 so that is spills down the column.
>
> In cell I12 add a data validation dropdown list based on the spilled unique list in cell K13.
>
> In cell I13 create a formula that can count based on the condition in cell I12.
>
> For the Product field, add conditional formatting that will add yellow fill based on the value in cell I12.
>
> No new records will be added, so we do not need to convert it to an Excel Table.

Figure 9.42 *The goals included in the worksheet PPCh09(3).*

	A	B	C	D	E	F	G	H	I	J	K
11											
12		Date	Company	Product	Net Sales ($)	Cost ($)		Select Product:	Quad		Product
13		01/01/2013	Gel Booms	Quad	1,232.44	591.58		Count Products Sold:			
14		01/02/2013	Tri Fly	V-Rang	451.20	212.08					
15		01/02/2013	Gel Booms	Carlota	357.50	193.06					
16		01/02/2013	Tri Fly	Darnell	1,957.60	1,037.55					
17		01/03/2013	Gel Booms	Quad	561.68	303.31					
18		01/03/2013	Gel Booms	Carlota	1,980.00	990.00					
19		01/05/2013	Gel Booms	Quad	4,536.00	2,358.72					
20		01/05/2013	Gel Booms	Bellen	503.10	251.56					
21		01/05/2013	Tri Fly	Darnell	3,938.40	1,890.40					
22		01/05/2013	Gel Booms	Bellen	464.96	237.12					
23		01/05/2013	Gel Booms	Carlota	1,650.00	792.00					
24		01/05/2013	Colorad Boom	Yanaki	114.00	55.86					
25		01/05/2013	Colorad Boom	Mt. Fun	1,008.72	504.36					
26		01/05/2013	Colorad Boom	Yanaki	730.20	365.10					
27		01/05/2013	Gel Booms	Sunset	3,174.00	1,713.96					
28		01/05/2013	Gel Booms	Quad	2,304.00	1,082.88					
29		01/05/2013	Gel Booms	Quad	2,744.98	1,317.61					
30		01/05/2013	Gel Booms	Quad	3,361.20	1,579.75					
31		01/05/2013	Colorad Boom	Crest	1,664.00	881.92					
32		01/06/2013	Colorad Boom	Yanaki	670.40	355.28					

Figure 9.43 *Setup provided for Practice Problem 3 in the worksheet named PPCh09(3).*

When you are done with this problem, you can check your work against the answer sheet named PPCh09(3an).

Practice Problem 4

In your Excel file for this chapter (Ch09-Excel365-GoldenRule.xlsx), go to the worksheet named PPCh09(4).

In your own words, see if you can answer these conceptual questions:

1. What are the benefits of following my Golden Rule for building Excel models?
2. What does conditional formatting do?
3. What does a data validation list do?
4. What is what-if analysis?
5. What is an Excel model?
6. What is an array function?

When you are done with this problem, you can check your work against the answer worksheet named PPCh09(4an).

Chapter 10: Knowing When to Use the ROUND Function

> **Note:** To follow along with the examples in this chapter, you can use the file named Ch10-Excel365-ROUND.xlsx.

Knowing when to use the ROUND worksheet function is an important skill that you must be fluent with in order to create effective and efficient Excel worksheet solutions. Figure 10.1 shows an employee payroll example where gross pay is multiplied by a tax rate. But which total is correct? Does 52.73 + 58.58 + 52.59 = 163.89? Or does 52.73 + 58.58 + 52.59 = 163.90?

The correct total is the one at the bottom of column E, where the ROUND function was used. If you add up the numbers yourself, you will see that 52.73 + 58.58 + 52.59 = 163.90. What you see in column D is a common error that people make when performing Excel tasks like handling employee payroll or sales invoicing: They forget to round when they need to round.

	A	B	C	D	E	F	G
6							
7			Tax Rate	7.65%			
8							
9				Did NOT use ROUND	Used ROUND function		
10							
11		Employee	Gross Pay	Tax Deduction	Tax Deduction		
12		Lillian Holt	$689.25	$52.73	$52.73		◄ $689.25 * 7.65%
13		Jasmine Phelps	$765.71	$58.58	$58.58		◄ $765.71 * 7.65%
14		Sadie Hudson	$687.43	$52.59	$52.59		◄ $687.43 * 7.65%
15			Total	$163.89	$163.90		◄ Add 3 calculations
16							
17				Which total is correct?			
18							

Figure 10.1 *Does 52.73 + 58.58 + 52.59 = 163.89? Or does 52.73 + 58.58 + 52.59 = 163.9?*

You can see the root cause of this error in Figure 10.2, where the Currency number format has been removed from the formulas that did not use the ROUND function. You can see many extra decimal places past the penny position that have not been removed with rounding, which of course is required when you are dealing with money.

	A	B	C	D	E
6					
7			Tax Rate	7.65%	
8					
9				Did NOT use ROUND	
10					
11		Employee	Gross Pay	Tax Deduction	
12		Lillian Holt	$689.25	52.727625	
13		Jasmine Phelps	$765.71	58.576815	
14		Sadie Hudson	$687.43	52.588395	
15			Total	163.892835	

Figure 10.2 *Applying the General number format to the range D7:D9 reveals that the numbers are not rounded.*

Before we can fully examine this issue, let's think about how to round a number by hand. There are several ways to round numbers. Although you will learn other methods for rounding later in this book, in this chapter we look at the standard rounding rule; this is the method you probably already know from school and that is used most often in business, economics, and other fields. Figure 10.3 illustrates the standard rounding rule and provides two examples of using it. Luckily, when you use Excel's ROUND function, you do not have to do all the steps shown in Figure 10.3, and if you have many numbers to round, you can create just one formula and then spill it down the column, and the ROUND function will instantly round all the numbers correctly!

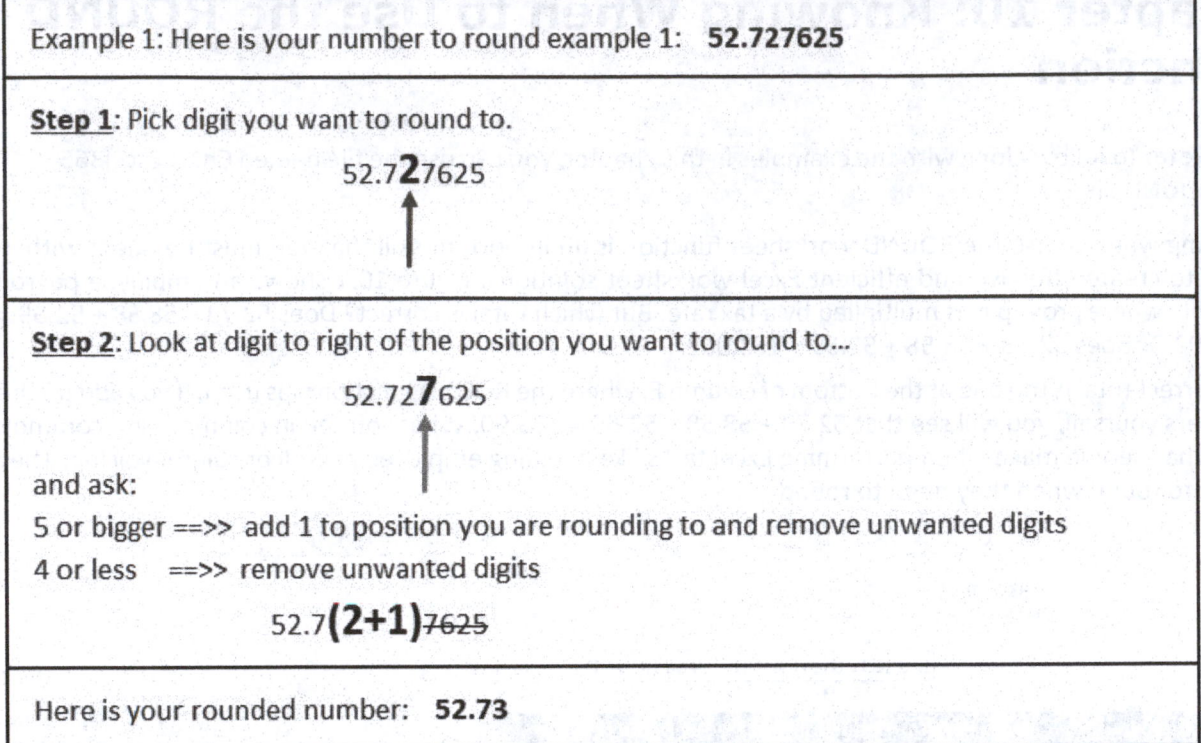

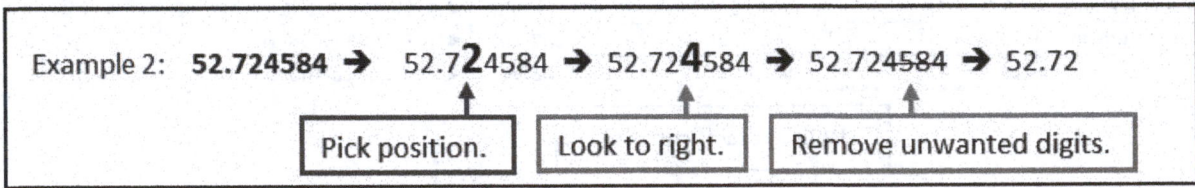

Figure 10.3 *Rules for standard rounding done by hand.*

Now before you create a formula and use ROUND, look back at Figure 10.1. Does it really matter if this Excel solution is a penny off? Yes, it does matter. When you are doing payroll for employees or creating a sales invoice for a customer, if you are a few pennies off, the employee or customer will not trust your ability to make accurate calculations. In addition, for systems like accounting systems, nothing will work unless everything balances to the penny!

> **Note:** In some cases, rounding is not very important, such as when you're creating a budget that estimates the unknown future. However, even though being a few pennies off in a budget is not very consequential, I still like to see everything add up correctly, and I therefore use the ROUND function in most situations were rounding is required.

Another thing to notice in Figure 10.1 is that the Currency number formatting in column D makes it appear as if the numbers are rounded. However, the numbers are not rounded; they are just displayed showing only two decimal places. As you can see in Figure 10.2, when the General number format is applied, the number formatting is wiped away, and you do not see legitimate money amounts. Because an employee payroll calculation is limited to pennies as the smallest unit of money, you *must* officially round each number to the penny *before* you add the numbers with the SUM function. If you do not round to get actual amounts with dollars and pennies, then when the SUM function adds the unrounded numbers, it adds all the extra decimal places, too. This is what leads to the wrong answer.

Further, don't be tricked by the fact that *sometimes* the unrounded numbers add up to the correct amount. If you do not properly round, sometimes you will get totals that are too large or too small, and then sometimes, by *accident*, the numbers will be correct. Also, remember what you learned about number formatting in Chapter 8:

- Number formatting is a façade.
- Formulas do not see number formatting.

Based on this information, you know that the SUM function did not use the numbers as they were displayed in column D, but instead it added up the unrounded numbers.

The ROUND Function Rule

Not all calculations require rounding. However, many do. To decide when rounding using the ROUND function is required, there is a rounding rule that you can use to determine exactly when you must use the ROUND function. When the answer to each of these three questions is *yes*, you must use the ROUND function:

- Are you are required to round (as with money)?
- Are there decimal places past the position that you want to round to?
- Will you use the formula result in other formulas?

Note: The ROUND function is available in both the Excel worksheet and the DAX formula language (used in Power Pivot and Power BI).

Consider these hints related to using the ROUND worksheet function:

- **Hint 1:** The first argument in the ROUND function is the *number* argument. This argument is where you put the number that needs to be rounded. You usually put a formula in this argument. The second argument is the *num_digits* argument. This is where you put the position of the number you want to round to. For example, 2 is for rounding to the penny, 0 is for rounding to the dollar, and -3 is for rounding to the $1,000 position.

- **Hint 2:** Start building your Excel solutions so that all formula input cells and cells that will have formulas have the General number format applied. This helps reveal calculation results that contain unwanted digits.

- **Hint 3:** If your formula results will not be used in other formulas and all you need to do is look at the formula results, then using number formatting to display the results in a specific way is sufficient, and you do not need to use the ROUND function.

- **Hint 4:** When you have individual amounts, like deductions from a paycheck or line item amounts in a sales invoice, you must round each individual number before adding the numbers. Rounding only the final total can yield inaccurate results.

- **Hint 5:** For money amounts, if you are multiplying or dividing with numbers that contain decimal places (rather than whole numbers or integers) and will use the formula results in other formulas, use the ROUND function.

The examples in the following sections give you practice using the ROUND worksheet function.

Example 1: Using the ROUND Function to Get Accurate Totals for Tax Deduction Calculations

Figure 10.4 lists three goals for an Excel model. After reading the goals, you can consider the three question to determine if you must use ROUND:

- Are you are required to round? *Yes*, because you are dealing with money amounts.
- Are there decimal places past the penny position? *Yes*, because you are multiplying numbers with decimal places. Specifically, the tax rate already has decimal places past the penny position before you even multiply tax rate by gross pay. You know even before you complete the multiplication that the result will yield decimal places past the penny position.
- Will you use the formula result in other formulas? *Yes*, because you are using the tax deduction results in the formula to determine total deductions.

In addition, Goal 3 states that no new employee records will be added, and so the Excel Table feature will not be required. This is important because it means you can use a spilled array formula rather than a formula with relative and absolute cell references, as you did earlier in the book (refer to Figure 8.92).

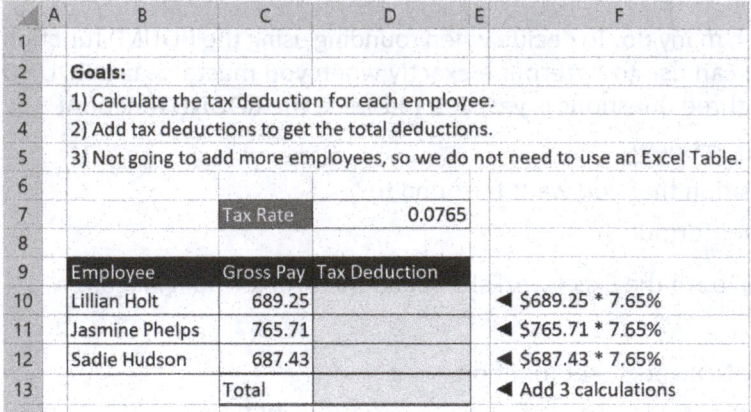

Figure 10.4 *Three goals for this tax deduction calculation.*

As shown in Figure 10.5, when you are making calculations that require rounding, it is best for all the cells that contain formula inputs or formulas to begin with the General number format. With the General number format applied to all cells, you can easily see any extra decimal places that show up. Even if you are not thinking about rounding, when you use the General number format and a formula yields extra decimal places for a money amount that will also be used in a subsequent formula, you immediately get a visual cue that can remind you to use the ROUND function.

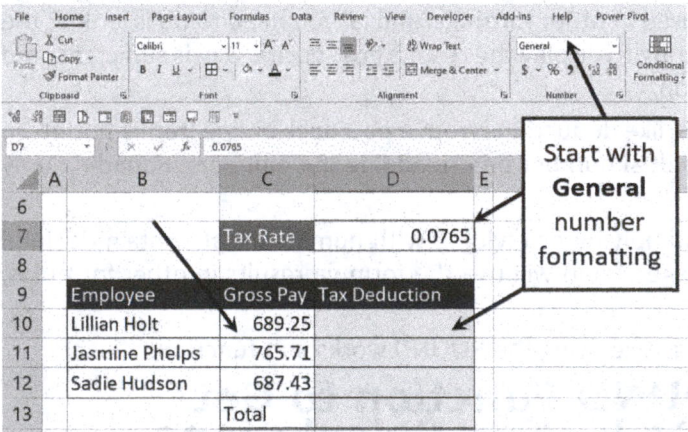

Figure 10.5 *For clarity and ease in formula building, always start with General number format applied to everything.*

To build a ROUND function solution, follow these steps:

1. Select the worksheet named Ch10(5-16).

2. Make sure the cells and ranges D7 (tax rate input), C10:C12 (gross pay input), D10:D12 (tax deduction formulas), and D12 (SUM function) have the General number format applied.

3. Select cell D10 and type an equal sign, and then select the range with the gross pay amounts, C10:C12, as shown in Figure 10.6. To quickly select the range, you can tap your LeftArrow key one time and then hold down the Shift key and tap the DownArrow key twice. At this point, you have given the formula an array of values to deal with.

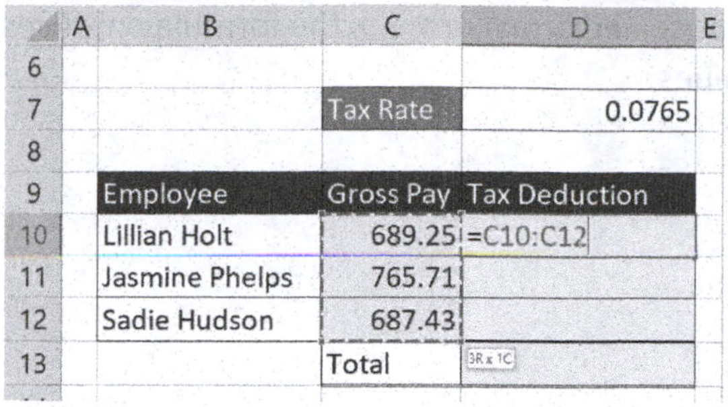

	A	B	C	D	E
6					
7			Tax Rate	0.0765	
8					
9		Employee	Gross Pay	Tax Deduction	
10		Lillian Holt	689.25	=C10:C12	
11		Jasmine Phelps	765.71		
12		Sadie Hudson	687.43		
13			Total	3R x 1C	

Figure 10.6 *The formula has a range of cells with three values.*

4. As shown in Figure 10.7, type an * (asterisk) for multiplication. Then select the cell with the tax rate (by tapping the UpArrow three times). Because you are multiplying an array of values with a single tax rate, the formula knows to make an array operation to multiply each individual gross pay amount by the tax rate.

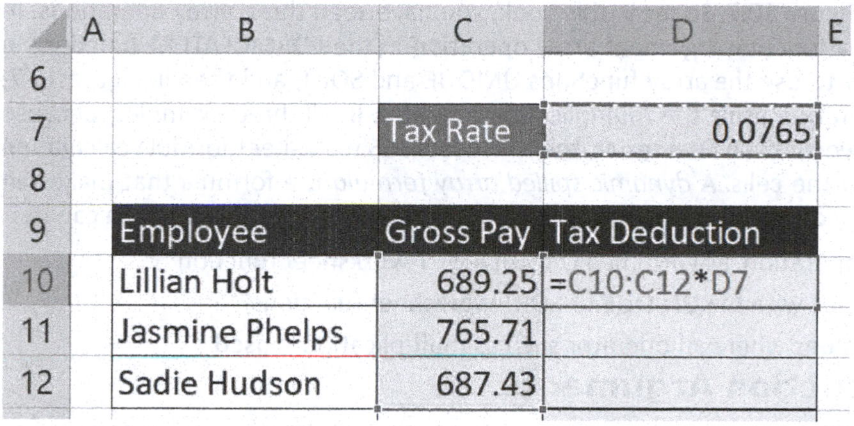

	A	B	C	D	E
6					
7			Tax Rate	0.0765	
8					
9		Employee	Gross Pay	Tax Deduction	
10		Lillian Holt	689.25	=C10:C12*D7	
11		Jasmine Phelps	765.71		
12		Sadie Hudson	687.43		

Figure 10.7 *The formula makes an array multiplication operation based on three gross pay values and a tax rate.*

5. Press Ctrl+Enter to put the formula in cell D10, keep the cell selected, and spill the answers down to the remaining employees. You can see the spilled values in Figures 10.8 and 10.9.

   Figure 10.8 shows the tax deduction calculations.

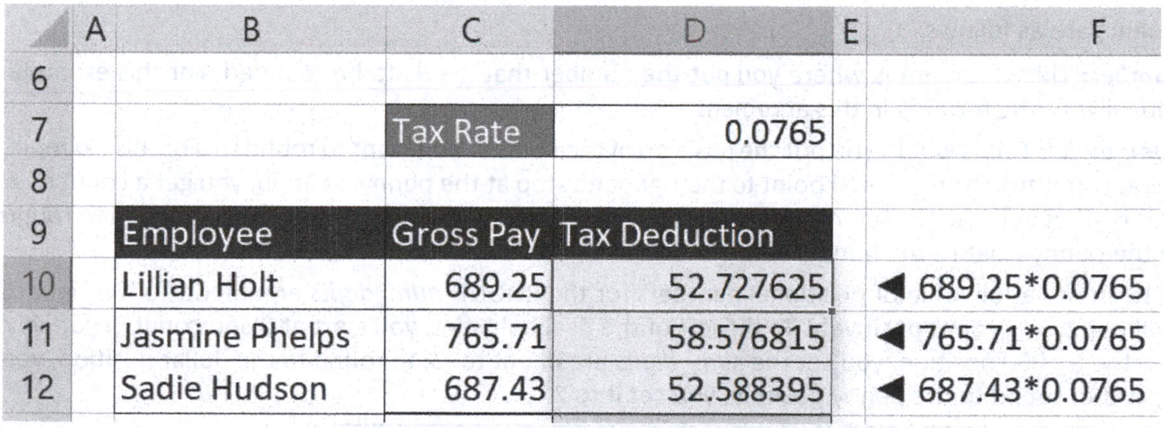

	A	B	C	D	E	F
6						
7			Tax Rate	0.0765		
8						
9		Employee	Gross Pay	Tax Deduction		
10		Lillian Holt	689.25	52.727625		◄ 689.25*0.0765
11		Jasmine Phelps	765.71	58.576815		◄ 765.71*0.0765
12		Sadie Hudson	687.43	52.588395		◄ 687.43*0.0765

Figure 10.8 *The three unrounded tax deductions are spilled into the worksheet.*

Figure 10.9 reminds you that when you create a dynamic spilled array formula, the formula only lives in the top cell, and the remaining cells show spilled values.

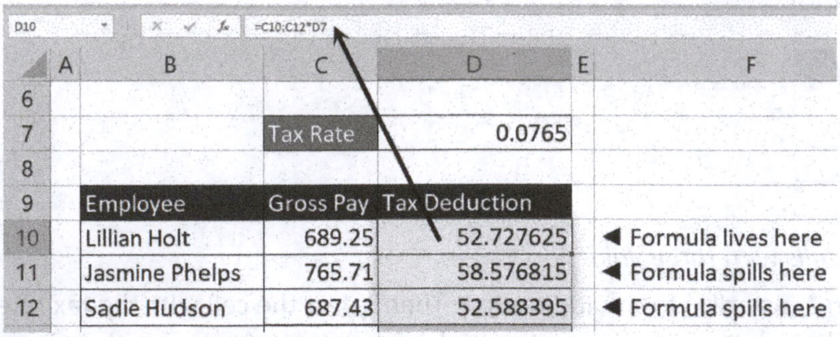

Figure 10.9 *The formula only lives in the top cell, cell D10.*

Defining a Dynamic Spilled Array Formula

You just saw an array operation in Figure 10.7. So far in this book, you have seen three array operations. In Figure 8.92, you saw how to make a function argument array operation in the FORMULATEXT function; in Figures 9.21 and 9.28, you saw how to use the array functions UNIQUE and SORT; and then in Figure 10.7, you saw how to make an array operation using the multiplication operator. In all three examples, because the formula delivered multiple answers as the final result, the Microsoft 365 worksheet formula calculation engine knew to spill the values into the cells. A *dynamic spilled array formula* is a formula that makes an array operation and delivers an array of final answers to the worksheet, where the array operation can be:

- A function argument array operation, as with the FORMULATEXT worksheet function
- An array function operation, as with the UNIQUE or SORT worksheet functions
- Operations on an array of values where an operator such as multiplication is used

ROUND Worksheet Function Arguments

Now that you have your array of spilled tax deductions, you need to use the ROUND worksheet function to round each amount. As shown in Figure 10.9, the unrounded tax deduction for Lillian Holt is 52.727625. The position that you have to round to when you are dealing with payroll tax deduction is the penny position. In order to get the ROUND function to work correctly, you have to communicate this position to the ROUND function. The ROUND function has the following syntax:

```
ROUND(number, num_digits)
```

The arguments are as follows:

- ***number***: This argument is where you put the number that needs to be rounded. For this example, you will put the formula in this argument.
- ***num_digits***: This is where you put the position of the number you want to round to. For this example, if you count from the decimal point to the right and stop at the penny position, you get a count of 2. This is what you must enter into the *num_digits* argument if you want the ROUND function to round to the penny (that is, the hundredths position).

Figure 10.10 shows a full table of positional numbers for the ROUND *num_digits* argument. To the right of the decimal point, you count positively. To the left of the decimal point, you start at 0 and count negatively. To round to the $1,000 position, you set the *num_digits* argument to -3; to round to the dollar position, you set it to 0; and to round to the penny position, you set it to 2.

Number	**Position of the number you want to round to for num_digit argument**								
52.727625	5	2	.	7	2	7	6	2	5
num_digits:	▲ -1	▲ 0	Decimal	▲ 1	▲ 2	▲ 3	▲ 4	▲ 5	▲ 6
		Dollar Position			*Penny Position*				

Figure 10.10 *The num_digits argument in the ROUND worksheet function is the position you want to round to.*

To round the array of numbers in this example, follow these steps:

1. As shown in Figure 10.11, select cell D10, where the spilled array formula lives, and press the F2 key to put the cell into edit mode. Place your insertion cursor after the equal sign and type **ROUND(**. The array formula now sits in the *number* argument of the ROUND worksheet function.

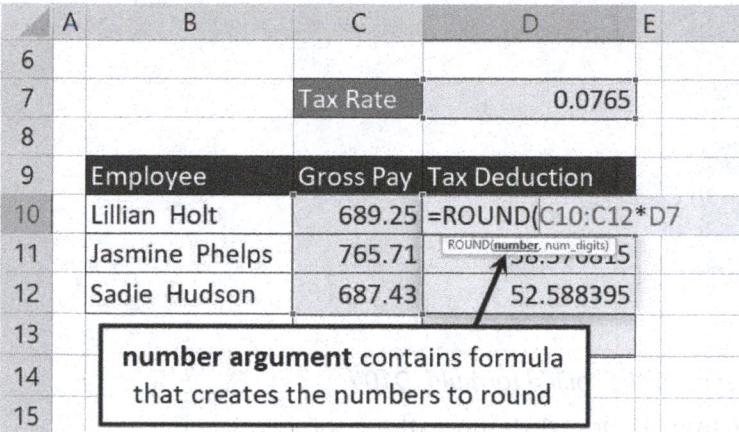

Figure 10.11 *The number argument is where the array formula sits.*

2. As shown in Figure 10.12, carefully use your I-beam cursor (not the selection cursor) to click at the end of the formula, directly after the D7 cell reference, and type a comma to get to the *num_digits* argument. Then type **2** and a close parenthesis. Finally, press Enter to spill the rounded values down the column. Figure 10.13 shows the result.

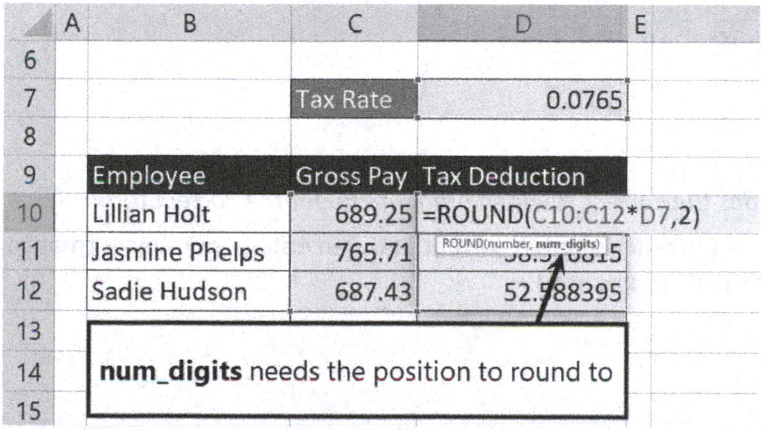

	A	B	C	D	E
6					
7			Tax Rate	0.0765	
8					
9		Employee	Gross Pay	Tax Deduction	
10		Lillian Holt	689.25	=ROUND(C10:C12*D7,2)	
11		Jasmine Phelps	765.71	ROUND(number, num_digits) 58.9~0815	
12		Sadie Hudson	687.43	52.588395	
13					
14		**num_digits** needs the position to round to			
15					

Figure 10.12 *You can round to the penny with a 2 in the num_digits argument.*

	A	B	C	D
9		Employee	Gross Pay	Tax Deduction
10		Lillian Holt	689.25	52.73
11		Jasmine Phelps	765.71	58.58
12		Sadie Hudson	687.43	52.59
13			Total	

Figure 10.13 *Correctly rounded tax deduction amounts.*

3. Press Enter twice to select the total deduction cell, D13. Then, as shown in Figure 10.14, use the keyboard shortcut Alt+= to invoke the SUM function. Notice that because you are adding all the results from a spilled array, the function includes the cell reference where the formula lives, cell D10, and the spilled range operator, the # symbol.

	A	B	C	D	E
6					
7			Tax Rate	0.0765	
8					
9		Employee	Gross Pay	Tax Deduction	
10		Lillian Holt	689.25	52.73	
11		Jasmine Phelps	765.71	58.58	
12		Sadie Hudson	687.43	52.59	
13			Total	=SUM(D10#)	
14				SUM(number1, [number2], ...)	

Figure 10.14 *The SUM function uses the reference to the spilled formula, D10#.*

4. Press Enter to enter the tax deduction total. Figure 10.15 shows the result.

	A	B	C	D	E
6					
7			Tax Rate	0.0765	
8					
9		Employee	Gross Pay	Tax Deduction	
10		Lillian Holt	689.25	52.73	
11		Jasmine Phelps	765.71	58.58	
12		Sadie Hudson	687.43	52.59	
13			Total	163.9	
14					

Figure 10.15 *The SUM function in cell D13 adds the correct rounded amounts to get the correct total.*

5. Using Figure 10.16 as a guide, add the Currency number format and Percentage number format to the appropriate cells and document the formulas used.

	A	B	C	D	E	F
1						
2		**Goals:**				
3		1) Calculate the tax deduction for each employee.				
4		2) Add tax deductions to get the total deductions.				
5		3) Not going to add more employees, so we do not need to use an Excel Table.				
6						
7			Tax Rate	7.65%		
8						
9		Employee	Gross Pay	Tax Deduction		**Formulas in Column:**
10		Lillian Holt	$689.25	$52.73		=ROUND(C10:C12*D7,2)
11		Jasmine Phelps	$765.71	$58.58		
12		Sadie Hudson	$687.43	$52.59		
13			Total	$163.90		=SUM(D10#)
14						

Figure 10.16 *Correctly rounded tax deduction solution.*

In this first example of how and when to use the ROUND worksheet function, you verified that the three conditions for using ROUND were met, removed all number formatting, created the formula to yield the correct rounded amounts, added the amounts, added number formatting for the dollar and percentage amounts, and documented the formulas used.

Example 2: Rounding to the Dollar

In some situations, money amounts need to be rounded to the dollar rather than to the penny. For example, as shown in Figure 10.17, U.S. federal income tax forms require that monetary amounts be rounded to the dollar.

To complete this example, follow these steps:

1. Select the worksheet named Ch10(17-19).

2. In cell D8, create the formula **=ROUND(C8:C12,0)**, as shown in Figure 10.17. Because you are rounding to the dollar position (that is, the ones position), you use a 0 in the *num_digits* argument of ROUND.

3. Press Enter to spill the formula results.

	A	B	C	D	E	F
1						
2		**Goals:**				
3		1) Round the federal income tax expense amounts to the dollar.				
4		2) Add to get the total expenses.				
5		3) Not going to add more expenses, so you do not need to use an Excel Table.				
6						
7		Expenses	Amounts	For Tax Form		
8		Auto	1689.51	=ROUND(C8:C12,0)		
9		Rent	12089.75	ROUND(number, **num_digits**)		
10		Office	1583.79			
11		Shipping	765.71			
12		COGS	25117.22			
13			Total			

Figure 10.17 *Rounding to the dollar requires a 0 in the second argument of ROUND.*

4. In cell D13, use the keyboard shortcut Alt+= to enter the SUM function, as shown in Figure 10.18.

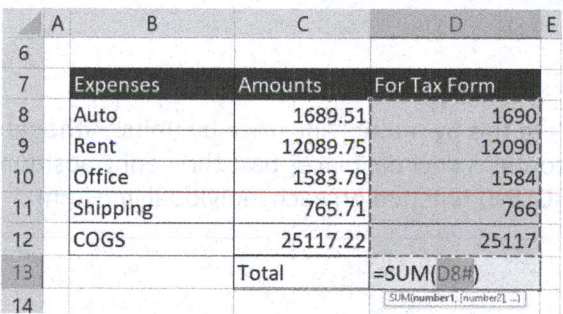

	A	B	C	D	E
6					
7		Expenses	Amounts	For Tax Form	
8		Auto	1689.51	1690	
9		Rent	12089.75	12090	
10		Office	1583.79	1584	
11		Shipping	765.71	766	
12		COGS	25117.22	25117	
13			Total	=SUM(D8#)	
14				SUM(**number1**, [number2], ...)	

Figure 10.18 *The formula SUM(D8#) adds all the spilled values from the formula in cell D8.*

5. Add number formatting and document the formulas as shown in Figure 10.19.

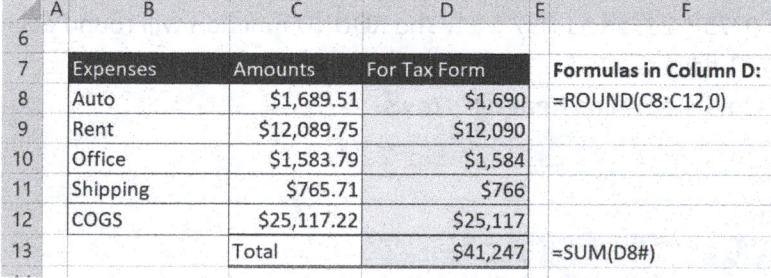

	A	B	C	D	E	F
6						
7		Expenses	Amounts	For Tax Form		Formulas in Column D:
8		Auto	$1,689.51	$1,690		=ROUND(C8:C12,0)
9		Rent	$12,089.75	$12,090		
10		Office	$1,583.79	$1,584		
11		Shipping	$765.71	$766		
12		COGS	$25,117.22	$25,117		
13			Total	$41,247		=SUM(D8#)

Figure 10.19 *Using the ROUND function with a 0 in the second argument allows SUM to calculate the correct total.*

Example 3: Rounding for a Sales Invoice

As shown in Figure 10.20, in this example, you need to complete a sales invoice, including calculations for line item sales, sales subtotal, tax amount, and invoice total. Because you will have to multiply money amounts that include decimal places, and you want accurate subtotal and total amounts, you must use the ROUND worksheet function. All three requirements for using the ROUND function are met:

- Rounding is required because these are money amounts.
- There are extra decimal places. The price and tax rate have decimal places past the penny.
- The formula results for line item sales and tax amount will be used in subsequent formulas.

	A	B	C	D	E	F	G
1							
2		**Goals:**					
3		1) Round line item sales and tax amount.					
4		2) Add to get the sales subtotal and invoice total.					
5		3) This is not a proper data set and so you can't use Excel Table feature.					
6							
7		**Sales Invoice Number:**		**#1025**			
8		**Item**	**Price ($)**	**Units**		**Line Sales ($)**	**Formulas Needed:**
9		1" screws	0.0513	31			◀Line Item Sale = 0.0513*31
10		2" screws	0.0775	21			◀Line Item Sale = 0.0775*21
11		6" lock pads	1.057	11			◀Line Item Sale = 1.057*11
12				**Sales Subtotal**			◀ Subtotal for Line Sales
13				**Tax**			◀ Subtotal * 0.0975
14				**Invoice Total**			◀ Total + Tax
15			**Thanks for your Order!**				
16							
17					**Tax Rate**		
18					0.0975		

Figure 10.20 *It takes four different formulas to complete this sales invoice.*

The first calculation to make is the line item sale; you complete this by multiplying price by units. Although you are multiplying whole numbers by price, because price contains decimal places past the penny position and you will need to add these numbers, you must use the ROUND function on each individual line item.

To complete this example, follow these steps:

1. Select the worksheet named Ch10(21-26).

2. Select cell E9 and create the spilled array formula **=ROUND(C9:C11*D9:D11,2)**, as shown in Figure 10.21. Notice that you are multiplying a range of three prices (C9:C11) by a range of three units (D9:D11). The Excel worksheet calculation engine will interpret this perfectly and then multiply each corresponding row: 0.0513 * 31, 0.0775 * 21, and 1.057 * 11. The ROUND function will round each value to the penny: 1.59, 1.63, and 11.63.

3. Press Enter to spill the three values to the new line item sales rows.

	A	B	C	D	E	F
6						
7		**Sales Invoice Number:**		**#1025**		
8		**Item**	**Price ($)**	**Units**	**Line Sales ($)**	
9		1" screws	0.0513	31	=ROUND(C9:C11*D9:D11,2)	
10		2" screws	0.0775	21	ROUND(number, num_digits)	
11		6" lock pads	1.057	11		
12				**Sales Subtotal**		

Figure 10.21 *The array operation is a three-row by one-column range multiplied by a second three-row by one-column range.*

4. As shown in Figure 10.22, select cell E12 and create a subtotal by using the SUM function keyboard shortcut Alt+=.

5. Press Enter to put the SUM function into cell E12 and move the selected cell down to cell E13.

	A	B	C	D	E
6					
7		Sales Invoice Number:		#1025	
8		Item	Price ($)	Units	Line Sales ($)
9		1" screws	0.0513	31	1.59
10		2" screws	0.0775	21	1.63
11		6" lock pads	1.057	11	11.63
12				Sales Subtotal	=SUM(E9#)
13				Tax	SUM(number1, [number2], ...)

Figure 10.22 *The SUM function picks up the correct spilled reference, E9#.*

6. In cell E13, create the formula **=ROUND(E12*E18,2)**, as shown in Figure 10.23. Notice that you are multiplying a single subtotal by a single tax rate. The Excel worksheet calculation engine will interpret this perfectly and deliver the single result 1.447875. Then the ROUND function will round that number to the penny, giving you 1.45.

	A	B	C	D	E	F
6						
7		Sales Invoice Number:		#1025		
8		Item	Price ($)	Units	Line Sales ($)	
9		1" screws	0.0513	31	1.59	
10		2" screws	0.0775	21	1.63	
11		6" lock pads	1.057	11	11.63	
12				Sales Subtotal	14.85	
13				Tax	=ROUND(E12*E18,2)	
14				Invoice Total	ROUND(number, num_digits)	
15			Thanks for your Order!			
16						
17					Tax Rate	
18					0.0975	

Figure 10.23 *You must use ROUND on the tax on the subtotal.*

7. Press Enter to put the tax calculation formula into cell E13 and move the selected cell down to cell E14.

8. As shown in Figure 10.24, create your invoice total formula by using the SUM function keyboard shortcut Alt+=. Notice that the SUM function does not grab the correct range of cells, E12:E13, that contains the subtotal and tax. This happens sometimes, and you must always verify that the range that the SUM function grabs is correct. Luckily, the dancing ants are still dancing around cell E13, which means you are in point mode and can use your mouse selection cursor or keyboard shortcuts to select the correct range.

	A	B	C	D	E	F
6						
7		Sales Invoice Number:		#1025		
8		Item	Price ($)	Units	Line Sales ($)	
9		1" screws	0.0513	31	1.59	
10		2" screws	0.0775	21	1.63	
11		6" lock pads	1.057	11	11.63	
12				Sales Subtotal	14.85	
13				Tax	1.45	
14				Invoice Total	=SUM(E13)	
15			Thanks for your Order!		SUM(number1, [number2], ...)	

Figure 10.24 *This time, the keyboard shortcut for the SUM function, Alt+=, grabs the wrong range!*

9. Using your mouse selection cursor, you can carefully select the range E12:E13. Or you can hold down the Shift key and click the UpArrow key one time to select the range E12:E13. Figure 10.25 shows the correct range for the SUM function.

	A	B	C	D	E
6					
7		Sales Invoice Number:		#1025	
8		Item	Price ($)	Units	Line Sales ($)
9		1" screws	0.0513	31	1.59
10		2" screws	0.0775	21	1.63
11		6" lock pads	1.057	11	11.63
12				Sales Subtotal	14.85
13				Tax	1.45
14				Invoice Total	=SUM(E12:E13)
15			Thanks for your Order!		SUM(number1, [number2], ...)

Figure 10.25 *Always be sure to verify that the SUM function grabs the correct range. In this case, E12:E13 is the correct range.*

10. Use number formatting to show two decimal places for the dollar amounts and use the Percentage number format for the tax rate. Document your formulas and set up the page for printing by excluding everything except the invoice in cells B7:E15. The finished worksheet should look as shown in Figure 10.26.

	A	B	C	D	E	F	G
1							
2		Goals:					
3		1) Round line item sales and tax amount.					
4		2) Add to get the sales subtotal and invoice total.					
5		3) This is not a proper data set and so you can't use Excel Table feature.					
6							
7		Sales Invoice Number:		#1025			
8		Item	Price ($)	Units	Line Sales ($)		Formulas Used:
9		1" screws	0.0513	31	1.59		=ROUND(C9:C11*D9:D11,2)
10		2" screws	0.0775	21	1.63		
11		6" lock pads	1.057	11	11.63		
12				Sales Subtotal	14.85		=SUM(E9#)
13				Tax	1.45		=ROUND(E12*E18,2)
14				Invoice Total	16.30		=SUM(E12:E13)
15			Thanks for your Order!				
16							
17					Tax Rate		
18					9.75%		

Figure 10.26 *You get an accurate invoice when you think carefully about where you need to round.*

Note: Notice that Figure 10.26 does not use the Currency number format for the cells containing money amounts. Rather than show a dollar sign in each cell to communicate the unit of money, the column headers at the top of the invoice indicate the monetary unit. By indicating the unit at the top of the column and not filling all the cells with $ signs, you can create a solution that is less cluttered and easier to read.

Example 4: Rounding a Percentage

As a final example of rounding, let's look at how to round a percentage. The hard part of rounding a percentage has to do with the fact that percentages are created with number formatting, and there is an underlying number that the formula works with (rather than working with the percentage itself). In Figure 10.27, you can see the number 0.85274 and the formatted percentage 85.274%. If you were given the directions "round to the nearest tenth of a percent," what would you put into the second argument of the ROUND function: 1 or 3? If you look at the percentage in Figure 10.27 and consider the words for the percentage digits, you might be tempted to say that 1 should be used in the second argument of ROUND. But that is incorrect because formulas cannot "see" number formatting. Remember that formulas act on the underlying numbers. So, although the directions are given to you as "nearest tenth of a percent," you have to realize that as a percentage, the position is a tenth, but that is for the formatted number. The underlying positional digit that sits under the "tenth of a percent" is located at the thousandth position, which, if you count left to right, is three places from the decimal point. As a result, the correct number to enter into the second argument of ROUND when you want to round to the "nearest tenth of a percent" is 3.

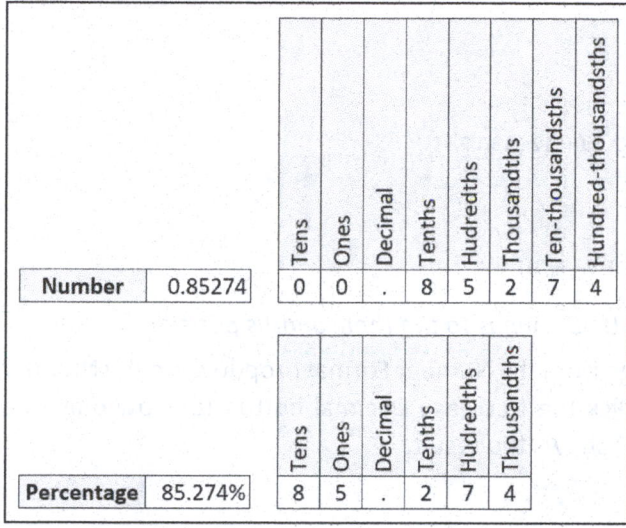

Figure 10.27 *Words for different digits in numbers and percentages.*

> **Note:** When using the ROUND worksheet function to round percentages, remember that you must look at the underlying number to determine the correct position to round to.

Figure 10.28 shows an example of a project that requires you to round percentage grades. Reading through the goals, you can see that all three requirements for using the ROUND worksheet function are met:

- Rounding is required, according to the rules in the syllabus.
- You have decimal places, and you are using the division operator, which creates a risk of extraneous decimals.
- The formula results will be used in the subsequent average calculation.

To complete this example, follow these steps:

1. Select the worksheet named Ch10(28-29).
2. Make sure the General number format is applied to the cells with formula input and cells that will get formulas.

3. Using Figure 10.28 as a guide, create the formula **=ROUND(C12:C15/C9,3)** in cell D12 and the formula **=AVERAGE(D12#)** in cell D16. When the student individual % grades are rounded correctly, they can be used by the AVERAGE function to calculate an overall average. (The AVERAGE worksheet function is programmed to add up the numbers and then divide by the count to calculate the average.) Because you are not going to use the result of the average calculation in any other formulas, you are not required to use the ROUND function for the average calculation. You can simply display it to show the percentage rounded to the tenth of a percent.

	A	B	C	D	E	F	G
1							
2		Goals:					
3		1) Calculate % Grade.					
4		2) Syllabus defines final grade as a percent, rounded to the tenth of a percent					
5				(or thousandths position for the decimal).			
6		3) Calculate the overall class average for % grade.					
7		4) We will not add new records.					
8							
9		Total Points Possible:	500				
10							
11		Student	Total Scores	% Grade			
12		Sioux Coolinator	426.37	0.853		=ROUND(C12:C15/C9,3)	
13		Chantel Williams	455.26	0.911			
14		Miki Yu	371.95	0.744			
15		Tyrone Zion	455.32	0.911			
16		Overall Class Average % Grade:		0.85475		=AVERAGE(D12#)	

Figure 10.28 *Using 3 in the num_digits argument of ROUND rounds to the thousandths position.*

4. Select the range D12:D16 and choose Percentage from the Number Format dropdown in the Number group in the Home tab of the Ribbon. Then click the Decrease Decimal button to show only one decimal place for the percentages. Figure 10.29 shows the result.

	A	B	C	D	E	F	G
8							
9		Total Points Possible:	500				
10							
11		Student	Total Scores	% Grade			
12		Sioux Coolinator	426.37	85.3%		=ROUND(C12:C15/C9,3)	
13		Chantel Williams	455.26	91.1%			
14		Miki Yu	371.95	74.4%			
15		Tyrone Zion	455.32	91.1%			
16		Overall Class Average % Grade:		85.5%		=AVERAGE(D12#)	

Figure 10.29 *There are no hidden decimal places in the range D12:D15, but there are hidden decimal places in cell D16.*

Note: In cell D16, you did not use the ROUND function but instead displayed the number the way you wanted it by using number formatting. It is fine to do it this way if all you are going to do is look at the number, report it on a form, or use it in discussions. As long as you will not use it in other formulas that require a number rounded to the tenth of a percent, displaying it with number formatting is sufficient.

Key Concepts in Chapter 10

*   To get accurate results in Excel, you must know **when to use the ROUND worksheet function**. If you are required to round a calculation and you might have unwanted decimal places and the results will be used in other formulas, you must use the ROUND function. The *number* argument in ROUND is where you put the number that needs to be rounded. The *num_digits* argument is where you put the position of the number you want to round to.

*   When using the ROUND worksheet function to **round percentages**, you must look at the underlying number to determine the correct position to round to.

- A **dynamic spilled array formula** is a formula that makes an array operation and delivers an array of final answers to the worksheet, where the array operation can be:
    - A function argument array operation, as with the FORMULATEXT worksheet function
    - An array function operation, as with the UNIQUE or SORT worksheet functions
    - A direct operator array operations, such as C10:C12 * D7

Practice Problems for Chapter 10

Practice Problem 1

In your Excel file for this chapter (Ch10-Excel365-ROUND.xlsx), go to the worksheet named PPCh10(1) and create the solution for this practice problem. Figure 10.30 shows the goals that are listed on the worksheet PPCh10(1).

	A	B	C	D	E	F	G	H
1								
2		**Goals:**						
3		In cell F11 change the number formatting so that it is not misleading.						
4		In the Gross Pay column, fix any numbers that are not numbers.						
5		In cell D11, create a formula that will calculate the correct Tax Deduction (Gross Pay * Tax Rate), then copy it down the column.						
6		In cell D21, create a formula to add all the tax deductions.						
7		We will not add more records later.						
8		Add page setup so range just the employee table prints out.						
9								
10		**Employee**	**Gross Pay**		**Tax Deduction**		**Tax Rate**	**Formulas in Tax Deduction Column:**
11		Tyrone Zion	3689..69				8%	
12		Chantel Williams	$3,862.41					
13		Terrilyn Ashmore	$2,979.29					
14		Tawana Hwang	$2,680.63					
15		Sioux Radcoolinator	$$3304.15					
16		Salley Janssen	$1,779.49					
17		Abdi Ali	3,,876.72					
18		Lavette Fournier	$2,748.74					
19		Diamond Quinones	$2,993.19					
20		Miki Yu	$1,612.36					
21			**Total Tax Deduction**					

Figure 10.30 *On the worksheet PPCh10(1), fix the data, fix the misleading number formatting, and be sure to round!*

When you are done with this problem, you can check your work against the answer sheet named PPCh10(1an).

Practice Problem 2

In the Excel file for this chapter (Ch10-Excel365-ROUND.xlsx), go to the worksheet named PPCh10(2) and create the solution for this practice problem. Figure 10.31 shows the goals that are listed on the PPCh10(2) worksheet.

	A	B	C	D	E
1					
2		**Goals:**			
3		1) Round the federal income tax expense amounts to the dollar.			
4		2) Add to get the total expenses.			
5		3) You do not need to use an Excel Table.			
6					
7		**Expenses**	**Amounts**	**For Tax Form**	
8		Cost of Goods Sold	$71,651,646.10		
9		Research Development	$4,455,821.83		
10		Selling, Marketing and Administrative	$3,122,656.27		
11		Interest Expense	$459,850.44		
12		Income Tax Expense	$950,359.69		
13		Other Expense	$228,465.49		
14			Total		

Figure 10.31 *On the worksheet PPCh10(2), your goal is to round to the dollar.*

When you are done with this problem, you can check your work against the answer sheet named PPCh10(2an).

Practice Problem 3

In your Excel file for this chapter (Ch10-Excel365-ROUND.xlsx), go to the worksheet named PPCh10(3) and create the solution for this practice problem. Figure 10.32 shows the goals that are listed on the PPCh10(3) worksheet.

◢	A	B	C	D	E
1					
2		**Goals:**			
3		1) Round the the percentages in the column to the hundredth of a percent.			
4		2) Although we are not using them in a subsequent formula right now,			
5		these are the type of percentages that could be used in a budget later.			
6		3) You do not need to use an Excel Table.			
7					
8		Expenses	Expenses As % of Revenue	% Used in Later Budgetting Process	
9		Cost of Goods Sold	52.9598757%		
10		Research Development	11.1640526%		
11		Selling, Marketing and Administrative	15.9181836%		
12		Interest Expense	3.4297380%		
13		Income Tax Expense	0.8881292%		
14		Other Expense	2.2135041%		
15					

Figure 10.32 *On the worksheet PPCh10(3), you need to round to the hundredth of a percent.*

When you are done with this problem, you can check your work against the answer sheet named PPCh10(3an).

Practice Problem 4

In your Excel file for this chapter (Ch10-Excel365-ROUND.xlsx), go to the worksheet named PPCh10(4).

In your own words, see if you can answer these conceptual questions:

1. When must you use the ROUND function?
2. When can you use number formatting to display numbers with a certain number of digits and leave some unwanted digits hidden by the number formatting?
3. When you are multiplying money amounts with decimals and you will use the formula result in subsequent formulas, is it a good idea to use ROUND? Explain your answer.
4. Why is it helpful to start with General number formatting on the cells with formula inputs and cells with formulas?

When you are done with this problem, you can check your work against the answer sheet named PPCh09(4an).

Chapter 11: Date and Time Number Formatting and Formulas

> **Note:** To follow along with the examples in this chapter, you can use the file named Ch11-Excel365-DateTime.xlsx.

This chapter covers date and time number formatting and formulas. All of us at one time or another have had to consider questions like these:

- How many days until school starts?
- How many days is the invoice past due?
- How many days outstanding is the loan?
- How many days did the project take?
- How many workdays are there?
- How many hours did the employee work?
- How many hours did the employee work on night shift?
- What is the time worked, rounded to the nearest 5 minutes?
- When is the loan due?
- What is the end date for the project?
- When does my pension plan vest?
- What is last day of next month?

All these questions deal with dates and times. And the way that you answer them by using Excel goes all the way back to when Bricklin and Frankston invented the spreadsheet. They ingeniously used date and time number formatting to make date and time math easy for Excel worksheet formulas to handle.

Figure 11.1 shows a preview of the 12 date and time formulas that you will learn in this chapter. Cell E3 shows that the formula to calculate the number of days between two dates is =D3-C3, which is 3/16/2020 – 2/27/2020. But how does a formula like this work to get the number 18 days? Similarly, cell E7 shows that the formula to calculate the number of hours between two times is =(D7-C7)*24, which is (1:00 PM – 8:30 AM) * 24. But how does a formula like this work to get the number 4.5 hours? The answers to these questions are related to the facts that number formatting is a façade, and formulas don't "see" number formatting.

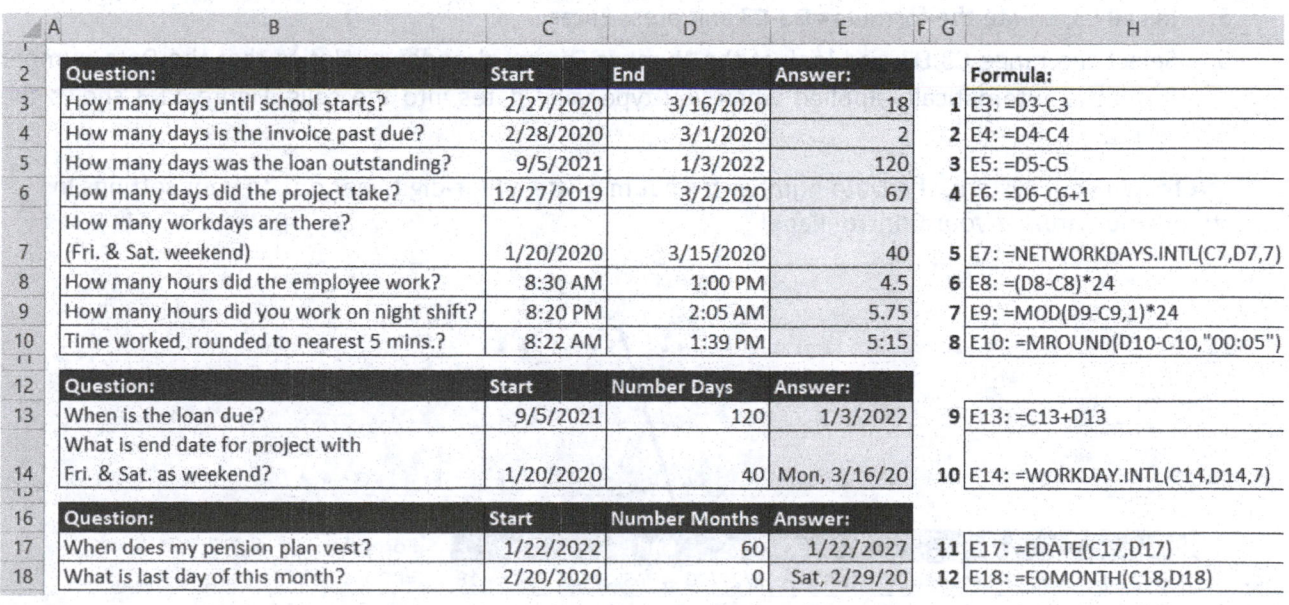

	A	B	C	D	E	F G	H
2		Question:	Start	End	Answer:		Formula:
3		How many days until school starts?	2/27/2020	3/16/2020	18	1	E3: =D3-C3
4		How many days is the invoice past due?	2/28/2020	3/1/2020	2	2	E4: =D4-C4
5		How many days was the loan outstanding?	9/5/2021	1/3/2022	120	3	E5: =D5-C5
6		How many days did the project take?	12/27/2019	3/2/2020	67	4	E6: =D6-C6+1
7		How many workdays are there? (Fri. & Sat. weekend)	1/20/2020	3/15/2020	40	5	E7: =NETWORKDAYS.INTL(C7,D7,7)
8		How many hours did the employee work?	8:30 AM	1:00 PM	4.5	6	E8: =(D8-C8)*24
9		How many hours did you work on night shift?	8:20 PM	2:05 AM	5.75	7	E9: =MOD(D9-C9,1)*24
10		Time worked, rounded to nearest 5 mins.?	8:22 AM	1:39 PM	5:15	8	E10: =MROUND(D10-C10,"00:05")
12		Question:	Start	Number Days	Answer:		
13		When is the loan due?	9/5/2021	120	1/3/2022	9	E13: =C13+D13
14		What is end date for project with Fri. & Sat. as weekend?	1/20/2020	40	Mon, 3/16/20	10	E14: =WORKDAY.INTL(C14,D14,7)
16		Question:	Start	Number Months	Answer:		
17		When does my pension plan vest?	1/22/2022	60	1/22/2027	11	E17: =EDATE(C17,D17)
18		What is last day of this month?	2/20/2020	0	Sat, 2/29/20	12	E18: =EOMONTH(C18,D18)

Figure 11.1 *These 12 useful date and time formulas combine number formatting and formula magic!*

Date Number Formatting, Date Serial Numbers, and Date Formulas

This section looks at how the Date number format interacts with a date formula.

When you enter a date value into a cell, you need to use the form that matches the regional settings in your Control Panel. Because my Control Panel specifies the U.S. settings, which use the date format *month/day/year*, I can type dates such as 02/27/2020, 2/27/20, 2-27-20, and so on.

> **Note:** As soon you type a number and a forward slash in a cell, Excel thinks that what you are typing is a date.

To see how to use Excel to calculate the number of days until school starts, follow these steps:

1. Select the worksheet named Ch11(2-13).
2. Select the range C3:D3 and notice that the Number Format dropdown (in the Number group on the Home tab of the Ribbon) shows that the range has the default General number format applied (see Figure 11.2).

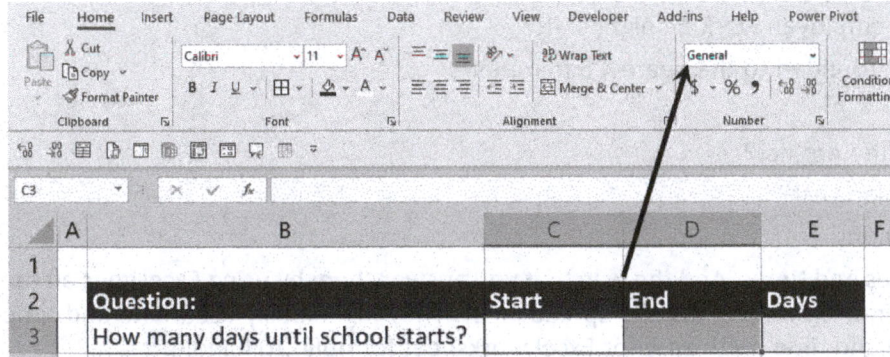

Figure 11.2 *Before you type dates, the cells have the General number format applied.*

3. Type the date **2/27/20** into cell C3 and press the Tab key to enter the date into cell C3 and move to cell D3.
4. Type the date **3/16/20** into cell D3 and press the Tab key to enter the date into cell D3 and move to cell E3.
5. In cell E3, create the formula **=D3-C3** and press Enter.
6. Select the range C3:D3 and look at the Number Format dropdown. Notice that the Date number format is automatically applied when you type valid dates into the cells. Figure 11.3 shows the results.

> **Note:** On your system, the Date number format may use a four-digit year due to your settings in the Region area of your Control Panel.

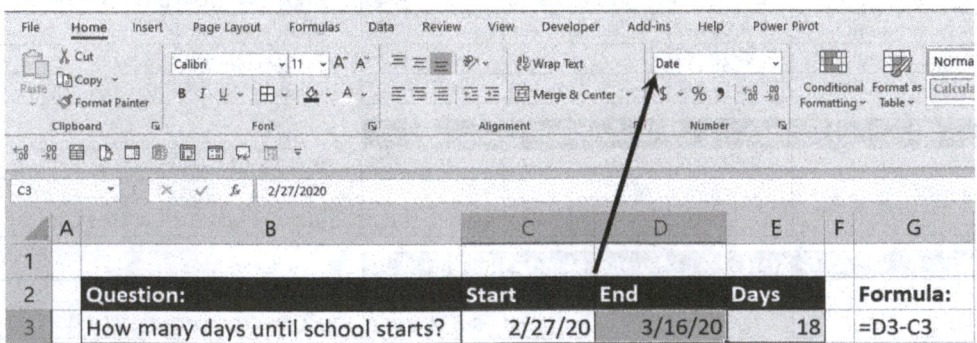

Figure 11.3 *When you type dates, Excel automatically applies the Date number format.*

7. With the range C3:D3 selected, choose the General number format from the Number Format drop-down, as shown in Figure 11.4. The General number format wipes away any Date number formatting that was applied and reveals the actual numbers that Excel stores in the cells.

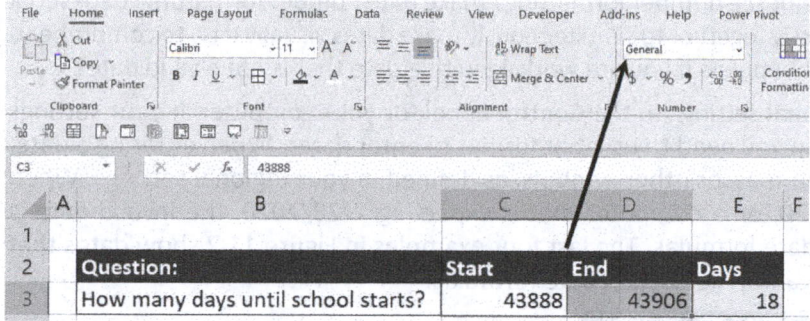

Figure 11.4 *Applying the General number format to dates reveals the underlying numbers that make the formulas work.*

Why does the date 2/27/2020 have the number 43888 under it? What is going on here? That number is called a *date serial number*, and it is there to help with date math. A date serial number is a whole number that represents the number of days since December 31, 1899, where January 1, 1900 = 1, January 2, 1900 = 2, January 3, 1900 = 3, and February 27, 2020 = 43888. These whole numbers for dates help you more easily perform math calculations like end date minus start date so you can get the difference between those two dates. Because formulas do not see number formatting, when you take the cells containing the dates 3/16/2020 and 2/27/2020 and make the formula 3/16/2020 – 2/27/2020, Excel sees the underlying serial numbers and makes the calculation 43905 – 43888 to properly get the answer 18. This design, which was Bricklin and Frankston's genius idea, means you can see and understand dates as dates, but underneath, the date serial numbers can be used to make the math calculations. Later in this section, you will see a list of dates and their related serial numbers.

8. To undo the application of the General number format to the range C3:D3, use the undo keyboard shortcut Ctrl+Z. Figure 11.5 shows the result.

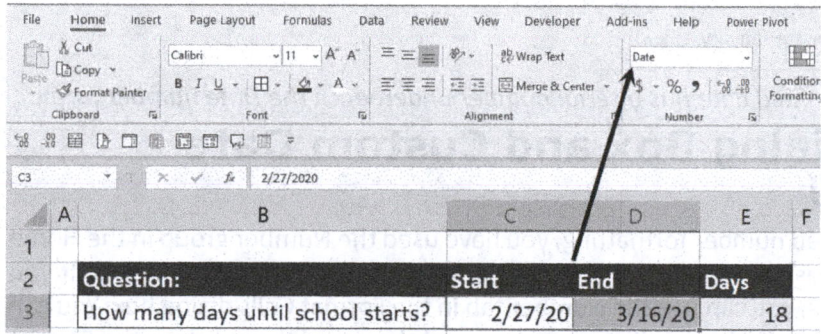

Figure 11.5 *Use Ctrl+Z to undo the application of the General number format.*

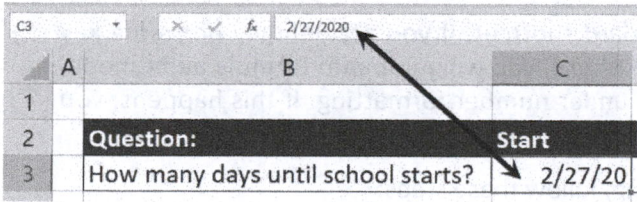

Figure 11.6 *You cannot look to the formula bar to find the date serial number.*

An important difference between number formats that display numbers (like Currency and Number) and the Date number format you just used is that when you use the Date number format, what you see in the cell and the formula bar are both dates, as shown in Figure 11.6. Look back at Figure 8.58, which shows that when you apply the Number number format, although you see 97 in a cell, the formula bar shows that the actual number stored in the cell is 9.67. This does not work with Excel dates. You cannot look at the date 2/27/20 in cell C3 and then look to the formula bar to find the serial number 43888. However, as you have just seen, you can apply the General number format in order to take a peek at what is really in the cell, and then you can use the Ctrl+Z keyboard shortcut to undo that formatting.

From this first investigation of dates in Excel, you can see that any time you type a valid date, such as 2/27/20, in a cell, Excel automatically applies the Date number format and stores the date serial number behind the scenes so that it can be used to make the date math calculations. You have seen that the key Excel concepts "number formatting is a façade" and "formulas do not see number formatting" make date number formatting, date serial numbers, and date formulas work seamlessly together to simultaneously make dates visually easy to comprehend and also work to do date math. But what happens if you are working with a date that is not a valid date?

Valid dates are determined by the regional settings in the Control Panel for your computer. If your settings require the format month/day/year, then you need to use that format to enter dates. When entering a date, you can use forward slashes, dashes, commas, or other symbols, as defined in your regional settings. When you enter an invalid date, like 28/7/2020, on a computer that is expecting 7/28/2020, the invalid date is considered text and cannot be used in date formulas. The last four examples in Figure 11.7 show dates that Excel considers text and that therefore cannot be used in date formulas.

Date	Serial Number Under the Date	Issue
1/1/1900	1	
1/3/1900	3	
Jan 1, 1900	1	
Jan 3, 1900	3	
10/24/1929	10890	
12/6/1969	25543	
2/29/2020	43890	
3/12/4369	901856	
7/28/20	44040	
7-28-20	44040	
Tuesday, July 28, 2020	44040	
Tue, 7/28/2020	44040	
July 28, 2020	44040	
8/2/2020	44045	
####################	44045	Column Not wide enough
8.2.2020	8.2.2020	Separator is not allowed
28/7/2020	28/7/2020	Day first is not allowed
11/1/1789	11/1/1789	Before January 1, 1900
12/31/1899	12/31/1899	

Figure 11.7 *Invalid dates are text. Each valid date has a serial number underneath the Date number format.*

The Format Cells Dialog Box and Custom Date Number Formatting

So far in the book, when you have applied number formatting, you have used the Number group in the Home tab of the Ribbon. The Number group is convenient for accessing commonly used number formats. If you want a larger variety of number formats, you can use the Number tab in the Format Cells dialog box. You can open the Format Cells dialog box by right-clicking a cell or range in a worksheet and then clicking the Format Cells option, or you can just use the keyboard shortcut Ctrl+1.

> **Note:** Be careful when you use the Ctrl+1 keyboard shortcut. If you accidentally press the key to the left of the number 1 key, the grave accent key (`), you will jump into formula audit mode, which shows all formulas and numbers that live under number formatting. If this happens, you need to press Ctrl+` again to toggle out of audit mode.

To display dates using different Date number formatting, follow these steps:

1. Select the worksheet named Ch11(2-13).

2. With the range C3:D3 selected, use the keyboard shortcut Ctrl+1 to open the Format Cells dialog box.

3. In the Format Cells dialog box, as shown in Figure 11.8, click on the Number tab, then click on Date in the Category list, and then, on the right, scroll down and click on 3/14/2012 in the Type list to display the year with four digits.

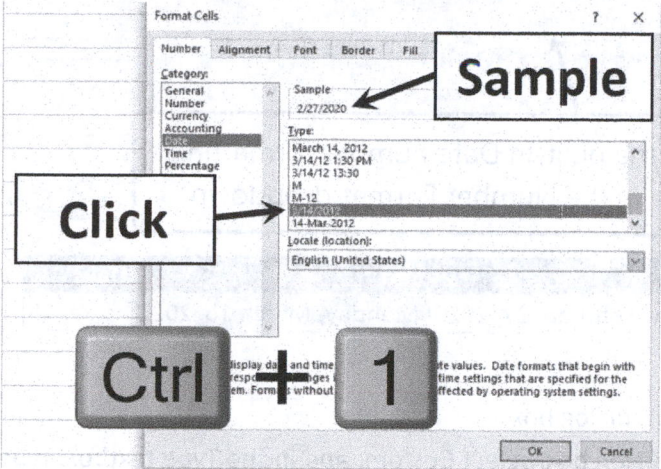

Figure 11.8 *Ctrl+1 is the keyboard shortcut to open the Format Cells dialog box.*

4. Click OK to close the Format Cells dialog box. Figure 11.9 shows the result of applying the Date number format to the range C3:D3.

> **Note:** If you see #### symbols when you try this, it means the columns are not wide enough, and you need to increase the column width enough to display the date.

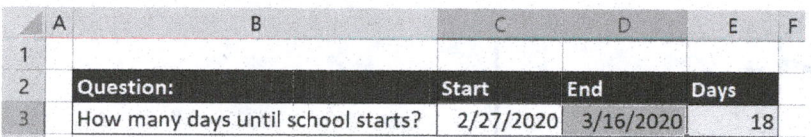

	A	B	C	D	E	F
1						
2		Question:	Start	End	Days	
3		How many days until school starts?	2/27/2020	3/16/2020	18	

Figure 11.9 *The Date format is displayed with four digits for the year.*

5. Press Ctrl+1 again to reopen the Format Cells dialog box.

6. In the Format Cells dialog box, click on the Number tab, click on Date in the Category list, and then, on the right, scroll down in the Type list and click on the date Wednesday, March 14, 2012 to display the date with weekday and month as words and day and year as numbers (see Figure 11.10).

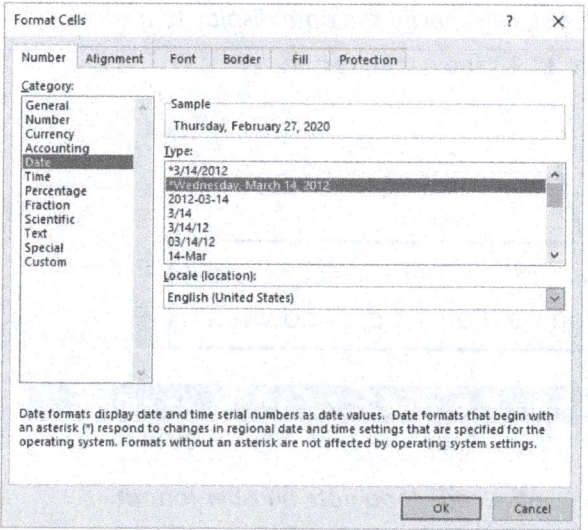

Figure 11.10 *You can display dates with day and month names, and the underlying serial numbers will not change.*

7. Click OK to close the Format Cells dialog box. Figure 11.11 shows the result of applying the Date number format to the range C3:D3.

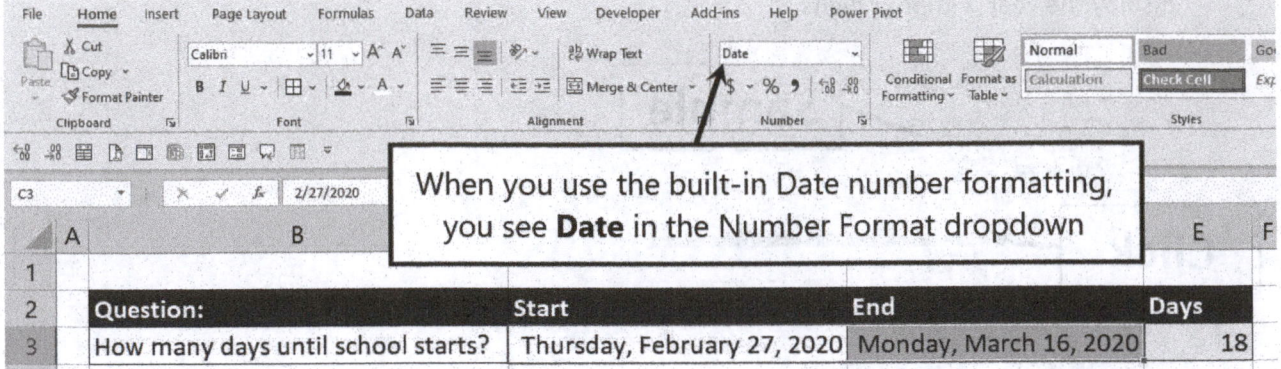

Figure 11.11 *Dates with day and month names.*

8. Press Ctrl+1 again to reopen the Format Cells dialog box.

9. From the Category list in the Format Cells dialog box, select Custom, and in the Type textbox, type the custom number format code **ddd, mmm d, yyyy**. The Sample area of the dialog box shows a preview of how dates will be displayed using this custom format (see Figure 11.12).

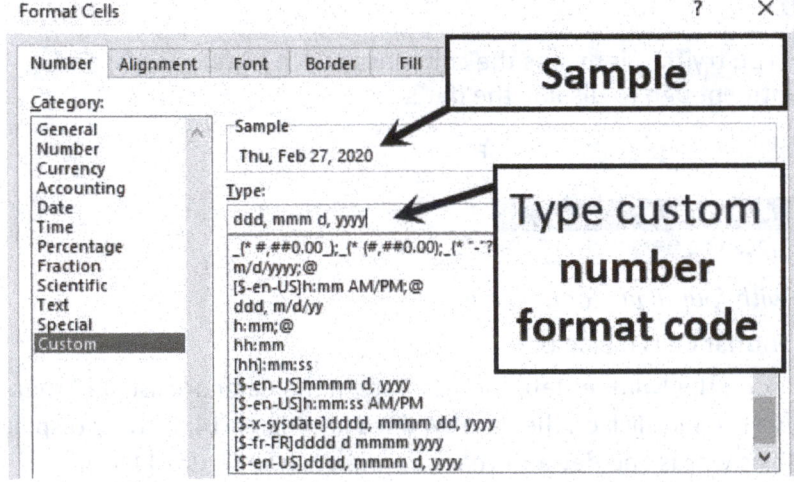

Figure 11.12 *By typing a custom date number format code, you can specify the date display to use.*

10. Click OK to close the Format Cells dialog box. Figure 11.13 shows the result.

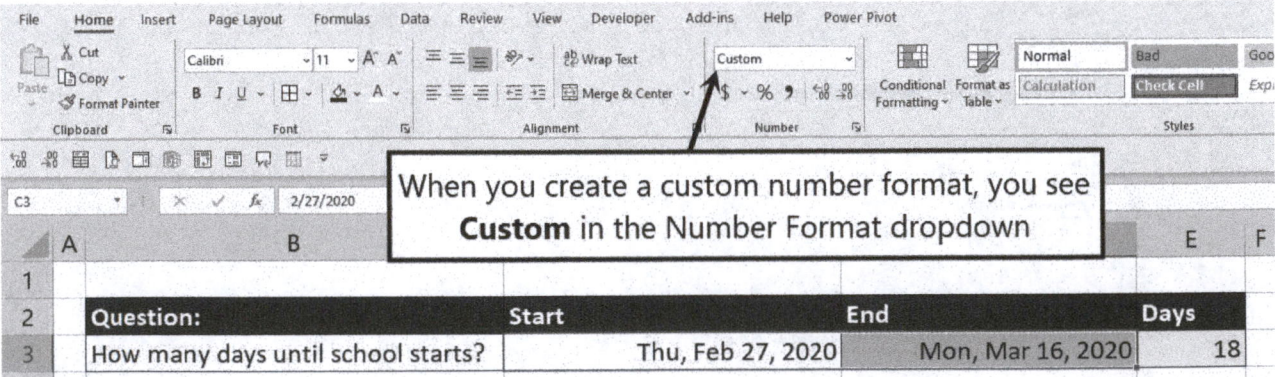

Figure 11.13 *The Number group shows Custom when you type the code for a date number format.*

As you have just seen, when creating custom date number formatting, you use the code **d** for day, **m** for month, and **y** for year. You can also use forward slashes, dashes, and commas when constructing custom date number formatting. Figure 11.14 shows examples of how to combine the codes into unique date number formats.

Code	Date = 3/16/2020	What Code Does
d	16	Day number
dd	16	Day number with leading zero
ddd	Mon	3 letter day
dddd	Monday	Full day name
m	3	Month number
mm	03	Month number with leading zero
mmm	Mar	3 letter month
mmmm	March	Full month name
y	20	Last 2 digits of year
yy	20	Last 2 digits of year
yyy	2020	4 digit year
yyyy	2020	4 digit year
m/d/yyy	3/16/2020	Forward slash okay
m-d-yyy	3-16-2020	Dash okay
ddd, m/d/yy	Mon, 3/16/20	Comma okay

Figure 11.14 *Custom date number formats allow more variety in how you can display dates.*

With custom date number formatting, you have the power to make your dates look exactly as you would like, and the serial number will still be there underneath to make date math possible.

Calculating the Difference Between Two Dates

Now that you understand how Date number formatting, serial numbers, and formulas interact, let's take a look at common date formulas. Figure 11.15 shows four common date calculations. The goal for each of them is to calculate the difference between a start date and an end date. The first three formulas do not include the start date in the final count of how many days are between a start date and an end date, but the last one does. When making typical date difference calculations for things like the number of days until school starts, the number of days an invoice is past due, or the number of days a loan is outstanding, you do not include the start date. For example, to determine how many days an invoice is past due, you do not include the start date because the invoice is not late until the day after the start date. However, if you are working on a project and work is done on the start date, the start date is included in the date difference count.

	A	B	C	D	E	F	G	H	I
1									
2		Question:	Start	End	Days:			Formula:	Notes:
3		How many days until school starts?	2/27/20	3/16/20	18		1	E3: =D3-C3	Difference between dates,
4		How many days is the invoice past due?	2/28/20	3/1/20	2		2	E4: =D4-C4	not including 1st day
5		How many days was the loan outstanding?	9/5/21	1/3/22	120		3	E5: =D5-C5	**= EndDate - StartDate**
6		How many days did the project take?	12/27/19	3/2/20	67		4	E6: =D6-C6+1	Difference between dates, including 1st day **= EndDate - StartDate + 1**

Figure 11.15 *Formulas for differences between dates.*

As shown in Figure 11.15, for most date difference calculations, you create the formula end date minus the start date, but for rare situations in which the first day is included in the count, you must create the formula end date minus the start date plus one.

In addition to the date formulas being easy to create, an added benefit to using Excel worksheet formulas for date math is that Excel knows about leap years, as evidenced in formula 2, where the two days that the invoice is past due are the dates 2/29/20 and 3/1/20.

To try the date formulas shown in Figure 11.15, follow these steps:

1. Select the worksheet Ch11(15).

2. In cell E3, create the formula **=D3-C3**.

3. In cell E4, create the formula **=D4-C4**.

4. In cell E5, create the formula **=D5-C5**.

5. In cell E6, create the formula **=D6-C6+1**.

Figure 11.15 shows the results.

Counting Workdays with NETWORKDAYS.INTL

Sometimes you need to calculate the difference between two dates, but your goal is to count workdays only, skipping weekends and holidays. Luckily, there is a built-in worksheet function for this in Excel: NETWORKDAYS. INTL. This function uses the following syntax:

```
=NETWORKDAYS.INTL(start_date, end_date, [weekend], [holidays])
```

This function includes both the start and end dates in the count. This function is only in the Excel worksheet and not in other tools, such as Power Query's M code formula language or the Data Model's DAX formula language.

To see how to use the NETWORKDAYS.INTL function, follow these steps:

1. Select the worksheet named Ch11(16-18).

2. As shown in Figure 11.16, create the formula with the start date in the first argument (*start_date*), the end date in the second argument (*end_date*), and the number 7 in the third argument (*weekend*). The 7 instructs the function to not count Fridays or Saturdays as workdays.

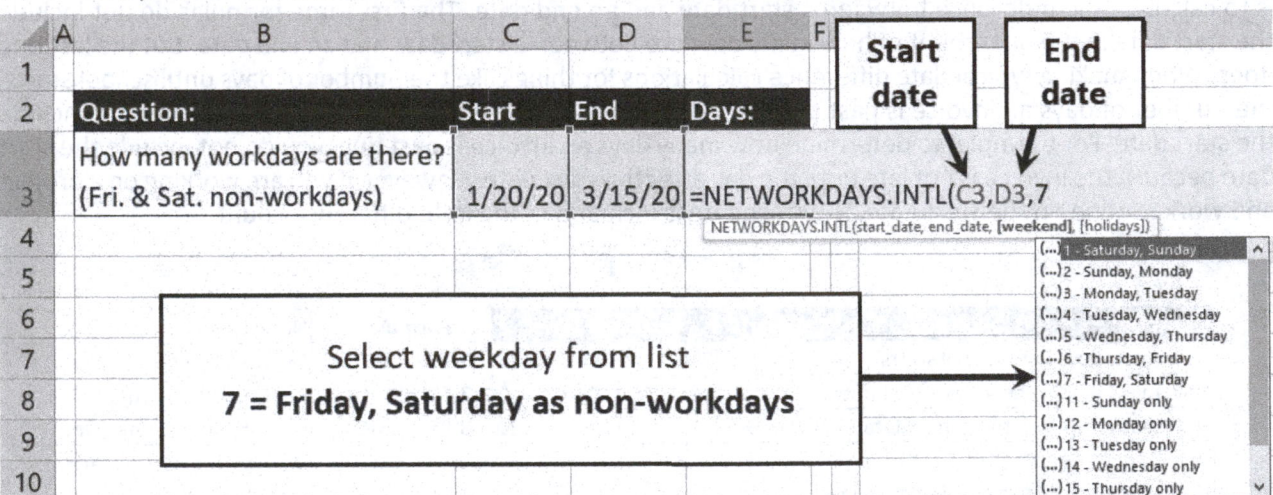

Figure 11.16 *The weekend argument in the NETWORKDAYS.INTL function provides a dropdown to select non-workdays.*

Note: The options available for the *weekend* argument are listed in Table 11.1. If the weekend pattern you need is not in this list, you can create your own custom pattern of workdays and non-workdays, as described shortly.

Table 11.1 The Options for the *weekend* Argument in the NETWORKDAYS.INTL and WORKDAY.INTL Functions

weekend Setting	Days Considered Weekend Days
1 or omitted	Saturday, Sunday
2	Sunday, Monday
3	Monday, Tuesday
4	Tuesday, Wednesday
5	Wednesday, Thursday
6	Thursday, Friday
7	Friday, Saturday
11	Sunday only
12	Monday only
13	Tuesday only
14	Wednesday only
15	Thursday only
16	Friday only
17	Saturday only

3. As shown in Figure 11.17, enter the list of holiday dates from the range J3:J6 into the *holidays* argument. This list of holiday dates instructs the function to not count dates from this list.

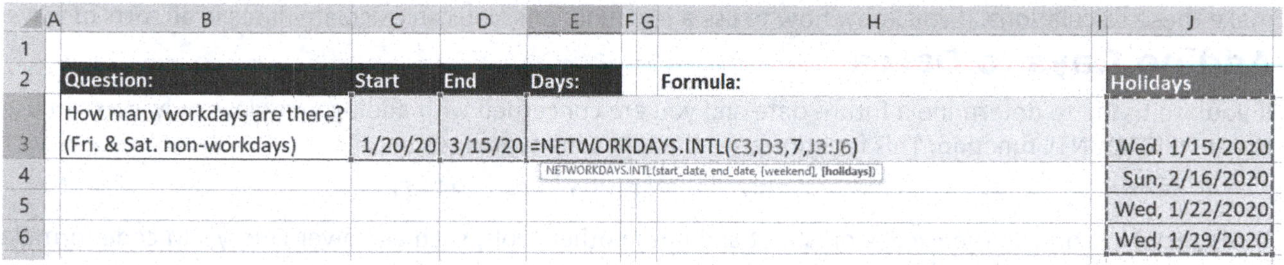

Figure 11.17 *You can specify holidays in the fourth argument of the NETWORKDAYS.INTL function.*

4. When you enter the formula, you should get a count of 37 workdays, as shown in Figure 11.18.

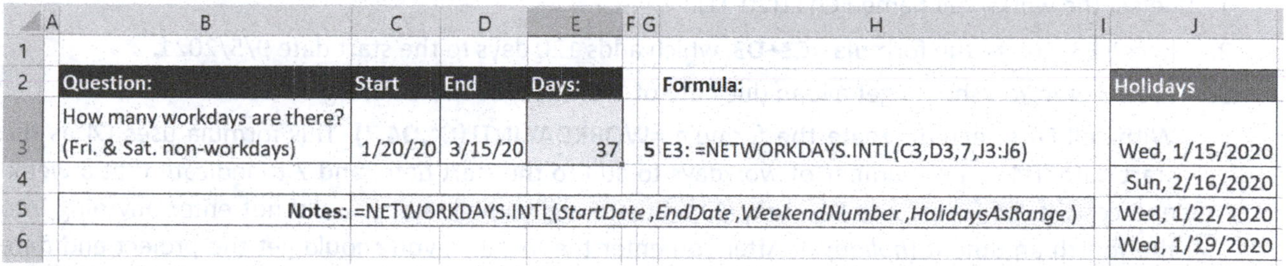

Figure 11.18 *The NETWORKDAYS.INTL function makes it easy to count workdays between a start date and an end date.*

Looking back at Table 11.1, you can see that there are only 17 possibilities for weekend combinations. As most working people know, schedules with workdays and non-workdays can be almost any possible combination. Luckily, you can define a custom pattern of workdays and non-workdays in the *weekend* argument by creating a seven-character text string that starts with Monday and uses 0 to indicate a workday and 1 a non-workday. Figure 11.19 shows an example of using the NETWORKDAYS.INTL function when the non-workdays are Wednesday and Sunday. To create this pattern, you use the string "0010001" in the *weekend* argument.

To see how this works, follow these steps:

1. Select the worksheet named Ch11(19).

2. In cell E3, create the formula **=NETWORKDAYS.INTL(C3,D3,"0010001",I3:I6)**.

3. After you enter the formula, you should get a net workday total of 40, as shown in Figure 11.19.

	A	B	C	D	E	F G	H	I	J
1									
2		Question:	Start	End	Days:		Formula:		Holidays
3		How many workdays are there? (Wed,. & Sun. non-workdays)	1/20/20	3/15/20	40	5	E3: =NETWORKDAYS.INTL(C3,D3,"0010001",J3:J6)		Wed, 1/15/2020
4									Sun, 2/16/2020
5				Notes:					Wed, 1/22/2020
6				=NETWORKDAYS.INTL(StartDate ,EndDate ,WeekendString ,HolidaysAsRange)					Wed, 1/29/2020
7				* weekend argumnet you can create any pattern of workdays / non-workdays.					
8				* 1 represents a non-workday and 0 represents a workday.					
9				* Must be 7 characters long. First character represents Monday.					
10				* Must be encased in quotes.					
11				* For example, "0010001" would result in a weekend that is Wednesday and Sunday.					

Figure 11.19 *"0010001" defines Wednesday and Sunday as non-workdays.*

Adding Days to Dates and Subtracting Days from Dates

If your goal is to add 120 days to the date 9/5/2021 to determine a future date, you are allowed to simply add the number 120 to that date. Because formulas always look at the underlying numbers below the number formatting, a calculation like this will add 120 to the date serial number and deliver the future date. Such calculations are common in tasks such as calculating a loan due date or a project end date. You can also use Excel to subtract dates in order to determine dates before the start date. For example, if you subtract 120 days from the date 1/3/22, you get the date answer 9/5/21. Behind the scenes, Excel uses data serial numbers to make these calculations. If you know how to use a few functions, you can calculate dates in all sorts of ways.

Adding Days to Dates

If you are trying to determine a future date and you are concerned with adding workdays only, you can use the WORKDAY.INTL function. This function uses the following syntax:

```
=WORKDAY.INTL(start_date, days, [weekend], [holidays]).
```

This function is only in the Excel worksheet and not in other tools, such as Power Query's M code formula language or the Data Model's DAX formula language.

To complete this example, follow these steps:

1. Select the worksheet named Ch11(20-21).

2. In cell E3, create the formula **=C3+D3**, which adds 120 days to the start date 9/5/2021.

3. Press Enter. You should get a loan due date of 1/3/2022, as shown in Figure 11.20.

4. With cell E4 selected, create the formula **=WORKDAY.INTL(C4,D4,7)**. This formula uses C4 as the start date, D4 as the number of workdays to add to the start date, and 7 to indicate that a weekend consists of Friday and Saturday. Since there are no holidays, you did not enter anything into the fourth argument (*holidays*). After you enter the formula, you should get the project end date 3/16/2020, as shown in Figure 11.20.

	A	B	C	D	E	F G	H	I
1								
2		Question:	Start	Number Days	Dates:		Formulas:	Notes:
3		When is the loan due?	9/5/21	120	1/3/22	9	E3: =C3+D3	← Calculate future date by adding days = **StartDate + NumberOfDays**
4		What is end date for project? (Fri. & Sat. non-workdays)	1/20/20	40	3/16/20	10	E4: =WORKDAY.INTL(C4,D4,7)	
5								↑ End date while excluding weekends and holidays **=WORKDAY.INTL(StartDate,NumberWorkDays, WeekendNumber,HolidayAsRange)**

Figure 11.20 *Because date formulas work with the underlying date serial numbers, you can add numbers to dates.*

Subtracting Days from Dates

In the two examples that you just completed, you added numbers to dates. You can also subtract numbers from dates to determine dates before the start date. For example, if you subtract 120 days from the date 1/3/22, you get the date answer 9/5/21. You can also enter a negative number of days into the WORKDAY. INTL function to count workdays backward from a start date.

To see how date subtraction works, follow these steps:

1. Select the worksheet named Ch11(20-21).

2. In cell E9, create the formula **=C9-D9**.

3. In cell E10, create the formula **=WORKDAY.INTL(C11,D11,7)**. Figure 11.21 shows the results.

A	B	C	D	E	F	G	H
8							
9	When is the loan due?	1/3/22	120	9/5/21		9	E9: =C9-D9
10							
11	What is start date for project? (Fri. & Sat. non-workdays)	3/16/20	-40	1/20/20		10	E11: =WORKDAY.INTL(C11,D11,7)

Figure 11.21 *You can subtract days from dates.*

Adding Months to Dates and Subtracting Months from Dates

If your goal is to add or subtract months to dates to yield a date on the same day of the month as the start date but in the future or past, you cannot simply add or subtract numbers to the dates. Since the underlying serial number is defined as "number of days," adding and subtracting days is mathematically allowed. However, with months, you can't add 1 to a date to jump one month ahead, and you can't add 30 days to jump one month ahead because not all months have 30 days. So, what can you do? Luckily, Microsoft provides several month-related date worksheet functions:

- **EDATE:** This function allows you to add or subtract months to a date.
- **EOMONTH:** This function calculates the end-of-the-month date for a given number of months in the future or past.

Both of these functions know how to deal with leap years.

The EDATE function uses the following syntax:

```
=EDATE(start_date, months)
```

The EOMONTH function uses the following syntax:

```
=EOMONTH(start_date, months)
```

The number of months for both functions can be positive (to jump into the future), negative (to jump into the past), or zero (for the same month as *start_date*). With the EDATE function, you can figure out payroll issues such as the pension vesting date if the hire date is 2/20/2020 and the pension vests in 60 months. With the EOMONTH function, you can figure out invoicing issues such as what day is considered the last day of the month if a contract says an invoice is due at the end of the current month.

To try using the month-related date functions EDATE and EOMONTH, follow these steps:

1. Open the worksheet named Ch11(22).

2. In cell E3, create the formula **=EDATE(C3,D3)**.

3. In cell E4, create the formula **=EOMONTH(C4,D4)**. Figure 11.22 shows the results. Notice that cell E4 has custom date number formatting and shows that the last day of February 2020 is Sat, 2/29/2020.

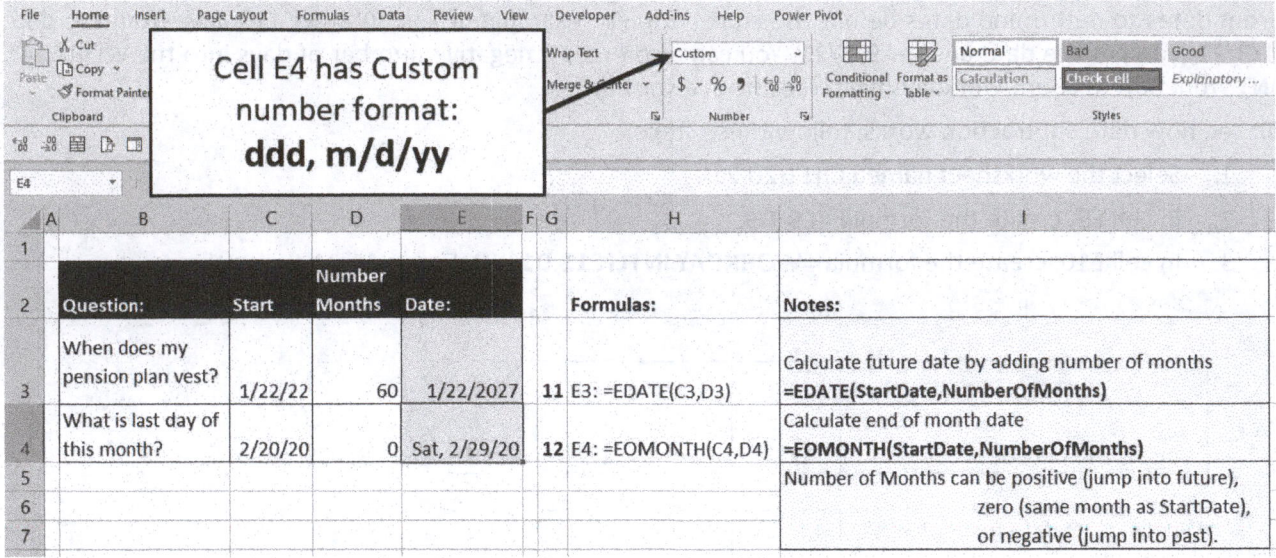

Figure 11.22 *To add or subtract months, you use worksheet functions like EDATE and EOMONTH.*

Now that you have learned all about date number formatting, date serial numbers, and date formulas, it is time to move on to the related time number formatting, time serial numbers, and time formulas.

Time Number Formatting, Time Serial Numbers, and Time Formulas

Much the same way Excel uses date serial numbers for making date formula calculations, it uses time serial numbers for making time formula calculations. However, as you will see, time serial numbers are very different from date serial numbers.

When you enter a time value into a cell, such as 8:00:00 a.m., you use the form *hh:mm:ss* AM/PM, where *h* = hour, *m* = minute, and *s* = seconds. A colon separates hours from minutes, and another colon separates minutes from seconds. You must enter a space between the time value and either AM or PM. If you do not type the AM or PM, the time value is entered as military time. Time values such as 8:00 AM and 8 AM, where you leave out seconds or minutes, are also valid time values.

The following sections present examples that walk you through the use of a variety of Excel time-related calculations.

Example 1: Calculating Hours Worked

Before we look closely at what a time serial number is, let's look at an example that helps illustrate time calculations in Excel. The goal of this example is to calculate the hours worked for the employee Shardae Fann and then multiply her hours worked by her wage per hour to find gross pay, as shown in Figure 11.23.

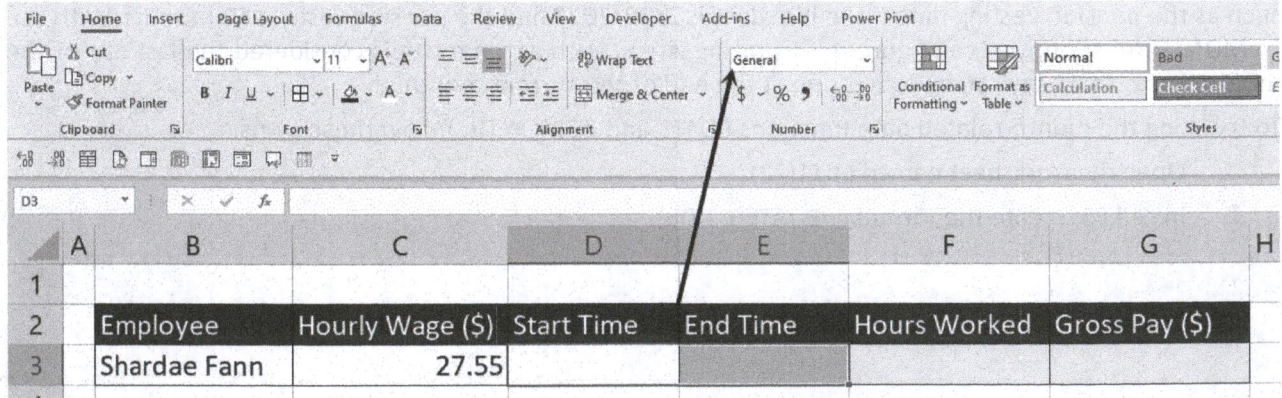

Figure 11.23 *Before you enter time values into cells, the default General number format is applied.*

To complete this example, follow these steps:

1. Open the worksheet named Ch11(23-33).

2. Select the range D3:E5. Look to the Number Format textbox, and you see that the General number format is applied (see Figure 11.23).

3. Select cell D3 and enter the invalid time value **8:00AM**. Press Ctrl+Enter to enter the value and keep cell D3 selected. As shown in Figure 11.24, you get a visual clue that the number is an invalid time value: The number is aligned to the left rather than to the right.

    Note: It is the missing space between the number and AM that makes 8:00AM an invalid time value.

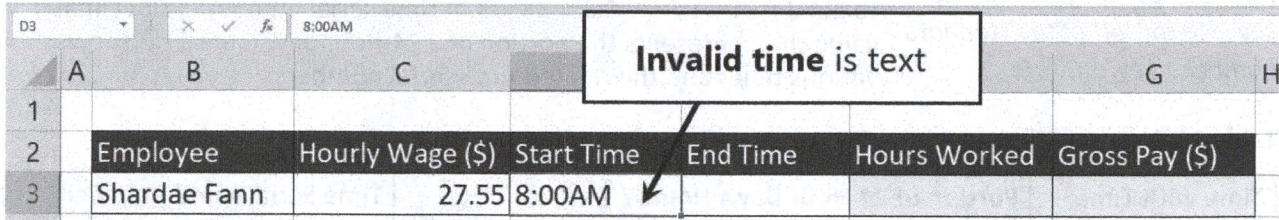

Figure 11.24 *Excel considers invalid time values to be text values.*

4. Enter a space to change the invalid value to the valid time value **8:00 AM**, as shown in Figure 11.25. Notice that the value is now right-aligned, which is a visual clue that Excel considers the item a number—specifically, in this case, a time value. Also notice that the Number Format textbox says Custom. This indicates that a custom time number format has been applied.

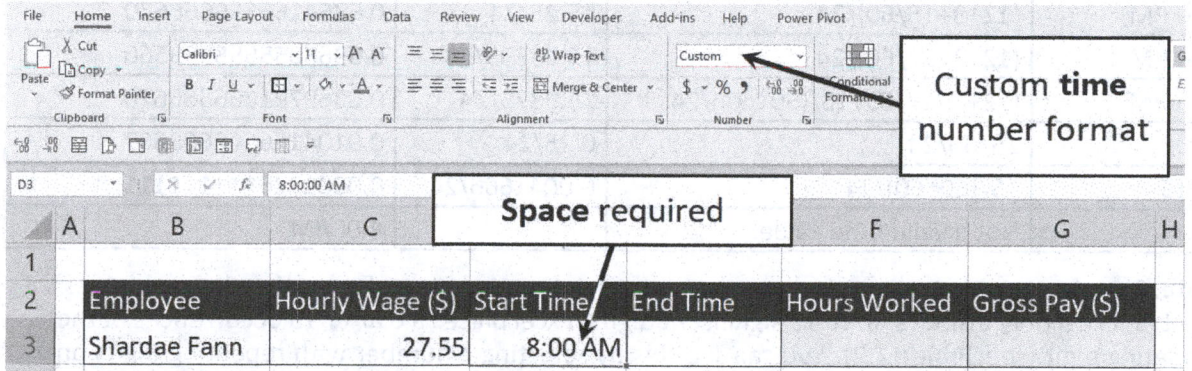

Figure 11.25 *When you type a time value, the Number Format textbox shows the Custom time number format.*

5. With cell D3 selected, apply the General number format by using the keyboard shortcut Ctrl+Shift+`. Figure 11.26 shows the application of the General number format to a time value.

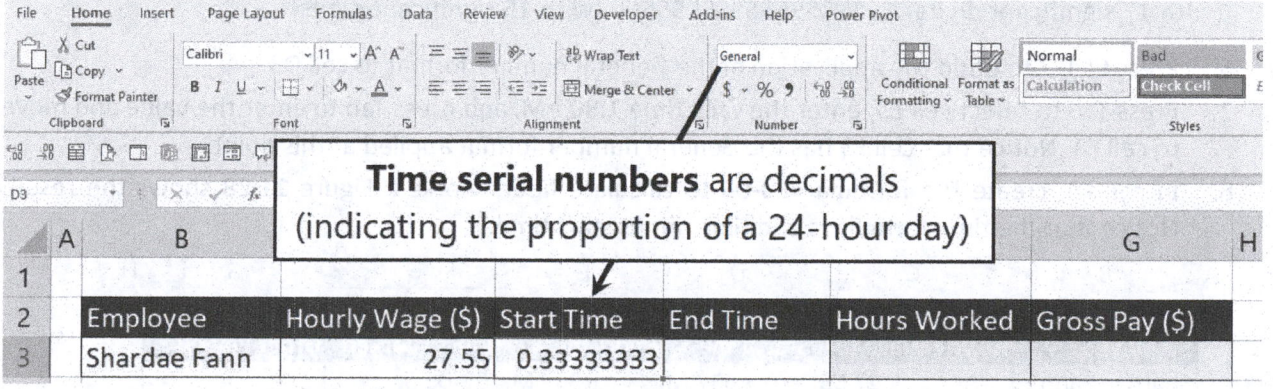

Figure 11.26 *Underneath time values are decimal values that represent portions of a 24-hour day.*

Figure 11.27 *The grave accent (`) key is to the left of the standard number 1 key.*

Note: The grave accent (`) key is to the left of the standard number 1 key, and it is also the tilde (~) key, as shown in Figure 11.27. (In Europe, the ` and ~ are on different keys.)

Note: How in the world does the number 0.33333333 represent 8:00 a.m.? Most Excel users in the world who see a time serial number for the first time are shocked. I know I was. But it is easy to overcome this shock when you realize that whenever you type a time value into a cell, behind the scenes, Excel divides that time by 24 hours. For the 8:00 a.m. time value, for example, Excel divides 8 hours by 24 hours to get 8 / 24 = 1 / 3 = 0.33333333. A time serial number is a decimal value that represents the portion of a 24-hour day. Table 11.2 shows various times and the related time serial numbers.

Table 11.2 Various Times and the Related Excel Time Serial Numbers

Time with Time Number Format	Portion of 24-Hour Day = Hours / 24 Hours	Fraction	Time Serial Number in Cell
12:00 AM	0		0.00
8:00 AM	8/24	1/3	0.3333333333333330
12:00 PM	12/24	1/2	0.50
3:00 PM	(12+3)/24	15/24	0.6250
3:15:00 PM	(12+3+15/60)/24	15.25/24	0.6354166666666670
3:17:00 PM	(12+3+17/60)/24	15.28333/24	0.6368055555555560
3:17:15 PM	(12+3+17/60+15/(60*60))/24	15.2875/24	0.6369791666666670
00:15:00	15/60/24	0.25/24	0.0104166666666667
00:00:15	15/(60*60)/24	0.0041666/24	0.0001736111111111
8:00AM	Not a valid time value.		8:00AM

Note: For a fraction that theoretically evaluates to an infinite number of repeating decimal values, like 1/3, Excel only displays up to 15 significant digits. Excel places a 0 after 15 occurrences of the repeating digit (see Table 11.2). You can see this by selecting a number with repeating digits on a worksheet and clicking the Increase Decimal button until Excel increases the number of digits past 15. In addition, if you try to enter a number with more than 15 significant digits into a cell, it will not work. Excel converts a number like 0.4577777777777777 (with 16 significant digits) to 0.457777777777777 (with 15 significant digits). It converts a number like 55555555555555555 (with 17 significant digits) to 55555555555555500 (with 15 significant digits).

6. Press Ctrl+Z to undo the application of the General number format to cell D3.

7. Press Tab to select cell E3, enter the valid time **1:30 PM**, and press Tab to enter the value and move to cell F3. Notice that cell F3 has the General number format applied at this point.

8. In cell F3, create the formula **=E3-D3** to calculate hours worked. Figure 11.28 shows the result. Notice that the time formula is end time minus start time.

◢ A	B	C	D	E	F	G	H
1							
2	Employee	Hourly Wage ($)	Start Time	End Time	Hours Worked	Gross Pay ($)	
3	Shardae Fann	27.55	8:00 AM	1:30 PM	=E3-D3		

Figure 11.28 *The formula is end time minus start time.*

9. Press Ctrl+Enter to enter the formula into cell F3 and keep this cell selected. What you see now, as shown in Figure 11.29, looks like the correct answer. Notice that because the formula input cells have the Time number format applied, Excel pulls that number formatting and applies it to cell F3. However, the number formatting on cell F3 is masking a problem with the formula.

	A	B	C	D	E	F	G	H
1								
2		Employee	Hourly Wage ($)	Start Time	End Time	Hours Worked	Gross Pay ($)	
3		Shardae Fann	27.55	8:00 AM	1:30 PM	5:30 AM		

Figure 11.29 *The Time number format is hiding a problem.*

10. With cell F3 selected, apply the General number format by using the keyboard shortcut Ctrl+Shift+`. Figure 11.30 shows the time serial number for the formula result.

	A	B	C	D	E	F	G	H
1								
2		Employee	Hourly Wage ($)	Start Time	End Time	Hours Worked	Gross Pay ($)	
3		Shardae Fann	27.55	8:00 AM	1:30 PM	0.229166667		

Figure 11.30 *Is this formula result correct?*

> **Note:** You can see in Figure 11.30 that the formula in this case did *not* perform the math calculation $(12 + 1.5) - 8 = 13.5 - 8 = 5.5$, as you might have expected it to. Remember that formulas cannot see number formatting. In this case, the formula acted on the underlying time serial numbers to perform the math calculation $13.5/24 - 8/24 = 0.333333333333333 - 0.5625 = 0.229166666666667$. This may seem like a confusing and crazy thing to have to deal with, but stop and think about how Excel created the time serial number in the first place. Because Excel took the hour values 8 and 13.5 and divided by 24 hours to reduce the result to a decimal value, when you create a formula for hours worked, you have to convert the decimal value back to hours by multiplying by 24. For this formula, the calculation would be $0.229166666666667 * 24 = 5.5$. This means that when you want your formula to correctly calculate the number of hours between two time values, you have to remember to multiply it by 24, using this formula $(EndTime - StartTime) * 24$.

11. Press the F2 key to put cell F3 into edit mode, amend the formula to **=(E3-D3)*24**, and then enter the formula by pressing Ctrl+Enter. Figure 11.31 shows that the Time number format is reapplied when you edit the formula in this way. The reapplication of the Time number format disguises the correct answer, 5.5, and shows 12:00 PM.

	A	B	C	D	E	F	G	H
1								
2		Employee	Hourly Wage ($)	Start Time	End Time	Hours Worked	Gross Pay ($)	
3		Shardae Fann	27.55	8:00 AM	1:30 PM	12:00 PM		
4								
5						F3: =(E3-D3)*24		

Figure 11.31 *The Time number format keeps getting in the way of effectively communicating the answer.*

> **Note:** It is very common for number formatting that is pulled from formula input cells to interfere with how an answer is shown—as illustrated in Figure 11.31. This happens often with number formats such as Time and Currency. This shows why knowing the keyboard shortcut that applies the General number format (Ctrl +Shift+`) is so important. You can use the General number format as an "eraser" on any number formatting that blocks you from seeing the true underlying number that lives in a cell.

12. To remove the incorrect number formatting on cell F3, press Ctrl+Shift+` to apply the General number format. As you can see in Figure 11.32, Excel now shows the correct number of hours worked: 5.5 hours.

	A	B	C	D	E	F	G
1							
2		Employee	Hourly Wage ($)	Start Time	End Time	Hours Worked	Gross Pay ($)
3		Shardae Fann	27.55	8:00 AM	1:30 PM	5.5	
4							
5					Formulas:	F3: =(E3-D3)*24	
6						Hours Worked = (EndTime - StartTime)*24	
7						Formula # 7 from list.	

Figure 11.32 *The correct formula for number of hours between two time values is (EndTime – StartTime) * 24.*

13. Press Tab to move to cell G3.

14. In cell G3, create the formula **=ROUND(F3*C3,2)** to multiply hours worked by wage per hour to get the gross pay for the employee (see Figure 11.33).

> **Note:** Technically, you do not have to round in this situation because you are not going to use the formula result in another formula in this case. However, when you calculate gross pay, you almost always use that gross pay in payroll deduction formulas, so it is just a good idea to round when you are multiplying a time hour value by a wage per hour.

	A	B	C	D	E	F	G
1							
2		Employee	Hourly Wage ($)	Start Time	End Time	Hours Worked	Gross Pay ($)
3		Shardae Fann	27.55	8:00 AM	1:30 PM	5.5	151.53
4							
5			Formula # 7 from list.		Formulas:	F3: =(E3-D3)*24	G3: =ROUND(F3*C3,2)
6							
7					Note:	↑ Number hours between two time values =	
8						(EndTime - StartTime)*24	

Figure 11.33 *The correct formula for hours worked when you have start and end times is (EndTime – StartTime) * 24.*

As shown in Figure 11.33, the final gross pay for Shardae is $151.53. To make time-related calculations like this, you must understand four things:

- Time number formatting is a façade.
- Time serial numbers under the number formatting are decimal values that represent portions of a 24-hour day.
- Formulas do not see number formatting but make their calculations based on time serial numbers.
- If you want hours as the result of a time calculation, you must multiply the result by 24.

Example 2: Calculating Hours Worked When There Is a Lunch Break

In this example, you will see how to calculate hours worked when there is a lunch break, how to use the Time number format to show hours greater than 24 hours, how to calculate hours worked for a night shift, and how to round a time value to within 5 minutes.

To complete this example, follow these steps:

1. Open the worksheet named Ch11(34).

2. In cell G3, create the formula **= (D3-C3+F3-E3)*24**. The first of the time calculations, D3-C3, calculates the time serial number for hours worked before lunch; the second calculation, F3-E3, calculates the time serial number for hours worked after lunch. The addition operator adds the before-lunch

and after-lunch amounts. Finally, the formula multiplies by 24 to translate the serial number back to the number of hours. Figure 11.34 shows the result.

> **Note:** Don't forget to use General number format when the Time number format disguises hours worked.

	Employee	Start Time	Lunch - Out	Lunch - IN	End Time	Hours Worked	Formulas for Hours Worked:
2	Employee	Start Time	Lunch - Out	Lunch - IN	End Time	Hours Worked	Formulas for Hours Worked:
3	Shardae Fann	8:30 AM	12:00 PM	12:30 PM	5:42 PM	8.7	=(D3-C3+F3-E3)*24

Figure 11.34 *This is the formula for hours worked with a lunch break.*

3. Open the worksheet named Ch11(35).

4. In cell H3, create the formula **= (E3:E7-D3:D7+G3:G7-F3:F7)*24**. This formula makes the same calculation as the previous formula, but rather than use single cell references with time values, it uses a range of cells with five time values. When the formula is complete, press Enter to spill the five hour amounts to new rows.

5. In cell H8, press Alt+= to enter the SUM function. Figure 11.35 shows the result.

	Employee	Day	Start Time	Lunch - Out	Lunch - IN	End Time	Hours Worked	Formulas for Hours Worked:
2	Employee	Day	Start Time	Lunch - Out	Lunch - IN	End Time	Hours Worked	Formulas for Hours Worked:
3	Shardae Fann	MONDAY	8:30 AM	12:00 PM	12:30 PM	5:42 PM	8.7	=(E3:E7-D3:D7+G3:G7-F3:F7)*24
4		TUESDAY	8:30 AM	12:00 PM	12:30 PM	5:00 PM	8	
5		WEDNESDAY	9:30 AM	12:10 PM	12:30 PM	4:00 PM	6.166666667	
6		THURSDAY	8:30 AM	12:00 PM	1:30 PM	5:30 PM	7.5	
7		FRIDAY	7:00 AM	10:30 AM	11:15 AM	3:00 PM	7.25	
8	TOTAL HOURS						37.61666667	=SUM(H3:H7)

Figure 11.35 *This spilled array formula calculates hours worked with a lunch break for all five days.*

Example 3: Using the Time Number Format to Show Hours Greater Than 24 Hours

Occasionally, you need to add time values that have not been converted to hour amounts and then display them as time values. For example, say that you want to show a 38.5-hour work week as 38:30 (38 hours, 30 minutes). How would you do this? Figure 11.36 shows what happens if you use the SUM function to add time values. The total 14:30 (14 hours, 30 minutes) is incorrect. This is because the standard Time number format *hh:mm* is programmed to only show hours that are greater than the last whole 24-hour period. Therefore, because 8:00 + 8:00 + 8:00 + 8:00 + 6:30 = 38:30, the standard Time number format can only show the amount greater than 24 hours, which is 38:30 − 24:00 = 14:30.

	Employee	Day	Start Time	Lunch - Out	Lunch - IN	End Time	Time Worked	
2	Employee	Day	Start Time	Lunch - Out	Lunch - IN	End Time	Time Worked	
3	Shardae Fann	MONDAY	8:30 AM	12:00 PM	12:30 PM	5:00 PM	08:00	
4		TUESDAY	8:30 AM	12:00 PM	12:30 PM	5:00 PM	08:00	
5		WEDNESDAY	8:30 AM	12:00 PM	12:30 PM	5:00 PM	08:00	
6		THURSDAY	8:30 AM	12:00 PM	12:30 PM	5:00 PM	08:00	
7		FRIDAY	8:30 AM	12:00 PM	12:30 PM	3:30 PM	06:30	
8	TOTAL HOURS						14:30	H8: =SUM(H3:H7)

Figure 11.36 *When you add time values that exceed 24 hours, Excel displays only the amount past the last whole 24-hour period—in this case, 14:30.*

To complete this example, follow these steps:

1. Open the worksheet named Ch11(36-38).

2. Select cell H8 and press Alt+= to enter the SUM function and then press Ctrl+Enter to enter the SUM function. As shown in Figure 11.37, if you apply the General number format to all the cells, you can see that the SUM function properly gets 1 for the first 24 hours and 0.604167 for the 14.5 hours. In this case, you need to create a custom number format.

	Employee	Day	Start Time	Lunch - Out	Lunch - IN	End Time	Time Worked		
2									
3	Shardae Fann	MONDAY	8:30 AM	12:00 PM	12:30 PM	5:00 PM	0.333333333		
4		TUESDAY	8:30 AM	12:00 PM	12:30 PM	5:00 PM	0.333333333		
5		WEDNESDAY	8:30 AM	12:00 PM	12:30 PM	5:00 PM	0.333333333		
6		THURSDAY	8:30 AM	12:00 PM	12:30 PM	5:00 PM	0.333333333		
7		FRIDAY	8:30 AM	12:00 PM	12:30 PM	3:30 PM	0.270833333		
8	TOTAL HOURS						1.604166667	H8: =SUM(H3:H7)	

Figure 11.37 *The General number format reveals that 1 represents 24 hours, and 0.604167 represents 14.5 hours.*

3. With cell H8 selected, press Ctrl+1 to open the Format Cells dialog box.

4. Click on the Number tab and, from the Category list, select Custom.

5. In the Type textbox, type the code **[hh]:mm** and click OK. Figure 11.38 shows the result of applying this code to cell H8.

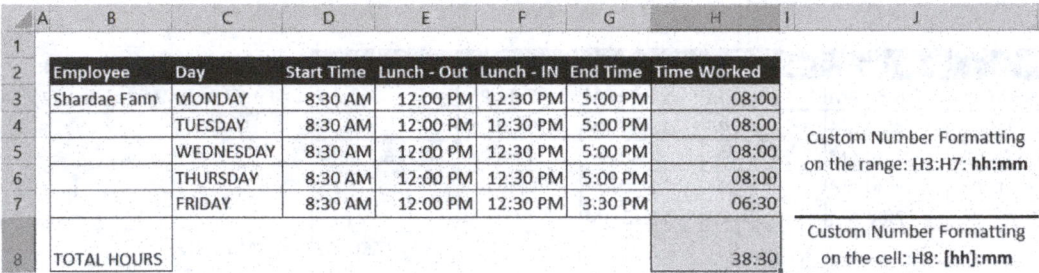

	Employee	Day	Start Time	Lunch - Out	Lunch - IN	End Time	Time Worked		
2									
3	Shardae Fann	MONDAY	8:30 AM	12:00 PM	12:30 PM	5:00 PM	08:00		Custom Number Formatting
4		TUESDAY	8:30 AM	12:00 PM	12:30 PM	5:00 PM	08:00		on the range: H3:H7: **hh:mm**
5		WEDNESDAY	8:30 AM	12:00 PM	12:30 PM	5:00 PM	08:00		
6		THURSDAY	8:30 AM	12:00 PM	12:30 PM	5:00 PM	08:00		
7		FRIDAY	8:30 AM	12:00 PM	12:30 PM	3:30 PM	06:30		Custom Number Formatting
8	TOTAL HOURS						38:30		on the cell: H8: **[hh]:mm**

Figure 11.38 *This custom time number format allows you to display cumulative hours greater than 24 hours.*

Table 11.3 shows a list of different time values and custom time number formats.

Table 11.3 Custom Time Number Formatting Codes

Time	Code Used	Time Serial Number
1:30 PM	h:mm AM/PM	0.5625
01:30 PM	hh:mm AM/PM	0.5625
1:30:00 PM	h:mm:ss AM/PM	0.5625
13:30	h:mm	0.5625
00:15:00	hh:mm:ss	0.010416667
00:00:15	hh:mm:ss	0.000173611
8 AM	h AM/PM	0.333333333
30:00:00	[hh]:mm:ss	1.25
30:00	[hh]:mm	1.25
78:30	[hh]:mm	3.270833333

Example 4: Calculating Hours Worked for a Night Shift

When creating hours worked formulas for employees who work the night shift, you see the #### error if the end time is smaller than the start time. As shown in Figure 11.39, an employee might start work at 8:20 p.m. and end work at 2:05 a.m. In this case, the end time 2:05 a.m. is smaller than the start time of 8:20 p.m. Figure 11.39 shows two possible formula solutions.

Note: In Chapter 13, you will learn about the logic behind the formulas shown in Figure 11.39. However, I show them here with the other time formulas so you can easily reference them all in one place. If you want to try to create these formulas, you can use the worksheet named Ch11(39).

	Question:	Start	End	Hours Worked:		Formula:	Notes:
3	How many hours did you work on night shift?	8:20 PM	2:05 AM	5.75	7	E3: =MOD(D3-C3,1)*24	Hours Worked on night shift = **MOD(EndTime - StartTime,1)*24**
4	How many hours did you work on night shift?	8:20 PM	2:05 AM	5.75	7	E4: =IF(D4<C4,D4-C4+1,D4-C4)*24	Hours Worked on night shift = **IF(EndTime<StartTime,EndTime-StartTime+1,EndTime-StartTime)*24**

Figure 11.39 *Hours worked formulas for situations where the end time is smaller than the start time.*

Example 5: Rounding a Time Value to Within 5 Minutes with the MROUND Function

In Chapter 10, you learned about the ROUND function and the standard rounding rule. Sometimes, however, you need to round to a certain amount or a certain multiple. In such situations, you can use the MROUND function, where the M is for *multiple*. The syntax of this function is as follows:

```
MROUND(number, multiple)
```

For example, if you need to round a time value to the nearest 5 minutes, you can use the formula MROUND(EndTime-StartTime,00:05). If you need to round a price for a product to the nearest $0.25, you can use the formula MROUND(Price,$0.25). Figure 11.40 shows an example of a time calculation that rounds to the nearest 5 minutes along with a few pricing examples.

			Multiple:	00:05		<< hh:mm	
	Question:	Start	End	Time Rounded:		Formula:	Notes:
5	Time worked, rounded to nearest 5 mins.?	8:22 AM	1:39 PM	5:15	8	E5: =MROUND(D5-C5,E2)	Rounding time = **MROUND(EndTime-StartTime,00:05)**
6							MROUND argumnets: **MROUND(number,multiple)**
7	**Other examples of MROUND:**						
	Question:	Price	Multiple	Time Rounded:			Notes:
10	Round to nearest $0.25	$24.43	$0.25	24.50		E10: =MROUND(C10,D10)	**MROUND(Amount , $0.25)**
11	Round to nearest $100	$47.00	$5.00	45.00		E11: =MROUND(C11,D11)	**MROUND(Amount , $5.00)**
12	Round to nearest $100	$48.00	$5.00	50.00		E12: =MROUND(C12,D12)	**MROUND(Amount , $5.00)**

Figure 11.40 *The MROUND function rounds a number to a certain multiple.*

To complete this example, follow these steps:

1. Open the worksheet named Ch11(40).
2. In cell E5, create the formula **=MROUND(D5-C5,E2)**.
3. In cell E10, create the formula **=MROUND(C10,D10)**.
4. In cell E11, create the formula **=MROUND(C11,D11)**.
5. In cell E12, create the formula **=MROUND(C12,D12)**.

Keyboard Shortcuts and Custom Date and Time Number Formatting

Excel provides a few date and time keyboard shortcuts and allows you to use custom date and time number formatting. These keyboard shortcuts can help you quickly enter date and time information in a worksheet:

Keyboard Shortcut	Description
Ctrl+;	Enters the current date
Ctrl+Shift+;	Enters the current time
Ctrl+; <space> Ctrl+Shift+;	Enters a date and time (for example, to mark the date and time when an event occurred)

If you need to show dates and times together in the same cell, such as to record the date and time for an event, you can use the custom date and time number formats shown in Table 11.4.

Table 11.4 Custom Data and Time Number Formats

Data Time	Custom Number Formatting	Time Serial Number in Cell
9/22/2017 6:00 AM	*m/d/yyyy h:mm AM/PM*	43000.25
1/1/20 6:00 PM	*m/d/yy h:mm AM/PM*	43831.75
7/31/20 16:51	*m/d/yy h:mm*	44043.70208

Key Concepts in Chapter 11

- **Date number formatting:** When you enter a date value into a cell, you need to use the form that matches the regional settings in your Control Panel. For example, with the U.S. settings, Excel defines a date format as *month/day/year*. As soon you type a number and a forward slash, Excel thinks that what you are typing is a date. When you type a valid date in a cell—for example, 2/27/20—Excel applies the Date number format and stores a date serial number behind the scenes so that it can be used in date math calculations. When you enter an invalid date—for example, 28/7/2020—on a computer that is expecting 7/28/2020, the invalid date is considered text and cannot be used in date formulas.

- You can create **custom number formats** with *d* for day, *m* for month, and *y* for year. For example, you could use the custom format *ddd, m/d/yyy* to show Mon, 3/16/2020.

- A **date serial number** is a whole number that represents the number of days since December 31, 1899, where January 1, 1900 = 1, January 2, 1900 = 2, January 3, 1900 = 3, and February 27, 2020 = 43888.

- **Time number formatting:** When you enter a time value into a cell, you use the form *hh:mm:ss AM/PM*, with *h* for hour, *m* for minute, and *s* for seconds. You must enter a space between the time value and either AM or PM. If you do not type the AM or PM, the time value is entered as military time. When you type a valid time in a cell—for example, 8:00 AM—Excel applies the Time number format and stores a time serial number behind the scenes so that it can be used in time math calculations. When you enter an invalid time, like 8:00AM (with no space), Excel considers the invalid time text and cannot use it in time formulas.

- You can create **custom number formats** for time values with *h* for hour, *m* for minute and *s* for seconds. For example, you could use the custom format *hh:mm AM/PM* to show 8:00 AM, *[hh]:mm* to show 38:30, or *m/d/yy h:mm* to show 7/31/20 15:51.

- A **time serial number** is a decimal value that represents the portions of a 24-hour day. For the 8 AM time value, for example, Excel divides 8 hours by 24 hours to give you 8 / 24 = 1 / 3 = 0.33333333.

- The **General number format** acts as an eraser, removing all applied number formatting and showing the number that is actually stored in a cell.

- For fractions like 1/3, which evaluate to infinitely repeating decimal values, Excel only displays up to **15 significant digits**.

Keyboard Shortcuts Learned in Chapter 11

Keyboard Shortcut	Description
Ctrl+1	Opens the Format Cells dialog box
Ctrl+Shift+`	Applies the General number format
Ctrl+`	Toggles the keyboard to jump into formula audit mode, which shows all formulas and numbers that live under number formatting
Ctrl+;	Enters the current date
Ctrl+Shift+;	Enters the current time
Ctrl+; <space> Ctrl+Shift+;	Enters the current data and time

Practice Problems for Chapter 11
Practice Problem 1

In your Excel file for this chapter (Ch11-Excel365-DateTime.xlsx), go to the worksheet named PPCh11(1) and create the solution for this practice problem. Figure 11.41 shows the goal that is listed on that worksheet.

	A	B	C	D	E	F	G	H	I
1									
2		Goal: Create a formula in cell G5 that calculates number of days it took to pay the invoice and that will spill down the column.							
3									
4		Customer	Invoice #	Amount Owed	Invoice Issue Date	Invoice Pay Date	Number Days To Pay Invoice		
5		Rafaela Sparkman	2693	$227.66	12/7/20	2/27/21			
6		Providencia Esposito	2867	$759.31	12/21/20	12/29/20			
7		Adrien Dougherty	3092	$303.89	12/24/20	7/17/21			
8		Marvis Block	3222	$459.95	12/30/20	6/12/21			
9		Drucilla Ragsdale	3247	$574.95	1/15/21	7/7/21			
10		Senaida Battles	3319	$315.25	2/11/21	5/24/21			
11		Ossie Kimbrough	3459	$181.82	2/16/21	3/1/21			
12		Elwood Koehler	3587	$177.74	2/19/21	10/23/21			
13		Corliss Coffin	3903	$581.59	3/14/21	5/5/21			
14		Claudette Barela	3950	$761.62	3/16/21	9/10/21			

Figure 11.41 *On the worksheet PPCh11(1), create a formula to calculate the number of days to pay each invoice.*

When you are done with this problem, you can check your work against the answer sheet named PPCh11(1an).

Practice Problem 2

In your Excel file for this chapter (Ch11-Excel365-DateTime.xlsx), go to the worksheet named PPCh11(2) and create the solution for this practice problem. Figure 11.42 shows the goal that is listed on that worksheet.

	A	B	C	D	E
1					
2		Goal: In cell E5, create a formula to calcualte the number of days to complete each project.			
3					
4		Project Address	Projected Start Date	Projected End Date	Number Of Days to Complete Project
5		9664 SE. Thomas St.	2/18/18	4/28/18	
6		92 Middle River Ave.	11/27/17	7/4/18	
7		7275 Belmont Lane	3/8/18	11/12/18	
8		9504 Grand St.	12/1/17	6/16/18	
9		8016 Applegate Court	2/10/18	3/24/18	
10		8 Canal Ave.	1/23/18	3/18/18	
11		28 Green Hill Lane	1/28/18	3/4/18	
12		26 West Purple Finch Ave.	12/17/17	8/6/18	
13		180 Augusta Ave.	10/22/17	4/11/18	
14		77 S. Sleepy Hollow Drive	1/8/18	9/2/18	

Figure 11.42 *On the worksheet PPCh11(2), create a formula to calculate the number of days to complete each project.*

When you are done with this problem, you can check your work against the answer sheet named PPCh11(2an).

Practice Problem 3

In your Excel file for this chapter (Ch11-Excel365-DateTime.xlsx), go to the worksheet named PPCh11(3) and create the solution for this practice problem. Figure 11.43 shows the goals that are listed on that worksheet.

	A	B	C	D	E	F	G
1							
2		**Goal #1:**	Using one of Excel's Date Functions, calculate the Due Date if the invoice				
3			contract says that the amount is due on the same day, two month's ahead.				
4							
5			InvoiceDate	11/3/21		Number Months	
6			Due Date				2
7							
8		**Goal #2:**	Using one of Excel's Date Functions, calculate the Due Date if the				
9			invoice contract says that the amount is due at the end of the month.				
10							
11			InvoiceDate	11/3/21		Number Months	
12			Due Date				0

Figure 11.43 *On the worksheet PPCh11(3), create the two formulas that calculate the correct invoice due dates.*

When you are done with this problem, you can check your work against the answer sheet named PPCh11(3an).

Practice Problem 4

In your Excel file for this chapter (Ch11-Excel365-DateTime.xlsx), go to the worksheet named PPCh11(4) and create the solution for this practice problem. Figure 11.44 shows the goal that is listed on that worksheet.

	A	B	C	D	E	F	G	H	I
1									
2		Goal: Create the formulas for the following columns: Hours Worked, Gross Pay, Deduction, and Day's Pay							
3									
4								Tax Rate	
5								0.0765	
6									
7		Employee	Wage	Time In	Time Out	Hours Worked	Gross Pay	Deduction	Day's Pay
8		Carroll Stanley	$24.94	8:00 AM	3:30 PM				
9		Anne Ramos	$18.14	9:00 AM	2:30 PM				
10		Blanche Sanchez	$17.94	7:30 AM	3:00 PM				
11		Karla Fletcher	$26.70	8:00 AM	1:30 PM				
12		Devin Smith	$24.30	9:00 AM	2:30 PM				
13		Edna Hansen	$22.85	8:00 AM	6:00 PM				
14		Moses Swanson	$26.98	6:30 AM	11:30 AM				
15		Sherman Moss	$17.71	8:00 AM	1:00 PM				
16		Amber Rios	$20.12	7:00 AM	4:30 PM				
17		Lindsey Powers	$23.69	8:00 AM	3:00 PM				

Figure 11.44 *On the worksheet PPCh11(4), create the four different formulas needed to complete this payroll project.*

When you are done with this problem, you can check your work against the answer sheet named PPCh11(4an).

Practice Problem 5

In your Excel file for this chapter (Ch11-Excel365-DateTime.xlsx), go to the worksheet named PPCh11(5) and create the solution for this practice problem. Figure 11.45 shows the goal that is listed on that worksheet.

	A	B	C	D	E	F	G	H
1								
2		**Goal:** In cell F8 create formula for a time value that is rounded to five minutes. In cell G8, calculate the						
3		hours worked. In cell H8, calculate the gross pay. Note: Some employees work the night shift.						
4								
5				Round to Nearest 00:05		0:05:00		
6								
7		Employee	Wage per Hour	Time In	Time Out	Time rounded to 00:05 min	Time in Hours	Gross Pay
8		Qiana Sisson	$38.34	9:02:00 PM	6:24:00 AM			
9		Loyd Forte	$28.59	8:31:00 AM	1:51:00 PM			
10		Pandora Lafleur	$39.70	4:47:00 PM	9:33:00 PM			
11		Gregorio Clapp	$31.73	9:25:00 PM	5:06:00 AM			
12		Madison Hooker	$34.76	7:10:00 PM	4:02:00 AM			
13		Nobuko Hobbs	$39.63	2:10:00 PM	6:38:00 PM			
14		Chere Shelley	$32.40	8:40:00 PM	4:35:00 AM			
15		Burl Crowe	$34.55	7:00:00 PM	12:15:00 AM			
16		Noreen Amaya	$29.60	11:53:00 AM	8:36:00 PM			
17		Jonna Lowery	$35.50	10:35:00 AM	6:30:00 PM			

Figure 11.45 *On the worksheet PPCh11(5), create calculations for the night shift and for rounding time values to the nearest 5 minutes.*

When you are done with this problem, you can check your work against the answer sheet named PPCh11(5an).

Practice Problem 6

In your Excel file for this chapter (Ch10-Excel365-ROUND.xlsx), go to the worksheet named PPCh10(6).

In your own words, see if you can answer these conceptual questions:

1. What does a date serial number represent?
2. What does a time serial number represent?
3. How is the General number format helpful?
4. What does the MROUND function do?
5. What does the EDATE function do?

When you are done with this problem, you can check your work against the answer sheet named PPCh09(6an).

Chapter 12: Worksheet Formula Types and Formula Elements

> **Note:** To follow along with the examples in this chapter, you can use the file named Ch12-Excel365-WorksheetFormulas.xlsx.

This chapter might be the most fun part of the whole book because it shows you all the different types of formulas you can use in a worksheet as well as examples of all the different formula elements that you are allowed to use in worksheet formulas. In this chapter, you will also learn about the order of operator precedence in worksheet formulas. This chapter gives you one place that you can come back to later when you need to get a refresher on how to do particular tasks with worksheet formulas.

In addition to being fun, this chapter also raises the level of difficulty over what you've seen so far in this book. The goal of this chapter is to demonstrate the full range of what is possible with Excel worksheet formulas, and it includes a lot of new content. It is a one-stop location for the full spectrum of formula fun!

Worksheet Formula Types

You can create a number of different types of formulas in a worksheet. Table 12.1 describes the major types of worksheet formulas.

Table 12.1 Worksheet Formula Types

Formula Type	Description
Number formula	Delivers number results (such as numbers, times, and dates).
Text formula	Delivers text results.
Logical formula	Delivers logical values, or Boolean values. A logical formula delivers either a TRUE or a FALSE.
Single-input/single-output formula	Operates on a single input and delivers a single answer. For this type of formula, you must:
	Consider what type of cell references (relative, absolute, or mixed) are required.
	Enter the formula into one cell.
	Manually copy the formula to other cells if the formula must be copied.
	This type of formula has a single value entered into a function argument (for example, =FORMULATEXT(B1) or has a single value on either side of a multiplication operator (for example, =A1*B1).
Array formula	Contains one or more array operations that deliver an array of answers rather than a single answer. An array operation can involve multiple values entered into a function argument (for example, =FORMULATEXT(B1:B4)), or there can be multiple values on one or more sides of an operator (for example, =A1*B1:B5, A1:A5*B1, or A1:A5*B1:B5). *Array formula* is the general term used to describe both types of array formulas.
Scalar array formula	Delivers a single scalar value as the final answer.
Dynamic spilled array formula	Delivers a spilled array to the worksheet as the final answer.
Aggregate formula	Operates on an array of values and delivers a single answer, as with adding, averaging, or running an AND logical test.
Lookup formula	Takes a lookup value, finds a match, and retrieves one or more values related to that match.

Worksheet Formula Elements

Table 12.2 lists all the different worksheet formula elements that are possible and provides examples of them.

Table 12.2 Excel Worksheet Formula Elements

Element	Description	Example
Equal sign (=)	As first character in cell, tells Excel you are making a formula.	=SUM(I2:I6)
Cell reference	Can be one of four types: relative, absolute, mixed with row locked, mixed with column locked.	G2, $G$2, G$2, $G2
Range of cells	Can be one of four types: relative, absolute, mixed with row locked, mixed with column locked.	G2:G5, $G$2:$G$5, G$2:G$5, $G2:$G5
Colon (:) reference operator	Used between two cell references, two sheet names, or two lookup functions to create a range of cells.	G2:G5, Jan:Apr!C3 XLOOKUP(V2,V3:Z3,V4:Z4):XLOOKUP(W2,V3:Z3,V4:Z4)
Comma (,) reference operator	Used to combine ranges. Works in FREQUENCY, IRR, INDEX, AREAS, LET, and aggregate functions such as SUM and LARGE. Works in defined names.	LARGE((V5:Z5,Sales),3)
Space ( ) reference operator	Used as an intersection operator to get the value at the intersection of two ranges.	G2:G6 F4:H4 yields "Quad"
Spilled range operator (#)	Allows you to refer to all items that are spilled from a cell with a spilled array formula.	C3#
Implicit intersection operator (@)	Allows you to get a corresponding item in the current row of a column or a parallel column. Most commonly seen in relative cell references in Excel Table columns.	fSales[@Product], @Product, @G2:G6
Data type, or dot (.), operator	For a cell that contains a record, allows you to specify what field you want to extract from the cell.	[@Stock].Price . B12.Price
Worksheet reference	Specifies the name of a worksheet (in single quotes if the name contains a space) with an exclamation point before the cell reference.	LookupTable!B3:B6 , 'Lookup Table'!B3:B6
Workbook reference	Same as worksheet reference with name of workbook in square brackets and full file path.	**If referenced workbook is open:** '[Ch12-Excel365-WorksheetFormulas.xlsx]Elements'!$G$5, **If referenced workbook is *not* open:** 'F:\[Ch12-Excel365-WorksheetFormulas.xlsx]Elements'!G5

Defined name	Represents a cell, a range of cells, or a formula. Defined names can be used in other formulas and features, including in Power Query and the Power Pivot Data Model.	Example 16 in Chapter 12: Defined name to define a cell: **CallRepConditionAnswer** ='Ch12(31-34an)'!$G$9 Example 16 in Chapter 14: Defined name to define formula: **LookupPicture** =XLOOK-UP('Ch14(38-40)'!$B$6,'Ch14(38-40)'!$B$9:$B$12,'Ch14(38-40)'!$D$9:$D$12)
Table formula nomenclature in an Excel Table	Full table	CallTable[#All]
	Records in table	CallTable
	Field names	CallTable[#Headers]
	Mixed with row locked column reference	CallTable[Rep]
	Locked column reference	CallTable[[Rep]:[Rep]]
	Selected columns	CallTable[[Rep]:[Calls]]
	Relative cell reference (using the implicit intersection operator)	CallTable[@Rep]
Worksheet function	Built-in function like SUM and ROUND that is programmed to make a defined calculation based on the formula inputs entered into the function's arguments.	SUM, COUNTIFS, SUMIFS, FORMULATEXT, ROUND, MROUND, UNIQUE, SORT, EDATE, EOMONTH, NETWORKDAYS.INTL, WORKDAY.INTL, AVERAGE, SEQUENCE, LARGE, RANK. EQ, XLOOKUP, FILTER and many more. More than 450 in all.
Function argument elements	Tells a function which type of calculation to make.	NETWORKDAYS.INTL(F2,F2,7)
Math operators	Used to create math calculations	+ Adding - Subtracting or negation * Multiplying / Dividing ^ Raising to an exponent ( ) Parentheses
Comparison operator	Used to create comparison calculations	= Equal: Are two things equal? <> Not: Are two things not equal? > Greater than: Is the left side greater than the right side? >= Greater than or equal to: Is the left side greater than or equal to the right side? < Less than: Is the left side less than the right side? <= Less than or equal to: Is the left side less than or equal to the right side?
Join operator (&)	Concatenates two items into one item.	C8&", "&B8 , "Item # "&C8:C12
Text within quotation marks	Text in formulas must be in quotes	C8&", "&B8 , "Item # "&C8:C12

| Hard-coded numbers | Numbers that will not change, like 12 months in a year or 24 hours in a day, and that you can hard code into formulas. | C10/12, (EndTime-StartTime)*24 |
| Array constants (hard-coded arrays) | Hard-coded tables, columns, or rows. Curly brackets ({}) house an array Comma (,) indicates a column Semicolon (;)indicates a row | {"Jan","Feb","Mar","Apr","-May";1,2,3,4,5} |

Order of Operator Precedence in Worksheet Formulas

To calculate an answer from the math expression 114 − 45 * 10, what do you do first: subtract 45 from 114 or multiply 45 by 110? If you do the former, you end up with the result 690, and if you do the latter, you end up with the result −336. These are very different results! To make it clear which operation takes place first in a formula with multiple operations, the math world consistently follows this *order of operator precedence*:

1. Parentheses

2. Exponents

3. Multiplication and division, from left to right

4. Addition and subtraction, from left to right

Based on this order, the math expression 114 − 45 * 10 is evaluated as 114 − (45 * 10) = 114 − 450 = −336 because the multiplication is performed before the subtraction.

Worksheet formulas can take advantage of formula operators and elements in addition to math operators and numbers. For example, there are operators such as the comma reference operator, the spilled range operator (#), the join operator (&), and other operators that the calculation engine must evaluate before returning a final answer. Just as you need to be aware of the order of operator precedence when doing math calculations, when Excel's worksheet formula calculation engine evaluates a formula, it must know the correct order in which to evaluate the operators. The order of precedence (or hierarchy) for worksheet formula operators is as follows:

1. Parentheses

2. Reference operators (:, <space>, , [comma], #, @, . (dot)), evaluated left to right

3. Negation (-) (for example, -2^4 = 16, -(2^4) = -16, and --2 + 1 = 3)

4. Conversion of percentages to numerals (for example, 1% to .01)

5. Exponents (^) (for example, 3^2 = 9, 8^(1/3) = 2)

6. Multiplication (*) and division (/), evaluated left to right

7. Addition (+) and subtraction (-), evaluated left to right

8. Concatenation (&)

9. Comparison symbols (=, <>, >=, <=, <, >), evaluated left to right

You must be familiar with the order of operator precedence because a formula like =(B2-C2)*D2 will yield a different answer than a formula like =B2-C2*D2, as you will see later in this chapter.

My Golden Rule, the ROUND Function, and Number Formatting As a Façade

Before you look at examples of the different types of formulas and formula elements in Excel, it is helpful to remember the crucial rules you have learned about formulas so far in the book:

- If an Excel solution input can change, you should put it into a cell, label it, and refer to it using a cell reference.

- Number formatting is a façade, and formulas act on the underlying numbers.

- If you are required to round, if you have extraneous digits, and if the formula result will be used in other formulas, you must use the ROUND function.

The following sections provide examples that illustrate the different types of worksheet formulas, formula elements, and order of operator precedence. You can follow along with each example and try it yourself using the worksheets in the file Ch12-Excel365-WorksheetFormulas.xlsx.

Example 1: Number Formula for Average Customer Ratings

Figure 12.1 shows customer ratings in column B. The goal of this formula is to gauge customer satisfaction by calculating the average customer ratings, rounded to the tenth. This is an example of an aggregate formula that delivers a number answer. In this example, you use the ROUND function because the result needs to be rounded and will be used in other formulas. Figure 12.1 shows the formula to use in cell D8, lists the formula types and formula elements, and describes the evaluation process.

You can try this example on the worksheet named Ch12(1).

	A	B	C	D	E	F	G	H	I
1									
2	Ex 1	**Goal:** Calculate the average customer rating, rounded to the tenth.							
3		The rounded value will be used in other formulas.							
4		**Type of Formula:** Number formula. Aggregate formula.							
5		**Formula Elements**: Equal sign, range of cells (cell references and colon reference operator),							
6		worksheet functions, hard coded number.							
7									
8		Customer Rating (1-5)		Average Customer Rating		**Formula in cell D9:**			
9		3		2.8		=ROUND(AVERAGE(B9:B17),1)			
10		2							
11		3		Steps in formula calculation process for **=ROUND(AVERAGE(B8:B16),1)**					
12		4		**1.** Colon reference operator with cell references get the range:					
13		1		=ROUND(AVERAGE(**{3;2;3;4;1;3;2;5;2}**),1)					
14		3		**2.** Worksheet function AVERAGE to add up & divide by count:					
15		2		=ROUND(**2.77777777777778**,1)					
16		5		**3.** Hard coded number 1 instructs ROUND function to round to tenth:					
17		2		=**ROUND**(2.77777777777778,1) ➔ **2.8**					

Figure 12.1 *The steps in the formula evaluation process.*

Figure 12.1 illustrates the steps in the formula evaluation process. However, if you would like to see Excel step through the formula evaluation process one step at a time, you can use Excel's Evaluate Formula feature. This feature helps you understand how the worksheet formula engine works and can help you track down errors in your formulas.

To use the Evaluate Formula feature for the formula in cell D8, follow these steps:

1. With cell D8 selected, click on the Formulas tab in the Ribbon, and then, in the Formula Auditing group, click the Evaluate Formula button. (Alternatively, use the keyboard shortcut Alt, M, V to open the Evaluate Formula dialog box.)

2. Click the Evaluate button to see the first step.

3. Keep clicking the Evaluate button to see the rest of the steps in the evaluation process.

4. When you are done with this problem, click Close in the Evaluate Formula dialog box.

Example 2: Using a Text Formula to Join First and Last Names in a Cell

Figure 12.2 shows a common human resources department task: The company database provided an employee's first and last names in two different cells, but a particular report requires that the last name and first name be in a single cell, separated by a comma and a space. This is an example of a single-input/single-output formula that delivers a text answer. Figure 12.2 shows the text formula to use in cell D7, lists the formula types and formula elements, and describes the evaluation process.

You can try this example on the worksheet named Ch12(2).

	A	B	C	D	E	F
1						
2	Ex 2	**Goal:** Join last name to comma and space and then to first name, like: Last, First.				
3		**Type of Formula:** Text formula. Single input-output formula.				
4		**Formula Elements**: Equal sign, cell references, join operator (&),				
5		Text within quotation marks.				
6						
7		Employee First	Employee Last	Last, First		**Formula in cell D8:**
8		Booker	Washington	Washington, Booker		=C8&", "&B8
9						
10		Steps in formula calculation process for **=C7&", "&B7**				
11		**1.** Retrieves what's in cell C7:				
12		="**Washington**"&", "&B7				
13		**2.** Joins comma and space to content of cell C7:				
14		="**Washington, **"&B7				
15		**3.** Retrieves what's in cell C7:				
16		="**Washington, **"&"**Booker**"				
17		**4.** Joins into one text item:				
18		**Washington, Booker**				

Figure 12.2 *Putting last name and first name in a single cell, separated by a comma and a space.*

Example 3: Using a Logical Formula to Determine Whether Accounts Are in Balance

Accounting professionals need to make sure everything is in balance by checking that the left side of the trial balance (debit) is equal to the right side (credit). Figure 12.3 shows that even though it looks like the number in cell B14 is equal to the number in cell C14, the logical formula in cell D7 delivers the result FALSE. The logical formula is correct that the two numbers are not in balance because formulas do not see number formatting. Recall that formulas act on the underlying numbers. The out-of-balance problem originates in cell B11, where number formatting is masking the true number. The formula bar shows that the actual number in the cell is 100.49, rather than the displayed 100.5.

Logical formulas that verify that amounts are in balance are very common. When there is a problem, such a formula reports FALSE to indicate that the numbers are not in balance. FALSE indicates that you should investigate. If a formula reports TRUE, then you know the numbers are in balance. In this case, you can assume that an error was made, and the correct number is 100.5. If you change the number in cell B11 to 100.5, the formula will report TRUE. In this case, you would also increase the decimal places for all numbers to show two decimal places. Doing this would also make the presentation clearer.

This is the first time in this book that you have encountered a *logical formula*, also known as a *Boolean formula*. (You will see a lot more of these formulas later in the book, including formulas that include the IF logical function.) This is an example of a single-input/single-output formula that delivers a Boolean answer. Figure 12.3 shows the logical formula you can use in cell E8, lists the formula types and formula elements, and describes the evaluation process.

You can try this example on the worksheet named Ch12(3).

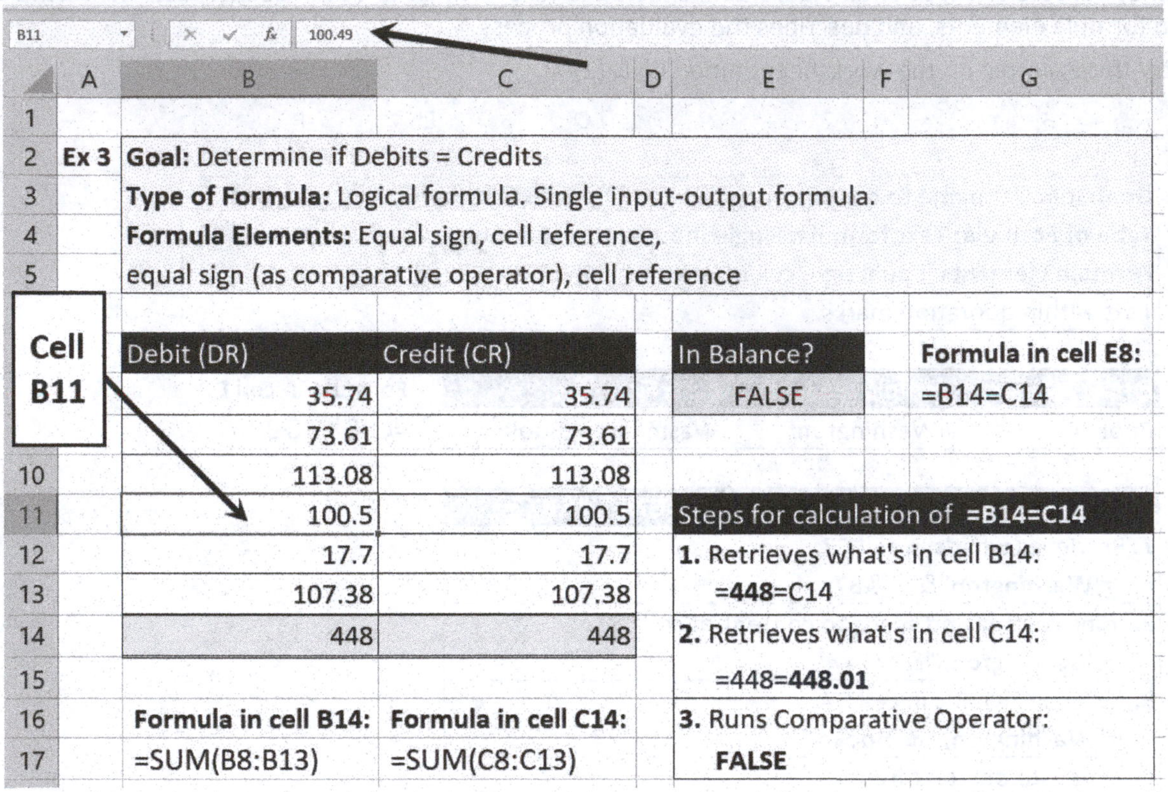
B11
100.49
A B C D E F G
Ex 3 Goal: Determine if Debits = Credits
Type of Formula: Logical formula. Single input-output formula.
Formula Elements: Equal sign, cell reference,
equal sign (as comparative operator), cell reference
Cell B11
Debit (DR)
Credit (CR)
In Balance?
Formula in cell E8:
35.74
35.74
FALSE
=B14=C14
73.61
73.61
113.08
113.08
100.5
100.5
Steps for calculation of =B14=C14
17.7
17.7
1. Retrieves what's in cell B14:
107.38
107.38
=448=C14
448
448
2. Retrieves what's in cell C14:
=448=448.01
Formula in cell B14:
Formula in cell C14:
3. Runs Comparative Operator:
=SUM(B8:B13)
=SUM(C8:C13)
FALSE

Figure 12.3 *Determining whether accounts are in balance.*

Examples 4 Through 6: Using a Cost of Goods Sold Formula with a Spilled Array, Relative Cell References, or Table Formula Nomenclature

When a business sells product inventory, at the end of each period, it must calculate the cost of the products sold. In accounting, this is called the *cost of goods sold*, or *COGS*. One method for calculating COGS is to subtract the number of units at the end of the period from the number of units at the beginning of the period to get the number of units sold and then multiply the number of units sold by the cost for each.

In Figure 12.4, the Aspen product in the first row shows beginning units of 114, ending units of 45, and a cost each of $10. If you were to make the left-to-right calculation 114 – 45 * 10, you would get the wrong answer because the worksheet formula engine (and the math order of operator precedence) would evaluate the multiplication before the subtraction, like this: 114 – (45 * 10) = 114 – 450 = –336. The correct formula must use parentheses to force the subtraction to occur before the multiplication. The correct math formula for the Aspen COGS is (114 – 45) * 10 = 69 * 10 = 690.

	A	B	C	D	E	F	G	H
2	Ex 4	**Goal:** Calculate Cost of Goods Sold (COGS) = (Begin Units - End Units)*Cost Each						
3		**Type of Formula:** Number formula. Dynamic spilled array formula.						
4		**Formula Elements:** Equal sign, range of cells (cell references and colon reference operator),						
5		math operators (parentheses, subtraction, multiplication)						
7		Product	Begin Units	End Units	Cost Each ($)	COGS ($)	**Formula in cell F8:**	
8		Aspen	114	45	10	690	=(C8:C12-D8:D12)*E8:E12	
9		Quad	146	117	20	580		
10		Carlota	108	102	15	90		
11		Bellen	61	47	10	140		
12		Sunset	54	51	12	36		
14		**Steps for calculation of =(C8:C12-D8:D12)*E8:E12**						
15		**1.** Calculate everything inside parentheses:						
16		=**(**C8:C12-D8:D12**)***E8:E12						
17		**2.** Evaluate Range 1 and Range 2:						
18		=({114;146;108;61;54}-{45;117;102;47;51})*E8:E12						
19		**3.** Subtract:						
20		=({114-45;146-117;108-102;61-47;54-51})*E8:E12						
21		**4.** To get:						
22		=**{69, 29, 6, 14, 3}***E8:E12						
23		**5.** Evaluate Range 3:						
24		=**{69;29;6;14;3}*{10;20;15;10;12}**						
25		**6.** Multiply:						
26		=**{69*10;29*20;6*15;14*10;3*12}**						
27		**7.** To get spilled result:						
28		=**{690;580;90;140;36}**						

Figure 12.4 *Using a dynamic spilled array formula to calculate cost of goods sold.*

Figure 12.4 shows the spilled array formula you can use in cell F8 to spill the correct COGS for each product. This is an example of a spilled array formula that delivers multiple number answers. Figure 12.4 also lists the formula types and formula elements and describes the evaluation process.

You can try this example on the worksheet named Ch12(4-5).

Figure 12.4 uses a dynamic spilled array formula to calculate the COGS for various products. If you had to add new products to the bottom of the table, it would be most efficient to use the Excel Table feature to convert the proper dataset to an Excel Table so that the formulas and formatting would automatically fill down when you add new records. The problem is that spilled array formulas are *not* allowed in Excel Tables.

You first learned about Excel Tables in Chapter 8. In this chapter, you will learn about the formulas that you can use in an Excel Table column. However, before you do that, you need to understand the error you get when you try to use a spilled array in an Excel Table. Figure 12.5 shows that you get a #SPILL! error when you convert a proper date set to an Excel Table that contains a spilled array. You can try this yourself by pressing Ctrl+T to convert the table to an Excel Table, and then, once you prove to yourself that the #SPILL! error does occur, use Ctrl+Z to undo the table conversion.

F8		× ✓ ƒx	=(C8:C12-D8:D12)*E8:E12							
	A	B	C	D	E	F	G	H	I	J
6										
7		Product ▾	Begin Units▾	End Units ▾	Cost Each ($)▾	COGS ($) ▾		COGS ($) Formula in cell F8:		
8		Aspen	114	45	10	#SPILL!		=(C8:C12-D8:D12)*E8:E12		
9		Quad	146	117	20					

Figure 12.5 *Converting a proper dataset with spilled array formulas leads to a #SPILL! error.*

Rather than use a spilled array COGS formula, you can use one of two alternatives:

- **Use single relative cell references:** As shown in Figure 12.6, you can use single relative cell references for the COGS formula in the first row and then copy it down the column. If you create the formula before you convert to an Excel Table, you can use your mouse or arrow keys to enter the cell references into the formula. (For a refresher on how to do this, see Chapter 8.) If you create the formula after you convert to an Excel Table, you must manually type out the cell references. This is because, as shown in Figure 12.7, if you create the formula after the table is already converted to an Excel Table, when you use your mouse or arrow keys to put a reference into a formula, rather than insert a cell reference (for example, C8), Excel inserts a table formula nomenclature relative cell reference (for example, [@[Begin Units]]).

Ex 5	Goal: Calculate Cost of Goods Sold (COGS) = (Begin Units - End Units)*Cost Each
	Type of Formula: Number formula. Single input-output formulas.
	Formula Elements: Equal sign, relative cell references, math operators (parentheses, subtraction, multiplication)

Product	Begin Units	End Units	Cost Each ($)	COGS ($)	COGS ($) Formula in cell F8:
Aspen	114	45	10	690	=(C8-D8)*E8
Quad	146	117	20	580	
Carlota	108	102	15	90	
Bellen	61	47	10	140	
Sunset	54	51	12	36	

Figure 12.6 *Using single relative cell references to find the cost of goods sold.*

- **Use table formula nomenclature:** As shown in Figure 12.7, you can use table formula nomenclature. The syntax for a relative cell reference in an Excel Table is the full column name in square brackets, [Begin Units], and then the implicit intersection operator, @[Begin Units], all encased in an outer set of square brackets: [@[Begin Units]]. The implicit intersection operator, the @ symbol, means "please get the item in the current row in the column [Begin Units]."

Ex 6	Goal: Calculate Cost of Goods Sold (COGS) = (Begin Units - End Units)*Cost Each
	Type of Formula: Number formula. Single input-output formulas.
	Formula Elements: Equal sign, table formula nomenclature relative cell reference with implicit intersection operator, math operators (parentheses, subtraction, multiplication)

Product	Begin Units	End Units	Cost Each ($)	COGS ($)	COGS ($) Formula in cell F8:
Aspen	114	45	10	690	=([@[Begin Units]]-[@[End Units]])*[@[Cost Each ($)]]
Quad	146	117	20	580	
Carlota	108	102	15	90	
Bellen	61	47	10	140	
Sunset	54	51	12	36	

Figure 12.7 *Table formula nomenclature.*

The table formula nomenclature only works in an Excel Table. Cell references, on the other hand, can work in an Excel Table or in worksheet cells. It is up to you which one to use. Either one is fine. In either case, when you add new records to the bottom of the table or when you delete rows, everything updates perfectly. Both formulas are examples of single-input/single-output formulas that deliver number answers. Figure 12.6 and 12.7 show the formulas and list the formula types and formula elements.

You can try these examples on the worksheets named Ch12(6) and 12(7).

Example 7: Dynamically Extracting the Top *N* Values by Using the Comma Reference Operator

Extracting the top values is a common Excel task in business, science, sports, and education. Sometimes it is the top 3 values that are desired; other times, it is the top 5 or top 10. In business, it might be the top sales values; in science, it might be the top experiment values; in sports, it might be the top averages; and in education, it might be the top test scores. Whatever the situation might be, worksheet formulas make a report like this easy to complete.

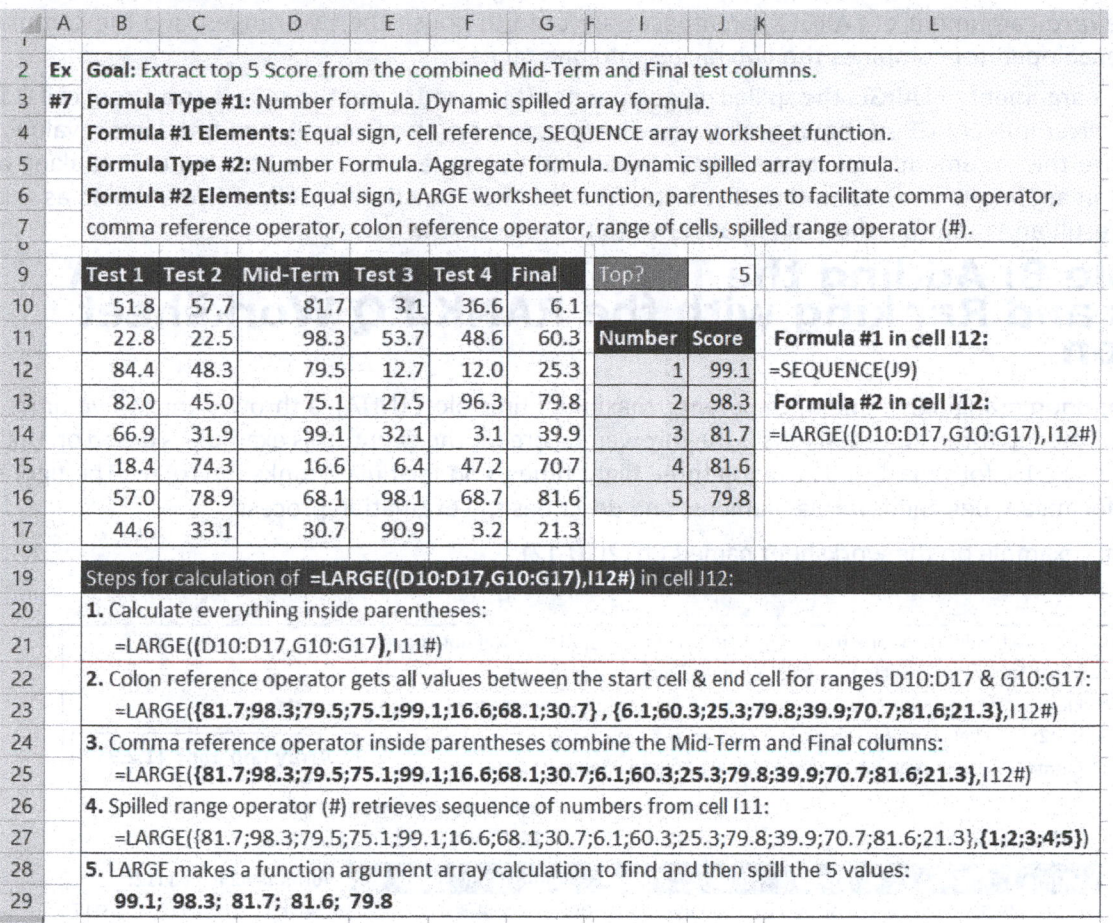

Figure 12.8 *Using the comma reference operator to dynamically extract the top N values.*

Figure 12.8 shows an example of extracting the top 5 test scores from the combined Mid-term and Final columns. It uses two spilled array formula that deliver multiple number answers. In addition, the LARGE function formula makes five separate aggregate operations. Figure 12.8 lists the formula types and formula elements and describes the evaluation process.

You can try this example on the worksheet named Ch12(8-9).

Consider these important notes about this example:

- To follow my Golden Rule, you put the top formula input number into cell J9 and label it. When you change the formula input to 3, the report immediately updates and shows only the top 3 scores.

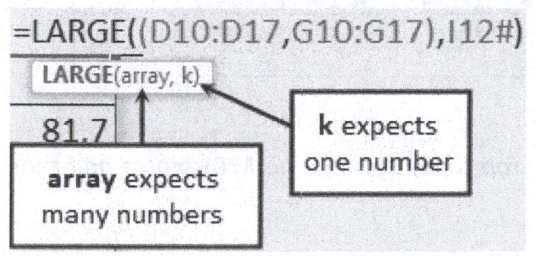

Figure 12.9 *Arguments for the LARGE worksheet function.*

- The SEQUENCE array function is programmed to deliver a sequence of numbers. In this example, SEQUENCE takes the formula input 5, and with its default argument settings, it delivers a spilled array from 1 to 5. The spilled array formula lives in cell I11 and spills the sequence of numbers from row 11 down to row 15.

- The LARGE function has two arguments, as shown in Figure 12.9. The first argument, *array*, expects an array of numbers that it can look through to find the specific *k*th largest value. The second argument, *k*, expects a single number, where *k* = 1 gets the largest value, *k* = 2 gets the second-largest value, *k* = 3 gets the third-largest value, and so on.

- For the two ranges of cells D10:D17 and G10:G17, the colon reference operator uses the start location (the cell before the colon) and the end location (the cell after the colon) as the two bookends to the range to then grab all the values in between the start and end cells. Importantly, because a colon operator uses start and end cell locations, if you ever insert rows between the start and end locations, the range of cells updates to get all values between the start and end locations.

- In the *array* argument of LARGE, parentheses are used to house the two ranges, and the comma reference operator combines the two ranges into one range.

- In the *k* argument of LARGE, the spilled range operator (#) is used to get the spilled array from cell I11 and deliver it to LARGE so that it can retrieve the first, second, third, fourth, and fifth largest values. Because this argument expects a single number, and you gave it five numbers, you are making a function argument array operation that instructs the LARGE function to deliver five answers as the final result and then spill those answers down to the rows below.

Example 8: Adding the Top Three Boomerang MTA Scores and Ranking with the RANK.EQ Worksheet Function

In the sport of boomeranging, in one of the events, maximum time aloft (MTA), a thrower throw five times, and the sum of the top three longest flights is the thrower's score for the event. This example is based on that event. In Figure 12.10, formula 1 adds the top three flight times, and formula 2 ranks the totals. The figure also lists the formula types and formula elements and describes the evaluation process.

You can try this example on the worksheet named Ch12(10-12).

	A	B	C	D	E	F	G	H	I	J	K
2	Ex	**Goal:** Add top three times. Then rank from biggest to smallest. "Top three" will not change.									
3	#8	**Formula Type #1:** Number formula. Aggregate Formula. Scalar array formula.									
4		**Formula #1 Elements:** Equal sign, SUM function, LARGE Function, relative range of cells, array constant.									
5		**Formula Type #2:** Number formula. Dynamic spilled array formula.									
6		**Formula #2 Elements:** Equal sign, RANK.EQ worksheet function, range of cells.							**Array Constant {1,2,3}**		
8								**Formula #1 in cell H12:**			
9			**Times in seconds:**					=SUM(LARGE(C12:G12,{1,2,3}))			
11		**Thrower**	**Time 1**	**Time 2**	**Time 3**	**Time 4**	**Time 5**	**Add Top 3**	**Rank**	**Formula #2 in cell I12:**	
12		Bower	0.00	86.87	92.40	80.89	85.09	264.36	2	=RANK.EQ(H12:H17,H12:H17)	
13		Kavanaugh	72.09	108.27	73.70	93.34	0.00	275.31	1		
14		Washington	55.26	85.96	89.82	34.85	31.66	231.04	5		
15		Rose	88.21	62.77	99.25	6.82	43.69	250.23	4		
16		Kinder	19.50	20.13	60.34	37.19	36.49	134.02	6		
17		Gix	78.30	47.64	104.85	68.31	13.35	251.46	3		
19		Steps for calculation of =SUM(LARGE(C12:G12,{1,2,3}))					Steps for calculation of =RANK.EQ(H12:H17,H12:H17)				
20		1. Array constant instructs LARGE to get the 3 biggest.					1. First argument in RANK.EQ contains numbers to rank.				
21		This is a function argument array calculation.					This is a function argument array calculation.				
22		=SUM(LARGE(C12:G12,**{1,2,3}**))					=RANK.EQ(**{264.36;275.31;231.04;113.38;134.02;251.46}**				
23		2. LARGE spills top 3 numbers into SUM function.					,H12:H17)				
24		=SUM(**{92.4,86.87,85.09}**)					2. Second argument in RANK.EQ has numbers to rank against.				
25		where:					=RANK.EQ({264.36;275.31;231.04;113.38;134.02;251.46},				
26		1st biggest = **92.4**					**{264.36;275.31;231.04;113.38;134.02;251.46}**)				
27		2nd biggest = **86.87**					3. RANK.EQ spills default rank of biggest to smallest.				
28		3rd biggest = **85.09**					**2; 1; 4; 6; 5; 3**				
29		3. SUM aggregates to get sum.									
30		**264.36**									

Figure 12.10 *Using the RANK.EQ worksheet function to add the top three boomerang MTA scores and rank them.*

There are six important takeaways from this example:

- You use array constants to hard code arrays of values into formulas. Figure 12.11 shows the correct syntax for creating array constants. Because retrieving the top three MTA scores is not a calculation requirement that can change, you used an array constant in the *k* argument of the LARGE function rather than the SEQUENCE function with a labeled formula input in a cell. According to my Golden Rule, when a formula input will not change, it is okay to hard code it into the formula.

Array constant syntax:

Curly Brackets house the array: { }

Comma means column ,

Semi-colon means row ;

Array constant of column values: D8: ={1,2,3}	1	2	3

Array constant of row values: D10: ={1;2;3}	1
	2
	3

Array constant of table values: D14: ={1,"Jan";2,"Feb";3,"Mar"}	1	Jan
	2	Feb
	3	Mar

Array constant = hard coded array of column values, row values or table values.

Figure 12.11 *Examples of syntax to create array constants.*

- The array constant in the *k* argument forces the LARGE function to make a function argument array operation and then spill the top three values into the SUM function *number1* argument. In specific, the LARGE function makes three separate aggregate operations—get the first biggest, get the second biggest, and get the third biggest—and then LARGE spills these numbers into the SUM function *number1* argument. The SUM function then adds the values to get a single answer. This is the first example you've seen of an array formula that does not spill into the cells. With this array formula, the array operation is made internally in the formula rather than as the last action in the calculation process. The last action in the evaluation process for this formula is the SUM function aggregate operation.

- Because the *number1* argument in the SUM function is programmed to make multiple numbers and make an aggregate operation to get one answer, you cannot make a function argument operation to get multiple answers to spill down the column. For this formula, you must enter the formula into cell H12 and then copy the formula down through the range H12:H17.

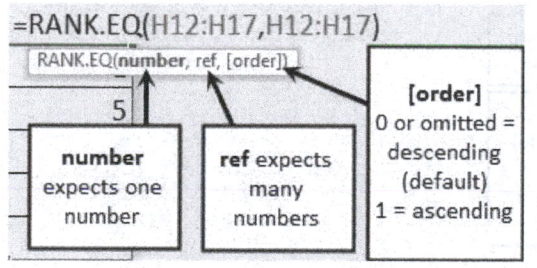

Figure 12.12 *Arguments for the RANK.EQ worksheet function.*

- The RANK.EQ worksheet function has three arguments, as shown in Figure 12.12. The first argument, *number*, expects a single number that it can rank against a set of numbers. The second argument, *ref*, expects the full set of numbers that it can use to find the relative rank for the number in the first argument. The third argument, *[order]*, provides a dropdown list from which you can select Descending (where the biggest is rank 1) or Ascending (where the smallest is rank 1). If you omit the third argument, RANK.EQ defaults to descending rank. If there are ties, the RANK.EQ function ranks each the same or equivalent (which is where the .EQ part of the function name comes from). If you want to average ties, you can use the RANK.AVE function. The RANK.EQ function is available in the DAX formula language as well as in the Excel worksheet; RANK.AVE is not.

- In the *number* argument of RANK.EQ, which expects a single number, you provide six numbers and make a function argument array operation that instructs the RANK.EQ function to deliver six ranks as the final result and then spill them down to the rows below.

- If you compare the SUM function, which you had to enter into a cell and then manually copy, and the RANK.EQ function, which automatically spilled its results down to the other rows, you can come to a useful conclusion about when formulas can spill their results and when they have to be manually copied. If a function is programmed to make an aggregate operation and deliver a single answer from many inputs, then you can only enter the formula to get a single answer; if copying is necessary, you must do it manually. On the other hand, if a function argument expects a single value and you give it multiple values, you make a function argument array operation that will cause the formula to spill the results and will not require that you manually copy the formula.

Example 9: Looking Up the Price for Invoicing by Using the XLOOKUP Worksheet Function

When creating invoices, it is common to have to look up product prices. Figure 12.13 shows the XLOOKUP worksheet function looking up the product Quad, finding a match in the third row of the Product column, and retrieving the price 43.95 from the third row of the Price column.

You can try this example on the worksheet named Ch12(13-16).

	A	B	C	D	E	F
2	Ex	**Goal:** Lookup product price using XLOOKUP function.				
3	#9	**Formula Type:** Lookup formula that delivers a number. Single input-output formula.				
4		**Formula Elements:** Equal sign, XLOOKUP function, cell reference, range of cells, text in quotes.				
6		**Invoicing Calculation:**				
8		**Product**	**Units**	**Price ($)**		**Formula in cell D9:**
9		Quad	144	43.95		=XLOOKUP(B9,B12:B15,D12:D15,"Not Found")
11		**Product**	**Flight Range (m)**	**Price ($)**	**Cost ($)**	**< == Lookup Table**
12		Aspen	25	24.95	13.47	
13		Carlota	22	26.95	12.67	
14		Quad	20	43.95	21.54	
15		Yanaki	30	27.95	14.81	

Figure 12.13 *Using the XLOOKUP worksheet function to look up prices for invoicing.*

Figure 12.14 shows the details for the XLOOKUP function's arguments. This is an example of a lookup formula that is also a single-input/single-output formula.

The XLOOKUP function is only in the Excel worksheet and is not available in other tools, such as Power Query's M code formula language or the Data Model's DAX formula language.

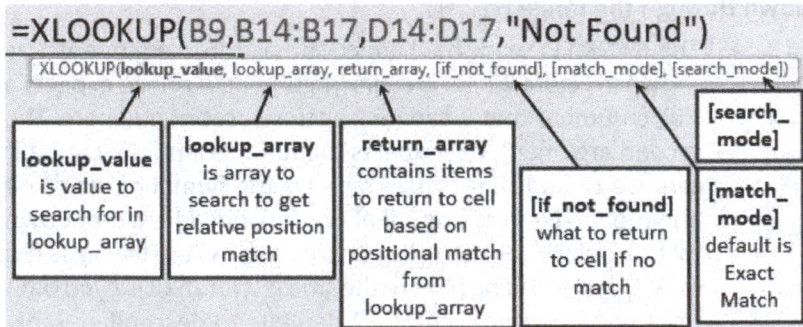

Figure 12.14 *There are six arguments in the worksheet lookup function XLOOKUP.*

These are the important takeaways from this first example of a lookup formula:

- *lookup_value* is the single item Quad from cell B9. XLOOKUP tries to find a Quad match in the *lookup_array* argument.

- XLOOKUP searches for Quad in the *lookup_array* Product column, in the range B12:B15. When XLOOKUP finds Quad in the third row, it internally records the relative position of the Quad as position 3.

- In the *return_array* argument, XLOOKUP searches through the Price column, in the range D12:D15, and uses the relative position 3 to retrieve the price 43.95 and then return it to cell D9.

- *lookup_array* and *return_array* must have the same number of rows (or number of columns) for XLOOKUP to work. If they do not, you get a #VALUE! error.

- The [*if_not_found*] argument lists the text "Not Found" (including the quotation marks). This is what is returned to cell D9 if there is no match for the *lookup value* in the *lookup array*. Try this test yourself: Type **Quad** followed by a space in cell B9, and you see that there is no match for these five characters in the Product column and that the formula returns "Not Found". If you do not enter an item into the [*if_not_found*] argument and there is no lookup value match in the lookup array, you will get an #N/A error. The [*if_not_found*] argument can contain text, numbers, formulas, or other values.

(...) 0 - Exact match
(...) -1 - Exact match or next smaller item
(...) 1 - Exact match or next larger item
(...) 2 - Wildcard character match

Figure 12.15 *Options for the [match_mode] argument in the XLOOKUP function.*

(...) 1 - Search first-to-last
(...) -1 - Search last-to-first
(...) 2 - Binary search (sorted ascending order)
(...) -2 - Binary search (sorted descending order)

Figure 12.16 *Options for the [search_mode] argument in the XLOOKUP function.*

- The [*match_mode*] argument provides a dropdown list of the different types of lookup modes, as shown in Figure 12.15. The default lookup match type is an exact match, which is what you did when you searched for exactly the four characters Quad. You will learn about the other match types in Chapter 14.

- The [*search_mode*] argument provides a dropdown list of the different types of lookup search modes, as shown in Figure 12.16. The default lookup search type is a first-to-last search, which is what you did when you searched through the Product column. You will learn about the other search modes in Chapter 14.

- The last three arguments have square brackets around them, which indicates that if you leave these arguments out, the defaults will kick in.

- When you use a lookup function such as XLOOKUP, and you are performing an exact match lookup from a lookup table, you can prevent typing errors and make your solution easy to use by implementing data validation on the cell containing the lookup value. Figure 12.13 shows that this was done on cell B9 in this example. (For a refresher on using data validation, see Example 4 in Chapter 9.)

Example 10: Looking Up All the Rows in a Column by Using the XLOOKUP Function

The XLOOKUP function can return a single item, all the rows in a column, or all the columns in a row. Figure 12.17 shows an example of looking up an entire column of row values and then adding them. The goal of the formula in cell H7 is to add all the values for the month in cell G7. XLOOKUP takes the single lookup value Feb and finds that it is in the second column position, in the range B6:E6; then, because the return array is a table with 4 columns and 11 rows, XLOOKUP returns the entire second column, with all 11 row values, to the SUM function so that it can add to get the correct Feb total of 160,301.25. This sort of lookup works only because there are four columns in the lookup array and four columns in the return array. The fact that there are 11 rows in the return array means you are doing a function argument array operation that forces the XLOOKUP function to return 11 values. However, these values do not spill into the cells; instead, they correctly spill into the SUM function, which makes an aggregate operation and delivers a single sum.

	A	B	C	D	E	F	G	H	I	J
2	Ex	Goal: Lookup a a Month Column, then Add.								
3	#10	Formula Type: Number Formula (that contains a lookup element). Scalar Array Formulas.								
4		Formula Elements: Equal Sign, SUM & XLOOKUP Worksheet Functions, Cell Reference, Range of Cells.								
6		Jan	Feb	Mar	Apr		Lookup Month	Feb Total		
7		21,704.52	10,672.77	11,987.75	11,654.43		Feb	160,301.25		
8		1,604.38	21,158.82	14,929.82	18,194.66					
9		3,536.33	7,226.97	13,059.04	25,213.06			Formula in cell H7:		
10		27,354.21	10,693.79	24,935.78	5,844.56			=SUM(XLOOKUP(G7,B6:E6,B7:E17))		
11		22,394.95	15,938.61	19,165.14	5,523.23					
12		2,820.34	22,778.17	12,240.00	10,999.83		Steps for calculation of =SUM(XLOOKUP(G7,B6:E6,B7:E17))			
13		11,432.23	4,272.76	19,785.72	4,032.27		1. XLOOKUP searches for "Feb" in column array B6:E6.			
14		16,217.27	21,835.95	24,855.78	9,270.93		Note: "Feb" is in the 2nd relative position,			
15		8,617.16	2,908.59	29,276.89	28,564.07		which is the 2nd column in the range B6:E6.			
16		2,095.04	28,853.64	27,587.91	7,965.32		=SUM(XLOOKUP(**"Feb"**,{"Jan",**"Feb"**,"Mar","Apr"},B7:E17))			
17		10,548.20	13,961.18	21,075.38	1,395.63		2. XLOOKUP looks for the 2nd column in the table array B7:E17,			
18							which has has 4 columns and 11 rows.			
19							XLOOKUP picks out the the second column and all 11 rows.			
20							=SUM({10672.77;21158.82;7226.97;10693.79;15938.61;			
21							22778.17;4272.76;21835.95;2908.59;28853.64;13961.18})			
22							4. Sum adds the 11 row values to get:			
23							160301.25			

Figure 12.17 *Using the XLOOKUP function to look up all the rows in a column.*

This is the first example you have seen of an array formula that does not spill into the cells. This is a scalar array formula, which is just a fancy way to say that it has an array operation inside the formula but delivers a single answer. This is also an example of a number formula (that contains a lookup element). Figure 12.17 lists the formula types and formula elements and describes the evaluation steps.

You can try this example on the worksheet named Ch12(17).

Example 11: Looking Up a List of Student Classes by Using the FILTER Function

In this book, you have already seen dynamic spilled array formulas that you enter into a single cell and that spill the results. This example shows a dynamic spilled array formula that you enter into a cell, and it spills, but then you need to copy the formula to other cells for new spilled results.

Figure 12.18 shows an example of a student data table in the range B7:D13. Figure 12.18 lists the formula types and formula elements and describes the evaluation process. The dynamic spilled array formula in cell F10 uses the FILTER array function. The arguments for FILTER are shown in Figure 12.19.

	A	B	C	D	E	F	G	H
2	Ex	**Goal:** List classes for each student.						
3	#11	**Formula Type:** Lookup formula that delivers text values. Dynamic spilled array formula that will be copied.						
4		**Formula Elements**: Equal sign, FILTER worksheet array function, absolute range of cells,						
5		comparative operator, relative cell reference.						
7		Student	Class	Grade		**List Classes For students:**		
8		Chantel Cann	Busn 101	3.1				
9		Chantel Cann	Busn 135	3.5		Chantel Cann	Ty Worthy	
10		Ty Worthy	Busn 135	3.5		Busn 101	Busn 135	
11		Ty Worthy	Busn 210	2.9		Busn 135	Busn 210	
12		Chantel Cann	Busn 216	3.4		Busn 216	ENGL 101	
13		Ty Worthy	ENGL 101	2.9				
14						**Formula entered into F10 & copied through F10:G10.**		
15						=FILTER($C$8:$C$13,$B$8:$B$13=F9)		
17		Steps for calculation of **=FILTER($C$8:$C$13,$B$8:$B$13=F9)** in cell F10:						
18		**1.** Second argumnet in FILTER funcion runs a logical test on the Student column and asks: Is student Chantel Cann?						
19		=FILTER($C$8:$C$13,						
20		{"Chantel Cann";"Chantel Cann";"Chantel Cann";"Ty Worthy";"Ty Worthy";"Ty Worthy"}="Chantel Cann")						
21		**2.** The Student column evaulates to TRUE for each row that where the student is "Chantel Cann".						
22		=FILTER($C$8:$C$13,**{TRUE;TRUE;TRUE;FALSE;FALSE;FALSE}**)						
23		**3.** FILTER sees the pattern of TRUE values and uses it to filter the Student column.						
24		=FILTER({**"Busn 135";"Busn 101";"Busn 216";**"ENGL 101";"Busn 135";"Busn 210"},						
25		**{TRUE;TRUE;TRUE;**FALSE;FALSE;FALSE})						
26		**4.** FILTER spilles the results down the rows: **Busn 101; Busn 135; Busn 216**						

Figure 12.18 *Using the FILTER function to look up a list of student classes.*

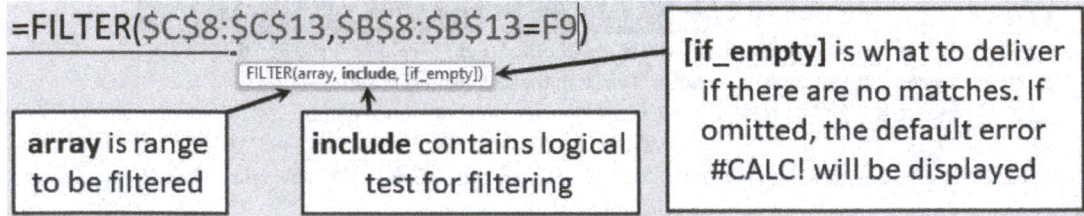

Figure 12.19 *Arguments for the FILTER worksheet function.*

The FILTER function is available only in the Excel worksheet, although similar functions are available in the DAX formula language (in Power Pivot and Power BI).

You can try this example on the worksheet named Ch12(18-19).

The FILTER array function can filter a table, a column, or a row based on one or more conditions. In this example, the FILTER function filters the Class column based on the student name in the Student column. Because the FILTER function sees the student name Chantel Cann in rows 1, 2, and 5 of the Student column, it knows to filter the Class column down to those corresponding rows. In cell F10, the spilled results are for the student Chantel Cann, but when you copy the formula from cell F10 to G10, the spilled results are for the student Ty Worthy. This is an example of a lookup formula that delivers text values and a dynamic spilled array formula that must be manually copied.

In this example, it is not possible to spill the formula to all six cells and avoid the manual copy process because the logical test based on both student names, =FILTER(C8:C13,B8:B13=F9:G9), would yield a rectangle of logical values in the second argument of FILTER that could not be interpreted correctly by FILTER. This is why you have to create the first spilled array formula in cell F10 using absolute ranges of cells and a relative cell reference before you copy the formula to cell G10.

Example 12: Using the SUMIFS Worksheet Function to Create a Sales and Costs Report by Product

Figure 12.20 shows a formula that is entered into cell H8 and copied to I8 to create a report for total sales and costs from the sales transaction table in the range B7:E22. This figure also lists the formula types and formula elements and describes the evaluation process.

You can try this example on the worksheet named Ch12(20-21).

	A	B	C	D	E	F	G	H	I	J
2	Ex	**Goal:** Create formula report for total sales and total costs.								
3	#12	**Formula Type:** Number formula. Dynamic spilled array formula that will be copied.								
4		**Formula Elements:** Equal sign, SUMIFS worksheet function, relative range of cells,								
5		absolute range of cells, absolute cell references with spilled range operator (#)								
7		Date	Product	Sales ($)	Cost ($)		Product	Total Sales ($)	Total Costs ($)	
8		8/12/20	Quad	4,024.80	2,092.32		Aspen	5,651.71	3,023.87	
9		8/12/20	Aspen	1,143.90	686.34		Carlota	7,678.79	3,980.87	
10		8/12/20	Sunshine	1,161.50	569.64		Quad	10,328.71	5,150.48	
11		8/12/20	Yanaki	1,640.00	770.80		Sunshine	5,543.37	3,019.35	
12		8/12/20	Carlota	2,616.25	1,099.00		Yanaki	8,070.18	4,293.04	
13		8/13/20	Quad	3,144.75	1,415.40					
14		8/13/20	Aspen	1,046.25	606.75					
15		8/13/20	Sunshine	1,671.60	986.16		**Formula entered into H8 & copied to I8.**			
16		8/13/20	Yanaki	1,632.00	979.20		=SUMIFS(D8:D22,$C$8:$C$22,$G$8#)			
17		8/13/20	Carlota	1,171.10	702.66					
18		8/17/20	Quad	3,159.16	1,642.76					
19		8/17/20	Aspen	3,461.56	1,730.78					
20		8/17/20	Sunshine	2,710.27	1,463.55					
21		8/17/20	Yanaki	4,798.18	2,543.04					
22		8/17/20	Carlota	3,891.44	2,179.21					
24		Steps for calculation of =SUMIFS(D8:D22,$C$8:$C$22,$G$8#) in cell H8:								
25		**1.** Second argument of SUMIFS evaluates the list of criteria for adding.								
26		This is a function argument array calculation, where SUMIFS adds to get total for each product.								
27		=SUMIFS(D8:D22,$C$8:$C$22,{"Aspen";"Carlota";"Quad";"Sunshine";"Yanaki"})								
28		**2.** SUMIFS uses the criteria to get a total for each product, then spills the values down the rows.								
29		**5651.71; 7678.79; 10328.71; 5543.37; 8070.18**								

Figure 12.20 *Using the SUMIFS worksheet function to create a sales and costs report by product.*

In this example, you use the SUMIFS worksheet function for the first time in this book. The arguments for this function are shown in Figure 12.21. The SUMIFS function is only available in the Excel worksheet and not in other tools, such as Power Query's M code formula language or the Data Model's DAX formula language. SUMIFS allows you to sum numbers with one or more conditions or criteria. For example, in cell H8 in Figure 12.20, the SUMIFS worksheet function is not adding all the numbers from the Sales column (D8:D22); instead, it is adding just the sales for the Aspen product from the cells D9, D14, and D19. This is an example of a number formula and a dynamic spilled array formula that must be manually copied.

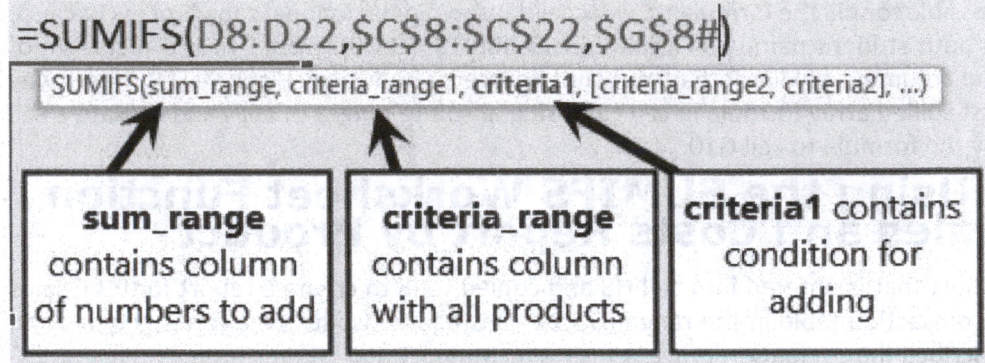

Figure 12.21 *Arguments for the SUMIFS function.*

The following formula elements in this example are noteworthy:

- The SUMIFS function is commonly used for adding with one or more conditions. In this example, you add with a single condition using the arguments *criteria_range1* and *criteria1*. The *criteria_range1* argument contains the column with all the product names, and the *criteria1* argument contains the specific condition used to determine which numbers to add. Even though you put multiple product names into the *criteria1* argument, and it might seem like you are adding with many conditions, for each one of the product names, the SUMIFS function adds with only one condition. For example, for the product Aspen, SUMIFS adds with the single condition Aspen to get the correct sum 5,651.71. Similarly, for the single condition Carlota, SUMIFS calculates the correct sum 5,651.71. (Later in this book, you will see examples of adding with two or more conditions.)

- The formula is entered into cell H8, where it spills the sales totals down the rows. Then the formula is copied to cell I8, where the formula spills a new set of numbers for the cost totals. This works because you enter the relative range of cells, D8:D17, which points to the sales column, into the *sum_range* argument of SUMIFS. When you copy the formula one column to the right, into cell I8, the range moves one column to the right, from the range D8:D17 (the Sales column) to E8:E17 (the Cost column).

- When you copy the formula, you have to lock both the Product column and the unique list of product names that is spilling from cell G8 so that both the sales and cost calculations can pick out the correct product names when they make the conditional sum calculation.

Example 13: Conducting a Customer Credit Analysis with the AND Function and Mixed Cell References

Businesses around the world extend credit to customers to enable those customers to buy goods immediately and pay for them later. Before a business extends credit, it must assess whether a customer is creditworthy. There are many ways to determine if a customer is reliable, and many different rules can be used. Figure 12.22 shows a situation where a company uses two different rules. The first rule looks at the customer's sales from the previous year and a credit rating issued from agency 1; the second rule uses the customer's same previous-year sales but looks at a second credit rating issued by a different agency. If either of the rules evaluates to TRUE, the business will extend credit to the customer.

This example uses a logical formula that is also a single-input/single-output formula. Figure 12.22 lists the formula type and formula elements and describes the evaluation process.

You can try this example on the worksheet named Ch12(22-24).

	A	B	C	D	E	F	G
2	Ex	**Goal:** Determine whether to extend credit to a customer based on last year's sales and a credit rating.					
3	**#13**	There are two rules that the company uses.					
4		**Formula Type:** Logical formula. Single input-output formula.					
5		**Formula Elements:** Equal sign, AND worksheet function, comparative operators (>=, >), mixed cell reference					
6		with column locked, absolute cell reference, relative cell reference, mixed cell reference with row locked.					
8		**Hurdles >>**	Sales	Rating1	Rating2		
9			50,000	2.5	4.5		
11				Customer Credit Analysis For Accounts Receivable			
12		Customer	Sales	Credit Rating 1	Credit Rating 2	Extend Credit Rule #1: Sales>=$50,000.00 Credit Rating 1>2.5	Extend Credit Rule #2: Sales>=$50,000.00 Credit Rating 2>4.5
13		Customer 1	90,550	5	7.4	TRUE	TRUE
14		Customer 2	41,255	5	5.9	FALSE	FALSE
15		Customer 3	56,241	3.3	4.4	TRUE	FALSE
16		Customer 4	69,920	1.2	2.4	FALSE	FALSE
18						**Formula entered into F13 & copied through F13:G16:**	
19						=AND($C13>=$C$9,D13>D$9)	
21		**Steps for calculation of =AND($C13>=$C$9,D13>D$9) in cell F13:**					
22		**1.** AND evaluates the first logical test.					
23		=AND(**$C13>=$C$9**,D13>D$9) ➔ =AND(**90550>=50000**,D13>D$9) ➔ =AND(**TRUE**,D13>D$9)					
24		**2.** AND evaluates the second logical test.					
25		=AND(TRUE,**D13>D$9**) ➔ =AND(TRUE,**5>2.5**) ➔ =AND(TRUE,**TRUE**)					
26		**3.** Because all the logical tests in the arguments of the AND function are TRUE, AND reports a TRUE.					
27		**TRUE**					

Figure 12.22 *Using the AND function and mixed cell references for customer credit analysis.*

In Figure 12.22, you can see that customer 1 and customer 2 will have credit extended to them. This figure shows the formula that you can enter into cell F13 and then manually copy through the rectangular range F13:G16. When you manually copy a formula through a rectangular range, you cannot complete the task with a single copy action. You must copy it one direction, stop, and then begin a second copy action with the selected range, using this process:

1. Use your angry rabbit cursor to copy cell F13 to G13 and then release the mouse.

2. Copy the highlighted cells down through the range F13:G16.

To implement this example as an Excel worksheet formula, you need to learn about the AND worksheet function, comparison operators, and mixed cell references. These are some of the basics you need to understand:

- The AND worksheet function runs an AND logical test, which requires that all logical tests are met before the AND function will deliver a TRUE value as the final result. When running two logical tests in the AND function, these are the four possibilities:
  - FALSE, FALSE
  - TRUE, FALSE
  - FALSE, TRUE
  - TRUE, TRUE (and this is the only possibility that yields a TRUE from the AND function)
- Figure 12.22 shows the evaluation process for customer 1, rule 1 in cell F13, where the AND function contains two TRUE values and therefore delivers a TRUE as the final output from the AND function.
- Because the AND function looks at multiple items and delivers a single answer, it is similar to aggregate functions, like the SUM function, which cannot spill results. In this example, it means you must enter the formula into a single cell and then manually copy it to the remaining cells. It is not possible to directly spill results from the AND function.

Note: Throughout my years of teaching about array formulas, I have often gotten the question "Why can't I use the AND function for an array operation?" The AND function can never spill an array because it is programmed to take multiple inputs and always deliver a single answer. In Chapter 13, when you learn about the FILTER function, you will see that there is a simple Boolean array operation workaround in which you need to create an AND logical test.

- Figure 12.23 details the arguments of the AND worksheet function and shows that this function can have up to 255 logical tests. However, it is rare to see more than 5 or 6 logical tests in an AND function.

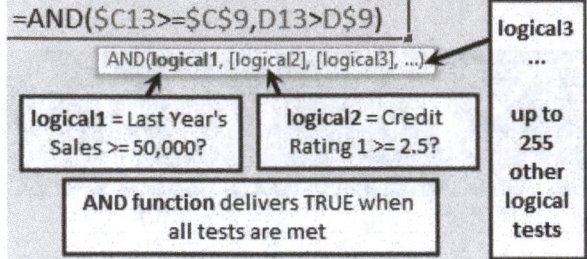

Figure 12.23 *AND worksheet function to run an AND logical test and deliver a single Boolean result.*

- In this AND logical test, you use two comparison operators. The greater-than-or-equal-to comparison operator (>=) must be entered as two successive characters: the greater-than operator, >, and then the equal sign operator, =. The greater-than operator is just the single character >. The difference is that with the >= operator, for a customer's previous year's sales of exactly 50,000, you would get a TRUE value, but with the > operator, you would get a FALSE. The AND function formula in this example uses the four different types of cell references: relative, absolute, mixed with column locked, and mixed with row locked (see Figure 12.24).

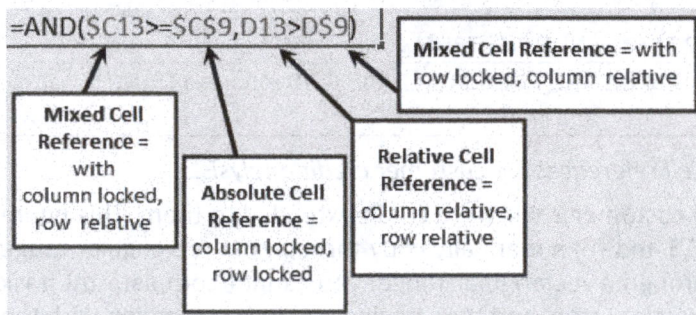

Figure 12.24 *Four types of cell references.*

- To toggle between the four different types of cell references—relative, absolute, mixed with column locked, and mixed with row locked—you can use the F4 key. You first learned about the F4 key in Chapter 8, when you learned to use it to convert a relative cell reference to an absolute cell reference. In this example, you can use it to toggle to any of the four types of cell references. The trick is that your insertion point cursor must be touching some part of the cell reference that you want to toggle. Then you can press the F4 key to move from one type of reference to the next. If you toggle too far, just keep pressing the F4 key until you toggle back to the one you want. The F4 key is sort of like a merry-go-round that keeps circling around and around.

Note: If you use the F4 key in situations other than for toggling cell references, Excel repeats that last action you performed.

- For the mixed cell reference with the column locked and the row left relative, $C13, the reference is locked as it is copied across the columns but allowed to move relatively when it is copied down across the rows. Specifically, the column C reference is locked so that when it is copied across the columns, the column C reference will not move, but the row 13 reference is left to move throughout the copy action so that when the formula is copied from row 13 down to row 14, the 13 moves to 14 so you get $C14. In Figure 12.22, you can see that $C13 references the customer 1 sales number, and when the formula is copied to row 14, the reference moves to $C14 to correctly point to the customer 2 sales number. However, when the formula is copied from column F to column G, the reference to the customer 1 sales number correctly remains locked on $C13.

- For the absolute cell reference, $C$9, the reference is locked in both directions so that the formula will correctly retrieve the sales hurdle number in every cell.

- For the relative cell reference, D13, the cell reference is allowed to move relatively, always looking two cells to the left of the cell containing the formula to correctly retrieve the customer rating.

- For the mixed cell reference with the row locked and the column left relative, D$9, the reference is locked as it is copied down across the rows but allowed to move relatively when it is copied across the columns. This is the correct reference to use to get the rating hurdle for each cell that the formula is copied to.

Example 14: Knowing When Mixed Cell References Are Required

If you are learning about mixed cell reference for the first time, I must report to you that this formula feature is just about the hardest formula feature to learn—at least that is what I have witnessed in over two decades of teaching Excel.

The good news is that because of the Microsoft 365 Excel calculation engine and dynamic spilled array formulas, there are not many situations that require mixed cell references anymore. It used to be that there were hundreds of applications for mixed cell references, but there are not very many of them today. There are, however, two common situations where mixed cell references are still required:

- With functions like AND and SUM that are not programmed to spill results
- With logical formulas for conditionally formatting a row

Figure 12.25 shows an example of a situation where mixed cell references used to be required but are not required now. This figure shows a common cross-tabulated report that adds the units from a transaction table based on the two conditions product and sales rep. The top formula is much more complicated to create because you have to carefully consider what type of cell references are required in the formula, and then you have to manually copy the formula with the two-step manual processes through the range G9:I11. The bottom formula does not require that you consider the different types of cell references or manually copy the formula. You just create the formula in cell F13 and press Enter, and you are done!

You can try this example on the worksheet named Ch12(25).

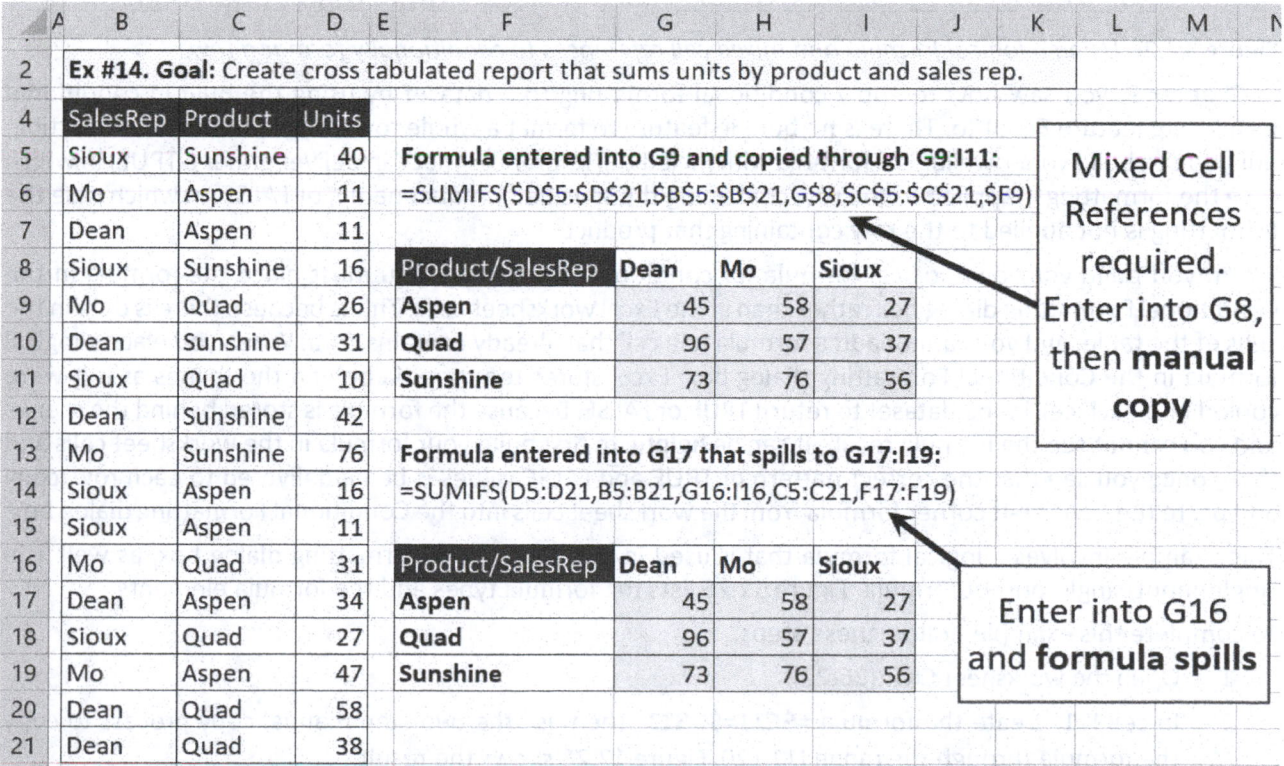

Figure 12.25 *A cross-tabulated report that adds the units from a transaction table based on two conditions: product and sales rep.*

Example 15: Conditionally Formatting a Row with a Logical Formula and Mixed Cell References

A common goal for visualizing data is to add conditional formatting to records in a dataset based on a condition in a cell. For example, Figure 12.26 shows that the product name Quad was entered into cell G11, and as a result, the records for the Quad product in the dataset are formatted with yellow fill color. If you change the product name from Quad to Sunshine, the conditional formatting changes to highlight the Sunshine records instead of the Quad records.

	A	B	C	D	E	F	G	H	I	J	K	L
2	Ex	**Goal:** Conditionally format row in table based on condition in cell G11.										
3	#15	**Formula Type:** Logical formula for conditional formatting dialog box. Single input-output formula.										
4		**Formula Elements:** Equal sign, mixed cell reference with column locked,										
5		comparative operators (=), absolute cell reference.										
7				**Formula entered into I11 and then manually copied through I11:L20:**								
8				=$C11=$G$11								
10		Date	Product	Sales ($)	Cost ($)		Product					
11		8/12/20	Quad	4,024.80	2,092.32		Quad		TRUE	TRUE	TRUE	TRUE
12		8/12/20	Aspen	1,143.90	686.34				FALSE	FALSE	FALSE	FALSE
13		8/12/20	Sunshine	1,161.50	569.64				FALSE	FALSE	FALSE	FALSE
14		8/12/20	Yanaki	1,640.00	770.80				FALSE	FALSE	FALSE	FALSE
15		8/12/20	Carlota	2,616.25	1,099.00				FALSE	FALSE	FALSE	FALSE
16		8/13/20	Quad	3,144.75	1,415.40				TRUE	TRUE	=$C16=$G$11	
17		8/13/20	Aspen	1,046.25	606.75				FALSE	FALSE	FALSE	FALSE
18		8/13/20	Sunshine	1,671.60	986.16				FALSE	FALSE	FALSE	FALSE
19		8/13/20	Yanaki	1,632.00	979.20				FALSE	FALSE	FALSE	FALSE
20		8/13/20	Carlota	3,891.44	2,179.21				FALSE	FALSE	FALSE	FALSE

Figure 12.26 *Using a logical formula and mixed cell references to conditionally format a row..*

In Chapter 9, you saw how to apply conditional formatting to a dataset by using the built-in conditional formatting feature Equal To. There is no built-in feature to format a whole row using conditional formatting, but you can build your own logical formula with mixed cell references that can deliver either a TRUE, in which case the formatting is applied to the row containing the specified product name, or FALSE, in which case the formatting is not applied to the row containing that product.

When you build your own logical formula for conditional formatting, you must place the formula in the Conditional Formatting dialog box rather than in the Excel worksheet cells. This is because there is data in the cells of the table, and you cannot add a formula to a cell that already contains data. When you place a logical formula in the Conditional Formatting dialog box, Excel stores the formula behind the scenes as if it were copied into each cell in the dataset to return TRUE or FALSE. Because the formula is stored behind the scenes and you cannot see the formula result, it can be helpful to first build your formula in the worksheet cells and then, once you see that the correct pattern of TRUE and FALSE values is being delivered to each row, copy and paste the upper-left corner formula from the worksheet cells into the Conditional Formatting dialog box.

This example involves a logical formula that is used in the Conditional Formatting dialog box, as well as a single-input/single-output formula. Figure 12.26 lists the formula types and the formula elements.

To complete this example, follow these steps:

1. Open the worksheet Ch12(26-27).

2. In cell I11, create the formula **=$C11=$G$11**. Then use the two-step manual copy process to copy the formula through the range I11:L20. Figure 12.26 shows the result.

Note: You should see the correct pattern of TRUE values only in the rows that contain the product that is listed in cell G11. Press the F2 key to put various cells into edit mode and check to see that the cell references are locked correctly. Figure 12.26 shows edit mode for cell K16.

3. Put cell I11 (the cell in the upper-left corner of the logical formula range) in edit mode. Highlight the whole formula in edit mode (=$C11:$G$11) and then press Ctrl+C to copy the formula.

4. Select the range B11:E20 with the active cell as cell B11 (the cell in the upper-left corner of the proper dataset).

Note: If your active cell in the selected dataset does not directly correspond to the formula you copied from the logical formula range, this conditional formatting trick will not work.

5. Select the Home tab of the Ribbon, go to the Style group, click the Conditional Formatting dropdown arrow, and select New Rule.

6. In the New Formatting Rule dialog box that appears, under Select a Rule Type, click Use a Formula to Determine Which Cells to Format (see Figure 12.27).

Note: Although Figure 12.27 shows the Edit Formatting Rule dialog box, the first time this box appears, it is called the New Formatting Rule dialog box. Every time you open it thereafter, its title is Edit Formatting Rule.

7. Under Edit the Rule Description, click the Format Values Where This Formula Is True textbox.

8. Press Ctrl+V to paste the formula.

9. Click the Format button.

10. In the Format Cells dialog box that appears, use the Fill tab to select yellow fill.

11. Click the OK button in the Format Cells dialog box.

12. Click the OK button in the New Formatting Rule dialog box.

Note: If you need to edit the formula or formatting later, go to Home tab of the Ribbon, find the Style group, and from the Conditional Formatting dropdown, select Manage Rule to open the Conditional Formatting Rules Manager.

13. Test your solution by changing the product name in cell G11.

14. Delete the formulas and clear the formatting from the range I11:L20. Theses formulas helped you create the solution but have no effect on the conditional formatting for the dataset.

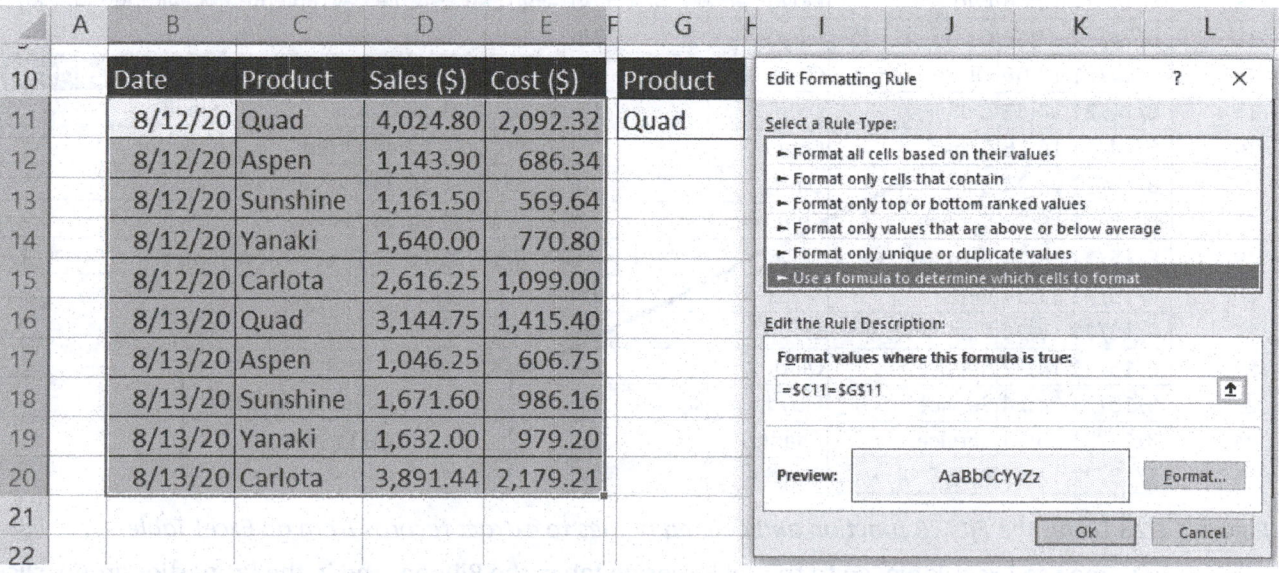

Figure 12.27 *Mixed cell reference are required when you conditionally format a whole row.*

Example 16: Extracting Records from an Excel Table with the FILTER Function and Defined Names

Extracting records from a table is a common task when you want to analyze a subset of records from a dataset. For example, in Figure 12.28, the call records for the call rep Floyd have been extracted into the range G15:J19. Your goal in this example is to build a solution so that a user can enter a call rep name into cell G9 and instantly see the extracted call records for that cell rep. In this example, you will also learn about the worksheet references for Excel Tables and defined names.

This example uses a dynamic spilled array lookup formula that can extract and display different types of data. Figure 12.28 lists the formula types and formula elements.

To complete this example, follow these steps:

1. Select the worksheet named Ch12(28-30).

2. Select cell G9.

3. To create a defined name, click in the name box and type **CallRepCondition** and then press Enter. The defined name you create in this step represents cell G9 and can be used throughout the workbook to refer to that cell.

4. To convert the proper dataset to an Excel Table, select one cell in the dataset and press Ctrl+T. In the Create Table dialog box that appears, make sure the My Table Has Headers checkbox is checked and click OK.

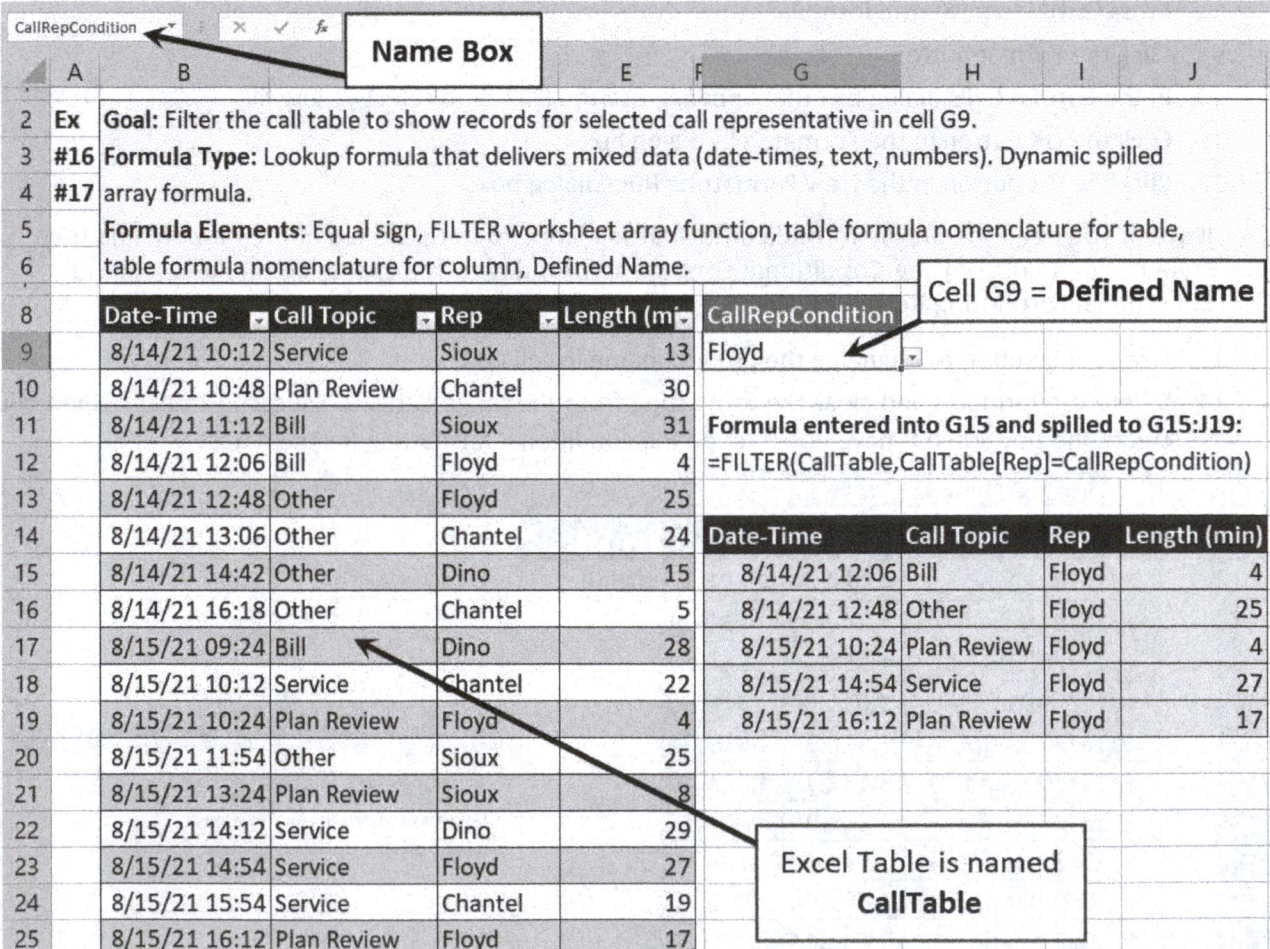

Figure 12.28 *Using the FILTER function and defined names to extract records from an Excel Table.*

5. To name the Excel Table, go to the Table Design tab in the Ribbon, and in the Properties group, click in the Table Name textbox, type the name **CallTable**, and then press Enter.

6. To create the field names for the record extract area, select cell G14 and type an equal sign. Then, using your selection cursor, select the field names in the Excel Table. When you do this, you should see the array formula =CallTable[#Headers], which is the table formula nomenclature for the field names in the Excel Table. When you press Enter, the field names spill to the right. (This formula is not pictured in Figure 12.28.)

7. In cell G15, create the formula **=FILTER(CallTable,CallTable[Rep]=CallRepCondition)**. When you are creating this formula, as you type the names of the references, notice that the names appear in the formula dropdown list, and you can select the correct reference after typing only the first few letters of the reference. For the column reference, type the table name first and then type an open square bracket, the field name, and a close square bracket. Figure 12.29 shows the FILTER function with the correct references.

Note: The way that this formula filters is by checking each row to see if the call rep name in cell G9 is equal to the call rep name in the Rep column. If you evaluate the formula, you will see this in step 4: =FILTER(CallTable,{FALSE;FALSE;FALSE;TRUE;TRUE;FALSE;FALSE; FALSE;FALSE;FALSE;TRUE;FALSE;FALSE;FALSE;TRUE;FALSE;TRUE}). It is from the TRUE and FALSE values that the FILTER functions knows which rows to display in the final spill.

8. When you are done creating the formula, press Enter to spill the formula into the cells.

9. Test your solution by changing the call rep name in cell G9.

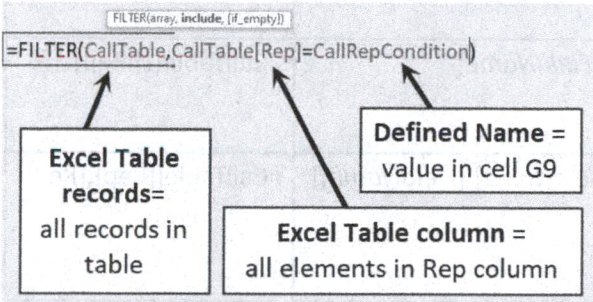

Figure 12.29 *Table formula nomenclature and defined names used in the FILTER function.*

Defined Names, Excel Tables, and the Name Manager

In this example, you have seen two types of named references: table formula nomenclature and defined names. As shown in Figure 12.29, these named references can make a formula easier to read and understand. Named references can also be easier to use in formulas because you can access them in any cell in a workbook by typing the first few letters of the name and then selecting the full name from the formula dropdown list. To see a full list of all named references in the workbook in this example, go to the Formula tab in the Ribbon, and in the Defined Name group, click the Name Manager button. You can also press Ctrl+F3 to open the Name Manager dialog box. In the Name Manager dialog box, you can create, edit, and delete defined names and edit the Excel Table names.

Note: When you name objects such as Excel Tables and defined names, you are not allowed to use spaces and other characters, including * /+- ( ) ^ < >+& % ~ ` |] [} { @ " ; : , ' $ # !.

Here are a couple more notes about named references:

- **Defined names:** A defined name can be used to reference a single cell, a range of cells, or even multiple noncontiguous ranges. Defined names are absolute references by default but can be changed in the Name Manager dialog box (which you open by pressing Ctrl+F3). Defined names can be used throughout an Excel workbook to reference those cells. Defined names can be used in all features in Excel except for Power Pivot. Defined names do not automatically expand and contract when new data is added, as an Excel Table does. If a defined name range changes, you must manually edit the range in the Name Manager dialog box. The most common use for defined names is when you have a single formula element, like the CallRepCondition defined name created in this example.

Note: If you copy a worksheet that contains a defined name and place it in the same workbook that you copied it from, a duplicate defined name is created that will work only on the copied sheet. The original defined name can be accessed anywhere in the workbook and is said to have *workbook scope*; the copied defined name is said to have *worksheet scope*. If you open the Name Manager dialog box, you can see the scope for each defined name listed.

- **Table formula nomenclature:** Table formula nomenclature is used when referencing a proper dataset that has been converted to an Excel Table. Table 12.3 shows a list of the table elements and the syntax for the table formula nomenclature for each of them. Table formula nomenclature can be used in any feature in an Excel workbook. The big advantage of using the Excel Table feature is that when new columns or rows are added to an Excel Table, the table formula nomenclature references automatically include the new data in the references.

Table 12.3 Table Formula Nomenclature for the Different Elements in an Excel Table

Table Element	Syntax	Example
Full table	*Table*[#All]	=CallTable[#All]
All records	*Table*	=CallTable
Field name	*Table*[#Headers]	=CallTable[#Headers]
Column (which is locked when it is copied down across rows and moves relatively as it is copied to the side across the columns)	*Table*[*FieldName*]	=CallTable[Rep]
Relative cell reference (where the implicit intersection operator works only when the reference is parallel to the column)	*Table*[@*FieldName*]	=CallTable[@Rep]
Absolute column reference (which you can lock by using the colon operator between two field names and placing that inside square brackets)	*Table*[[*FieldName*]:[*FieldName*]]	=CallTable[[Rep]:[Rep]]
Total row (to access the totals in the last row)	*Table*[#Totals]	=CallTable[#Totals]

Example 17: Conditional Formatting for Dynamic Spilled Array Formulas

In Example 16, you created a dynamic spilled array formula to extract records based on a condition. However, when you change the condition in cell G9, the size of the spilled array changes. How do you format a table that can expand and contract so that only the spilled cells have formatting applied? This sound like a job for conditional formatting based on the logical test "Is the cell not empty?" If a cell is not empty, the logical test evaluates to TRUE, and the formatting is applied; if the cell is empty, the logical test evaluates to FALSE, and the formatting is not applied.

This is an example of a logical formula that is used in the Conditional Formatting dialog box, and it is also a single-input/single-output formula. Figure 12.30 lists the formula types and formula elements.

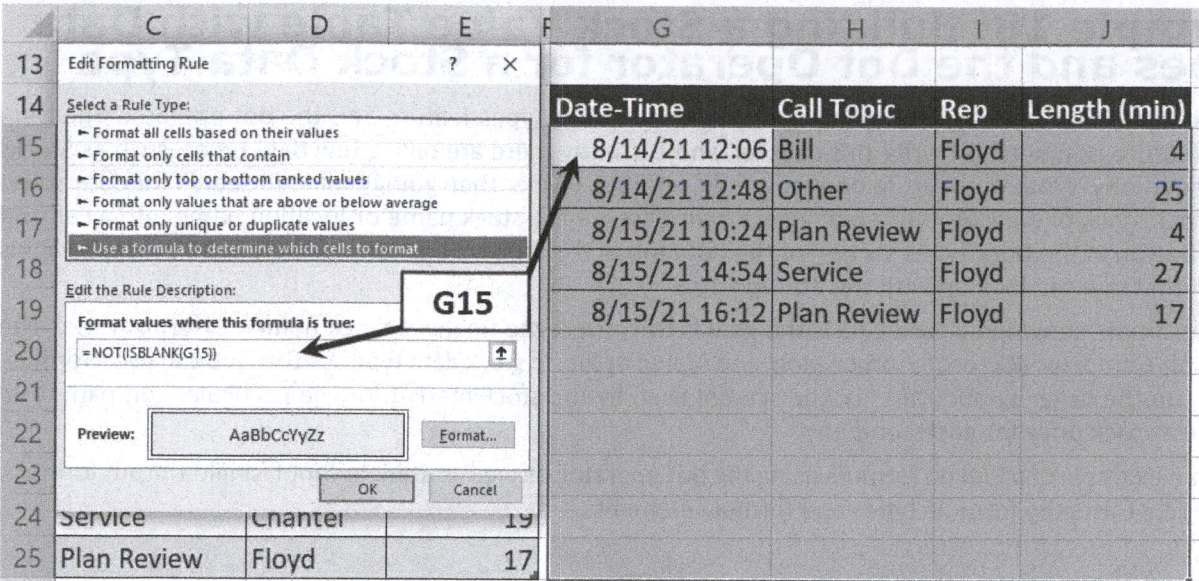

Figure 12.30 *Conditional formatting for dynamic spilled array formulas.*

To complete this example, follow these steps:

1. Select the worksheet named Ch12(28-30).

2. With G15 as the active cell, select the worksheet range G15:J25. This range will accommodate the maximum number of spilled call rep records for this dataset. When using conditional formatting on a spilled array, the number of cells you highlight for the conditional formatting range should accommodate the maximum number of potential extracted records.

3. Go to the Home tab of the Ribbon, and in the Style group, click the Conditional Formatting dropdown arrow and select New Rule.

4. In the New Formatting Rule dialog box that appears, under Select a Rule Type, click Use a Formula to Determine Which Cells to Format.

    Note: Recall from earlier in this chapter that although I show the Edit Formatting Rule dialog box here, you will actually see the title New Formatting Rule the first time you open this dialog box.

5. Under Edit the Rule Description, click the Format Values Where This Formula Is True textbox.

6. Create the logical formula **=NOT(ISBLANK(G15))**. If you use your selection cursor to select cell G15 while in the textbox, the cell reference appears in the formula as an absolute cell reference, which is not what you want. You want a relative cell reference. Press the F4 key to toggle to a relative cell reference.

7. Click the Format button.

8. In the Format Cells dialog box that appears, in the Fill tab, select a green fill. Then go to the Border tab and click the Outline button.

9. Click the OK button in the Format Cells dialog box.

10. Click the OK button in the New Formatting Rule dialog box.

    Note: If you need to edit the formula or formatting later, go to Home tab of the Ribbon, find the Style group, and from the Conditional Formatting dropdown, select Manage Rule to open the Conditional Formatting Rules Manager.

11. Test your solution by changing the product name in cell G9.

Example 18: Building a Stock Value Table with Data Types and the Dot Operator for a Stock Data Type

This example shows you the brand-new Microsoft 365 Data Types feature and the dot operator. The Data Types feature is in beta as I write this chapter, and currently there are only a few data types, such as Stocks and Geography. What this feature does is simply amazing. Rather than going online to search for data about a financial stock or a geographic area, you can simply type the stock name or location name into a cell and click a button in the Data Types section of the Data tab of the Ribbon; the cell instantly populates with fields of data that you can look up with the dot operator.

In the example shown in Figure 12.31, the goal is to convert the financial stock names Caterpillar Inc., The Coca-Cola Company, Microsoft Corporation, and Alphabet Inc. to stock data types so that you can use a formula to look up the ticker symbol (that is, the symbol used by the stock market for the particular company) and the latest stock price for each company.

This is an example of a lookup formula using the dot operator, as well as a single-input/single-output formula. Figure 12.31 lists the formula types and formula elements.

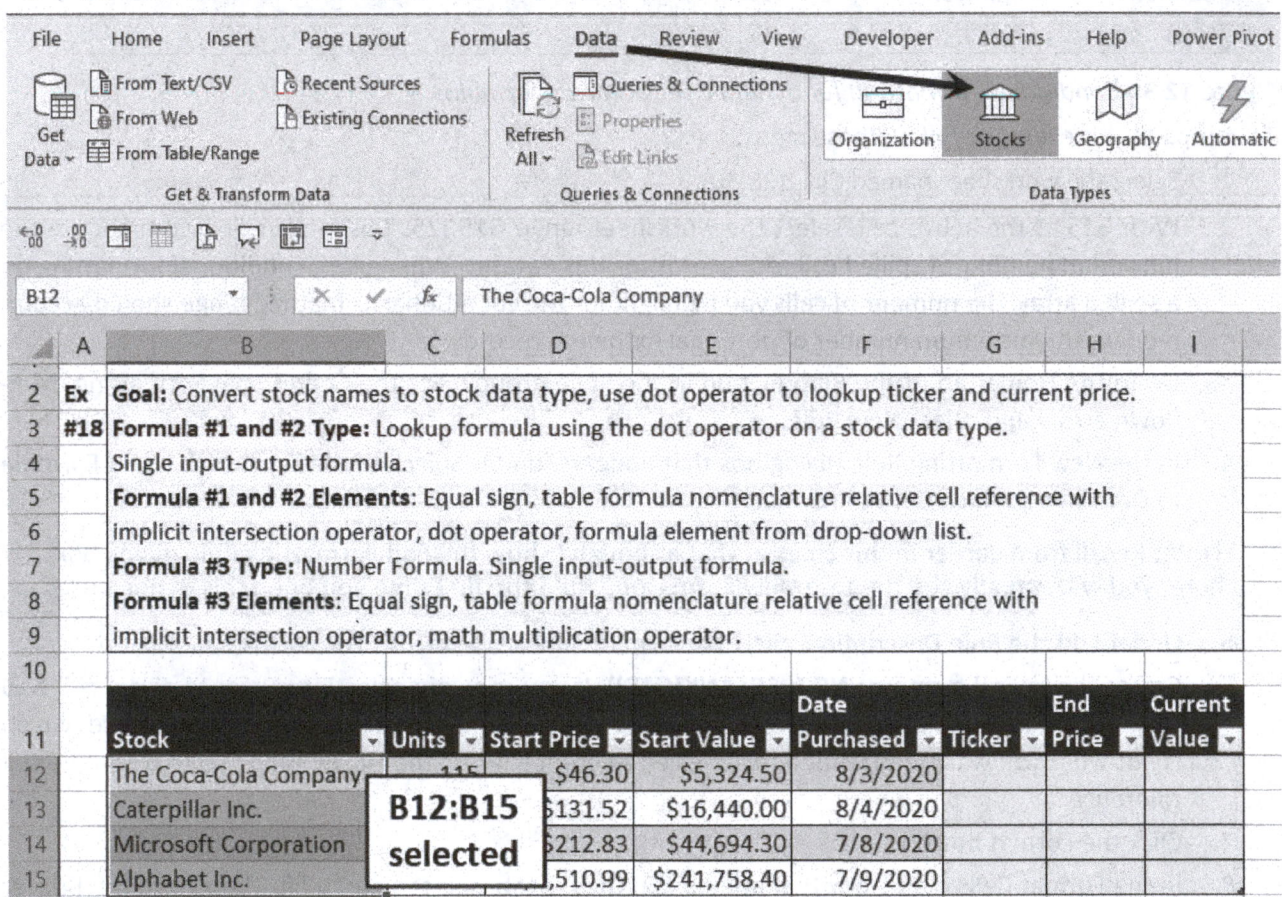

Figure 12.31 *Building a stock value table with data types and the dot operator for a stock data type.*

To complete this example, follow these steps:

1. Open the worksheet named Ch12(31-33).

2. To convert a column of stock names to the Stocks data type, select the range B12:B15 in the Stock column in the Excel Table.

3. Go to the Data tab of the Ribbon, and in the Data Types group, click the Stocks button (refer to Figure 12.31). As shown in Figure 12.32, the names of the companies are converted to Stocks data types. Each one has a financial market symbol on the left side of the cell, followed by the full name of the stock company, and, in parentheses, the name of the stock exchange that the stock is traded on, a colon, and the ticker symbol for the stock.

4. As shown in Figure 12.32, in cell G12 (the first cell in the Ticker column), type an equal sign and select the first cell in the Stock column. After Excel inserts the table formula nomenclature for a relative cell reference, type a dot (period). Because the Stock column contains a Stocks data type, the dot operator opens a dropdown list of all the fields that are available in the stock record that are stored in the cell. Scroll down (using the ArrowDown key for speed) and select the ticker symbol field. (Once this field is highlighted in blue, you can double-click with your mouse or use the Tab key to insert the ticker symbol after the dot operator.) You end up with the formula =[@Stock].[Ticker symbol].

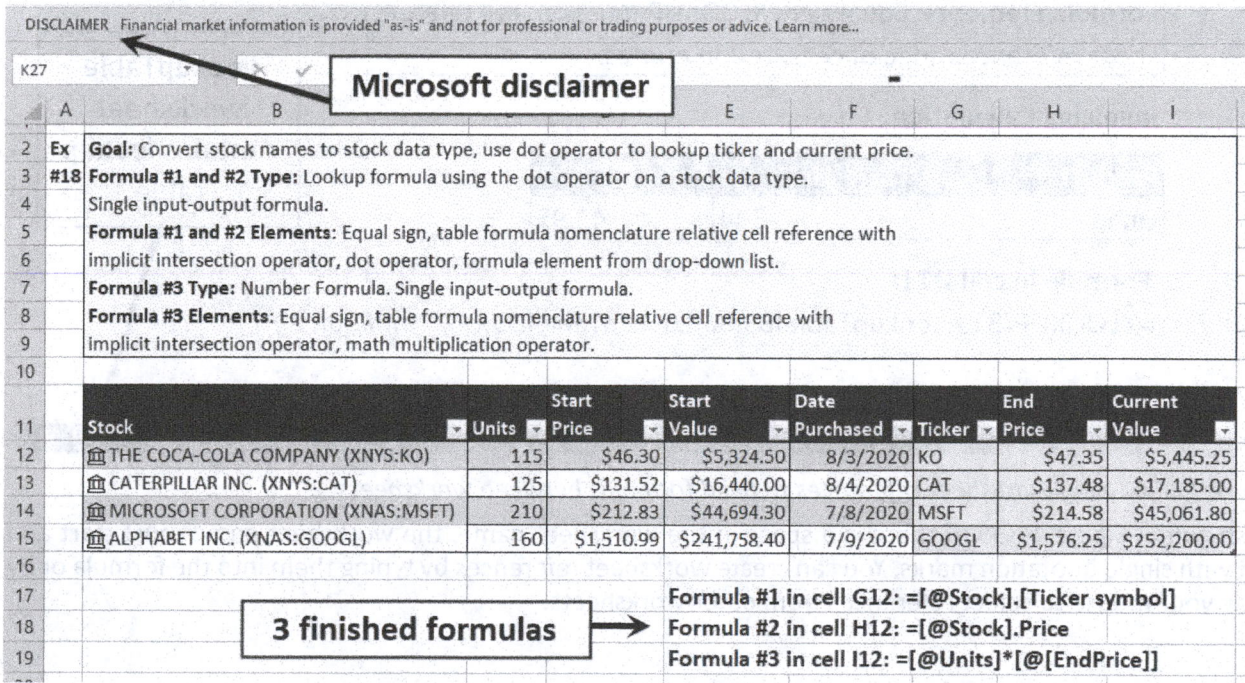

	Stock	Units	Start Price	Start Value	Date Purchased	Ticker	End Price	Current Value
11								
12	🏛 THE COCA-COLA COMPANY (XNYS:KO)	115	$46.30	$5,324.50	8/3/2020	=[@Stock].		
13	🏛 CATERPILLAR INC. (XNYS:CAT)	125	$131.52	$16,440.00	8/4/2020			
14	🏛 MICROSOFT CORPORATION (XNAS:MSFT)	210	$212.83	$44,694.30	7/8/2020			
15	🏛 ALPHABET INC. (XNAS:GOOGL)	160	$1,510.99	$241,758.40	7/9/2020			

Dropdown list fields: Name, Official name, Open, P/E, Previous close, Price, Price (Extended hours), Shares outstanding, Ticker symbol, Volume, Volume average, Year incorporated

Figure 12.32 *With the Stocks data type in the range B12:B15, you can use the dot operator to look up stock data.*

5. With the formula =[@Stock].[Ticker symbol] in cell G12, press Enter to populate the stock ticker formula into the column. (This is an Excel Table, so formulas automatically copy down the column after you press Enter.) Together, the Stocks data type and the dot operator allow you to look up the stock ticker symbol (which is the abbreviation used on the stock market for that stock).

6. As shown in Figure 12.33, create the formulas for the End Price column and the Current Value column.

DISCLAIMER Financial market information is provided "as-is" and not for professional or trading purposes or advice. Learn more...

Microsoft disclaimer

K27

	A	B			E	F	G	H	I
2	Ex	**Goal:** Convert stock names to stock data type, use dot operator to lookup ticker and current price.							
3	#18	**Formula #1 and #2 Type:** Lookup formula using the dot operator on a stock data type.							
4		Single input-output formula.							
5		**Formula #1 and #2 Elements:** Equal sign, table formula nomenclature relative cell reference with							
6		implicit intersection operator, dot operator, formula element from drop-down list.							
7		**Formula #3 Type:** Number Formula. Single input-output formula.							
8		**Formula #3 Elements:** Equal sign, table formula nomenclature relative cell reference with							
9		implicit intersection operator, math multiplication operator.							
10									

	Stock	Units	Start Price	Start Value	Date Purchased	Ticker	End Price	Current Value
11								
12	🏛 THE COCA-COLA COMPANY (XNYS:KO)	115	$46.30	$5,324.50	8/3/2020	KO	$47.35	$5,445.25
13	🏛 CATERPILLAR INC. (XNYS:CAT)	125	$131.52	$16,440.00	8/4/2020	CAT	$137.48	$17,185.00
14	🏛 MICROSOFT CORPORATION (XNAS:MSFT)	210	$212.83	$44,694.30	7/8/2020	MSFT	$214.58	$45,061.80
15	🏛 ALPHABET INC. (XNAS:GOOGL)	160	$1,510.99	$241,758.40	7/9/2020	GOOGL	$1,576.25	$252,200.00
16								

3 finished formulas →

Formula #1 in cell G12: =[@Stock].[Ticker symbol]
Formula #2 in cell H12: =[@Stock].Price
Formula #3 in cell I12: =[@Units]*[@[EndPrice]]

Figure 12.33 *Right-clicking the range B12:B15 and selecting the Refresh option updates stock prices.*

7. Because you used the Stocks data type, which is connected to the internet, you can right-click any cell in the range B12:B15 and click on the Refresh option to update the stock prices. If the stock markets are open, the prices update after you refresh.

Note: Notice in Figure 12.33 that Microsoft presents a disclaimer about using financial market data for professional trading.

The new Data Types feature in Excel gives you an exciting way to build formulas that can look up data. As an experiment, try to type some geographic locations, like country names or state names, and convert them to data types; then see if you can use the dot operator to look up the populations for those geographic locations.

Microsoft says it will add many more data types to Excel in the near future and will allow you to look up even more data from the internet live with Excel formulas! In addition, Microsoft says that eventually a company will be able to use its own data in the Data Types feature.

Example 19: Building Formulas Between Worksheets by Using Worksheet References

When you build Excel formulas, the cell references and ranges of cells that you use in formulas can be from any worksheet in an Excel workbook. It is common when building a large Excel solution that spans many worksheets for formula inputs or lookup tables to be located on a specific worksheet that is different from the worksheet containing the formulas. The logic for keeping all the formula inputs on a separate worksheet is that it is organizationally easier to have a single location that you can go to when you need to change the formula inputs. Luckily, it is easy to reference cells and ranges from other worksheets.

Figure 12.34 shows a worksheet like the one you used in Example 9 in this chapter, but now the lookup table is on a different worksheet than the worksheet containing the formula. When you refer to a cell or range of cells on a different worksheet, you are required to use the worksheet name followed by an exclamation point and then the cell reference or range of cells. For example, if the *lookup_array* argument of the XLOOKUP function requires the range B3:B6 from the worksheet named LookupTable, rather than use the range B3:B6, you must use LookupTable!B3:B6.

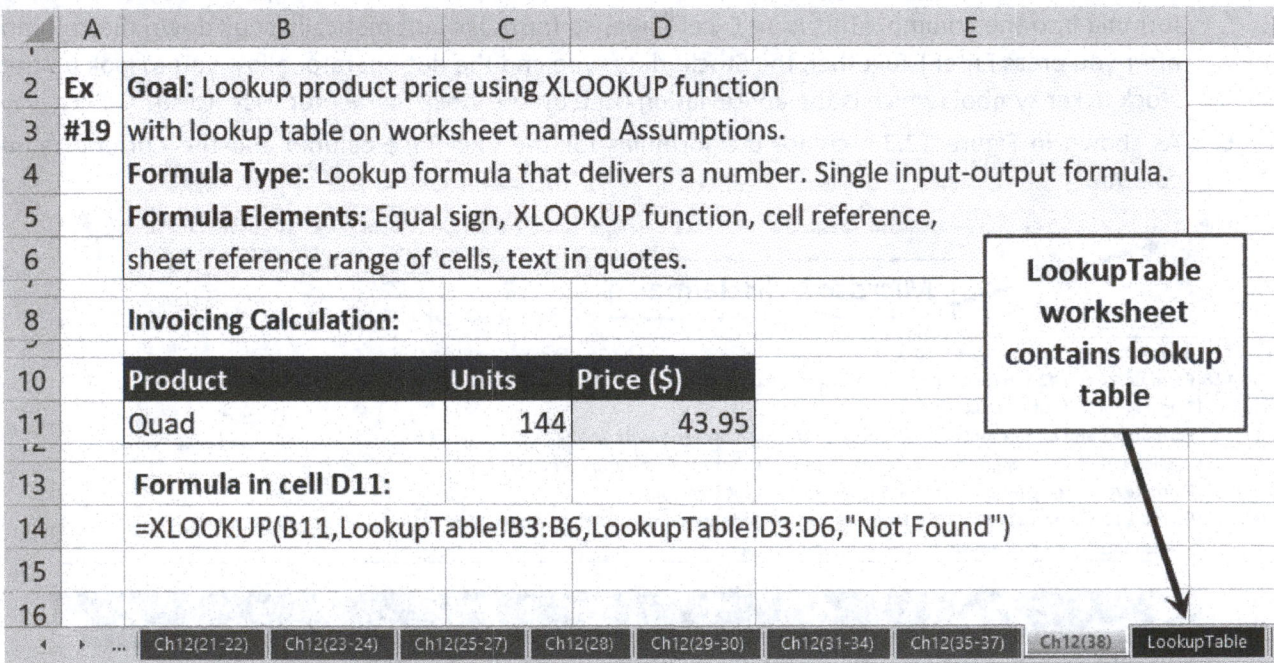

Figure 12.34 *Using worksheet references to build formulas between worksheets.*

As shown in Figure 12.35, if there is a space in the worksheet name, the worksheet name must start and end with single quotation marks. You can create worksheet references by typing them into the formula or by using your mouse to select references from other worksheets.

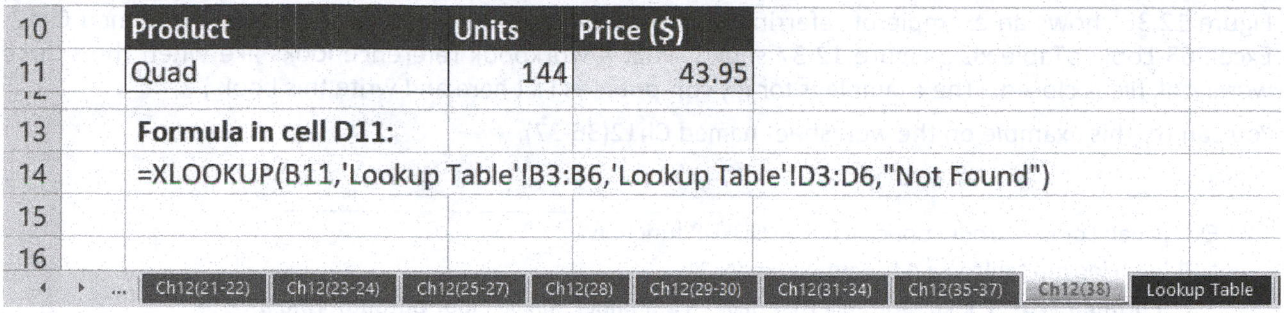

10	Product		Units	Price ($)			
11	Quad		144	43.95			
12							
13	**Formula in cell D11:**						
14	=XLOOKUP(B11,'Lookup Table'!B3:B6,'Lookup Table'!D3:D6,"Not Found")						
15							
16							

◄ ► ... Ch12(21-22) Ch12(23-24) Ch12(25-27) Ch12(28) Ch12(29-30) Ch12(31-34) Ch12(35-37) Ch12(38) Lookup Table

Figure 12.35 *A worksheet name that contains a space must be enclosed in single quotation marks.*

To complete this example, follow these steps:

1. Select the worksheet named Ch12(34-35).

2. Select cell D11 and start your formula by typing **=XLOOKUP(**.

3. Select cell B11 for the *lookup_value* argument of XLOOKUP. Notice that when you select a cell on the same worksheet as the formula, the only thing that is entered into the formula is the cell reference.

4. Type a comma to get to the *lookup_array* argument, click on the worksheet named LookupTable, and select the range B3:B6. Notice that the syntax for the worksheet reference is automatically put into the formula as LookupTable!B3:B6.

5. Type a comma to get to the *return_array* argument and select the range D3:D6. Notice that the syntax for the worksheet reference is automatically put into the formula as LookupTable!D3:D6.

6. Type a comma to get to the [*if_not_found*] argument and then type **"Not Found")**.

7. Press Enter to enter the lookup formula and jump back to the worksheet containing the formula.

> **Note:** Notice that you press the Enter key on the LookupTable worksheet, and Excel simultaneously enters the formula and jumps you back to the original worksheet. People commonly make the mistake of trying to click back on the original sheet to jump back to the original worksheet. You do not want to do that. Just press the Enter key.

8. As an experiment, change the LookupTable worksheet name from LookupTable (no space) to Lookup Table (with a space). When you do this, notice that the worksheet reference syntax changes from LookupTable!B3:B6 to 'Lookup Table'!B3:B6. When you have spaces in worksheet names, the single quotation marks are required to make the worksheet reference legitimate.

Examples 20 and 21: Building Formulas Between Workbooks by Using Workbook References

> **Note:** For this example, you will have to open the two Excel files. Ch12-Excel365-WorksheetFormulas.xlsx is the destination file, which contains the formula. Ch12-Excel365-LookupTable.xlsx is the source file, which is an external file that you will reference.

In Example 19, you saw how to use a worksheet reference when you need a range of cells from a different worksheet. These two examples take it a step further and show how you can refer to a cell reference or range of cells from a different source workbook file.

Figure 12.36 shows an example of referring to a lookup table from an open workbook file named Ch12-Excel365-LookupTable.xlsx. Figure 12.37 shows what a workbook reference looks like when the source workbook file is closed. (The example is for my computer as I sit here and write this book.)

You can try this example on the worksheet named Ch12(36-37).

	A	B	C	D	E
2	Ex	**Goal:** Lookup product price using XLOOKUP function			
3	#20	with lookup table in a different workbook file.			
4		**Formula Type:** Lookup formula that delivers a number. Single input-output formula.			
5		**Formula Elements:** Equal sign, XLOOKUP function, cell reference,			
6		workbook reference range of cells, text in quotes.			
8		**Invoicing Calculation:**			
10		Product	Units	Price ($)	
11		Quad	144	43.95	
13		**Formula in cell D11:**			
14		=XLOOKUP(B11, '[Ch12-Excel365-LookupTable.xlsx]LookupTable'!$B$3:$B$6, '[Ch12-Excel365-LookupTable.xlsx]LookupTable'!$D$3:$D$6, "Not Found")			

Figure 12.36 *Using workbook references to build formulas between workbooks.*

10	Product	Units	Price ($)	
11	Quad	144	43.95	
13	**Formula in cell D11:**			
14	=XLOOKUP(B11, 'C:\Users\mgirvin\Desktop\TheOnlyAppThatMatters\Ch12\[Ch12-Excel365-LookupTable.xlsx]LookupTable'!$B$3:$B$6, 'C:\Users\mgirvin\Desktop\TheOnlyAppThatMatters\Ch12\[Ch12-Excel365-LookupTable.xlsx]LookupTable'!$D$3:$D$6, "Not Found")			

Figure 12.37 *When you close the source workbook file, the workbook reference shows the full file path.*

When the source file is closed, the destination workbook file (that is, the file containing the formula) shows the full file path, including the worksheet name and cell references. When you create a workbook reference, you start with both files open and work between the two files to create the formula. By default, when you highlight a cell or range in a different workbook, the references are locked and absolute. You can change a reference to a relative or mixed cell reference by pressing the F4 key to toggle between the different cell reference types.

To try this example, you need to have both workbooks open. You need to start the formula in the destination file and then navigate to the source file by using your mouse and the taskbar, select the ranges in the source file, and then finally navigate back to the destination file to finish your formula and press Enter. When you close the source file, the full file path in the destination file will reflect the path on your computer.

Note: Workbook references are not common, but you still you need to learn about workbook references in case you encounter a situation where they are required.

In some situations, it might be necessary to have multiple users refer to one central workbook file, such as for a central product pricing table that all users are required to use. In such a case, you might have to use a workbook reference. The main drawback to workbook references is that if the source workbook file is moved, the workbook reference in the destination workbook file will be broken. When you open a workbook with an external workbook reference, Excel asks if you want to update the data from the link. If you click OK and the link is broken, you can go to the Data tab in the Ribbon, find the Queries & Connections group, and click the Edit Links button to reestablish the link.

Note: You can control the type of message that you receive when you open a workbook with workbook references by going to the File menu and selecting Options, Trust Center, Trust Center Settings, External Content tab.

The other drawback to workbook references is that if you use them in functions like SUMIFS and COUNTIFS, you get an error if the source workbook file is closed—and that is inconvenient. (There is a known SUMPRODUCT function workaround for this error that you will see shortly, in Figure 12.38.)

Figures 12.37 and 12.38 list the formula types and formula elements for these workbook reference examples. You can try this example on the worksheet named Ch12(38).

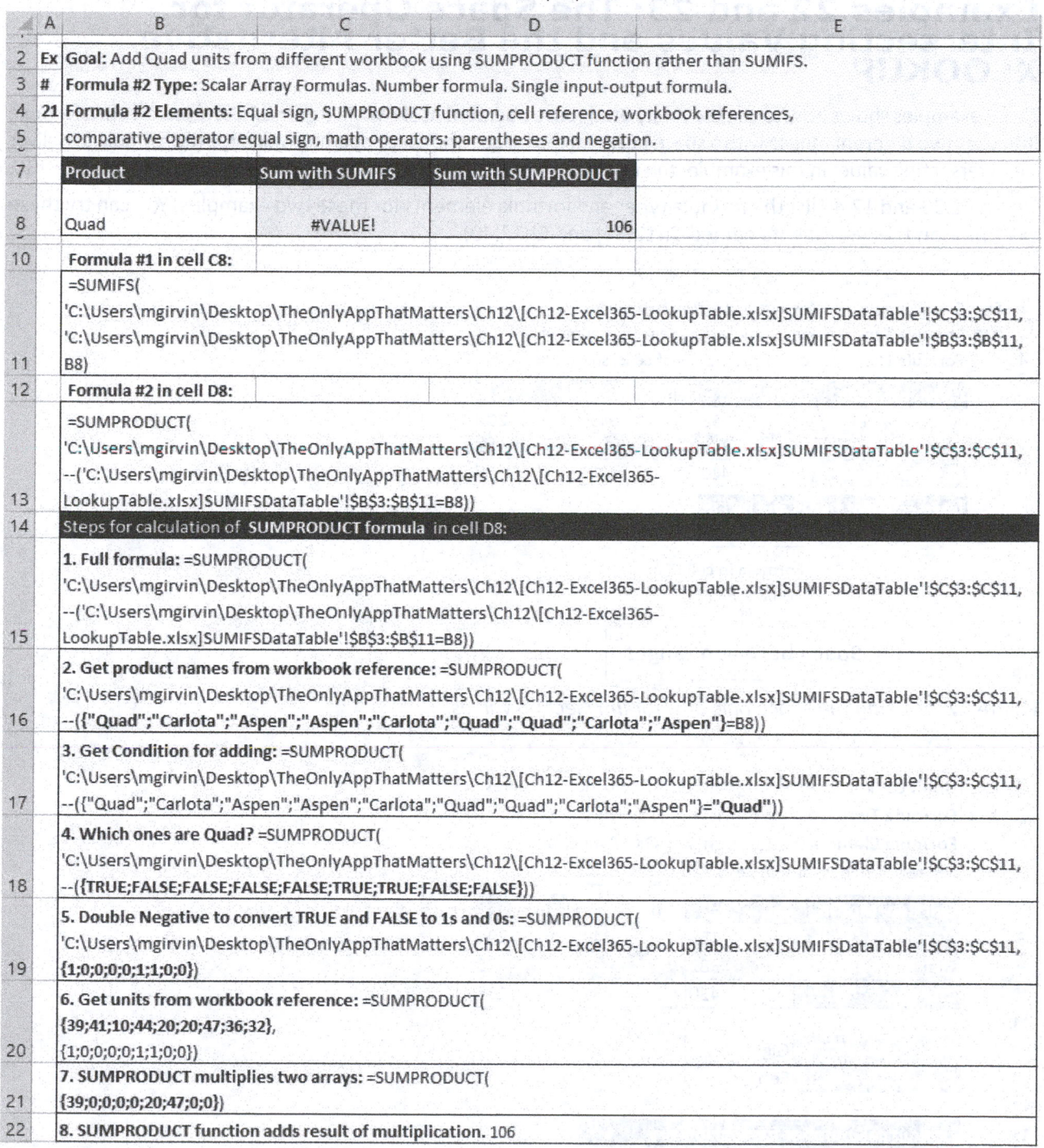

Figure 12.38 content (cell grid):

	A	B	C	D	E
2	Ex	**Goal:** Add Quad units from different workbook using SUMPRODUCT function rather than SUMIFS.			
3	#	**Formula #2 Type:** Scalar Array Formulas. Number formula. Single input-output formula.			
4	21	**Formula #2 Elements:** Equal sign, SUMPRODUCT function, cell reference, workbook references,			
5		comparative operator equal sign, math operators: parentheses and negation.			
7		**Product**	**Sum with SUMIFS**	**Sum with SUMPRODUCT**	
8		Quad	#VALUE!	106	
10		**Formula #1 in cell C8:**			
11		=SUMIFS('C:\Users\mgirvin\Desktop\TheOnlyAppThatMatters\Ch12\[Ch12-Excel365-LookupTable.xlsx]SUMIFSDataTable'!$C$3:$C$11, 'C:\Users\mgirvin\Desktop\TheOnlyAppThatMatters\Ch12\[Ch12-Excel365-LookupTable.xlsx]SUMIFSDataTable'!$B$3:$B$11, B8)			
12		**Formula #2 in cell D8:**			
13		=SUMPRODUCT('C:\Users\mgirvin\Desktop\TheOnlyAppThatMatters\Ch12\[Ch12-Excel365-LookupTable.xlsx]SUMIFSDataTable'!$C$3:$C$11, --('C:\Users\mgirvin\Desktop\TheOnlyAppThatMatters\Ch12\[Ch12-Excel365- LookupTable.xlsx]SUMIFSDataTable'!$B$3:$B$11=B8))			
14		**Steps for calculation of SUMPRODUCT formula in cell D8:**			
15		**1. Full formula:** =SUMPRODUCT('C:\Users\mgirvin\Desktop\TheOnlyAppThatMatters\Ch12\[Ch12-Excel365-LookupTable.xlsx]SUMIFSDataTable'!$C$3:$C$11, --('C:\Users\mgirvin\Desktop\TheOnlyAppThatMatters\Ch12\[Ch12-Excel365- LookupTable.xlsx]SUMIFSDataTable'!$B$3:$B$11=B8))			
16		**2. Get product names from workbook reference:** =SUMPRODUCT('C:\Users\mgirvin\Desktop\TheOnlyAppThatMatters\Ch12\[Ch12-Excel365-LookupTable.xlsx]SUMIFSDataTable'!$C$3:$C$11, --({"Quad";"Carlota";"Aspen";"Aspen";"Carlota";"Quad";"Quad";"Carlota";"Aspen"}=B8))			
17		**3. Get Condition for adding:** =SUMPRODUCT('C:\Users\mgirvin\Desktop\TheOnlyAppThatMatters\Ch12\[Ch12-Excel365-LookupTable.xlsx]SUMIFSDataTable'!$C$3:$C$11, --({"Quad";"Carlota";"Aspen";"Aspen";"Carlota";"Quad";"Quad";"Carlota";"Aspen"}="Quad"))			
18		**4. Which ones are Quad?** =SUMPRODUCT('C:\Users\mgirvin\Desktop\TheOnlyAppThatMatters\Ch12\[Ch12-Excel365-LookupTable.xlsx]SUMIFSDataTable'!$C$3:$C$11, --({TRUE;FALSE;FALSE;FALSE;FALSE;TRUE;TRUE;FALSE;FALSE}))			
19		**5. Double Negative to convert TRUE and FALSE to 1s and 0s:** =SUMPRODUCT('C:\Users\mgirvin\Desktop\TheOnlyAppThatMatters\Ch12\[Ch12-Excel365-LookupTable.xlsx]SUMIFSDataTable'!$C$3:$C$11, {1;0;0;0;0;1;1;0;0})			
20		**6. Get units from workbook reference:** =SUMPRODUCT({39;41;10;44;20;20;47;36;32}, {1;0;0;0;0;1;1;0;0})			
21		**7. SUMPRODUCT multiplies two arrays:** =SUMPRODUCT({39;0;0;0;0;20;47;0;0})			
22		**8. SUMPRODUCT function adds result of multiplication.** 106			

Figure 12.38 *You can use SUMPRODUCT rather than SUMIFS to avoid errors if the source workbook file is closed.*

The syntax for a workbook reference when the source file (external file) is closed is as follows:

'file_path [workbook_name] worksheet_name'!cell_references

> **Note:** When it comes to worksheet and workbook references in worksheet formulas, I tend to use worksheet references when I have formulas that span many worksheets in the same workbook so I have one location where I can place all the formula inputs. I do this, for example, with some of my large budget and financial models. However, I tend not to use workbook references very often because it is easier to manage an Excel solution when everything is in the same workbook file.

Examples 22 and 23: The Space Operator for Intersecting Values and the Better Alternative, XLOOKUP

These examples shows how to use the rarely used space operator. As shown in Figure 12.39, if you create a formula that uses two different ranges with a space between the ranges, the space operator will force the formula to deliver the intersecting value. In this example, the two ranges intersect at cell D8, so the formula delivers the value 180.

Figure 12.39 and 12.40 list the formula types and formula elements for these two examples. You can try these examples on the worksheets named Ch12(39) and Ch12(40).

	A	B	C	D	E
2	Ex	Goal: Lookup intersecting value from two ranges.			
3	#22	Formula Type: Lookup formula that delivers a number.			
4		Formula Elements: Equal sign, range of cells, space operator.			
6		Call Rep/Month	Jan	Feb	Mar
7		Floyd	158	349	204
8		Gigi	382	180	416
9		Chantel	420	484	135
11		Intersection of D6:D9 and B8:E8:			
12			180		
14			Formula in cell C12:		
15			=D6:D9 B8:E8		
16			↑		
17			**Space between ranges**		
18					

Figure 12.39 *Using the space operator for intersecting values.*

	A	B	C	D	E
2	Ex	Goal: Lookup intersecting value from two lookup values.			
3	#23	Formula Type: Lookup formula that delivers a number.			
4		Formula Elements: Equal sign, XLOOKUP function,			
5		cell reference, range of cells.			
7		Call Rep/Month	Jan	Feb	Mar
8		Floyd	158	349	204
9		Gigi	382	180	416
10		Chantel	420	484	135
11					
12		Row Header	Gigi		
13		Column Header	Feb		
14					
15		Lookup call number for Gigi in Feb:			
16		180			
18		Formula in cell B16:			
19		=XLOOKUP(C12,B8:B10,XLOOKUP(C13,C7:E7,C8:E10))			

Figure 12.40 *Using XLOOKUP for intersecting values.*

Note: The only possible use that I can think of for the space operator is if you have a large lookup table, and you want the intersecting value between a row and a column. If you wanted to do this sort of two-way lookup for an efficient Excel solution, then you would use a two-way lookup formula, as shown in Figure 12.40. However, I only use the space operator as an Excel party trick that I can show someone as an example of something silly that is possible in Excel.

Example 24: Using the Colon Reference Operator and 3D Cell References to Add Across Multiple Worksheets

In this example, you'll learn how to add the same cell across multiple sheets using a 3D cell reference. In Figure 12.41, you can see four cross-tabulated tables that show the same sales reps at the front of each row and the same products at the top of each column, each on a different monthly worksheet. The goal is to consolidate or summarize the four tables into one table that shows the same sales reps as the row headers and products as column headers, with totals from across the four sheets (see Figure 12.42). To understand the goal more specifically, look at cell C5 on the four different worksheets in Figure 12.41. The goal here is to add the numbers from all the C5 cells across the four sheets. You want to add the units for the sales rep Sioux and the product Quad for January to April: 12 + 55 + 44 + 66 = 177. You can see this summary number in cell C9 in Figure 12.42.

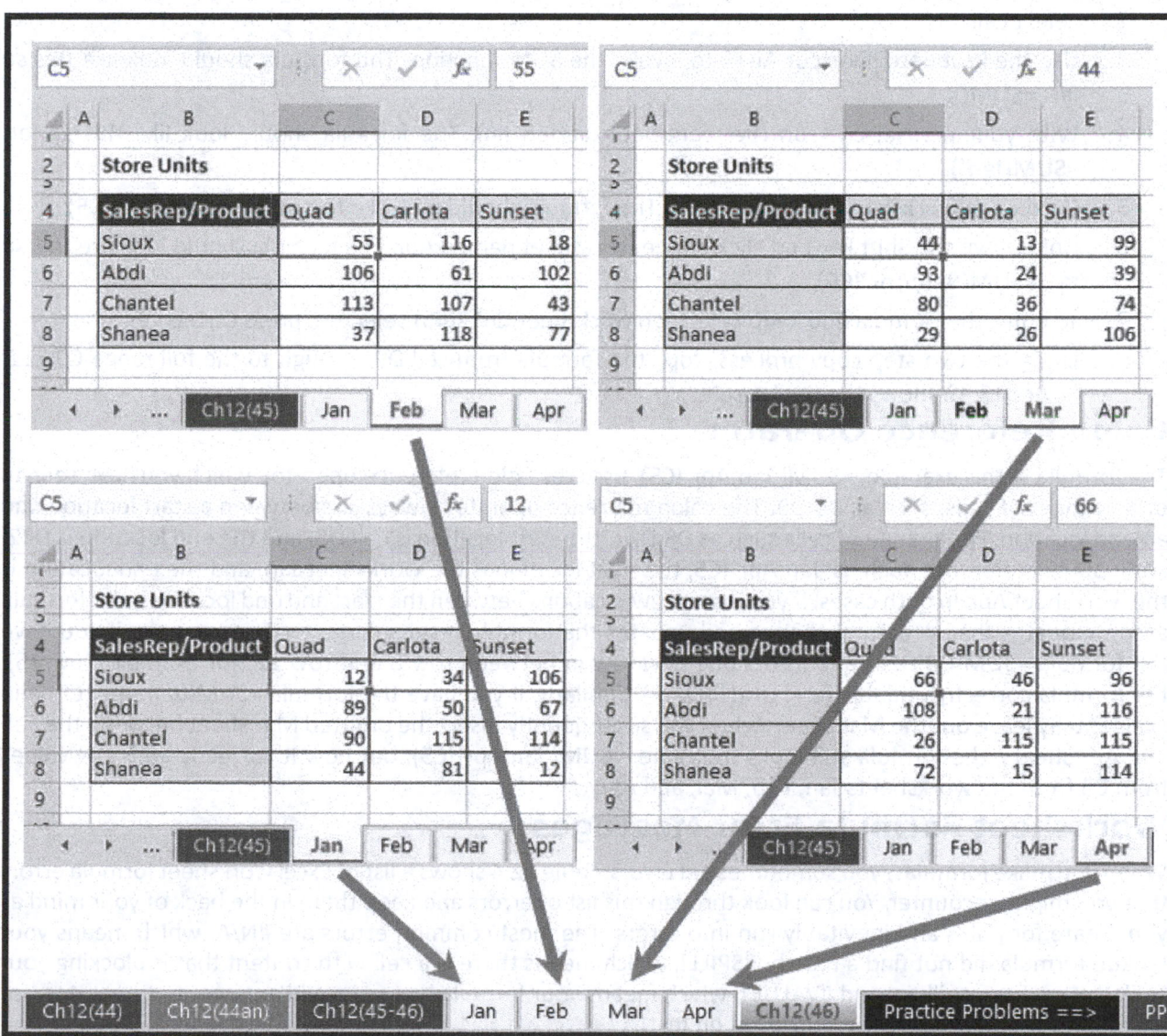

Figure 12.41 *There are four worksheets, all with same-sized Sales Rep/Product Units tables.*

This 3D cell reference formula is an example of an aggregate formula that delivers a number answer. Figure 12.42 lists the formula types and the formula elements.

	A	B	C	D	E
2	Ex	**Goal:** Add units by sales rep & product for Jan. to Apr.			
3	#24	**Formula Type:** Aggregate formula. Number formula.			
4		**Formula Elements:** Equal sign, SUM function,			
5		3-D cell reference across worksheets,			
6		worksheet names with colon operator.			
8		**SalesRep/Product**	Quad	Carlota	Sunset
9		Sioux	177	209	319
10		Abdi	396	156	324
11		Chantel	309	373	346
12		Shanea	182	240	309
14		**Formula in cell C9, manually copied to range C9:E12:**			
15		=SUM(Jan:Apr!C5)			

Figure 12.42 *Formula types and the formula elements for adding across multiple worksheets.*

To complete this example, follow these steps:

1. Select the worksheet named Ch12(42).

2. Select cell C9.

3. Use the keyboard shortcut Alt+= to invoke the SUM function. The formula should look like this so far: **=SUM()**.

4. With your mouse, click on the worksheet named Jan. The formula should look like this so far: **=SUM(Jan!)**.

5. On the Jan worksheet, click on cell C5. The formula should look like this so far: **=SUM(Jan!C5)**.

6. Hold Down the Shift key and click on the worksheet named Apr. The formula should look like this so far: **=SUM('Jan:Apr'!C5)**.

7. To enter the formula and keep cell C9 on worksheet Ch12(45) selected, press Ctrl+Enter.

8. Using the two-step copy process, copy the formula from cell D9 through to the full range C9:E12. Figure 12.42 shows the final result.

Colon Reference Operator

The formula in this example, =SUM('Jan:Apr'!C5), uses the colon reference operator, which you have seen in other ranges of cells, such as D6:D9. The colon reference operator always sits between a start location and an end location. For a range of cells such as D8:D22, the start location is cell D8, and the end location is D22. For a 3D cell reference such as 'Jan:Apr'!C5, the start location is the worksheet Jan, and the end location is the worksheet Apr. In both cases, if you insert new locations between the start and end locations, the formula accommodates that structural change and updates the formula results correctly. For example, if you have the formula =SUM(D8:D22) and insert one new row in between row 8 and row 22 (for example, row 15), the formula correctly updates to =SUM(D8:D23). Similarly, if you have the formula =SUM('Jan:Apr'!C5) and accidentally leave out the Mar sheet, when you subsequently insert the omitted Mar sheet between the Feb and Apr sheets, the formula still looks the same, =SUM('Jan:Apr'!C5), but now it correctly adds the values from C5 from the worksheets Jan, Feb, Mar, and Apr.

Worksheet Formula Error Messages

When you make formulas, you sometimes get errors. Table 12.4 shows a list of Excel worksheet formula errors that you might encounter. You can look through this list of errors and keep them in the back of your mind as you create formulas and inevitably run into errors. The most common errors are #N/A, which means your lookup formula did not find a match, #SPILL!, which means there is a cell with content that is blocking your spilled array from spilling, and #VALUE!, which means your formula has an invalid argument or operator (for example, a multiplication operator used on text).

Table 12.4 Errors You May Encounter in Excel Worksheets

Error Message	What It Means
#DIV/0!	A divide-by-zero error has occurred.
#REF!	The formula is using a cell reference that has been deleted or an otherwise invalid cell reference.
#NAME?	An Excel built-in function or defined name is misspelled or word data in a formula is not in double quotation marks.
#N/A	A not available error has occurred, such as when VLOOKUP can't find a match.
#VALUE!	An invalid operator or argument (such as ="Red"*12 or =VLOOKUP(12,"Red",2,0) or array formula was entered without Ctrl+Shift+Enter.
#NULL!	There is no intersection for a space operator lookup.
#NUM!	The number is too big or small (and not between −1*10^307 and 1*10^307), a formula or function contains invalid numeric values, or an iterative function such as IRR cannot find an answer.
#######	The column is not wide enough to display data (values) or a date or time is a negative value.
Circular cell reference	A formula contains a reference to the cell the formula sits in. This would occur, for example, if =SUM(A1:A3) were in cell A1. The formula doesn't know what to do because it is looking at itself.
#SPILL!	Something in a cell is blocking a dynamic spilled array formula from spilling the full array of values.
#CALC!	An array formula cannot make a calculation, such as when the formula tries to calculate an array within an array, which is not allowed.
#BUSY!	The data type dot operator is waiting to get an answer, as with a stock price for a Stocks data type or a population number for a Location data type.

Worksheet Function Screentips and What the Square Brackets Mean

Earlier in this chapter, you saw the screentips for the FILTER and RANK.EQ functions. They are shown again in Figure 12.43. Notice that the FILTER function has an argument named [*if_empty*], and the RANK.EQ function has an argument named [*order*]. In both cases, the argument name appears in square brackets. Any time you see a function argument name in brackets in a screentip, it means the argument is not required, and if you omit the argument, the default value will be used. For example, if you omit the [*if_error*] argument in the FILTER function, when the FILTER function filters the dataset down to an empty filter (that is, no matches), the default error value #CALC! is delivered by the FILTER function. As another example, if you omit the [*order*] argument in the FILTER function, the default descending sort order is used.

> **Note:** In general, Microsoft has programmed the default settings with the most commonly used options so that you can leave out the arguments and create formulas more quickly and with less typing.

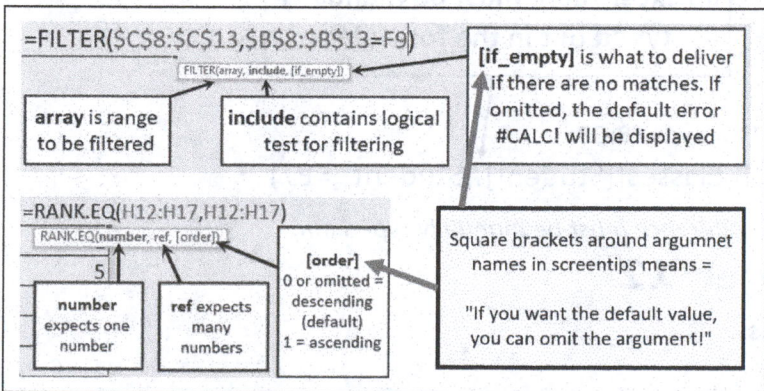

Figure 12.43 *Screentip arguments with square brackets mean the arguments are not required, and Excel will use the defaults.*

Example 25: Using Table Formula Nomenclature Absolute and Mixed References

Earlier in this chapter, in Table 12.3, you saw a list of the different types of table formula nomenclature references. You also learned about the syntax for creating an Excel Table absolute column reference. By default, when you highlight an Excel Table column, the syntax is *Table*[*FieldName*]—that is, the table name followed by the column name in square brackets. This default table formula nomenclature for a column reference remains absolute when copied down across rows but moves relatively when you copy it across columns. This means that the default behavior is to work like a mixed reference that is locked as you copy the column across rows but that is relative when you copy it side to side across columns.

If you want to convert a default column reference to an absolute reference so the reference is locked in all directions throughout the copy action, you must use the syntax *Table*[[*FieldName*]:[*FieldName*]]—that is, open square bracket, field name in square brackets, colon, field name in square brackets repeated a second time, then close square bracket.

Figure 12.44 shows an example of using an Excel Table absolute column reference in a formula, where the goal is to list, below a student's name, the classes the student has taken. You can use the FILTER array function and an Excel Table absolute column reference for this task: Enter the formula into cell E8 and then copy the formula through the range E8:G8. The hard part of this formula is the table formula nomenclature absolute reference. What makes it hard is that there is no special keystroke to convert the reference to an absolute reference, as there is for column ranges, where you can use the F4 key. When you use a column from an Excel Table and you want the column to be locked, you must type out the double square brackets and colon. Typing it out just takes time.

> **Note:** Excel users have for years begged Microsoft to program the F4 key so that it converts an Excel Table column name to an absolute reference, but so far, Microsoft has not done it.

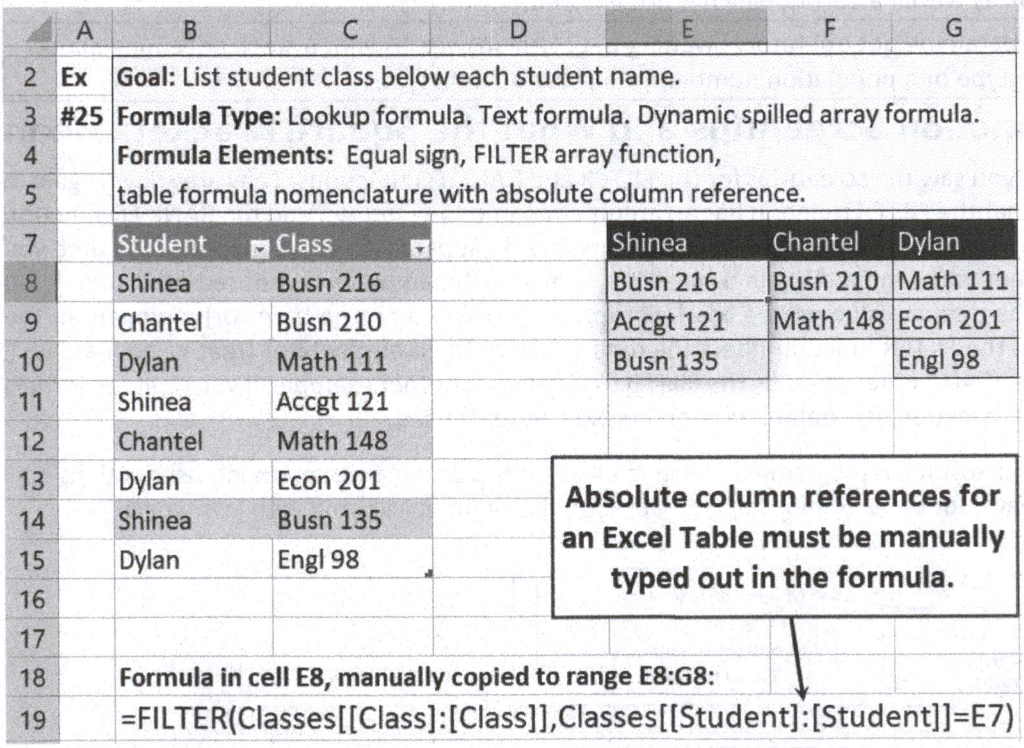

	A	B	C	D	E	F	G
2	Ex	Goal: List student class below each student name.					
3	#25	Formula Type: Lookup formula. Text formula. Dynamic spilled array formula.					
4		Formula Elements: Equal sign, FILTER array function,					
5		table formula nomenclature with absolute column reference.					
7		Student	Class		Shinea	Chantel	Dylan
8		Shinea	Busn 216		Busn 216	Busn 210	Math 111
9		Chantel	Busn 210		Accgt 121	Math 148	Econ 201
10		Dylan	Math 111		Busn 135		Engl 98
11		Shinea	Accgt 121				
12		Chantel	Math 148				
13		Dylan	Econ 201				
14		Shinea	Busn 135				
15		Dylan	Engl 98				
16							
17							
18		Formula in cell E8, manually copied to range E8:G8:					
19		=FILTER(Classes[[Class]:[Class]],Classes[[Student]:[Student]]=E7)					

Absolute column references for an Excel Table must be manually typed out in the formula.

Figure 12.44 *An Excel Table absolute column reference must be manually typed out.*

Key Concepts in Chapter 12

- Excel has a number of **formula types:**
  - Number formulas
  - Text formulas
  - Logical formulas

- Single-input/single-output formulas
- Scalar array formulas
- Dynamic spilled array formulas
- Aggregate formulas
- Lookup formulas

- Excel formulas can include a number of **formula elements:**
  - Equal sign
  - Cell references: relative, absolute, mixed with row locked, mixed with column locked
  - Range of cells: relative, absolute, mixed with row locked, mixed with column locked
  - Reference operators: colon, comma, space
  - Spilled range operator (#)
  - Implicit intersection operator (@)
  - Data type operator (dot)
  - Worksheet reference
  - Workbook reference
  - Defined name
  - Table formula nomenclature
  - Worksheet functions (more than 450 of them)
  - Function argument elements
  - Math operators (() , ^ , * , / ,+,-)
  - Comparison operators (= , <> ,> ,>= ,< ,<=)
  - Join operator (&)
  - Quotation marks
  - Numbers (if they won't change)
  - Array constants (if data won't change)

- Excel uses a particular order of operator precedence for evaluating worksheet formulas:
1. Parentheses
2. Reference operators (:, <space>, , [comma], #, @, . (dot)), evaluated left to right
3. Negation (-) (for example, -2^4 = 16, -(2^4) = -16, and --2 + 1 = 3)
4. Conversion of percentages to numerals (for example, 1% to .01)
5. Exponents (^) (for example, 3^2 = 9, 8^(1/3) = 2)
6. Multiplication (*) and division (/), evaluated left to right
7. Addition (+) and subtraction (-), evaluated left to right
8. Concatenation (&)
9. Comparison symbols (=, <>, >=, <=, <, >), evaluated left to right
   - To watch Excel step through the formula evaluation process and see the worksheet formula order of operator precedence in action, you can select the cell containing a formula and then use the **Evaluate Formula feature**, which helps you understand how the worksheet formula engine works and can help you track down errors in formulas.
   - If a built-in function is programmed to make an aggregate operation and deliver a single answer from many inputs, you can only enter the formula to get a single answer; if copying is necessary, you must do it manually. On the other hand, if a function argument expects a single value and you give it multiple values, you need to make a function argument array operation that will cause the formula to spill the results; in this case, you do not need to manually copy the formula. Some examples of worksheet **functions that cannot spill** because they are only programmed to deliver a single answer are SUM, AVERAGE, AND, and OR.

- **Dynamic spilled array functions** like UNIQUE, SORT, and FILTER are specifically programmed to spill results in a worksheet. Dynamic spilled array formulas are not allowed in Excel Tables.
- You can open the **Name Manager dialog box** by pressing Ctrl+F3 or by going to the Formulas tab in the Ribbon, and then, in the Defined Names group, clicking the Name Manager button. The Name Manager dialog box lists the defined name references and Excel Table name references and allows you to create, edit, or delete defined names.

Keyboard Shortcuts Learned in Chapter 12

Keyboard Shortcut	Description
Alt, M, V	Opens the Evaluate Formula dialog box
F4 key in formula edit mode while touching a cell reference	Toggles between the four different types of cell references: relative, absolute, mixed with column locked and mixed with row locked
F4 key when you are not in formula edit mode	Enacts the repeat command and repeat that last action that you performed
Ctrl+F3	Opens the Name Manager dialog box

Practice Problems for Chapter 12

Practice Problem 1

In your Excel file for this chapter (Ch12-Excel365-WorksheetFormulas.xlsx), go to the worksheet named PPCh12(1) and create the solution for this practice problem. Figure 12.45 shows the goals that are listed on that worksheet.

	A	B	C	D	E	F	G	H
2		**Goal:** Create a formula is cell G7 that can spill through the range G7:H16 and calculate						
3		the correct total sales and total costs.						
4		**Hints:** For the first record, line sales = 144*27.25 = 4,024.80 and line costs = 144*14.53.						
6		Date	Product	Units	Sales Price	Cost	Line Sales ($)	Line Costs ($)
7		8/13/20	Quad	144	27.95	14.53		
8		8/13/20	Aspen	82	13.95	8.37		
9		8/13/20	Sunshine	101	11.5	5.64		
10		8/13/20	Yanaki	164	10	4.7		
11		8/13/20	Carlota	175	14.95	6.28		
12		8/12/20	Quad	105	29.95	13.48		
13		8/12/20	Aspen	75	13.95	8.09		
14		8/12/20	Sunshine	168	9.95	5.87		
15		8/12/20	Yanaki	136	12	7.2		
16		8/12/20	Carlota	98	11.95	7.17		

Figure 12.45 *On the worksheet PPCh12(1), create the spilled formula in cell G6 for line sales and line costs.*

When you are done with this problem, you can check your work against the answer sheet named PPCh12(1an).

Practice Problem 2

In your Excel file for this chapter (Ch12-Excel365-WorksheetFormulas.xlsx), go to the worksheet named PPCh12(2) and create the solution for this practice problem. Figure 12.46 shows the goals that are listed on that worksheet.

	A	B	C	D
2		**Goal:** Create formula in cell D7 that will spill down column and add the		
3		text prefix "Item # " to each number. For example, the first number		
4		**Hint #1:** The first number 517231 should be converted to: Item # 517231.		
5		**Hint #2:** "Item # " will not change, so we are not violating Excel's Golden Rule.		
6				
7		Product	Item Number	Item # & Number
8		Aspen	517231	
9		Quad	469890	
10		Carlota	162451	
11		Bellen	114541	
12		Sunset	832593	

Figure 12.46 *On the worksheet PPCh12(2), create a text formula in cell D7 that can spill down the column.*

When you are done with this problem, you can check your work against the answer sheet named PPCh12(2an).

Practice Problem 3

In your Excel file for this chapter (Ch12-Excel365-WorksheetFormulas.xlsx), go to the worksheet named PPCh12(3) and create the solution for this practice problem. Figure 12.47 shows the goals that are listed on that worksheet.

	A	B	C	D	E	F	G
1							
2		**Goal:** In cell C4, add calls for Day 1 and Day 2.					
3							
4		Total Day 1 and Day 5:					
5							
6		Center	Calls Day 1	Calls Day 2	Calls Day 3	Calls Day 4	Calls Day 5
7		Center #1	962	166	254	698	760
8		Center #2	849	142	442	407	575
9		Center #3	306	458	776	509	524
10		Center #4	1004	155	192	401	1147
11		Center #5	383	535	643	710	925
12		Center #6	926	382	657	360	905
13		Center #7	886	445	130	466	442

Figure 12.47 *On the worksheet PPCh12(3), create the aggregate formula for cell C4.*

When you are done with this problem, you can check your work against the answer sheet named PPCh12(3an).

Practice Problem 4

In your Excel file for this chapter (Ch12-Excel365-WorksheetFormulas.xlsx), go to the worksheet named PPCh12(4) and create the solution for this practice problem. Figure 12.48 shows the goals that are listed on that worksheet.

	A	B	C	D	E	F	G	H
1								
2		Goal: In cell E4, create a formula that will spill to display top 3 call amounts from Day 1 and Day 5:						
3								
4		Display top 3 call amounts from Day 1 and Day 5:						
5								
6		Center	Calls Day 1	Calls Day 2	Calls Day 3	Calls Day 4	Calls Day 5	
7		Center #1	962	166	254	698	760	
8		Center #2	849	142	442	407	575	
9		Center #3	306	458	776	509	524	
10		Center #4	1004	155	192	401	1147	
11		Center #5	383	535	643	710	925	
12		Center #6	926	382	657	360	905	
13		Center #7	886	445	130	466	442	

Figure 12.48 *On the worksheet PPCh12(4), create the dynamic spilled array formula in cell E4.*

When you are done with this problem, you can check your work against the answer sheet named PPCh12(4an).

Practice Problem 5

In your Excel file for this chapter (Ch12-Excel365-WorksheetFormulas.xlsx), go to the worksheet named PPCh12(5) and create the solution for this practice problem. Figure 12.49 shows the goals that are listed on that worksheet.

	A	B	C	D	E	F	G
1							
2		Goal: In cell E4, Add top 3 call amounts from Day 1 and Day 5:					
3							
4		Add top 3 call amounts from Day 1 and Day 5:					
5							
6		Center	Calls Day 1	Calls Day 2	Calls Day 3	Calls Day 4	Calls Day 5
7		Center #1	962	166	254	698	760
8		Center #2	849	142	442	407	575
9		Center #3	306	458	776	509	524
10		Center #4	1004	155	192	401	1147
11		Center #5	383	535	643	710	925
12		Center #6	926	382	657	360	905
13		Center #7	886	445	130	466	442

Figure 12.49 *On the worksheet PPCh12(5), create the scalar array formula in cell E4.*

When you are done with this problem, you can check your work against the answer sheet named PPCh12(5an).

Practice Problem 6

In your Excel file for this chapter (Ch12-Excel365-WorksheetFormulas.xlsx), go to the worksheet named PPCh12(6) and create the solution for this practice problem. Figure 12.50 shows the goals that are listed on that worksheet.

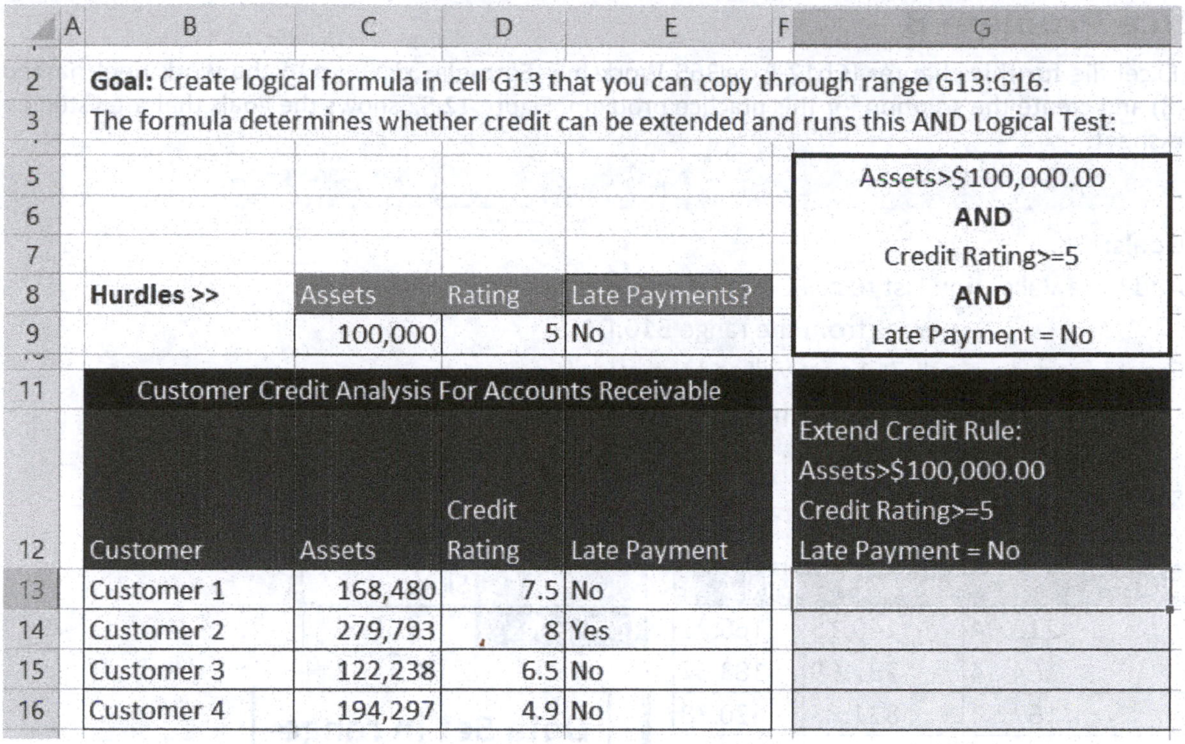

	A	B	C	D	E	F	G
2		**Goal:** Create logical formula in cell G13 that you can copy through range G13:G16.					
3		The formula determines whether credit can be extended and runs this AND Logical Test:					
5							Assets>$100,000.00
6							**AND**
7							Credit Rating>=5
8		Hurdles >>	Assets	Rating	Late Payments?		**AND**
9			100,000	5	No		Late Payment = No
11		Customer Credit Analysis For Accounts Receivable					
12		Customer	Assets	Credit Rating	Late Payment		Extend Credit Rule: Assets>$100,000.00 Credit Rating>=5 Late Payment = No
13		Customer 1	168,480	7.5	No		
14		Customer 2	279,793	8	Yes		
15		Customer 3	122,238	6.5	No		
16		Customer 4	194,297	4.9	No		

Figure 12.50 *On the worksheet PPCh12(6), create the logical formula in cell G13 that you copy to G13:G16.*

When you are done with this problem, you can check your work against the answer sheet named PPCh12(6an).

Practice Problem 7

In your Excel file for this chapter (Ch12-Excel365-WorksheetFormulas.xlsx), go to the worksheet named PPCh12(7) and create the solution for this practice problem. Figure 12.51 shows the goals that are listed on that worksheet.

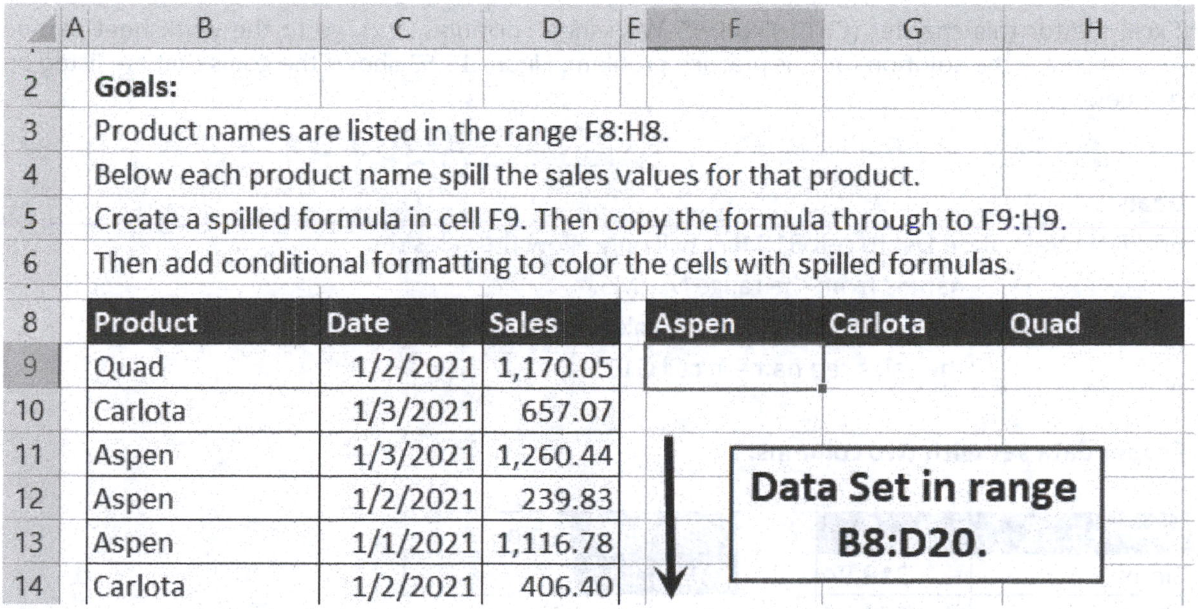

	A	B	C	D	E	F	G	H
2		**Goals:**						
3		Product names are listed in the range F8:H8.						
4		Below each product name spill the sales values for that product.						
5		Create a spilled formula in cell F9. Then copy the formula through to F9:H9.						
6		Then add conditional formatting to color the cells with spilled formulas.						
8		Product	Date	Sales		Aspen	Carlota	Quad
9		Quad	1/2/2021	1,170.05				
10		Carlota	1/3/2021	657.07				
11		Aspen	1/3/2021	1,260.44				
12		Aspen	1/2/2021	239.83				
13		Aspen	1/1/2021	1,116.78				
14		Carlota	1/2/2021	406.40				

Data Set in range B8:D20.

Figure 12.51 *On the worksheet PPCh12(7), create the spilled array formula in cell F9.*

When you are done with this problem, you can check your work against the answer sheet named PPCh12(7an).

Practice Problem 8

In your Excel file for this chapter (Ch12-Excel365-WorksheetFormulas.xlsx), go to the worksheet named PPCh12(8) and create the solution for this practice problem. Figure 12.52 shows the goals that are listed on that worksheet.

	A	B	C	D	E	F	G
2		**Goals:**					
3		Add Data Validation List to cell G10 that will only allow the sales rep					
4			names from the range B10:D10.				
5		Create formula in cell G11 that will add the sales for					
6			the sales rep name in cell G10.				
7							
8		**Sales for each Sales Rep:**					
9							
10		Sioux	Chantel	Miki		Sales Rep:	Sioux
11		218.94	149.15	166.22		Total Sales	
12		164.34	237.69	183.67			
13		167.54	821.86	320.78		**Data Set in range**	
14		147.9	305.3	364.48		**B10:D20.**	
15		352.12	290.7	378.52			
16		131.95	279.5	164.85			

Figure 12.52 *On the worksheet PPCh12(8), create the aggregate and lookup formula in cell G11.*

When you are done with this problem, you can check your work against the answer sheet named PPCh12(8an).

Practice Problem 9

In your Excel file for this chapter (Ch12-Excel365-WorksheetFormulas.xlsx), go to the worksheet named PPCh12(9) and create the solution for this practice problem. Figure 12.53 shows the goals that are listed on that worksheet.

	A	B	C	D	E	F	G	H
2		**Goals:**						
3		Add Data Validation List to cell G10 that will only allow the sales rep						
4			names from the range M3:M5.					
5		Create formula in cell G11 that will add the sales for						
6			the sales rep name in cell G10.					
7								
8		**Proper data set with two columns:**						
9								
10		Sales Rep	Sales			Sales Rep:	Sioux	
11		Sioux	218.94			Total Sales		
12		Sioux	164.34					
13		Sioux	167.54			**Data Set in range**		
14		Sioux	147.9			**B10:C40.**		
15		Sioux	352.12					
16		Sioux	131.95					

Figure 12.53 *On the worksheet named PPCh12(9), create the aggregate formula in cell G11.*

When you are done with this problem, you can check your work against the answer sheet named PPCh12(9an).

Practice Problem 10

In your Excel file for this chapter (Ch12-Excel365-WorksheetFormulas.xlsx), go to the worksheet named PPCh12(10).

In your own words, see if you can answer these conceptual questions:

1. List the different types of worksheet formulas and give an example of each.
2. Describe the difference between what you did in Practice Problem 8 and in Practice Problem 9.
3. When can a formula spill?
4. List all the different types of references that you can use in an Excel formula.

When you are done with this problem, you can check your work against the answer sheet named PPCh12(10an).

Chapter 13: Logical Tests and Related Functions (AND, ISNUMBER, IF, IFS, FILTER, SUMIFS, and More)

Logic pervades everything you do in all the tools in Excel and Power BI, whether you're making calculations or performing data analysis. So far in this book, you have created 11 logical tests in Excel worksheets:

Logical Test	Description	Chapter and Example
Product Column = Quad	Using the COUNTIFS function to count how many Quad products were sold. In this example, you counted with one condition.	Chapter 9, Example 3
Product Name in Cell = Product Name in Valid List	Using the Data Validation feature to verify that the product name entered into the cell was from a valid list of product names. In this example, you validated data based on a list.	Chapter 9, Example 4
Product in Cell = Quad	Locating a cell that contained the product Quad using the Conditional Formatting feature. In this example, you added formatting based on one condition.	Chapter 9, Example 5
Debits Cell = Credits Cell	Determining whether the two sides of the accounts were in balance using a logical formula. In this example, you checked if two cell values were equal.	Chapter 12, Example 3
Student Column = Student Name	Looking up a student's list of classes and spilling results using the FILTER function. In this example, you extracted class names based on one condition.	Chapter 12, Example 11
Product Column = Aspen	Adding the sales values and then the cost values for the product Aspen. In this example, you added based on one condition.	Chapter 12, Example 12
Last Year's Sales >= Sales Hurdle AND Credit Rating > Rating Hurdle	Determining whether a customer is extended credit based on last year's sales and a credit rating. In this example, you ran an AND logical test to deliver a single TRUE or FALSE.	Chapter 12, Example 13
Product Column = Aspen AND Sales Rep Column = Dean	Adding sales for the product Aspen and the sales rep Dean. In this example, you added using an AND logical test with two criteria.	Chapter 12, Example 14
Product Column Cell for Record = Quad	Conditionally formatting the row in a transaction dataset when the cell in the product column is equal to Quad. In this example, you applied formatting to a row based on the Product column value.	Chapter 12, Example 15
Rep Column = Floyd	Extracting call records from the proper dataset for the sales rep Floyd. In this example, you extracted records based on one condition.	Chapter 12, Example 16
NOT(ISBLANK(Cell))	Adding conditional formatting to a cell when the cell is not empty. In this example, you added formatting where the cell was not empty (that is, the cell had content).	Chapter 12, Example 17

In these 11 examples, you performed the following Excel tasks based on logical tests: counting, validating, formatting, adding, delivering logical values (TRUE or FALSE), and filtering columns and tables. Much of what you do in Excel involves logical tests. It is more common to count, add, and format based on logical tests than it is to simply add, count, or format all the values. However, most of the logical tests that you have learned about so far have involved a single condition and the equal sign comparison operator.

In this chapter you will expand your ability to run logical tests by learning about the different types of comparison operators, logical tests that involve multiple conditions, and a number of worksheet logical functions, including IF, AND, OR, ISNUMBER, and MAXIFS. You will also learn a little about how logical tests work in Power Query, Power Pivot, and Power BI.

Note: To follow along with the examples in this chapter, you can use the file named Ch13-Excel365-LogicalFormulas.xlsx.

Comparison Operators

Comparison operators allow you to compare items, such as comparing whether two items are equal or whether a sales number is greater than 50,000. There are six different comparison operators that you can use to create logical tests, as shown in Table 13.1. These comparison operators work in worksheet formulas, PivotTables, the Filter feature, Power Query M code formulas, Data Model DAX formulas, and more.

Any time you use a comparison operator in a formula, you are creating a logical formula that results in either a TRUE or FALSE value. Sometimes the trickiest part of creating a logical test is converting the description of the logical test into the correct comparison operator. Table 13.1 can help you choose the correct comparison operator for a logical test.

Table 13.1 Comparison Operators Used in Logical Tests

	Comparison Operator					
	=	>	>=	<	<=	<>
Name	Equals	Greater than	Greater than or equal to	Less than	Less than or equal to	Not equal to
Alternative names and phrases	Equal to Same as	More than Above	At least No more than X or more	Below Under	At most No more than X or less	Not Complement of
Examples based on the condition 2000	Equals 2000 Equal to 2000 Same as 2000	Greater than 2000 More than 2000 Above 2000	Greater than or equal to 2000 At least 2000 No less than 2000 2000 or more	Less than 2000 Below 2000 Under 2000	Less than or equal to 2000 At most 2000 No more than 2000 2000 or less	Not equal to 2000 Not 2000 Complement of 2000

Logical Tests

A *logical test* is an expression that evaluates to one of only two possible values: TRUE or FALSE. These two possible outcomes are called *Boolean values*, named for the 19th-century mathematician George Boole. A logical test, or Boolean test, can have one or more requirements called *conditions* or *criteria*. For example, the logical test Product Column = Quad (which answers the question "Is product name equal to Quad?") has the single condition =Quad, whereas the logical test Sales >= 50,000 AND Rating > 2.5 (which answers the question "Are sales no less than 50,000 and is the rating above 2.5?") has the two conditions Sales >= 50,000 and Rating >2.5.

Logical tests can be created in Excel by using comparison operators, logical worksheet functions (such as COUNTIFS and ISBLANK), or built-in features like conditional formatting, data validation, filtering, or PivotTables. Logical tests are also used extensively in the Power Query, Power Pivot, and Power BI tools. Any time you make a calculation or perform data analysis with one or more conditions or criteria, you are running a logical test.

You need to be aware of a couple other important topics regarding logical tests:

- When you run logical tests in an Excel worksheet or in Power Pivot or Power BI, the logical tests are not case-sensitive. This means that the logical test "busn" = "BUSN" evaluates to TRUE because the formula does not consider case. The lowercase letter *b* is equivalent to the uppercase letter *B*. Power Query, on the other hand, is case-sensitive, as you will see later in this book. Three functions in an

Excel worksheet and in the DAX formula language in Power Pivot and Power BI are case-sensitive: EXACT, FIND, and SUBSTITUTE. In addition, as you will see later in the book, in an Excel worksheet, the XLOOKUP and XMATH functions have a case-sensitive option.

- When you create logical formulas in a worksheet and with DAX, any nonzero number will be interpreted as TRUE, and zero will be interpreted as FALSE. The fact that any nonzero number is interpreted as TRUE and zero is interpreted as FALSE may seem like a strange attribute of the calculation engines, but this fact leads to short and efficient solutions when using conditional formatting and the IF function, as you will see later.

The following sections provide examples that show a variety of the most common logical tests, such as logical tests with a single condition, AND logical tests with two or more conditions, OR logical tests with two or more conditions, and NOT logical tests.

Example 1: Creating a Logical Test with a Single Condition

Figure 13.1 shows some examples of using comparison operators to create logical formulas. For each formula, the item on the left is being compared to the condition or hurdle on the right. Logical tests with comparison operators can be created in any of the tools in Excel. Notice that the last example in Figure 13.1 shows that text numbers are not equal to numbers. The text number five, which is surrounded by quotation marks ("5"), is not equivalent to the number 5. In Example 12 in Chapter 14, you will see how text numbers can cause problems and how to convert them to actual numbers so there are no problems.

Select the worksheet named Ch13(1) and try the logical test examples shown in Figure 13.1.

	A	B	C	D	E	F	G	H
1								
2	Ex	Item #1	Item #2	Comparative Operator		Logical Test	Result	Formula
3	#1	Busn	Busn	=	Equal	"Busn" = "Busn"	TRUE	=B3=C3
4		busn	BUSN	=	Equal	"busn" = "BUSN"	TRUE	=B4=C4
5		Econ	Busn	=	Equal	"Econ" = "Busn"	FALSE	=B5=C5
6		12.11	12.111	=	Equal	12.11 = 12.111	FALSE	=B6=C6
7		Econ	Busn	<>	Not equal to	"Econ" <> "Busn"	TRUE	=B7<>C7
8		Busn	Busn	<>	Not equal to	"Busn" <> "Busn"	FALSE	=B8<>C8
9		3.2	3	>=	Greater than or equal to	3.2 >= 3	TRUE	=B9>=C9
10		z	a	>	Greater than	"z" > "a"	TRUE	=B10>C10
11		10	10	>	Greater than	10 > 10	FALSE	=B11>C11
12		5	5	<=	Less than or equal to	5 <= 5	TRUE	=B12<=C12
13		5	2	<	Less than	5 < 2	FALSE	=B13<C13
14		z	a	<	Less than	"z" < "a"	FALSE	=B14<C14
15		5	5	=	Equal	"5" = "5"	TRUE	=B15=C15
16		5	5	=	Equal	5 = 5	TRUE	=B16=C16
17		5	5	=	Equal	5 = "5"	FALSE	=B17=C17

Figure 13.1 *When you use a comparison operator, you are creating a logical formula that will deliver the result TRUE or FALSE.*

Example 2: Using Math Operations to Convert TRUE to 1 and FALSE to 0

In most digital systems in the world—phones, computers, and TVs, for example—TRUE can be represented by the number 1, and FALSE can be represented by the number 0. This is also the case in Excel. When building formulas in Excel, sometimes you need to convert TRUE to 1 and FALSE to 0. With worksheet formulas and DAX formulas (in Power Pivot and Power BI), you can make this conversion with any math operation that does not change the value from 1 for TRUE or 0 for FALSE. Figure 13.2 shows a list of these possible conversions. You can try the examples shown in Figure 13.2 on the worksheet named Ch13(2).

In Power Query, everything is data type specific, so numbers cannot equate to logical values because number values and logical values are different data types. If you need to convert numbers to Boolean values in Power Query, you have to use the Power Query M code function Logical.From. You will learn about M code in Power Query in Chapters 18 and 19.

	A	B	C	D	E
1					
2	Ex	Math Operation	Boolean Value Result		Formula
3	#2	Double Negative	TRUE	1	=--C3
4		Times 1	TRUE	1	=C4*1
5		Divide by 1	TRUE	1	=C5/1
6		Exponent 1	TRUE	1	=C6^1
7		Double Negative	FALSE	0	=--C7
8		Times 1	FALSE	0	=C8*1
9		Divide by 1	FALSE	0	=C9/1
10		Exponent 1	FALSE	0	=C10^1

Figure 13.2 *Math operations that convert TRUE to 1 and FALSE to 0.*

Example 3: Using IS Worksheet Functions

Many logical tests can be created using comparison operators, but some cannot. For example, you cannot use comparison operators to check whether a value is a number or whether a cell contains a formula. For these logical tests, you need the IS functions. An IS function allows you to ask a question and get a TRUE or FALSE answer. IS functions yield information about a value, such as the data type or whether it is an error, a formula, a reference, or an even number or odd number. An IS function can deliver a single Boolean value, or it can spill results.

Table 13.2 lists the IS functions that are available in an Excel worksheet. Most of these functions are also available in the Power Pivot and Power BI DAX formula language.

Table 13.2 The IS Functions Available in an Excel Worksheet

Worksheet IS Function	Question the Function Answers
ISNUMBER	Is the value a number?
ISTEXT	Is the value text?
ISBLANK	Is the cell empty?
ISERROR	Is the value an error (#DIV/0!, #REF!, #NAME?, #N/A, #VALUE!, #NULL!, #NUM!, #SPILL!, #CALC!, or #BUSY!)?
ISNA	Is the value an #N/A error?
ISERR	Is the value an error other than #N/A?
ISNONTEXT	Is the value *not* text?
ISLOGICAL	Is the value a logical value?
ISFORMULA	Does the cell contain a formula?
ISREF	Is the value a reference?
ISEVEN	Is the number even?
ISODD	Is the number odd?

As you have probably guessed by now, Power Query is different from Power Pivot and Power BI. In Power Query, there are no IS functions. Instead, you use the single Power Query M code function Value.Is and specify the data type you are interested in. (You will learn more about Power Query M code in Chapters 18 and 19.)

Figure 13.3 shows examples of the IS worksheet functions. You can try the examples shown in Figure 13.3 on the worksheet named Ch13(3). Throughout this book, you will see practical examples of these IS functions, such as using the ISBLANK function to see if someone has entered data into a cell, using the ISNUMBER function to check if a value is a valid number, or using ISNA to check whether a value results in an #N/A error.

	A	B	C	D	E
1					
2	Ex	What's in C Column?	Value	Result	Formula
3	#3	43	43	TRUE	=ISNUMBER(C3)
4		43	43	FALSE	=ISTEXT(C4)
5		43	43	FALSE	=ISBLANK(C5)
6		#N/A	#N/A	TRUE	=ISERROR(C6)
7		43	43	FALSE	=ISNA(C7)
8		#N/A	#N/A	FALSE	=ISERR(C8)
9		TRUE	TRUE	TRUE	=ISNONTEXT(C9)
10		TRUE	TRUE	TRUE	=ISLOGICAL(C10)
11		=SUM({1,2,3})	6	TRUE	=ISFORMULA(C11)
12		=C11	6	TRUE	=ISREF(C12)
13		43	43	FALSE	=ISEVEN(C13)
14		43	43	TRUE	=ISODD(C14)

Figure 13.3 *IS functions deliver TRUE or FALSE results, based on data type, object type, or content.*

Types of Logical Tests: Single Condition, Contains, NOT, AND, BETWEEN, and OR

In general, you can either have a logical test with a single condition or a logical test with two or more conditions. In specific, the types of logical tests that you will study in this chapter are single condition, contains, NOT, AND, BETWEEN, and OR. The following subsections provide details about these different types of logical tests.

Logical Test with a Single Condition

A logical test with a single condition evaluates to TRUE or FALSE. In general, the item on the left is being checked against a condition or hurdle on the right. Single-condition logical tests may use the IS functions.

Contains, or "Partial Text," Logical Test

A contains test is a logical test with a single condition that checks whether text is located within a second text item. For example, if you ask whether "Cola" is contained in "Coca Cola," you get a TRUE answer, but if you ask whether "Cola" is in "7-Up," you get a FALSE answer. There are various ways to perform this type of logical test, as you will see in the upcoming examples.

NOT Logical Test

A NOT logical test is a test with a single condition that checks whether two items are *not* equal. A NOT logical test can also take a logical test with two or more conditions and reverse the outcome so that TRUE becomes FALSE or FALSE becomes TRUE.

With Excel worksheet formulas, Power Query's M code formulas or the Data Model's DAX formulas, the comparison operator for a NOT logical test is <>, which is a less-than symbol followed by a greater-than symbol. This comparison operator checks whether two items are not equal (that is, not the same). For example, the logical test "Econ"<>"Busn" evaluates to TRUE, whereas "Busn"<>"Busn" evaluates to FALSE.

You can use the NOT function in an Excel worksheet and in the DAX formula language. The NOT function converts a TRUE value to FALSE and a FALSE value to TRUE. For example, the logical test =NOT(FALSE) evaluates to TRUE. Although this seems like a bizarre logical test to need, it is quite useful when you are checking whether a number of logical tests all come out FALSE, but then you want to convert the FALSE to a TRUE to verify that yes, they are all FALSE. Example 7, later in this chapter, illustrates this sort of "none are TRUE" logical test.

In the Power Query M code formula language, you can use the not operator, which converts a TRUE value to FALSE and a FALSE value to TRUE. You will see this in Chapter 19.

AND Logical Test

An AND logical test has two or more conditions. The goal of this type of test is to run two or more logical tests to determine if all logical tests evaluate to TRUE.

Two common examples of using an AND logical test to solve problems are for adding numbers with two or more criteria and for filtering a dataset with two or more criteria.

For an AND logical test with only two tests, there are four possible answers:

- FALSE, FALSE
- TRUE, FALSE
- FALSE, TRUE
- TRUE, TRUE

Only the last one (TRUE, TRUE) yields a TRUE value from an AND logical test.

The AND worksheet and DAX function is a logical function that can run up to 255 logical tests; only when all tests evaluate to TRUE does the AND function deliver a TRUE as the final result. The AND function cannot spill an array of answers because it is programmed to deliver a single scalar result.

In Power Query, you use the and operator, which runs an AND logical test and results in a true value only when all tests evaluate to true.

In an Excel worksheet, a number of aggregate worksheet functions can perform AND logical tests:

- **SUMIFS:** Adds numbers with two or more conditions or criteria
- **COUNTIFS:** Counts with two or more conditions or criteria
- **AVERAGEIFS:** Averages numbers with two or more conditions or criteria
- **MAXIFS:** Finds the maximum number with two or more conditions or criteria
- **MINIFS:** Finds the minimum number with two or more conditions or criteria

In addition, D functions are database worksheet functions that require a specific setup and can be used for single-cell and logical test calculations.

In math and statistics worksheet formulas and DAX formulas, you can perform an AND logical test by using the math multiplication operator. When you create an AND logical test using multiplication, you are creating a *Boolean math formula*. For example, you could test to see if 3>2 AND 5<9 by using either of these formulas:

- **AND function solution:** =AND(3>2,5<9) = AND(TRUE,TRUE) = TRUE
- **Boolean formula solution:** =(3>2)*(5<9) = (TRUE)*(TRUE) = 1*1 = 1

Boolean AND logical tests are often used in array formulas because you cannot use the AND function to deliver an array of answers. For example, if you want to find the answer to the logical question "Which records have the product Quad AND the sales rep Chantel?" you can create the AND logical test using multiplication, like this:

```
(Product Column = Quad)*(Sales Rep Column = Chantel)
```

If you are trying to filter a dataset with the FILTER function, the formula looks like this:

```
=FILTER(DataSetRecords, (Product Column = "Quad")*(Sales Rep Column =
"Chantel"))
```

You will see more examples of this type of test later in this chapter.

AND logical tests are *very* common, and there are many different terms used to refer to an AND logical test, including *and, conjunction, concurrent, intersection, joint, both, all conditions*, and *multiplication*. Many of these terms come from math and statistics.

BETWEEN Logical Test

When you run a BETWEEN logical test, you are running an AND logical test with a lower limit and an upper limit. Most of the time, the lower and upper limits are numbers, but text values are also allowed. For example, you can count how many students have between 46 and 90 school credits. For a student to be counted, you would use:

```
Credits >= Lower Limit of 46 AND Credits <= Upper Limit of 90
```

Whether or not you include the equal signs for both the upper and lower limits often depends on whether the numbers are whole numbers (in which case you include an equal sign with both the upper and lower limits) or decimal numbers (in which case you include an equal sign on only one side). However, every time you create a BETWEEN logical test, you must consider whether the lower and upper limits are included. If a limit is included, then you must use an equal sign; if it is not, you do not use an equal sign. In the data analysis and PivotTable sections of this book (Chapters 17, 18, and 19), you will see many examples of BETWEEN logical tests for tasks like adding between an upper date and a lower date and counting between an upper number and a lower number.

OR Logical Test

An OR is a logical test that has two or more conditions. The goal of an OR logical test is to run two or more logical tests to determine whether at least one test evaluates to TRUE. Another way to say this is that you run two or more logical tests to determine whether one or more of the logical tests evaluate to TRUE.

Two common examples of using an OR logical test to solve problems are for adding numbers with two or more criteria and for filtering a dataset with two or more criteria.

For an OR logical test with two tests, you can get these possible answers:

- FALSE, FALSE
- TRUE, FALSE
- FALSE, TRUE
- TRUE, TRUE

Only the first one (FALSE, FALSE) yields a FALSE value from an OR logical test. The last three all have at least one TRUE value; therefore, for an OR logical test, all three results yield the final answer TRUE. Notice that for an OR logical test with two tests, you can have one TRUE, the other TRUE, or both TRUE, and an OR logical test evaluates to TRUE.

The OR worksheet and DAX function is a logical function that can run up to 255 logical tests, and when one or more logical test evaluates to TRUE (that is, at least one TRUE), the OR function delivers TRUE as the final result. The OR function cannot spill an array of answers because it is programmed to deliver a single scalar result.

In Power Query, you use the or operator, which runs an OR logical test and results in a true value when at least one test evaluates to true.

When creating OR logical tests for aggregate operations, there are no specific built-in worksheet or DAX functions to use, as there are for AND logical tests (such as SUMIFS). Technically, there are D functions that can run OR logical tests, but they are inefficient. However, you can create your own OR logical test formulas to count, add, average, and filter when an OR logical test is needed.

In math and statistics worksheet formulas and DAX formulas, you can perform an OR logical test by using the math addition operator. When you create an OR logical test using addition, you are creating a *Boolean math formula*. For example, you could test to see if 1>2 OR 5<9 by using either of these formulas:

- **OR function solution:** =OR(1>2,5<9) = OR(FALSE,TRUE) = TRUE
- **Boolean formula solution:** =(1>2)+(5<9) = (FALSE)+(TRUE) = 0+1 = 1

Boolean OR logical tests are often used in array formulas because you cannot use the OR function to deliver an array of answers. For example, if you want to find the answer to the logical question "Which records have sales made by the sales rep Miki or the sales rep Jojo?" you can create the OR logical test using addition, like this:

```
(Sales Rep Column = Miki)+(Sales Rep Column = Jojo)
```

If you want to filter a dataset with the FILTER function, the formula looks like this:

```
=FILTER(DataSetRecords, (Sales Rep Column = "Miki")+(Sales Rep Column =
"Jojo"))
```

You will see more examples of this type of test later in this chapter.

OR logical tests are *very* common, and there are many different terms used to refer to OR logical tests, including *or, inclusive, disjunction, alternation, union, at least one, one or more,* and *adding.* Many of these terms come from math and statistics.

Logical Functions That Deliver a Single Scalar Boolean Value: AND, OR, and NOT

There are a number of Excel worksheet and DAX (Power Pivot and Power BI) functions that can deliver a single Boolean value, TRUE or FALSE. The most important of these are the AND, OR, and NOT functions:

- **AND:** The AND function runs an AND logical test and delivers a single scalar Boolean value.
- **OR:** The OR function runs an OR logical test and delivers a single scalar Boolean value.
- **NOT:** The NOT function changes FALSE to TRUE or TRUE to FALSE.

The AND and OR functions can have up to 255 logical tests entered as arguments, separated by commas. The order in which you enter logical tests into the arguments of these two functions does not matter because both functions are simply looking at how many TRUE values there are, not the order in which they occur. Unlike the AND and OR functions, the NOT function accepts only one argument. The arguments in all three functions interpret any nonzero number as TRUE and interpret zero as FALSE. All three functions can accept logical tests created with comparison operators, numeric values, the IS functions, or any other function or formula that delivers a Boolean or numeric value. It follows from this that you can nest any of these logical functions into arguments of other logical functions, as shown in Examples 8 and 9 in this chapter. Finally, you are not allowed to spill results from the AND, OR, or NOT functions because they are each programmed to deliver a single scalar Boolean value. When you use these functions in a column, you must enter the formula in the top cell and then manually copy the formula down; alternatively, you can use an Excel Table, which automatically fills formulas down to the rows below.

Example 4: Using an AND Function to Run an AND Logical Test

For this example, you need to use the AND function with two criteria to check whether a student is eligible for a scholarship when they have 45 or more credits and a GPA over 2.5 (see Figure 13.4).

You can try this example on the worksheet named Ch13(4).

G15			f_x	=AND(E15>=$C$11,F15>$C$12)		

	A	B	C	D	E	F	G
2	Ex	**Task:** Students are eligible for scholarship if:					
3	#4	They have completed 45 or more credits AND have GPA more than 2.5.					
4		**Goal:** Create logical formula (T/F) that shows if they are eligible for the scholarship.					
6		**Translate words into comparative operators:**					
7		"45 or more credits" logical test is: **Credits >= 45**					
8		"GPA more than 2.5" logical test is: **GPA > 2.5**					
10					**Formula in cell G15:**		
11		Credit Hurdle:	45		=AND(E15>=$C$11,F15>$C$12)		
12		GPA Hurdle:	2.5		Then copied to rows below.		
14		**Student**	**Start Date**	**Major**	**Credits**	**GPA**	**Eligible?**
15		Carey, Zada	9/29/2020	Business	45	1.7	FALSE
16		Emmons, Christi	7/14/2018	Accounting	135	2.3	FALSE
17		Lear, Vania	9/3/2020	Chemistry	45	3	TRUE
18		Meador, Corazon	11/21/2019	Accounting	90	3.1	TRUE
19		Mohamed, Abdi	1/28/2021	Business	23	1.6	FALSE
20		Nga, Luong	7/7/2020	Physics	45	2.4	FALSE
21		Robinson, Chantel	4/12/2020	History	70	4	TRUE
22		Rouse, Sioux	6/30/2020	Chemistry	40	2.4	FALSE
23		Simone, Alanna	8/2/2019	Physics	60	3.5	TRUE
24		Thornburg, Tyrone	12/27/2019	Sociology	75	3.9	TRUE

Figure 13.4 *An AND function to run an AND logical test.*

Example 5: Using an OR Function to Run an OR Logical Test

For this example, you need to use the OR function with two criteria to check whether a student is eligible for a scholarship when their major is either history or sociology (see Figure 13.5).

You can try this example on the worksheet named Ch13(5).

When you create the OR logical test inside the OR function, notice that for each student, the formula has to check the cell with the student's major twice: once to compare the cell to the history condition and a second time to compare the cell to the sociology condition. This means that in your formula, you need to use the cell reference D14 twice. When you run an OR logical test on a single column, this is the correct procedure.

When you are checking whether an item is equal to more than two different items, rather than use the OR function, you can use the XMATCH function, which tries to match an item in a list. You will see how to do this in Example 12, later in this chapter.

G14	▾	× ✓ fx	=OR(D14=$C$10,D14=$C$11)			

	A	B	C	D	E	F	G
2	Ex	Task: Students are eligible for scholarship if their major is history OR sociology.					
3	#5	Goal: Create logical formula (T/F) that shows if they are eligible for the scholarship.					
5		Translate words into comparative operators:					
6		"Major is history" logical test is: Major = History					
7		"Major is sociology" logical test is: Major = Sociology					
9					Formula in cell G14:		
10		Major:	History		=OR(D14=$C$10,D14=$C$11)		
11		Major:	Sociology		Then copied to rows below.		
13		Student	Start Date	Major	Credits	GPA	Eligible?
14		Carey, Zada	9/29/2020	Business	45	1.7	FALSE
15		Emmons, Christi	7/14/2018	Accounting	135	2.3	FALSE
16		Lear, Vania	9/3/2020	Chemistry	45	3	FALSE
17		Meador, Corazon	11/21/2019	Accounting	90	3.1	FALSE
18		Mohamed, Abdi	1/28/2021	Business	23	1.6	FALSE
19		Nga, Luong	7/7/2020	Physics	45	2.4	FALSE
20		Robinson, Chantel	4/12/2020	History	70	4	TRUE
21		Rouse, Sioux	6/30/2020	Chemistry	40	2.4	FALSE
22		Simone, Alanna	8/2/2019	Physics	60	3.5	FALSE
23		Thornburg, Tyrone	12/27/2019	Sociology	75	3.9	TRUE

Figure 13.5 *An OR function to run an OR logical test.*

Example 6: Creating an AND Boolean Math Formula to Run an AND Logical Test

As discussed earlier in this chapter, an AND logical test can be created by using the AND function or by using a Boolean math formula with the multiplication operator. For an AND logical test with only two tests, there are four possible answers for a Boolean AND logical test using the multiplication operator:

- FALSE * FALSE = 0
- TRUE * FALSE = 0
- FALSE * TRUE = 0
- TRUE * TRUE = 1

Only when all logical tests evaluate to TRUE does a Boolean AND logical test evaluate to 1, which Excel interprets as TRUE. Figure 13.6 shows how you can create a spilled array formula that runs an AND logical test and delivers a 1 value for TRUE and a 0 value for FALSE. Using a Boolean math AND logical test can be preferable to using the AND function if you want to spill your formula (which means you avoid locking cell references and manually copying the formula). As you will see later in this chapter, you might also want to use a Boolean math AND logical test to create array formulas, such as when you use the IF or FILTER functions.

You can try this example on the worksheet named Ch13(6).

G11			f_x	=(E11:E20>=C7)*(E11:E20>C8)		

	A	B	C	D	E	F	G
2	Ex	**Task:** Students are eligible for scholarship if:					
3	#6	They have completed 45 or more credits AND have GPA more than 2.5.					
4		**Goal:** Create Boolean logical formula that shows a 1 if they are eligible & 0 if not.					
6					**Formula in cell G11:**		
7		Credit Hurdle:	45		=(E11:E20>=C7)*(E11:E20>C8)		
8		GPA Hurdle:	2.5		Formula spills to rows below.		
10		**Student**	**Start Date**	**Major**	**Credits**	**GPA**	**Eligible?**
11		Carey, Zada	9/29/2020	Business	45	1.7	1
12		Emmons, Christi	7/14/2018	Accounting	135	2.3	1
13		Lear, Vania	9/3/2020	Chemistry	45	3	1
14		Meador, Corazon	11/21/2019	Accounting	90	3.1	1
15		Mohamed, Abdi	1/28/2021	Business	23	1.6	0
16		Nga, Luong	7/7/2020	Physics	45	2.4	1
17		Robinson, Chantel	4/12/2020	History	70	4	1
18		Rouse, Sioux	6/30/2020	Chemistry	40	2.4	0
19		Simone, Alanna	8/2/2019	Physics	60	3.5	1
20		Thornburg, Tyrone	12/27/2019	Sociology	75	3.9	1
22		**Steps for calculation of =(E11:E20>=C7)*(E11:E20>C8) in cell G11:**					
23		**1.** For a Boolean AND logical test use multiplication.					
24		=(E11:E20>=C7)*(E11:E20>C8)					
25		**2.** The first array of Boolean values evaluates.					
26		=({TRUE;TRUE;TRUE;TRUE;FALSE;TRUE;TRUE;FALSE;TRUE;TRUE})*(E11:E20>C8)					
27		**3.** The second array of Boolean values evaluates.					
28		=({TRUE;TRUE;TRUE;TRUE;FALSE;TRUE;TRUE;FALSE;TRUE;TRUE})* ({TRUE;TRUE;TRUE;TRUE;TRUE;TRUE;TRUE;TRUE;TRUE;TRUE})					
29		**4.** Only when there is a corresponding TRUE*TRUE, does the resultant array get a 1.					
30		={1;1;1;1;0;1;1;0;1;1}					

Figure 13.6 *An AND Boolean math multiplication formula to run an AND logical test.*

Example 7: Creating an OR Boolean Math Formula to Run an OR logical Test

As discussed earlier in this chapter, an OR logical test can be created using the OR function or by using a Boolean math formula with the addition operator. For an OR logical test with only two tests, there are four possible answers for a Boolean OR logical test using the addition operator:

- FALSE + FALSE = 0
- TRUE + FALSE = 1
- FALSE + TRUE = 1
- TRUE + TRUE = 2

When at least one logical test evaluates to TRUE, the Boolean OR logical test evaluates to a nonzero number, which Excel interprets as TRUE. Figure 13.7 shows how you can create a spilled formula that runs an OR logical test and delivers a 1 value for TRUE and a 0 value for FALSE. Using a Boolean OR logical test can be preferable to using the OR function when you want to spill your results or create other array formulas by using functions like IF and FILTER.

You can try this example on the worksheet named Ch13(7).

G10	▼	:	×	✓	fx	=(D10:D19=C6)+(D10:D19=C7)		

	A	B	C	D	E	F	G
2	Ex	**Task:** Students are eligible for scholarship if their major is history OR sociology.					
3	#7	**Goal:** Create logical formula (T/F) that shows if they are eligible for the scholarship.					
5					**Formula in cell G10:**		
6		Major:	History		=(D10:D19=C6)+(D10:D19=C7)		
7		Major:	Sociology		Formula spills to rows below.		
9		**Student**	**Start Date**	**Major**	**Credits**	**GPA**	**Eligible?**
10		Carey, Zada	9/29/2020	Business	45	1.7	0
11		Emmons, Christi	7/14/2018	Accounting	135	2.3	0
12		Lear, Vania	9/3/2020	Chemistry	45	3	0
13		Meador, Corazon	11/21/2019	Accounting	90	3.1	0
14		Mohamed, Abdi	1/28/2021	Business	23	1.6	0
15		Nga, Luong	7/7/2020	Physics	45	2.4	0
16		Robinson, Chantel	4/12/2020	History	70	4	1
17		Rouse, Sioux	6/30/2020	Chemistry	40	2.4	0
18		Simone, Alanna	8/2/2019	Physics	60	3.5	0
19		Thornburg, Tyrone	12/27/2019	Sociology	75	3.9	1
21		Steps for calculation of =(D10:D19=C6)+(D10:D19=C7) in cell G10:					
22		**1.** For a Boolean OR logical test use addition.					
23		=(D10:D19=C6)+(D10:D19=C7)					
24		**2.** The first array of Boolean values evaluates.					
25		=({FALSE;FALSE;FALSE;FALSE;FALSE;FALSE;TRUE;FALSE;FALSE;FALSE})+(D10:D19=C7)					
26		**3.** The second array of Boolean values evaluates.					
27		=({FALSE;FALSE;FALSE;FALSE;FALSE;FALSE;TRUE;FALSE;FALSE;FALSE})+ ({FALSE;FALSE;FALSE;FALSE;FALSE;FALSE;FALSE;FALSE;FALSE;TRUE})					
28		**4.** FALSE+TRUE or TRUE+FALSE both will create a 1 in the resultant array.					
29		{0;0;0;0;0;0;1;0;0;1}					

Figure 13.7 *An OR Boolean math addition formula to run an OR logical test.*

Example 8: Nesting the OR Function Inside the AND Function to Run a Complex Logical Test

Sometimes logical tests can be complex because they have more than two criteria or you might have to combine different types of logical tests together, such as by running an OR logical test inside an AND logical test. Figure 13.8 shows a situation in which there are three conditions that must be met before a student is eligible for a scholarship. The rule for eligibility is that the student must have a start date before 1/1/2020, and their major must be business or accounting. When you get a logical test like this, you can break it down piece by piece. In this case, the second part to the rule is "major is business or accounting." This is an OR logical test because it includes the word *or*.

When you try this example on the worksheet Ch13(8), you can first create the formula OR(D16=$C$12,D16=$C$13) in cell G16 to check whether the first student's major is business or accounting. Notice that for this OR logical test, you must check the same cell twice: once to see if it is equal to business and a second time to see if it is equal to accounting. You can enter the formula into cell G16 and then copy it down to see if it works. Then, looking back at the full eligibility rule, notice that the "start date before 1/1/2020" part of the rule sits before the word *and*. This means you need to create an AND logical test that uses the "start date before 1/1/2020" and the OR logical test result. Editing the formula in cell G16, you can create the full logical test formula:

```
=AND(C16<$C$11,OR(D16=$C$12,D16=$C$13))
```

> **Note:** Remember that the order in which logical tests are entered does not matter. The formula =AND (C16<$C$11,OR(D16=$C$12,D16=$C$13)) is just as valid as =AND(OR(D16=$C$12,D16=$C$13), C16<$C$11) or =AND(C16<$C$11,OR(D16=$C$13, D16=$C$12)).

G16			× ✓ fx	=AND(C16<$C$11,OR(D16=$C$12,D16=$C$13))				
⊿	A	B	C	D	E	F	G	H
2	Ex	**Task:** Students are eligible for scholarship if:						
3	#8	Their start date is before 1/1/2020 AND their major is business OR accounting.						
4		**Goal:** Create logical formula (T/F) that shows if they are eligible for the scholarship.						
6		**Translate words into comparative operators:**						
7		"Start date is before 1/1/2020" logical test is: **Start Date < 1/1/2020**						
8		"Major is business" logical test is: **Major = Business**						
9		"Major is accounting" logical test is: **Major = Accounting**						
11		Start Date:	1/1/2020		Formula in cell G16:			
12		Major:	Business		=AND(C16<$C$11,OR(D16=$C$12,D16=$C$13))			
13		Major:	Accounting		Then copied to rows below.			
15		**Student**	**Start Date**	**Major**	**Credits**	**GPA**	**Eligible?**	
16		Carey, Zada	9/29/2020	Business	45	1.7	FALSE	
17		Emmons, Christi	7/14/2018	Accounting	135	2.3	TRUE	
18		Lear, Vania	9/3/2020	Chemistry	45	3	FALSE	
19		Meador, Corazon	11/21/2019	Accounting	90	3.1	TRUE	
20		Mohamed, Abdi	1/28/2021	Business	23	1.6	FALSE	
21		Nga, Luong	7/7/2020	Physics	45	2.4	FALSE	
22		Robinson, Chantel	4/12/2020	History	70	4	FALSE	
23		Rouse, Sioux	6/30/2020	Chemistry	40	2.4	FALSE	
24		Simone, Alanna	8/2/2019	Physics	60	3.5	FALSE	
25		Thornburg, Tyrone	12/27/2019	Sociology	75	3.9	FALSE	

Figure 13.8 *Using the OR function inside the AND function to run a complex logical test.*

Example 9: Using a None Are True Logical Test or a NOT NOT Logical Test

Figure 13.9 shows a situation in which a student can be eligible for a scholarship if their major is *not* business or accounting. When you are checking whether an item (in this case, a major) is not equal to two other items, you have two equally good ways to solve the problem. The first approach is to read the words in the rule literally. If you read the scholarship rule literally, you read "major is not business or accounting," and you can see the word *not* and then the word *or*. This makes it straightforward to identify the two types of logical tests that you need to combine. Further, because the word *or* comes after the word *not*, you know that the OR logical test will go inside the NOT function.

When you try this example on the worksheet Ch13(9), you can first create the formula =OR(D13=$G$9,D13=$G$10) in cell G13 to check whether the first student's major is business or accounting. Then you can place the Boolean result from the OR function inside the NOT function to create the final formula you can copy down:

```
=NOT(OR(D13=$G$9,D13=$G$10))
```

When you place the OR function inside the NOT function, it can be thought of as a "none are true" logical test because when OR reports a FALSE value, the student's major matches neither of the criteria (business or accounting), and therefore neither part is TRUE. An OR logical test only results in a FALSE value when all the tests come out FALSE. Then, to convert the OR logical test FALSE to TRUE, you use the NOT function.

The second approach to solving this problem is to think of the logical test as two consecutive NOT logical tests that both must come out TRUE. First, you check whether the student's major is not business, and then you check whether the student's major is not accounting; then you put those two logical tests inside the AND function. The formula for the second example in Figure 13.9 is:

`=AND(D13<>$G$9,D13<>$G$10)`

Either one of the formulas is sufficient and efficient for situations like these.

There is a third way to solve the problem in Figure 13.9. Can you figure it out?

> **Note:** In learning Excel with this book and in your career, whenever you can think of multiple ways to solve a problem, you are expanding your thought process and your ability to find the best solution for a given situation. Thinking of multiple ways to solve a problem increases your insights into how Excel works and your ability to solve problems.

| G13 | | f_x | =NOT(OR(D13=$G$9,D13=$G$10)) | | | | | |

	A	B	C	D	E	F	G	H	I	J
2	Ex	**Task:** Students are eligible for scholarship if their major is NOT business OR accounting.								
3	#9	**Goal:** Create logical formula (T/F) that shows if they are eligible for the scholarship.								
5		**Translate words into comparative operators:**								
6		"Major is business" logical test is: **Major = Business**								
7		"Major is accounting" logical test is: **Major = Accounting**								
9					Major:		Business			
10					Major:		Accounting			
12		**Student**	**Start Date**	**Major**	**Credits**	**GPA**	**Eligible?**	**Eligible?**	**Formula in cell G13:**	
13		Carey, Zada	9/29/20	Business	45	1.7	FALSE	FALSE	=NOT(OR(D13=$G$9,D13=$G$10))	
14		Emmons, Christi	7/14/18	Accounting	135	2.3	FALSE	FALSE	Then copied to rows below.	
15		Lear, Vania	9/3/20	Chemistry	45	3	TRUE	TRUE		
16		Meador, Corazon	11/21/19	Accounting	90	3.1	FALSE	FALSE	**Alternative:**	
17		Mohamed, Abdi	1/28/21	Business	23	1.6	FALSE	FALSE	**Formula in cell H13:**	
18		Nga, Luong	7/7/20	Physics	45	2.4	TRUE	TRUE	=AND(D13<>$G$9,D13<>$G$10)	
19		Robinson, Chantel	4/12/20	History	70	4	TRUE	TRUE	Then copied to rows below.	
20		Rouse, Sioux	6/30/20	Chemistry	40	2.4	TRUE	TRUE		
21		Simone, Alanna	8/2/19	Physics	60	3.5	TRUE	TRUE		
22		Thornburg, Tyrone	12/27/19	Sociology	75	3.9	TRUE	TRUE		

Figure 13.9 *Two methods to run a "none are true" logical test. A third way is possible, too, as described in Example 29.*

Example 10: Using a BETWEEN Logical Test

Figure 13.10 shows a situation in which a student can be eligible for a scholarship if they are in their second year of study, which is defined as having completed between 46 and 90 credits. Because there are upper and lower limits to this AND logical test, it is called a BETWEEN logical test. For a student to be eligible, their credits must be simultaneously greater than or equal to 46 and less than or equal to 90. Notice that you must check the cell with the student's credits against both the lower limit and the upper limit. Further, you cannot run a single-condition test that simply checks against the lower limit because then you would get everything greater than or equal to 45, but you would also get everything bigger than 90. For this reason, you must add the second constraint to make sure that there are no numbers counted that are above the upper limit.

Whenever you do a BETWEEN logical test, you must check the item against both the lower limit and the upper limit. In this example, the credits are whole numbers with no decimal places, and the definition of a second-year student allows students to have exactly 46 credits or exactly 90 credits. For this reason, you have to use an equal sign with both the lower and upper limits:

```
Credits >= 45 AND Credits <= 90
```

If there were some reason that your presentation needed to show the logical test as "credits must be greater than 45 and no more than 90," the logical test would be constructed with no equal sign on the lower limit and an equal sign on the upper limit, like this:

```
Credits > 45 AND Credits <= 90
```

You would get exactly the same pattern of TRUE and FALSE values for the student dataset with either logical test. As you will see in Chapters 17 through 19, between criteria are very common, and each time you run a BETWEEN logical test, you must be diligent and pay attention to where the equal signs are placed.

You can try this example on the worksheet named Ch13(10).

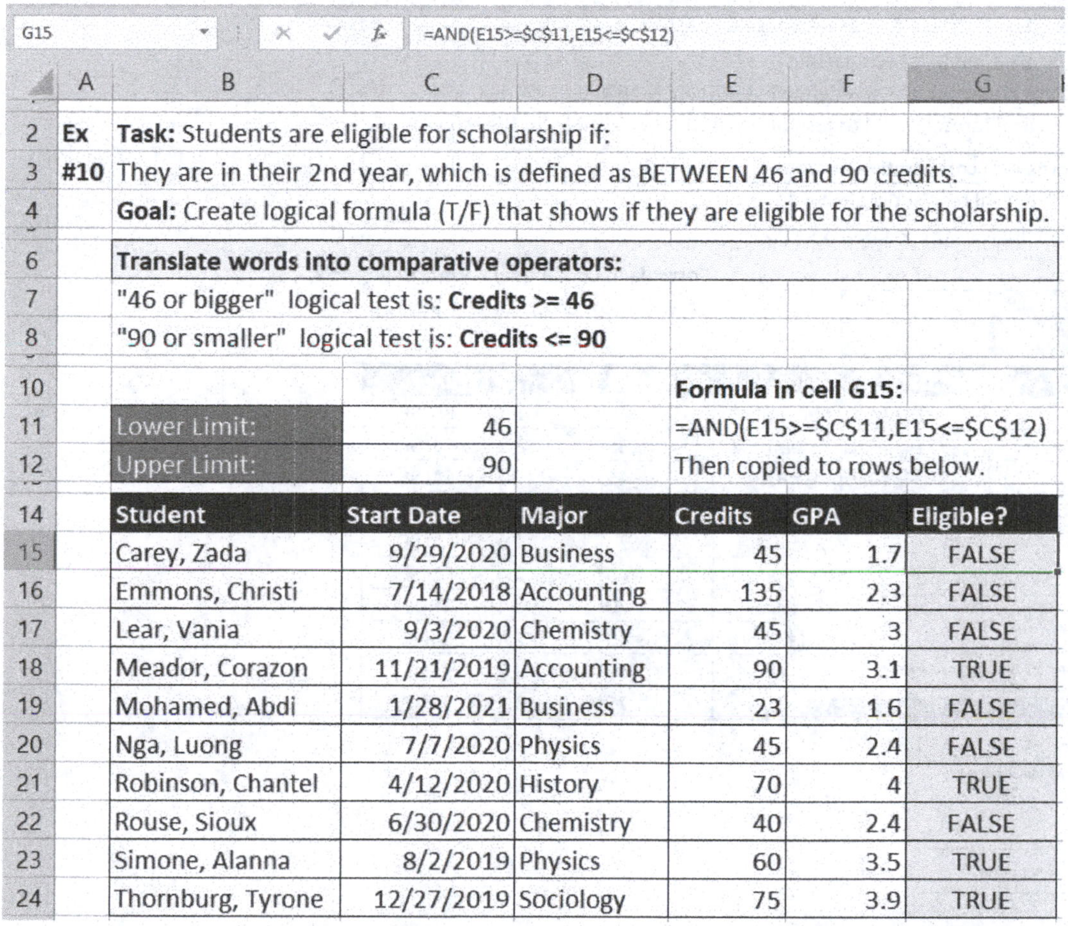

Figure 13.10 *A BETWEEN logical test runs an AND logical test with upper and lower limits.*

Example 11: Conditionally Formatting a Row with an AND Logical Test and Mixed Cell References

As you learned in Example 17 in Chapter 12, if you want to conditionally format a row in a dataset based on conditions from a particular column, you need to use mixed cell references. Figure 13.11 shows how to conditionally format the rows in the student dataset where the student is a second-year student. The trick is to carefully select the range B15:F24 in the worksheet with the active cell set as cell B15 and then, in the Edit Formatting Rule dialog box, use a similar formula to the formula in Example 8; however, rather than use relative cell references, you need to use mixed cell references with the column locked. This is the formula to use in this case:

```
=AND($E13>=$G$9,$E13<=$G$10)
```

You can try this example on the worksheet named Ch13(11). If you need to be reminded about the specific steps for applying a logical formula for conditionally formatting a row, you can look back at Example 17 in Chapter 12.

	A	B	C	D	E	F	G	H
2	Ex	**Task:** Students are eligible for scholarship if:						
3	#11	They are in their 2nd year, which is defined as BETWEEN 46 and 90 credits.						
4		**Goal:** Create logical formula (T/F) to format row if they are eligible for the scholarship.						
6		**Translate words into comparative operators:**						
7		"46 or bigger" logical test is: **Credits >= 46**						
8		"90 or smaller" logical test is: **Credits <= 90**						
10						**Formula in Conditional Format dialog box:**		
11		Lower Limit:	46			=AND($E15>=$C$11,$E15<=$C$12)		
12		Upper Limit:	90					
14		**Student**	**Start Date**	**Major**	**Credits**	**GPA**	**Eligible?**	
15		Carey, Zada	9/29/2020	Business	45	1.7	FALSE	
16		Emmons, Christi	7/14/2018	Accounting	135	2.3	FALSE	
17		Lear, Vania	9/3/2020	Chemistry	45	3	FALSE	
18		Meador, Corazon	11/21/2019	Accounting	90	3.1	TRUE	
19				ness	23	1.6	FALSE	
20				ics	45	2.4	FALSE	
21				ory	70	4	TRUE	
22				nistry	40	2.4	FALSE	
23				ics	60	3.5	TRUE	
24				ology	75	3.9	TRUE	

Edit Formatting Rule   ?   X

Select a Rule Type:
- Format all cells based on their values
- Format only cells that contain
- Format only top or bottom ranked values
- Format only values that are above or below average
- Format only unique or duplicate values
- Use a formula to determine which cells to format

Edit the Rule Description:

Format values where this formula is true:

=AND($E15>=$C$11,$E15<=$C$12)

Preview: AaBbCcYyZz   Format...

OK   Cancel

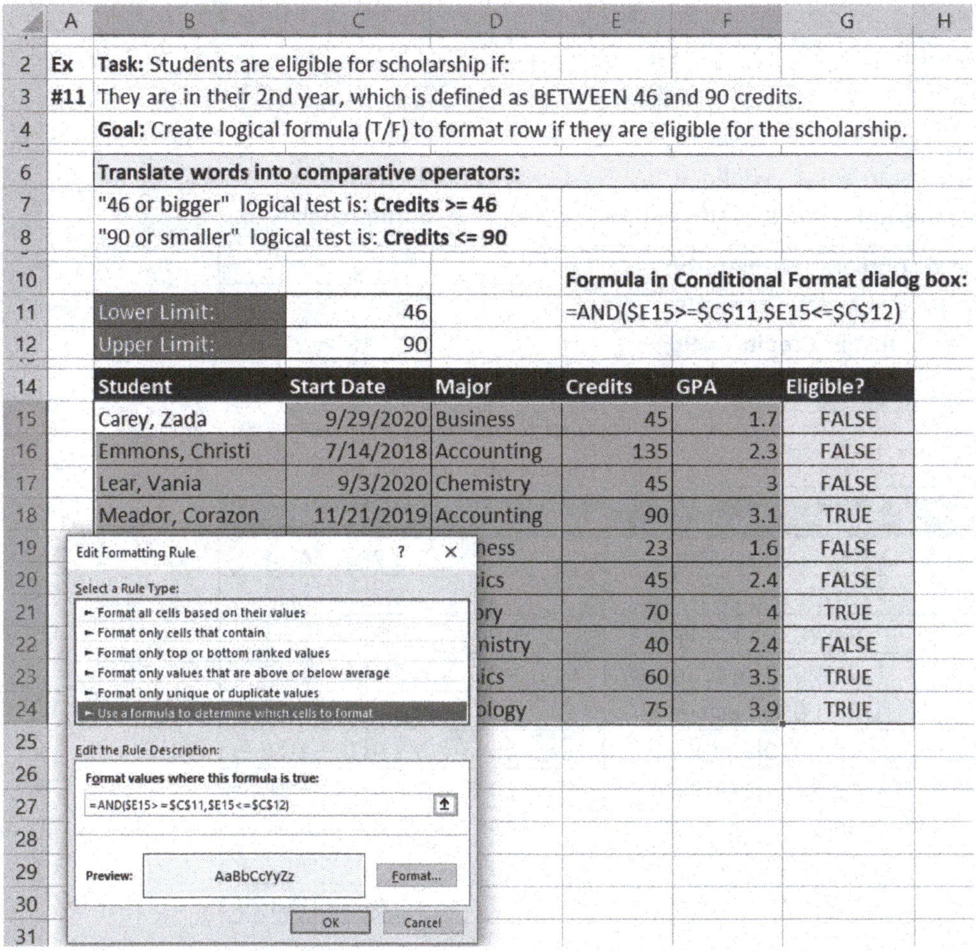

Figure 13.11 *Mixed cell references with the column reference are required to conditionally format a row.*

Example 12: Creating a Test Where Any Nonzero Number Is Considered a TRUE Value

Figure 13.12 shows a customer dataset where the goal is to determine whether a thank-you e-mail should be sent, based on whether the Total Paid column amount is greater than zero and the customer's account status is excellent. You could use the logical test:

```
Total Paid > 0 AND Account Status = Excellent
```

However, if you know the intricacies of how logical tests work in Excel and remember that any nonzero number is interpreted as TRUE, you can shorten the formula and reduce the number of calculations that the formula calculation engine makes. When you do this, the logical test for the Total Paid column can use Total Paid Cell rather than Total Paid Cell > 0. So rather than using the AND logical test =AND(D16>0,C16=$B$13), you can simply use

```
=AND(D16,C16=$B$13)
```

It is a shorter formula to type out, and the formula engine can make one fewer calculation for each cell that contains a formula. Although this may seem insignificant, when you start to create larger models and Excel solutions, these sorts of small details can add up to significant efficiencies.

You can try this example on the worksheet named Ch13(12).

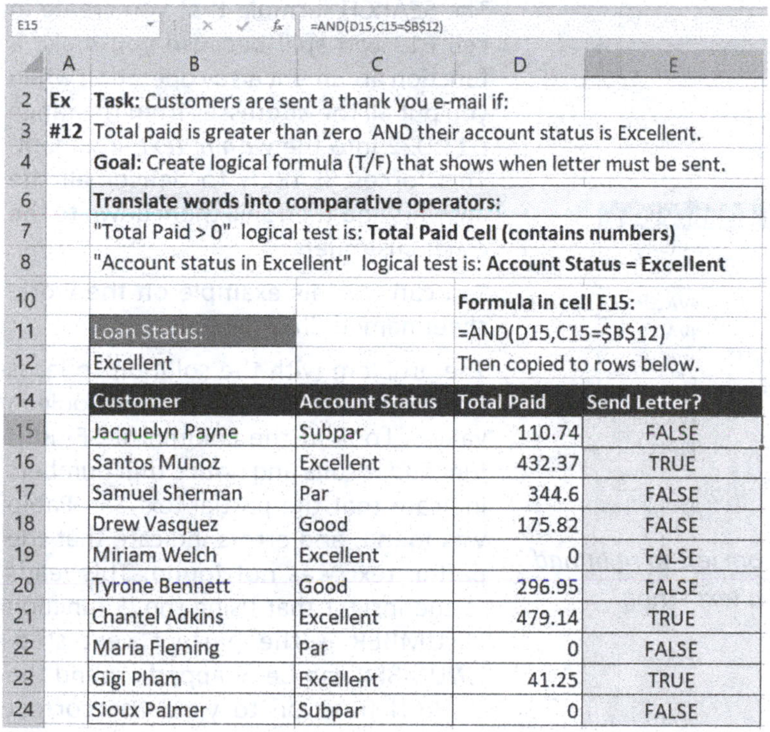

E15		× ✓ fx	=AND(D15,C15=$B$12)		
	A	B	C	D	E
2	Ex	**Task:** Customers are sent a thank you e-mail if:			
3	#12	Total paid is greater than zero AND their account status is Excellent.			
4		**Goal:** Create logical formula (T/F) that shows when letter must be sent.			
6		**Translate words into comparative operators:**			
7		"Total Paid > 0" logical test is: **Total Paid Cell (contains numbers)**			
8		"Account status in Excellent" logical test is: **Account Status = Excellent**			
10				**Formula in cell E15:**	
11		Loan Status:		=AND(D15,C15=$B$12)	
12		Excellent		Then copied to rows below.	
14		**Customer**	**Account Status**	**Total Paid**	**Send Letter?**
15		Jacquelyn Payne	Subpar	110.74	FALSE
16		Santos Munoz	Excellent	432.37	TRUE
17		Samuel Sherman	Par	344.6	FALSE
18		Drew Vasquez	Good	175.82	FALSE
19		Miriam Welch	Excellent	0	FALSE
20		Tyrone Bennett	Good	296.95	FALSE
21		Chantel Adkins	Excellent	479.14	TRUE
22		Maria Fleming	Par	0	FALSE
23		Gigi Pham	Excellent	41.25	TRUE
24		Sioux Palmer	Subpar	0	FALSE

Figure 13.12 *Any nonzero number is interpreted as TRUE, and zero is interpreted as FALSE.*

EXCEL – THE ONLY APP THAT MATTERS

Example 13: Using the SEARCH and ISNUMBER Functions in a Contains Logical Test

Figure 13.13 shows a common situation in which you need to identify whether a customer lives on a particular street. In this example, you need a logical formula that will tell you when a customer lives on San Pablo Ave. The problem with this logical test is that the Address column contains the street name and number address. So you cannot directly match the text San Pablo with any of the address in the Address column. What you need to do is search for the subtext string, or partial text (San Pablo), within the larger text string (the full address). You can do this with the SEARCH function.

The SEARCH worksheet function checks whether the specified text is located within a second text item and reports the position where it finds the specified text, counting characters from left to right. Figure 13.13 shows the arguments for the SEARCH function, where *find_text* is the partial text to find and *within_text* is the text to search within. In Figure 13.13, you can see that in cell E18, SEARCH finds San Pablo in the fifth character position from the left.

The SEARCH function is not case-sensitive. If you need to accomplish a case-sensitive search, you use the FIND worksheet function (with the same *find_text* and *within_text* arguments). Both SEARCH and FIND are in the DAX formula language that you will learn about later in this book.

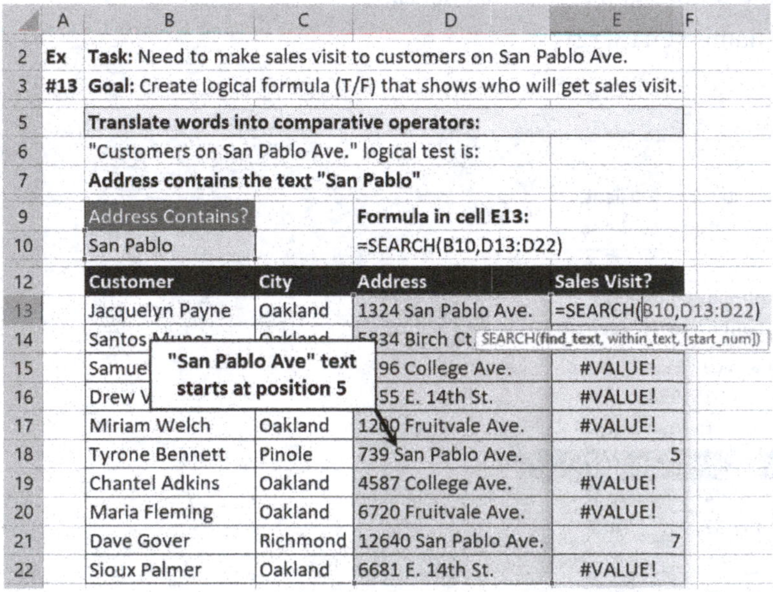

The SEARCH formula that you create in cell E13 can spill because you make a function argument array operation when you put all the addresses from the range D13:D22 into the *within_text* argument. This forces SEARCH to deliver all the answers and then spill them down to the other customers.

You can try this example on the worksheet named Ch13(13-14).

The problem with the solution so far is that it does not yield the desired Boolean values. Look at the column of SEARCH function results and notice that numbers indicate that the partial text San Pablo was found, and errors indicate that the partial text was not found. This leads to the insight that using the IS function ISNUMBER is the perfect next step. ISNUMBER can be wrapped around the SEARCH function to yield the correct Boolean values. Figure 13.14 shows the final logical formula with SEARCH inside the ISNUMBER function.

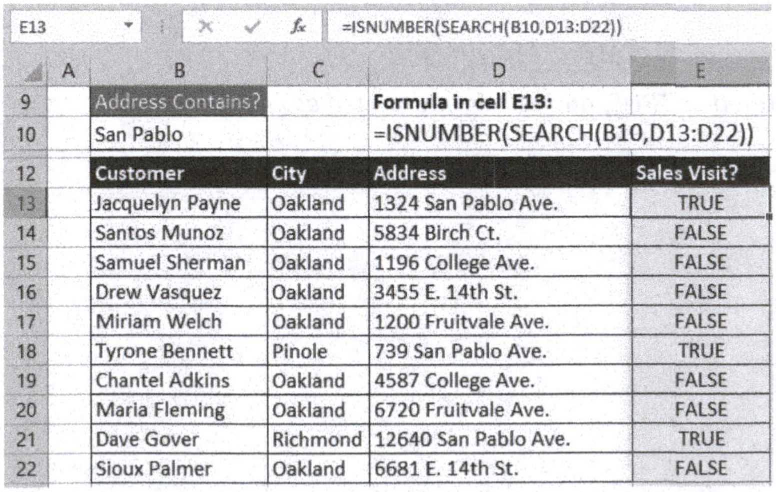

It is helpful to notice that the IS functions are different from the AND, OR, and NOT functions because they can spill results. Further, if you examine this problem a bit more, notice that if you were interested in the customers not on San Pablo Ave., the errors would indicate a match, and you would use ISERROR rather than ISNUMBER.

Figure 13.13 *The SEARCH function counts from left to right and reports the position of specified text within a text string.*

Figure 13.14 *ISNUMBER reports TRUE when it finds a number.*

Example 14: Using Formula Wildcards to Create a Contains Logical Test Inside the COUNTIFS Worksheet Function

In Example 13, you used the SEARCH function to check whether the text San Pablo was in a larger text address. If you were interested in making an aggregate count operation rather than showing Boolean values, you would use the COUNTIFS worksheet function to count with a single condition and the asterisk wildcard character to create the contains criteria.

As shown in Figure 13.15, the contains condition inside the COUNTIFS function is *San Pablo* (in cell F7), rather than just San Pablo (as in Example 13).

A few special characters can help you conduct searches in an Excel worksheet:

- **Asterisk (*):** The * is a wildcard character that represents any set of zero or more characters.
- **Question mark (?):** The ? is a wildcard character that represents exactly any one single character.
- **Tilde (~):** The ~ is used to convert the wildcards * and ? to actual characters.

By placing the asterisk character at the front and back of the text San Pablo, you are telling Excel to find text items such as 1324 San Pablo (where there are 5 characters before San Pablo), San Pablo Ave. (where there are 5 characters after San Pablo), 1324 San Pablo Ave. (where there are 5 characters before and 5 characters after San Pablo), or simply San Pablo (where there are 0 characters before or after San Pablo). Conveniently in this example, you could type the partial text condition *San Pablo* into the cell and simply use the cell reference F7 in the *criteria1* argument of the COUNTIFS function. You could do this because you do not need the text San Pablo for any other calculations. Sometimes, however, you need a condition for one calculation to be exact (for example, San Pablo), and you need partial text (for example, *San Pablo Ave*) for a different calculation. In this case, you can simply type **San Pablo** into the cell and then add the wildcards in the formula, like this (see the bottom of Figure 13.15):

```
=COUNTIFS(D9:D18,"*"&F15&"*")
```

With this version of the formula, you must put both asterisk wildcards in double quotation marks and then use the join operator (the ampersand) to join them to the beginning and end of the cell with the exact condition San Pablo.

You can try this example on the worksheet named Ch13(15).

	A	B	C	D	E	F	G
2	Ex	**Task:** Need to make sales visit to customers on San Pablo Ave.					
3	#14	**Goal:** Count how many sales visits to make using a contains condition.					
5		**Translate words into condition for COUNTIFS function:**					
6		"On San Pablo Ave." condition is:				Wild card in cell	
7		***San Pablo***				*San Pablo*	
9		**Customer**	**City**	**Address**		No. San Pablo addresses	
10		Jacquelyn Payne	Oakland	1324 San Pablo Ave.		3	
11		Santos Munoz	Oakland	5834 Birch Ct.		**Formula in cell F10:**	
12		Samuel Sherman	Oakland	1196 College Ave.		=COUNTIFS(D10:D19,F7)	
13		Drew Vasquez	Oakland	3455 E. 14th St.			
14		Miriam Welch	Oakland	1200 Fruitvale Ave.		Wild card in formula	
15		Tyrone Bennett	Pinole	739 San Pablo Ave.		San Pablo	
16		Chantel Adkins	Oakland	4587 College Ave.			
17		Maria Fleming	Oakland	6720 Fruitvale Ave.		No. San Pablo addresses	
18		Dave Grover	Richmond	12640 San Pablo Ave.		3	
19		Sioux Palmer	Oakland	6681 E. 14th St.		**Formula in cell F18:**	
20						=COUNTIFS(D10:D19,"*"&F15&"*")	

Figure 13.15 *The asterisk wildcard character represents zero or more characters.*

Logical Worksheet Functions That Deliver Values: IF, IFS, IFNA, IFERROR, and FILTER

One of the most widely used functions in Excel's 40-year history is the IF function. The IF function is a logical function, but rather than delivering TRUE or FALSE, it can deliver one of two items (numbers, text, formulas, ranges, and more). Given that you have already studied 14 logical test examples, you are ready to learn about the IF function, which uses a logical test in its first argument, and then the second and third arguments are simply the items you want to deliver when you get a TRUE or FALSE, respectively. The syntax of the IF functions is as follows:

```
IF(logical_test, value_if_true, value_if_false)
```

When a formula requires one of two items, you use the IF function. The IF function is also available in the DAX formula language in Power Pivot and Power BI.

Example 15: Using the IF Function to Deliver One of Two Number Values: 750 or 0

The best example I know to illustrate the power of the IF function is an employee incentive bonus situation (see Figure 13.16). For example, say that an employee's contract states that if the employee makes sales for the company of $20,000 or more, they will get a $750 bonus; otherwise, they do not get a bonus. The incentive is in place to entice the employee to make sales that equal or exceed the hurdle $20,000. If you need to make a formula that automatically determines whether this hurdle has been reached, you use the IF function because only one of two different values can go in the cell: 750 or 0. You know you need to do the logical test Employee Sales >= 20,000, which can evaluate to TRUE or FALSE. Therefore, this is the formula you use:

```
=IF(Employee Sales >= 20,000,750,0)
```

This formula runs the logical test and delivers the number 750 to the cell when the logical test evaluates to TRUE and delivers the number 0 when it evaluates to FALSE.

You can try this example on the worksheet named Ch13(16).

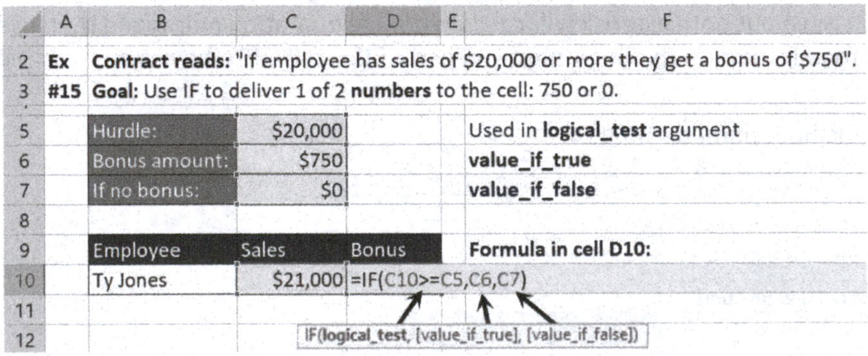

Figure 13.16 *The IF function is used when the goal is to deliver one of two items to a cell or formula.*

In Figure 13.16, notice that the employee must jump over the hurdle 20,000 (in cell C5) to get a bonus. Because you use an equal sign as part of the comparison operator, the employee will get a bonus if their sales are exactly equal to 20,000 or any other number above that. When you try this example, change the employee sales number in cell C10 to a number below 20,000, use the number 20,000, and also use a number greater than 20,000. By checking all three possibilities (less than, equal to, and greater than), you can verify that the formula is working correctly. For the formula to be correct, the IF function must deliver the 750 value to the cell for any number greater than or equal to 20,000 and a 0 value for any number less than 20,000.

Example 16: Using the IF Function to Deliver One of Two Text Values: Over or Under

Whereas in Example 15, you used the IF function to deliver one of two number values, in this example, you need to use the IF function to deliver one of two text values to a cell. For the example in Figure 13.17, you need to use the IF function to deliver the text Over when the customer's cell phone data usage is over or equal to 1 GB and Under when it is less than 1 GB. In this example, you use the IF function to deliver one of two text values. Be sure to check whether the IF function works in all three situations (over, equal to, and over the hurdle).

You can try this example on the worksheet named Ch13(17).

	A	B	C	D	E	F	G	H
	D10		✕ ✓ *fx*	=IF(C10<C5,C7,C6)				
2	Ex	**Contract reads:** "If data is under 1 GB per month you do not pay extra".						
3	#16	**Goal:** Use IF to deliver 1 of 2 **text** items to each cell: "Under" or "Over"						
5		Hurdle (GB):		1		Use in **logical_test** argument		
6		Hurdle or more:	Over			**value_if_true**		
7		Less than hurdle:	Under			**value_if_false**		
9		Customer	Usage (GB)	Usage?		Formula in cell D10:		
10		Dino Jones	0.97	Under		=IF(C10<C5,C7,C6)		

Figure 13.17 *The IF function can be used to deliver one of two text values to a cell or formula.*

Examples 17 and 18: Using the IF Function to Deliver a Formula or Show Nothing

When building invoices in an Excel worksheet, your goal is to have formulas automatically appear when the user enters sales data. If the user does not enter data, then the formulas should not appear. For example, in Figure 13.18, if the invoice user enters a product name into cell B15, you want the price to appear in cell D15. Similarly, if the invoice user enters the units number into cell C15, you want the correctly calculated sales amount to appear in cell E15. You can accomplish this with the IF function, where for each cell you either want a formula or you want to show nothing. The formulas for the price and sales columns are shown in Figure 13.18.

For the Price column formula, the *logical_test* argument of the IF function uses the ISBLANK function to check whether the cells in the Product column are empty. If the cells are empty, the *value_if_true* argument uses the two-double-quotation-marks formula syntax for showing nothing in the cell; otherwise, if the cell is not empty, the *value_if_false* argument uses the XLOOKUP formula.

For the Sales column formula, the *logical_test* argument of the IF function uses the ISNUMBER function to check whether the cells in the Units Sold column contain numbers. If the cells contain numbers, the *value_if_true* argument uses a formula that multiplies the Units Sold column value by the spilled range of prices; otherwise, if the cell is not a number, the *value_if_false* argument uses the two-double-quotation-marks formula syntax to show nothing.

Because you use IS functions in both formulas for the *logical_test* arguments, you can place the full columns into the IS function arguments to cause the formulas to spill.

You can try this example on the worksheet named Ch13(18).

	A	B	C	D	E	F	G	H
	D12		✕ ✓ *fx*	=IF(ISBLANK(B12:B17),"",XLOOKUP(B12:B17,G12:G17,H12:H17))				
2		**Task:** Create Invoice that can lookup price and calculate sales						
3		based on whether data is entered into a cell.						
4		**Goal:** Use IF to deliver 1 of 2 items, either a formula or "" (show nothing).						
6	Ex	**Formula in cell D12:**						
7	#17	=IF(ISBLANK(B12:B17),"",XLOOKUP(B12:B17,G12:G17,H12:H17))						
8		**Formula in cell E12:**						
9	#18	=IF(ISNUMBER(C12:C17),C12:C17*D12#,"")						
11		Product	Units Sold	Price ($)	Sales ($)		Product	Price
12		Yanaki	12	27.95	335.4		Quad	43.95
13		Sunshine	44	19.95	877.8		Carlota	26.95
14		Aspen	34	25.95	882.3		Aspen	25.95
15							Yanaki	27.95
16							Sunshine	19.95
17							FastCatch	31.95
19				**Prove it to yourself:**				
21		Empty cell =>		TRUE	Formula in cell D21: =ISBLANK(C21)			
22		"" =>		FALSE	Formula in cell D22: =ISBLANK(C22)			
23		"" =>		TRUE	Formula in cell D23: =ISTEXT(C23)			
24		"" =>		0	Formula in cell D24: =LEN(C24)			

Figure 13.18 *Formulas use zero-length text strings to show nothing in a cell, even though it is something.*

Surprisingly, the most conceptually difficult part of the formulas in Figure 13.18 is the method for showing nothing in an Excel worksheet formula. The formula syntax for showing nothing in a cell requires that you use two double quotation marks, like this: "" (and not four single quotation marks and not spaces between the double quotation marks). Remember from Chapter 12 that all text in formulas must be placed in double quotation marks, but for this particular use, you just use the double quotation marks with nothing inside them.

When you use two double quotation marks in a formula, you are using a *zero-length text string* because Excel considers it text that has zero length. You can prove this to yourself by trying the functions ISBLANK (which reports TRUE when the cell is empty), ISTEXT (which reports TRUE when the cell contains text), and LEN (which tells how many characters are in a cell), as shown in the bottom of Figure 13.18. Most of the time, you do not need to think about this technical side of using two double quotation marks. You just use them when you need your formula to show nothing in the cell. However, occasionally, a zero-length text string in a cell can cause trouble. For example, if you are using a math formula on a cell with a zero-length text string and you are expecting the empty cell to evaluate to zero, you will get a #VALUE! error because the cell really contains text. In fact, this is exactly what would happen in the Sales column in Figure 13.18 if you did not use the IF function.

Examples 19 and 20: Using the AND and OR Functions Inside the IF Function

Figures 13.19 and 13.20 show examples of using the AND and OR functions, respectively, in the *logical_test* argument of the IF function. In both examples, the text values in the *value_if_true* and *value_if_false* arguments are hard coded into the formula because they are values that the scholarship department determined will not change. Unlike in Example 18, where you used IS functions in the *logical_test* argument and were allowed to spill the formulas, in these examples you cannot spill the results because functions like AND and OR cannot spill results.

You can try these two examples on the worksheets named Ch13(19) and Ch13(20).

G14		✕ ✓ ƒx	=IF(AND(E14>=$C$6,F14>$C$7),"Eligible","Not Eligible")				
	A	B	C	D	E	F	G
2	Ex	**Task:** Students are eligible for scholarship if:					
3	#19	They have completed 45 or more credits AND have GPA more than 2.5.					
4		**Goal:** Create formula that shows "Eligible" or "Not Eligible"					
6		Credit Hurdle:	45				
7		GPA Hurdle:	2.5				
9		**Formula in cell G14:**					
10		=IF(AND(E14>=$C$6,F14>$C$7),"Eligible","Not Eligible")					
11		Then copied to rows below.					
13		**Student**	**Start Date**	**Major**	**Credits**	**GPA**	**Eligible?**
14		Carey, Zada	9/29/2020	Business	45	1.7	Not Eligible
15		Emmons, Christi	7/14/2018	Accounting	135	2.3	Not Eligible
16		Lear, Vania	9/3/2020	Chemistry	45	3	Eligible
17		Meador, Corazon	11/21/2019	Accounting	90	3.1	Eligible
18		Mohamed, Abdi	1/28/2021	Business	23	1.6	Not Eligible
19		Nga, Luong	7/7/2020	Physics	45	2.4	Not Eligible
20		Robinson, Chantel	4/12/2020	History	70	4	Eligible
21		Rouse, Sioux	6/30/2020	Chemistry	40	2.4	Not Eligible
22		Simone, Alanna	8/2/2019	Physics	60	3.5	Eligible
23		Thornburg, Tyrone	12/27/2019	Sociology	75	3.9	Eligible

Figure 13.19 *You can use the AND function inside the logical_test argument of IF.*

G13 | : | × ✓ *fx* | =IF(OR(D13=$C$5,D13=$C$6),"Eligible","Not Eligible")

	A	B	C	D	E	F	G
2	Ex	**Task:** Students are eligible for scholarship if their major is history OR sociology.					
3	#20	**Goal:** Create formula that shows "Eligible" or "Not Eligible"					
5		Major:	History				
6		Major:	Sociology				
8		**Formula in cell G13:**					
9		=IF(OR(D13=$C$5,D13=$C$6),"Eligible","Not Eligible")					
10		Then copied to rows below.					
12		**Student**	**Start Date**	**Major**	**Credits**	**GPA**	**Eligible?**
13		Carey, Zada	9/29/2020	Business	45	1.7	Not Eligible
14		Emmons, Christi	7/14/2018	Accounting	135	2.3	Not Eligible
15		Lear, Vania	9/3/2020	Chemistry	45	3	Not Eligible
16		Meador, Corazon	11/21/2019	Accounting	90	3.1	Not Eligible
17		Mohamed, Abdi	1/28/2021	Business	23	1.6	Not Eligible
18		Nga, Luong	7/7/2020	Physics	45	2.4	Not Eligible
19		Robinson, Chantel	4/12/2020	History	70	4	Eligible
20		Rouse, Sioux	6/30/2020	Chemistry	40	2.4	Not Eligible
21		Simone, Alanna	8/2/2019	Physics	60	3.5	Not Eligible
22		Thornburg, Tyrone	12/27/2019	Sociology	75	3.9	Eligible

Figure 13.20 *You can use the OR function inside the logical_test argument of IF.*

Example 21: Creating an AND Logical Test That Can Spill Results

If you need to run an AND logical test in the first argument of the IF function, and you want to spill your formula so you can avoid having to lock cell references and manually copy the formula, you can create a Boolean math AND logical test, as shown in Figure 13.21.

You can try this example on the worksheet named Ch13(21).

	A	B	C	D	E	F	G
2	Ex	**Task:** Students are eligible for scholarship if:					
3	#21	They have completed 45 or more credits AND have GPA more than 2.5.					
4		**Goal:** Create formula that shows "Eligible" or "Not Eligible"					
6		Credit Hurdle:	45				
7		GPA Hurdle:	2.5				
9		**Formula in cell G14:**					
10		=IF((E14:E23>=C6)*(F14:F23>C7),"Eligible","Not Eligible")					
11		Formula spills to rows below.					
13		**Student**	**Start Date**	**Major**	**Credits**	**GPA**	**Eligible?**
14		Carey, Zada	9/29/2020	Business	45	1.7	Not Eligible
15		Emmons, Christi	7/14/2018	Accounting	135	2.3	Not Eligible
16		Lear, Vania	9/3/2020	Chemistry	45	3	Eligible

Figure 13.21 *Using Boolean math for an AND logical test inside the IF function allows you to spill your results.*

Example 22: Using the IFS Function When You Have Three or More Things to Put in a Cell

With the IF function, you can put one of two items into a cell. But what if you want to put one of three items into a cell? In that case, you can use the IFS function, which can put three or more items into a cell, based on a series of logical tests. In Figure 13.22, the goal of the formula in cell B12 is to show the report label "Net Loss" when revenues are less than expenses, "Break Even" when revenue is equal to expenses, and "Net Income" when revenues are greater than expenses.

The IFS function can have up to 127 pairs of arguments. For example, the first pair of arguments consists of the arguments *logical_test1* and *value_if_true1*. You use these arguments for the first logical test and for the item that you want to put into the cell if that logical test evaluates to TRUE. The next pair of arguments, the third and fourth arguments, are *logical_test2* and *value_if_true2*. These two arguments are presented in the screentip in square brackets ([*logical_test2*, *value_if_true2*]) to indicate that they are a pair: a logical test and an item that should be put into the cell if that matched logical test evaluates to TRUE.

The major difference between the IFS function and the IF function is that there is no *value_if_false* argument in the IFS function, as there is in the IF function. As a result, if you have a final value that is the default when all previous logical tests evaluate to FALSE, then for the last matched pair of arguments, you can put a TRUE value in the *logical_test* argument and the final item in the *value_if_true* argument, as shown in Figure 13.22. In this example, it would be fine to use Revenue > Total Expenses as C6>C11 for the third logical test because it is the only other option possible; however, this test involves more typing and a longer formula to achieve the same goal as simply using a TRUE value. The IFS function is unique to the Excel worksheet and is not available in Power Query's M code formula language or the Data Model's DAX formula language.

You can try this example on the worksheet named Ch13(22).

B12		✕ ✓ *fx*	=IFS(C6<C11,"Net Loss",C6=C11,"Break Even",TRUE,"Net Income")				
	A	B	C	D	E	F	G
2	Ex	**Goal:** Report must have the label: "Net Loss", Net Income" or "Break Even",					
3	#22	based on whether revenues are less than, equal to or bigger than expenses.					
4		**IFS** to deliver 1 of 3 Text Items to the cell: "Net Loss" or "Break Even" or "Net Income"					
6		Revenue	$65,000				
7		COGS Expense	29,500				
8		Operations Expense	12,750				
9		Admin Expense	5,750				
10		Other Expense	6,950				
11		Total Expenses	$54,950		**Formula in cell C11:**	=SUM(C7:C10)	
12		Net Income	$10,050		**Formula in cell C12:**	=ABS(C6-C11)	
14		**Formula in cell B12:**					
15		=IFS(C6<C11,"Net Loss",C6=C11,"Break Even",TRUE,"Net Income")					
16		IFS(**logical_test1**, value_if_true1, [logical_test2, value_if_true2], [logical_test3, value_if_true3], [logical_test4, …])					

Figure 13.22 *The IFS function allows you to deliver three or more items to a cell or formula.*

Examples 23 and 24: Using the IFNA Function to Replace the #N/A Error with Something Different

So far in this book, you have often documented your formulas using the FORMULATEXT function. However, if you have tried to use the FORMULATEXT function on an empty cell, you have noticed that you get an #N/A error, which means not available. When building Excel solutions and templates to use, it would be convenient to put the FORMULATEXT function into the cells before you enter the formulas. Then, when a formula is entered into a cell, the documentation will automatically happen.

As shown in Figure 13.23, you can put the FORMULATEXT function into the first argument of the IFNA worksheet function, and you can put the formula syntax to show nothing (two double quotation marks) into the second argument of IFNA. With this IFNA formula in cell G6, if a user puts a formula into cell E6, FORMULATEXT can show the formula; if the user does not put a formula in cell E6, the FORMULATEXT function will deliver an #N/A error, and IFNA will deliver a zero-length text string to cell G6, and nothing will be displayed.

You can try this example on the worksheet named Ch13(23). When you try it, be sure to test both possibilities: a formula cell E6 and no formula in cell C6.

G6			× ✓ fx	=IFNA(FORMULATEXT(E6),"")			

	A	B	C	D	E	F	G	H
2	Ex	Goal: Show formula in cell if user creates a formula in that cell, otherwise show nothing.						
3	#23	Use IF to deliver 1 of 2 items, either a **formula** or "" (**show nothing**).						
5		Product	Price	Units	Units		Formula in cell E6:	
6		Quad	43.95	32	$1,406.40		=C6:C8*D6:D8	
7		Carlota	26.95	25	$673.75			
8		Aspen	25.95	44	$1,141.80		Formula in cell G6:	
9							=IFNA(FORMULATEXT(E6),"")	
10							IFNA(**value**, value_if_na)	
11								

Figure 13.23 *You can use the IFNA worksheet function to show nothing rather than the #N/A error.*

Figure 13.24 shows a common use for the IFNA function: to deliver the message "Product Not Valid" when the user enters the incorrect product name for the XLOOKUP lookup function. Figures 13.25 and 13.26 show that the IFNA function is perfect when you use functions, like FORMULATEXT and XLOOKUP, that deliver the #N/A error when there is a problem and you want to show something different than the error value.

You can try this example on the worksheet named Ch13(24). When you try it, be sure to test both possibilities: a valid product name in cell B6 and an invalid product name in cell B6.

The IFNA function is unique to the Excel worksheet and is not available in Power Query's M code formula language or the Data Model's DAX formula language.

D6			× ✓ fx	=IFNA(XLOOKUP(B6,F4:F7,G4:G7),"Product Not Valid")		

	A	B	C	D	E	F	G
2	Ex	Goal: Lookup formula that inicates				Lookup Table:	
3	# 24	when product not valid.				Product	Price
4						Quad	43.95
5		Product	Units Sold	Price ($)		Carlota	26.95
6		Quuad	12	Product Not Valid		Aspen	25.95
7						Yanaki	27.95
8		**Formula in cell D6:**					
9		=IFNA(XLOOKUP(B6,F4:F7,G4:G7),"Product Not Valid")					

Figure 13.24 *You can use the IFNA worksheet function to report a message rather than show the #N/A error.*

Examples 25: Using the IF Function Instead of IFERROR

Figure 13.25 shows an example that you first saw back in Chapter 12, in Example 8, where you need to add the three longest boomerang flight times for the maximum time aloft boomerang event. The formula used in cell H15 is an array formula that adds the three biggest numbers. For the template shown here, there are only three throwers' scores entered. For the empty rows, the formula yields an unsightly error. It would be great if you could avoid the errors in rows where data has not been entered. Figure 13.25 shows two formulas that can accomplish this goal:

- The formula used in cell I15 uses the IFERROR function to either show the formula result or show nothing. The IFERROR function is similar to the IFNA function except that, rather than just check for the #N/A error, it checks for all formula error types.

- The formula in cell J15 uses the IF function and a more specific logical test to look for an answer to the question "Are there more than two numbers in the row?" The logical test uses the COUNT worksheet function, which counts how many numbers are in a range, which is perfect in this situation because the times entered are numbers. The full logical test, COUNT(C15:G15)>2, will get a TRUE value only when three or more numbers have been entered.

You can try this example on the worksheet named Ch13(25).

J15		▼	× ✓ *fx*	=IF(COUNT(C15:G15)>2,SUM(LARGE(C15:G15,{1,2,3})),"")						

	A	B	C	D	E	F	G	H	I	J
2	Ex	Goal: Create array formula that calculates when 3 or more scores have been entered.								
3	# 25									
5		Formula in cell H15:								
6		=SUM(LARGE(C15:G15,{1,2,3}))								
8		Formula in cell I15:								
9		=IFERROR(SUM(LARGE(C15:G15,{1,2,3})),"")								
11		Formula in cell J15:								
12		=IF(COUNT(C15:G15)>2,SUM(LARGE(C15:G15,{1,2,3})),"")								
14		Thrower	Time 1	Time 2	Time 3	Time 4	Time 5	Add Top 3	Add Top 3	Add Top 3
15		Bower	0.00	86.87	92.40	80.89	85.09	264.36	264.36	264.36
16		Kavanaugh	72.09	108.27	73.70	93.34	0.00	275.31	275.31	275.31
17		Washington	55.26	85.96	89.82	34.85	31.66	231.04	231.04	231.04
18								#NUM!		
19								#NUM!		
20								#NUM!		

Figure 13.25 *Three formulas to add the top three scores.*

The disadvantage of using the IFERROR function in this situation is that IFERROR must calculate the array formula in every cell to determine whether to show the formula results or show nothing. For larger array formulas that span many cells in a column, this can sometimes slow performance (that is, formula calculation time) to the point where you have to wait for a column of formulas to finish calculating before you move on to the next task.

Note: The advantage of the IFERROR function is that it requires less typing and time to create than the IF function formula. The advantage of the IF function is that it must calculate the logical test in every cell, but then that test determines whether to run the array formula or simply deliver the zero-length text string to the cell. This means that if the logical test formula element can calculate more quickly than the array formula element, using the IF formula alternative will be more efficient. My rule of thumb is that if an alternative logical test exists, and I don't have to run the array formula to get an error, I go with the IF function version rather than the IFERROR version. In my years of consulting, I have seen significant improvements when users change their IFERROR formulas to IF formulas.

Examples 26: Using the IF Function Inside an Aggregate Function to Make a Conditional Calculation

When doing a sum, a count, or an average aggregate operation with one or more conditions, you can use the built-in functions SUMIFS, COUNTIFS, and AVERAGEIFS, respectively. However, for some aggregate operations, such as the standard deviation calculation in statistics, there is no built-in function. The IF function can come to the rescue in such a situation.

The steps for the calculation of the formula =STDEV.S(IF($B$8:$B$20=E8,$C$8:$C$20)) in Figure 13.26 show that the IF function can deliver the correct numbers for the specified Quad product to the STDEV.S function to calculate the sample standard deviation, which is a common statistical calculation to express the variation in the data points and the reliability of the average for those data points.

You can try this example on the worksheet named Ch13(26).

> **Note:** I hid rows 16 to 19 in Figure 13.26 to better fit the figure on the page. However, they are not hidden in the file you use to follow along.

| G8 | ▾ | × ✓ *fx* | =STDEV.S(IF($B$8:$B$20=E8,$C$8:$C$20)) |

	A	B	C	D	E	F	G	H
2	**Ex**	**Goal:** Calculate Standard Deviation for each product.						
3	**# 26**	Standard Deviation tells you how reliable the average is.						
4		Small standard deviation = reliable average.						
5		Large standard deviation = less reliable average.						
7		Product	Units Sold		Product	Average Units	Standard Deviation	
8		Quad	154		Quad	67.3333	78.50053078	
9		Carlota	12		Carlota	63.75	44.31986011	
10		Quad	1					
11		Sunshine	256		**Formula in cell F8:**			
12		Aspen	1		=AVERAGEIFS($C$8:$C$20,$B$8:$B$20,E8)			
13		Aspen	57		**Formula in cell G8:**			
14		Sunshine	249		=STDEV.S(IF($B$8:$B$20=E8,$C$8:$C$20))			
15		Quad	47		Then formulas copied down.			
20		Aspen	32					
21								
22		Steps for calculation of **=STDEV.S(IF($B$8:$B$20=E8,$C$8:$C$20))** in cell G8:						
23		**1.** We use the IF function inside an aggregate function to select specified values.						
24		=STDEV.S(**IF(B8:B20=E8,C8:C20)**)						
25		**2.** The logical test argument checks to see which products are "Quad".						
26		=STDEV.S(IF({**TRUE**;FALSE;**TRUE**;FALSE;FALSE;FALSE;FALSE;**TRUE**;FALSE; FALSE;FALSE;FALSE;FALSE},{**154**;12;**1**;256;1;57;249;**47**;120;66;57;250;32}))						
27		**3.** IF function delivers resultant array of Quad numbers and FALSE values.						
28		=STDEV.S({**154**;FALSE;**1**;FALSE;FALSE;FALSE;FALSE;**47**;FALSE;FALSE;FALSE;F ALSE;FALSE})						
29		**4.** STDEV.S is programmed to ignore FALSE and uses only: 154, 1, 47.						
30		Sample Standard Deviation = **78.5005307837682**						

Figure 13.26 *You can select only specified values using the IF function and use the resultant array in other functions.*

Examples 27: Putting a Boolean AND Logical Test Inside the FILTER Function to Filter a Dataset

As shown in Figure 13.27, a Boolean AND logical test can be constructed using multiplication in the second argument of the FILTER array function to filter the dataset down to records where the sales rep is Chantel and the product is Quad.

You can try this example on the worksheet named Ch13(27).

> **Note:** I hid some of the rows in Figure 13.27 to help fit the large dataset on the page. Those rows are not hidden in the file you use to follow along.

| G14 | ▼ | : | × | ✓ | *fx* | =FILTER(B8:E36,(C8:C36=H10)*(D8:D36=H11),"None") |

	A	B	C	D	E	F	G	H	I	J	K
2	Ex	Goals:									
3	# 27	Extract records based on specified sales rep in cell H10 and product in cell H11.									
4		When you change conditions in cells, solution must instantly update.									
5		Use a Boolean AND logical test in the second argument of the FILTER array function.									
7		Date	Sales Rep	Product	Sales		Formula in cell G14:				
8		9/9/21	Sioux	Quad	$1,045.98		=FILTER(B8:E36,(C8:C36=H10)*(D8:D36=H11),"None")				
9		9/8/21	Ty	Aspen	$1,533.89						
10		9/10/21	Chantel	Quad	$1,904.66		Sales Rep	Chantel			
11		9/10/21	Sioux	Carlota	$690.16		Product	Quad			
12		9/8/21	Ty	Carlota	$1,029.52						
13				Aspen	$642.89		Date	Sales Rep	Product	Sales	
14		**Hidden rows**		Carlota	$883.31		9/10/21	Chantel	Quad	$1,904.66	
15		9/8/21	Miki	Carlota	$528.14		9/10/21	Chantel	Quad	$771.90	
28		9/9/21	Chantel	Carlota	$1,065.58						
29		9/10/21	Chantel	Quad	$771.90						
36		9/9/21	Gigi	Carlota	$376.29						
37											
38		Steps for calculation of =FILTER(B8:E36,(C8:C36=H10)*(D8:D36=H11),"None") in cell G14:									
39		**1.** Multiplication is used for an AND logical test.									
40		=FILTER(B8:E36,(C8:C36=H10)*(D8:D36=H11),"None")									
41		**2.** TRUE values in Sales Rep column AND TRUE values in Product column.									
42		=FILTER(B8:E36,({FALSE;FALSE;**TRUE**;FALSE;FALSE;FALSE;TRUE;FALSE;FALSE;FALSE;FALSE;FALSE;TRUE;FALSE;FALSE;FALSE;FALSE;FALSE;FALSE;FALSE;TRUE;**TRUE**;TRUE;FALSE;FALSE;FALSE;FALSE;FALSE;FALSE;FALSE})*({TRUE;FALSE;**TRUE**;FALSE;FALSE;FALSE;FALSE;FALSE;TRUE;TRUE;FALSE;FALSE;FALSE;FALSE;FALSE;TRUE;FALSE;TRUE;FALSE;TRUE;FALSE;**TRUE**;FALSE;FALSE;FALSE;FALSE;FALSE;TRUE;FALSE}),"None")									
43		**3.** Only when there is a TRUE*TRUE is the result 1.									
44		=FILTER(B8:E36,{0;0;1;0;0;0;0;0;0;0;0;0;0;0;0;0;0;0;0;0;0;1;0;0;0;0;0;0;0;0},"None")									
45		**4.** FILTER array function uses pattern of 0s and 1s to filter the table to matching records.									
46		Filtered table: {9/10/21,"Chantel","Quad",1904.66;9/10/21,"Chantel","Quad",771.9}									

Figure 13.27 *A Boolean math multiplication AND logical test inside the FILTER function.*

Examples 28: Putting a Boolean OR Logical Test Inside the FILTER Function to Filter a Dataset

As shown in Figure 13.28, a Boolean OR logical test can be constructed using addition in the second argument of the FILTER array function to filter the dataset down to records where the sales rep is Miki OR Jojo.

You can try this example on the worksheet named Ch13(28).

Note: I hid some of the rows in Figure 13.28 to help fit the large dataset on the page. Those rows are not hidden in the file you use to follow along.

| G14 | | | ✕ ✓ fx | =FILTER(B8:E36,(C8:C36=H10)+(C8:C36=H11),"None") | | | | | |

	A	B	C	D	E	F	G	H	I	J	K
2	Ex	Goals:									
3	# 28	Extract records based on specified sales reps in cell H10 and H11.									
4		When you change conditions in cells, solution must instantly update.									
5		Use a Boolean OR logical test in the second argument of the FILTER array function.									
7		Date	Sales Rep	Product	Sales		Formula in cell G14:				
8		9/9/21	Sioux	Quad	$1,045.98		=FILTER(B8:E36,(C8:C36=H10)+(C8:C36=H11),"None")				
9		9/8/21	Ty	Aspen	$1,533.89						
10		9/10/21	Chantel	Quad	$1,904.66		Sales Rep	Miki			
11		9/10/21	Sioux	Carlota	$690.16		Sales Rep	Jojo			
12		9/8/21	Ty	Carlota	$1,029.52						
13		9/8/21	Miki	Aspen	$642.89		Date	Sales Rep	Product	Sales	
14		9/10/21	Chantel	Carlota	$883.31		9/8/21	Miki	Aspen	$642.89	
15		9/8/21	Miki	Carlota	$528.14		9/8/21	Miki	Carlota	$528.14	
16		9/8/21	Jojo	Quad	$574.41		9/9/21	Jojo	Quad	$574.41	
17		9/9/21	Sioux	Quad	$309.18		9/8/21	Miki	Carlota	$1,033.92	
18		9/8/21	Ty	Aspen	$771.07		9/9/21	Miki	Quad	$1,217.02	
19		9/8/21	Miki	Carlota	$1,033.92		9/9/21	Miki	Aspen	$674.16	
20		9/9/21		ta	$290.43		9/8/21	Jojo	Carlota	$529.20	
21		9/	**Hidden rows**		$1,756.26		9/10/21	Jojo	Quad	$809.31	
36		9/		ta	$376.29						
38		Steps for calculation of **=FILTER(B8:E36,(C8:C36=H10)+(C8:C36=H11),"None")** in cell G14:									
39		**1.** Addition is used for an OR logical test.									
40		=FILTER(B8:E36,(C8:C36=H10)+(C8:C36=H11),"None")									
41		**2.** TRUE value in Sales Rep column OR TRUE value in Product column.									
		=FILTER(B8:E36,({FALSE;FALSE;FALSE;FALSE;FALSE;**TRUE**;FALSE;**TRUE**;FALSE;FALSE;FALSE; **TRUE**;FALSE;FALSE;FALSE;**TRUE**;**TRUE**;FALSE;FALSE;FALSE;FALSE;FALSE;FALSE;FALSE;FALSE ;FALSE;FALSE;FALSE;FALSE})+({FALSE;FALSE;FALSE;FALSE;FALSE;FALSE;FALSE;FALSE;**TRUE**; FALSE;FALSE;FALSE;FALSE;FALSE;FALSE;FALSE;FALSE;FALSE;FALSE;FALSE;FALSE;FALSE;FALS									
42		E;FALSE;FALSE;FALSE;**TRUE;TRUE**;FALSE}),"None")									
43		**3.** TRUE + FALSE = 1 or FALSE + TRUE = 1..									
44		=FILTER(B8:E36,{0;0;0;0;0;0;**1**;0;**1;1**;0;0;**1**;0;0;0;**1;1**;0;0;0;0;0;0;0;0;0;**1;1**;0},"None")									
45		**4.** FILTER array function uses pattern of 0s and 1s to filter the table to matching records.									

Figure 13.28 A Boolean math addition OR logical test inside the FILTER function.

Example 29: Comparing Two Lists and Extracting Results Using XMATCH and Other Functions

One of the most common tasks in the everyday lives of employees is to compare two lists. You might, for example, need to compare two lists of customer names or two lists of product parts or two lists of library books. For any of these situations, you usually do one of two things: compare the two lists and keep the items that are in both lists or compare the two lists and keep the items that are not in both lists.

In the example shown in Figure 13.29, you need to compare two lists and show the items that are not in both lists. The goal here is to find the missing library books after a physical inventory is completed. List 1 shows the library books that are in the computer system and that should be on the shelf. List 2 shows the books counted from the shelves in the physical inventory.

You can try this example on the worksheet named Ch13(29).

B10		✕ ✓ fx	=FILTER(B17:B26,ISNA(XMATCH(B17:B26,D17:D23)),"None")	
◢	A	B	C	D
2	Ex	**Goals:**		
3	**# 29**	Extract list of missing library books		
4		Show book titles from list #1 that are not in List #2.		
6		**Formula in cell B10:**		
7		=FILTER(B17:B26,ISNA(XMATCH(B17:B26,D17:D23)),"None")		
9		**Missing:**		
10		Cool Drink of Water (Maya d Angelo)		
11		East of Eden (John Steinbeck)		
12		Catch-22 (Joseph Heller)		
14		Are items in List #1 in List #2?		
16		**List #1: Books listed in computer system**		**List #2: Books counted during inventory**
17		Cool Drink of Water (Maya d Angelo)		The Lord of the Rings: Two Towers (Tolkien)
18		The Lord of the Rings: Two Towers (Tolkien)		Stomping the Blues (Albert Murray)
19		Stomping the Blues (Albert Murray)		The Da Vinci Code (Dan Brown)
20		The Da Vinci Code (Dan Brown)		Angela's Ashes (Frank McCourt)
21		East of Eden (John Steinbeck)		Life of Pi (Yann Martel)
22		Angela's Ashes (Frank McCourt)		The Grapes of Wrath (John Steinbeck)
23		Life of Pi (Yann Martel)		Bible
24		The Grapes of Wrath (John Steinbeck)		
25		Catch-22 (Joseph Heller)		
26		Bible		
28		**Steps for calculation of =FILTER(B17:B26,ISNA(XMATCH(B17:B26,D17:D23)),"None") in cell B10:**		
29		**1.** XMATCH function asks are books from List #1 in List #2?		
30		=FILTER(B16:B25,ISNA(**XMATCH(B17:B26,D17:D23)**),"None")		
31		**2.** XMATCH reports the relative position from List #2, otherwise report #N/A.		
32		=FILTER(B16:B25,ISNA(**{#N/A;1;2;3;#N/A;4;5;6;#N/A;7}**),"None")		
33		**3.** #N/A error indicates that book from List #1 is NOT in List #2, so you use ISNA function.		
34		=FILTER(B16:B25,**{TRUE;FALSE;FALSE;FALSE;TRUE;FALSE;FALSE;FALSE;TRUE;FALSE}**,"None")		
35		**4.** FILTER picks books from List #1 where there is a TRUE value.		
36		**{"Cool Drink of Water (Maya d Angelo)";"East of Eden (John Steinbeck)";"Catch-22 (Joseph Heller)"}**		

Figure 13.29 *Using the XMATCH, ISNA, and FILTER functions to extract items in List 1 that are not in List 2.*

Any time you want to compare two lists using Excel worksheet formulas, the most efficient way to accomplish this is to use the XMATCH function. The XMATCH function is a lookup function that looks up and reports the relative position of an item in a list. For example, with List 1, if you ask the question "Is the first book *Cool Drink of Water* located in List 2?" you get the XMATCH answer #N/A, which means not available (that is, it did not find it). Starting in List 1 again, If you ask the question "Is the second book *The Lord of the Rings* located in List 2?" you get the XMATCH answer 1 because it is in the first position of List 2. If then you ask "Is the last book in List 1, the Bible, in List 2?" you get the XMATCH answer 7 because it is in the seventh position of List 2.

Because the goal is to extract a list of missing library books, you need to filter List 1 to show only the books that are missing from List 2. You can filter data with the FILTER array function. With the FILTER function, you need a resultant array of TRUEs and FALSEs in the second argument, where TRUE tells you the book is missing. The XMATCH function can help you to do this.

The first two arguments in the XMATCH function are *lookup_value* and *lookup_array*. These are the same first two arguments as in the lookup function XLOOKUP. The trick for the library books formula is to make a function argument array operation in the *lookup_value* argument and list all the books from List 1 and then list the books from List 2 in the *lookup_array* argument, like this:

```
XMATCH(B17:B26,D17:D23)
```

If you evaluate just the XMATCH part of the formula, you see this:

```
{#N/A;1;2;3;#N/A;4;5;6;#N/A;7}
```

This is a pattern of #N/A errors and numbers that perfectly corresponds in size (1 column and 10 rows) to List 1. All you need to do now is convert the #N/A errors to TRUE values. The ISNA function is perfect for this task. Once you wrap the ISNA function on the outside of XMATCH and then place that in the second argument of FILTER, your formula is:

```
=FILTER(B17:B26,ISNA(XMATCH(B17:B26,D17:D23)),"None")
```

If you needed to instead extract books that are in both lists, the formula would use ISNUMBER rather than ISNA, like this:

```
=FILTER(B17:B26,ISNUMBER(XMATCH(B17:B26,D17:D23)),"None")
```

Because comparing two lists is such a common task, you need to remember that the key worksheet formula starting point is the XMATCH function. Then you use ISNA when you want to get the items in List 1 that are not in List 2, or you use ISNUMBER to get the items in both lists. You will learn more about XMATCH in Chapter 14.

Using IFS Aggregate Functions (COUNTIFS, SUMIFS, AVERAGEIFS, MINIFS, and MAXIFS) to Calculate Based on an AND Logical Test

When you make reports and perform analysis, you often need to do aggregate operations like counting, adding, averaging, or finding the minimum or maximum values. However, most of the time you do not perform the calculations on all the records in a dataset but rather make the calculations on a subset of records based on conditions and criteria.

For example, if the goal is to add all the sales for the product bananas to the customer Safeway in the month July, then you are adding with three conditions. If you need a worksheet formula to accomplish this, the SUMIFS worksheet function will work to add with the three conditions.

As shown in Figure 13.30, there are five worksheet functions that can make aggregate operations with up to 127 conditions or criteria in an AND logical test (although you would rarely use more than 5 criteria):

- **COUNTIFS:** Counts matches
- **SUMIFS:** Adds numbers
- **AVERAGEIFS:** Averages numbers
- **MINIFS:** Finds the smallest number
- **MAXIFS:** Finds the biggest number

These functions only exist in the Excel worksheet and are not available in Power Query's M code formula language or the Data Model's DAX formula language.

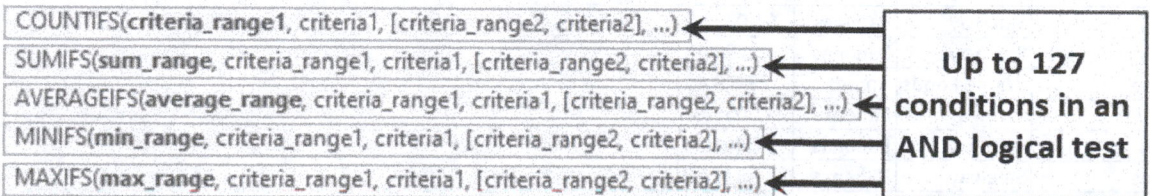

Figure 13.30 *Screentips with arguments for the COUNTIFS, SUMIFS, AVERAGEIFS, MINIFS, and MAXIFS worksheet functions.*

The important requirements for these functions are as follows:

- All five functions have matching pairs of *criteria_range* and *criteria arguments* that increment as *criteria_range1* and *criteria1*, *criteria_range2* and *criteria2*, and so on. These matching pairs expect a range of values in the *criteria_range* argument and the condition for the logical test in the *criteria* argument.

- The COUNTIFS function contains only paired *criteria_range* and *criteria* arguments because it counts how many times matches are made.

- SUMIFS, AVERAGEIFS, MINIFS, and MAXIFS all contain a first argument that expects a range of number values.

- The dimensions for the number ranges and criteria ranges must be the same; if they are not, you get a #VALUE! error.

- Array operations are not allowed in the number ranges and criteria ranges (for example, *sum_range*, *criteria_range1*).

- Array operations are allowed in the criteria arguments (for example, *criteria1*, *criteria2*).

- When you use two or more criteria arguments (*critera2* or more), these functions run an AND logical test.

- You can force these functions to make an OR logical test by placing an array of values into the *criteria* argument.

Example 30: Using IFS Aggregate Functions to Make Calculations with Three Criteria

Figure 13.31 shows the SUMIFS function in cell C10 adding with three conditions. For the SUMIFS formula, the logical test for adding sales is:

```
product = bananas AND customer = Safeway AND month = July
```

You can try all five of these aggregate functions to make calculations with three criteria on the worksheet named Ch13(31).

C10		fx	=SUMIFS(E16:E35,B16:B35,C5,C16:C35,C6,D16:D35,C7)		

	A	B	C	D	E
2	Ex	Goals:			
3	# 30	Count, add, average, find max & min for the banana sales in July made to Safeway.			
5		Month	July		
6		Customer	Safeway		
7		Product	Bananas		
9		Count records	5	Formula in C9:=COUNTIFS(B16:B35,C5,C16:C35,C6,D16:D35,C7)	
10		Add Sales	$4,881.05	Formula in C10:=SUMIFS(E16:E35,B16:B35,C5,C16:C35,C6,D16:D35,C7)	
11		Average Sales	$976.21	Formula in C11:=AVERAGEIFS(E16:E35,B16:B35,C5,C16:C35,C6,D16:D35,C7)	
12		Min Sale	$290.43	Formula in C12:=MINIFS(E16:E35,B16:B35,C5,C16:C35,C6,D16:D35,C7)	
13		Max Sale	$1,461.60	Formula in C13:=MAXIFS(E16:E35,B16:B35,C5,C16:C35,C6,D16:D35,C7)	
15		Month	Customer	Product	Sales
16		June	Whole Foods	Apples	$1,533.89
17		June	Whole Foods	Bananas	$690.16
18		July	Safeway	Bananas	$1,029.52
19		July	Whole Foods	Apples	$642.89
20		June	Safeway	Bananas	$883.31
21		July	Whole Foods	Bananas	$528.14
22		June	Safeway	Apples	$771.07
23		July	Safeway	Bananas	$1,033.92
24		July	Safeway	Bananas	$290.43
28		June	Whole Foods	Apples	$449.45
29		July	Safeway	Bananas	$1,065.58
30		July	Safeway	Bananas	$1,461.60
35		June	Safeway	Bananas	$376.29

Figure 13.31 *COUNTIFS, SUMIFS, AVERAGEIFS, MINIFS, and MAXIFS calculating with three conditions in an AND logical test.*

Example 31: Taking a Closer Look at Using the SUMIFS Function to Run an AND Logical Test with Three Criteria

This example takes a closer look at the sum calculation with three criteria. Figure 13.32 shows that the SUMIFS function has to look through the Month column to find July AND look through the Customer column to find Safeway AND look through the Product column to find Bananas; only when SUMIFS has found that a record meets all three conditions does it finally select the corresponding sales numbers from the Sales column to make the final aggregate operation:

$$\$1,029.52 + \$1,033.92 + \$290.43 + \$1,065.58 + \$1,461.60 = \$4,881.05$$

Notice that you use SUMIFS to calculate a single answer in cell C10.

You can try this example on the worksheet named Ch13(32).

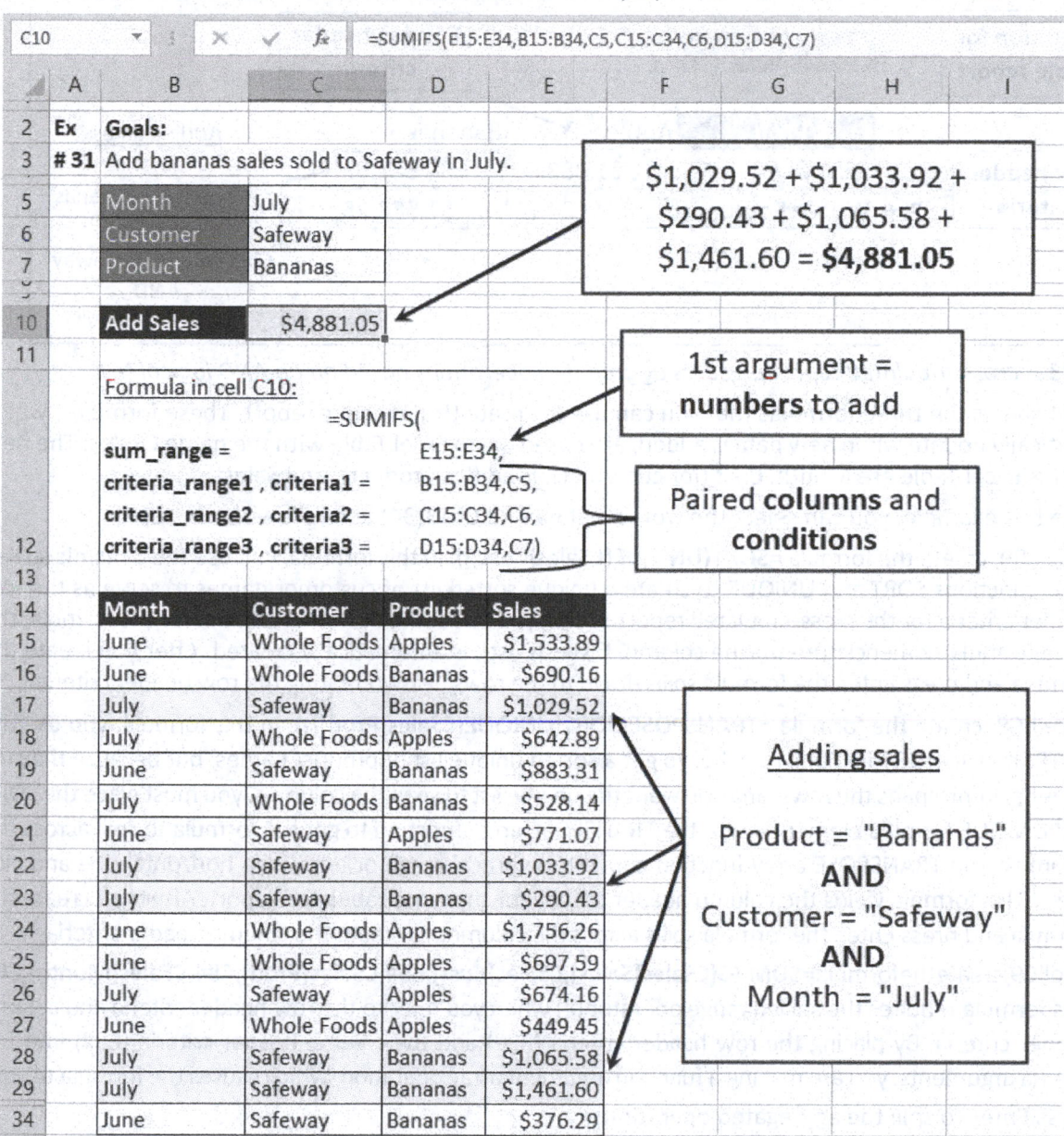

Figure 13.32 *SUMIFS runs an AND logical test with three conditions to select the correct sales numbers to add.*

Example 32: Using the SUMIFS Function with Three Criteria in a Cross-Tabulated Report

Often it is the case that you need to use the SUMIFS and other IFS aggregate functions to create reports that spill to more than one cell. Figure 13.33 shows a common summary report called a *cross-tabulated report*. A cross-tabulated report shows aggregate results calculated with two or more conditions, with criteria at the head of each row, criteria at the top of each column, and conditions for the whole report above the report. It is called a cross-tabulated, or cross-tab, report because the column header and row header criteria form a sort of cross (like a plus symbol) that intersect at the aggregated operation.

In Figure 13.33, the Bananas column and the Safeway row intersect where the SUMIFS function calculates the sum of sales for the product Bananas AND the customer Safeway AND the month July:

$1,029.52 + $1,033.92 + $290.43 + $1,065.58 + $1,461.60 = $4,881.05

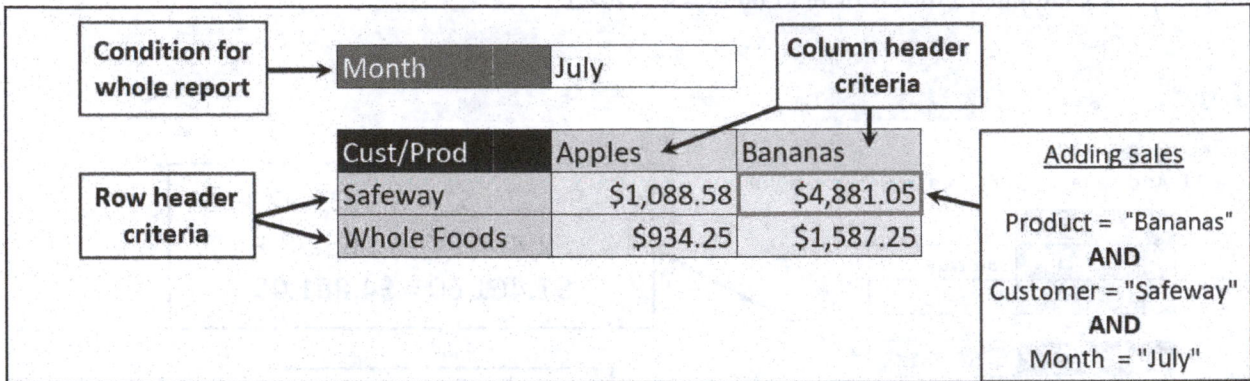

Figure 13.33 *A cross-tabulated report presents aggregated operations based on an AND logical test.*

Figure 13.34 shows the three formulas that you can use to create this dynamic report. These formulas, which will automatically update when new data is added, are based on an Excel Table with the name CSales. The field names for this Excel Table are Month, Cust (for customer), Prod (for product), and Sales.

To complete this example, you can select the worksheet named Ch13(34) and follow these steps:

1. In cell B9, create the formula **=SORT(UNIQUE(CSales[Cust]))**. In this formula, you use the dynamic spilled array functions SORT and UNIQUE to create a unique sorted list of customer names to serve as the row header criteria for the cross-tabulated report. When you select the customer column for the formula, the table formula nomenclature for the column, CSales[Cust], is automatically created. After you create the formula and press Enter, the formula spills down to the rows below, creating the row header criteria.

2. In cell C8, create the formula **=TRANSPOSE(SORT(UNIQUE(CSales[Prod])))**. In this formula, you use the SORT and UNIQUE functions together to get a sorted unique list of product names, but because the customer column spans the rows, and you want the unique list to span the columns, you must place the SORT and UNIQUE formula element inside the TRANSPOSE array function to get the formula to spill across the columns. The TRANSPOSE array function converts a vertical range or array to a horizontal one and vice versa. This formula yields the column header criteria for the cross-tabulated report. After you create the formula and press Enter, the formula spills across the columns to create the column header criteria.

3. In cell C9, create the formula **=SUMIFS(CSales[Sales],CSales[Cust],B9#,CSales[Prod],C8#,CSales[Month],C6)**. This formula requires the spilled range operator (#) when you refer to the row header criteria and column header criteria. By placing the row header criteria (B9#) and the column header criteria (C8#) into the criteria arguments, you are making a function argument array operation, which causes the formula to spill.

4. Press Enter to spill the aggregated operations.

> **Note:** Figure 13.34 shows the report and the documentation of the formulas created directly above the report. I set it up this way so that the figure would fit on the book page. However, because this report will automatically expand when new data is added, it would be better to create it off to the side of the Excel Table or on an entirely different worksheet. You can try this yourself by cutting and pasting the report off to the side, typing a few new records at the bottom of the Excel Table, and watching your report instantly update.

	A	B	C	D	E	F	G	H	I
2	Ex	Goals:							
3	# 32	Use SUMIFS function to add sales by customer, product and month.							
4		Create cross tabulated report that adds with three conditions.							
6		Month	July						
8		Cust/Prod	Apples	Bananas					
9		Safeway	$1,088.58	$4,881.05					
10		Whole Foods	$934.25	$1,587.25					
11									
12		Formula in cell B9:=SORT(UNIQUE(CSales[Cust]))							
13		Formula in cell C8:=TRANSPOSE(SORT(UNIQUE(CSales[Prod])))							
14		Formula in cell C9:=SUMIFS(CSales[Sales],CSales[Cust],B9#,CSales[Prod],C8#,CSales[Month],C6)							
15									
16		Month	Cust	Prod	Sales				
17		June	Whole Foods	Apples	$1,533.89				
18		June	Whole Foods	Bananas	$690.16				
19		July	Safeway	Bananas	$1,029.52				
20		July	Whole Foods	Apples	$642.89				
21		June	Safeway	Bananas	$883.31				
22		July	Whole Foods	Bananas	$528.14				
23		June	Safeway	Apples	$771.07				
24		July	Safeway	Bananas	$1,033.92				
25		July	Safeway	Bananas	$290.43				
26		June	Whole Foods	Apples	$1,756.26				
27		June	Whole Foods	Apples	$697.59				
28		July	Safeway	Apples	$674.16				
29		June	Whole Foods	Apples	$449.45				
30		July	Safeway	Bananas	$1,065.58				
31		July	Safeway	Bananas	$1,461.60				
32		July	Whole Foods	Bananas	$1,059.11				
33		July	Safeway	Apples	$414.42				
34		July	Whole Foods	Apples	$291.36				
35		June	Whole Foods	Bananas	$529.20				
36		June	Safeway	Bananas	$376.29				

Figure 13.34 *Adding with three criteria in a cross-tabulated report: sales by month, customer, and product.*

Example 33: Using a BETWEEN Logical Test with SUMIFS and MAXIFS in a Monthly Sales Report

One of the reports most commonly used in businesses is a monthly sales report. A sales dataset typically contains a date column with daily dates rather than a month column with month names. So, if you want to create an aggregate operation by month, you must use a BETWEEN logical test where the lower limit is the first of the month and the upper limit is the end of the month. If you are creating a BETWEEN logical test for January 2021, for example, the logical test would be "Is the daily date between the first of the month and the end of the month, inclusive?" or "Is the daily date greater than or equal to the first of the month AND is the daily date less than or equal to the end of the month?" The notation for this logical test might look like this:

```
Date >= 1/1/2021 AND Date <= 1/31/2021
```

So far in this book, any time you have created a logical test using comparison operators, you have used the comparison operator between the item to be tested and the hurdle, as in these four formulas:

- **Chapter 12, Example 11:** =FILTER($C$8:$C$13,$B$8:$B$13=F9)
- Chapter 12, Example 13: =AND($C13>=$C$9,D13>D$9)
- Chapter 13, Example 15: =IF(C10>=C5,C6,C7)
- **Chapter 13, Example 25:** =IF(COUNT(C15:G15)>2,SUM(LARGE(C15:G15,{1,2,3})),"")

In all four of these examples, the comparison operator could directly touch the item to be tested and the hurdle or condition, as highlighted above. Why does this matter? Because you are *not* allowed to do this in any of the IFS aggregate functions, such as COUNTIFS, SUMIFS, AVERAGEIFS, MINIFS, and MAXIFS. It seems strange that Microsoft would program the IFS aggregate functions to work totally differently than all the other formulas that you will make, but that is the way it is. When you use comparison operators with the IFS aggregate functions, you must join them together, either in a cell or in a formula, by using the join operator. For example, if you want to create the lower limit condition for the month of January 2021, you have to type >=1/1/2021 into a cell or type the date 1/1/2021 into cell E9 and then create this formula element: ">="&E9.

Joining a Comparison Operator to a Cell with Criteria Inside SUMIFS, MAXIFS, and Other IFS Aggregate Functions

Figure 13.35 shows how to create a monthly sales report using the SUMIFS and MAXIFS functions in two different ways. The top report joins the comparison operator inside double quotes to the range of dates for both the lower and upper limits. The bottom report joins the comparison operators to the dates in the cells and then refers to those cells in the criteria argument inside the formula. For this example, the date range, B8:B27, has been given the defined name Date, and the sales range, C8:C27, has been given the defined name Sales.

To complete this example, select the worksheet named Ch13(35) and follow these steps:

1. Select cell G9 and type **=SUMIFS(**.

2. In the *sum_range* argument of SUMIFS, select the sales range C8:C27. Excel inserts the defined name Sales into the formula, so your formula should now look like this: =**SUMIFS(Sales**.

3. Type a comma. Then, in the *criteria1_range* argument, select the date range B8:B27. Your formula should now look like this: **=SUMIFS(Sales,Date**.

4. Type a comma. Then, in the *criteria1* argument, type the greater-than-or-equal comparison operator inside double quotes: **">="**. Your formula should now look like this: **=SUMIFS(Sales,Date,">="**. What you have typed so for in the *criteria1* argument is only the comparison operator.

5. To join the comparison operator to the cells with the lower-limit dates, type the join operator, **&**, and then select the range of lower-limit dates, E9:E12. Now your formula should look like this: **=SUMIFS(Sales,Date,">="&E9:E12**. Because you highlighted the fours lower-limit date cells, E9:E12, you are making a function argument array operation that will give the four individual lower-limit conditions to the SUMIFS function.

6. Type a comma. Then, in the *criteria2_range* argument, select the date column. Your formula should look like this: **=SUMIFS(Sales,Date,">="&E9:E12,Date**.

Note: When you do a BETWEEN logical test and you have to repeat the column that contains the numbers to which you are comparing the lower and upper limits, you repeat the Date column.

7. Type a comma. Then, in the *criteria2* argument, finish the formula by creating the upper-limit conditions. The finished formula should now look like this: **=SUMIFS(Sales,Date,">="&E9:E12,Date,"<="&F9:F12)**.

8. Press Enter, and the four answers spill down to the rows below.

9. Select cell H9 and create the MAXIFS formula: =MAXIFS(Sales,Date,">="&E9:E12,Date,"<="&F9:F12).

10. As shown in Figure 13.35, in cells G20 and H20, enter the formulas that use the upper and lower limits created with both the comparison operator and dates in the same cell.

G9   =SUMIFS(Sales,Date,">="&E9:E12,Date,"<="&F9:F12)

	A	B	C	D	E	F	G	H	I
2		**Ex**	**Goals:**						
3		**# 33**	Use SUMIFS & MAXIFS functions to create a monthly sales report.						
4			Create a BETWEEN logical test with a lower and upper limit.						
5			The lower limit is the first of the month & upper limit is end of the month.						
7		**Date**	**Sales ($)**		**1st of Month**	**End of Month**			
8		4/14/21	1,533.89		**Lower Limit**	**Upper Limit**	**Add Sales**	**Max Sale**	
9		3/12/21	690.16		1/1/2021	1/31/2021	$5,608.23	$1,461.60	
10		2/22/21	1,029.52		2/1/2021	2/28/2021	$3,234.22	$1,029.52	
11		3/5/21	642.89		3/1/2021	3/31/2021	$3,763.47	$1,756.26	
12		4/4/21	883.31		4/1/2021	4/30/2021	$3,572.43	$1,533.89	
13		2/16/21	528.14						
14		2/12/21	771.07		Formula in cell G9:=SUMIFS(Sales,Date,">="&E9:E12,Date,"<="&F9:F12)				
15		1/30/21	1,033.92		Formula in cell H9:=MAXIFS(Sales,Date,">="&E9:E12,Date,"<="&F9:F12)				
16		1/18/21	290.43		Formulas spill down to rows below.				
17		3/24/21	1,756.26						
18		1/28/21	697.59		**1st of Month**	**End of Month**			
19		3/28/21	674.16		**Lower Limit**	**Upper Limit**	**Add Sales**	**Max Sale**	
20		4/21/21	449.45		>=1/1/2021	<=1/31/2021	$5,608.23	$1,461.60	
21		1/25/21	1,065.58		>=2/1/2021	<=2/28/2021	$3,234.22	$1,029.52	
22		1/8/21	1,461.60		>=3/1/2021	<=3/31/2021	$3,763.47	$1,756.26	
23		1/15/21	1,059.11		>=4/1/2021	<=4/30/2021	$3,572.43	$1,533.89	
24		4/22/21	414.42						
25		4/22/21	291.36		Formula in cell G20:=SUMIFS(Sales,Date,E20:E23,Date,F20:F23)				
26		2/5/21	529.20		Formula in cell H20:=MAXIFS(Sales,Date,E20:E23,Date,F20:F23)				
27		2/20/21	376.29		Formulas spill down to other rows.				

Figure 13.35 *Monthly sales report using a BETWEEN logical test and defined names in the SUMIFS and MAXIFS functions.*

It may take a while to get used to joining the comparison operators to the hurdle values or conditions when you use the IFS aggregate functions. However, these functions are very common, and you will have to remember to join the comparison operator with the condition, even though all the other formulas that use comparison operators do not require this convention.

> **Note:** Of the two reports created in Figure 13.35, the bottom one is less common; having the comparison operators visible in the cells makes a report very busy. Later in the book, when you study data analysis and learn how to create PivotTables, you will learn that a monthly sales report is much more easily created by using the PivotTable feature. The main reason that you would create a report like this with formulas is because formulas update instantly when source data changes, and PivotTables do not (although it is easy to refresh a PivotTable report).

Aggregate Operations That Require OR Logical Tests

When you need to make an OR logical test rather than an AND logical test for an aggregate operation, things get complicated. With an AND logical test, there are built-in IFS aggregate functions like SUMIFS and MAXIFS. When you use an IFS aggregate functions to conduct an AND logical test, it does not matter if you are running the logical test on a single column (as for a BETWEEN logical test to add sales for a month) or on three different columns (as when adding the sales of bananas to Safeway in July), and it does not matter which of the five calculations you want to make: count, sum, average, minimum, or maximum. In all cases, you just choose the correct IFS aggregate function—COUNTIFS, SUMIFS, AVERAGEIFS, MINIFS, or MAXIFS—and then create the formula. It is not so easy when you need to make an aggregate operation based on an OR logical test.

There are no good built-in functions to make an OR logical test. The formula that you use for an OR logical test depends on how many columns you are analyzing and what type of calculation you are making—as you will see in the following examples.

Example 34: Using the SUMIFS Function to Do an OR Logical Test on a Single Column

Figure 13.36 shows a common situation where a sales team is made up of three individual sales reps, and you need to add all the sales from the Sales column for each of the sales reps on the team to get a single total. In this case, you need to run an OR logical test on the SalesRep column to determine which numbers to add. The OR logical test you need is "Is the sales rep in the SalesRep column Gigi OR Sioux OR Tyrone?" In this situation, there are two different SUMIFS function methods that you can use for adding with an OR logical test that runs on a single column.

Figure 13.36 shows the first SUMIFS method in cell G10. Since the goal is to add all the sales for Sales Team 1, you can create a new SUMIFS function formula element for each sales rep and then add each of the SUMIFS results with the plus operator. The full formula would be:

```
=SUMIFS(D7:D26,C7:C26,G7)+SUMIFS(D7:D26,C7:C26,G8)+SUMIFS(D7:D26,C7:C26,G9)
```

This gives you the correct answer, but it takes a long time to type out the formula, and if you had a very large list of conditions for your OR logical test, the formula could get huge!

	A	B	C	D	E	F	G	H
	G11		:	× ✓ f_x	=SUM(SUMIFS(D7:D26,C7:C26,G7:G9))			
2	Ex	Goals:						
3	# 34	Add sales for Sales Team 1.						
4		Create aggregate calculations using an OR logical test.						
6		Date	SalesRep	Sales			Sales Team 1	
7		4/14/21	Sioux	1,533.89			Gigi	
8		3/12/21	Gigi	690.16			Sioux	
9		2/22/21	Tyrone	1,029.52			Tyrone	
10		3/5/21	Abdi	642.89		Sum	$9,898.28	
11		4/4/21	Chantel	883.31		Sum	$9,898.28	
12		2/16/21	Sioux	528.14				
13		2/12/21	Chantel	771.07			Formula in G10:	
14		1/30/21	Miki	1,033.92			=SUMIFS(D7:D26,C7:C26,G7)+	
15		1/18/21	Abdi	290.43				
16		3/24/21	Gigi	1,756.26			SUMIFS(D7:D26,C7:C26,G8)+	
17		1/28/21	Tyrone	697.59			SUMIFS(D7:D26,C7:C26,G9)	
18		3/28/21	Sioux	674.16				
19		4/21/21	Tyrone	449.45			Formula in G11:	
20		1/25/21	Sioux	1,065.58			=SUM(	
21		1/8/21	Chantel	1,461.60				
22		1/15/21	Gigi	1,059.11			SUMIFS(D7:D26,C7:C26,G7:G9))	
23		4/22/21	Tyrone	414.42				
24		4/22/21	Miki	1,291.36				
25		2/5/21	Chantel	529.20				
26		2/20/21	Abdi	376.29				

Figure 13.36 *Using multiple SUMIFS functions is inefficient. Using SUM and SUMIFS is more efficient.*

A much more efficient formula for adding when there is an OR logical test is shown in cell G11 in Figure 13.36. The trick is to use all three sales rep names in the *criteria1* argument to force a function argument array operation that will cause the SUMIFS function to deliver three sales total answers—one for each sales rep name. The SUMIFS formula element with the function argument array operation is SUMIFS(D7:D26,C7:C26,G7:G9).

Because you put the range G7:G9 into the *criteria1* argument, SUMIFS delivers three answers: $3,505.53 (for Gigi's sales total), $3,801.77 (for Sioux's sales total), $2,590.98 (for Tyrone's sales total). Now, if you entered the SUMIFS formula element into a cell, the three answers would spill into the cells—but that is not what you want. The goal is to add the three numbers. To do this, you place the SUMIFS formula element into the SUM function so it can add the three numbers to get the sales team total. The final formula for adding with an OR logical test that is run on a single column is:

```
=SUM(SUMIFS(D7:D26,C7:C26,G7:G9))
```

You can try these two formulas on the worksheet named Ch13(36).

Example 35: Carrying Out Aggregate Operations with an OR Logical Test on a Single Column

When you need to run an OR logical test on a single column for any of the aggregate operations count, minimum, and maximum, you can use a construction similar to the two-function construction used in Example 34.

Figure 13.37 shows the aggregate operations sum, count, maximum, and minimum for Sales Team 1 and Sales Team 2. For addition, you use SUM and SUMIFS. To find the maximum value, you use MAX and MAXIFS. To find the minimum value, you use MIN and MINIFS. For counting, you cannot use the COUNT function because that function counts numbers. For Sales Team 1, the COUNTIFS function with the function argument array operation delivers {3;4;4}, which shows the number of sales for Gigi (3), for Sioux (4), and for Tyrone (4). If you used COUNT instead, you would get the incorrect total 3 rather than the correct total 11 (= 3 + 4 + 4) for Sales Team 1. When you place the COUNTIFS formula element into the SUM function, the SUM function can add the individual counts to get the correct total, 11.

Therefore, for any of the aggregate operations sum, count, minimum, and maximum, you can use the two functions shown in Figure 13.37 and a function argument array operation when you want to do an OR logical test on a single column.

You can try these calculations on the worksheet named Ch13(37).

G11		▼	:	× ✓	fx	=SUM(COUNTIFS(C7:C26,G7:G9))						
	A	B	C	D	E	F	G	H	I	J	K	L
2	Ex	Goals:										
3	#35	Make aggregate calculations for each Sales Team.										
4		Create aggregate calculations using an OR logical test.										
6		Date	SalesRep	Sales			Sales Team 1	Sales Team 2				
7		4/14	Sioux	1,533.89			Gigi	Abdi				
8		3/12	Gigi	690.16			Sioux	Chantel				
9		2/22	Tyrone	1,029.52			Tyrone	Miki				
10		3/5	Abdi	642.89	Sum		$9,898.28	$7,280.07				
11		4/4	Chantel	883.31	Count		11	9				
12		2/16	Sioux	528.14	Max		$1,756.26	$1,461.60				
13		2/12	Chantel	771.07	Min		$414.42	$290.43				
14		1/30	Miki	1,033.92	Average		$899.84	$808.90				
15		1/18	Abdi	290.43	Standard Deviation		$437.90	$399.71				
16		3/24	Gigi	1,756.26								
17		1/28	Tyrone	697.59	Formula in G10: =SUM(SUMIFS(D7:D26,C7:C26,G7:G9))							
18		3/28	Sioux	674.16	Formula in G11: =SUM(COUNTIFS(C7:C26,G7:G9))							
19		4/21	Tyrone	449.45	Formula in G12: =MAX(MAXIFS(D7:D26,C7:C26,G7:G9))							
20		1/25	Sioux	1,065.58	Formula in G13: =MIN(MINIFS(D7:D26,C7:C26,G7:G9))							
21		1/8	Chantel	1,461.60								
22		1/15	Gigi	1,059.11	Formula in G14: =AVERAGE(FILTER(D7:D26,ISNUMBER(XMATCH(C7:C26,G7:G9))))							
23		4/22	Tyrone	414.42	Formula in G15: =STDEV.S(FILTER(D7:D26,ISNUMBER(XMATCH(C7:C26,G7:G9))))							
24		4/22	Miki	1,291.36								
25		2/5	Chantel	529.20	All 6 formulas are entered into cell & copied from the G column to the H column.							
26		2/20	Abdi	376.29								

Figure 13.37 *OR logical tests run on a single column for various aggregate operations.*

An OR Logical Test on a Single Column: A "Comparing Two Lists" Situation

But what about the average calculation? For some aggregate operations, such as averaging and calculating the standard deviation, the two-function method (such as using SUM and SUMIFS for adding) will not work. You cannot find the average for each sales rep (with AVERAGEIFS and the function argument array operation) and then average those values (with AVERAGE) because the final average calculation must have all the individual numbers from the original sales column. For standard deviation, there is no STDEV.SIFS function. The solution to this problem is to use the FILTER function.

For calculations like averaging and calculating the standard deviation when you are running an OR logical test on a single column, you can use the same "comparing two lists" trick that you learned in Example 29. Inside either AVERAGE or STDEV.S (or any other aggregate function), you can filter the sales column by using the FILTER array function to get the correct numbers based on your OR logical test. In Example 29, you learned that when you want to check whether the items in one list exist in a second list, you can use the ISNUMBER and XMATCH function to generate the correct pattern of TRUEs and FALSEs to then use in the FILTER function to filter and get the correct items. Notice what this implies: When you run an OR logical test on a single column, you are really comparing two lists.

In the averaging example in Figure 13.37, the first list is the full SalesRep column, with all the possible sale rep names, and the second list is the list of sales reps on a given team. For the calculation in cell G14, you can use the XMATCH function with the full SalesRep column in the *lookup_value* argument and the range G7:G9 (the Sales Team 1 names) in the *lookup_array* argument, like this: XMATCH(C7:C26,G7:G9). Because the lookup value is the SalesRep column, and it has the same dimensions as the sales column (1 column, 20 rows), the resultant array of error values and relative positions will be as follows: {2;1;3;#N/A;#N/A;2;#N/A;#N/A;#N/A;1;3;2;3;2;#N/A;1;3;#N/A;#N/A;#N/A}. Notice that the relative positions 1, 2, and 3 are the only numbers because the list of sales rep names is only three entries long. Because the numbers indicate a match, you place the XMATCH function inside the ISNUMBER function, like this:

```
ISNUMBER(XMATCH(C7:C26,G7:G9))
```

When you evaluate the ISNUMBER formula element, you get:

```
{TRUE;TRUE;TRUE;FALSE;FALSE;TRUE;FALSE;FALSE;FALSE;TRUE;TRUE;TRUE;TRUE;-
FALSE;TRUE;TRUE;FALSE;FALSE;FALSE}
```

This pattern of TRUEs and FALSEs is exactly what you need inside the FILTER array function, so you create the following formula:

```
FILTER(D7:D26,ISNUMBER(XMATCH(C7:C26,G7:G9)))
```

This formula evaluates to 1533.89, 690.16, 1029.52, 528.14, 1756.26, 697.59, 674.16, 449.45, 1065.58, 1059.11, 414.42, which are the correct individual numbers needed in either the AVERAGE or STDEV.S functions for the OR logical test.

The final formula for the OR logical test on a single column average calculation is:

```
=AVERAGE(FILTER(D7:D26,ISNUMBER(XMATCH(C7:C26,G7:G9))))
```

This yields the final answer $899.84 as the average transactional sales amount for Sales Team 1. This same method can be used for the standard deviation calculation.

You can try these calculations on the worksheet named Ch13(37).

> **Note:** For simplicity, you can use this "comparing two lists inside FILTER" method inside any aggregate function when the OR logical test is on a single column. My personal preference is to use the two-function method (such as SUM and SUMIFS for adding) when making the sum, count, minimum, or maximum calculation because it involves only two functions. Then, to get the numbers needed for the OR logical test, when I make other aggregate function operations based on the OR logical test on a single column, I switch over to the "comparing two lists inside FILTER" method, like this: FILTER(*FullNumberColumn*,ISNUMBER(XMATCH(*FullConditionColumn*,*ORCriteriaList*))).

Example 36: Conducting Aggregate Operations with an AND and OR Logical Test

Occasionally, you may need to make an OR logical test on a single column combined with an AND logical test. For example, Figure 13.38 shows a sales team report based on country. In cell G13, the total sales figure $3,681.58 represents the sum of sales for Sales Team 1 in the country USA. To create the formula to accomplish this, you must understand the full logical test, which consists of an AND logical test combined with an OR logical test. To get the correct sales numbers, you need to get the formula to execute this full logical test:

Gigi AND USA

OR

Sioux AND USA

OR

Tyrone AND USA

By just looking at the dataset, you can pick out the numbers that match this logical test and add them: $1,533.89 + $674.16 + $1,059.11 + $414.42 = $3,681.58.

Luckily, however, you do not have to do this just by looking at the data. You can combine what you have learned so far about how to use SUMIFS to make an AND logical test and an OR logical test. As shown in Figure 13.38, the full formula for this calculation in cell G13 is:

```
=SUM(SUMIFS(Sales_,Country,$F13,SalesRep,G$10:G$12))
```

This formula uses defined names for the columns. A formula like this cannot spill because there are multiple criteria for the OR logical test at the top of each column. For this cross-tabulated report where the column header criteria constitutes an OR logical test, you have to create a formula with mixed cell references, enter the formula in G13, and then manually copy the formula through the range G13:H15.

You can try this formula on the worksheet named Ch13(38).

| G13 | ▼ | ✕ ✓ *fx* | =SUM(SUMIFS(Sales_,Country,$F13,SalesRep,G$10:G$12)) |

	A	B	C	D	E	F	G	H
2	Ex	Goals:						
3	# 36	Create sales report by country and sales team.						
4		Create aggregate calculations using an AND logical test and an OR logical test.						
6		Country	SalesRep	Sales_				
7		USA	Sioux	1,533.89		Sales Report by Country and Sales Team		
8		Mexico	Gigi	690.16				
9		Canada	Tyrone	1,029.52			Sales Team 1	Sales Team 2
10		Canada	Abdi	642.89			Gigi	Abdi
11		USA	Chantel	883.31			Sioux	Chantel
12		Canada	Sioux	528.14			Tyrone	Miki
13		USA	Chantel	771.07		USA	$3,681.58	$5,970.46
14		USA	Miki	1,033.92		Canada	$2,704.70	$642.89
15		Mexico	Abdi	290.43		Mexico	$3,512.00	$666.72
16		Mexico	Gigi	1,756.26				
17		Canada	Tyrone	697.59		Formula in cell G13:		
18		USA	Sioux	674.16		=SUM(		
19		Canada	Tyrone	449.45		SUMIFS(Sales_,		
20		Mexico	Sioux	1,065.58				
21		USA	Chantel	1,461.60		Country,$F13,		
22		USA	Gigi	1,059.11		SalesRep,G$10:G$12))		
23		USA	Tyrone	414.42		Copied through range G13:H15.		
24		USA	Miki	1,291.36				
25		USA	Chantel	529.20				
26		Mexico	Abdi	376.29				

Figure 13.38 *An AND Logical test combined with an OR logical tests to create a sales team report by country.*

Example 37: Conducting Aggregate Operations with an OR Logical Test on Two Columns

This example looks at how to make aggregate operations when an OR logical test works across two columns. In such a case, you can use a Boolean math OR logical test with the addition operator. When you run a Boolean math OR logical test on a single column, the only two possible outcomes are 0 and 1. When you run a Boolean math OR logical test on two different columns, the possible outcomes are 0, 1, and 2, as shown here:

- FALSE + FALSE = 0
- TRUE + FALSE = 1
- FALSE + TRUE = 1
- TRUE + TRUE = 2

The good news is that, as you learned earlier in this chapter, the logical features in Excel interpret any nonzero number as TRUE and zero as FALSE. This means you can use the FILTER array function with a Boolean math OR logical test to filter a column of numbers, and then you can place the FILTER function resultant array into any aggregate function you like.

Figure 13.39 shows five different aggregate operations based on an OR logical test run across two columns.

C9	▼	:	×	✓	fx	=AVERAGE(FILTER(B18:B28,(C18:C28=B7)+(D18:D28=D7)))		
	A	B	C	D	E	F	G	H	I

	A	B	C	D	E	F	G	H
2	Ex	Goals:						
3	#37	OR logical test where product = Quad OR sales rep = Abdi.						
4		Create aggregate calculations using an OR logical test based on two different columns.						
6		Product	OR	Sales Rep				
7		Quad		Abdi				
9		Average	30	Formula in C9: =AVERAGE(FILTER(B18:B28,(C18:C28=B7)+(D18:D28=D7)))				
10		Sum	120	Formula in C10: =SUM(FILTER(B18:B28,(C18:C28=B7)+(D18:D28=D7)))				
11		Count	4	Formula in C11: =COUNT(FILTER(B18:B28,(C18:C28=B7)+(D18:D28=D7)))				
12		Max	50	Formula in C12: =MAX(FILTER(B18:B28,(C18:C28=B7)+(D18:D28=D7)))				
13		Min	10	Formula in C13: =MIN(FILTER(B18:B28,(C18:C28=B7)+(D18:D28=D7)))				
15		Boolean OR logical test on two columns can result in 0, 1, or 2:						
17		Sales	Product	Sales Rep		Product	Sales Rep	Result
18		50	Quad	Abdi		TRUE	TRUE	TRUE + TRUE = 2
19		30	Bellen	Khawi		FALSE	FALSE	FALSE + FALSE = 0
20		50	Sunshine	Gigi		FALSE	FALSE	FALSE + FALSE = 0
21		30	Aspen	Pham		FALSE	FALSE	FALSE + FALSE = 0
22		10	Aspen	Abdi		FALSE	TRUE	FALSE + TRUE = 1
23		50	Quad	Abdi		TRUE	TRUE	TRUE + TRUE = 2
24		10	Quad	Khawi		TRUE	FALSE	TRUE + FALSE = 1
25		50	Bellen	Khawi		FALSE	FALSE	FALSE + FALSE = 0
26		30	Bellen	Pham		FALSE	FALSE	FALSE + FALSE = 0
27		30	Sunshine	Gigi		FALSE	FALSE	FALSE + FALSE = 0
28		20	Aspen	Gigi		FALSE	FALSE	FALSE + FALSE = 0

Figure 13.39 *OR logical tests based on two different columns for various aggregate operations.*

> **Note:** This example show how to do the calculation with two columns, but you can extend the logic to as many columns as you would like by adding a new logical test in parentheses with a new plus operator for each new OR logical test criteria.

You can try these formulas on the worksheet named Ch13(39).

Example 38: Using Database Worksheet Functions

Since almost the beginning of Excel's history, there has been a class of worksheet functions called *database worksheet functions*, that include functions like DSUM, DCOUNT, DMIN, and DSTDEV. These functions, also known as *D functions*, can perform various aggregate operations with any type of logical test that you can dream up. However, there is a significant flaw in the database functions: Most of the time, you cannot copy these functions to other cells. Since many situations require that you copy a formula result to other cells, D functions are rarely the most efficient for worksheet solutions. However, this example looks at the different database worksheet functions and describes the rules for setting up the criteria area so that if you encounter an Excel file that is already using D functions, you will be familiar with them. In addition, it is helpful to understand how to set up the criteria area for these functions because the criteria area works the same way for the Advanced Filter feature.

> **Note:** The *criteria area* is a place in a worksheet where you list the field names and then the conditions or criteria below the field names (see Figures 13.40 and 13.41).

Table 13.3 lists and describes the database worksheet functions.

Table 13.3 The Database Worksheet Functions

Function	Description
DSUM	Adds numbers
DCOUNT	Counts numbers
DCOUNTA	Counts non-empty cells
DSTDEV	Calculates the standard deviation of a sample
DSTDEVP	Calculates the standard deviation of a population
DMAX	Finds the maximum number
DMIN	Finds the minimum number
DAVERAGE	Finds the average
DPRODUCT	Multiplies numbers
DVAR	Calculates the variation in a sample
DVARP	Calculates the variation in a population
DGET	Looks up a value when there are two lookup values and one matching record

A database worksheet function has the following syntax:

```
D_FUNCTION(database, field, criteria)
```

These are the arguments in a D function:

- **database:** A proper dataset with field names
- **field:** A field from the *database* argument that you want to make a calculation on, specified either as "*field name*" in double quote or as the relative position of the field name among all the field names (for example, either "Sales" or 3 if the third field is named Sales)
- **criteria:** The criteria area with a field name and comparison operator and condition below each field name typed into a range of cells.

You need to keep in mind a few rules for the *criteria* argument to a database worksheet functions:

- The criteria area must have the field names above the cell that contains the comparison operator and the condition.
- If field names in the criteria area are not exactly the same as in the database, the calculation will not work.
- The criteria area must include a comparison operator, such as '=USA (that is, equals USA) or >600 (that is, greater than 600).
- To enter an equal sign with *criteria*, use a single quotation mark before the equal sign when you type the comparison operator and condition into a cell, like this: '=Chantel.
- If you enter text into a cell as *criteria* without an equal sign comparison operator, like USA, Excel will do a "contains" logical test.

- AND logical test criteria must be in the same row.
- OR logical test criteria must be in different rows.

Figure 13.40 and Figure 13.41 show all the database worksheet functions and many of the possible logical tests that you can set up.

> **Note:** Data worksheet functions exist only in the Excel worksheet and not in other tools, such as Power Pivot and Power BI.

You can try these examples on the worksheet named Ch13(40-41). However, given that these functions are rarely used, you do not have to try them. The red answer worksheet named Ch13(40-41an) includes all these formulas, and you can reference it if you encounter a need for these worksheet functions.

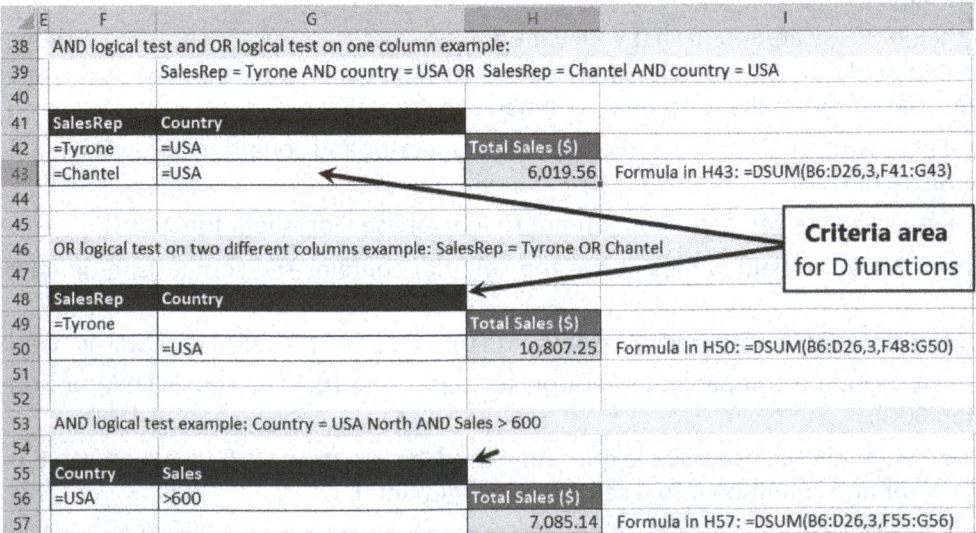

Figure 13.40 *For database worksheet functions, you need to set up a criteria area with field names and criteria.*

	E	F	G	H	I
38		AND logical test and OR logical test on one column example:			
39			SalesRep = Tyrone AND country = USA OR SalesRep = Chantel AND country = USA		
40					
41		SalesRep	Country		
42		=Tyrone	=USA	Total Sales ($)	
43		=Chantel	=USA	6,019.56	Formula in H43: =DSUM(B6:D26,3,F41:G43)
44					
45					
46		OR logical test on two different columns example: SalesRep = Tyrone OR Chantel			
47					
48		SalesRep	Country		
49		=Tyrone		Total Sales ($)	
50			=USA	10,807.25	Formula in H50: =DSUM(B6:D26,3,F48:G50)
51					
52					
53		AND logical test example: Country = USA North AND Sales > 600			
54					
55		Country	Sales		
56		=USA	>600	Total Sales ($)	
57				7,085.14	Formula in H57: =DSUM(B6:D26,3,F55:G56)

Figure 13.41 *Whereas OR logical test conditions sit in different rows, AND logical test conditions sit in the same row.*

Table 13.4 shows the equivalent Microsoft 365 Excel formula for each database worksheet function presented in Figures 13.40 and 13.41. Whereas the database worksheet functions cannot be copied to other cells to create reports, all of the Microsoft 365 Excel formulas can be copied to other cells. All of these formulas can be seen in the R column on the worksheet Ch13(40-41).

> **Note:** In the second and third Microsoft 365 Excel formulas shown in Table 13.4, <> is used as a condition that means that the cell is not empty.

Table 13.4 Database Worksheet Functions and Their Equivalent Microsoft 365 Excel Formulas

Database Worksheet Formula	Microsoft 365 Excel Formula
=DSUM(B6:D26,3,F60:G61)	=SUMIFS($D$7:$D$26,$B$7:$B$26,T8,$C$7:$C$26,U8)
=DCOUNT(B6:D26,3,F5:G6)	=COUNTIFS($B$7:$B$26,T9,$C$7:$C$26,U9,$D$7:$D$26,"<>")
=DCOUNTA(B6:D26,2,F5:G6)	=COUNTIFS($B$7:$B$26,T10,$C$7:$C$26,U10,$C$7:$C$26,"<>")
=DSTDEV(B6:D26,3,F5:G6)	=STDEV.S(FILTER($D$7:$D$26,($B$7:$B$26=T11)*($C$7:$C$26=U11)))
=DSTDEVP(B6:D26,3,F5:G6)	=STDEV.P(FILTER($D$7:$D$26,($B$7:$B$26=T12)*($C$7:$C$26=U12)))
=DMAX(B6:D26,3,F5:G6)	=MAXIFS($D$7:$D$26,$B$7:$B$26,T13,$C$7:$C$26,U13)
=DMIN(B6:D26,3,F5:G6)	=MINIFS($D$7:$D$26,$B$7:$B$26,T14,$C$7:$C$26,U14)
=DAVERAGE(B6:D26,3,F5:G6)	=AVERAGEIFS($D$7:$D$26,$B$7:$B$26,T15,$C$7:$C$26,U15)
=DPRODUCT(B6:D26,3,F5:G6)	=PRODUCT(FILTER($D$7:$D$26,($B$7:$B$26=T12)*($C$7:$C$26=U12)))
=DVAR(B6:D26,3,F5:G6)	=VAR.S(FILTER($D$7:$D$26,($B$7:$B$26=T17)*($C$7:$C$26=U17)))
=DVARP(B6:D26,3,F5:G6)	=VAR.P(FILTER($D$7:$D$26,($B$7:$B$26=T18)*($C$7:$C$26=U18)))
=DGET(B6:D26,3,F20:G21)	=FILTER($D$7:$D$26,($B$7:$B$26=T23)*($C$7:$C$26=U23))
=DSUM(B6:D26,3,F26:G27)	=SUMIFS($D$7:$D$26,$B$7:$B$26,"*"&T27&"*",$C$7:$C$26,U27)
=DSUM(B6:D26,3,F33:F35)	=SUM(SUMIFS($D$7:$D$26,$C$7:$C$26,T34:T35))
=DSUM(B6:D26,3,F41:G43)	=SUM(SUMIFS($D$7:$D$26,$B$7:$B$26,U43,$C$7:$C$26,T43:T44))
=DSUM(B6:D26,3,F48:G50)	=SUM(FILTER($D$7:$D$26,($B$7:$B$26=T50)+($C$7:$C$26=U50)))
=DSUM(B6:D26,3,F55:G56)	=SUM(FILTER($D$7:$D$26,($B$7:$B$26=T57)*(D7:D26>U57)))

Key Concepts in Chapter 13

- There are six **comparison operators** that allows you to make comparisons in Excel:
    - Equals: =
    - Greater than: >
    - Greater than or equal to: >=
    - Less Than: <
    - Less than or equal to: <=
    - Not: <>
- A **logical test** is an expression that evaluates to one of only two possible **Boolean values**: TRUE or FALSE. There are several types of logical tests:
    - **Logical test with a single condition:** One test evaluates to TRUE or FALSE.
    - **Contains, or "partial text," logical test:** This is a logical test with a single condition that checks whether text is located within a second text item.
    - **NOT logical test:** This is a logical test with a single condition that checks whether two items are not equal.
    - **AND logical test:** This is a logical test with two or more conditions. The goal of an AND logical test is to run two or more logical tests to determine if all logical tests evaluate to TRUE.
    - **BETWEEN logical test:** When you run a BETWEEN logical test, you are running an AND logical test with a lower limit and an upper limit.

- **OR logical test:** This is a logical test with two or more conditions. The goal of an OR logical test is to run two or more logical tests to determine whether at least one test evaluates to TRUE or, said a different way, whether one or more logical tests evaluate to TRUE.

- **Complex logical test:** This is a logical test and combines any of the above logical tests into a single logical test.

- **Boolean values can be converted** from TRUE to 1 and FALSE to 0 with any math operation that does not change the value away from the 1 for TRUE or the 0 for FALSE.

- The formula syntax for showing nothing in a cell involves using two double quotation marks with no space in between: "" (not four single quotes). When you use two double quotation marks in a formula, you are using a **zero-length text string** because Excel considers it text that has zero length.

- Excel worksheet functions, Excel features, and the DAX formula language (Power Pivot and Power BI) consider any **nonzero number to be TRUE and zero to be FALSE**.

- Excel logical worksheet functions can be used to deliver **Boolean values** or **non-Boolean values**. In addition, a number of database worksheet functions can make various **aggregate operations** when you have a proper dataset and the correct criteria area set up.

- You can use **wildcards** to represent variable characters in formulas. The asterisk character (*) is used to represent any set of zero or more characters, the question mark character (?) is used to represent exactly one character, and the tilde character (~) is used to convert the wildcards * and ? to actual characters.

Practice Problems for Chapter 13

Practice Problem 1

In your Excel file for this chapter (Ch13-Excel365-LogicalFormulas.xlsx), go to the worksheet named PPCh13(1) and create the solution for this practice problem. Figure 13.42 shows the goal that is listed on that worksheet.

	Customer	Account Status	Pay 1	Pay 2	Pay 3	Pay 4	Pay 5	Total Paid	Letter?
2	**Goal:** Customers are sent a letter after then missed their last 5 payments AND account status in Subpar.								
3	Mark customer record with a TRUE when a letter must be sent and FALSE if no letter is required.								
4	Hint: You must follow Excel's Golden Rule.								
6									
8	Customer	Account Status	Pay 1	Pay 2	Pay 3	Pay 4	Pay 5	Total Paid	Letter?
9	Jacquelyn Payne	Subpar	0	13.8	0	97	0	110.74	
10	Santos Munoz	Par	145	5.72	13.7	131	137	432.37	
11	Samuel Sherman	Par	76.4	59.8	77.3	47.6	83.6	344.6	
12	Drew Vasquez	Par	29.8	47.8	56.9	33.8	7.49	175.82	
13	Miriam Welch	Subpar	0	0	0	0	0	0	
14	Tyrone Bennett	Subpar	72.5	118	14.7	24.4	67.2	296.95	
15	Chantel Adkins	Par	142	46.2	148	125	18.5	479.14	
16	Maria Fleming	Par	0	0	0	0	0	0	
17	Gigi Pham	Par	3.68	0	28.3	7.76	1.54	41.25	
18	Sioux Palmer	Subpar	0	0	0	0	0	0	

Figure 13.42 *On the worksheet PPCh13(1), create a logical formula in J9 and then copy it down to all customers.*

When you are done with this problem, you can check your work against the answer sheet named PPCh13(1an).

Practice Problem 2

In your Excel file for this chapter (Ch13-Excel365-LogicalFormulas.xlsx), go to the worksheet named PPCh13(2) and create the solution for this practice problem. Figure 13.43 shows the goal that is listed on that worksheet.

	A	B	C	D	E	F	G	H
2		**Goal:** Create Formula that runs a checkbook balance formula if a date is entered in the date column.						
3		Use IF to deliver 1 of 2 items, either a formula or "" (show nothing - zero length text string).						
4		Create formula in cell G8 and then copy through range G8:G18.						
6		Date	Check #/Trans #	Description	Add		Subtract	Checkbook Balance
7		10/1/21	Bal. Forward					$ 5,000.00
8		10/3/21	Ch. 1034	Rent			$ 500.00	
9		10/4/21	Dept 5458	Pay	$ 950.00			
10		10/4/21	Ch 1035				$ 55.25	
11		10/5/21	Dept 5511	Pay	$ 150.45			
12								
13								
14								
15								
16								
17								
18								

Figure 13.43 *On the worksheet PPCh13(2), create the checkbook balance formula in cell G8 and then copy it down.*

When you are done with this problem, you can check your work against the answer sheet named PPCh13(2an).

Practice Problem 3

In your Excel file for this chapter (Ch13-Excel365-LogicalFormulas.xlsx), go to the worksheet named PPCh13(3) and create the solution for this practice problem. Figure 13.44 shows the goals that are listed on that worksheet.

	A	B	C	D	E	F	G	H	I	J	K
2		**Goal:**									
3		Create Boolean formula that will deliver TRUE or FALSE in cell H16 that spills to the rows below, and tests each '% Enrollment' number to see if it is 70.00% or above.									
4		Create Boolean formula that will deliver TRUE or FALSE in cell I16 that spills to the rows below, and tests each '% Enrollment' number to see if it is past the hurdle of 70.00%.									
5		Use the IF function in cell J16 that spills to the rows below, and tests each '% Enrollment' number to see if it is 70.00% or above.									
6		If it is 70.00% or above, the IF should deliver 'Target Met', otherwise 'No'.									
7		Use the IF function in cell K16 that spills to the rows below, and tests each '% Enrollment' number to see if it is past the hurdle of 70.00%.									
8		If it is past the hurdle of 70.00%, the IF should deliver 'Target Met', otherwise 'No'.									
9		For the two IF function formulas, the text values of 'Target Met' and 'No' will not change so you can hard code them into formula.									
13					Target	70.00%					
14								70.00% included	70.00% NOT included	70.00% included	70.00% NOT included
15		Quarter	Dept	Class	Student Cap	Enrollment	% Enrolled	Met Target? T/F.	Met Target? T/F.	Met Target? "Target Met" or "No"	Met Target? "Target Met" or "No"
16		Q1	Math	Busn 101	30	21	70.0%				
17		Q1	Engl	Busn 303	30	21	70.0%				
18		Q1	Ast	Busn 401	25	12	48.0%				
19		Q1	Read	Busn 107	25	10	40.0%				
20		Q2	Math	Busn 101	25	20	80.0%				
21		Q2	Engl	Busn 303	25	15	60.0%				
22		Q2	Ast	Busn 401	25	16	64.0%				
23		Q2	Read	Busn 107	25	19	76.0%				
24		Q3	Math	Busn 101	25	15	60.0%				
25		Q3	Engl	Busn 303	25	20	80.0%				
26		Q3	Ast	Busn 401	25	20	80.0%				
27		Q3	Read	Busn 107	25	12	48.0%				
28		Q4	Math	Busn 101	25	22	88.0%				
29		Q4	Engl	Busn 303	25	16	64.0%				
30		Q4	Ast	Busn 401	25	19	76.0%				
31		Q4	Read	Busn 107	25	14	56.0%				

Figure 13.44 *On the worksheet PPCh13(3), create four formulas to determine if the percentage enrolled is above the hurdle.*

When you are done with this problem, you can check your work against the answer sheet named PPCh13(3an).

Practice Problem 4

In your Excel file for this chapter (Ch13-Excel365-LogicalFormulas.xlsx), go to the worksheet named PPCh13(4) and create the solution for this practice problem. Figure 13.45 shows the goals that are listed on that worksheet.

	A	B	C	D	E	F	G	H
2	**Goals:**							
3	In cell F12 spill prospective customer names that made it into our master list.							
4	In cell H12 spill prospective customer names that did NOT make it into our master list (and we still need to contact them							
5	Add conditional formatting to both spilled lists that adds a border and green fill for cells that have a spilled value.							
7	**List 1 = Master List.**			**List 2 = Customers we have made sales calls to.**				
9	Master Customer List			Prospective Customers				
11	List 1			List 2		Items in List 2 that are in List 1		Items in List 2 that are in NOT in List 1
12	Fran's Produce			Produce Fast And Fresh				
13	Produce Fast And Fresh			Healthy Garden Produce				
14	Veggies And Fruit Delight			Veggies And Fruit Delight				
15	Fruit & Veggie Delights			Best For U				
16	Clean & Neat Produce			Julie's Produce				
17	Julie's Produce			Fruit & Veggie Inc.				
18	Fruits And Nuts R Us			Health Choice Fruit				
19	Table Ready Produce			Fresh Delights				
20	Freshy Produce			CA Produce				
21	Veggie Are THE Way			Gigi'S Produce				
22	Greens Delight			Delight & Health				
23	Garden Fresh			Garden Health				
24	Garden Ready							
25	Best Garden Produce							
26	Fresh Produce Inc.							
27	Fresh Delights							
28	Down To Earth							
29	Fruit & Veggie Health							
30	Garden Fresh Produce							
31								

Figure 13.45 *On the worksheet PPCh13(4), create the two "compare lists" formulas with conditional formatting.*

When you are done with this problem, you can check your work against the answer sheet named PPCh13(4an).

Practice Problem 5

In your Excel file for this chapter (Ch13-Excel365-LogicalFormulas.xlsx), go to the worksheet named PPCh13(5) and create the solution for this practice problem. Figure 13.46 shows the goal that is listed on that worksheet.

	A	B	C	D	E	F
2		Goal: Calculate the total, max and average sales for each team.				
4			Team 1	Team 2	Team 3	Team 4
5			Sioux	Min	Marco	Ian
6			Chin	Tyrone	Maria	Pham
7			Ty	Washington	Syntela	Mandi
8			Chantel	Gigi	Twanisha	Tim
9			Mento	Kiki	Han	Lim
10			Carmel	Kip	Pops	Mario
11		Sum ($)				
12		Max ($)				
13		Average ($)				
15			SalesRep	Sales		
16			Twanisha	769.76		
17			Tyrone	1296.22		
18			Twanisha	335.27		
19			Chin	240.84		
36100			Pops	1168.21		
36101			Min	196.89		
36102			Kiki	595.62		
36103			Tyrone	819.66		
36104			Twanisha	505.31		
36105			Washington	762.14		

Figure 13.46 *On the worksheet PPCh13(5), create the aggregate formulas for each sales team.*

When you are done with this problem, you can check your work against the answer sheet named PPCh13(5an).

Practice Problem 6

In your Excel file for this chapter (Ch13-Excel365-LogicalFormulas.xlsx), go to the worksheet named PPCh13(6) and create the solution for this practice problem. Figure 13.47 shows the goal that is listed on that worksheet.

	A	B	C	D	E	F	G	H
2		Goal: Make the aggregate calculations sum, count, average and max based on the AND logical test:						
3		Sales must be for the Customer Whole Foods AND the Product Apples.						
5		Customer	Product	Sales		Customer	Product	
6		Whole Foods	Apples	1533.89		Whole Foods	Apples	
7		Whole Foods	Bananas	690.16				
8		Safeway	Bananas	1029.52		Aggregate Calc.		
9		Whole Foods	Apples	642.89			<= Add	
10		Safeway	Bananas	883.31			<= Count	
11		Whole Foods	Bananas	528.14			<= Average	
12		Safeway	Apples	771.07			<= Max	
13		Safeway	Bananas	1033.92				
14		Safeway	Bananas	290.43				
15		Whole Foods	Apples	1756.26				

Figure 13.47 *On the worksheet PPCh13(6), create the four aggregate formulas and the conditional format required.*

When you are done with this problem, you can check your work against the answer sheet named PPCh13(6an).

Practice Problem 7

In your Excel file for this chapter (Ch13-Excel365-LogicalFormulas.xlsx), go to the worksheet named PPCh13(7) and create the solution for this practice problem. Figure 13.48 shows the goal that is listed on that worksheet.

	A	B	C	D	E	F	G	H
1								
2	Goal: Create formula report that will count how many sales are between the following categories:							
3		0 up to but not including 250						
4		250 up to but not including 500						
5		500 up to but not including 750						
6		750 up to but not including 1000						
7								
8	Customer		Product	Sales				
9	Whole Foods		Apples	533.89				
10	Whole Foods		Bananas	690.16				
11	Safeway		Bananas	29.52				
12	Whole Foods		Apples	642.89				
13	Safeway		Bananas	883.31				
14	Whole Foods		Bananas	528.14				
15	Safeway		Apples	771.07				
16	Safeway		Bananas	33.92				
17	Safeway		Bananas	290.43				
18	Whole Foods		Apples	756.26				

Figure 13.48 *On the worksheet named PPCh13(7), create a report that shows the count of sales between an upper limit and a lower limit.*

When you are done with this problem, you can check your work against the answer sheet named PPCh13(7an).

Practice Problem 8

In your Excel file for this chapter (Ch13-Excel365-LogicalFormulas.xlsx), go to the worksheet named PPCh13(8).

In your own words, see if you can answer these conceptual questions:

1. Describe an AND logical test.
2. Describe an OR logical test.
3. Describe a NOT logical test.
4. Describe a BETWEEN logical test.
5. For an aggregate operation that uses an OR logical test, what are the two types of situations that you must be aware of when creating a worksheet formula?
6. What does the IF function do? What does the IFS function do?
7. How do Excel logical functions interpret a negative number?
8. What is a zero-length text string, and how is it used?
9. What do the ISNUMBER and ISNA functions do?

When you are done with this problem, you can check your work against the answer sheet named PPCh13(8an).

Chapter 14: Worksheet Lookup Functions and Formulas

Note: To follow along with the examples in this chapter, you can use the file named Ch14-Excel365-LookupFormulas.xlsx.

Creating lookup formulas is one of the most common tasks that Excel users have had to do over the past 40 years, and this will continue to be the case for the next 40 years. All the way back in 1979, when Bricklin and Frankston invented the first spreadsheet, VisiCalc, they included the LOOKUP function as 1 of the original 25 worksheet functions because they said they wanted to be able to do their taxes with a spreadsheet.

Over the years, many new lookup functions have been added to Excel, including VLOOKUP, MATCH, INDEX, and CHOOSE. The Microsoft 365 Excel lookup function XLOOKUP is designed to be a single function that replaces many of the various other lookup functions. Other Excel 365 lookup tools—such as the XMATCH function, the SWITCH function, the FILTER array function, and the new Data Types feature with the dot operator—have helped revolutionize how Excel users create lookup formulas. A few old-school lookup functions are still useful, including INDEX, CHOOSE, and LOOKUP, as you will see in this chapter.

You might wonder how prevalent lookup formulas are. One lookup function, VLOOKUP, historically ranked in the top five most commonly used worksheet functions. There is a famous story in Microsoft Excel lore about how Bill "MrExcel" Jelen made the succinct post "Can do VLOOKUP in my sleep" in an online accounting job forum and received multiple job offers the next day. As this story illustrates, at that time, potential employers really valued VLOOKUP skills. VLOOKUP is now mostly a thing of the past, and employers instead want to make sure interviewees can do XLOOKUP in their sleep. The XLOOKUP function is a new function that replaces VLOOKUP as well as some other lookup functions.

Note: Chapter 1 presents a comparison of VLOOKUP and XLOOKUP and shows why XLOOKUP is the more efficient option for many lookup formulas. Chapter 1 also shows how the FILTER function can be used to replace the complicated lookup formulas of the past to accomplish the "one lookup value to return multiple items" scenario.

So far in this book, you have created nine lookup formulas in Excel worksheets:

Function or Feature	What the Formula Does	Chapter and Example
XLOOKUP	Looks up a product price	Chapter 12, Example 9
XLOOKUP	Looks up all the rows in a column	Chapter 12, Example 10
FILTER	Looks up a list of student classes	Chapter 12, Example 11
FILTER	Uses one lookup value to return multiple records	Chapter 12, Example 16
Data Types feature	Uses the Data Types feature and dot operator to look up a stock's price and ticker symbol	Chapter 12, Example 18
Two XLOOKUP functions	Does a two-way lookup or intersection lookup	Chapter 12, Example 23
FILTER	Uses two lookup values (in an AND logical test) to return multiple records	Chapter 13, Example 27
FILTER	Uses two lookup values (in an OR logical test) to return multiple records	Chapter 13, Example 28
XMATCH, ISNA, and FILTER	Retrieves items in List 1 that are not in List 2	Chapter 13, Example 29

Already in this book, you have seen some of the great lookup formulas that you can create with the new Microsoft 365 worksheet functions XLOOKUP, XMATCH, and FILTER. This chapter takes closer look at those three functions, as well as a few others, to help you learn about the many types of lookup formulas you can create in an Excel worksheet.

Note: All of the lookup techniques presented in this chapter are for creating worksheet formula solutions. When you learn about Power Query, Power Pivot, and Power BI later in this book, you will explore the different lookup techniques used in those tools, including merges and relationships.

Exact Match Versus Exact Match or Next Smaller Item Lookups

A *lookup* involves using a lookup value to retrieve a related bit of data. Although there are many different types of lookup situations, these are the most common lookup types:

- **Exact match lookup:** When you perform an *exact match lookup*, you try to find a match for the exact characters in the lookup value. For example, If the lookup value is Quad, which contains only the four characters q, u, a, d (remember that worksheet formulas are not case-sensitive), an exact match lookup can only make a match when it finds exactly those four characters. Even Quad followed by a space will not yield a match. Figure 14.1 shows an exact match in which Quad is used to get the price of the Quad product: $43.95.

Note: You typically use exact match lookups with lookup tables such as product tables, employee tables, customer tables, and parts tables.

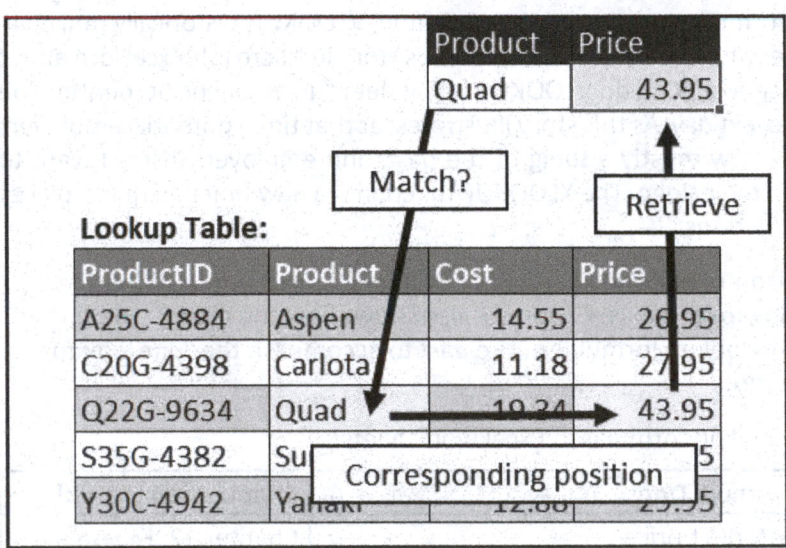

Figure 14.1 *An exact match lookup.*

- **Exact match or next smaller item lookup:** When you perform an exact match or next smaller item lookup, you are trying to find a match, but if there is no exact match, the next smaller value is considered a match. For example, the goal in Figure 14.2 is to look up the tax rate for weekly payroll earnings of $1,200. If the lookup value $1,200 cannot be found, the next smaller value, $1,000, becomes the match. In this example, each number in the Weekly Earnings Lower Limit column implies a category with a lower limit and an upper limit. For example, in the fourth row, the number $1,000 represents all numbers from $1,000 up to but not including the next biggest number, $2,000. Because this example deals with money, the number $1,000 represents all the numbers from $1,000 to $1,999.99. Based on what you learned about logical tests in Chapter 13, you know that the more correct category description for the number $1,000 is the BETWEEN logical test category: $1,000 <= Weekly Earnings < $2,000. Here the lower limit is included, and the upper limit is not included. This means that in the Weekly Earnings Lower Limit column, each number is the lower limit for the category that extends all the way up to, but does not include, the next biggest number.

Note: You typically use exact match or next smaller item lookups for lookup tables such as tax rate tables, commission rate tables, and grading tables.

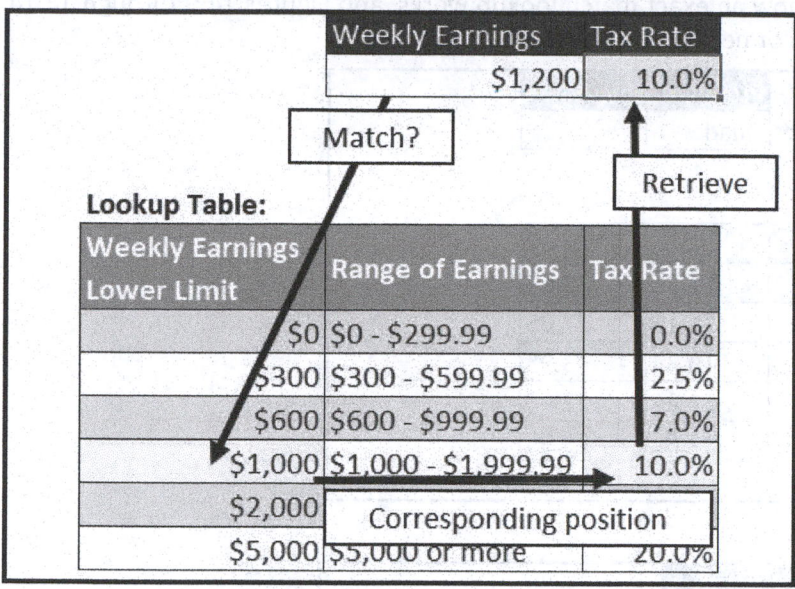

Figure 14.2 *An exact match or next smaller item lookup.*

The "exact match or next smaller item" match mode is a huge improvement over the "approximate match" match mode that exists in all versions of Excel before Microsoft 365—in two ways. First, whereas the term *approximate match* is ambiguous and leaves some users wondering how it works, with exact match or next smaller item, there is no ambiguity: The term says exactly how it works and implies the full category, with its lower and upper limits. Second, in older versions of Excel, you have to have the values in the range where you are searching for a match sorted from smallest to biggest; without this sorting, the approximate match lookup does not work correctly. With exact match or next smaller item match mode, the values in the range where you search for a match do not need to be sorted in any particular order.

A lookup involves these basic steps:

1. Determine a lookup value.

2. Try to match the lookup value in a lookup range (that is, a list of items used to find a match).

3. Note the relative position of the match.

4. Go to the corresponding relative position in the return range (that is, the potential items to retrieve).

5. Get the item from the relative position in the return range and bring it back to a particular cell or larger formula.

As mentioned earlier, whereas an exact match tries to match an exact set of characters, an exact match or next smaller item match tries to find an exact match or accepts the next smaller value as a match. Figures 14.3 through 14.8 further demonstrate how an exact match lookup works, and Figures 14.9 through 14.14 further demonstrate how an exact match or next smaller item lookup works.

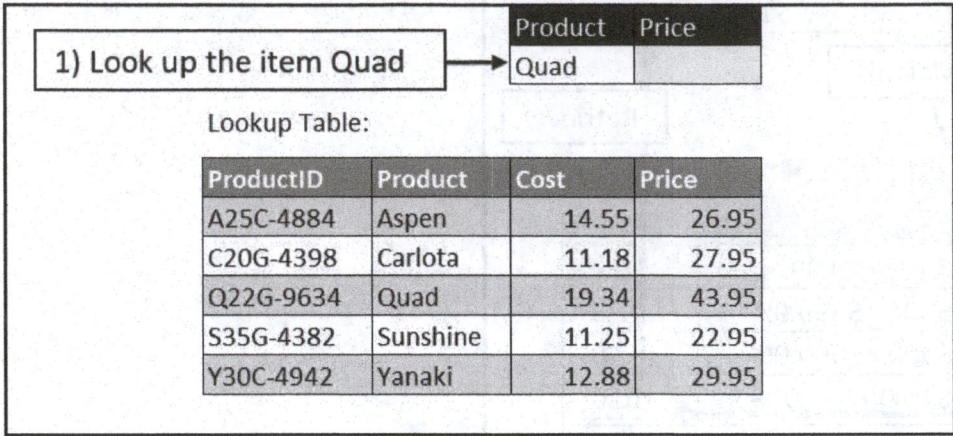

Figure 14.3 *Exact match lookup, step 1.*

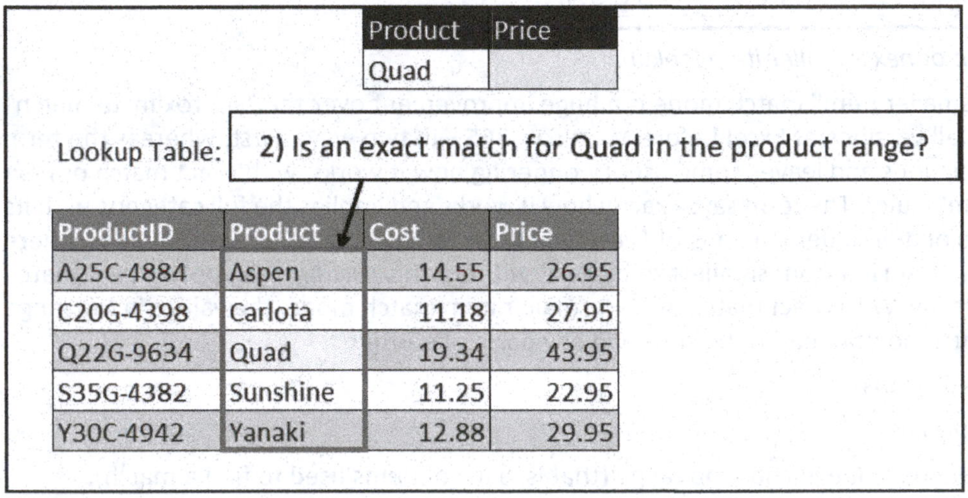

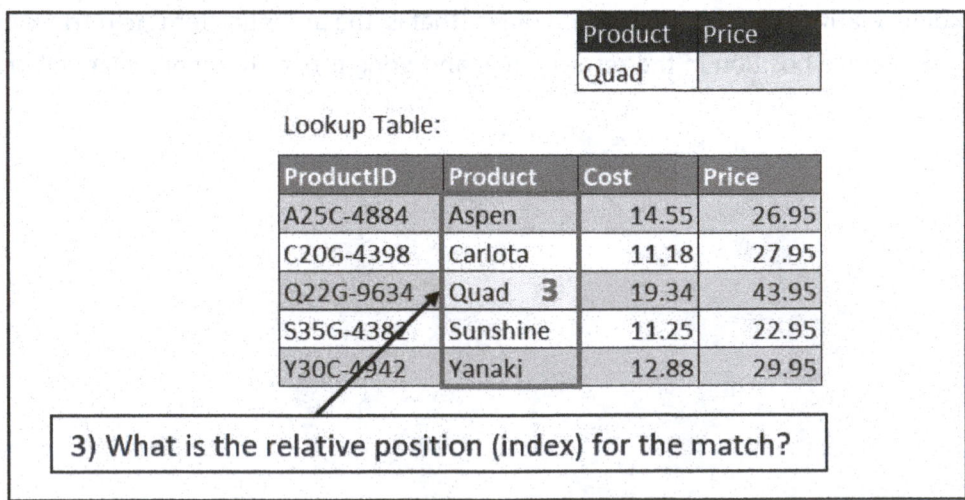

Figure 14.4 *Exact match lookup, step 2.*

Figure 14.5 *Exact match lookup, step 3.*

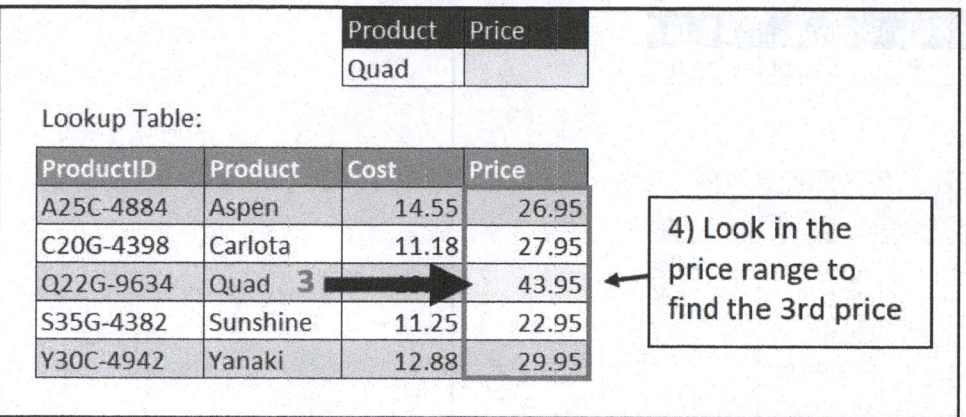

Figure 14.6 *Exact match lookup, step 4.*

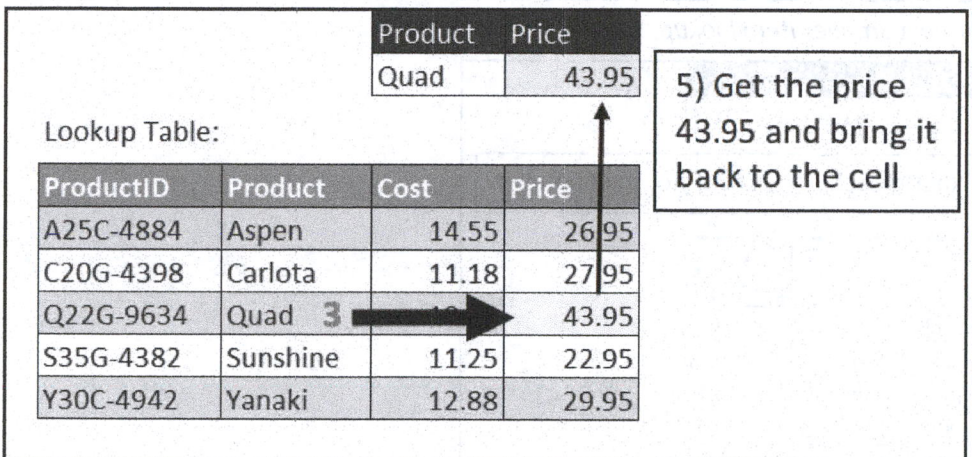

Figure 14.7 *Exact match lookup, step 5.*

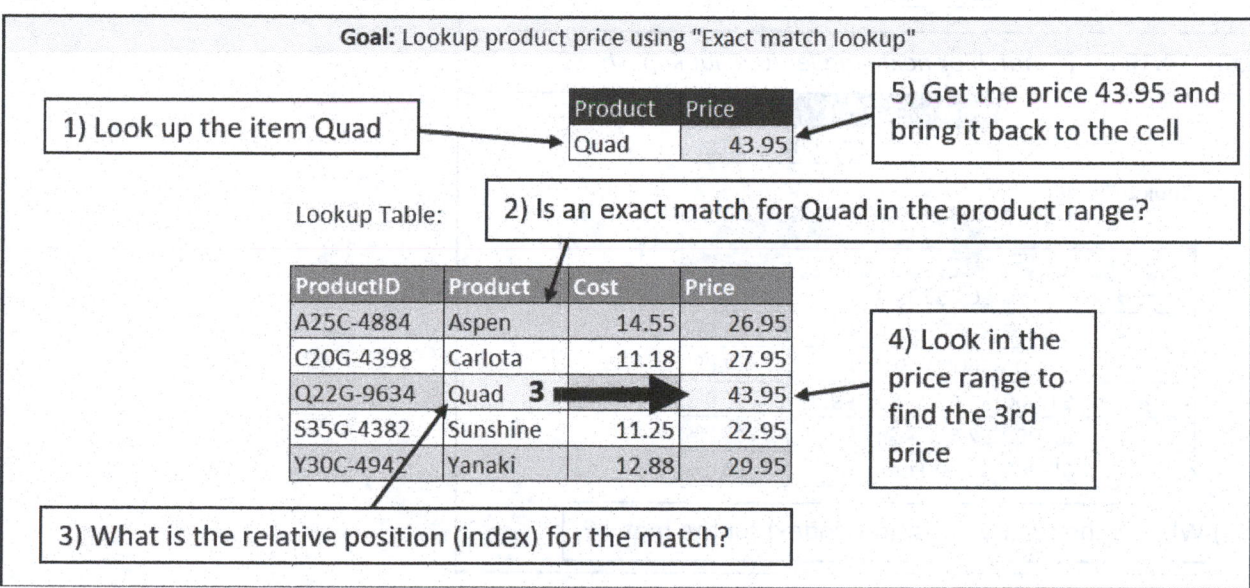

Figure 14.8 *Summary of an exact match lookup.*

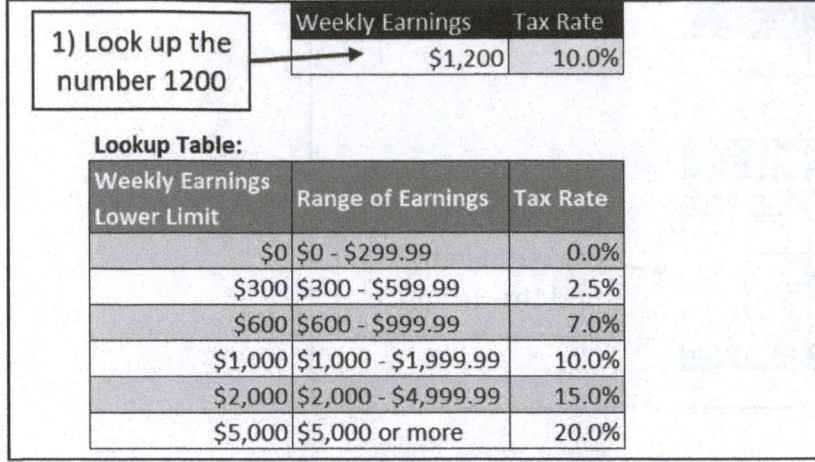

1) Look up the number 1200

Weekly Earnings	Tax Rate
$1,200	10.0%

Lookup Table:

Weekly Earnings Lower Limit	Range of Earnings	Tax Rate
$0	$0 - $299.99	0.0%
$300	$300 - $599.99	2.5%
$600	$600 - $999.99	7.0%
$1,000	$1,000 - $1,999.99	10.0%
$2,000	$2,000 - $4,999.99	15.0%
$5,000	$5,000 or more	20.0%

Figure 14.9 *Exact match or next smaller item lookup, step 1.*

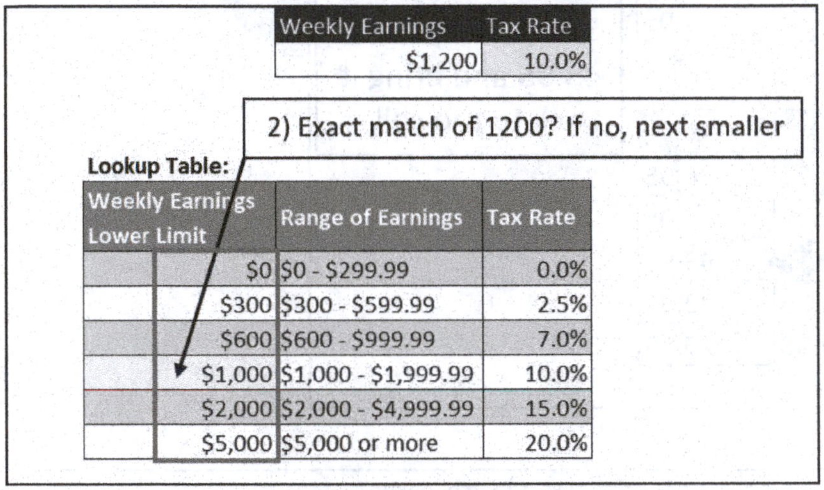

Weekly Earnings	Tax Rate
$1,200	10.0%

2) Exact match of 1200? If no, next smaller

Lookup Table:

Weekly Earnings Lower Limit	Range of Earnings	Tax Rate
$0	$0 - $299.99	0.0%
$300	$300 - $599.99	2.5%
$600	$600 - $999.99	7.0%
$1,000	$1,000 - $1,999.99	10.0%
$2,000	$2,000 - $4,999.99	15.0%
$5,000	$5,000 or more	20.0%

Figure 14.10 *Exact match or next smaller item lookup, step 2.*

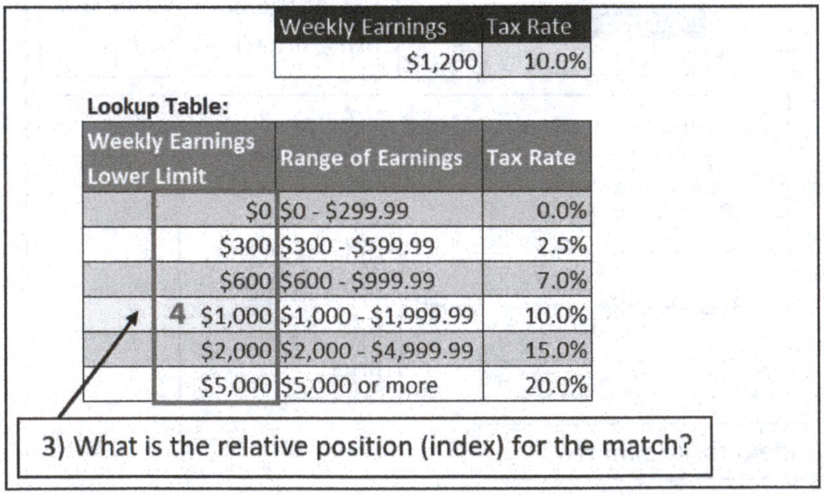

Weekly Earnings	Tax Rate
$1,200	10.0%

Lookup Table:

Weekly Earnings Lower Limit	Range of Earnings	Tax Rate
$0	$0 - $299.99	0.0%
$300	$300 - $599.99	2.5%
$600	$600 - $999.99	7.0%
4 $1,000	$1,000 - $1,999.99	10.0%
$2,000	$2,000 - $4,999.99	15.0%
$5,000	$5,000 or more	20.0%

3) What is the relative position (index) for the match?

Figure 14.11 *Exact match or next smaller item lookup, step 3.*

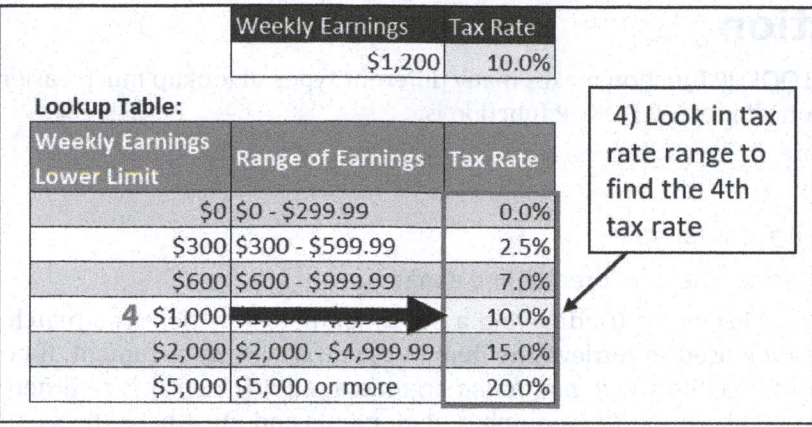

Figure 14.12 *Exact match or next smaller item lookup, step 4.*

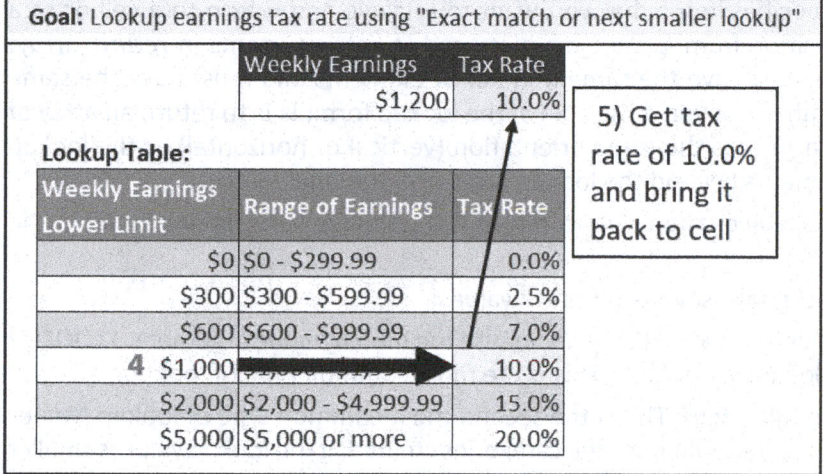

Figure 14.13 *Exact match or next smaller item lookup, step 5.*

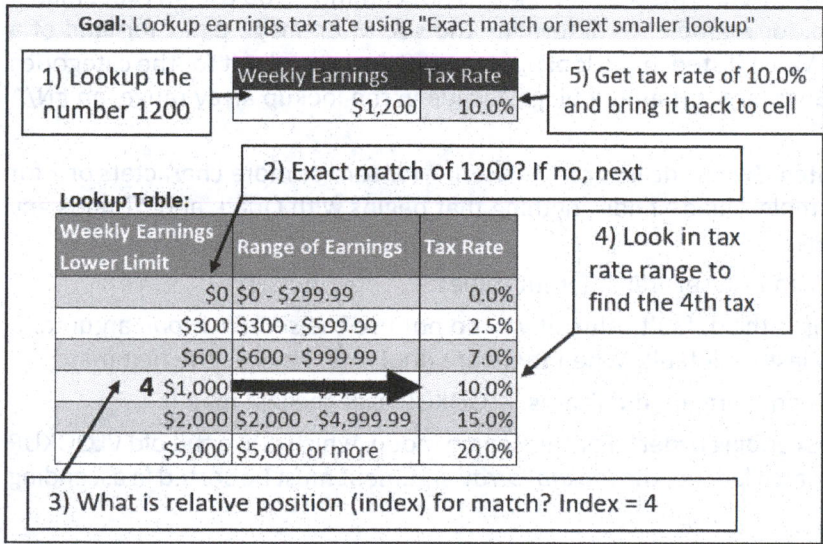

Figure 14.14 *Summary of exact match or next smaller item lookup.*

The XLOOKUP Function

Luckily, with Microsoft 365 Excel, the XLOOKUP function makes many different types of lookup much easier than in earlier versions of Excel. The syntax for the XLOOKUP function is:

```
XLOOKUP(lookup_value, lookup_array, return_array, [if_not_found], [match_
mode], [search_mode])
```

The arguments of the XLOOKUP function are as follows:

- ***lookup_value***: This argument specifies the item used to find a match.
- ***lookup_array***: This argument specifies items used to find a potential match. If there is a match, XLOOKUP yields the relative position used to retrieve the item in the *return_array* argument. If no is match found and nothing is entered into the *if_not_found* argument, an #N/A error is returned. *lookup_array* and *return_array* must have the same number of elements and must have the same orientation (vertical or horizontal). A lookup array does not have to be sorted in a particular order.
- ***return_array***: This argument specifies items that you want to retrieve and return to a cell or to a larger formula. The relative position from *lookup_array* is used to retrieve items in *return_array*. *return_array* and *lookup_array* must have the same number of elements and must have the same orientation (vertical or horizontal). However, if the goal of the lookup formula is to return an array of answers, as long as the return array has the same orientation (vertical or horizontal) as the lookup array, it can have additional elements beyond the lookup array orientational match.
- **[*if_not_found*]**: This argument specifies the value to return if the lookup value is not found in the lookup array.
- **[*match_mode*]**: This argument can take several different values:
    - **0 - Exact match:** This is the default value. If you do not use the *match_mode* argument, XLOOKUP performs an exact match lookup by default. This is the most common type of lookup.
    - **-1 - Exact match or next smaller item:** This is the second-most-common type of lookup. Values listed in a lookup array are the lower limit for the categories created. If the lookup value is smaller than the smallest value in the lookup array range, an #N/A error is returned.
    - **1 - Exact match or next larger item:** This sort of lookup is not common. You use an exact match or next larger item lookup, for example, to determine the size of drainage pipes for land of a particular square footage. Values listed in the lookup array are the upper limit for the categories created. If the lookup value is bigger than the biggest value in the lookup array range, an #N/A error is returned.
    - **2 - Wildcard character match:** Two wildcards can be used: * for zero or more characters or ? for a single character. For example, Quad* finds anything that begins with Quad, and *? finds any text (at least one character).
- **[*search_mode*]**: This argument can take several different values:
    - **1 - Search first-to-last:** This is the default value. If you do not use the *search_mode* argument, XLOOKUP searches first to last by default. When there are duplicates, it uses the first match.
    - **-1 - Search last-to-first:** When there are duplicates, XLOOKUP uses the last match.
    - **2 - Binary search (sorted ascending order):** For this search mode, which is like the old VLOOKUP and MATCH approximate match lookup, the *lookup_array* argument must be sorted in ascending order.
    - **-2 - Binary search (sorted descending order):** For this search mode, which is like the old MATCH -1 approximate match lookup, the *lookup_array* argument must be sorted in descending order.

The screentips for the [*match_mode*] argument, as shown in Figure 14.15, are quite helpful.

0 - Exact match	Return the index of the Exact match, if none return #N/A
-1 - Exact match or next smaller item	
1 - Exact match or next larger item	
2 - Wildcard character match	

0 - Exact match	
-1 - Exact match or next smaller item	Return the index of the Exact match, if not found return the index of the next smaller item
1 - Exact match or next larger item	
2 - Wildcard character match	

0 - Exact match	
-1 - Exact match or next smaller item	
1 - Exact match or next larger item	Return the index of the Exact match, if not found return the index of the next larger item
2 - Wildcard character match	

0 - Exact match	
-1 - Exact match or next smaller item	
1 - Exact match or next larger item	
2 - Wildcard character match	Return the index of a wildcard match where *, ? and ~ have special meaning

Figure 14.15 *Screentips for the [match_mode] argument of the XLOOKUP function.*

The screentips for the [*search_mode*] argument, as shown in Figure 14.16, are also quite helpful. Note that with this argument, the last two binary search options are not really needed if you use the second and third options in the [*match_mode*] argument instead. The binary search option just adds the unnecessary requirement of sorting the column. These arguments were included for backward compatibility with the approximate match lookup in earlier Excel versions. Rather than use a binary search (sorted in ascending order), you can just use the [*match_mode*] argument option -1 - Exact match or next smaller item. Rather than use a binary search (sorted in descending order), you can just use the [*match_mode*] argument option 1 - Exact match or next larger item.

1 - Search first-to-last	Perform a search starting at the first item
-1 - Search last-to-first	
2 - Binary search (sorted ascending order)	
-2 - Binary search (sorted descending order)	

1 - Search first-to-last	
-1 - Search last-to-first	Perform a reverse search starting at the last item
2 - Binary search (sorted ascending order)	
-2 - Binary search (sorted descending order)	

1 - Search first-to-last	
-1 - Search last-to-first	
2 - Binary search (sorted ascending order)	Perform a binary search that relies on lookup_array being sorted in ascending order.
-2 - Binary search (sorted descending order)	

1 - Search first-to-last	
-1 - Search last-to-first	
2 - Binary search (sorted ascending order)	
-2 - Binary search (sorted descending order)	Perform a binary search that relies on lookup_array being sorted in descending order.

Figure 14.16 *Screentips for the [search_mode] argument of the XLOOKUP function.*

Example 1: Using the XLOOKUP Function to Look Up Product Price Based on an Exact Match Lookup and Data Validation List

Whenever you do an exact match lookup and the lookup table is easily accessible, you should use the Data Validation feature to add a dropdown list of the potential lookup values from the lookup array range to the cell with the lookup value input. By doing this, you make your solution robust by allowing only items that are from the lookup array list to be entered into the lookup value input cell. This prevents the XLOOKUP function from failing to find matches that do exist and thus prevents errors.

For the example in Figure 14.17, the goal is to allow the user to look up any product and retrieve its price. The lookup table has already been converted to an Excel Table named ProductTable.

To see how to use the XLOOKUP function to perform an exact match lookup, go to the worksheet Ch14(17-21) and follow these steps:

1. Select cell B5 and use the Data Validation feature to add a dropdown list with the Product column from the lookup table as the source list. (For a refresher on the Data Validation feature, refer to Chapter 9.)

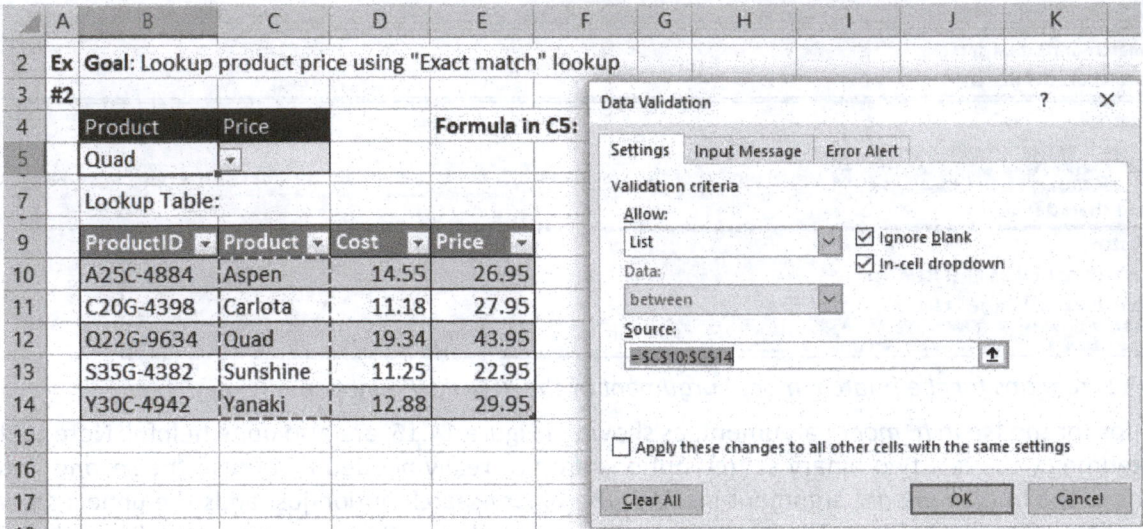

Figure 14.17 *When performing an exact match lookup, use the Data Validation feature to make the solution robust.*

2. Select cell C5. As shown in Figure 14.18, use the XLOOKUP function and enter cell B5 into the *lookup_value* argument. Because you already added data validation to cell B5, the XLOOKUP function will always be assured of finding a match. The formula so far should look like this: **=XLOOKUP(B5**.

	A	B	C	D	E	F	G	H	I	J
2	Ex	**Goal**: Lookup product price using "Exact match" lookup								
3	#2									
4		Product	Price		Formula in C5:					
5		Quad	=XLOOKUP(B5							
			XLOOKUP(**lookup_value**, lookup_array, return_array, [if_not_found], [match_mode], [search_mode])							
7		Lookup Table:								
9		ProductID ▼	Product ▼	Cost ▼	Price ▼					
10		A25C-4884	Aspen	14.55	26.95					
11		C20G-4398	Carlota	11.18	27.95					
12		Q22G-9634	Quad	19.34	43.95					
13		S35G-4382	Sunshine	11.25	22.95					
14		Y30C-4942	Yanaki	12.88	29.95					

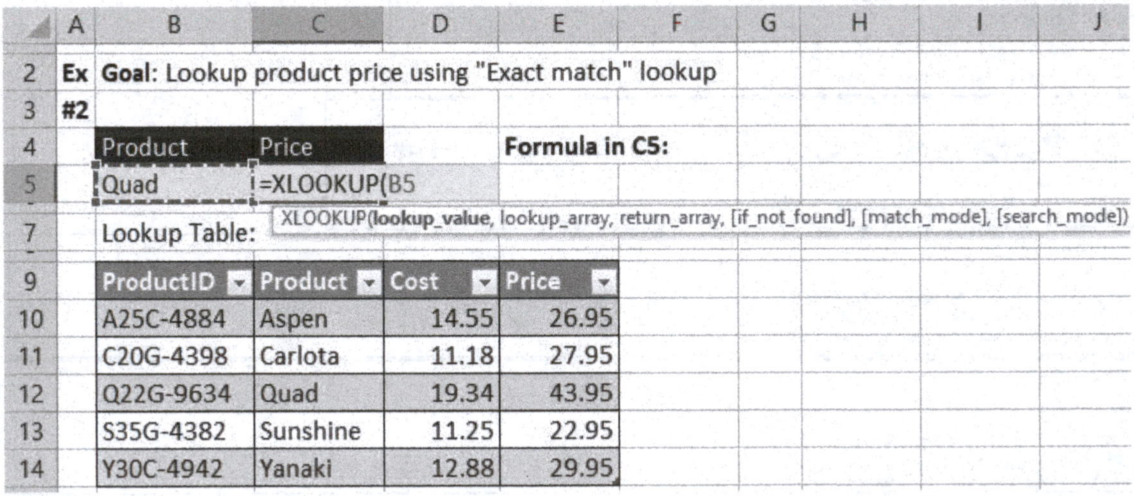

Figure 14.18 *The lookup value contains Quad.*

3. As shown in Figure 14.19, type a comma to move to the *lookup_array* argument. Select the Product column. The formula should now look like this: **=XLOOKUP(B5,ProductTable[Product]**.

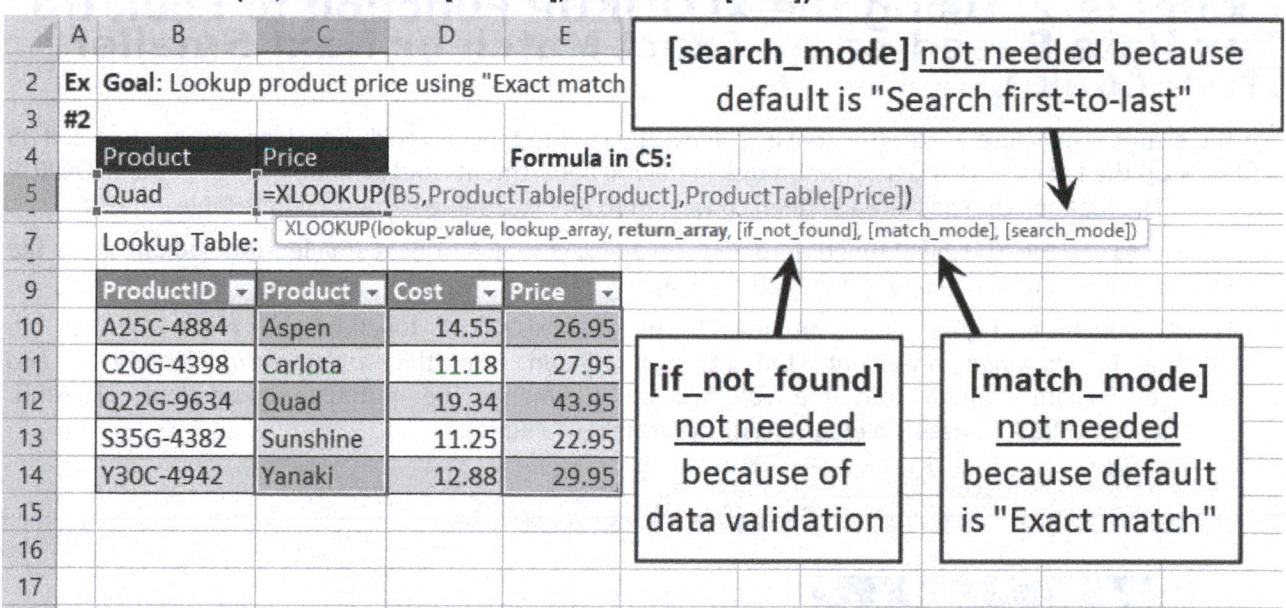

	A	B	C	D	E	F	G	H	I	J
2	Ex	**Goal:** Lookup product price using "Exact match" lookup								
3	#2									
4		Product	Price			**Formula in C5:**				
5		Quad	=XLOOKUP(B5,ProductTable[Product]							
7		Lookup Table:		XLOOKUP(lookup_value, **lookup_array**, return_array, [if_not_found], [match_mode], [search_mode])						
9		ProductID ▾	Product ▾	Cost ▾	Price ▾					
10		A25C-4884	Aspen	14.55	26.95					
11		C20G-4398	Carlota	11.18	27.95					
12		Q22G-9634	Quad	19.34	43.95					
13		S35G-4382	Sunshine	11.25	22.95					
14		Y30C-4942	Yanaki	12.88	29.95					

Figure 14.19 *The lookup array contains the Product column.*

4. As shown in Figure 14.20, type a comma to move to the *return_array* argument. Select the Price column and then type a close parenthesis. The formula should now look like this: **=XLOOKUP(B5,ProductTable[Product],ProductTable[Price])**.

	A	B	C	D	E		
2	Ex	**Goal:** Lookup product price using "Exact match					
3	#2						
4		Product	Price			**Formula in C5:**	
5		Quad	=XLOOKUP(B5,ProductTable[Product],ProductTable[Price])				
7		Lookup Table:		XLOOKUP(lookup_value, lookup_array, **return_array**, [if_not_found], [match_mode], [search_mode])			
9		ProductID ▾	Product ▾	Cost ▾	Price ▾		
10		A25C-4884	Aspen	14.55	26.95		
11		C20G-4398	Carlota	11.18	27.95		
12		Q22G-9634	Quad	19.34	43.95		
13		S35G-4382	Sunshine	11.25	22.95		
14		Y30C-4942	Yanaki	12.88	29.95		
15							
16							
17							

[search_mode] not needed because default is "Search first-to-last"

[if_not_found] not needed because of data validation

[match_mode] not needed because default is "Exact match"

Figure 14.20 *The return array contains the Price column, and the last three arguments are not needed.*

Note: As shown in Figure 14.20, you should not enter anything into the last three arguments of the XLOOKUP function. You do not need to add an error message in the [*if_not_found*] argument because you will not get errors, thanks to the data validation you added to cell B5. You do not need to enter anything into the [*match_mode*] argument because the default is 0 - Exact match. You do not need to enter anything into the [*search_mode*] argument because the default is 1 - Search first-to-last.

5. Press Enter to enter the formula. Figure 14.21 shows the XLOOKUP result: $43.95.

6. Test your solution by using the dropdown in cell B5 to try different product names.

C5		▼	:	×	✓	fx	=XLOOKUP(B5,ProductTable[Product],ProductTable[Price])			
	A	B	C	D	E	F	G	H	I	J
2	Ex	Goal: Lookup product price using "Exact match" lookup								
3	#2									
4		Product	Price			Formula in C5:				
5		Quad	43.95			=XLOOKUP(B5,ProductTable[Product],ProductTable[Price])				
7		Lookup Table:								
9		ProductID ▼	Product ▼	Cost ▼	Price ▼					
10		A25C-4884	Aspen	14.55	26.95					
11		C20G-4398	Carlota	11.18	27.95					
12		Q22G-9634	Quad	19.34	43.95					
13		S35G-4382	Sunshine	11.25	22.95					
14		Y30C-4942	Yanaki	12.88	29.95					

Figure 14.21 *Only the first three arguments are needed when you do an exact match lookup and use data validation.*

Example 2: Using the XLOOKUP Function to Look Up Tax Rate Based on an Exact Match or Next Smaller Item Lookup

For the example in Figure 14.22, the goal is to allow the user to type a weekly earnings number into cell B5 and look up the tax rate. This is a common task in payroll departments and is made easy with the XLOOKUP function. The lookup table has already been converted to an Excel Table named TaxRateTable.

To see how to use the XLOOKUP function to perform an exact match or next smaller item lookup, go to the worksheet named Ch14(22-25) and follow these steps:

1. As shown in Figure 14.22, in cell C5, use the XLOOKUP function and enter cell B5 into the *lookup_value* argument, the Earnings column into the *lookup_array* argument, and the TaxRate column into the *return_array* argument. The formula should look like this: **=XLOOKUP(B5,TaxRateTable[Earnings],TaxRateTable[TaxRate]**.

	A	B	C	D	E	F	G	H	I
2	Ex	Goal: Lookup earnings tax rate using "Exact match or next smaller lookup"							
3	#2								
4		Earnings	TaxRate			Formula in C5:			
5		$1,200	=XLOOKUP(B5,TaxRateTable[Earnings],TaxRateTable[TaxRate]						
7		Lookup Table:	XLOOKUP(lookup_value, lookup_array, **return_array**, [if_not_found], [match_mode], [search_mode])						
9		Earnings ▼	Range ▼	TaxRate ▼					
10		$0	$0 - $299.99	0.0%					
11		$300	$300 - $599.99	2.5%					
12		$600	$600 - $999.99	7.0%					
13		$1,000	$1,000 - $1,999.99	10.0%					
14		$2,000	$2,000 - $4,999.99	15.0%					
15		$5,000	$5,000 or more	20.0%					

Figure 14.22 *Using XLOOKUP to look up weekly earnings and return a tax rate.*

2. Type a comma and enter the number **0** into the [*if_not_found*] argument (see Figure 14.23). This zero tax rate will be returned if a user enters a negative number into cell B5. Because the smallest number in the earnings column (refer to Figure 14.22) is 0, the XLOOKUP function would not be able to find an exact match or next smaller if the user entered a negative number. If the user enters a

negative number without a zero in the [*if_not_found*] argument, XLOOKUP delivers an #N/A error. With the 0 in the [*if_not_found*] argument, the correct tax rate of 0 will be delivered if a negative number is entered in cell B5.

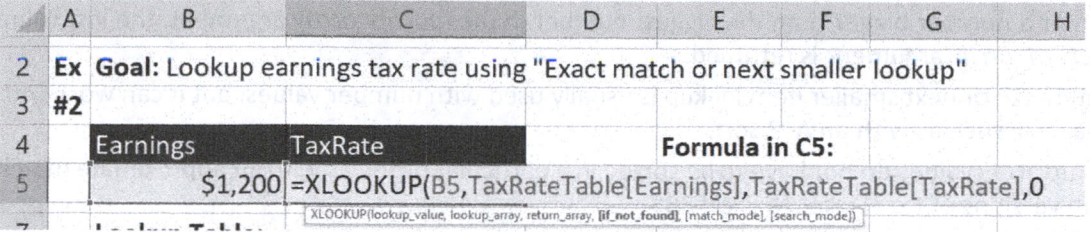

Figure 14.23 *A zero tax rate from the [if_not_found] argument is delivered if a negative number in entered in cell B5.*

3. Type a comma to move to the [*match_mode*] argument. As shown in Figure 14.24, select the second option from the dropdown list, -1 - Exact match or next smaller item.

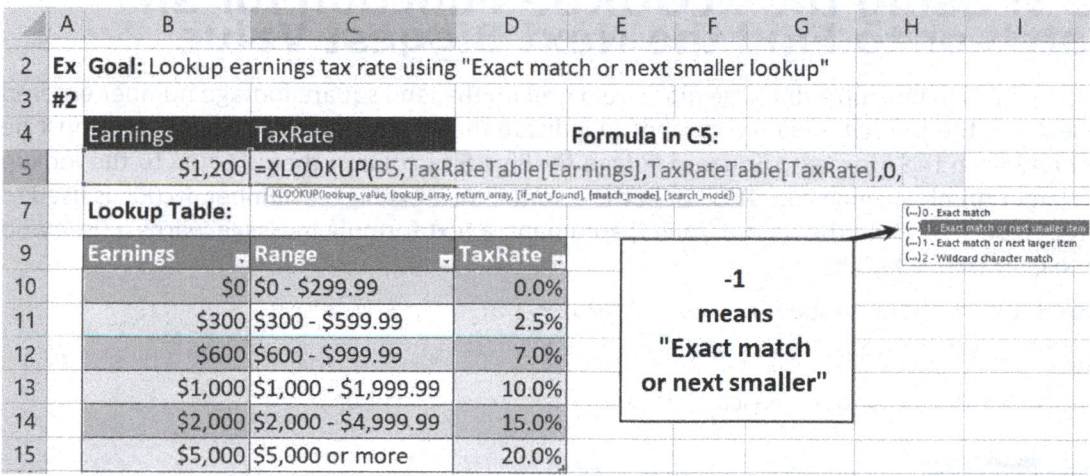

Figure 14.24 *-1 in the [match_mode] argument instructs XLOOKUP to do and exact match or next smaller item lookup.*

4. Since the default for the [*search_mode*] argument is to search from first to last, and that is what you want, type a close parenthesis. The final formula should look like this: **=XLOOKUP(B5,TaxRateTable[Earnings],TaxRateTable[TaxRate],0,-1)**.

5. Press Enter. The XLOOKUP formula should retrieve the correct tax rate, 10%, as shown in Figure 14.25.

6. Test your formula by trying different numbers in cell B5.

C5		× ✓ *fx*	=XLOOKUP(B5,TaxRateTable[Earnings],TaxRateTable[TaxRate],0,-1)							

	A	B	C	D	E	F	G	H	I	J	K
2	Ex	Goal: Lookup earnings tax rate using "Exact match or next smaller lookup"									
3	#2										
4		Earnings	TaxRate		Formula in C5:						
5		$1,200	10.0%		=XLOOKUP(B5,TaxRateTable[Earnings],TaxRateTable[TaxRate],0,-1)						
7		Lookup Table:									
9		Earnings	Range	TaxRate							
10		$0	$0 - $299.99	0.0%							
11		$300	$300 - $599.99	2.5%							
12		$600	$600 - $999.99	7.0%							
13		$1,000	$1,000 - $1,999.99	10.0%							
14		$2,000	$2,000 - $4,999.99	15.0%							
15		$5,000	$5,000 or more	20.0%							

Figure 14.25 *When you do an exact match or next smaller item lookup, the Earnings column can be sorted in any order.*

Consider these key points related to doing an exact match or next smaller item lookup:

- If *lookup_value* is smaller than the smallest number in the lookup array, you will get an #N/A error unless you enter something in the [*if_not_found*] argument.
- If you enter a number bigger than the biggest number in the *lookup_array* argument, the last value in the *return_array* argument is returned.
- An exact match or next smaller item lookup is usually used with number values, but it can work with text data also, such as with an A–Z sort.
- The lookup array values do not have to be sorted in a particular order, as with an approximate match lookup in versions of Excel prior to Excel 365.
- *lookup_array* and *return_array* must have the same number of elements and must have the same orientation (vertical or horizontal).
- An exact match or next smaller item lookup is a common lookup type for lookup tables such as tax tables, commission tables, and grading tables.

Example 3: Using the XLOOKUP Function for an Exact Match or to Find the Next Biggest Value

In Figure 14.26, the goal is to look up a drainage pipe size based on the land square footage number entered in cell C4. You use a 1 in the [*match_mode*] argument to indicate that the square footage number must be matched with a number in the Max Land Square Footage for Pipe Size column that is equal to the lookup value or the next larger number. Since 23,000 is not in the column, the next bigger number 46,000 is used to pick out the correct pipe size, 8". In the [*if_not_found*] argument, a text formula message warns a user who enters a number bigger than 238,000.

You can try this example on the worksheet named Ch14(26).

	A	B	C	D	E	F	G	H
2	Ex	**Goal:** Retrieve land square footage based on pipe size.						
3	#3							
4		Land Square Footage	23,000		**Formula in C5:**			
5		Pipe Size Required	8"		=XLOOKUP(C4,B8:B14,C8:C14,"Enter value "&B8&" or smaller",1)			
6								
7		Max Land Square Footage for Pipe Size	Drain Pipe Size (in.)		**Implied category:**			
8		238,000	16"		238,000 >= Pipe Size > 134,000			
9		134,000	12"		134,000 >= Pipe Size > 83,000			
10		83,000	10"		83,000 >= Pipe Size > 46,000			
11		46,000	8"		46,000 >= Pipe Size > 22,000			
12		22,000	6"		22,000 >= Pipe Size > 14,000			

Figure 14.26 *An exact match or next bigger item lookup to determine the drainage pipe size based on land square footage.*

Example 4: Using the XLOOKUP Function to Do a Wildcard Lookup

Figure 14.27 shows a lookup situation where you use a 2 in the [*match_mode*] argument so you can use wildcards with the lookup value. The goal is to type just part of the company name, such as *Coca Cola*, and get a match with the full company name *Coca Cola Inc*. As you learned in Chapter 13, Example 14, the wildcard asterisk (*) represents zero or more characters. When you use the join operator (&) to join an asterisk in double quotes to the front and back of the cell reference B6, you are asking to make a match with any text in the *lookup_array* argument that contains *Coca Cola*. The formula also includes the text "Not Found" in the [*if_not_found*] argument so that XLOOKUP can return that message if the user types some text that is not contained in any of the values in the *lookup_array* argument.

	A	B	C	D	E	F	G	H	I
2	Ex	Goal: Lookup Coca Cola and get a match for Coca Cola Inc.							
3	#4	Example of: Wildcard lookup (partial text lookup, fuzzy lookup)							
5		Company (partial text)	City			Formula in C6:			
6		Coca Cola	Atlanta			=XLOOKUP("*"&B6&"*",B11:B14,C11:C14,"Not Found",2)			
8		Lookup Table:							
10		Company (full text)	City						
11		Coca Cola Inc.	Atlanta						
12		Pepsi Cola Inc.	NY						
13		RC Cola	KC						
14		Shasta Drinks	Calistoga						

Figure 14.27 *A wildcard lookup based on a partial text lookup value.*

The drawback to using wildcards is that it is not guaranteed that the formula can always return the correct value. For example, if you type **Cola** into cell B6, the formula will not know whether you want Coca Cola Inc., Pepsi Cola Inc., or RC Cola. However, because the default is to return the first item when there are duplicates, if you enter **Cola**, the formula will return the city of Atlanta because Coca Cola Inc. is the first company name that contains Cola. This sort of lookup is never 100% guaranteed to work.

You can try this example on the worksheet named Ch14(27).

Example 5: Using the XLOOKUP Function to Get the First Item When There Are Duplicates

In some lookup situations, you need to get the first match when there are duplicates. For example, Figure 14.28 shows a template where an x means an employee worked on the project on the specified date at the top of the column. To look up the first work date for each employee, you can look up x in the relative range to the right of the employee name and then return the date from the column header dates, which is an absolute locked range. When you don't enter anything into the [*match_mode*] or [*search_mode*] arguments, XLOOKUP defaults to an exact match and searches from first to last. With these settings, XLOOKUP will always get the first match when there are duplicates. If you follow my Golden Rule, in this formula you hard code the lookup value x into the formula because this input will not change. Because you have a single lookup value rather than a range of values, this formula will not spill, and you must enter the formula and then manually copy it to the rows below.

You can try this example on the worksheet named Ch14(28).

C12			▼	:	× ✓ fx	=XLOOKUP("x",D12:H12,$D$11:$H$11,"Didn't work")		

	A	B	C	D	E	F	G	H
2	Ex	Goal: Lookup first date worked on project.						
3	#5	"Get First" when there are duplicates.						
5		Formula in C12:						
6		=XLOOKUP("x",D12:H12,$D$11:$H$11,"Didn't work")						
7		Enter and copy to rows below.						
9		"x" marks when employee worked on project.						
11		Employee	First Date Worked	10/4/21	10/5/21	10/6/21	10/7/21	10/8/21
12		Chin	10/6/21			x	x	x
13		Gigi	10/5/21		x		x	
14		Sioux	10/5/21		x	x	x	
15		Chantel	10/4/21	x	x	x	x	x
16		Billy	10/7/21				x	x

Figure 14.28 *When you use an exact match and a first-to-last search, XLOOKUP gets the first match when there are duplicates.*

Example 6: Using the XLOOKUP Function to Get the Last Item When There Are Duplicates

When you need to look up the last matched value in a range, you can use the option -1 - Search last-to-first in the [*search_mode*] argument. This forces XLOOKUP to get the last value when there are duplicates. In Figure 14.29, the goal for the lookup formula is to look up the last sale for each sales rep. Notice that the formula requires that you type commas to skip over and accept the defaults for the fourth and fifth arguments. Also notice that you can enter both employee names into the *lookup_value* argument to force the formula to spill the results.

You can try this example on the worksheet named Ch14(29).

| G6 | ▼ | : | ✕ | ✓ | *fx* | =XLOOKUP(F6:F7,C6:C15,D6:D15,,,-1) |

	A	B	C	D	E	F	G	H	I	J	K	L
2	**Ex**	**Goal:** Lookup last sale for each sales rep.										
3	**#6**	"Get Last" when there are duplicates.										
5		Date	Sales Rep	Sales		Sales Rep	Last Sale	Formula in G6:				
6		10/3/21	Sioux	$640.56		Sioux	311.12	=XLOOKUP(F6:F7,C6:C15,D6:D15,,,-1)				
7		10/3/21	Chin	$706.02		Chin	765.99	Enter and it spills down to rows below.				
8		10/3/21	Chin	$589.69								
9		10/3/21	Chin	$695.31								
10		10/3/21	Sioux	$474.26								
11		10/3/21	Sioux	$786.13								
12		10/3/21	Sioux	$311.12								
13		10/3/21	Chin	$483.25								
14		10/3/21	Chin	$696.97								
15		10/3/21	Chin	$765.99								

Figure 14.29 *When you use an exact match and a last-to-first search, XLOOKUP gets the last match when there are duplicates.*

Example 7: Using the XLOOKUP Function to Look Up All the Rows in a Column

In Example 10 in Chapter 12, you saw how to use the XLOOKUP function to look up all the rows in a column and then add the results inside the SUM function. However, I include a second example here for completeness.

Figure 14.30 shows that a user can select a day from the data validation dropdown in cell C5, and Excel updates which column the XLOOKUP function looks up and then delivers it to the SUM function in cell C6. The key to getting the XLOOKUP function to look up all the rows in a column is that the lookup array must be a single row, and it must contain the same number of columns as the return array. In this example, the lookup array is the range C10:F10 (which is 1 row by 4 columns), and the return array is C11:F22 (which is 12 rows by 4 columns), so things work correctly. It just so happens that these two ranges span the columns C to F, but that is not what causes such a lookup to work. It is the number of columns—in this case, 4 columns in both the lookup array and return array—that determines whether this sort of lookup is successful.

The number of rows returned is determined by how many rows are in the return array. In this case, because there are 12 rows, XLOOKUP returns the 12 rows of numbers for Day 2 to the SUM function so it can aggregate and add.

You can try this example on the worksheet named Ch14(30).

	A	B	C	D	E	F
2	Ex	**Goal:** Lookup column and then aggregate as sum.				
3	#7	Add total units by Day selected in cell C5.				
5		Select Day:	Day 2		**Formula in C6:**	
6		Total Units	11,792		=SUM(XLOOKUP(C5,C10:F10,C11:F22))	
8		**Units by Day:**				
10		**Hour**	**Day 1**	**Day 2**	**Day 3**	**Day 4**
11		6:00 AM	373	1,646	1,606	738
12		7:00 AM	38	1,198	1,719	1,888
13		8:00 AM	300	1,828	1,285	816
14		9:00 AM	1,221	265	484	1,277
15		10:00 AM	930	780	246	15
16		11:00 AM	914	227	409	443
17		12:00 PM	1,271	945	1,924	715
18		1:00 PM	1,840	617	144	887
19		2:00 PM	966	1,824	268	378
20		3:00 PM	672	1,208	1,946	528
21		4:00 PM	1,177	822	323	760
22		5:00 PM	304	432	495	364

looup_array
1 row x
4 columns

return_array
12 rows x
4 columns

Figure 14.30 *You can look up a full column can by using the XLOOKUP function.*

Example 8: Using the XLOOKUP Function to Look Up a Record (All Columns in a Row)

Figure 14.31 shows the formula to look up and spill an employee record based on the employee ID in cell B5. This formula looks up all the columns in a row. For this to work, the lookup array must be a single column with the same number of rows as there are in the return array. In this example, the lookup array is B10:B13 (which is 1 column by 4 rows), and the return array is C10:G13 (which is 5 columns by 4 rows); the two arrays contain the same number of rows, so the record can be returned. When you enter the formula into cell D5, the record spills.

You can try this example on the worksheet named Ch14(31).

	A	B	C	D	E	F	G	H
2	Ex #8	**Goal:** Lookup employee record based on EmployeeID in cell B5.						
4		**EmployeeID**		**First**	**Last**	**StartDate**	**CellPhone**	**Department**
5		4369-4774		Ty	Smithe	40862	435-398-5510	Finance
7		**Formula in D5:**		=XLOOKUP(B5,B10:B13,C10:G13)				
8								
9		**EmployeeID**	**First**	**Last**	**StartDate**	**CellPhone**	**Department**	
10		4369-9084	Sioux	Chin	10/6/12	206-767-2190	Accounting	
11		4369-4774	Ty	Smithe	11/15/11	435-398-5510	Finance	
12		4369-2234	Gigi	Sy	2/3/18	206-337-0288	Accounting	
13		4369-3979	Kip	Hensel	10/6/20	206-821-4452	Maintenance	

Figure 14.31 *XLOOKUP can be used to look up an employee record.*

Examples 9 and 10: Using the XLOOKUP Function to Do a Two-Way Lookup

A two-way lookup is a common type of lookup that finds a row header match and a column header match and then looks up the interesting value. A typical example is the payroll situation where you must look up an employee's gross pay and number of allowances (which is basically the number of people in the household for tax purposes) to retrieve a federal tax withholding amount for the deduction on a paycheck.

As shown in Figure 14.32, if an employee's gross pay is $705 and number of allowances is 2, the intersecting withholding amount of $45 is the tax deduction for this employee. When doing this sort of two-way lookup with the XLOOKUP function, you use XLOOKUP two times in the same formula, nesting the inner XLOOKUP in the outer XLOOKUP.

To start this formula, you can use the inner XLOOKUP function to look up the column header variable (number of allowances = 2) to return all the rows for that column. Then you use that inner XLOOKUP in the *return_array* argument in the outer XLOOKUP. The outer XLOOKUP then looks up the $705 amount as an exact match or next smaller item lookup to get the 700-710 row and then return the $45 withholding tax amount.

> **Note:** For payroll taxes, there are a wide variety of tax tables. In this example, I show a very specific table for the marital status single, no allowances greater than 7, and a gross pay range from $450 to $720.

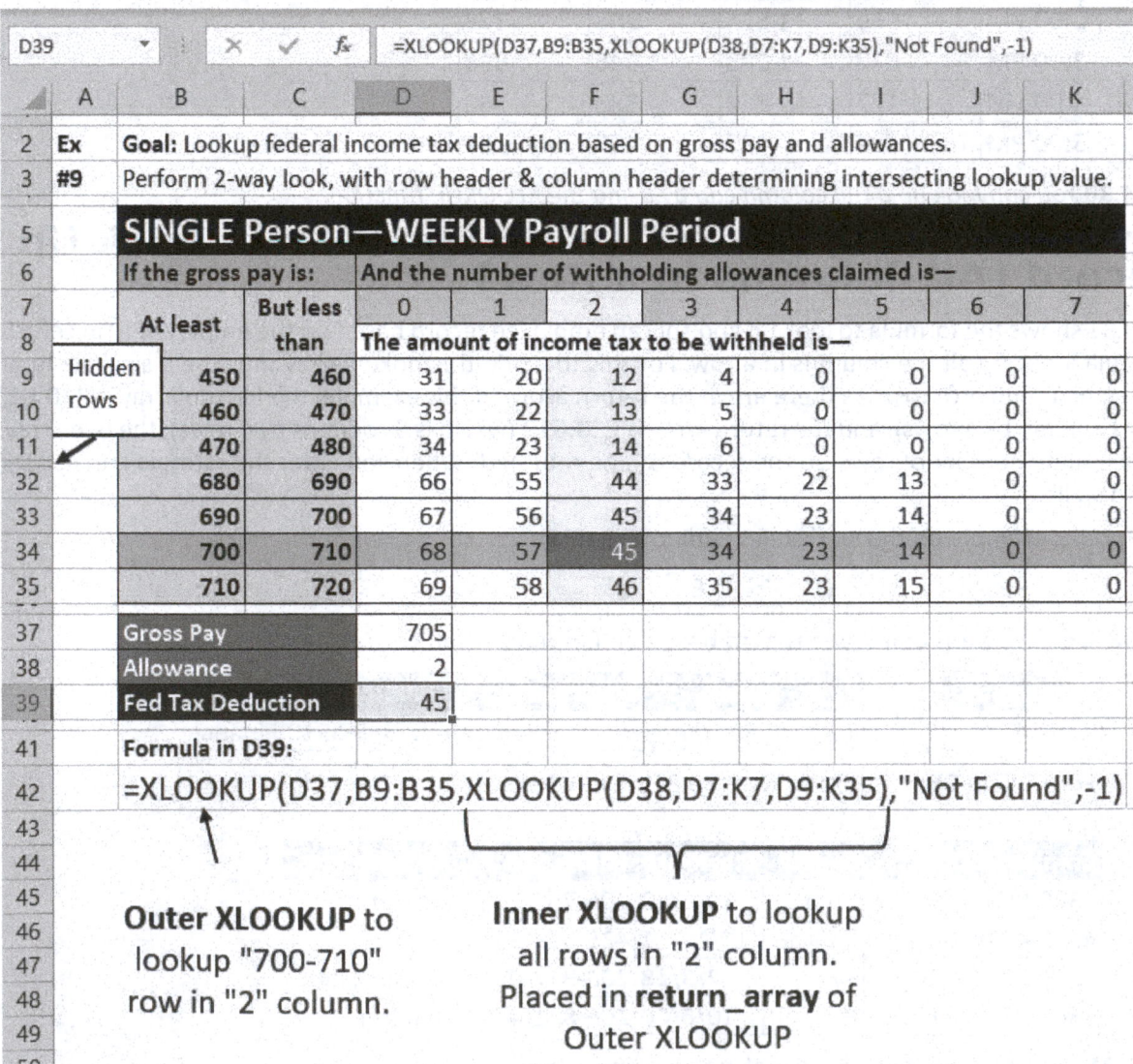

Figure 14.32 *A two-way lookup with two nested XLOOKUP functions to get federal tax withholding.*

Figure 14.33 shows a second example of performing a two-way lookup. In this example, a roofing company needs to look up the maximum roof square footage allowed for a given pipe size and rainfall per hour. In this example, both input cells for pipe size (cell C4) and hourly rainfall (cell C5) use data validation to ensure that the lookup values for both XLOOKUP functions are from the row and column header area. As a result, you can use two exact match nested XLOOKUP functions to perform this two-way lookup.

	A	B	C	D	E	F	G	H	I	J	K	L
2	Ex	**Goal:** Lookup "Roof Sq. Ft." based on "Pipe Size (in.)" and "Hourly Rainfall (in.).										
3	#10	Perform 2-way look, with row header & column header determining intersecting lookup value.										
5		Pipe Size (in.)	4									
6		Hourly Rainfall (in.)	3		**Formula in C7:**							
7		Total Sq. Ft. Covered Per Drain	6,130		=XLOOKUP(C6,C10:L10,XLOOKUP(C5,B12:B17,C12:L17))							
9								Hourly Rainfall (in.)				
10			1	1.5	2	2.5	3	4	5	6	7	8
11		Pipe Size (in.)					Total Sq. Ft. Covered Per Drain					
12		2	2,880	1,920	1,440	115	960	720	575	480	410	360
13		3	8,800	5,860	4,400	3,520	2,930	2,200	1,760	1,470	1,260	1,100
14		4	18,400	12,700	9,200	7,360	6,130	4,600	3,680	3,070	2,630	2,300
15		5	34,600	23,050	17,300	13,840	11,530	8,650	6,920	5,765	4,945	4,325
16		6	54,000	3,600	27,000	21,600	18,000	13,500	10,800	9,000	7,715	6,750
17		8	116,000	77,400	58,000	46,400	38,660	29,000	23,200	19,315	16,570	14,500

Figure 14.33 *A two-way lookup to get roof square footage using two nested XLOOKUP functions.*

When creating a two-way lookup formula using the XLOOKUP function, you can nest two XLOOKUP functions together to create the final formula. In our payroll example, the inner XLOOKUP function returns all the rows in a column, and that inner XLOOKUP is used in the second XLOOKUP's *return_array* argument. In our roofing square footage example, the inner XLOOKUP function returns all the columns in a row, and that inner XLOOKUP is used in the second XLOOKUP's *return_array* argument. However, the order in which you nest the XLOOKUP functions is arbitrary. You can either look up all the rows in a column with the inner XLOOKUP or look up all the columns in a row. The result will be the same in either case.

You can try these two examples on the worksheets named Ch14(32) and Ch14(33).

Example 11: Using the XLOOKUP Function with Two Lookup Values

Most lookup tables have a unique identifier column that allows a user to look up and find a single match. In some lookup situations, you do not have a single column that can serve as a unique list but instead must use two columns joined together to create a unique list that allows a user to find a single match to return the desired value.

If the goal is to look up the Quad product price for the store in Seattle, as shown in Figure 14.34, then rather than just use the single lookup value Quad for the *lookup_value* argument, you can join the store name and product name together to convert two separate lookup values into a single lookup value. Similarly, rather than use a single column in the *lookup_array* argument, you can join the Store and Product columns together to convert two separate columns into a single column for the *lookup_array* argument.

In versions of Excel prior to Excel 365, this is much harder to do because you have to use two different functions, and you need to use a special keystroke to enter the array formula. With Microsoft 365 Excel and XLOOKUP, this lookup formula and many others are much easier to create.

You can try this example on the worksheet named Ch14(34).

	A	B	C	D	E	F
2	Ex	**Goal:** Lookup price based on product & store.				
3	#11	Two value lookup to determine price.				
5		Store	Seattle			
6		Product	Quad			
7		Price	39.95			
9		**Formula in C7:**				
10		=XLOOKUP(C5&C6,B13:B21&C13:C21,D13:D21)				
12		Store	Product	Price		
13		Oakland	Quad	43.95		
14		Oakland	Aspen	27.95		
15		Oakland	Carlota	25.95		
16		Seattle	Quad	39.95		
17		Seattle	Aspen	24.95		
18		Seattle	Carlota	26.95		
19		Tacoma	Quad	30.95		
20		Tacoma	Aspen	27.95		
21		Tacoma	Carlota	25.95		

Figure 14.34 *You can join the two lookup values and the two columns for the lookup array right in the formula.*

Example 12: Using the XLOOKUP Function to Do a Lookup Left

When Excel people use the term *lookup left*, they may mean either of two things. Both meanings are illustrated in the example shown in Figure 14.35, where the goal of the lookup formula is to look up the flight range for a boomerang and return the boomerang product name:

- **First meaning:** You have a lookup value and need to compare it not against an entire column but against just the first few characters on the left side of each element in that column. In Figure 14.35, the goal is to match the number 45 against the first two characters in the Flight Range column. By manually performing this lookup, you can see that the closest match using an exact match or next smaller item lookup is the "40 - m flight" item in the fifth position.

- **Second meaning:** The return array (in this case, the Boomerang Product column) is to the left of the lookup array (in this case, the Flight Range column). For XLOOKUP, this is not a problem at all. But in versions of Excel prior to Excel 365, the most commonly used lookup function, VLOOKUP, is notorious for being unable to easily deal with this second type of "lookup left" scenario.

	A	B	C	D	E	F	G	H	I
2	Ex	**Goal:** Lookup boomerang product based on flight range.							
3	#12	**Issue #1:** Need to match lookup_value, 45, with the first two characters for each item in flight range column.							
4		**Issue #2:** With match in flight range column, lookup to the left and get boomerang product name.							
6		Flight Range		45					
7		Boomerang Product	Majestic Beaut						
9		**Formula in D7:**							
10		=XLOOKUP(D6,--LEFT(E13:E19,2),C13:C19,"Range must be 20 or bigger",-1)							
12		Boomerang Product	Price		Flight Range				
13		Quad	$43.95	20 - m flight					
14		Aspen	$27.95	25 - meters					
15		Yanaki	$30.95	30 - meters					
16		Sunshine	$35.95	35 - m flight					
17		Majestic Beaut	$40.95	40 - m flight					
18		Phenolic Sunshine	$75.00	50 - m flight					
19		Manu Distance	$100.00	70 - apex (m)					
21		**Steps for calculation of =XLOOKUP(D6,--LEFT(E13:E19,2),C13:C19,"20 or bigger",-1)**							
22		**1.** The LEFT function makes function argument array calculation on flight range column:							
23		=XLOOKUP(D6,--LEFT(**E13:E19**,2),C13:C19,"20 or bigger",-1)							
24		**2.** LEFT function delivers the two left characters from columns as text numbers:							
25		=XLOOKUP(D6,--**{"20";"25";"30";"35";"40";"50";"70"}**,C13:C19,"20 or bigger",-1)							
26		**3.** Any math operation performed on text numbers will convert them back to numbers:							
27		=XLOOKUP(D6,**--**{"20";"25";"30";"35";"40";"50";"70"},C13:C19,"20 or bigger",-1)							
28		**4.** The flight range, as numbers, now sits in lookup_array argument:							
29		=XLOOKUP(D6,**{20;25;30;35;40;50;70}**,C13:C19,"20 or bigger",-1)							
30		**5.** XLOOKUP looks up product name in a column that is to the left of the lookup_array:							
31		=XLOOKUP(D6,{20;25;30;35;40;50;70},**C19:C19**,"20 or bigger",-1)							
32		**6.** The "Exact match or next smaller lookup" returns "Majestic Beaut" boomerang.							

Figure 14.35 *A double "lookup left" can be accomplished with the LEFT and XLOOKUP functions.*

The XLOOKUP formula to accomplish the double "lookup left" task in this example is shown in cell D7 in Figure 14.35. The key to getting this formula to work is to place the Flight Range column, E13:E19, into the first argument of the LEFT function to make a function argument array operation to extract the first two characters from the left for each flight range description. You enter the number **2** into the second argument of LEFT to instruct LEFT to get only the first two characters from the left. You do not violate Excel's Golden Rule when you hard code the number 2 into the formula because all boomerangs have a flight range of two digits.

When the LEFT function delivers the two leftmost characters, it delivers them as text. If you were to try to match the number 45 against a column of text numbers, you would get no match. As you saw in Example 1 in Chapter 13, text numbers and numerals are not equivalent. However, if the goal is to create a match, you can convert the text numbers to numerals to help create a match. In an Excel worksheet (as well as in DAX formulas in Power Pivot and Power BI), any math operation that does not change the value of the number will convert text numbers to numerals.

In Example 2 in Chapter 13, you saw a list of all the different math operations that can be used, but in this example, you want to use a double negative in front of the resultant array of text numbers to convert it to an array of numbers that can be used to make a match. Figure 14.35 shows the complete formula and the calculation steps.

You can try this example on the worksheet named Ch14(35).

Example 13: Using the XLOOKUP Function to Perform a Vertical or Horizontal Grade Lookup

With a vertical lookup, you search for a match in a vertical column to pick out a certain row. With a horizonal lookup, you search for a match in a horizontal row to pick out a certain column. Whereas vertical lookups are very common, horizontal lookups are rare. Almost every example you will encounter will involve vertical lookup tables, such as tax tables, product price tables, customer tables, employee tables, and commission tables. This is why the old-school lookup function VLOOKUP (whose *V* refers to *vertical*) was so prevalent. In fact, in the old days, you had to use a different function to do horizonal lookups. You had to either use the HLOOKUP function or the combined functions INDEX and MATCH. Today you can instead use the superhero lookup function XLOOKUP. It can do both vertical and horizontal lookups, as shown in Figure 14.36. In this example, the goal is to perform an exact match or next smaller item lookup to look up a student's letter grade based on the percentage grade earned in the class.

	A	B	C	D	E	F	G	H	I	J
2	Ex	**Goal:** XLOOKUP can use vertical or horizontal lookup tables.								
3	#13									
4		Student:	Gigi		Student:	Chantel				
5		% Grade:	83.5%		% Grade:	0.94				
6		Letter Grade:	B		Letter Grade:	A				
8		**Formula in C6:**				**Formula in F6:**				
9		=XLOOKUP(C5,B14:B18,C14:C18,,-1)				=XLOOKUP(F5,F13:J13,F14:J14,,-1)				
10										
11		**Vertical Lookup Table:**				**Horizontal Lookup Table:**				
13		% Grade	Letter Grade			% Grade	90.0%	80.0%	70.0%	60.0%	50.0%
14		90.0%	A			Letter Grade	A	B	C	D	F
15		80.0%	B								
16		70.0%	C								
17		60.0%	D								
18		50.0%	F								

Figure 14.36 *XLOOKUP can perform vertical and horizontal lookups.*

With the VLOOKUP function, in situations with grade lookup tables (as shown in Figure 14.36), the first column always has to be sorted ascending to get the approximate match lookup to work correctly. This is inconvenient because the grade lookup table has to be sorted descending for the display in the syllabus. With the XLOOKUP function and the new-and-improved exact match or next smaller item lookup, the sort of the first column does not matter. The column can be sorted in any order, including descending. This means you can use the sorted descending grade lookup table for both of your formulas and for the final display in the syllabus.

You can try this example on the worksheet named Ch14(36).

Example 14: Using the XLOOKUP Function with a Lookup Cell Reference

Figure 14.37 illustrates a situation where the goal is to let the user select a state, a start month, and an end month and then add all the COVID-19 cases for that period. For example, if the user selects the state NV for the months May to Aug, the formula will need to add the numbers 3,595, 9,863, 2,9632, and 2,1140 to get the total number of cases: 64,230. The key to this type of lookup is to first reduce the table of case numbers from all the months, Mar to Sep, to just the months May to Aug; then, within that smaller lookup table, you look up the row of numbers for just the state NV. Looking at Figure 14.37 and manually picking out the table of numbers for May to Sep, you would pick out the range E6:H10. Notice that the first cell reference in that range is E6, and the last one is H10. The colon operator instructs Excel to get the two bookend cell references E6 and H10 and then all the cells between them, with all of their numbers.

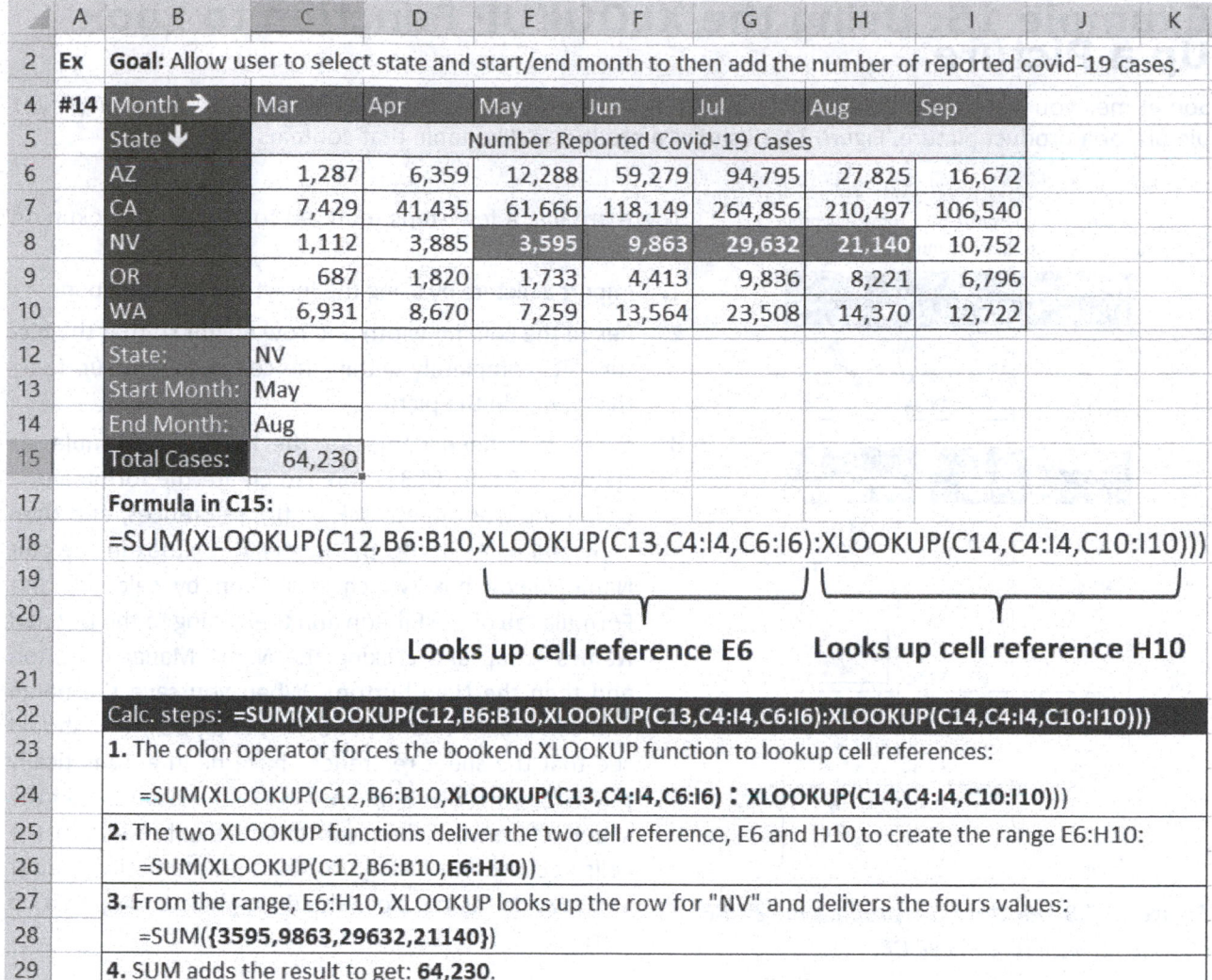

	A	B	C	D	E	F	G	H	I	J	K
2	Ex	**Goal:** Allow user to select state and start/end month to then add the number of reported covid-19 cases.									
4	#14	Month →	Mar	Apr	May	Jun	Jul	Aug	Sep		
5		State ↓			Number Reported Covid-19 Cases						
6		AZ	1,287	6,359	12,288	59,279	94,795	27,825	16,672		
7		CA	7,429	41,435	61,666	118,149	264,856	210,497	106,540		
8		NV	1,112	3,885	3,595	9,863	29,632	21,140	10,752		
9		OR	687	1,820	1,733	4,413	9,836	8,221	6,796		
10		WA	6,931	8,670	7,259	13,564	23,508	14,370	12,722		
12		State:	NV								
13		Start Month:	May								
14		End Month:	Aug								
15		Total Cases:	64,230								

17 **Formula in C15:**

18 =SUM(XLOOKUP(C12,B6:B10,XLOOKUP(C13,C4:I4,C6:I6):XLOOKUP(C14,C4:I4,C10:I10)))

Looks up cell reference E6   **Looks up cell reference H10**

22 **Calc. steps: =SUM(XLOOKUP(C12,B6:B10,XLOOKUP(C13,C4:I4,C6:I6):XLOOKUP(C14,C4:I4,C10:I10)))**

23 **1.** The colon operator forces the bookend XLOOKUP function to lookup cell references:

24   =SUM(XLOOKUP(C12,B6:B10,**XLOOKUP(C13,C4:I4,C6:I6) : XLOOKUP(C14,C4:I4,C10:I10)**))

25 **2.** The two XLOOKUP functions deliver the two cell reference, E6 and H10 to create the range E6:H10:

26   =SUM(XLOOKUP(C12,B6:B10,**E6:H10**))

27 **3.** From the range, E6:H10, XLOOKUP looks up the row for "NV" and delivers the fours values:

28   =SUM(**{3595,9863,29632,21140}**)

29 **4.** SUM adds the result to get: **64,230**.

Figure 14.37 *XLOOKUP can look up cell references when used with the colon operator.*

The good news is that you do not have to do this manually. You can simply use the XLOOKUP function to look up the start cell reference and end cell reference in the range E6:H10. When you use the formula element XLOOKUP(C13,C4:I4,C6:I6):XLOOKUP(C14,C4:I4,C10:I10), the colon operator between the two XLOOKUP functions forces the XLOOKUP functions to look up cell references rather than the values from those cells. The formula element delivers the range E6:H10. Then you use that delivered range in the *return_array* argument for the outermost XLOOKUP function, which then looks up the correct row for NV, with the values 3,595, 9,863, 2,9632, and 2,1140. The SUM function then adds those numbers to get the total number of reported COVID-19 cases in NV for the months May to Aug.

You can try this example on the worksheet named Ch14(37).

Example 15: Using the XLOOKUP Function to Look Up a Picture

Sometimes you want to be able to look up pictures. For example, you might want to look up an employee picture or a product picture. Figure 14.38 shows a product lookup table that contains pictures.

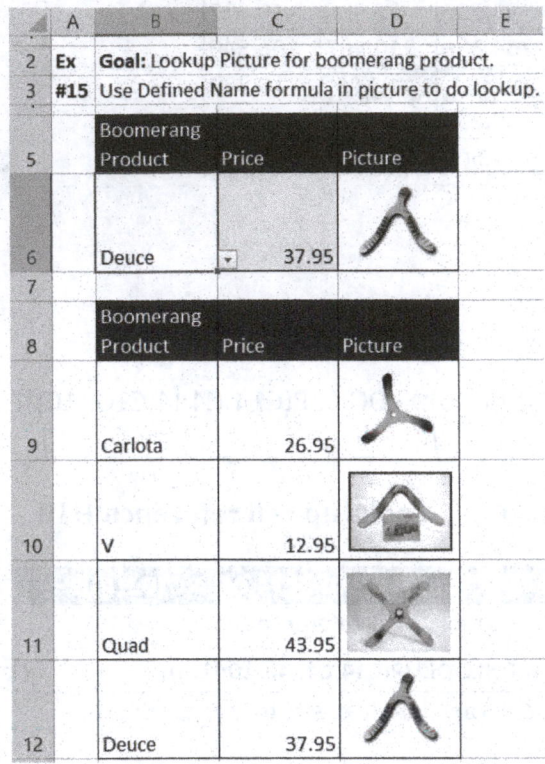

Figure 14.38 *Selecting the product in cell B6 changes the picture in cell D6.*

There are just a few steps required to perform a lookup on a picture:

1. Import a picture by using the Insert tab of the Ribbon.

2. Resize the column width and row height so that the picture sits completely within the cell in the lookup table that will hold the picture.

3. Create a defined name for the XLOOKUP formula, as shown in Figure 14.39. You can create the formula in a cell in the worksheet, lock all the references, and then copy and paste it into the Refers To textbox in the Edit Name dialog box (which you open by selecting the Formula tab of the Ribbon and then going to the Defined Names group and clicking the Name Manager button and then the New button). When you save the name and come back and look at the dialog box, you should see that the sheet references have been automatically put in for you (which means you do not have to add the sheet references when you create the formula in the cells because the dialog box does it automatically after you save the name, close the dialog box, and open it up later).

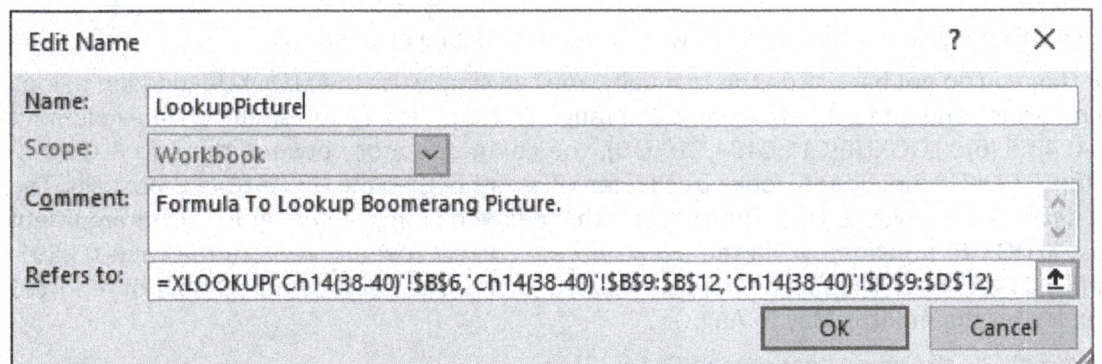

Figure 14.39 *Create a defined name to define the XLOOKUP formula.*

4. Paste one of the pictures into cell D6. Then, with that picture selected, click in the formula bar and create the formula that uses the defined name, as shown in Figure 14.40.

You can try this example on the worksheet named Ch14(38-40).

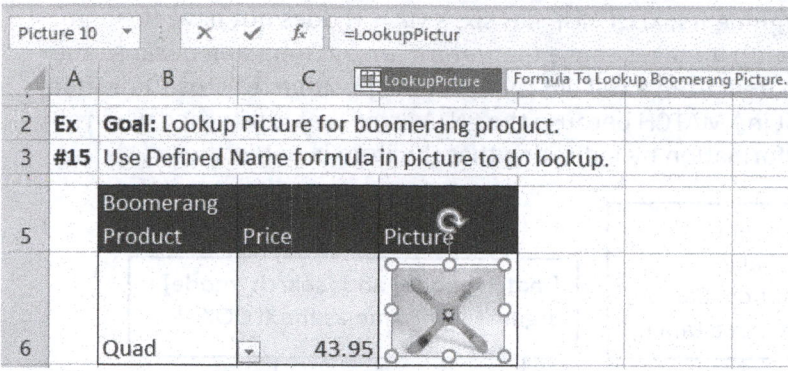

Figure 14.40 *Using the formula bar, create a formula with a defined name in the picture itself.*

Example 16: Using the XMATCH Function to Deliver the Relative Position of an Item in a List

It is often the case that you need to determine the relative position of an item in a list. For example, you might want to be able to determine the position of Sioux in the list of employee names Ty, Gigi, Sioux, Chantel. In this case, the relative position of Sioux in the list is 3. Or you might need to know the relative position of the field name E-mail in the list of field names ID, First, Last, Hire Date, E-mail, Phone. In this case, the relative position of E-mail in the list is 5.

In an Excel worksheet, when you need to look up the relative position of an item in a one-way list (for example, a column or a row but not a table), you can use the XMATCH function to do this. The XMATCH function arguments, as shown in the following syntax, are like the XLOOKUP function arguments (see Figure 14.41):

```
XMATCH(lookup_value, lookup_array, [match_mode], [search_mode])
```

The arguments of the XMATCH function are as follows:

- **lookup_value**: This argument specifies the item to look up.
- **lookup_array**: This argument is used to search for the lookup value to yield the relative position. It can be a column or a row but not a table.
- **[match_mode]**: As with XLOOKUP, this argument can take several different values:
  - **0 - Exact match:** This is the default value. If you do not use the *match_mode* argument, XMATCH performs an exact match lookup by default. This is the most common type of lookup.
  - **-1 - Exact match or next smaller item:** This is the second-most-common type of lookup. Values listed in a lookup array are the lower limit for the categories created. If the lookup value is smaller than the smallest value in the lookup array range, an #N/A is returned.
  - **1 - Exact match or next larger item:** This sort of lookup is not common. Values listed in the lookup array are the upper limit for the categories created. If the lookup value is bigger than the biggest value in the lookup array range, an #N/A is returned.
  - **2 – Wildcard character match:** Two wildcards can be used: * for zero or more characters or ? for a single character. For example, Quad* finds anything that begins with Quad, and *? finds any text (at least one character).
- **[search_mode]**: As with XLOOKUP, this argument can take several different values:
  - **1 - Search first-to-last:** This is the default value. If you do not use the *search_mode* argument, XMATCH searches first to last by default. When there are duplicates, it uses the first match.
  - **-1 - Search last-to-first:** When there are duplicates, it uses the last match.
  - **2 - Binary search (sorted ascending order):** For this search mode, which is like the old VLOOKUP and MATCH approximate match lookup, the *lookup_array* argument must be sorted in ascending order.
  - **-2 - Binary search (sorted descending order):** For this search mode, which is like the old MATCH -1 approximate match lookup, the *lookup_array* argument must be sorted in descending order.

Note: Whereas XMATCH has four arguments, XLOOKUP has six. XMATCH does not have the arguments *return_array* and *[if_not_found]*. It makes sense that *return_array* is missing because the goal of XMATCH is not to retrieve an item from a cell but to report the position. Microsoft did not include the *[if_not_found]* argument in XMATCH because the #N/A error that is returned when an item is not found provides useful information by indicating that the item is not in the list.

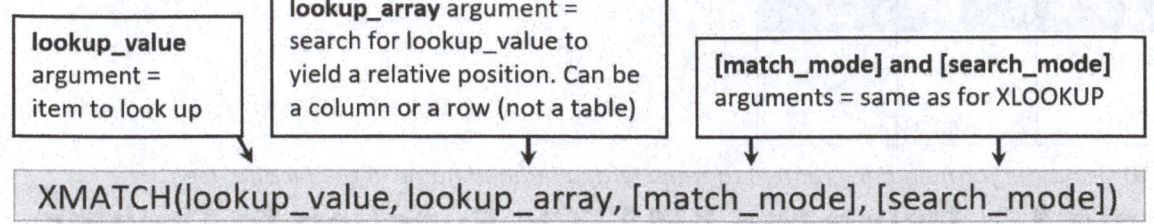

Figure 14.41 *Arguments for the XMATCH lookup function.*

Back in Example 29 in Chapter 13, you saw how to use the XMATCH and ISNA functions together to check whether an item is not in a list. In that example, you also saw that you can use the XMATCH and ISNUMBER functions to check whether an item is in a list. Although the XMATCH function is a lookup function, it can deliver only one of two values: a number (the relative position) or an #N/A error. If XMATCH returns a number, it means the item is in the list, and if it returns an error, it means the item is not in the list.

Note: Just as XLOOKUP replaces most of what the old-school VLOOKUP function does, XMATCH replaces most of what the old-school MATCH function does.

There are four typical uses for the XMATCH function:

- Determine the relative position of an item in a list. For example, you might want to know the position of a specific name in an ordered list of names. Figure 14.42 shows an example of this. You can try this example on the worksheet Ch14(42).

- Compare two lists to determine if an item is in a list or is not in a list (refer to Example 29 in Chapter 13).

- Use XMATCH in the INDEX function, where the INDEX function is a lookup function that requires relative positions for a row index or a column index (see Example 19, later in this chapter).

- Create a logical formula to compare two lists and apply conditional formatting (see Example 17).

C5		▼	:	×	✓	*fx*	=XMATCH(C4,B8:B11)	

◢	A	B	C	D	E
2	Ex	**Goal:** Find the relative position of "Sioux" in the signup list.			
3	#16				
4		Contestant	Sioux		**Formula in C5:**
5		Relative Position?	3		=XMATCH(C4,B8:B11)
6					
7		**Signups**			
8		Ty			
9		Gigi			
10		Sioux			
11		Chantel			

Figure 14.42 *XMATCH is a lookup function that reports the relative position of an item in a list.*

Example 17: Using the XMATCH Function to Add Conditional Formatting When Comparing Two Lists

Say that you want to conditionally format items in one list that are also in a second list. Figure 14.43 shows a list of names for a Sunday event and a list of names for a Saturday event. The goal is to conditionally format names in the Sunday list that are also in the Saturday list. This means you must answer the question "Are any of the names in the Sunday list also in the Saturday list?"

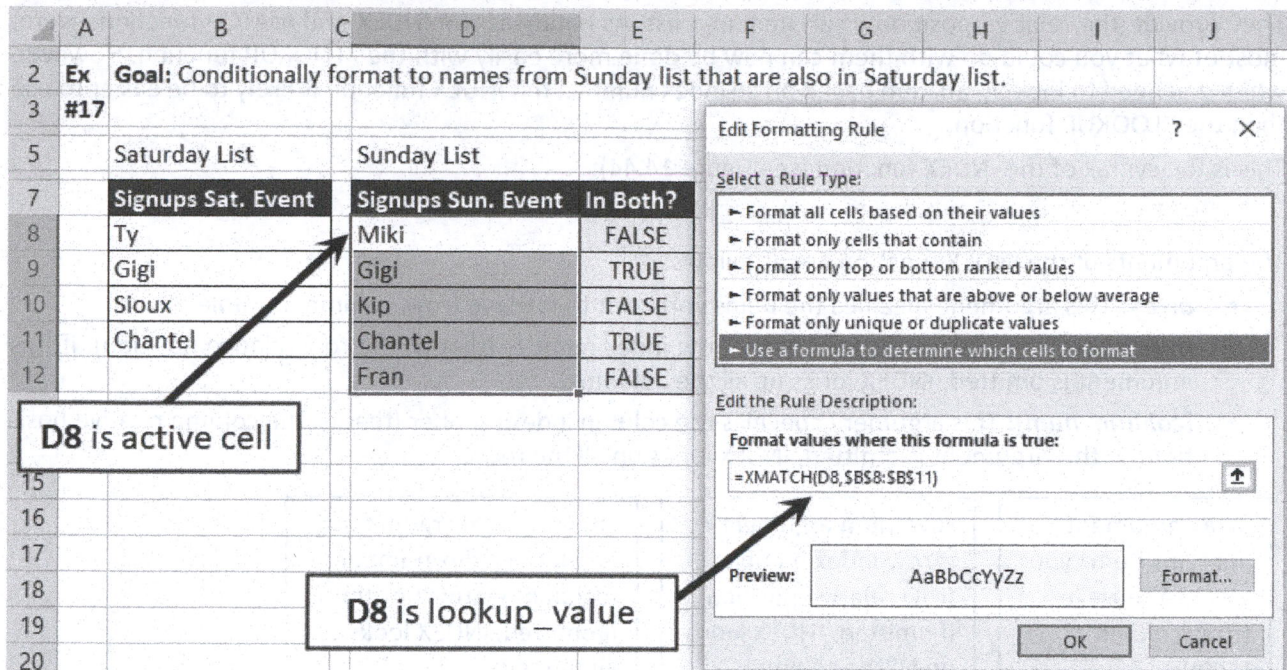

Figure 14.43 *The Edit Formatting Rule dialog box interprets any nonzero number as TRUE and zero and errors as FALSE.*

Any time you compare two lists, you start with XMATCH. If XMATCH finds a match, it returns a number; otherwise, it returns an #N/A error. In Example 29 in Chapter 13, when you wanted a TRUE value when an item was in two lists, you put XMATCH into the ISNUMBER function. However, when you use the Edit Formatting Rule dialog box to create a formula, the Conditional Formatting feature interprets any nonzero number as TRUE and zero or an error value as FALSE. This means that the formula to conditionally format the items in both lists is the XMATCH function without the ISNUMBER function.

You can try this example on the worksheet named Ch14(43) by following these steps:

1. As shown in Figure 14.43, select the range D8:D12, with D8 as the active cell.

2. Go to the Home tab of the Ribbon, and in the Styles group, click the Conditional Formatting drop-down arrow and then click New Rule.

3. Click Use a Formula to Determine Which Cells to Format and then click in the Format Values Where This Formula Is True textbox and create the formula =XMATCH(D8,$B$8:$B$11). Figure 14.43 shows this formula.

4. Click the Format button and then add formatting.

5. Click OK in the Format Cells dialog box. Click OK in the New Rule (or Edit Formatting Rule) dialog box.

The INDEX Function

As mentioned at the beginning of this chapter, for decades, if you wanted to get a business-related job, saying things like "Can do VLOOKUP in my sleep" would get you in the door for an interview, and inevitably during the interview, an employer would ask you about the VLOOKUP function. But an employer that *really* wanted to see if you were great with Excel worksheet formulas would also ask you about the INDEX function. Although the VLOOKUP function was the most commonly used lookup function, it could not do all types of lookups (such as lookup lefts or exact match or next bigger item lookups). However, by using INDEX with the old-school MATCH function, you could do an exotic lookup left, an exact match or next bigger item lookup, and almost any other type of lookup—including everything that VLOOKUP could do.

The INDEX function also has the great distinction of having been invented before the VLOOKUP function. It was one of the original functions in Microsoft's precursor to Excel, the Multiplan Spreadsheet program, in the early 1980s. What makes INDEX unique as a lookup function is that it can perform a lookup based on a row index number and a column index number. This means that you can directly look up things by their positions. Of course, this is why the old MATCH and the new XMATCH functions work perfectly in tandem with INDEX:

They provide the relative position of an item in a list. As handy as the INDEX and MATCH functions were, most of what you could do with them can now be done more easily with the XLOOKUP function. However, when you need to look up an item based on an index number, the INDEX function is likely to be easier to use than the XLOOKUP function.

This is the syntax of the INDEX function (see Figure 14.44):

```
INDEX(array, row_num, [column_num])
```

The arguments of the INDEX function are as follows:

- **array**: This argument specifies the items you want to retrieve (row, column, or table).
- **row_num**: This argument specifies the row index number (that is, the row relative position). If this argument is omitted, INDEX looks up all the columns.
- **[column_num]**: This argument specifies the column index number (that is, the column relative position). If this argument is omitted, INDEX looks up all the rows.

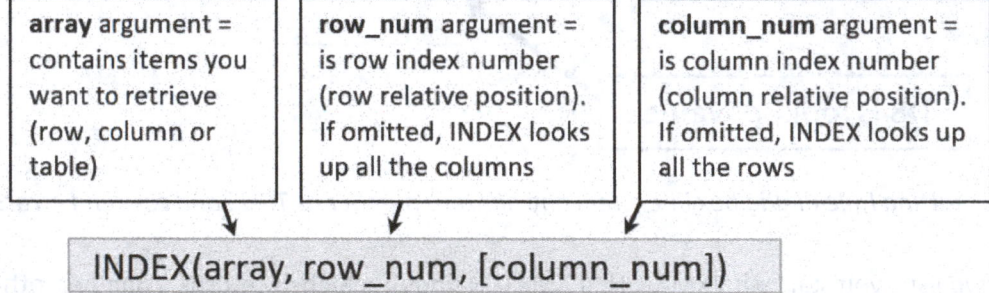

Figure 14.44 *Arguments for the INDEX lookup function.*

As you will see in the following examples, you can use the INDEX function to randomly look up a name and also to select and rearrange columns from a proper dataset.

Example 18: Looking Up Random Data with the INDEX and RANDBETWEEN Functions

As shown in Figure 14.45, the goal of this example is to randomly draw an employee name from a list of names. The column of employee names, in the range B6:B15, spans 10 rows and is placed in the first argument of the INDEX function. Because the goal is to randomly pick a name from rows 1 to 10, the second argument of the INDEX function uses the RANDBETWEEN function, which can randomly choose between a bottom number and a top number. When the bottom number 1 and the top number 10 are placed inside the RANDBETWEEN function, the function will randomly generate a number between 1 and 10 that INDEX can use to pick an employee name from the list of 10 names.

	A	B	C	D	E	F
2	Ex	Goal: Select random employee name (so they can win a prize).				
3	#18					
5		Office Employees		Random Draw		
6		Constance Bryant		Lee Hale		
7		Santiago Lloyd				
8		Daryl West		Formula in D6:		
9		Elsie Manning		=INDEX(B6:B15,RANDBETWEEN(1,10))		
10		Richard Woods				
11		Clay Cruz		* F9 Key re- calculates formulas.		
12		Irma Hubbard				
13		Kelly Christensen				
14		Lee Hale				
15		Maxine Cook				

Figure 14.45 *Using INDEX and RANDBETWEEN to randomly choose a name.*

After you enter the formula into cell D6, you can press the F9 key to recalculate the formula. Each time you press F9, the formula randomly selects a new name. Technically, the F9 key recalculates all formulas in the workbook. You can use the keyboard shortcut Shift+F9 if you want to recalculate just the worksheet rather than the whole workbook.

You can try this example on the worksheet named Ch14(45).

Example 19: Performing a Lookup and Rearranging Columns with the INDEX, SEQUENCE, ROWS, and XMATCH Functions

Sometimes a table has many columns, and you need to extract a few of the columns off to the side of the table. For example, the Excel Table named pt in Figure 14.46 has many columns, and the goal is to extract and spill just the Product, Product ID, and Price columns as a new table. You can use the INDEX function to do all this. The trick is that you need to give the function an array of row numbers (relative positions) that represent all the rows in the table and an array of just the desired column numbers (relative positions). The formula might look like this:

```
=INDEX(pt,{1;2;3;4;5},{2,1,7})
```

In this case, the second argument of INDEX contains an array constant of row numbers separated by semicolons, and the third argument contains an array constant of column numbers separated by commas.

⊿	A	B	C	D	E	F	G	H	I
2	Ex #19	**Goal:** Extract Product, ProductID and Price columns from the Excel Table with the name **pt**.							
4		ProductID ⯆	Product ⯆	Supplier ⯆	State ⯆	Category ⯆	Cost ⯆	Price ⯆	
5		A25C-4884	Aspen	Col. Boom	CO	Beginner	14.55	26.95	
6		C20G-4398	Carlota	Gel Boom	CA	Freestyle	11.18	27.95	
7		Q22G-9634	Quad	Gel Boom	CA	Freestyle	19.34	43.95	
8		Y30C-4942	Yanaki	Col. Boom	CO	Intermediate	12.88	29.95	
10		**Extract & rearrange columns so results spills from cell B13:**							
12		Product	ProductID	Price					
13		Aspen	A25C-4884	26.95					
14		Carlota	C20G-4398	27.95					
15		Quad	Q22G-9634	43.95					
16		Yanaki	Y30C-4942	29.95					
18		**Formula in B13:**							
19		=INDEX(pt,SEQUENCE(ROWS(pt)),XMATCH(B12:D12,pt[#Headers]))							
21		Steps for calculation of =INDEX(pt,SEQUENCE(ROWS(pt)),XMATCH(B12:D12,pt[#Headers]))							
22		**1.** ROWS counts how many rows are in **pt** Excel Table.							
23		=INDEX(pt,SEQUENCE(**ROWS(pt)**),XMATCH(B12:D12,pt[#Headers]))							
24		=INDEX(pt,SEQUENCE(**5**),XMATCH(B12:D12,pt[#Headers]))							
25		**2.** SEQUENCE(5) delivers array of row positions, 1 to 5 separated by semi-colons:							
26		=INDEX(pt,**{1;2;3;4;5}**,XMATCH(B12:D12,pt[#Headers]))							
27		**3.** B12:D12 spans columns, so XMATCH delivers an array of column positions separated by commas:							
28		=INDEX(pt,{1;2;3;4;5},**XMATCH(B12:D12,pt[#Headers])**)							
29		=INDEX(pt,{1;2;3;4;5},**{2,1,7}**)							
30		**4.** With the correct array syntax, INDEX lookups the rows 1 to 5 for each of the columns 2, 1 and 7:							
31		=INDEX(pt,**{1;2;3;4;5},{2,1,7}**)							
32		**5.** INDEX delivers all the rows for each of the columns Product, ProductID, Price.							

Figure 14.46 *The spilled array formula =INDEX(B5:H9,{1;2;3;4;5},{2,1,7}) selects all rows in columns 2, 1, and 7.*

As you saw for the first time in Figure 12.11 in Chapter 12, in an array constant, you use semicolons with rows and commas with columns. The INDEX formula shown above does not work unless the row positions are separated by semicolons and the column positions are separated by commas. The formula =INDEX(pt,{1;2;3;4;5},{2,1,7}) asks the full product table to retrieve five rows in the second column, five rows in the first column, and five rows in the seventh column and then spill the new table out from cell B13.

Although viewing the array constants from the outset here helps you understand how the formula works, if you want everything to be dynamic, you should not hard code the array constants into the formula. Instead, you need to use the formula element SEQUENCE(ROWS(pt)) to generate the rows {1;2;3;4;5} and XMATCH(B13:D13,pt[#Headers]) to generate the columns {2,1,7}.

For the SEQUENCE(ROWS(pt)) formula element, the ROWS function delivers the number of rows from the table, 5, to the first argument, *rows*, in SEQUENCE, to produce the correct array syntax with semicolons to get the relative position of the rows as {1;2;3;4;5}.

For the XMATCH(B13:D13,pt[#Headers]) formula element, XMATCH makes a function argument array operation with the range B13:D13 to look up the desired field names in the header range from the Excel Table. Because the lookup value, B13:D13, spans columns, XMATCH creates the correct array syntax with commas to get the relative position of the columns as {2,1,7}.

Figure 14.46 lists all the calculation steps for this "lookup and rearrange columns" formula.

Figure 14.47 shows an alternative for this "lookup and rearrange columns" formula that uses the XLOOKUP function. This XLOOKUP formula is less complicated to create, but it cannot spill the full table. Instead, this formula must be entered into cell B37 and then manually copied through the range B37:D37.

	A	B	C	D	E	F	G	H	I	J
34		**Alternative:**								
36	Ex	Product	ProductID	Price		Formula in B37:				
37	#19	Aspen	A25C-4884	26.95		=XLOOKUP(B36,$B$4:$H$4,$B$5:$H$8)				
38		Carlota	C20G-4398	27.95		Spills down to rows. Copied across columns to range B37:D37				
39		Quad	Q22G-9634	43.95						
40		Yanaki	Y30C-4942	29.95						

Figure 14.47 *This alternative formula to select all rows in columns 2, 1, and 7 requires a manual copy action.*

You can try these examples on the worksheet named Ch14(46-47).

The FILTER Array Function

So far in this book, you have seen multiple examples of how to use the FILTER array function to filter datasets and deliver dynamic spilled arrays of results. You can primarily think of the FILTER function as a means to filter data based on conditions and criteria. However, you can also think of this function as a lookup function because the FILTER function solves one of the most perplexing lookup problems in Excel of all time: how to look up an item and return multiple records when lookup functions like VLOOKUP and XLOOKUP ignore all duplicate values except the first one. There has always been a way to do this, but the solution (as shown in Figures 1.17 and 14.46) is complex to create and understand. In fact, in my second book, *Ctrl+Shift+Enter: Mastering Excel Array Formulas*, I spent several chapters explaining its complexities. Now that FILTER has hit the scene, all those complexities have been replaced with the simplicity and beauty of FILTER. The following examples show how to use the FILTER function to look up and return multiple records when there are duplicate matches for the lookup value.

Example 20: Using the FILTER Function with One Lookup Value to Return Multiple Records

In Figure 14.48, the goal is to look up the grade records for a particular student. The first argument of the FILTER function contains all the student records, and the second argument contains a logical test array operation that asks the question "Which student names in the Student column are equal to the student name in cell G6?" When you change the name in cell G6, the dynamic spilled array instantly updates.

You can try this example on the worksheet named Ch14(48).

	A	B	C	D	E	F	G	H	I	J	K	L	M
2	Ex	Goal: Extract student class records.											
3	#20	Famous Excel task: One lookup value, return multiple items/records.											
5		Student	Class	Department	Grade		Student						
6		Sioux Chin	Acc 121	Accounting	1.7		Gigi Dmitri						
7		Chantel Mimms	Busn 216	Business	3.1								
8		Dylan Franks	Busn 101	Business	2.1		Class	Department	Grade		Formula in G9:		
9		Sioux Chin	Acc 201	Accounting	4		Busn 210	Business	2.6		=FILTER(C6:E17,B6:B17=G6)		
10		Chantel Mimms	Busn 218	Business	3.8		Econ 202	Economics	2				
11		Dylan Franks	Eng 201	English	2								
12		Sioux Chin	Econ 201	Economics	2.6								
13		Chantel Mimms	Busn 210	Business	3.3								
14		Dylan Franks	Busn 216	Business	1.9		Class	Department	Grade				
15		Gigi Dmitri	Busn 210	Business	2.6		Busn 210	Business	2.6				
16		Chantel Mimms	Eng 201	English	3.1		Econ 202	Economics	2				
17		Gigi Dmitri	Econ 202	Economics	2								
19							Formula 'before we had FILTER' in G15:						
20							=IF(ROWS(G$15:G15)>COUNTIFS($B$6:$B$17,$G$6),"",						
21							INDEX(C$6:C$17,AGGREGATE(15,6,(ROW($B$6:$B$17)-						
22 23							ROW($B$6)+1)/($B$6:$B$17=$G$6),ROWS(G$15:G15))))						

Figure 14.48 *The classic "one lookup value, return multiple records" is made easy with the FILTER lookup function!*

Example 21: Using the FILTER Function with Two Lookup Values to Return Multiple Records

In Figure 14.49, the goal is to look up the grade records for a particular student with classes from a particular department. In this example, there are two lookup values: one for the student name and one for the department. The FILTER formula here differs from the one in the previous example in that you must join the two lookup values and two lookup arrays when you make your logical test array operation.

You can try this example on the worksheet named Ch14(49).

	A	B	C	D	E	F	G	H	I	J	K
2	Ex	Goal: Extract student class records.									
3	#21	Famous Excel task: One lookup value, return multiple items/records.									
5		Student	Class	Department	Grade		Student	Department			
6		Sioux Chin	Acc 121	Accounting	1.7		Sioux Chin	Accounting			
7		Chantel Mimms	Busn 216	Business	3.1						
8		Dylan Franks	Busn 101	Business	2.1		Formula in G12:				
9		Sioux Chin	Acc 201	Accounting	4		=FILTER(C6:E17,B6:B17&D6:D17=G6&H6)				
10		Chantel Mimms	Busn 218	Business	3.8						
11		Dylan Franks	Eng 201	English	2		Class	Department	Grade		
12		Sioux Chin	Econ 201	Economics	2.6		Acc 121	Accounting	1.7		
13		Chantel Mimms	Busn 210	Business	3.3		Acc 201	Accounting	4		

Figure 14.49 *Using two lookup values is easy: Just join the two lookup values and two lookup arrays.*

LOOKUP: The Original Lookup Function for Spreadsheets

Although VLOOKUP is the most-used lookup function in Excel history, this book does not even have a section about how to use it because the XLOOKUP function can more efficiently accomplish everything that you used to do with the VLOOKUP function. This section covers the LOOKUP function, which is a much less commonly used lookup function than VLOOKUP but that can do a few things that XLOOKUP cannot do.

The first thing to note about the LOOKUP function is that it has two options—in essence giving you two different functions in one function (see Figure 14.50):

- **Option 1:** LOOKUP(lookup_value, lookup_vector, [result_vector])
- **Option 2:** LOOKUP(*lookup_value*, *array*)

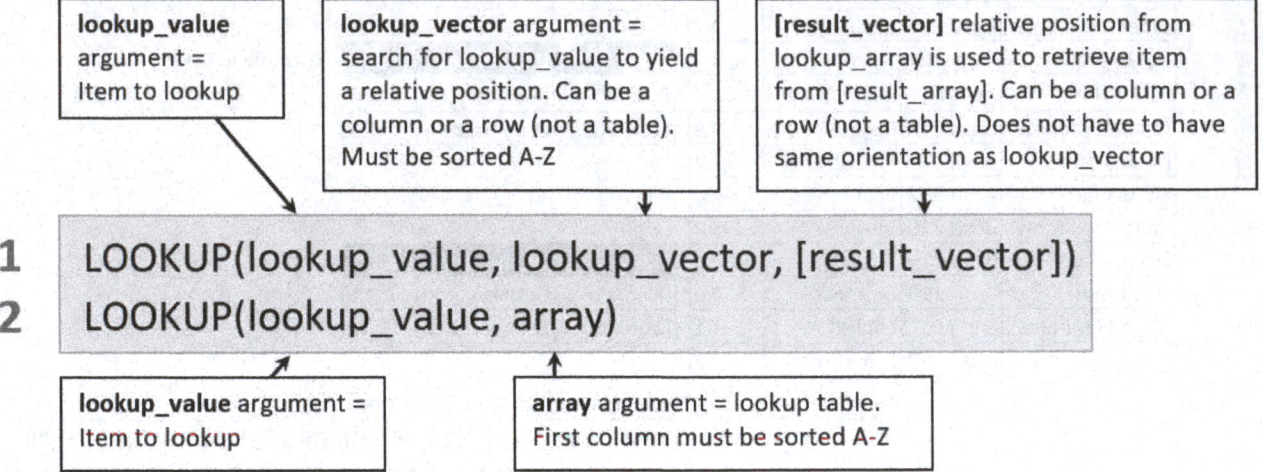

Figure 14.50 *The LOOKUP function is two functions in one.*

The second thing to note about the LOOKUP function is that it can *only* do an approximate match lookup, which is like an exact match or next smaller item lookup, but the column that you use to make a match *must* be sorted smallest to largest (A–Z). Although there are ways to force the LOOKUP function to do an exact match lookup, they are overly complicated. If you need to do an exact match lookup, you should instead use the XLOOKUP function.

The second argument of LOOKUP, *lookup_vector* or *array*, is the trigger for the function to determine whether to run Option 1 or Option 2. If you put a one-way array (column or row, but not table) into the second argument, Option 1 is executed; if you put a table (rows and columns) into the second argument, Option 2 is executed.

Consider the following information about Option 1, LOOKUP(*lookup_value*, *lookup_vector*, [*result_vector*]):

- This option searches for the lookup value in the ascending-sorted lookup vector to find a match and yield a relative position that it uses to then retrieve the corresponding element in the argument [*result_vector*].
- The lookup vector must be sorted ascending, A–Z.
- The *lookup_vector* and [*return_vector*] argument values must be one-way arrays. These one-way arrays do not have to have the same orientation or the same number of elements. This is different from how the second and third arguments in XLOOKUP work.
- The advantage that this option has over the XLOOKUP function is that the *lookup_vector* and [*return_vector*] argument values can be oriented differently (both horizontal, both vertical, or one vertical and one horizontal). The XLOOKUP *lookup_array* and *return_array* arguments cannot do this.

Consider the following information about Option 2, LOOKUP(*lookup_value*, *array*):

- This option allows the user to search for the lookup value in a lookup table rather than look up a lookup vector.
- The *array* argument allows you to either use a vertical lookup table or a horizontal lookup table.
- If the number of rows in the lookup table is greater than or equal to the number of columns, LOOKUP does a vertical lookup. With a vertical lookup, the first column of the table must be sorted ascending, A–Z. The LOOKUP function tries to find a match and yields a relative position that it then uses to retrieve the corresponding element from the last column in the vertical lookup table.

- If the number of columns in the lookup table is greater than the number of rows, LOOKUP does a horizontal lookup. With a horizontal lookup, the first row of the table must be sorted ascending, A–Z. The LOOKUP function tries to find a match and yields a relative position that it then uses to retrieve the corresponding element from the last row in the horizontal lookup table.

- The advantage that this option has over the XLOOKUP function is that if you have a table that is sorted correctly (like most tax tables, commission tables, and other tables), you only have to enter two arguments when using the LOOKUP function rather than enter five with the XLOOKUP function.

There are two situations in which it can be more efficient to use the LOOKUP function than the XLOOKUP function, as illustrated in Examples 22 and 23.

Example 22: Using the LOOKUP Function to Do Half Vertical/Half Horizontal Lookups

If you want to have the lookup vector oriented vertically and the results array oriented horizontally, you can use LOOKUP function Option 1. The XLOOKUP function cannot accomplish this type of lookup. Figure 14.51 shows an example of this.

You can try this example on the worksheet named Ch14(51).

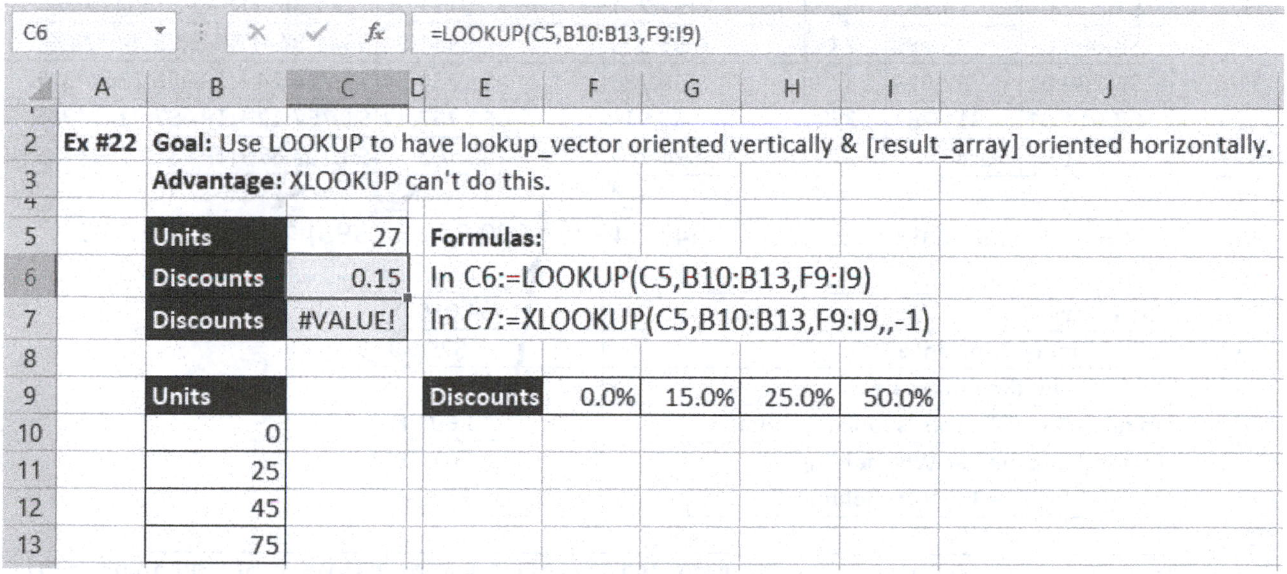

C6			f_x	=LOOKUP(C5,B10:B13,F9:I9)					
	A	B	C	D E	F	G	H	I	J
2	Ex #22	**Goal:** Use LOOKUP to have lookup_vector oriented vertically & [result_array] oriented horizontally.							
3		**Advantage:** XLOOKUP can't do this.							
4									
5		Units	27	Formulas:					
6		Discounts	0.15	In C6:=LOOKUP(C5,B10:B13,F9:I9)					
7		Discounts	#VALUE!	In C7:=XLOOKUP(C5,B10:B13,F9:I9,,-1)					
8									
9		Units		Discounts	0.0%	15.0%	25.0%	50.0%	
10		0							
11		25							
12		45							
13		75							

Figure 14.51 *This sort of situation is rare, but if you need to do it, LOOKUP can handle it, and XLOOKUP can't.*

Example 23: Using LOOKUP to Create Approximate Match Lookup Formulas More Quickly Than with XLOOKUP

If you are performing an exact match or next smaller item lookup and the first column of a lookup table is always sorted ascending (as in a tax table), you can use LOOKUP rather than the XLOOKUP function. With LOOKUP, you enter only two arguments rather than the five that XLOOKUP requires, which means you can create the formula more quickly. This can save a lot of time for complicated tax formulas where you must use multiple lookup functions. Figure 14.52 shows an example of this. In this figure, if the lookup value for an exact match or next smaller item lookup were taxable pay of $3,690.80, the correct row in the lookup table would contain three different numbers that must be used in the formula.

You can try this example on the worksheet named Ch14(52).

| F21 | ▾ | : | × ✓ fx | =LOOKUP(F20,B6:F13)+(F20-LOOKUP(F20,B6:E13))*LOOKUP(F20,B6:D13) |

◢	A	B	C	D	E	F	G
2	Ex	**Goal:** "Approximate match" lookup when 1st column sorted & we want item from last column.					
3	#23	**Advantage:** Enter fewer arguments, as compared to XLOOKUP. Faster to create formula with LOOKUP.					
4							
5		Taxable Pay Lower Limit	Taxable Pay Upper Limit	Tax Rate	Upper Limit Previous Category	Cumulative Tax From Previous Categories	Tax Rule in Full:
6		$0.00	$222	0%	$0	$0.00	
7		$222.01	$588	10%	$222	$0.00	$0.00 +(TP - $222) *10%
8		$588.01	$1,711	12%	$588	$36.60	$36.60 +(TP - $588) *12%
9		$1,711.01	$3,395	22%	$1,711	$171.36	$171.36 +(TP - $1,711) *22%
10		$3,395.01	$6,280	24%	$3,395	$541.84	$541.84 +(TP - $3,395) *24%
11		$6,280.01	$7,914	32%	$6,280	$1,234.24	$1,234.24 +(TP - $6,280) *32%
12		$7,914.01	$11,761	35%	$7,914	$1,757.12	$1,757.12 +(TP - $7,914) *35%
13		$11,761.01	more	37%	$11,761	$3,103.57	$3,103.57 +(TP - $11,761) *37%
14							
15		If we make calculation manually: $541.84 + ($3,690.80 - $3,395) * 24% = $612.83					
16							
17		**Gross Pay**				$4,010.00	
18		**Withholding Allowance**				$79.80	
19		**# of Withholding Allowances**				4	
20		**Taxable Pay (TP). This is lookup_value:**				$3,690.80	
21		**Federal Income Tax Withholdings?**				$612.83	
22		**Federal Income Tax Withholdings?**				$612.83	
23							
24		Formula in F21:=LOOKUP(F20,B6:F13)+(F20-LOOKUP(F20,B6:E13))*LOOKUP(F20,B6:D13)					
25		Formula in F22:=XLOOKUP(F20,B6:B13,F6:F13,,-1)+(F20-XLOOKUP(F20,B6:B13,E6:E13,,-1)) *XLOOKUP(F20,B6:B13,D6:D13,,-1)					

Figure 14.52 *The one tax calculation needs to look up three values from the lookup table.*

Example 24: Determining Whether to Use Multiple Lookup Tables and the SWITCH or FILTER Function

Sometimes you have more than one lookup table. For example, Figure 14.53 shows three different units transaction lookup tables: one for the Bellen product, one for the Quad product, and a default lookup table. If the goal in the units transaction table is to create a formula to look up the correct price discount based on the number of units for a given product, the formula needs to use a different lookup table in each row. For example, in the first row, the formula has to use the lookup table for the Bellen product in the range J8:K10; in the second row, the formula has to use the default lookup table in the range J18:K20; and so on.

	A	B	C	D	E	F	(	H	I	J	K	L	M	N	O
2	Ex	**Goal:** Lookup correct lookup table based on product name.													
3	#24	Use lookup table to perform "approximate match" lookup.						**Situation #1:**				**Situation #2:**		
4								Multiple lookup tables.				One Lookup Table.		
5		**Units Transaction Table:**						Use SWITCH.				Use FILTER.		
7		Product	Price	Units Sold	Price Discount	Price Discount	Bellen	Units		P. Discount		Product	Units	Price Discount
8		Bellen	26.95	24	0.25	0.25		0		0%		Bellen	0	0%
9		Aspen	28.95	60	0.5	0.5		15		25%		Bellen	15	25%
10		Bellen	26.95	50	0.4	0.4		45		40%		Bellen	45	40%
11		Quad	43.95	5	0	0						Quad	0	0%
12		Quad	43.95	25	0.2	0.2	Quad	Units		P. Discount		Quad	20	20%
13		Bellen	26.95	96	0.4	0.4		0		0%		Quad	60	45%
14		Yanaki	30.95	8	0	0		20		20%		Default	0	0%
15		Quad	43.95	124	0.45	0.45		60		45%		Default	15	30%
16		Bellen	26.95	55	0.4	0.4						Default	25	50%
17		Bellen	26.95	2	0	0	Default	Units		P. Discount				
18		Quad	43.95	5	0	0		0		0%				
19		Yanaki	30.95	19	0.3	0.3		15		30%				
20								25		50%				

22	Formula in E8:=LOOKUP(D8,SWITCH(B8,$H$7,$J$8:$K$10,$H$12,$J$13:$K$15,$J$18:$K$20))
23	Formula in F8:=LOOKUP(D8,FILTER($N$8:$O$13,$M$8:$M$13=B8,$N$14:$O$16))
24	Formulas entered, and manually copied to the rows below.

Figure 14.53 *With multiple lookup tables, you can use either the SWITCH function or the FILTER function.*

You can try this example on the worksheet named Ch14(53).

In general, when dealing with multiple lookup tables, there are two situations that you will encounter (refer to Figure 14.53):

- **Situation 1:** The lookup tables are separate and distinct. In this situation, it is usually better to use the SWITCH function to look up the correct lookup table.

- **Situation 2:** You have a single lookup table. In this situation, it is usually better to use the FILTER function to look up the correct lookup table.

Of these two situations, it is more common to encounter lookup tables that are separate and distinct than it is to encounter a single table. The separate and distinct lookup tables tend to be easier to understand and maintain than a single large lookup table. However, if you can combine the individual lookup tables into one lookup table, the formula is easier to create, especially if you have many different lookup tables.

The specifics of the SWITCH function are explained in the next section. However, it is important to note that although there are other functions that can be used to look up distinct and separate lookup tables (for example, INDEX, IF, IFS, and CHOOSE), the SWITCH function is the least complicated of all these function options. Finally, when you create a formula that internally delivers a full table in each cell (that is, delivers an array of values), it is not possible to spill the formula, and instead you enter the formula in the top cell and manually copy the formula down to the rows below.

The SWITCH Function

The SWITCH lookup function is the Swiss Army knife of the lookup function family because it is not limited to values in cells, ranges, or arrays (as the XLOOKUP and LOOKUP functions are). With the SWITCH function, you can look up tables, formulas, functions, text values, number values, values in cells, and any other type of formula element that you can dream up. Because it is a function that can look up any type of formula element or value, SWITCH is also an efficient substitute for the IF or IFS functions in some situations.

The syntax of the SWITCH function is as follows (see Figure 14.54):

`SWITCH(expression, value1, result1, [default_or_value2, result2], …)`

The arguments of the SWITCH function are as follows:

- **expression**: This argument specifies the lookup value.
- **value1, value2, etc.**: These arguments specify the values to match.
- **result1, result2, etc.**: These arguments specify the values returned.
- **default**: This argument is delivered when no matches are found in the *value* arguments.

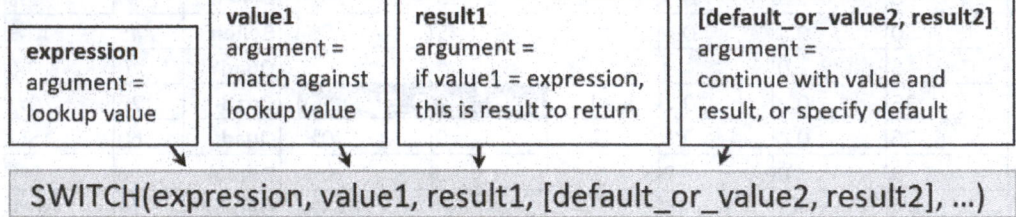

| expression argument = lookup value | value1 argument = match against lookup value | result1 argument = if value1 = expression, this is result to return | [default_or_value2, result2] argument = continue with value and result, or specify default |

SWITCH(expression, value1, result1, [default_or_value2, result2], …)

Figure 14.54 *Arguments of the SWITCH function.*

Figure 14.55 shows a close-up of the SWITCH function used in Example 24, where you had to look up different lookup tables based on a product name. The relative cell reference B6 contains the name of the product sold. If the product in cell B6 is Bellen, then the table in the range J6:K8 is used; if the product is Quad, the table in the range J11:K13 is used; finally, if the product is not Bellen or Quad, the default table from the range J16:K18 is used.

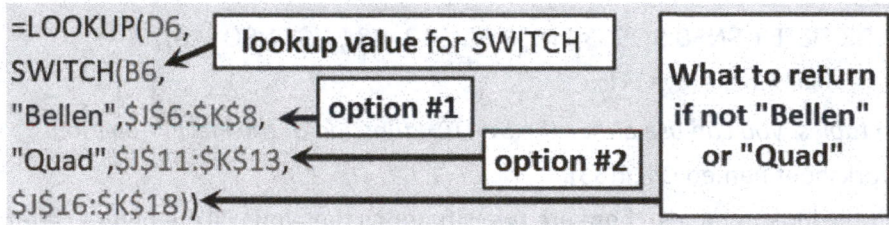

```
=LOOKUP(D6,
SWITCH(B6,
"Bellen",$J$6:$K$8,
"Quad",$J$11:$K$13,
$J$16:$K$18))
```

lookup value for SWITCH

option #1

option #2

What to return if not "Bellen" or "Quad"

Figure 14.55 *Using the SWITCH function to look up the correct lookup table in the second argument of LOOKUP.*

Example 25: Using SWITCH with Lookup Formulas

As a second example of this Swiss Army knife lookup function, Figure 14.56 shows how to use SWITCH to deliver different formulas to each cell. In this example, you need to determine whether to extend credit to a customer based on three different rules: Rule 1, Rule 2, and a default rule for other situations. For each of these rules, there is a different formula that is used to determine whether the customer is extended credit:

- **Rule 1:** Sales Last Year >$250,000 AND Asset Value >$300,000

  =AND(C12>$C$9,D12>$D$9)

- **Rule 2:** At least 1 of the credit ratings is exceeded.

  =OR(E12>$E$9,F12>$F$9)

- **Default rule:** Credit 1 >= 4 AND Credit 2 >=8

  =AND(E12>=$E$9,F12>=$F$9)

The full table with the customer information is listed in the range B11:G17.

The SWITCH function is perfect for a situation like this, where you need to run a different formula in each cell, based on the value in the Rule Used column.

As shown in Figure 14.56, the SWITCH function can be entered into cell H12 and then manually copied to the rows below. As you learned in Chapter 13, logical functions like AND and OR cannot be spilled because they are programmed to each deliver a single scalar value. With the formula in this example, each cell in the Credit? SWITCH column looks up a different formula, based on the value in the Rule Used column.

You can try this example on the worksheet named Ch14(56).

	A	B	C	D	E	F	G	H
2	Ex	Goal: Determine whether we should extend credit to customers based on one of 3 rules.						
3	#25							
4		Rule #1:	Sales Last Year >$250,000 AND Asset Value >$300,000					
5		Rule #2:	At least 1 of the credit ratings is exceeded.					
6		Default:	Credit 1 >= 4 AND Credit 2 >=8					
8			Sales Last Year	Asset Value	Credit Rating 1	Credit Rating 2		
9			$250,000	$300,000	4	8		
11		Name	Sales Last Year	Asset Value	Credit Rating 1	Credit Rating 2	Rule Used	Credit? SWITCH
12		Birch Stores Inc.	$250,000	$370,000	2.4	7	Rule 2	FALSE
13		RAD Web Design	$430,313	$292,808	3.1	9	Rule 2	TRUE
14		Blue Acorn Design	$280,396	$111,622	3.7	7.1	Not specified	FALSE
15		Shark Logistics Co.	$280,306	$370,448	2.9	5	Rule 1	TRUE
16		Foggy Camel Vacations	$454,172	$369,208	3.5	6.8	Rule 1	TRUE
17		Battalion's Moving Inc.	$270,797	$277,251	4	9		TRUE

Formula in H12:
=SWITCH(G12,   ← lookup value
"Rule 1",AND(C12>$C$9,D12>$D$9),   ← option #1
"Rule 2",OR(E12>$E$9,F12>$F$9),   ← option #2
AND(E12>=$E$9,F12>=$F$9))   ← default

Formulas entered, and manually copied to the rows below.

Figure 14.56 *Using the SWITCH function to look up different formulas.*

Note: In Chapter 16, you will learn about another great use for the SWITCH function: to look up different sections of a report and append them, one on top of the other.

Example 26: Combining Columns with the CHOOSE Function

CHOOSE is a lookup function where the lookup value is an index number such as 1, 2, and so on. The syntax of the CHOOSE function is as follows (see Figure 14.57):

```
CHOOSE (index_num, value1, [value2], …)
```

The arguments of the CHOOSE function are as follows:

- ***index_num:*** This argument specifies lookup values as index numbers (1, 2, and so on).

- ***value1, value2, etc.:*** These arguments specify the values to return if index numbers match. Index 1 retrieves *value1*, index 2 retrieves *value2*, and so on.

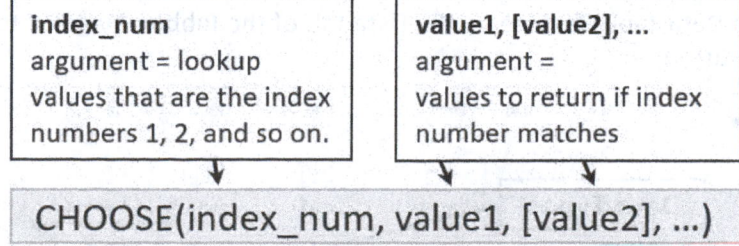

Figure 14.57 *Arguments of the CHOOSE function.*

Although many of the lookup formulas you can create with the CHOOSE function can be created more easily using the SWITCH function, there is still one great lookup situation that the CHOOSE function can perform more efficiently than any of the other lookup functions: It is best to use CHOOSE when you need to look up multiple columns and join them together, side-by-side, into a table.

In Figure 14.58, the goal is to look up the three different columns of names (F6:F10, I6:I9, and I14:I19) from the three different classes and join them together side-by-side into a table. CHOOSE can perform this task easily. Because you need to simultaneously look up the three columns, you can place the array constant {1,2,3} into the first argument of the CHOOSE function, *index_num*, and then place the three columns into the three subsequent arguments *value1*, [*value2*], and [*value3*]. If you enter the CHOOSE function into cell B6, the table will spill into the worksheet. To remove the #N/A errors from the columns that have fewer names than the column with the most names, you can place the CHOOSE function into the IFNA function and then, in the *value_if_na* argument, you create the syntax for showing nothing: a zero-length text string using two double quotes.

You can try this example on the worksheet named Ch14(58).

| B6 | ▼ | ⋮ | × | ✓ | *fx* | =IFNA(CHOOSE({1,2,3},F6:F10,I6:I9,I14:I19),"") |

▲	A	B	C	D	E	F	G	H	I	J
2	Ex	**Goal:** Combine three separate columns into a table.								
3	#26						Class #1		Class #2	
5		Class 1	Class 2	Class 3		Names	Scores	Names	Scores	
6		Mozella Chatman	Fran Taber	Lucinda Mimms		Mozella Chatman	68	Fran Taber	89	
7		Earline Kinsey	Sioux Almeida	Britt Clem		Earline Kinsey	104	Sioux Almeida	99	
8		Chantel Southern	Velda Currier	Jerlene Calderon		Chantel Southern	73	Velda Currier	77	
9		Delicia Haggard	Ouida Crain	Dawna Guthrie		Delicia Haggard	59	Ouida Crain	27	
10		Lucrecia Treadway		Amal Rhoades		Lucrecia Treadway	104			
11				Felisha Nugent				Class #3		
12										
13		Formula in B6:						Names	Scores	
14		=IFNA(CHOOSE({1,2,3},F6:F10,I6:I9,I14:I19),"")						Lucinda Mimms	89	
15								Britt Clem	55	
16								Jerlene Calderon	75	
17								Dawna Guthrie	108	
18								Amal Rhoades	81	
19								Felisha Nugent	79	

Figure 14.58 *Using CHOOSE to simultaneously look up three columns and join them together, side-by-side, into a table.*

Example 27: Using Data Types and the Dot Operator to Perform a Lookup

Back in Example 18 in Chapter 12, you learned about using the Data Types feature and the dot operator to look up a stock market ticker symbol and stock price by using the Stocks data type. In this example, the goal is to use the Zip Code data type and the dot operator to look up the average house value and median household income, based on zip codes in the United States.

As shown in Figure 14.59, you can access the Data Types feature on the Data tab of the Ribbon by going to the Data Types group and clicking the More button.

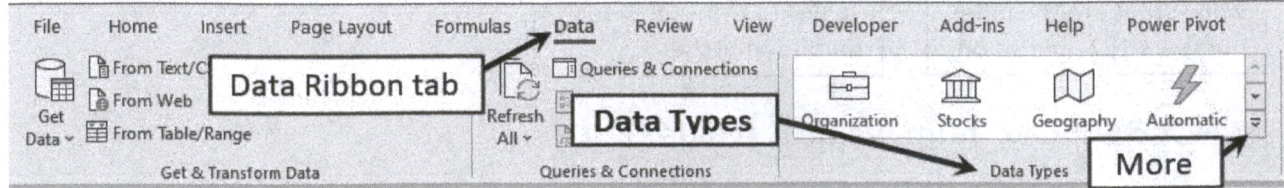

Figure 14.59 *The Data Types feature is in the Data tab of the Ribbon.*

To follow along with this example, you can select the worksheet named Ch14(59-62) and follow these steps:

1. As shown in Figure 14.60, select the range containing the zip codes, D6:D8, and then, in the Data tab, go to the Data Types group, click the More button, and then click the Zip Code button. Excel converts the zip codes from numbers in cells to numbers that have the Zip Code data type, which allows you to look up commonly used data from the internet that is related to particular zip codes. You can look up data such as latitude, longitude, average house value for the zip code, median household income for the zip code, and many other bits of common zip code–related data.

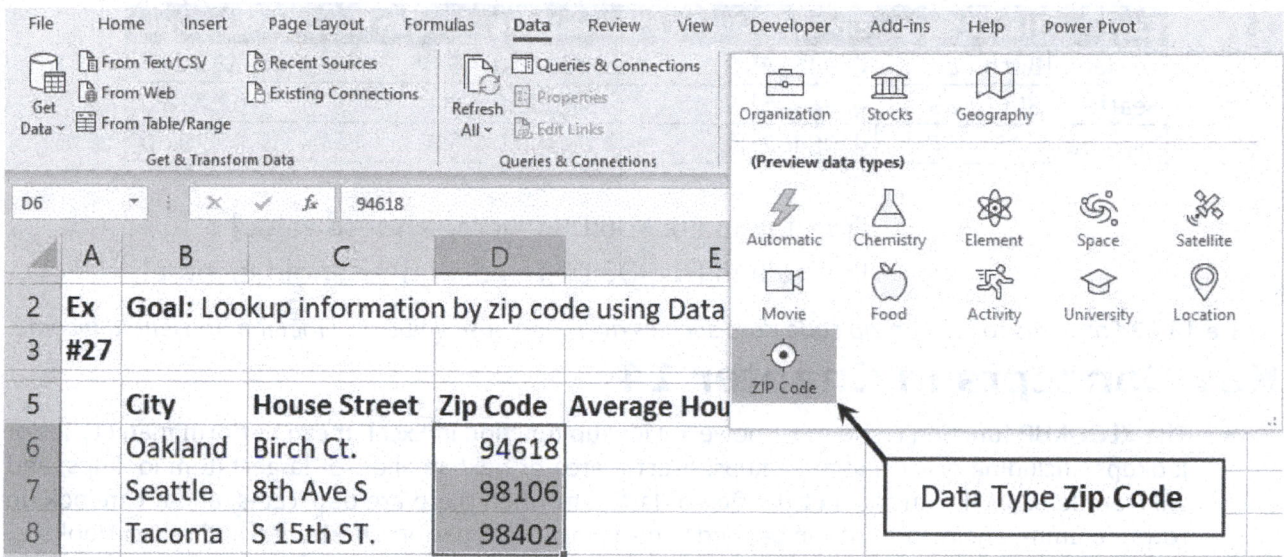

Figure 14.60 *The Zip Code data type allows you to look up data by zip code.*

2. To look up data based on zip code, select cell E6 and create the formula **=D6:D8**.

3. Type the dot operator after the range D6:D8. As shown in Figure 14.61, a large dropdown list appears, with all the possible items you can look up for a given zip code.

4. From the dropdown, select the Average House Value option. You can use your arrow keys and the Tab key to select the item, or you can use your mouse to double-click the item you want to look up. The final formula should look like this: **=D6:D8.[average house value]**.

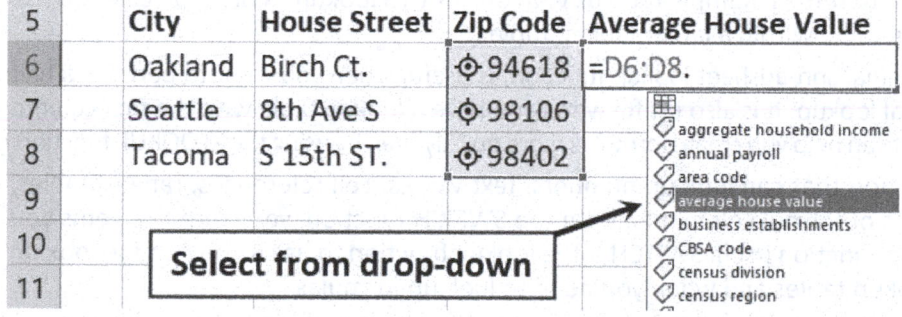

Figure 14.61 *The dot operator works with data types to look up data from the internet.*

5. Press the Tab key to spill the formula to the rows below.

6. In cell F6, create the formula **=D6:D8.[median household income]**.

7. Press the Enter key to spill the formula to the rows below. Figure 14.62 shows the final results.

E6	▼	:	×	✓	*fx*	=D6:D8.[average house value]	

▲	A	B	C	D	E	F
2	Ex	**Goal:** Lookup information by zip code using Data Types and Dot Operator.				
3	#27					
5		City	House Street	Zip Code	Average House Value	Median Household Income
6		Oakland	Birch Ct.	◈ 94618	$ 1,030,000	$ 133,125
7		Seattle	8th Ave S	◈ 98106	$ 157,600.0	$ 62,726.0
8		Tacoma	S 15th ST.	◈ 98402	$ 129,800.0	$ 45,797.0
9						
10				Formula in E6: =D6:D8.[average house value]		
11				Formula in F6: =D6:D8.[median household income]		

Figure 14.62 *Formulas to look up zip code data such as average house value and median household income.*

Key Concepts in Chapter 14

- The **XLOOKUP** function is the most powerful lookup function in Excel. It can perform many types of lookups, including exact match lookups, exact match or next smaller (or larger) item lookups, and wildcard lookups. It can also get the first or last item when there are duplicates, and it can look up rows, columns, and records. It can be used to do a lookup left, perform horizontal and vertical lookups, look up cell references, and look up pictures.

- **XMATCH** is a lookup function that can determine the relative position of an item in a list. XMATCH is the function to use when you need to compare two lists. You can use XMATCH and ISNA to determine whether an item is not in a list. You can use XMATCH and ISNUMBER to determine whether an item is in a list.

- **INDEX** is a lookup function that can look up an item in a row, a column, or a table and that uses index numbers to complete the lookup. INDEX can be used to look up values from a range with index numbers, look up random data, and look up and rearrange columns.

- **FILTER** is a useful lookup function for creating an array of TRUE and FALSE values to help look up values. You can use FILTER to return multiple records with one or two lookup values. You can also use it to look up a sub-lookup table within a larger lookup table.

- **LOOKUP**, which is the original spreadsheet lookup function, is useful when you want to perform a half vertical and half horizontal lookup. It is also useful when you have a lookup table with the first column sorted ascending, A–Z, as it can help you create formulas more quickly than by using the XLOOKUP function.

- **SWITCH** is a lookup function that can look up numbers, text values, cell references, ranges, tables, formulas, and other types of formula elements. With the SWITCH function, you store the items you need to look up inside the function itself. SWITCH is the lookup function to use if you need to look up distinct and separate lookup tables and when you need to look up formulas.

- **CHOOSE** is a lookup function that uses index numbers to determine which of the items stored in a *value* argument to look up and retrieve. This lookup function is useful when you need to look up columns and combine them side-by-side in a table.

- You can use **data types** and the **dot operator** to perform lookups that retrieve common data from the internet.

- In this chapter, you have seen how to **convert text numbers to numerals** with math operations. Any math operation that does not change the value of a numeral can change a text number back to a numeral.

Keyboard Shortcuts Learned in Chapter 14

Keyboard Shortcut	Description
F9	Causes all formulas in the workbook to be recalculated
Shift+F9	Causes all formulas in the active worksheet to be recalculated

Practice Problems for Chapter 14

Practice Problem 1

In your Excel file for this chapter (Ch14-Excel365-LookupFormulas.xlsx), go to the worksheet named PPCh14(1) and create the solution for this practice problem. Figure 14.63 shows the goals that are listed on that worksheet.

	A	B	C	D	E	F	G	H
2	**Goals:** Add a Data Validation dropdown list to cell B6 based on the E-mails in the range G11:G17.							
3	In cell C8, create a formula to lookup Employee ID based on the e-mail in cell B6.							
5	E-mail							
6								
8	Employee ID:							
10	**Employee ID**	**First**		**Last**	**Start Date**	**E-mail**	**Start Position**	**BirthDate**
11	880-245-3400	Jo		Jones	11/22/10	JJ10@gb.com	C1	11/27/90
12	880-245-3401	Mo		Abdi	10/31/14	MA14@gb.com	A1	11/8/83
13	880-245-3402	Phil		Kips	12/23/15	PK15@gb.com	A1	12/30/86
14	880-245-3403	Ty		Mimms	1/31/16	TM16@gb.com	C1	2/6/89
15	880-245-3404	Lin		Chinn	2/1/16	LC16@gb.com	D1	2/9/63
16	880-245-3405	Hien		Pham	8/24/17	HP17@gb.com	A1	9/3/78
17	880-245-3406	Sam		Fix	8/9/18	SF18@gb.com	D2	8/14/97

Figure 14.63 *On the worksheet PPCh14(1), you can create a formula to look up employee ID based on e-mail address.*

When you are done with this problem, you can check your work against the answer sheet named PPCh14(1an).

Practice Problem 2

In your Excel file for this chapter (Ch14-Excel365-LookupFormulas.xlsx), go to the worksheet named PPCh14(2) and create the solution for this practice problem. Figure 14.64 shows the goals that are listed on that worksheet.

	A	B	C	D	E	F	G	H	I
2	**Goals:** Add a Data Validation dropdown list to cell B6 based on the Employee IDs in the range B11:B17.								
3	In cell C8, create a formula to lookup the full record for the Employee ID selected in cell B6.								
5	Employee ID								
6									
8	Lookup Record:								
10	**Employee ID**		**First**	**Last**	**Start Date**	**E-mail**		**Start Position**	**BirthDate**
11	880-245-3400		Jo	Jones	11/22/10	JJ10@gb.com		C1	11/27/90
12	880-245-3401		Mo	Abdi	10/31/14	MA14@gb.com		A1	11/8/83
13	880-245-3402		Phil	Kips	12/23/15	PK15@gb.com		A1	12/30/86
14	880-245-3403		Ty	Mimms	1/31/16	TM16@gb.com		C1	2/6/89
15	880-245-3404		Lin	Chinn	2/1/16	LC16@gb.com		D1	2/9/63
16	880-245-3405		Hien	Pham	8/24/17	HP17@gb.com		A1	9/3/78
17	880-245-3406		Sam	Fix	8/9/18	SF18@gb.com		D2	8/14/97

Figure 14.64 *On the worksheet PPCh14(2), you can create a formula to look up employee record.*

When you are done with this problem, you can check your work against the answer sheet named PPCh14(2an).

Practice Problem 3

In your Excel file for this chapter (Ch14-Excel365-LookupFormulas.xlsx), go to the worksheet named PPCh14(3) and create the solution for this practice problem. Figure 14.65 shows the goals that are listed on that worksheet.

	A	B	C	D	E	F	G	H
2		**Goals:** In the grade column create the % Grade for each student.						
3		In the Decimal Grade column create formula to lookup the correct decimal grade.						
5		Max Points for Class:	650					
7		Student	Score for class	% Grade	Decimal Grade		% Grade	Decimal Grade
8		Abdi Linberger	491				0.95	4
9		Kip Berkeley	404				0.94	3.9
10		Gigi Pham	525				0.93	3.8
11		Chantel Mimms	632				0.92	3.7
12		Fred Dean	566				0.91	3.6
13		Dino Hipster	45				0.9	3.5
14		Tyrone Spawn	612				0.89	3.4
15							0.88	3.3
16							0.87	3.2
41							0.62	0.7
42							0	0

Figure 14.65 *On the worksheet PPCh14(3), you can create grade formulas.*

When you are done with this problem, you can check your work against the answer sheet named PPCh14(3an).

Practice Problem 4

In your Excel file for this chapter (Ch14-Excel365-LookupFormulas.xlsx), go to the worksheet named PPCh14(4) and create the solution for this practice problem. Figure 14.66 shows the goals that are listed on that worksheet.

	A	B	C	D	E	F	G	H
2		**Goals:** Create a lookup formula in the commission column that can						
3		lookup the commission bonus based on the employee's sales.						
4		Create the formula two different ways.						
5								
6		Employee	Sales	Commission Bonus	Commission Bonus		Sales	Commission Bonus
7		Akilah Delaney	338,922				$0	$0
8		Asa Crain	230,965				$125,000	$750
9		Vern Coppola	210,205				$175,000	$1,250
10		Sharilyn Mahaffey	221,499				$225,000	$2,000
11		Jackson Rizzo	215,074				$275,000	$3,000
12		Sarina Parnell	131,933				$325,000	$3,750
55		Shane Southern	309,112					
56		Felice Cherry	158,108					

Figure 14.66 *On the worksheet PPCh14(4), you can create the commission bonus formula two different ways.*

When you are done with this problem, you can check your work against the answer sheet named PPCh14(4an).

Practice Problem 5

In your Excel file for this chapter (Ch14-Excel365-LookupFormulas.xlsx), go to the worksheet named PPCh14(5) and create the solution for this practice problem. Figure 14.67 shows the goal that is listed on that worksheet.

	A	B	C	D	E	F	G
2		Goals: In cell C5 create lookup formula to look up correct Vent Size based on Room Sq. Ft.					
4		Room Sq. Ft.	414		Room Sq. Ft.	Vent Size (inch)	
5		Vent Size:			0		6
6					5		8
7		Hint: use "Exact match or next larger" lookup.			20		12
8					100		14
9					200		16
10					300		20
11					500		25
12					700		30

Figure 14.67 *On the worksheet PPCh14(5), you can create a lookup formula to perform an exact match or next larger item lookup.*

When you are done with this problem, you can check your work against the answer sheet named PPCh14(5an).

Practice Problem 6

In your Excel file for this chapter (Ch14-Excel365-LookupFormulas.xlsx), go to the worksheet named PPCh14(6) and create the solution for this practice problem. Figure 14.68 shows the goal that is listed on that worksheet.

	A	B	C	D	E	F	G	H	I	J	K	L	M	N	O	P
2		Goals: In cell C5 create formula to add the total calls for the month name in cell C4.														
4		Month	Dec		Calls by Month:											
5		Total Calls:														
6					Jan	Feb	Mar	Apr	May	Jun	Jul	Aug	Sep	Oct	Nov	Dec
7					145	23	133	163	164	112	161	93	125	115	51	86
8					117	51	76	161	123	95	21	107	131	56	111	84
9					160	40	123	131	50	144	103	84	13	48	121	89
10					88	66	52	148	44	151	139	70	106	101	161	94
29					215	89	113	72	168	91	22	53	132	84	127	12
30					287	105	47	123	37	73	83	10	45	97	89	21

Figure 14.68 *On the worksheet PPCh14(6), you can create a formula to add calls for the month selected in cell C5.*

When you are done with this problem, you can check your work against the answer sheet named PPCh14(6an).

Practice Problem 7

In your Excel file for this chapter (Ch14-Excel365-LookupFormulas.xlsx), go to the worksheet named PPCh14(7) and create the solution for this practice problem. Figure 14.69 shows the goals that are listed on that worksheet.

	B	C	D	E	F	G	H	I	J	K	L	M	N	O	P	Q
2	**Goals:** In cell C11 create formula to add the academic credits taken per quarter for the student listed in cell C8 and for the															
3	period start quarter to end quarter as listed in cell C9 and C10, respectively.															
4	Create conditional formatting for range of cells with credits (F9:Q24) using a logical formula that will															
5	highlight the student's credits taken from the start to end quarter (this is an advanced formula).															
7					Fal 20	Win 20	Spr 20	Sum 20	Fal 21	Win 21	Spr 21	Sum 21	Fal 22	Win 22	Spr 22	Sum 22
8	Room Sq. Ft.	Etsuko Redd		Student				Academic Credits Taken per Quarter:							
9	**Start Quarter:**	Fal20		Temika Weis	2	15	0	5	0	15	0	15	3	10	3	0
10	**End Quarter:**	Spr21		Stephen Witherspoon	5	7	12	0	2	3	10	15	2	10	15	5
11	Vent Size:			Breann Dang	15	10	0	5	0	15	15	0	15	15	15	10
12				Arlette Dancy	2	10	15	0	2	0	15	12	15	15	0	0
13				Etsuko Redd	7	0	15	0	15	15	10	15	15	15	2	12
23				Porsha Caudle	2	2	12	15	5	0	0	12	0	0	10	15
24				Florentina Hummel	5	15	7	10	0	0	10	15	10	3	15	15

Figure 14.69 *On the worksheet PPCh14(7), you can create a formula to add a student's credits from the starting quarter to the ending quarter.*

When you are done with this problem, you can check your work against the answer sheet named PPCh14(7an).

Practice Problem 8

In your Excel file for this chapter (Ch14-Excel365-LookupFormulas.xlsx), go to the worksheet named PPCh14(8) and create the solution for this practice problem. Figure 14.70 shows the goals that are listed on that worksheet.

	B	C	D	E	F
2	**Goals:** 1) Create column next to Winter 2020 list of student names that contains				
3	a logical formula that says whether student was also in the Fall 2020 Class.				
4	2) Create conditional formatting to highlight student in				
5	Winter 2020 class that was also in Fall 2020 class.				
7		Accounting 121 Class		Accounting 121 Class	
9		Fall 2020		Winter 2020	
10		Temika Weis		Cheryl Estrada	
11		Stephen Witherspoon		Judy Douglas	
25		Florentina Hummel		Cesar Dunn	
26		Luz Caldwell		Allan Nguyen	
27		Judy Douglas		Roderick Mendez	
28				Blanche Stanley	

Figure 14.70 *On the worksheet PPCh14(8), you can create a logical formula to show names that are in both lists.*

When you are done with this problem, you can check your work against the answer sheet named PPCh14(8an).

Practice Problem 9

In your Excel file for this chapter (Ch14-Excel365-LookupFormulas.xlsx), go to the worksheet named PPCh14(9) and create the solution for this practice problem. Figure 14.71 shows the goals that are listed on that worksheet.

	A	B	C	D	E	F	G
2		**Goals:** Create formula in cell G8 to extract and spill names in Winter 2020 class that are not in Fall 2020 class:					
3		Add conditional formatting to spilled range that adds a border and green fill if the cell shows a spilled value.					
4							
5			Accounting 121 Class		Accounting 121 Class		
6							
7			Fall 2020		Winter 2020		Extract names in Winter 2020 class that are not in Fall 2020 class:
8			Temika Weis		Cheryl Estrada		
9			Stephen Witherspoon		Judy Douglas		
10			Breann Dang		Wade Grant		
11			Arlette Dancy		Isaac Owens		
24			Luz Caldwell		Allan Nguyen		
25			Judy Douglas		Roderick Mendez		
26					Blanche Stanley		

Figure 14.71 *On the worksheet PPCh14(9), you can extract names in the winter class that are not in fall class.*

When you are done with this problem, you can check your work against the answer sheet named PPCh14(9an).

Practice Problem 10

In your Excel file for this chapter (Ch14-Excel365-LookupFormulas.xlsx), go to the worksheet named PPCh14(10) and create the solution for this practice problem. Figure 14.72 shows the goals that are listed on that worksheet.

	A	B	C	D	E	F	G	H	I	J
2		**Goals:** Create formula to extract records for World Series Games from start year in cell C7 to end year in cell C8.								
3		Solve this problem in two ways:								
4		1) In cell G13 spill the result using the FILTER function.								
5		2) In cell L13 spill the result using the XLOOKUP function.								
6										
7		Start Year:	1970							
8		End Year:	1979							
9										
10		Baseball World Series Teams from 1903 to 2019:								
11										
12		Year	Winning team	Losing team	Games		Year	Winning team	Losing team	Games
13		1903	Boston Americans	Pittsburgh Pirates	5–3					
14		1904	No World Series	No World Series	No WS					
15		1905	New York Giants	Philadelphia Athletics	4–1					
126		2016	Chicago Cubs	Cleveland Indians	4–3					
127		2017	Houston Astros	Los Angeles Dodgers	4–3					
128		2018	Boston Red Sox	Los Angeles Dodgers	4–1					
129		2019	Washington Nationals	Houston Astros	4–3					

Figure 14.72 *On the worksheet PPCh14(10), you can look up World Series baseball teams between a start year and an end year.*

When you are done with this problem, you can check your work against the answer sheet named PPCh14(10an).

Practice Problem 11

In your Excel file for this chapter (Ch14-Excel365-LookupFormulas.xlsx), go to the worksheet named PPCh14(11) and create the solution for this practice problem. Figure 14.73 shows the goal that is listed on that worksheet.

	A	B	C	D	E	F	G	H	I	J	K	L
2		**Goals:** In cell H7, spill the records for the product listed in cell I4.										
3												
4		Date	Sales	Web Site	Product	Time		Product:	Quad			
5		1/30/21	Amazon	Amazon	Quad	1:00 AM						
6		1/27/21	Gel.com	Amazon	Quad	10:24 PM		Date	Sales	Web Site	Product	Time
7		1/24/21	Boom.com	Amazon	Aspen	7:18 PM						
8		1/4/21	Amazon	Amazon	Carlota	5:54 PM						
9		1/14/21	E-Bay	Amazon	Aspen	12:24 PM						
10		1/22/21	Gel.com	Amazon	Quad	5:06 PM						
55		1/28/21	Boom.com	Amazon	Quad	8:00 PM						

Figure 14.73 *On the worksheet PPCh14(11), you can create a formula to extract multiple records based on one lookup value.*

When you are done with this problem, you can check your work against the answer sheet named PPCh14(11an).

Practice Problem 12

In your Excel file for this chapter (Ch14-Excel365-LookupFormulas.xlsx), go to the worksheet named PPCh14(12) and create the solution for this practice problem. Figure 14.74 shows the goal that is listed on that worksheet.

	A	B	C	D	E	F	G	H	I	J	K
2		**Goals:** Create formula in cell C7 to lookup price of shipping based on weight and shipper name.									
4							**Standard Ship Prices:**				
5		Standard Pack Weight:	25								
6		Shipper:	DHL		**UPS**		Weight (lbs.)	Price ($)			
7		Price:					0	11.95			
8							5	16.95			
9							15	29.95			
11						**Fed X**	Weight (lbs.)	Price ($)			
12							0	9.95			
13							2	13.95			
14							10	29.95			
15							25	45.95			
17						**DHL**	Weight (lbs.)	Price ($)			
18							0	16.95			
19							7	20.95			
20							20	29.95			

Figure 14.74 *On the worksheet PPCh14(12), you can create a formula that can do a lookup from multiple tables.*

When you are done with this problem, you can check your work against the answer sheet named PPCh14(12an).

Practice Problem 13

In your Excel file for this chapter (Ch14-Excel365-LookupFormulas.xlsx), go to the worksheet named PPCh14(13) and create the solution for this practice problem. Figure 14.75 shows the goal that is listed on that worksheet.

When you are done with this problem, you can check your work against the answer sheet named PPCh14(13an).

	A	B	C	D	E	F	G	H
2		**Goals:** Create formula in cell F7 to lookup last 3 records in table.						
4		Date	Price ($)	Stock		Last		3
5		10/1/20	212.46	MSFT				
6		10/5/20	210.38	MSFT		Date	Price ($)	Stock
7		9/30/20	210.33	MSFT				
8		10/7/20	209.83	MSFT				
9		9/28/20	209.44	MSFT				
14		10/6/20	205.91	MSFT				
15		9/24/20	203.19	MSFT				
16		9/23/20	200.59	MSFT				

Figure 14.75 *On the worksheet PPCh14(13), you can create formula to extract the last three records in a table.*

Practice Problem 14

In your Excel file for this chapter (Ch14-Excel365-LookupFormulas.xlsx), go to the worksheet named PPCh14(14).

In your own words, see if you can answer these conceptual questions:

1. Name all the different types of lookups you can do by using the XLOOKUP function.
2. What does the XMATCH function do?
3. When do you use the INDEX function?
4. What are three good uses for the FILTER function?
5. What makes SWITCH different from the other lookup functions, such as XLOOKUP and VLOOKUP?

When you are done with this problem, you can check your work against the answer sheet named PPCh14(14an).

Chapter 15: Worksheet Array Formulas: Just Enter!

Note: To follow along with the examples in this chapter, you can use the file named Ch15-Excel365-ArrayFormulas.xlsx.

You have learned a lot about worksheet array formulas and the new Microsoft 365 Excel worksheet calculation engine in Chapters 8 through 14. You have already learned about more than 40 array formulas, including these:

Function or Feature	What the Formula Does	Chapter and Example
FORMULATEXT	Spills documentation results	Chapter 8, FORMULATEXT example
UNIQUE	Creates and spills a unique list of product names	Chapter 9, Example 4
ROUND	Spills accurate totals for tax deduction calculations	Chapter 10, Example 1
SUM and LARGE	Add the top three scores	Chapter 12, Example 8
AND and OR	Use Boolean math to create and spill the results from these logical tests	Chapter 13, Examples 6 and 7
OR	Uses a Boolean logical test with aggregate functions	Chapter 13, Examples 35 and 36
FILTER	Looks up and spills records based on a single lookup value	Chapter 14, Example 20

What is so amazing about the array formulas in the new Excel 365 worksheet calculation engine is that you just create and enter an array formula, and everything works. If you are learning Excel for the first time, you will never have to deal with the difficulties of array formulas that existed in all prior versions of Excel. When you create array formulas in older versions of Excel, you have to remember to execute these requirements:

- For most array formulas, you have to enter the formula into the worksheet with the keystroke Ctrl+Shift+Enter. If you do not use this keystroke, you get either an error message or the wrong answer.
- You have to pre-highlight the correct number of cells for spilled formulas.
- You have to know which functions require Ctrl+Shift+Enter and which ones do not.

Note: Array formulas used to be so difficult that in 2012, I wrote a 300-page book all about the intricacies and complexities of array formulas, titled *Ctrl+Shift+Enter: Mastering Excel Array Formulas*.

Thanks to the new and amazing Excel 365 worksheet formula calculation engine, you do not have to worry about those complexities. You don't need to use any special keystroke or pre-highlight cells or memorize lists of functions. You can just make an array formula, enter the formula, and everything works.

Note: Joe McDaid, the Microsoft program manager for the worksheet calculation engine, says that all formulas are array formulas; it is just that some array formulas deliver only one answer.

Everything you learn in this chapter works in the Excel worksheet only. Power Query, Power Pivot, and Power BI also have arrays (called *lists* or *table objects*) and array formulas, but the concepts and mechanics are different from those used with worksheet array formulas.

What Is a Worksheet Array?

An *array* is a collection of two or more items. The items, or values, that are allowed in a worksheet array are numbers, text, Boolean values, formula errors, and empty cells.

There are several types of worksheet arrays:

- **Range reference:** A range reference is an array that can include a range of cells, an Excel Table element, or a defined name with two or more items. For example, Figure 15.1 shows that the range reference B3:B9 is an array in the array formula =SORT(UNIQUE(B3:B9)).

	B	C	D	E
2	Product	Sales		Unique List Products:
3	Quad	326.17		Aspen
4	Carlota	251.57		Carlota
5	Quad	374.03		Quad
6	Aspen	256.22		
7	Aspen	171.21		**Formula in cell E3:**
8	Carlota	446.2		=SORT(UNIQUE(B3:B9))
9	Quad	236.06		

Figure 15.1 *B3:B9 is an array in the array formula shown here.*

- **Array constant:** An array constant is an array of column values, row values, or table values that are hard coded into a formula. Figure 15.2 shows the syntax used for array constants. Figure 15.3 shows that the array constant {1,2,3} is an array in the array formula =SUM(LARGE(C3:G3,{1,2,3})).

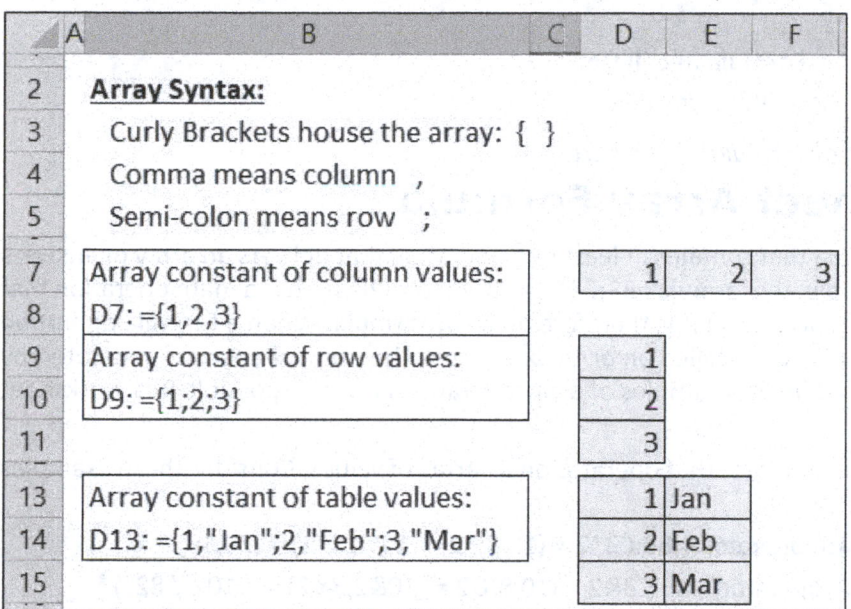

Figure 15.2 *Syntax for array constants and resultant arrays.*

	B	C	D	E	F	G	H
2	Thrower	Time1	Time2	Time3	Time4	Time5	Total of Top 3
3	Stevie	143s	78s	43s	169s	118s	430s
5					**Formula in cell H3:**		
6					=SUM(LARGE(C3:G3,{1,2,3}))		

Figure 15.3 *{1,2,3} is an array in the array formula shown here.*

- **Resultant array:** A resultant array is an array created by a formula element. For example, Figure 15.4 shows that the formula element LARGE(C3:G3,{1,2,3}) evaluates to the resultant array {169,143,118}, which is used by the SUM function.

A	B	C	D	E	F	G	H
2	Thrower	Time1	Time2	Time3	Time4	Time5	Total of Top 3
3	Stevie	143s	78s	43s	169s	118s	430s
5	**Formula in cell H3:**						
6	=SUM(LARGE(C3:G3,{1,2,3})) = SUM({169,143,118})						

Figure 15.4 *The formula element LARGE(C3:G3,{1,2,3}) evaluates to the resultant array {169,143,118}.*

- **Spilled array:** A spilled array is an array that uses the spilled range operator #. For example, Figure 15.5 shows the spilled range B6# in the formula =SUM(B6#*D3).

A	B	C	D	E
2	Quad Cost	Aspen Cost	Tax Rate	
3	10	8	0.1	
5	Quad Cost*2	Aspen Cost*2	Tax Amount	
6	20	16	3.6	
8	**Formula in cell B6:**		**Formula in cell D6:**	
9	=B3:C3*2		=SUM(B6#*D3)	

Figure 15.5 *B6# is an array in the array formula shown here.*

Defining a Worksheet Array Formula

A *worksheet array formula* is a formula that contains at least one operation that delivers an array of answers rather than a single answer. For example, the formula =B3:C3*2 = {10,8}*2 = {20,16} has a math operation that delivers an array of answers (two answers), and it is therefore an array formula. When a formula operation delivers an array of answers, the operation is called an *array operation*. The array of answers generated by an array operation is called a *resultant array*. Examples of array operations that are possible in a worksheet are as follows:

- Direct array operation with an operator that operates on an array of values: Consider these examples (see Figure 15.6):
    - This example uses a math operator: =B3:C3*2 = {10,8}*2 = {10*2,8*2} = {20,16}
    - This example uses a join operator: =B3:C3&2 = {10,8}&2 = {10&2,8&2} = {"102","82"}
    - This example uses a comparison operator: =B3:C3>=2 = {10,8}>=2 = {10>=2,8>=2} = {TRUE,TRUE}

A	B	C	D	E	F	G	H	I
2	Quad Cost	Aspen Cost						
3	10	8						
4								
5	**Math Operator:**			**Join Operator:**			**Comparative Operator:**	
6	Quad Cost*2	Aspen Cost*2		Quad Cost&2	Aspen Cost&2		Quad Cost>=2	Aspen Cost>=2
7	20	16		102	82		TRUE	TRUE
9	**Formula in cell B7:**			**Formula in cell E7:**			**Formula in cell H7:**	
10	=B3:C3*2			=B3:C3&2			=B3:C3>=2	

Figure 15.6 *Examples of direct array operations with operators working on arrays of values.*

- **Function argument array operation, where the argument expects a single value, and you give it an array of values:** A function argument array operation forces the function to deliver an array of answers. Consider these examples (see Figure 15.7):
    - =ROUND(C5:C7*D9,2) = ROUND({249.80445;276.20985;197.89875},2) = {249.8;276.21;197.9}
    - =XMATCH(H5:H8,F5:F7) = {#N/A;1;2;#N/A}

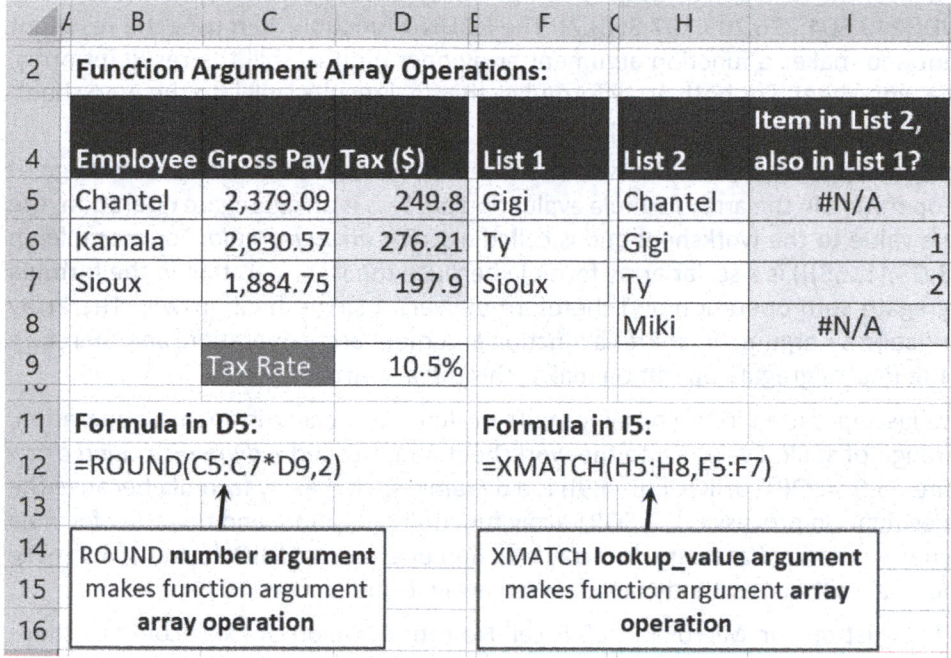

Figure 15.7 *An array of values placed into an argument that expects one value creates a function argument array operation.*

- Array function operation (using a function such as UNIQUE, TRANSPOSE, SEQUENCE, or MMULT), which is programmed to deliver an array of answers: Consider these examples (see Figure 15.8):
    - =UNIQUE(B5:B11) = {Quad; Carlota; Aspen}
    - =TRANSPOSE(E5#) = TRANSPOSE({Quad; Carlota; Aspen}) = {Quad, Carlota, Aspen}
    - =SEQUENCE(3) = {1;2;3}
    - =MMULT(B5:D5,C10:D12) = {$1,183.00, $1,157.00}

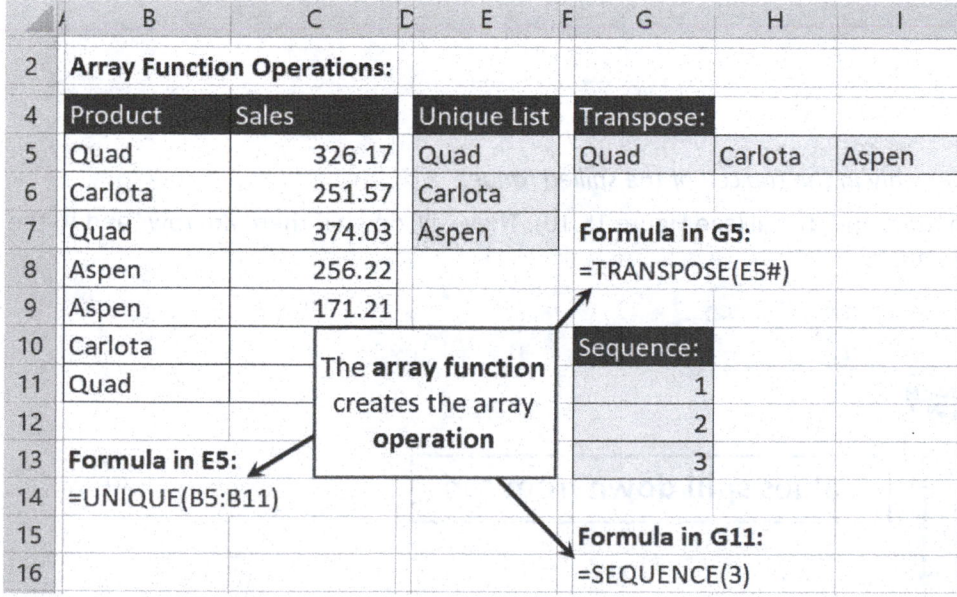

Figure 15.8 *Examples of array function operations.*

When you create an array formula with an array operation that yields a resultant array, that resultant array can either be the final answer that Excel spills into the worksheet cells or it can be used as a formula element within a larger formula. For example, in Figure 15.8, the array formula =UNIQUE(B5:B11) makes an array function operation to deliver the resultant array {Quad;Carlota;Aspen}, which is then spilled into the worksheet. On the other hand, in cell D5 in Figure 15.7, the array formula =ROUND(C5:C7*D9,2) makes the math array operation C5:C7*D9 to deliver the resultant array {249.804;276.209;197.898}, which is then used in the larger array formula, =ROUND({249.804;276.209;197.898},2). The ROUND function then uses the resultant array in the *number* argument and makes a function argument array operation to spill the resultant array, {249.8;276.21;197.9}, into the worksheet. For both array formulas, the final results spill into the worksheet. The results do not always spill into the worksheet, though.

For an array formula, the final answer delivered to the worksheet can either be a single value or a range of spilled values. When the last operation in the array formula evaluation process is an aggregate operation, the array formula delivers a single value to the worksheet and is called a *scalar array formula*. For example, in Figure 15.3, =SUM(LARGE(C3:G3,{1,2,3})) is a scalar array formula because the last operation in the formula evaluation process is an aggregate sum operation and therefore delivers a single final answer. The array constant used in the LARGE function's *k* argument creates a function argument array operation, and therefore this is an array formula, but the final aggregate operation makes this a scalar array formula.

On the other hand, when the last operation in the array formula evaluation process is an array operation, the array formula delivers a range of spilled values into the worksheet and is called a *dynamic spilled array formula*. For example, in Figure 15.9, =SORT(UNIQUE(B3:B9)) is a dynamic spilled array formula because the last operation in the formula evaluation process is the SORT array function operation, and the array formula delivers a range of spilled values as the final answer. The array function operations UNIQUE and SORT make this an array formula, and the final spill makes it a dynamic spilled array formula.

Dynamic spilled array formulas exist only in Microsoft 365 Excel. No other version of Excel contains these revolutionary formulas. Dynamic spilled array formulas have a number of important characteristics:

- The top-left cell in a spilled range contains the formula (see Figure 15.9). The remaining cells do not contain formulas.

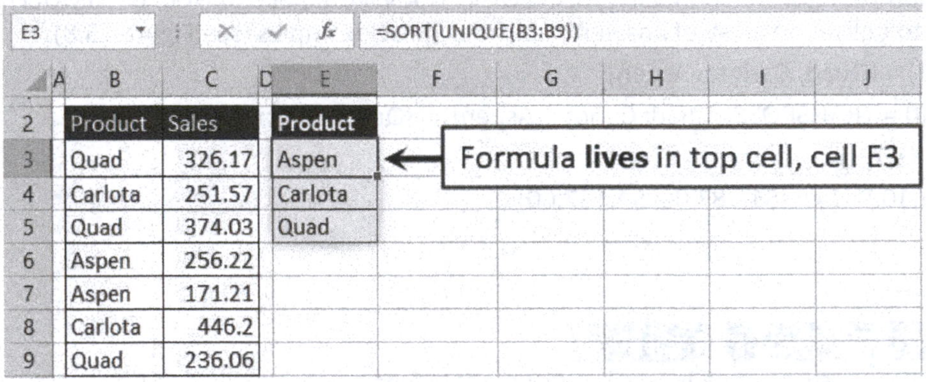

Figure 15.9 *The formula exists only in the top cell of the spilled range.*

- The values spill from that top-left cell (see Figure 15.10). They spill down if there are rows and to the right if there are columns.

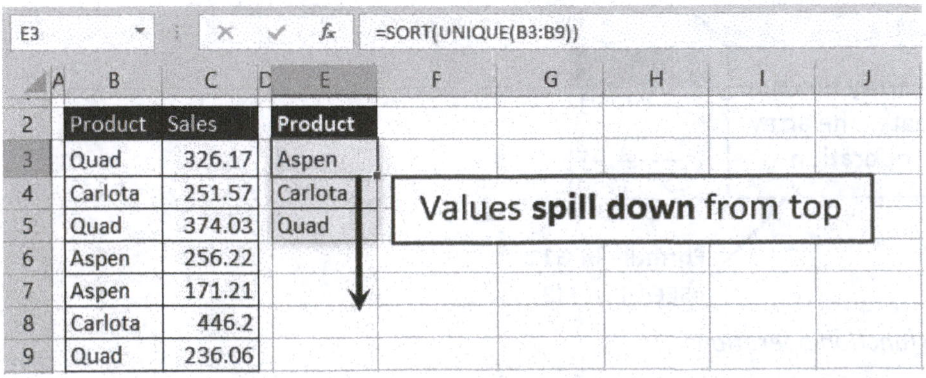

Figure 15.10 *Values from the dynamic spilled array formula emanate from the top cell in the spilled range.*

- If you need to edit a dynamic spilled array formula, you must do it in the top-left cell of the spilled range. As shown in Figure 15.11, when you select the top cell, you can edit the formula in the cell or in the formula bar.

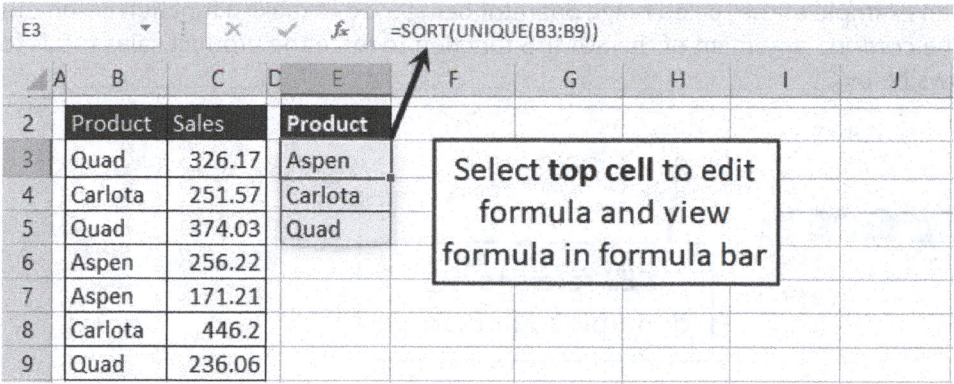

Figure 15.11 *The formula bar displays the formula (and it is not grayed out).*

- If you select a cell in the spilled range that is not the top-left cell, the formula in the formula bar is grayed out, or "ghosted," and you cannot edit it (see Figure 15.12).

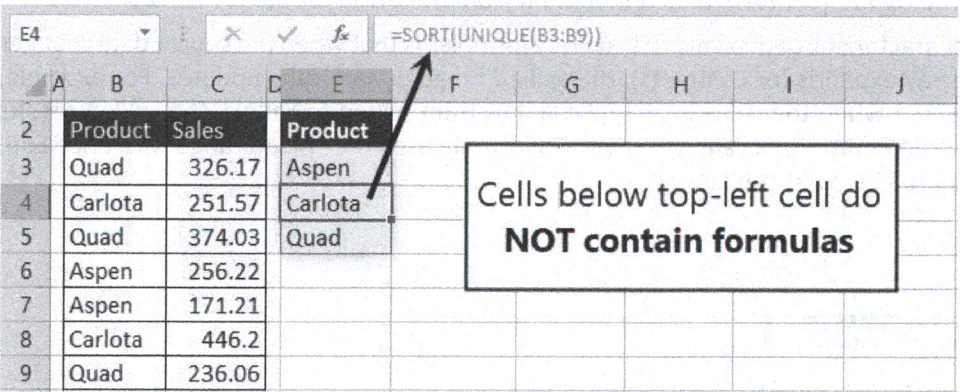

Figure 15.12 *"Ghosted" is the term Microsoft uses to describe a cell that shows a spilled value and no formula.*

- If there is preexisting data in the spilled range, the top-left cell displays a #SPILL! error (see Figure 5.13).

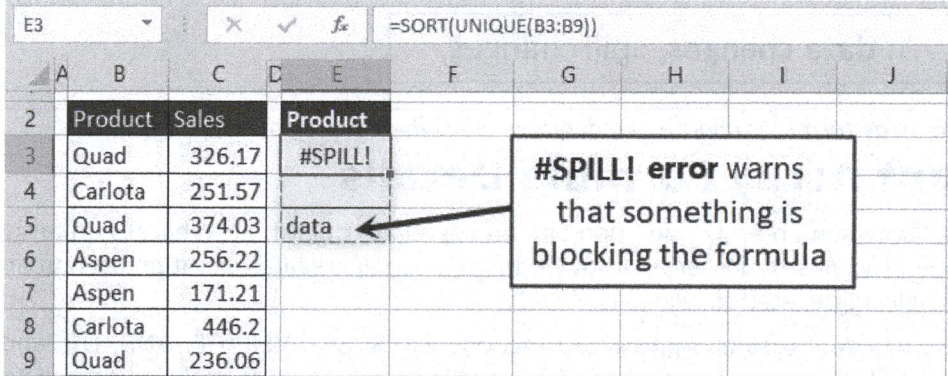

Figure 15.13 *If something is in the way of the spilled result, the #SPILL! error says "I don't have enough room!"*

- When you refer to the full spilled range in other formulas, you refer to the top-left cell address (since that is where the formula lives) and then use the # spilled range operator. For example, if you want to refer to a spilled range of values created by the array formula in cell E3, you use the spilled range E3#. Figure 15.14 shows an example of the spilled range operator being used to make a function argument array operation in the *criteria1* argument of the SUMIFS function to force the product sales totals to spill down to the rows below.

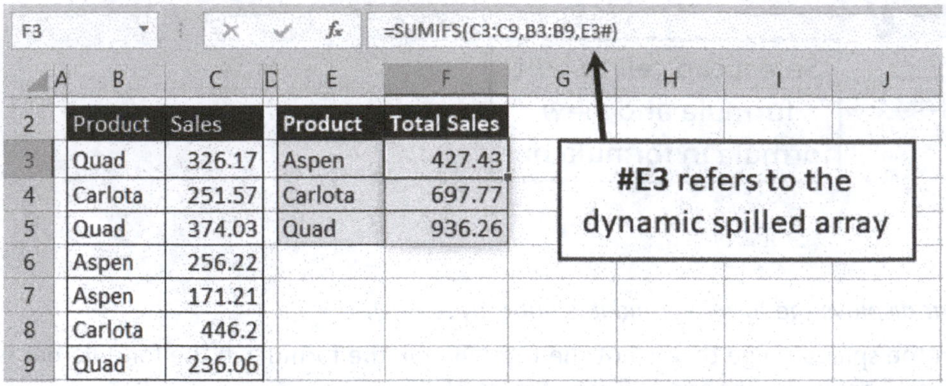

F3		× ✓ *fx*	=SUMIFS(C3:C9,B3:B9,E3#)					
A	B	C	D E	F	G	H	I	J
2	Product	Sales	Product	Total Sales				
3	Quad	326.17	Aspen	427.43				
4	Carlota	251.57	Carlota	697.77				
5	Quad	374.03	Quad	936.26				
6	Aspen	256.22						
7	Aspen	171.21						
8	Carlota	446.2						
9	Quad	236.06						

#E3 refers to the dynamic spilled array

Figure 15.14 *E3# refers to the dynamic spilled range emanating from the array formula in cell E3.*

- The most amazing characteristic of dynamic spilled array formulas is that when the source data changes and the resultant array expands (or contracts), the spilled range dynamically updates. For example, Figure 15.15 shows that when the value in cell B7 changes from Aspen to Yanaki, the spilled results now spill four values. In addition, because the SUMIFS formula uses the spilled range reference E3#, the SUMIFS function spilled totals update also.

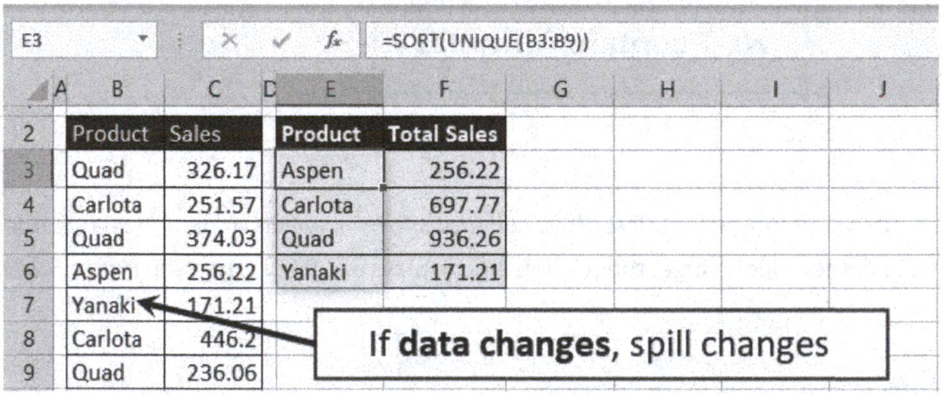

E3		× ✓ *fx*	=SORT(UNIQUE(B3:B9))					
A	B	C	D E	F	G	H	I	J
2	Product	Sales	Product	Total Sales				
3	Quad	326.17	Aspen	256.22				
4	Carlota	251.57	Carlota	697.77				
5	Quad	374.03	Quad	936.26				
6	Aspen	256.22	Yanaki	171.21				
7	Yanaki	171.21						
8	Carlota	446.2						
9	Quad	236.06						

If data changes, spill changes

Figure 15.15 *Dynamic spilled array formulas update in a dynamic way when source data changes.*

Other Important Array Formula Details

It is important to distinguish between an array operation and an aggregate operation. Whereas an array operation can act on an array of values to deliver an array of answers, an aggregate operation acts on an array of values to deliver a single aggregated answer.

Not all worksheet functions can spill results. Aggregate functions like SUM, AVERAGE, AND, OR, and SUMPRODUCT cannot deliver spilled arrays. Each of these functions is programmed to make an aggregate operation and deliver a single scalar answer from a range or from an array of inputs.

Spilled array formulas are not allowed in Excel Tables. If you try to create a dynamic spilled array formula in an Excel Table, you will get a #SPILL! error.

Some function arguments do not allow function argument array operations:

- The *range* argument of the functions SUMIF, COUNTIF, and AVERAGEIF
- The *criteria_range* argument of the functions SUMIFS, COUNTIFS, AVERAGEIFS, MINIFS, and MAXIFS
- The first argument of the functions SUMIFS, AVERAGEIFS, MINIFS, and MAXIFS

Almost all array operations involve operations on multiple formula inputs, such as C5:C7*D9, where a column of values is multiplied by a single value. The exceptions are array functions like SEQUENCE, RANDARRAY, and MUNIT, which are each programmed to generate an array of answers from a single input (for example, =SEQUENCE(3) = {1;2;3}).

Most of the time when you are creating formulas, your cue that you have moved from a non-array formula to an array formula is that the operation involves multiple values. For example, in Figure 15.16, the formula =E3-D3 is not an array formula because there are single values on either side of the subtraction operator. On the other hand, in Figure 15.17, the formula =E3:E5-D3:D5 is an array formula because one of the values on either side of the subtraction operator is an array of values. In this case, both the values on the left and the right of the operator are ranges of cells. As another example, look back at Figure 15.7, where =XMATCH(H5,F5:F7) is not an array formula because the lookup value, H5, is a single value, and the operation from the *lookup_value* argument involves looking up a single value and delivering a single answer. On the other hand, =XMATCH(H5:H8,F5:F7) is an array formula because the lookup value, H5:H8, is an array of values, which forces XMATCH to look up two items and deliver two answers.

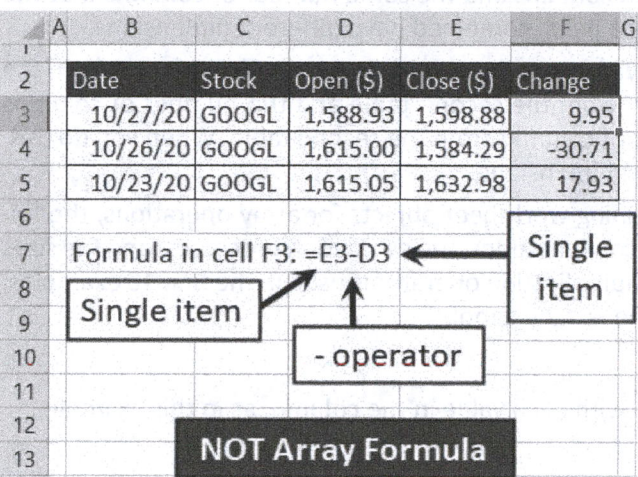

Figure 15.16 *This is not an array formula because there are single values on either side of the subtraction operator.*

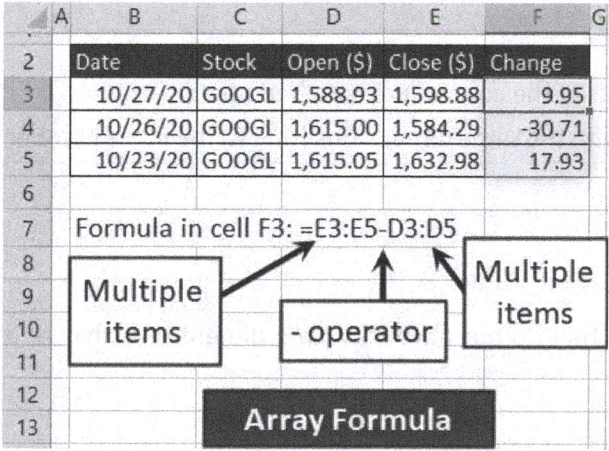

Figure 15.17 *This is an array formula because there are multiple values on at least one side of the subtraction operator.*

Array operations can involve many elements. The more elements involved, however, the more time it takes the Microsoft 365 Excel calculation engine to cycle through all the elements. For a single-cell array formula that delivers a single answer, it might seem that Excel would always do the processing quickly, but if the engine must deal with a large dataset, the overall calculation time may be much greater than expected.

Array Operation Configurations, the Evaluation Process, and the Size of the Resultant Array

In an Excel worksheet, you can operate on a cell, a column, a row, or a table (that is, rows and columns). You can combine these objects for direct array operations or function argument array operations if you follow these guidelines:

- You can combine a cell with any of the other objects (a column, a row, or a table). When you do this, the two objects being combined have different dimensions.

- When you use two columns, the number of rows in each column must be equivalent. When you do this, the two objects being combined have the same dimensions.

- When you use two rows, the number of columns in the rows must be equivalent. When you do this, the two objects being combined have the same dimensions.

- When you combine a row with a column or a column with a row, Excel delivers a cross-tabulated table with the same number of rows that the column contains and the same number of columns that the row contains. When you do this, the two objects being combined have different dimensions.

- When you combine a table with a table, Excel yields a table, as long as the number of rows from the first table is equivalent to the number of rows from the second table and the number of columns from the first table is equivalent to the number of columns from the second table. When you do this, the two objects being combined have the same dimensions.

To demonstrate the different possibilities when combining worksheet objects for array operations, the following subsections show the different array operation configurations, the evaluation processes, and the sizes of the resultant arrays for 12 different scenarios. The multiplication operator is used in the first 10 examples, and a function argument array operation is used for the last 2 examples.

Cell Times a Column

For a cell times a column, the cell value is matched up with each value in the column, as in this example:

```
=D7*C3:C4
=2*{10;20} = {2*10;2*20} = {20;40}
=Cell (1R x 1C) * Column (2R x 1C) = Column (2R x 1C)
```

The worksheet Ch15Config(1) shows this example.

Column Times a Column

For a column times a column, the corresponding elements in the column are matched up.

The following example shows multiplication of columns with the same dimensions (that is, the same number of rows in each column):

```
=B11:B12*C11:C12
={2;5}*{5;4} = {2*5;5*4} = {10;20}
=Column (2R x 1C) * Column (2R x 1C) = Column (2R x 1C)
```

The following example shows multiplication of columns that do not have the same dimensions (that is, a different number of rows in each column):

```
=B19:B20*C19:C21
={2;5}*{5;4;2} = {2*5;5*4; #N/A*4} = {10;20;#N/A}
=Column (2R x 1C) * Column (3R x 1C) = Error because columns do not contain
same number of rows
```

The worksheet Ch15Config(1) shows these examples.

Cell Times a Row

For a cell times a row, the cell value is matched up with each value in the row, as in this example:

```
=D5*C2:D2
=2*{10,20} = {2*10,2*20} = {20,40}
=Cell (1R x 1C) * Row (1R x 2C) = Row (1R x 2C)
```

The worksheet Ch15Config(2) shows this example.

Row Times a Row

For a row times a row, the corresponding elements in the row are matched up.

The following example shows multiplication of rows that have the same dimensions (that is, the same number of columns in each row):

```
=C10:D10*C11:D11
={2,5}*{5,4} = {2*5,5*4} = {10,20}
=Row (1R x 2C) * Row (1R x 2C) = Row (1R x 2C)
```

The following example shows multiplication of rows that do not have the same dimensions (that is, a different number of columns in each row):

```
=C18:D18*C19:E19
={2,5}*{5,4,2} = {2*5,5*4, #N/A*4} = {10,20,#N/A}
=Row (1R x 2C) * Row (1R x 3C) = Error because rows do not contain same
number of columns.
```

The worksheet Ch15Config(2) shows these examples.

Column Times a Row

For a column times a row, each row element from the column is matched with each column element from the row to create a cross-tabulated result, as in this example:

```
=B3:B5*C2:D2
={2;1;3}*{10,20} = {2*10,2*20;1*10,1*20;3*10,3*20} = {20,40;10,20;30,60}
=Column (3R x 1C) * Row (1R x 2C) = Table (3R x 2C)
```

The worksheet Ch15Config(3) shows this example.

Row Times a Column

For a row times a column, each column element from the row is matched with each row element from the column to create a cross-tabulated result, as in this example:

```
=C10:E10*B11:B12
={2,1,3}*{10;20} = {2*10,1*10,3*10;2*20,1*20,3*20} = {20,10,30;40,20,60}
=Column (3R x 1C) * Row (1R x 2C) = Table (3R x 2C)
```

The worksheet Ch15Config(3) shows this example.

Table Times a Table

For a table times a table, the corresponding elements are matched up.

The following example shows multiplication of tables with the same dimensions, where the number of rows in the first table is equivalent to the number of rows in the second table and the number of columns in the first table is equivalent to the number of columns in the second table:

```
=B22:C24*B26:C28
={2,5;4,3;1,6}*{7,2;1,5;3,4} = {2*7,5*2;4*1,3*5;1*3,6*4} = {14,10;4,15;3,24}
Table (3R x 2C) * Table (3R x 2C) = Table (3R x 2C)
```

With multiplication of tables that do not have the same dimensions—where the number of rows in the first table is not equivalent to the number of rows in the second table, or the number of columns in first table is not equivalent to the number of columns in the second table—the resultant array yields #N/A errors.

The worksheet Ch15Config(3) shows this example.

Row Times a Column Times a Table

For a row times a column times a table, each column element from the row is matched with each row element from the column to create a cross-tabulated resultant array (table) and then each corresponding element in that resultant array is matched with each corresponding element in the table, as in this example:

```
=C3:C5*D2:E2*D3:E5
={1;2;1}*{1,4}*{1,3;5,1;1,2} = {1*1,1*4;2*1,2*4;1*1,1*4}*{1,3;5,1;1,2} =
{1,4;2,8;1,4}*{1,3;5,1;1,2} = {1*1,4*3;2*5,8*1;1*1,4*2] = {1,12;10,8;1,8}
=Column (3R x 1C) * Row (1R x 2C) * Table (3R x 2C) = Table (3R x 2C)
```

The worksheet Ch15Config(4) shows this example.

Function Argument Array Operation

For a function argument array operation, the same rules apply as with direct operations.

For a function argument array operation that uses a column and a row, each row element from the column is matched with each column element from the row to create a cross-tabulated result, as in this example:

```
=SUMIFS(D4:D9,B4:B9,F4:F5,C4:C9,G3:H3)
```

```
=SUMIFS(D4:D9,B4:B9,{"Aspen";"Quad"},C4:C9,{"Sioux","Ty"})
```

The two function argument array operations in the *criteria1* and *criteria2* arguments are F4:F5, Column (2R x 1C), and G3:H3, Row (1R x 2C), respectively, which results is a table (2R x 2C) delivered by SUMIFS.

SUMIFS delivers a cross-tabulated table like this: {20,40;20,20}.

For a function argument array operation that uses two rows that do not have the same number of columns, the elements cannot be matched, and the formula yields an error, as in this example:

```
=SEARCH(F9:F10,B4:B9)
```

```
=SEARCH({"Carlota";"Quad"},{"Quad";"Aspen";"Quad";"Aspen";"Aspen";"Quad"})
```

The two function argument array operations in the *find_text* and *within_text* arguments are F9:F10, Column (2R x 1C), and B4:B9, Column (6R x 1C), respectively. This results in an error because the columns do not contain the same number of rows.

The worksheet Ch15Config(5) shows these examples.

Examples 1 Through 3: Doing Financial Calculations Using the Direct Array Operation Column * Row * Table

In the field of finance, array calculations in Excel worksheets are very common. For example, in Figure 15.18, the goal is to estimate the returns of two stocks (Stock A and Stock B), given assumptions about the state of the economy. To make this calculation, you would have to create in cell G6 a formula that multiplies the probability of an economic state (the column range C6:C8) by the weights of each stock in the portfolio of stocks (the row range D4:E4) by the estimated stock returns (the table range D6:E8) to estimate the contribution each stock makes to the expected portfolio rate of return. Because the number of rows in the column and table are equivalent and the number of columns in the table and row are equivalent, you can create the formula =C6:C8*D4:E4*D6:E8 in cell G6, and when you press Enter, the correct returns spill from cell G6 down and to the right into the full spilled range G6:H8.

G6	▼	:	×	✓	*fx*	=C6:C8*D4:E4*D6:E8		
◢	A	B	C	D	E	F G	H	
2		Ex #1	Goal: Estimate returns for stock A & B in a portfolio of stocks.					
4		Weight of Stock in Portfolio:		0.6	0.4			
5		Probability of Economic State		Stock A Full Estimated Return	Stock B Full Estimated Return	Stock A Contribution to Portfolio	Stock B Contribution to Portfolio	
6		Bad	0.5	0.01	-0.15	0.003	-0.03	
7		OK	0.4	0.05	0.05	0.012	0.008	
8		Great	0.1	0.1	0.2	0.006	0.008	
10						Formula in cell G6:		
11						=C6:C8*D4:E4*D6:E8		

Figure 15.18 *Array formulas like this one are very common in the field of finance.*

Figure 15.19 illustrates the error that occurs if you create an array operation between a column, a table, and a row, and the number of rows in the columns and table are not equivalent.

	A	B	C	D	E	F	G	H
2	Ex #2	Goal: Estimate returns for stock A & B in a portfolio of stocks.						
4		Weight of Stock in Portfolio:			0.6	0.4		
5		Probability of Economic State		Stock A Full Estimated Return	Stock B Full Estimated Return		Stock A Contribution to Portfolio	Stock B Contribution to Portfolio
6		Bad	0.5	0.0	-0.15		=C6:C7*D4:E4*D6:E8	
7		OK	0.4	0.05	0.05		0.012	0.008
8		Great	0.1	0.1	0.2		#N/A	#N/A
10							Formula in cell G6:	
11							=C6:C7*D4:E4*D6:E8	

Figure 15.19 *When an array operation involves rows on both sides of the operator, the rows must be equivalent.*

You can try these examples on the worksheets named Ch15(18) and Ch15(19).

What is most amazing about the financial formula calculation in cell G6 in Figure 15.18 is that you simply create the formula and press Enter, and the formula spills the results. This type of financial calculation to estimate the expected portfolio rate of return is a common calculation that has been made often throughout Excel's 40-year history. Before Excel 365's dynamic spilled array formulas, however, such calculations were not so easy to make. Figure 15.20 shows the formula that was used before spilled array formulas were available (see cell G6). This formula is difficult because you have to use mixed cell references and then enter the formula before manually copying the formula down and to the right. As you've just seen, with dynamic spilled array formulas, you can accomplish this common financial calculation task much more easily.

G6			✕ ✓	f_x	=$C6*D6*D$4			
	A	B	C	D	E	F	G	H
2	Ex #3	Goal: Estimate returns for stock A & B in a portfolio of stocks.						
4		Weight of Stock in Portfolio:			0.6	0.4		
5		Probability of Economic State		Stock A Full Estimated Return	Stock B Full Estimated Return		Stock A Contribution to Portfolio	Stock B Contribution to Portfolio
6		Bad	0.5	0.01	-0.15		0.003	-0.03
7		OK	0.4	0.05	0.05		0.012	0.008
8		Great	0.1	0.1	0.2		0.006	0.008
10							Formula in cell G6:	
11							=$C6*D6*D$4	

Figure 15.20 *Before dynamic spilled array formulas, stock portfolio return formulas were more difficult.*

You can try this example on the worksheet named Ch15(20).

Example 4: Using Array Formulas to Build More Compact Excel Solutions

In finance, when you analyze a portfolio of stocks, usually you are interested in finding the sum of all the individual contributions that the stocks make to the expected portfolio rate of return rather than viewing those individual contributions in the worksheet. Sometimes, you create a dynamic spilled array formula, as shown in cell G6 in Figure 15.21, and then you add the spilled results from the cells by using the SUM function in a second formula, as shown in cell G10. However, more often, you skip over that intermediate step and go straight to the formula, as shown in cell E10. With this formula, the array operation creates a resultant array that the SUM function uses to add to get the expected portfolio returns. This is called a *scalar array formula* because, although the formula contains array operations internally, the final aggregated answer is a scalar value. You can use a scalar array formula to create an Excel solution more compactly. When the intermediate steps are not needed, it is most efficient to create a single cell scalar array formula like the one in cell E10 in Figure 15.21.

You can try this example on the worksheet named Ch15(21).

E10	▾	:	× ✓	fx	=SUM(C6:C8*D4:E4*D6:E8)			
◢	A	B	C	D	E	F	G	H
2		Ex #4	**Goal:** Calculate the expected portfolio of stocks return.					
4		**Weight of Stock in Portfolio:**		0.6	0.4			
5		**Probability of Economic State**		**Stock A Full Estimated Return**	**Stock B Full Estimated Return**		Stock **A** Contribution to Portfolio	Stock **B** Contribution to Portfolio
6		Bad	0.5	0.0	-0.15		0	-0.03
7		OK	0.4	0.05	0.05		0.012	0.008
8		Great	0.1	0.1	0.2		0.006	0.008
10		Expected Portfolio Returns:			0.004		2-Step Formula:	0.004
12		Formula in cell E10:					Formula in cell G6:	
13		=SUM(C6:C8*D4:E4*D6:E8)					=C6:C8*D4:E4*D6:E8	
15							Formula in cell H10:	
16							=SUM(G6#)	

Figure 15.21 *Cell E10 contains a single-cell formula to find an expected portfolio's return.*

Examples 5 and 6: Using the SUMPRODUCT Function to Multiply Same-Size Arrays and Add the Resultant Array

The formula in cell E10 in Figure 15.21 takes three arrays with different dimensions, performs multiplication, and then adds the results. If your goal is to take arrays with the same dimensions, perform multiplication, and then add the results rather than use the multiplication operator and the SUM function, it can be more efficient to use the SUMPRODUCT function.

The SUMPRODUCT function is a unique aggregate function that can multiply same-sized arrays and then add the result to get an aggregated sum. As Microsoft succinctly describes it, this function "calculates the sum of the products of corresponding arrays." The arguments in the SUMPRODUCT function are *array1*, *array2*, *array3*, and so on, up to 255 arrays. The *array* arguments must all contain arrays with the same dimensions— for example, two columns, each with five rows, or two tables, each with five rows and three columns. If the dimensions of the arrays are not the same, SUMPRODUCT delivers a #VALUE! error.

For multiplying and then adding same-sized arrays, using the SUMPRODUCT function offers two advantages over using the SUM function and a direct multiplication operator:

- SUMPRODUCT tends to calculate more quickly on larger datasets. For example, as shown in Figure 15.22, if the goal is to create a single-cell formula to calculate total sales based on the Price column and the Units column, where Units times Price yields a sales amount, you can use the formula =SUM(C5:C100556*D5:D100556) or the formula =SUMPRODUCT(C5:C100556,D5:D100556). For this example, there are more than 100,000 rows of data. When I timed the two formulas, the SUMPRODUCT formula was about 10% faster. This alone is no big deal, but if you have many similar formulas in a workbook file, the formula calculation time savings can add up.

Note: When I have a choice between different methods of accomplishing a task, I tend to use the more efficient method—not because it yields tangible benefits in every case but because then I get in the good habit of always deploying the most efficient method. For this reason, I tend to use SUMPRODUCT when multiplying and then adding same-sized arrays.

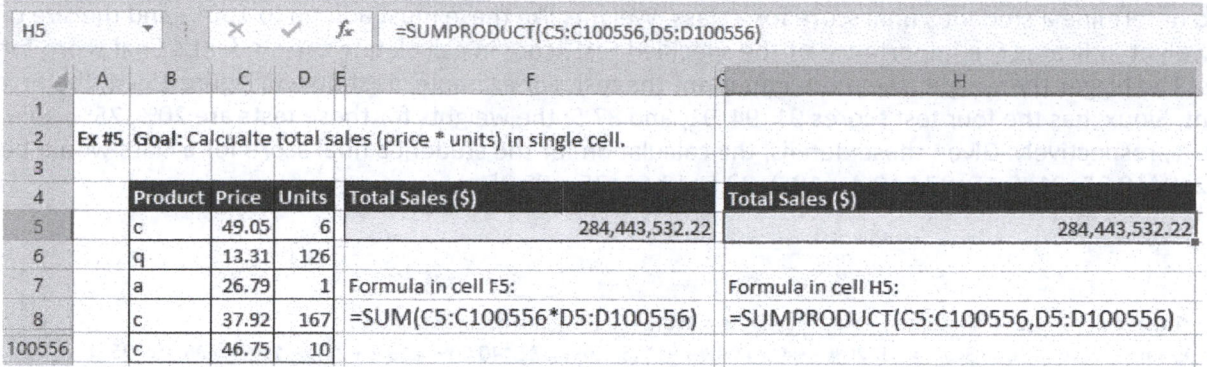

H5			× ✓ f_x	=SUMPRODUCT(C5:C100556,D5:D100556)			

	A	B	C	D	E	F	G	H
1								
2		Ex #5	Goal: Calcualte total sales (price * units) in single cell.					
3								
4			Product	Price	Units	Total Sales ($)		Total Sales ($)
5			c	49.05	6	284,443,532.22		284,443,532.22
6			q	13.31	126			
7			a	26.79	1	Formula in cell F5:		Formula in cell H5:
8			c	37.92	167	=SUM(C5:C100556*D5:D100556)		=SUMPRODUCT(C5:C100556,D5:D100556)
100556			c	46.75	10			

Figure 15.22 *Over large datasets, the SUMPRODUCT function is more efficient than the SUM function.*

- The SUMPRODUCT function and all other aggregate functions are programmed to ignore text values, whereas a direct math operation does not ignore text values and causes a formula error. Figure 15.23 shows a situation where missing prices are recorded as NA. In specific, cell C9 shows the text NA because the price for the Yanaki is not known. If your goal is to multiply the Price and Units columns and ignore records with text values, then the SUMPRODUCT function in cell H5 will work, but the SUM function with the direct array multiplication operator in cell F5 will not work. Even though the SUM function is programmed to ignore text values, it is the direct multiplication operator (which cannot ignore text) that causes the formula to yield an error.

H5			× ✓ f_x	=SUMPRODUCT(C5:C12,D5:D12)			

	A	B	C	D	E	F	G	H
1								
2		Ex #6	Goal: Calculate total sales (price * units) in single cell, have formula ignore text.					
3								
4			Product	Price	Units	Total Sales ($)		Total Sales ($)
5			Carlota	49.05	9	#VALUE!		1,529.64
6			Quad	13.31	7			
7			Aspen	26.79	10	Formula in cell F5:		Formula in cell H5:
8			Aspen	37.92	2	=SUM(C5:C12*D5:D12)		=SUMPRODUCT(C5:C12,D5:D12)
9			Yanaki	NA	2			
10			Carlota	40.37	5			
11			Quad	25.83	7			
12			Aspen	44.77	6			

Figure 15.23 *SUMPRODUCT is programmed to ignore text values. The multiplication operator cannot ignore text.*

You can try these two examples on the worksheets named Ch15(22) and Ch15(23).

Finally, if you look back at Figure 12.39 in Chapter 12, you will see another good reason to use the SUMPRODUCT function. In that example, the SUMPRODUCT function works with workbook references when a workbook is closed; the SUMIFS function cannot work with workbook references when a workbook is closed.

When you are multiplying arrays and then adding the results and the dimensions of the arrays are not the same, you should use the SUM function and a direct multiplication operator. When the dimensions of the arrays that you are multiplying and then adding are the same, you can use either method, but using SUMPRODUCT offers these benefits:

- It works efficiently with large datasets.
- It ignores text values.
- Workbook references do not yield errors when the source workbook file is closed.

Examples 7 Through 12: Using the SUMPRODUCT Function for Weighted Average Test Scores

As a final example of using the SUMPRODUCT function, let's look at how to use this function to calculate a weighted average. Weighted averages are common calculations in many fields. For example, in academia, you might want to calculate the weighted average of four tests that are given the weights 20%, 25%, 15%, and

40% to determine a student's final score for a class. Weights like these must add up to 100%, and the size of each weight indicates the importance of the specified test score in calculating the student's final score for a class. The bigger the weight, the more important the test. For example, as shown in Figure 15.24, the first student, Sioux, has the four test scores 91, 94, 91, and 87.5; the weights for these tests are 20%, 25%, 15%, and 40%, respectively. Given these details, the calculation for the student's final score for a class would be 91*0.2+94*0.25+91*0.15+87.5*0.4 = 18.2+23.5+13.65+35 = 90.35.

G8			✕	✓	fx	=SUMPRODUCT(C8:F8,$C$5:$F$5)						
	A	B	C	D	E	F	G	H	I	J	K

2	Ex	**Goal:** Multiply each test score by each test weight and then add to get student total score.									
3	#7	Example: Sioux's Total Score = 91*20% + 94*25.00% + 91*15.00% + 87.5*40.00% = 18.2 + 23.5 + 13.65 + 35 = 90.35									
5		Weights:	20%	25%	15%	40%					
7		Name	Test 1	Test 2	Test 3	Test 4	Weighted Average				
8		Sioux	91	94	91	87.5	90.35				
9		Chin	98	87.5	79	86	87.73				
10		Ty	73	36	56	78	63.20				
11		Mo	65	70	72	84	74.90				
13						Formula in cell G8: =SUMPRODUCT(C8:F8,$C$5:$F$5)					
15		Longhand formula: =C8*$C$5+D8*$D$5+E8*$E$5+F8*$F$5 = 90.35									

Figure 15.24 *SUMPRODUCT makes creating a weighted average formula easy.*

If the weights and tests scores are contained in ranges of cells with the same dimensions, you can use the formula =SUMPRODUCT(C8:F8,$C$5:$F$5), as shown in cell G8 in Figure 15.24. Because this is an aggregate formula, you need to be sure to lock the correct cell references and manually copy the formula down to the rows below. The SUMPRODUCT function takes the weights from the range C5:F5 (1R x 4C) and multiplies them by the test scores from the range C8:F8 (1R x 4C) and then adds to find the result. You could create the formula manually, like this:

=C8*$C$5+D8*$D$5+E8*$E$5+F8*$F$5

However, it would take a lot more time to create this formula, and you would need to pay careful attention to the tedious details of getting the multiplication and plus operators in the right places.

You can try this example on the worksheet named Ch15(24).

Matrix Multiplication Using the MMULT Array Function

At this point, you have learned two methods for multiplying arrays and then adding the results: using the SUM function with a direct multiplication operator and using the SUMPRODUCT function. However, there is a third method, and it involves matrix multiplication from linear algebra and the MMULT array function.

Wait a second. Linear algebra? This is a book about Excel! Well, in the second book I wrote (*Ctrl+Shift+Enter: Mastering Excel Array Formulas*), I had a whole chapter on the MMULT array function, including a section on solving systems of linear algebra equations. In this chapter, you will just look at a few practical business examples where the MMULT function can really make your Excel life a lot easier. The following three examples show how the MMULT array function can help you create more efficient formulas.

If you again consider the weighted average test scores example from Figure 15.24, but this time the range of cells for the weights does not have the same dimensions as the range of cells that contains the test scores, things get a little tricky. As shown in Figure 15.25, the test scores in the range C6:F6 have the dimensions 1 row by 4 columns, and the weights in the range C12:C15 have the dimensions 4 rows by 1 column. In this case, you can't use the SUMPRODUCT function because the arrays do not have the same dimensions; as shown in Figure 15.25, if you try to use SUMPRODUCT here, you get a #VALUE! error. If you try to make a direct array multiplication operation inside the SUM function, as shown in Figure 15.26, this will also not work because the resultant array contains 16 numbers, which is 12 too many. The 16-number result is due to the fact that with a direct array operation on a row and a column, the result is a table—in this case, (1R x 4C) * (4R x 1C) = (4R x 4C). As you can see in Figure 15.26, the totals are much too big.

	A	B	C	D	E	F	G	H	I	J
2	Ex	Goal: Multiply each test score by each test weight and then add to get student total score.								
3	#8	Example: Sioux's Total Score = 91*20% + 94*25% + 91*15% + 87.5*40% = 18.2 + 23.5 + 13.65 + 35 = 90.35								
5		Name	Test 1	Test 2	Test 3	Test 4	Weighted Average			
6		Sioux	91	94	91	87.5	=SUMPRODUCT(C6:F6,$C$12:$C$15)			
7		Chin	98	87.5	79	86	#VALUE!			
8		Ty	73	36	56	78	#VALUE!			
9		Mo	65	70	72	84	#VALUE!			
11		Test	Weights				Formula in cell G6: =SUMPRODUCT(C6:F6,$C$12:$C$15)			
12		Test 1	20%							
13		Test 2	25%							
14		Test 3	15%							
15		Test 4	40%							

Figure 15.25 *SUMPRODUCT does not work with arrays of different sizes.*

	A	B	C	D	E	F	G	H	I	J
2	Ex	Goal: Multiply each test score by each test weight and then add to get student total score.								
3	#9	Example: Sioux's Total Score = 91*20% + 94*25% + 91*15% + 87.5*40% = 18.2 + 23.5 + 13.65 + 35 = 90.35								
5		Name	Test 1	Test 2	Test 3	Test 4	Weighted Average			
6		Sioux	91	94	91	87.5	=SUM(C6:F6*C12:C15)			
7		Chin	98	87.5	79	86	280.40			
8		Ty	73	36	56	78	133.65			
9		Mo	65	70	72	84	116.40			
11		Test	Weights				Formula in cell G6: =SUM(C6:F6*C12:C15)			
12		Test 1	20%							
13		Test 2	25%							
14		Test 3	15%							
15		Test 4	40%							

Figure 15.26 *A direct array operation will not work because resultant array yields 16 elements rather than 4.*

As shown in Figure 15.27, you can create a longhand formula that gives you the correct answer, but creating the formula takes a long time and requires careful attention to many details, and you must manually copy it to the rows below.

	A	B	C	D	E	F	G	H	I	J
2	Ex	Goal: Multiply each test score by each test weight and then add to get student total score.								
3	#10	Example: Sioux's Total Score = 91*20% + 94*25% + 91*15% + 87.5*40% = 18.2 + 23.5 + 13.65 + 35 = 90.35								
5		Name	Test 1	Test 2	Test 3	Test 4	Weighted Average			
6		Sioux	91	94	91	87.5	=C6*$C$12+D6*$C$13+E6*$C$14+F6*$C$15			
7		Chin	98	87.5	79	86	87.73			
8		Ty	73	36	56	78	63.20			
9		Mo	65	70	72	84	74.90			
11		Test	Weights				Formula in cell G6: =C6*$C$12+D6*$C$13+E6*$C$14+F6*$C$15			
12		Test 1	20%							
13		Test 2	25%				Then manually copy down ↓			
14		Test 3	15%							
15		Test 4	40%							

Figure 15.27 *A longhand formula yields the correct answer, but it is difficult to create and must be manually copied.*

Figure 15.28 shows a spilled version of the longhand formula, but it also takes a long time to create. You can try this example on the worksheet named Ch15(28).

	A	B	C	D	E	F	G	H	I	J
2	Ex	Goal: Multiply each test score by each test weight and then add to get student total score.								
3	#11	Example: Sioux's Total Score = 91*20% + 94*25% + 91*15% + 87.5*40% = 18.2 + 23.5 + 13.65 + 35 = 90.35								
5		Name	Test 1	Test 2	Test 3	Test 4	Weighted Average			
6		Sioux	91	94	91	87.5	=C6:C9*C12+D6:D9*C13+E6:E9*C14+F6:F9*C15			
7		Chin	98	87.5	79	86	87.73			
8		Ty	73	36	56	78	63.20			
9		Mo	65	70	72	84	74.90			
11		Test	Weights		Formula in cell G6: =C6:C9*C12+D6:D9*C13+E6:E9*C14+F6:F9*C15					
12		Test 1	20%							
13		Test 2	25%		Spills down ⬇					
14		Test 3	15%							
15		Test 4	40%							

Figure 15.28 *This spilled longhand formula yields the correct answer, but it is difficult to create.*

In this case, the best solution is to use the MMULT array function formula, as shown in cell G6 in Figure 15.29, which is accurate and easy to create. Compared to the longhand formulas, the MMULT array function formula is a short formula that yields the correct answer and automatically spills the results down to the rows below. But how in the world does it work? What are the inner mechanics that make the MMULT array function calculate the correct spilled results? To understand this, you must learn about matrix multiplication.

	A	B	C	D	E	F	G	H	I	J
2	Ex	Goal: Multiply each test score by each test weight and then add to get student total score.								
3	#12	Example: Sioux's Total Score = 91*20% + 94*25% + 91*15% + 87.5*40% = 18.2 + 23.5 + 13.65 + 35 = 90.35								
5		Name	Test 1	Test 2	Test 3	Test 4	Weighted Average			
6		Sioux	91	94	91	87.5	=MMULT(C6:F9,C12:C15)			
7		Chin	98	87.5	79	86	87.73	MMULT(array1, array2)		
8		Ty	73	36	56	78	63.20			
9		Mo	65	70	72	84	74.90			
11		Test	Weights		Formula in cell G6: =MMULT(C6:F9,C12:C15)				2 arguments:	
12		Test 1	20%						**array1**	
13		Test 2	25%		Spills down ⬇				**array2**	
14		Test 3	15%							
15		Test 4	40%							

Figure 15.29 *This MMULT array function performs matrix multiplication to create a solution in the easiest way.*

You can try this example on the worksheet named Ch15(29).

The first M in the MMULT array function name stands for *matrix*, and the MULT in MMULT stands for *multiplication*. The MMULT array function has two arguments: *array1* and *array2*. To perform matrix multiplication on two arrays using the MMULT array function, these conditions must be met:

- Array 1 and array 2 can contain no empty cells.
- The number of columns in array 1 must be equal to the number of rows in the array 2.
- You must multiply each row from array 1 by each column in array 2 and the add the results.
- The dimensions of the desired spilled array must have the same number of rows as are in array 1 and the same number of columns as are in array 2.

Figure 15.30 shows how these four conditions apply to the weighted average student grade calculation from Figure 15.29. Here you can see that you need to have the same number of columns in array 1 as you have rows in array 2 because when you multiply the row by the column, you need to match up the elements for multiplication—and you can't do that if you don't have the same number of elements in the row as in the column.

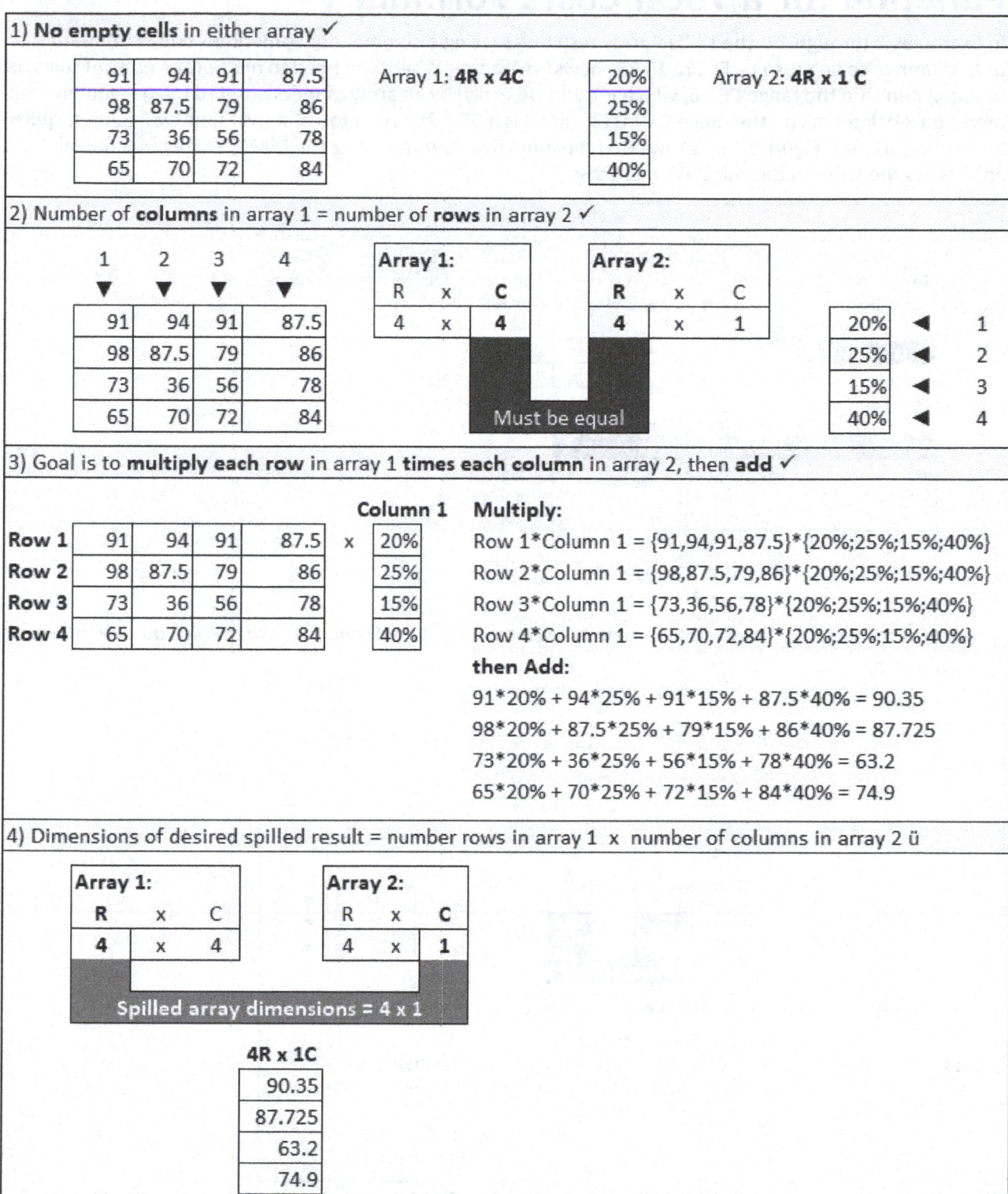

Figure 15.30 *Requisite conditions and process for the matrix multiplication weighted average grade example.*

Examples 13 and 14: Using the MMULT Array Function for a Total Costs Formula

In Examples 7 through 12, the spilled array result was a single column, but sometimes you want more than one column of spilled results. Figure 15.31 shows an example where you need to multiply an array of costs for baseball items (in the range C6:E6, which is a 1R x 3C array) by an array of units ordered by the women's and men's baseball teams (in the range C10:D12, which is a 3R x 2C array) to get a resultant two-column spilled array of total costs. Figure 15.32 shows that the four conditions for using the MMULT array function are met and shows the steps in the calculation process.

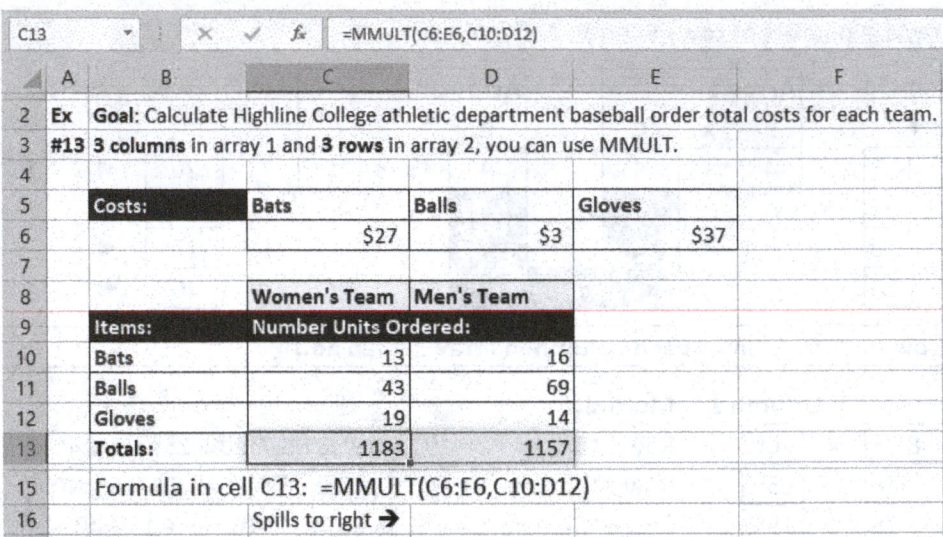

Figure 15.31 *The MMULT array function can be used to create an efficient formula to calculate the total costs for each team.*

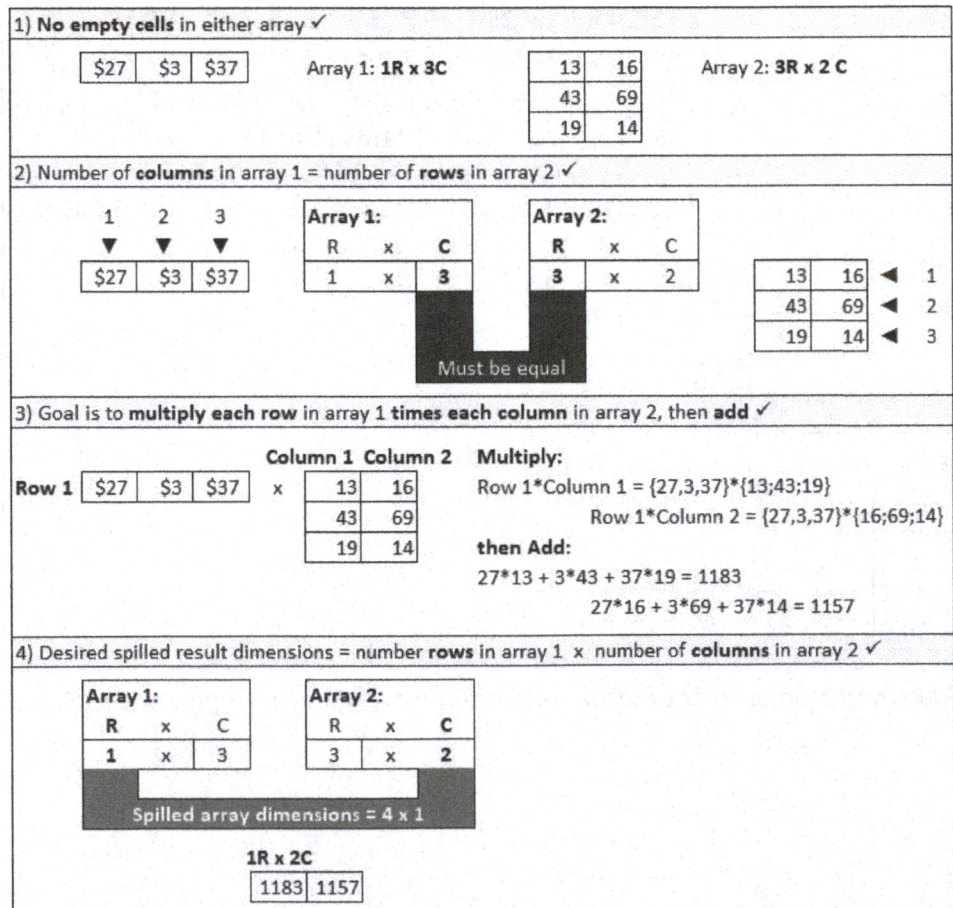

Figure 15.32 *Requisite conditions and process for the matrix multiplication total cost by category example.*

You can use the MMULT function for the solution shown in Figure 15.31 because of the orientation and layout of the arrays: You have the same number of columns in array 1 as you have rows in array 2. Figure 15.33 shows a different layout of the same arrays of numbers. In this example, because the number of columns in the first array of costs (one column) is not equivalent to the number of rows in the second array of units (three rows), you cannot use MMULT to spill the results. In this case, you would use the SUMPRODUCT function and enter the formula into cell D10 and then copy the formula to the right. However, if you want to spill the results with the layout shown in Figure 15.33, you can flip the vertical range of costs to a horizontal range by using the TRANSPOSE array function, as shown in cell D15.

	A	B	C	D	E	F
2	Ex	**Goal**: Calculate Highline College athletic department baseball order total costs for each team.				
3	#14	Parallel arrays, then you can use SUMPRODUCT, or TRANSPOSE and MMULT.				
5				**Women's Team**	**Men's Team**	
6		**Items:**	**Costs:**	**Number Units Ordered:**		
7		Bats	$27	13	16	
8		Balls	$3	43	69	
9		Gloves	$37	19	14	
10			**Totals:**	1183	1157	
12		Formula in cell D10: =SUMPRODUCT(D7:D9,$C$7:$C$9)				
13				Then manually copy to right →		
14		OR				
15			**Totals:**	1183	1157	
17		Formula in cell D15: =MMULT(TRANSPOSE(C7:C9),D7:E9)				
18				Spills to right →		

Figure 15.33 *The layout of the model determines what solutions are possible.*

You can try these two examples on the worksheets named Ch15(31) and Ch15(33).

Example 15: Using the MMULT Array Function to Spill Row Totals for a Table

In Chapter 8, you saw how to create row totals by using the aggregate function SUM. Figure 15.34 shows that with the SUM function, if you want totals in each row, you must enter the formula in the top cell and then copy the formula down to the rows below. If you want to spill aggregate row totals rather than manually copy the formula, as shown in Figure 15.35, you cannot simply highlight the whole table containing numbers because aggregate functions are programmed to deliver a single answer and cannot spill results.

	A	B	C	D	E	F	G	H	I
4		Name	Test 1	Test 2	Test 3	Test 4	Total Test Points		
5		Sioux	91	94	91	87.5	363.50	◄ =SUM(C5:F5)	
6		Chin	98	87.5	79	86	350.50	◄ =SUM(C6:F6)	
7		Ty	73	36	56	78	243.00	◄ =SUM(C7:F7)	
8		Mo	65	70	72	84	291.00	◄ =SUM(C8:F8)	
10					Formula in cell G5: =SUM(C5:F5)				
12					Then manually copy down ↓				

Figure 15.34 *An aggregate function cannot spill. You must enter a single formula and then copy to the rows below.*

	A	B	C	D	E	F	G
4		Name	Test 1	Test 2	Test 3	Test 4	Total Test Points
5		Sioux	91	94	91	87.5	=SUM(C5:F8)
6		Chin	98	87.5	79	86	
7		Ty	73	36	56	78	
8		Mo	65	70	72	84	

Figure 15.35 *If you try to make an aggregate calculation on all the numbers, the formula will not spill.*

If the need to spill aggregate row totals arises, you can use the MMULT array function to spill the correct row totals for each row in a table. However, to do this, you have to get a little tricky. Figure 15.36, which is repeated from Example 12 in this chapter (refer to Figure 15.29), shows the dimensions of array 1 and array 2 in the weighted average test score example. Array 1 has the dimensions 4R x 4C. Array 2 had the dimensions 4R x 1C. The arrays were the correct dimensions and gave you the correct weighted average score in Example 12. But what if, rather than have percentages that added up to 100%, you just put the number 1 in place of each weight? Figure 15.37 shows this scenario. With the array 2 column of 1 values, MMULT performs matrix multiplication, multiplying each number in the row by 1, and then adds to come up with the result. In order to determine how many 1s you need in the column, you simply count how many columns are in the array 1 table.

	A	B	C	D	E	F	G	H
2	Ex	Goal: Create a formula that can spill weighted average.						
3	#12	Example: Sioux's Total Score = 91*20% + 94*25% + 91*15% + 87.5*40% = 18.2 + 23.5 + 13.65 + 35 = 90.35						
5		Name	Test 1	Test 2	Test 3	Test 4	Weighted Average	
6		Sioux	91	94	91	87.5	=MMULT(C6:F9,C12:C15)	
7		Chin	98	87.5	79	86	87.73	MMULT(array1, array2)
8		Ty	73	36	56	78	63.20	
9		Mo	65	70	72	84	74.90	
11		Test	Weights		Formula in cell G6: =MMULT(C6:F9,C12:C15)			
12		Test 1	20%					
13		Test 2	25%		Spills down ↓			
14		Test 3	15%					
15		Test 4	40%					

Figure 15.36 *Looking back at Example 12, you can get an idea of how to spill row totals.*

G6	▼	:	✕ ✓ *fx*	=MMULT(C6:F9,C12:C15)				
	A	B	C	D	E	F	G	H
2	Ex	Goal: Create a formula that can spill row totals for each row in table.						
3	#15	Example: Sioux's Total Score = 91*1 + 94*1 + 91*1 + 87.5*1 = 91 + 94 + 91 + 87.5 = 363.5						
5		Name	Test 1	Test 2	Test 3	Test 4	Total Test Points	
6		Sioux	91	94	91	87.5	363.50	
7		Chin	98	87.5	79	86	350.50	
8		Ty	73	36	56	78	243.00	
9		Mo	65	70	72	84	291.00	
11		Test	Weights		Formula in cell G6: =MMULT(C6:F9,C12:C15)			
12		Test 1	1					
13		Test 2	1		Spills down ↓			
14		Test 3	1					
15		Test 4	1					

Figure 15.37 *A vertical array of 1s in the array2 argument of MMULT allows you to spill row totals.*

You can try this example on the worksheets named Ch15(36) and Ch15(37).

Technically, what you are doing here is inferring the dimensions of array 2. As shown in Figure 15.38, for the inference process, you use the number of columns from array 1 (4 columns) to determine the number of rows in array 2; then you use the number of columns from the known spilled array result (1 column) to determine the number of columns in array 2, to get the dimensions of array 2: 4R x 1C. Then you simply fill the cells with 1 values.

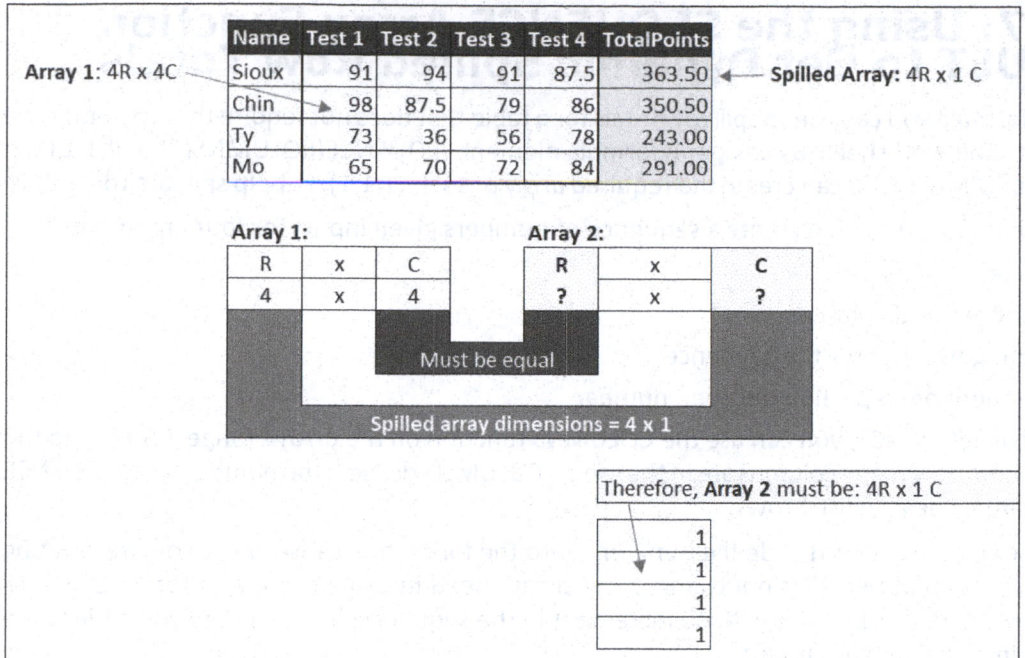

Figure 15.38 *You can infer the size of the array with 1 values.*

Example 16: Using MMULT to Find the Standard Deviation of Expected Portfolio Returns

Why go through the complications of using the MMULT function to spill row totals when using the SUM function and manually copying the formula is so easy? Most of the time, you can just use the SUM function and manually copy the results. However, in advanced array formulas in statistics and finance and other analytic fields, it is common to do this as an internal step within a larger array formula. In such cases, you need MMULT, which (unlike SUM) enables you to spill row totals. Figure 15.39 shows an example of using MMULT to calculate a column of row totals internally inside a larger financial stock portfolio example.

> **Note:** The financial and statistical mechanics of this formula are beyond the scope of this book; however, this formula is explained in Chapter 18 of my book *Ctrl+Shift+Enter: Mastering Excel Array Formulas*.

You can try this example on the worksheet named Ch15(39).

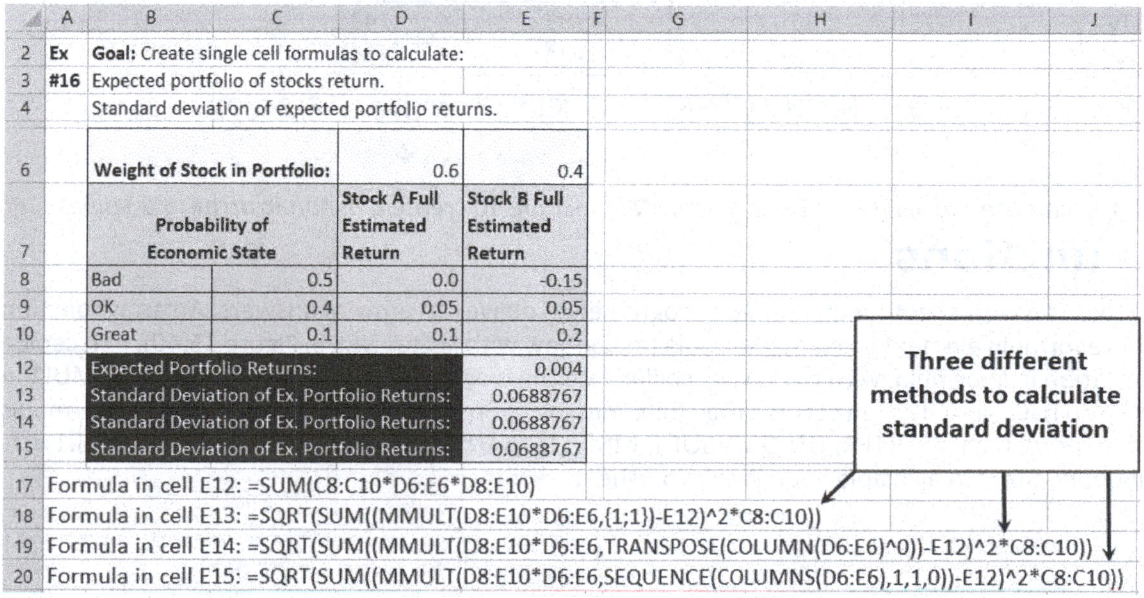

	A	B	C	D	E	F	G	H	I	J
2	Ex	**Goal:** Create single cell formulas to calculate:								
3	#16	Expected portfolio of stocks return.								
4		Standard deviation of expected portfolio returns.								
6		**Weight of Stock in Portfolio:**		0.6	0.4					
7		**Probability of Economic State**		**Stock A Full Estimated Return**	**Stock B Full Estimated Return**					
8		Bad	0.5	0.0	-0.15					
9		OK	0.4	0.05	0.05					
10		Great	0.1	0.1	0.2					
12		Expected Portfolio Returns:			0.004					
13		Standard Deviation of Ex. Portfolio Returns:			0.0688767					
14		Standard Deviation of Ex. Portfolio Returns:			0.0688767					
15		Standard Deviation of Ex. Portfolio Returns:			0.0688767					
17	Formula in cell E12: =SUM(C8:C10*D6:E6*D8:E10)									
18	Formula in cell E13: =SQRT(SUM((MMULT(D8:E10*D6:E6,{1;1})-E12)^2*C8:C10))									
19	Formula in cell E14: =SQRT(SUM((MMULT(D8:E10*D6:E6,TRANSPOSE(COLUMN(D6:E6)^0))-E12)^2*C8:C10))									
20	Formula in cell E15: =SQRT(SUM((MMULT(D8:E10*D6:E6,SEQUENCE(COLUMNS(D6:E6),1,1,0))-E12)^2*C8:C10))									

Three different methods to calculate standard deviation

Figure 15.39 *Using the MMULT array function to calculate a column of row totals as part of a larger financial stock portfolio formula.*

Example 17: Using the SEQUENCE Array Function Inside MMULT to Get Dynamic Spilled Row Totals

Figure 15.40 shows a formula you can use to spill row totals for a table that does not require that you enter the column of 1 values into the worksheet. By using the formula element SEQUENCE(COLUMNS(C5:F8),1,1,0) in the *array2* argument of MMULT, you can create the required array of 1s, {1;1;1;1}, to help spill the row totals.

SEQUENCE is an array function that can create a sequence of numbers given inputs for four arguments:

- *row*: The number of rows
- *columns*: The number of columns
- *start*: The starting number for the sequence
- *step*: The increment or step value between number

In the *rows* argument of SEQUENCE, you can use the COLUMNS function on the *array1* range, C5:F8, and the COLUMNS function counts how many columns are in the range. COLUMNS delivers the number 4 to SEQUENCE to instruct it to generate an array with 4 rows.

In the *columns* argument, you can hard code the number 1 into the formula because when you are creating a column of row totals, this number does not change: You always need just one column of totals. Similarly, because you will always need the 1 values with no increment in the sequence, you can hard code 1 into the *start* argument and 0 into the *step* argument.

The good thing about using the SEQUENCE formula element in the *array2* argument of MMULT is that if you insert a new column with a new test between the Test 1 column and the Test 4 column, the formula automatically updates with the correct row totals.

> **Note:** you will learn more about the SEQUENCE array function later in this chapter, in Examples 39 through 39.

You can try this example on the worksheet named Ch15(40).

G5	▼	:	×	✓	fx	=MMULT(C5:F8,SEQUENCE(COLUMNS(C5:F8),1,1,0))	

◢	A	B	C	D	E	F	G	H
2	**Ex #17**	**Goal:** Spill Row Totals using MMULT, SEQUENCE and COLUMNS functions.						
4		Name	Test 1	Test 2	Test 3	Test 4	Total Test Points	
5		Sioux	91	94	91	87.5	363.5	
6		Chin	98	87.5	79	86	350.5	
7		Ty	73	36	56	78	243	
8		Mo	65	70	72	84	291	
10		Formula in cell G5: =MMULT(C5:F8,SEQUENCE(COLUMNS(C5:F8),1,1,0))						
12							Spills down ⬇	

Figure 15.40 *You can use the SEQUENCE and COLUMNS functions to create a dynamic array of 1 values.*

Array Functions

An *array function* is a worksheet function that is programed to deliver an array of answers. An array function can be used as a formula element in a larger formula (as you saw with SEQUENCE in Figure 15.40), or it can be the final calculation in a formula, with the results spilled into the worksheet cells (as you saw with MMULT in Figure 15.40). You have already seen several array functions in action and completed some amazing formulas using array functions such as FILTER, UNIQUE, SORT, MMULT, TRANSPOSE, and SEQUENCE. Table 15.1 lists the array functions that are available in an Excel worksheet.

Table 15.1 The Array Functions Available in an Excel Worksheet

Array Function	Description
FILTER	Filters a dataset based on conditions and criteria that you specify in a Boolean array logical test.
RANDARRAY	Creates an array of random numbers based on a uniform distribution and lower and upper boundaries.
SEQUENCE	Generates a sequence of numbers in a row, a column, or a table, based on a start value and an increment value.
SORT	Sorts a row, a column, or a table in ascending or descending order.
SORTBY	Sorts an array by the values in one or more corresponding arrays.
UNIQUE	Creates a unique list of values or records.
TRANSPOSE	Converts a vertical array into a horizontal array or vice versa.
FREQUENCY	Counts how many values are in each category, given the upper limit for each category, and returns the counts in a vertical array.
MODE.MULT	Calculates the mode for a set of numbers, where the mode is the number that occurs most frequently. If there are multiple modes, MODE.MULT lists all modes in a vertical array.
TREND	Using the least-squares method for best-fitting data to a straight line, returns an array of y-values, given these formula inputs: known y-values, known x-values, and an array of x-values used to estimate the array of y-values.
LINEST	Returns a set of statistics for single or multiple regression, using the least-squares method for best fitting data to a straight line.
MMULT	Returns the matrix product of two arrays.
MUNIT	Returns the unit matrix, given a single number.
MINVERSE	Returns the inverse matrix, given a matrix.
GROWTH	Calculates predicted exponential growth by using existing data. GROWTH returns the y-values for a series of new x-values that you specify by using existing x-values and y-values. You can also use the GROWTH worksheet function to fit an exponential curve to existing x-values and y-values.
LOGEST	In regression analysis, calculates an exponential curve that fits the data and returns an array of values that describes the curve.

Note: Look for these new array functions that should be out by the time this book is printed: VSTACK, HSTACK, CHOOSEROWS, CHOOSECOLS, TOCOL, TOROW, and VECTORWRAP.

Examples 18 Through 23: Using the FILTER Array Function with Different Logical Tests in the *include* Argument

You have already seen the full spectrum of uses for the FILTER array function. Here is a list of the examples you have already seen:

Function or Feature	What the Formula Does	Chapter and Example
FILTER	Looking up the records for Quad	Chapter 1, Figure 1.8
FILTER	Looking up a list of student classes	Chapter 12, Example 11
FILTER and defined names	Extracting records from an Excel Table	Chapter 12, Example 16
FILTER and Boolean AND logical test	Filtering a dataset	Chapter 13, Example 27
FILTER and Boolean OR logical test	Filtering a dataset	Chapter 13, Example 28
XMATCH and other functions	Comparing two lists and extracting results	Chapter 13, Example 29

OR logical test	Running aggregate operations on a single column	Chapter 13, Example 35
OR logical test	Running aggregate operations on two columns	Chapter 13, Example 37
FILTER and one lookup value	Returning multiple records	Chapter 14, Example 20
FILTER and two lookup values	Returning multiple records	Chapter 14, Example 21

I encourage you to go back and review what you have already learned. However, because FILTER is one of the most important and versatile functions, this section reviews, summarizes, and provides all the technical details of the FILTER array function.

The FILTER array function filters a dataset based on conditions and criteria that you specify in a Boolean array logical test to deliver a resultant array of answers. (For a review of Boolean array logical tests, see Chapter 13.) The FILTER array function has the following syntax (see Figure 15.41):

```
FILTER(array, include, [if_empty])
```

The arguments of the FILTER function are as follows:

- **array**: This argument contains the table, column, or row that you want to filter.
- **include**: This argument contains a Boolean array logical test that indicates which items to include and which items to not include in the resultant array of answers. This array must have the same number of rows or columns as the array that is being filtered.
- **[if_empty]**: This argument contains the value you want the formula to return when the result of the filter is an empty filter (that is, with no records). Here are two examples.
    - Single-cell message: =FILTER(B5:D11,(B5:B11=F5)*(C5:C11=F8),"NA")
    - Three-column message: =FILTER(B5:D11,(B5:B11=F5)*(C5:C11=F8),{"None,"-","-"})

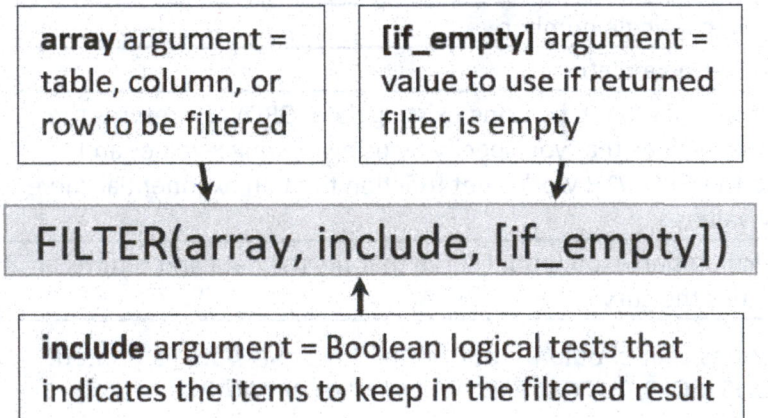

Figure 15.41 *Arguments in the FILTER array function.*

A Boolean array logical test must evaluate to an array of TRUE, FALSE, or number values. If there are other values in the logical test resultant array, such as text values or errors, the FILTER function delivers a #VALUE! error. A TRUE value or any nonzero number means that the item should be included in the filtered array of answers. A FALSE value or zero means that the item should not be included in the filtered array of answers. Consider these examples:

- =FILTER({"Q";"C";"Q";"A"},{TRUE;FALSE;TRUE;FALSE}) = {"Q";"Q"}
- =FILTER({"Q";"C";"Q";"A"},{1;0;1;0}) = {"Q";"Q"}
- =FILTER({"Q";"C";"Q";"A"},{43;0;-2;0}) = {"Q";"Q"}
- =FILTER({"Q";"C";"Q";"A"},{TRUE;0;-2;0}) = {"Q";"Q"}
- =FILTER({"Q";"C";"Q";"A"},{TRUE;"";-2;"Text"}) = #VALUE!

If you are filtering by rows, a Boolean array logical test must contain a single column that contains the same number of rows as there are in the item being filtered in the *array* argument. If the numbers of rows in the *array* and *include* arguments are not equivalent, the result is a #VALUE! error. Consider these examples:

- =FILTER({"Q";"C";"Q";"A"},{TRUE;FALSE;TRUE;FALSE}) = {"Q";"Q"}
- =FILTER({"Q";"C";"Q";"A"},{TRUE;FALSE;TRUE}) = #VALUE!

If you are filtering by columns, a Boolean array logical test must contain a single row that contains the same number of columns as there are in the item being filtered in the *array* argument. If the number of columns in the array and *include* arguments are not equivalent, the result is a #VALUE! error. Consider these examples:

- =FILTER({"Q","C","Q","A"},{TRUE,FALSE,TRUE,FALSE}) = {"Q","Q"}
- =FILTER({"Q","C","Q","A"},{TRUE,FALSE,TRUE}) = #VALUE!

A Boolean array logical tests can involve any of the logical tests that you learned about in Chapter 13, such as a single-condition logical test, an AND logical test, an OR logical test, a NOT logical test, a logical test based on numbers, and a logical test that compares two lists. Consider these examples:

- Single-condition logical test: =FILTER(B5:D11,B5:B11=F5)
- **AND logical test using multiplication:** =FILTER(B5:D11,(B5:B11=F5)*(C5:C11=F8))
- **OR logical test using addition:** =FILTER(B5:D11,(B5:B11=F5)+(C5:C11=F8))
- **NOT logical test:** =FILTER(B5:D11,B5:B11<>F5)
- Test to filter out rows with no numbers: =FILTER(B5:D11,D5:D11)
- **Test to get items in two lists:** =FILTER(B5:F11,ISNUMBER(XMATCH(B4:F4,H4:I4)))

In Chapter 8, you learned a little about the filter feature that is available in the Data tab in the Ribbon. (You will learn more about this feature in Chapter 16.) Although the filter feature is easier to use than the FILTER function, the results from the filter feature do not instantly update when source data changes. Because the FILTER array function is used in worksheet formulas, if the source data or any of the formula inputs change, the results from the FILTER function update instantly. If you want a quick and easy filtered dataset, you can use the filter feature. If you want a dynamic solution that updates when inputs change, you should use the FILTER array function.

Figure 15.42 shows an example of a single-condition logical test, where the Boolean array logical test evaluates to an array of TRUE and FALSE values. The filtered result spills into the worksheet cells. If you change the product name in cell F5, the filter results automatically update.

	A	B	C	D	E	F	G	H	I	J	K
2		**Ex #18**	**Goal**: Extract "Quad" product records.								
4		Product	Color	Sales		Product		Product	Color	Sales	
5		Quad	Blue	326.17		Quad		Quad	Blue	326.17	
6		Carlota	Red	251.57				Quad	Blue	374.03	
7		Quad	Blue	374.03				Quad	Clear	236.06	
8		Aspen	Red	256.22							
9		Aspen	Blue	171.21							
10		Carlota	Red	446.2		Formula in cell H5: =FILTER(B5:D11,B5:B11=F5)					
11		Quad	Clear	236.06		Spills down ⬇					
12											
13		Steps for calculation of **=FILTER(B5:D11,B5:B11=F5)**									
14		**1.** Which row in the product column is a "Quad"?									
15		=FILTER(B5:D11,B5:B11="Quad")									
16		**2.** The single condition Boolean test evaluates to TRUEs and FALSEs.									
17		=FILTER(B5:D11,{**TRUE**;FALSE;**TRUE**;FALSE;FALSE;FALSE;**TRUE**})									
18		**3.** TRUE indicates that the row must be returned in the resultant array of answers.									

Figure 15.42 *The include argument contains a single-condition logical test. TRUE and FALSE values filter the dataset.*

You can try this example on the worksheet named Ch15(42).

Figure 15.43 shows an example of an AND logical test, where the Boolean array logical test evaluates to an array of 1s and 0s. The filtered result spills into the worksheet cells. If you change the product name in cell F5 to Aspen and the color name in cell F8 to Clear, the filter results automatically update to show NA (not available), which is the value from the [*if_empty*] argument.

	A	B	C	D	E	F	G	H	I	J	K
2	Ex	Goal: Extract records that contain the product "Quad" AND the color "Blue".									
4	#19	Product	Color	Sales		Product		Product	Color	Sales	
5		Quad	Blue	326.17		Quad		Quad	Blue	326.17	
6		Carlota	Red	251.57				Quad	Blue	374.03	
7		Quad	Blue	374.03		Color					
8		Aspen	Red	256.22		Blue					
9		Aspen	Blue	171.21							
10		Carlota	Red	446.2		Formula in cell H5: =FILTER(B5:D11,(B5:B11=F5)*(C5:C11=F8),"NA")					
11		Quad	Clear	236.06		Spills down ⬇					
12											
13		Steps for calculation of =FILTER(B5:D11,(B5:B11=F5)*(C5:C11=F8),"NA")									
14		**1.** Which row in the product column has a "Quad"? Which row in the color column has a "Blue"?									
15		=FILTER(B5:D11,(B5:B11="Quad")*(C5:C11="Blue"),"NA")									
16		**2.** A TRUE in the first array and a TRUE in the corresponding position in the second array indicates that									
17		the record meets both conditions and should be included in the result.									
18		=FILTER(B5:D11,{**TRUE**;FALSE;**TRUE**;FALSE;FALSE;FALSE;**TRUE**}*{**TRUE**;FALSE;**TRUE**;FALSE;TRUE;FALSE;FALSE})									
19		=FILTER(B5:D11,{**TRUE*TRUE**;FALSE*FALSE;**TRUE*TRUE**;FALSE*FALSE;FALSE*TRUE;FALSE*FALSE;TRUE*FALSE})									
20		=FILTER(B5:D11,{**1**;0;**1**;0;0;0;0})									
21		**3.** Multiplication yields a one when both conditions are met.									
22		=FILTER(B5:D11,{1;0;1;0;0;0;0})									
23		**4.** 1 indicates that the row must be returned in the resultant array of answers.									

Figure 15.43 *The include argument contains an AND logical test. 1s and 0s filter the dataset.*

You can try this example on the worksheet named Ch15(43).

Figure 15.44 shows an example of a OR logical test, where the Boolean array logical test evaluates to an array of 1s, 2s, and 0s. A 0 value indicates that neither condition was met, a 1 value indicates that one of the conditions was met, and a 2 value indicates that both conditions were met. With an OR logical test, it is not important which test was met or whether both tests were met. All that matters is that at least one test was met. Because the worksheet calculation engine recognizes any nonzero number as TRUE, all rows with a 1 or a 2 are returned in the resultant array of answers. The filtered result spills into the worksheet cells.

	A	B	C	D	E	F	G	H	I	J	K
2	Ex	Goal: Extract records that contain the product "Quad" OR the color "Blue".									
4	#20	Product	Color	Sales		Product		Product	Color	Sales	
5		Quad	Blue	326.17		Quad		Quad	Blue	326.17	
6		Carlota	Red	251.57				Quad	Blue	374.03	
7		Quad	Blue	374.03		Color		Aspen	Blue	171.21	
8		Aspen	Red	256.22		Blue		Quad	Clear	236.06	
9		Aspen	Blue	171.21							
10		Carlota	Red	446.2		Formula in cell H5: =FILTER(B5:D11,(B5:B11=F5)+(C5:C11=F8))					
11		Quad	Clear	236.06		Spills down ⬇					
12											
13		Steps for calculation of **=FILTER(B5:D11,(B5:B11=F5)+(C5:C11=F8))**									
14		**1.** Which row in the product column has a "Quad"? Which row in the color column has a "Blue"?									
15		=FILTER(B5:D11,(B5:B11="Quad")+(C5:C11="Blue"))									
16		**2.** A TRUE in the first array or a TRUE in the second array indicates that record should be included in result.									
17		=FILTER(B5:D11,{**TRUE**;FALSE;**TRUE**;FALSE;FALSE;FALSE;**TRUE**}+{**TRUE**;FALSE;**TRUE**;FALSE;**TRUE**;FALSE;FALSE})									
18		=FILTER(B5:D11,{**TRUE+TRUE**;FALSE+FALSE;**TRUE+TRUE**;FALSE+FALSE;FALSE+TRUE;FALSE+FALSE;**TRUE+FALSE**})									
19		=FILTER(B5:D11,{**2**;0;**2**;0;**1**;0;**1**})									
20		**3.** Addition yields a one if one of the conditions is met and a two if both conditions are met.									
21		=FILTER(B5:D11,{**2**;0;**2**;0;**1**;0;**1**})									
22		**4.** 1 or 2 indicates that the row must be returned in the resultant array of answers.									

Figure 15.44 *The include argument contains an OR logical test where 1s, 2s, and 0s filter the dataset.*

You can try this example on the worksheet named Ch15(44).

Figure 15.45 shows an example of a NOT logical test, where the Boolean array logical test evaluates to an array of TRUE and FALSE values.

	A	B	C	D	E	F	G	H	I	J	K
2		Ex #21 Goal: Extract records where the product is NOT "Quad".									
4		Product	Color	Sales		Product		Product	Color	Sales	
5		Quad	Blue	326.17		Quad		Carlota	Red	251.57	
6		Carlota	Red	251.57				Aspen	Red	256.22	
7		Quad	Blue	374.03				Aspen	Blue	171.21	
8		Aspen	Red	256.22				Carlota	Red	446.2	
9		Aspen	Blue	171.21							
10		Carlota	Red	446.2		Formula in cell H5: =FILTER(B5:D11,B5:B11<>F5)					
11		Quad	Clear	236.06		Spills down ↓					
12											
13		Steps for calculation of =FILTER(B5:D11,B5:B11<>F5)									
14		1. Which row in the product column is NOT a "Quad"?									
15		=FILTER(B5:D11,B5:B11<>"Quad")									
16		2. The single condition Boolean test evaluates to TRUEs and FALSEs.									
17		=FILTER(B5:D11,{FALSE;TRUE;FALSE;TRUE;TRUE;TRUE;FALSE})									
18		3. TRUE indicates that the row must be returned in the resultant array of answers.									

Figure 15.45 *The include argument contains a NOT logical test where TRUE and FALSE values filter the dataset.*

You can try this example on the worksheet named Ch15(45).

In the example in Figure 15.46, the goal is to filter out records where a sales number was not entered. Because Excel interprets any nonzero number as TRUE and empty cells as 0 values, you can simply place the Sales column in the *include* argument as the Boolean array logical test. The Sales column in the range D5:D11 evaluates to the resultant array {326.17;0;0;0;171.21;0;236.06} and achieves the filter goal perfectly.

	A	B	C	D	E	F	G	H	I	J	K
2		Ex	Goal: Filter out records where no sale is entered.								
4	#22	Product	Color	Sales		Product		Product	Color	Sales	
5		Quad	Blue	326.17		Quad		Quad	Blue	326.17	
6		Carlota	Red					Aspen	Blue	171.21	
7		Quad	Blue					Quad	Clear	236.06	
8		Aspen	Red								
9		Aspen	Blue	171.21							
10		Carlota	Red			Formula in cell H5: =FILTER(B5:D11,D5:D11)					
11		Quad	Clear	236.06		Spills down ↓					
12											
13		Steps for calculation of =FILTER(B5:D11,D5:D11)									
14		1. Which row in the sales column has a number?									
15		=FILTER(B5:D11,{**326.17**;0;0;0;**171.21**;0;**236.06**})									
16		2. Any non-zero number indicates that the row must be returned in the resultant array of answers.									

Figure 15.46 *The include argument contains a column of numbers and empty cells.*

You can try this example on the worksheet named Ch15(46).

In the example shown in Figure 15.47, the goal is to filter by columns and show only the Product and Sales columns. In the *include* argument of FILTER, you can use the XMATCH and ISNUMBER functions together to check whether the field names in the dataset match either of the specified field names in the range H4:I4. (For a reminder of how to use the XMATCH and ISNUMBER functions to compare two lists, see Example 29 in Chapter 13.) When you use the XMATCH and ISNUMBER functions, if you change the names of the fields in the range H4:I4, Excel updates the filtered result by filtering to get the new columns. If you want to hard code the column selection into the formula, you can use this less complicated formula:

```
=FILTER(B5:F11,{0,1,0,0,1})
```

	A	B	C	D	E	F	G	H	I	J
2	Ex	**Goal:** Filter data set to show only the "Product" and "Sales" columns.								
4	**#23**	Sales Rep	Product	Color	Date	Sales		Product	Sales	
5		Sioux	Quad	Blue	12/2/20	326.17		Quad	326.17	
6		Chantel	Carlota	Red	12/2/20	251.57		Carlota	251.57	
7		Chin	Quad	Blue	12/2/20	374.03		Quad	374.03	
8		Chantel	Aspen	Red	12/2/20	256.22		Aspen	256.22	
9		Chin	Aspen	Blue	12/2/20	171.21		Aspen	171.21	
10		Sioux	Carlota	Red	12/2/20	446.2		Carlota	446.2	
11		Sioux	Quad	Clear	12/2/20	236.06		Quad	236.06	
13		Formula in cell H5: =FILTER(B5:F11,ISNUMBER(XMATCH(B4:F4,H4:I4)))								
14		Spills down ⬇								
15										
16		Steps for calculation of **=FILTER(B5:F11,ISNUMBER(XMATCH(B4:F4,H4:I4)))**								
17		**1.** XMATCH looks up the table field names within range H4:I4 to determine the relative position of 1 or 2.								
18		=FILTER(B5:F11,ISNUMBER(XMATCH({"Sales Rep","Product","Color","Date","Sales"},{"Product","Sales"})))								
19		**2.** XMATCH returns #N/A when field name not found and relative position when field name is found.								
20		=FILTER(B5:F11,ISNUMBER({#N/A,**1**,#N/A,#N/A,**2**}))								
21		**3.** ISNUMBER converts numbers to TRUE and all other data types to FALSE.								
22		=FILTER(B5:F11,{FALSE,**TRUE**,FALSE,FALSE,**TRUE**})								
23		**4.** TRUE indicates that the column must be returned in the resultant array of answers.								

Figure 15.47 *The include argument contains the XMATCH and ISNUMBER functions to dynamically filter by columns.*

You can try this example on the worksheet named Ch15(47).

Examples 24 Through 28: Using the UNIQUE Array Function in Different Ways

You have already used the UNIQUE function several times in this book, but in each case, you only used the first argument in the function. Now you will see how to use all three arguments.

The UNIQUE array function can deliver either a distinct set of items or a unique set of items from a table, a column, or a row:

- A *distinct* set of items has all duplicates in the set removed, leaving only one of each item.
- A *unique* set of items lists only items that occur exactly one time in the dataset.

The UNIQUE function has the following syntax (see Figure 15.48):

```
UNIQUE(array, [by_col], [exactly_once])
```

The arguments of the UNIQUE function are as follows:

- **array:** This argument contains the table, column, or row that you want to filter:
  - When you provide a table, the function generates a unique/distinct set of records.
  - When you provide a column, the function generates a unique/distinct list of items in a column.
  - When you provide a row, the function generates a unique/distinct list of items in a row.

- **[by_col]**: This argument can take one of two possible values:
  - TRUE or 1: Returns all unique/distinct columns from the array.
  - FALSE or omitted or 0: Returns all unique/distinct rows from the array. This the default.
- **[exactly_once]**: This argument can take one of two possible values:
  - TRUE or 1: Returns a unique set (that is, returns only return rows or columns that appear exactly once in the array).
  - FALSE or 0 or omitted: Returns a distinct set (that is, returns every distinct row or column in the array), much like the Remove Duplicates feature. This the default.

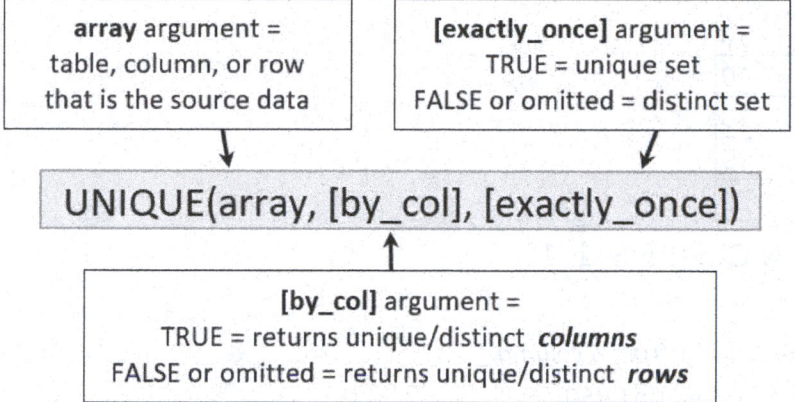

Figure 15.48 *Arguments of the UNIQUE array function.*

The most common use of the UNIQUE array function is to create a distinct list from a column. However, when people say "I want unique list," they typically mean they want a distinct list with duplicates removed and showing just one of each item. This is a less common way to use the UNIQUE function.

Figure 15.49 shows an example of creating a distinct list of sales rep names, where the UNIQUE function removes all duplicates and spills one of each sale rep name. You can enter the Sales Rep column, B5:B11, into the first argument, and then because the goal is to extract all distinct rows, you accept the defaults for the second and third arguments.

	A	B	C	D	E	F
2	**Ex #24**	**Goal:** Extract a distinct list of sales rep names.				
4		Sales Rep	Product	Sales		Sales Rep
5		Sioux	Quad	10		Sioux
6		Chantel	Carlota	20		Chantel
7		Chin	Quad	30		Chin
8		Chantel	Carlota	10		Dino
9		Chantel	Quad	30		
10		Sioux	Carlota	10		
11		Dino	Quad	20		
13		Formula in cell F5: =UNIQUE(B5:B11)				
14		Spills down ⬇				

Figure 15.49 *Using UNIQUE to return a distinct list from a column. In everyday language, this is a "unique list."*
You can try this example on the worksheet named Ch15(49).

Figure 15.50 shows how to create a unique list of sales rep names. You can enter the Sales Rep column, B5:B11, into the first argument, omit the second argument, and put a 1 value (or TRUE) into the third argument to instruct the UNIQUE function to deliver a list of sales rep names that occur exactly one time.

◢	A	B	C	D	E	F
2	Ex #25	Goal: Extract a unique list of sales rep names.				
4		Sales Rep	Product	Sales		Sales Rep
5		Sioux	Quad	10		Chin
6		Chantel	Carlota	20		Dino
7		Chin	Quad	30		
8		Chantel	Carlota	10		
9		Chantel	Quad	30		
10		Sioux	Carlota	10		
11		Dino	Quad	20		
13		Formula in cell F5: =UNIQUE(B5:B11,,1)				
14		Spills down ⬇				

Figure 15.50 *Using UNIQUE to return a unique list from a column.*

You can try this example on the worksheet named Ch15(50).

Figure 15.51 shows that if you enter a table into the first argument of the UNIQUE array function and accept the defaults for the second and third arguments, the result is a table with a distinct set of records or rows.

◢	A	B	C	D	E	F	G	H
2	Ex #26	Goal: Extract a distinct list of records (distinct rows).						
4		Sales Rep	Product	Sales		Sales Rep	Product	Sales
5		Sioux	Quad	100		Sioux	Quad	100
6		Chantel	Carlota	200		Chantel	Carlota	200
7		Chantel	Carlota	200		Chantel	Quad	100
8		Chantel	Carlota	200				
9		Chantel	Quad	100				
10		Sioux	Quad	100				
11		Sioux	Quad	100				
13		Formula in cell F5: =UNIQUE(B5:D11)						
14		Spills down ⬇						

Figure 15.51 *Using UNIQUE to return a distinct set of records from a table.*

You can try this example on the worksheet named Ch15(51).

Figure 15.52 shows that if you place a row of names into the first argument of the UNIQUE function and use a 1 value (or TRUE) in the second argument, Excel delivers a unique list of names from the row (or a unique list of items from the columns).

◢	A	B	C	D	E	F	G	H	I
2	Ex #27	Goal: Extract a distinct list of names from a row.							
3									
4		Sales Rep	Sioux	Chantel	Chin	Chantel	Chantel	Sioux	Dino
5									
6		Sales Rep	Sioux	Chantel	Chin	Dino			
7									
8		Formula in cell C6: =UNIQUE(C4:I4,1)							
9		Spills to right ➡							

Figure 15.52 *Using UNIQUE to return a distinct list from a row.*

You can try this example on the worksheet named Ch15(52).

Finally, one of the most revolutionary uses for the UNIQUE function is to create a dynamic set of distinct criteria for either the SUMIFS function or the COUNTIFS function. Figure 15.53 shows the spilled range reference F5# in the *criteria1* argument of SUMIFS and the spilled range reference I5# in the *criteria1* argument of COUNTIFS. In each case, the *criteria1* argument is pointing to a cell that contains the spilled product name results of the UNIQUE array function. The revolutionary aspect of this is that if you add to an Excel Table a new record with a new product name, the UNIQUE array function will spill new results, and both the SUMIFS and COUNTIFS functions will spill new results as well.

	A	B	C	D	E	F	G	H	I	J
2		Ex #28 Goal: Create two reports: 1) product sales report, and, 2) product count (frequency distribution) report.								
4		Sales Rep	Product	Sales		Product	Total Sales		Product	Count (Frequency)
5		Sioux	Quad	10		Quad	90		Quad	4
6		Chantel	Carlota	20		Carlota	40		Carlota	3
7		Chin	Quad	30						
8		Chantel	Carlota	10		Formula in cell F5: =UNIQUE(st[Product])				
9		Chantel	Quad	30		Formula in cell G5: =SUMIFS(st[Sales],st[Product],F5#)				
10		Sioux	Carlota	10		Both spill down ↓				
11		Dino	Quad	20						
12						Formula in cell I5: =UNIQUE(st[Product])				
13						Formula in cell J5: =COUNTIFS(st[Product],I5#)				
14						Both spill down ↓				

Figure 15.53 *The UNIQUE array function has revolutionized how SUMIFS and COUNTIFS are used.*

You can try this example on the worksheet named Ch15(53).

Examples 29 Through 33: Using the SORT Array Function in Different Ways

You have already used the SORT function several times in this book, but in each case, you only used the first argument of the function. Now you will see how to use all four arguments.

The SORT array function can sort a row, a column, or a table in ascending or descending order. It can also sort by more than one column. The SORT function has the following syntax (see Figure 15.54):

```
SORT(array, [sort_index], [sort_order], [by_col])
```

The arguments of the SORT function are as follows:

- ***array***: This argument contains the table, column, or row that is the source data.
- **[*sort_index*]**: You use this argument when you have more than two columns or rows and you want to specify which column or row should be used for sorting. This argument indicates the relative position of the column or columns that you want to sort by. When this argument is omitted, if you are sorting a table by rows, the first column in the table is used to sort the records; if you are sorting a table by columns, the first row in the table is used to sort the records. Consider these examples:
  - Sort by column 2: =SORT(D5:E10,2)
  - Sort by column 1 and then by column 3: =SORT(C5:E10,{1,3})
- **[*sort_order*]**: This argument can take the following values:
  - 1 or omitted: A–Z, or smallest-to-largest, sort. This is the default.
  - -1: Z–A, or largest-to-smallest, sort.

  If you want to sort two or more columns, each with a different sort, use array syntax, such as =SORT(C5:E10,{3,1},{1,-1}), where column 3 gets an A–Z sort and column 1 gets a Z–A sort.
- **[*by_col*]**: This argument can take one of two values:
  - TRUE: Sort by columns. Use this option when you are sorting a row of values.
  - FALSE or omitted: Sort by rows. Use this option when you are sorting a column. This is the default.

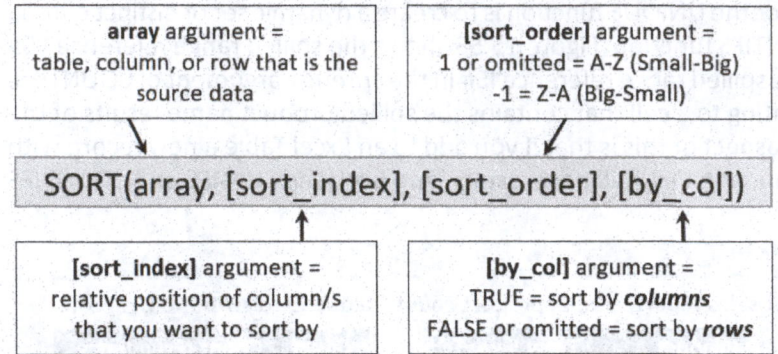

Figure 15.54 *Arguments in the SORT array function.*

Figure 15.55 shows how to sort a column into a distinct list from A to Z. The UNIQUE array function result is placed into the first argument of SORT, and the defaults for the last three arguments are accepted. When you omit the last three arguments, the function sorts the single column A–Z.

	A	B	C	D	E	F	G
2		**Ex #29**	**Goal:** Sort the column distinct list A-Z.				
4		Sales Rep	Sales Rep				
5		Sioux	Chantel				
6		Chantel	Chin				
7		Chin	Dino				
8		Chantel	Sioux				
9		Chantel					
10		Sioux					
11		Dino					
13		Formula in cell D5: =SORT(UNIQUE(B5:B11))					
14		Spills down ⬇					

Figure 15.55 *Using SORT to sort a column A–Z.*

You can try this example on the worksheet named Ch15(55).

Figure 15.56 shows how to sort a column into a distinct list from Z to A. The first argument contains the distinct list. The second argument is left empty because you have only one column and do not need to specify which column to sort. You use a -1 in the third argument to specify that you want to sort Z–A.

	A	B	C	D	E	F	G
2		**Ex #30**	**Goal:** Sort the column distinct list Z-A.				
4		Sales Rep	Sales Rep				
5		Sioux	Sioux				
6		Chantel	Dino				
7		Chin	Chin				
8		Chantel	Chantel				
9		Chantel					
10		Sioux					
11		Dino					
13		Formula in cell D5: =SORT(UNIQUE(B5:B11),,-1)					
14		Spills down ⬇					

Figure 15.56 *Using SORT to sort a column Z–A.*

You can try this example on the worksheet named Ch15(56).

Figure 15.57 shows how to sort a row into a distinct list from A to Z. The first argument contains the distinct list. The second argument is left empty because you have only one row and do not need to specify which row to sort. The third argument is left empty to accept the A–Z default setting. You use a 1 in the fourth argument to specify that you want to sort the columns within the row of names.

	A	B	C	D	E	F	G	H	I
2		Ex #31	**Goal:** Sort the row distinct list A-Z.						
4			**Sales Rep**	Sioux		Chantel	Chin	Chantel	Chantel	Sioux	Dino
5										
6			**Sales Rep**	Chantel	Chin		Dino	Sioux		
8			Formula in cell C6: =SORT(UNIQUE(C4:I4,1),,,1)							
9			Spills to right ➔							

Figure 15.57 *Using SORT to sort a row A–Z.*

You can try this example on the worksheet named Ch15(57).

Say that you want to analyze racing times. To do so, you might need to sort a dataset to show the fastest racing times at the top. Figure 15.58 shows how to sort a table with Racer and Time(s) columns from smallest to largest, based on the Time(s) column. You can enter the Racer and Time(s) columns from the range D5:E10 into the first argument of the SORT function, and then you can enter a 2 value into the second argument to instruct the SORT function to sort the table by the second column. When you omit the third and fourth arguments, SORT will sort the records in the table from smallest to largest, based on the time values in the second column.

This example illustrates an advantage that the SORT array function has over the sort feature that you learned about in Chapter 8: If you convert the source dataset to an Excel Table and add new records, the SORT formula automatically updates and shows the fastest racers on top. Using the SORT function is a better solution than sorting and unsorting the original source dataset to see the fastest racers on top.

	A	B	C	D	E	F	G	H	I
2		Ex #32	**Goal:** Select the racer & time columns and sort the records by time, smallest to biggest.						
4			**Date**	**Track**	**Racer**	**Time(s)**	**Racer**	**Time(s)**	
5			8/5/22	SeaTac	Isaac	38.8	Isaac	35.1	
6			8/5/22	SeaTac	Zaine	38.2	Ella	36.5	
7			8/5/22	SeaTac	Ella	38.1	Zaine	37.5	
8			8/6/22	Everett	Zaine	37.5	Ella	38.1	
9			8/6/22	Everett	Isaac	35.1	Zaine	38.2	
10			8/6/22	Everett	Ella	36.5	Isaac	38.8	
12						Formula in cell G5: =SORT(D5:E10,2)			
13						Spills down ⬇			

Figure 15.58 *Using SORT to sort a table from smallest to largest, based on the second column.*

You can try this example on the worksheet named Ch15(58).

Figure 15.59 shows how to sort based on two columns, using the formula =SORT(C5:E10,{1,3},{-1,1}). The goal of this formula is to sort the track names Z–A and then to show, for each track, the times sorted from smallest to largest. In the figure, you can see that Ella had the fastest time at the SeaTac track, and Isaac had the fastest time at the Everett track. Because you are dealing with two columns and two different sort orders, you must enter {1,3} into the [*sort_index*] argument to instruct the SORT function to sort by column 1 and then by column 3, and you must enter {-1,1} into the [*sort_order*] argument to instruct the SORT function to sort column 1 from largest to smallest and to sort column 3 A–Z.

	A	B	C	D	E	F	G	H	I
2		Ex #33	**Goal:** Sort records by the times (small-big) for each track (Z-A).						
4			**Date**	**Track**	**Racer**	**Time(s)**	**Track**	**Racer**	**Time(s)**
5			8/5/22	SeaTac	Isaac	38.8	SeaTac	Ella	38.1
6			8/5/22	SeaTac	Zaine	38.2	SeaTac	Zaine	38.2
7			8/5/22	SeaTac	Ella	38.1	SeaTac	Isaac	38.8
8			8/6/22	Everett	Zaine	37.5	Everett	Isaac	35.1
9			8/6/22	Everett	Isaac	35.1	Everett	Ella	36.5
10			8/6/22	Everett	Ella	36.5	Everett	Zaine	37.5
12			Formula in cell G5: =SORT(C5:E10,{1,3},{-1,1})						
13			Spills down ⬇						

Figure 15.59 *Using SORT to sort by the Track column, Z–A, then by the Time(s) column, from smallest to largest.*

You can try this example on the worksheet named Ch15(59).

Example 34: Using the SORTBY Array Function

You can achieve the same result achieved with the SORT function in Figure 15.59 by using the SORTBY function. As shown in Figure 15.60, the difference is that rather than use curly brackets and numbers, as you do with the SORT function, with SORTBY, you list the range of the column to sort by followed by a number to indicate the sort order, where 1 yields A–Z (or smallest to largest) and -1 yields Z–A (or largest to smallest). In Figure 15.60, you can see that the first argument of the SORTBY function contains the array to sort. The second and third arguments indicate that the Track column, range C5:C10, should be sorted Z–A. The fourth and fifth arguments indicate that the Time(s) column, range C5:C10, should be sorted from smallest to largest. This example shows a sort based on 2 columns, but you can have up to 126 pairs of arguments.

	A	B	C	D	E	F	G	H	I
2		Ex #34	**Goal:** Sort the times for each track smallest to biggest.						
4			**Date**	**Track**	**Racer**	**Time**	**Track**	**Racer**	**Time(s)**
5			8/5/22	SeaTac	Isaac	38.8	SeaTac	Ella	38.1
6			8/5/22	SeaTac	Zaine	38.2	SeaTac	Zaine	38.2
7			8/5/22	SeaTac	Ella	38.1	SeaTac	Isaac	38.8
8			8/6/22	Everett	Zaine	37.5	Everett	Isaac	35.1
9			8/6/22	Everett	Isaac	35.1	Everett	Ella	36.5
10			8/6/22	Everett	Ella	36.5	Everett	Zaine	37.5
12			Formula in cell G5: =SORTBY(C5:E10,C5:C10,-1,E5:E10,1)						
13			Spills down ⬇						

Figure 15.60 *Using SORTBY to sort by the Track column, Z–A, then by the Time(s) column, from smallest to largest.*

You can try this example on the worksheet named Ch15(60).

Sorting Mixed Data

All the sorting examples you have seen so far in this chapter involve columns or rows of data with a single data type, such as a range with just text or just numbers. In these cases, you automatically know what the order should be. But if you have mixed data types, you need to know about Excel's sort order.

When you sort A–Z or from smallest to largest by using the SORT function or the sort feature in the Data tab in the Ribbon, the sort order is based on the 255 ASCII characters, each of which corresponds with a number from 1 to 255, as well as other elements, such as empty cells, error values, and Boolean values. In general, when sorting ascending (that is, A–Z, or smallest to largest), the sort order is as follows:

1. Numbers
2. Text (including zero-length text strings)
3. FALSE
4. TRUE
5. Errors in the order in which they occur
6. Empty cells

For sorting Z–A, or largest to smallest, the order is reversed, but empty cells are still at the very bottom, just as with the A–Z sort.

Let's look at an example of sorting based on the full set of ASCII characters. The ASCII character 5 corresponds to the ASCII number 53, and the ASCII character S corresponds to the ASCII number 83. If you use the A–Z sort order for a column that contains the number 5 and the letter S, the number 5 appears above S because 53 is smaller than 83.

You can easily view all 255 ASCII characters by placing the formula =CHAR(SEQUENCE(255)) in a cell. The CHAR function delivers an ASCII character based on a number input. The formula element SEQUENCE(255) delivers a column with the numbers 1 to 255. Because an array of the numbers 1 to 255 is placed in CHAR, CHAR spills a list of all the ASCII characters. Figure 15.61 shows an example of sorting mixed data.

	Start		Sort A-Z		Sort Z-A
Number>	43	→	43	→	#DIV/0!
Text>	{@J2*&%				TRUE
Zero Length Text String >			{@J2*&%		FALSE
Empty Cell >			rad		rad
TRUE>	TRUE		FALSE		{@J2*&%
Text>	rad		TRUE		
FALSE>	FALSE		#DIV/0!		43
Error>	#DIV/0!				

Figure 15.61 *A–Z and Z–A sorts on mixed data.*

Example 35: Finding the Top Three Scores, Including Ties, with the FILTER, LARGE, and SORT Functions

This last example of the SORT function involves extracting the records with the top three scores, including any records involved if there is a tie for third.

The first step in solving this problem is to use the LARGE function to get the third-largest value. In Figure 16.62, cell G5 contains the LARGE function, which pulls the third-largest value, 22. Then, in cell I5, you use the FILTER array function to filter, or extract, the records where the score is greater than or equal to the third-largest value in cell G5. Finally, you wrap the SORT function around the FILTER function with a 2 in the [*sort_index*] argument to instruct SORT to sort the records by the Score column and with a -1 in the [*sort_order*] argument to instruct SORT to sort from largest to smallest.

> **Note:** This way of extracting the top values formula is common in business to get the top customer sales, in science to get the top values in an experiment, in sports to get the top-scoring games, and in many other types of situations.

I5		:	× ✓ *fx*	=SORT(FILTER(ScoreTable,ScoreTable[Score]>=G5),2,-1)						

	A	B	C	D	E	F	G	H	I	J	K
2	Ex #35	**Goal:** Extract top 3, including records if there is a tie for third.									
4		Name ▼	Score ▼		Top		Top 3 hurdle		Name	Score	
5		Shinea	25		3		22		Shinea	25	
6		Phil	10						Hue	23	
7		Pham	10						Chantel	22	
8		Gigi	19						Sammi	22	
9		Ty	6								
10		Chantel	22								
11		Chin	15								
12		Hue	23		Formula in cell G5: =LARGE(ScoreTable[Score],E5)						
13		Miki	10		Formula in cell I5: =SORT(FILTER(ScoreTable,ScoreTable[Score]>=G5),2,-1)						
14		Abdi	15								
15		Tyrone	15								
16		Sammi	22								

Figure 15.62 *Using the LARGE, FILTER, and SORT functions to extract the top three scores.*

You can try this example on the worksheet named Ch15(62).

Examples 36 Through 39: Using the SEQUENCE Array Function

The SEQUENCE array function generates a sequence of numbers in a row, a column, or a table, based on the formula inputs for the number of rows in the final sequence, the number of columns in the final sequence, a start value, and an increment value. The SEQUENCE function has the following syntax (see Figure 15.63):

```
SEQUENCE(rows, [columns], [start], [step])
```

The arguments of the SEQUENCE function are as follows:

- **rows**: This argument contains the number of rows you want in sequence. If you use the [*columns*] argument and leave the *rows* argument empty, *rows* defaults to 1.
- **[columns]**: This argument contains the number of columns you want in sequence. The default value is 1.
- **[start]**: This argument contains the start number for the sequence. The default value is 1.
- **[step]**: This argument contains the increment amount to add to calculate the next number in the sequence. The default value is 1.

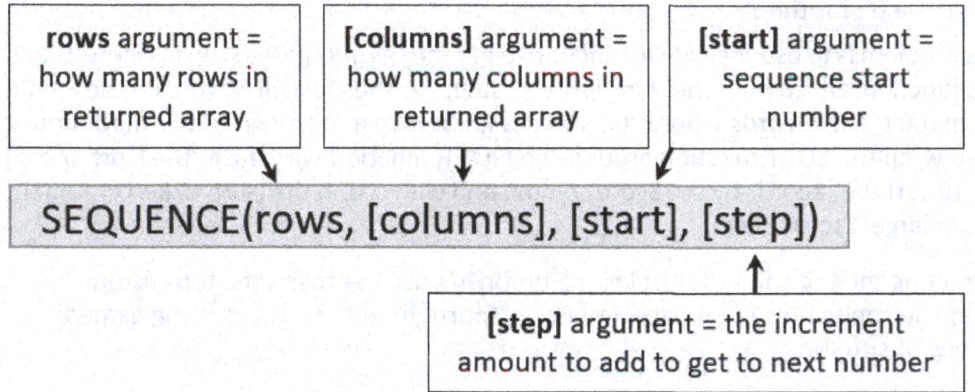

Figure 15.63 *Arguments of the SEQUENCE array function.*

The SEQUENCE function is useful because a formula solution may require a certain pattern of numbers. For example, in Figure 15.40, earlier in this chapter, you needed a sequence of repeating 1 values inside the MMULT *array2* argument. In that example, you used the formula element SEQUENCE(4,,1,0) to generate the sequence {1;1;1;1}, where you wanted a sequence with four rows that started at 1 and had an increment, or step value, of 0. In addition, in Figure 14.46, you saw how to use the formula element SEQUENCE(5) to generate the sequence {1;2;3;4;5}, which you then used inside the *row_index* argument of the INDEX function to look up the first five rows in a dataset.

Figures 15.64 through 15.67 show various sequences that you can create inside larger worksheet formulas. You can try these examples on the worksheets named Ch15(64), Ch15(65), Ch15(66), and Ch15(67).

	A	B	C	D	E	F
2	Ex #36	**Goal:** Demonstrate various types of number sequences.				
4		rows	6	6	6	6
5		[columns]				
6		[start]		-15	0	1
7		[step]			2	0
9			Start at 1, Step 1	Start at -15, Step 1	Start at 0, Step 2	All 1s
10			1	-15	0	1
11			2	-14	2	1
12			3	-13	4	1
13			4	-12	6	1
14			5	-11	8	1
15			6	-10	10	1
16						
17			C10: =SEQUENCE(C4)	D10: =SEQUENCE(D4,,D6)	E10: =SEQUENCE(E4,,E6,E7)	F10: =SEQUENCE(F4,,F6,F7)

Figure 15.64 *Various sequences of numbers created using the SEQUENCE array function.*

	A	B	C	D	E	F
2	**Ex #37**	**Goal:** Demonstrate rectangular sequence.				
4		rows	4			
5		[columns]	4			
6		[start]				
7		[step]				
9			1	2	3	4
10			5	6	7	8
11			9	10	11	12
12			13	14	15	16
13						
14			C9: =SEQUENCE(C4,C5)			

Figure 15.65 *The SEQUENCE array function with rows and [columns] arguments and default settings for the remaining arguments.*

	A	B	C	D	E	F
2	**Ex #38**	**Goal:** Demonstrate repeating number sequences.				
4		Size:	3			
5		rows	6			All in one formula:
7			Step 1	Step 2	Step 3	**Repeat**
8			1	0.333333333	1	1
9			2	0.666666667	1	1
10			3	1	1	1
11			4	1.333333333	2	2
12			5	1.666666667	2	2
13			6	2	2	2
14						
15			C8: =SEQUENCE(C5)	D8: =C8#/C4	E8: =ROUNDUP(D8#,0)	F8: =ROUNDUP(SEQUENCE(C5)/C4,0)

Figure 15.66 *Repeating blocks of numbers are commonly used in INDEX lookup formulas.*

	A	B	C	D	E	F
2	**Ex #39**	**Goal:** Demonstrate cyclical number sequences.				
4		Size:	3			
5		rows	6			
6		start	0			All in one formula:
8			Step 1	Step 2	Step 3	**Cyclical**
9			0	0	1	1
10			1	1	2	2
11			2	2	3	3
12			3	0	1	1
13			4	1	2	2
14			5	2	3	3
15						
16			C9: =SEQUENCE(C5,,C6)	D9: =MOD(C9#,C4)	E9: =D9#+1	F9: =MOD(SEQUENCE(C5,,0),C4)+1
18		**** Note:** MOD gives you the remainder after performing division. For example MOD(4,3) = 1 because 4/3 = 1 R 1.				

Figure 15.67 *Cyclical blocks of numbers are commonly used in INDEX lookup formulas.*

Frequency Distributions

A *frequency distribution* is a list of a set of categories and counts items from a dataset to show how many items occur in each category. For example, in Figure 15.68, you can see a list of products (categories) and the counts for each product. (You also saw this type of product frequency distribution in Figure 15.53.)

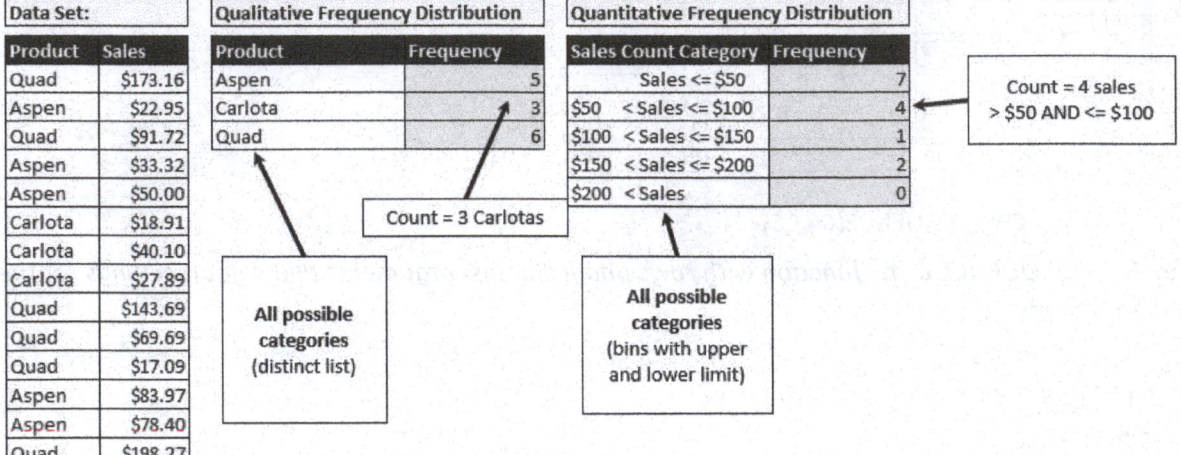

Figure 15.68 *Frequency distributions are commonly used for both qualitative and quantitative data.*

Formally, a *frequency distribution* is a list of mutually exclusive and collectively exhaustive categories that are used to count items from a dataset, where *mutually exclusive* means an item that is counted can only fit into one category, and *collectively exhaustive* means you have enough categories to count everything from the dataset. Figure 15.68 shows two different types of frequency distributions:

- **Qualitative frequency distribution:** This type of distribution counts non-numeric text data (that is, qualitative data).

- **Quantitative frequency distribution:** This type of distribution counts numeric data (that is, quantitative data) based on number categories with lower and upper limits.

The key to a frequency distribution is that it includes all possible categories or enough categories that you can count all items from the original dataset without missing any data points. For example, for the qualitative frequency distribution shown in Figure 15.68, if you use only the categories Aspen and Carlota, you end up missing all the counts for the product Quad. To count all the products from this source data, you need all three (collectively exhaustive and mutually exclusive) categories: Aspen, Carlota, and Quad. For the quantitative frequency distribution shown in Figure 15.68, if you use only the sales upper limits $50, $100, and $150, you end up missing all the counts for the sales from $150 up to $200. To count all the sales numbers from this source data, you need the whole (collectively exhaustive and mutually exclusive) list of upper limits: $50, $100, $150, and $200.

Example 40: Using SORT, UNIQUE, and COUNTIFS to Create a Qualitative Frequency Distribution

When creating the full list of categories for a qualitative frequency distribution, the task is relatively easy if you use the UNIQUE function, which is programmed to create a full distinct list and which updates if data changes. As shown in Figure 15.69, you can use the functions SORT, UNIQUE, and COUNTIFS to create a qualitative frequency distribution to count the number of each product sold.

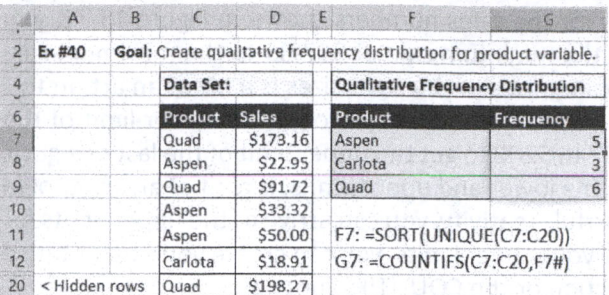

Figure 15.69 *A frequency distribution to count product transactions.*

You can try this example on the worksheet named Ch15(69).

Example 41: Using the FREQUENCY Array Function to Create a Quantitative Frequency Distribution

The FREQUENCY array function creates a vertical quantitative frequency distribution that counts how many numbers occur within a set of categories based on an upper limit for each category. The syntax of the FREQUENCY function is as follows (see Figure 15.70):

```
FREQUENCY(data_array, bins_array)
```

The arguments of the FREQUENCY function are as follows:

- *data_array*: This argument contains the table, column, or row with the number source data that you want to count. FREQUENCY only counts numbers and ignores empty cells and text.
- *bins_array*: This argument contains the upper limit numbers, sorted from smallest to largest, for the counting categories. The upper limits are sorted to help reveal patterns in the number data.

Keep in mind the following about categories with the FREQUENCY function:

- Categories are automatically created. There is no visual indication of how the categories are structured.
- The first category counts all the numbers less than or equal to the first upper limit.
- The middle categories count between the lower limit (the previous category upper limit) and the given upper limit. Numbers that match the lower limit are not included in the count. Numbers that match the upper limit are included in the count.
- The last category catches all the values that are greater than the last upper limit.
- There is always one more category than there are bins.

Note: FREQUENCY delivers a vertical array. If you need a horizontal array, use the TRANSPOSE function, like this: TRANSPOSE(FREQUENCY(*data*, *bins*)).

Note: If there are duplicate bins, the duplicates get a count of 0.

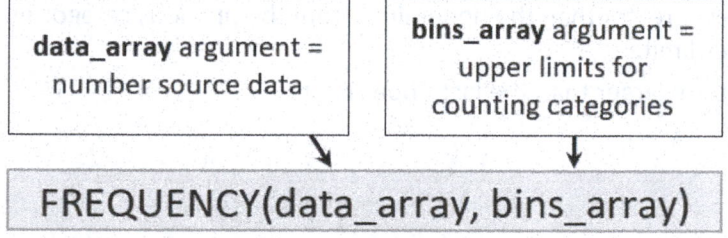

Figure 15.70 *Arguments of the FREQUENCY array function.*

When creating the full list of categories for a quantitative frequency distribution, the task is a bit involved because you have to create number categories, or number bins, with lower and upper limits. In addition, you have to make sure that you have enough categories so that all numbers are counted from the minimum to the maximum value in the original dataset. For example, for the sales numbers shown in Figure 15.71, you have to create your categories so that all numbers from the minimum sale of $17.09 to the maximum sale of $198.27 will be counted. The process of creating the categories of the right sizes is a bit of an art. In this case, it makes sense to round down from the minimum value of $17.09 to $0 to get the lower limit of the first category and round up the maximum value of $198.27 to $200 to get the upper limit of the last category. Choosing the width of each bin, or the distance between the lower and upper limits, is a bit of an art, too. In this case, an easy choice would be to use $50. With that artful creativity, you can arrive at the upper limits for each category: $50, $100, $150, and $200. Once you have your upper limits, you can create your quantitative frequency distribution by using the FRQUENCY array function or the COUNTIFS function.

	A	B	C	D	E	F	G	H
2	Ex #41	**Goal:** Create quantitative frequency distribution for sales variable.						
4		**Data Set:**			**Quantitative Frequency Distribution**			
5								
6		**Product**	**Sales**		**$ Sales Upper Limit (included)**	**Frequency**		
7		Quad	$173.16		$50	=FREQUENCY(C7:C20,E7:E10)		
8		Aspen	$22.95		$100	4	FREQUENCY(data_array, **bins_array**)	
9		Quad	$91.72		$150	1		
10		Aspen	$33.32		$200	2		
11		Aspen	$50.00			0	< extra category that FREQUENCY	
12		Carlota	$18.91				creates to catch any values	
13		Carlota	$40.10				bigger than last upper limit	
20		Quad	$198.27		< Hidden data rows			

Figure 15.71 *A quantitative frequency distribution to count sales based on categories with upper limits.*

Figure 15.71 shows the upper limits typed into the range E7:E10, from smallest to largest, and the FREQUENCY function entered into cell F7. The *data_array* argument contains the dataset, and the *bins_array* argument contains the upper limits. Notice that the FREQUENCY array function creates five counts in the range G7:F11, even though you only gave it four upper limits. The last count is for any values in the dataset that might be bigger than the last upper limit.

> **Note:** If you are careful in how you determine your upper limits, as you were when you rounded up from the maximum value to the upper limit for the last category, you will always get a 0 in this last category. If you have a few larger outlier data points, you might want to set the upper limit for the last category below the maximum value in the dataset.

You can try this example on the worksheet named Ch15(71).

The FREQUENCY array function always creates one more counting category than the number of upper limits you give it. Figure 15.71 shows the categories that are automatically created for the four upper limits in this example. The first and last categories are different from the middle categories:

- The first category counts anything equal to or less than the first upper limit.
- The middle categories count any numbers greater than the upper limit from the previous categories and less than or equal to the given upper limit.
- The last category counts any values that are larger than the last upper limit.

Microsoft designed the categories this way so that all numbers in the dataset will be counted, no matter what upper limits you set. In addition, the categories created are mutually exclusive because the equal sign is used only on the upper limit and not on the lower limit. For example, the sales value $50 is counted only in the first category, and it does not get counted in the second category. The categories created are also collectively exhaustive so that no number is left out of the count. The way the first and last categories are created ensures that all numbers below the first lower limit are counted and all numbers above that last upper limit are counted.

$ Sales Upper Limit (included)	Frequency	Categories created by FREQUENCY:
$50	7	Sale <= $50
$100	4	$50 < Sales <= $100
$150	1	$100 < Sales <= $150
$200	2	$150 < Sales <= $200
	0	$200 < Sales

Figure 15.72 *Categories are automatically created by the FREQUENCY array function.*

Example 42: Removing the Last Category by Using the INDEX, SEQUENCE, and ROWS Functions

If you do not want the last counting category that the FREQUENCY array function creates to appear in a report, you can remove it. Figure 15.73 shows how to remove the last category by using the INDEX, SEQUENCE, and ROWS functions. The formula element SEQUENCE(ROWS(E7:E10)) creates the vertical array of row numbers {1;2;3;4} that the INDEX function can use in the *row_num* argument to dynamically look up all the rows that FREQUENCY delivers except the last one.

	A	B	C	D	E	F	G	H
2		Ex #42	**Goal:** Remove last counting category that FREQUENCY array function creates.					
4			**Data Set:**		**Quantitative Frequency Distribution**			
5								
6			**Product**	**Sales**	**$ Sales Upper Limit (included)**	**Frequency**		
7			Quad	$173.16	$50	7		
8			Aspen	$22.95	$100	4		
9			Quad	$91.72	$150	1		
10			Aspen	$33.32	$200	2		
11			Aspen	$50.00				
12			Carlota	$18.91	Formula in cell F7:			
13			Carlota	$40.10	=INDEX(FREQUENCY(C7:C20,E7:E10),SEQUENCE(ROWS(E7:E10)))			
14			Carlota	$27.89				
20			Quad	$198.27	< Hidden data rows			

Figure 15.73 *Using INDEX, SEQUENCE, and ROWS to remove last category.*

You can try this example on the worksheet named Ch15(73).

Example 43: Using FREQUENCY in Formulas to Create Upper Limits

When you create upper limits, you typically want to use Excel formulas to determine the upper limits. Figure 15.74 shows the formula that you can use to create the upper limits. Keep in mind that it is helpful to label the column with the upper limits with something like $ Sales Upper Limit (Included) to make it clear that the upper limits represent dollar sales amounts and that the upper limits are included in the count for that category. Finally, if you do use the last category, it is best to label it. In cell E20 in Figure 15.74, you can see the text formula =">$"&E19 that is used to create the label. I right-aligned cell E20 to get the text value to align with the numbers.

	A	B	C	D	E	F	G	H
2		Ex #43	Goal: Full process to create quantitative frequency distribution for sales variable.					
4		Data Set:			Min	$17.09	◄ cell F4: =MIN(C7:C20)	
5					Max	$198.27	◄ cell F5: =MAX(C7:C20)	
6		Product	Sales		Lower limit of 1st category	$0.00	◄ cell F6: =FLOOR(F4,F8)	
7		Quad	$173.16		Upper limit last category	$200.00	◄ cell F7: =CEILING(F5,F8)	
8		Aspen	$22.95		Width of each bin	50		
9		Quad	$91.72		rows	4	◄ cell F9: =F7/F8	
10		Aspen	$33.32		start	$50.00	◄ cell F10: =F8	
11		Aspen	$50.00		step	$50.00	◄ cell F11: =F8	
12		Carlota	$18.91					
13		Carlota	$40.10		Quantitative Frequency Distribution			
14		Carlota	$27.89					
15		Quad	$143.69		$ Sales Upper Limit (included)	Frequency		
16		Quad	$69.69		$50	7		
17		Quad	$17.09		$100	4		
18		Aspen	$83.97		$150	1		
19		Aspen	$78.40		$200	2		
20		Quad	$198.27		>$200	0		
21								
22					Formula in cell E16: =SEQUENCE(F9,,F10,F11)			
23					Formula in cell F16: =FREQUENCY(C7:C20,E16#)			
24					Formula in cell E20: =">$"&E19			

Figure 15.74 *The full process to create a quantitative frequency distribution.*

You can try this example on the worksheet named Ch15(74).

Example 44: Using Formulas to Create Logical Labels for Counting Categories

You may want to create logical labels for a quantitative frequency distribution report, and Figure 15.75 shows the text formulas to accomplish this. The DOLLAR function is similar to the ROUND function except that, rather than deliver a number result, it delivers a text result formatted with currency number formatting.

	F	G	H	I	J
15	Frequency		Categories created by FREQUENCY:		
16	7		Sale <= $50	◀ Formula in cell H16: ="	Sale <= "&DOLLAR(E16,0)
17	4		$50 < Sales <= $100	◀ Formula in cell H17: =DOLLAR(E16,0)&" < Sales <= "&DOLLAR(E17,0)	
18	1		$100 < Sales <= $150	◀ Formula in cell H18: =DOLLAR(E17,0)&" < Sales <= "&DOLLAR(E18,0)	
19	2		$150 < Sales <= $200	◀ Formula in cell H19: =DOLLAR(E18,0)&" < Sales <= "&DOLLAR(E19,0)	
20	0		$200 < Sales	◀ Formula in cell H20: =DOLLAR(E19,0)&" < Sales"	

Figure 15.75 *Formulas to create logical labels for the counting categories.*

You can try this example on the worksheet named Ch15(75).

Example 45: Using the COUNTIFS Function to Create Custom Counting Categories for a Quantitative Frequency Distribution

You may not like the categories created by the FREQUENCY function. Figure 15.76 shows how you can use the COUNTIFS function to choose which limit you want to include in the counting category. In Figure 15.76, for example, the lower limit for each category is included in the count, but the upper limit is not included.

	A	B	C	D	E	F	G	H	I	J	K
2	Ex #45	**Goal:** Create quantitative frequency distribution for sales variable with COUNTIFS function.									
4		**Data Set:**			**Quantitative Frequency Distribution**						
5											
6		**Product**	**Sales**		**Lower Limit (included)**	**Upper Limit (not included)**	**Frequency**		**Categories for COUNTIFS:**		
7		Quad	$173.16		$0	$50	6		$0 >= Sales < $50		
8		Aspen	$22.95		$50	$100	5		$50 >= Sales < $100		
9		Quad	$91.72		$100	$150	1		$100 >= Sales < $150		
10		Aspen	$33.32		$150	$200	2		$150 >= Sales < $200		
11		Carlota	$18.91								
12		Carlota	$40.10								
13		Carlota	$27.89						**Inputs for SEQUENCE:**		
14		Quad	$143.69						rows	start	step
15		Aspen	$50.00		Formula in cell E7: =SEQUENCE(I15,,J15,K15)				4	0	50
16		Quad	$69.69		Formula in cell F7: =SEQUENCE(I16,,J16,K16)				4	50	50
17		Quad	$17.09								
18		Aspen	$83.97		Formula in cell G7: =COUNTIFS(C7:C20,">="&E7#,C7:C20,"<"&F7#)						
19		Aspen	$78.40								
20		Quad	$198.27								

Figure 15.76 *The COUNTIFS function, unlike FREQUENCY, can create any type of upper and lower limits.*

You can try this example on the worksheet named Ch15(76).

Frequency distributions, which help reveal patterns in data, are used in a great variety of professions and endeavors. Figure 15.77 shows a student grade dataset and a target sales dataset with a frequency distribution and a histogram column chart for each dataset. (You'll learn how to create the chart in Chapter 19.) By creating a set of sorted (smallest to largest) counting categories and calculating the frequencies, you can search for patterns in the data. The frequency distribution helps reveal a bell-shaped pattern in the student data and a descending frequency shape with a skew to the right and a few large outlier values in the sales data. Both of these are typical patterns. (For example, it makes sense that in a store like Target, there are fewer large sales and many small sales.)

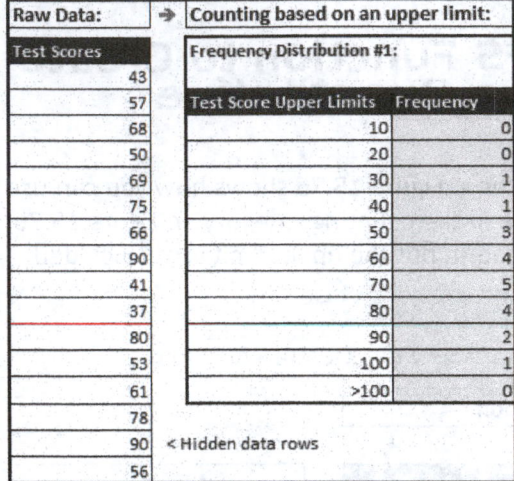

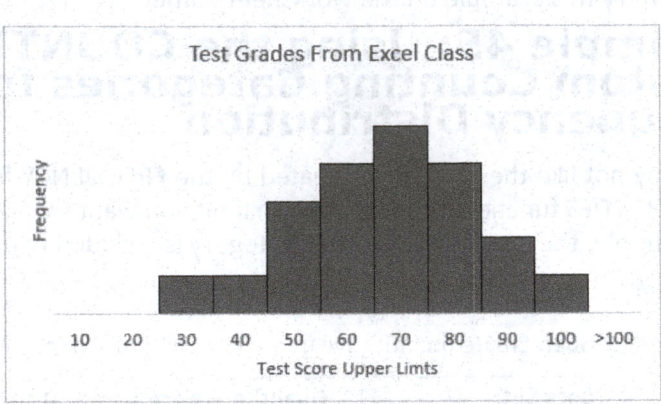

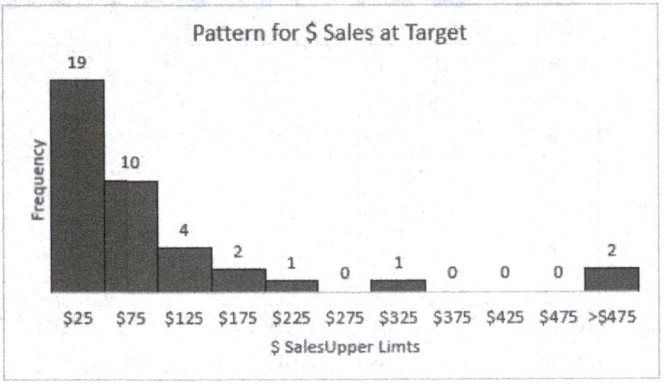

Figure 15.77 *Frequency distributions help reveal patterns in data.*

Key Concepts in Chapter 15

- A **worksheet array** is a collection of two or more items, or values. The items that are allowed in a worksheet array are numbers, text, Boolean values, formula errors, or empty cells. There are a few types of worksheet arrays:
  - A range **reference** is an array such as a range of cells, an Excel Table element, or a defined name with two or more items.
  - An **array constant** is an array of column values, row values, or table values that are hard coded into a formula.
  - A **resultant array** can be created by a formula element.
  - A **spilled array** uses the spilled range operator #.
- A **worksheet array formula** is a formula that contains one or more array operations. An **array operation** is an operation that delivers a **resultant array** of answers rather than a single answer. The array operations include math, join, comparative, function argument, and array function operations. The resultant array can be internal in a larger formula or can be the result of the final array operation that spills into the worksheet cells.

- An array formula known as a **scalar array formula** delivers a single answer.
- A **dynamic spilled array formula** delivers a spilled array of answers. A dynamic spilled array formula lives in the top-left cell of the spilled range and must be edited in that cell. The spilled values can be dynamically referred to with the cell address of the top-left cell in the spilled range and the spilled range operator, #. Dynamic spilled array formulas are dynamic because when the source data changes and the spilled array expands or contracts, the values emanating from the top-left cell expand and contract accordingly.
- The **SUMPRODUCT function** is an aggregate function that can multiply same-sized arrays and then add the result to get an aggregated sum. When working with large datasets or when you have text values you need to ignore, using the SUMPRODUCT function is more efficient than using the SUM function with a direct array operation. The SUMPRODUCT function can also be a substitute for the SUMIFS function.
- To perform matrix multiplication on two arrays using the **MMULT array function**, these conditions must be met:
  - Array 1 and array 2 can contain no empty cells.
  - The number of columns in array 1 must be equal to the number of rows in the array 2.
  - You must multiply each row from array 1 by each column in array 2 and the add the results.
  - The dimensions of the desired spilled array must have the same number of rows as are in array 1 and the same number of columns as are in array 2.
- The **FILTER array function** filters a dataset based on conditions and criteria that you specify in a Boolean array logical test to deliver a resultant array of answers. The FILTER function has many applications, such as filtering a dataset, using a single lookup value to return multiple items, filtering a dataset and using the resultant array in an OR logical test conditional calculation, and filtering a dataset and using the resultant array as a lookup table in a lookup formula.
- The **UNIQUE array function** can deliver either a distinct set of items or a unique set of items from a table, a column, or a row.
- The **SORT array function** can sort a row, a column, or a table in ascending or descending order. It can also sort by more than one column.
- The **SEQUENCE array function** generates a sequence of numbers in a row, a column, or a table, based on the formula inputs for the number of rows in the final sequence, the number of columns in the final sequence, a start value, and an increment value.
- The **FREQUENCY array function** creates a vertical quantitative frequency distribution that counts how many numbers occur within a set of categories based on an upper limit for each category.

Practice Problems for Chapter 15

Practice Problem 1

In your Excel file for this chapter (Ch15-Excel365-ArrayFormulas.xlsx), go to the worksheet named PPCh15(1) and create the solution for this practice problem. Figure 15.78 shows the goal that is listed on that worksheet.

A	B	C	D	E	F	G	H	I	J	K	L
2	**Goal:**	In cell D7 create a formula that calculates the total bank deposit based on the bills and number of bills.									
3											
4		Bills ($ currency)		$1	$5	$10	$20	$50	$100		
5		Number Bills		75	25	22	142	5	43		
6											
7		Total Deposit									

Figure 15.78 *On the worksheet PPCh15(1), create a formula to total the bank deposit.*

When you are done with this problem, you can check your work against the answer sheet named PPCh15(1an).

Practice Problem 2

In your Excel file for this chapter (Ch15-Excel365-ArrayFormulas.xlsx), go to the worksheet named PPCh15(2) and create the solution for this practice problem. Figure 15.79 shows the goal that is listed on that worksheet.

	A	B	C	D	E	F	G
2		**Goal:**		In cell E14 create a formula that calculates the expected portfolio returns.			
3				Formula should sum:			
4				'probability of economic state' * 'weight of stock in portfolio' * 'estimates returns'.			
5				For extra credit, see if you can calculate the standard deviation in cell E15.			
6							
7		**Weight of Stock in Portfolio:**			0.3	0.4	0.3	
8		**Probability of Economic State**			**Stock A Full Estimated Return**	**Stock B Full Estimated Return**	**Stock C Full Estimated Return**	
9		Bad		0.15	0.00	-0.15	-0.20
10		OK		0.3	0.03	-0.02	0.01
11		Good		0.35	0.05	0.11	0.08
12		Great		0.2	0.10	0.20	0.20
13							
14		Expected Portfolio Returns:					
15		Standard Deviation of Ex. Portfolio Returns:					

Figure 15.79 *On the worksheet PPCh15(2), create a formula to calculate the expected portfolio return.*

When you are done with this problem, you can check your work against the answer sheet named PPCh15(2an).

Practice Problem 3

In your Excel file for this chapter (Ch15-Excel365-ArrayFormulas.xlsx), go to the worksheet named PPCh15(3) and create the solution for this practice problem. Figure 15.80 shows the goal that is listed on that worksheet.

	A	B	C	D	E	F	G	H
2			**Goal:** Create a formula in cell H5: to spill a column of row totals.					
3								
4			Sales Rep	Week 1 Units Sold	Week 2 Units Sold	Week 3 Units Sold	Week 4 Units Sold	Totals
5			Chun	44	11	218	13	
6			Xiaver	249	138	212	105	
7			Shinia	150	239	188	33	
8			Billy	46	119	67	90	

Figure 15.80 *On the worksheet PPCh15(3), create a formula to spill row totals.*

When you are done with this problem, you can check your work against the answer sheet named PPCh15(3an).

Practice Problem 4

In your Excel file for this chapter (Ch15-Excel365-ArrayFormulas.xlsx), go to the worksheet named PPCh15(4) and create the solution for this practice problem. Figure 15.81 shows the goal that is listed on that worksheet.

	A	B	C	D	E	F	G	H	I	J	K
2		Goal:	Create a formula in cell J5: extract the Sales Rep column and the Week 2 Units Sold Column.								
3											
4			Sales Rep	Week 1 Units Sold	Week 2 Units Sold	Week 3 Units Sold	Week 4 Units Sold	Totals		Sales Rep	Week 2 Units Sold
5			Chun	44	11	218	13	286			
6			Xiaver	249	138	212	105	704			
7			Shinia	150	239	188	33	610			
8			Billy	46	119	67	90	322			

Figure 15.81 *On the worksheet PPCh15(4), create a formula to extract the two desired columns.*

When you are done with this problem, you can check your work against the answer sheet named PPCh15(4an).

Practice Problem 5

In your Excel file for this chapter (Ch15-Excel365-ArrayFormulas.xlsx), go to the worksheet named PPCh15(5) and create the solution for this practice problem. Figure 15.82 shows the goal that is listed on that worksheet.

	A	B	C	D	E	F	G	H	I	J	K	L
2		Goal:	Somewhere in the worksheet create a formula report that shows the total call times for each sales rep.									
3			Add conditional formatting that formats the report depending on how many rows are spilled in the report.									
4												
5			Sales Rep	Date	Time on Calls (min)							
6			Chun	1/1/22	218							
7			Xiaver	1/1/22	418							
8			Shinia	1/1/22	332							
9			Billy	1/1/22	248							
10			Chun	1/2/22	343							
11			Xiaver	1/2/22	183							
12			Shinia	1/2/22	223		< Hidden Rows					
20			Shinia	1/4/22	122							

Figure 15.82 *On the worksheet PPCh15(5), use two formulas to create a report of total call time by sales reps.*

When you are done with this problem, you can check your work against the answer sheet named PPCh15(5an).

Practice Problem 6

In your Excel file for this chapter (Ch15-Excel365-ArrayFormulas.xlsx), go to the worksheet named PPCh15(6) and create the solution for this practice problem. Figure 15.83 shows the goal that is listed on that worksheet.

	A	B	C	D	E	F	G	H	I	J
2		**Goal:**	Using the FILTER function, filter the data set to show records that contains a time value.							
3			Format the filtered data set.							
4										
5			Sales Rep	Date	Time on Calls (min)		Sales Rep	Date	Time on Calls (min)	
6			Chun	1/1/22	218					
7			Xiaver	1/1/22	418					
8			Shinia	1/1/22	332					
9			Billy	1/1/22						
10			Chun	1/2/22	343					
11			Xiaver	1/2/22	183					
12			Shinia	1/2/22	223					
13			Billy	1/2/22						
19			Xiaver	1/4/22	217		< Hidden Rows			
20			Shinia	1/4/22	122					

Figure 15.83 *On the worksheet PPCh15(6), create a formula to filter out rows that do not have time values.*

When you are done with this problem, you can check your work against the answer sheet named PPCh15(6an).

Practice Problem 7

In your Excel file for this chapter (Ch15-Excel365-ArrayFormulas.xlsx), go to the worksheet named PPCh15(7) and create the solution for this practice problem. Figure 15.84 shows the goal that is listed on that worksheet.

	A	B	C	D	E	F	G	H	I	J
2		**Goal:**		Extract records with top 5 scores, including records if there is a tie for 5th						
3				Sort result by the numbers, biggest to smallest.						
4										
5		Name	Score		Top		Top 5 hurdle		Name	Score
6		Shinea	25		5					
7		Phil	10							
8		Pham	10							
9		Gigi	19							
16		Tyrone	19		< Hidden Rows					
17		Sammi	22							

Figure 15.84 *On the worksheet PPCh15(7), create a formula to extract and sort the top five records.*

When you are done with this problem, you can check your work against the answer sheet named PPCh15(7an).

Practice Problem 8

In your Excel file for this chapter (Ch15-Excel365-ArrayFormulas.xlsx), go to the worksheet named PPCh15(8) and create the solution for this practice problem. Figure 15.85 shows the goal that is listed on that worksheet.

	A	B	C	D	E	F	G	H	I
2		Goal:			With the two data sets below, create two different qualitative frequency distributions.				
3					Use the worksheet to make calculations and create your final reports.				
4									
5		Data Set #1			Data Set #1				
6									
7		Test Grades			$ Sales at Target				
8		43			$15.21				
9		57			$8.80				
10		68			$22.26		More data below		
11		50			$35.30		v v v		
12		69			$15.53				
13		75			$19.12				
14		66			$25.53				
15		90			$27.58				
16		41			$182.88				
17		37			$5.47				

Figure 15.85 *On the worksheet PPCh15(8), create two quantitative frequency distributions.*

When you are done with this problem, you can check your work against the answer sheet named PPCh15(8an).

Practice Problem 9

In your Excel file for this chapter (Ch15-Excel365-ArrayFormulas.xlsx), go to the worksheet named PPCh15(9).

In your own words, see if you can answer these conceptual questions:

1. List the different types of arrays you can have in a worksheet.
2. In your own words, define *array formula*.
3. What is the difference between a SUM function that contains a direct array multiplication operation, the SUMPRODUCT function, and the MMULT array function?
4. What is the difference between a distinct set of items and a unique set of items?
5. What does the SEQUENCE array function do?
6. What does the FREQUENCY array function do?

When you are done with this problem, you can check your work against the answer sheet named PPCh15(9an).

Chapter 16: The LET and LAMBDA Functions

> **Note:** To follow along with the examples in this chapter, you can use the file named Ch16-Excel365-LETandLAMBDA.xlsx.

So far in this book, you have seen new game-changing features and functions (such as dynamic spilled array formulas, the XLOOKUP function, and the FILTER array function) that have dramatically expanded what you can do with Excel. This chapter looks at two more game-changing functions: LET and LAMBDA.

The LET function allows you to define variables and is helpful in reducing formula calculation time when you have repeating formula elements within a formula; it can help make complex formulas easier to read. The LAMBDA function allows you to define your own custom functions that you can reuse; it is helpful for performing calculations for which a built-in function does not already exist and for making complex formulas easier to use. Both of these worksheet functions exist only in Microsoft Excel 365.

The LET Worksheet Function

You can define variables within the LET worksheet function and then use those variables to create final calculations that are delivered to the worksheet or internally in other formulas. There are several advantages to using the LET function to create worksheet solutions:

- A variable is evaluated a single time, and the result is stored in memory so that it can be used throughout a formula. For formulas with repeating formula elements, this can reduce overall calculation time by preventing duplication of evaluation procedures.
- Formulas with repeating elements are easy to edit because you have to edit in only one location.
- Complex formulas can be visually easy to read because each element has a name and can be placed on a different line with the line feed keyboard shortcut, Alt+Enter.
- You can condense reports made up of multiple formulas into a single-cell formula that spills the complete report into the worksheet.

The syntax of the LET function is as follows (see Figure 16.1):

```
LET(name1, name_value1, name2, name_value2, …, name_n, name_value_n,
calculation)
```

The arguments of the LET function are as follows:

- **name1:** This argument specifies the name of variable 1.

> **Note:** Just like defined names and Excel Table names, *name* arguments to the LET function cannot include spaces and other characters, including * /+- ( ) ^ < >+& % ~ ` |] [} { @ " ; : , ' $ # !.

- **name_value1:** This argument specifies a worksheet element, such as a reference, number, or function.
- **name2:** This argument specifies the name of variable 2.
- **name_value2:** This argument specifies a worksheet element or any previously defined variable. Previously defined variables appear in a dropdown list along with defined names, table names, and worksheet function names when you type the first few letters of a variable name in a formula.
- **name_n** and **name_value_n:** These arguments specify further variables and their corresponding worksheet elements. You can list up to 126 variables.
- *calculation:* This argument specifies a formula that can use worksheet elements and any previously defined variables. This is the final result that is delivered by LET.

```
LET(
name1, name_value1,        name argument = variable name.
name2, name_value2, ...    name_value argument = variable formula element.
                                   Up to 126 variables
name_n, name_value_n,
calculation)               calculation argument = final result that is delivered by LET
```

Figure 16.1 *Arguments of the LET worksheet function.*

Examples 1 Through 3: Using the LET Worksheet Function When There Are Repeating Formula Elements

Figure 16.2 shows the formula =MID(B7,SEARCH("/",B7)+2,SEARCH(":",B7)-SEARCH("/",B7)-2). The goal of this formula is to extract the region text West from the full description text Carlota / West: 658. This can be accomplished by using a combination of the MID and SEARCH functions:

- The MID function can extract a partial text string from a larger text string based on a start digit number (in the *start_num* argument) and the number of characters to extract (in the *num_char* argument).

- As you first saw in Chapter 13, the SEARCH function reports the position of the specified text within a second text item, counting characters from left to right.

	A	B	C	D	E	F
2	Ex #1	Goal: Extract Region from Description:				
4			Repeat Elements:	LET:		
6		Description	Region	Region		
7		Carlota / West: 658	=MID(B7,SEARCH("/",B7)+2,SEARCH(":",B7)-SEARCH("/",B7)-2)			
8				MID(text, start_num, num_chars)		
9						
10				Repeated formula elements		
11						

Figure 16.2 This formula has the repeated formula element SEARCH("/",B7).

In this example, the formula element SEARCH("/",B7) determines that the / character is in the 9th position. This position number is then added to 2 (9 + 2), to yield 11, which is the starting position the MID function uses for extracting the text. The number of characters to extract from that 11th position is determined by the formula element SEARCH(":",B7)-SEARCH("/",B7)-2, which evaluates to $15 - 9 - 2 = 4$.

In the final evaluation step for the formula =MID("Carlota / West: 658",11,4), MID counts 11 characters from the left and then takes the 4 characters West. The original full formula, however, has the repeated formula element SEARCH("/",B7), which the Excel worksheet calculation engine must process two times. By using the LET function, as shown in Figure 16.3, you can remove the unnecessary repeated calculation steps by defining the variable Description to represent cell B7 and defining the variable SlashDigit to represent SEARCH("/",B7).

Note: When you type this formula into cell C7, you can use the keyboard shortcut Alt+Enter to add a line break after each variable and make the formula easier to read and understand.

	A	B	C	D	E	F	G	H	I
2	Ex #1	Goal: Extract Region from Description:							
4			Repeat Elements:	LET:					
6		Description	Region	Region					
7		Carlota / West: 658	West	=LET(					
8			Variable 1	Description,B7,					
9			Variable 2	SlashDigit,SEARCH("/",Description),					
10			Final Calculation	MID(Description,SlashDigit+2,SEARCH(":",Description)-SlashDigit-2))					
11				LET(name1, name_value1, calculation_or name2, [name_value2, calculation_or_name3], [name_value3, calculation_or_name4], [name_value4, ...])					
12				1	2	Final Calculation			

Figure 16.3 The LET function is used because there are repeated formula elements in the original formula.

When you define these two variables, the LET function evaluates each variable one time, stores the result in memory, and uses the result when necessary later in the formula for either a subsequent variable or in the final calculation. Although the amount of formula calculation time saved is not a lot for this single formula, if you had a large column of data, the time savings could be significant. For those in statistics, finance, economics, science, and other fields that often work with large formulas that have many repeated formula elements, using the LET function can be particularly beneficial in helping avoid unnecessary repeated calculation steps and making complex formulas easier to read.

You can try this example on the worksheet named Ch16(2-3).

In Figure 16.3, I chose to name my variables using full names. The advantage to this approach is that the variable names explicitly communicate the meanings of the variables and therefore make understanding the formula easier. There is less ambiguity in the meaning of the formula when you give variables informative names. The downside of this approach is that it can make formulas long and difficult to read. Figure 16.4 shows a different approach: using very short variable names. The advantages to this approach are that the formula is concise, and it looks less busy. The disadvantage is that it may be harder to understand because the meaning of a variable is not communicated in its name.

	A	B	C	D
2	**Ex #2**	**Goal:** Extract Region from Description:		
4			LET:	
6		**Description**	**Region**	
7		Carlota / West: 658	=LET(	
8			d,B7,	
9			sd,SEARCH("/",d),	
10			MID(d,sd+2,SEARCH(":",d)-sd-2))	
11			LET(name1, name_value1, calculation_or_name2, [name_value2, **calculation_or_name3**]	

Figure 16.4 This naming approach yields shorter and more concise formulas.

You can try this example on the worksheet named Ch16(4).

Editing the LET function formula is easy. As shown in Figure 16.5, if your goal for the formula changes from making a calculation on a single cell to making a calculation on a column of values, you can simply edit the formula by changing the Description variable value from cell B7 to the range B7:B10. The results then spill down the column.

	A	B	C	D	E	F	G	H
2	**Ex #3**	**Goal:** Extract Region from Description for full column:						
4			LET:					
6		**Description**	**Region**					
7		Carlota / West: 658	=LET(					
8		Aspen / South: 345	Description,B7:B10,					
9		Carlota / East: 23.5	SlashDigit,SEARCH("/",Description),					
10		Quad / West: 399.95	MID(Description,SlashDigit+2,SEARCH(":",Description)-SlashDigit-2))					
11			LET(name1, name_value1, calculation_or_name2, [name_value2, **calculation_or_name3**], [name_value3, calculation_or_name4], [name_value4, ...)					

Figure 16.5 *By editing the variable Description, you can have the formula spill a column of results.*

You can try this example on the worksheet named Ch16(5).

Examples 4 Through 7: Using the LET Worksheet Function to Create Single-Cell Reports

Another great way to use the LET function is to create a single-cell formula to deliver a full report. Figure 16.6 shows data in the range B7:B46 from a survey about customer preference for a particular soft drink. The reporting goal is to create a frequency distribution that shows the count for each ranking category, sorted from largest to smallest. The final report is in the range G7:H11 and shows that the Superior category received the most votes, at 11. This solution requires two initial formulas spilling from cells D7 and E7 and then a final report formula in cell G7.

	A	B	C	D	E	F	G	H
2		**Ex #4**	**Goal:** Create frequency distribution for soft drink rank data, sorted by count:					
4		Survey Results:					**Final Frequency Distribution:**	
6		**Rank Soft Drink by Category**		**Rank Soft Drink by Category**	**Count**		**Rank Soft Drink by Category**	**Count**
7		Superior		Superior	11		Superior	11
8		Superior		Poor	4		Great	10
9		Poor		Good	8		Good	8
10		Good		Great	10		Okay	7
11		Great		Okay	7		Poor	4
12		Good						
45		Superior		< Hidden Rows				
46		Superior						
48		**Formula 1:**		Cell D7: =UNIQUE(B7:B46)				
49		**Formula 2:**		Cell E7: =COUNTIFS(B7:B46,D7#)				
50		**Formula 3:**		Cell G7: =SORT(D7:E11,2,-1)				

Figure 16.6 *This sorted frequency distribution report requires three formulas in three different cells.*

Figure 16.7 shows how you can use the LET function to condense the three separate columns of calculations for the report into a single-cell formula. Inside the LET function, the UNIQUE and COUNTIFS functions create the two initial columns needed for the report; then the CHOOSE function simultaneously looks up both columns and delivers them as a two-column table. (You first saw how to use CHOOSE in this way in Example 26 in Chapter 14.) CHOOSE then delivers the final calculation to the LET function, and the SORT function sorts the two-column table from largest to smallest, based on the Count column.

	A	B	C	D	E	F
2		**Ex #5**		**Goal:** Create frequency distribution for soft drink rank data, sorted by count:		
4		Survey Results:		**Frequency Distribution:**		
6		**Rank Soft Drink by Category**		**Rank Soft Drink by Category**	**Count**	
7		Superior		=LET(		
8		Superior		Data,B7:B46,		
9		Poor		UniqueList,UNIQUE(Data),		
10		Good		Counts,COUNTIFS(Data,UniqueList),		
11		Great		Report,CHOOSE({1,2},UniqueList,Counts),		
12		Good		SORT(Report,2,-1))		

LET(name1, name_value1, calculation_or_name2, [name_value2, calculation_or_name3], [name_value3, calculation_or_name4], [name_value4, **calculation_or_name5**], [name_value6, ...])

	A	B	C	D	E	F
14		Good		**Result**	v v v	
15		Good		**Rank Soft Drink by Category**	**Count**	
16		Great		Superior	11	
17		Poor		Great	10	
18		Great		Good	8	
19		Okay		Okay	7	
20		Okay		Poor	4	
45		Superior				
46		Superior		< Hidden Rows		

Figure 16.7 When you use the LET function this way, the sorted frequency distribution report spills from a single cell.

As an alternative to using this LET formula, you could simply use this formula:

```
=SORT(CHOOSE({1,2},UNIQUE(B7:B46),COUNTIFS(B7:B46, UNIQUE(B7:B46))),2,-1)
```

Although this alternative has repeated formula elements, on a small dataset, it is a perfectly acceptable formula. However, the LET formula does have two advantages: It is easier to read because the variable names communicate the purpose of the formula elements, and it does not have to go through unnecessary formula evaluation steps.

You can try these two examples on the worksheets named Ch16(6) and Ch16(7).

Figure 16.8 shows a method to spill a frequency distribution report from a single cell that also includes the column headers and a total row. You can try this example on the worksheet named Ch16(8).

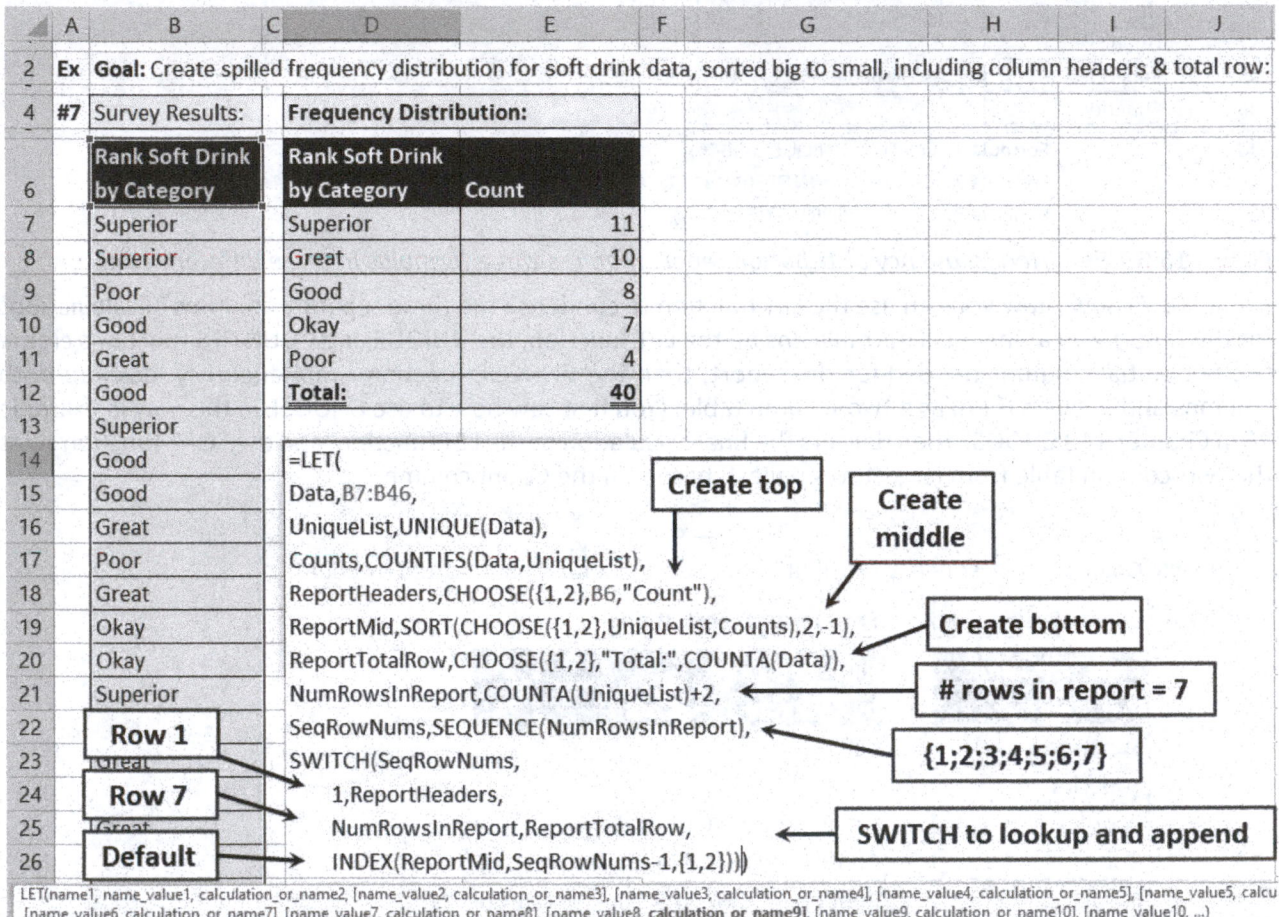

Figure 16.8 This LET function formula delivers the full report with column headers and a total row.

This type of formula is usually overkill and not necessary. A spilled frequency distribution report like the one in Figure 16.7 is usually sufficient for making a dynamic report. However, if you could construct a complex formula like the one in Figure 16.8 and then reuse it for multiple different datasets, that would be efficient and convenient. The LAMBDA function—another new Excel 365 function that's discussed later in this chapter—allows you to define your own custom reusable functions.

The basic idea of this formula is that you must create the three sections of the report (top, middle, and bottom) and then use the SWITCH lookup function (or the IFS function) to append the three sections, one on top of the other. (To review how to use SWITCH, see Chapter 14.) Figure 16.8 shows the three sections in the context of the full formula, and Figure 16.9 shows a close-up of the formulas used to create the top, middle, and bottom parts of the report.

Part	Variable Name	Formula	Result	
Top	ReportHeaders	=CHOOSE({1,2},B6,"Count")	Rank Soft Drink by Category	Count
Middle	ReportMid	=SORT(CHOOSE({1,2},UNIQUE(B7:B46), COUNTIFS(B7:B46,UNIQUE(B7:B46))),2,-1)	Superior	11
			Great	10
			Good	8
			Okay	7
			Poor	4
Bottom	ReportTotalRow	=CHOOSE({1,2},"Total:",COUNTA(B7:B46))	Total:	40

Figure 16.9 The formula elements for the top, middle, and bottom parts of the spilled report.

Before you can append the three sections, you must create variables for the total number of rows in the report and a sequence of numbers from 1 to the total number of rows in the report, as shown in Figure 16.8. To append the three tables, you can use the SWITCH function, where the first argument, *expression*, contains the sequence {1;2;3;4;5;6;7}, representing the seven rows in the report. Then, using the remaining arguments in SWITCH, you can place the top part of the report into row 1 and the bottom part of the report into row 7; the middle part of the report is then placed into the *default* argument of SWITCH. However, because the middle part of the report (the ReportMid variable) is a table with more than one row, you cannot simply place it into the *default* argument in SWITCH (as you did when you placed the single-row top and bottom parts of the report into SWITCH's arguments). If you did this, the first row of the ReportMid variable table would be cut off.

To get the ReportMid variable table to fit into the second row of the final report, you have to convert the 5R x 2C ReportMid variable table to a 7R x 2C table. As shown in Figure 16.10, you can use the INDEX lookup function to accomplish this by placing the ReportMid variable into the *array* argument, {0;1;2;3;4;5;6} into the *row_num* argument, and {1,2} into the *column_num* argument (refer to Example 19 in Chapter 14). For the resulting 7R x 2C table output from the INDEX function, the duplicate in the first row is caused by the row 0 number, which is a valid row number for pulling the first row. Then the full ReportMid variable gets placed into row 2 because the 1 value is in the second position in the *row_num* argument, as shown here:

$$\{0;1;2;3;4;5;6\}$$

Subsequently, the second through fifth rows from the ReportMid variable are selected and spilled. Finally, the last row shows error values because there is no 6th row in the ReportMid variable table. When the INDEX function fully evaluates and delivers the 7R x 2C table to the *default* argument in the SWITCH function, the SWITCH function pulls it into row 2 in the final report. Because the top and bottom parts were previously selected by SWITCH, they sit on top of the duplicate value and error row in the final 7R x 2C report.

Note: If you are appending tables, the key idea is to place the number 1 in the correct location in the array of row numbers that you use in the *row_num* argument of the INDEX function. For example, if you needed to place the ReportMid variable table in the third row rather than the second row, you would use this array of row numbers: {-1;0;1;2;3;4;5}. Otherwise, if the appended item contains just a single row or is a table placed in the first row of the final spilled result, you do not need to use the INDEX function. Practice Problem 1 at the end of this chapter involves appending multiple tables using the INDEX and IFS functions. You can expand your skills related to appending formulas by attempting that problem and looking at the answer sheet.

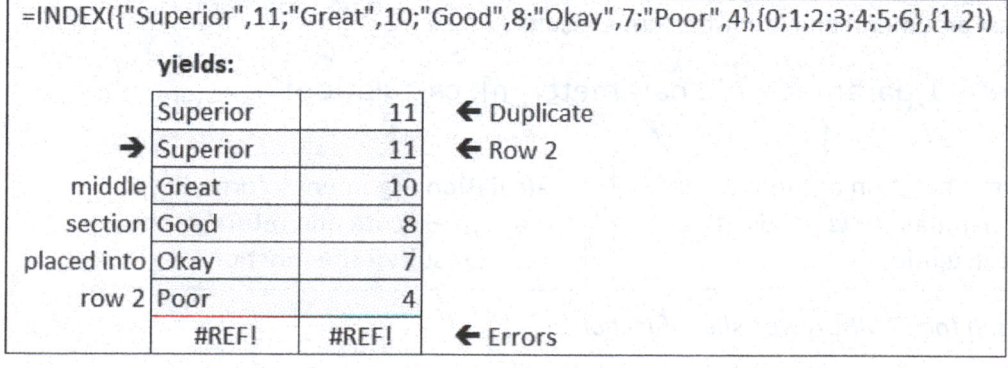

Figure 16.10 *Using INDEX to convert a 5R x 2C table into a 7R x 2C table.*

Figure 16.11 shows a close-up of the final LET formula used in this example.

```
=LET(
Data,B7:B46,
UniqueList,UNIQUE(Data),
Counts,COUNTIFS(Data,UniqueList),
ReportHeaders,CHOOSE({1,2},B6,"Count"),
ReportMid,SORT(CHOOSE({1,2},UniqueList,Counts),2,-1),
ReportTotalRow,CHOOSE({1,2},"Total:",COUNTA(Data)),
NumRowsInReport,COUNTA(UniqueList)+2,
SeqRowNums,SEQUENCE(NumRowsInReport),
SWITCH(SeqRowNums,
    1,ReportHeaders,
    NumRowsInReport,ReportTotalRow,
    INDEX(ReportMid,SeqRowNums-1,{1,2})))
```

Figure 16.11 The final LET worksheet function formula to create a sorted frequency distribution report.

Note: When you study Power Query in Chapter 18 and beyond, you will learn that Power Query uses a let expression that is similar to the LET worksheet function. Both the LET worksheet function and the Power Query let expression allow you to define variables, use the variables throughout the process, and then deliver a final value.

The LAMBDA Function

The LAMBDA function allows you to define a custom function that you can reuse. You might want to use this function, for example, when you need to make the same calculation repeatedly in a particular workbook or when you want to make complex formulas easier to use. The LAMBDA function creates a function value that you copy from the worksheet and then use to create a defined name in the Create Name dialog box. Once the LAMBDA function defined name formula has been saved, the function is available in the worksheet as a reusable function. In addition, although we don't discuss it in this book, it is worth mentioning that a defined function created by LAMBDA is recursive, which just means the function can be called within itself to make iterative calculations.

Note: The one downside of custom reusable functions (as of this writing) is that Excel does not provide screentips to help you with the function arguments.

The LAMBDA function has the following syntax (see Figure 16.12):

```
LAMBDA([parameter1, parameter2, …, parameter_n], calculation)
```

The arguments of the LAMBDA function are as follows:

- **parameter1, parameter2, parameter_n**: These optional arguments are function arguments in the returned function. You can enter up to 253 parameters..
- **calculation**: This argument is the formula you want to execute and return as a result of the function. It must be the last argument, and it must return a result.

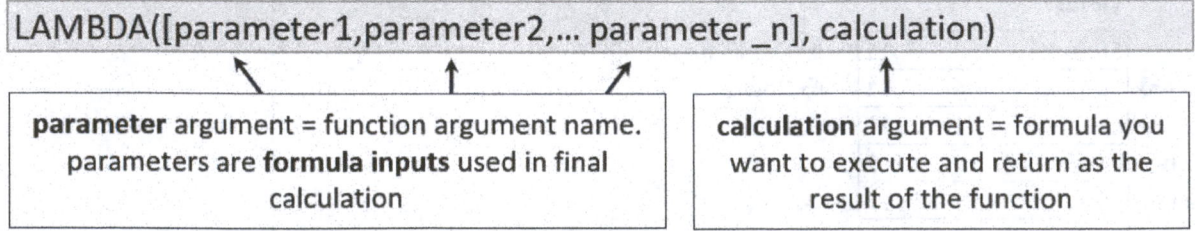

Figure 16.12 *Arguments in the LAMBDA worksheet function.*

Examples 8 and 9: Using the LAMBDA Worksheet Function to Create Reusable Functions for Common Calculations

When you use the LAMBDA function to create a function, you follow four steps:

1. Create a worksheet formula.

2. Create the LAMBDA function in the worksheet and test it.

3. Copy the LAMBDA function (without the test part), paste it into the name manager, and give it a descriptive name.

4. Test the defined-name LAMBDA function.

Figure 16.13 shows an example of creating a function that calculates the percentage change between a start amount and an end amount and then using the TEXT function to convert the answer to a text value by applying the custom number formatting 0.00% to show a percentage with two decimal places.

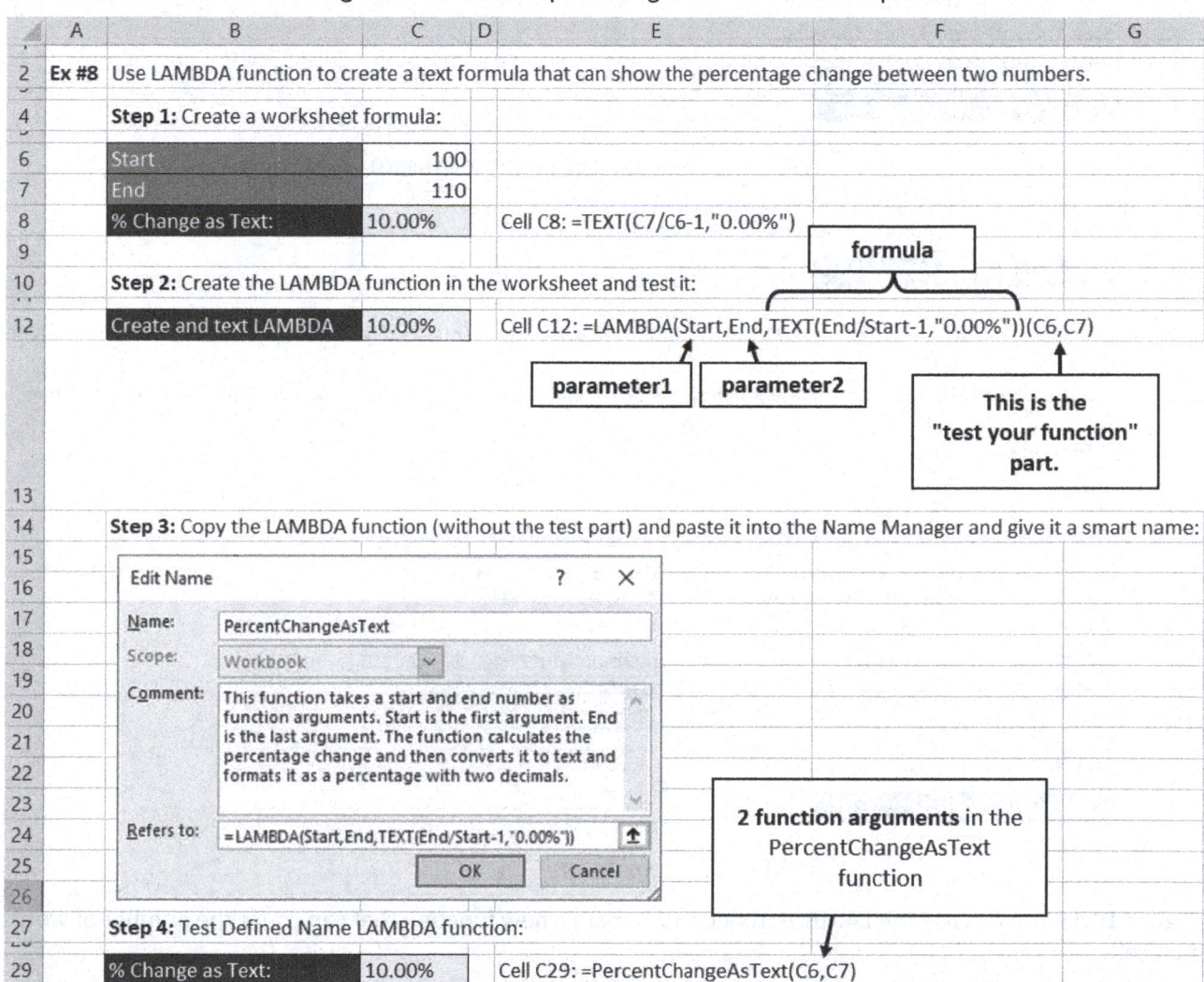

Figure 16.13 *A LAMBDA function to create a reusable function.*

You can try this example on the worksheet named Ch16(13).

LAMBDA can be very helpful in formulas that you tend to use all the time. For example, if you often need to count the number of words in a cell, where words are separated by spaces, you can create this formula:

```
=LAMBDA(Text,LEN(TRIM(Text))-LEN(SUBSTITUTE(TRIM(Text)," ",""))+1)
```

In this formula, the TRIM function removes all spaces except single spaces between words. Then the SUBSTITUTE function removes all spaces to leave only the characters. The LEN function counts the number of characters in both the text with the single spaces between words and the text without spaces. Finally, the formula calculates the difference between the two counts and adds 1 to get a final count of the number of words in the cell.

In this formula, you might notice that there is formula element repetition and that it is possible to refine the LAMBDA function by using the LET function, as shown in Figure 16.14. You can define a single parameter in LAMBDA named Text, and then, inside the LET function, rather than define a variable that points to a cell, you can define a variable that points to the LAMBDA function's parameter. Figure 16.15 shows the full process.

```
=LAMBDA(Text,
LET(t,Text, tt,TRIM(t),
LEN(tt)-LEN(SUBSTITUTE(tt," ","")))+1)(C6)
```

Figure 16.14 *You can use the LET function inside LAMBDA to make the formula more efficient.*

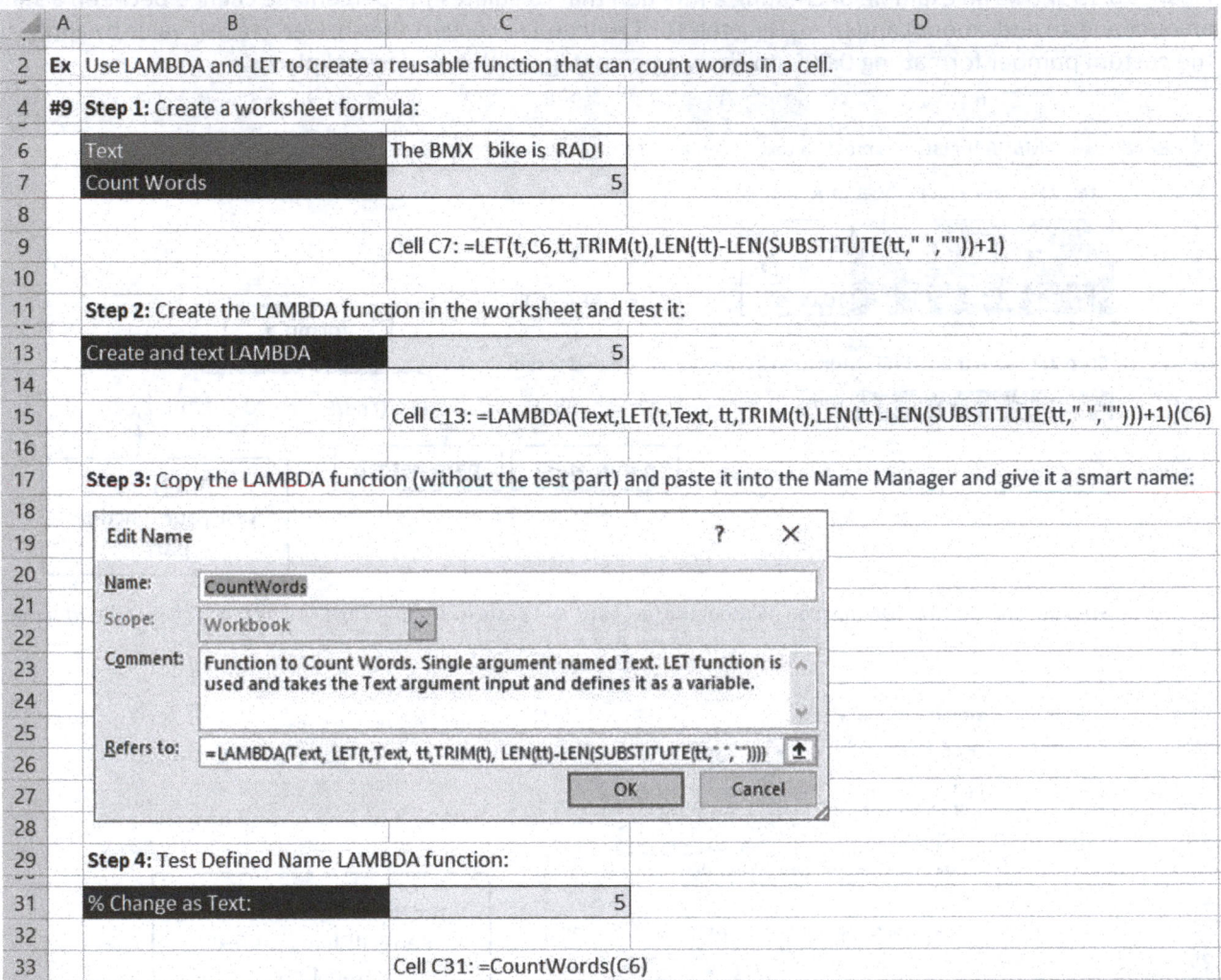

	A	B	C	D
2	Ex	Use LAMBDA and LET to create a reusable function that can count words in a cell.		
4	#9	**Step 1:** Create a worksheet formula:		
6		Text	The BMX bike is RAD!	
7		Count Words	5	
8				
9			Cell C7: =LET(t,C6,tt,TRIM(t),LEN(tt)-LEN(SUBSTITUTE(tt," ","")))+1)	
10				
11		**Step 2:** Create the LAMBDA function in the worksheet and test it:		
13		Create and text LAMBDA	5	
14				
15			Cell C13: =LAMBDA(Text,LET(t,Text, tt,TRIM(t),LEN(tt)-LEN(SUBSTITUTE(tt," ","")))+1)(C6)	
16				
17		**Step 3:** Copy the LAMBDA function (without the test part) and paste it into the Name Manager and give it a smart name:		

Edit Name ? ✕

Name: CountWords

Scope: Workbook

Comment: Function to Count Words. Single argument named Text. LET function is used and takes the Text argument input and defines it as a variable.

Refers to: =LAMBDA(Text, LET(t,Text, tt,TRIM(t), LEN(tt)-LEN(SUBSTITUTE(tt," ","")))) ⬆

OK   Cancel

29		**Step 4:** Test Defined Name LAMBDA function:		
31		% Change as Text:	5	
32				
33			Cell C31: =CountWords(C6)	

Figure 16.15 *You can use the LAMBDA function to create a new function that can count the number of words in a cell.*

You can try this example on the worksheet named Ch16(14-15).

Examples 10 and 11: Using the LAMBDA Worksheet Function to Simplify Complex Formula Reports

The two examples you just completed illustrate how you can use LAMBDA to build functions for calculations that you perform often. Another great use for LAMBDA is to make complex formulas easier to use.

Figure 16.16 shows how you can use the LAMBDA function with two parameters to make the spilled sorted frequency distribution LET formula you saw back in Figure 16.8 easier to use. By defining two function arguments (that is, parameters) in LAMBDA and then using them in LET, you can create a custom function that requires only two argument inputs to spill the complete report.

You can try this example on the worksheet named Ch16(16). The LET function is already on this sheet, and you just need to use the LAMBDA function and the Define Name feature to create a new custom function with the name SortedFrequencyDistribution.

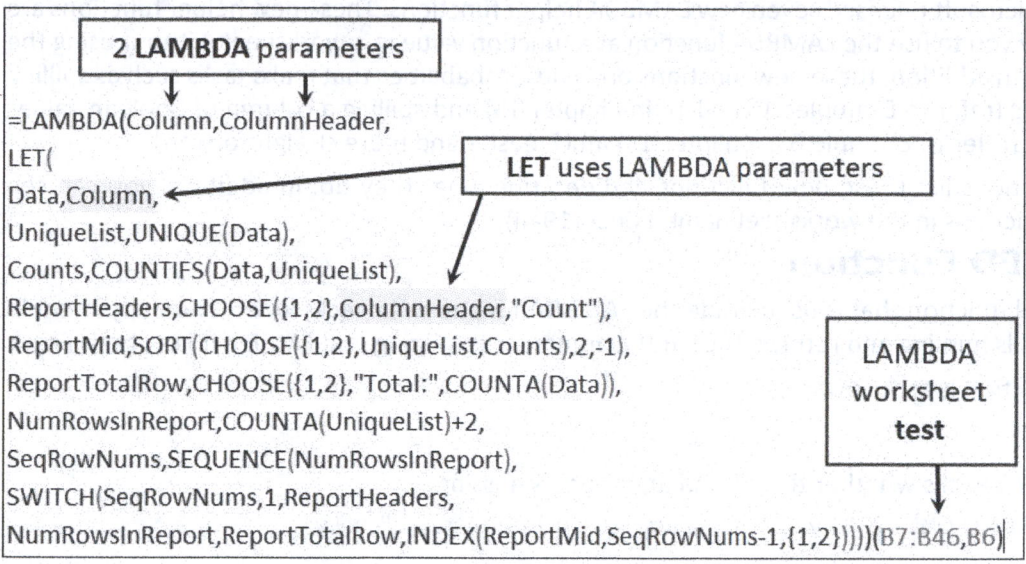

2 LAMBDA parameters

```
=LAMBDA(Column,ColumnHeader,
LET(
Data,Column,
UniqueList,UNIQUE(Data),
Counts,COUNTIFS(Data,UniqueList),
ReportHeaders,CHOOSE({1,2},ColumnHeader,"Count"),
ReportMid,SORT(CHOOSE({1,2},UniqueList,Counts),2,-1),
ReportTotalRow,CHOOSE({1,2},"Total:",COUNTA(Data)),
NumRowsInReport,COUNTA(UniqueList)+2,
SeqRowNums,SEQUENCE(NumRowsInReport),
SWITCH(SeqRowNums,1,ReportHeaders,
NumRowsInReport,ReportTotalRow,INDEX(ReportMid,SeqRowNums-1,{1,2})))))(B7:B46,B6)
```

LET uses LAMBDA parameters

LAMBDA worksheet test

Figure 16.16 *The LET function uses the two parameters from the LAMBDA function.*

Once you have created the SortedFrequencyDistribution function, you can try it on a new dataset on the worksheet named Ch16(17-18).

Figure 16.17 shows the simplicity of the new function. All you have to do is enter the column of new data into the first argument and the data column header name into the second argument. When you press the Enter key, the full report spills into the worksheet, as shown in Figure 16.18.

	A	B	C	D	E
2	Ex #11	Goal: Use SortedFrequencyDistribution function on new data set.			
4		Autos Sold At Dealer		=SortedFrequencyDistribution(B5:B383,B4)	
5		Toyota			
6		Chevy			
7		Honda			
8		Ford			
9		Ford			
10		Chevy			
382		Toyota			
383		Subaru			

Figure 16.17 *This LAMBDA function allows users to use complicated formulas without seeing the complexity.*

D4		× ✓ fx	=SortedFrequencyDistribution(B5:B383,B4)	

	A	B	C	D	E
2	Ex #11	Goal: Use SortedFrequencyDistribution function on new data set.			
4		Autos Sold At Dealer		Autos Sold At Dealer	Count
5		Toyota		Toyota	106
6		Chevy		Subaru	93
7		Honda		Ford	65
8		Ford		Honda	63
9		Ford		Chevy	52
10		Chevy		Total:	379
382		Toyota			
383		Subaru			

Figure 16.18 The SortedFrequencyDistribution can now be used on any column of data.

New LAMBDA Helper Functions That Allow You to Use a LAMBDA Function Value in the Worksheet

At the end of 2021, Microsoft released seven new LAMBDA helper functions. These new helper functions are amazing as they allow you to use the LAMBDA function as a function value in a worksheet without using the Define Name feature. In addition, these new functions bring new capabilities that make tasks such as spilling a column of row totals (refer to Examples 15 and 16 in Chapter 15) and spilling a column of Boolean values in an AND logical test (refer to Example 6 in Chapter 13) much easier and more straightforward.

The following subsections list these new functions and describe what they do. In addition, you can see examples of these functions in the worksheet named Ch16(19an).

The ISOMITTED Function

ISOMITTED is a logical function that is used inside the LAMBDA function. It checks whether an argument in the LAMBDA function is missing and returns TRUE if the argument is missing and FALSE if it is not missing.

The syntax of this function is as follows:

```
=ISOMITTED(argument)
```

The following example checks whether the second argument is missing:

```
=LAMBDA(x,y, IF(ISOMITTED(y),"Missing second argument",x+y))
```

The following example checks whether the first argument, the second argument, or both arguments are missing:

```
=LAMBDA(Start,End,IFS(AND(ISOMITTED(Start),ISOMITTED(End)),"Enter Both Start
and End Amounts",ISOMITTED(Start),"Please Enter Start",ISOMITTED(End),"Please
Enter End",TRUE,End/Start-1))
```

The MAKEARRAY Function

MAKEARRAY is a function that spills a calculated array of a specified row and column size, based on a scalar LAMBDA function result. MAKEARRAY uses the LAMBDA function in its last argument. The LAMBDA function must deliver a scalar value, not an array of values.

The syntax of this function is as follows:

```
=MAKEARRAY(rows, cols, LAMBDA(row, col, formula))
```

The following example generates a 2x2 array with random numbers that fit a bell-shaped distribution:

```
=MAKEARRAY(2,2,LAMBDA(r,c,ABS(ROUND(NORM.INV(RAND(),45,10),2)))).
```

The following example multiplies the corresponding row or column position to generate an array:

```
=MAKEARRAY(2,2,LAMBDA(r,c,r*c))
```

The BYROW Function

The BYROW function spills a single column of row values by applying a LAMBDA function to each row in the array listed in the first argument of BYROW. BYROW uses the LAMBDA function in its last argument. The LAMBDA function must deliver a scalar value, not an array of values.

The syntax of this function is as follows:

```
=BYROW(array, LAMBDA(row, formula))
```

The following example generates a spilled column of row totals for a table:

```
=BYROW(C5:E7, LAMBDA(r, SUM(r)))
```

The following example generates a spilled column of row totals by summing the result from multiplying a single-row table by each row in the array in the first argument of BYROW:

```
=BYROW(M31:N33, LAMBDA(r, SUM(r*M29:N29)))
```

The BYCOL Function

The BYCOL function spills a single row of column values by applying a LAMBDA function to each column in the array listed in the first argument of BYCOL. BYCOL uses the LAMBDA function in its last argument. The LAMBDA function must deliver a scalar value, not an array of values.

The syntax of this function is as follows:

```
=BYCOL(array, LAMBDA(column, formula))
```

The following example generates a spilled row of column totals for a table:

```
=BYCOL(T31:V33, LAMBDA(c, SUM(c)))
```

The MAP Function

The MAP function spills an array of the same size as the array (or arrays) listed in the arguments of MAP by applying a LAMBDA function to each item in the array (or arrays) listed. The MAP function can have one or more arrays listed in its arguments, and the LAMBDA function is listed as the last argument. The LAMBDA function works over a single array or in parallel across multiple arrays when more than one array is listed. The LAMBDA function must deliver a scalar value, not an array of values.

The syntax of this function is as follows:

```
=MAP(array, LAMBDA(items, formula))
```

For more than one array, the syntax is as follows:

```
=MAP(array1, array2, …arrayN, LAMBDA(items1, items2, …itemN, formula))
```

The following example generates an array of squared number values:

```
=MAP(J13:L15,LAMBDA(item,item^2))
```

The following example generates a column of TRUE/FALSE values based on an AND logical test:

```
=MAP(D19:D22,E19:E22, LAMBDA(cr,gpa, AND(cr>=E15,gpa>=E16)))
```

The SCAN Function

The SCAN function spills an array of the same size as the array listed in the second argument of SCAN by applying an accumulating LAMBDA function to each item in the array listed. If you use the SCAN function to add, you generate a running total or a list of accumulated values. SCAN and REDUCE are similar in that they accumulate values. However, whereas SCAN lists each intermediate values in the accumulation process, REDUCE delivers only the final value calculated in the accumulation process. SCAN uses the LAMBDA function in its last argument. The LAMBDA function must deliver a scalar value, not an array of values.

The syntax of this function is as follows:

```
=SCAN (initial_value, array, LAMBDA(accumulator, item, formula))
```

The following example successively *adds* the numbers in the array to spill an array of intermediate accumulated amounts:

```
=SCAN(0,E10:E13, LAMBDA(acc,i,acc+i))
```

The following example successively *multiplies* the numbers in the array to spill an array of intermediate accumulated amounts:

```
=SCAN(1,E10:E13, LAMBDA(acc,i,acc*i))
```

The following example successively *joins* the items in the array to spill an array of intermediate accumulated amounts:

```
=SCAN("",D10:D13, LAMBDA(acc,i,acc&i))
```

The REDUCE Function

REDUCE works that same way as SCAN, but it delivers the final result only after all items in the array have been accumulated. If you run the same calculation using REDUCE and using SCAN, REDUCE will deliver only the last value in the array that the SCAN function spills. REDUCE uses the LAMBDA function in its last argument. The LAMBDA function must deliver a scalar value, not an array of values.

The syntax of this function is as follows:

```
=REDUCE (initial_value, array, LAMBDA(accumulator, item, formula))
```

Example 12: Three Examples of LAMBDA Helper Functions

Figure 16.19 shows examples of how to use the BYROWS function to spill a column of row totals, the SCAN function to spill a list of running total amounts, and the MAP function to spill a column of AND logical test results. This figure also shows the old-school formulas that were used before these new functions were introduced.

You can try this example on the worksheet named Ch16(19).

	A	B	C	D	E	F	G	H	I	J	K
2		Ex #12		Goal: Learn about BYROW, SCAN and MAP functions.							
4		Date/Product	Aspen	Bellen	Quad	Spilled Row Totals:		BYROW			
5		8/11/21	120.79	125.11	18.8	264.7		Cell F5: =BYROW(C5:E7, LAMBDA(r, SUM(r)))			
6		8/12/21	225	154.05	288.73	667.78		What we used before BYROW:			
7		8/13/21	178.73	247.21	313.95	739.89		=MMULT(C5:E7,ROW(B5:B7)^0)			
9			Sales		Counts	Spilled Running Total:		SCAN			
10			0 up to 25		15	15		Cell F10: =SCAN(0,E10:E13, LAMBDA(acc,i,acc+i))			
11			25 up to 50		8	23		What we used before SCAN:			
12			50 up to 75		5	28		=SUBTOTAL(9,OFFSET(E10,,,ROW(E10:E13)-ROW(E9)))			
13			Over 75		4	32					
14											
15				Credit Hurdle:	45						
16				GPA Hurdle:	2.5						
18		Student	Major	Credits	GPA	Spilled AND Test:		MAP			
19		Sim, Chantel	History	70	4	TRUE		Cell F19: =MAP(D19:D22,E19:E22, LAMBDA(cr,gpa, AND(cr>=E15,gpa>=E16)))			
20		Carey, Zada	Business	45	1.7	FALSE		What we used before MAP:			
21		Nga, Luong	Physics	45	2.4	FALSE		=IF((D19:D22>=E15)*(E19:E22>=E16),TRUE)			
22		Kins, Tyrone	Sociology	75	3.9	TRUE					

Figure 16.19 *Examples of three of the seven LAMBDA helper functions: BYROW, SCAN, and MAP.*

Key Concepts in Chapter 16

- With the **LET function**, you can define variables within the function itself and use variables to create a final calculation that is delivered to the worksheet or internally to other formulas. The LET function has a number of advantages:
  - A variable is evaluated a single time, and the result is stored in memory so that it can be used throughout the formula. For formulas with repeating formula elements, this can reduce overall calculation time by preventing duplication of evaluation procedures.
  - Formulas with repeating elements are easy to edit because there is only one location to edit.
  - Complex formulas can be visually easy to read because each element has a name, and elements can be placed on different lines.
  - You can condense reports made up of multiple formula columns into a single-cell formula that spills the complete report into the worksheet.
- The **LAMBDA function** allows you to define a reusable custom function that can be helpful when you need to make the same calculation multiple times in a specific workbook or when you want to make a more user-friendly function for complex calculations. You can also use LAMBDA to define a function value that you can use in related functions, such as MAP and BYROW.
- There are seven **LAMBDA helper functions** that work with the LAMBDA function exclusively: ISOMITTED, MAKEARRAY, BYROW, BYCOL, MAP, SCAN, and REDUCE.
- Although the process is complex, you can **append tables by using worksheet formulas**; it is much easier to do this with the various Power Query append tools. However, there are some situations where a formula append may be required, such as when you're appending the different parts of a report into a single report. You can use the SWITCH or IFS functions for appending tables. If the table being appended is the top table in the append or is a table with a single row, you can use the table

directly. If there are two or more rows in the table, you can use the INDEX function with an array of row numbers where the row 1 number is in the correct relative position.

Practice Problems for Chapter 16

Practice Problem 1

In your Excel file for this chapter (Ch16-Excel365-LETandLAMBDA.xlsx), go to the worksheet named PPCh16(1) and create the solution for this practice problem. Figure 16.20 shows the goal that is listed on that worksheet.

	A	B	C	D	E	F	G	H	I	J	K	L	M	N
2		Goal:		This formula in cell J9: =FILTER(FILTER(C9:F15,(C9:C15=H9)+(C9:C15=H10)),ISNUMBER(XMATCH(C8:F8,J8:K8)))										
3				filters the records by the specified product names and then filters to show just the product and sales columns.										
4				Using the LET worksheet function in cell M9, remove the duplicate references and make the formula easier to										
5				understand with smart variable names.										
6										Original Formula:			LET function:	
8		Sales Rep	Product	Color	Date	Sales		Product Criteria		Product	Sales		Product	Sales
9		Sioux	Quad	Blue	12/2/20	326.2		Carlota		Quad	326.17			
10		Chantel	Yanaki	Red	12/2/20	251.6		Quad		Quad	374.03			
11		Chin	Quad	Blue	12/2/20	374				Carlota	446.2			
12		Chantel	Aspen	Red	12/2/20	256.2				Quad	236.06			
13		Chin	Aspen	Blue	12/2/20	171.2								
14		Sioux	Carlota	Red	12/2/20	446.2								
15		Sioux	Quad	Clear	12/2/20	236.1								

Figure 16.20 *On the worksheet named PPCh16(1), remove the formula element repetition by using the LET function.*

When you are done with this problem, you can check your work against the answer sheet named PPCh16(1an).

Practice Problem 2

In your Excel file for this chapter (Ch16-Excel365-LETandLAMBDA.xlsx), go to the worksheet named PPCh16(2) and create the solution for this practice problem. Figure 16.21 shows the goal that is listed on that worksheet.

	A	B	C	D	E	F	G	H	I	J	K	L
2		Goal:					Use LET function to remove formula element repetition from the advanced statistics calculation in cell H15.					
3							Create your LET worksheet function formula in cell H21.					
5		2011	2012	2013	2014		Question: Executive at HMO wanted to check Patient Record Data accuracy and see					
6		Yes	Yes	No	No		if the proportion error rate was different between the years 2011 - 2014.					
7		No	No	No	No							
8		No	No	No	No				Alpha		0.05	
9		No	No	No	No		Observed Frequencies = f_{ij} :					
10		Yes	No	No	No		Errors in Form/Year		2011	2012	2013	2014 Total
11		Yes	No	Yes	No		Yes		39	43	45	41	168
12		No	No	No	No		No		304	223	271	341	1139
13		No	No	No	No		Total		343	266	316	382	1307
14		Yes	No	No	No							
15		No	No	No	No		Test Statistic Chi-Square = χ^2 =		=SUM((H11:K12-L11:L12/L13*H13:K13)^2/(L11:L12/L13*H13:K13))			
16		No	No	No	No		k = count populations =		4			
17		No	No	No	No		df		3			
18		No	No	No	No		p-value =		0.147605801			
19		No	No	No	No		Chi Critical Value		7.814727903			
20		No	No	No	No							
21		No	No	No	Yes		Test Statistic Chi-Square = χ^2 =			←	LET function	

Figure 16.21 *On the worksheet PPCh16(2), remove the formula element repetition from the statistics formula.*

When you are done with this problem, you can check your work against the answer sheet named PPCh16(2an).

Practice Problem 3

The goal of this problem is to redo Example 16 in Chapter 15 and replace MMULT in the standard deviation of expected portfolio returns calculation with the BYROW and LAMBDA functions. There is no picture for this practice problem. In your Excel file for this chapter (Ch16-Excel365-LETandLAMBDA.xlsx), go to the worksheet named PPCh16(3) and create the solution for this practice problem.

When you are done with this problem, you can check your work against the answer sheet named PPCh16(3an).

Practice Problem 4

In your Excel file for this chapter (Ch16-Excel365-LETandLAMBDA.xlsx), go to the worksheet named PPCh16(4) and create the solution for this practice problem. Figure 16.22 shows the goal that is listed on that worksheet.

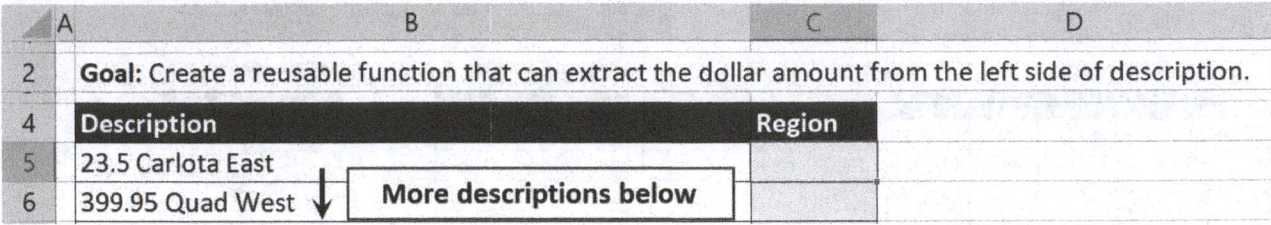

	A	B	C	D
2	**Goal:** Create a reusable function that can extract the dollar amount from the left side of description.			
4	**Description**		**Region**	
5	23.5 Carlota East			
6	399.95 Quad West ↓	**More descriptions below**		

Figure 16.22 On the worksheet named PPCh16(4), create a reusable function to extract the dollar amount from the description.

When you are done with this problem, you can check your work against the answer sheet named PPCh16(4an).

Practice Problem 5

In your Excel file for this chapter (Ch16-Excel365-LETandLAMBDA.xlsx), go to the worksheet named PPCh16(5) and create the solution for this practice problem. Figure 16.23 shows the goal that is listed on that worksheet.

	A	B	C	D	E	F	G	H	I
2	**Goal:** Create a reusable function that can create a Product Sales Total Report.								
4	**Product**		**Sales**		**Product**	**Sales**			
5	Quad		326.17						
6	Carlota		251.57 ↓		**More records below**				
7	Quad		374.03 ▼						

Figure 16.23 *On the worksheet named PPCh16(5), create a reusable function that delivers a product sales report.*

When you are done with this problem, you can check your work against the answer sheet named PPCh16(5an).

Practice Problem 6

In your Excel file for this chapter (Ch16-Excel365-LETandLAMBDA.xlsx), go to the worksheet named PPCh16(6) and create the solution for this practice problem. Figure 16.24 shows the goal that is listed on that worksheet.

	A	B	C	D	E	F	G	H	I	J	K	L
2	**Goal:** Append the three tables with a formula.											
4	**Array 1:**				**Array 2:**			**Array 3:**			**More**	
5											**records**	
6	Shawnta Gable		3.9		Marica Perryman	3.6		Cinda Jacobsen		1.5	**below**	
7	Rina Tejeda		4.0		Jarrod Neville	3.5		Nam Duffy		1.9 ↓		
8	Gus Cornelius		2.3		Edwina Nutt	3.1		Sherika Perales		4.0		

Figure 16.24 On the worksheet named PPCh16(6), create a formula that appends tables with student names and grade data.

When you are done with this problem, you can check your work against the answer sheet named PPCh16(6an).

Practice Problem 7

In your Excel file for this chapter (Ch16-Excel365-LETandLAMBDA.xlsx), go to the worksheet named PPCh16(7) and create the solution for this practice problem. Figures 16.25 and Figure 16.26 show the goal for the problem and two possible solutions.

E6   fx   =INDEX(I6:M10,XMATCH(D6:D42,H6:H10),XMATCH(C6:C42,I5:M5))*B6:B42

2 Goal: Convert amounts in the Amount field from source to target currency using conversion table.
3   Create a formula in cell E7 that can spill the two-way lookup results.

	Amount	Source currency	Target currency	Amount in target currency			Source				
							USD	GBP	CAD	EUR	AUD
6	705.51	CAD	GBP	333.08		USD	1.00	1.86	0.88	1.25	0.75
7	389.29	EUR	CAD	554.75		GBP	0.54	1.00	0.47	0.67	0.41
8	568.64	GBP	EUR	845.19		CAD	1.14	2.12	1.00	1.43	0.86
9	408.72	USD	GBP	219.67		EUR	0.80	1.49	0.70	1.00	0.60
10	743.76	USD	EUR	594.15		AUD	1.33	2.47	1.17	1.66	1.00
11	296.37	EUR	USD	370.99							
12	509.32	CAD	GBP	240.46							
13	632.68	AUD	EUR	380.93							
14	698.64	CAD	USD	613.70							
15	144.42	AUD	EUR	86.95							
16	148.72	AUD	GBP	60.25							
17	227.55	GBP	EUR	338.22							
42	470.98	EUR	GBP	316.87							

Formula you can use in cell E7:
```
=INDEX(
    I7:M11,
    XMATCH(D7:D43,H7:H11),
    XMATCH(C7:C43,I6:M6)
    )*B7:B43
```

Figure 16.25 On the worksheet named PPCh16(7), this is one way (solution 1) to create a two-way lookup formula that can spill results.

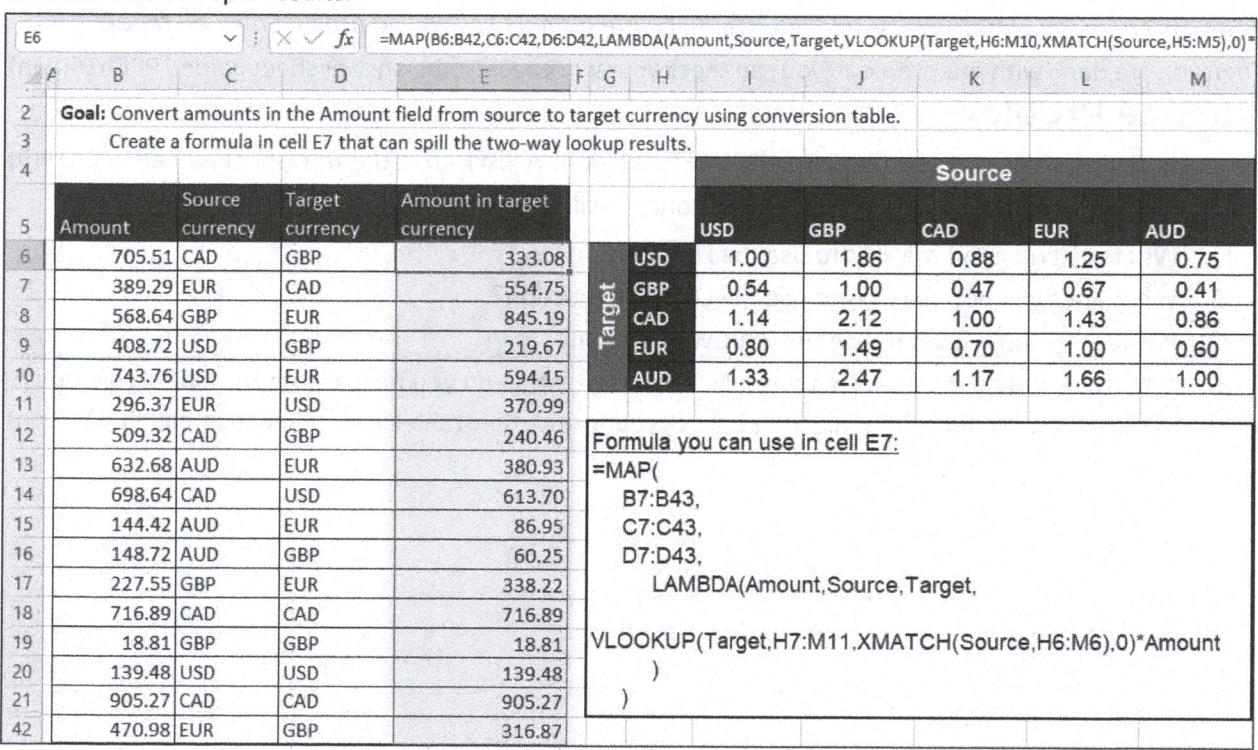

E6   fx   =MAP(B6:B42,C6:C42,D6:D42,LAMBDA(Amount,Source,Target,VLOOKUP(Target,H6:M10,XMATCH(Source,H5:M5),0)*

2 Goal: Convert amounts in the Amount field from source to target currency using conversion table.
3   Create a formula in cell E7 that can spill the two-way lookup results.

	Amount	Source currency	Target currency	Amount in target currency			Source				
							USD	GBP	CAD	EUR	AUD
6	705.51	CAD	GBP	333.08		USD	1.00	1.86	0.88	1.25	0.75
7	389.29	EUR	CAD	554.75		GBP	0.54	1.00	0.47	0.67	0.41
8	568.64	GBP	EUR	845.19		CAD	1.14	2.12	1.00	1.43	0.86
9	408.72	USD	GBP	219.67		EUR	0.80	1.49	0.70	1.00	0.60
10	743.76	USD	EUR	594.15		AUD	1.33	2.47	1.17	1.66	1.00
11	296.37	EUR	USD	370.99							
12	509.32	CAD	GBP	240.46							
13	632.68	AUD	EUR	380.93							
14	698.64	CAD	USD	613.70							
15	144.42	AUD	EUR	86.95							
16	148.72	AUD	GBP	60.25							
17	227.55	GBP	EUR	338.22							
18	716.89	CAD	CAD	716.89							
19	18.81	GBP	GBP	18.81							
20	139.48	USD	USD	139.48							
21	905.27	CAD	CAD	905.27							
42	470.98	EUR	GBP	316.87							

Formula you can use in cell E7:
```
=MAP(
    B7:B43,
    C7:C43,
    D7:D43,
        LAMBDA(Amount,Source,Target,

VLOOKUP(Target,H7:M11,XMATCH(Source,H6:M6),0)*Amount
        )
    )
```

Figure 16.26 *On the worksheet named PPCh16(7), this is another way (solution 2) to create a two-way lookup formula that can spill results.*

When you are done with this problem, you can check your work against the answer sheets named PPCh16(7-INDEXan) and PPCh16(7-MAPan).

Practice Problem 8

In your Excel file for this chapter (Ch16-Excel365-LETandLAMBDA.xlsx), go to the worksheet named PPCh16(8) and create the solution for this practice problem. Figure 16.27 shows the goal for the problem.

	A	B	C	D	E	F	G	H	I	J	K
2		**Goal:**	Create a single cell report in cell E5, that spills a sorted unique list of product name and median values.								
3			For the aggregate calculation you can use MEDIAN function.								
4			Hint: aggregate functions cannot spill. So this is where you can use LAMBDA and BYROWS functions.								
5			Finished result should look like the range E15:F17.								
6											
7		Product	Values		Product	Median					
8		Quad	26								
9		Aspen	96								
10		Carlota	60								
11		Quad	40								
12		Quad	30								
13		Aspen	72								
14		Carlota	11		Product	Median					
15		Carlota	45		Aspen	87.5					
16		Carlota	97		Carlota	52.5					
17		Aspen	96		Quad	35					
18		Aspen	79								
19		Quad	69								

Figure 16.27 *On the worksheet named PPCh16(8), create a single-cell spilled product median report.*

When you are done with this problem, you can check your work against the answer sheet named PPCh16(8an).

Practice Problem 9

In your Excel file for this chapter (Ch16-Excel365-LETandLAMBDA.xlsx), go to the worksheet named PPCh16(9).

In your own words, see if you can answer these conceptual questions:

5. What are two good reasons to use the LET function?
6. What are two good reasons to use the LAMBDA function?
7. What is a good reason to use the BYROWS function?
8. When appending tables with a formula, in what situation do you have to use the INDEX function?

When you are done with this problem, you can check your work against the answer sheet named PPCh16(9an).

Chapter 17: Data Analysis Basics: Standard Pivot Tables, Sorting, Filtering, Visualizations, and More

Note: To follow along with the examples in this chapter, you can use the file named Ch17-Excel365-IntroDataAnalysis.xlsx.

As you learned in Chapter 3, *data analysis* involves converting raw data into useful information for decision making. *Business intelligence* is very similar to data analysis except that the data and decision making are in a business context. For both data analysis and business intelligence, you need *useful information*—that is, reports, visuals, and other presentations of data that can help people make data-driven, evidence-based decisions.

So far in this book, you have already seen a number of examples of data analysis tasks, such as using a transactional sales table to create a sales report (Example 23 in Chapter 12; see Figure 17.1), converting survey results into a frequency distribution (Example 5 in Chapter 16; see Figure 17.2), sorting bike racing records to show the fastest times for each track on top (Example 59 in Chapter 15; see Figure 17.3), and filtering a table of sales records to show only the sales for the blue Quad product (Example 19 in Chapter 15; see Figure 17.4). In all four of these examples, worksheet formulas were used to create the useful information. In this chapter, you will learn that there are many other tools that you can use to create useful information from raw data.

Raw Data → Useful Information

Date	Product	Sales ($)	Cost ($)
8/12/20	Quad	4,024.80	2,092.32
8/12/20	Aspen	1,143.90	686.34
8/12/20	Sunshine	1,161.50	569.64
8/12/20	Yanaki	1,640.00	770.80
8/12/20	Carlota	2,616.25	1,099.00
8/13/20	Quad	3,144.75	1,415.40
8/13/20	Aspen	1,046.25	606.75
8/13/20	Sunshine	1,671.60	986.16
8/13/20	Yanaki	1,632.00	979.20
8/13/20	Carlota	1,171.10	702.66
8/17/20	Quad	3,159.16	1,642.76
8/17/20	Aspen	3,461.56	1,730.78
8/17/20	Carlota	3,891.44	2,179.21

Product	Total Sales ($)	Total Costs ($)
Aspen	5,651.71	3,023.87
Carlota	7,678.79	3,980.87
Quad	10,328.71	5,150.48
Sunshine	5,543.37	3,019.35
Yanaki	8,070.18	4,293.04

Formula in cell G5:
=SORT(UNIQUE(C5:C19))
Formula in cell H5:
=SUMIFS(D5:D19,$C$5:$C$19,$G$5#)
Formula in cell I5:
=SUMIFS(E5:E19,$C$5:$C$19,$G$5#)
< Hidden Rows

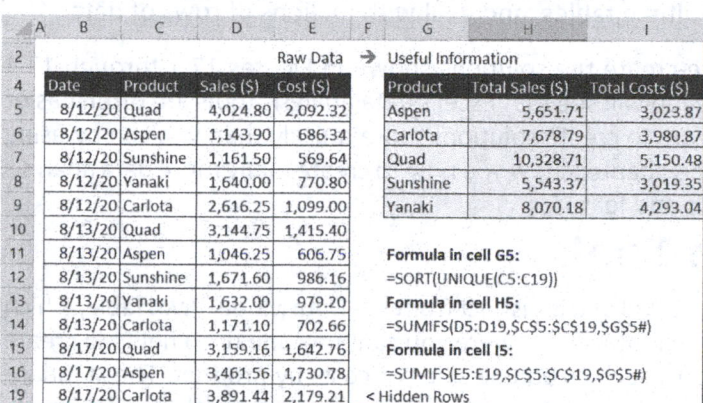

Figure 17.1 *Example 23 in Chapter 12: Converting sales data into a sales report.*

Raw Data → Useful Information

Rank Soft Drink by Category
Superior
Superior
Poor
Good
Great
Good
Superior
Good
Good
Great
Poor
Great
Okay
Okay
Superior

Rank Soft Drink by Category	Count
Superior	11
Great	10
Good	8
Okay	7
Poor	4

Formula in cell D5:
=LET(Data,B5:B44,
UniqueList,UNIQUE(Data),
Counts,COUNTIFS(Data,UniqueList),
Report,CHOOSE({1,2},UniqueList,Counts),
SORT(Report,2,-1))

< Hidden Rows

Figure 17.2 Example 5 in Chapter 16: Converting customer survey data into counts to see which rank got the most votes.

Raw Data → Useful Information

Date	Track	Racer	Time
8/5/22	SeaTac	Isaac	38.8
8/5/22	SeaTac	Zaine	38.2
8/5/22	SeaTac	Ella	38.1
8/6/22	Everett	Zaine	37.5
8/6/22	Everett	Isaac	35.1
8/6/22	Everett	Ella	36.5

Track	Racer	Time(s)
SeaTac	Ella	38.1
SeaTac	Zaine	38.2
SeaTac	Isaac	38.8
Everett	Isaac	35.1
Everett	Ella	36.5
Everett	Zaine	37.5

Formula in cell G5:
=SORT(C5:E10,{1,3},{-1,1})

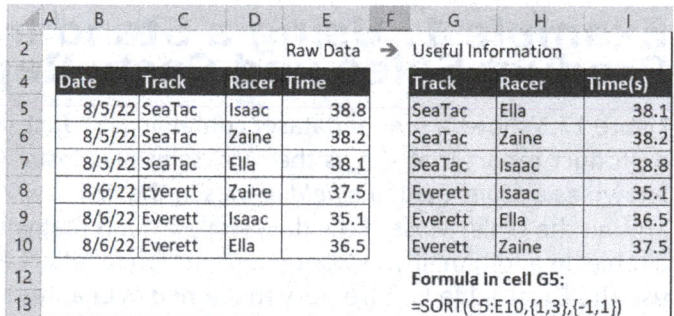

Figure 17.3 *Example 59 in Chapter 15: Sorting racing records to show fastest times for each track on top.*

Raw Data → Useful Information

Product	Color	Sales
Quad	Blue	326.17
Carlota	Red	251.57
Quad	Blue	374.03
Aspen	Red	256.22
Aspen	Blue	171.21
Carlota	Red	446.2
Quad	Clear	236.06

Product
Quad

Color
Blue

Product	Color	Sales
Quad	Blue	326.17
Quad	Blue	374.03

Formula in cell H5:
=FILTER(B5:D11,(B5:B11=F5)*(C5:C11=F8),"NA")

Figure 17.4 *Example 19 in Chapter 15: Filtering sales records to show only sales for the blue Quad product.*

The advantage of using formulas to perform data analysis is that when the source data changes, the formulas instantly update to reflect the new data. This is the hallmark of worksheet formulas. None of the other data analysis tools discussed in this book (such as Power Query and the Data Model) instantly update when source data changes. However, many data analysis tools (such as standard PivotTables, Power Query, and the Data Model) are much easier to use than formulas and can perform tasks that formulas cannot handle. In addition, most of the time, it is not hard to update the output from data analysis tools to reflect new data: You simply click a refresh button, and your solution updates.

This chapter focuses on the standard Excel data analysis tools that work well on small proper datasets that are stored in an Excel worksheet (with about 50,000 rows of data or less). Standard PivotTables, Excel charts, and conditional formatting are some examples of the data analysis tools covered in this chapter.

> **Note:** In Chapter 18, you will continue learning about data analysis, focusing on data analysis terms and data modeling tools such as Power Query, Power Pivot, and Power BI Desktop, which help you clean and transform data, work with multiple tables, and deal with millions of rows of data.

To begin the examples in this chapter, you will re-create the solutions shown in Figures 17.1 through 17.4 using non-formula data analysis tools. As you do, you will see that Excel's data analysis tools are often easier to use than worksheet formulas, and they allow you to create solutions more quickly than you can by using worksheet formulas. The rest of the examples in this chapter show you how to create many more data analysis solutions using Excel's amazing data analysis tools and features.

The Standard PivotTable Tool

The standard PivotTable tool has been around since 1993 and is distinct from the Data Model PivotTable, which was invented in 2009. Both tools have the same user interface, where you can drag and drop fields to create summary reports based on conditional calculations, such as adding sales or costs by product. The standard PivotTable tool is a commonly used quick and easy ad hoc data analysis tool; it is useful with small datasets (under around 50,000 rows) for simple calculations such as adding, counting, or calculating percentages. It makes these tasks easy and fun.

> **Note:** When you are working with a lot of data (about 50,000 rows or more) or need to make complex calculations, you should use the Data Model PivotTable tool, which is discussed in Chapters 18 and 19.

When you use the standard PivotTable tool, the data you use it on must be stored in a proper dataset (as a table). The standard PivotTable tool does not work on data that does not have field names.

Example 1: Using a Standard PivotTable to Create a Product Sales and Costs Report

Figure 17.5 shows a proper dataset containing product sales and cost data. The data analysis goal is to create a product report that shows the total sales and costs. As you learned in Chapter 8, a *proper dataset*, also known as a *table*, contains *field names* in the first row, *records* of data in subsequent rows, and empty cells around the table. Most of the data analysis tools that you will learn about require that you store your data in a table. In addition, if you want your solution to reflect any new data that is added to the table, you need to use the Excel Table feature. As you learned in Chapter 8, the Excel Table feature creates a table object that is referenced by the table name and has dynamic ranges so that if you add new rows or columns, the Excel Table can be refreshed to reflect the new data.

To complete this example, follow these steps on the worksheet named Ch17(5-18):

1.   Select a single cell inside the table (or select the entire table).

2.   Press Ctrl+T to open the Create Table dialog box. As shown in Figure 17.5, the Create Table dialog box grabs the correct range for the table.

3.   Click the OK button.

> **Note:** When you use data analysis tools such as an Excel Table, the standard PivotTable Sort tool, and the Filter tool, you can select a single cell inside a table, and the tool finds the complete table. To do so, the tool searches outward from the selected cell until it bumps into a complete range of empty cells or the worksheet column or row headers. If a table contains a row or column that is completely empty, however, this mechanism does not work.

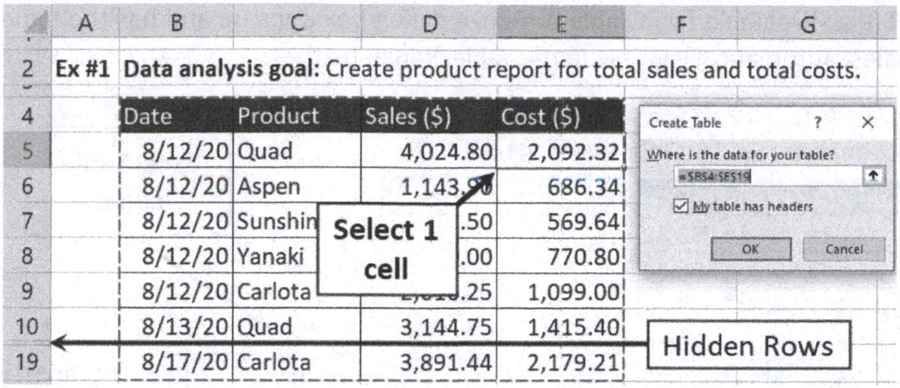

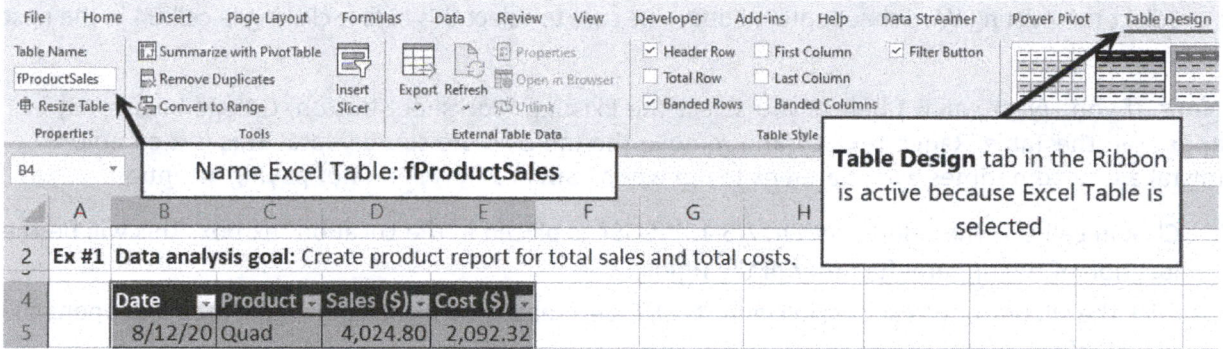

Figure 17.5 *If your table is stored in an Excel worksheet, convert it to an Excel Table to create a dynamic data source.*

4. To name the Excel Table object, as shown in Figure 17.6, click on the Table Design tab of the Ribbon and then, in the Properties group, click in the Table Name textbox and type **fProductSales**. Then press **Enter**. The Excel Table object now has the name fProductSales, and this name can be used throughout the Excel workbook file to refer to the dynamic table object.

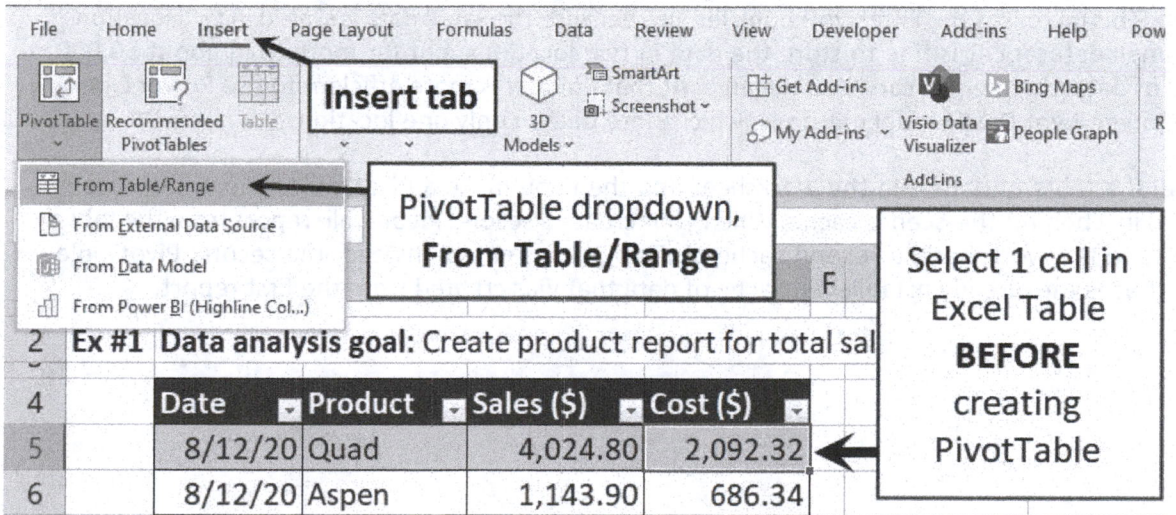

Figure 17.6 *Always name your Excel Tables.*

5. As shown in Figure 17.7, to create a standard PivotTable report, select a cell in the fProductSales table, click on the Insert tab of the Ribbon, and then, in the PivotTables group, click the PivotTable drop-down arrow and select From Table/Range.

Figure 17.7 *Click in one cell and then use the standard PivotTable tool.*

As shown in Figure 17.8, the PivotTable from Table or Range dialog box pops up and has the table object name, fProductSales, automatically visible in the Table/Range textbox.

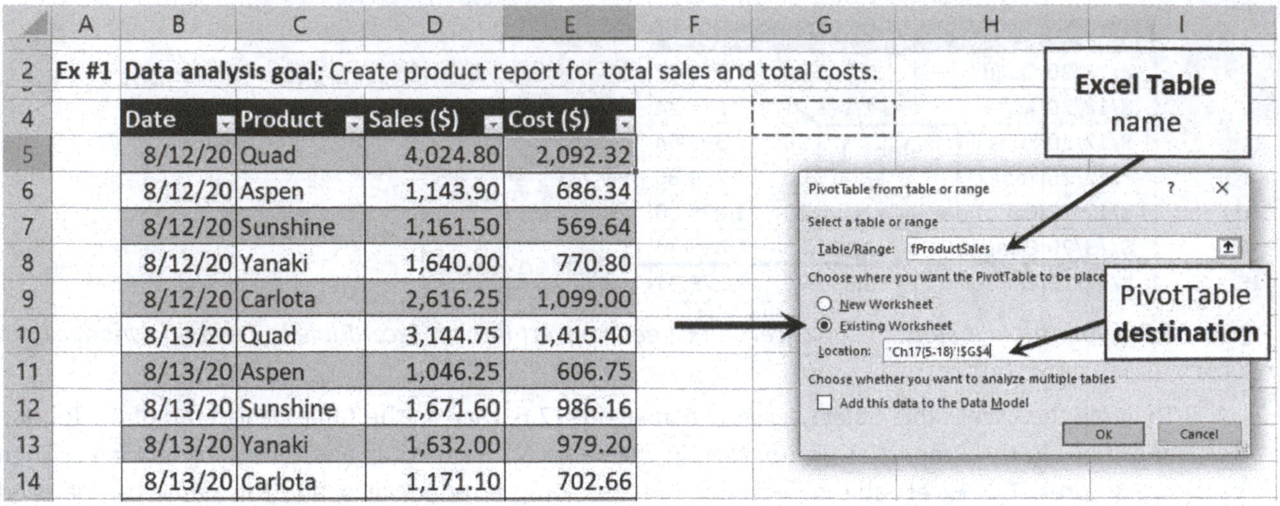

Figure 17.8 *Select the location (destination) for the report in the PivotTable from Table or Range dialog box.*

6. Select the Existing Worksheet option button. Be sure to select this *before* clicking in cell G4 in the next step.

    Note: If you select cell G4 before you select the Existing Worksheet button, G4 will incorrectly appear in the Table/Range textbox and remove the table as the source data. This is a common mistake that sometimes even happens to me when I am in a hurry and not paying attention.

7. Click in cell G4. The reference 'Ch17(5-18)'!$G$4 is placed in the Location textbox. This will be the location of the upper-left corner of the report.

8. Click the OK button. As shown in Figure 17.9, Excel creates the PivotTable report area and opens the PivotTable Fields task pane.

    Note: When you click the OK button in the PivotTable from Table or Range dialog box, the standard PivotTable tool stores the data from the table in a behind-the-scenes location called the standard PivotTable cache. When you store data in the Excel worksheet and then make a standard PivotTable based on that data, the data is stored in two locations: the worksheet and the standard PivotTable cache. This increases the Excel workbook file size because the same data is stored in two locations. For small datasets, it is fine to store the data in two locations, but for more than about 50,000 rows of data, the file size can become large. At that point, it is more efficient to use Power Query and Power Pivot Data Model methods, which store data in only one location.

    Note: If a table of data is in the worksheet and then you make a PivotTable report, the data is stored in a behind-the-scenes cache. When your create a second PivotTable report from the table of data in the worksheet, a second cache of data is not created; instead, the second PivotTable report uses the already established cache of data that was created from the first report.

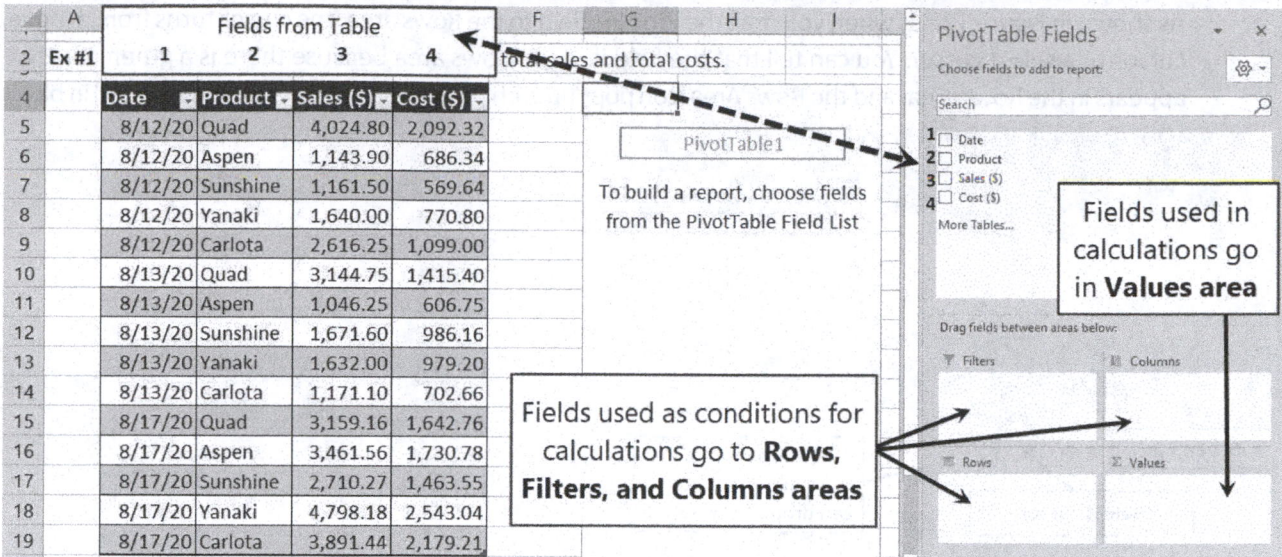

Figure 17.9 *The PivotTable Fields task pane lists all fields from the Excel Table.*

Note: In Figure 17.9, notice that the fields from your Excel Table are listed vertically at the top of the PivotTable Fields task pane. The list of fields is called a *field list*. You can drag fields from the field list to the Rows, Filters, Columns, and Values areas in the bottom section of the PivotTable Fields task pane. Fields dragged to the Values area will be used to make calculations, like summing the sales field or counting items in the product field. Fields dragged to the Rows, Filter, or Columns areas become the conditions or criteria for calculations; for example, the Product field can be used as a condition for adding sales from the Sales column. You can use the checkboxes next to the field names to place fields into the Rows, Filter, Columns, or Values areas in the bottom of the PivotTable Fields task pane. However, Excel does not always place the fields in the correct location. Therefore, I like to drag and drop my fields from the top of the PivotTable Fields task pane to the Rows, Filter, Columns, or Values areas. When you drag fields, you have more control over how the report is created because the fields will almost always be used in the correct spots.

9.   As shown in Figure 17.10, hover your cursor over the Product field in the field list and click and drag it down to the Rows area.

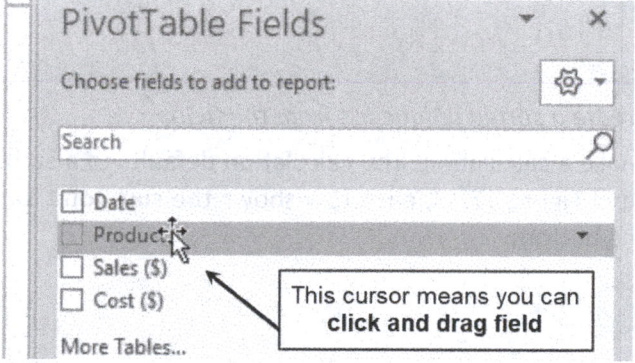

Figure 17.10 *When you see the move cursor, it indicates that you can click and drag the field.*

As shown in Figure 17.11, when you drag the Product field to the Rows area, the cursor turns from a move cursor to a select cursor. You can tell that the field is in the Rows area because there is a green bar that appears in the Rows area, and the Rows Area icon pops up with the row area of the icon highlighted in blue.

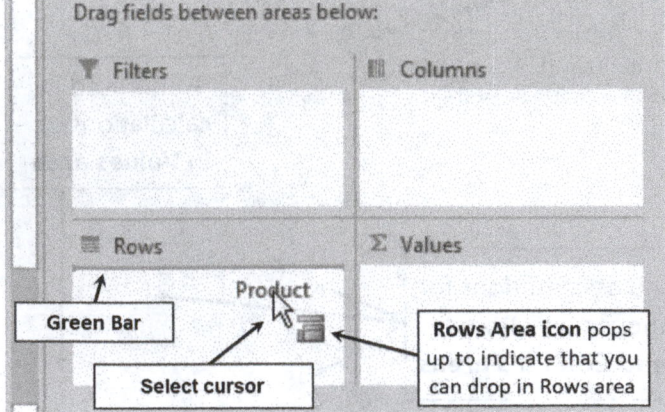

Figure 17.11 *Drop the Product field into the Rows area.*

As shown in Figure 17.12, when you drop the Product field in the Rows area, a sorted unique list of product names from the full Product column is created in the Rows area of the PivotTable report. Each product name is now a condition for the calculations that will be made in each row.

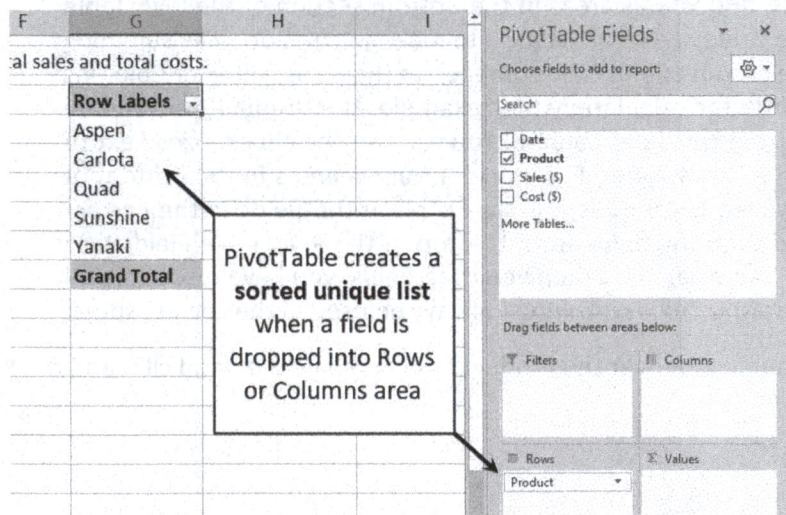

Figure 17.12 *Fields in the Rows or Columns areas will create a sorted unique list from the field.*

10. Drag the Sales ($) field to the Values area to make a calculation. The calculation defaults to a sum because the field contains numbers. As shown in Figure 17.13, each row shows the sum total for each product, and the grand total appears at the bottom.

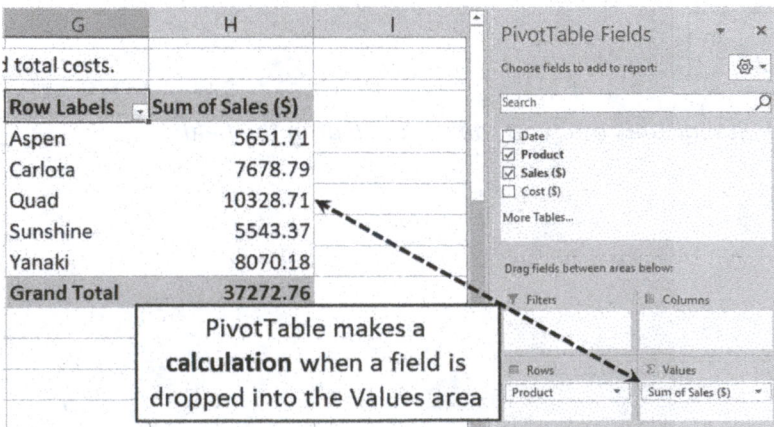

Figure 17.13 *Sum of Sales ($) for each product and a grand total calculation at the bottom of the report.*

Note: When a field is dragged to the Values area, a calculation is made on that field. If the field contains numbers, the default calculation is addition. If the field contains text, the default calculation is counting. The calculations can be easily changed, as you will learn later in this chapter. But the addition calculation is what you want in this case, so you should not change it here. Because the product name sits in each row of the standard PivotTable, the Sum of Sales ($) calculation adds the total sales for each product. Specifically, addition is done with a single-condition logical test where the product name is the condition for the logical test. *Fundamentally, this is what all PivotTables do:* They make calculations with conditions or criteria, where the criteria can come from the Rows, Columns, or Filters areas of the PivotTable report.

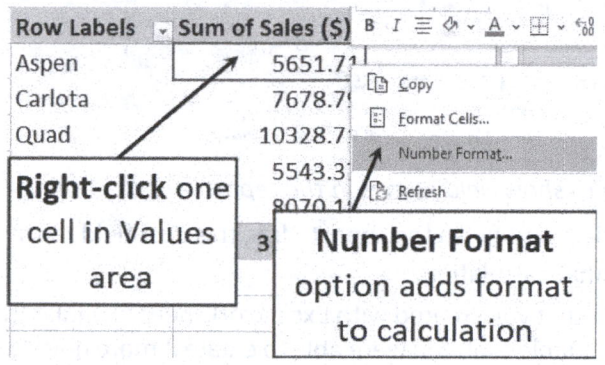

Figure 17.14 *Right-click in the Values area of the report and select Number Format.*

11. Examine the standard PivotTable in Figure 17.13 and notice that there are two problems. First, the numbers are hard to read without number formatting, and second, the ambiguous column title Row Labels would be more helpful if it showed the field name, Product. When you add helpful number formatting and show the field names in the report rather than using ambiguous labels, the report is more effective. As shown in Figure 17.14, to add number formatting to the Sum of Sales ($) calculation, select one cell in the Values area of the standard PivotTable, right-click to open the context-sensitive menu, and click on the Number Format option.

Note: When right-clicking in the Values area to add number formatting, do not select the Format Cells option above the Number Format option. The Format Cells option adds formatting to the selected cells only and might not accommodate future changes to the report. You want the Number Format option, which adds number formatting to the PivotTable calculation and allows the PivotTable report to retain the correct number formatting when conditions are changed in the Rows or Columns area. As shown in Figure 17.15, when you select the Number Format option, the Format Cells dialog box appears. What? Why is the dialog box for the Number Format option called Format Cells? Microsoft made a mistake in naming this dialog box; it really should be called the Values Calculation Number Format dialog box. However, you can tell that it is the correct dialog box because there is only one tab—the Number tab—whereas the Excel worksheet Format Cells dialog box has five tabs.

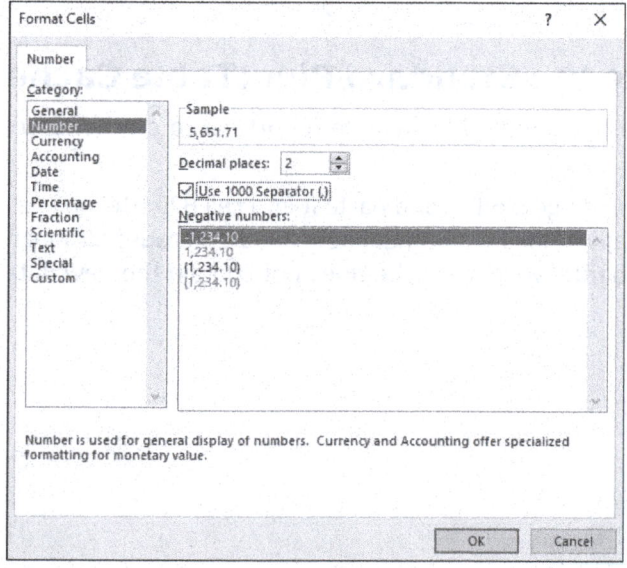

Figure 17.15 *Adding number formatting to the calculation helps make the report easier to read.*

12. As shown in Figure 17.15, in the Category list, select Number to add number formatting to the Sum of Sales ($) calculation. You could select other options, such as Currency or Accounting, which would show dollar signs, but because the unit in this case (dollars) is indicated in the label at the top of the column, you can create a less cluttered report by choosing the Number category to avoid adding more dollar signs.

13. On the right side of the Format Cells dialog box, check the checkbox Use 1000 Separator (,). The rest of the defaults in this dialog box are okay, but you can change them if you want. For example, you might want to show zero decimal places if the penny detail is not important and you want to make the report less cluttered and more direct.

14. Click OK.

15. To use the Product field name as a column label in the report rather than using the default Row Labels, make sure the PivotTable is selected and then, as shown in Figure 17.16, click on the Design tab of the Ribbon, and in the Layout group, click the Report Layout dropdown and select Show in Tabular Form. As shown in Figure 17.17, the Row Labels column header changes to Product.

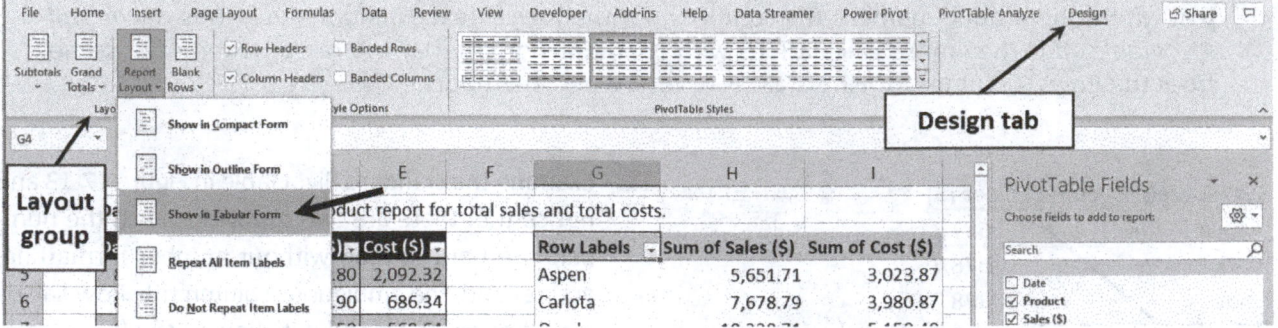

Figure 17.16 *Show in Tabular Form causes the PivotTable to show field names in the report.*

16. To make the conditional calculation on the Cost field and finish the report, drag the Cost field to the Values area and then add number formatting to that calculation.

Figure 17.17 shows the final report. This is the same report that you created with Excel worksheet formulas in Chapter 12 (refer to Figure 17.1). By using the standard PivotTable tool, you were able to create it more quickly.

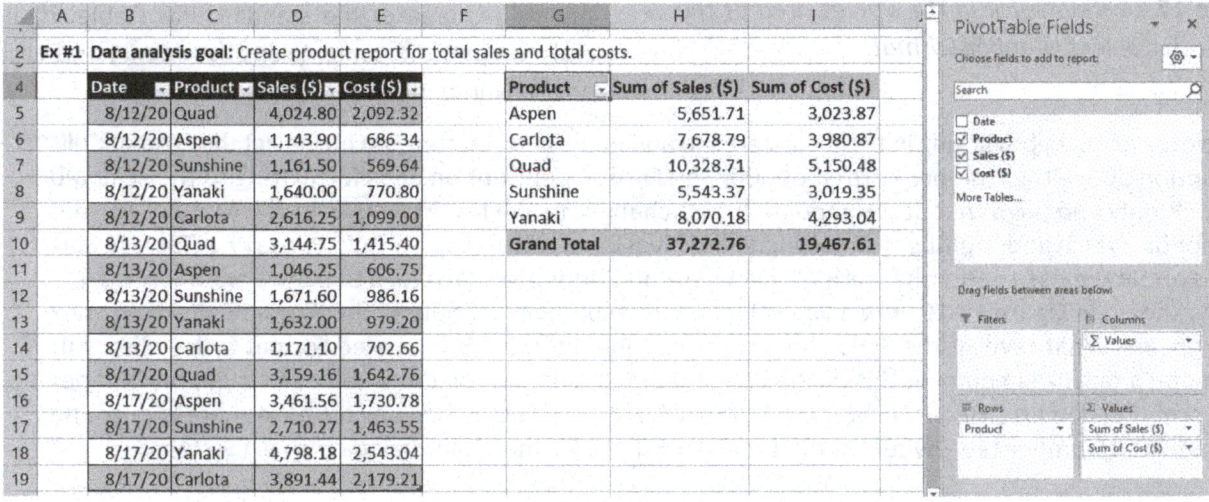

Figure 17.17 *Final Sales and Cost by Product report.*

Using the Refresh Button to Update the Standard PivotTable Cache

You can add new data to an Excel Table and then refresh a standard PivotTable report based on that Excel Table. To learn how, follow these steps:

1. As shown in Figure 17.18, copy new data from the range I26:L30 and paste it into cell B20 (the first cell in the row directly below the Excel Table). The report does not immediately update because although the Excel Table contains the new data, the standard PivotTable cache does not contain the new data until you refresh it.

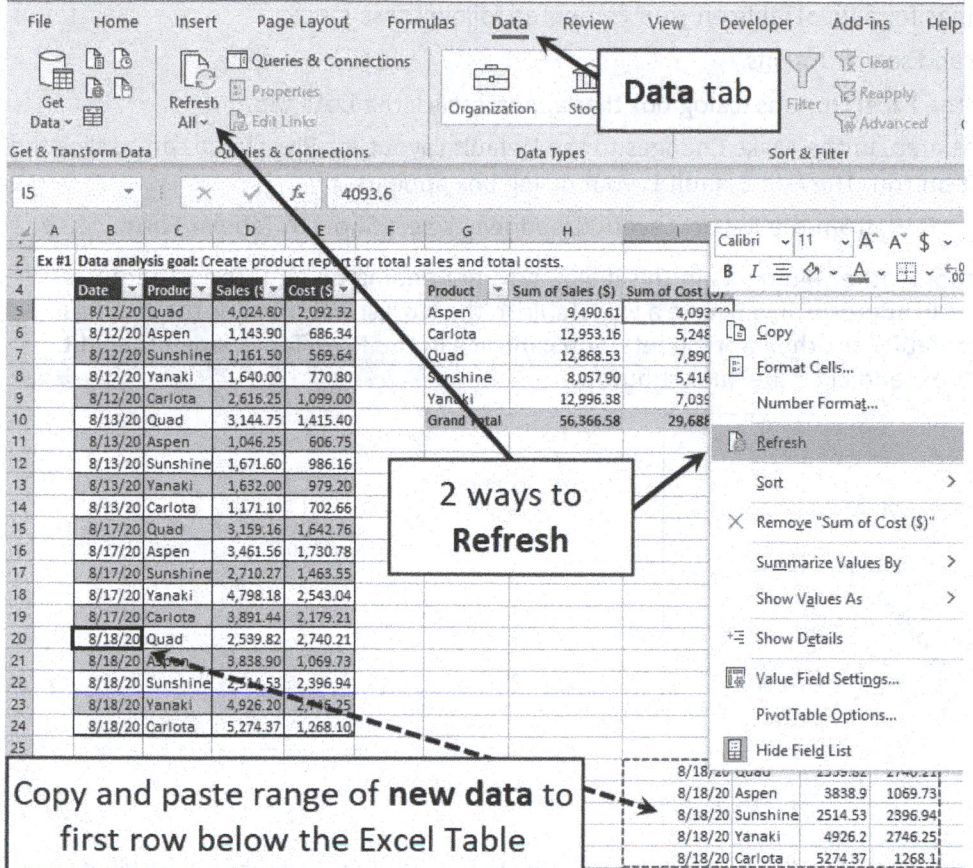

Figure 17.18 *When new data is added to the Excel Table, you must refresh the PivotTable report.*

2. To refresh the PivotTable report to reflect the new data from the Excel Table object, select the Data tab of the Ribbon, and, in the Queries and Connections group, click Refresh All (which refreshes everything in the Excel file) or right-click the PivotTable report and then click the Refresh option in the context-sensitive menu (which refreshes this specific report).

When you refresh a standard PivotTable, you are updating the standard PivotTable cache. When you add new data to an Excel Table, you always need to remember to refresh the report. In addition, if you have multiple Excel Tables in an Excel workbook file and you make standard PivotTables based on each one of those tables, the standard PivotTable cache stores the data table for each one of the tables separately. If you refresh an individual report, only the table associated with that report will be updated. When you click the Refresh All button, Excel refreshes all the tables that are stored in the cache as well as any Power Query or Power Pivot data sources. If you have many data source connections, it is usually fastest to update only the individual report that has the new data.

Setting the Default for PivotTable Reports to Show in Tabular Form

Earlier in this chapter (refer to Figure 17.16), you manually changed the PivotTable layout to Show in Tabular Form. You almost always want to make this change because using field names in a report rather than using the generic Row Labels head indicates more clearly what fields are being used and helps create a more effective report. Similarly, by default when you use a field in the Columns area of a PivotTable, the Column Labels head shows up. You can also change the default setting to show a specific name instead. A report can almost always communicate its message more effectively if you use field names rather than nondescript labels.

With Excel 365, Microsoft has added an option that allows you to set the default report layout to either Show in Tabular Form or Show in Outline Form. Though these two options look slightly different, both of them show field names rather than generic labels. I use Show in Tabular Form, but either one is fine. You make the change in the Edit Default Layout dialog box, and then all future standard or Data Model PivotTables created on your computer will reflect the change.

To change the default settings for a PivotTable on your computer, follow these steps:

1. Click the File menu and select Options.

2. On the left side of the Excel Options dialog box that appears, click the Data tab.

3. In the Data Options area, in the Make Changes to the Default Layout for PivotTables area, click the Edit Default Layout button. The Edit Default Layout dialog box appears.

4. As shown in Figure 17.19, from the Report Layout dropdown, select Show in Tabular Form.

> **Note:** You can also change other elements in this dialog box, depending on your report requirements and preferences. In addition, if you have a PivotTable in the worksheet that has the settings you want to use as a default for other worksheets, you can click in the PivotTable, open the Edit Default Layout dialog box, and click the Import button.

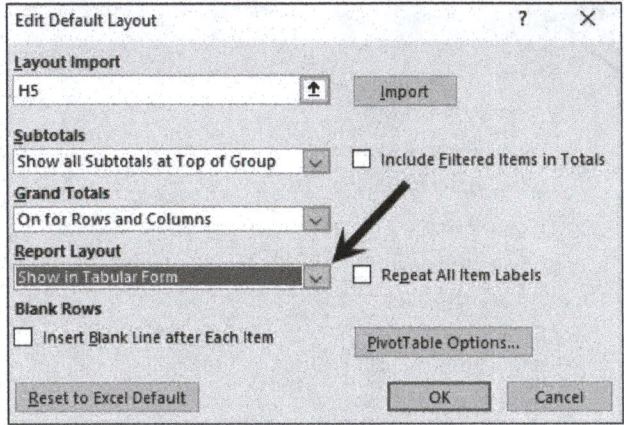

Figure 17.19 Changing the default PivotTable Report Layout setting to Show in Tabular Form causes PivotTables to show field names.

5. Click OK in the Edit Default Layout dialog box. Then click OK in the Excel Options dialog box.

Worksheet Formulas Versus a Standard PivotTable

Figure 17.20 shows the finished Product Sales and Costs report created with the standard PivotTable tool and worksheet formulas in this example. In most cases, it is easy to decide when to use worksheet formulas for reporting and when to use a PivotTable:

*   If you need a report to update instantly when new data arrives, you have to use worksheet formulas.

*   If you want to create a report quickly and do not need the data analysis results to update instantly and you don't mind manually refreshing to get a report to reflect new data, then use the standard PivotTable tool. It gives you results with just a few clicks and is a much less time-consuming process than creating worksheet formula solutions.

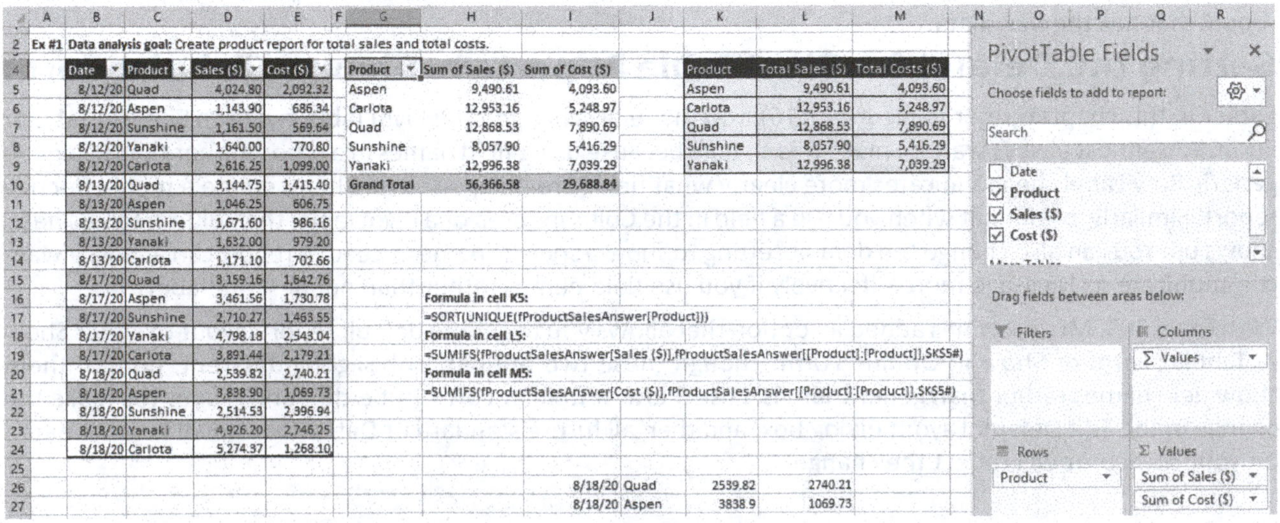

Figure 17.20 *A product sales and costs report can be created with worksheet formulas or a standard PivotTable.*

You have already learned that there are more than 450 different worksheet functions. As you will learn shortly, the PivotTable tool has 11 aggregate functions and 14 Show Values As calculations. So you have many more calculation options with worksheet functions, but for many reporting conditional calculations that sum, count, or make percentage calculations, it is hard to beat the speed and simplicity of the standard PivotTable tool.

Example 2: Creating a Frequency Distribution from Customer Survey Data with the Standard PivotTable Tool

Figure 17.21 shows a table with a single column that contains the results from a survey that asked customers to rank a soft drink product by selecting one of these five categories: Superior, Great, Good, Okay, or Poor. The goal of this data analysis example is to create a frequency distribution that shows the count for each ranking category and the percentage of total for each count. In frequency distribution terms, you want to calculate the frequency and percent frequency. For this data analysis task, you will never get more data, so you do not need to convert the source data to an Excel Table to create dynamic ranges. This will be a one-time report, and you can simply make the report from a proper dataset.

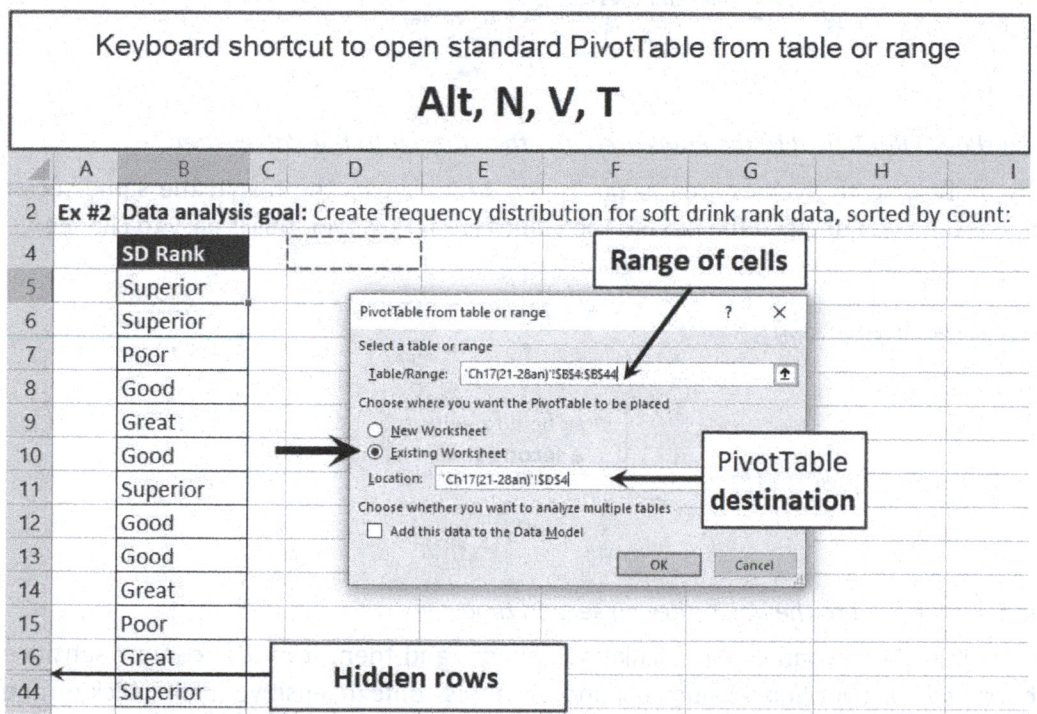

Figure 17.21 *It is common to create a report from a table with only one field.*

To complete this example, follow these steps on the worksheet named Ch17(21-28):

1.   Select cell B5 inside the table.

2.   Open the PivotTable from Table or Range dialog box by using the keyboard shortcut Alt, N, V, T. As shown in Figure 17.21, the dialog box pops up with the range of cells for the table automatically placed in the Table/Range textbox.

> **Note:** Alt, N, V, T is a *succession keyboard shortcut*, so you press the keys one after the other rather than holding them down simultaneously, as you do with shortcuts such as Ctrl+C or Ctrl+Shift+Enter.

3.   Select the Existing Worksheet option button (*before* clicking in cell D4 in the next step).

4.   Click in cell D4. The reference 'Ch17(21-28)'!$D$4 is placed in the Location textbox. This will be the location of the upper-left corner of the report.

5.   Click the OK button to add the data to the standard PivotTable cache. In the PivotTable Fields task pane, you now see only one field, SD Rank, in the field list.

6. As shown in Figure 17.22, drag the SD Rank field to the Rows area in the bottom part of the PivotTable task pane to create a unique list of soft drink rank categories in the Rows area of the PivotTable report.

7. Drag the SD Rank field to the Values area in the bottom part of the PivotTable task pane to create a count calculation for each row in the PivotTable report. Figure 17.22 shows the result. Because the field contains text values, the calculation defaults to counting. The standard PivotTable tool creates a conditional counting calculation for each row, where a single-condition logical test is created to count how many of each of the soft drink rank categories occurred.

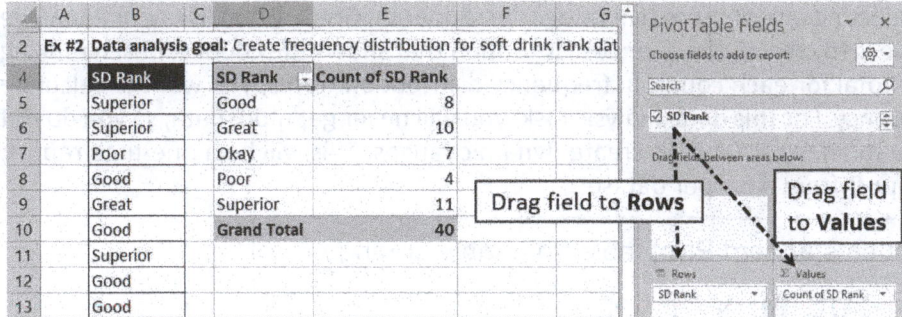

Figure 17.22 *First, drag the SD Rank field to the Rows area and then drag it to the Values area.*

8. Drag the SD Rank field to the Values area again. Figure 17.23 shows the result: the same set of counts as the first time you dragged the field to the Values area. However, this is easy to change.

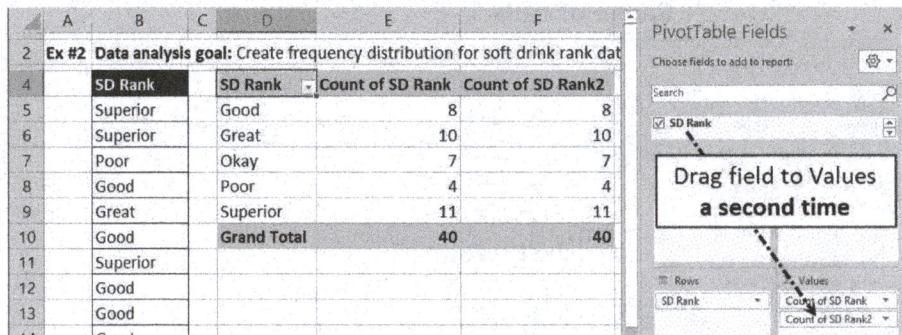

Figure 17.23 *Drag the SD Rank field to the Values area a second time.*

9. Right-click any cell in the second count calculation column, and then, from the context-sensitive menu, hover your cursor over Show Values As, and from this context-sensitive menu, click on the % of Column Total option (see Figure 17.24). Figure 17.25 shows the % of Column Total calculation result.

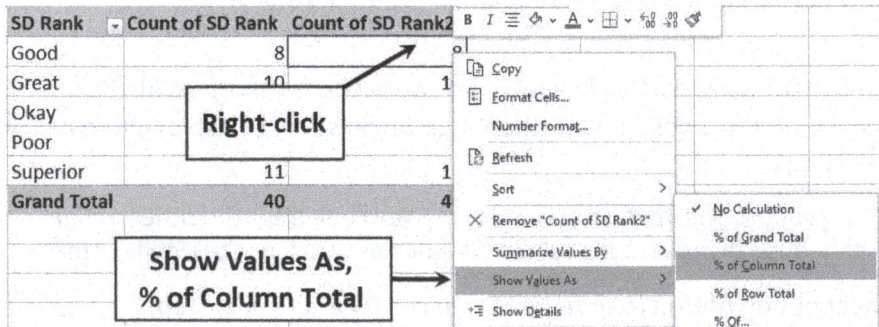

Figure 17.24 *The Show Values As option offers a lot of amazing calculations.*

	A	B	C	D	E	F
2	Ex #2	Data analysis goal: Create frequency distrib			**Type** new labels for report	
4		SD Rank		SD Rank ⌄	Frequency	% Frequency
5		Superior		Good	8	20.00%
6		Superior		Great	10	25.00%
7		Poor		Okay	7	17.50%
8		Good		Poor	4	10.00%
9		Great		Superior	11	27.50%
10		Good		**Grand Total**	**40**	**100.00%**

Figure 17.25 *You can type new labels for the report as long as each new label is different from a field name.*

10. Click in cell E4, type **Frequency**, and press Tab.

11. Click in cell F4, type **% Frequency**, and press Enter. Excel adds the column labels, as shown in Figure 17.25.

> **Note:** When you use the Show Values As, % of Column Total option on the Count of SD Rank2 column, internally the PivotTable compares each one of the soft drink rank counts to the total at the bottom of the column by using division. Then it adds the Percentage number format. For example, for the Good rank, it makes the math calculation 8 / 40 = 0.20 and then formats it with the Percentage number format to display it as 20.00%. For the Great rank, it calculates 10 / 40 = 0.25 and then formats it to display 25.00%. The Show Values As feature works with the column's existing aggregate calculation to make a second calculation. In this case, the aggregate calculation Count is used to count the number of survey results and then, as a second calculation, % of Column Total compares each individual count to the column total at the bottom of the columns.

12. To sort the PivotTable to show the highest frequency on top, as shown in Figure 17.26, at the top of the Rows area in the PivotTable report, click the Sort & Filter dropdown arrow and select More Sort Options. The Sort (SD Rank) dialog box appears.

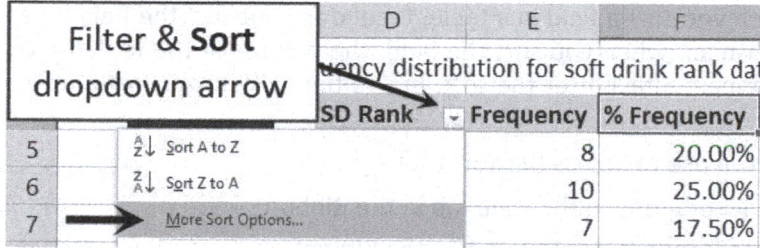

Figure 17.26 *PivotTables have dropdowns for sorting and filtering.*

13. As shown in Figure 17.27, in the Sort (SD Rank) dialog box, select the Descending (Z to A) By option button. Then, from the dropdown under that button, select Frequency.

14. Click OK in the Sort (SD Rank) dialog box.

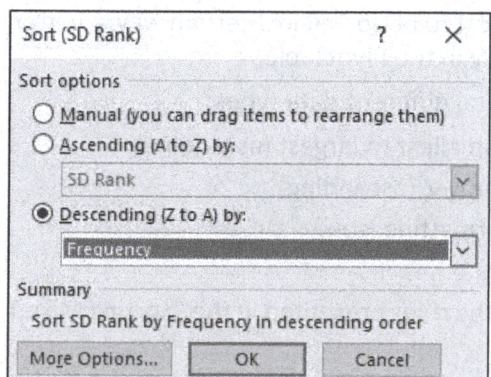

Figure 17.27 *This is the dialog box for sorting a PivotTable.*

Figure 17.28 shows the final report. This is the same report you created with Excel worksheet formulas in Chapter 16 (refer to Figure 17.2), but by using the standard PivotTable tool in this case, you were able to create it much more quickly. Converting survey data into a frequency distribution report like this is a common task, and you can see how quickly and easily you can do it with a PivotTable. If you are ever given survey results without a field name, you can just type a field name at the top of the column of values and create the report in about six clicks. Your boss or co-worker will be amazed at how quickly this can be done. I have taught a *lot* of people how to create this type of report over the past two decades, and every time it is the same: They are amazed by how easy it is to convert their survey data into useful information.

	A	B	C	D	E	F	G	H	I
2	Ex #2	**Data analysis goal:** Create frequency distribution for soft drink rank data, sorted by count:							
4		SD Rank		SD Rank	Frequency	% Frequency			
5		Superior		Superior	11	27.50%			
6		Superior		Great	10	25.00%			
7		Poor		Good	8	20.00%			
8		Good		Okay	7	17.50%			
9		Great		Poor	4	10.00%			
10		Good		**Grand Total**	**40**	**100.00%**			

Figure 17.28 *In about six clicks, you can create the most common report for survey data.*

Example 3: Using the Sort Tool to Sort the Fastest Race Times to the Top for Each Track

Sorting is an important data analysis task that allows you to arrange or order a list of values in a column. You can, for example, sort alphabetically, numerically, or by color. (You can also sort rows, although that is rarely required.) You might, for example, need to sort sales so that the biggest sales appear at the top of a sales dataset.

You can sort a single column or a table. When you sort a field in a table, Excel does not sort the field independently of the other fields in the table; instead, when you sort the field, the records in the table move with the sorted values so that the records remain intact after the sort. In addition, when you sort a table, you can sort by one or more fields.

In a worksheet, there are four methods you can use to access the Sort tool:

- Use the Sort dialog box in the Sort & Filter group in the Data tab in the Ribbon
- Use the Sort buttons in the Sort & Filter group in the Data tab in the Ribbon
- Use the Excel Table Sort & Filter dropdown arrows
- Right-click any cell and select Sort from the context-sensitive menu

In this book, you have already learned how to sort by using the SORT array function. And that is the method to use when you need your sorting results to update instantly when the source data changes. However, if you want to do a quick sorting task or want your final PivotTable report to be sorted in a certain way, a better option is to use the Sort tool in the Data tab in the Ribbon or directly in the PivotTable.

In an Excel worksheet, you can sort a column of data based on several different data types:

- Numbers can be sorted largest to smallest (descending) or smallest to largest (ascending).
- Text values can be sorted alphabetically, Z–A (descending) or A–Z (ascending).
- Cells can be sorted by cell color, font color, or conditional formatting icon.
- Values can be sorted using a custom list (like Jan, Feb, Mar, etc.).
- You can sort mixed data ascending or descending, based on the rules presented in the "Sorting Mixed Data" section in Chapter 15.

In Example 59 in Chapter 15, you saw how to use the SORT array function to sort the fastest race times to the top for each racetrack (refer to Figure 17.3). In this example, you will use the Sort dialog box to sort the fastest race times to the top for each racetrack.

Figure 17.29 shows a proper dataset with Date, Track, Racer, and Time (sec) fields. The goal of this data analysis example is to sort the fastest BMX race times to the top for each track. For this sorting task, you must sort the two fields Track and Time (sec).

To complete this example, follow these steps on the worksheet named Ch17(29-34):

1. Click in any cell in the Excel Table.

2. To open the Sort dialog box, click on the Data tab in the Ribbon and then, in the Sort & Filter group, click the Sort button. As shown in Figure 17.29, the Sort dialog box pops up.

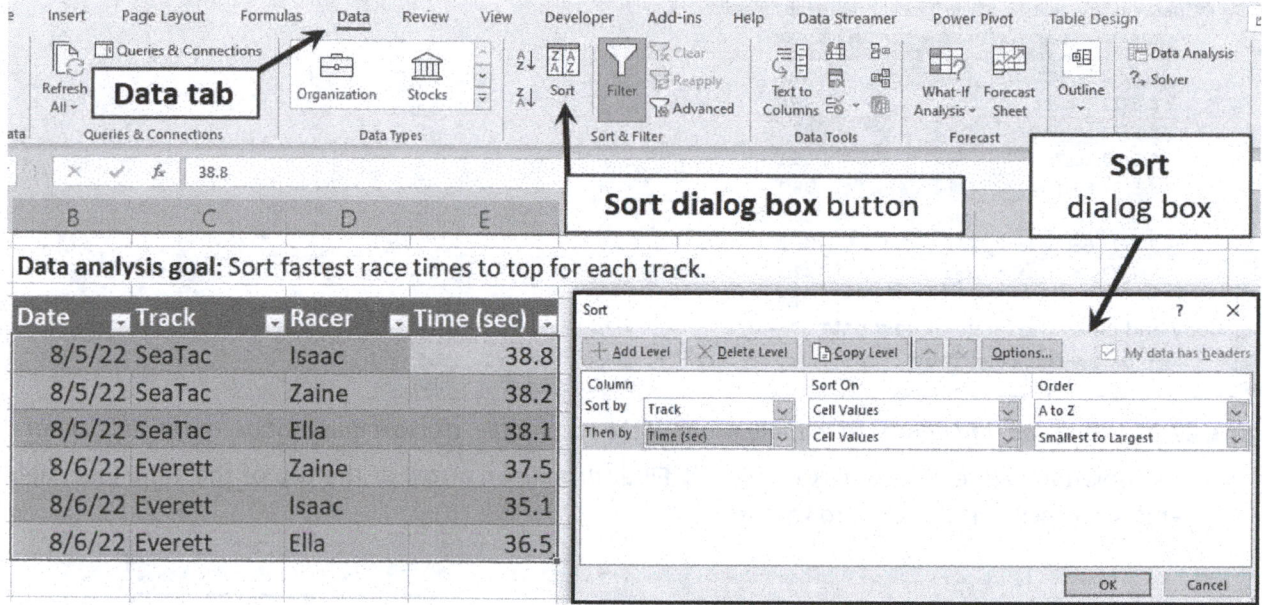

Figure 17.29 *The Sort dialog box makes it easy to sort by multiple columns.*

3. In the Sort dialog box, for the Sort By row, select the Track field for the Column option, select Cell Values for the Sort On option, and select A to Z for the Order option.

4. Click the Add Level button.

5. For the Then By row, select the Time (sec) field for the Column option, select Cell Values for the Sort On option, and select Smallest to Largest for the Order option.

6. Click OK. Figure 17.30 illustrates the mechanics of what happens when you sort by two columns. In the Sort dialog box, you sorted the Track field A-Z and then the Time (sec) field smallest to largest to show the fastest BMX bike racing times for each track. It is as if the Time (sec) field gets two separate sorts, while the Track field gets just one sort. In this case, the Track field is called the *major sort*, and the Time (sec) field is called the *minor sort*. You can say that the race times are sorted within the Track field.

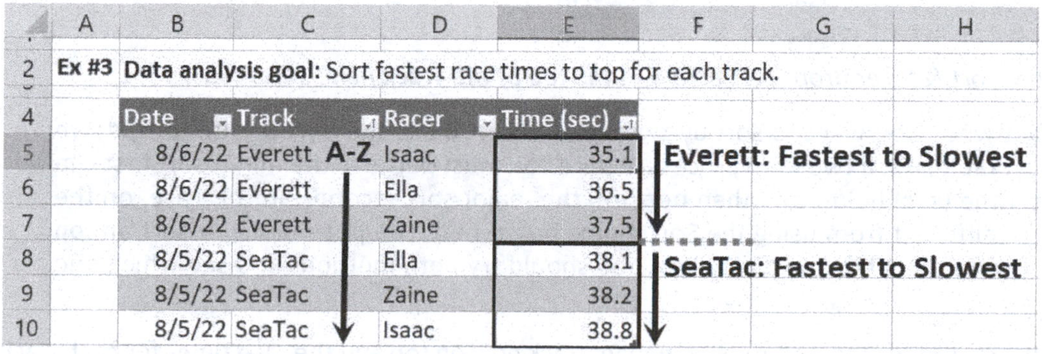

Figure 17.30 The Time (sec) field sorted within the Track field.

Note: Because you are sorting the source dataset, if you add new data to the bottom, the table will not automatically be updated. In the following steps, you will add some new data and then see how to use the Sort & Filter dropdown arrows at the top of each field in the Excel Table to sort the table by two fields.

7. To add new data to the Excel Table, copy the new data from the range G14:J16 and then paste it into cell B11, the first cell in the row below the Excel Table object. Figure 17.31 shows the result.

	A	B	C	D	E	F	G	H	I	J
2		Ex #3	Data analysis goal: Sort fastest race times to top for each track.							
4		Date	Track	Racer	Time (sec)					
5		8/6/22	Everett	Isaac	35.1					
6		8/6/22	Everett	Ella	36.5					
7		8/6/22	Everett	Zaine	37.5					
8		8/5/22	SeaTac	Ella	38.1					
9		8/5/22	SeaTac	Zaine	38.2					
10		8/5/22	SeaTac	Isaac	38.8					
11		8/7/22	Bellingham	Ella	45.4					
12		8/7/22	Bellingham	Isaac	47.9					
13					1.9					
14		Copy and paste the range of **new data**					8/7/22	Bellingham	Ella	45.4
15		below the Excel Table					8/7/22	Bellingham	Isaac	47.9
16							8/7/22	Bellingham	Zaine	41.9

Figure 17.31 *When you add new data to the bottom of the Excel Table, the sort does not automatically update.*

8. As shown in Figure 17.32, click the Sort & Filter dropdown arrow at the top of the Time (sec) field and then click Sort Smallest to Largest.

	A	B	C	D	E	F	G	H
2		Ex #3	**Data analysis goal:** Sort fastest race times to top for each				Sort	
4			Date	Track	Racer	Time (sec)	Time (sec) field	
5			8/6/22 Everett	Sort Smallest to Largest			**first**	
6			8/6/22 Everett	Sort Largest to Smallest				

Figure 17.32 *Using the Sort & Filter dropdown arrow at the top of the Time (sec) field, sort smallest to largest.*

9. As shown in Figure 17.33, click the Sort & Filter dropdown arrow at the top of the Track field and then click Sort A to Z.

	A	B	C	D				H
2		Ex #3	**Data analysis goal:** Sort fastest race		Sort Track field **second**			
4			Date	Track	Racer	Time (sec)		
5			Sort A to Z		Isaac	35.1		
6			Sort Z to A		Ella	36.5		

Figure 17.33 *Using the Sort & Filter dropdown arrow at the top of the Track field, sort A–Z.*

Note: Notice that when you want to sort by two fields and you use the Sort & Filter dropdown arrows in an Excel Table, it is a two-step process, where you must perform the minor sort first—in this case on the Time (sec) field—and then perform the major sort second—in this case, on the Track field. This is different from using the Sort dialog box, where you put the major sort on top and the minor sort below, all in one dialog box. You should try both methods and see which one you prefer.

Figure 17.34 shows the sorted results with the Bellingham track now on top and the race times for each track sorted fastest to slowest. In the Time (sec) field, there are three separate sorts—one for each track. Now if you stop and think about this, a coach who is entering new data each day may want to keep the historical records in the table sorted by date. In this case, it might be better to use Excel worksheet formulas, as shown in Figure 17.3 (and as described in Example 59 in Chapter 15). With formulas, you would gain two benefits:

The results would instantly update when new data is added, and the original order of the records based on the date would be maintained. However, if you need a quick sort, the Sort dialog box or the sorting option in the Excel Table are better options.

	Date	Track A-Z	Racer	Time (sec)	
4					
5	8/7/22	Bellingham	Zaine	41.9	**Bellingham: Fastest to Slowest**
6	8/7/22	Bellingham	Ella	45.4	
7	8/7/22	Bellingham	Isaac	47.9	
8	8/6/22	Everett	Isaac	35.1	**Everett: Fastest to Slowest**
9	8/6/22	Everett	Ella	36.5	
10	8/6/22	Everett	Zaine	37.5	
11	8/5/22	SeaTac	Ella	38.1	**SeaTac: Fastest to Slowest**
12	8/5/22	SeaTac	Zaine	38.2	
13	8/5/22	SeaTac	Isaac	38.8	

Figure 17.34 *Three separate sorts in the Time (sec) field within the Track field.*

Sorting is a very common task. You will see sorting in almost all the tools you use, from the worksheet, to PivotTables, to Power Query and Power BI Desktop. You will see a lot more sorting throughout your data analysis study.

Example 4: Sorting by Color

As shown in Figure 17.35, an employee call record table has the cell fill colors red and yellow in the Length (min) field. It is common for Excel users to add fill color to mark records in tables. If your goal is to sort the colors to the top after marking all the records, you can use the Sort dialog box to accomplish this data analysis goal.

> **Note:** Although it would be better to have a separate field in the table where the user could indicate what the meaning of the fill color is, many users still use ambiguous color coding to mark records. In this particular example, users are likely to know what the colors mean, so a legend, or key to the colors, is not crucial here.

To sort the colors to the top of the Length (min) field, follow these steps on the worksheet named Ch17(35-36):

1. As shown in Figure 17.35, with a single cell in the proper dataset selected, click on the Data tab in the Ribbon and then, in the Sort & Filter group, click the Sort button.

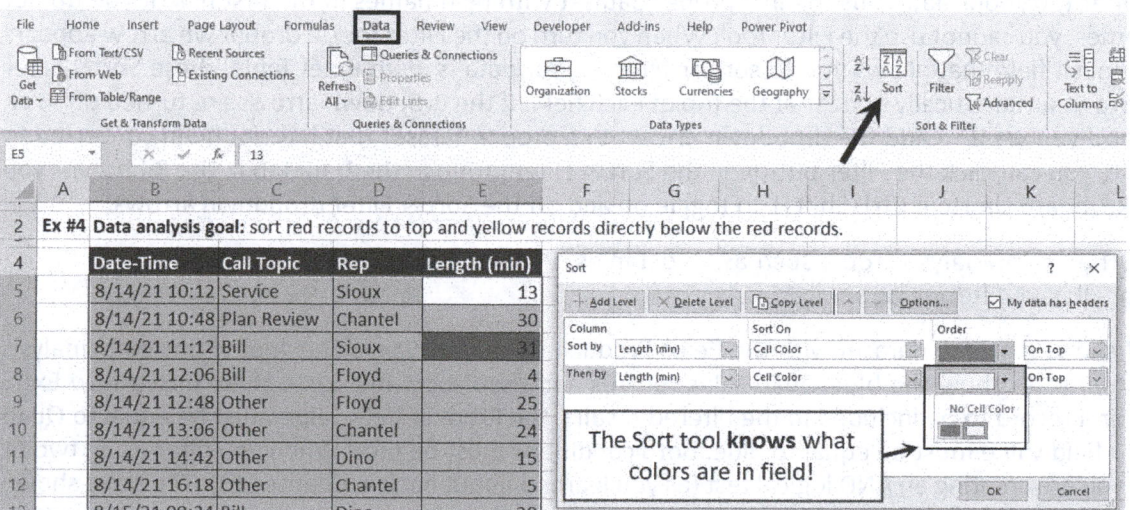

Figure 17.35 *The Sort dialog box allows you to sort by cell color.*

2. In the Sort dialog box that appears, for the Sort By row, select the Length (min) field for the Column option, select Cell Color for the Sort On option, select the color red for the Order option, and then select the On Top option in the last dropdown.

3. Click the Add Level button.

4. For the Then By row, select the Length (min) field for the Column option, select Cell Color for the Sort On option, select the color yellow for the Order option, and then select the On Top option in the last dropdown.

5. Click OK. Figure 15.36 shows the sorted table results.

	A	B	C	D	E	F	G	H	I
2		Ex #4	**Data analysis goal:** sort red records to top and yellow records directly below the red records.						
4		Date-Time	Call Topic	Rep	Length (min)				
5		8/14/21 11:12	Bill	Sioux	31				
6		8/15/21 15:54	Service	Chantel	19				
7		8/14/21 12:48	Other	Floyd	25				
8		8/15/21 09:24	Bill	Dino	28				
9		8/14/21 10:12	Service	Sioux	13				
10		8/14/21 10:48	Plan Review	Chantel	20				

Figure 17.36 *As a result of the sort, cells in the Length (min) field with red fill are on top, followed by cells with yellow fill and then cells with no fill.*

Example 5: Using the Filter Tool to Extract the Blue Quad Sales Records

Earlier in this book, you learned how to filter with the FILTER array function. When you need your filtering results to update instantly when the source data changes or when you have a complex filter, such as a filter that compares two lists (refer to Example 29 in Chapter 13), using the FILTER array function is the best option. But if you have a quick filtering task, the Filter tool in the Data tab in the Ribbon is the way to go.

Filtering is an important data analysis task that allows you to specify one or more conditions in a proper dataset to show only records that match those conditions. For example, you might need to show sales records for a specified product so you can e-mail the records to your boss. When you filter a table, you specify conditions in a logical test, and then the records that do not match are hidden, leaving only the matching records. This is different from sorting a dataset. Sorting does not hide records; instead, it leaves all records showing and reorders the records based on a sorting condition. Filtering hides records that do not match the filtering conditions and shows only records that match the conditions.

To use the Filter tool, your data must be in a proper dataset with field names in the first row. If you do not have field names, you cannot use the Filter tool. When you turn on the Filter tool, a dropdown arrow appears at the top of each field that allows you to sort or filter. If your data is in an Excel Table, these Sort& Filter dropdown arrows automatically appear at the top of each field. If the dropdown arrows are turned off in an Excel Table or if you want to add the dropdown arrows to a proper dataset that has not been converted to an Excel Table, you can click the Filter button in the Sort & Filter group in the Data tab in the Ribbon or you can use the keyboard shortcut Ctrl+Shift+L to toggle on and off the Sort & Filter dropdown arrows.

> **Note:** Other data analysis, tools such as PivotTables, Power Query, Power Pivot, and Power BI Desktop, all have filtering options.

Figure 17.37 shows a proper dataset with the fields Product, Color, and Sales. The goal of this data analysis example is to filter to show the blue Quad sales records and then copy and paste them into a new Excel workbook. For a record to be included in the filtered results, the Product field value must be equal to Quad *and* the Color field value must be equal to Blue. Both conditions must be met. When you filter using two or more fields, you are creating an AND logical test (as you learned about back in Chapter 13). The table shown in Figure 17.37 has not been converted to an Excel Table, and it therefore does not automatically show the Sort & Filter dropdown arrows. In this case, you will not get new records, so there is no need to use the Excel Table tool. Instead, you can add Sort & Filter dropdown arrows to the proper dataset by using the Filter tool.

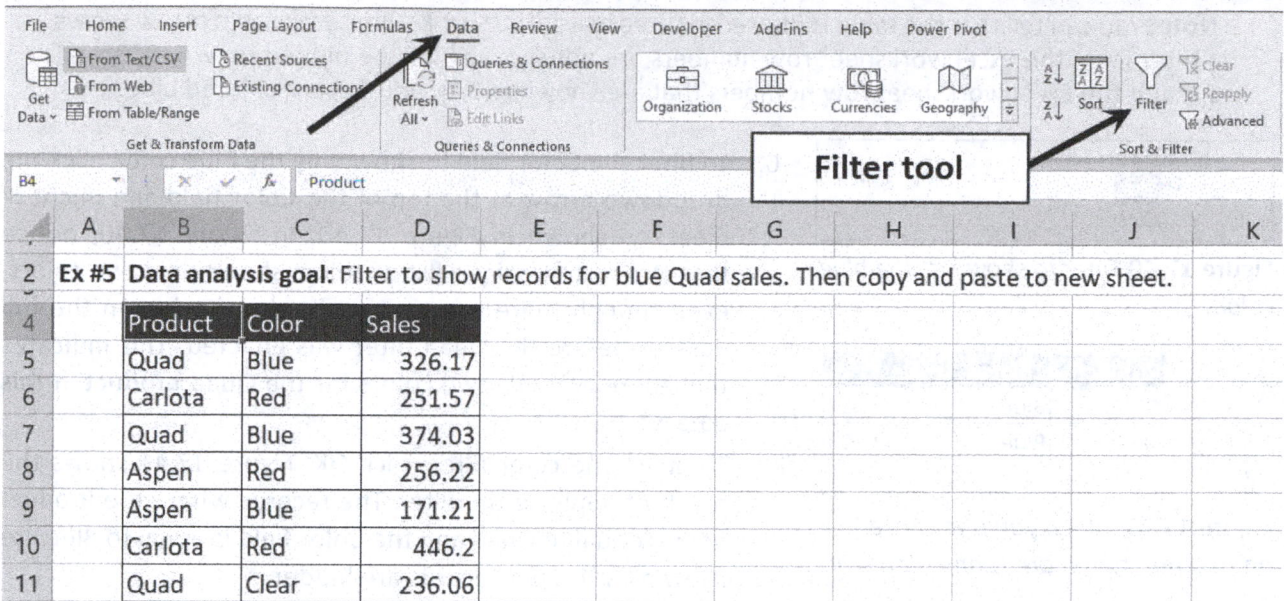

Figure 17.37 *Click the Filter button to add the Sort & Filter dropdown arrows to each field.*

To complete this example, follow these steps on the worksheet named Ch17(37-47):

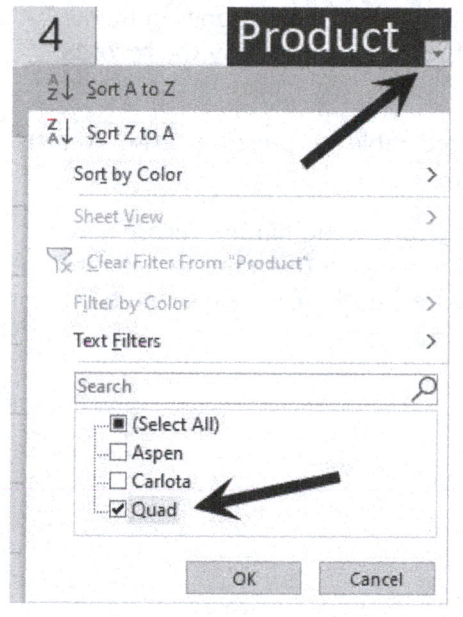

Figure 17.38 *From the sorted unique list of items in the Sort & Filter menu, check only the Quad product.*

1. Select one cell in the proper dataset.

2. To turn on the Sort & Filter tool for the proper dataset and show a dropdown arrow next to each field name, click on the Data tab in the Ribbon and then, in the Sort & Filter group, click the Filter button. Once you click the Filter button, as shown in Figure 17.37, you see the dropdown arrows at the top of each field.

3. To open the Sort & Filter menu for the Product field, click the dropdown arrow at the top of the Product field, as shown in Figure 17.38.

    Note: One of the amazing side benefits of using the Sort & Filter tool is that when you open the Sort & Filter menu for any field, the bottom part of the menu shows a sorted unique list of items in the field. In Figure 17.38, you can see that the sorted unique items in this field are Aspen, Carlota, and Quad. This aspect of the Filter tool occurs in all the data analysis tools that you will encounter. If you are in a hurry and need to see a unique list of items for any field, if the Sort & Filter dropdown arrows are showing, you can just click one and get a quick glance at the unique items in that field.

4. To filter the Product field to show only Quad product records, uncheck the (Select All) checkbox and check the Quad checkbox, as shown in Figure 17.38.

5. Click OK. Figure 17.39 shows the result of this filter. By selecting the Quad checkbox in the Sort & Filter menu, you have hidden all records in the table where the product is not Quad. By checking only the Quad product, you create a single-condition logical test that determines whether the product in the Product field equals Quad. The hidden records are still part of the dataset, but they are temporarily hidden until you clear the filter. To complete the AND logical test, you must next filter the Color field.

	A	B	C	D
2	Ex #5	Filter to show records for blue Q		
4		Product	Color	Sales
5		Quad	Blue	326.17
7		Quad	Blue	374.03
11		Quad	Clear	236.06

Figure 17.39 *Filtering to show Quad records hides all records where the product is not Quad.*

Note: You can tell that the table is filtered in three ways: The Sort & Filter dropdown arrow shows a filter icon; the Excel worksheet row numbers are not showing for the hidden rows 6, 8, 9, and 10; and the Excel worksheet row numbers that are showing (5, 7, and 11) are colored blue.

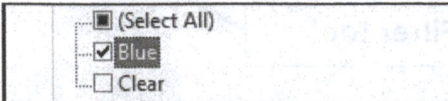

Figure 17.40 *Filter to show just the blue color.*

4	Product	Color	Sales
5	Quad	Blue	326.17
7	Quad	Blue	374.03
12			

Figure 17.41 *When you filter based on two fields, you are running an AND logical test.*

6. To filter the Color field to show only the blue color, click the dropdown arrow at the top of the Color field and uncheck Clear, as shown in Figure 17.40. In Figure 17.40, notice that the sorted unique list of colors shows only two colors, even though there were originally three colors in the full dataset before the Quad filter was enacted. This indicates that there are only two colors for the Quad product in this dataset.

7. To enact the color filter, click OK. Figure 17.41 shows the result of applying the filter. The records where the Product field is equal to Quad and the Color field is equal to Blue are showing. All other records are hidden.

Note: When you filter, it is often the case that your goal is to copy and paste the records. A crucial thing to remember when you have done some filtering is that there are some hidden rows. This means that if you try to copy and paste the filtered records to the side of the table, you may be pasting the copied records to hidden rows. To avoid this, you can paste the records above or below the table, to a new worksheet, or to a new workbook file. In this case, you will copy the records to a new workbook file.

8. To copy the table with the filtered records, select the filtered table by pressing Ctrl+* (that is, Ctrl+Shift+8) and then copy the filtered table by pressing Ctrl+C.

Note: When you copy a filtered table, only the visible cells are copied. The hidden records are not copied. You can tell that only the filtered records are copied because the dancing ants are dancing around only the visible records, as shown in Figure 17.42, rather than around the outside of the table.

◢	A	B	C	D
2	**Ex #5**	Filter to show records for blue Q		
4		Product	Color	Sales
5		Quad	Blue	326.17
7		Quad	Blue	374.03

Figure 17.42 *When you copy a filtered table, you are copying only the visible rows.*

9. To open a new Excel workbook file, press Ctrl+N (or select the File menu and then click New).

10. In the new workbook, on the first sheet, select cell A1 and paste the records by pressing Ctrl+V.

11. Rename the worksheet and then save and name the file by using the Save As command keyboard shortcut F12. Figure 17.43 shows the result.

Note: This example shows the same set of records that you created with Excel worksheet formulas in Figure 17.4, but the Filter tool allowed you to extract the desired records much more quickly. For a one-time data extraction task, the Filter tool cannot be beat. In addition, filtering to get just the data you want and pasting it into a new workbook and sending it off to a boss or colleague is a common task. By using the Filter tool and some handy keyboard shortcuts, you can accomplish a task like this in less than a minute.

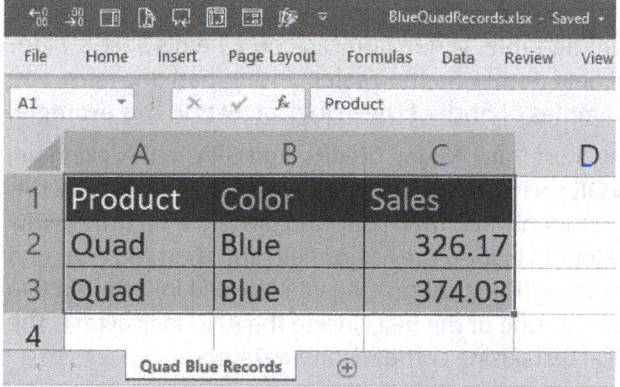

Figure 17.43 *Name the worksheet and file so that the person receiving it knows what records they are getting.*

To clear an individual filter on a field, you can use the Clear Filter option from the specified field's Sort & Filter menu, as shown in Figure 17.44. If you want to clear all filters from a table, you can use the Clear button in the Sort & Filter group in the Data tab in the Ribbon, as shown in Figure 17.45.

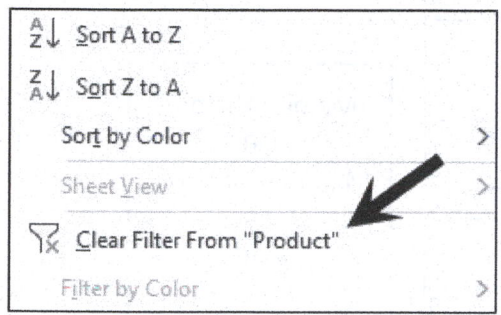

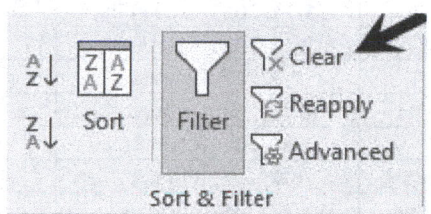

Figure 17.44 *The dropdown filter arrow for each field has a Clear Filter option.*

Figure 17.45 *The Clear button in the Sort & Filter group in the Data tab of the Ribbon clears all filters from a table.*

Example 6: Filtering to Extract Student Records Based on AND and OR Logical Tests

Another amazing aspect of the Filter tool is that for text, number, and date data fields, there are many powerful data-specific filters available from the dropdown arrows. For example, Figure 17.46 shows some of the possible logical test filters that you can use for text data. These options are available after you click the dropdown arrow on a field that contains text data. Figure 17.47 shows some of the possible logical test filters that you can use for number data. These options are available after you click the dropdown arrow on a field that contains number data. All the logical test theory that you learned about in Chapter 13 can be applied by using these filters. These logical test filters are also available in the other data analysis tools, such as standard PivotTables, Data Model PivotTables, Power Query, and Power BI Desktop.

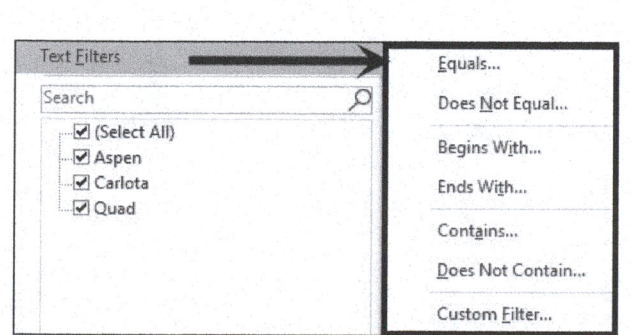

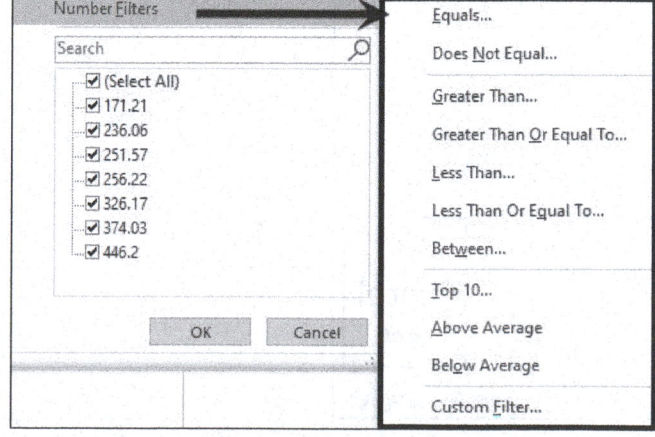

Figure 17.46 *For text data, the Text Filters option offers many logical tests for filtering a dataset.*

Figure 17.47 *For number data, the Number Filters option offers many logical tests for filtering a dataset.*

When you use two or more fields to filter a proper dataset, you are creating an AND logical test, where records are included only when all tests are met for a given row in the table. When you click on a field's Sort & Filter dropdown and then use the sorted unique checkbox list of field items and then select more than one item, you are running an OR logical test on that field. You will see examples of both of these logical tests in this example.

Figure 17.48 shows a student dataset with the fields Student, Start Date, Major, Credits, and GPA. In this example, a student is eligible for a scholarship if their major is history OR sociology AND their GPA is >= 2.5. The goal of this data analysis example is to filter the records to show eligible students and then copy and paste the records below the dataset. To accomplish this goal, you have to run an OR logical test on the Major field and then run a second logical test on the GPA field. By using two fields, you create an AND logical test. As you learned in Example 8 in Chapter 13, this means that you are running an OR logical test as one of the tests inside the AND logical test. The right side of Figure 17.48 illustrates the two combined logical tests using comparison operators.

	A	B	C	D	E	F	G	H	I
2	Ex #6	**Scholarship:** Students are eligible for scholarship if their major is history OR sociology AND their GPA is >= 2.5.							
3		**Data analysis goal:** Filter to show eligible student records, then copy and paste below data set.							
5	Student	Start Date	Major	Credits	GPA				
6	Carey, Zada	9/29/2020	History	45	1.7				
7	Emmons, Christi	7/14/2018	Sociology	135	2.3				
8	Lear, Vania	9/3/2020	Chemistry	45	3				
9	Meador, Corazon	11/21/2019	Accounting	90	3.1	Major = History			
10	Mohamed, Abdi	1/28/2021	Business	23	1.6	OR			
11	Nga, Luong	7/7/2020	Physics	45	2.4	Major = Sociology			
12	Robinson, Chantel	4/12/2020	History	70	4				
13	Rouse, Sioux	6/30/2020	Chemistry	40	2.4	AND			
14	Simone, Alanna	8/2/2019	Physics	60	3.5				
15	Thornburg, Tyrone	12/27/2019	Sociology	75	3.9				
16						GPA >= 2.5			
17			Paste records below table						
18									

Figure 17.48 *The goal is to extract records for scholarship-eligible students.*

To complete this example, follow these steps on the worksheet named Ch17(48-54):

1. Select a single cell in the Excel Table.

2. As shown in Figure 17.49, click the Sort & Filter dropdown for the Major field, uncheck the (Select All) checkbox, and check the checkboxes for History and Sociology. This filter will run the OR logical test "is the major equal to history or sociology?"

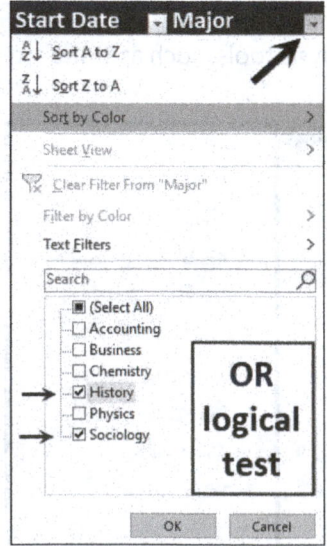

Figure 17.49 *When you select more than one item from a unique list of items, you are running an OR logical test.*

Figure 17.50 shows that the dataset has been filtered to show student records where the major is history or sociology. From those records, you must filter a second time to show results where the GPA is greater than or equal to 2.5.

5	Student	Start Date	Major	Credits	GPA
6	Carey, Zada	9/29/2020	History	45	1.7
7	Emmons, Christi	7/14/2018	Sociology	135	2.3
12	Robinson, Chantel	4/12/2020	History	70	4
15	Thornburg, Tyrone	12/27/2019	Sociology	75	3.9

Figure 17.50 *Filtered results of the OR logical test.*

3. As shown in Figure 17.51, click the Sort & Filter dropdown for the GPA field. Because this is a number field, the data type–specific menu option Number Filters appears in the menu.

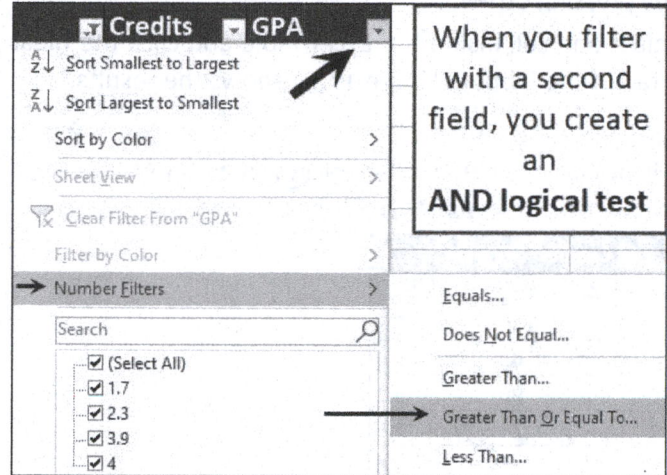

Figure 17.51 *The GPA field contains number data, so the data type–specific Number Filters option is available.*

4. Hover your cursor over the Number Filters options and then, from the submenu, click the Greater Than or Equal To option.

5. As shown in Figure 17.52, in the Custom AutoFilter dialog box that appears, type **2.5** in the textbox to the right of the Is Greater Than or Equal To option.

> **Note:** In Figure 17.52, you need to take note of a few things. First, when you type a value into the Custom AutoFilter dialog box, you are hard coding that number into the dialog box. There is no way to link this textbox to a cell in the worksheet. If you need to change the value, you must follow the same path (GPA dropdown arrow, Number Filters, Greater Than or Equal To) to open the Custom AutoFilter dialog box again and edit it. Second, notice that there are And and Or option buttons; you can select one run an AND or OR logical test. These option buttons affect the outcome of the filter only when you use the second row of textboxes below these option buttons. Third, in the lower-left corner, the dialog box reminds you about wildcards (which you learned about in Example 14 in Chapter 13).

Figure 17.52 *Enter **2.5** into the textbox to filter to show GPA .>= 2.5.*

6. To enact the GPA filter, in the Custom AutoFilter dialog box, click OK. Figure 17.53 shows the filtering results. It looks like Chantel Robinson and Tyrone Thornburg are eligible for the scholarship.

	Student	Start Date	Major	Credits	GPA
5					
12	Robinson, Chantel	4/12/2020	History	70	4
15	Thornburg, Tyrone	12/27/2019	Sociology	75	3.9

Figure 17.53 *Records where major is history or sociology and GPA is greater than or equal to 2.5.*

7. To extract the records and paste them below the table, select the filtered table by pressing Ctrl+* (that is, Ctrl+Shift+8).

8. Copy the filtered table by pressing Ctrl+C.

9. Click in cell B18 and then paste the records by pressing Ctrl+V.

10. To clear the filter on the student dataset, select one cell inside the Excel Table and click the Clear button in the Sort & Filter group in the Data tab of the Ribbon. Figure 17.54 shows the results.

	A	B	C	D	E	F	G	H	I
2		Scholarship: Students are eligible for scholarship if their major is history OR sociology AND their GPA is >= 2.5.							
3	Ex #6	Data analysis goal: Filter to show eligible student records, then copy and paste below data set.							
5		Student	Start Date	Major	Credits	GPA			
6		Carey, Zada	9/29/2020	History	45	1.7			
7		Emmons, Christi	7/14/2018	Sociology	135	2.3			
8		Lear, Vania	9/3/2020	Chemistry	45	3			
9		Meador, Corazon	11/21/2019	Accounting	90	3.1			
10		Mohamed, Abdi	1/28/2021	Business	23	1.6			
11		Nga, Luong	7/7/2020	Physics	45	2.4			
12		Robinson, Chantel	4/12/2020	History	70	4			
13		Rouse, Sioux	6/30/2020	Chemistry	40	2.4			
14		Simone, Alanna	8/2/2019	Physics	60	3.5			
15		Thornburg, Tyrone	12/27/2019	Sociology	75	3.9			
16									
17									
18		Student	Start Date	Major	Credits	GPA			
19		Robinson, Chantel	4/12/2020	History	70	4			
20		Thornburg, Tyrone	12/27/2019	Sociology	75	3.9			

Figure 17.54 *The scholarship-eligible student records have been successfully extracted and pasted below the full table.*

More About the Fast and Easy Standard PivotTable Tool

You have already seen two reports that you can create with the standard PivotTable tool. But there are more amazing standard PivotTable features that make reporting and charting fast and easy. In the following sections, you will create five more common standard PivotTable reports and, in the process, solidify your understanding of some important standard PivotTable features. You have already learned about some of the following capabilities in the standard PivotTable tool, and you will learn about the rest of them shortly:

• Dragging a field to the Rows, Columns, or Filters area creates a sorted unique list from all the values in the field.

• From the sorted unique list, the values in the Rows area become the conditions for the calculation in the row, and the values in the Columns area become the conditions for the calculation in the column.

• By default, dragging a field that contains numbers to the Values area makes an aggregate sum calculation and dragging a field that contains text values to the Values area makes an aggregate counting calculation.

- Using the Summarize Values By option allows you to change the aggregate calculation to 1 of 11 different functions, such as Sum, Count, or Average.

- Using the Show Values As option allows you to make 1 of 14 different calculations, such as % of Grand Total, % of Column Total, Difference From, or % Difference From.

- Using the Number Format option allows you to add number formatting to the Values area calculation.

- Dragging a field that contains dates to the Rows area causes Excel to automatically group the dates by year, quarter, and month, allowing you to create common reports such as yearly, quarterly, or monthly sales reports.

- Dragging a field to the Filters area allows you to select a condition or criterion that is used by all calculations in the report. For example, selecting the year 2021 in the Filters area would convert all calculations in the report to calculations for the year 2021.

- The PivotTable Slicer option allows you to filter the entire report with an easy-to-use user interface.

- When a field is placed into the Filters area and you use the Show Report Filter Pages feature, you create a new standard PivotTable for each selected item in the Filters area sorted unique list. This feature allows you to make many reports with a single click.

- You can create a cross-tabulated report by dragging one field to the Rows area and a second field to the Columns area. In the Values area, each cell contains a calculation based on an AND logical test where the Rows area condition is one condition and Columns area condition is the other condition.

Figure 17.55 shows a net revenue Excel Table named fNetRevenue, which contains the fields Date, Sales Rep, Units, Product, Region, and Net Revenue. In the following examples, you will be creating a number of reports from this dataset.

	Date	Sales Rep	Units	Product	Region	Net Revenue
	12/10/20	Tynia Malone	1	Quad	West	$43.49
	11/14/20	Chantel Mims	13	Majestic Beaut	West	$448.20
Hidden rows	10/30/20	Janis Figueroa	9	Quad	South	$177.21
	12/8/22	Hien Pham	6	Quad	MidWest	$275.59
	12/2/22	Kiki Sho	50	Majestic Beaut	NorthWest	$1,318.07

Ex #7-11 **Data analysis goal:** Create 5 reports from data set using the Standard PivotTable tool.

Figure 17.55 *This dataset contains more than 5,000 rows of net revenue data.*

Net revenue is the metric that shows the total sales for the transaction minus any returns, allowances, and discounts. There are more than 5,000 records in the table, which spans the years 2020 to 2022. You will use the table of data to create the following standard PivotTable reports and visualizations:

- A report that calculates average and total net revenue and transactional count for each sales rep (see Figure 17.56)

Sales Rep	Ave. Net Revenue ($)	Net Revenue ($)	Transactional Count
Chantel Mims	2,458	4,164,291	1694
Hien Pham	2,382	4,059,094	1704
Janis Figueroa	2,316	1,836,407	793
Tynia Malone	2,268	1,973,179	870
Kiki Sho	2,244	1,851,206	825
Grand Total	2,359	13,884,178	5886

Figure 17.56 *Create three different aggregate calculations for each sales rep.*

- A report that shows the amount change and percentage change in net revenue by year (see Figure 17.57)

Years	Sum of Net Revenue ($)	$ Change from Previous Year	% Change From Previous Year
2020	4,823,962		
2021	4,357,559	-466,403	-9.67%
2022	4,702,657	345,098	7.92%
Grand Total	13,884,178		

Figure 17.57 *Group transactions by year and show the year-over-year changes.*

- A report that calculates total units by product, filtered by region using a slicer (see Figure 17.58)

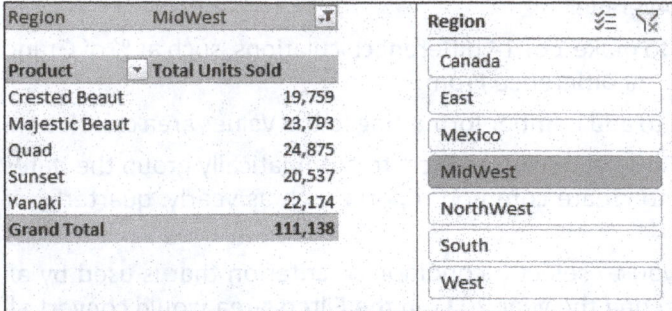

Figure 17.58 *Filter a report by region by using a slicer.*

- Seven separate regional total units by product reports created with a single click (see Figure 17.59)

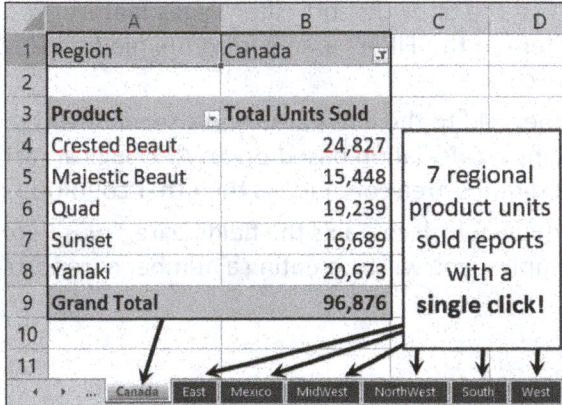

Figure 17.59 *Each report shows total units sold by product for a different region.*

- A cross-tabulated report and visualization for 2021 transactional count by product and sales rep (see Figure 17.60)

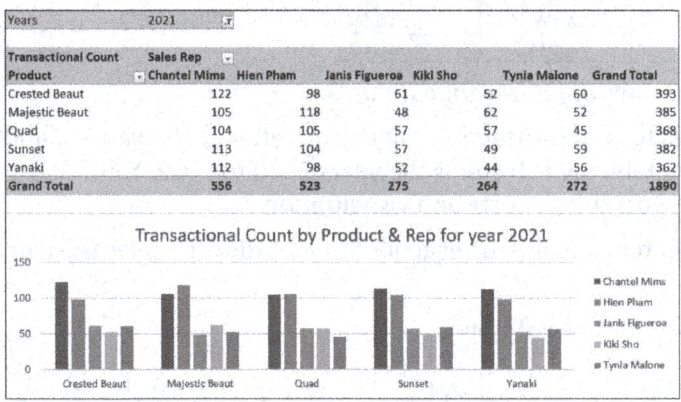

Figure 17.60 *Create a cross-tabulated report and visualization.*

Example 7: Changing the Functions in a Standard PivotTable by Using Summarize Values By

The goal for the first report is to calculate the average net revenue, total net revenue, and transactional count for each sales rep. As you do this, you will learn how to change the aggregate function by using the Summarize Values As feature in the standard PivotTable.

To complete this example, follow these steps on the worksheet named Ch17(55-117):

1. Click in a single cell in the Excel Table.

2. To open the PivotTable from Table or Range dialog box, use the keyboard shortcut Alt, N, V, T.

3. When the dialog box opens, as shown in Figure 17.61, notice that the default setting for the PivotTable location is New Worksheet. To accept this default location, you can click the OK button or press Enter.

Note: When your goal is to create a standard PivotTable on a new worksheet, if you have a single cell selected in a table, you can use the keyboard shortcut Alt N, V, T, Enter. This keyboard shortcut seems long, but when you get used to it, it is lightning quick! This is a keyboard shortcut you can show off to your coworkers and boss to get extra speed style points.

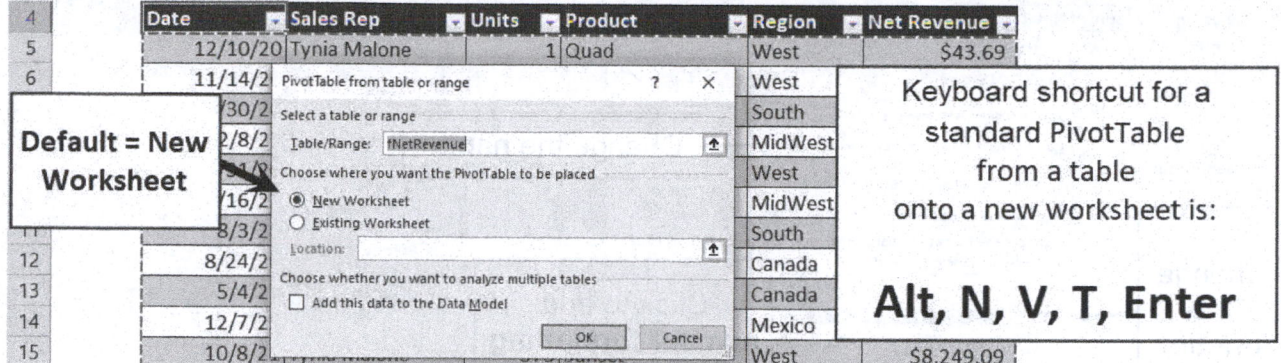

Figure 17.61 *Keyboard shortcut to start a standard PivotTable on a new worksheet.*

4.   Name the new worksheet that contains the standard PivotTable **SalesRep3Calcs** (see Figure 17.62).

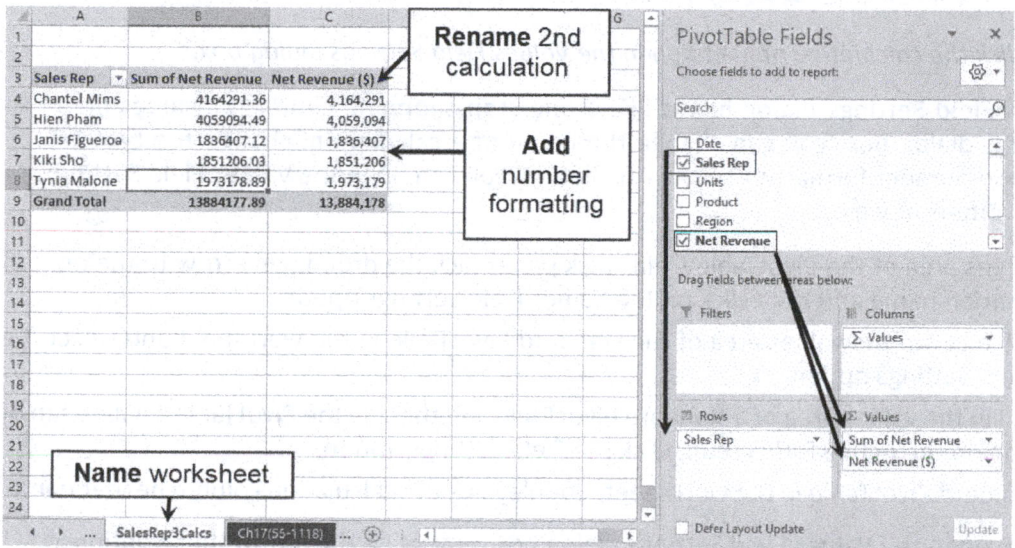

Figure 17.62 *To make different calculations on the same field, you drag the field multiple times.*

5.   In the PivotTable Fields task pane, drag the Sales Rep field to the Rows area, drag the Net Revenue field to the Values area, and then drag the Net Revenue field to the Values area a second time. By dragging the Net Revenue field to the Values area two times, you get a duplicate Sum of Net Revenue calculation. In this case, you will change the first one to an average calculation and leave the second one as a sum calculation.

6.   To add number formatting to the sum calculation, select a cell in the PivotTable Values area for the second Sum of Net Revenue calculation (column C in the worksheet) and right-click and select the Number Format option. Change the number formatting to show a comma separator and zero decimal places.

7.   To rename the sum calculation, select cell C3, press the F2 key to put the cell in edit mode, highlight the existing text, and type **Net Revenue ($)**. Then press Enter. Figure 17.62 shows the report progress so far.

8. Open the Values Field Settings dialog box by double-clicking the calculation name in cell B3 (see Figure 17.63).

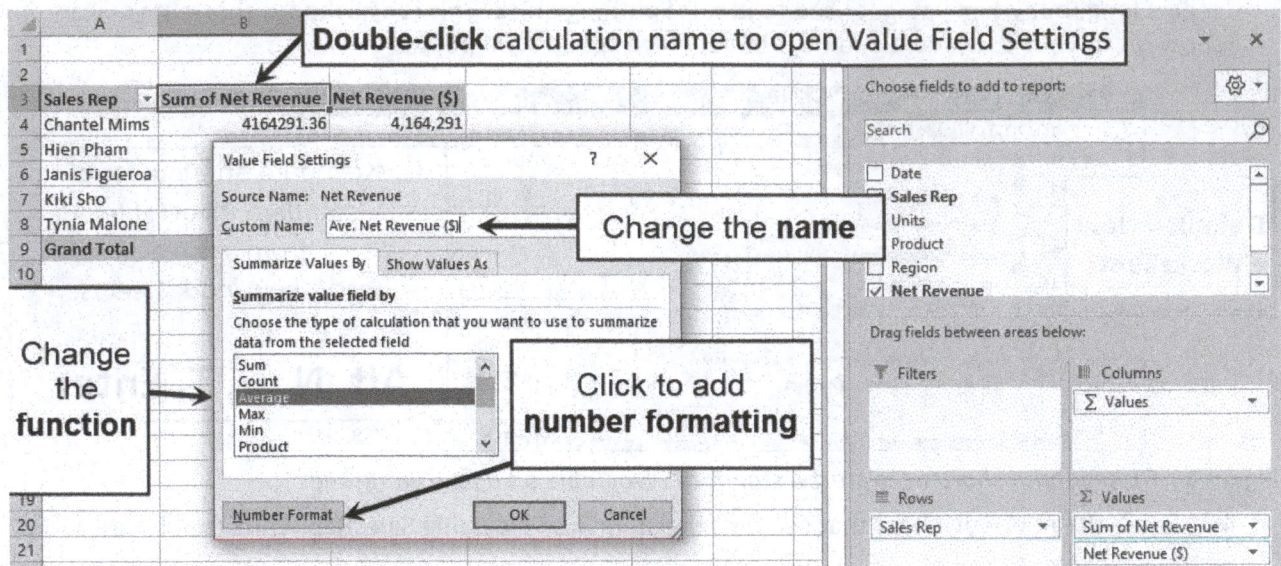

Figure 17.63 *Double-click the calculation name to open the Values Field Settings dialog box.*

Note: The Values Field Settings dialog box is like a one-stop shopping center for Values area calculations. In this dialog box, you can change the name of a calculation, change the type of calculation, and add number formatting to the calculation. You can open the Values Field Setting dialog box in four different ways:

- In the Values area of the PivotTable Fields task pane, click the dropdown arrow to the right of the calculation name and then click on the Values Field Settings option.
- Right-click a cell in the values area of the standard PivotTable in the worksheet and select the Values Field Settings option.
- Click a cell in the values area of a standard PivotTable and then, in the PivotTable Analyze tab of the Ribbon, in the Active Field group, click the Field Settings option.
- In the standard PivotTable in the worksheet, double-click the calculation column header name.

The fastest way to open the Values Field Settings dialog box is by using the last of these options, but I tend to use all of them, depending on where my cursor happens to be. Since this is such a helpful dialog box, you should try all four and see which one you prefer.

9. In the Summarize Values By tab, select the Average function from the list of available functions. Table 17.1 shows the 11 aggregate functions that are available in a standard PivotTable.

Table 17.1 The Aggregate Functions Available in a Standard PivotTable Using the Summarize Values By Feature

Value Field Settings Dialog Box Function	Equivalent Worksheet Function	Description
Average	AVERAGE	Calculates the arithmetic mean
Count Numbers	COUNT	Counts numbers
Count	COUNTA	Counts on-empty cells
Max	MAX	Finds the largest value

Min	MIN	Finds the smallest value
Product	PRODUCT	Multiplies numbers
Stdev	STDEV	Finds the standard deviation for a sample
Stdevp	STDEVP	Finds the standard deviation for a population
Sum	SUM	Adds numbers
Var	VAR	Finds the variation for a sample
Varp	VARP	Finds the variation for a sample

10. In the Custom Name textbox, type the calculation name **Ave. Net Revenue ($)**.

Note: You must type the calculation name after you select the function. If you type a name and then change the function, the typed name will disappear.

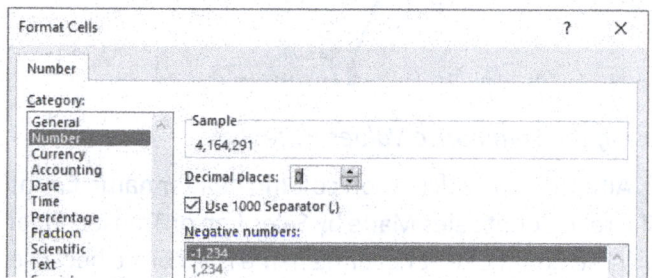

Figure 17.64 *Add number formatting to the average calculation.*

3	Sales Rep	▼	Ave. Net Revenue ($)	Net Revenue ($)
4	Chantel Mims		2,458	4,164,291
5	Hien Pham		2,382	4,059,094
6	Janis Figueroa		2,316	1,836,407
7	Kiki Sho		2,244	1,851,206
8	Tynia Malone		2,268	1,973,179
9	**Grand Total**		**2,359**	**13,884,178**

Figure 17.65 *Two aggregate calculations for each sales rep.*

11. To add number formatting to the average calculation, click the Number Format button in the lower-left corner of the Values Field Settings dialog box (refer to Figure 17.63). The Format Cells dialog box appears, and you can use it to add number formatting to the Values area calculation.

12. As shown in Figure 17.64, in the Format Cells dialog box, select the Number option from the Category list, set Decimal Places to 9, and check the checkbox to add a comma separator.

13. Click OK in the Format Cells dialog box.

14. Click OK in the Values Field Setting dialog box. Figure 17.65 shows the two completed aggregate calculations that you have created so far. Next, you need to count the number of transactions that each sales rep made.

Note: When you create a count calculation in a PivotTable, you can get the correct answer with any field in the PivotTable list. This is because when you are counting, what you are actually counting is how many times each Rows area condition occurs in the dataset. To prove this, and to gain an accurate understanding of the counting mechanism in a standard PivotTable, in this example, you will make this counting calculation two different ways. Once you do that, you can decide which one you prefer.

15. As shown in Figure 17.66, drag the Net Revenue field to the Values area. Because this field contains number data, the calculation defaults to Sum.

16. To change the function from Sum to Count, right-click a cell in the Values area of the standard PivotTable, select Summarize Values By, and then select Count. (Although you could use the Values Field Setting dialog box to change the function, because all you need to do in this case is change the function for the calculation, it is faster to use this right-click method.)

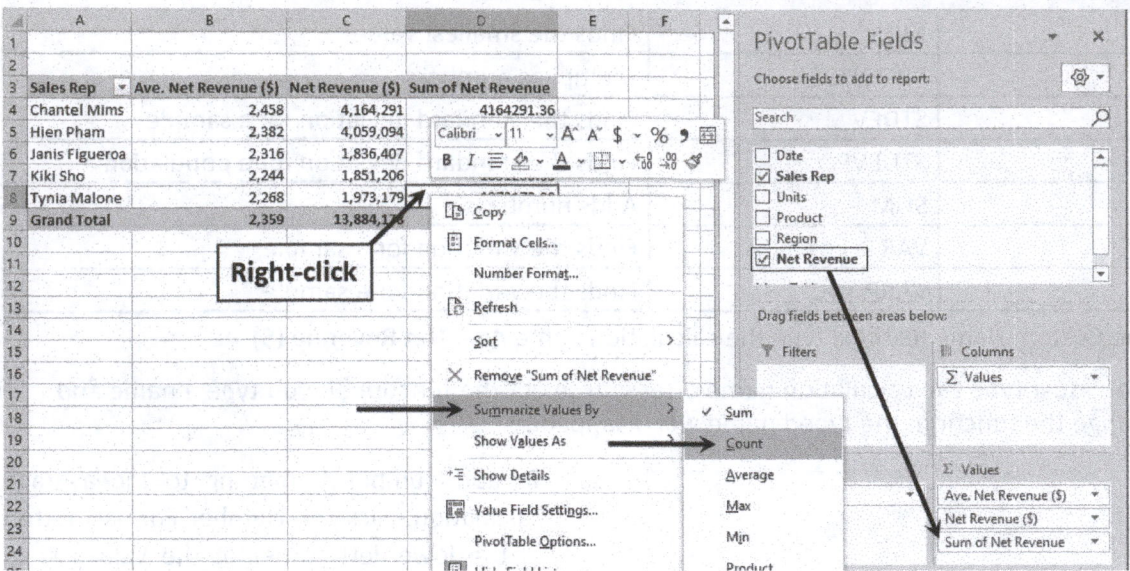

Figure 17.66 *You can change the default function by using the Summarize Values By feature.*

The count calculation is shown in Figure 17.67. Although the calculation column header name Count of Net Revenue is accurate, it would be better if it read Count Sales Made by Sales Rep or Transactional Count by Sale Rep or simply Transactional Count. The Count of Net Revenue name is accurate because the calculation counted the number of numbers in the Net Revenue field where the Sales Rep field contains the given sales rep's name. This means that the effect of any counting calculation in a standard PivotTable is to count how many times the Rows area condition occurred in the dataset. For counting, it does not matter which field you drag to the Values area; when you change the function to Count, all fields get the same answer.

Note: When I make a count calculation in a standard PivotTable, my rule is to drag a text field to the Values area because text fields default to the count calculation. Then all I have to do is rename the calculation column header name and add number formatting. You'll try this method next.

	Sales Rep	Ave. Net Revenue ($)	Net Revenue ($)	Count of Net Revenue
4	Chantel Mims	2,458	4,164,291	1694
5	Hien Pham	2,382	4,059,094	1704
6	Janis Figueroa	2,316	1,836,407	793
7	Kiki Sho	2,244	1,851,206	825
8	Tynia Malone	2,268	1,973,179	870
9	Grand Total	2,359	13,884,178	5886

When you use the **Count aggregate function**, it is counting how many times the Rows area condition occurred in the data set

Figure 17.67 *A better name for this calculation would be Count Sales Made by Sales Rep or Transactional Count.*

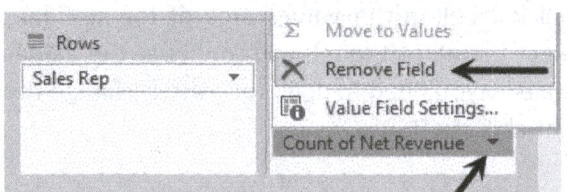

Figure 17.68 *Click the dropdown next to the calculation in the Values area of task pane and then click Remove Field.*

17. As shown in Figure 17.68, to remove the Count of Net Revenue calculation from the report, in the Values area of the PivotTable Fields task pane, click the dropdown arrow next to the calculation name and then click Remove. (An alternative method for removing the calculation is to click the calculation name in the Values area of the PivotTable Fields task pane and then drag it to the worksheet.)

18. To start the Values area count calculation again, drag the Product field to the Values area of the PivotTable Fields task pane. Because it is a text field, the calculation is count.

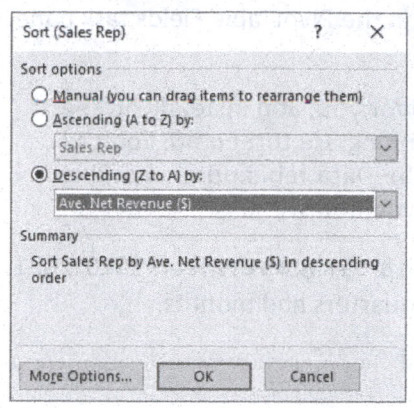

Figure 17.69 *Sort the report by the Ave. Net Revenue ($) calculation.*

19. To open the Values Field Settings dialog box for the count calculation, double-click the Count of Product calculation column header name.

20. Change the name of the calculation to **Transactional Count** and then add number formatting to show a comma separator and zero decimal places.

21. In the Rows area of the report, click the Sales Rep Sort and Filter dropdown arrow and select More Sort Options to open the Sort (Sales Rep) dialog box.

22. In the Sort (Sales Rep) dialog box, select the Descending option button and from the dropdown below it, select the Ave. Net Revenue ($) calculation, as shown in Figure 17.69.

23. Click OK. Figure 17.70 shows the final report.

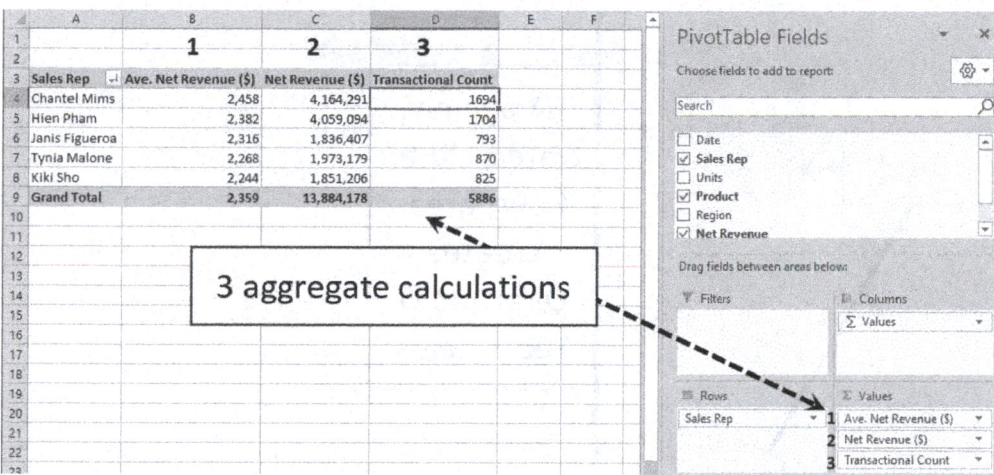

Figure 17.70 *Using a standard PivotTable to make multiple aggregate calculations for a set of conditions is easy and fast.*

Example 8: Using the Standard PivotTable Group Feature to Create a Yearly Sales Report

The goal for this report is to use transactional sales amounts recorded by date and calculate yearly sales totals, year-over-year amount of change, and year-over-year percentage change. As you create this report, you will learn how to use the standard PivotTable Group feature and the Show Values As Difference From and % Difference From calculations.

One of the most beloved features of the standard PivotTable tool is the Group feature. This feature allows you to use number values, such as dates, and group them into categories, such as month and year. This feature is beloved because it makes it easy to roll sales transactions listed by date into totals for month and year to create yearly or monthly sales reports. This feature works with a standard PivotTable; with a Data Model PivotTable, it either does not work at all or works inefficiently (as you'll see later in this chapter).

In this example, you will first use the Group feature to create the month and year categories, then you will sum sales to get the yearly totals, and finally you will use the Show Values As feature to calculate the year-over-year changes.

To complete this example, follow these steps on the worksheet named Ch17(55-117):

1. Select one cell in the Excel Table fNetRevenue.

2. To create a new standard PivotTable on a new worksheet, use the keyboard shortcut Alt, N, V, T, Enter.

3. Name the new worksheet **YearlyNetRevenue**.

4. Drag the Date field to the Rows area in the PivotTable Fields task pane. As shown in Figure 17.71, when you drag the Date field to the Rows area (or Columns area) in the PivotTable Fields task pane, two new fields are created, named Quarters and Years.

> **Note:** If the Quarters and Years fields are not automatically created for you, and instead you see a list of daily dates, then the default settings for date and time grouping are turned off. You can change these default settings by going to File, Options, selecting the Data tab, and unchecking the option Disable Automatic Grouping of Date/Time columns in PivotTables.

In the PivotTable report in the worksheet, you can see that the Rows area shows the years 2020, 2021, and 2022. The Years field is collapsed so that you cannot see the quarters and months.

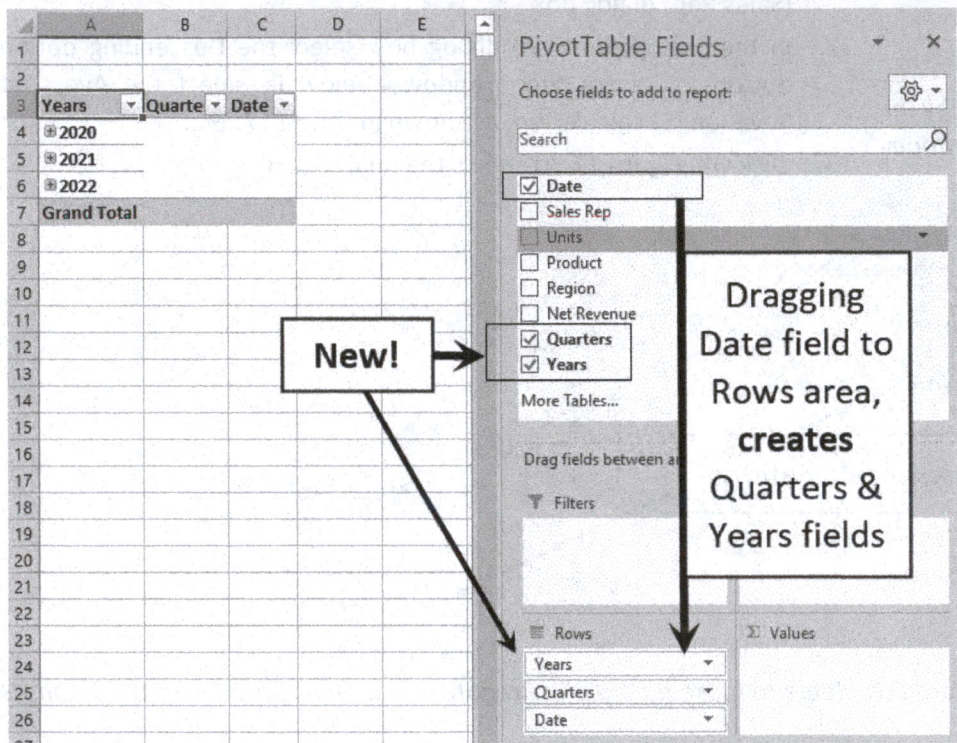

Figure 17.71 *By dragging Date to the Rows area, you create the new fields for Months (temporarily named Date), Quarters, and Years.*

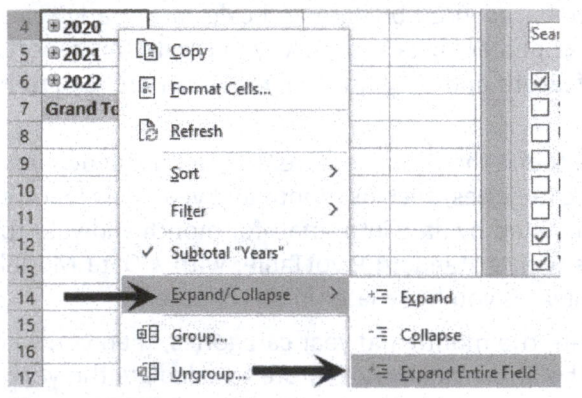

Figure 17.72 *Expand Entire Year field.*

5. To expand the Years field so that you can see quarters, right-click a cell in the Rows area that contains the Years field and select Expand/Collapse and then Expand Entire Field (see Figure 17.72). The Quarters field is now visible.

6. To expand the Quarters field so that you can see quarters, right-click a cell in the Rows area that contains the Quarters field and select Expand/Collapse and then Expand Entire Field. The Date field, which is showing Month names, is now visible.

Figure 17.73 shows the fully expanded Rows area of the PivotTable. When you use the Group feature, the standard PivotTable cache of data stores the new fields. If you build any other standard PivotTable from the fNetRevenue table, these new fields appear in the PivotTable Fields task pane. In addition, if you go back to the first PivotTable report that you created from the fNetRevenue table and refresh it, these new fields become part of that field list also.

Note: If you do not want the new fields to appear in the PivotTable Fields task pane, you have to create a standard Pivot Table based on a new cache of data by using the standard PivotTable three-step wizard. This is an older feature that is not available in the Ribbon but that can be accessed with the keyboard shortcut Alt, D, P.

As shown in Figure 17.73, you have the fields Years, Quarters, and Date. For the final report, you do not need the Quarters field. To override the automatic grouping categories, you can manually group the date fields into the time and date categories that best fit your goals by using the Grouping dialog box.

7.   To open the Grouping dialog box, right-click in any cell in the Rows area and then select Group (see Figure 17.74).

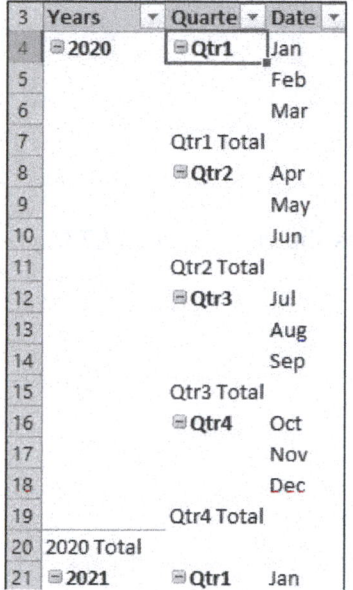

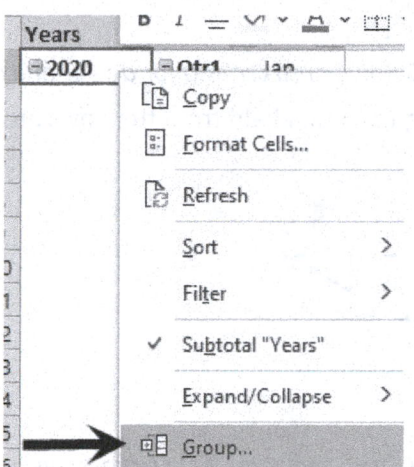

Figure 17.73 *Now you have Years, Quarters, and Months Rows area criteria for adding net revenue.*

Figure 17.74 *Right-click the Years field in the Rows area and then click Group.*

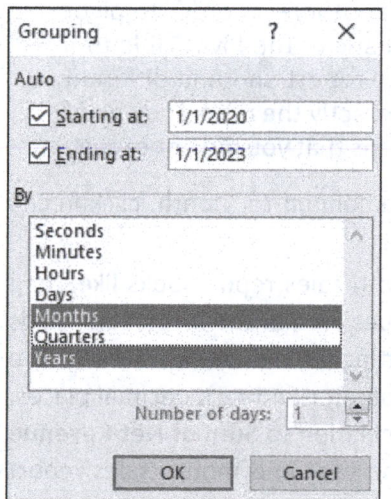

Figure 17.75 *The Grouping dialog box allows you to group by seven different time or date groupings.*

8.   In the Grouping dialog box, click on Quarters to deselect it as a grouping option. Figure 17.75 shows that only Months and Years are selected as grouping categories.

The Grouping dialog box allows you to create Rows (or Columns) area conditions based on dates and time that can be used as conditions for your calculations. You can select one to seven of the date and time categories, and Excel adds them to the field list so you can drag and drop them to build your reports. The term "grouping" comes from the database world, where the SQL term "group by" refers to grouping together records that match the date and time categories to make conditional calculations. For this report, you only need to group by months and years, but notice that, depending on the type of data you have, you could group by hours, minutes, and even seconds. The Hours grouping category is particularly good for creating reports to analyze the peak hours for sales or website activity. You can use the Grouping dialog box on any number values, including time values and number values. You will see other examples of grouping numbers later in this book.

9. Click OK in the Grouping dialog box, and you see the year and month Rows area conditions shown in Figure 17.76.

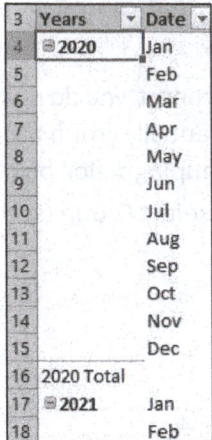

3	Years	▾	Date	▾
4	⊟ 2020		Jan	
5			Feb	
6			Mar	
7			Apr	
8			May	
9			Jun	
10			Jul	
11			Aug	
12			Sep	
13			Oct	
14			Nov	
15			Dec	
16	2020 Total			
17	⊟ 2021		Jan	
18			Feb	

Figure 17.76 *Rows area criteria for a year and month net revenue report.*

10. Drag the Years field from the Rows area to the Columns area, as shown in Figure 17.77.

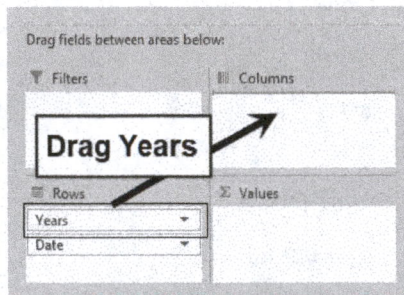

Figure 17.77 *Drag the Years field from Rows area to the Columns area.*

Figure 17.78 shows a cross-tabulated PivotTable with Months in the Rows area and Years in the Columns area.

Note: This ability to drag a field from one location in a PivotTable to another—in order to pivot the report—gave the PivotTable tool its name. The pivoting characteristic of the PivotTable tool allows you to change a report and investigate different layouts for the report and find different conditions for your calculations. This exploratory aspect helps you get exactly the report you want to match your initial goals or to discover a new layout or set of calculations that you did not expect.

2					
3		Years ▾			
4	Date ▾	2020	2021	2022	Grand Total
5	Jan				
6	Feb				
7	Mar				
8	Apr				
9	May				
10	Jun				
11	Jul				
12	Aug				
13	Sep				
14	Oct				
15	Nov				
16	Dec				
17	Grand Total				

Figure 17.78 *Months in the Rows area and Years in the Columns area.*

11. To change the name of the Data column to Month, click in cell A4, type **Month**, and press Enter.

12. To explore what a year and month sales report looks like, drag the Net Revenue field to the Values area of the PivotTable Fields task pane, add number formatting to the Values area in the worksheet to show a comma separator and zero decimal places, and change the name of the calculation to **Sum of Net Revenue ($)**. Figure 17.79 shows what the year and month sales report looks like with these changes.

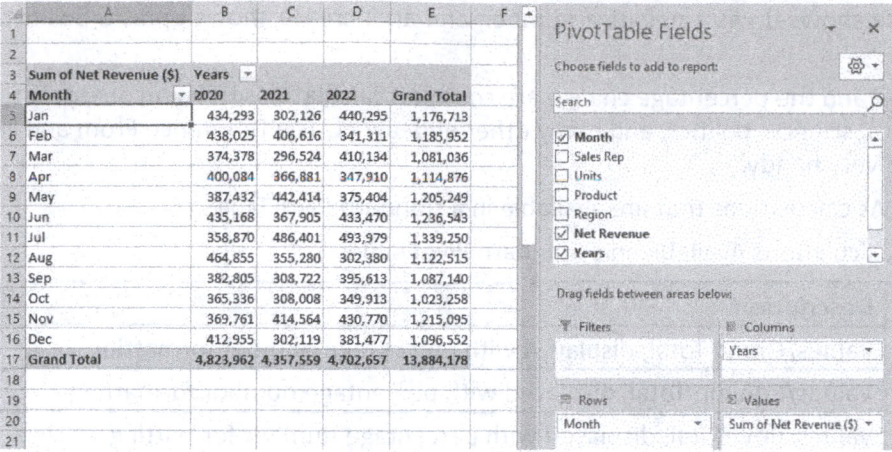

Figure 17.79 *Year/month cross-tabulated net revenue report from transactional records.*

13. To remove the Month field from the Rows area, uncheck the Month checkbox in the PivotTable Fields field list.

14. To add the Years condition to the Rows area, click the Years field in the Columns area and then drag and drop it into the Rows area. Figure 17.80 shows the pivoted result.

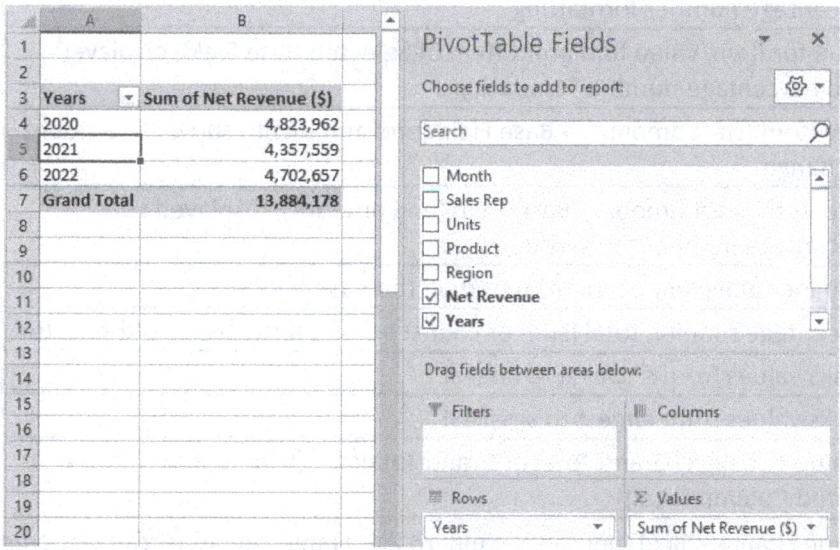

Figure 17.80 *Remove the Month condition and then drag Years to the Rows area.*

Show Values As Calculation for Difference From and % Difference From

Now that the report shows the yearly amounts, next you want to make the calculations to show the year-over-year amount of change and percentage of change. Luckily, in a standard PivotTable, you can use the Show Values As feature to make these calculations. The Difference From calculation will determine the amount of change between an end amount, known as the *base field*, and a start amount, known as the *base item*. The calculation is as follows:

```
End Amount – Start Amount = Amount of Change
```

The % Difference From calculation will determine the percentage of change between the end amount (base field) and the start amount (base item). The % Difference From calculation automatically applies percentage number formatting to the Values area of the report to display the answer as a percentage. The calculation is as follows:

```
(End Amount – Start Amount)/Start Amount = Change/Start Amount = Percentage
Change
```

You may know this calculation by its mathematical equivalent:

```
End/Start – 1 = Percentage Change
```

For both calculations, a decrease shows up as a negative number, and an increase shows up as a positive number.

Calculating the amount of change and the percentage change are common calculations that you are likely to encounter in business, economics, science, politics, and many other endeavors. The Difference From and % Difference From calculations are very handy.

Table 17.2 lists the Show Values As calculations that are available in a standard PivotTable.

Table 17.2 The Show Values As Calculations Available in a Standard PivotTable

Show Values As Calculation	Description
% of Grand Total	Values/Grand Total, displayed with percentage number formatting
% of Column Total	Values/Column Total, displayed with percentage number formatting
% of Row Total	Values/Row Total, displayed with percentage number formatting
% Of	Field Values/Specified Value, displayed with percentage number formatting
% of Parent Row Total	Value for Item/Value for Parent Item in the Rows Area, displayed with percentage number formatting
% of Parent Column Total	Value for Item/Value for Parent Item in the Columns Area, displayed with percentage number formatting
% of Parent Total	Value for Item/Value for Parent Item of Selected Base Field, displayed with percentage number formatting
Difference From	Base Item (start amount) – Base Field (end amount)to show the amount of change
% Difference From	Base Item (start amount)/Base Field (end amount), displayed with percentage number formatting
Running Total in	Running total (sum or count) based on the base field selected
% Running Total in	Percentage running total (sum or count) based on the base field selected
Rank Smallest to Largest	Ranks values from smallest to largest
Rank Largest to Smallest	Ranks values from largest to smallest
Index	((Value in Cell) x (Grand Total of Grand Totals)) / ((Grand Row Total) x (Grand Column Total))

To make the year-over-year net revenue change calculations in a standard PivotTable, you must calculate the sum of net revenue first and then add your Show Values As calculations to the sum of net revenue calculation. You can start with the difference from calculation:

1. Drag the Net Revenue field down to the Values area a second time. Drop the field below the Sum of Net Revenue ($) calculation.

2. As shown in Figure 17.81, in the Values area of the report for the second calculation (column C), right-click any cell and select Show Values As and then Difference From. The Show Values As (Sum of Net Revenue) dialog box appears.

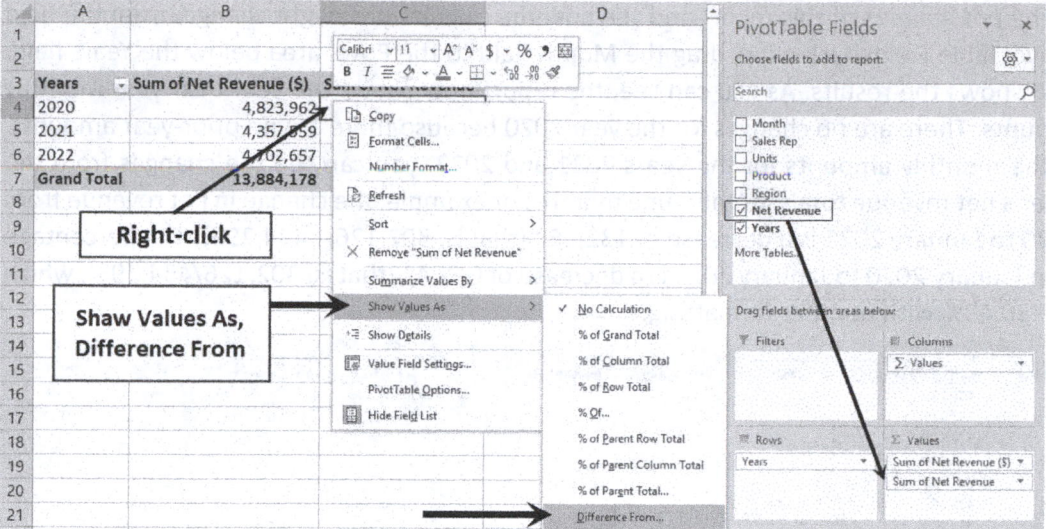

Figure 17.81 *The Show Values, Difference From calculation to determine the amount of change.*

3. As shown in Figure 17.82, in the Show Values As (Sum of Net Revenue) dialog box, select Years for Base Field and select (previous) for Base Item and then click OK.

3	Years	Sum of Net Revenue ($)	Sum of Net Revenue
4	2020	4,823,962	4823961.97
5	2021	4,357,559	4357558.97
6	2022	4,702,657	4702656.95
7	Grand Total	13,884,178	13884177.89

Show Values As (Sum of Net Revenue)   ?   ✕

Calculation: Difference From
Base Field: Years
Base Item: (previous)

OK   Cancel

Figure 17.82 *Calculate the amount of change from the previous year.*

4. Add consistent number formatting that matches the previous calculation and type the new calculation name **$ Change From Previous Year** in cell C3. Figure 17.83 shows the result.

5. To create the % Difference From calculation, drag the Net Revenue field to the Values area and create a Show Values As, % Difference From calculation with Base Field set to Years and Base Item set to (previous).

3	Years	Sum of Net Revenue ($)	$ Change From Previous Year
4	2020	4,823,962	
5	2021	4,357,559	-466,403
6	2022	4,702,657	345,098
7	Grand Total	13,884,178	

Figure 17.83 *Add number formatting and change the calculation name at the top of the column.*

6. In cell D3, type the new calculation name **% Change From Previous Year**. Figure 17.84 shows the completed calculation in the year-over-year report. Look at cell C5 in the report, and you can see that the change in net revenue from 2020 to 2021 is a decrease of $466,403 (that is, 4,357,559 – 4,823,962) . In cell D5, the percentage change from 2020 to 2021 is a decrease of 9.67% (that is, 4,357,559/4,823,962).

	A	B	C	D
1				
2				
3	Years	Sum of Net Revenue ($)	$ Change From Previous Year	% Change From Previous Year
4	2020	4,823,962		
5	2021	4,357,559	-466,403	-9.67%
6	2022	4,702,657	345,098	7.92%
7	Grand Total	13,884,178		

Figure 17.84 *Standard PivotTable Show Values As Difference From and % Difference From calculations.*

7. To explore the possibilities of this report and see how the calculations might change, from the field list in the PivotTable Fields task pane, drag the Month field to the Rows area below the Years field. Figure 17.85 shows the results. As you can see, the report now shows the year-over-year monthly change amounts. There are no changes for the year 2020 because there are no prior-year amounts. But for all the monthly amounts for the years 2021 and 2022, you can see the changes from the previous year's net revenue totals for the same month. For example, the change in net revenue from January 2020 to January 2021 is a decrease of 132,167 (that is, 302,126 – 434,293). The percentage change from January 2020 to January 2021 is a decrease of 0.3043 (that is, 302,126/434,293), which appears as –30.43% with number formatting.

Years	Month	Sum of Net Revenue ($)	$ Change From Previous Year	% Change From Previous Year
⊟ 2020	Jan	434,293		
	Feb	438,025		
	Mar	374,378		
	Apr	400,084		
	May	387,432		
	Jun	435,168		
	Jul	358,870		
	Aug	464,855		
	Sep	382,805		
	Oct	365,336		
	Nov	369,761		
	Dec	412,955		
2020 Total		4,823,962		
⊟ 2021	Jan	302,126	-132,167	-30.43%
	Feb	406,616	-31,409	-7.17%
	Mar	296,524	-77,854	-20.80%
	Apr	366,881	-33,203	-8.30%
	May	442,414	54,982	14.19%
	Jun	367,905	-67,263	-15.46%
	Jul	486,401	127,531	35.54%
	Aug	355,280	-109,575	-23.57%
	Sep	308,722	-74,084	-19.35%
	Oct	308,008	-57,329	-15.69%
	Nov	414,564	44,802	12.12%
	Dec	302,119	-110,835	-26.84%
2021 Total		4,357,559	-466,403	-9.67%
⊟ 2022	Jan	440,295	138,169	45.73%

PivotTable Fields

Choose fields to add to report:

Search

- ☑ Month
- ☐ Sales Rep
- ☐ Units
- ☐ Product
- ☐ Region
- ☑ Net Revenue
- ☑ Years

Drag fields between areas below:

▼ Filters

▥ Columns
Σ Values

▦ Rows
Years
Month

Σ Values
Sum of Net Revenu... ▼
$ Change From Pre... ▼
% Change From Pr... ▼

Figure 17.85 *This report shows the year-over-year monthly and yearly change amounts.*

8. To pivot the report back to just showing years in the Rows area, remove the Month field from the Rows area. The report should once again look as shown in Figure 17.84.

Example 9: Filtering a Standard PivotTable Report Using a Slicer

In this example, you will create a total units sold by product report that allows a user to filter the report to show different regions. When you filter a standard PivotTable report based on one or more conditions, you are adding the conditions to every calculation in the PivotTable. This is different from a Rows area condition, which adds a condition only to the calculations in the row in the report, or a Columns area condition, which adds a condition only to the calculations in the column in the report.

You can add a filter to a standard PivotTable by dragging a field to the Filters area of the PivotTable Fields task pane or by adding a slicer from the Filter group in the PivotTable Analyze tab in the Ribbon.

To complete this example, follow these steps on the worksheet named Ch17(55-117):

1. Select one cell in the Excel Table fNetRevenue.

2. To create a new standard PivotTable on a new worksheet, use the keyboard shortcut Alt, N, V, T, Enter.

3. Name the new worksheet **UnitsSoldByProduct**.

4. Drag the Product field to the Rows area in the PivotTable Fields task pane.

5. Drag the Units field to the Values area of the PivotTable Fields task pane, add number formatting (a comma separator and zero decimal places showing) to the Values area in the worksheet, and change the name of the calculation to **Total Units Sold**.

6. Drag the Region field to the Filters area in the PivotTable Fields task pane.

Figure 17.86 shows the total units sold by product report with the Region filter dropped into the Filters area. Cell A1 shows the field that was dropped into the Filters area of the task pane. Cell B1 shows the word (All) and indicates that no filter has been applied to the calculations in the report. In cell B4, you can see that there were 138,782 Crested Beaut boomerang products sold over the entire time period of the dataset.

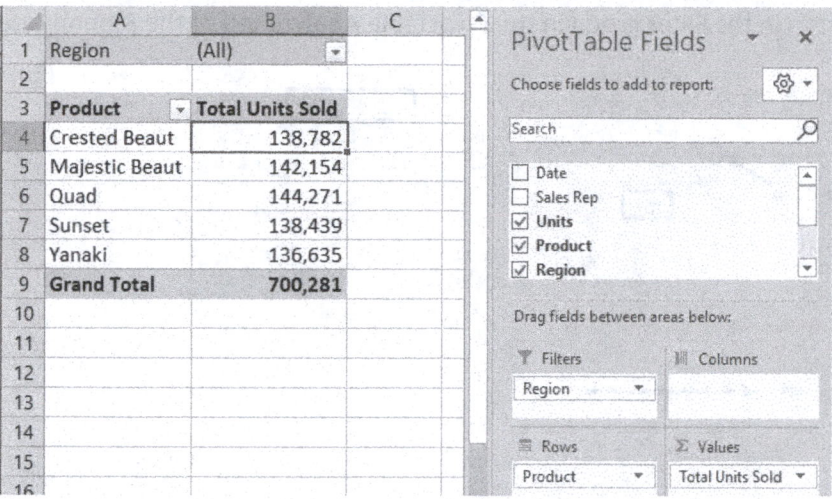

Figure 17.86 *Total units sold by product report with a filter for Region that has not been enacted.*

7. To filter the calculations for just the NorthWest region, in cell B1, click the Filter dropdown arrow, select NorthWest, and click the OK button (see Figure 17.87).

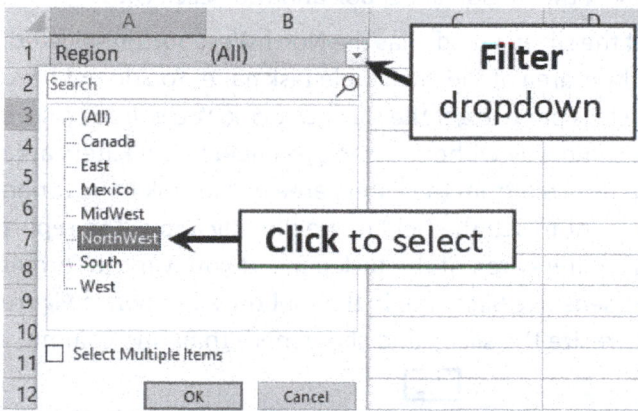

Figure 17.87 *Use the Filter dropdown to filter the calculations in the report.*

Figure 17.88 shows that all six calculations in the report now have the condition NorthWest region applied to them. In cell B4, the sum of total units sold for the Crested Beaut product in the NorthWest region is 21,264; in cell B6, the sum of total units sold for the Quad product in the NorthWest region is 18,357; and in cell B9, the sum of total units sold in the NorthWest region is 97,525. For each row in the report (except the grand total cell), an AND logical test is used to sum total units sold based on the product and the region NorthWest.

	A	B	C	D	E	F	G
1	Region	NorthWest					
2							
3	**Product**	**Total Units Sold**					
4	Crested Beaut	21,264	◄ Total Units Sold for Crested Beaut in the NorthWest				
5	Majestic Beaut	18,637	◄ Total Units Sold for Majestic Beaut in the NorthWest				
6	Quad	18,357	◄ Total Units Sold for Quad in the NorthWest				
7	Sunset	19,040	◄ Total Units Sold for Sunset in the NorthWest				
8	Yanaki	20,227	◄ Total Units Sold for Yanaki in the NorthWest				
9	**Grand Total**	**97,525**	◄ Total Units Sold in the NorthWest				

Figure 17.88 *When you add a filter, the condition is used in all calculations in the report.*

The Filter feature in a standard PivotTable is quite amazing. However, when you drop a field into the Filters area in the PivotTable Fields task pane, you must use a dropdown arrow to expose the sorted unique list of items that the report user can select from. This is okay, but if you want a more user-friendly and visually appealing way to filter a report, you can use a slicer.

8. To add a slicer for the Region field to the standard PivotTable report, select one cell in the report and click the Insert Slicer button in the Filter group in the PivotTable Analyze tab of the Ribbon (see Figure 17.89).

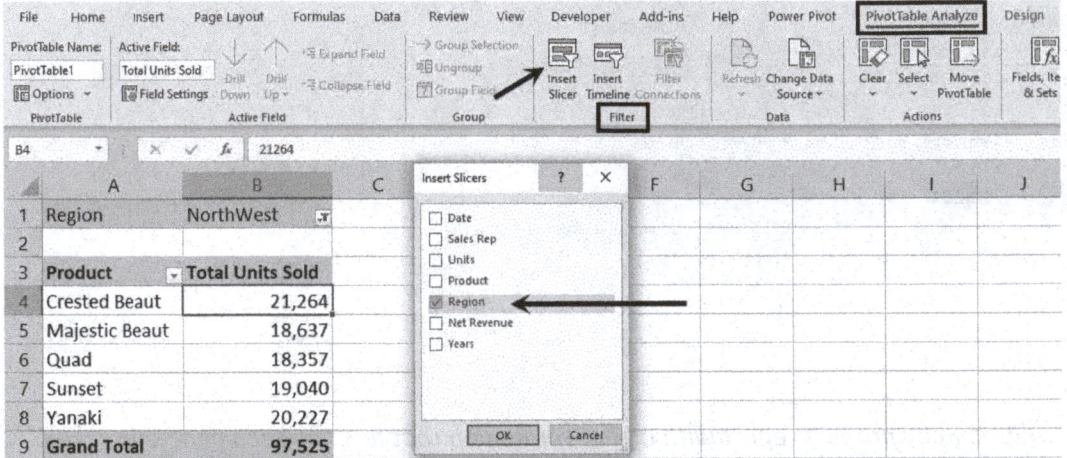

Figure 17.89 *Checking a field name adds a slicer for that field.*

9. In the Insert Slicers dialog box that appears, check the Region checkbox and then click OK.

Figure 17.90 shows the slicer added. Notice that the slicer already has the NorthWest button selected; this is because you left the Region field in the Filters area of the PivotTable task pane. You do not have to keep the Region field in the Filters area of the task pane to get the slicer to work. You will see a little later (in Figure 17.94) that the slicer works the same way without the Region field in the Filters area of the task pane. Most of the time, you remove the field from the Filters area of the task pane (or do not add it at all) before you add a slicer. If you want to see the field name directly above the report and listed in a cell, you can keep the field in the Filters area of the task pane. If you want to format your slicer, select the slicer and use the context-sensitive Slicer tab in the Ribbon, as shown in Figure 17.90. You can use this tab to change the style, resize the slicer, and show more than one column.

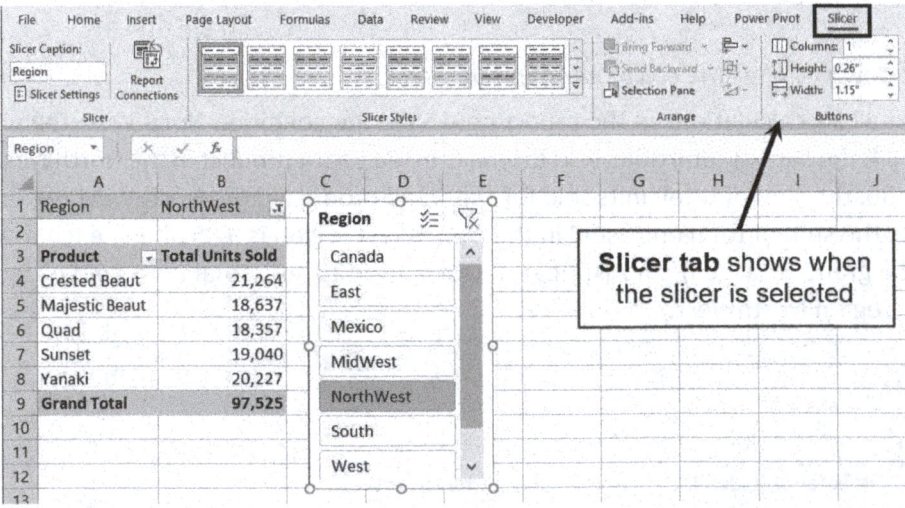

Figure 17.90 *You can format and change the size and structure of the slicer in the Slicer tab in the Ribbon.*

10. To test the slicer, click on the East region. Figure 17.91 shows that all calculations in the report now show the amounts for the East region. To select more than one item from the slicer, you can select a first item, hold down the Ctrl key, and select the remaining items. You can also use the Multiple Items button at the top of the Slicer, as shown in Figure 17.92.

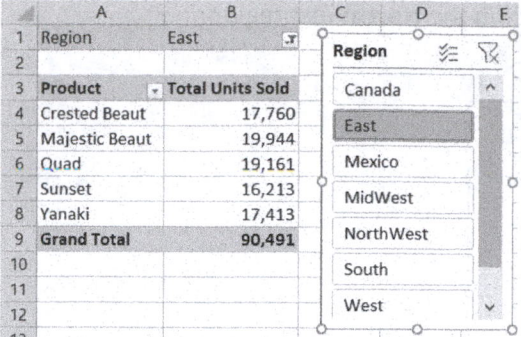

Figure 17.91 *Click to select the East region.*

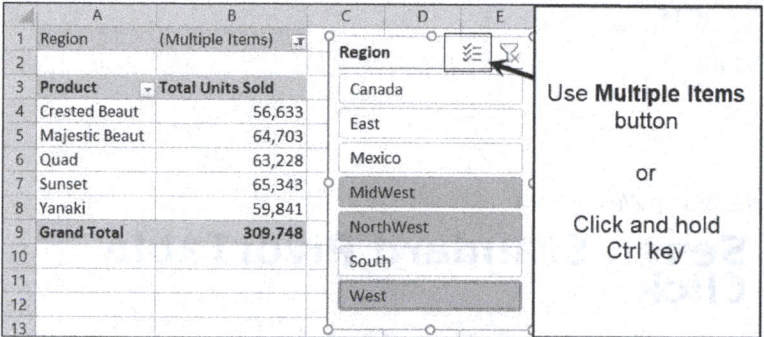

Figure 17.92 *When you select more than one field in a slicer, you create an OR logical test.*

11. To select only the regions that contain west, click West, hold down the Ctrl key, click NorthWest, and then click MidWest. Figure 17.92 shows the OR logical test results. In cell B4, you can see the total units sold amount of 56,633 units. The logical test used on the dataset is: "add the units sold when the product is equal to Crested Beaut AND the Region is West OR NorthWest OR MidWest."

12. As shown in Figure 17.93, click the Clear Filter button at the top of the slicer to show calculated amounts for all regions.

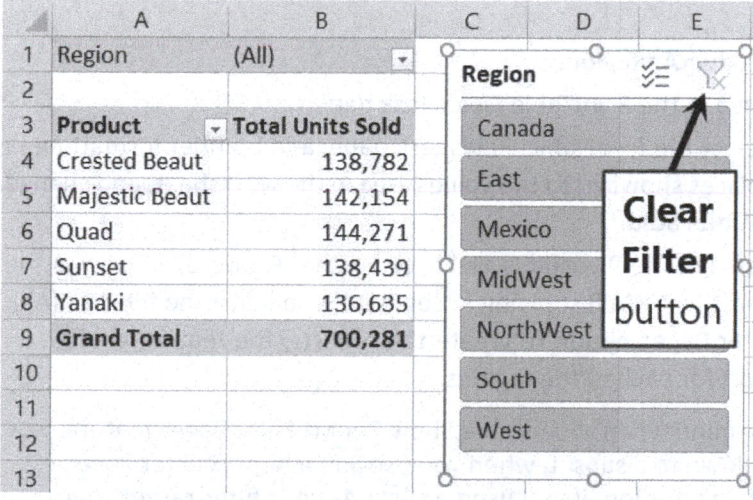

Figure 17.93 *Clear Filter button in the slicer.*

13. To remove the Region field from the Filters area of the task pane, uncheck the checkbox for the Region field in the PivotTable Fields task pane field list.

14. To show calculations for only the NorthWest region, click NorthWest in the slicer.

Figure 17.94 shows the final report for total units sold by product in the NorthWest region.

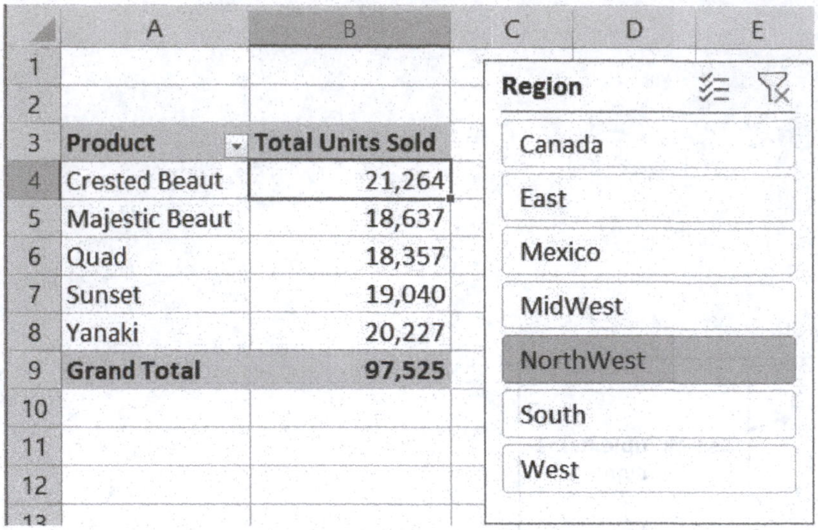

Figure 17.94 *Total units sold by product for the NorthWest region.*

Example 10: Creating Seven Standard PivotTable Reports with a Single Click

Say that your boss asks you to create seven reports like the one in Figure 17.94—one for each region. You can do this in one click by using the Show Report Filter Pages feature, which is one of the most amazing features in a standard PivotTable. This feature only works on a standard PivotTable and does not work on a Data Model PivotTable.

This example walks through how to create seven separate regional reports showing total units by product. To complete this example, follow these steps on the worksheet named Ch17(55-117):

1. Select one cell in the Excel Table fNetRevenue.

2. To create a new standard PivotTable on a new worksheet, use the keyboard shortcut Alt, N, V, T, Enter.

3. Name the new worksheet **UnitsByProductAllRegion**.

4. Drag the Product field to the Rows area in the PivotTable Fields task pane.

5. Drag the Units field to the Values area of the PivotTable Fields task pane, add number formatting (a comma separator and zero decimal places showing) to the Values area in the worksheet, and change the name of the calculation to **Total Units Sold**.

6. Drag the Region field to the Filters area in the PivotTable Fields task pane. Figure 17.95 shows the initial total units sold by product report, with (All) showing in cell B1. If you leave the filter as (All), when you click the Show Report Filter Pages option to create the reports, the feature creates an individual total units by product report for each of the regions.

> **Note:** There are several things to keep in mind when you use the Show Report Filter Pages feature. If you used the filter to filter the report down to a subset, when you use Show Report Filter Pages, only a subset of reports will be created. In addition, if you used a slicer as your filter rather than drag the Region field to the Filters area in the PivotTable Fields task pane, this feature will not work. Finally, this feature is notoriously hard to find. To find the correct dropdown menu to access the Show Report Filter Pages feature, you go to Options dropdown arrow in the PivotTable group in the context-sensitive PivotTable Analyze tab in the Ribbon, as shown in Figure 17.95.

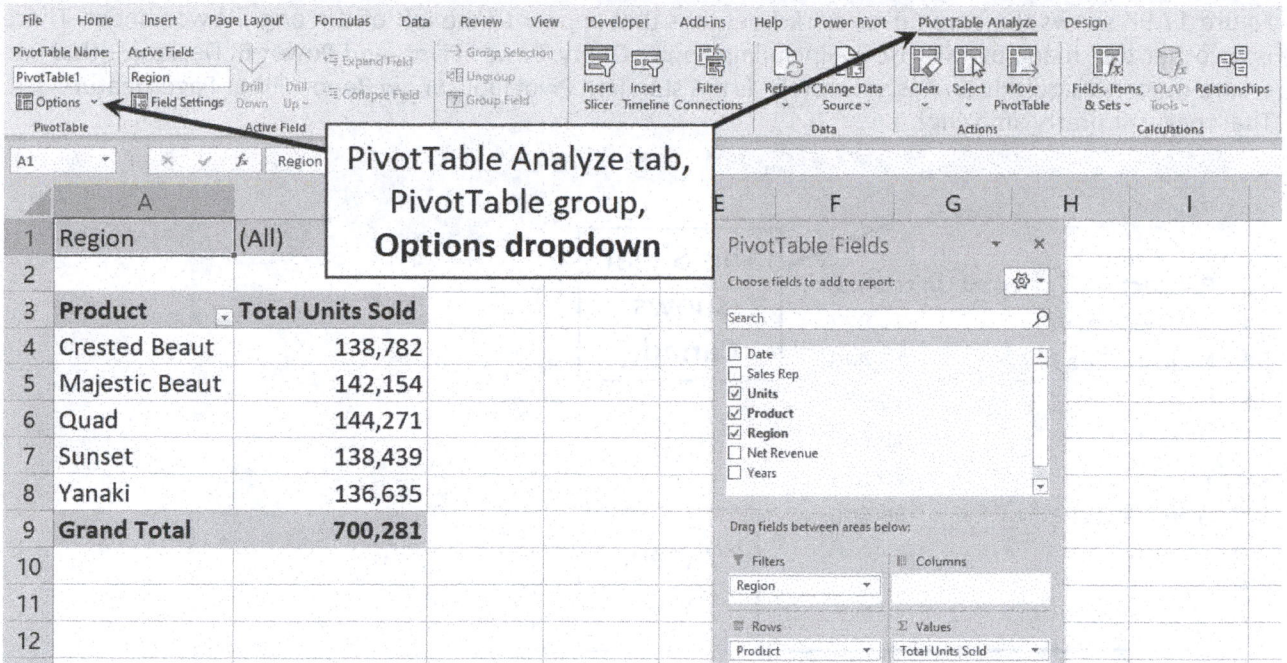

Figure 17.95 *Once you get the total units sold by product for all regions, you must find the Options dropdown arrow.*

7. Select one cell in the PivotTable, click on the PivotTable Analyze tab in the Ribbon, and then, in the PivotTable group, click the Options dropdown arrow and click on Show Report Filter Pages option, as shown in Figure 17.96.

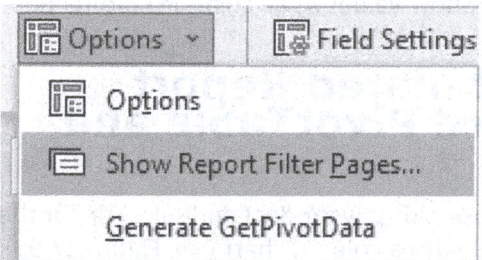

Figure 17.96 *From the Options dropdown arrow, click Show Report Filter Pages.*

8. In the Show Report Filter Pages dialog box that appears, select the Region filter and click OK (see Figure 17.97).

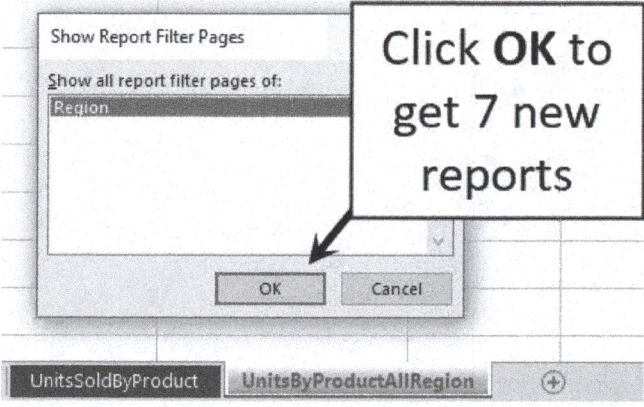

Figure 17.97 *The Show Report Filter Pages dialog box.*

Figure 17.98 shows the seven new worksheet tabs that appear to the left of the original worksheet. There is no other tool made by Microsoft—including Power Query, Power Pivot, and Power BI Desktop—that can create reports as quickly and as accurately as the standard PivotTable Show Report Filter Pages feature can. That makes it pretty amazing!

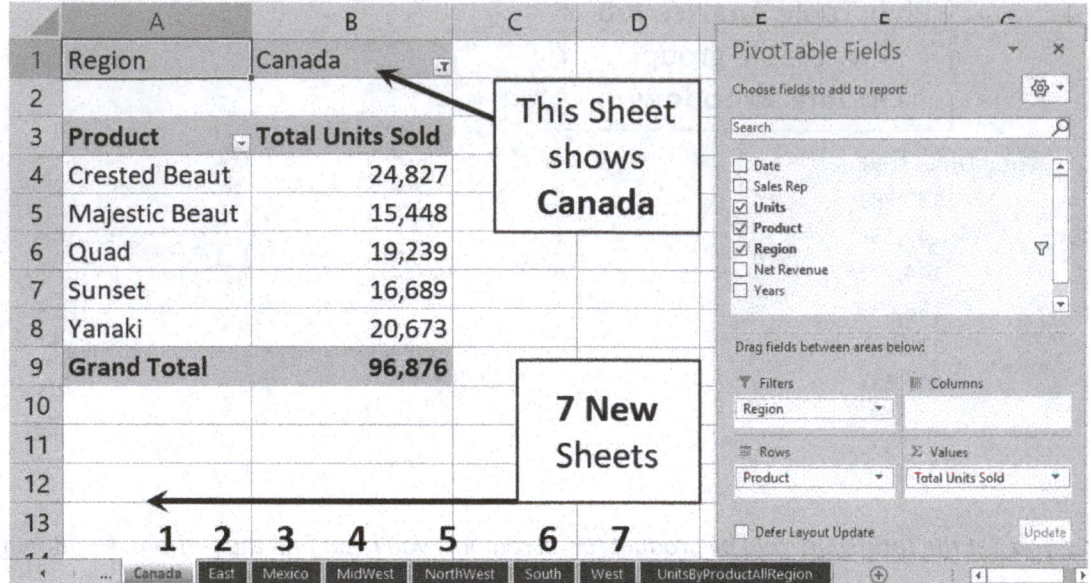

Figure 17.98 *Seven new reports created with a single click and the Show Report Filter Pages option.*

When deciding whether to use a standard PivotTable as opposed to worksheet formulas or a Data Model PivotTable to make non-big data reports with summary calculations like adding, counting, and percentages, the Show Report Filter Pages feature, the Grouping feature, and the Show Values As calculation feature make the decision easy: Choose the standard PivotTable!

Example 11: Creating a Cross-Tabulated Report and Visualization Using a Standard PivotTable and PivotChart

The goal for this data analysis project is to count the number of transactions by product and sales rep for the year 2021 and show the detailed counts in a cross-tabulated report with a column chart (see Figure 17.99). A *cross-tabulated report*, as you first saw in Chapter 12, is a compact means to show calculations when you have two or more conditions for the AND logical test calculation, where the row header is the condition for each row, the column header is the condition for each column, and the value at the top of the report is used as a condition in all calculations.

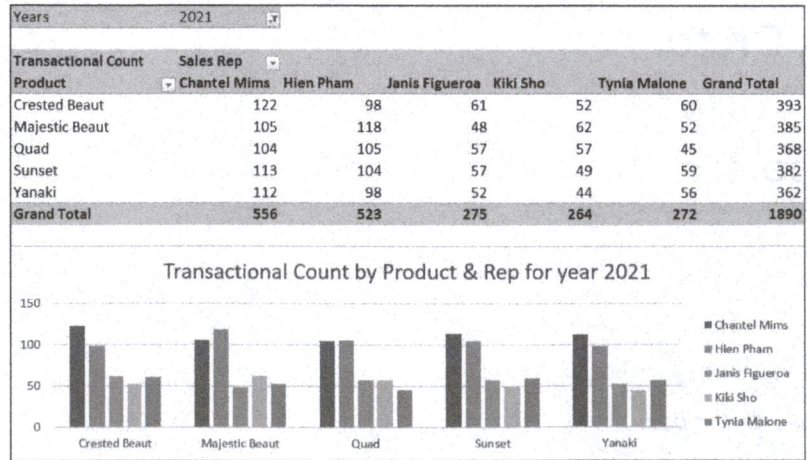

Figure 17.99 *Completed cross-tabulated report and chart.*

Whereas reports are great at presenting number details, visualizations are great at giving the viewer a quick visual impression of the data. For example, a *column chart* is an effective visualization for emphasizing differences across categories.

To complete this example, follow these steps on the worksheet named Ch17(55-117):

1. Select one cell in the Excel Table fNetRevenue.

2. To create a new standard PivotTable on a new worksheet, use the keyboard shortcut Alt, N, V, T, Enter.

3. Name the new worksheet **CrossTabAndChart**.

4. Drag the Product field to the Rows area in the PivotTable Fields task pane.

5. Drag the Sales Rep field to the Columns area in the PivotTable Fields task pane.

6. Drag the Year field to the Filters area in the PivotTable Fields task pane; then select the year 2021 as the filter.

7. Drag the Sales Rep field to the Values area of the PivotTable Fields task pane, add number format-ting (a comma separator and zero decimal places showing) to the Values area in the worksheet, and change the name of the calculation to **Transactional Count**. Figure 17.99 shows the completed report with the cross-tabulated counts.

8. To create a column chart based on the cross-tabulated PivotTable, select a single cell in the PivotTable, click the Insert tab of the Ribbon and then, in the Charts group, click the Column Chart dropdown arrow, as shown in Figure 17.100.

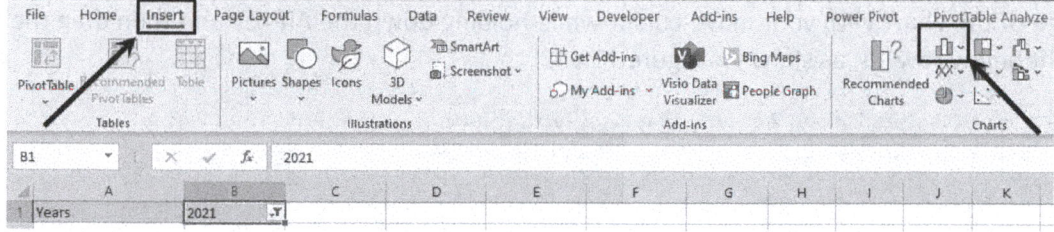

Figure 17.100 Column Chart dropdown arrow in the Chart group in the Insert tab of the Ribbon.

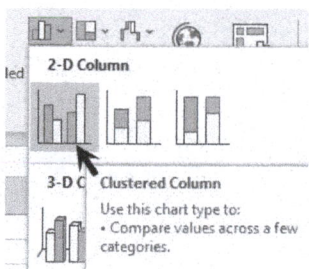

Figure 17.101 *Select the Clustered Column option.*

9. As shown in Figure 17.101, from the Column Chart dropdown, select the first option, Clustered Column.

Figure 17.102 shows the standard PivotChart that Excel creates. On the right side of the chart, a color-coded legend lists the sales rep names. The product names are listed along the horizonal axis. For each product name, the color-coded columns are clustered together to show the relative heights for the sales reps. The height of each column represents the number of transactions that each sales rep had for each product. This sort of clustered column chart is perfect for when you want to show the relative sizes of the transactional counts for each sales rep within each product and emphasize the difference between the counts across sale rep categories. For example, in this case, you can quickly see that the sales rep Chantel Mims had the largest number of transactions for the products Crested Beaut, Sunset, and Yanaki, and Kiki Sho had the fewest transactions for the products Crested Beaut, Sunset, and Yanaki. The chart contains gray buttons for the Year, Product, and Sales Rep fields. These buttons can be used to filter the PivotChart.

If you use the field filter buttons on the PivotChart, the PivotChart and the PivotTable will become filtered. Similarly, if you use the field filter buttons in the PivotTable, the PivotChart will become filtered. In this way, the standard PivotTable and the standard PivotChart are connected and always contain the same fields, filters, and calculations. If you ever need a chart and a report to be filtered in different ways or contain different calculations, you can use the Data Model PivotTable and PivotChart tool, as you will learn Example 2 in Chapter 18.

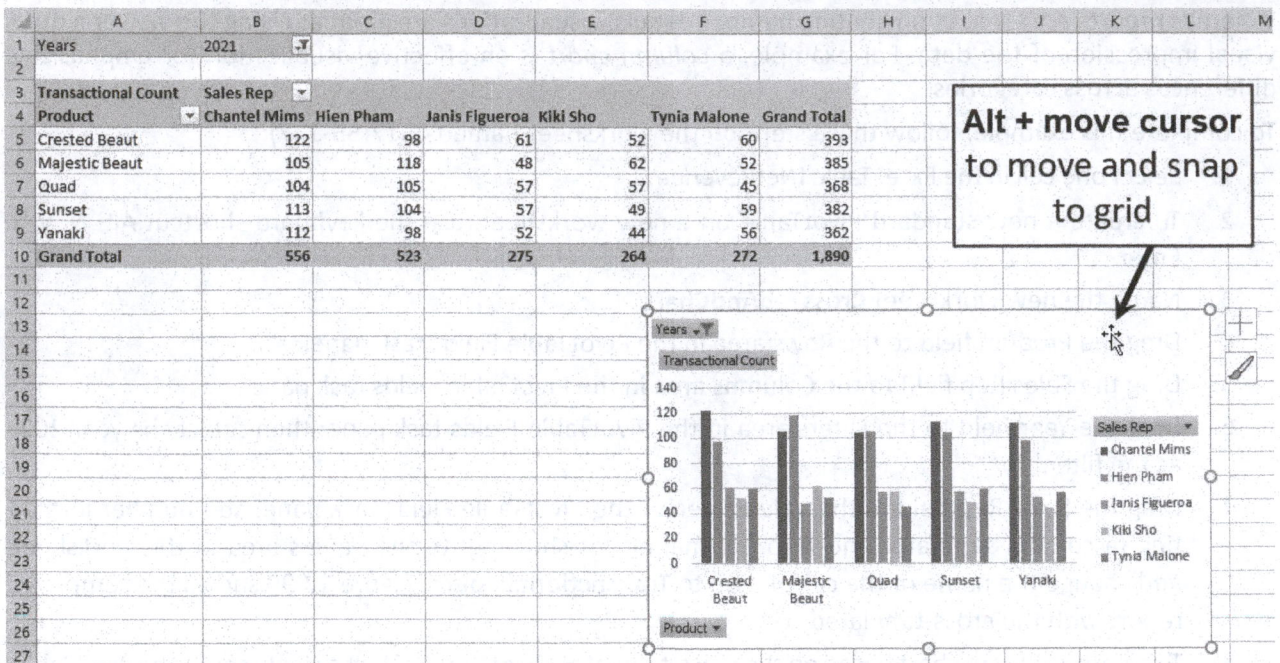

Figure 17.102 Move the chart to the left side of the worksheet, directly below row 11.

10. As shown in Figure 17.102, to move the chart and snap to the worksheet gridlines, click on the outside edge of the chart with your move cursor while holding down the Alt key and then drag the chart to right below row 11, as shown in Figure 17.103.

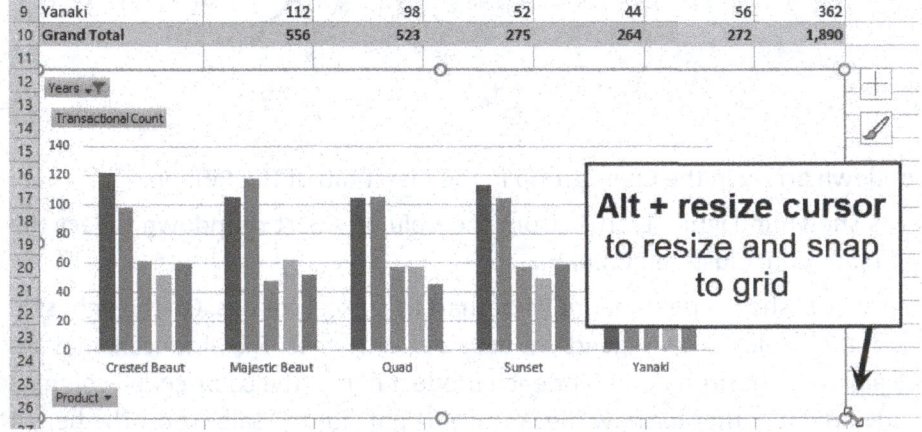

Figure 17.103 *Resize the chart and snap it to column G and down through row 26.*

11. As shown in Figure 17.103, to resize the chart and snap to the worksheet gridlines, click on the white circle in the lower-right corner with your mouse while holding down the Alt key and then use the resize cursor to drag the chart edge to the edge of column G and down through row 26, as shown in Figure 17.103.

12. Because you will not need to use the gray field buttons or the gray Transactional Count calculation button, remove these buttons by right-clicking each one and selecting Hide All Field Buttons on Chart (see Figure 17.104). (The option to hide all field buttons is also available in the Show/Hide group in the PivotChart Analyze context-sensitive tab of the Ribbon.)

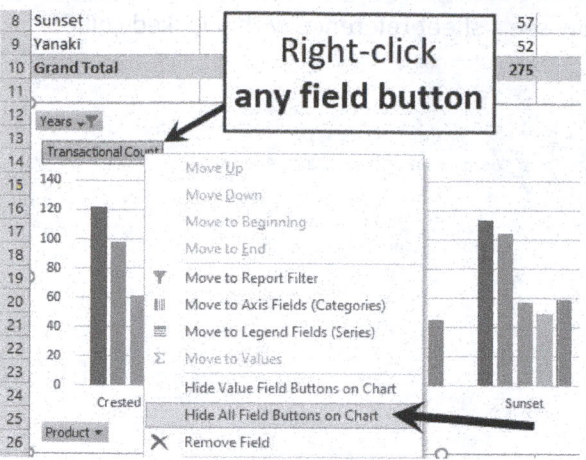

Figure 17.104 *Hide All Field Buttons on Chart.*

13. To insert a chart title for the chart, as shown in Figure 17.105, near the upper-right corner of the chart, click the green Add/Remove Chart Elements plus icon to open the list of chart elements and check the Chart Title checkbox.

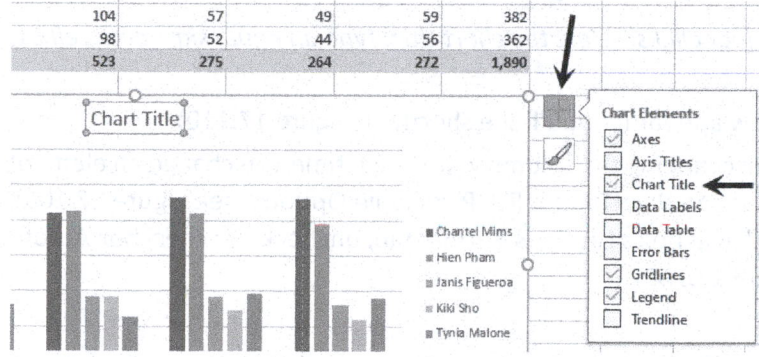

Figure 17.105 *Click the green plus icon to add chart elements.*

14. As shown in Figure 17.106, in cell D1, type **Chart Title:**.

15. To create a dynamic chart title that is linked to the criteria in the PivotTable, in cell E1 create the formula shown in Figure 17.106 and press Enter.

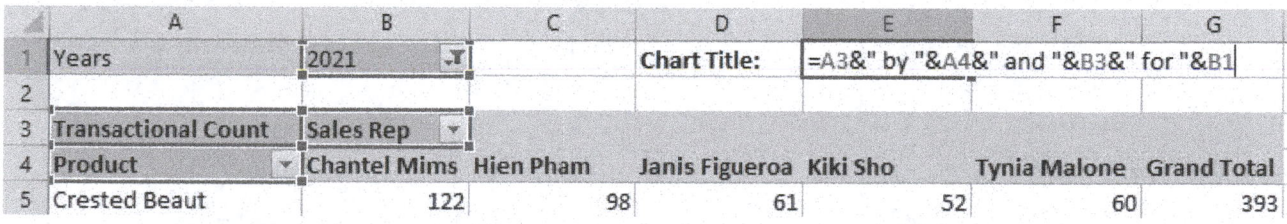

	A	B	C	D	E	F	G
1	Years	2021		Chart Title:	=A3&" by "&A4&" and "&B3&" for "&B1		
2							
3	Transactional Count	Sales Rep					
4	Product	Chantel Mims	Hien Pham	Janis Figueroa	Kiki Sho	Tynia Malone	Grand Total
5	Crested Beaut	122	98	61	52	60	393

Figure 17.106 *Worksheet formula to create a dynamic chart title.*

16. To link the chart title to the formula in cell E1, select the chart title (making sure the outside edge of the chart title is a solid line rather than a dashed line).

17. Type an equal sign (which jumps you up to the formula bar).

18. Click on cell E1. As shown in Figure 17.107, you now see a sheet reference with a locked cell E1.

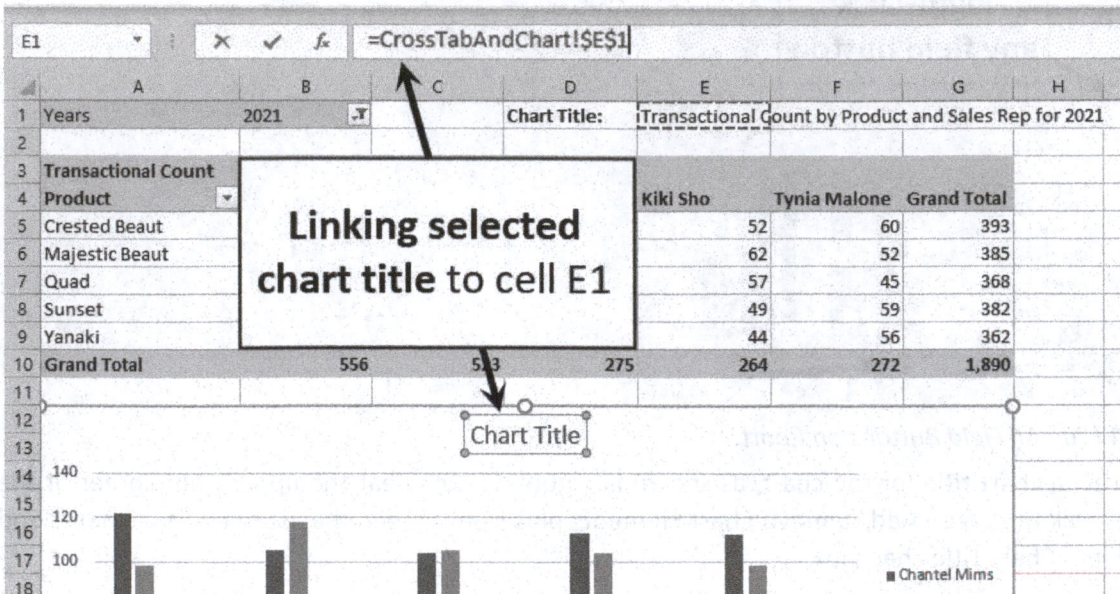

Figure 17.107 *Linking a chart title to a cell in four clicks: select the chart title, type an equal sign, click cell E1, and press Enter.*

19. Press Enter. The chart title should now appear (as you'll see shortly, in Figure 17.110).

20. To prevent the PivotTable report from changing the column width each time you change an element in the PivotTable, right-click any cell in the PivotTable, click PivotTable Options (see Figure 17.108), and then, in the PivotTable Options dialog box's Layout & Format tab, uncheck the checkbox Autofit Column Widths on Update (see Figure 17.109).

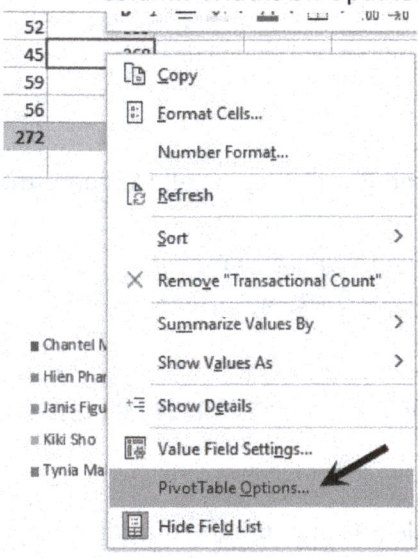

Figure 17.108 Right-click any cell in the PivotTable to access the PivotTable Options dialog box.

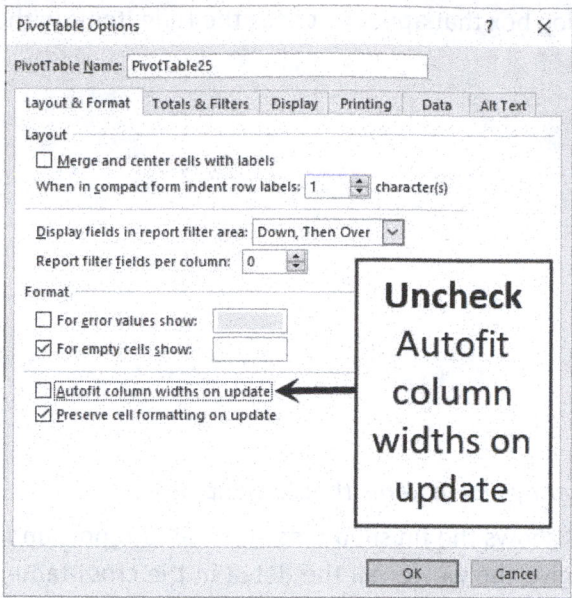

Figure 17.109 *This allows you to set column widths and prevents the annoying automatic column width changes.*

21. Click the OK button in the PivotTable Options dialog box.

22. To add a slicer to the PivotTable, select any cell in the PivotTable, click the context-sensitive PivotTable Analyze tab of the Ribbon, and then, in the Filter group, click the Insert Slicer button.

23. In the Insert Slicer dialog box that appears, select the Year field and click OK. Figure 17.110 shows that the slicer has some ghost buttons.

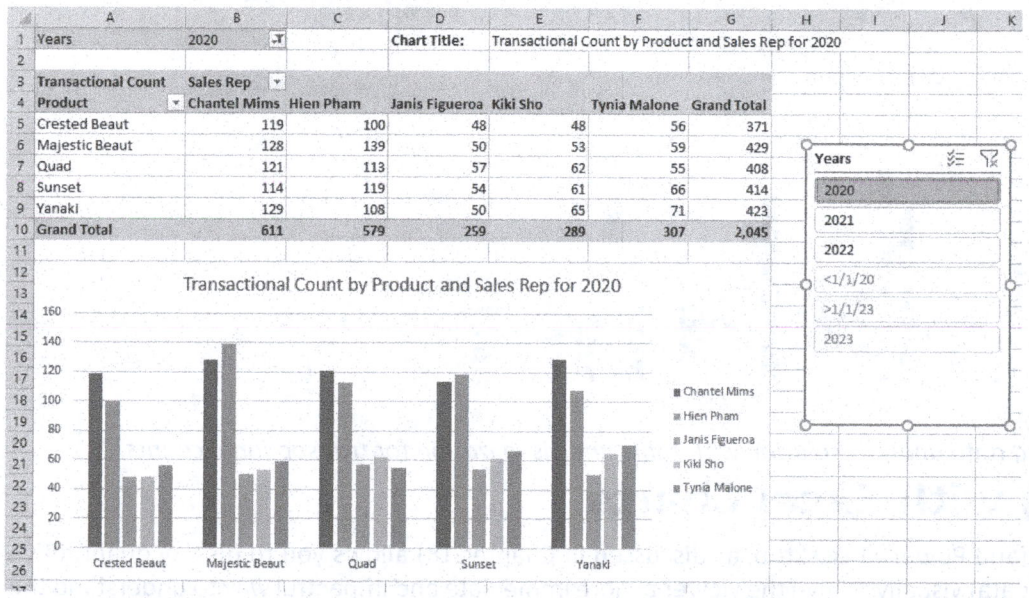

Figure 17.110 *Add a slicer for the Years field and select the year 2021.*

24. To hide the ghost buttons on the slicer and make the data analysis solution look tidy, right-click any part of the slicer and click on Slicer Settings, as shown in Figure 17.111.

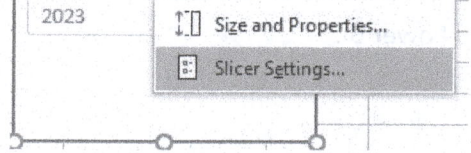

Figure 17.111 *Right-click the slicer to get to Slicer Settings.*

25. As shown in Figure 17.112, in the Slicer Settings dialog box that appears, check the Hide Items with No Data checkbox and click OK.

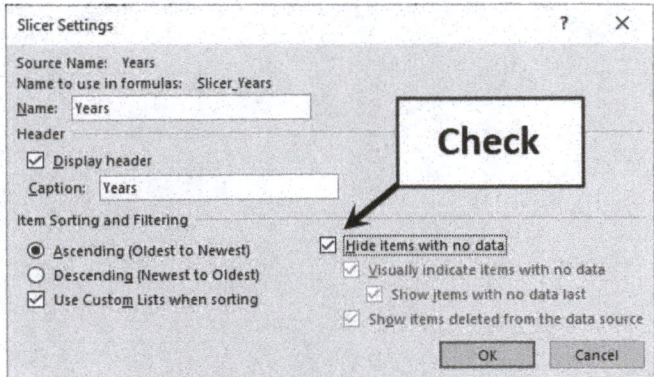

Figure 17.112 *You need to hide the ghost buttons on the slicer by hiding items that have no data.*

26. From the slicer, select the year 2022. Figure 17.113 shows the finished cross-tabulated report and visualization. With this data analysis solution, you give the viewer all the detail in the cross-tabulated report as well as a quick visual impression of the same data, using a clustered column chart.

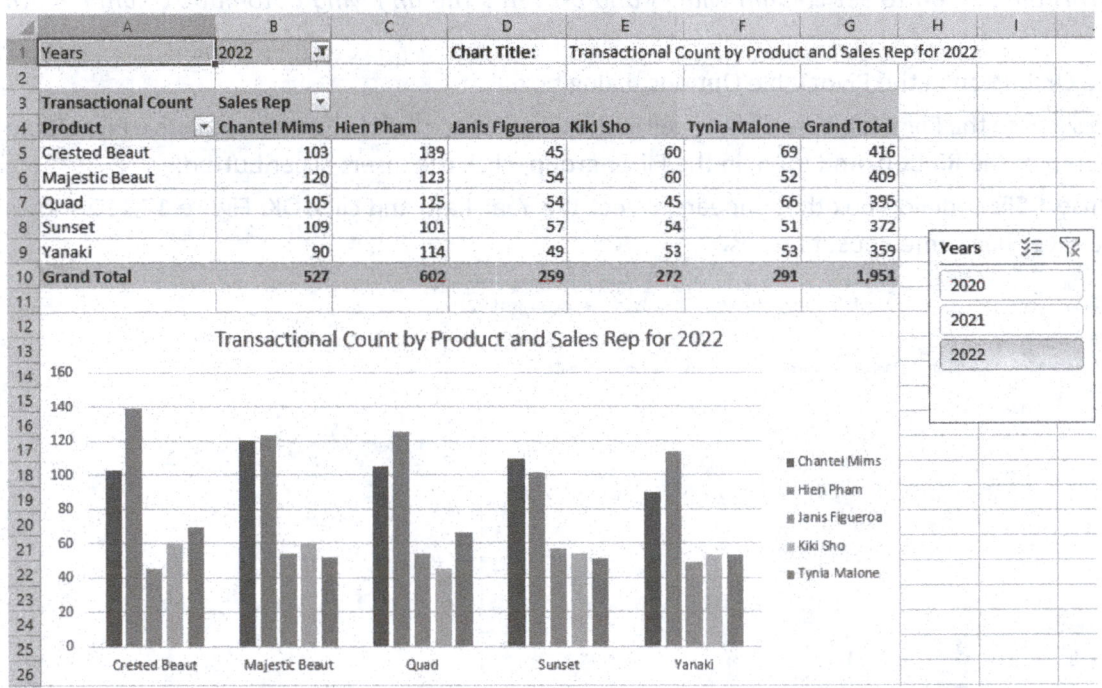

Figure 17.113 *Finished data analysis solution with table and visualization for transactional counts.*

Visualizing with Excel Charts

Using charts in Excel (and Power BI Desktop, as discussed in Chapter 18) allows you to display quantitative data (that is, number data) visually to give the viewer a more immediate and impactful way to understand the data. Whereas reports are great at presenting detailed numbers, visualizations are great at giving the viewer a quick visual impression and can help to reveal patterns and trends. As you just saw with the column chart in Example 11, it is much easier to pick out the largest or smallest amounts from a visual like a column chart than it is to try to hunt through the numbers in a report to find the largest or smallest number.

Table 17.3 lists and describes some of the charts available in Excel and Power BI.

Table 17.3 Charts Available in Excel and Power BI

Type of Chart	Description
Column chart	Used to compare relative differences across categories. The height of a column conveys the number.
Bar chart	Used to compare relative differences across categories. The length of a bar conveys the number.
Stacked column/bar chart	Good for displaying cross-tabulated numbers, with an emphasis on axis categories.
Clustered column/bar chart	Good for displaying cross-tabulated numbers, with an emphasis on legend categories.
Histogram	A specific type of column or bar chart that is used for counting numbers between a lower limit and an upper limit. No gap between columns or bars indicates that there are no numbers between the upper limit of a given category and the lower limit of the following category.
Line chart	Used to plot a number variable over equidistant categories (usually time) to show changes or trends.
X-Y scatter	Used to show relationship between two numbers (x- and y-variables).
X-Y scatter with straight lines	Use to show changes or trends for a time or number variable over non-equidistant categories.
Break-even chart	A specific type of X-Y scatter chart that shows the break-even crossover lines for revenue and costs.
Map	Used for geographic data, like sales by zip code, sates, or country.

As you create charts and other visualizations, the most important rule for visualizing data is *to eliminate all extraneous elements in your visualization that do not help deliver the message*. The world-renowned visualization expert Edward R. Tufte states this rule in two succinct phrases: "No chart junk" (which means that if a chart contains an element that does not help deliver the message, delete it) and "Use a high data-to-ink ratio" (which means emphasize the data over non-data elements such as lines, boxes, and busy colors).

The two charts most commonly used to visualize quantitative data are:

- **Column or bar charts:** To emphasize relative size differences across categories. Research has shown that column and bar charts are more effective than pie charts at conveying differences across categories.
- **Line charts:** To show changes or trends in a number variable across time categories.

There are many other types of charts and visualizations, but often what people need from a visual is either to compare number amounts across categories or to show changes and trends over time. The next two examples look at the differences between the four charts you can use when you have a cross-tabulated report with a single number variable and two conditions for the calculation:

- Clustered column chart
- Stacked column chart
- Clustered bar chart
- Stacked bar chart

Example 12: Visualizing with a Clustered Column Chart or a Stacked Column Chart

In this example, you will learn about a column chart that is slightly different from the clustered column chart you created in Example 11. In this example, you will convert that chart from a clustered column chart to a stacked column chart.

To complete this example, follow these steps on the worksheet named CrossTabAndChart:

1. Select the outside edge of the clustered column chart you created on the worksheet named CrossTabAndChart and copy it by pressing Ctrl+C.

2. Select cell M3.

3. To paste the copied chart, press Ctrl+V.

4. Change the chart type from clustered column to stacked column by right-clicking anywhere on chart and selecting Change Chart Type, as shown in Figure 17.114.

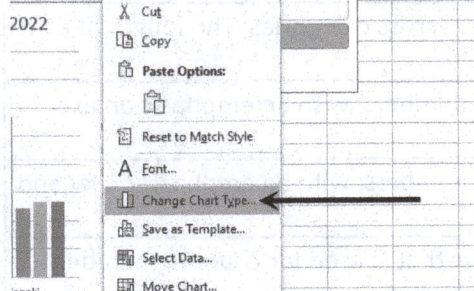

Figure 17.114 *Select this option to open the Change Chart Type dialog box.*

5. As shown in Figure 17.115, from the left side of the Change Chart Type dialog box that appears, select the Column option and then, at the top right of the dialog box, select the second option, Stacked Column.

6. Click the OK button in the Change Chart Type dialog box.

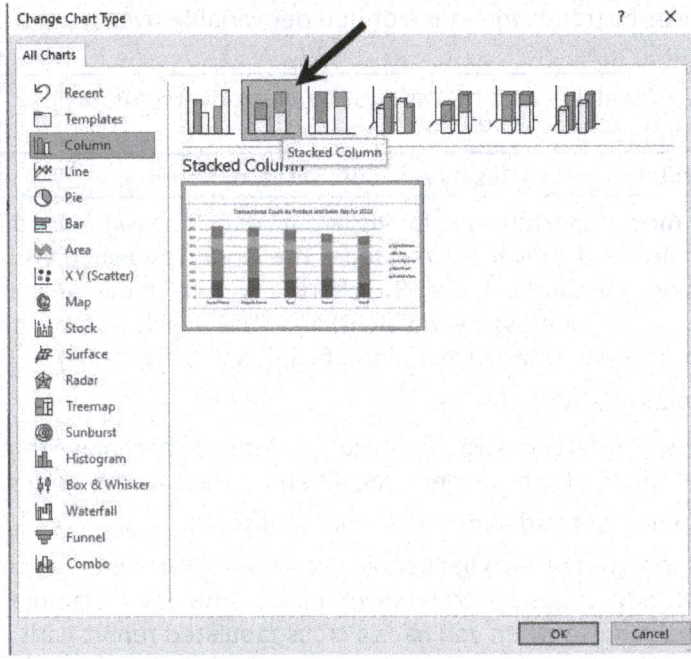

Figure 17.115 *Use the Change Chart dialog box to change the chart type to Stacked Column.*

You can see the difference between the clustered column chart and the stacked column chart in Figure 17.116. Whereas with a clustered column chart the emphasis is on comparing the items in the legend against each other for each product, with a stacked column chart the emphasis is on comparing the items in the horizontal axis against each other. In this example, with the clustered column chart, you can clearly see that Hien Pham had the biggest count for all products except the Sunset. With the clustered column chart, the emphasis is on comparing the items in the legend against each other—that is, comparing the sales rep counts against each other for each product. However, with the clustered column chart, it is hard to see which product had the overall largest total transactional counts.

If your goal is to still see all the detail of both cross-tabulated variables (sales rep and product) but the emphasis is on quickly knowing which products had the largest count, then the stacked column chart is the better choice for a visual. With the stacked column chart in this example, you can clearly see that the Crested Beaut had the largest number of transactions. With the stacked column chart, the emphasis is on comparing the items in the horizontal axis against each other—that is, comparing the product total counts.

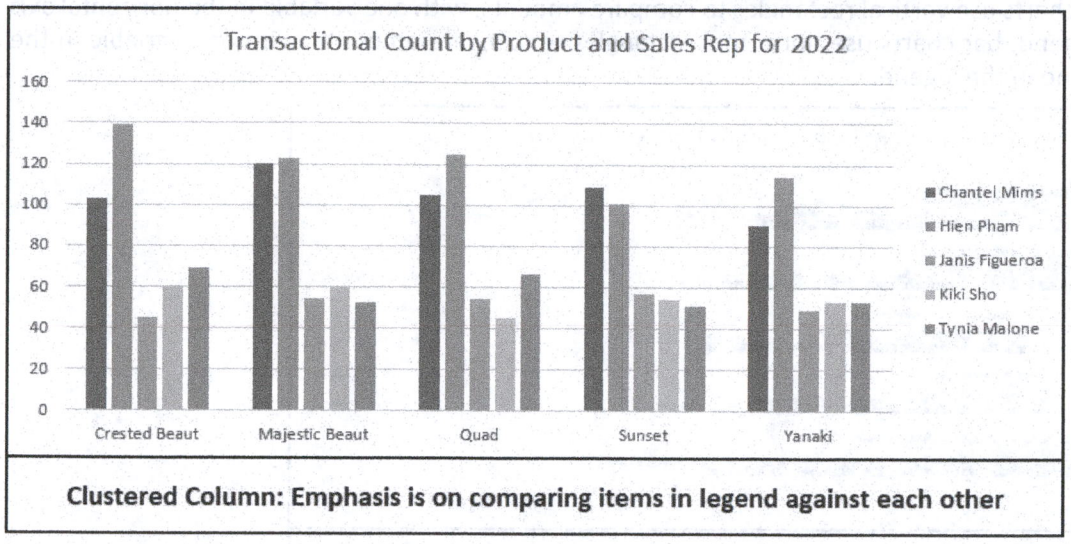

Clustered Column: Emphasis is on comparing items in legend against each other

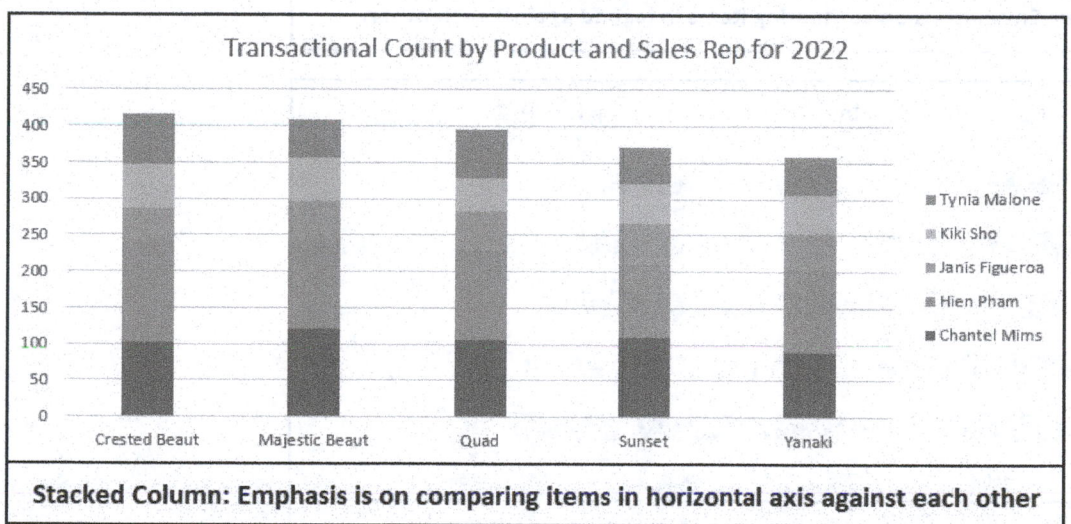

Stacked Column: Emphasis is on comparing items in horizontal axis against each other

Figure 17.116 *Both charts contain the same variables and data, but they have slightly different emphases.*

Example 13: Visualizing with a Clustered Bar Chart or a Stacked Bar Chart

The *clustered bar chart* and the *stacked bar chart* are similar to the clustered column chart and stacked column chart. You can see the difference between the clustered bar chart and the stacked bar chart in Figure 17.117. Whereas column charts use vertical rectangles to compare amounts, with one variable in the horizontal axis and one in the legend, bar charts use horizontal rectangles to compare amounts, with one variable in the vertical axis and one in the legend.

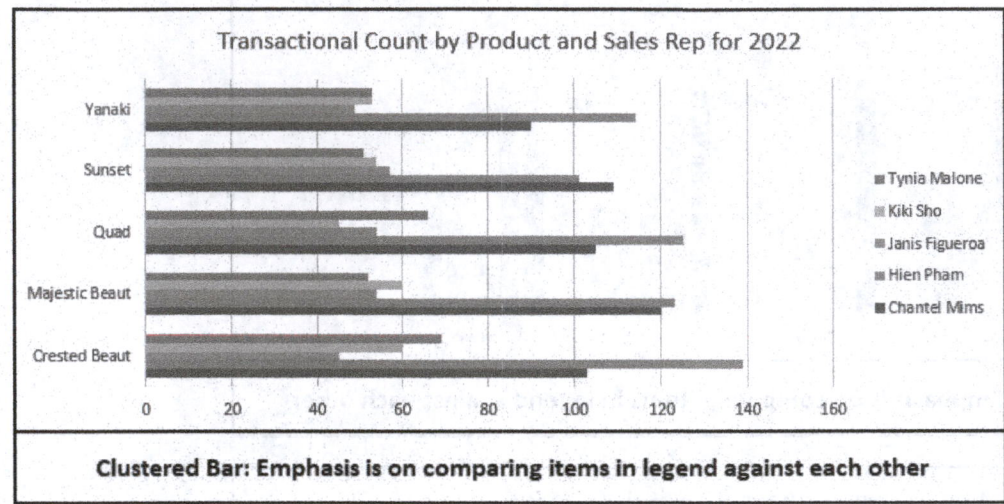

Clustered Bar: Emphasis is on comparing items in legend against each other

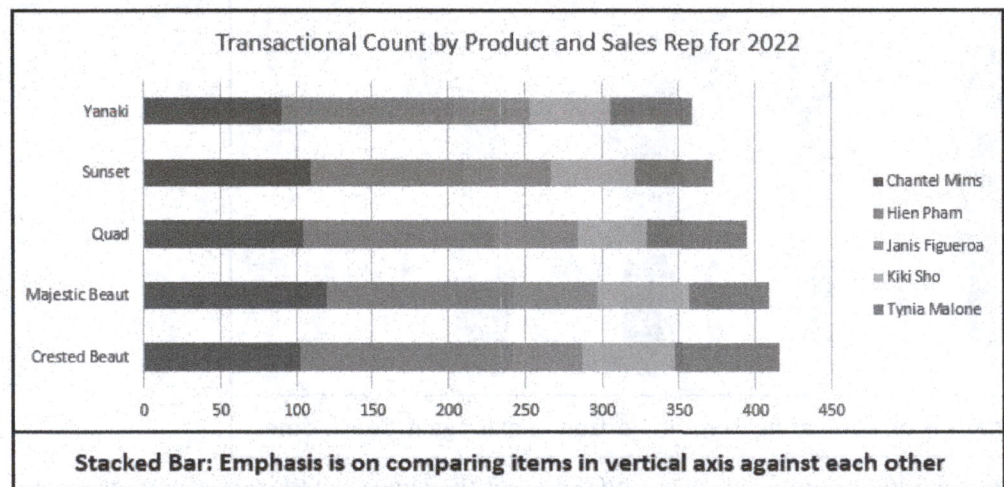

Stacked Bar: Emphasis is on comparing items in vertical axis against each other

Figure 17.117 *Both charts contain the same variables and data, but they have slightly different emphases.*

Column charts and bar charts are very similar, and both effectively emphasize relative sizes and differences in amounts across categories. However, compared to a column chart, a bar chart can more forcefully emphasize differences across categories because of the horizontal orientation, and it can accommodate long category names in a less cluttered way than can column charts.

To create the two bar charts shown here, follow these steps on the worksheet named CrossTabAndChart:

1. Copy the clustered column chart from Example 12.

2. Paste the clustered column chart into the worksheet.

3. Use the Change Chart Type dialog box to change the chart type to Clustered Bar Chart or Stacked Bar Chart.

Using a Column Chart or a Bar Chart to Plot a Number Variable Summarized with One Condition

When you created a clustered column chart in Example 11, you plotted a number variable based on two conditions: one condition used in the axis and one used in the legend. When you plot a number summarized with a single variable condition, either with a column chart or a bar chart, the single condition is used in the axis, and there is no variable in the legend. In addition, because there is just one condition, the Clustered Column/Bar Chart and Stacked Column/Bar Chart options will yield the same chart.

Both a column chart and a bar chart are effective visualizations for comparing the relative differences for a plotted number across categories. However, whereas column charts use vertical rectangles to compare amounts across one condition in the horizontal axis, bar charts use horizontal rectangles to compare amounts across one condition in the vertical axis. The difference between the two charts is that the bar chart can more forcefully emphasize differences across categories and can accommodate longer category names.

> **Note:** In some statistics and math textbooks, authors refer to both column charts and bar charts as *bar charts*. However, in Excel and Power BI Desktop, column charts use vertical rectangles, and bar charts use horizonal rectangles.

As shown in Figure 17.118, in general, there are three situations that can arise when using a column chart or a bar chart to plot a number variable summarized with a single condition for a calculation:

- Plot the number variable summarized with a single qualitative variable (non-numeric) as the condition for the calculation. The qualitative variable appears on the axis, and the size of the column or bar conveys the relative size of the plotted number. In Figure 17.118, the chart on the left is an example.

- Plot the number variable summarized with a single discrete quantitative variable (with gaps between numbers) as the condition for calculation. The discrete quantitative variable appears on the axis, and the size of the column or bar conveys the relative size of the plotted number. In Figure 17.118, the chart in the middle is an example.

- Plot the number variable summarized with a single continuous quantitative variable with lower and upper limits for each axis category as the condition for calculation. The continuous quantitative variable categories appear on the axis, and the size of the column or bar conveys the relative size of the plotted number. The lower and upper limit categories must be mutually exclusive so that plotted numbers appear in only one category and are collectively exhaustive so that all numbers in the dataset are included. In Figure 17.118, the chart on the right is an example. This type of chart is called a *histogram*.

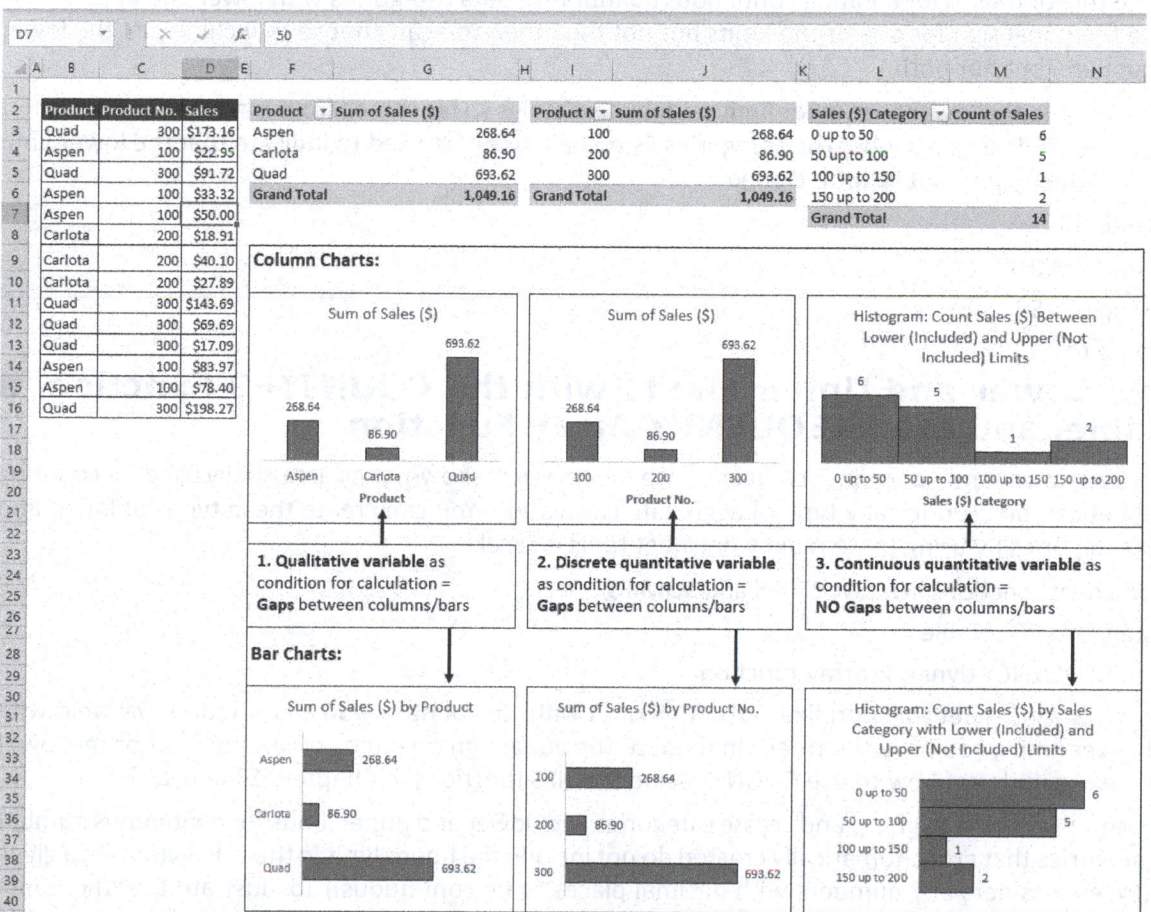

Figure 17.118 *Three possibilities for column charts or bar charts for number calculations with one condition.*

Using Histogram Column Charts with Lower and Upper Limits for Counting Continuous Quantitative Variables

An important visual element when using column or bar charts is the gap width between the columns or bars. For qualitative variables and discrete quantitative variables, you should leave a gap between the columns or bars to visually indicate that the variables are not continuous. For continuous qualitative variables, you should leave no gap between the columns to visually indicate that the variables are continuous and that no numbers can fit between the axis categories.

When creating the axis categories for a continuous variable, you must create mutually exclusive categories. Categories for counting sales values such as the ones listed below are *not* mutually exclusive and risk double counting because the upper limit of one category is the same as the lower limit of the following category:

- 0 <= Count <= 50
- 50 <= Count <= 100
- 100 <= Count <= 150
- 150 <= Count <= 200

For example, a sales amount of exactly $50 would be counted in both the first and second categories.

Categories for counting sales values such as the ones listed below are mutually exclusive and do *not* risk double counting because the categories do not include overlapping values:

- 0 <= Count < 50
- 50 <= Count < 100
- 100 <= Count < 150
- 150 <= Count < 200

For example, a sales amount of exactly $50 would be counted only in the second category. The difference between this set of categories and the previous one is in how the equal sign is used in the comparison operator. The rule of thumb for creating continuous quantitative data categories with lower and upper limits is to include the equal sign for one of the limits but not the other. You can choose to include just the lower or just the upper—but not both.

The notation used in the lower and upper limit category examples so far comes from math and is usually not used in reporting and visualizations. The categories listed below can be used to indicate that the lower limit is included and the upper limit is not included:

- 0 up to 50
- 50 up to 100
- 100 up to 150
- 150 up to 200

Creating Lower and Upper Limits with the COUNTIFS Function, a PivotTable, and the FREQUENCY Array Function

When you create lower and upper limit categories like the ones just shown, they are usually used for counting and adding but can be used for any type of aggregate calculation. You can create these types of lower and upper limit categories by using three main worksheet tools is Excel:

- Worksheet functions like COUNTIFS and SUMIFS
- A standard PivotTable
- The FREQUENCY dynamic array function

When you use a worksheet function like COUNTIFS or SUMIFS to count or add a continuous variable with upper and lower limits, you have the freedom to place the equal sign on either the upper limit or the lower limit. (You saw examples of how to use COUNTIFS and SUMIFS functions in Chapters 13 and 15.)

When you use a PivotTable to group and create categories with lower and upper limits for continuous number data, the categories that are automatically created do not include the upper limit in the calculation for a given category. (Excel considers any numbers with decimal places to be continuous.) To illustrate that the upper limit is not included in the count when you use a PivotTable, in Figure 17.118, notice the sales amount $50 in cell D7. That $50 is *not* counted in the first category of 0 up to 50; instead, it is counted in the category 50 up to 100. The five values that are counted in the 50 up to 100 category are $91.72, $50.00, $69.69, $83.97, and $78.40.

As you learned in Chapter 15, the FREQUENCY worksheet array function automatically creates categories where the upper limit is included in the calculation for that given category—except for the last catch-all category. Look back at Figure 15.68 in Chapter 15, which illustrates that the upper limit *is* included in the count when you use the FREQUENCY array function to automatically create the counting category 50 < Sales <= 100. In that figure, the same dataset is used as in Figure 17.118 so that you can see that the different tools in Excel can count with slightly different upper and lower limits. In Figure 15.68, the four values that are counted in the 50 < Sales <= 100 category are $91.72, $69.69, $83.97, and $78.40.

> **Note:** In the following example, you will learn how to create the histogram chart shown in Figure 17.118. If you would like to try to create column or bar charts for the qualitative variable or the discrete quantitative variable, you can use the dataset in the worksheet Ch17(119-132). This chapter does not provide step-by-step instructions, but you have enough experience creating similar charts that you should be able to figure it out.

Example 14: Creating a Frequency Distribution and Histogram Chart with a PivotTable and a PivotChart

Figure 17.119 shows a proper dataset with three fields that show retail sales transactions. The goal in this data analysis example is to use the Sales field to create a frequency distribution PivotTable report and a histogram column chart to visualize how the frequencies of sales amounts are distributed across sales categories.

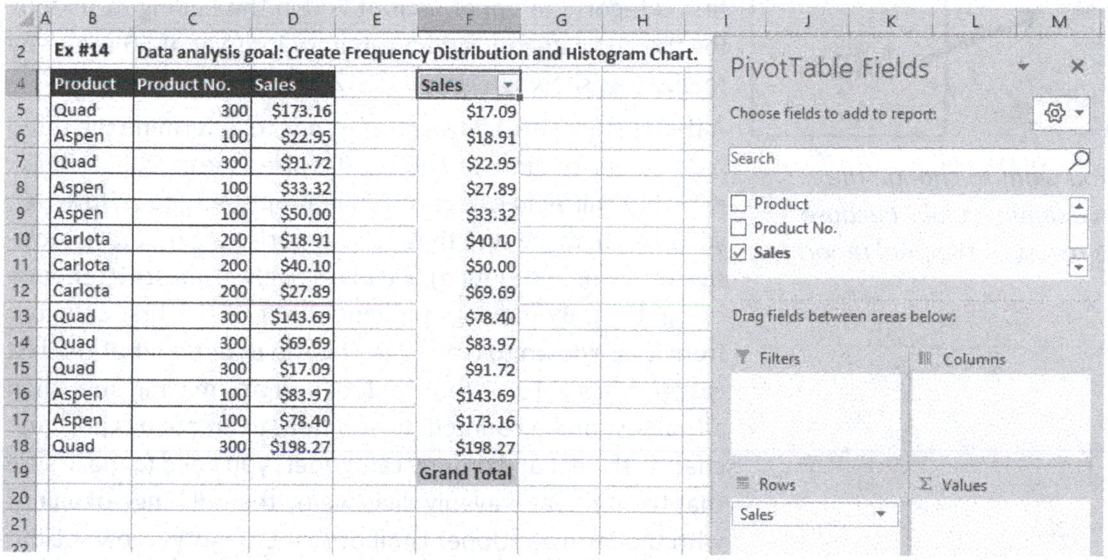

Figure 17.119 *The goal is to create a frequency distribution and histogram from the unique list of sales values.*

> **Note:** When you create a histogram chart, you usually do not want to use the built-in histogram chart that Microsoft offers in its list of chart types. The built-in histogram chart assumes that the data is based on a normal distribution, which is not always the case, and it does not allow you to set the lower limit for the first category. Therefore, when you create a histogram, you should use the Clustered Column Chart option and manually build a histogram based on that.

To complete this example, follow these steps on the worksheet named Ch17(119-132):

1. Select one cell in the proper dataset on this worksheet.

2. Create a new standard PivotTable on the existing worksheet in cell F4.

3. Drag the Sales field to the Rows area in the PivotTable Fields task pane. As shown in Figure 17.119, when you drag the Sales field to the Rows area, a unique list of values is created. This is not what you want. You want to group the numbers into categories.

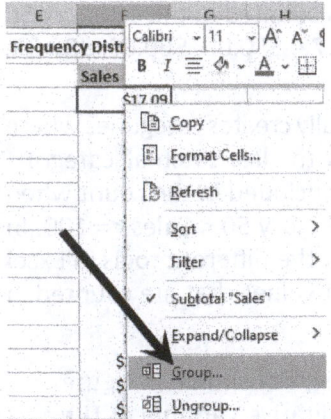

Figure 17.120 *In the Rows area in the PivotTable report, right-click and then click Group.*

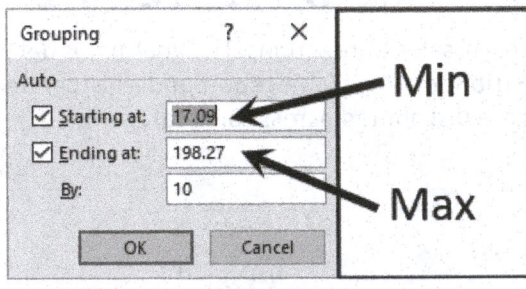

Figure 17.121 *You want to change the minimum and maximum values because they would look messy in the final report and chart.*

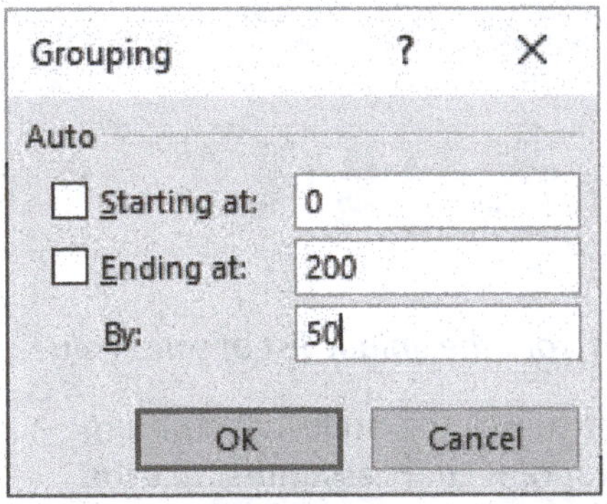

Figure 17.122 *Create starting and ending amounts that will accommodate all values in the dataset.*

4. To group the numbers into categories such as 0 up to 50, 50 up to 100, and so on, right-click the unique list of values in the Rows area of the PivotTable report and select Group, as shown in Figure 17.120. The Grouping dialog box appears.

The Grouping dialog box contains three settings that determine how the lower and upper limits for each category are created (see Figure 17.121): The Starting At textbox determines the lower limit for the first category, the Ending At textbox determines the upper limit for the last category, and the By textbox determines the interval between the lower and upper values (that is, the width for each category). By default, the minimum value from the Sales field is listed in the Starting At textbox, the maximum value from the Sales field is listed in the Ending At textbox, and a suggested category interval of 10 is listed in the By textbox. If you use the default settings to create your grouping categories, you get messy categories such as 17.09–27.09, 27.09–37.09, and so on. Messy categories like these yield a cluttered report and chart. In this case, it would better to use a lower limit of 0 in the Starting At textbox for the first category, an upper limit of 200 in the Ending At textbox for the last category, and a category interval of 50 in the By textbox, as shown in Figure 17.122.

Although there are statistical methods to determine the three parameters for these categories, it is often the case that a quick estimate will yield categories that are just as good. However, you need to make sure that the categories are *mutually exclusive* (no double counting) and *collectively exhaustive* (enough categories). By moving the lower limit of the first category from 17.09 down to 0 and moving the upper limit of the last category from 198.27 up to 200, you are making sure than all values can be counted. In addition, to create a report and chart with neat and orderly categories, you need to make sure that the interval is evenly divisible by the full range of values with the formula (Upper Limit of Last Category – Lower Limit of First Category)/(Category Interval). This formula determines the number of categories and should yield a whole number with no remainder. In this example, you would get (200 – 0)/50 = 4 categories.

Finally, if you create a lower limit for the first category that is bigger than the smallest value in the dataset, the Group feature will create an automatic category such as < Lower Limit so that it can count all values. Similarly, if you create an upper limit that is smaller than the biggest value in the dataset, the Group feature will create an automatic category such as > Upper Limit so that it can count all values. As you will see in the following steps, you can change the default settings in the Grouping dialog box to get better results.

5. As shown in Figure 17.122, type **0** into the Starting At textbox, type **200** into the Ending At textbox, and type **50** into the By textbox.

6. Click the OK button. Figure 17.123 shows the four categories that are created in the Rows area of the PivotTable report.

> **Note:** When the source data contains number values with decimal places, the categories shown in Figure 17.123 are created. Because the source data is numbers with decimals, and not whole numbers or integers, internally, the PivotTable Group feature creates continuous quantitative categories where the lower limit of a given category is equal to the upper limit of the following category. However, for each category, the lower limit is included, and the upper limit is not included; this ensures that there is no double counting, and the categories are mutually exclusive. In this example, the $50 sales amount will be counted in the second category, not in the first category. On the other hand, if you used the same parameters for this PivotTable Group feature, but you had whole numbers rather than decimal numbers, the automatic categories that would be created would be 0–49, 50–99, and so on. For whole numbers or integers, there is no ambiguity in the category labels. However, as shown in Figure 17.123, because you have continuous quantitative numbers, the automatic grouping labels are ambiguous. Someone viewing the report or chart might not know that the upper limits are not included in the categories. In such a case, it would be better to edit the category labels and make them less ambiguous. You can use the Replace feature to quickly change the labels.

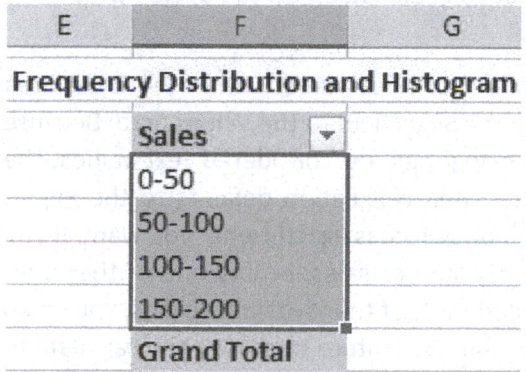

Figure 17.123 *The default categories are ambiguous because the viewer is not sure which limits are included.*

7. To edit the category labels, select the Rows area of the PivotTable report in the range F5:F8.

8. To open the Replace dialog box, in the Home tab of the Ribbon, in the Editing group, click the Find & Select dropdown arrow and select Replace. Or use the keyboard shortcut Ctrl+H.

9. As shown in Figure 17.124, type a hyphen followed by a space (-) in the Find What textbox and type **up to** followed by a space (**up to**) in the Replace With textbox.

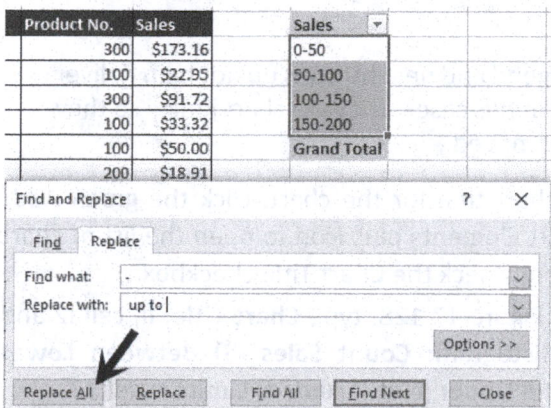

Figure 17.124 *You can use the Replace feature to create less ambiguous row area category labels.*

10. Click the Replace All button. Excel changes the category labels as shown in Figure 17.125.

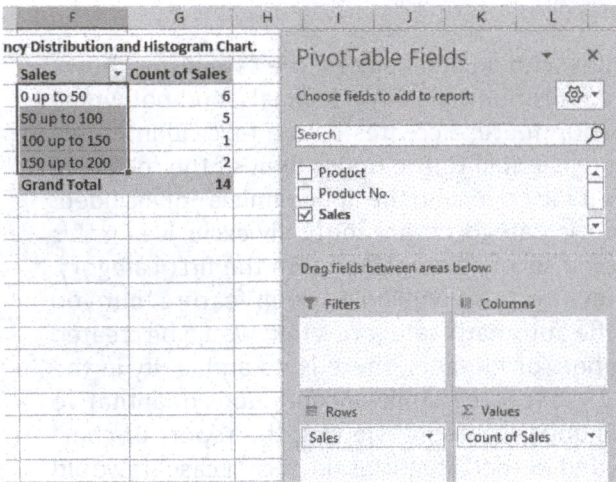

Figure 17.125 *The counts include the lower limits up to but not including the upper limits.*

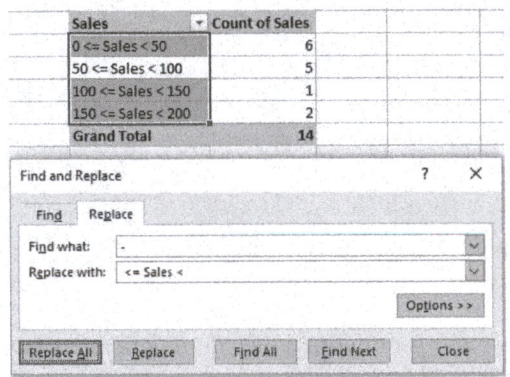

Figure 17.126 *Categories with math notation and comparison operators shows the exact logic for each category.*

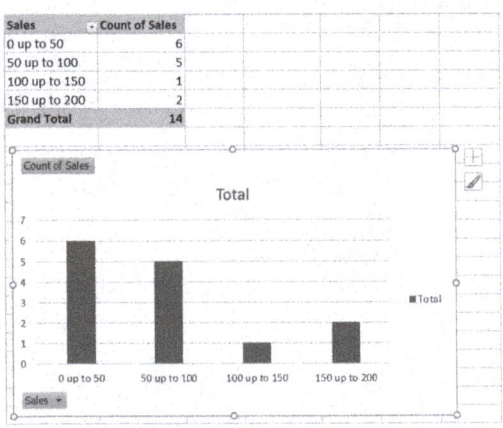

Figure 17.127 *Use a clustered column chart to create the histogram visualization.*

11. To create the count of sales values within the Rows area categories, drag the Sales field to the Values area. Because the Rows area categories are considered text values, the PivotTable Values area calculation defaults to the aggregate Count function, which is exactly what you want. If you wanted to see the sum of sales, or any one of the other aggregate calculations that the PivotTable offers, you could use Summarize Value By feature to change the calculation.

12. To start the histogram chart, click in a single cell in the PivotTable and then, from the Insert tab in the Ribbon, in the Charts group, click the Column Chart dropdown arrow and select Clustered Column Chart, as shown in Figure 17.127.

13. To remove the legend, click on the legend and press the Delete key. To remove the field buttons, right-click any field button in the chart and select Hide All Field Buttons on Chart.

14. To insert a chart title for the chart, click the green Add/Remove Chart Elements plus icon to open the list of chart elements. Then check the Chart Title checkbox.

15. As shown in Figure 17.128, type **Chart Title:** in cell I2 and then type **Histogram: Count Sales ($) Between Lower (Included) and Upper (Not Included) Limits** in cell J2.

16. To create a dynamic chart title that is linked to the chart title in cell J2, select the chart title (making sure the outside edge of the chart title is a solid line rather than a dashed line), type an equal sign (which jumps you up to the formula bar), click on cell J2, and press Enter. The chart title should appear like the chart title in Figure 17.128.

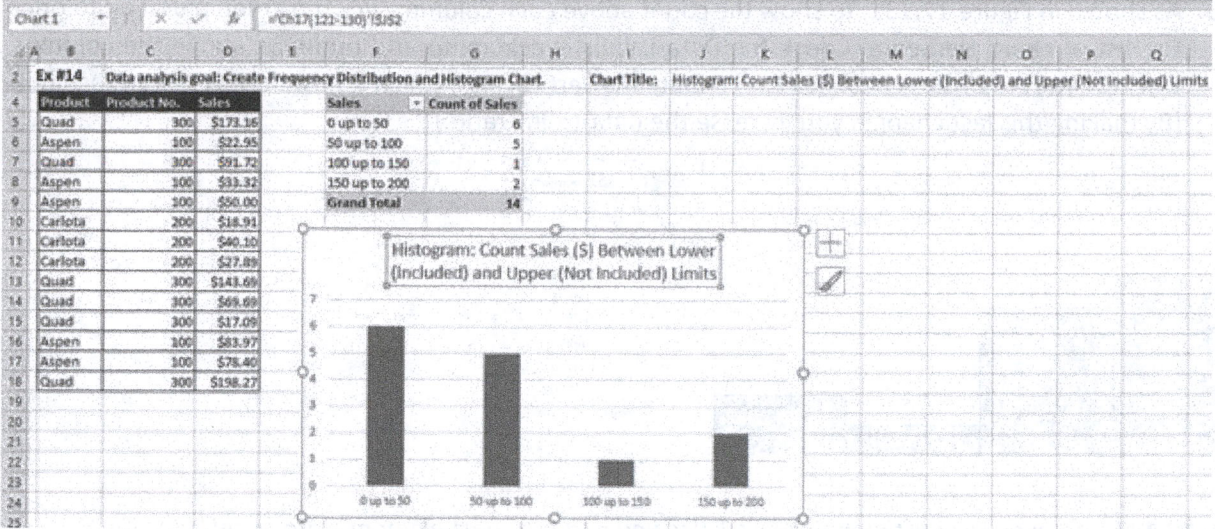

Figure 17.128 *Clean up the chart and give it a proper chart title.*

17. To visually indicate that the variable in the horizontal axis is a continuous quantitative variable, you need to reduce the gap width between the columns to zero so click any column (to select all the columns) and press Ctrl+1 to open the Format Data Series task pane.

18. As shown in Figure 17.129, in the Series Options area, slide the Gap Width bar to 0%.

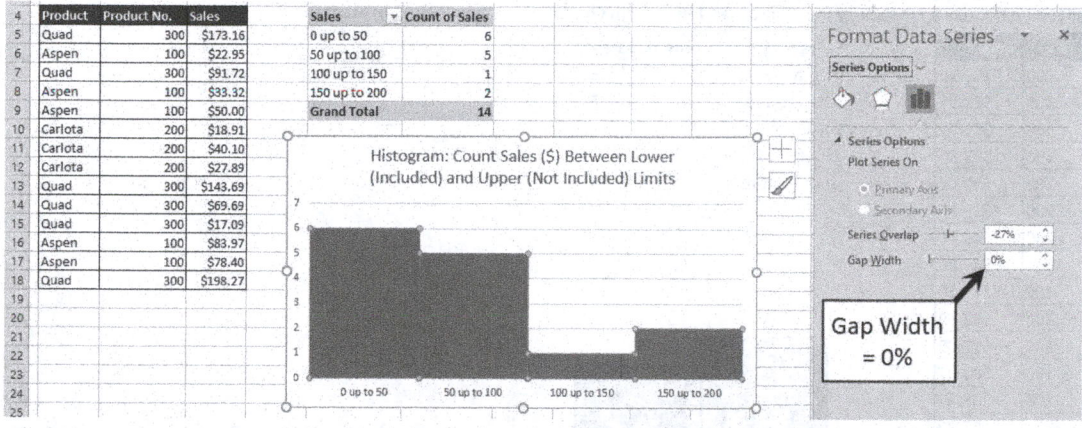

Figure 17.129 *Change the column gap width to 0%.*

19. As shown in Figure 17.130, with the columns in the chart still selected, click the paint bucket icon to open the Fill tab. Then, under Border, click the Solid Line option button, use the Color dropdown arrow to set the color to black, and set Width to 1.5 pt.

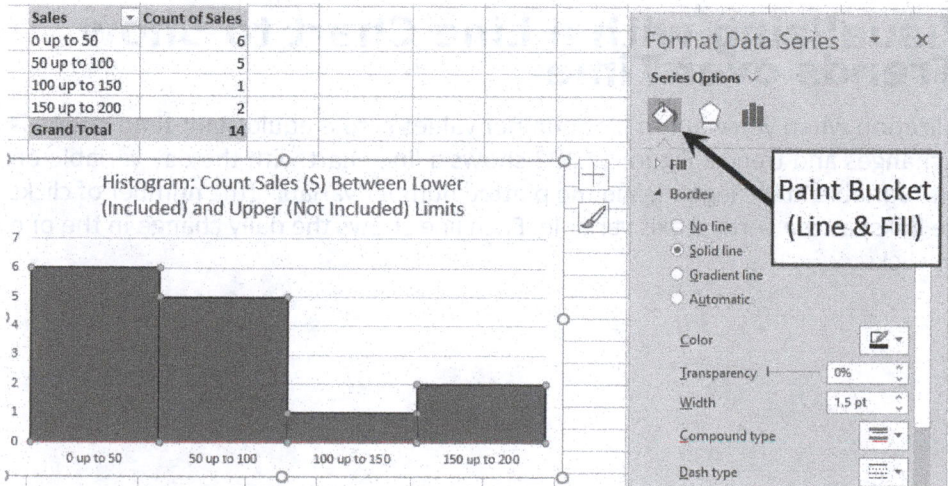

Figure 17.130 *Add borders to columns for clarity.*

20. As shown in Figure 17.131, to show the count above each column, click the green plus icon to open the list of chart elements. Check the Data Labels checkbox to add numbers above the columns. Uncheck the Axis Titles checkbox to eliminate the vertical axis, which is now unnecessary chart junk. (By making this last change, you increase the data-to-ink ratio.)

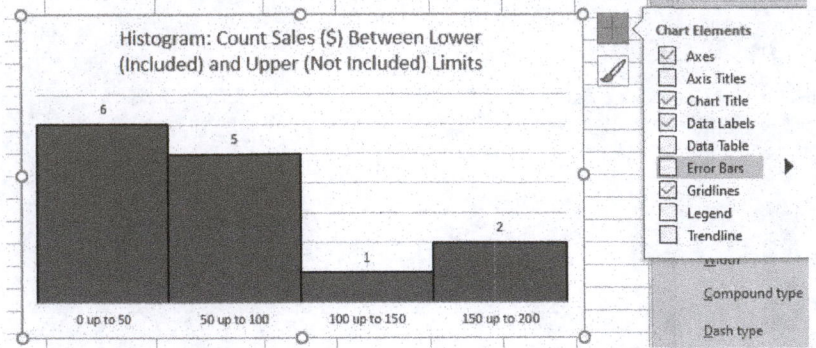

Figure 17.131 *Remove the chart element Axis Titles and add the chart element Data Labels.*

Figure 17.132 shows the finished frequency distribution and histogram chart. The histogram visual reveals a typical pattern in retail sales, with a larger number of customers making small dollar amount purchases and a smaller number making larger dollar amount purchases. In addition, you can see that the frequency tends to decrease as the dollar amount categories increase.

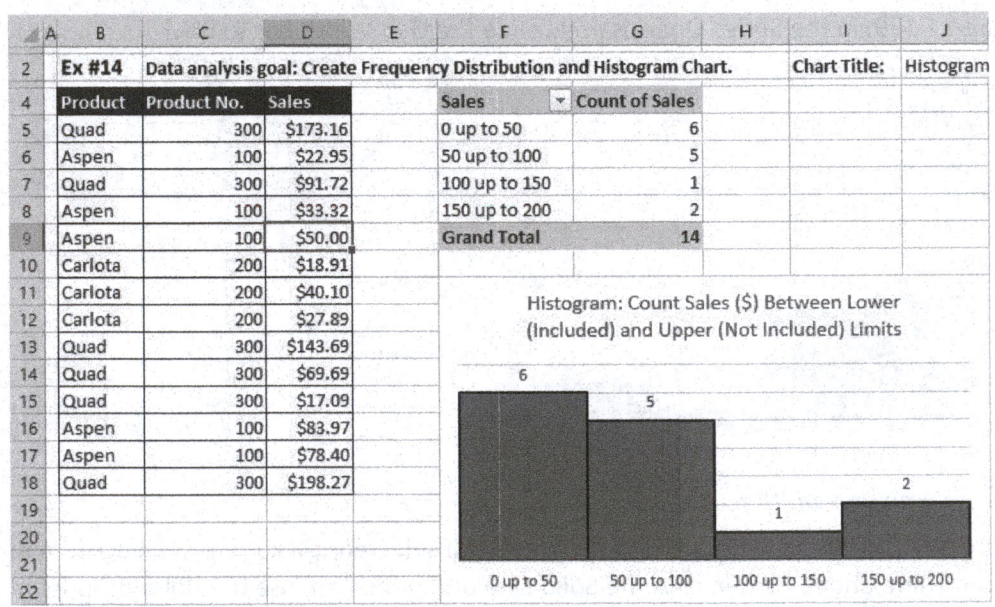

Figure 17.132 *The completed frequency distribution and histogram chart.*

Example 15: Visualizing with a Line Chart to Show Changes and Trends over Time

A line chart is a perfect visualization when you want to plot number values across equidistant time intervals or other categories to show changes and trends. Figure 17.133 shows a line chart with the day variable on the horizontal axis, the website variable in the legend, and the plotted number variable (the number of clicks on automobile listing website links) as the vertical axis variable. Each line shows the daily change in the one vertical axis variable: website clicks.

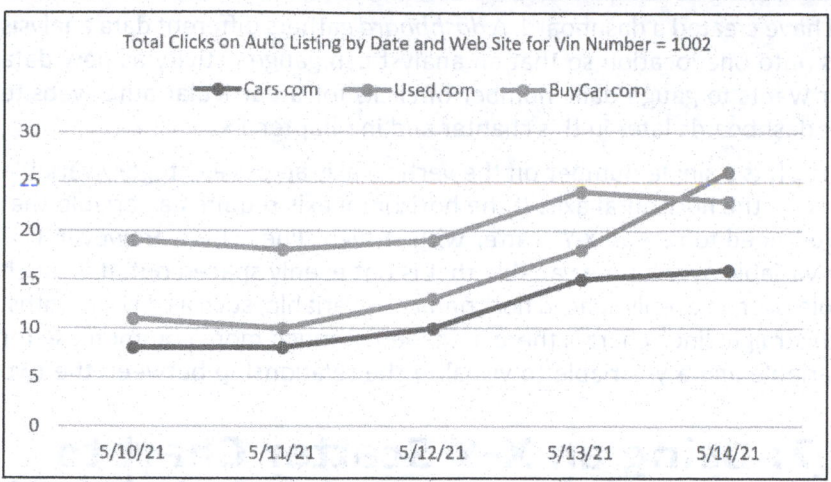

Figure 17.133 *Line chart showing changes and trends in the daily number of clicks on auto listing website links.*

To plot one number variable across equidistance categories, such as time, you should use a line chart, although people commonly make the mistake of using an X-Y scatter chart for this task. The line connects the plotted vertical axis variable to show the up and down daily changes. For example, Figure 17.133 shows that from 5/13/21 to 5/14/21, Cars.com had a modest increase in clicks, the Used.com website had the biggest increase, and BuyCar.com had a modest decrease. You can also see the overall trends: Whereas the Used.com website was consistently trending upward, both of the other websites had a less dramatic upward trend.

The line chart in Figure 17.133 was created from the Excel Table (named fClicks) shown in Figure 17.134. This table contains the fields Date, Vin Number, Web Site, and Clicks on Auto Listing. Each record in the table shows the daily number of clicks on a website auto listing, which is linked to the car's vehicle identification number (VIN).

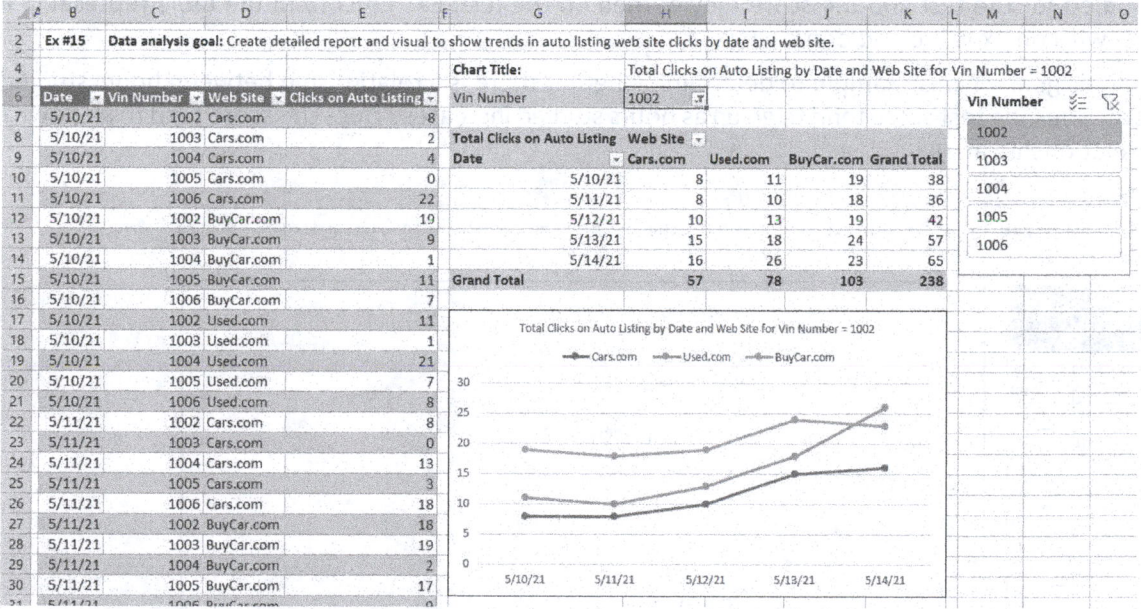

Figure 17.134 *An Excel Table of data, a cross-tabulated PivotTable, a slicer, and a line chart PivotChart.*

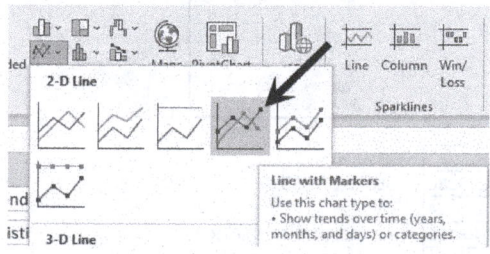

Figure 17.135 *Insert tab in the Ribbon, Charts group, Line with Markers.*

To try this example, you can go to the worksheet named Ch17(133-135). There are no step-by-step instructions for you to follow in this section. However, the steps are almost identical to the steps in Example 11, where you created a cross-tabulated report with the standard PivotTable tool and a slicer, as well as a clustered column chart with the standard PivotChart tool. The only difference here is that you need to choose Line with Marker from the Line Chart dropdown arrow in the Charts group in the Insert tab of the Ribbon, as shown in Figure 17.135, and then change the name of the PivotTable Values sum calculation in cell G5 to **Total Clicks on Auto Listing**, as shown in Figure 17.134.

When you complete this task, you will have created a dashboard. A *dashboard* gathers different data analysis solutions, such as reports and visuals, into one location so that an analyst can gauge activity as new data arrives. In this example, the manager wants to gauge daily number of clicks for a particular auto website listing. You will learn a lot more about dashboards later in this chapter and in Chapter 18.

It is important to note that a line chart plots a single number on the vertical axis across a category variable that is placed at equidistance intervals on the horizontal axis. If the horizontal axis requires a variable that is not spaced out at even intervals, you need to use an X-Y scatter with straight lines chart. However, it is uncommon to need to plot a number variable over a time variable that is not evenly spaced out. It is much more common to plot a number variable over an evenly spaced horizontal axis variable, such as days, months, or years. However, the X-Y scatter with straight lines chart is there if needed. A much more common use for the X-Y scatter chart is to plot an x-variable and a y-variable to visualize the relationship between the two quantitative variables.

Examples 16 and 17: Using an X-Y Scatter Chart to Visualize the Relationship Between Two Quantitative Variables

If your analysis involves linear algebra or linear regression and you need to visualize the relationship between a set of paired x-values and y-values, you can use an X-Y scatter chart. In addition, if you are a student in school, you will inevitably have to use this visualization in your math and analytics classes. So this is a good visualization to know how to use. This visualization is in both Excel (as an Excel chart) and Power BI (as a visualization).

An X-Y scatter chart plots two quantitative variables with one x-variable (the independent, or predictor, variable) and one y-variable (the dependent, or predicted, variable). (In contrast, in Example 15, you plotted one quantitative variable with a line chart.) Figure 17.136 shows a proper dataset with an x-variable, hours studied, and a y-variable, test score. Each record in the table represents the number of hours the student says they studied for the test and the score they earned on the test. Each record in the table represents a matched pair with one x-value and one y-value.

The data analysis goal for this example to determine whether there is a relationship between hours studied and test score. Does the test score tend to go up as hours studied increases? Does the score tend to go down? Is there no relationship at all?

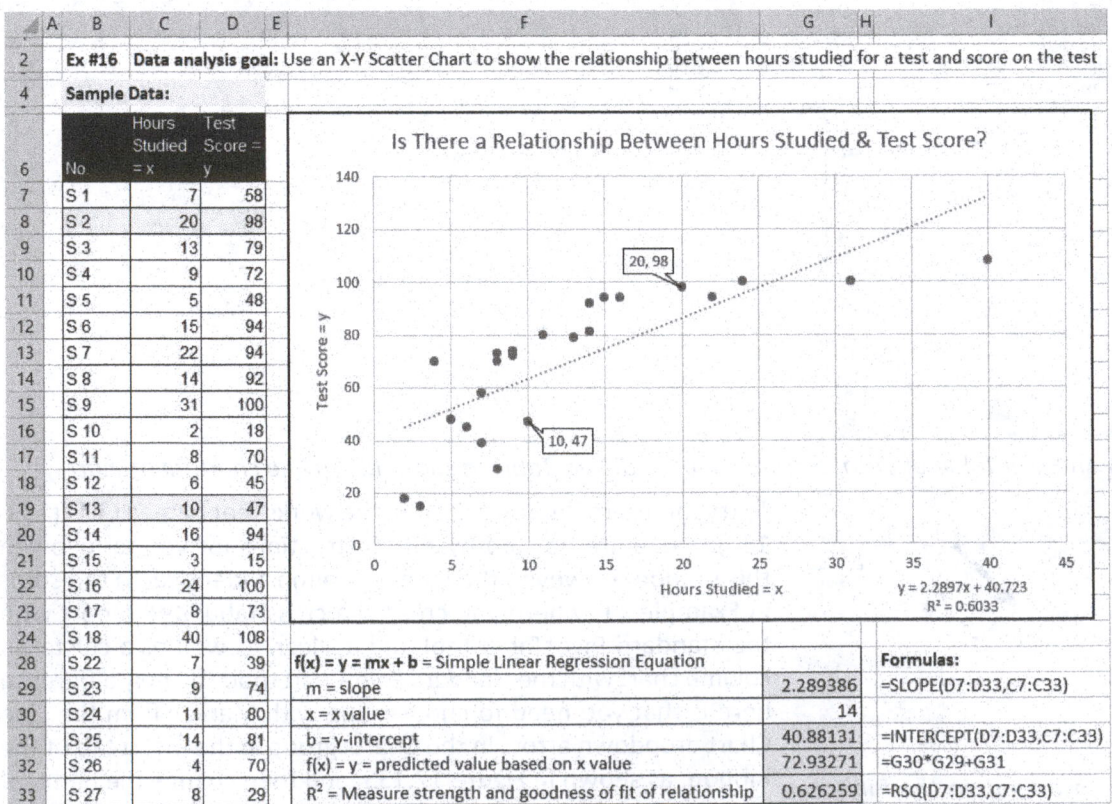

Figure 17.136 *This X-Y scatter chart shows a direct relationship between hours studied and test score.*

In addition to showing the dataset, Figure 17.136 shows an X-Y scatter chart with the x-variable plotted on the horizontal axis and the y-variable plotted on the vertical axis. Each marker, or dot, is determined by a matched x, y pair. For example, the table in Figure 17.136 shows that student 13 studied 10 hours and earned a test score of 47 points. To determine the marker on the chart, you must start with the x-value and move, left to right, out along the horizontal axis to the 10 hours spot. Then, from that 10 hours spot, you use the matched y-value and move up along the vertical axis to the 47 points location. That becomes the marker for the matched x, y pair. Figure 17.136 shows a callout next to this marker with the matched pairs notation (10, 47). As another example, student 2 studied 20 hours and earned a test score of 98 points. To plot this marker, move out the horizontal axis to the 20 hours spot and then move up the vertical axis to the 98 points spot. Figure 17.136 shows a callout next to this marker with the matched pairs notation (20, 98).

When each pair of values is plotted, the X-Y scatter chart reveals the trend, or pattern, for the relationship. In this example, the chart shows that as the hours studied variable increases from left to right, the test score variable tends to increase upward from a low score to a higher score. The visual reveals that there is a direct, or positive, relationship: As the hours studied increases, the test score increases. The chart also shows a straight line moving left to right. This line, called a *trendline*, is created using linear regression and is represented by the famous linear algebra equation y = mx+b. This line and equation can be shown on the chart with just a few clicks. The line is used to visualize the relationship, and the equation can be used to make predictions over the range of x-values from the dataset.

As a second example of an X-Y scatter chart, say that you need to determine whether there is a relationship between how much a bicycle weighs (the predictor variable) and the bike's price (the predicted variable). Figure 17.137 shows an example of a proper dataset with the three fields—for bike type, bike weight, and price. The finished X-Y scatter chart shows the bike weight variable plotted on the horizontal axis and the price plotted on the vertical axis. The visual shows that as the bike weight variable increases from left to right, the price variable decreases from a high price to a low price. The visual reveals that there is an indirect, or negative, relationship: As the bike weight increases, the price decreases.

> **Note:** At the bottom of both Figures 17.136 and 17.137, you can see formulas used to build simple linear regression models. If you have studied statistics, you might want to try them on the worksheet named Ch17(137). However, the goal of this part of the book is to learn how to create the X-Y scatter charts shown in Figures 17.136 and 17.137, and working with the statistics formulas is optional.

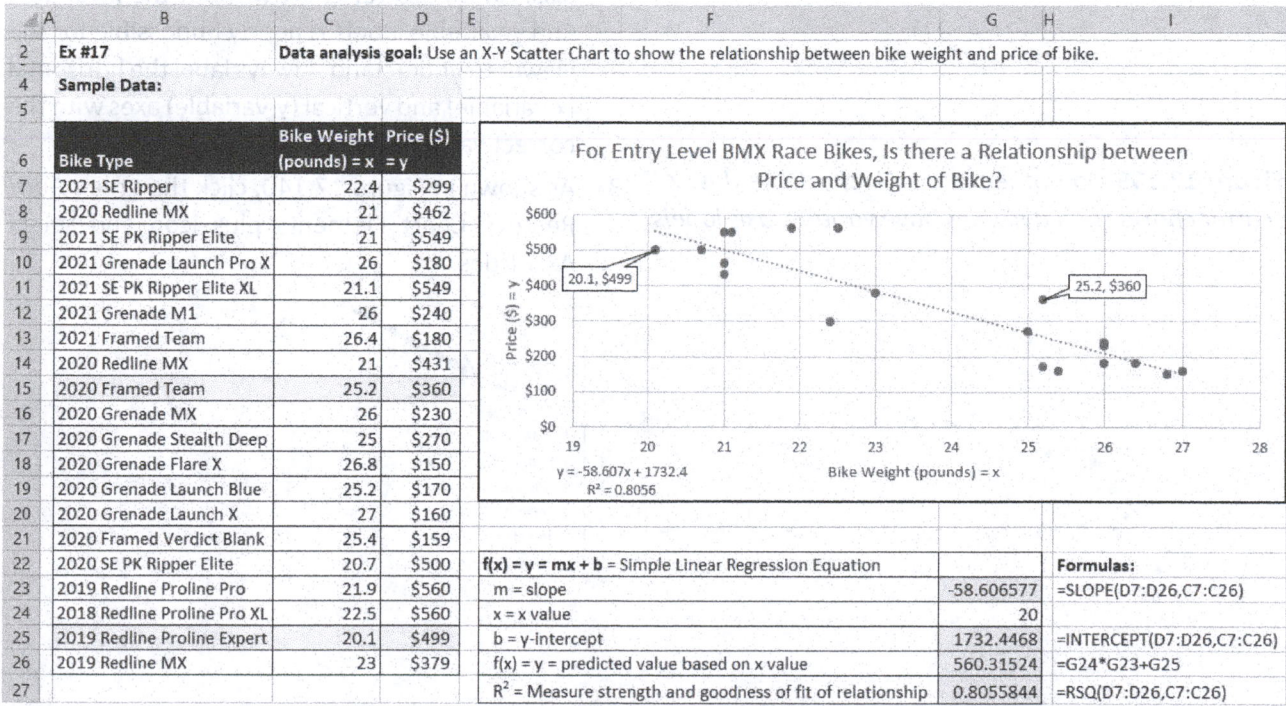

Figure 17.137 *X-Y scatter chart showing an inverse relationship between bike weight and price.*

In order to create an X-Y scatter chart, you must have columns of x-variable data and y-variable data that are collected so that each y-value is matched to its associated x-value. For the hours studied and test score dataset, students were asked to report how many hours they studied before the test. After the test, each student's test score was recorded with the associated reported hours studied number to create one record for each student in the proper dataset. For the bike weight and price dataset, the bike price was recorded with the associated bike weight number to create one record in the proper dataset for each unique bike.

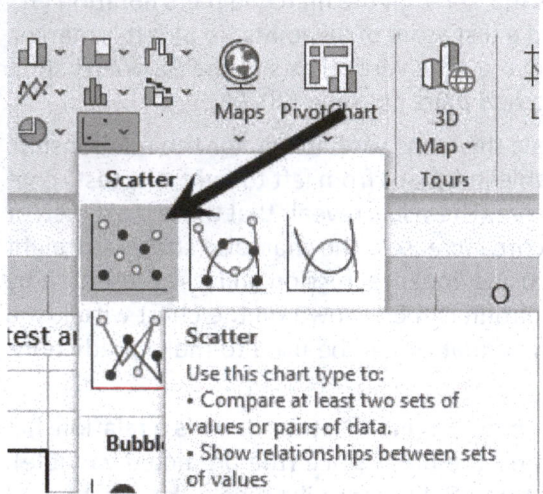

Figure 17.138 *Click the Scatter dropdown arrow to create an X-Y scatter chart.*

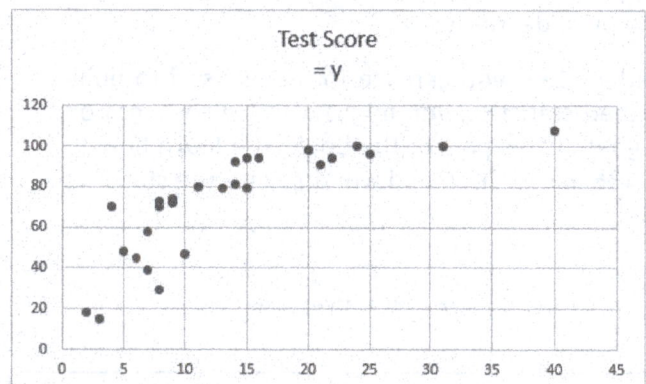

Figure 17.139 *Do not leave an X-Y chart like this. X-Y scatter charts should always have variable axis labels.*

Once you have the x-value and y-value data recorded in a proper dataset, it is best to place the two columns side-by-side, with the x-variable field listed first and then the y-variable field. When you organize the proper dataset in this way, the charting engine knows to place the x-variable data on the horizontal axis and the y-variable data on the vertical axis. In addition, when the proper dataset has more fields than just the x- and y-variable fields, you must pre-highlight the x-variable and y-variable data fields (the field names and all the data) before staring the chart so that the charting engine understands that you are plotting only those two fields and not the full dataset.

To complete this example, follow these steps on the worksheet named Ch17(138-148):

1. Select the range C6:D33 (that is, the field names and data for the x- and y-variables).

2. As shown in Figure 17.138, from the Insert tab of the Ribbon, in the Charts group, click the Scatter dropdown arrow and then select Scatter.

   Figure 17.139 shows that the resulting chart does not list the x-variable name along the horizontal axis or the y-variable name along the vertical axis. An X-Y scatter chart without the x-variable and y-variable labels is nearly impossible for the viewer to understand. Always label the horizontal (x-variable) and vertical (y-variable) axes with the correct variable labels.

3. As shown in Figure 17.140, click the green Add/Remove Chart Elements plus icon and select Axis Titles.

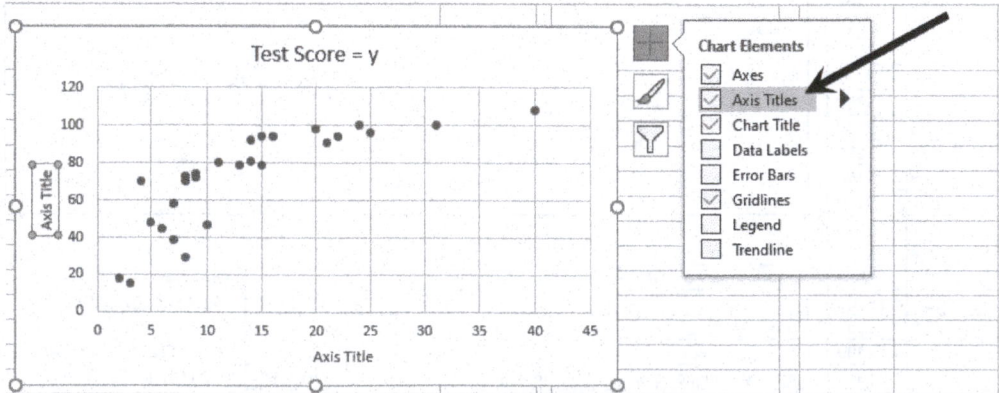

Figure 17.140 *Always add axis titles to an X-Y scatter chart!*

4. To link the vertical y-axis label to the y-variable label in cell D6, select the vertical axis label, type an equal sign (which jumps your cursor up to the formula bar), click on cell D6, and press Enter.

5. To link the horizontal x-axis label to the x-variable label in cell C6, select the horizontal axis label, type an equal sign, click on cell C6, and press Enter.

6. To link the chart title to the title text in cell L4, select the chart title, type an equal sign, click on cell L4, and press Enter.

Figure 17.141 shows the correctly linked axis labels and chart title.

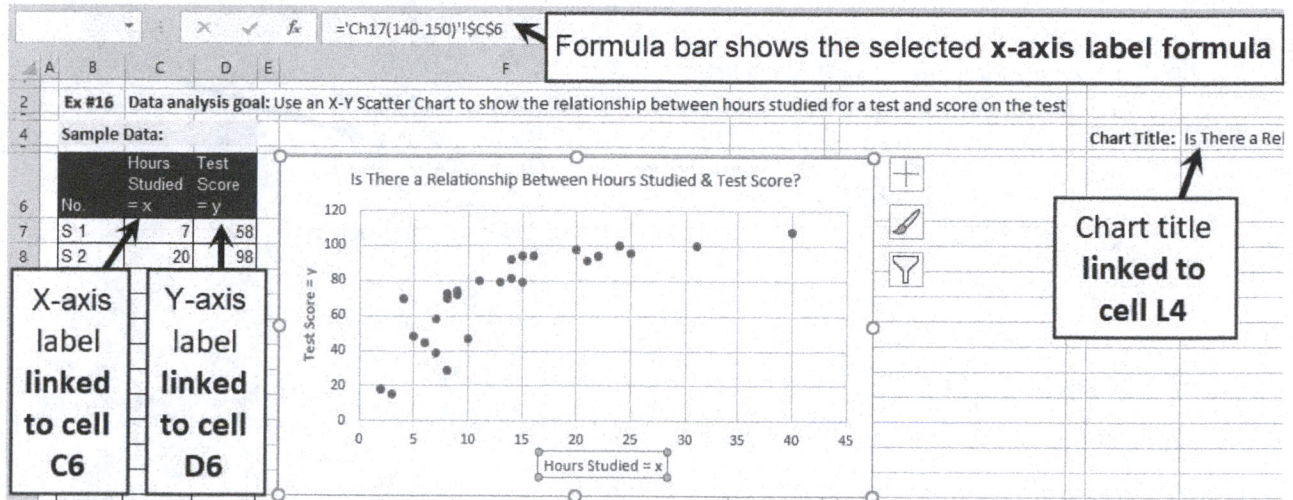

Figure 17.141 *Using a formula, link the axis labels and chart title to the correct labels and titles in the worksheet cells.*

7. As shown in Figure 17.142, to add a trendline to the chart, right-click any one of the data points and click Add Trendline. (There are other ways to add a trendline, but this right-click methods is convenient because it adds the line and opens the Format Trendline task pane, which allows you to access all options for the trend line.)

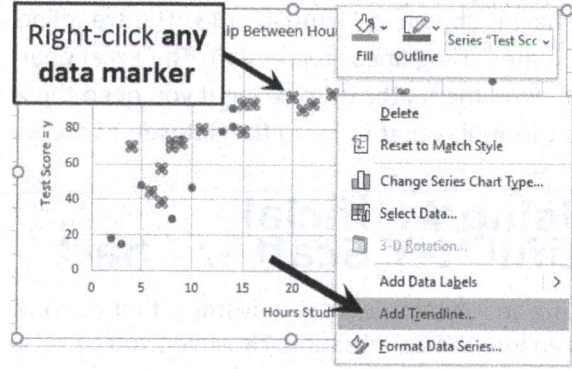

Figure 17.142 *Right-click a data marker to add a regression trendline.*

8. As shown in Figure 17.143, in the Format Trendline task pane, under Trendline Options, select the bar chart icon and then select the Linear option button (if it is not already selected by default). Check the Display Equation on Chart checkbox and then check the Display R-Squared Value on Chart checkbox.

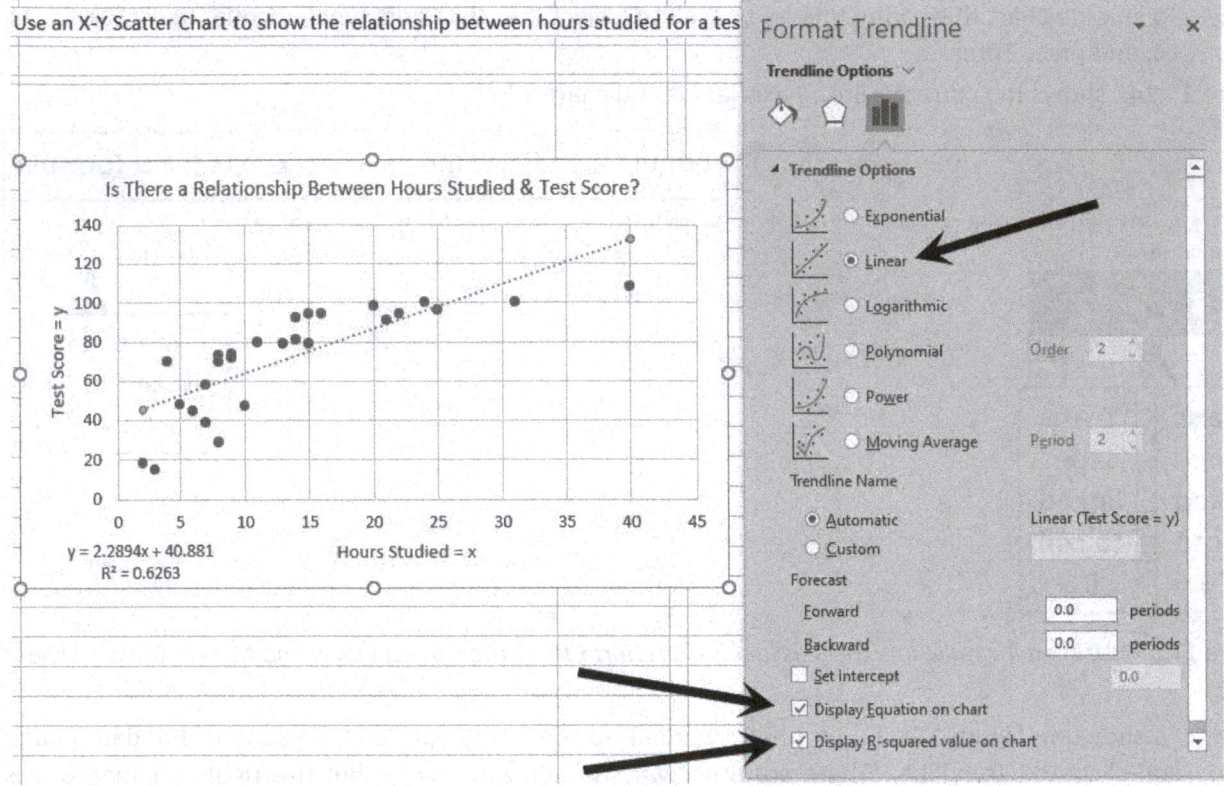

Figure 17.143 *In the Format Trendline task pane, check the checkboxes for equation and R-squared.*

9. To move the textbox with the equation and R-squared value, select the textbox and then drag it to the lower-left corner of the chart. The finished chart is shown in Figure 17.143. The trendline, equation, and R-squared value in this example are created using linear regression. The Excel Chart tool creates these values automatically and shows them in the textbox. However, if you need these values to use in formulas, you must create worksheet formulas that point to the dataset, as shown back in the bottom portion of Figure 17.136.

Example 18: Analyzing Data Using Artificial Intelligence to Create a Beautiful X-Y Scatter Chart

You have already learned the step-by-step method for creating an X-Y scatter chart. It is important to know this method as it gives you control over all the elements that go into the visualization. However, you can also use the new Microsoft 365 Excel Analyze Data button to create an X-Y scatter chart with a single click (see Figure 17.144).

The Analyze Data feature uses artificial intelligence (that is, automatic algorithms to detect patterns and trends) to create reports and visualizations. Because it is an automatic feature that builds finished solutions for you, you do not have as much control over the finished result as you have if you create a solution manually. In my experience, sometimes the Analyze Data feature gets things right, but other times it produces finished reports and visuals that are not helpful. However, every time I have used this feature on x, y data from a proper dataset, the X-Y scatter charts have come out beautiful. Therefore, I must show you this amazing feature.

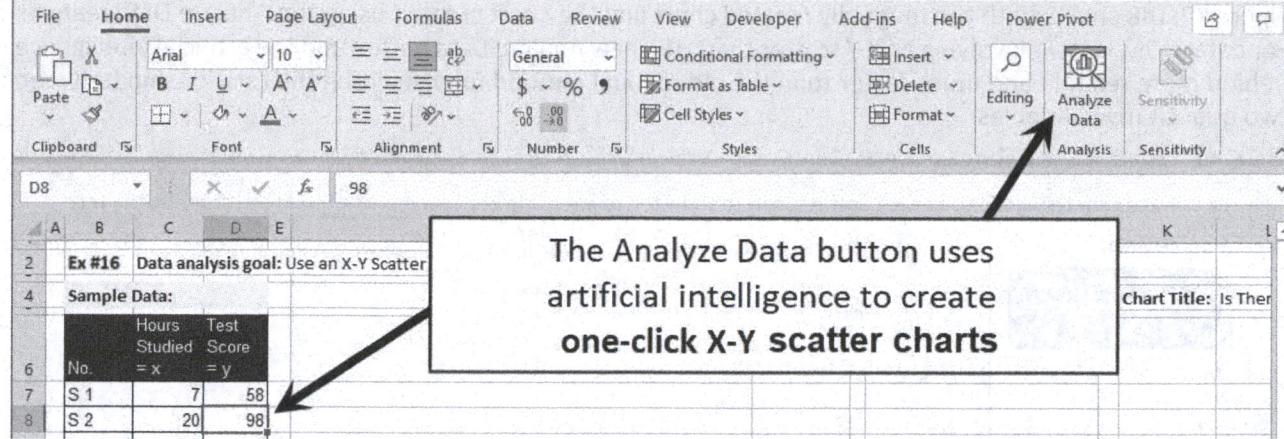

Figure 17.144 *The Analyze Data button is in the Analysis group in the Home tab of the Ribbon.*

To use the Analyze Data feature, you must have your data stored in a proper dataset. When you use this feature, the Analyze Data task pane offers you various finished PivotTable reports and Excel chart visualizations. Some of the offerings will have nothing to do with your data analysis goals or may even be ineffectual data analysis solutions. So you must be careful when you look through the list of offered solution and make sure to select results that you are sure will match your data analysis goals.

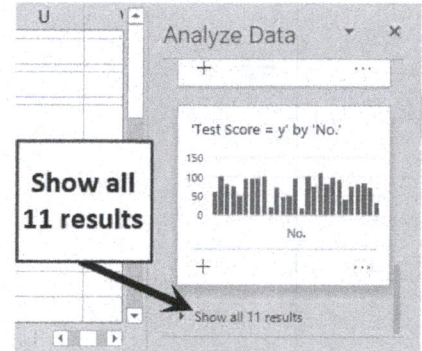

Figure 17.145 *Scroll down to find Show All 11 Results.*

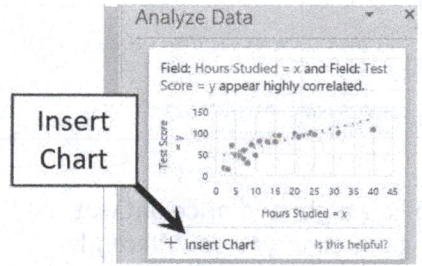

Figure 17.146 *Click Insert Chart for the X-Y scatter option.*

Note: The Analyze Data feature works best if you have some data analysis skills and know how to select the correct solutions for your goals. This feature is not a safe tool for users who have no data analysis experience.

To complete this example, follow these steps on the worksheet named Ch17(138-148):

1. Select a single cell in the proper dataset. Then, in the Home tab of the Ribbon, go to the Analysis group and click the Analyze Data button.

2. As shown in Figure 17.145, in the Analyze Data task pane, scroll down and click the Show All 11 Results link.

3. As shown in Figure 17.146, scroll down and then click on the Insert Chart option below the X-Y scatter chart.

4. To increase the data-to-ink ratio, select the chart and then click the green plus icon to remove the horizontal and vertical gridlines. Figure 17.147 shows the resulting X-Y scatter chart with informative axis labels, a helpful chart title, and a trendline. The Analyze Data feature even created an insightful chart title, which concludes that the two variables are highly correlated.

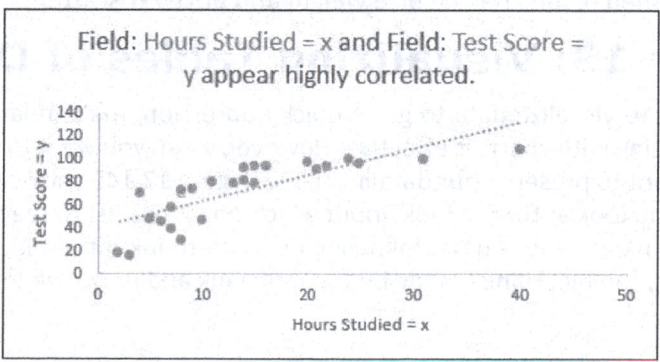

Figure 17.147 *With one click, you get plotted data points, correct labels, and a trendline.*

Figure 17.148 shows both the manually created chart and the chart created using the Analyze Data feature. For data analysis tasks involving an X-Y scatter chart, the new Analyze Data button and the artificial intelligence behind it are reliable and much faster than the old manual method for visualizing the relationship between two quantitative variables.

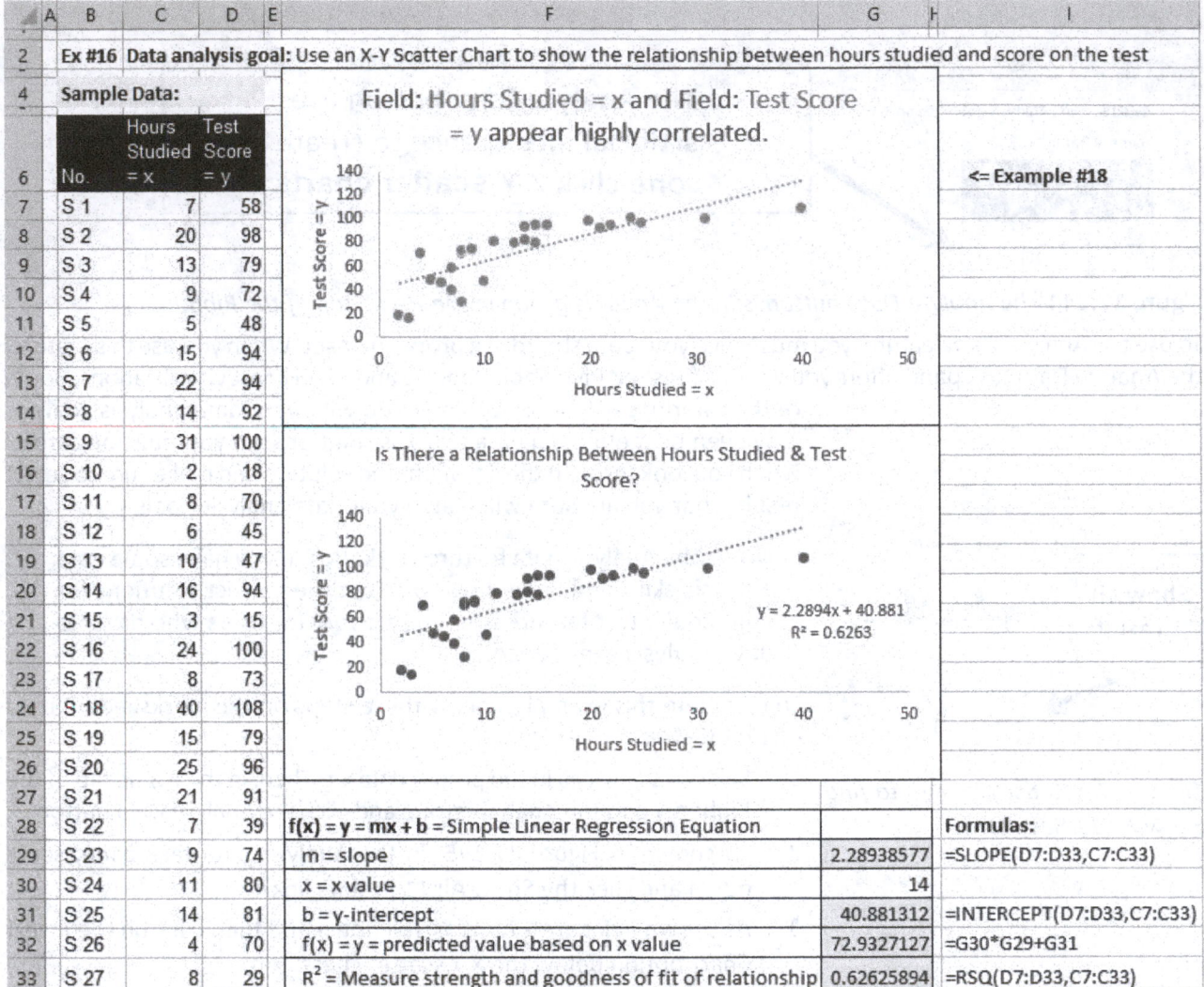

Figure 17.148 *Finished analysis for hours studied and test score data.*

> **Note:** If you would like to try to create the X-Y scatter chart for the bike weight and price dataset, you can use the dataset on the worksheet named Ch17(137). One thing you can try to do differently is to set a minimum value for the horizontal axis. To do this, you can select the horizontal axis, press Ctrl+1 to open the Axis task pane, and then set the minimum for Axis Options Bounds to 19. The finished results for the bike weight and price X-Y scatter chart are shown in Figure 17.137.

Example 19: Visualizing Tables of Data

When you want to visualize data to get a quick impression, make relative comparisons, or see trends and patterns, visualizing with charts is effective. However, when you want to see details for a more exact analysis, you probably want to present your data in a table. Figure 17.149 shows three examples of data presented in table form. As you look at them, think about which one is easiest to read. You are likely to pick the last table, which uses less ink and more data, following the data-to-ink ratio rule. The table in the middle is okay, but for some people, the black lines many be too much ink and may look too busy.

Ex #19 Data analysis goal: Format the table of data so the detail is easy to see.

SalesRep	2015 Total Sales ($)	2016 Total Sales ($)	% Change	Customer Accounts	Years with Company
Hien Loung Pham	30346.7	32291.9235	0.0641	8	2
Carl Levin	53363.33	42338.4660	-0.2066	18	2
Wilford Snell	366373.12	348750.5729	-0.0481	74	10
Chantel Mimms	264435.35	320539.0819	0.2122	89	11
Tyrone Ways	483572.75	594527.0949	0.2294	113	15
Terica Mcswain	247830.8	257136.9282	0.0376	45	10

SalesRep	2015 Total Sales ($)	2016 Total Sales ($)	% Change	Customer Accounts	Years with Company
Hien Loung Pham	30,347	32,292	6.41	8	2
Carl Levin	53,363	42,338	-20.66	18	2
Wilford Snell	366,373	348,751	-4.81	74	10
Chantel Mimms	264,435	320,539	21.22	89	11
Tyrone Ways	483,573	594,527	22.94	113	15
Terica Mcswain	247,831	257,137	3.76	45	10

SalesRep	2015 Total Sales ($)	2016 Total Sales ($)	% Change	Customer Accounts	Years with Company
Hien Loung Pham	30,347	32,292	6.41	8	2
Carl Levin	53,363	42,338	-20.66	18	2
Wilford Snell	366,373	348,751	-4.81	74	10
Chantel Mimms	264,435	320,539	21.22	89	11
Tyrone Ways	483,573	594,527	22.94	113	15
Terica Mcswain	247,831	257,137	3.76	45	10

Figure 17.149 *Which table do you find easiest to read?*

As you format a table, keep in mind the following principles:

- The data-to-ink ratio should be high.
- Horizontal lines are generally necessary only for separating column titles from data values or when indicating that a calculation has taken place.
- In large tables, light shading can be used to differentiate columns.
- Numbers should be right-aligned (because right-alignment is a visual cue that something is a number).
- Text should be left-aligned (because left-alignment is a visual cue that something is text).
- All numbers should have the same number of decimal places.
- Units must be indicated either with number formatting or labels.
- You can make a table report significantly less cluttered and increase the data-to-ink ration by indicating the unit in the labels at the top of the column rather than in each cell of the report.
- Large numbers may be rounded to the dollar or to the thousand, million, and so on.
- You can hide the default worksheet gridlines in the Show group in the View tab of the Ribbon.

You can try out these principles by formatting the tables in Figure 17.149 on the worksheet named Ch17(149).

Example 20: Using PivotTable Styles

All the PivotTables you have created so far have used the default PivotTable style. Figure 17.150 shows an example of a PivotTable report that uses the default PivotTable style. Notice that this style follows the table formatting principles listed in the previous section. Although the default style is an effective style to use, you may want to change the style of a PivotTable report. In such a case, you can use one of the many built-in PivotTable styles, or you can create your own PivotTable style. When you create your own PivotTable style, you can reuse it and even set it as the default style for future PivotTables.

Years	2020								
Sum of Units		Region							
Sales Rep	Product	Canada	East	Mexico	MidWest	NorthWest	South	West	Grand Total
⊟ Chantel Mims	Crested Beaut	1,214	1,203	835	3,380	1,958	2,104	2,247	12,941
	Majestic Beaut	1,114	1,032	1,409	2,325	1,926	4,126	3,637	15,569
	Quad	3,173	2,335	2,225	1,106	2,426	3,447	1,958	16,670
	Sunset	1,937	1,861	1,305	1,961	2,344	2,851	2,950	15,209
	Yanaki	1,562	2,616	2,188	2,615	2,303	1,530	2,565	15,379
Chantel Mims Total		9,000	9,047	7,962	11,387	10,957	14,058	13,357	75,768
⊟ Hien Pham	Crested Beaut	4,229	1,330	1,208	1,575	1,404	1,567	316	11,629
	Majestic Beaut	2,447	3,173	1,911	3,523	2,677	2,164	3,088	18,983
	Quad	316	1,553	2,591	5,080	1,637	1,927	1,039	14,143
	Sunset	942	592	2,753	2,500	1,939	998	3,414	13,138
	Yanaki	828	1,163	1,322	3,141	752	1,675	1,025	9,906
Hien Pham Total		8,762	7,811	9,785	15,819	8,409	8,331	8,882	67,799
⊟ Tynia Malone	Crested Beaut	1,006	763	199	326	955	1,063	678	4,990
	Majestic Beaut	814	1,902	1,131	1,132	619	1,560	894	8,052
	Quad	746	1,057	1,138	1,586	1,699	1,849	1,543	9,618
	Sunset	365	786	668	1,725	449	1,311	668	5,972
	Yanaki	1,719	1,572	720	1,617	1,680	1,052	758	9,118
Tynia Malone Total		4,650	6,080	3,856	6,386	5,402	6,835	4,541	37,750
Grand Total		22,412	22,938	21,603	33,592	24,768	29,224	26,780	181,317

Figure 17.150 *The default PivotTable style follows table formatting principles.*

To complete this example, follow these steps on the worksheet named Ch17(150-157):

1. Select a single cell in the existing PivotTable.

2. As shown in Figure 17.151, click on the More button in the PivotTable Styles group in the Design tab of the Ribbon. A large list of built-in PivotTable styles appears. You can apply any of these styles by clicking on it in this list. However, in this case, you do not want to do select an existing style. You want to create our own style.

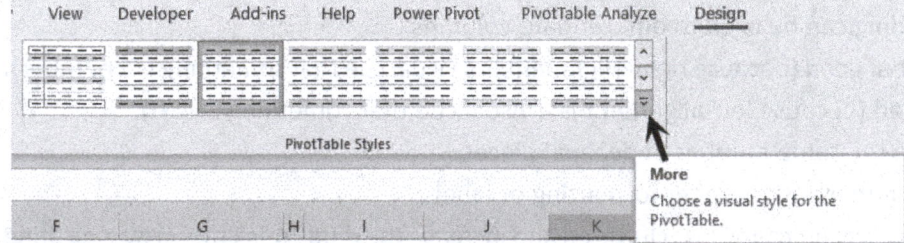

Figure 17.151 *Click the More button to see more PivotTable styles and the New Pivot Style option.*

3. Scroll to the bottom of the list of built-in PivotTable styles and click the New PivotTable Style option (see Figure 17.152).

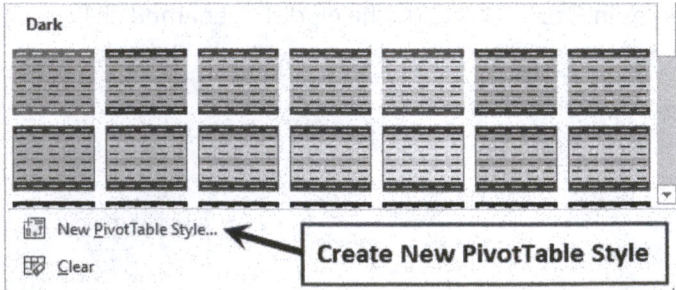

Figure 17.152 *The New PivotTable Style button is at the very bottom of the list of built-in styles.*

4. In the New PivotTable Style dialog box that appears, in the Name textbox type **Dark Blue PivotTable Style** (see Figure 17.153).

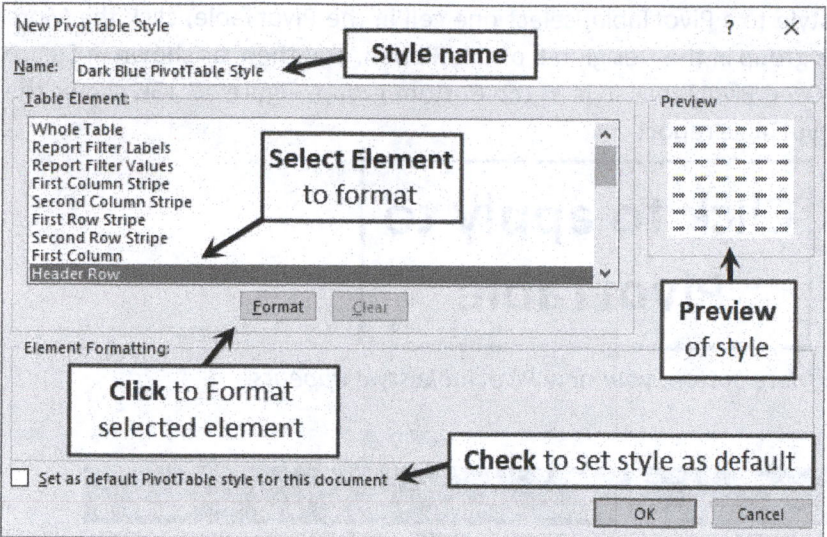

Figure 17.153 *The New PivotTable Style dialog box.*

5. From the Table Element list, select Header Row.

6. Click the Format button.

7. In the Formatting dialog box that appears, add the formatting white font, bold font, and a dark blue fill color. Then click the OK button. Figure 17.154 shows that after you click the OK button in the Formatting dialog box, the New PivotTable Style dialog box shows that the table element appears in bold, a description of the formatting applied is listed under the title Element Formatting, and the Preview area shows a preview of the formatting applied.

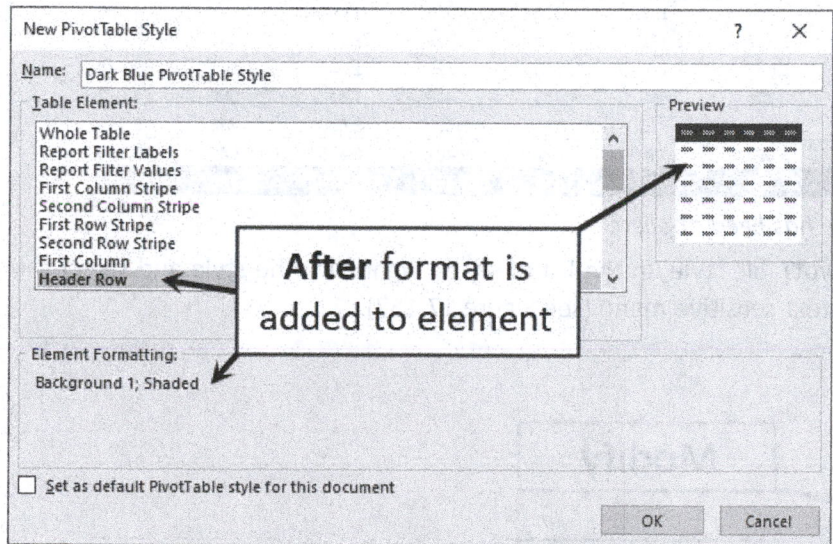

Figure 17.154 *The formatted element appears in bold, with a description and a preview.*

8. Select the PivotTable elements from the Table Element list and then format them as you like. These are the elements that I formatted:

   • **Report Filter Labels:** White font, bold font, and dark blue fill

   • **Report Filter Values:** Thin black border

   • **Header Row:** White font, bold font, and dark blue fill

   • **Subtotal Row 1:** Bold font and thin black border at top and bottom

   • **Grand Total Row:** White font, bold font, and dark blue fill

9. When you are done formatting the PivotTable elements, click the OK button in the New PivotTable Style dialog box.

10. To apply the new PivotTable style to a PivotTable, select one cell in the PivotTable, click the More button in the PivotTable Styles group in the Design tab of the Ribbon, and then, as shown in Figure 17.155, click on the newly created PivotTable style in the Custom group. Figure 17.156 shows the new style applied to the full PivotTable report.

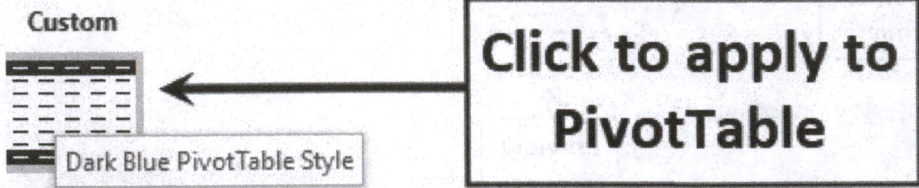

Figure 17.155 *Now when you click the More button, your new PivotTable style appears.*

Sum of Units	Region								
Sales Rep	Product	Canada	East	Mexico	MidWest	NorthWest	South	West	Grand Total
⊟Chantel Mims	Crested Beaut	1,214	1,203	835	3,380	1,958	2,104	2,247	12,941
	Majestic Beaut	1,114	1,032	1,409	2,325	1,926	4,126	3,637	15,569
	Quad	3,173	2,335	2,225	1,106	2,426	3,447	1,958	16,670
	Sunset	1,937	1,861	1,305	1,961	2,344	2,851	2,950	15,209
	Yanaki	1,562	2,616	2,188	2,615	2,303	1,530	2,565	15,379
Chantel Mims Total		**9,000**	**9,047**	**7,962**	**11,387**	**10,957**	**14,058**	**13,357**	**75,768**
⊟Hien Pham	Crested Beaut	4,229	1,330	1,208	1,575	1,404	1,567	316	11,629
	Majestic Beaut	2,447	3,173	1,911	3,523	2,677	2,164	3,088	18,983
	Quad	316	1,553	2,591	5,080	1,637	1,927	1,039	14,143
	Sunset	942	592	2,753	2,500	1,939	998	3,414	13,138
	Yanaki	828	1,163	1,322	3,141	752	1,675	1,025	9,906
Hien Pham Total		**8,762**	**7,811**	**9,785**	**15,819**	**8,409**	**8,331**	**8,882**	**67,799**
⊟Tynia Malone	Crested Beaut	1,006	763	199	326	955	1,063	678	4,990
	Majestic Beaut	814	1,902	1,131	1,132	619	1,560	894	8,052
	Quad	746	1,057	1,138	1,586	1,699	1,849	1,543	9,618
	Sunset	365	786	668	1,725	449	1,311	668	5,972
	Yanaki	1,719	1,572	720	1,617	1,680	1,052	758	9,118
Tynia Malone Total		**4,650**	**6,080**	**3,856**	**6,386**	**5,402**	**6,835**	**4,541**	**37,750**
Grand Total		**22,412**	**22,938**	**21,603**	**33,592**	**24,768**	**29,224**	**26,780**	**181,317**

Figure 17.156 *The new PivotTable style has been applied.*

11. If you need to modify your PivotTable style, in the list of styles, right-click the style and select the option you want from the context-sensitive menu (see Figure 17.157).

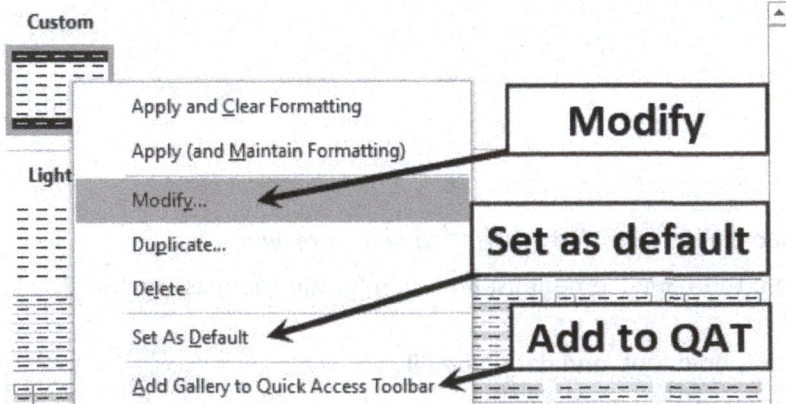

Figure 17.157 *To modify the style or perform other actions on a style, just right-click and select the option you want.*

Example 21: Using Conditional Formatting to Add a Heat Map or Color Scales to a Table Report

Conditional formatting allows you to set a rule that determines when and how to apply formatting. You have already seen numerous examples of how to use conditional formatting to visualize data in Chapters 9, 12,

13, and 15. For example, in Chapter 12, Example 15, you saw how to conditionally format a row in a table based on a specified condition, and then in Chapter 12, Example 17, you saw how to conditionally format a dynamic spilled array report based on the spilled results from a formula. In both of those examples, you used logical formulas to apply the conditional formatting.

In the following examples, you will see that there are many useful built-in conditional formatting options that are perfect for table reports, including color scales to apply a gradient of colors to rank values from smallest to largest, formatting for only the top five values, and data bars to visualize the relative sizes of values.

The top half of Figure 17.158 shows an unformatted table report, and the bottom half shows the table with style formatting and color scales conditional formatting applied to the percentage change values. With a color scale, also known as a heat map, you can apply a color gradient to a range of values so that, for example, the lightest fill colors represent the largest numbers and the darkest fill colors represent the smallest numbers. A color scale helps the reader of a table report pick out the relative sizes of the numbers.

> **Note:** The numbers in this example are all negative (representing percentage decreases in COVID-19 deaths), and the darkest fill colors are applied to the biggest decreases.

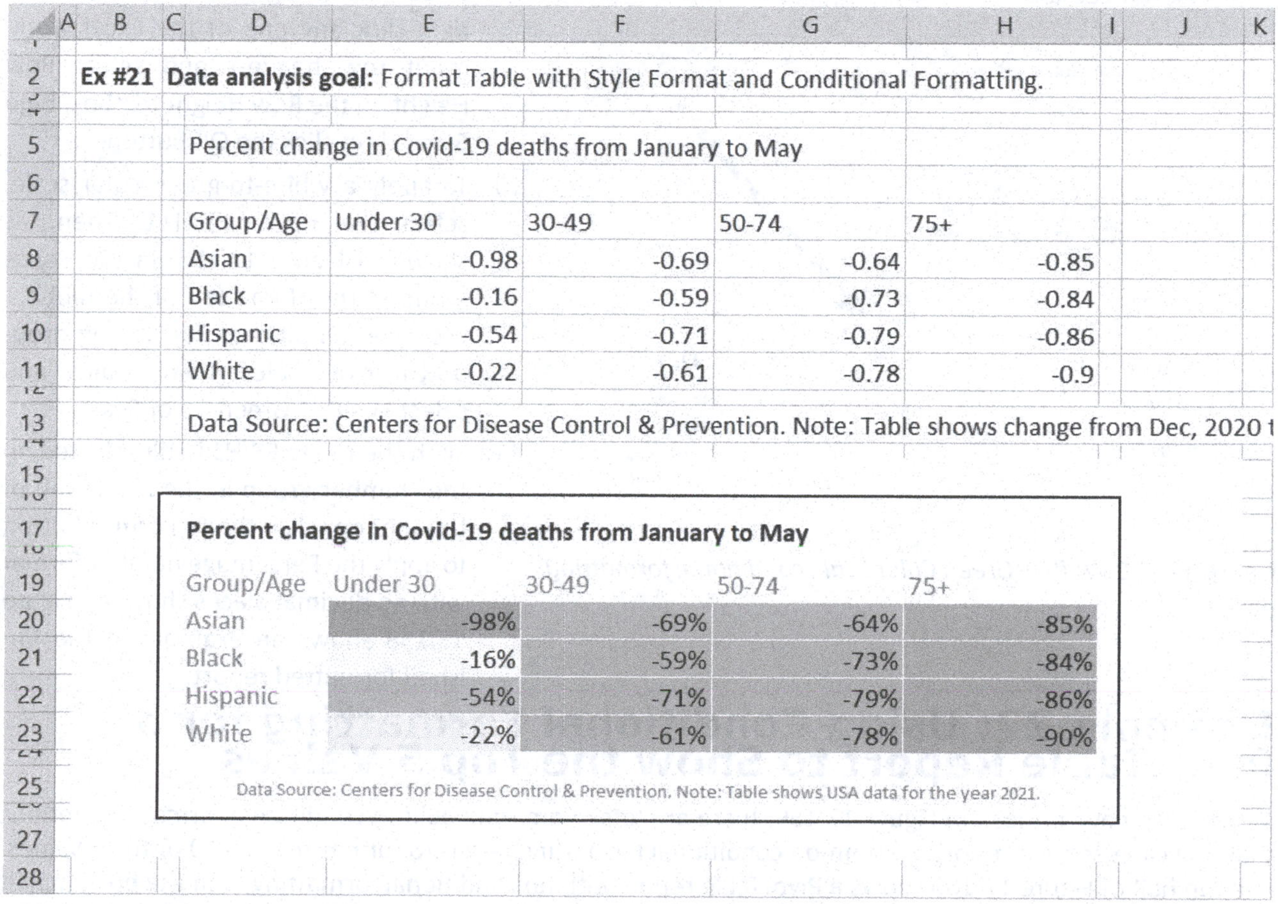

	Group/Age	Under 30	30-49	50-74	75+
	Asian	-0.98	-0.69	-0.64	-0.85
	Black	-0.16	-0.59	-0.73	-0.84
	Hispanic	-0.54	-0.71	-0.79	-0.86
	White	-0.22	-0.61	-0.78	-0.9

Ex #21 **Data analysis goal:** Format Table with Style Format and Conditional Formatting.

Percent change in Covid-19 deaths from January to May

Data Source: Centers for Disease Control & Prevention. Note: Table shows change from Dec, 2020 t

Percent change in Covid-19 deaths from January to May

Group/Age	Under 30	30-49	50-74	75+
Asian	-98%	-69%	-64%	-85%
Black	-16%	-59%	-73%	-84%
Hispanic	-54%	-71%	-79%	-86%
White	-22%	-61%	-78%	-90%

Data Source: Centers for Disease Control & Prevention. Note: Table shows USA data for the year 2021.

Figure 17.158 *You can use style formatting and conditional formatting to make a report easier to read.*

To complete this example, follow these steps on the worksheet named Ch17(158-159):

1. To format the title, select cell D4 and press Ctrl to apply bold font.

2. To format the note at the bottom, select the range D13:H13 and use the keyboard shortcut Ctrl+1 to open the Format Cells dialog box. On the Alignment tab, select Center Across Selection from the Text Alignment Horizontal dropdown arrow. To close the dialog box and apply the formatting, click the OK button.

3. With the range D13:H13 still selected, in the Home tab of the Ribbon, in the Font group, change the font size to 8 and the font color to a medium gray color.

4. Select the range D8:D11 and change the font color to a medium gray color.

5. Select the range E7:H7 and change the font color to a medium gray color.

6. To remove lines and increase the data-to-ink ratio for the report, highlight the range C4:I14 and open the Format Cells dialog box by pressing Ctrl+1. On the Borders tab, in the Line area, select white from the Color dropdown list. In the Presets area, click the buttons Outline and Inside.

7. To add more border formatting to the outside edge of the report, still in the Borders tab, in the Line area, from the Color dropdown list, select black. In the Styles area, select the think black solid line. In the Presets area, click the Outline button.

8. Click the OK button in the Format Cells dialog box.

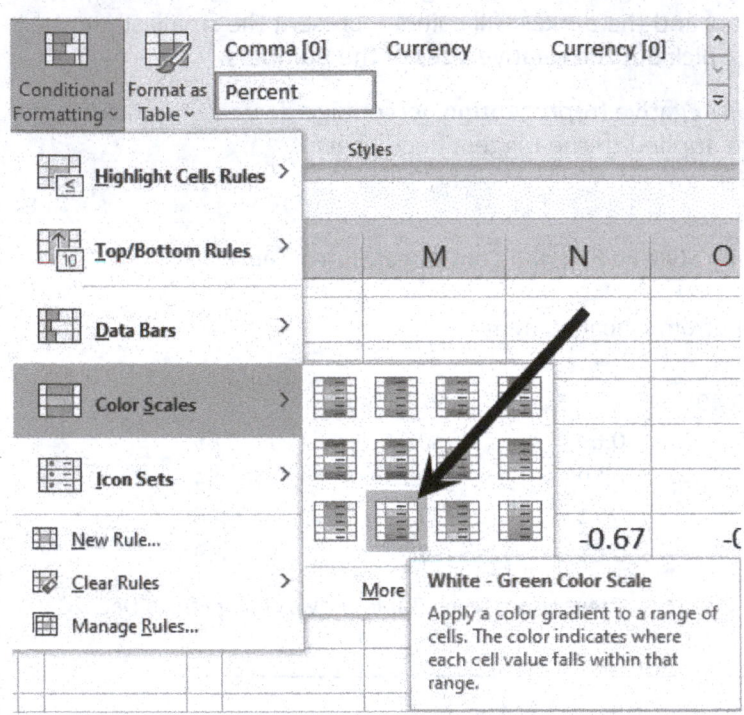

Figure 17.159 *White – Green Color Scale conditional formatting option.*

9. To change the height of rows 4, 12, and 14, select the Excel worksheet row header 4 and then, holding down the Ctrl key, click on the Excel worksheet row header 12 and then 14. With the three noncontiguous rows selected, right-click any one of the Excel worksheet row headers and select Row Height. In the Row Height textbox, type **6** and then click the OK button.

10. To apply a white-to-green color scale, select the range E8:H11. Then, as shown in Figure 17.159, in the Styles group in the Home tab of the Ribbon, click the Conditional Formatting dropdown arrow, select Color Scales, and select White – Green Color Scale.

11. With the range E8:H11 still selected, in the Number group in the Home tab of the Ribbon, click the % Format button to apply the Percentage number format with no decimal places showing. Figure 17.158 shows an example of the finished formatted report.

Example 22: Using Conditional Formatting for a PivotTable Report to Show the Top 5 Values

As you may have noticed in Figure 17.159, there are lots of amazing built-in conditional formatting options that you can use for a report. A common conditional formatting task is to format the top 10 or top 5 values. The top half of Figure 17.160 shows a PivotTable report with no conditional formatting, and the bottom half of the figure shows the same report with the top 5 numbers formatted in a light red. In addition, because it is a PivotTable, if you pivot the report, the conditional formatting is dynamic and automatically adjusts to whatever pivot you apply to the report.

Sum of Units	Product						
Sales Rep	Crested Beaut	Majestic Beaut	Quad	Sunset	Yanaki		Grand Total
Chantel Mims	40,059	39,577	44,792	45,150	40,911		210,489
Hien Pham	41,845	43,762	42,048	40,420	36,078		204,153
Janis Figueroa	17,093	19,074	20,915	17,047	17,143		91,272
Kiki Sho	18,826	19,501	17,656	17,512	20,011		93,506
Tynia Malone	20,959	20,240	18,860	18,310	22,492		100,861
Grand Total	138,782	142,154	144,271	138,439	136,635		700,281

Ex #22 Data analysis goal: Add Conditional Formatting to Top 5 values in PivotTable.

Sum of Units	Product						
Sales Rep	Crested Beaut	Majestic Beaut	Quad	Sunset	Yanaki		Grand Total
Chantel Mims	40,059	39,577	44,792	45,150	40,911		210,489
Hien Pham	41,845	43,762	42,048	40,420	36,078		204,153
Janis Figueroa	17,093	19,074	20,915	17,047	17,143		91,272
Kiki Sho	18,826	19,501	17,656	17,512	20,011		93,506
Tynia Malone	20,959	20,240	18,860	18,310	22,492		100,861
Grand Total	138,782	142,154	144,271	138,439	136,635		700,281

Figure 17.160 *The top 5 values in the bottom PivotTable are formatted using conditional formatting.*

To complete this example, follow these steps on the worksheet named Ch17(160-165):

1. Select any one cell inside the PivotTable.

2. As shown in Figure 17.161, in the Styles group in the Home tab of the Ribbon, click the Conditional Formatting dropdown arrow, select Top/Bottom Rules, and then select Top 10 Items.

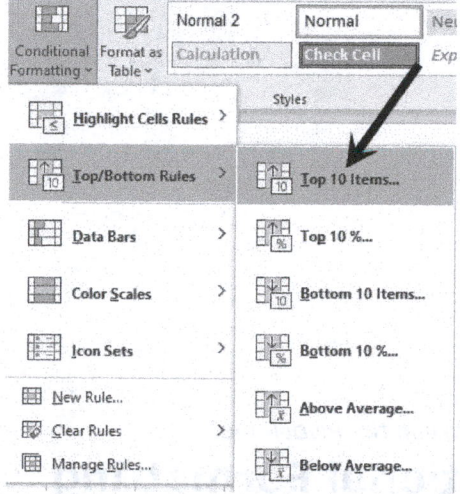

Figure 17.161 *Top 10 Items can be changed to Top 5 or Top 20 or any other number.*

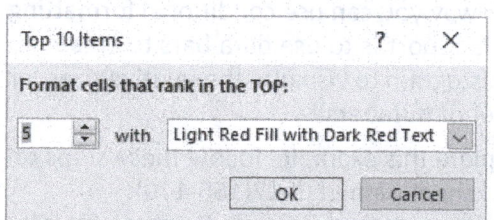

Figure 17.162 *Set the top rank number and the formatting that you would like.*

3. In the Top 10 Items dialog box that appears, change 10 to 5, as shown in Figure 17.162. For this example, you should accept the default, Light Red Fill with Dark Red Text, from the dropdown, but if you want to create your own set of formats to apply, click the dropdown and then select Custom Format. Click the OK button.

4. When you apply conditional formatting to a PivotTable, a special formatting options smart tag appears, as shown in Figure 17.163. Click the dropdown arrow on this smart tag.

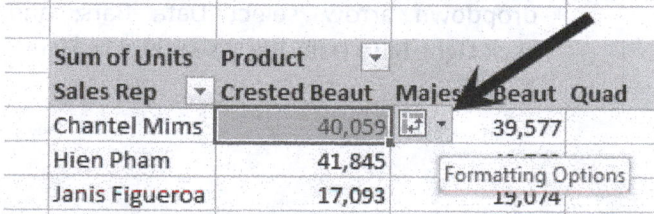

Figure 17.163 *Formatting options smart tag in a PivotTable.*

5. As shown in Figure 17.164, select the last option, All Cells Showing "Sum of Units" Values for "SalesRep" and "Product", to format only the values on the inside of the cross-tabulated report. The calculations on the inside of the report are based on the AND logical test, and therefore so is the conditional formatting.

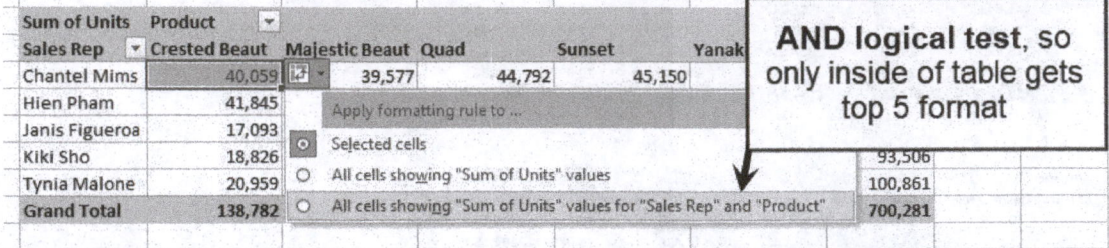

Figure 17.164 *Choose the option for the inside of the cross-tabulated report.*

6. In the PivotTable Fields task pane, drag the Product field from the Columns area to above the Sales Rep field in the Rows area. As shown in Figure 17.165, when you pivot the PivotTable like this, the conditional formatting is dynamic and continues to work as an AND logical test to format the top 5 Sum of Units values for Sale Rep and Product.

Product	Sales Rep	Sum of Units
⊟ Crested Beaut	Chantel Mims	40,059
	Hien Pham	41,845
	Janis Figueroa	17,093
	Kiki Sho	18,826
	Tynia Malone	20,959
Crested Beaut Total		**138,782**
⊟ Majestic Beaut	Chantel Mims	39,577
	Hien Pham	43,762
	Janis Figueroa	19,074
	Kiki Sho	19,501
	Tynia Malone	20,240
Majestic Beaut Total		**142,154**
⊟ Quad	Chantel Mims	44,792
	Hien Pham	42,048
	Janis Figueroa	20,915
	Kiki Sho	17,656
	Tynia Malone	18,860
Quad Total		**144,271**
⊟ Sunset	Chantel Mims	45,150
	Hien Pham	40,420

Figure 17.165 *Conditional formatting adjusts to any pivot you may make in the PivotTable.*

Example 23: Using Data Bars Conditional Formatting to Make an In-Cell Histogram

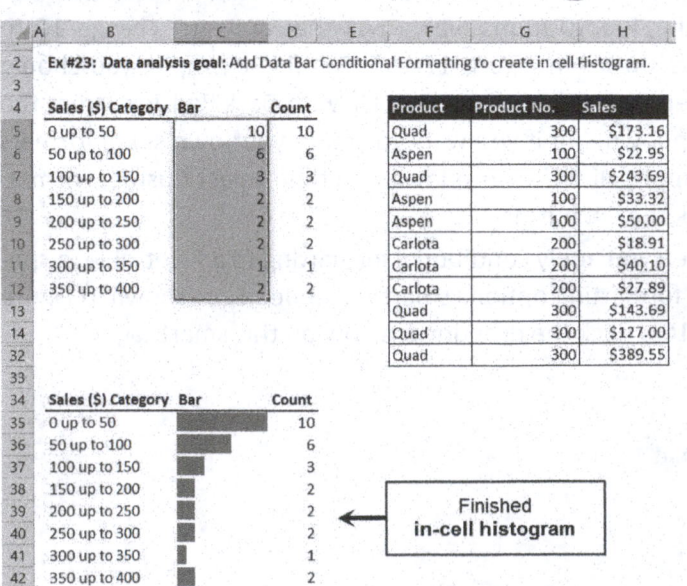

Another way you can use conditional formatting in a table report is to use data bars to create an in-cell histogram to visualize the relative sizes for a give set of numbers.

To complete this example, follow these steps on the worksheet named Ch17(166-170):

1. Select the range C5:C12 (see Figure 17.166).

2. In the Styles group in the Home tab of the Ribbon, click the Conditional Formatting dropdown arrow, select Data Bars, and click Light Blue Data Bar, as shown in Figure 17.167.

Figure 17.166 *Select the range with the count values.*

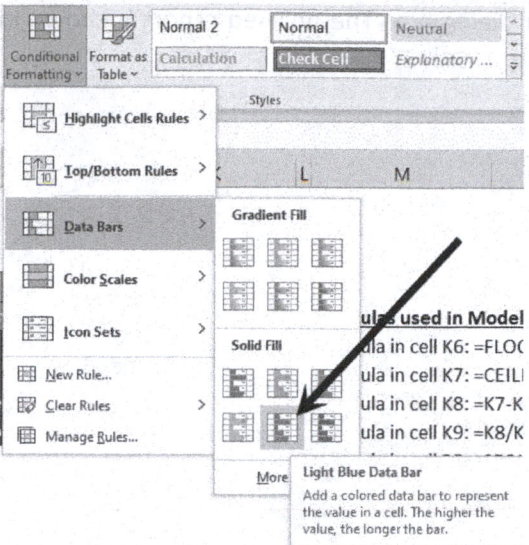

Figure 17.167 *The Data Bars conditional formatting option can create an in-cell histogram.*

3.   To edit the conditional formatting rule to show the conditional formatting bars without the numbers, with the range C5:C12 still selected, click the Conditional Formatting dropdown arrow and then select the Manage Rules option (see Figure 17.168).

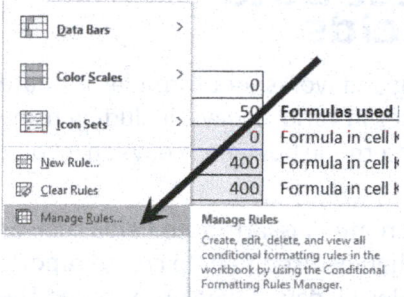

Figure 17.168 *Manage Rules allows you to edit, delete, or move any of your conditional formatting rules.*

4.   In the Conditional Formatting Rules Manager dialog box that appears, select the rule and then click the Edit Rule button (see Figure 17.169).

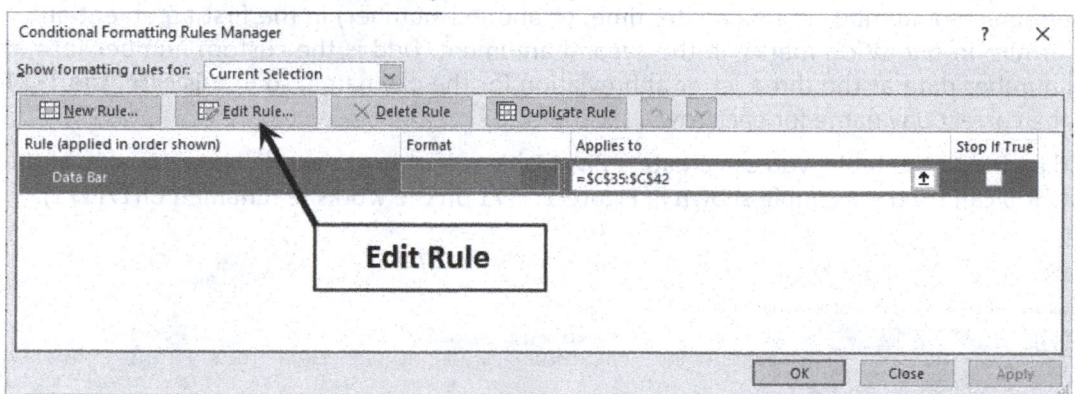

Figure 17.169 *Conditional Formatting Rules Manager dialog box.*

5.   In the Edit Formatting Rule dialog box that appears, to hide the number values and show only the bar in each cell, check the Show Bar Only checkbox (see Figure 17.170).

6.   Click OK in the Edit Formatting Rule dialog box.

7. Click OK in the Conditional Formatting Rules Manager dialog box. The finished report is shown in Figure 17.166.

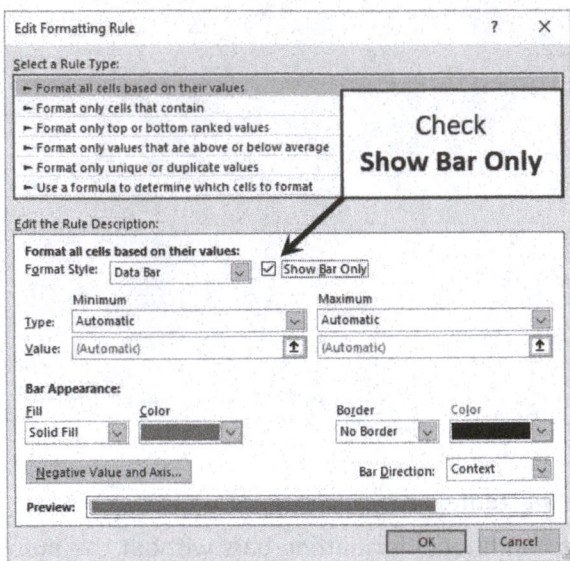

Figure 17.170 *Select Show Bar Only to hide the number value.*

Examples 24 and 25: Using Worksheet Date Formulas to Create Date Attribute Fields

Back in Chapter 11, you learned how to use and create number formatting and worksheet formulas for date and time values. In that chapter, you learned how to format dates and times in various ways, including using custom number formatting, and you learned how to make calculations to determine how many days an invoice is past due and how many hours an employee worked.

In data analysis, sometimes it is important to use worksheet formulas to create date attribute fields such as "day of the week" or "fiscal period" in a proper dataset. These fields can then be used to help create reports and visualizations. For example, if your data analysis goal is to create a sales by day of week report and the only date field in the table is a serial number date, as shown in Figure 17.171, you need to add a date attribute field to mark each record in the table with the name of the day before you can make your report.

As shown in Figure 17.171, you can use the TEXT function to create the day name from a serial number date. The TEXT function requires a number value (a date, time, or another number) in the first argument and a custom number format, in quotation marks, in the second argument. Ddd is the custom number format to display a serial number date as the three-letter abbreviation for the day name, so in this case, the TEXT function delivers the correct day name for each row.

With the new field added to the table, you can create a PivotTable report to show sales totals by day of the week and product. You can try the example shown in Figure 17.171 on the worksheet named Ch17(171).

E5			fx	=TEXT([@Date],"ddd")										
A	B	C	D	E	F	G	H	I	J	K	L	M	N	O
2	Ex #24	**Data analysis goal:** Create Sales by Day of Week Report												
4	Date	Product	Sales ($)	Day of Week		Formula:		Sum of Sales ($)	Product					
5	8/9/22	Yanaki	2,580.02	Tue		◄ =TEXT([@Date],"ddd")		Day of Week	Aspen	Bellen	Carlota	Quad	Yanaki	Grand Total
6	10/14/21	Carlota	1,530.77	Thu				Sat	36,060	52,825	49,252	94,322	77,608	310,068
7	11/16/22	Yanaki	895.13	Wed				Mon	32,031	36,861	37,645	82,211	95,010	283,759
8	8/3/21	Yanaki	502.66	Tue				Fri	36,794	31,276	41,278	66,580	99,387	275,315
9	10/10/22	Quad	3,912.13	Mon				Wed	32,533	37,206	41,394	66,602	83,573	261,307
10	11/10/21	Yanaki	2,075.11	Wed				Thu	37,612	22,945	54,746	73,906	58,324	247,533
11	1/25/23	Yanaki	154.36	Wed				Tue	32,070	48,759	22,453	46,428	78,398	228,108
12	12/28/22	Aspen	572.00	Wed				Sun	23,203	32,294	33,508	48,965	70,253	208,223
13	10/30/21	Yanaki	3,328.19	Sat				**Grand Total**	230,302	262,167	280,277	479,013	562,554	1,814,313
14	1/20/22	Quad	318.31	Thu										
1212	11/11/22	Bellen	279.46	Fri										

Figure 17.171 *The TEXT function can convert a number value to a text value based on a custom number format.*

Figure 17.172 shows 12 common worksheet date formulas you can use to create date attribute fields that are often needed for reporting and visualizing data. The fiscal quarter and fiscal year formulas are used for accounting purposes where the start of the year is defined as some month other than January. Fiscal periods are defined by the reporting entity and are selected so that the end of the year corresponds with the least busy time of the year to help provide more time for year-end reporting duties.

Date	DayNum	ShortDay Name	LongDay Name	Month Num	ShortMonth Name	LongMonth Name	CalendarQuarter	CalendarYear	Fiscal Quarter4	Fiscal Year4	Fiscal Quarter7	Fiscal Year7
Day Num	Day Name "ddd"	Day Name "dddd"	Month Num.	Month Name "mmm"	Month Name "mmmm"	Calendar Quarter Start = 1/1	Calendar Year Start =1/1	Fiscal Quarter Start = 4/1	Fiscal Year Start = 4/1	Fiscal Quarter Start =7/1	Fiscal Year Start = 7/1	
4/1/21	1	Thu	Thursday	4	Apr	April	2	2021	Q 1	2021	Q 4	2020
5/1/21	1	Sat	Saturday	5	May	May	2	2021	Q 1	2021	Q 4	2020
6/1/21	1	Tue	Tuesday	6	Jun	June	2	2021	Q 1	2021	Q 4	2020
7/1/21	1	Thu	Thursday	7	Jul	July	3	2021	Q 2	2021	Q 1	2021
8/1/21	1	Sun	Sunday	8	Aug	August	3	2021	Q 2	2021	Q 1	2021
9/1/21	1	Wed	Wednesday	9	Sep	September	3	2021	Q 2	2021	Q 1	2021
10/1/21	1	Fri	Friday	10	Oct	October	4	2021	Q 3	2021	Q 2	2021
11/1/21	1	Mon	Monday	11	Nov	November	4	2021	Q 3	2021	Q 2	2021
12/1/21	1	Wed	Wednesday	12	Dec	December	4	2021	Q 3	2021	Q 2	2021
1/1/22	1	Sat	Saturday	1	Jan	January	1	2022	Q 4	2021	Q 3	2021
2/1/22	1	Tue	Tuesday	2	Feb	February	1	2022	Q 4	2021	Q 3	2021
3/1/22	1	Tue	Tuesday	3	Mar	March	1	2022	Q 4	2021	Q 3	2021
4/1/22	1	Fri	Friday	4	Apr	April	2	2022	Q 1	2022	Q 4	2021
5/1/22	1	Sun	Sunday	5	May	May	2	2022	Q 1	2022	Q 4	2021
6/1/22	1	Wed	Wednesday	6	Jun	June	2	2022	Q 1	2022	Q 4	2021
7/1/22	1	Fri	Friday	7	Jul	July	3	2022	Q 2	2022	Q 1	2022
8/1/22	1	Mon	Monday	8	Aug	August	3	2022	Q 2	2022	Q 1	2022
9/1/22	1	Thu	Thursday	9	Sep	September	3	2022	Q 2	2022	Q 1	2022
10/1/22	1	Sat	Saturday	10	Oct	October	4	2022	Q 3	2022	Q 2	2022
11/1/22	1	Tue	Tuesday	11	Nov	November	4	2022	Q 3	2022	Q 2	2022
12/1/22	1	Thu	Thursday	12	Dec	December	4	2022	Q 3	2022	Q 2	2022
1/1/23	1	Sun	Sunday	1	Jan	January	1	2023	Q 4	2022	Q 3	2022
2/1/23	1	Wed	Wednesday	2	Feb	February	1	2023	Q 4	2022	Q 3	2022
3/1/23	1	Wed	Wednesday	3	Mar	March	1	2023	Q 4	2022	Q 3	2022

Formulas:

DayNum =DAY([@Date])

ShortDayName =TEXT([@Date],"ddd")

LongDayName =TEXT([@Date],"dddd")

MonthNum =MONTH([@Date])

ShortMonthName =TEXT([@Date],"mmm")

LongMonthName =TEXT([@Date],"mmmm")

CalendarQuarter =ROUNDUP([@MonthNum]/3,0)

CalendarYear =YEAR([@Date])

FiscalQuarter4 ="Q "&IF([@CalendarQuarter]=1,4,[@CalendarQuarter]-1)   Fiscal year starts 4/1

FiscalYear4 =IF([@CalendarQuarter]=1,[@CalendarYear]-1,[@CalendarYear])   Fiscal year starts 4/1

FiscalQuarter7 ="Q "&IF([@CalendarQuarter]<3,[@CalendarQuarter]+2,[@CalendarQuarter]-2)   Fiscal year starts 7/1

FiscalYear7 =IF([@CalendarQuarter]<3,[@CalendarYear]-1,[@CalendarYear])   Fiscal year starts 7/1

Fiscal Period Notes:

Fiscal Year is defined as any 12-month period that the company uses for accounting purposes.

The end for the fiscal year is usually chosen as the least busy part of the year so that the company has more time to complete the year end accounting duties.

Figure 17.172 *Common worksheet date formulas for creating date attribute fields.*

If you are dealing with a small proper dataset in a worksheet (that is, about 50,000 or fewer rows), it can be efficient to use worksheet functions to add these fields to your single proper data source. However, as you will learn in Chapter 18, in other situations, such as with large datasets, it can be more efficient to build a separate date table. In Chapter 19, you will learn how to create a separate date table using tools such as Power Query and DAX formulas.

The good news is that the formulas shown in Figure 17.172 are either identical to or nearly identical to the formulas you will learn about when you build separate date tables using DAX formulas. Using your worksheet formula skills from Chapters 8 through 15, you can try to create the formulas shown in the following list on the worksheet named Ch17(172):

- DayNum =DAY([@Date])
- ShortDayName =TEXT([@Date],"ddd")
- LongDayName =TEXT([@Date],""""dddd"""")

- MonthNum =MONTH([@Date])
- ShortMonthName =TEXT([@Date],"mmm")
- LongMonthName =TEXT([@Date],"mmmm")
- CalendarQuarter =ROUNDUP([@MonthNum]/3,0)
- CalendarYear =YEAR([@Date])
- FiscalQuarter4 ="Q "&IF([@CalendarQuarter]=1,4,[@CalendarQuarter]-1)
- FiscalYear4 =IF([@CalendarQuarter]=1,[@CalendarYear]-1,[@CalendarYear])
- FiscalQuarter7 ="Q "&IF([@CalendarQuarter]<3,[@CalendarQuarter]+2,[@CalendarQuarter]-2)
- FiscalYear7 =IF([@CalendarQuarter]<3,[@CalendarYear]-1,[@CalendarYear])

Cleaning and Transforming Data by Recognizing Patterns in the Data: Worksheet Formulas, Flash Fill, Power Query, or DAX?

When performing data analysis, it is often the case that the data you get is not in the final form you need to create a report or visual. In such a case, you need to clean and perhaps transform the data before you can perform the analysis. For example, in Figure 17.173, the first field in the table, State-Zip, combines the state abbreviation and zip code. If you need to make a summary calculation based on state or sort the table by zip code, it will be extremely difficult to accomplish that with the combined field. You need to break the state abbreviation and zip code into two separate fields. To do this, you need to recognize a pattern in the data that you can use to clean and transform the data. If you are extracting the state abbreviation, for example, the pattern for extracting is the two characters from the left side of the text string. If you are extracting the zip code, the pattern for extracting is the five characters from the right side of the text string.

State-Zip	Sales Rep	Description	Web Site	SS #	ISO Date
CA-94704	Chantel Mullins	Carlota / West: 658	Amazon	047-58-9096	20160715
WA-98106	Tanika Parker	Aspen / South: 345	Gel-boomerangs	022-84-1275	20160229
OR-96011	Christy Hogan	Yanaki / South: 19.5	E-bay	044-99-8241	20160822
CA-98702	Sophia Maxwell	FlatTop / South: 987.75	Amazon	095-16-8959	20160817
WA-98108	Salvador Craig	Carlota / South: 56	Amazon	041-29-5981	20160605
WA-98112	Wanda Stevens	Carlota / East: 23.5	E-bay	068-16-8345	20160206
OR-96011	Chin Pham	Carlota / West: 321	Gel-boomerangs	033-78-7677	20160610
CA-94600	Miki Su	Yanaki / East: 1209.5	Amazon	082-13-8237	20160515

State	Zip	First Name	Last Name	Product	Amount	Web Site	Date
CA	94704	Chantel	Mullins	Carlota	658	Amazon	7/15/16
WA	98106	Tanika	Parker	Aspen	345	Gel-boomerangs	2/29/16
OR	96011	Christy	Hogan	Yanaki	19.5	E-bay	8/22/16
CA	98702	Sophia	Maxwell	FlatTop	987.75	Amazon	8/17/16
WA	98108	Salvador	Craig	Carlota	56	Amazon	6/5/16
WA	98112	Wanda	Stevens	Carlota	23.5	E-bay	2/6/16
OR	96011	Chin	Pham	Carlota	321	Gel-boomerangs	6/10/16
CA	94600	Miki	Su	Yanaki	1209.5	Amazon	5/15/16

Formula for State in cell B15:   =LEFT(B5,2)
Formula for Zip in cell C15:   =RIGHT(B5,5)
Formula for First Name in cell D15:   =LEFT(C5,SEARCH(" ",C5)-1)
Formula for Last Name in cell E15:   =SUBSTITUTE(C5,D15&" ","")
Formula for Product in cell F15:   =LEFT(D5,SEARCH("/",D5)-2)
Formula for Amount in cell G15:   =RIGHT(D5,LEN(D5)-SEARCH(":",D5))+0
Formula for Web Site in cell H15:   =TRIM(E5)
Formula for Date in cell I15:   =TEXT(G5,"0000-00-00")+0

Figure 17.173 *Examples of worksheet text formulas for cleaning data and creating text attribute fields.*

Now look at the second field in the table, Sales Rep. If your goal is to list the first name in one field and the last name in another field, the pattern you need to recognize for the first name is everything before the space; for the last name, the pattern is everything after the space.

As a third example, notice that the Web Site field seems to have extra spaces. Here you don't need to look for a pattern to transform the data; rather, you need to just clean it by removing the extra spaces.

In all three of these examples, as a data analyst, you need to clean and transform the data before you begin the analysis by recognizing the patterns that can help you or determining the actions that are necessary to create a proper dataset that has the correct attribute fields for analysis. There are four main Excel tools that you can use to clean and transform data:

- **Worksheet formulas:** If you have small datasets in a worksheet (with around 50,000 or fewer rows of data) and you want your solution to update instantly when the source data changes, you can use worksheet formulas to create these attribute fields (as illustrated in Example 26).

- **Flash Fill:** If you have a quick one-time data cleaning task, you can use the Flash Fill tool (as illustrated in Example 27).

- **Power Query:** If you have large datasets or complex data cleaning and transforming tasks, you may need to use Power Query. Power Query is the most powerful and versatile tool for cleaning and transforming data because it is designed to do almost any task that can be dreamed up, it has a user interface that creates formulas for you, and it can be used as part of the data importing process. You will learn more about Power Query in Chapter 18.

- **DAX formulas:** If you have large datasets or complex data cleaning and transformation tasks, you may need to use DAX formulas. DAX can also be used to clean data in some cases in Power Pivot and Power BI. You will learn how to use DAX formulas in Chapter 18.

Example 26: Using Worksheet Text Formulas to Clean and Transform Data and Create Text Attribute Fields

Table 17.4 lists some of the text worksheet functions that perform data cleaning and transformation tasks and deliver text value results.

Table 17.4 Worksheet Functions for Data Cleaning and Transformation

Function	Description
LEFT	Extracts a given number of characters from the left of a text string.
RIGHT	Extracts a given number of characters from the right of a text string.
MID	Extracts text from the middle of a text string, given a character starting position and the number of characters to extract.
SEARCH	Counting characters left to right, reports the starting position of text that you specify within a second text string. For example, in the text string "start", the text r is in position 4. SEARCH is not case-sensitive.
FIND	Counting characters left to right, reports the starting position of text that you specify within a second text item. For example, in the text string "Rad", the text R is in position 1. FIND is not case-sensitive.
LEN	Counts the number of characters or digits in a cell.
REPLACE	Replaces part of a text string with text you specify, given a starting number and the number of characters.
SUBSTITUTE	Finds some text and replaces it with different text.
TRIM	Removes all spaces from a text string except for single spaces between words.
TEXT	Converts a number value to a text value based on the specified custom number formatting.

Figure 17.173 shows eight examples of worksheet text formulas that can be used to clean and transform data. Using your worksheet formula skills from Chapters 8 through 15, you can try to create the formulas shown in that list on the worksheet named Ch17(173).

Example 27: Using Flash Fill to Perform One-Time Cleaning Tasks Where the Pattern Is Consistent

Flash Fill has been one of the most beloved data analysis tools since it debuted in Excel 2013. If you have a one-time data cleaning task, and the pattern for extracting data is the same for every row in the table, then Flash Fill is the tool you want to use. However, if the pattern is not consistent in every row, then Flash Fill can be hard to use and may even give you incorrect results, especially if you have a large dataset where it is hard to determine whether a perceived pattern is the same in every row. In addition, when Flash Fill cleans data, the solution created does not automatically update if the source data changes, so Flash Fill is usually not a good tool for data analysis solutions that will later be updated with new data. (Power Query and worksheet formulas are designed specifically for situations where you will get new data later and you need the solution to update.) Nevertheless, for separating first and last names or getting a sales number from a description, there is no other tool as fast and easy as Flash Fill.

To use Flash Fill, you simply type one or two examples of the cleaned data that you want in the column directly to the right of the table, and the tool automatically spills the results down the column. Microsoft calls the process that Flash Fill uses "programming by example," which just means that after you give it an example of the cleaned data that you want, behind the scenes, Excel creates a program to automatically clean the data.

The figures in this example show a dataset with data that needs to be cleaned. Importantly, each cleaning task in each row has a consistent pattern for extracting the data.

To complete this example, follow these steps on the worksheet named Ch17(174-178):

1. To find the state portion of the text in the State-Zip column, select cell E5, type **CA**, and press the Enter key.

2. Type **W**. As shown in Figure 17.174, a ghost list appears, offering you a suggested list of cleaned data. In this case, the pattern is simple: Always get the two leftmost characters. The Flash Fill ghost list shows exactly what you want.

	A	B	C	D	E	F	G	H	I	J
2		Ex# 27	Examples of data cleaning and transforming using Flash Fill.							
4		State-Zip	Sales Rep	Description	State	Zip	First Name	Last Name	Product	Amount
5		CA-94704	Chantel Mullins	Carlota / West: 658	CA					
6		WA-98106	Tanika Parker	Aspen / South: 345	WA					
7		OR-96011	Christy Hogan	Yanaki / South: 19.5	OR					
8		CA-98702	Sophia Maxwell	FlatTop / South: 987.75	CA					
9		WA-98108	Salvador Craig	Carlota / South: 56	WA					
10		WA-98112	Wanda Stevens	Carlota / East: 23.5	WA					
11		OR-96011	Chin Pham	Carlota / West: 321	OR					
12		CA-94600	Miki Su	Yanaki / East: 1209.5	CA					
13										

Figure 17.174 *When there a consistent pattern in the data, when you give Flash Fill two examples, it knows what to do.*

3. To accept the list of suggested cleaned data points, press Enter. Figure 17.175 shows the new field of cleaned data.

	A	B	C	D	E	F	G	H	I	J
2		Ex# 27	Examples of data cleaning and transforming using Flash Fill.							
4		State-Zip	Sales Rep	Description	State	Zip	First Name	Last Name	Product	Amount
5		CA-94704	Chantel Mullins	Carlota / West: 658	CA					
6		WA-98106	Tanika Parker	Aspen / South: 345	WA					
7		OR-96011	Christy Hogan	Yanaki / South: 19.5	OR					
8		CA-98702	Sophia Maxwell	FlatTop / South: 987.75	CA					
9		WA-98108	Salvador Craig	Carlota / South: 56	WA					
10		WA-98112	Wanda Stevens	Carlota / East: 23.5	WA					
11		OR-96011	Chin Pham	Carlota / West: 321	OR					
12		CA-94600	Miki Su	Yanaki / East: 1209.5	CA					

Figure 17.175 *To accept the ghost list of suggested values, press Enter.*

4. To find the zip code portion of the State-Zip column, select cell F5, type **94704**, and press the Enter key.

5. As shown in Figure 17.176, because you are 100% sure that the pattern "always get the five right-most characters" is correct, you can use the keyboard shortcut for Flash Fill: Ctrl+E. As shown in Figure 17.177, Flash Fill correctly creates a column filled with clean zip codes.

	A	B	C	D	E	F	G	H	I	J
2		Ex# 27	Examples of data cleaning and transforming using Flash Fill.							
4		State-Zip	Sales Rep	Description	State	Zip	First Name	Last Name	Product	Amount
5		CA-94704	Chantel Mullins	Carlota / West: 658	CA	94704				
6		WA-98106	Tanika Parker	Aspen / South: 345	WA		Invoke Flash Fill with:			
7		OR-96011	Christy Hogan	Yanaki / South: 19.5	OR		**Ctrl + E**			
8		CA-98702	Sophia Maxwell	FlatTop / South: 987.75	CA					
9		WA-98108	Salvador Craig	Carlota / South: 56	WA					
10		WA-98112	Wanda Stevens	Carlota / East: 23.5	WA					
11		OR-96011	Chin Pham	Carlota / West: 321	OR					
12		CA-94600	Miki Su	Yanaki / East: 1209.5	CA					

Figure 17.176 *When there is a consistent pattern in the data, you can use the keyboard shortcut Ctrl+E for Flash Fill.*

	A	B	C	D	E	F	G	H	I	J
2		Ex# 27	Examples of data cleaning and transforming using Flash Fill.							
4		State-Zip	Sales Rep	Description	State	Zip	First Name	Last Name	Product	Amount
5		CA-94704	Chantel Mullins	Carlota / West: 658	CA	94704				
6		WA-98106	Tanika Parker	Aspen / South: 345	WA	98106				
7		OR-96011	Christy Hogan	Yanaki / South: 19.5	OR	96011				
8		CA-98702	Sophia Maxwell	FlatTop / South: 987.75	CA	98702				
9		WA-98108	Salvador Craig	Carlota / South: 56	WA	98108				
10		WA-98112	Wanda Stevens	Carlota / East: 23.5	WA	98112				
11		OR-96011	Chin Pham	Carlota / West: 321	OR	96011				
12		CA-94600	Miki Su	Yanaki / East: 1209.5	CA	94600				

Figure 17.177 *After just one example and the keyboard shortcut Ctrl+E, Flash Fill delivers the correct result.*

6. For the remaining four fields, use Flash Fill to clean the data and create the new field. Figure 17.178 shows the correct results for the remaining four fields after using Flash Fill.

	A	B	C	D	E	F	G	H	I	J
2		Ex# 27	Examples of data cleaning and transforming using Flash Fill.							
4		State-Zip	Sales Rep	Description	State	Zip	First Name	Last Name	Product	Amount
5		CA-94704	Chantel Mullins	Carlota / West: 658	CA	94704	Chantel	Mullins	Carlota	658
6		WA-98106	Tanika Parker	Aspen / South: 345	WA	98106	Tanika	Parker	Aspen	345
7		OR-96011	Christy Hogan	Yanaki / South: 19.5	OR	96011	Christy	Hogan	Yanaki	19.5
8		CA-98702	Sophia Maxwell	FlatTop / South: 987.75	CA	98702	Sophia	Maxwell	FlatTop	987.75
9		WA-98108	Salvador Craig	Carlota / South: 56	WA	98108	Salvador	Craig	Carlota	56
10		WA-98112	Wanda Stevens	Carlota / East: 23.5	WA	98112	Wanda	Stevens	Carlota	23.5
11		OR-96011	Chin Pham	Carlota / West: 321	OR	96011	Chin	Pham	Carlota	321
12		CA-94600	Miki Su	Yanaki / East: 1209.5	CA	94600	Miki	Su	Yanaki	1209.5

Figure 17.178 *One-time data cleaning tasks with Flash Fill when the pattern for cleaning is simple.*

Example 28: Using Dashboards to Gauge Activity as New Data Arrives

A *dashboard*—which can include summary reports, visualizations, and other elements all in one location—allows user to monitor activity as new data arrives. Just like the dashboard in a car, a dashboard in Excel should present information that is required for making good decisions. A dashboard allows you to gather various tables, reports, charts, visualizations, and other useful information and pin them in one location so that decision makers can view and interact with the information to gauge performance, see patterns and trends, and gain insights. You already saw a dashboard in Example 15 in this chapter. Figure 17.179 shows the dashboard that you created in that example and also shows new data that can be added to update the dashboard.

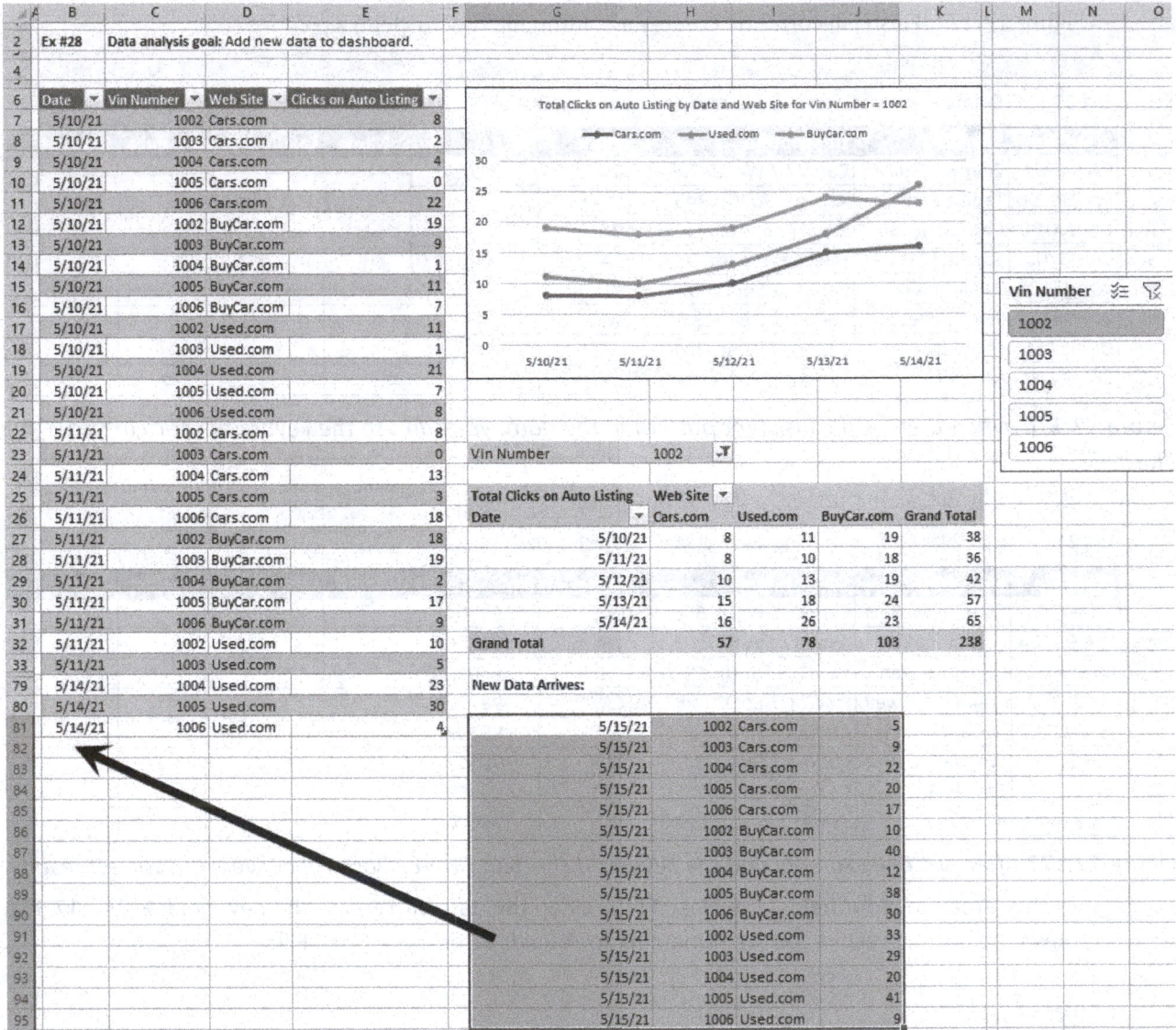

Figure 17.179 *The new data for 5/15/21 can be added to the bottom of the Excel Table.*

The purpose of the dashboard in this example is to allow an auto sales website manager to gauge the number of clicks that a particular auto listing gets as the presentation of the auto at the website changes. For example, the manager changed the picture of the automobile with VIN 1002 at the website Used.com on 5/13/21. In Figure 17.179, you can see that the day after the picture was changed at Used.com, the number of clicks increased. At the other two websites, where the picture was not changed, the number of clicks tended not to increase that day. Figure 17.180 shows the dashboard after the new data for the date 5/15/21 has been added. After the PivotTable is refreshed, the new data helps reveal that the number of clicks for the website with the new picture dramatically increased, whereas for the websites that did not have the picture changed, there was a significant decrease in clicks.

Although there are many variables involved in driving people to click on a link, and it may or may not be because of a single action like changing a picture, as the dashboard is updated each day, the changing information helps the manager consider why the trends are occurring and make better decisions based on data.

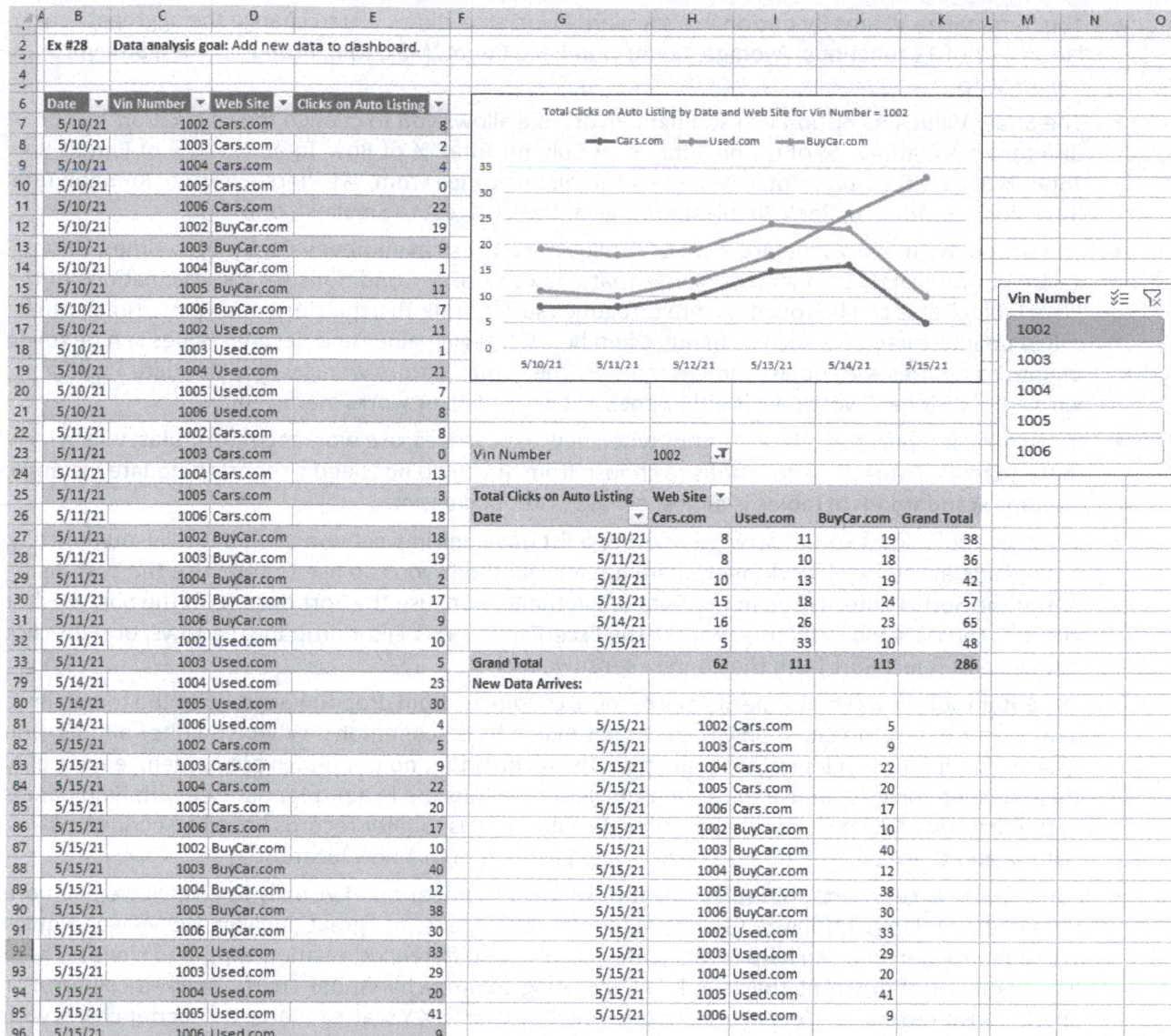

Figure 17.180 *After you refresh the PivotTable, the dashboard updates to show new trends.*

Key Concepts in Chapter 17

- **Data analysis** involves converting raw data into useful information for decision makers. **Business intelligence** involves converting raw data into useful information for decision makers in a business context. **Useful information** includes reports, visuals, and other presentations of data that can help people make data-driven, evidence-based decisions.

- The **standard PivotTable** tool has been around since 1993 and is distinct from the **Data Model PivotTable**, which was released in 2009. These two tools use the same user interface that allows users to drag and drop fields to create summary reports based on conditional calculations, such as adding sales or costs by product. The standard PivotTable is considered the definitive quick and easy, ad hoc data analysis tool because it is very easy to use. It is a popular tool for making simple calculations like adding, counting, or calculating percentages. However, with a lot of data (about 50,000 or more rows) or when you need to make complex calculations, you should use the Data Model PivotTable tool.

- When you store the data in an Excel worksheet and then make a standard PivotTable, the data is stored in two locations: the worksheet and the **standard PivotTable cache**. Storing the same data in two locations increases the file size of the Excel workbook. For small datasets (under about 50,000 rows of data), it is fine to store the data in two locations. When you create a second PivotTable report from the table of data in the worksheet, a second cache of data is not created; instead, the second PivotTable report uses the already established cache of data that was created from the first report.

- The **Summarize Values By option** in a standard PivotTable allows you to change the aggregate calculation to 1 of 11 functions: Average, Count Numbers, Count, Max, Min, Product, Stdev, Stdevp, Sum, Var, or Varp.

- The **Show Values As option** in a standard PivotTable allows you to change the calculation to 1 of 14 different calculations: % of Grand Total, % of Column Total, % of Row Total, % Of, % of Parent Row Total, % of Parent Column Total, % of Parent Total, Difference From, % Difference From, Running Total In, % Running Total In, Rank Smallest to Largest, Rank Largest to Smallest, or Index.

- The **Group feature** in a standard PivotTable allows you to group number values (dates, times, decimal values, or integers) to create categories that you can use as conditions for the calculations in the PivotTable. Dates can be rolled up into categories such as months, quarters, and years. Times can be rolled up into categories such as minutes and hours. Integer values and decimal values can be rolled up into categories with upper and lower limits. The Group feature works with a standard PivotTable; with a Data Model PivotTable, it either does not work at all or works inefficiently.

- If you need a report to update instantly when new data arrives, use **worksheet formulas**, which have more than 450 worksheet functions to choose from. If you do not need a report to update instantly, creating **standard PivotTables** is almost always faster and easier.

- The **Sort tool** allows you to arrange or order a list of values in a column alphabetically, numerically, or by color. In the Excel worksheet, there are four methods you can use to sort: Use the Sort dialog box in the Sort & Filter group in the Data tab in the Ribbon, use the Sort buttons in the Sort & Filter group in the Data tab in the Ribbon, use the Excel Table Sort & Filter dropdown arrows, or right-click any cell and select Sort from the context-sensitive menu.

- The **Filter tool** allows you to specify one or more conditions from dropdown arrows at the top of fields in a proper dataset to show only records that match those conditions. When you filter a table, you specify conditions in a logical test, and then the records that do not match are hidden, leaving only the matching records. To use the Filter tool, your data must be in a proper dataset with field names in the first row. The most common use for the Filter tool is to filter records based on conditions and criteria and then copy the filtered records and paste them to a new location.

- You can use **Excel charts** to display quantitative data (number data) visually to give viewers a more immediate and impactful way to understand the data. Charts are great at giving the viewer a quick visual impression and can help reveal patterns, relative differences, relationships, and trends. There are a number of different charts in Excel, including column charts, bar charts, stacked column/bar charts, clustered column/bar charts, histograms, line charts, X-Y scatter charts, X-Y scatter charts with straight lines, break-even charts, and maps.

- The **overriding rule for visualizing data** is to eliminate all extraneous elements in a visualization that do not help deliver the message. The world-renowned visualization expert Edward R. Tufte stated this rule in two succinct phrases: "No chart junk," which means that if a chart contains an element that does not help deliver the message, delete it, and "Use a high data-to-ink ratio," which means emphasize the data over non-data elements such as lines, boxes, and busy colors.

- When you create **categories with upper and lower limits for a quantitative variable** for reports and visualizations, you must make sure to create categories that are mutually exclusive so that included numbers appear in only one category and collectively exhaustive so that all numbers in the dataset are included in the calculations. How the lower and upper limits are created for different tools in Excel varies.

- The **Analyze Data** feature uses artificial intelligence to create reports and visualizations from proper datasets. This feature is not a safe tool for users who have no data analysis experience.

- When you want to present all the numeric details in an data analysis solution, use a **table report**.

- **PivotTable styles** can be used to create reusable table styles.

- **Conditional formatting** can be used to help visualize data. You can build your own logical formulas to apply the formatting, and you can also use built-in conditional formatting rules such as the Color Scales, Top 10, and Data Bars rules.

- **Cleaning and transforming data** is the process of converting unusable data into data that you can use for reports and visuals. The four main Excel tools that you can use to clean and transform data are worksheet formulas, Flash Fill, Power Query, and DAX formulas. Worksheet formulas are good for small datasets when you want the solution to update instantly. Flash Fill is good when you have one-time data cleaning tasks and the pattern for the cleaning task is consistent. Power Query is the most powerful and versatile data cleaning and transformation tool. DAX can be a good tool for cleaning and transforming big data.

- A **dashboard** allows you to gather various tables, reports, charts, visualizations, and other useful information and pin them in one location so that decision makers can view and interact with the information to gauge performance, see patterns and trends, and gain insights.

Keyboard Shortcuts Learned in Chapter 17

Keyboard Shortcut	Description
Alt, N, V, T	When a single cell is selected in a table in the worksheet, opens the PivotTable from the Table/Range dialog box
Alt, N, V, T, Enter	When a single cell is selected in a table in the worksheet, creates a new standard PivotTable on a new worksheet
Alt, D, P	Opens the legacy standard PivotTable three-step wizard to create a new cache of data
Ctrl+Shift+L	Toggles the Sort & Filter dropdown arrows on and off for each field in a table
Ctrl+H	Opens the Replace dialog box
Ctrl+E	Invokes Flash Fill
Ctrl+1	Opens the Format Chart Element task pane for the selected chart element

Practice Problems for Chapter 17

Practice Problem 1

In your Excel file for this chapter (Ch17-Excel365-IntroDataAnalysis.xlsx), go to the worksheet named PPCh17(1) and create the solution for this practice problem. Figure 17.181 shows the goal that is listed on that worksheet.

	A	B	C	D	E	F
2		Goal:	Create Frequency Distribution Report. "Count of Phones Purchased Report & % Phones Purchased" Report.			
3			This is an example of:			
4			1) A small data set.			
5			2) Built-in Calculations in a Standard PivotTable are perfect for the task at hand.			
6			3) We do not need report to update instantly when source data changes.			
7			4) This is a one time sample of data that we do not need to refresh			
8						
9			Data = about 560 rows =			
10			From sample of Phone Purchases			
11						
12			Phones Purchased			
13			Apple iPhone 9			
14			Apple iPhone 9			
15			Apple iPhone 9			
16			Samsung Galaxy S8			
17			Apple iPhone 10			
18			Samsung Galaxy S5			
19			Samsung Galaxy S5			
570			Pixel			
571			Apple iPhone 10			

Figure 17.181 *On the worksheet PPCh17(1), create a formula to total the bank deposit.*

When you are done with this problem, you can check your work against the answer sheet named PPCh17(1an).

Practice Problem 2

In your Excel file for this chapter (Ch17-Excel365-IntroDataAnalysis.xlsx), go to the worksheet named PPCh17(2) and create the solution for this practice problem. Figure 17.182 shows the goal that is listed on that worksheet.

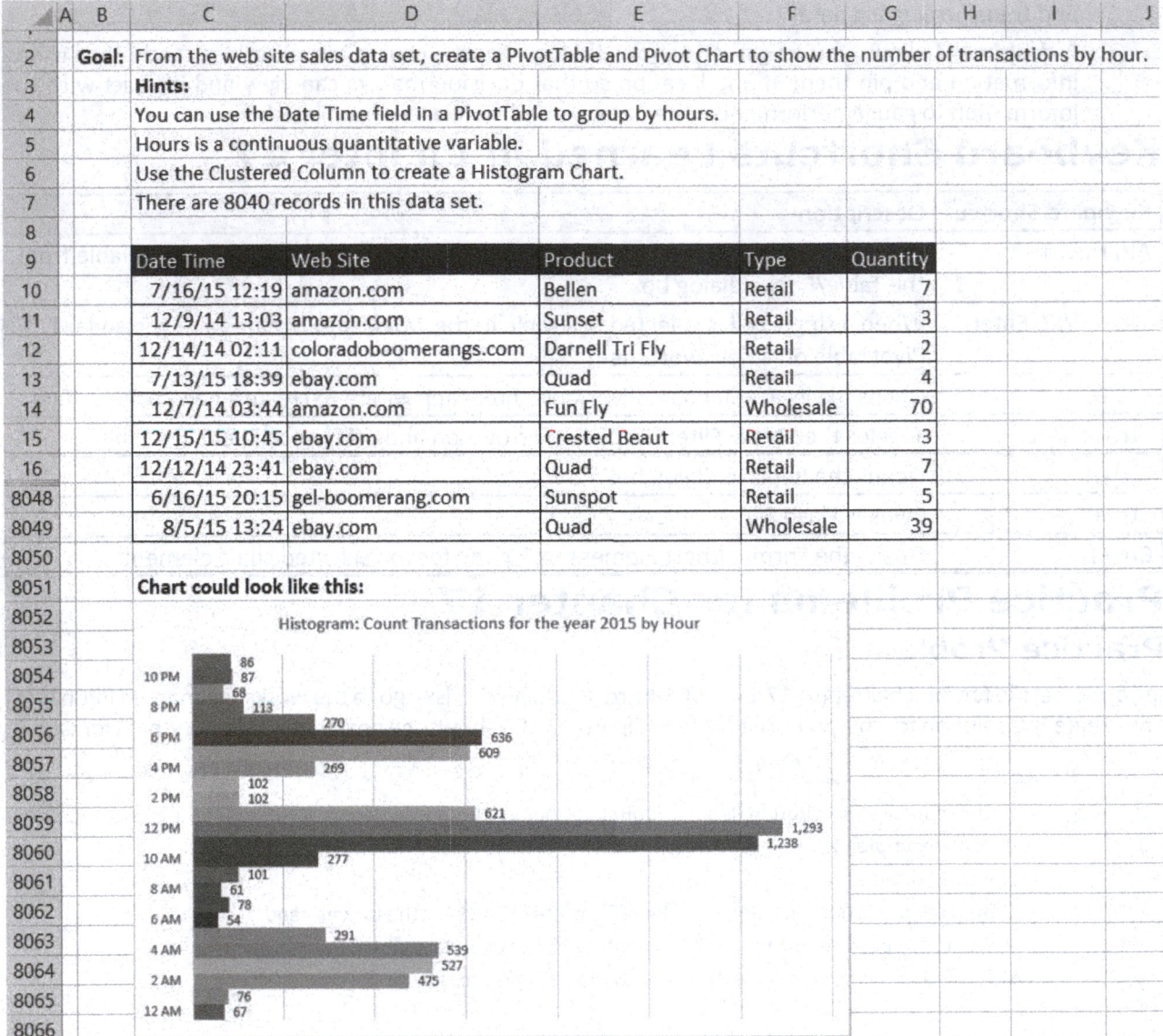

Figure 17.182 *On the worksheet PPCh17(2), create a histogram to count transactions by hour.*

When you are done with this problem, you can check your work against the answer sheet named PPCh17(2an).

Practice Problem 3

In your Excel file for this chapter (Ch17-Excel365-IntroDataAnalysis.xlsx), go to the worksheet named PPCh17(3) and create the solution for this practice problem. Figure 17.183 shows the goal that is listed on that worksheet.

	A	B	C	D	E	F	G	H	I

Goal: Create Dashboard to monitor month sales and sales rep COGS by Region.

Steps: 1) Create a PivotTable on this sheet that adds Sales for each Month in each Year. Name your PivotTable.

2) Then add a Slicer for the Region Column.

3) Create a second PivotTable on this sheet that adds COGS for each Sales Rep. Name the PivotTable.

4) Then Connect the Slicer to this second PivotTable.

5) Add Formatting and present it as a dashboard.

Hints: To name a PivotTable, right-click PivotTable report, click PivotTable Options,

then in PivotTable Options dialog box, use PivotTable Name textbox.

To connect both PivotTable to one Slicer, right-click the Slicer, click on Report Connections,

then check the checkbox for both PivotTable.

There are 1,999 records in the below table.

Date	Region	Sales Rep	Customer	Product	COGS	Sales
10/7/18	SouthEast	Luke	Amazon.com	AIM Item	$3,641.63	$6,278.68
10/26/17	West	Jeri	Costco	UYR Item	$3,188.92	$7,416.09
5/20/18	North	Sheliadawn	Home Depot	XOU Item	$3,636.08	$6,269.11
9/24/17	MidWest	Jon	Whole Foods	ILP Item	$2,982.53	$5,422.79
1/14/18	MidWest	Steven	McLendon's Hardware	LXS Item	$6,385.73	$6,829.66
4/3/17	West	Sheliadawn	Whole Foods	MFB Item	$1,174.98	$2,611.06
1/20/18	NorthEast	Jeri	Nature Company	NEE Item	$2,790.65	$4,811.47
2/26/17	SouthEast	Jeri	Home Depot	JHF Item	$15.06	$22.15
12/24/18	NorthEast	Chin	The Economist	BFQ Item	$435.40	$1,012.56

Finished dashboard could look like this:

Month Report, Sales Rep Report

Years	Date	Sum of Sales ($)
⊟ 2017	Jan	122,141
	Feb	53,982
	Mar	73,950
	Apr	82,211
	May	34,561
	Jun	66,706
	Jul	72,840
	Aug	60,449
	Sep	55,968
	Oct	41,487
	Nov	55,810
	Dec	71,218
2017 Total		**791,323**
⊟ 2018	Jan	73,028
	Feb	60,958
	Mar	101,747
	Apr	60,090
	May	94,077
	Jun	78,836
	Jul	71,294
	Aug	39,386
	Sep	51,253
	Oct	85,841
	Nov	42,484
	Dec	101,183
2018 Total		**860,179**
Grand Total		**1,651,502**

Region

- MidWest
- North
- NorthEast
- SouthEast
- West

Sales Rep	Sum of COGS ($)
Chin	158,162
Jeri	134,551
Jon	144,159
Luke	129,775
Rhonda	143,313
Sheliadawn	111,124
Steven	97,104
Troung	146,450
Grand Total	**1,064,639**

Figure 17.183 *On the worksheet PPCh17(3), create a monthly sales and COGS dashboard.*

When you are done with this problem, you can check your work against the answer sheet named PPCh17(3an).

Practice Problem 4

In your Excel file for this chapter (Ch17-Excel365-IntroDataAnalysis.xlsx), go to the worksheet named PPCh17(4) and create the solution for this practice problem. Figure 17.184 shows the goal that is listed on that worksheet.

	A B	C	D	E	F	N
2	Goal:	Using the "table visualization principles", make this table more effective:				
3		To display the numbers in millions, you can use the Custom Number Formatting: #,###,,				
4						
5		GDP/breakdown at constant 2005 prices in US Dollars (all countries)				
6						
7		Country	2000	2001	2002	2010
8		Argentina	201,962,716,310.6	193,058,497,457.6	172,025,773,978.4	293,702,179,733.4
9		Belgium	355,035,280,793.6	358,316,769,281.8	363,904,793,271.8	412,181,652,726.6
10		Brazil	768,855,134,604.8	778,951,115,997.1	799,656,369,540.0	1,096,449,538,478.6
11		Canada	1,030,602,342,820.8	1,045,009,504,940.3	1,073,203,622,405.6	1,234,996,659,985.3
12		Finland	179,902,129,035.5	184,544,968,412.7	187,645,998,109.7	212,913,371,138.6
13		France	2,029,983,087,101.4	2,069,666,218,972.3	2,092,809,530,915.8	2,289,832,363,328.9
14		Germany	2,777,363,467,542.2	2,824,447,709,015.7	2,824,751,452,450.8	3,037,693,759,017.1
15		Greece	204,952,992,090.7	212,611,923,593.5	219,335,920,011.9	244,188,802,666.3
16		Greenland	1,527,406,281.9	1,546,789,610.3	1,531,767,530.8	1,868,795,763.2
17		Ireland	165,931,285,098.8	174,682,021,353.8	184,880,332,774.0	211,702,532,107.1
18		Italy	1,768,788,613,639.8	1,800,146,122,469.3	1,804,660,622,792.6	1,825,019,275,730.0
19		Luxembourg	31,791,026,215.0	32,426,876,585.6	33,489,155,847.4	41,349,425,458.9
20		Mexico	788,246,519,932.4	787,987,769,283.2	794,070,620,626.4	952,037,461,072.8
21		Norway	276,894,377,648.0	282,668,537,410.8	286,732,484,021.1	323,262,710,846.6
22		Panama	12,523,862,775.4	12,595,783,928.5	12,876,529,746.5	23,122,705,775.9
23		Peru	61,705,803,374.4	62,087,078,797.9	65,473,015,607.0	106,185,066,601.4
24		Poland	262,992,731,637.2	266,162,582,612.6	270,004,636,092.5	383,287,772,563.6
25		Portugal	188,974,536,610.5	192,646,903,601.8	194,127,912,503.9	203,428,770,843.8
26		Saudi Arabia	258,610,834,969.3	260,026,971,690.8	260,359,146,865.2	435,993,880,532.9
27		Slovakia	38,278,398,188.2	39,550,521,367.3	41,415,097,698.9	61,401,650,486.4
28		Slovenia	30,461,740,243.5	31,360,185,920.5	32,563,216,768.6	39,591,559,883.1
29		Spain	979,526,062,985.8	1,018,717,818,112.4	1,048,054,809,786.9	1,219,911,122,126.1
30		Sweden	341,717,395,402.3	347,059,840,287.9	354,256,394,050.4	420,871,356,306.8
31		Switzerland	378,377,143,051.9	383,850,698,282.4	384,401,146,039.9	454,938,016,491.1
32		Turkey	386,584,134,135.9	364,558,594,063.9	387,029,401,185.4	565,098,632,773.9
33		United Arab Emirate	139,150,824,019.6	141,065,061,316.3	144,497,703,072.0	203,434,946,892.6
34		United Kingdom	2,087,472,757,637.1	2,143,094,196,538.3	2,195,648,906,230.7	2,477,504,671,262.6
35		United States	11,553,315,901,319.6	11,666,074,165,730.0	11,874,444,226,541.1	13,599,255,645,064.3
36		Venezuela	128,278,574,764.1	132,632,652,467.3	120,887,172,490.0	174,550,915,575.9

Figure 17.184 *On the worksheet PPCh17(4), format the table to make it more effective.*

When you are done with this problem, you can check your work against the answer sheet named PPCh17(4an).

Practice Problem 5

In your Excel file for this chapter (Ch17-Excel365-IntroDataAnalysis.xlsx), go to the worksheet named PPCh17(5) and create the solution for this practice problem. Figure 17.185 shows the goal that is listed on that worksheet.

	A	B	C	D	E	F	G	H	I	J
2		Goals:	From the proper data set below, create the report shown here:							
3		Hints:	Use the Show Values As calculation: "% of Parent Total" for Customer.							
4			There are 1,999 records in the below table.							
5										
6		Sales Rep	Customer	Product	Sales		Customer ⌕	Sales Rep ▾	Total Sales ($)	Sales Rep Sales as % of Customer Total
7		Luke	Amazon.com	AIM Item	$6,278.68		Amazon.com	Chin	92,828	11.80%
8		Jeri	Costco	UYR Item	$7,416.09			Jeri	118,225	15.03%
9		Sheliadawn	Home Depot	XOU Item	$6,269.11			Jon	132,248	16.82%
10		Jon	Whole Foods	ILP Item	$5,422.79			Luke	92,790	11.80%
11		Steven	McLendon's Hardware	LXS Item	$6,829.66			Rhonda	80,610	10.25%
12		Sheliadawn	Whole Foods	MFB Item	$2,611.06			Sheliadawn	100,472	12.78%
13		Jeri	Nature Company	NEE Item	$4,811.47			Steven	94,309	11.99%
14		Jeri	Home Depot	JHF Item	$22.15			Troung	74,865	9.52%
15		Jeri	Amazon.com	LII Item	$8,206.48		Amazon.com Total		786,347	100.00%
16		Jeri	Costco	FSJ Item	$8,449.61		Google	Chin	125,591	17.25%
17		Jeri	Yahoo	HVH Item	$2,143.19			Jeri	85,245	11.71%
18		Chin	Sherman Williams	YVD Item	$6,111.65			Jon	79,590	10.93%
19		Luke	Google	TTM Item	$271.58			Luke	75,958	10.43%
20		Rhonda	Costco	MKA Item	$2,552.46			Rhonda	80,542	11.06%
21		Troung	McLendon's Hardware	EVO Item	$9,828.64			Sheliadawn	110,524	15.18%
22		Rhonda	The Economist	EYG Item	$4,452.68			Steven	74,091	10.18%
23		Luke	Yahoo	LVD Item	$322.21			Troung	96,445	13.25%
24		Luke	Nature Company	BCD Item	$1,024.66		Google Total		727,986	100.00%
25		Jon	Costco	UGN Item	$2,004.95		Yahoo	Chin	124,946	17.22%
26		Chin	Solar and Wind Inc.	PET Item	$8,150.36			Jeri	83,180	11.47%
27		Jeri	ExcellsVeryFun.com	AIU Item	$6,991.91			Jon	75,327	10.38%
28		Steven	The Economist	XIM Item	$5,837.66			Luke	76,219	10.51%
29		Jeri	Amazon.com	AIZ Item	$923.44			Rhonda	89,555	12.34%
30		Chin	The Economist	VBF Item	$2,442.61			Sheliadawn	80,300	11.07%
31		Rhonda	Costco	VCN Item	$3,989.02			Steven	71,138	9.81%
32		Troung	ExcellsVeryFun.com	GHH Item	$8,701.78			Troung	124,836	17.21%
33		Jeri	Home Depot	WPD Item	$5,414.79		Yahoo Total		725,501	100.00%
34		Chin	Costco	YWP Item	$1,298.25		Grand Total		2,239,834	
35		Sheliadawn	Home Depot	BPJ Item	$1,238.20					

Figure 17.185 *On the worksheet PPCh17(5), create a sales rep by customer sales report.*

When you are done with this problem, you can check your work against the answer sheet named PPCh17(5an).

Practice Problem 6

In your Excel file for this chapter (Ch17-Excel365-IntroDataAnalysis.xlsx), go to the worksheet named PPCh17(6) and create the solution for this practice problem. Figure 17.186 shows the goal that is listed on that worksheet.

	A	B	C	D	E	F	G	H	I	J	K
2		**Goal:**	Using Conditional Formatting, Format Numbers by Month and Sales Rep so that								
3			the largest 1/3 are blue, the smallest 1/3 are red and the middle 1/3 are white.								
4		**Hint:**	For the range D7:I16, apply the Conditional Formatting "Blue-White-Red Color Scale".								
5											
6			Sales Rep	Jan	Feb	Mar	Apr	May	Jun	Total	
7			Ivelisse Peel	696	420	722	428	279	349	2,894	
8			Sigrid Grooms	429	419	146	253	730	473	2,450	
9			Majorie Flaherty	563	325	197	229	664	275	2,253	
10			Stevie Fisk	710	287	209	485	459	498	2,648	
11			Nova Bolduc	767	283	624	149	156	460	2,439	
12			Naoma Moyer	220	282	390	714	563	783	2,952	
13			Eric Minter	231	735	416	378	368	353	2,481	
14			Dotty Dorn	229	496	519	309	616	405	2,574	
15			Kandice Hussey	752	773	483	220	597	175	3,000	
16			Cleo Nixon	255	567	237	692	245	472	2,468	
17			Total	4,852	4,587	3,943	3,857	4,677	4,243	26,159	

Figure 17.186 *On the worksheet PPCh17(6), add Color Scales conditional formatting to make the table more effective.*

When you are done with this problem, you can check your work against the answer sheet named PPCh17(6an).

Practice Problem 7

In your Excel file for this chapter (Ch17-Excel365-IntroDataAnalysis.xlsx), go to the worksheet named PPCh17(7) and create the solution for this practice problem. Figure 17.187 shows the goal that is listed on that worksheet.

	A	B	C	D	E	F	G	H	I
2		**Goal:**	Create a chart that shows the trend over time (year).						
3		**Hint:**	If the horizontal axis does not show years, use the Select Data dialog box to						
4			edit the horizontal categories (axis labels).						
5			You can access the Select Data dialog box by right-clicking the chart.						
6									
7			Year	Sales					
8			2005	$577,023					
9			2006	$566,239					
10			2007	$580,987					
11			2008	$603,500					
12			2009	$605,821					
13			2010	$669,356					
14			2011	$664,569					
15			2012	$717,832					
16			2013	$700,144					

Figure 17.187 *On the worksheet PPCh17(7), create a chart to show the sales changes over years.*

When you are done with this problem, you can check your work against the answer sheet named PPCh17(7an).

Practice Problem 8

In your Excel file for this chapter (Ch17-Excel365-IntroDataAnalysis.xlsx), go to the worksheet named PPCh17(8) and create the solution for this practice problem. Figure 17.188 shows the goals that are listed on that worksheet.

	A	B	C	D	E	F	G	H	I
2		Goal:	Create a date attribute field for day of the week.						
3			Create a field that extracts the state abbreviation from the Sate-Zip field.						
4			Create a field that extracts the zip code from the Sate-Zip field.						
5			Sort the table by zip code, smallest to largest.						
6			Create a PivotTable report that shows sales by day of the week and state.						
7			There are 64 records in the table.						
8									
9									
10		Date	State-Zip	Sales ($)					
11		7/5/22	CA-94704	1297.57					
12		6/6/22	WA-98106	430.35					
13		9/13/22	OR-96011	1199.78					
14		7/1/22	CA-98702	283.03					
15		5/16/22	WA-98108	492.31					
16		2/14/22	WA-98112	764.97					
17		9/10/22	OR-96011	924.26					
18		10/29/22	CA-94600	714.74					
19		6/11/22	CA-94704	1068.68					
20		2/5/22	WA-98106	1010.11					
21		2/22/22	OR-96011	509.87					

Figure 17.188 *On the worksheet PPCh17(8), create a report that shows sales by day of the week and state.*

When you are done with this problem, you can check your work against the answer sheet named PPCh17(8an).

Practice Problem 9

In your Excel file for this chapter (Ch17-Excel365-IntroDataAnalysis.xlsx), go to the worksheet named PPCh17(9).

In your own words, see if you can answer these conceptual questions:

1. Define data analysis.
2. What makes the PivotTable tool so useful?
3. If you group dates in a PivotTable, what happens to the PivotTable cache?
4. What is a frequency distribution?
5. List three Show Values As calculations.
6. How is visualizing data different from creating a report based on data?
7. When you want to compare differences across categories, which type of visualization should you use?
8. When you want to show how a variable value changes over time, which type of chart should you use?
9. What does conditional formatting do?

When you are done with this problem, you can check your work against the answer sheet named PPCh17(9an).

Chapter 18: Advanced Data Analysis with Power Query, Power Pivot, Power BI, M Code, and DAX

You just finished an epic chapter all about the standard data analysis tools that you can use in the Excel worksheet. This chapter takes a deeper dive into the field of data analysis and business intelligence, more rigorously defining data analysis terms and describing the new Microsoft 365 power tools for data analysis and business intelligence.

It is important to understand that *data* and *information* are not the same thing. You might hear someone ask, "Can you import the information from the database?" when what they are asking you to import is the raw data. Or you might hear someone say "the table stores the information" when what they mean is that the table stores the data. Whereas *data* is unorganized raw data and alone is not very useful or insightful, *information* is created from raw data and is organized and presented in such a way that it helps users make decisions, find patterns, and gain insights. Figure 18.1 illustrates the difference between data and information.

Note: Remember that *data* is the unorganized starting point, and *information* is created from data.

Raw **Data**:

Date	Product	Sales ($)
Mar	Quad	560
Apr	Quad	781
May	Quad	612
Jun	Quad	714
Jul	Quad	932
Aug	Quad	717
Sep	Quad	718
Oct	Quad	1203
Nov	Quad	1445
Dec	Quad	1334

Convert into ==>>

Useful **Information**:

Question: What is trend in Quad Sales?

Answer = **Information** created from Raw **Data**

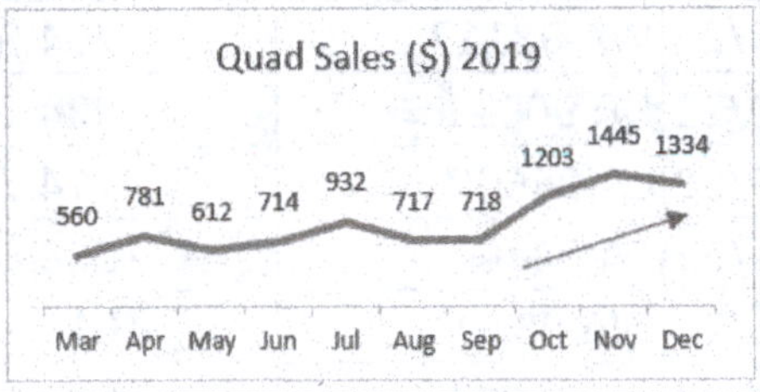

Figure 18.1 *Data and information are not interchangeable words.*

Data analysis (or *data analytics*) is the process of converting raw data into useful, actionable, and updatable information. Rather than make decisions based on historical precedence or intuition or just guessing, decision makers should use information based on data to make intelligent decisions. Sometimes data analysis can be an exploratory process without a stated goal, where you explore the data in various ways to try to discover patterns or trends and gain unexpected insights. Other times, it is undertaken to solve a particular problem.

Note: As you learned in Chapter 17, *business intelligence* is a synonym for *data analysis* but applies in the context of business data and business decision making. Microsoft calls many of its data analysis tools *business intelligence tools*. Although the tools are well suited for business analysis, they are also well suited for most other data analysis tasks in non-business fields.

When decision makers have useful information, they can:

- Make data-driven decisions
- Make evidence-based decisions
- Discover patterns and trends
- Gain insights

Useful Information: Summary Reports, Visualizations, and Dashboards

The useful information that you obtain through the data analysis process can take many forms, but the three most common are summary reports, visualizations, and dashboards.

A *summary report* is an account of a particular subject or topic that has been carefully prepared and presented. A summary report contains detailed numbers with labels, and the numbers are almost always metrics that help gauge performance or help make some decision. Further, the numbers are almost always conditional calculations based on logical tests (discussed in Chapter 13).

Figure 18.2 shows an example of a two-year gross profit report for the company Boomerang Incorporated. The subject of the report is yearly gross profit, which is a metric the company uses to gauge its efficiency in using labor and supplies to produce and sell products. The three conditional calculations in this report are total revenue, total COGS, and total gross profit. The conditions for the calculations are year and month.

Year	Total Revenue ($)	Total COGS ($)	Total Gross Profit ($)
⊟ 2018	418,005,988	238,740,341	179,265,647
January	5,059,290	2,874,258	2,185,032
February	4,500,011	2,519,552	1,980,459
March	4,962,490	2,771,769	2,190,721
April	4,935,400	2,814,529	2,120,871
May	42,399,220	24,099,422	18,299,798
June	55,563,855	31,560,686	24,003,169
July	57,638,454	32,729,149	24,909,305
August	44,145,411	25,332,067	18,813,344
September	4,903,118	2,819,009	2,084,109
October	5,105,360	2,925,338	2,180,022
November	86,838,107	49,837,217	37,000,890
December	101,955,272	58,457,345	43,497,928
⊟ 2019	597,442,594	346,343,675	251,098,920
January	5,131,800	2,932,780	2,199,019
February	4,446,305	2,559,693	1,886,612
March	18,851,636	10,814,188	8,037,447
April	23,463,452	13,482,700	9,980,752
May	24,114,739	13,882,597	10,232,142
June	23,577,820	13,505,596	10,072,224
July	24,395,718	13,997,343	10,398,375
August	24,465,457	14,082,390	10,383,067
September	23,567,695	13,485,680	10,082,015
October	24,240,498	14,060,530	10,179,967
November	212,228,551	123,559,228	88,669,323
December	188,958,923	109,980,948	78,977,975
Total	1,015,448,583	585,084,016	430,364,567

Figure 18.2 *A two-year gross profit report.*

Whereas reports like swathe Boomerang gross profit report present detailed numbers, or quantitative values, *visualizations* present quantitative values in a visual way that helps users quickly see patterns and trends and gain insights. Visualizations such as bar charts, column charts, line charts, and word clouds can often communicate more quickly than can numbers alone. Humans can process visual images faster than they can process rows of numbers. As the old saying goes: A picture paints a thousand words.

To illustrate the power of a visualization, Figure 18.3 shows a line chart based on the Boomerang data from Figure 18.2. You can see in this visualization how the numbers are changing over the years and months, and you can immediately identify a pattern: At Boomerang Incorporated, the largest revenues and COGS occur in the months November and December. You can also see that the trend for the gross profit is downward across the entire time period. These patterns and trends are immediately evident with the visualization but really hard to pick out and see in the report alone.

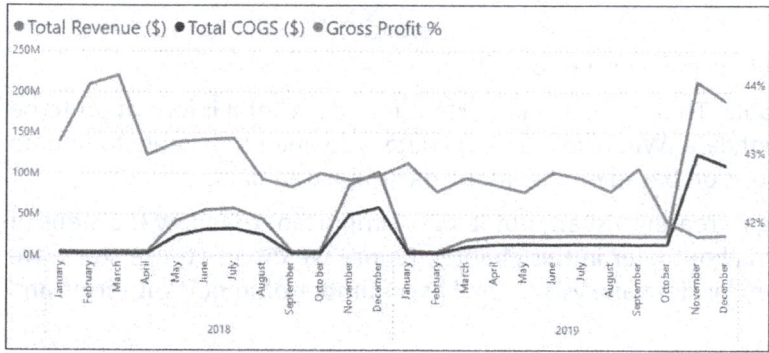

Figure 18.3 *Using a line chart to visualize total revenue, total COGS, and gross profit percentage over time.*

You can create a *dashboard* by putting summary reports, visualizations, and other elements together in one location to enable decision makers to better monitor activity as new data arrives. A decision maker can view and interact with the information in a dashboard to gauge performance, see patterns and trends, and gain insights. A dashboard should refresh if new data is available, and it should be easy to share with interested parties.

Figure 18.4 shows a gross profit dashboard for Boomerang Incorporated that includes the summary report and the line chart you've already seen, as well two bar charts. This dashboard shows gross profit by year, month, country, and product. The dashboard shows data for 2020 (which we can assume is the current year in this example) as well as for the two preceding years. The line chart shows that the pattern of high revenues in November and December from the two previous years is continuing and accelerating. It looks like the managers took notice of the downward trend of the gross profit percentage and made changes to stabilize it at around 41%. In the bar charts, you can see that the product Quad and the country United States have the top gross profit amounts. The different elements of the dashboard work together to present detailed number data as well as visualizations that help decision makers at Boomerang Incorporated quickly form impressions of the situation.

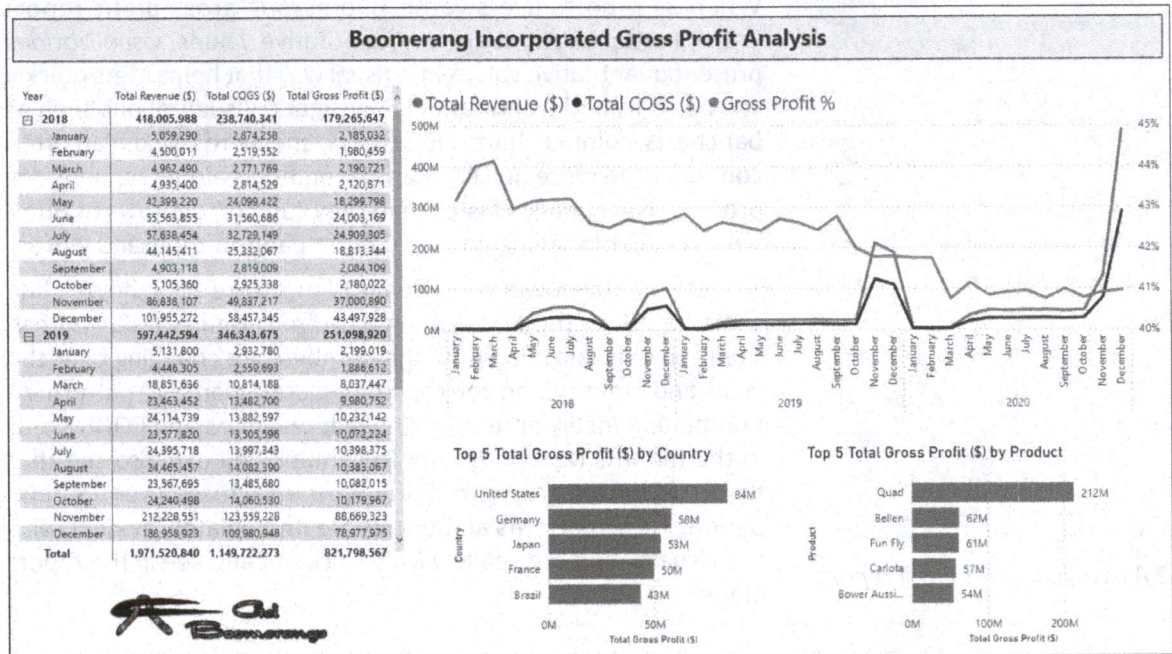

Figure 18.4 *Dashboard to monitor gross profit activity as new data arrives.*

Better decisions are possible with current data. Therefore, it is important for your useful information to be updatable so that it reflects the most current data. When you get new data, you need to be able to update your reports and visuals so you can make decision based on the latest, most updated data.

It may be tempting to jump right in and begin creating visuals, but it's very important to follow the steps of the data analysis process, which you'll learn about later in this chapter. Before we discuss those steps, we need to talk about the tools Microsoft offers for data analysis as well as a number of important terms and concepts related to data analysis.

Microsoft's Data Analysis Tools

As you have just seen, the useful information created in the data analysis process might be a single calculation result, a summary report, a visualization such as a bar chart, a dashboard that contains multiple informative elements, or some other type of useful information. Microsoft has long offered a number of tools that can be used for data analysis, including worksheet formulas and PivotTables. (In this book, especially in Chapters 8 through 17, you have already seen a number of examples of using these old favorites for data analysis.) In addition, Microsoft 365 offers a number of new data analysis tools that make performing data analysis easier than ever, even on data with different structures or different sources and on small and big datasets alike.

In this chapter, you will learn about these new Microsoft 365 data analysis tools:

- **Power Query:** You can use this tool to import, clean, transform, and load data into an Excel worksheet, the standard PivotTable cache, or a data model in Power Pivot or Power BI Desktop. Power Query is available both in the Excel app and in the Power BI Desktop app.

- **M code:** This is the functional language that is used in Power Query.

- **Data Model PivotTables created with Excel Power Pivot:** You can use Power Pivot to create summary reports that contain conditional calculations when you have big data (50,000 rows of data or more) or when you need more advanced calculations than are possible with a standard PivotTable.

- **Microsoft Power BI Desktop and Power BI Online:** You can use these two tools to create reports, visualizations, and dashboards when you want interactive reports and visualizations that you can share online. The Power BI Desktop app is used to build data models, reports, and visualizations, and Power BI Online is used to share reports, dashboards, and datasets. In this book, the emphasis is on building data analysis solutions, and so you will spend most of your time building solutions in Power BI Desktop. However, you will also learn how to share Power BI Desktop results to the Power BI Online website. The Power BI Desktop app is a separate Microsoft tool (outside the Excel app) that you can download for free. This app contains Power Query and the Data Model, which are almost identical to the same tools in the Excel app. If you are familiar with Power Query and Power Pivot, it is easy to learn Power BI Desktop.

- **DAX:** This is the functional language that is used in Power Pivot and Power BI Desktop.

Thanks to these tools, data analysis to make data-driven decisions has never been as effective, efficient, and fun as it is today.

You will see very detailed examples of using these tools later in this chapter. The following pages provide a preview of the types of analysis you can perform with Microsoft data analysis tools.

Figure 18.5 shows an example of data analysis using worksheet formulas to answer the question "Which product is most profitable?" The raw data on the left is used to create the useful information on the right and find the answer. As you can see here, the Quad product is most profitable.

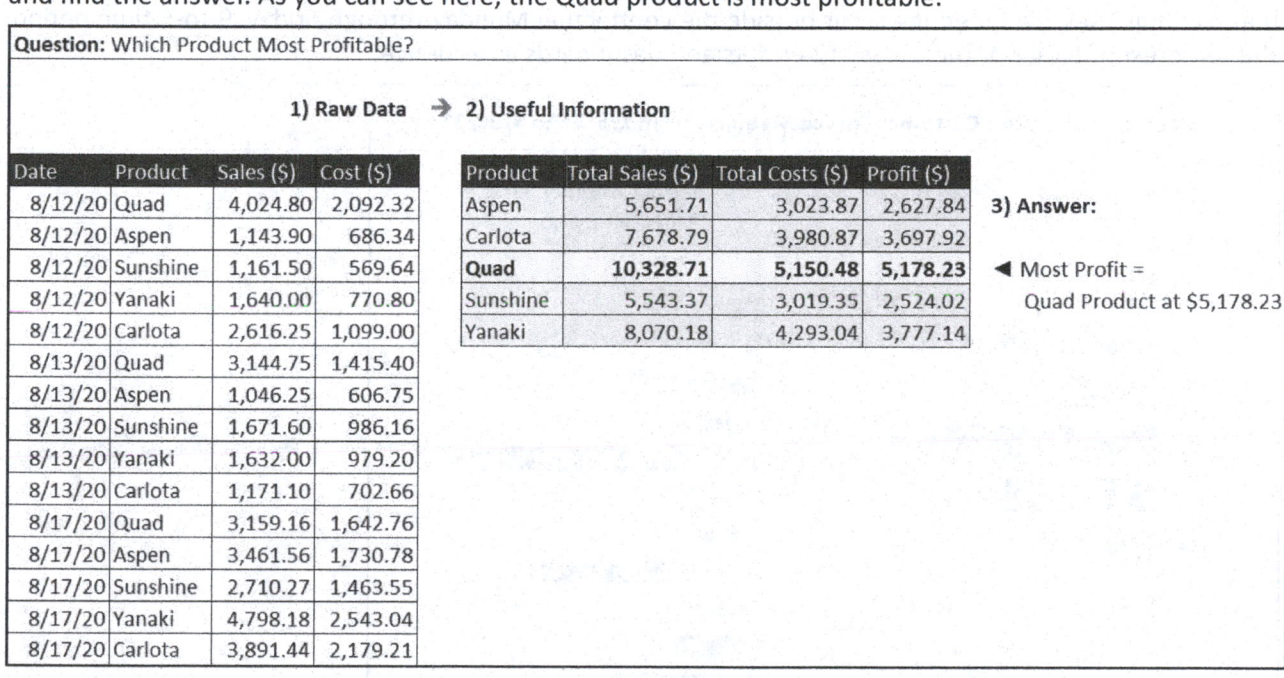

Figure 18.5 *You perform data analysis on the raw data to get the one desired number.*

Figure 18.6 shows an example of a standard PivotTable created to help make a decision about which product a company should debut. The customer survey data on the left is converted to the useful information on the right. The PivotTable indicates that Double BBQ Chicken should be the new product to debut.

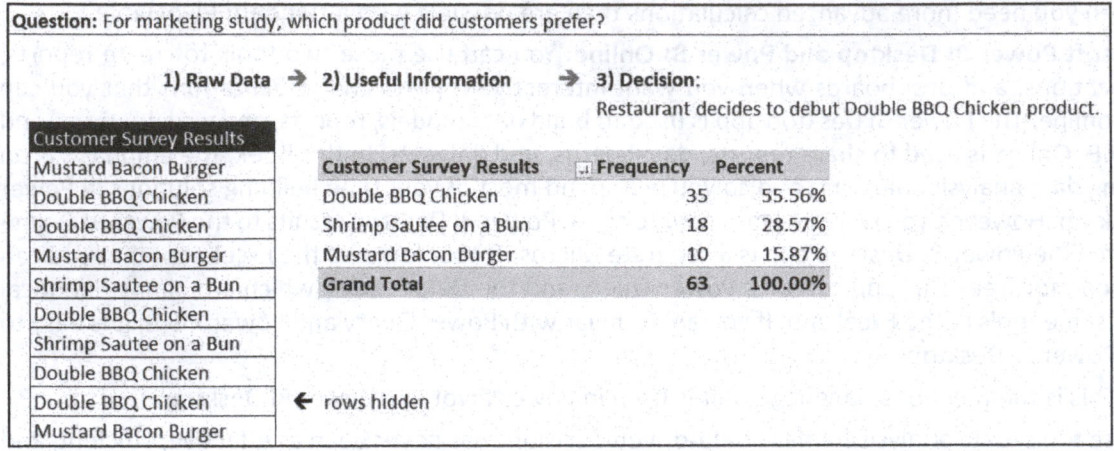

Figure 18.6 *You perform data analysis on the raw data to help make a decision.*

Figures 18.7 and 18.8 show two customer service dashboards that contain detailed reports and bar chart visualizations. The dashboards, which resulted from the data analysis process, present up-to-date information about the customer service calls that Chantel Washington is managing. Chantel and her managers can use the useful information presented in either dashboard to gauge what type of issues customers are having and to assess the distribution of meetings across days and times. For example, if Chantel needs to present evidence that customer service meetings occur outside the contractual Monday-through-Friday, 9-to-5 time period, she can present either of these easy-to-understand dashboards as evidence.

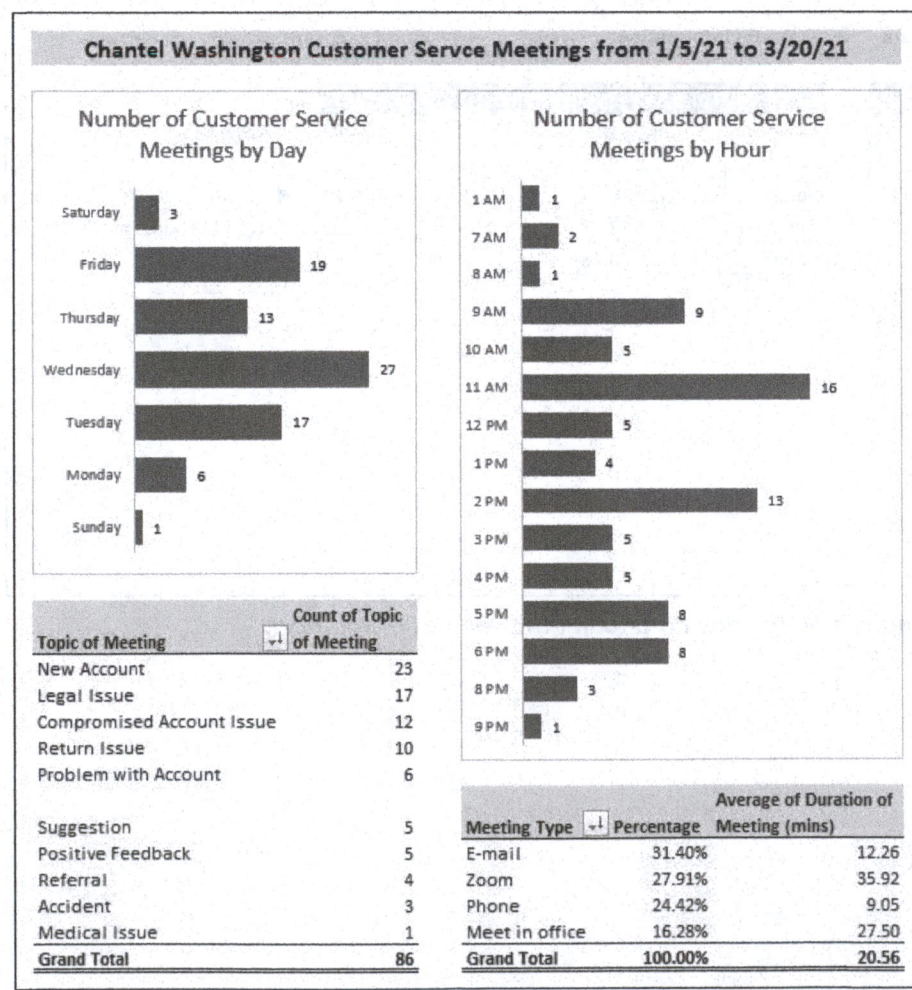

Figure 18.7 *Customer service dashboard created with the Excel app.*

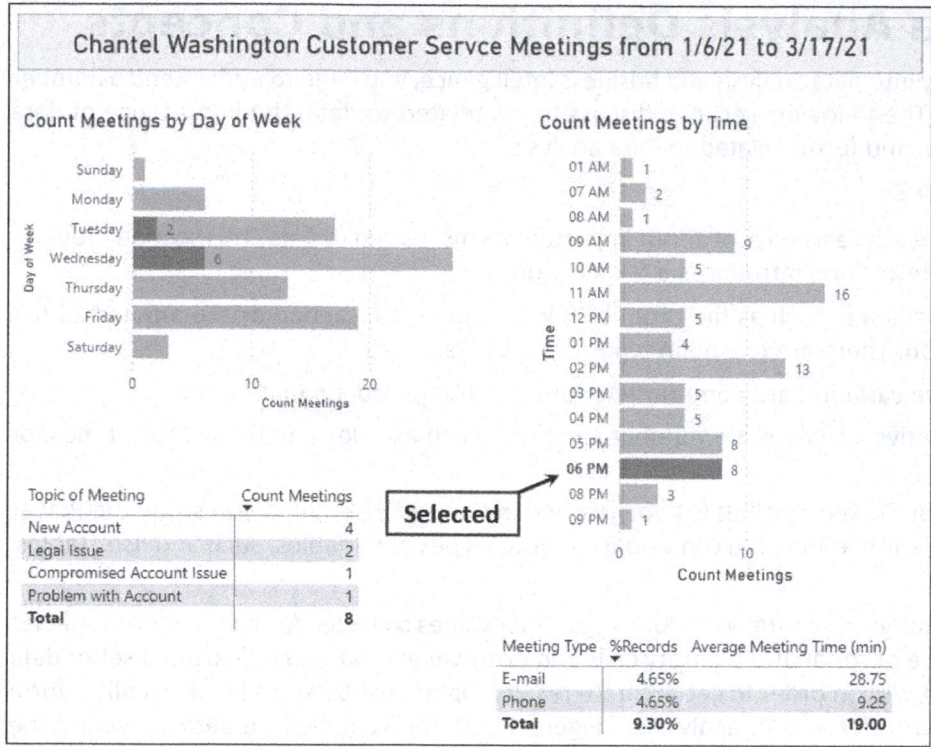

Figure 18.8 *Interactive customer service dashboard created with the Power BI Desktop app.*

The dashboard in Figure 18.7 was created using the Excel app, and the dashboard in Figure 18.8 was created using the Power BI Desktop app. Although you will study much more later about the differences between these two apps, in general, the Excel app with its standard PivotTable feature tends to be easier to use than the Power BI Desktop app; however, the Power BI Desktop app can create more interactive and shareable results than the Excel app. For example, Figure 18.8 shows that with the Power BI Desktop app, when the 6 PM bar is selected, other elements in the dashboard are automatically filtered to show data for the 6 PM time period. Achieving this sort of interactivity between the elements of a dashboard is simple in Power BI, but it is very difficult or even impossible with an Excel worksheet.

> **Note:** You will work with this Chantel Washington example as a practice problem at the end of Chapter 19.

Figure 18.9 shows a product sales dashboard that is used to analyze product sales. It was created from over 7 million rows of data from an SQL database. This is an example of data analysis on big data, using the Power Query and Data Model tools in both Excel and Power BI Desktop.

> **Note:** You will work with this big data example in a practice problem at the end of Chapter 19.

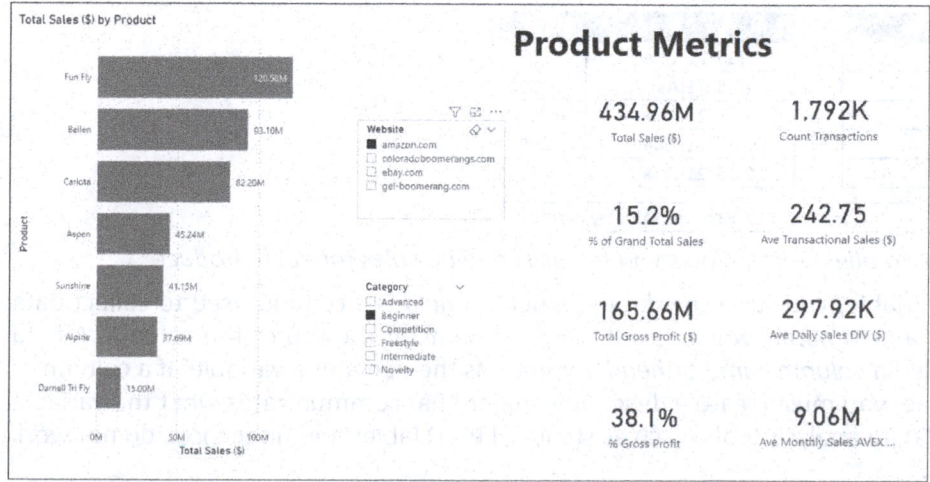

Figure 18.9 *Over 7 million rows of data converted into a dashboard in the Power BI Desktop app.*

Important Data Analysis Definitions and Concepts

Before we can really get deeply into data analysis and business intelligence, you need to understand a number of basic terms and concepts. The following sections discuss terms related to data, the importance of data types, text files and delimiters, and terms related to data analysis.

Data-Related Terms

In earlier chapters, you have already learned a lot about important terms related to data. This section provides a refresher on many of those terms and introduces a few new ones.

A *variable* is a value that can change, such as the product sold in a sales transaction or the amount of the sale made in a sales transaction. There are two main types of variables:

- **Qualitative:** Qualitative variables are non-numeric variables like product names.
- **Quantitative:** Quantitative variables are number variables, such as sales amounts, dates, times, or integer counts.

Variables can also be logical, or *Boolean*, values (as you learned in Chapter 13). When you study the Power Query tool in Chapter 19, you will see that you can also have other types of variables, such and lists, tables, and files.

Raw data, or just *data*, is qualitative, quantitative, Boolean, or other values collected for one or more variables and kept together for reference or for analysis. Empty cells and error values can also be part of a set of data and must be tracked and dealt with in order to get accurate results. Data must be stored in its smallest form so that it can be easily used for reference or analysis. In Figure 18.10, for example, the data shown on the left side is not stored as raw data (that is, in its smallest form): The address, city, state, and zip code are all stored in a single cell. If the address data is not stored in its smallest form, it is hard to perform data analysis such as sorting by zip code. But once you break the address, city, state, and zip code into separate columns, as shown on the right side of Figure 18.10, it is easy to perform the data analysis task of sorting by zip code.

Data that needs to be transformed to be useful		Raw Data stored in smallest form				
Addresses		CustomerID	Address	City	State	Zip
20324, 313 173rd Blvd, Kent, WA 98121		20324	313 173rd Blvd	Kent	WA	98121
20325, 316 66th Blvd, Kent, WA 98124		20325	316 66th Blvd	Kent	WA	98124
20326, 4358 23rd St, Kent, WA 98122		20326	4358 23rd St	Kent	WA	98122
20327, 2977 66th Lane, Seattle, WA 98117		20327	2977 66th Lane	Seattle	WA	98117
20328, 3392 23rd St, Seattle, WA 98113		20328	3392 23rd St	Seattle	WA	98113
Hard to sort by Zip Code		**Easy to sort by Zip Code**				

Figure 18.10 *Storing data in its smallest form allows for easier analysis, such as sorting by zip code.*

Figure 18.11 shows a similar problem with sales transaction data. Performing the data analysis task of adding sales for each product is very difficult with the data on the left but very easy with the data on the right.

Data that needs to be transformed to be useful	Raw Data stored in smallest form		
Date-Product-Sales	Date	Product	Sales
2/15/2021-Quad-287.7	2/15/21	Quad	287.7
2/15/2021-Aspen-89.85	2/15/21	Aspen	89.85
2/15/2021-Aspen-239.6	2/15/21	Aspen	239.6
2/15/2021-Quad-239.75	2/15/21	Quad	239.75
2/15/2021-Quad-239.75	2/15/21	Quad	239.75
Hard to add sales by Product	**Easy to add sales by Product**		

Figure 18.11 *Storing data in its smallest form allows you to easily add up sales for each product.*

When you collect data for a variable, you store the data in a field. A *field* is a column used to collect data for a variable that always has a *field name*, which is a descriptive name at the top of the column. A field name—which may also be called a *column name* or *header name*—is the name of a variable. If a column of data does not have a field name, you must create a descriptive name that communicates what the variable represents. A number of Excel data analysis tools, such as standard PivotTables and filter tools, do not work on data that lacks field names.

The data that is placed into a field must be *consistent data*, such as dates in a date field or sales amounts in a sales field. As shown on the left side of Figure 18.12, the data for dates is stored in a column with the field name Date, the data for the product IDs is stored in a column with the field name ProductID, and the data for the sales is stored in a column with the field name Sales ($). In an Excel worksheet, a field sometimes contains inconsistent data, and this can cause problems. For example, it is not uncommon to get a sales dataset where the date field contains inconsistent dates, such as a mixture of serial number dates and text dates (refer to Chapter 11). In an Excel worksheet, you do not get a warning that there is inconsistent data in a field. However, if you try to use a field that contains inconsistent data, some of the data analysis tools do not work correctly; this is the case, for example, when you try to use a date field with inconsistent data in a standard PivotTable. Fields with error values such as #N/A can also cause problems. One of the important tasks that you will learn about shortly, called *data cleaning*, is a process used to catch data inconsistencies.

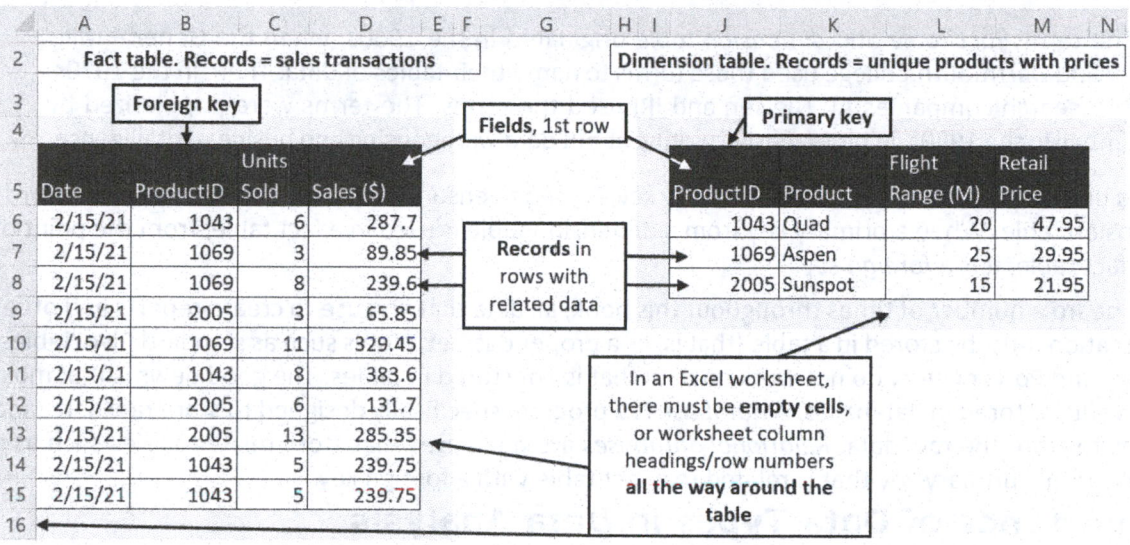

Figure 18.12 *A table contains field names in the first row and records in subsequent rows.*

> **Note:** When you are not storing data in a worksheet but are instead storing data in Power Query or the Power Pivot Data Model or Power BI Desktop Data Model, you will encounter fewer data inconsistency problems because Power Query and the Data Model have better tools for preventing data inconsistencies (as you will see shortly).

Data that is stored properly—usually in table format—is called a *proper dataset*. A *table* is a collection of one or more fields that contains rows of related data. Field names are always in the first row, and records of related data are in subsequent rows. In an Excel worksheet, you must have empty cells or worksheet column headings (A, B, C, and so on) or row numbers (1, 2, 3, and so on) all the way around the table. Figure 18.12 shows two examples of tables that are in proper dataset form.

> **Note:** Importantly, for tables that are stored in an Excel worksheet, you are not allowed to place any cell content, such as rogue bits of nonrelated data or formulas, directly next to a table without leaving at least one row or column between that item and the table. If you accidentally place rogue cell content next to a table, some Excel data analysis tools, such as the standard PivotTable and Excel Table tools, will not work correctly. This is not an issue with Power Query tables and Power Pivot or Power BI Desktop tables because in these tools, it is not possible to place stray data or rogue formulas next to a table.

The rows below the first row of field names in a table are called records. A *record* is a row of related data within a table, such as the date, product ID, units sold, and sales amount for a sales transaction, or a product ID, product name, flight range, and price of a product for a company's boomerang product.

Figure 18.12 illustrates the two most common types of tables:

- **Fact table:** A *fact table* contains the data that you want to summarize or measure (such as sales amounts or units sold). Examples of fact tables are tables that store sales transactions, tables that store baseball data for baseball games, tables that store customer clicks at a website, and tables that store observations from an experiment. The facts are the measurements of activities, such as the amount of a sale, the number of balls and strikes in a baseball game, the start and end times for someone who visits a website, and the temperature size in an experiment. Fact tables can sometimes be very large; they may contain 100,000 rows, 1 million rows, or even 100 million rows or more.

- **Dimension table:** A *dimension table* contains a field with a unique list of entities (such as product IDs) with attributes in subsequent fields for conditional calculations (such as product names) or lookup items (such as product prices). The term *dimension table* is used in data analysis to refer to a lookup table. Remember from Chapter 14 that a lookup table always has a unique list of items in the first column of the table (the primary key); it is the same with dimension tables. For example, a product dimension table has a unique identifier, usually in the first column, such as product name or product ID; an employee dimension table has a unique identifier in the first column, such as employee ID or employee name. Dimension tables are usually much smaller than fact tables.

Note: The terms *fact table* and *dimension table* originated in the 1960s, when the General Mills company and Dartmouth College used these terms to name their tables of data. Then, in the 1970s, the data research companies AC Nielsen and IRI used the terms. The terms were popularized by Ralph Kimball in the 1980s, in his extensive writing about data warehousing and business intelligence.

A field with a unique list of entities, called a *primary key*, is used to ensure that there are no duplicate records in the dimension table. When a primary key from a dimension table is used in a fact table, from the point of view of the fact table, it is a *foreign key*.

As you have heard a number of times throughout this book, all data that you use to create reports and other useful information must be stored in a table (that is, as a proper dataset). Tools such as standard PivotTables, filtering tools, and Power Query do not work on data that is not stored in tables. The good news is that most data in the world is stored in databases. A *database* is a program specifically designed to store raw data, and it uses tables to store the raw data. *Relational databases* are databases that store related tables such as a product table with a primary key that is related to a fact table with a foreign key.

The Importance of Data Types in Data Analysis

To ensure that a table contains consistent data, you can use data types. A *data type* is a specific type of data that is allowed in a field, such as a decimal number, a whole number, a date, a text value, a list value, or a binary value. Once you define a data type for a field, only data of that specified data type is allowed to be entered into the field. Specifying a data type for a field is a safeguard that helps ensure data consistency and accuracy for your reports, visualizations, and other useful information that you create.

Note: There is a famous saying in the database world: "Garbage in, garbage out." This is a catchy way of saying that inconsistent and inaccurate data will create inaccurate and unhelpful reports and visuals. Data types are important in data analysis because they help ensure data consistency. When you have consistent data, you can create more consistent reports and visuals. Therefore, data types prevent garbage from going in.

In an Excel worksheet, you can use data validation to limit the type of data that can go into a field; you can also create data types by using Power Query. Power Query is the preferred tool to use to declare data types for the fields in a table before you load the table to an Excel worksheet, a PivotTable cache, the Power Pivot Data Model, or the Power BI Desktop Data Model. (You will learn more about Power Query later in this chapter and in Chapter 19.)

Note: Remember from Chapters 8 and 11 that you can use number formatting in an Excel worksheet to display data in a certain way but that number formatting is cosmetic and does not enforce a consistent data type for a field.

Tables show up in all of the data analysis tools. These tables look slightly different from each other and treat data types in different ways. The following pages show examples of the following tools and tables and help you understand the importance of data types in a number of scenarios:

- Excel worksheets
- Excel Tables created with the Excel Table tool
- The Power Query Editor window
- Power Query output loaded to an Excel worksheet as an Excel Table

- The Power Pivot Data Model Data View window
- The Power BI Desktop Data Model Data View window
- Text files exported from data storage systems

Inconsistent data is possible when you store data in an Excel worksheet. Figure 18.13 shows a proper dataset in table form that is stored in an Excel worksheet but not in an Excel Table. This table does not have declared data types, as you would see in a Power Query table, and therefore, it cannot enforce data integrity. Date number formatting has been applied to the Date field to make the dates appear to have a consistent format, but remember that number formatting is cosmetic only: It does not affect how Excel stores the data and does not prevent users from entering text dates. As you can see in Figure 18.13, the Date field contains many serial number dates and one text date. Inconsistent data like this will prevent some data analysis tools, like the standard PivotTable tool, from working correctly.

	A	B	C	D	E	F
2			Excel Worksheet			
4			Date	ProductID	Units Sold	Sales ($)
5			2/15/19	1043	6	287.7
6			2/15/19	1069	3	89.85
7			2/15/19	1069	8	239.6
8			2/15/19	2005	3	65.85
9	Serial Number Date ==>>		2/15/19	1069	11	329.45
10	Text Date ==>>		15/2/2019	1043	8	383.6
11			2/15/19	2005	6	131.7
12			2/15/19	2005	13	285.35
13			2/15/19	1043	5	239.75
14			2/15/19	1043	5	239.75

Figure 18.13 *The Excel worksheet allows you to enter inconsistent data.*

Another problem with storing data in an Excel worksheet table is that the table is not dynamic, and reports and charts that are pointing to the table will not update when new data is added. (As you will see later on, unlike a table in an Excel worksheet, an Excel Table is dynamic.)

Storing data in an Excel worksheet is the least desirable method for storing data. However, if a table of data will not get new records, if you do not need to use it in other tools like Power Query or Power Pivot, and if a simple standard PivotTable report or chart is required, this method of storing data is acceptable.

Figure 18.14 shows a proper dataset that is stored in an Excel Table created using the Excel Table tool. The Excel Table tool does not allow you to declare data types for the fields in the table. In Figure 18.14, you can see that inconsistent data is possible when you store data in an Excel Table, leading to the same issues as with tables stored in a worksheet. The benefit of storing data in an Excel Table is that the Excel Table object is dynamic, so when you add new data to the Excel Table (such as new rows or new columns), any report, visual, or other tool that is pointing to the table as its source data will be updated.

	A	B	C	D	E	F
2			Excel Table (using Excel Table feature)			
4			Date	ProductID	Units Sold	Sales ($)
5			2/15/19	1043	6	287.7
6			2/15/19	1069	3	89.85
7			2/15/19	1069	8	239.6
8			2/15/19	2005	3	65.85
9	Serial Number Date ==>>		2/15/19	1069	11	329.45
10	Text Date ==>>		15/2/2019	1043	8	383.6
11			2/15/19	2005	6	131.7
12			2/15/19	2005	13	285.35
13			2/15/19	1043	5	239.75
14			2/15/19	1043	5	239.75
16			Excel Table object name = **fTransaction**			

Figure 18.14 *An Excel Table is a dynamic data source, but it allows you to enter inconsistent data.*

If you want to bring data from an Excel worksheet into the Power Query or Power Pivot tools, you must first store the data in an Excel Table. This requirement ensures that the solutions you build with the Power Query and Power Pivot data analysis tools can always be updated when new data arrives.

Another benefit of storing data in an Excel Table is that the name of the Excel Table and all its field names are available throughout the Excel workbook file, and you can use them in worksheet formulas, standard PivotTable reports, charts, Power Query, and other Excel tools.

> **Note:** As you learned in Chapter 8, it is crucial that objects such as tables and fields have names that help communicate the meaning and significance of the objects. For example, the name of the table in Figure 18.14 is fTransaction, where the lowercase *f* stands for *fact table*, and Transaction indicates sales transactions.

Figure 18.15 shows a proper dataset in the Power Query Editor window. When you bring data into the Power Query Editor, if it is not in proper dataset form, Power Query assigns generic field names (Column 1, Column 2, Column 3, and so on) that are almost always not very useful. Power Query has some built-in data consistency tools that allow you to explicitly declare data types for the fields to ensure consistency. For example, in Figure 18.15, you can see a data type icon to the left of each field name that indicates the declared data type for that field. In addition, there is a Column Quality tool below each field name that shows the percentage of errors and empty cells in that column. In this example, the date data type is applied to the Date field. As a result, proper serial number dates are stored as dates, and text dates are stored as errors. These errors are warnings to fix the issues.

It is important to choose the correct data type for a field. For example, if you accept the default data type for the Date field in Figure 18.15, which is text, calculations involving dates will not work correctly. If you load the Power Query table to the worksheet with text dates, you will not be able to make date calculations such as subtracting one date from another to find the difference between the dates, and you will not be able to make monthly sales reports.

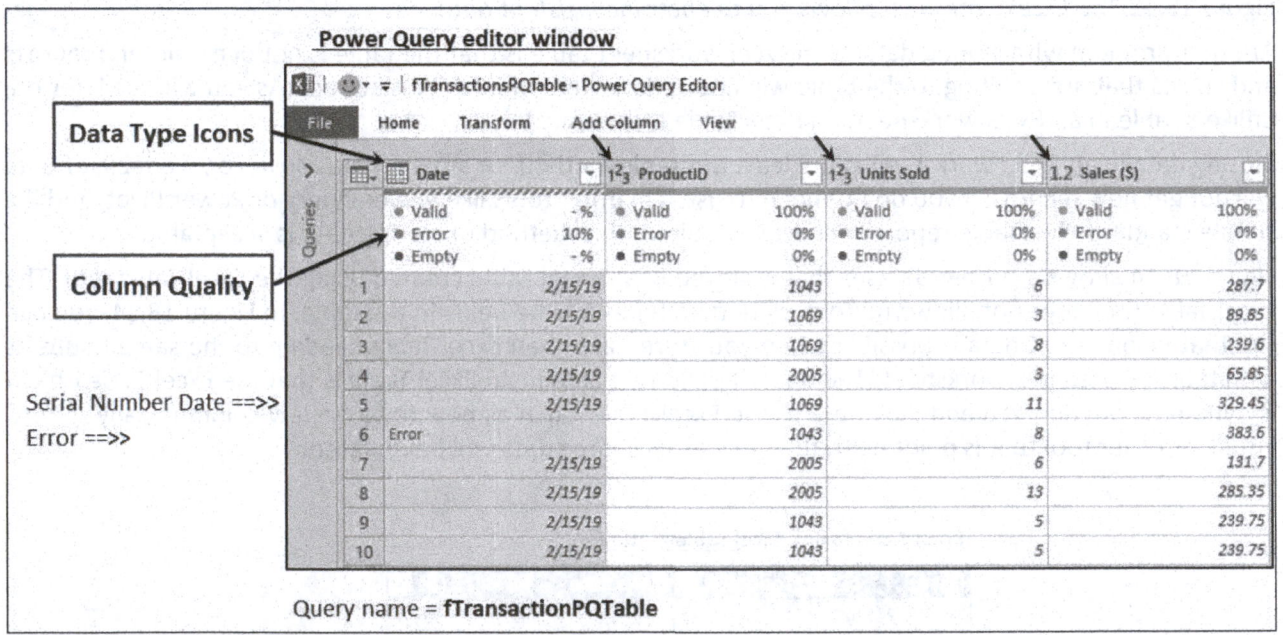

Figure 18.15 *In the Power Query Editor, inconsistent data leads to errors that warn you to fix the data.*

> **Note:** In Power Query, you must give each query a name that communicates the purpose and meaning of the query. For example, I named the query in Figure 18.15 fTransactionPQTable to indicate that it is a Power Query fact table showing sales transactions.

Once you have completed a query in the Power Query Editor, you can load it to an Excel worksheet as an Excel Table (as shown in Figure 18.16), to a PivotTable cache, or to the Data Model in Excel Power Pivot or Power BI Desktop; in all three cases, the error value will show up as an empty cell.

	A	B	C	D	E	F	G	H
2			**Power Query output when it is loaded to the Excel worksheet as an Excel Table**					
4			Date ▾	ProductID ▾	Units Sold ▾	Sales ($) ▾		
5			2/15/19	1043	6	287.7		
6			2/15/19	1069	3	89.85		
7			2/15/19	1069	8	239.6		
8			2/15/19	2005	3	65.85		
9	Serial Number Date ==>>		2/15/19	1069	11	329.45		
10	Empty Cell ==>>			1043	8	383.6		
11			2/15/19	2005	6	131.7		
12			2/15/19	2005	13	285.35		
13			2/15/19	1043	5	239.75		
14			2/15/19	1043	5	239.75		
16			Excel Table name is same as Query Name = **fTransactionsPQTable**					

Figure 18.16 *The error from the Power Query Editor window is converted to an empty cell when the data is loaded to an Excel worksheet.*

Figure 18.17 shows an example of data that is loaded from an Excel Table directly into the Power Pivot Data Model and then viewable in the Power Pivot Data View widow. When you import a table directly from an Excel Table into Power Pivot and there is inconsistent data in a field, the whole field is usually considered text. In this example, the inconsistent text date in row 6 causes the whole field to be converted to text values. (Remember that you can tell immediately that these are text values because they're left-aligned.) The Power Pivot Data View widow has a data type feature that you can use to convert the Date field to a date data type, but the text date may or may not be converted correctly. The data type feature in Power Pivot is not as robust as it is in Power Query.

Power Pivot data model Data View window

	Date	ProductID	Units Sold	Sales ($)	Add Column
1	2/15/19	1043	6	287.7	
2	2/15/19	1069	3	89.85	
3	2/15/19	1069	8	239.6	
4	2/15/19	2005	3	65.85	
5	2/15/19	1069	11	329.45	
6	15/2/2019	1043	8	383.6	
7	2/15/19	2005	6	131.7	
8	2/15/19	2005	13	285.35	
9	2/15/19	1043	5	239.75	
10	2/15/19	1043	5	239.75	

All data in Date field Text data type ==>>

Figure 18.17 *In the Power Pivot Data Model Data View window, inconsistent date data appears as text.*

When you load a table of data directly from an Excel Table to the Power BI Desktop tool, you can also get strange results from inconsistent data. Figure 18.18 shows that inconsistent date data also shows up as text, which will prevent you from making reports and visuals based on dates. To avoid inconsistent data and to gain the ability to create all desired reports and visuals, it is usually best to bring data through Power Query first, define a date data type, deal with the errors, and then load it into the Power Pivot or Power BI Desktop Data Model.

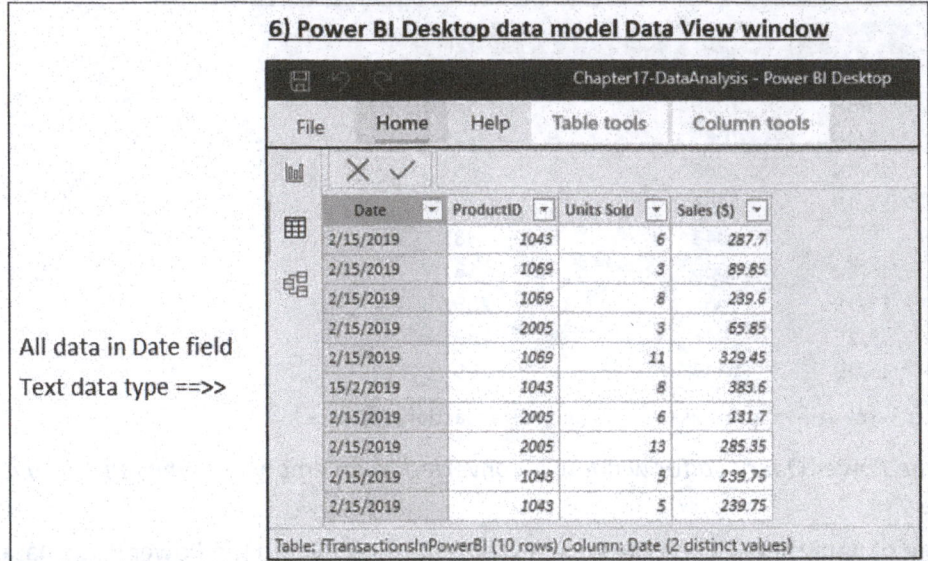

Figure 18.18 *In the Power BI Desktop Data Model Data View window, inconsistent date data appears as text.*

Text Files and Delimiters

You are likely to import tables of data from many different types of systems, including SQL databases, websites, and other Excel workbooks. When moving tables of data from one such system to another, you often use a *text file* as an intermediate place to store data. As shown in Figure 18.19, a text file stores data in a unique way, and delimiters are needed to separate the fields of data.

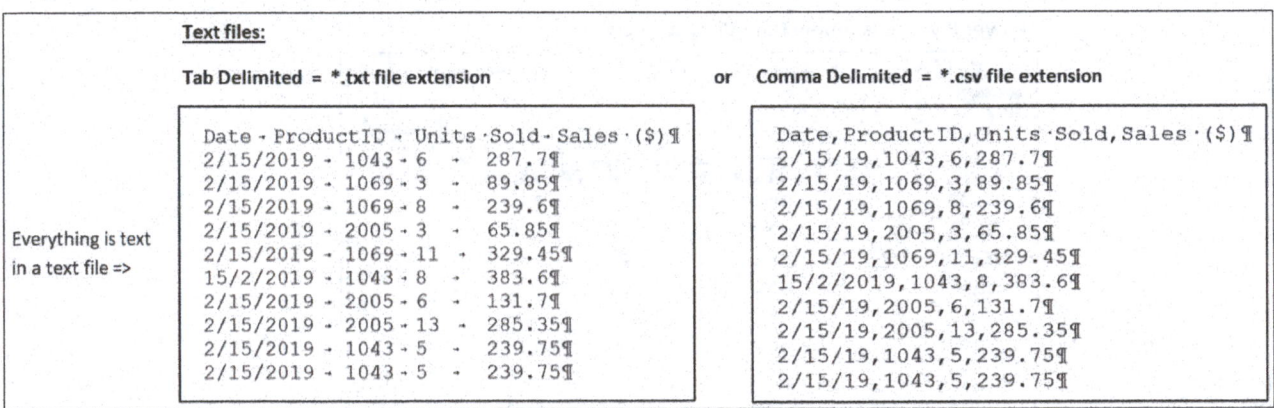

Figure 18.19 *It is common to use text files when transferring data from one system to another.*

A *delimiter*—which can be just about any combination of one or more characters but is typically a tab or a comma—signals to the computer system where the data should be split into separate fields or columns. In Figure 18.19, the table on the left uses a tab delimiter, which is represented by the arrow character, to separate columns; it uses a hard return, which is represented by the paragraph character, to separate rows. For tab-delimited tables, the file extension .txt (which stands for *text*) is used at the end of the filename.

The table on the right in Figure 18.19 uses a comma delimiter to separate columns and a paragraph character to separate rows. For comma-delimited tables, the file extension .csv (which stands for *comma-separated values*) is used at the end of the filename.

Note: In addition to .txt and .csv file extensions for structured table data, you may also encounter .xml (which stands for Extensible Markup Language) and .json (which stands for JavaScript Object Notation) file types, which allow structured tables of data to be transported from one system to another.

Delimiters are signals that allow most data systems, including the Excel and Power BI Desktop apps, to interpret a file as a proper dataset. A file that is a proper dataset is said to have a consistent *structure*, or *schema*, that allows other systems to interpret the file as a table.

Note: If you receive a text file and want to view the delimiters, you can open the file in Microsoft Word and then click the Show/Hide Non-Printing Characters button (which looks like a paragraph symbol) in the Paragraph group in Home tab of the Ribbon.

In a text file, all data is initially stored as the text data type. Using Power Query, you can import text data and then add data types to each field before loading it to the desired location for analysis.

Data Analysis–Related Terms

Now that you have learned a lot of data-related terms and background information about storing data so it can be used in data analysis, you're ready to get into data analysis. This section defines a number of important terms involved in the data analysis process.

A *query* is a command that you create to do something to data, such as retrieve data from a data source, clean or transform data, combine two tables into one table, change the data type of a field of data, or otherwise manipulate data or make calculations from data before loading it to a final location. Almost anything that you do with raw data, from importing data to creating the final useful information, is a query that you make against the raw data.

Note: The tool that is usually most efficient for building queries is (as you might guess from its name) Power Query. Power Query is available in the Excel app and in the Power BI Desktop app. The Excel app also includes several other query tools for the Excel worksheet, such as Sort, Filter, Flash Fill, and worksheet formulas, but they are not as powerful or robust as the Power Query tool. However, as you learned in Chapter 17, those tools are extremely useful when you have a small dataset or need to do a simple task or a quick one-time task in a worksheet.

As mentioned earlier, when you create a query, you can do many things, such as import, clean, and transform data. *Importing data* involves accessing external data and loading it into either Excel or Power BI Desktop. Power Query can be used to get data from almost any external data source, such as Excel files, text files, SQL databases, websites, and other sources.

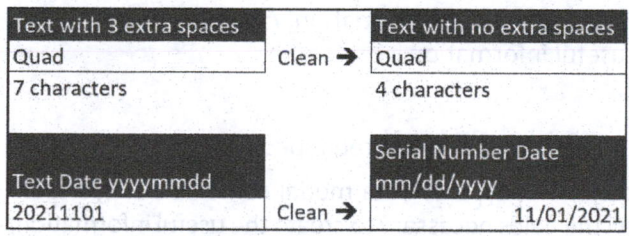

Figure 18.20 *Example of cleaning data.*

Cleaning data involves fixing unusable raw data before loading it to the final location. You clean data so that it can be used to perform data analysis. Figure 18.20 shows two common examples of cleaning data. In the top example, cleaning means removing extra spaces from a text value. As you first learned in Chapter 9, if there are extra spaces in text values, your calculations will not be correct. For example, the value Quad, with four characters, cannot be matched with the value Quad followed by three spaces, which totals seven characters. In the bottom example in Figure 18.20, cleaning means changing the data type by turning a text date into a proper serial number date that can be used in calculations. As you learned in Chapter 11, date calculations are possible only on data that is in proper serial number date format.

Transforming data involves changing the structure of the data so that it can more easily be used for data analysis. Figure 18.21 shows three common examples of transforming data. In the top example, records that are stored in cells are split into separate columns to create a proper dataset. In the middle example, a cross-tabulated table is transformed into a proper dataset. In the bottom example, the yearly data stored in different Excel files is transformed into a single fact table. In all three examples, the original data has to be transformed into a proper dataset before it can be loaded and then used to create the useful information.

Date-Product-Sales
2/15/2019-Quad-287.7
2/15/2019-Aspen-89.85
2/15/2019-Aspen-239.6

Transform ➔

Date	Product	Sales
2/15/19	Quad	287.7
2/15/19	Aspen	89.85
2/15/19	Aspen	239.6

Sales	1/12/21	1/13/21	1/15/21
Quad	291.65	745.58	253.76
Carlota	296.45	407.73	786.67

Transform ➔

Date	Product	Sales
1/12/21	Quad	291.65
1/13/21	Quad	745.58
1/15/21	Quad	253.76
1/12/21	Carlota	296.45
1/13/21	Carlota	407.73
1/15/21	Carlota	786.67

FlyingBoom-2014.xlsx
FlyingBoom-2015.xlsx
FlyingBoom-2016.xlsx
FlyingBoom-2017.xlsx
FlyingBoom-2018.xlsx

Transform ➔

Field 1	Field 2	Field 3
data	data	data
data	data	data
data	data	data

Figure 18.21 *Examples of transforming data.*

Data Modeling Basics

Data modeling involves getting and transforming data from the original source (such as a database, a text file, or data in a worksheet) into a source data structure (such as a single table, two or more tables, or a more complex structure) that can be used to create useful information. The final source data used to create the useful information is called the *data model*.

As you will learn later in this chapter, you create a data model by accessing, cleaning, transforming, and loading data as proper datasets and then, if necessary, further preparing the data by building relationships between related tables and creating the formulas necessary to measure the activities, gauge performance, and provide the numeric information needed to make decisions. The final data model must be an accurate, reliable, and updatable source of data that you can use to create useful information. After you create a data model, you can use it as the final source data to create useful information.

Types of Data Models

A wide variety of data models can be created, but they all fall into roughly three types:

ProductID ▼	UnitsSold ▼	Sales($) ▼	Product ▼
1043	6	287.7	Quad
1069	3	89.85	Aspen
1069	8	239.6	Aspen
2005	3	65.85	Sunspot
1069	11	329.45	Aspen
1043	8	383.6	Quad
2005	6	131.7	Sunspot
2005	13	285.35	Sunspot
1043	5	239.75	Quad
1043	5	239.75	Quad

Figure 18.22 *A flat table.*

- **Flat table:** This type of data model contains a single table with all the fields necessary to create the useful information, including both fact and dimension fields. There may be other tables in the data model that are used to create the flat table, but the one flat table is the final source data for the useful information. Standard PivotTables work well with a flat table data model. Figure 18.22 shows an example of a flat table.

- **Star schema:** This type of data model contains one fact table along with one or more dimension tables, and it features relationships between the tables and premade reusable formulas. Figure 18.23 shows an example of a star schema data model. This type of data model is designed to work efficiently with big data and complex calculations in the Power Pivot or Power BI Desktop Data Model.

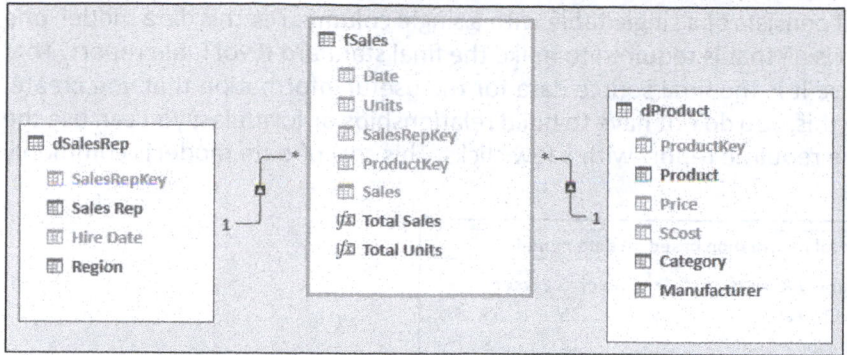

Figure 18.23 *A star schema data model.*

- **Snowflake:** This type of data model contains one fact table with several dimension tables, and there may be sub-dimension tables that split off from the main dimension table. Figure 18.24 shows an example of a snowflake data model. Snowflake data models are common in databases, but they can lead to unnecessary complications when you're building formulas (because you have attribute fields in two or more tables rather than in just one table), and they prevent some features from working correctly (such as the hierarchy feature). Power Pivot and Power BI Desktop are designed to work efficiently with the star schema data model. If you encounter a snowflake data model, you can transform it into a star schema data model by using Power Query. For example, if you used Power Query to transform the snowflake data model in Figure 18.24 into a star schema data, you would end up with the data model shown in Figure 18.23.

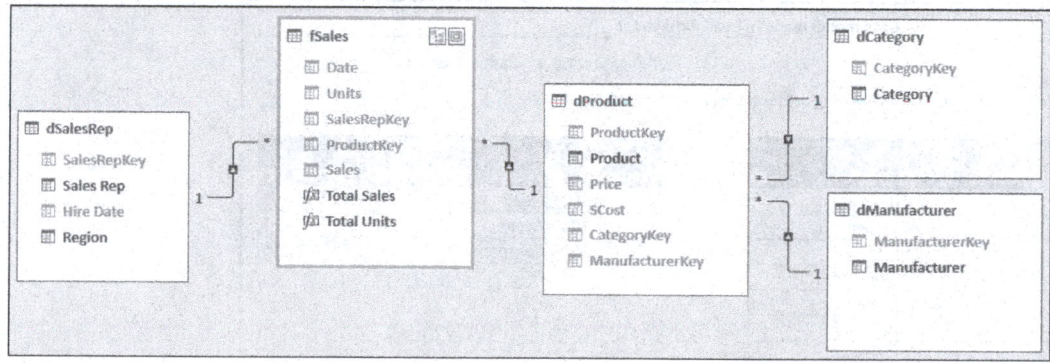

Figure 18.24 *A snowflake data model.*

Additional types of data models are possible, but they are not used nearly as frequently as the three types just described.

Later in this chapter, you'll see a number of example of data models that you can create using Excel tools. No matter which type you choose to create, make sure it has these characteristics:

- It contains the data necessary for the end solution.
- It is easy for a decision maker to use.
- It allows formulas to calculate quickly.
- The reports and visualizations are easy to update when new data is available.
- The data model is easy to update when the situation changes.

Let's look at a few example of the data models you can create and the useful information you might get from each one.

Figure 18.25 shows a data model that consists of a single table with a single column. For this data model, one single fact table with a single column is all that is required to make the final standard PivotTable report. That single table is the data model because it is the final source data for the useful information that you create. For simple data analysis projects like this, you do not have to build relationships or formulas; you can use the standard PivotTable tool to create the required report with a few clicks. This sort of data model is commonly used with single-column survey data.

Data model	Useful information based on data model		
Customer Survey Results	**Customer Survey Results**	**Frequency**	**Percent**
Mustard Bacon Burger	Double BBQ Chicken	35	55.56%
Double BBQ Chicken	Shrimp Sautee on a Bun	18	28.57%
Double BBQ Chicken	Mustard Bacon Burger	10	15.87%
Mustard Bacon Burger	**Grand Total**	**63**	**100.00%**
Shrimp Sautee on a Bun			
Mustard Bacon Burger	← rows hidden		

Figure 18.25 *A single table can be a data model that you use to create a standard PivotTable report.*

Figure 18.26 shows a data model that consists of two tables and worksheet formulas. For this data model, one fact table, one dimension table, and two worksheet lookup formula fields are used to make the final standard PivotTable report. The two tables and the worksheet formulas are considered the data model, but the fact table alone serves as the final source data for the useful information that you create. You would use this sort of data model when you have a small amount of data, the data is already located in the worksheet, and only simple calculations, such as adding or calculating percentages, are required.

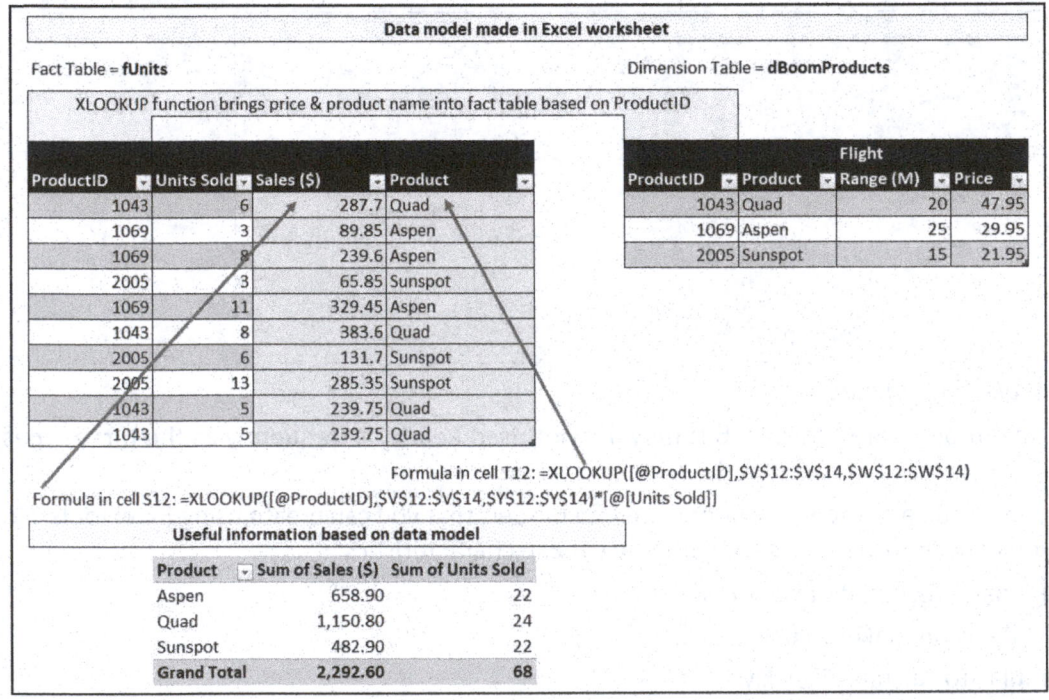

Figure 18.26 *One fact table and one dimension table with the XLOOKUP function creating a one-to-many relationship.*

There are two important characteristics of this data model that you should note:

- The XLOOKUP function is used in the fact table to look up the product price and name from the dimension table. This creates a *relationship* between the two tables. Without the product dimension table, you cannot create the Sales and Product fields necessary to create the final report. Both tables and the relationship created by the XLOOKUP function are required to create the final useful information.

- A single fact table contains fact fields (Units and Sales), and a dimension field (Product) is used as the final source data for the final report. This is a *flat table* that mixes facts and dimensions. Remember that a flat table has all the fields necessary for the useful information in one table. The product sales report shown at the bottom of Figure 18.26 uses the Product field (a dimension field) and Sales field (a fact field) from the flat table to create the useful information.

Using the sort of worksheet formula data modeling shown in Figure 18.26 to create a single flat table was common practice for most of spreadsheet history. However, this sort of data modeling does not work efficiently when you have a lot of data or when you have complex calculations. In addition, using flat tables that require many intermediate formula calculation steps to create the final fact columns is usually less efficient than using the Power Pivot or Power BI Desktop tools. You can build a flat table data model with about a million rows of data stored in an Excel worksheet, but having that much data and that many formulas in the worksheet unnecessarily slows the formula calculation time and increases the file size. When you have more than about 50,000 rows of data, it is more efficient to use the Power Pivot or Power BI Desktop tools, which give you faster formula calculation time and smaller file sizes. Microsoft 365 Excel and Power BI Desktop offer the Data Model tool as an alternative to the traditional worksheet formula flat table data model. This Data Model tool allows you to import multiple tables and create relationships between related tables, using the DAX formula language.

Figure 18.27 shows a data model that consists of two tables with a relationship and two DAX formulas. It is based on the same initial data as the data model in Figures 18.26 and also shows the same resulting report; however, these two data models use different methods:

- Figures 18.26 uses the flat table data model method with worksheet formulas and a standard PivotTable.
- Figure 18.27 uses the star schema data model method with a relationship and a DAX formula, as well as a Data Model PivotTable.

Given the initial small dataset and the simple useful information requirement in this case, either method is fine. You should try both and determine your preferred method for this type of situation.

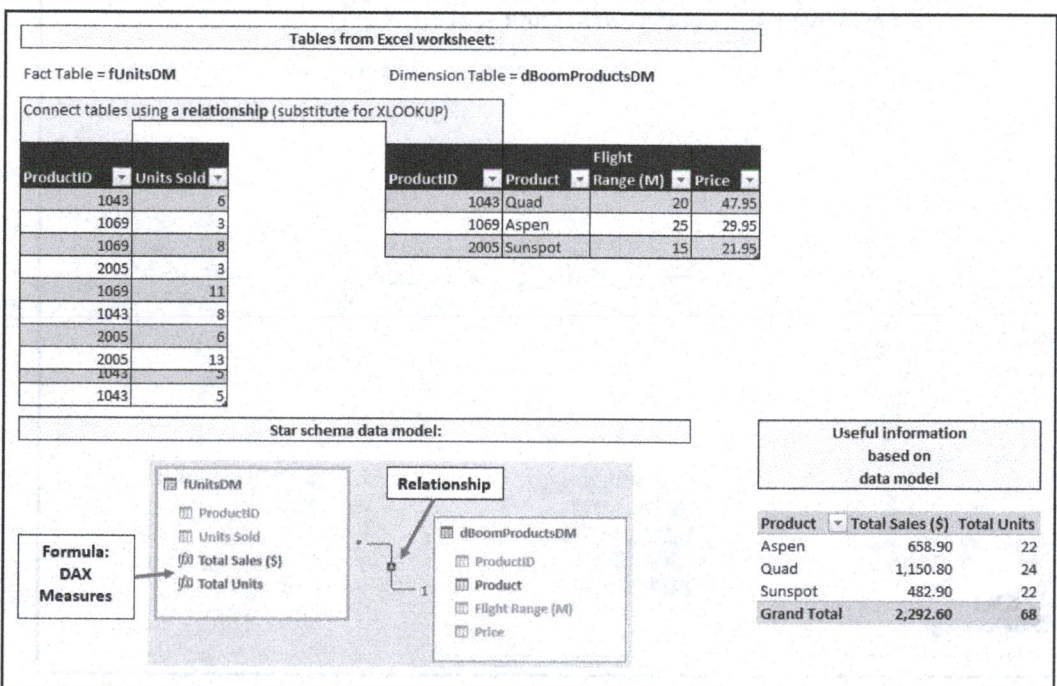

Figure 18.27 *One fact table and one dimension table with two DAX measures.*

If you have big data (50,000 rows of data or more) or complex calculations or if you want more interactive and shareable useful information, you should use a star schema data model in either Power Pivot or the Power BI Desktop Data Model. Figure 18.28 shows an example of such a data model, which consists of many tables, relationships, and DAX formulas based on millions of rows of data. This is a big data star schema data model created in the Power BI Desktop app, where the goal is to take a million rows of data from five different Excel files and create a gross profit dashboard.

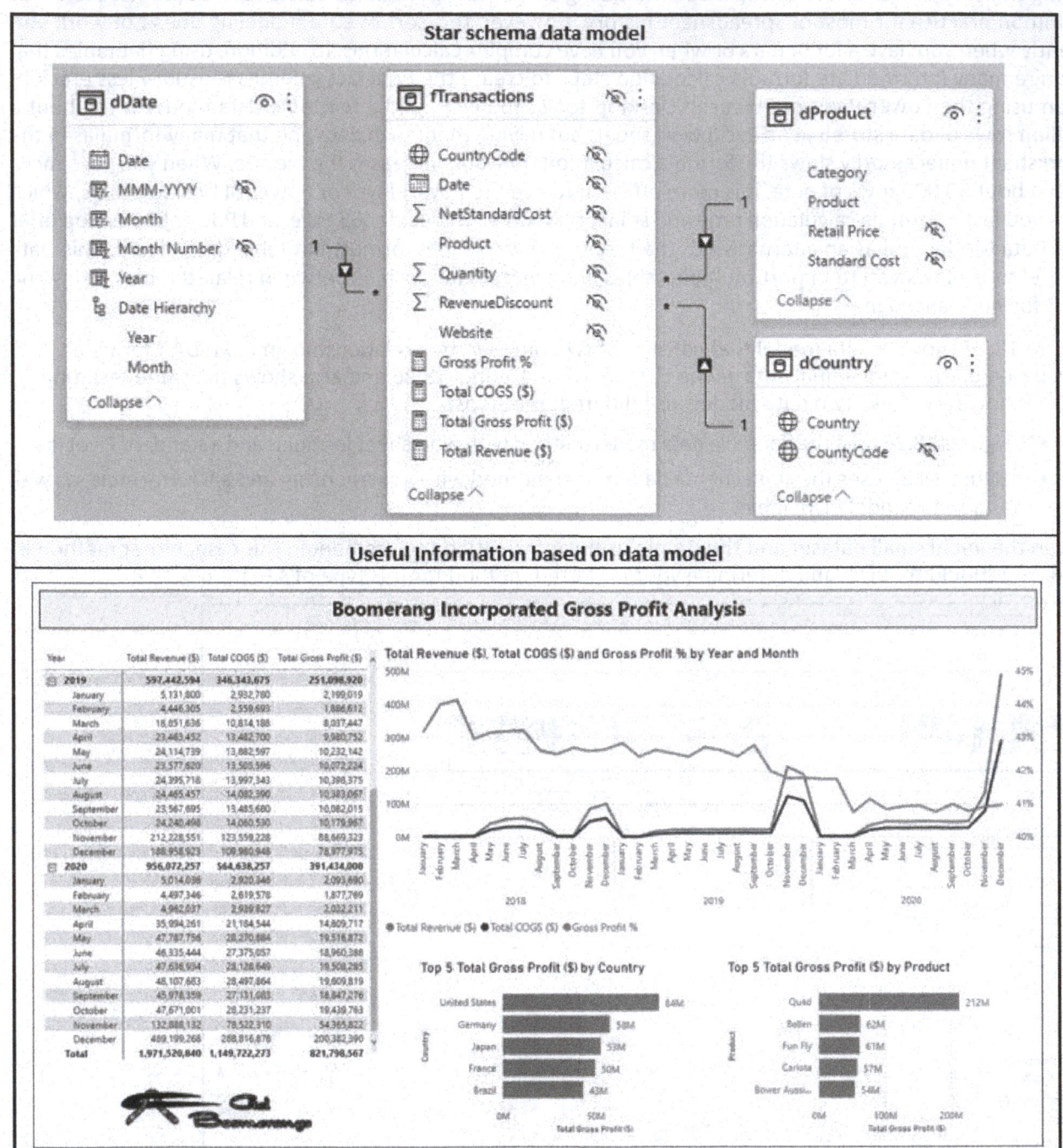

Figure 18.28 *A more complex data model with multiple tables, relationships, and DAX formulas.*

> **Note:** In Excel Power Pivot and Power BI Desktop, the *Data Model tool* is where you store the data models you create.

As you have already begun to see, your choice of data model type should be based on the source data you are working with and the goals of your project. In addition, you need to choose the most appropriate Excel tool for the type of data model you want to create. For example, if you have a small amount of data in an Excel worksheet and you want to make simple calculations such as adding and calculating percentages, then a flat data model and the standard PivotTable tool would be appropriate. If you have a lot of data and multiple lookup tables, or if you need to make complex calculations such as an average monthly sales calculation based on daily transactional sales amounts, then it would make sense to create a data model using Power Pivot or Power BI Desktop. If you want interactive and shareable reports and visualizations, then it makes sense to create a data model using the Power BI Desktop tool. You will see examples of using these tools later in this chapter.

Relationships in Data Models

In Figure 18.26, the XLOOKUP function is used to create a relationship between the ProductID field in the dimension table, which is the primary key (with a unique identifier for each product), and the ProductID field in the fact table, which is the foreign key (as has many duplicates). A relationship like this is called a *one-to-many relationship*. The primary key in the dimension table represents the one-side, and the foreign key in the fact table represents the many-side. This relationship makes sense because on the one-side, the business has exactly one of each product, and on the many-side, the business wants to sell many of each of the products.

One-to-many is the most common type of relationship, but there are other types of relationships:

- **Many-to-many relationship:** In this type of relationship, both columns can have duplicate values. As an example, say that you have a sales order fact tables and an invoice fact table, where an order can show up on many invoices, and an invoice can contain many orders.

- **One-to-one relationship:** In this type of relationship, each column contains a unique list, as with company cars that are each issued to only one employee or student IDs that are each issued to only one student.

For the data model in Figure 18.27, a star schema data model is used to make the final Data Model PivotTable report. As you've already seen, a star schema data model contains one fact table surrounded by dimension tables with relationships between related tables; it can also have reusable DAX formulas listed in the fact table. A star schema data model sometimes has more than one fact table, such as when you have budgeted amounts in one fact table and actual amounts in a second fact table. However, most of the time, there is just one fact table. The top part of Figure 18.27 shows one fact table and one dimension table. You can use Power Query to import the tables into the Power Pivot Data Model. Then, rather than use XLOOKUP to create a one-to-many relationship, you use the Relationship feature to connect the tables by using the one-side ProductID field from the dimension table and the many-side ProductID field from the fact table. (You will learn how to create relationships in Examples 2 and 3, later in this chapter.) With the relationship created, you can more easily and efficiently look up product attributes, such as price, or use fields from the dimension table in your report, such as the Product field from the Product dimension table.

Relationships improve efficiency when working with big data. When you use relationships rather than the XLOOKUP worksheet function, you avoid having many lookup function formulas in the Excel worksheet; this is beneficial because lookup function formulas in the Excel worksheet increase formula calculation time and file size.

DAX Formulas in Data Models

In addition to adding relationships to a data model, you can create formulas in the fact table and other parts of the data model by using the Data Model formula language DAX. There are three types of DAX formulas:

- **DAX calculated columns:** These columns are similar to helper columns used with formulas in Excel.

- **DAX measures:** These reusable formulas can be used in reports, visuals, and other areas in the Data Model.

- **DAX tables:** These formulas create tables.

Note: *DAX stands for Data Analysis Expressions, where the word expressions is a synonym for formulas.*

The bottom part of Figure 18.27 shows two DAX measures: one to calculate total sales and one to calculate total units. These two DAX measures are not fields in the table. Rather, they are premade, reusable formulas that you can drag and drop into reports and visuals, and they function like the standard PivotTable Values area calculations that you learned how to create in Chapter 17. By using these measures, you can make many more types of calculations than you can make by using the standard PivotTable Values area calculations, and you can use them as many times as you like, in as many different reports and visuals as you like.

There are four main advantages to using DAX formulas:

- You can create reusable, preformatted formulas, called measures, that you can drag and drop into PivotTables and PivotCharts.

- DAX formulas are specifically designed to work with the compressed data in the Data Model to calculate much more quickly than worksheet formulas.

- There are many more functions available in the DAX formula language than there are in a standard PivotTable; there are more than 250 DAX functions.

- The DAX formula language makes it easy and efficient to use tables with different granularities within a formula, which can reduce the number of intermediate steps in a complex formula.

The *granularity* (or *grain*) of a table is the size of the aggregation for each number in each row, such as a sales amount that can be calculated at the transaction, day, month, or year level. As you move from transaction granularity to year granularity, the granularity gets larger. Granularity is important for calculations like the average calculation, where numbers at a transaction level can yield the average transaction amount but cannot yield the average monthly amount. If your goal is to calculate the average monthly amount from numbers at a transaction level, you need to pre-aggregate to get the monthly totals, and then you can use those numbers in your average calculation. DAX formulas are particularly good at this type of pre-aggregation to get the correct granularity. (You will see how to use DAX formulas to pre-aggregate to get the correct granularity in the Chapter 19.)

DAX table formulas can also aggregate with other types of conditions and criteria, which can help reduce intermediate steps for complex calculations. When you have a lot of data or complex calculations, DAX formulas work with the compressed data and relationships to make data analysis on big data much more efficient than is possible with worksheet solutions.

The Data Model Tool in Excel Power Pivot and Power BI Desktop

The two places that you will use the Data Model tool are Excel Power Pivot and Power BI Desktop. The user interfaces in these two tools present data models slightly differently. Figure 18.29 compares the two interfaces, showing the same data model in the two different tools.

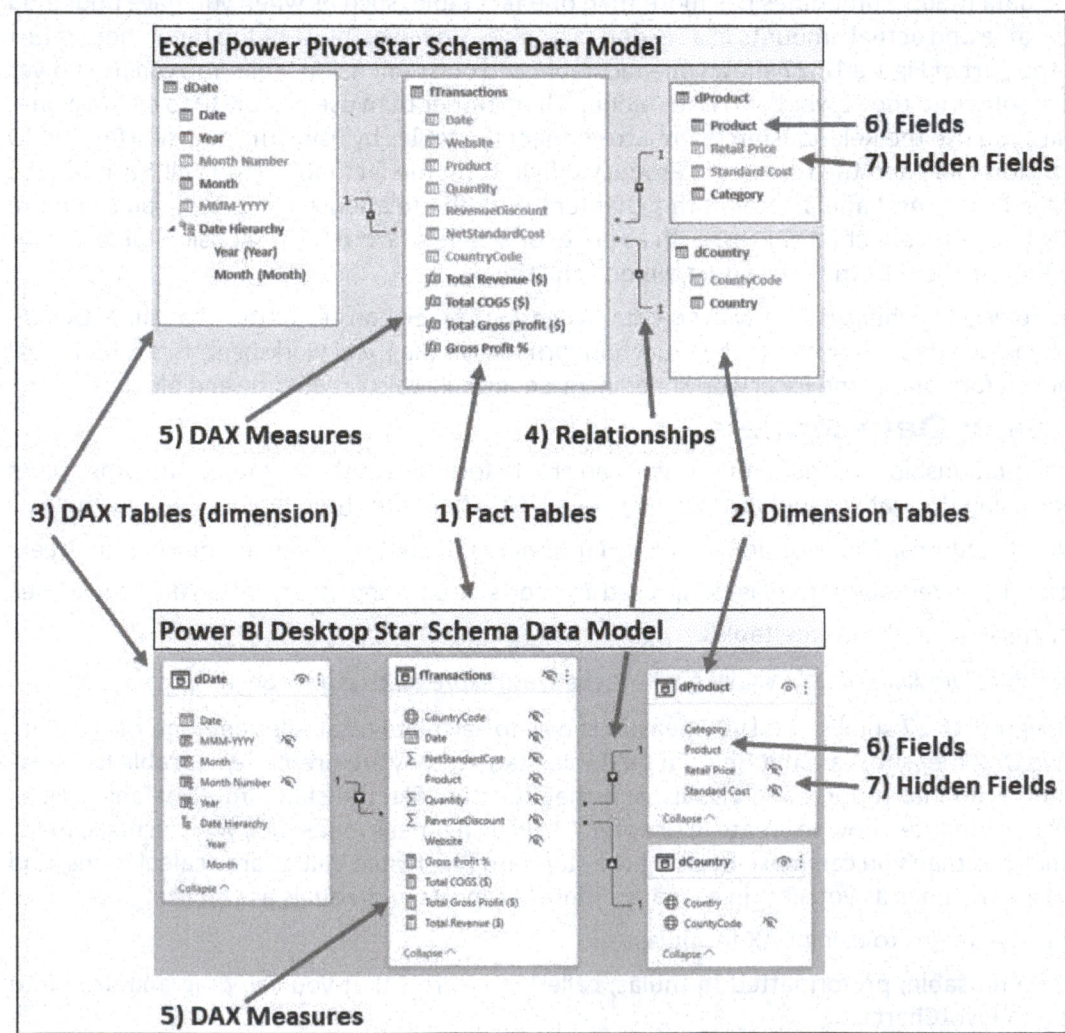

Figure 18.29 *A data model in Excel Power Pivot (top) and a data model in Power BI Desktop (bottom).*

The top half of Figure 18.29 shows an Excel Power Pivot star schema data model in the Data Model Design view window with one fact table and three dimension tables. The bottom half of Figure 18.29 shows the same star schema data model but in the Model view in the Power BI Desktop Data Model. The two tools depict the data model similarly: in a rectangle format, with the table name at the top and field names and DAX measure names listed below the table name. Fields and DAX measures that are not needed in the final reports, visuals, and dashboards are grayed out. One-to-many relationships are represented with arrowed lines, pointing from the one-side dimension table to the many-side fact table. The one-side is represented by the number 1, and the many-side is represented by an asterisk (*).

However, these tools take different approaches to displaying DAX measures and hidden columns. In Power BI Desktop, the DAX measures are shown with a handheld calculator icon, and the hidden fields are shown with what looks like an eyeball with a line through it. In Excel Power Pivot, the DAX measures are shown with a function icon (fx) that looks like the function icon for worksheet functions, and the hidden fields are shown grayed out.

The advantage of using the Data Model for big data is that you can load more than 1 million rows of data, and the data is significantly compressed to a much smaller size, which causes formulas to be calculated more quickly and file sizes to be much smaller. The Data Model contains a behind-the-scenes RAM *columnar database* that compresses and stores the data and also allows DAX formulas to work efficiently with big data. (Like the standard PivotTable cache that you learned about in Chapter 17, the columnar database is not a location that you can view and examine.)

The Process of Turning Data into Information: The 10-Step Data Analysis Process

Sometimes the data analysis process involves a single table and requires a simple report, and other times it is more involved and takes a long time. There are 10 basic steps involved in turning data into information. The first 8 steps are related to creating a *data model* (which, as you have already seen in this chapter, is the final source data), and the last 2 steps have to do with creating *useful information* (such as reports and visuals) based on that model and updating the data model as new data becomes available. Everything in the data analysis process, including designing the data model, starts with figuring out what questions need to be answered and what decisions need to be made.

> **Note:** Sometimes designing and building the data model is the most difficult and time-consuming part of the data analysis process.

These are the steps in the data analysis process:

1. **Determine the goals of the analysis.** Figure out what questions need answers and what decisions need to be made. Sometimes you just want to explore the data without an initial goal or question.

2. **Determine where the data is.** Figure out where the data is located (for example, a database, an Excel file, a text file, a website).

3. **Determine how much data exists.** Figure out how much data there is.

4. **Determine which tool or tools to use.** Figure out which tool or tools will work best, given your goals and the data involved. In general, as you have already seen in this chapter, there are five tools you can use in Excel:

   - **Worksheet formulas:** When data analysis results must update instantly when source data changes, you need to use formulas. Worksheet formulas are flexible and can work with data from anywhere in the worksheet, and when you use them, your data model does not have to be structured in any formal way.

   - **Standard PivotTables:** When you have a small dataset and simple calculations, you can use a standard PivotTable and Excel worksheet visualizations. The data model must be a flat table stored in the worksheet as an Excel Table or stored directly in the PivotTable cache.

   - **Mixed tools:** When you have many rows of data in a flat table and need to do simple calculations such as finding the frequency or percentage frequency, you can use a standard PivotTable and Excel worksheet visualizations. The data model can be a flat table stored in the Power Pivot Data Model.

- **Excel Power Pivot:** When you have many rows of data or multiple tables and need to make complex calculations but you do not need the visualization and sharing capabilities of Power BI, you can use Power Query and Power Pivot to build Data Model PivotTables and PivotCharts, using a star schema.
- **Power BI Desktop and/or Power BI Online:** When you have many rows of data or multiple tables and need to make complex calculations and you want interactive visualizations and/or sharing capabilities, you can use Power BI Desktop and/or Power BI Online, using a star schema data model.

5. **Import the data.** Bring the data into the tool you want to use, such as the Excel app or the Power BI Desktop app.

6. **Clean and transform the data.** Clean and transform the data into a proper dataset.

7. **Load the data.** Load the data into an Excel worksheet, a PivotTable cache, the Data Model, or some other location. When using Power Query, you must load the Power Query tables, using one of the following options:
   - Connection only (when the data is an intermediate step toward the final tables)
   - A PivotTable cache
   - An Excel worksheet
   - The Data Model in Power Pivot
   - The Data Model in Power BI Desktop

8. **Create a data model.** Create a data model to serve as the final source data for the analysis. Often this involves creating relationships between tables; adding helper columns to make row-by-row calculations or add attribute columns; and creating metrics, calculations, and other formulas that can help answer questions and fulfill goals. For small datasets, you can use worksheet formulas. But in most cases you will use the Data Model tool to perform these tasks:
   - Create DAX date or time dimension tables or other helper tables, if necessary.
   - Create DAX calculated columns (like date attribute columns or sales columns).
   - Create relationships between fact tables and dimension tables.
   - Create DAX measures (which are premade, reusable-metric formulas).
   - Hide fields and tables that are not required in the reporting visualization area.

9. **Create useful information.** Create reports, visualizations, and dashboards.

10. **Update the data model based on new data.** Refresh your data model and reports, visualizations, and dashboards when new data becomes available.

As you analyze data, you often need to repeat some or all of these steps. For example, you might need to add more data later, make adjustments to the cleaning and transforming data steps, create new metrics using DAX measures, or create new reports and visuals. With tools such as Power Query and the Data Model, these types of changes are easy to accomplish.

> **Note:** When you get new data, you need to add it to your data model and then refresh the reports and visualizations. For example, if you have data in an Excel Table in the worksheet, you can add new data to the bottom of the Excel Table and then refresh the standard PivotTable. If you have data in an on-premises file or folder or in an SQL database, and you use Power Query to import it, you can refresh the query, and the Data Model will receive the new data and then feed it to the reports and visualizations.

Data Analysis Examples

Now that you have learned all about data analysis—from the tools you can use to the terminology to the steps involved—you are ready to see examples of data analysis in action. To get familiar with Microsoft's data analysis tools, in the following sections you will use the small fact table and dimension table shown in Figures 18.26 and 18.27 to complete three examples:

- **Example 1:** You will use worksheet formulas, a standard PivotTable, and an Excel chart to create a product sales report and visualization.
- **Example 2:** You will use the Excel app with Power Query, a Power Pivot Data Model PivotTable, and an Excel chart to create a product sales report and visualization.

- **Example 3:** You will use Power BI Desktop and Power BI Online with Power Query, the Data Model, and visualizations to create a product sales report.

Example 1: Using Worksheet Formulas, a Standard PivotTable, and an Excel Chart to Create a Product Sales Report and Visualization

Note: For this example, you can use the file named Ch18-Excel365-AdvancedDataAnalysisEx1-62.xlsx.

Figure 18.30 shows a fact table with product units sold for each transaction and a product dimension table that you can use to look up product price and product name. Both tables have been converted to Excel Tables. The fact table is named fUnits, and the dimension table is named dProduct. The data analysis goal in this case is to create a report that shows total sales and total units sold by product and to create a visualization that shows total sales by product, sorted largest to smallest.

	A	B	C	D	E	F	G	H	I	J
2	Ex #1	Source Data: Excel Tables on this worksheet.								
3		Data analysis goal: Create product total sales and total units sold report with visualization.								
4		Other facts: We will create the solution using the Old School methods. We will use worksheet formulas to create flat table.								
5		With a small data set and simple calculations, this is an acceptable method.								
7		Fact Table = fUnits								
9		ProductID	UnitsSold				Dimension Table = dProducts			
10		1043	6							
11		1069	3				ProductID	Product	FlightRange(M)	Price
12		1069	8				1043	Quad	20	47.95
13		2005	3				1069	Aspen	25	29.95
14		1069	11				2005	Sunspot	15	21.95
15		1043	8							
16		2005	6							
17		2005	13							
18		1043	5							
19		1043	5							

Figure 18.30 *One small fact table and one small dimension table. Both are Excel Tables in the worksheet.*

	A	B	C	D
7		Fact Table = fUnits		
9		ProductID	UnitsSold	Sales($)
10		1043	6	
11		1069	3	
12		1069	8	

Figure 18.31 *Type the new field name directly to the right of the last field name in the Excel Table.*

	A	B	C	D
9		ProductID	UnitsSold	Sales($)
10		1043	6	
11		1069	3	
12		1069	8	
13		2005	3	
14		1069	11	
15		1043	8	
16		2005	6	
17		2005	13	
18		1043	5	
19		1043	5	

Figure 18.32 *When you press Enter, a new field is added to the dynamic Excel Table object.*

In this example, you will use worksheet formulas to create a flat fact table that you can then use to create a standard PivotTable report and a PivotChart visualization. This is the method used throughout most of Excel data analysis history. Learning this old-school method is helpful for a couple reasons:

- It provides a reference point as you move to the newer data analysis tools.

- For some small datasets, it can still be an efficient method.

To follow along, complete these steps on the worksheet named Ch18(30-62):

11. As shown in Figure 18.31, click in cell D9 and type the new field name **Sales($)**.

12. As shown in Figure 18.32, when you press the Enter key to enter the field name into the cell, the Excel Table object automatically expands to include the new field.

13. As shown in Figure 18.33, click in cell D10 and create a lookup formula to look up the product ID in the dProduct dimension table and return the product price. (You learned how to use the XLOOKUP function in Chapter 14 and how to use table formula nomenclature in Chapter 12.)

7	Fact Table = fUnits									
9	ProductID	UnitsSold	Sales($)			Dimension Table = dProducts				
10	1043		6	=XLOOKUP([@ProductID],dProducts[ProductID],dProducts[Price])						
11	1069	3				ProductID	Product	FlightRange(M)		Price
12	1069	8				1043	Quad	20		47.95
13	2005	3				1069	Aspen	25		29.95
14	1069	11				2005	Sunspot	15		21.95

Figure 18.33 *XLOOKUP is the worksheet function you use to create a lookup formula.*

14. As shown in Figure 18.34, when you press Enter to enter the worksheet lookup formula name into the cell, the Excel Table object automatically copies the formula down to all rows in the table.

7	Fact Table = fUnits		
9	ProductID	UnitsSold	Sales($)
10	1043	6	47.95
11	1069	3	29.95
12	1069	8	29.95
13	2005	3	21.95
14	1069	11	29.95
15	1043	8	47.95
16	2005	6	21.95
17	2005	13	21.95
18	1043	5	47.95
19	1043	5	47.95

Figure 18.34 *In an Excel Table, when you create a formula, it is automatically copied down to the rows below.*

Note: The new Sales($) field is not like the spilled array formulas that you learned about in Chapter 15. Remember that spilled array formulas are not even allowed in Excel Tables. The reason the formula automatically fills down in this case is that the Excel Table feature is programmed to copy a formula down when you create the formula in the first row of the table. This is called an *Excel Table calculated column*. If you do not like this Excel Table ability, you can turn it off by going to File, Options, Proofing, AutoCorrect Options; then, in the AutoFormat As You Type tab, uncheck Fill Formulas in Table to Create Calculated Columns. I love this feature: It is very convenient, and it is similar to how calculated columns work in Power Query, Power Pivot, and Power BI Desktop, as you'll learn later in this chapter.

15. As shown in Figure 18.35, to complete the Sales($) field formula for calculating sales for each transaction, click in the top cell in the field, press the F2 key to put the cell in edit mode, multiply the XLOOKUP function by the units sold for the first row, and press the Enter key to populate the edited formula down to the rows below.

7	Fact Table = fUnits						
9	ProductID	UnitsSold	Sales($)			Dimension Table = dProducts	
10	1043		6	=XLOOKUP([@ProductID],dProducts[ProductID],dProducts[Price])*[@UnitsSold]			

Figure 18.35 *The formula for sales is the price delivered by XLOOKUP multiplied by UnitsSold.*

Note: Importantly, for the formula in Figure 18.35, you did not have to use the ROUND function (which you learned about in Chapter 10) because, although you will use the results in subsequent formulas, your multiplication calculation will never get decimal places past the penny position when you multiply a whole number by a money amount with two decimal places.

Figure 18.36 shows the completed Sales($) calculated column field. You can also see how the fact table and dimension table can communicate with each other to create a relationship by using the XLOOKUP function. With worksheet formulas, you use a lookup function such as XLOOKUP to make a connection and create a relationship from the one-side (the primary key side) in the dimension table to the many-side (the foreign key side) in the fact table.

	The two tables are connected through the ProductID field (relationship)								
7									
8									
9	**ProductID**	**UnitsSold**	**Sales($)**						
10	1043	6	287.7						
11	1069	3	89.85		**ProductID**	**Product**	**FlightRange(M)**	**Price**	
12	1069	8	239.6		1043	Quad	20	47.95	
13	2005	3	65.85		1069	Aspen	25	29.95	
14	1069	11	329.45		2005	Sunspot	15	21.95	
15	1043	8	383.6						
16	2005	6	131.7		^ ^ ^				
17	2005	13	285.35		* One-side				
18	1043	5	239.75						
19	1043	5	239.75						
20									
21	^ ^ ^								
	* Many-side								

Figure 18.36 *The ProductID field connects the tables and creates a worksheet formula relationship.*

16. As shown in Figure 18.37, create a second field, named Product, in the fUnits fact table to look up the product name.

7	Fact Table = fUnits							
9	**ProductID**	**UnitsSold**	**Sales($)**	**Product**	**Dimension Table = dProducts**			
10	1043	6	287.7	=XLOOKUP([@ProductID],dProducts[ProductID],dProducts[Product])				
11	1069	3	89.85	Aspen	**ProductID**	**Product**	**FlightRange(M)**	**Price**
12	1069	8	239.6	Aspen	1043	Quad	20	47.95
13	2005	3	65.85	Sunspot	1069	Aspen	25	29.95
14	1069	11	329.45	Aspen	2005	Sunspot	15	21.95

Figure 18.37 *Creating a Product field in the fact table.*

Data Modeling with Worksheet Formulas

As shown in Figure 18.38, you now have a flat fact table with a foreign key (ProductID), two fact fields (UnitsSold and Sales($)), and a dimension field (Product) that you can use as the source data for a PivotTable report and PivotChart visualization. Together, the dimension table, the worksheet formulas, and the flat fact table constitute a data model that you can use to achieve the data analysis goals in this example. I still sometimes use this old-school method in two situations:

- **With a small dataset:** When there is not a lot of data, there are not a lot of formulas in the worksheet, and, therefore, slow formula calculation is not an issue. Because I am comfortable with worksheet formulas, I can create a data model like this quickly, so this old-school method is a good option.

- **With millions of rows of data and a complex data model:** I often build a small parallel dataset and data model with Power Query, Power Pivot, and Power BI Desktop to test a data model before I try the data model techniques on the big dataset. I also build a solution using worksheet formulas to double-check my work and see if I can yield the same answers with worksheet formulas. (You will see an example of this in Chapter 19.)

7	Fact Table = fUnits							
9	**ProductID**	**UnitsSold**	**Sales($)**	**Product**	**Dimension Table = dProducts**			
10	1043	6	287.7	Quad				
11	1069	3	89.8		**ProductID**	**Product**	**FlightRange(M)**	**Price**
12	1069	8			1043	Quad	20	47.95
13	2005			Sunspot	1069	Aspen	25	29.95
14	1069		329.45	Aspen	2005	Sunspot	15	21.95
15		8	383.6	Quad				
16		6	131.7	Sunspot				
17	2005	13	285.35	Sunspot				
18	1043	5	239.75	Quad				
19	1043	5	239.75	Quad				
20								
21	Both tables together are **the data model**							
22								

Flat fact table

Figure 18.38 *The data model created consists of one dimension table and one flat fact table.*

Creating a PivotTable from a Flat Table

Next, from the flat fact table, you can create the PivotTable report. For this small initial example, you will create the report and visualization on the same worksheet as the dataset so you can see all the connected pieces of the project. Follow these steps:

1. As shown in Figure 18.39, click in one cell in the fact table. Then use the keyboard shortcut Alt, N, V, T to open the PivotTable from Table or Range dialog box. When the dialog box pops up, the table name automatically appears in the Table/Range textbox.

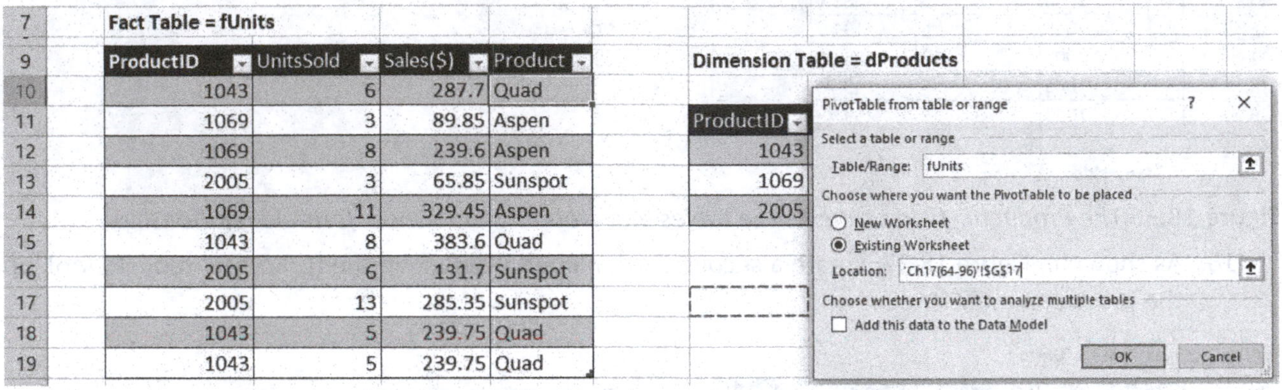

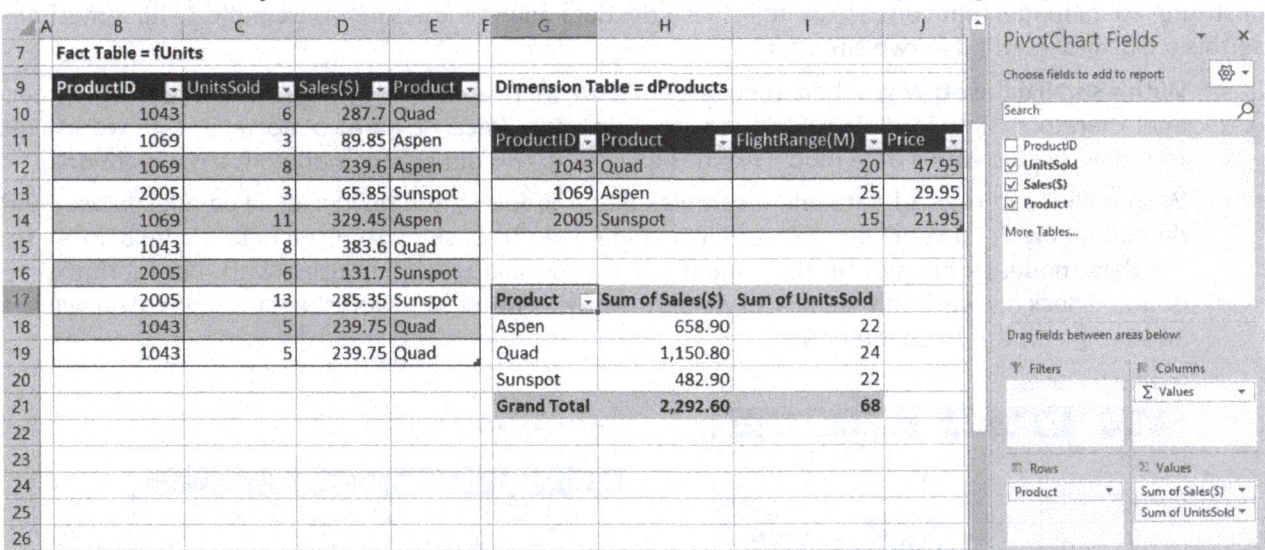

Figure 18.39 *Create a standard PivotTable from the flat fact table.*

2. Select the Existing Worksheet option button.

3. Click in cell G17.

4. Click OK to add the data to the standard PivotTable cache.

5. As shown in Figure 18.40, to create the report using the PivotChart Fields task pane, drag the Product field to the Rows area, drag the Sales($) field to the Values area, and then drag the UnitsSold field to the Values area below the Sales($) field.

6. Add number formatting to the Sales($) calculation. Figure 18.40 shows the finished report. As you can see, with just a few clicks, the standard PivotTable tool can do amazing things!

Figure 18.40 *Using the PivotChart Fields task pane, you drag and drop fields to create a report.*

Next, you need to create a visualization for total sales by product. As you can see in Figure 18.40, you already have a calculation that shows the total sales for each product. So why do you need a visualization to show total sales by product? Because visualizations have a more immediate impact, enabling a decision maker to quickly see which item has the largest Sum of Sales($) amount. However, if you use an Excel chart to visualize the Sum of Sales($) calculation from the existing PivotTable, the chart will include both calculations because the PivotTable is considered a single object—and that is not what you want. You want just Sum of Sales($) in the visualization. You can accomplish this by initiating the charting process from the fact table. Because the fact table does not have summarized data, and you need the data to be summarized, you can use the PivotChart tool, which summarizes the data before charting it.

Using the Excel Chart Tools to Visualize Data with Bar and Column Charts

You need to compare the different total sales for each product name. As you learned in Chapter 17, charts can be used to visually portray quantitative data in a more immediate way than can numbers alone. The visualization that best communicates amounts across categories is either a *column chart* or a *bar chart*, where the lengths of the bars or heights of the columns communicate the relative sizes of the numbers. In an Excel worksheet, you can use the *Excel chart tools* to create visualizations.

Follow these steps to first create a column chart and then create a bar chart:

1. As shown in Figure 18.41, select a single cell in the fact table, click the Insert tab in the Ribbon, click the PivotChart dropdown arrow in the Charts group, and select PivotChart.

    In the PivotChart dropdown list in Figure 18.41, you can see two options: PivotChart and PivotChart & PivotTable. It might seem as if they are two different options, where the first one creates just a PivotChart and the second one creates both a PivotTable and a PivotChart. For a standard PivotTable, both options will do the same thing, though: create a PivotTable in the worksheet and a PivotChart that is based on that PivotTable. Later, however, if you use the Data Model for your source data, the bottom option will be grayed out, and only the top option will be available. Further, if you look at the Charts group in the Insert tab in Figure 18.41, you can see that there are many charting options besides the PivotChart button. Whereas the PivotChart button is for summarizing data and then making a chart, as you learned in Chapter 17, the other buttons are for making charts from data that is already summarized or from raw data.

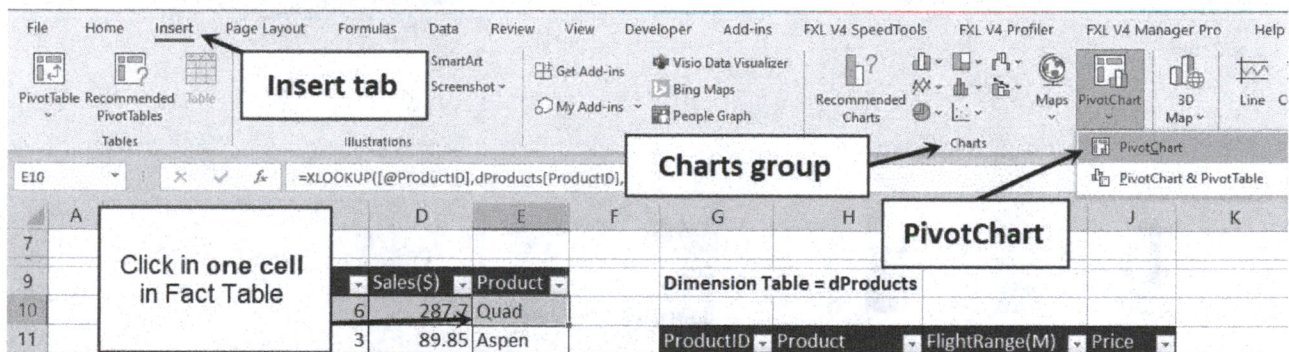

Figure 18.41 *From the flat fact table, you want to create a PivotChart to show total sales by product.*

2. When the Create PivotChart dialog box pops up and you see the that the Table/Range textbox shows the fact table name (see Figure 18.42), select the Existing Worksheet option button, click in cell G17, and click OK to access the PivotTable cache that has already been stored for this fact table.

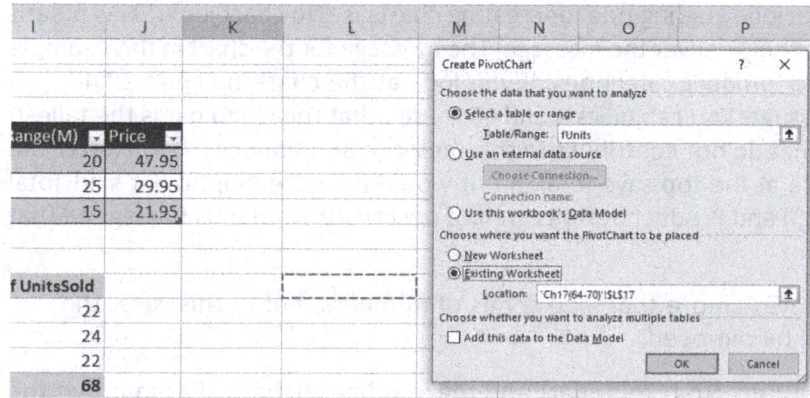

Figure 18.42 *Place a PivotChart in cell L17.*

As shown in Figure 18.43, a standard PivotTable and a PivotChart are created on the worksheet, and the PivotChart Fields task pane appears on the right. Importantly, when you created this second PivotTable/PivotChart from the fUnits table, the data did not get placed in a second PivotTable cache. As you learned in Chapter 17, the PivotTable/PivotChart conveniently accessed the PivotTable cache of data that already existed for the fUnits table when you created the first PivotTable. Using the existing cache of data in this way helps reduce file size.

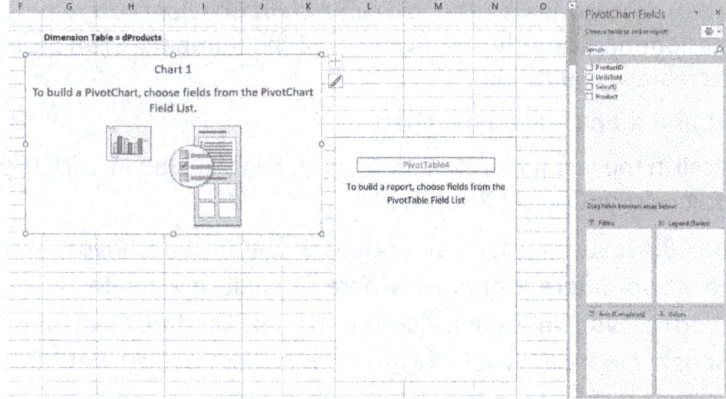

Figure 18.43 *When you are not using the Data Model, a PivotChart creates a standard PivotTable as the source data.*

3. As shown in Figure 18.44, drag the Product field to the Axis (Categories) area and the Sales($) field to the Values area to simultaneously create the PivotTable and PivotChart. The default PivotChart chart type is a column chart—and that is the visualization you want.

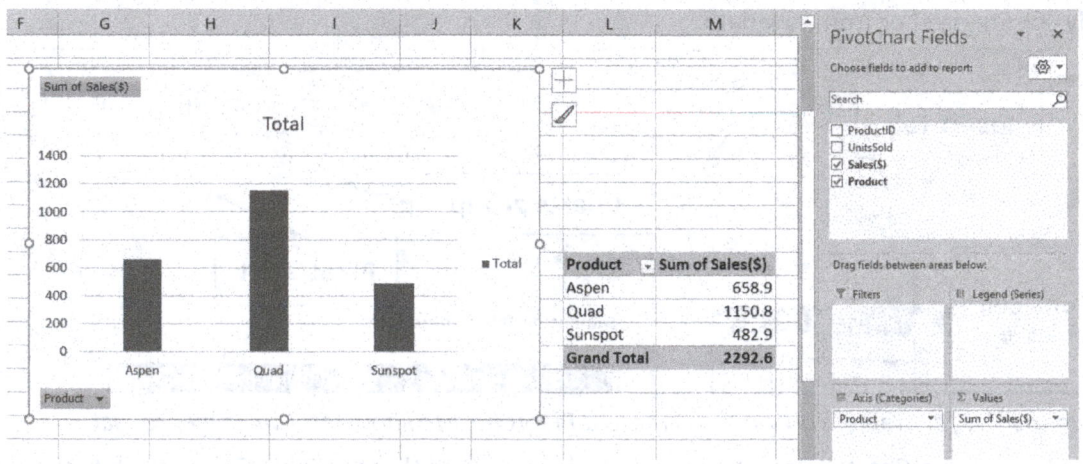

Figure 18.44 *Using the PivotChart Fields task pane, you create the report and chart simultaneously.*

Making your Chart More Effective

As you learned in Chapter 17, the number-one guiding rule for creating charts is "No chart junk." This means you must remove all elements that do not help deliver the message. The message for the chart in this example is simple: Compare sales amounts across product categories. If you look at the chart in Figure 18.44, you can see that you have delivered this message: You can quickly and easily see that the Quad bar is the tallest. However, there are multiple elements that do not contribute to this message and unnecessarily clutter the visualization. For example, the chart title at the top says Total, but it would be more helpful if it said Total Sales by Product. The gray Sum of Sales($) and Product buttons are not necessary. Neither is the legend that shows a blue square and the word Total.

> **Note:** Legends are useful when there is more than one series of numbers, but in this case, the legend is not necessary and should be removed.

Follow these steps to remove the chart junk from this chart and make other changes that improve the effectiveness of the chart:

1. As shown in Figure 18.45, to remove the Sum of Sales($) and Product buttons, right-click either one of them and then click on the option Hide All Field Buttons on Chart.

Note: The Hide All Field Buttons on Chart option is also available in the PivotChart Analyze tab in the Ribbon, in the Show/Hide group.

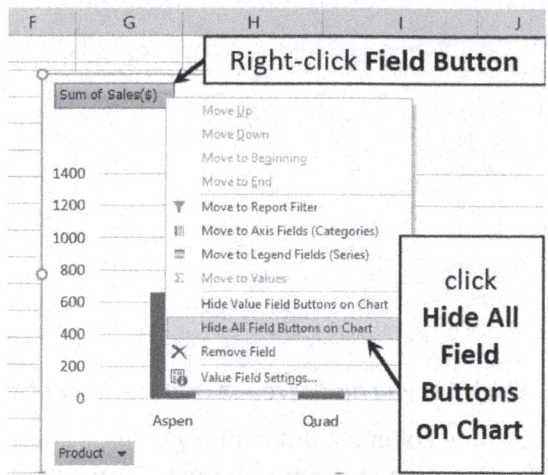

Figure 18.45 *Usually the field buttons on a PivotChart do not look good in the final presentation.*

2. To remove the legend, as shown in Figure 18.46, click the legend and press the Delete key.

Note: You can also delete the legend by clicking the green Add/Remove Chart Elements plus icon that hovers on the right side of a selected chart.

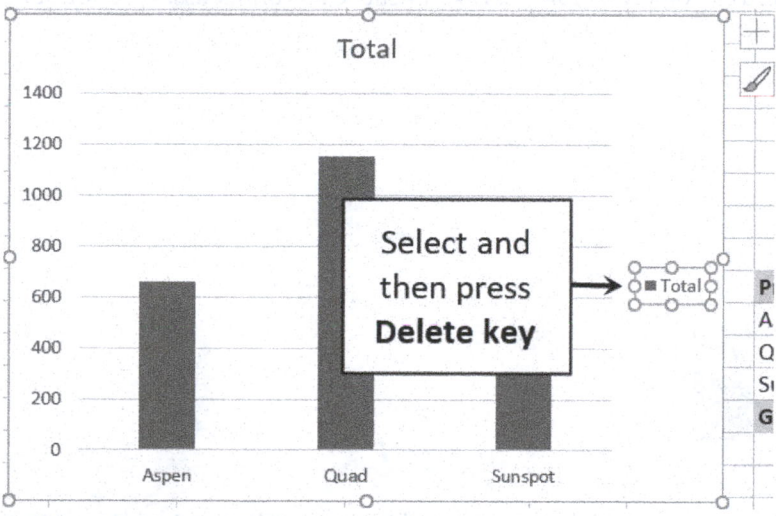

Figure 18.46 *Because there is only one series of numbers, the legend is chart junk and should be removed.*

3. To edit the chart title, slowly click it two times to put the title in edit mode. When the outside edge of the chart title is a dashed line, as shown in Figure 18.47, you know the title is in edit mode. Then select the text and type **Total Sales by Product**. To enter the text as a new chart title, click outside the edge of the chart title.

Note: Another way to edit the chart title is to click it one time (making sure the outside edge is not a dashed line but instead a solid line) and then type a new title in the formula bar or type an equal sign and click on a cell that contains the chart title. To enter the title in the formula bar, press the Enter key.

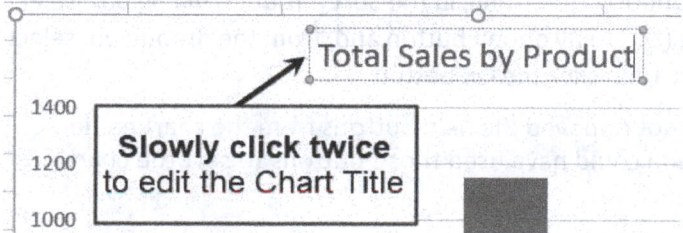

Figure 18.47 *Slowly click two times to put the chart title in edit mode and then type a new chart title.*

4. To add data labels, as shown in Figure 18.48, click on the green Add/Remove Chart Elements plus icon that hovers on the right side of the selected chart and select the Data Labels checkbox.

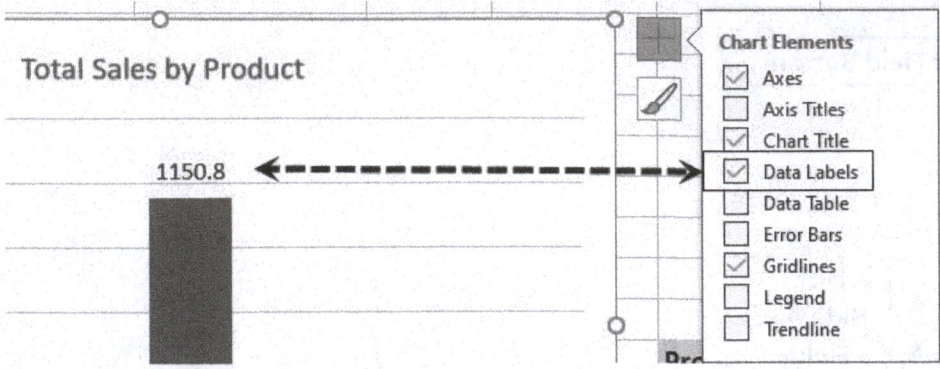

Figure 18.48 *To the right of all Excel charts is the green plus icon, which lets you add or remove chart elements.*

When you add data labels, Excel shows the numbers above the columns. But in many cases, a chart includes numbers on the vertical axis and gridlines that make it easy to compare the heights of the columns (see Figure 18.49). In many cases you don't need labels on both the vertical axis and the columns. The numbers at the top of the columns show the exact numbers; when you use them, the relatively sized columns have an immediate impact, and the exact numbers provide more specific details. You don't usually want to include numbers both on the axis and at the top of each columns. But it is a judgment call. For this chart, you can delete the vertical axis because it is unnecessary repetition.

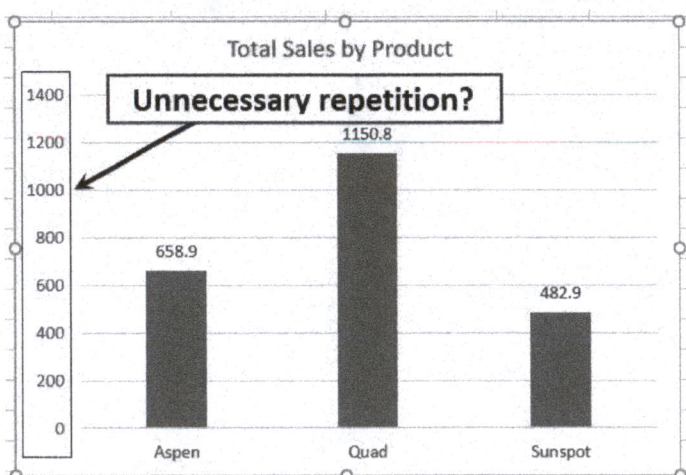

Figure 18.49 *When you add data labels, you must consider whether or not showing numbers in two locations is necessary.*

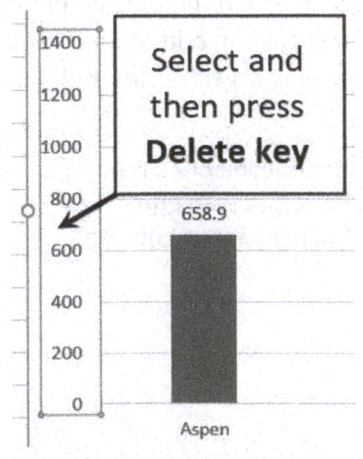

5. To remove the vertical axis, click to select it and press the Delete key (see Figure 18.50).

    Note: You can also remove the axis by clicking the green Add/Remove Chart Elements plus icon and deselecting Axis Labels.

6. To sort the columns from largest to smallest, click the dropdown arrow in the Rows area of the PivotTable, as shown in Figure 18.51, and click the More Sort Options item. Then, in the Sort (Product) dialog box, select the Descending (Z to A) By option button and, from the dropdown, select Sum of Sales($). Then click the OK button.

    Note: If you had not removed the field buttons from the chart earlier in this process, you could have used those buttons to sort the chart.

Figure 18.50 *To delete any chart element, you can select it and press the Delete key.*

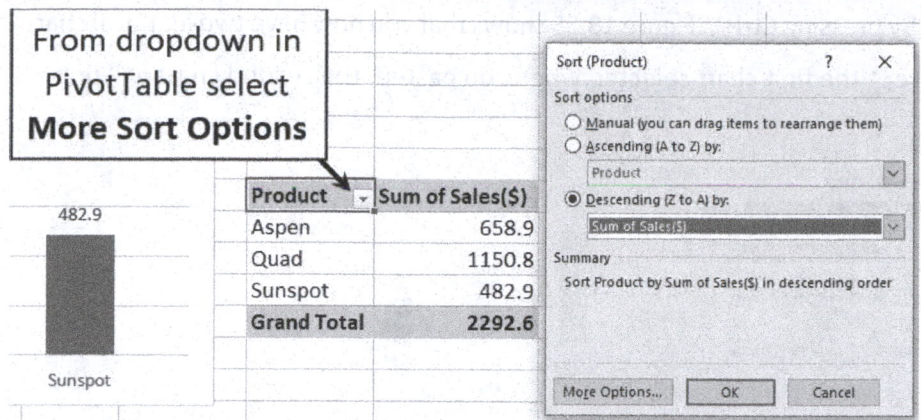

Figure 18.51 *If you want to sort the columns from largest to smallest, you must sort the PivotTable.*

The sorted column chart is shown in Figure 18.52.

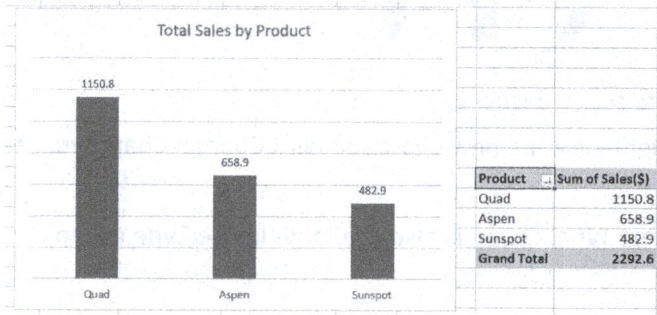

Figure 18.52 *When you sort the PivotTable, the chart is also sorted.*

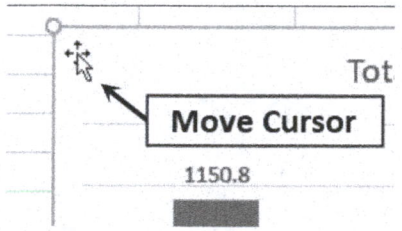

Figure 18.53 *If you want to move a chart, carefully point to the outside edge of the chart and use the move cursor.*

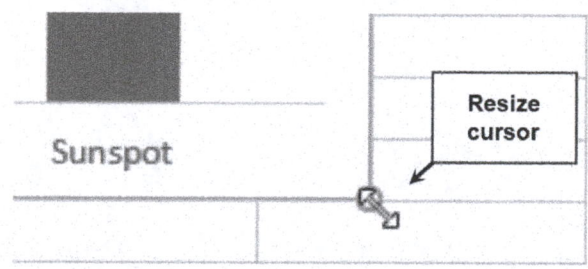

Figure 18.54 *If you want to resize a chart, use the resize cursor on the corner of the chart.*

7. As shown in Figure 18.53, to move the chart, point to the outside edge of the chart and click and drag using the move cursor.

Note: When you move a chart, you must be careful to point to the very outside edge of the chart. If you try to use the move cursor on the middle part of the chart, you might grab a column or a label or the whole series of numbers (columns) and accidentally move those instead. Also, if you want to move a chart and snap the chart to the edge of a column or row, you can hold the Alt key and then move the chart. This can help you line things up and make everything look neat. Figure 18.54 shows how you can resize a chart and make it bigger or smaller by using the resize cursor.

Next, you need to create a bar chart and compare it to the column chart you've already created. Follow these steps:

1. Copy your column chart by clicking on the outside edge of the chart and pressing Ctrl+C.

2. Select a cell in the worksheet, such as L24.

3. Paste the copied chart by pressing Ctrl+V. Figure 18.55 shows that you now have two identical charts.

> **Note:** If you accidentally kept the first chart selected when you pasted, the second chart will not be created.

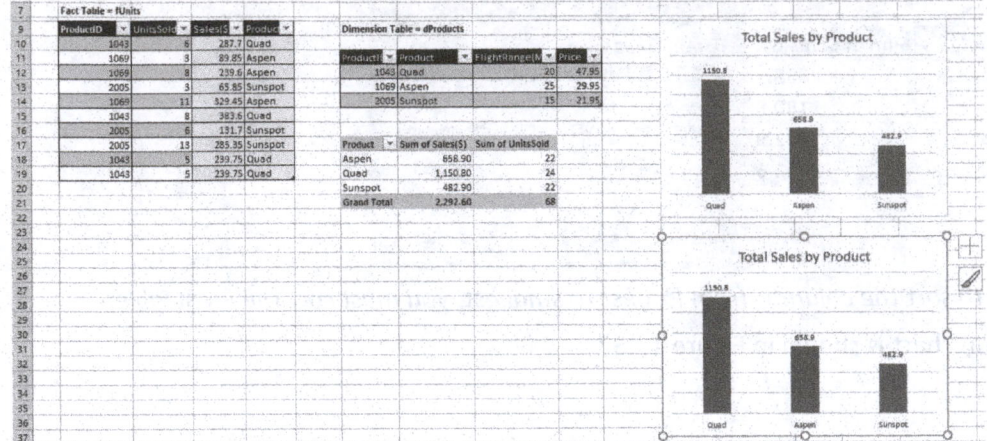

Figure 18.55 *Copy the first chart and then paste it into the worksheet.*

4. To change the chart type of the new chart, right-click the new chart and click Change Chart Type, as shown in Figure 18.56.

> **Note:** When a chart is selected, the Change Chart Type option is also available in the Type group on the Design tab of the Ribbon.

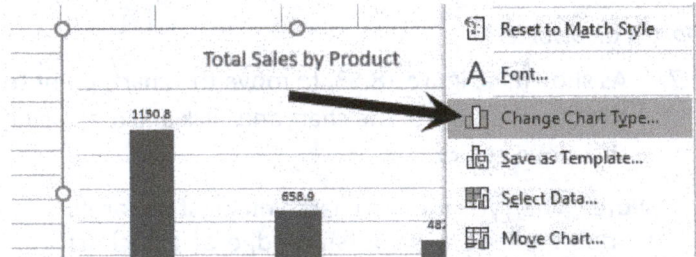

Figure 18.56 *Right-click the PivotChart to change the type of the chart.*

5. As shown in Figure 18.57, in the Change Chart Type dialog box, select Bar on the left, on the right select Clustered Bar, and then click the OK button.

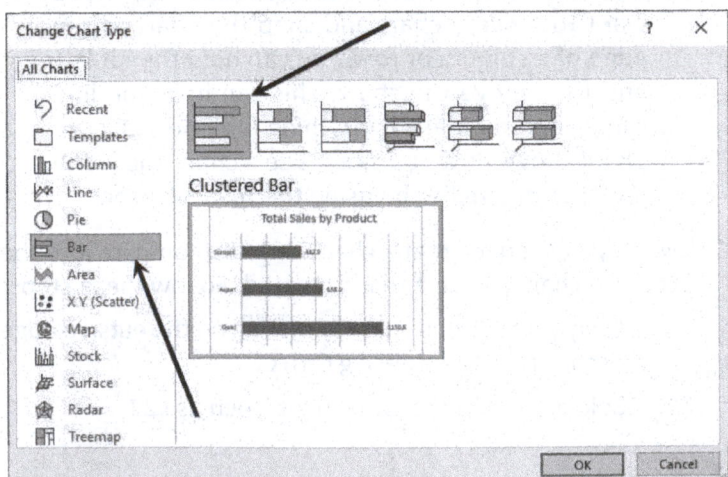

Figure 18.57 *Select Clustered Bar chart.*

6. To remove the vertical gridlines from the bar chart, click the green Add/Remove Chart Elements plus icon on the right side of the chart and uncheck Gridlines (not pictured).

7. To change the size of the gap between the bars, click any one of the bars to select all of them and then press Ctrl+1, as shown in Figure 18.58. The Format Data Series task pane appears.

> **Note:** Another way to open the Format Data Series task pane is to right-click a bar and select the Chart Formatting option. Also, note that the title at the top of this task pane changes, depending on what chart element you have selected. The pane that is called the Format Data Series task pane here may instead be called the Format Chart Element task pane or the Format Axis task pane, for example. This is a pretty cool feature of Excel charts because as soon as you open the task pane, you can simply click on different chart elements to bring up a different formatting task pane.

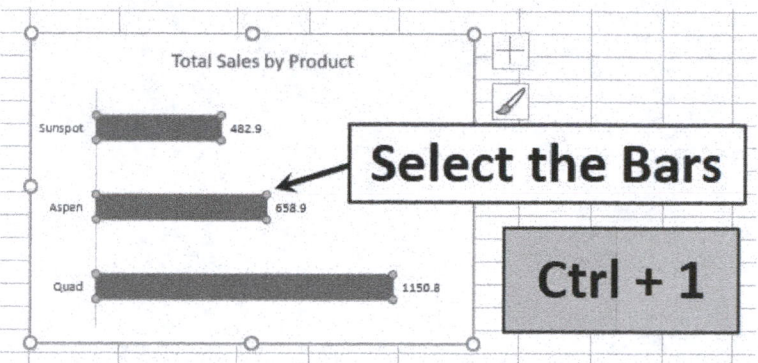

Figure 18.58 *Select a bar in a chart and then press Ctrl+1 to open the Format Data Series task pane.*

8. As shown in Figure 18.59, slide the Gap Width bar to 100%.This will cause the gridlines to be removed and the gap between the bars (the data series) to be reduced.

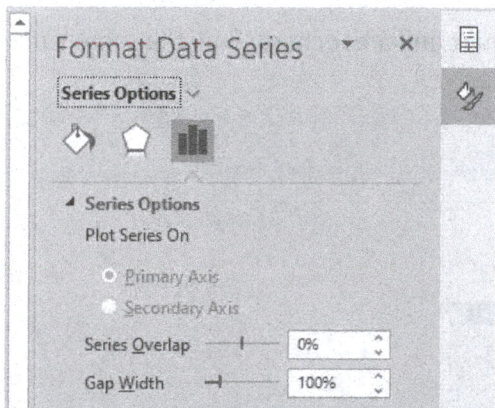

Figure 18.59 *The task pane shows the term Format Data Series because data series is the term Microsoft uses to refer to the numbers in a chart.*

To open the Format Axis task pane, click on the vertical axis that lists the product names, as shown in Figure 18.60.

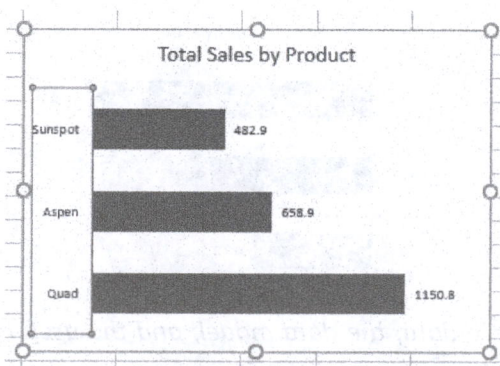

Figure 18.60 *Select the vertical axis to show the Format Axis task pane.*

9. As shown in Figure 18.61, in the Format Axis task pane, check the Categories in Reverse Order checkbox.

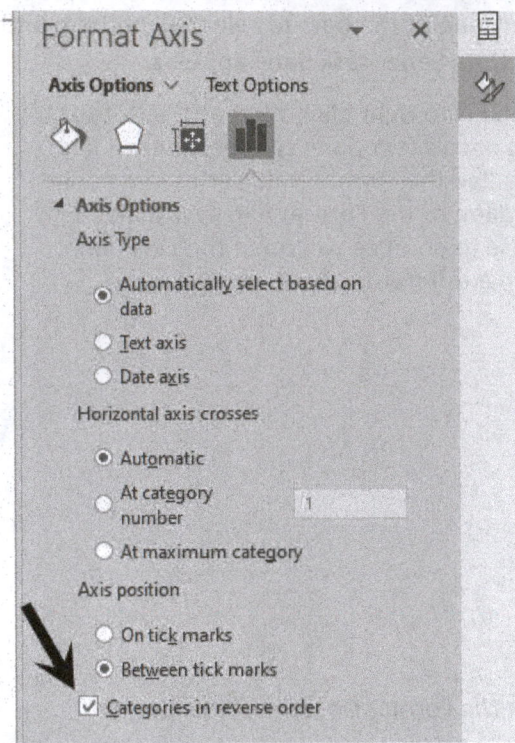

Figure 18.61 *The Categories in Reverse Order option reverses the order so the largest Sum of Sales($) amounts are on top.*

Figure 18.62 shows the final data analysis results. In it, a column chart and a bar chart show the same summarized data.

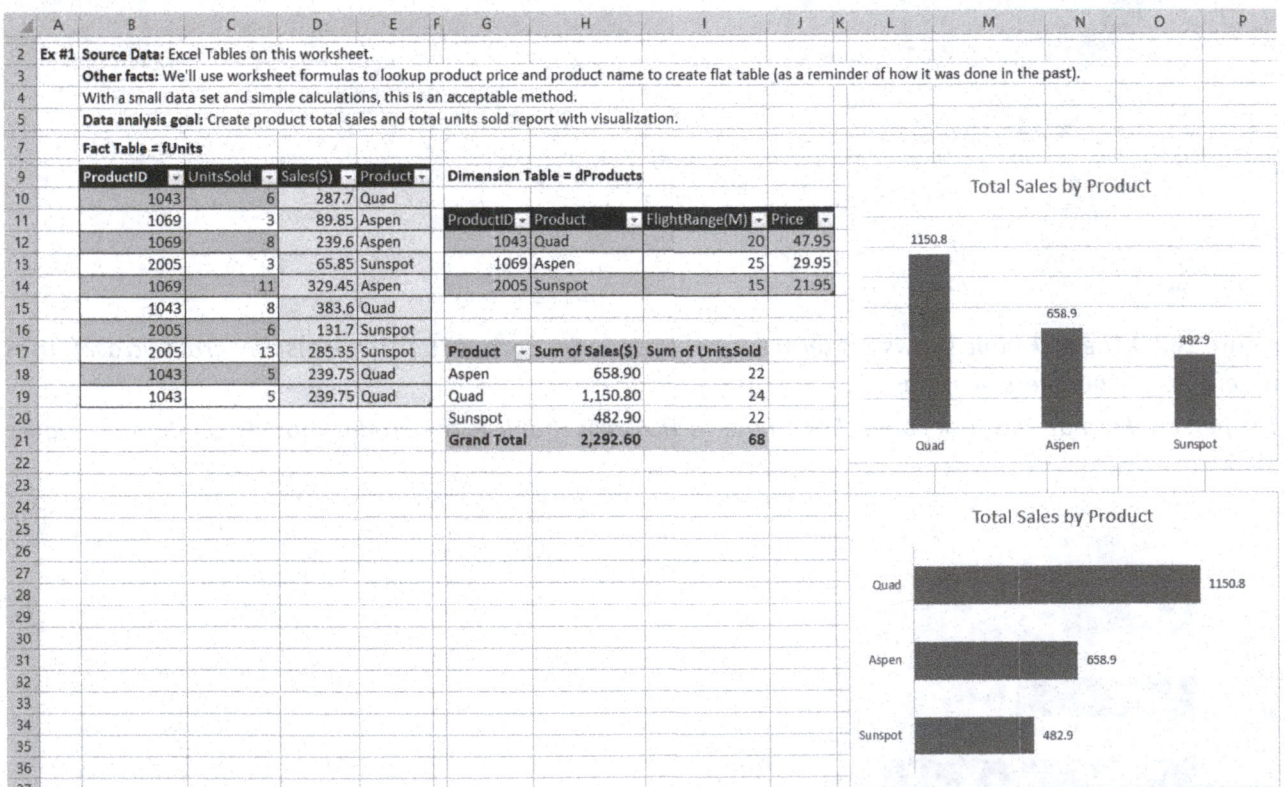

Figure 18.62 *In this small example, you can see the original source data, the data model, and the useful information.*

As you learned in Chapter 17, column charts and bar charts are very similar, but there are two subtle differences:

- A bar chart can emphasize the difference between categories more forcefully than can a column chart because of the horizontal orientation.
- A bar chart can present longer category labels in a less cluttered way than can a column chart.

And remember that both column charts and bar charts show information more clearly than do pie charts. Column charts and bar charts use rectangles to compare heights rather than wedged pie pieces, and our eyes can gauge the differences between rectangles more quickly than they can determine the differences between wedges of a pie.

Example 1 Summary

Table 18.1 summarizes this example according to the 10-step data analysis process described earlier in this chapter.

Table 18.1 Example 1 Data Analysis Process Summary

Step	How Step Is Carried Out in This Example
1. Determine the goals of the analysis	Create a total sales and total units report and a sorted total sales visualization.
2. Determine where the data is	The data is in an Excel Table in a worksheet.
3. Determine how much data exists	There is a small amount of data.
4. Determine which tool or tools to use	Use worksheet formulas and a standard PivotTable.
5. Import the data	It is already in an Excel worksheet.
6. Clean and transform the data	Use worksheet formulas.
7. Load the data	Load the data to the PivotTable cache.
8. Create a data model	Use an Excel Table and worksheet formulas.
9. Create useful information	Use a standard PivotTable and a PivotChart.
10. Update the data model based on new data	You do not yet have any new data.

Example 2: Using the Excel App with Power Query, a Power Pivot Data Model PivotTable, and an Excel Chart to Create a Product Sales Report and Visualization

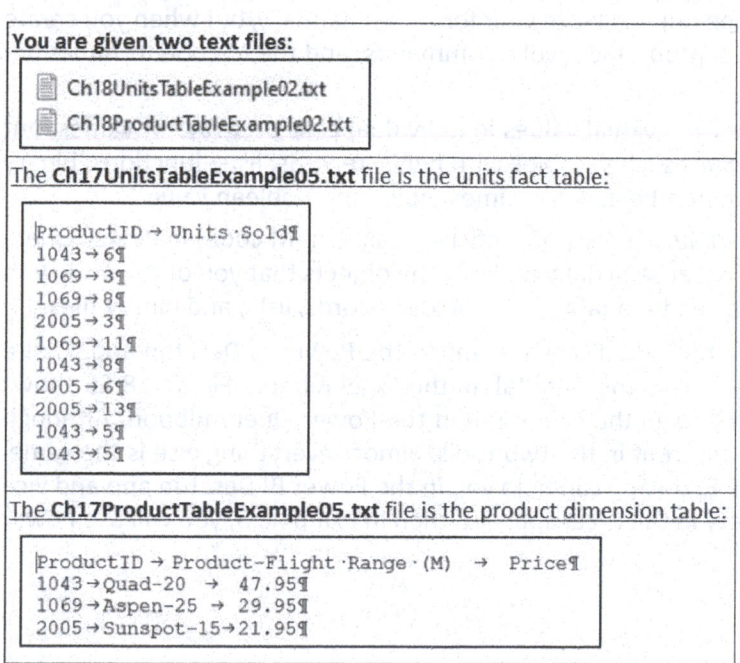

You are given two text files:

📄 Ch18UnitsTableExample02.txt
📄 Ch18ProductTableExample02.txt

The **Ch17UnitsTableExample05.txt** file is the units fact table:

```
ProductID → Units ·Sold¶
1043→6¶
1069→3¶
1069→8¶
2005→3¶
1069→11¶
1043→8¶
2005→6¶
2005→13¶
1043→5¶
1043→5¶
```

The **Ch17ProductTableExample05.txt** file is the product dimension table:

```
ProductID → Product-Flight ·Range ·(M)  →  Price¶
1043→Quad-20  →  47.95¶
1069→Aspen-25 →  29.95¶
2005→Sunspot-15→21.95¶
```

Figure 18.63 *Text files are commonly used to transfer data from one system to another.*

Note: For this example, you will use the following files: Ch18-Excel365-AdvancedDataAnalysisStartEx63-153.xlsx, Ch18UnitsTableExample02.txt, and Ch18ProductTableExample02.txt.

When you get data, you need to be able to recognize what you're looking at. Recall from earlier in this chapter that delimiters signal to a computer system where a dataset should be split into separate fields or columns. The data for this example is the same data as in the previous example, except that in this case, it is not provided in an Excel worksheet but is instead provided as two tab-delimited text files. In Figure 18.63, you can see that there is a single tab in each row of the fact table to indicate that there are only two columns. The three-column dimension table also uses tab delimiters, and the product name and product flight range are combined with a dash. In this example, you will see how to use Power Query tool to import the data and split it into four fields, using the tab and dash delimiters.

The data analysis goal in this example is the same as in Example 1: Create a report that shows total sales and total units sold by product and create a visualization that shows the total sales by product. In this example, however, you will use the Power Query tool to import, transform, and load the data to the Power Pivot Data Model, and then you will use the Power Pivot tool to create relationships and DAX formulas to create a star schema data model. Finally, you will use your data model to build a Data Model PivotTable and PivotChart. Before beginning this example, though, let's take a closer look at the Power Query and Power Pivot tools.

Power Query

Power Query was first introduced in Excel in 2013, exactly 20 years after the PivotTable was invented. And as it turns out, Power Query is the greatest invention in Excel since the PivotTable. When you have to deal with data, Power Query is a dream tool that can do everything. In Excel 365, most data analysis projects start with Power Query, which is a perfect tool for all the data preparation you need to do before you use a PivotTable to create summary reports with conditional calculations.

Power Query can connect to data sources such as text files, databases, websites, other Excel files, and XML files. It can also bring data into the Power Query Editor window, which is an interface you can use to invoke commands to import, clean, transform, and manipulate data. Finally, Power Query can load data to locations such as the worksheet, the PivotTable cache, or the Data Model in the Excel app; and to the Data Model in the Power BI Desktop app. Power Query can also perform many other tasks that involve data, such as financial and statistical calculations that are not related to reporting, visualizations, and dashboards.

When you use the Power Query user interface to do things like import data, add a data type, or combine multiple tables, behind the scenes Power Query records every step for you so that you can go back and see previous steps or even go back and edit previous steps in the query. Power Query records these steps using a case-sensitive, function-based formula programming language called *M code*, were M stands for *data mashup*. There are more than 700 functions in the M code language, but none of them are identical to Excel worksheet functions. Luckily, most of the time you can use the Power Query user interface to create queries by clicking on buttons and commands, and Power Query will write the M code for you. Sometimes, however, the best option is to write your own M code. In this chapter, you will learn how to create queries both ways.

As you begin to learn how to use Power Query, it is helpful to understand that Power Query queries are different from Excel worksheet formulas in two main ways:

- With worksheet formulas, you must type out and write your formulas manually, but when you create a query, most of the time you click on buttons and invoke commands, and the M code formulas are written for you.

- In a worksheet, formulas mostly deliver individual values in individual cells or arrays of values, but in Power Query, M code can deliver *values* such as tables with fields, records, lists, functions, binary files, and individual values such as text, numbers, dates, times, nulls, and Boolean values.

You can work with more types of objects (or *values*, as they are officially called in M code) in Power Query than in an Excel worksheet. This makes sense because in data analysis, the objects that you often work with are not simply numbers, text, and dates but instead are tables with fields, records, lists, and binary files.

Luckily, Microsoft put the Power Query tool in both the Excel app and in the Power BI Desktop app. Figure 18.64 shows that in the Excel app, Power Query is in the Data tab in the Excel Ribbon. Figure 18.65 shows that in the Power BI Desktop app, Power Query is in the Home tab in the Power Query Ribbon. Although the Power Query user interface is somewhat different in the two tools, almost everything else is the same. Whatever you learn about Power Query in the Excel app can help you in the Power BI Desktop app and vice versa. In this example, you will use Power Query in the Excel app, and then in Example 3, you will use Power Query in the Power BI Desktop app.

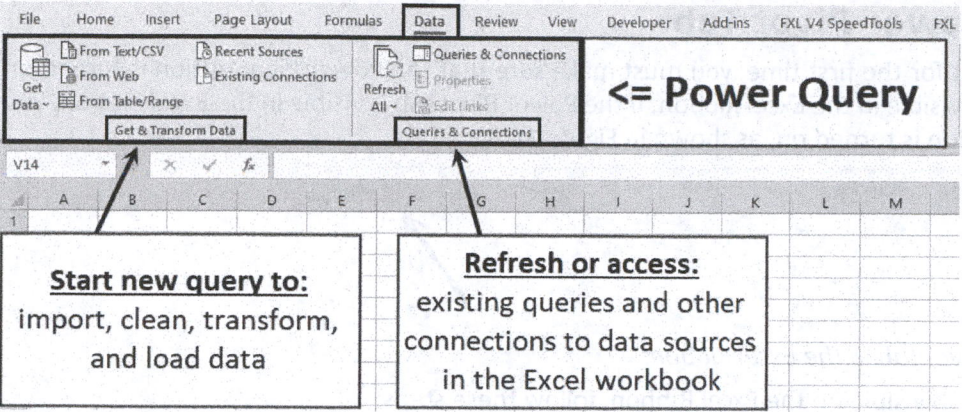

Figure 18.64 *Power Query in Excel.*

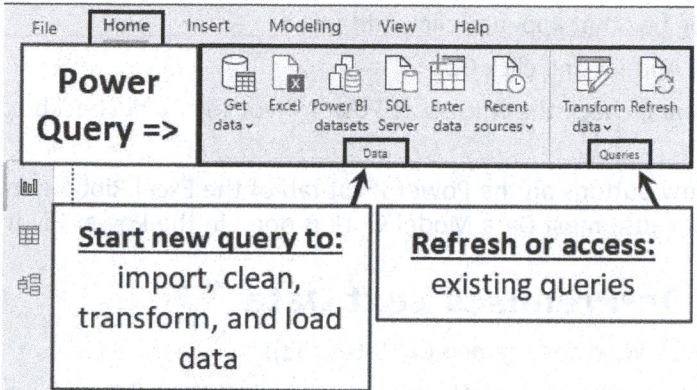

Figure 18.65 *Power Query in Power BI Desktop.*

Power Pivot

Microsoft introduced the Power Pivot tool in 2009 to help deal with big datasets and complex calculations involving multiple tables. When you are working with a dataset that has 50,000 rows of data or more and you want to create summary PivotTable reports with conditional calculations, or when you have multiple tables that work together to create reports and visualizations, it can be worthwhile to use Power Pivot. However, as you will see in this example, even when you have a small dataset, there are some advantages that make using the Power Pivot tool worthwhile.

Power Pivot consists of three components that together are considered the *Data Model*, which is the source of data for Data Model PivotTable reports and PivotChart visualizations:

- **In-RAM columnar database:** This database efficiently compresses data to a small file size and stores data so that DAX formulas can work quickly with big data. When you load data to the Data Model, the behind-the-scenes columnar database is where the data is stored.

- **Relationships:** Relationships are created between related tables and can replace worksheet lookup formulas. Relationships help reduce the complexity of DAX formulas, allow you to drag and drop fields from multiple tables in a PivotTable report, and work as a filtering mechanism to reduce the size of tables when DAX formulas are evaluated.

- **DAX (Data Analysis Expressions):** DAX is a function-based formula programming language that contains more than 250 functions and works in conjunction with the columnar database and relationships to create efficient formulas. DAX formulas are programmed to work efficiently with big data and can significantly reduce the number of intermediate steps in complex calculations by creating columns and tables within formulas. DAX formulas can deliver *DAX measures* (which are premade, preformatted, drag-and-drop formulas), *DAX calculated columns* (which are fields in tables), or *DAX tables*. DAX includes many functions that are almost identical to Excel worksheet functions, such as SUM, AVERAGE, and EOMONTH, as well as functions that are unique to DAX, such as RELATED, SUMX, and CALCULATE.

Activating the Power Pivot Tab

When you use Power Pivot for the first time, you must make sure that the Power Pivot option is turned on and the Power Pivot tab is visible in the Excel Ribbon. If the Power Pivot tab is visible in the Excel Ribbon, you know the Power Pivot option is turned on, as shown in Figure 18.66.

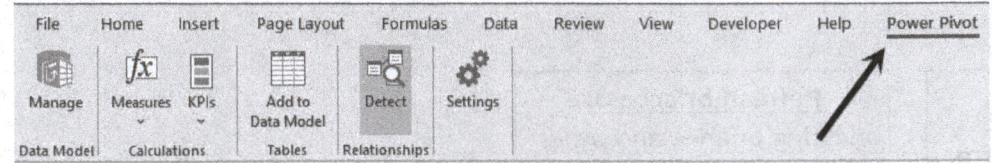

Figure 18.66 *The Power Pivot tab in the Excel Ribbon.*

To make the Power Pivot tab visible on the Excel Ribbon, follow these steps:

1. Click on the File menu and select Options.

2. On the left side of the Excel Options dialog box that appears, click Add-ins.

3. From the Manage dropdown, select COM Add-ins and click Go.

4. In the COM Add-ins dialog box that appears, check the Microsoft Power Pivot for Excel checkbox and click OK.

As you can see in Figure 18.66, there are only a few buttons on the Power Pivot tab of the Excel Ribbon. In general, you will not have to use this tab much because most Data Model work is done in the Power Pivot for Excel window.

Using Power Query to Import On-Premises Text Data

To complete this example, follow these steps on the worksheet named Ch18(67-153):

1. To import the fact table text file, click on the Data tab in the Excel Ribbon and then, in the Get & Transform Data group, click the From Text/CSV button, as shown in Figure 18.67.

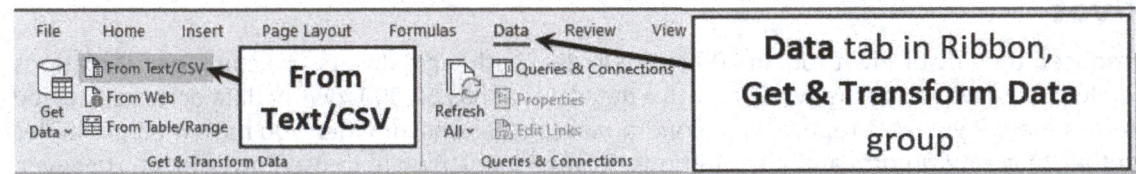

Figure 18.67 *To import a text file, you can click the From Text/CSV button.*

2. In the Import Data dialog box that appears, navigate to and select the text file named Ch18UnitsTableExample02.txt, as shown in Figure 18.68.

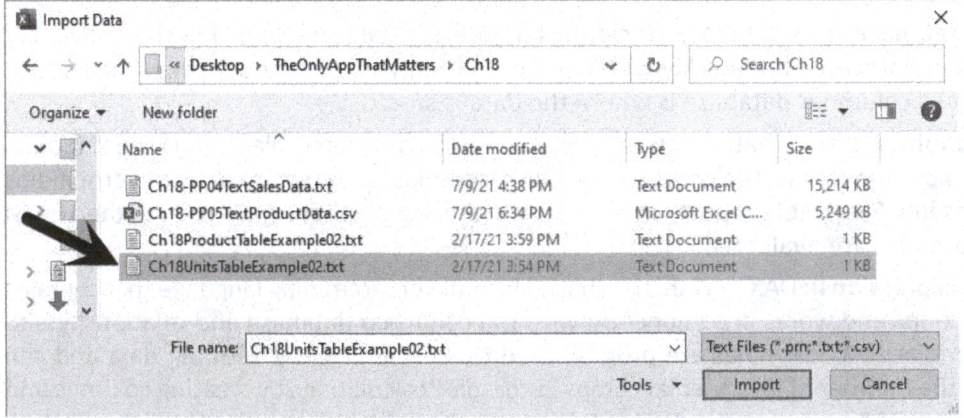

Figure 18.68 *Select the file to import.*

Note: Before clicking the Import button, if you want to see the folder path that Power Query will use for importing this file, you can click in the address bar at the top of the dialog box, as shown in Figure 18.69. The full file path that Power Query memorizes is the folder path and filename together—in this case, C:\Users\mgirvin\Desktop\TheOnlyAppThatMatters\Ch18\ Ch18UnitsTableExample02.txt. However, the folder path in Figure 18.69 is not the folder path that you will see on your computer.

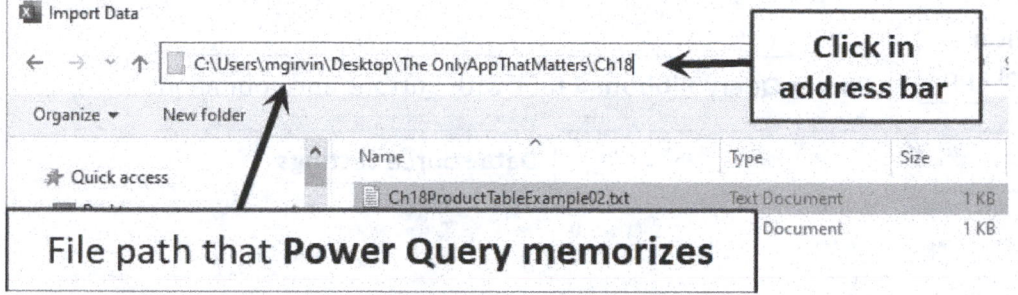

Figure 18.69 *Power Query stores this folder path in the M code so it knows where the data came from.*

3.   To initiate the import process, click the Import button in the Import Data dialog box (refer to Figure 18.68).

4.   In the dialog box that appears (see Figure 18.70), make sure the delimiter dropdown is set to Tab.

5.   To bring the text file into the Power Query Editor window, click the Transform Data button.

Note: As shown in Figure 18.70, you usually do not want to click the Load button because doing so loads the data without opening the Power Query Editor. You almost always want to bring the data through the Power Query Editor first, before loading it, so that you can check to see if the automatic steps that Power Query creates are correct. If you click the Load button rather than the Transform Data button, your data may not be converted to a proper dataset.

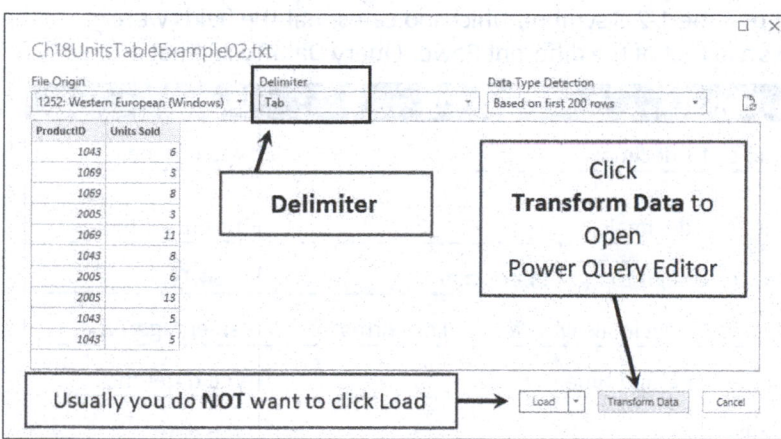

Figure 18.70 *Click the Transform Data button.*

Using the Power Query Editor Window and User Interface

Figure 18.71 shows the Power Query Editor window and the Power Query Ribbon with the File menu and four tabs: Home, Transform, Add Column, and View. The Power Query Editor opens as a new window that sits on top of the Excel app window. In the Query Settings task pane on the right, you can see the default query name in the Name textbox and the three query steps that Power Query automatically created in the Applied Steps list. The last step in this list, Changed Type, automatically changed the data type for both fields.

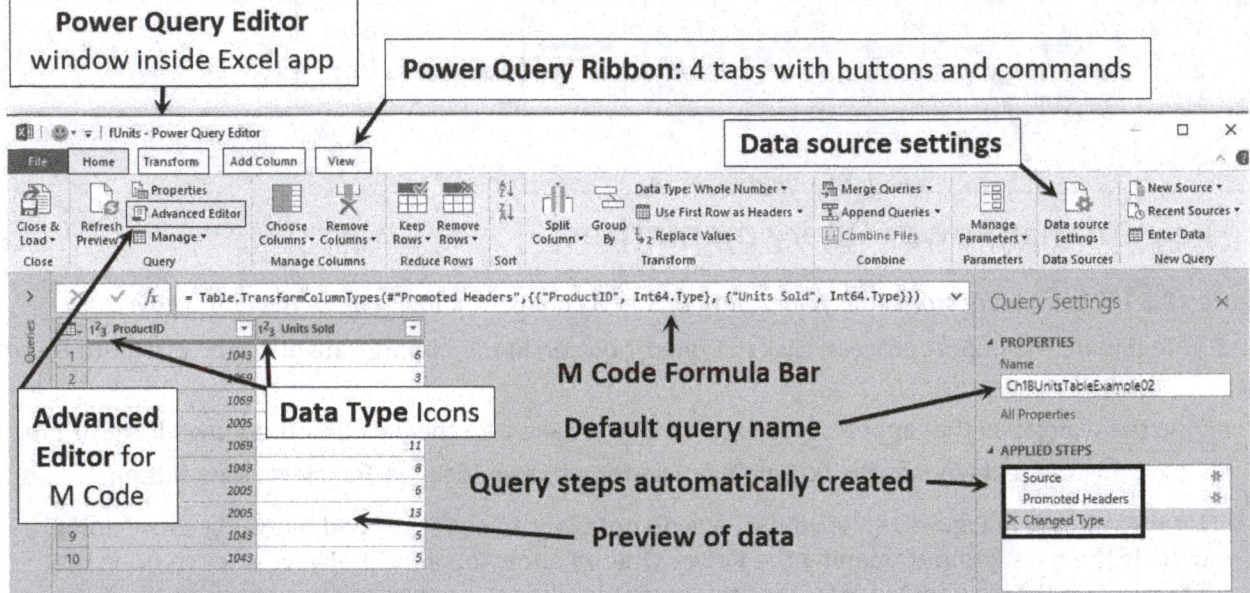

Figure 18.71 *The Power Query Editor with the Power Query Ribbon*

At the top of each field in the data preview, to the left of the field name, you can see the Data Type icon. For both of the fields in this example, the icon shows the 1-2-3 symbol, which indicates that the fields were given the whole number data type. Figure 18.72 shows a full list of the different Power Query Data Types that are possible.

Data Type	Icon	Short Description	M Code
Decimal number	1.2	Number up to 15 decimals	type number
Currency (Fixed decimal number)	$	Number up to 4 decimals	Currency.Type
Whole number	$1^2{}_3$	Number with no digit to right of decimal	Int64.Type
Percentage	%	Number up to 15 decimals with % Number Format	Percentage.Type
Date/Time	🕑	Serial number date and time together	type datetime
Date	🔲	Serial number date	type date
Time	🕐	Serial number time	type time
Date/Time/Timezone	🌐	Represents a UTC date/time with a time-zone offset	type datetimezone
Duration	⏱	Serial Number Length of Date and Time	type duration
Text	$A^B{}_C$	Text	type text
True/False	✗✓	Boolean	type logical
Binary	▤	File like Excel file or Text file	type binary
Any	ABC 123	Sets numbers such as dates and decimals according to regional settings	type any

Figure 18.72 *Data types in Power Query.*

In the middle of the Power Query Editor window, you can see the formula bar and the formula that was automatically created for the selected query step. Notice that in this case, Power Query used an M code function named Table.TransformColumnTypes to change the field data types. In the Home tab of the Power Query Ribbon, you can see the Advanced Editor button, which you can click to see the complete M code created for this query.

Looking at the Applied Steps in the Query

To look at the steps in the query Power Query created for you, follow these steps:

1. As shown in Figure 18.73, in the Applied Steps list, click on the Promoted Headers step.

   Note: In the Applied Steps list, clicking the X to the left of a step deletes the step. Clicking the gear icon to the right of a step opens the dialog box for that step.

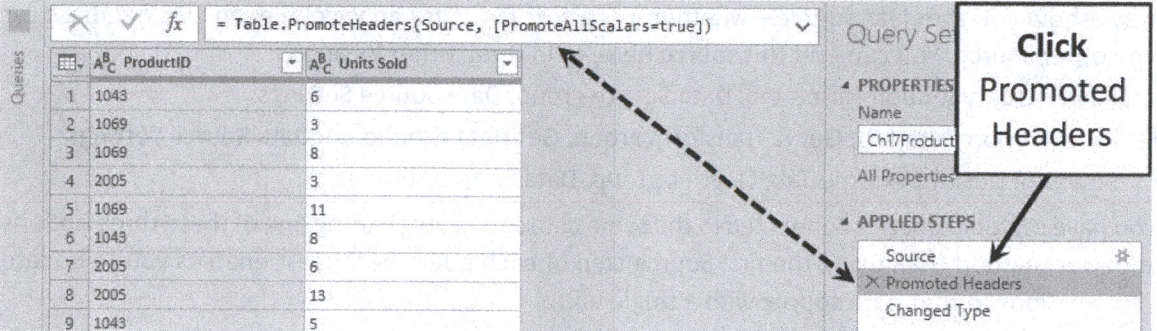

Figure 18.73 *When you select an applied step, you can see the M code function that was used in the formula bar.*

After you select the Promoted Headers query step, in the formula bar you can see the M code function named Table.PromoteHeaders. This function took the first row of field names from the text file and promoted them to official table field names.

Note: Notice that each Power Query M code function has a commonsense name that lists the type of value it is working on (for example, table) and the action it will take (for example, promote headers). Also notice that a Power Query M code function is a combination of upper- and lowercase letters, with periods between some of the words. In contrast, Excel worksheet functions (and DAX functions, too) use uppercase letters only. These M code functions are case-sensitive, so that, for example, the function Table.PromoteHeaders would not work if you typed Table.promoteheaders.

2. As shown in Figure 18.74, in the Applied Steps list, click on the gear icon to the right of the Source step. Figure 18.74 shows the dialog box that appears and allows you to edit the inputs for this data import process, including the file path and delimiter. The file path that you identified during the data import process (refer to Figure 18.69) is shown in both the dialog box and the formula bar.

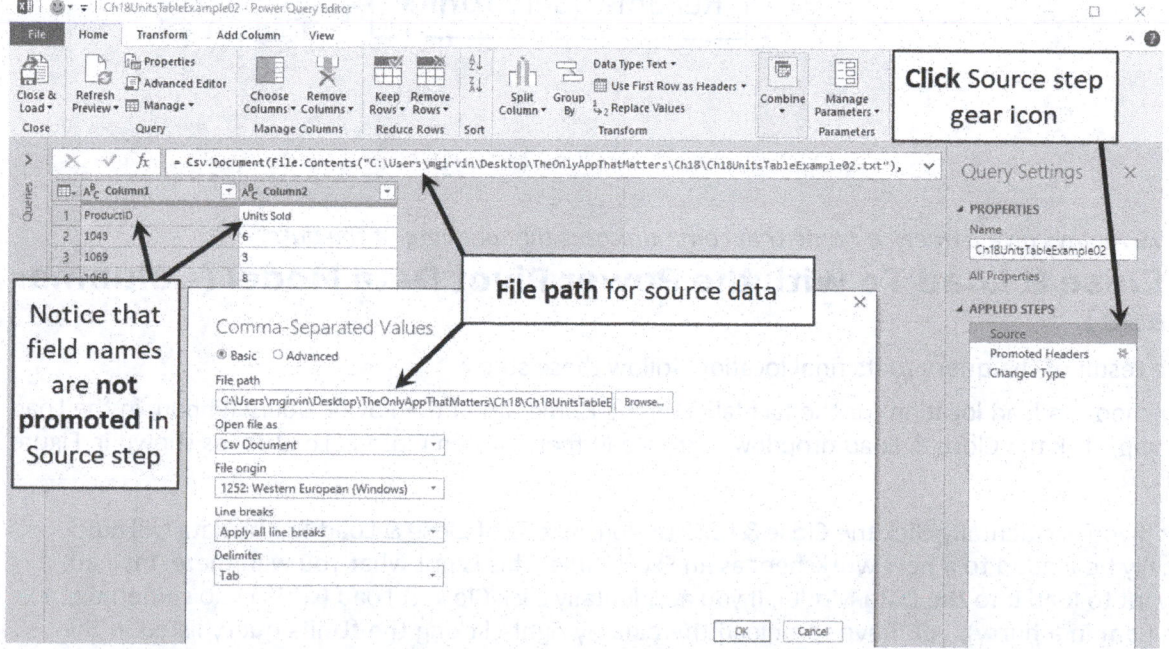

Figure 18.74 *Clicking the Source step gear icon opens a dialog box where you can change the import parameters.*

This file path, C:\Users\mgirvin\Desktop\TheOnlyAppThatMatters\Ch18\Ch18UnitsTableExample02. txt, is called an *on-premises location* because the file is on the local computer (mine in this case); with an *in-the-cloud location*, in contrast, the data is stored on a server computer in a data center that is always connected to the internet. With an on-premises file path, if the file moves or if the file is shared, Power Query will not be able to find the data. If you do not need to refresh or edit a query, an on-premises file path is okay because the data has been loaded and can be used for your data analysis task. If you need to refresh or edit the query, however, then you need to know how to change this location. The good news is that the first step in all queries is the Source step, and it will always show you the data source—whether it is a text file path, an Excel file, an SQL database, or some other source. You can edit this source here, or in three other locations:

- Power Query Ribbon Home tab, Data Source group, Data Source Settings
- Excel Ribbon Data tab, Get & Transform group, Get Data dropdown, Data Source Settings
- Power BI Desktop, Home Tab, Queries group, Data Source Settings

If you have multiple queries connected to the same data source, then using one of these three options is a better method than using the first Source step of each query because it enables you to update all connections to that data source with a single edit.

> **Note:** In Figure 18.74, notice that the preview of the dataset on the left shows that the field names are not promoted. This is because the Source step is selected, and the field names are not promoted until the following query step. The ability to look backward through a query is convenient; it helps you learn how the steps were constructed and gives you the freedom to edit steps, if necessary. As you will learn later, however, if you edit a step, your changes will influence the remining steps, so care must be taken.

3. As shown in Figure 18.75, to change the default query name, in the Query Settings task pane, under Properties, click in the Name textbox and rename the query **fUnits**.

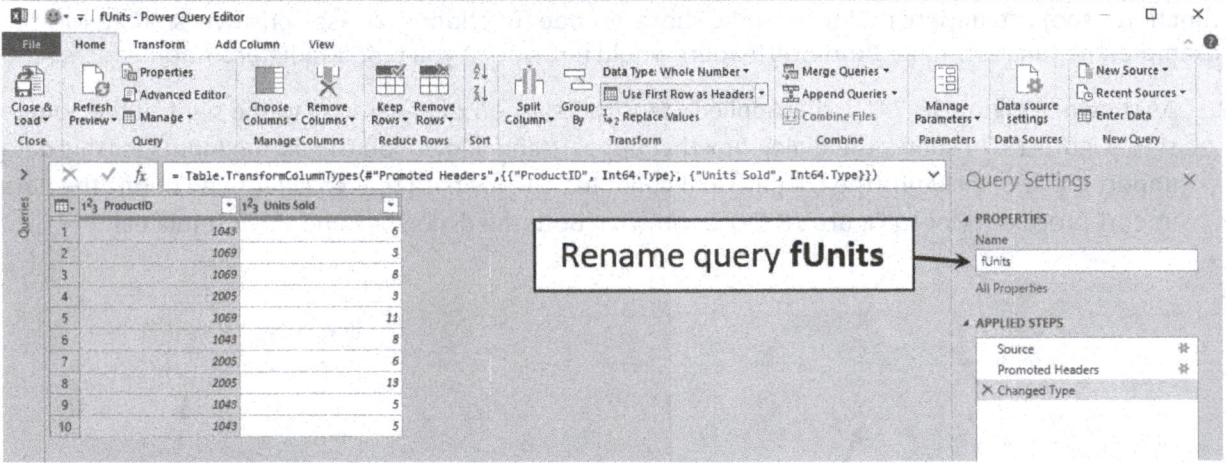

Figure 18.75 *Always give a query a name that communicates the meaning of the data.*

Using Close & Load To with the Power Pivot Data Model (Columnar Database)

To load the result of the query to its final location, follow these steps:

1. To choose a load location for the fact table, in the Home tab of the Power Query Ribbon, in the Load group, click the Close & Load dropdown arrow and then click on Close & Load To, as shown in Figure 18.76.

> **Note:** If you accidentally click the Close & Load option instead of Close & Load To, the data will automatically be loaded to a new worksheet as an Excel Table. This is not what you want here. Instead, you want to load it to the Data Model. If you accidentally click Close & Load (which I do sometimes when I am in a hurry), you have to unload the data by right-clicking the fUnits query listed in the Queries & Connections task pane and then click on the Load To option to reset the load location.

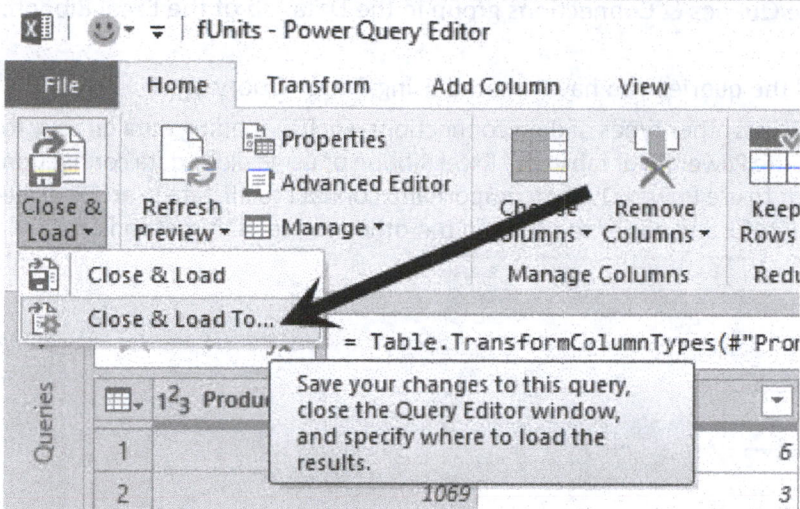

Figure 18.76 *Use the Close & Load To option to choose where the data is loaded.*

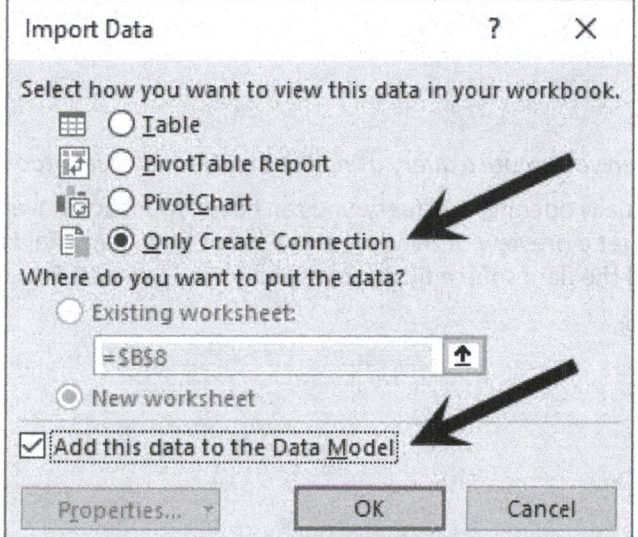

Figure 18.77 *When you load to the Data Model, you must select both of these options.*

2. In the Import Data dialog box that appears, to load the table to the Power Pivot Data Model, select the Only Create Connection option button and check the Add This Data to the Data Model checkbox, as shown in Figure 18.77.

3. Click OK in the Import Data dialog box. The fact table is loaded into the Data Model's columnar database, and you are taken back to the Excel app window.

Take a closer look at the Import Data dialog box in Figure 18.77. The top four options allow you to select how to view the data in the Excel workbook file:

- **Table:** The query is loaded as an Excel Table in the worksheet

- **PivotTable Report:** The query is loaded into the PivotTable cache.

- **PivotChart:** The query is loaded into the PivotTable cache.

- **Only Create Connection:** The query is not loaded to the worksheet or the PivotTable cache. This option allows Power Query to run the query steps on the source data in the Power Query Editor but then pass the data along to other queries—or, in this case, pass the data into the Data Model's columnar database.

> **Note:** A *columnar database* is a special type of behind-the-scenes data storage location that is loaded into random access memory (RAM) when you open an Excel file. A columnar database compresses the data into a smaller size and stores the data one column at a time (hence the "columnar" name). For each column of data that is stored, the columnar database stores a unique list of items. The more unique items in any given column, the larger the size of the stored column in the database. The database also stores a type of mapping that allows it to reconstruct records of data from the columns of unique lists that are stored in the columnar database. This database was specifically designed by Microsoft to work efficiently with big data for data analysis and is part of the Power Pivot Data Model tool.

After you click the OK button in the Import Data dialog box, you jump back to the Excel app window, and the Queries & Connections task pane opens, as shown in Figure 18.78. This task pane lists all the queries that are in the Excel workbook file. You use this task pane to open the Power Query Editor to look at or edit a query or to get basic information about the query. If this task pane is not open, you can open it by clicking the Queries & Connections button in the Queries & Connections group in the Data tab of the Excel Ribbon. This task pane has two tabs:

- **Queries:** The Queries tab lists all the queries you have created using Power Query.
- **Connections:** The Connections tab lists other types of data connections, such as loading data directly to the Power Pivot Data Model using the Power Pivot tab in the Excel Ribbon or using older data connection tools. In general, it is more efficient to use Power Query to import and connect to all data in an Excel file because Power Query is more powerful and easier to use than the other connection methods.

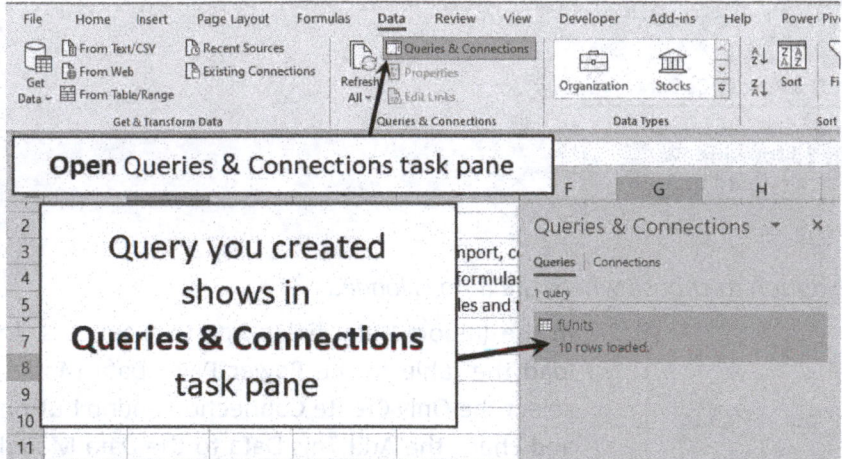

Figure 18.78 *The Queries & Connections pane opens when you create a query using the Excel Power Query tool.*

If you want to see information about a query without actually opening the query, you can hover your cursor over the query in the Queries & Connections task pane and get a preview of the data and a list of how many fields (that is, columns) are in the table, the load location, and the data source file path, as shown in Figure 18.79.

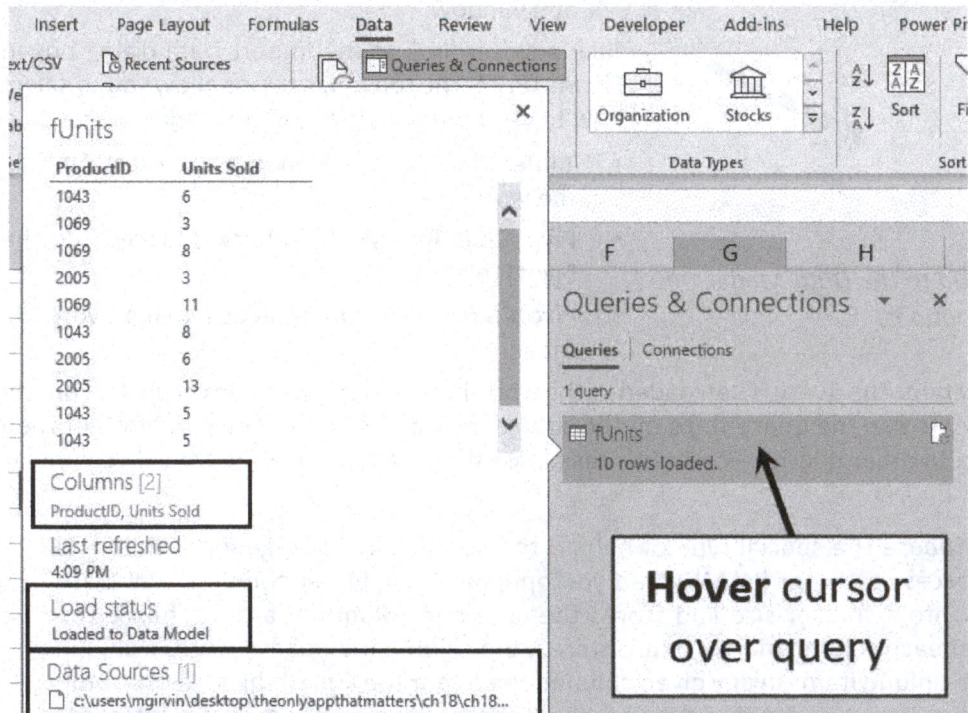

Figure 18.79 *When you hover over a query, you can see the file path, the load location, and other details.*

Before using Power Query to import the second text file, let's look at fUnits table in the Power Pivot window. The following section gives you a preview of the data that has been loaded to the Data Model.

Viewing the Power Pivot Data Model

After you use Power Query to load a table to the Data Model, you can open the Power Pivot for Excel window and see a preview of the table by clicking the Manage Data Model button in one of two locations:

- The Data Tools group in the Data tab of the Excel Ribbon, as shown in Figure 18.80
- The Data Model group in the Power Pivot tab in the Excel Ribbon, as shown in Figure 18.81

> **Note:** I tend to use the Manage Data Model button in the Data tab because I often have that tab open. Also, the keyboard shortcut for the Manage Data Model button in the Data tab is Alt, A, D, M, which is easy to remember because it includes **D** (Data) and **M** (Model).

Figure 18.80 To view the Data Model, you can use the Manage Data Model button in the Excel app Data tab.

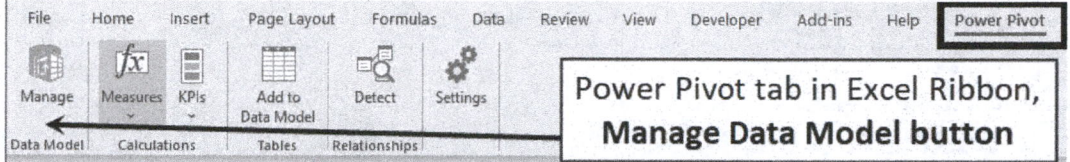

Figure 18.81 To view the Data Model, you can use the Manage Data Model button in the Excel app Power Pivot tab.

The Power Pivot for Excel Window and User Interface

To take a look at the Power Pivot for Excel window, follow these steps:

1. To view the Data Model and open the Power Pivot for Excel window, click the Manage Data Model button or use the keyboard shortcut Alt, A, D, M. Figure 18.82 shows the Power Pivot for Excel window.

   In this figure, you can see the Power Pivot Ribbon with the File menu and three tabs: Home, Design, and Advanced. The Power Pivot for Excel window opens as a new window that sits on top of the Excel app window. This window is where you work directly with the Data Model to preview data that is stored in a columnar database, create relationships, create DAX formulas, and carry out other data modeling tasks. When you open the Power Pivot for Excel window, the Data View button is selected by default so that you have a preview of the table.

   The table you loaded in this case contains only 10 rows of data, so you can preview the whole table. When you use the Power Pivot for Excel window to view a table that contains millions of rows of data, you see only a preview of some of the data that is compressed in the columnar database.

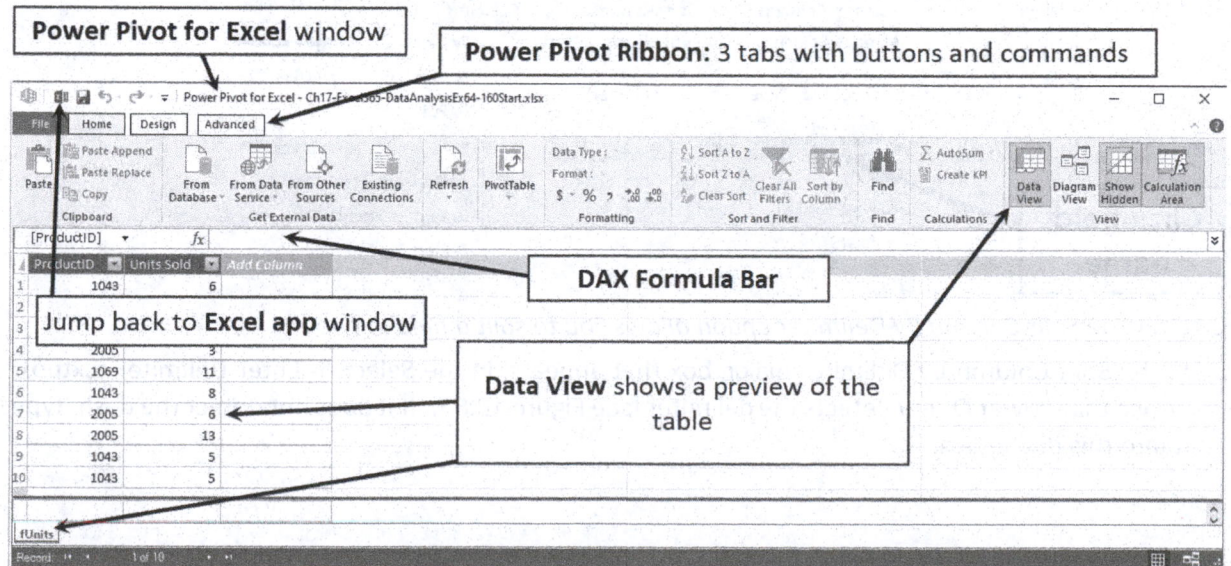

Figure 18.82 The Power Pivot for Excel window shows a preview of the table that was loaded to the Data Model.

2. To jump back to the Excel app window, you can click the Excel icon in the upper-left corner of the Power Pivot for Excel window title bar, as shown in Figure 18.82, or you can use the keyboard shortcut Alt+Tab to jump back to the last used window.

3. To import the on-premises dimension table text file, click on the Data tab in the Excel Ribbon and then, in the Get & Transform group, click the From Text/CSV button.

4. In the Import Data dialog box, navigate to the text file named Ch18ProductTableExample02.txt and select this file.

5. To initiate the import process, click the Import button in the Import Data dialog box.

6. In the dialog box that pops up, showing the filename at the top, make sure the delimiter textbox lists Tab. Then to bring the text file into the Power Query Editor window, click the Transform Data button.

7. When the Power Query Editor window opens, name the query **dProduct**, as shown in Figure 18.83.

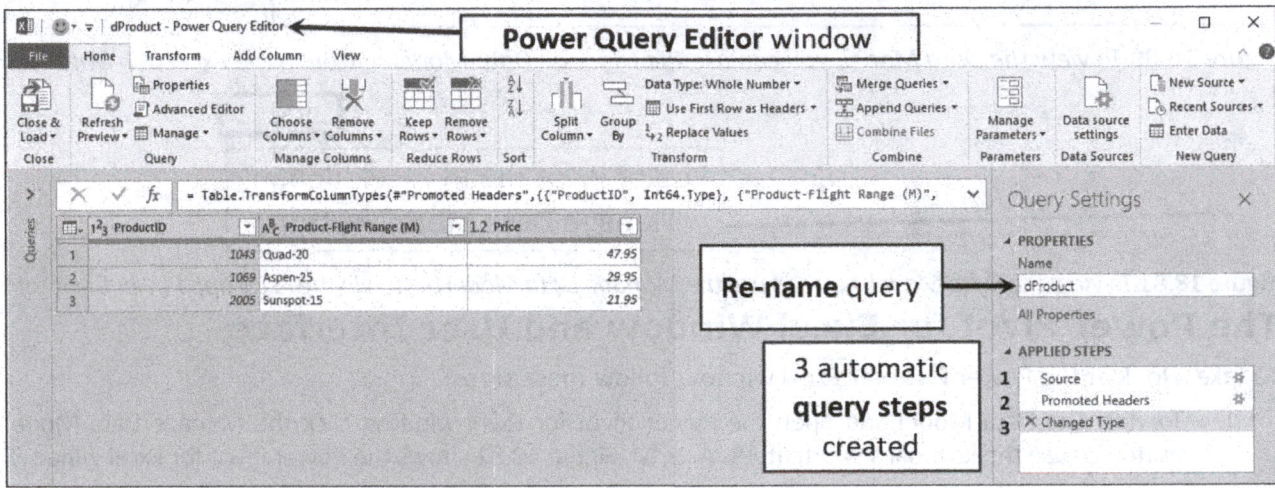

Figure 18.83 *Rename the query dProduct.*

8. To split the Product-Flight Range (M) field into two separate fields, click the field name Product-Flight Range (M) and then, in the Home tab in the Power Query Ribbon, in the Transform group, click the Split Column dropdown arrow and select the By Delimiter option (see Figure 18.84).

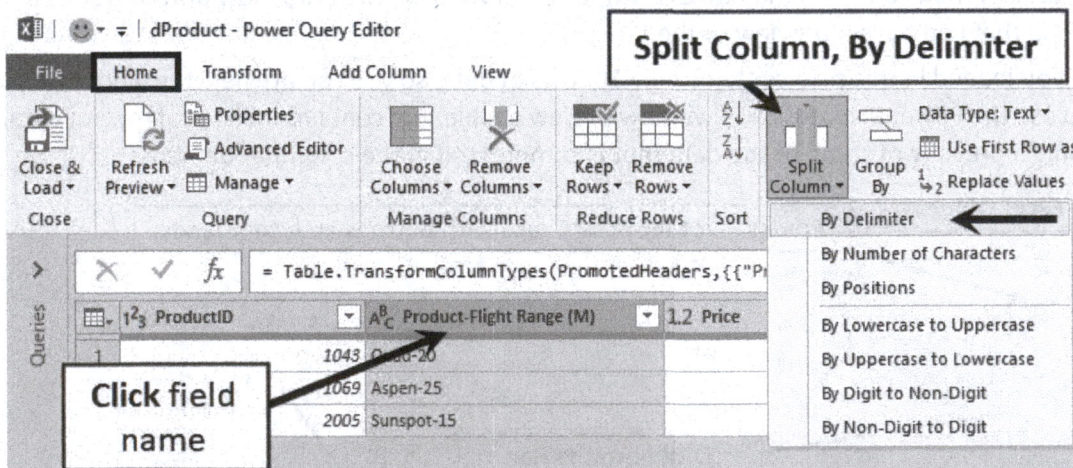

Figure 18.84 *The Split Column By Delimiter option allows you to split a field in two.*

9. In the Split Column by Delimiter dialog box that appears, in the Select or Enter Delimiter textbox, notice that Power Query detects the delimiter (see Figure 18.85). If it does not detect the dash, type it into this dialog box.

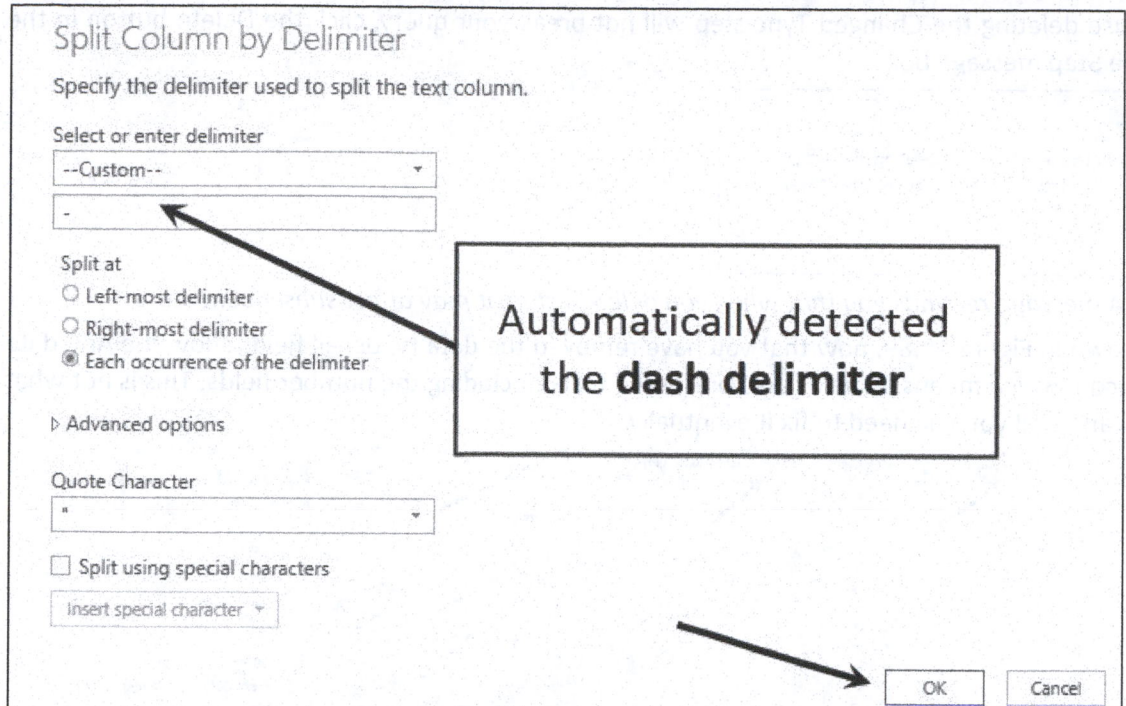

Figure 18.85 *Power Query detects the dash as the delimiter.*

10. Click the OK button in the Split Column by Delimiter dialog box. Figure 18.86 shows the result.

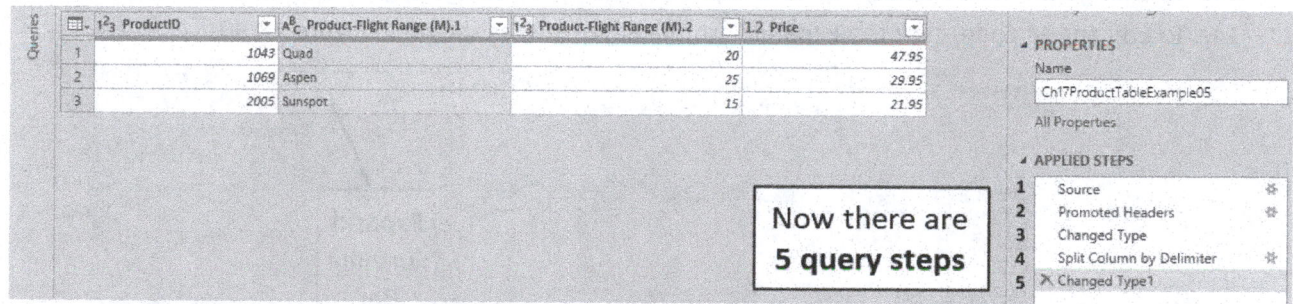

Figure 18.86 *The Split Column by Delimiter command allowed you to turn three fields into four fields.*

As you can see in the Applied Steps box in Figure 18.86, there are five query steps. The last two steps, Split Column by Delimiter and Changed Type1, were added when you used the Split Column by Delimiter command. Notice that the third step is named Changed Type, and the fifth step is named Changed Type1. Both of these steps change the data types for the fields. It might be more efficient, however, to change the data types for the fields in only one step. You can accomplish both tasks by editing the query steps and the underlying M code. However, when you edit query steps, you must be careful to ensure that your edits will not adversely affect subsequent steps. Next, you will make two edits, and you will see that the first of them will not adversely affect subsequent steps, but the second one will.

11. As shown in Figure 18.87, in the Applied Steps list, click the X next to Changed Type1 to delete this step. A polite message box pops up when you try to delete a query step, reminding you that deleting a step might break your query (see Figure 18.88).

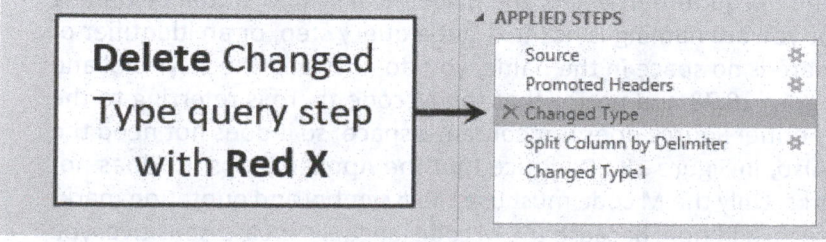

Figure 18.87 *Click the X to delete this query step.*

12. Because deleting the Changed Type step will not break your query, click the Delete button in the Delete Step message box.

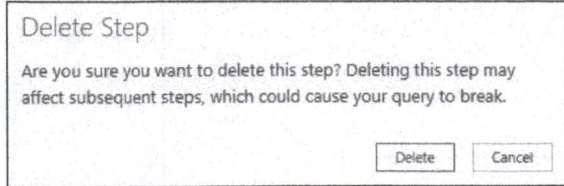

Figure 18.88 *A message reminds you that when you delete a step, it may affect subsequent steps.*

As shown in Figure 18.89, now that you have removed the data types, all fields show the ABC data type icon, which means all fields are considered text—including the number fields. This is not what you want, and you will need to fix it eventually.

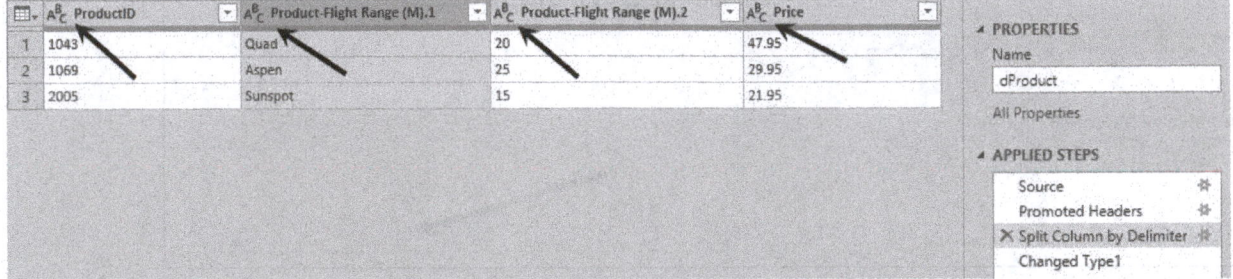

Figure 18.89 *When you remove the Changed Type step, all fields are considered to have the text data type.*

13. To change the field names, select the Split Column by Delimiter step in the Applied Steps list.

14. To edit the M code, click the Expand Formula Bar arrow, as shown in Figure 18.90.

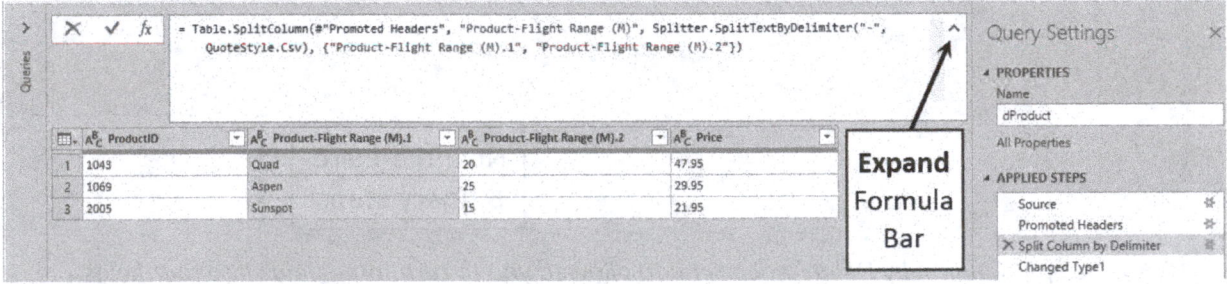

Figure 18.90 *Expanding formula bar allows you to edit the M Code more easily.*

Taking a First Look at Power Query M Code

After expanding the formula bar, notice in Figure 18.90 that the Split Column by Delimiter query step uses the Table.SplitColumn M code function. This is a table function that can split a table field into two or more new fields. Figure 18.91 shows the four arguments in this function:

- **#"Promoted Headers":** The first argument of this function requires a table value. The previous step, named Promoted Headers, is a table value and was automatically placed into the first argument.

> **Note:** Why does the first argument have the strange syntax with a # symbol? In Power Query M code, *quotation marks* are reserved for text values, as can be seen in the second argument of this function, where the field name of the column to split is given as the text value "Product-Flight Range (M)". When you name a query step—or any other Power Query value—if there is a space in the name, you must put the name in quotation marks and place the # symbol at the beginning of the name to indicate that what you are naming is not text but a query step, or an identifier of the new Power Query value. If there is no space in the name, you do not need the # symbol and quotation marks. Look back at Figure 18.73 and notice that the M code there is referring to the first query step as Source. The identifier Source does not contain a space, so it does not need the # symbol and quotation marks. Also, in Figure 18.90, notice that the Applied Steps list does not show # symbol and quotation marks. Only the M code must use the # symbol and quotation marks when an identifier contains a space. In addition, because the M code language is case-sensitive, you must be careful to get the case of the letters correct when you create and refer to the identifiers.

- **"Product-Flight Range (M)":** The second argument in the Table.SplitColumn function indicates the column that should be split.
- **Splitter.SplitTextByDelimiter:** The third argument in the Table.SplitColumn function requires that you use a second M code function to split the fields. Power Query automatically uses the Splitter. SplitTextByDelimiter function in this case. There are many splitter functions that Power Query can put into this third argument, depending on how you choose to split. Notice that this splitter splits using a dash.
- **{"Product-Flight Range (M).1", "Product-Flight Range (M).2"}:** The fourth argument in the Table. SplitColumn function is the one that you are interested in editing. This is where the names of the two new fields are defined. In this case, Power Query automatically entered two text field names, each in double quotes, as a list. A *list* value in Power Query is a one-dimensional list of values that must include open and close curly brackets and have the values in the list separated by commas. You need to carefully edit this list of text field names.

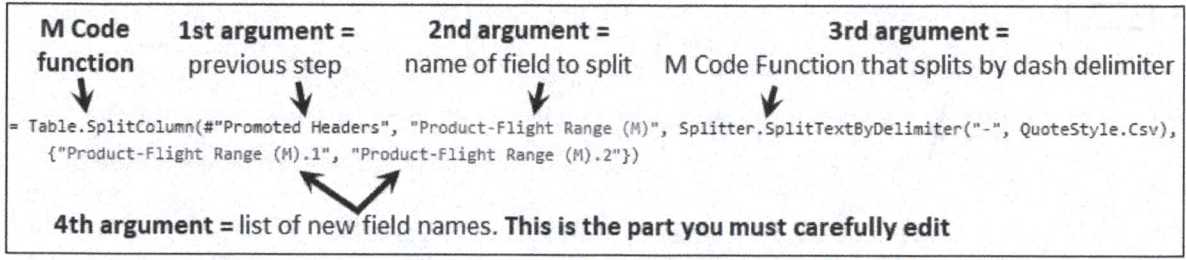

Figure 18.91 *This Power Query M code function has four arguments.*

Editing M Code

The following steps show how to edit the M code directly:

1. Click in the formula bar and change the two field names in the fourth argument to **"Product"** and **"Flight Range (M)"**. Be careful to create the correct list value syntax in this fourth argument: {**"Product", "Flight Range (M)"**}.

2. When you are done editing, press Enter. Figure 18.92 shows that the field names have been changed.

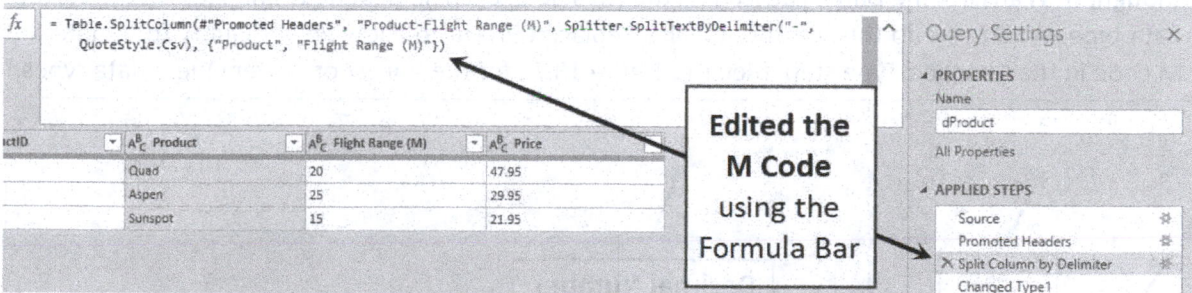

Figure 18.92 *Changing the field names inside the Table.SplitColumn function changes the field names in the table.*

3. After you edit the M code for the Table.SplitColumn function, click on the Changed Type1 step in the Applied Steps list. When you do this, a yellow error message pops up. In this case, as shown in Figure 18.93, the error message says that you broke the query when you changed the field names. If you look closely at the figure, you can see that the Table.TransformColumnTypes function is still using the old field names. You could edit the formula and change the field names to the correct names, but in this case, it would be easier to delete the step and create it again using the Detect Data Type option.

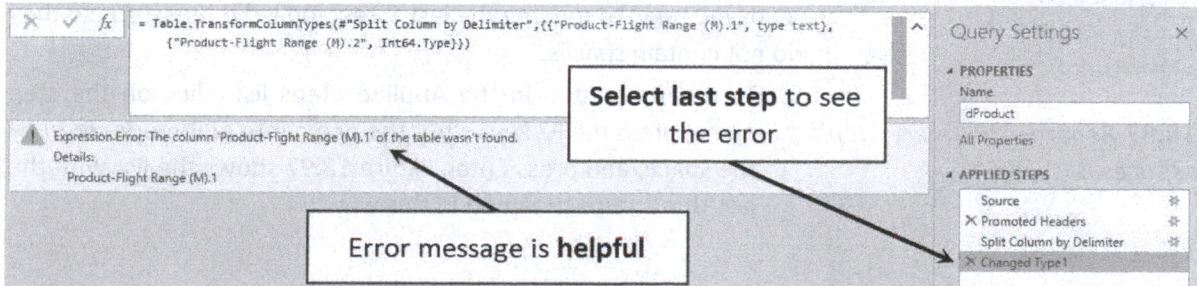

Figure 18.93 *When you click on the last step, you can see that the edited M code caused an error.*

4.   In the Applied Steps list, click the X next to Changed Type1 to delete this step (see Figure 18.94).

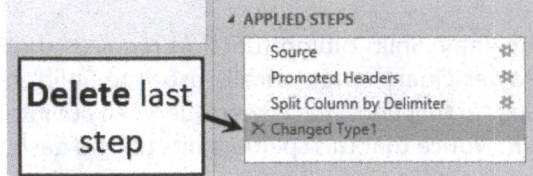

Figure 18.94 *Although you could fix the error, in this case, it is easier to just delete the last step.*

5.   As shown in Figure 18.95, select all four fields in the table and then, with the Split Column by Delimiter step in the Applied Steps list selected, click on the Transform tab in the Power Query Ribbon and, in the Any Column group, click the Detect Data Type button.

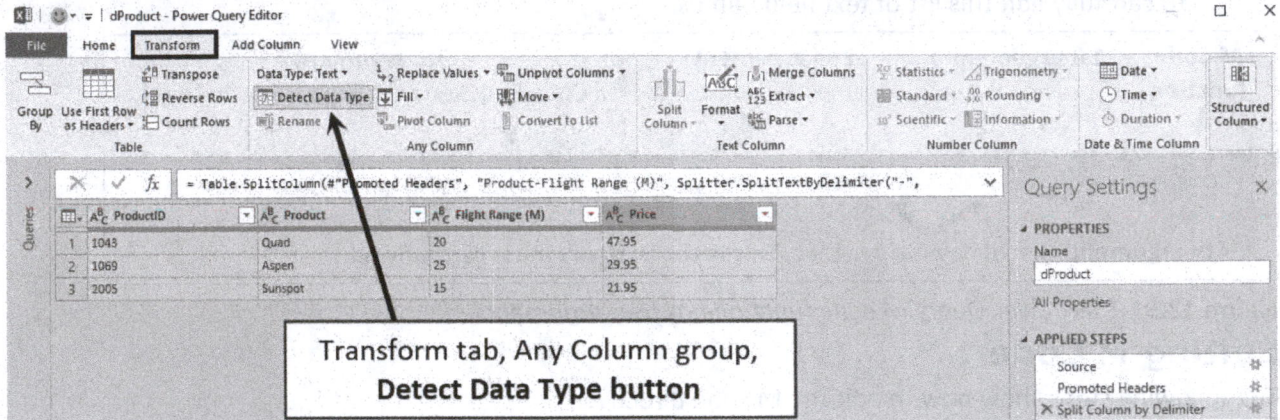

Figure 18.95 *The Detect Data Type command usually creates the correct data types.*

Figure 18.96 shows that the Detect Data Type option applies the correct data types to the fields. The Detect Data Type option is pretty good at detecting the correct data types. If it guesses wrong, though, you can click the Data Type icon on the left side of each field name to change it to the correct data type. When you do this, be sure to click Replace Current to allow Power Query to update the M code in the Changed Type step. (Refer to Figure 18.72 for the full list of Power Query data types.)

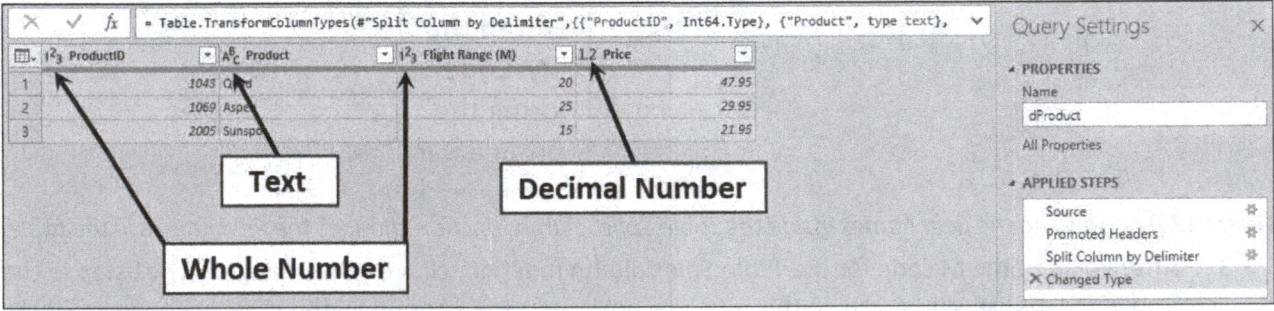

Figure 18.96 *The Detect Data Type command got the correct data types for all four fields.*

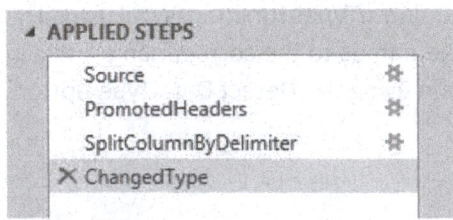

Figure 18.97 *Rename the query step without spaces.*

As noted a few pages ago, query step names, or identifiers, that contain spaces must use a more complicated syntax than query identifiers that do not contain spaces. So, to make the M code easier to read, you need to rename the last three applied query steps so they do not contain spaces.

6.   To rename a step in the Applied Steps list, click on the step name, press the F2 key to put the name into edit mode, remove the space, and press Enter. Figure 18.97 shows the list with the last three steps renamed in this way.

Using the M Code Advanced Editor and Let Expressions

Finally, before you load the table to the Data Model, you need to look at all of the M code that was written for you, including the editing that you performed. You can view it in the Advanced Editor.

To open the Advanced Editor, click on the Advanced Editor button in the Query group in the Home tab of the Power Query Ribbon.

As you can see in Figure 18.98, the Advanced Editor shows all the Power Query M code in a let expression. But what is a let expression? A *let expression* allows Power Query to combine all the query steps that you created into a single statement that can deliver the final value.

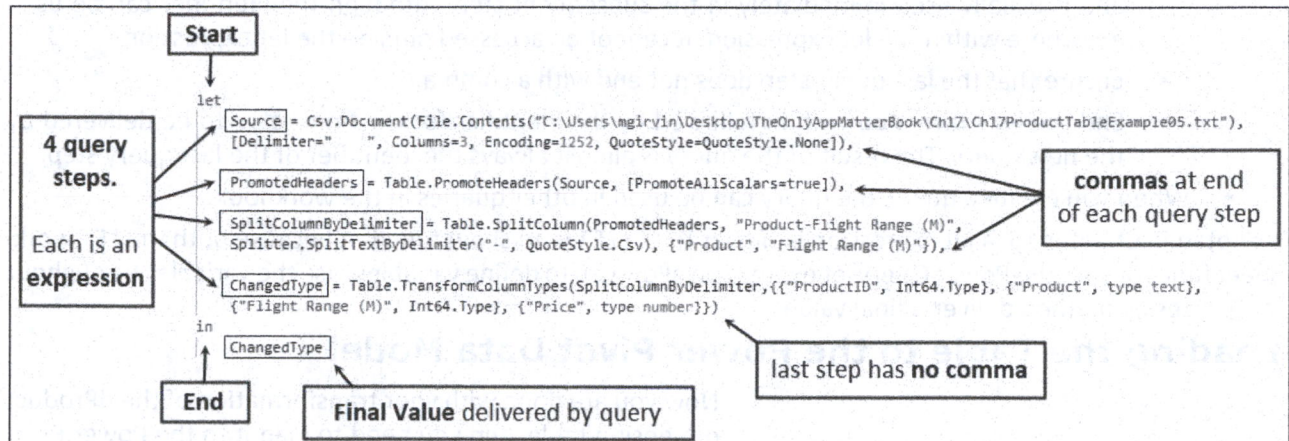

Figure 18.98 *The Advanced Editor shows the full let expression that combines all query steps to deliver a final value.*

To help you understand let expressions, the following list defines a number of important M code terms:

- An *expression* is any M code that results in a value. There are a number of types of expressions, including:
  - The let expression
  - A function like *Table.ColumnNames(TableName)*
  - A query step
  - A list
  - A number
- The *values* possible in Power Query M code are:
  - **Table:** A proper dataset with fields dataset
  - **Record:** A row from a table
  - **List:** For example, {1,2,3} or {"Quad","Aspen"}
  - **Function:** A user-built custom function
  - **Binary:** A file such as an Excel, text, or CSV file
  - **Data Type:** A data validation control for fields, such as *type number* for the decimal data type
  - **Text:** For example, Quad
  - **Number:** For example, 43
  - **Date:** For example, 10/01/2021 or #date(2021,10,01)
  - **Time:** For example, 11:10:57 or #time(11,10,57)
  - **DateTime:** For example, 10/01/21 11:10:57 AM or #datetime(2021,10,01,11,10,57)
  - **DateTimeZone:** For example, #datetimezone(2021,10,01,11,10,57.09,00)
  - **Duration:** A length of time, like 1 day and 1 hour 10 minutes or #duration(01,01,10,0))
  - **Null value:** null
  - **Boolean Value:** Either true or false

- A *new query* that is created with the Power Query tool uses a let expression.
- A *let expression* is designed to combine all query steps (that is, expressions) to deliver a final value. The final value delivered by the let expression is what the query delivers as its result.
- The *rules for a let expression* are:
  - Start the let expression with **let**.
  - Start each query step with an identifier (the query step name), followed by an equal sign, then an expression, then (if it is not the last step) a comma to indicate that the query step delivers a reusable value (a variable). The identifier can be used in other locations in the let expression and is usually used immediately in the subsequent step. Although the identifier can be used anywhere within the let expression, it cannot be accessed outside the let expression.
  - Ensure that the last query step does not end with a comma.
  - End the let expression with **in** followed by the identifier for the final value to be delivered by the new query. The result of the query is almost always the identifier of the last query step.
- When you create a query, the query can be used in other queries in the workbook.

As noted in Chapter 16, a let expression is similar to the LET worksheet function because both the LET worksheet function and the Power Query let expression allow you to define variables, use the variables throughout the process, and then deliver a final value.

Loading the Table to the Power Pivot Data Model

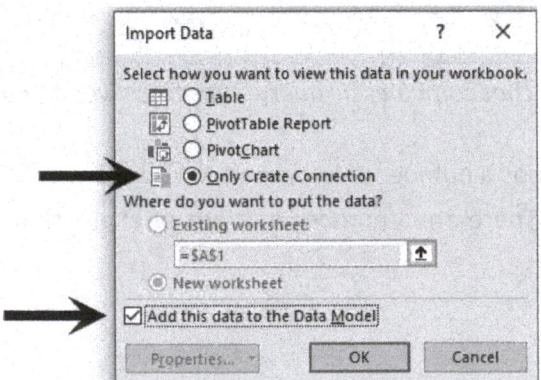

Figure 18.99 *To load the dimension table to the Data Model, you must select two items in Import Data dialog box.*

Now you are done with your transformation of the dProduct dimension table, and you need to load it to the Power Pivot Data Model. To do so, follow these steps:

1. In the Home tab of the Power Query Ribbon, in the Load group, click the Close & Load dropdown arrow and select Close & Load To. The Import Data dialog box appears.

2. In the Import Data dialog box, to load the table to the Power Pivot Data Model, select the Only Create Connection option button and check the Add This Data to the Data Model checkbox, as shown in Figure 18.99.

3. Click OK in the Import Data dialog box. The dimension table is loaded into the Data Model's columnar database, and you are taken back to the Excel app window.

In the Queries & Connections task pane, you can now see two queries that you have loaded to the Power Pivot Data Model (see Figure 18.100).

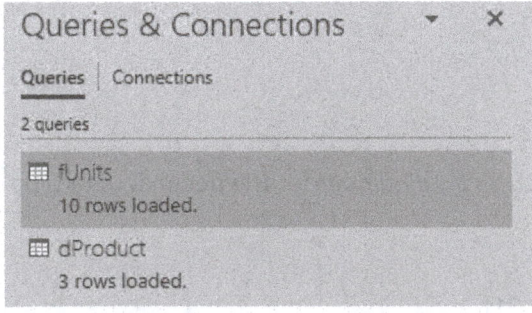

Figure 18.100 *After you load the dimension table to the Data Model, the Queries & Connections task pane shows both queries.*

Using Power Pivot to Create a One-to-Many Relationship

Now you need to verify that both the fact table and the dimension table are in the Data Model and build relationships and DAX formulas in the Power Pivot for Excel window. Follow these steps:

1. To jump back to the previously opened Power Pivot for Excel window, press Alt+Tab.

> **Note:** If you accidentally closed the Power Pivot for Excel window, click the Manage Data Model button in either the Data tab or the Power Pivot tab.

2. As shown in Figure 18.101, in the View group in the Home tab of the Power Pivot Ribbon, click the Diagram View button. You can see in this figure that both tables were loaded to the Data Model.

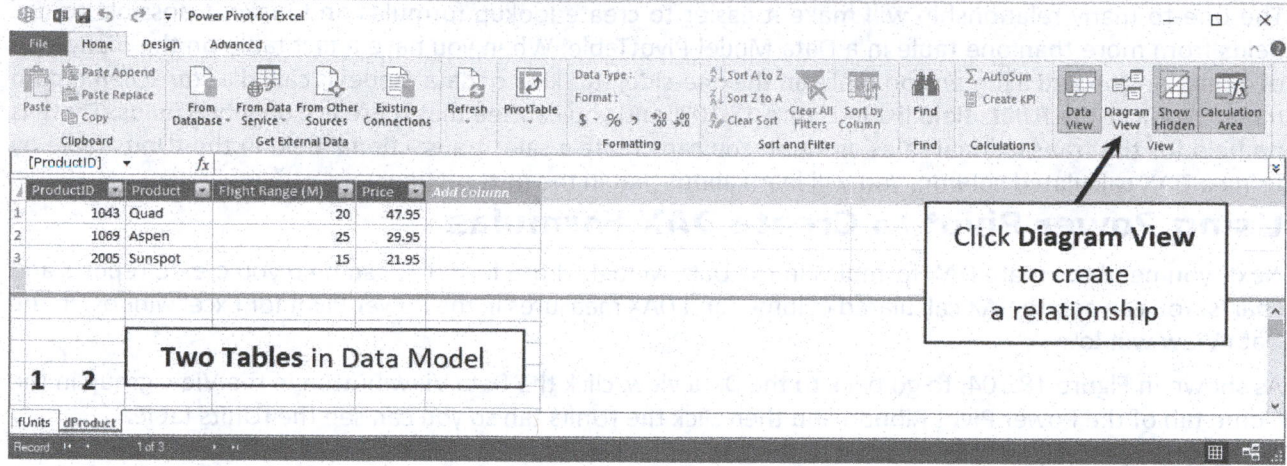

Figure 18.101 *You can see both tables in the Power Pivot for Excel window.*

3. As shown in Figure 18.102, to create the one-to-many relationship, click and drag the ProductID field from under dProduct over and on top of the ProductID field in the fUnits table and then let go of your mouse.

> **Note:** You can also drag the field from fUnits to dProduct and get the same result.

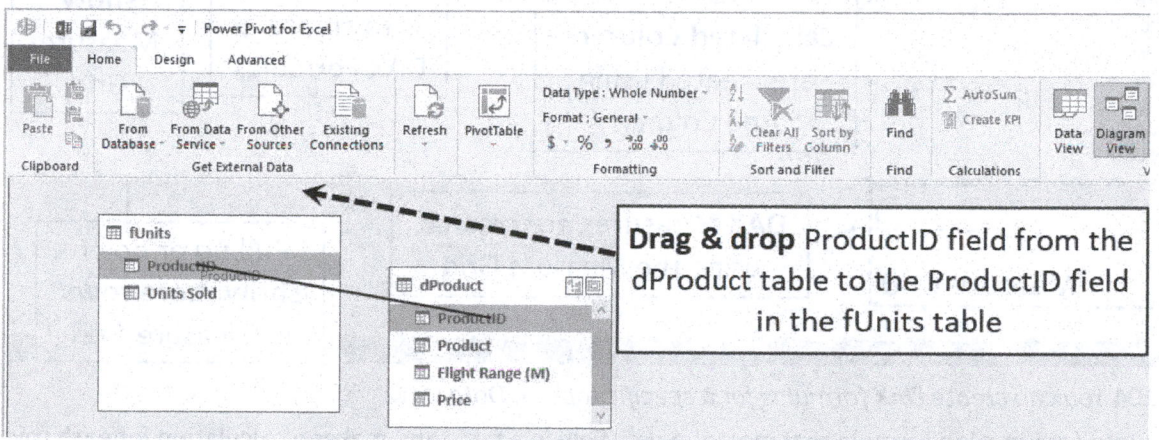

Figure 18.102 *In Diagram view, you can drag and drop the ProductID field to create a one-to-many relationship.*

As shown in Figure 18.103, a *one-to-many relationship* is created from the one-side—the dProduct table with the primary key—to the many-side—the fUnits table with the foreign key. The relationship line that is created between the two tables has the number 1 on the one-side, an asterisk (*) on the many-side, and an arrow indicating that the conditions or criteria applied in formulas, called *filters*, flow from the one-side to the many-side. This mechanism, as you will learn in full detail later, is called *filter context*, and it helps reduce formula calculation times for big data.

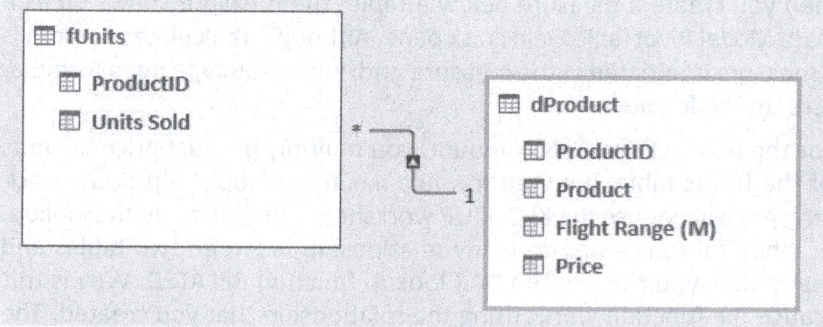

Figure 18.103 *A one-to-many relationship is created from the one-side (primary key) to the many-side (foreign key).*

The one-to-many relationship will make it easier to create lookup formulas and make it possible to use fields from more than one table in a Data Model PivotTable. When you have a fact table on the many-side of a relationship and a dimension table on the one-side, this kind of data model is called a *star schema data model*. Look at the fUnits field list in Figure 18.103, and you can see that there are only two fields. There is no field for the transactional sales amount. You can create a sales transactional field in the fUnits table by using a DAX calculated column. You will learn about that in the next section.

Using Power Pivot to Create DAX Formulas

Next, you need to create DAX formulas in the Data Model. These formulas can help you create reports and charts. You can create DAX calculated columns and DAX measures in the Power Pivot for Excel window in the Data View window.

As shown in Figure 18.104, to go back to the Data view, click the Data View button in the View group in the Home tab of the Power Pivot Ribbon and then click the fUnits tab so you can see the fUnits table.

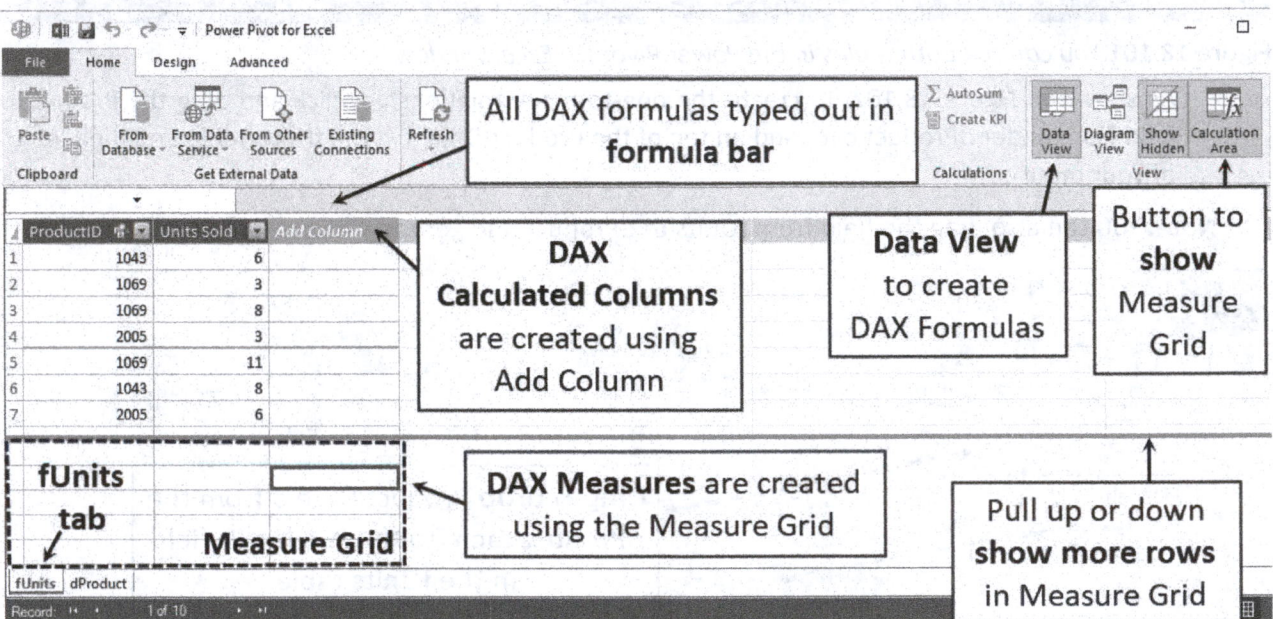

Figure 18.104 *You can create DAX formulas for a specific table in Data view.*

A *DAX calculated column* is a formula that creates a new field in a table and makes a calculation for each row in the table. In this example, you will use a DAX calculated column to create a sales field in the fUnits table that will calculate the transaction sales amount for each row. As illustrated in Figure 18.104, you create a DAX calculated columns by using the Add Column header to the right of the table where you want the new field. A *DAX measure* is a premade, preformatted formula that you drag and drop into Data Model PivotTables or PivotCharts to make conditional calculations. In this example, you will create two DAX measures: one for total sales and one for total units sold.

As illustrated in Figure 18.104, you create a DAX measure in the area below the table, which is called the *measure grid*, or *calculation area*. When you create a measure below a table, the measure shows up as a drag-and-drop formula in that table's Data Model PivotTable Fields task pane. Although a calculated column is initiated in the Add Column area and a measure is initiated in the measure grid, when you type out a formula, you must use the DAX formula bar to create the formula.

To create the DAX calculated column for the transactional sales amount, you multiply product price by units sold. The units sold are in each row of the fUnits table, but your formula has to look up the product price based on the ProductID in each row. Here you will not use the XLOOKUP worksheet function to do the lookup. Instead, in the DAX formula language, when there is a one-to-many relationship between two tables and you need to look up an item on the many-side, you can use the DAX lookup function RELATED. Why is this DAX RELATED function so named? Because the function works using the relationship that you created. The amazing thing about this function is that it only requires one argument! If you place the product price field from the dProduct table into RELATED, the function will automatically use the foreign key for each row to find a match in the primary key field and return the product price. This illustrates one of the magical benefits of using relationships between tables and shows that using DAX formulas instead of worksheet formulas makes lookup formulas easier to create.

These are the basic steps involved in creating a DAX calculated column:

1. Double-click the Add Column header to the right of the table where you want your calculated column.

2. Type the field name and press Enter.

3. Click in the formula bar, type your formula, and press Enter.

4. Click Add Formatting in the Formatting group in the Home tab of the Power Pivot Ribbon.

5. To edit the calculated column, select the calculated column and then edit it in the formula bar.

Creating a DAX Calculated Column for Transactional Sales Using the DAX RELATED Lookup Function

To create the Sales ($) calculated column, follow these steps:

1. As shown in Figure 18.105, double-click the Add Column header, type **Sales ($)**, and press Enter. An equal sign is automatically entered into the formula bar, where you must type out the formula.

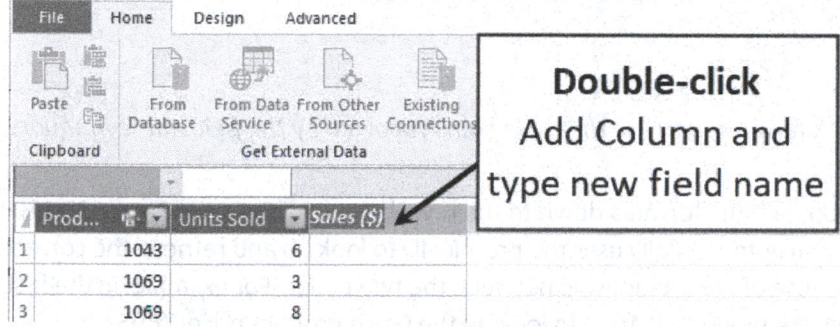

Figure 18.105 *Create a DAX calculated column for transactional sales.*

2. As shown in Figure 18.106, click in the formula bar to start to type the formula.

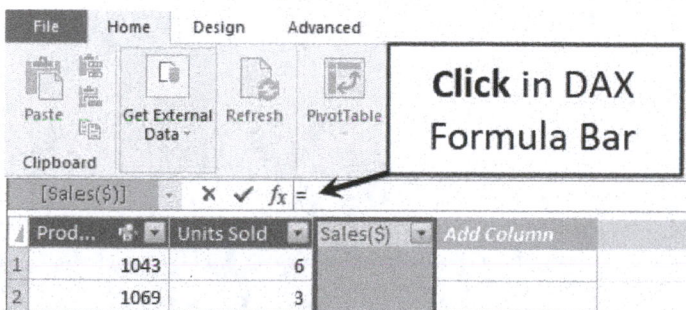

Figure 18.106 *After typing the field name and pressing Enter, click in the formula bar.*

3. As shown in Figure 18.107, type **rel**. Then, when the RELATED function is highlighted in blue in the dropdown function list, press the Tab key to enter the function into the formula bar.

> **Note:** When you are creating DAX formulas, you can use the dropdown lists, arrow keys, and Tab key shortcuts to enter functions, field names, measures, and other formula elements, just as you can in the Excel worksheet.

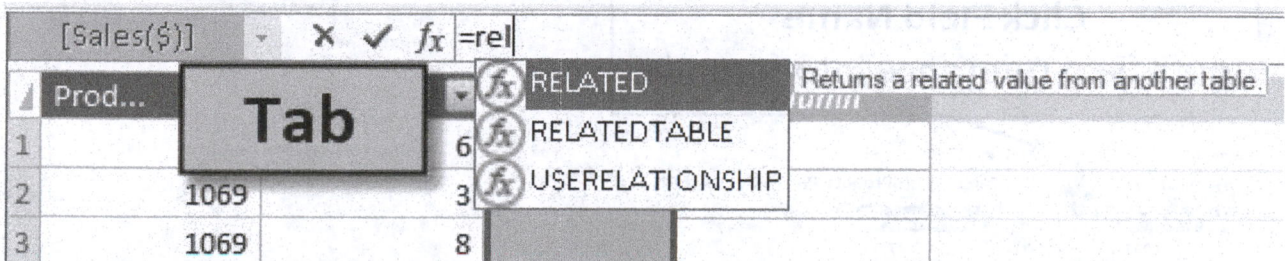

Figure 18.107 *Press the Tab key to enter the selected function into your formula.*

4. Notice that only fields from the one-side dProduct table are presented in the dropdown list inside the RELATED function (see Figure 18.108). Using your arrow keys, arrow down and select the dProduct[Price] field and then press the Tab key to enter this field into RELATED.

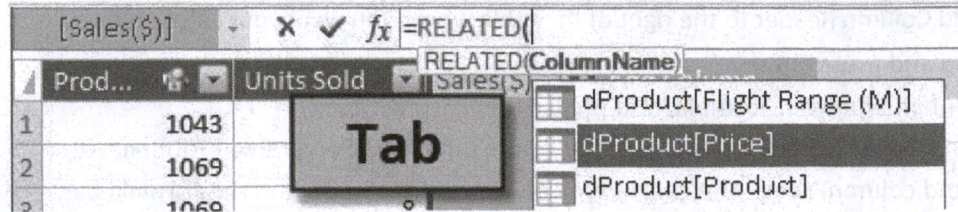

Figure 18.108 *There is a one-to-many relationship, and only the fields from the one-side table appear in the dropdown.*

5. As shown in Figure 18.109, type a close parenthesis.

[Sales($)]	× ✓ *fx* =RELATED(dProduct[Price])

Prod...	Units Sold	Sales($)	Add Column
1	1043	6	

Figure 18.109 *To refer to a field in a DAX formula, you use the table name followed by the field name in square brackets.*

6. Press Enter to automatically populate the formula down to the rows below. As shown in Figure 18.110, in each row, the RELATED function automatically uses the product ID to look up and retrieve the correct product price; it can do this because of the relationship between the two tables. For example, in the first row, the RELATED function uses the product ID 1043 to look up the Quad product price 47.95.

[Sales($)]	*fx* =RELATED(dProduct[Price])

	Prod...	Units Sold	Sales($)	Add Column
1	1043	6	47.95	
2	1069	3	29.95	
3	1069	8	29.95	
4	2005	3	21.95	
5	1069	11	29.95	
6	1043	8	47.95	
7	2005	6	21.95	
8	2005	13	21.95	
9	1043	5	47.95	
10	1043	5	47.95	

Figure 18.110 *The RELATED DAX lookup function uses the product ID in each row to look up the correct price.*

7. As shown in Figure 18.111, to complete the formula, click back in the formula bar, at the end of the formula type the multiplication operator * (asterisk), and then hover your cursor over the Units Sold field name, and when you see the solid black downward-pointing arrow, click to insert the field name into the formula.

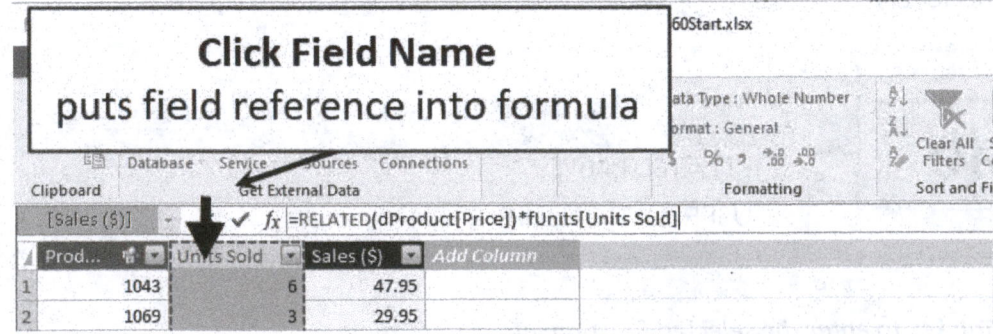

Figure 18.111 *The transaction sales formula is price multiplied by units sold.*

8.   Press Enter. The DAX calculated column is created, as shown in Figure 18.112.

[Sales ($)] ▼			fx =RELATED(dProduct[Price])*fUnits[Units Sold]	
Prod... 🔐 ▼	Units Sold ▼	Sales ($) ▼	Add Column	
1	1043	6	287.7	
2	1069	3	89.85	
3	1069	8	239.6	
4	2005	3	65.85	
5	1069	11	329.45	
6	1043	8	383.6	
7	2005	6	131.7	
8	2005	13	285.35	
9	1043	5	239.75	
10	1043	5	239.75	

Figure 18.112 *DAX calculated columns use row context, rather than cell references, to see values in each row.*

Look at Figure 18.112 and notice these important things about DAX formulas:

- When you refer to a field in a DAX formula, you must list the table name and then the field name in square brackets. This is the same syntax you use to refer to Excel Table fields in worksheet formulas.

- In a DAX calculated column, when you create a formula, it is automatically copied down to the rows below; this works very much like a formula with a calculated column in an Excel Table in the Excel worksheet. With DAX calculated columns, you never have to manually copy a formula down to the rows below. (Technically, in a DAX calculated column, there is one formula that applies to all rows. The formula is not actually copied down.)

- In DAX formulas, you cannot reference a cell value directly, as you can with worksheet formulas. With worksheet formulas, you can use a cell reference like B2 in the worksheet or [@UnitsSold] in an Excel Table. In DAX, you are limited to referring to fields and tables. However, in a DAX calculated column, the formula automatically picks out the correct row value in each row by using *row context*. For example, in Figure 18.112, the formula element fUnits[Units Sold] uses row context to get the Units Sold value 6 in the first row, 3 in the second row, and so on. As a second example, the RELATED function uses row context to automatically use the correct lookup value of ProductID 1043 in the first row, 1069 in the second row, and so on. In DAX formulas, row context is automatically generated when you use calculated columns or when you use *iterator functions* that simulate calculated columns, such as the SUMX function, which you will learn about shortly.

- When you create a DAX calculated column, the values become part of the data that is stored in the in-RAM columnar database. When there are not many unique items in a stored column, storing the values in the in-RAM columnar database does not increase the size of the stored database very much. The more unique items that need to be stored, the more the stored column will increase the size of the database. When you work with big data, this is something to track carefully.

Steps to Create a DAX Measure

To create a DAX measure, you follow these basic steps:

1.   In the View group in the Home tab of the Power Pivot Ribbon, make sure that the Calculation Area button is selected. This button hides/unhides the measure grid.

2.   Select the table tab where you want to create the measure. The measure you create will appear under this table name in the Data Model PivotTable Fields task pane.

3.   Click in a cell in the measure grid below the table.

4. Type the name of the measure. When you type the name, you are automatically moved to the formula bar. (DAX formulas can only be typed out in the formula bar.) The name you typed will appear in the Data Model PivotTable Fields task pane, so be sure to use a name that the user will understand.

5. Type the assignment operator **:=** (a colon followed by an equal sign).

> **Note:** An *assignment operator* is a symbol used to tell a program that everything after it is the formula. Whereas Excel worksheet formulas, Power Query M code formulas, and Power BI DAX formulas all use an equal sign as the assignment operator, Power Pivot uses a colon followed by an equal sign.

6. Type your DAX formula and then press Enter.

7. Add number formatting to the formula from the Formatting group in the Home tab of the Power Pivot Ribbon. You can also right-click the cell in the measure grid that contains the formula and select Format.

> **Note:** The number formatting you add to the cell in the measure grid that contains the measure is attached to the formula and will show up any time you use the measure in a report or visualization.

8. If you want to add a description, right-click the cell in the measure grid that contains the formula, click on Description, and enter a description.

9. To edit the measure, go back to the measure grid or navigate to the Calculations group in the Power Pivot tab in the Excel Ribbon, click the Measure dropdown arrow and select Manage Measures, and then, in the Manage Measures dialog box, select the measure and click the Edit button.

As you can see in these steps, when you create a DAX measure, you create the name of the measure, type the assignment operator, and type the formula all in one place (that is, *Name of Measure := Formula*). In addition, although you can create measures in the measure grid, there is a dialog box for creating measures that you can access from the Power Pivot tab in the Excel Ribbon. I rarely use this dialog box, though, because it does not let me decide where to place the measure in the measure grid. I like to manually place my measures in the measure grid so that I can neatly organize them in different rows.

Creating a DAX Measure for Total Sales Using SUM

Now you are ready to create the Total Sales ($) measure, which will add the transactional sales from the Sales ($) field. To create the Total Sales ($) measure, follow these steps:

1. Make sure the Calculation Area button is selected in the View group in the Home tab of the Power Pivot Ribbon.

2. Select the fUnits tab.

3. Select a cell in the measure grid below the Sales ($) field, as shown in Figure 18.113.

4. As also shown in Figure 18.113, type the field name and the assignment operator: **Total Sales ($):=**.

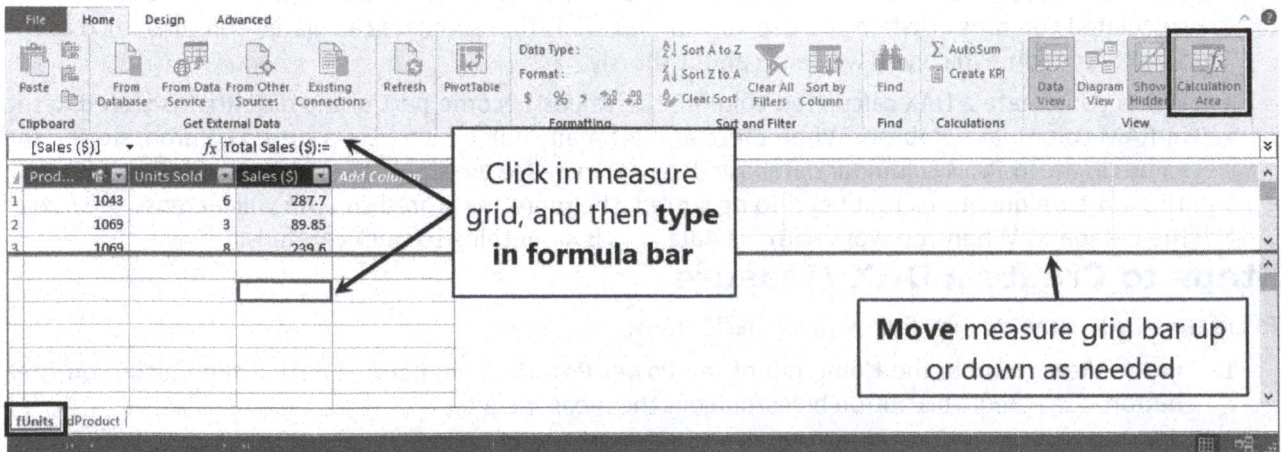

Figure 18.113 *Start your DAX measure.*

5. As shown in Figure 18.114, create the formula **SUM(fUnits[Sales ($)])**.

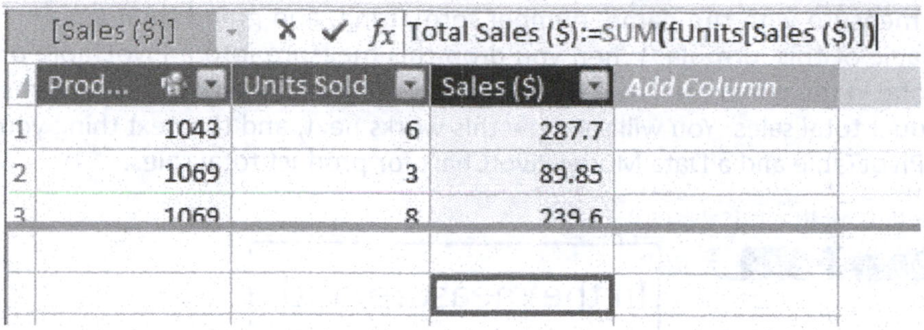

[Sales ($)]	▾	✕ ✓	f_x	Total Sales ($):=SUM(fUnits[Sales ($)])

	Prod...	📌 ▾	Units Sold ▾	Sales ($) ▾	Add Column
1	1043		6	287.7	
2	1069		3	89.85	
3	1069		8	239.6	

Figure 18.114 *Use the DAX SUM function to add sales from the fUnits[Sales ($)] field.*

6. Press Enter to enter the formula in the measure grid. In Figure 18.115, you can see the whole formula in the formula bar and only partially in the measure grid.

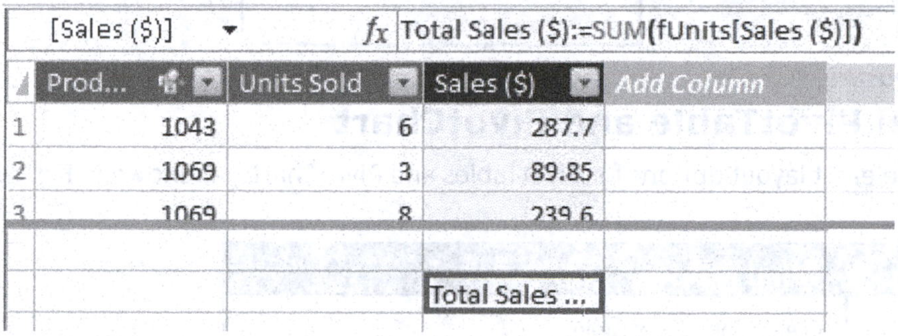

[Sales ($)]	▾		f_x	Total Sales ($):=SUM(fUnits[Sales ($)])

	Prod...	📌 ▾	Units Sold ▾	Sales ($) ▾	Add Column
1	1043		6	287.7	
2	1069		3	89.85	
3	1069		8	239.6	
				Total Sales ...	

Figure 18.115 *Enter the formula in the measure grid.*

7. Use the white double-sided horizontal arrow to resize the field so that you can see the full measure name and overall total sales amount in the measure grid (see Figure 18.116).

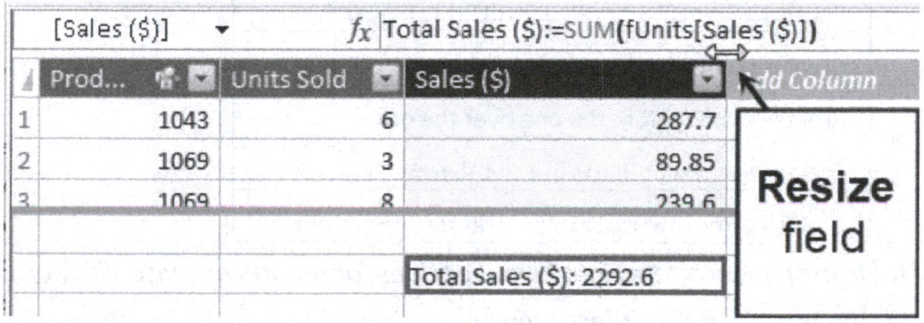

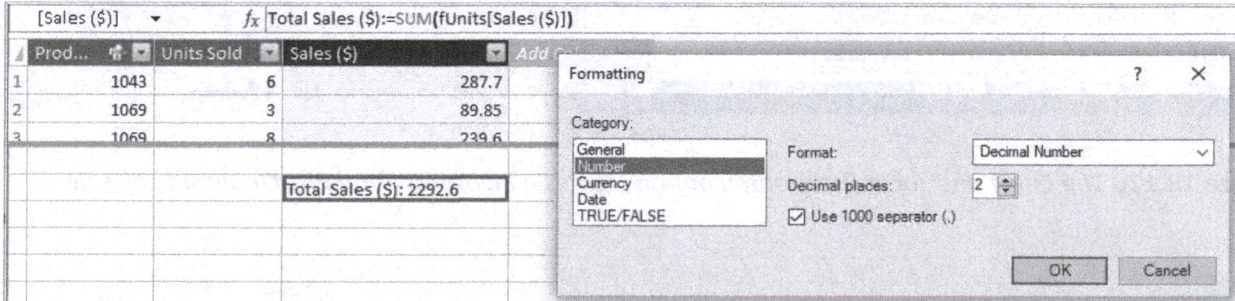

Figure 18.116 *Adjust the field width so that you can see the measure result in the measure grid.*

8. Right-click the cell that contains the measure and select Format.

9. In the Formatting dialog box that appears, as shown in Figure 18.117, select Number from the Category list, check the Use 1000 Separator (,) checkbox, and click OK to apply the number formatting to the measure.

> **Note:** When you apply number formatting to a measure, the formatting will appear any time you use the measure.

Figure 18.117 *With DAX, when you add number formatting to a measure, that formatting will appear any time you use the measure.*

Figure 18.118 shows the finished measure with the name, number formatting, and grand total amount. However, you can't yet see the magic of this formula: When you drop this measure into a PivotTable or PivotChart, it will show the grand total in the grand total row, but in the rows containing product names, the measure will show the correct product total sales. You will see how this works next, and the next thing you need to do is create a Data Model PivotTable and a Data Model PivotChart for product total sales.

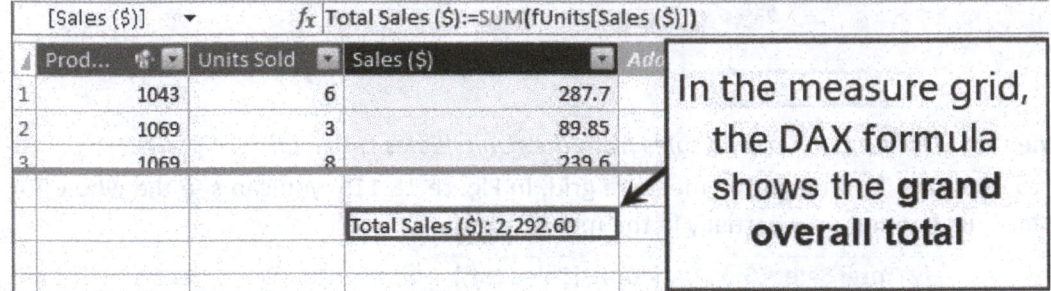

Figure 18.118 *The finished DAX measure.*

Creating a Data Model PivotTable and PivotChart

With the Power Pivot tool, you have eight layout options for PivotTables and PivotCharts, as shown in Figure 18.119.

Dropdown Icon		What is does
	PivotTable	Creates one PivotTable
	PivotChart	Creates one PivotChart
	Chart and Table (Horizontal)	Creates a PivotChart and a PivotTable side by side
	Chart and Table (Vertical)	Creates a PivotChart with a PivotTable below it
	Two Charts (Horizontal)	Creates two PivotCharts side by side
	Two Charts (Vertical)	Creates two PivotCharts, one over the other
	Four Charts	Creates four PivotCharts in a two-by-two square
	Flattened PivotTable	Creates a PivotTable with row criteria filled down

Figure 18.119 *The Power Pivot PivotTable dropdown offers eight layout options for reports and visualizations.*

To create a PivotChart and PivotTable side by side, follow these steps:

10. As shown in Figure 18.120, to start your Data Model PivotTable, in the Home tab of the PowerPivot Ribbon, click the PivotTable dropdown to reveal the eight reporting and visualization layout options and select the third item in the list, Chart and Table (Horizontal).

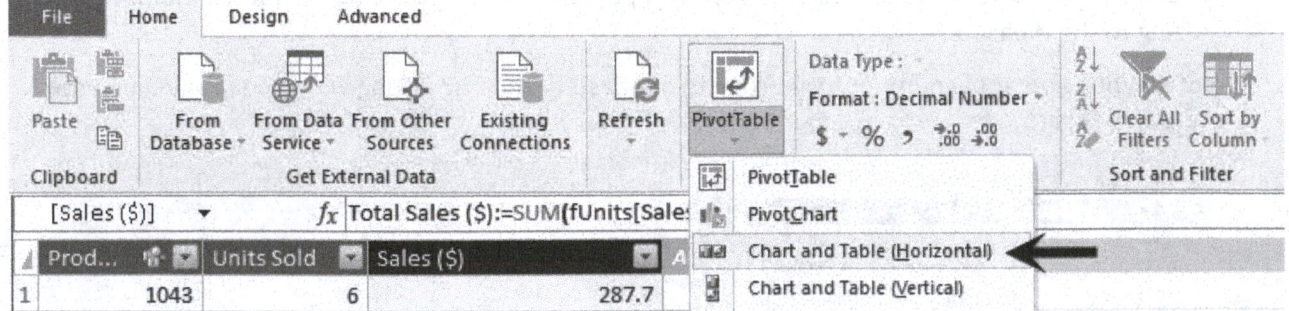

Figure 18.120 *The Chart and Table (Horizontal) option creates a PivotChart and PivotTable side by side.*

11. In the Create PivotChart and PivotTable (Horizontal) dialog box that appears, as shown in Figure 18.121, click the Existing Worksheet option button and then click the collapse button.

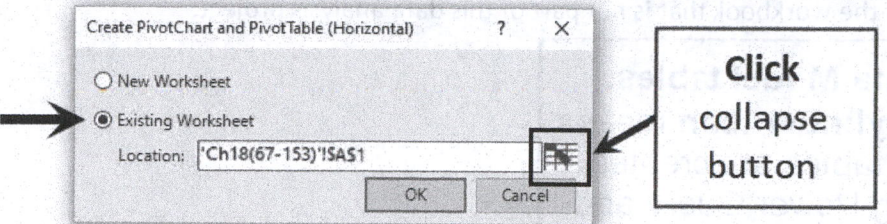

Figure 18.121 *Be sure to click the collapse button to open the next dialog box.*

12. In the Range Selection dialog box that appears, as shown in Figure 18.122, make sure the sheet Ch18(67-153) is selected, click in cell B8, and click OK.

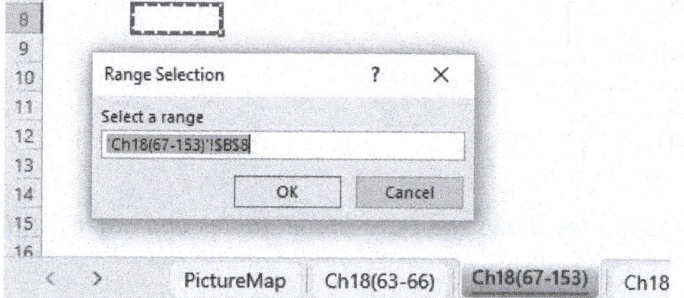

Figure 18.122 *The Range Selection dialog box allows you to select the destination for the chart and report.*

13. As shown in Figure 18.123, back in the Create PivotChart and PivotTable (Horizontal) dialog box, click OK. The PivotChart and PivotTable appear in the worksheet, and the PivotChart is initially selected.

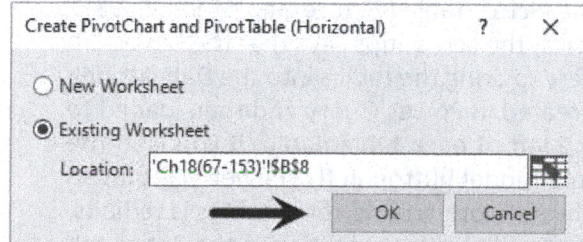

Figure 18.123 *Click OK in the Create PivotChart and PivotTable (Horizontal) dialog box.*

14. To select the PivotTable reporting area in the worksheet, click in cell J8, as shown in Figure 18.124. This figure shows the worksheet with an area to build a chart and report and the PivotTable task pane with three tables listed. This is one more table than you need for your report!

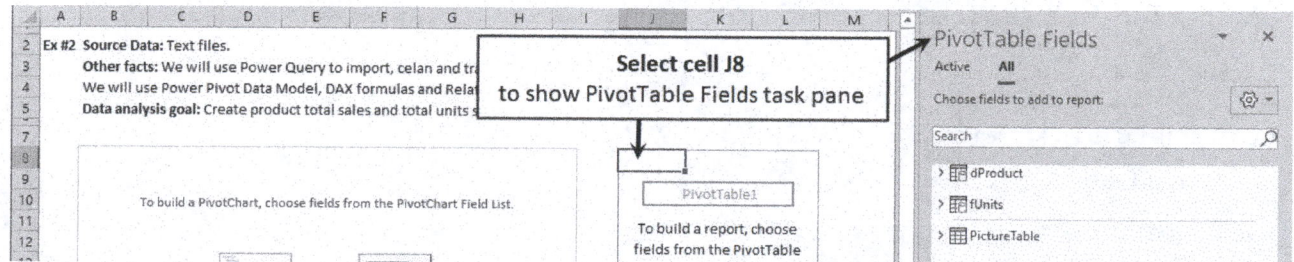

Figure 18.124 *The PivotTable is selected, and, on the right, you can see the PivotTable task pane.*

Figure 18.125 shows a closeup of the task pane with the three tables in the All tab (which is the tab that shows up by default). The top two tables are the Data Model tables, and the bottom table is an Excel Table from within the workbook that is not part of this data analysis project.

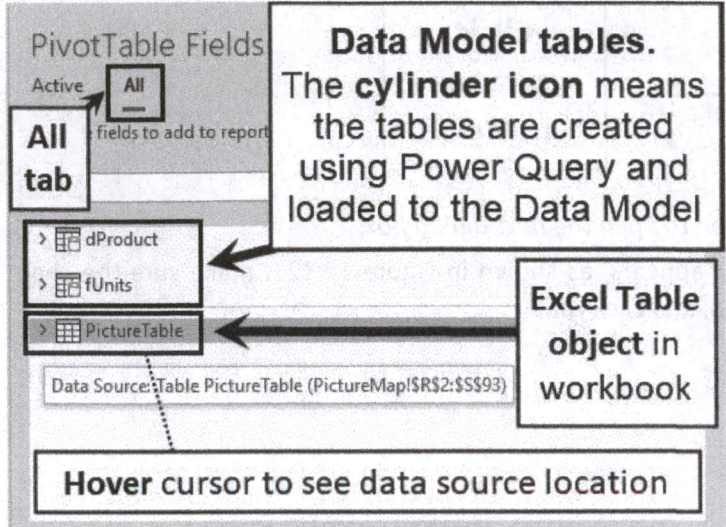

Figure 18.125 *The All tab in the PivotTable Fields task panes shows the Data Model tables and other Excel Tables.*

Note: When you create a Data Model PivotTable or PivotChart, all the Data Model tables and Excel Tables from within the workbook show up in the PivotTable Fields task pane. If you are not sure where the tables are located in the workbook, you can hover your cursor over a table name to bring up a screentip that indicates where the table is located. In Figure 18.125, the screentip for the last table shows the message "Data Source: Table PictureTable (PictureMap!$R$2:$S$93)." If you hover your cursor over either of the top two tables, the screentips says that the tables are from Power Query. This is because you used Power Query to bring the tables into the Data Model. You can also tell that the top two tables were tables created in Power Query and then loaded to the Data Model because a cylinder icon is listed to the left of each table name. If you load the tables directly to the Data Model using the Load to Data Model button in the Power Pivot tab in the Excel Ribbon, this icon will not appear. Finally, trying to work around three tables is tedious, so you want to show the two Data Model tables that you will use for reporting in the Active tab in the PivotTable Fields task pane.

15. To show the dProduct Data Model table in the Active tab, right-click the table name and click on Show in Active Tab (see Figure 18.126).

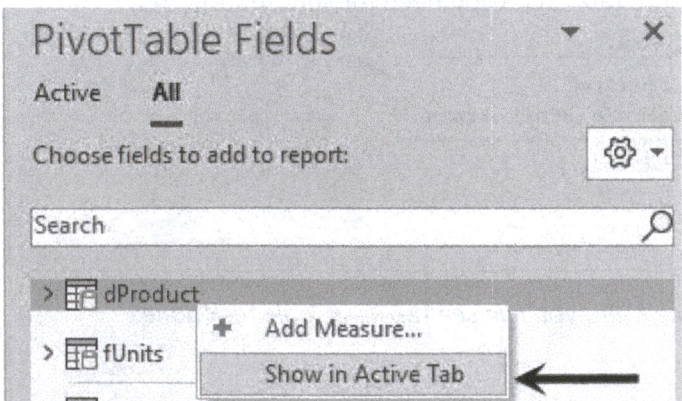

Figure 18.126 *To show a table in the Active tab, right-click the table in the PivotTable Fields task pane and select Show in Active Tab.*

16. Right-click the fUnits Data Model table name and click on Show in Active Tab.

17. To see the two Data Model tables in the Active tab, select the Active tab in the PivotTable Fields task pane. As shown in Figure 18.127, the Active tab shows the dProduct table with four field names and the fUnits table with three field names and one measure.

Note: This Data Model PivotTable Fields task pane is very different from the standard PivotTable Fields task pane because it allows you to show multiple tables, allows you to drag and drop fields from any of the tables into the same report/chart, and allows measures to be listed and then dragged and dropped into reports/charts.

Note: The fx next to an item in this pane indicates that the item is a measure.

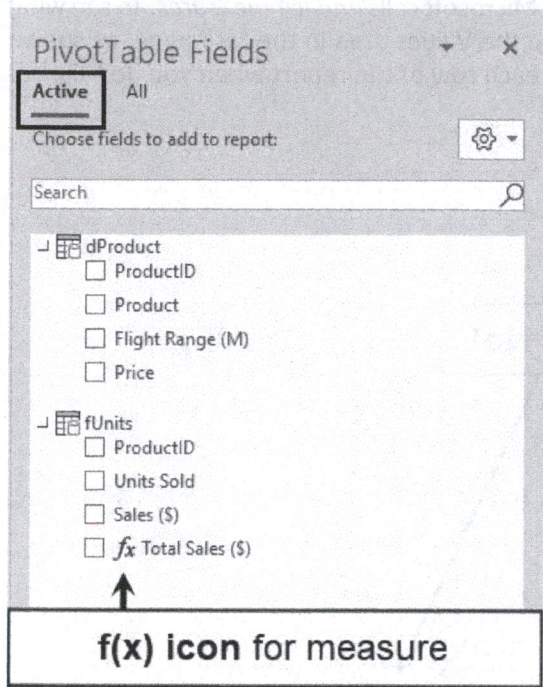

Figure 18.127 *The Active tab in the PivotTable Fields task pane lists the Data Model tables.*

18. To build a PivotTable report from the two tables, in the PivotTable Fields task pane, drag the Product field from the dProduct table down to the Rows area and then drag the measure from the fUnits table down to the Values area (see Figure 18.128).

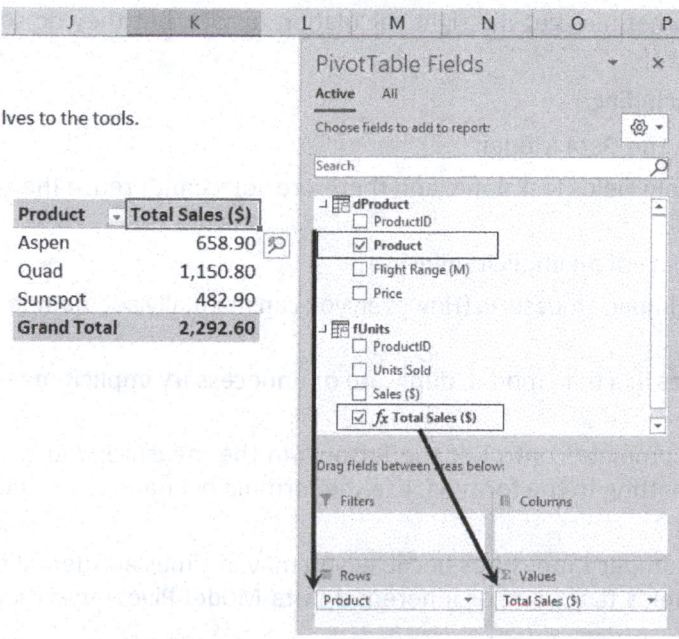

Figure 18.128 *Drag and drop one field and one measure.*

Figure 18.128 shows the correct product sales report. Already, you can see two benefits of this data modeling approach as compared to using the flat table standard PivotTable approach described in Example 1. The first benefit is that you can directly drag the Product field from the dProduct table into the report rather than having to create the XLOOKUP formula in the fact table. The second benefit is that you can drag a premade formula (a measure) to the report, and it already contains number formatting. There are some other benefits, but before we look at them, I want to show you a Data Model mistake so you can learn about a potential drawback to a Data Model PivotTable/PivotChart.

Implicit Measures: Why They're Problematic and When to Use Them

The mistake I just mentioned has to do with creating something Microsoft calls *implicit measures*. To see what happens, drag the Sales ($) field from the fUnits table down to the Values area in the task pane, as shown in Figure 18.129. You get the correct product sales amounts in each row of the report when you do this, but there are a number of drawbacks.

Product	Total Sales ($)	Sum of Sales ($)
Aspen	658.90	658.9
Quad	1,150.80	1150.8
Sunspot	482.90	482.9
Grand Total	2,292.60	2292.6

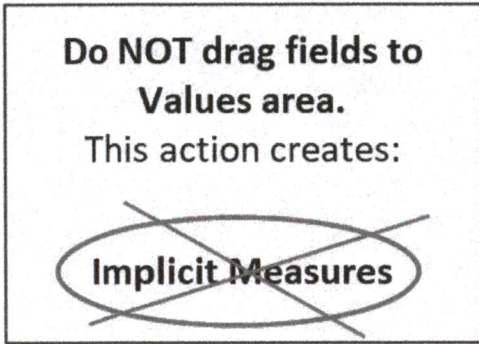

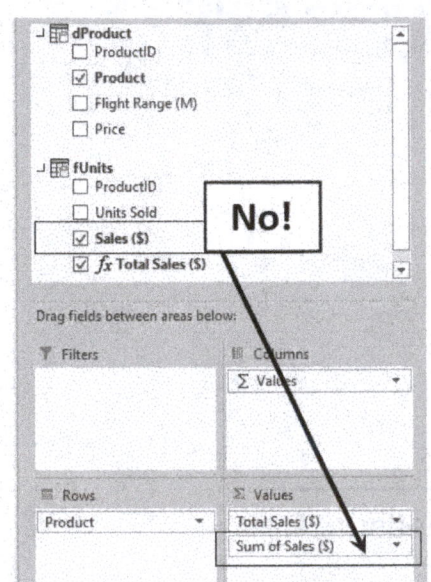

Figure 18.129 *When you drag a field to the Values area, an inefficient implicit measure is created.*

When you drag a field from a table into the Values area of a Data Model PivotTable, Power Pivot creates a read-only measure in a hidden behind-the-scenes location. Microsoft calls this hidden measure an *implicit measure*. When you author your own measure, as you did with the Total Sales ($) measure, Microsoft calls that an *explicit measure*. Implicit measures can sometimes get the right calculation results, but they do so in an inefficient way.

Implicit measures have a number of drawbacks, including:

- By default, implicit measures are hidden in the Data Model.
- The measures do not appear in the PivotTable Fields task pane, and therefore you cannot reuse them in other reports or visuals.
- You cannot edit the name or the formula part of an implicit measure.
- You cannot attach number formatting to an implicit measure. (However, you can manually add number formatting in the report or chart.)
- When you create multiple implicit measures in a data model, duplicate or unnecessary implicit measures may be created.

When you create an explicit measure, you have complete control of the formula in the measure: You can edit the name, edit the formula, add number formatting to the formula, use the formula over and over, and share your data model online.

It is important to know how to look for and delete implicit measures because you may at times accidentally drag fields to the Values area of the PivotTable Fields task pane or inherent a Data Model PivotTable that contains implicit measures. Here's the process:

1. As shown in Figure 18.130, to show the implicit measure for the fUnits table, click the Show Implicit Measures button in the Advanced tab of the Power Pivot Ribbon. The implicit measures are now highlighted in the measure grid.

2. Select the cell that contains the implicit measure. Notice in the formula bar that everything is grayed out and cannot be edited, including the number formatting. You can see the grayed-out measure in the formula bar in Figure 18.130.

3. To delete the implicit measure, select the cell that contains the implicit measure and press Delete. In the Confirm dialog box, click the Delete from Model button.

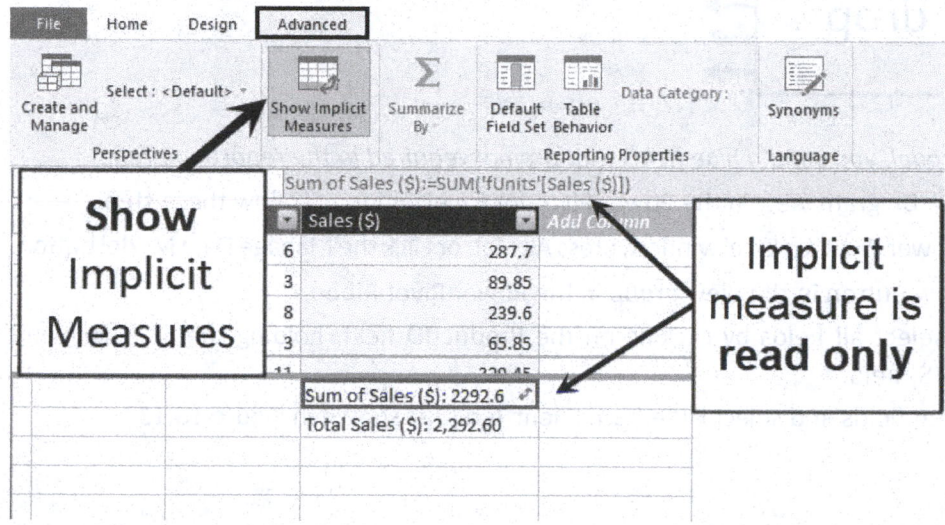

Figure 18.130 *The Show Implicit Measure button is in the Advanced tab of the Power Pivot Ribbon.*

When you delete an implicit measure, it is removed from the measure grid and from the Data Model PivotTable. In general, as you work in the Data Model, it is a good idea to have the Show Implicit Measure button selected in case you encounter implicit measures.

You have already seen that implicit measures are inefficient, but there are some situations where they're useful. For example, if you have some big data datasets and you just want a quick report, it can be okay to load a big data flat table to the Data Model and use implicit measures. For example, say that you get a large amount of single-column text data, and you want to quickly create a frequency distribution that shows counts and percentages by category. (You saw an example of this sort of frequency distribution in Example 2 in Chapter 17.) In this case, you can import the data by using Power Query, load it to the Data Model, and drag the text field to the Values area, thereby creating an implicit measure for the frequency calculation. Then you can drag the text field to the Values area a second time and use the standard PivotTable Show Values As, % of Column Total feature to create the percentage frequency calculation. In this case, you would be mixing and matching a Data Model PivotTable with a standard PivotTable. Specifically, you would be creating a Data Model implicit measure for counting and a standard PivotTable Show Values As, % of Column Total calculation for the percentage calculation. In this example, the potential benefits of the quick-and-easy Show Values As calculation outweigh any inefficiencies of the implicit measure. (You will see this again in Practice Problem 6 at the end of this chapter.)

Hiding Fields to Enable User-Friendly Reporting

Let's now consider the PivotTable Fields task pane as the user interface for creating reports and visualizations. In Power Pivot, the PivotTable Fields task pane is called the client tool area, and in Power BI, it is called the report view area. As you learned earlier in this chapter, a good data model has a user interface that is easy for a decision maker to use. To increase make a data model's interface usable, you often need to hide some fields, including ones the user will never use (such as ProductID, which only exists to create the relationship) and those that can create implicit measures (such as Price, Units Sold, and Sales ($)), as shown in Figure 18.131.

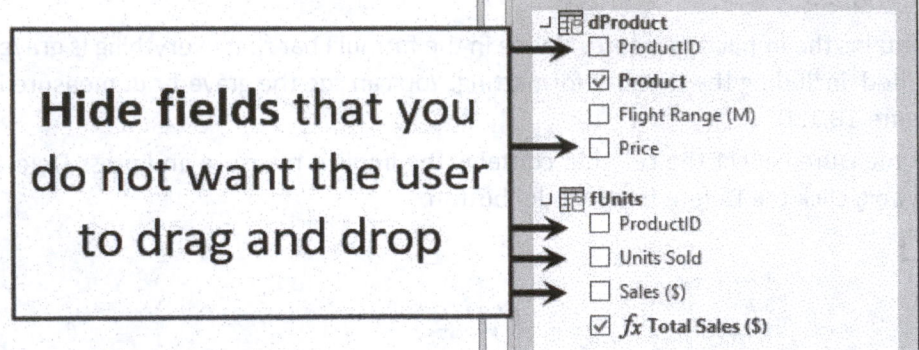

Figure 18.131 *With a data model, you should hide fields that are not required in the reporting area.*

To hide fields, you can use the Diagram view in the Power Pivot for Excel window. Follow these steps:

1. To jump back to the Power Pivot for Excel window, press Alt+Tab or click the Manage Data Model button.

2. Click the Diagram View button in the View group in the Power Pivot Ribbon.

3. In the fUnits table, select all fields by clicking on the ProductID field, holding the Shift key, and clicking on the Sales ($) field.

4. Right-click the selected fields and select Hide from Client Tools, as shown in Figure 18.132.

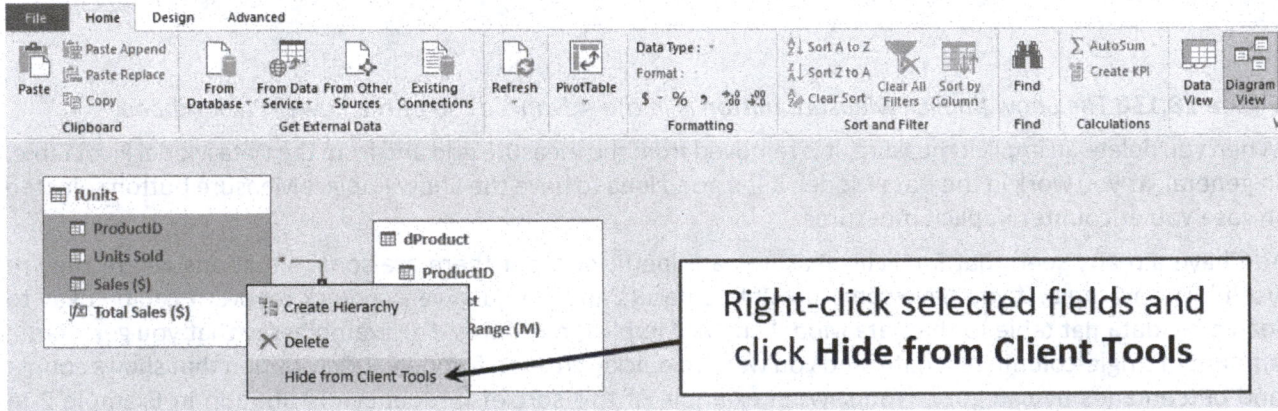

Figure 18.132 *In Diagram view in the Power Pivot for Excel window, you can hide fields.*

5. In the dProduct table, select the first and last fields by clicking on the ProductID field, holding the Ctrl key, and clicking on the Price field.

6. Right-click the selected fields and select Hide from Client Tools. Figure 18.133 shows that the hidden fields are now grayed out. This indicates that these fields will not show up in the PivotTable Fields task pane.

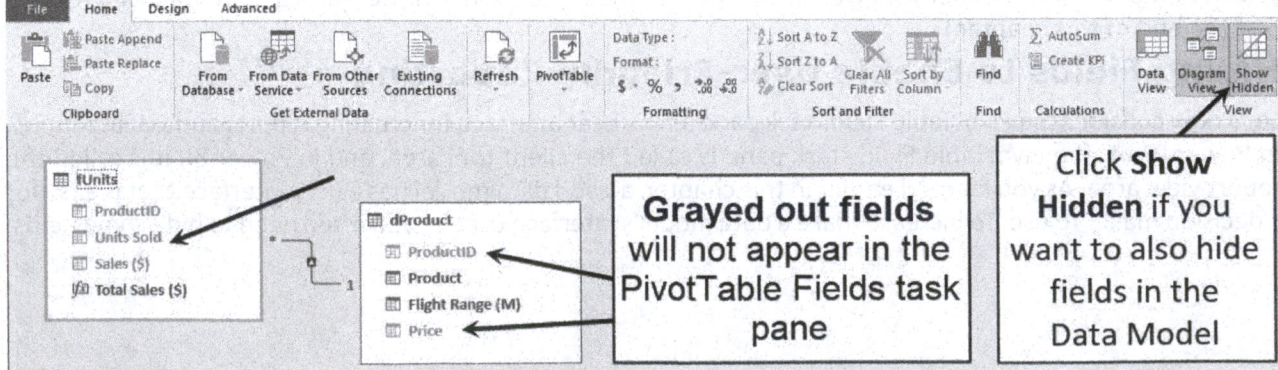

Figure 18.133 *Grayed-out fields in the field list will not show up in the reporting area.*

Figure 18.134 shows that the PivotTable Fields task pane now lists only the fields and measures that you will use for reporting and charting. Notice that because the fUnits table had all the fields hidden, a Greek sigma icon now appears. This indicates that there are only measures in this list.

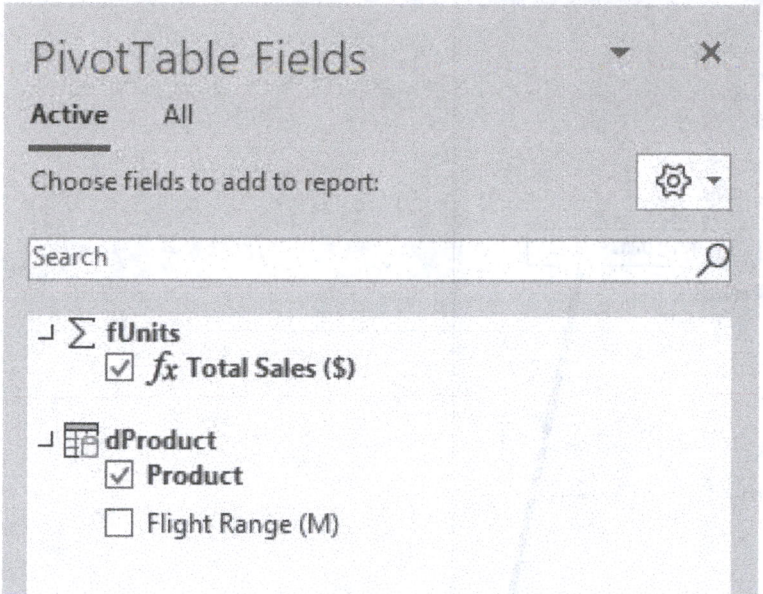

Figure 18.134 *A neat and tidy PivotTable Fields task pane.*

Creating a Measure in the Measure Grid

The next task is to create a total units measure in the measure grid below the fUnits table. Follow these steps:

1. In the Power Pivot for Excel window, click the Data View button and then click the fUnits tab.

2. As shown in Figure 18.135, in the measure grid below the fUnits table, create the Total Units Sold measure: **Total Units Sold:=SUM(fUnits[Units Sold])**.

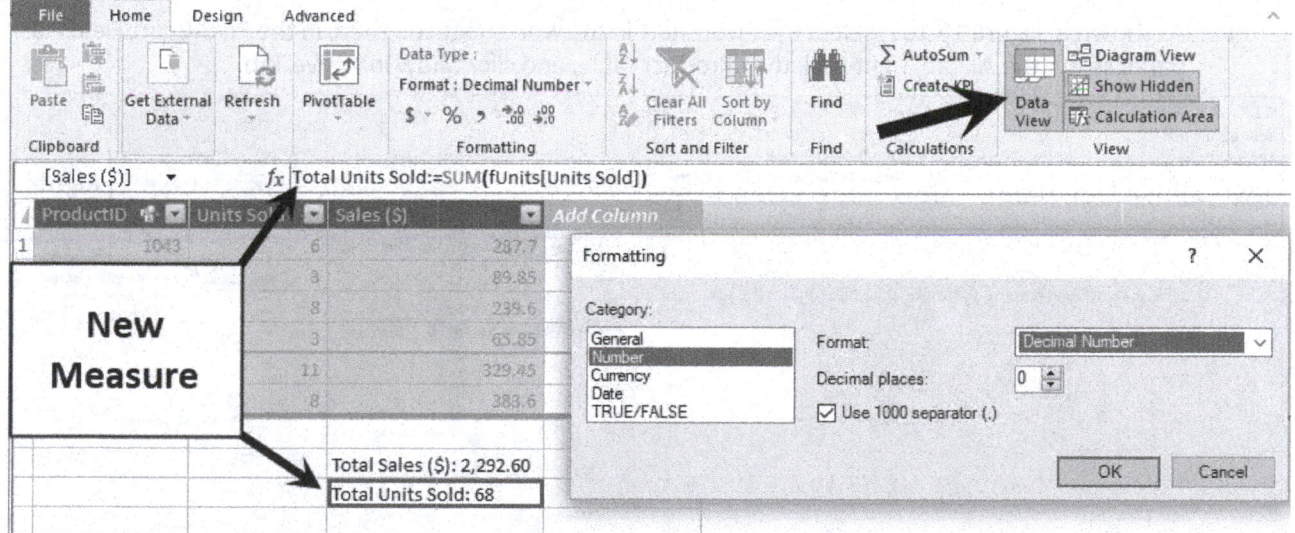

Figure 18.135 *Create the Total Units Sold measure to add units from the Units Sold field.*

3. Right-click the cell that contains the measure and select Format.

4. Use the Formatting dialog box that appears to add number formatting with a comma separator and zero decimal places showing and then click OK.

5. Press Alt+Tab to jump back to the Excel window. With the PivotTable still selected, notice that the new measure appears in the PivotTable Fields task pane, as shown in Figure 18.136.

6. Drag the Total Units Sold measure down to the Values area. Figure 18.136 shows resulting PivotTable report.

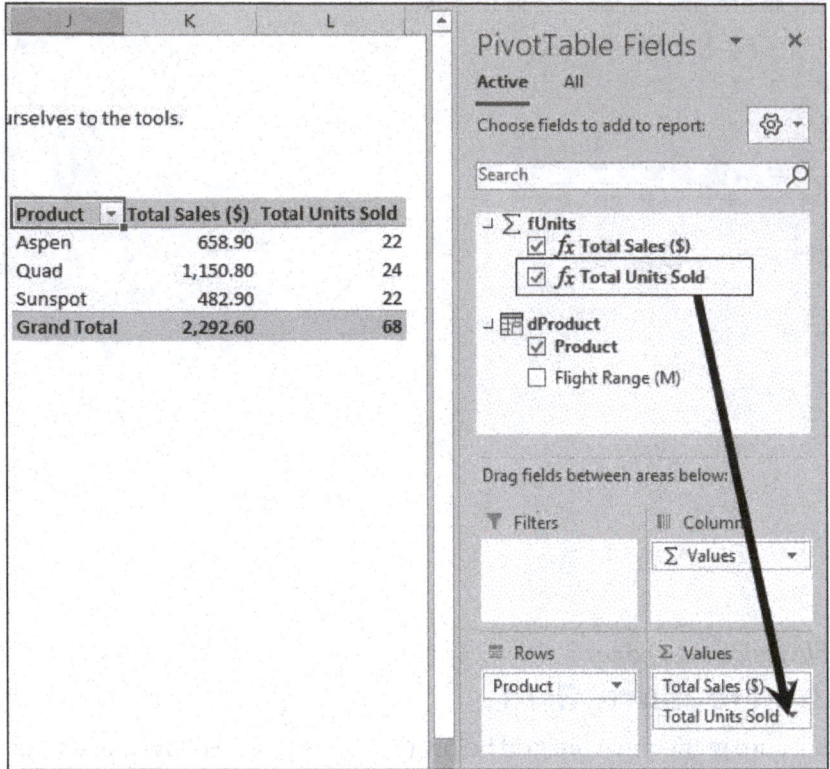

Figure 18.136 *Drag the Total Units Sold measure to the Values area.*

Creating a PivotChart

To create the PivotChart for total sales by product, follow these steps:

1. As shown in Figure 18.137, select the PivotChart in the worksheet and then, in the PivotChart Fields task pane, select the All tab, right-click the dProduct table, and click Show in Active Tab.

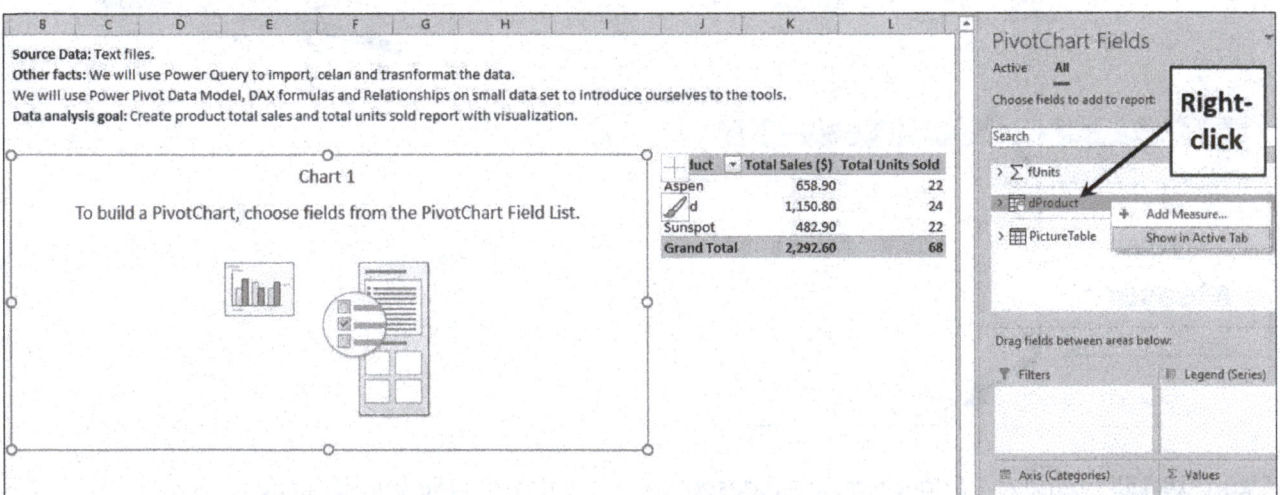

Figure 18.137 *In the PivotChart Fields task pane All tab, add the dProduct table to the Active tab for the PivotChart.*

2. Click on the Active tab in the PivotChart Fields task pane. You should see the dProduct table and the list of measures (see Figure 18.138).

3. As indicated in Figure 18.138, drag the Product field to the Axis area and the Total Sales ($) measure to the Values area.

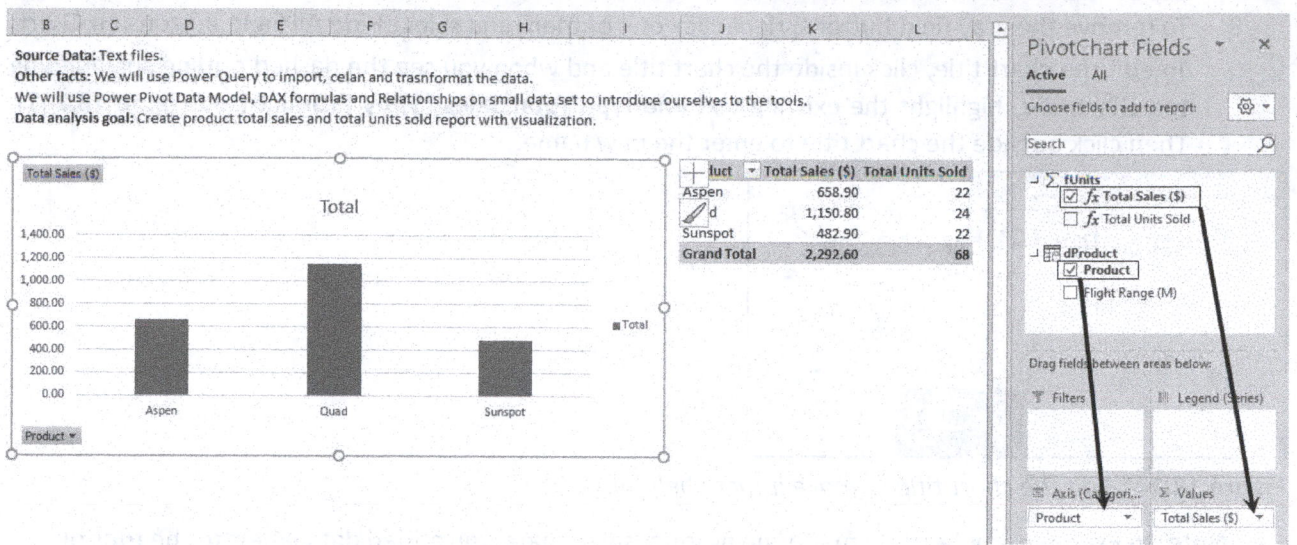

Figure 18.138 *Drag the Product field to the Rows area and the Total Sales ($) measure to the Values area.*

4. To begin cleaning up the chart junk in the report, remove the "Total" legend by selecting the legend and clicking the Delete button.

5. To sort the columns from largest to smallest, based on the total sales amounts, click the Product field button dropdown arrow and select More Sort Options, as shown in Figure 18.139.

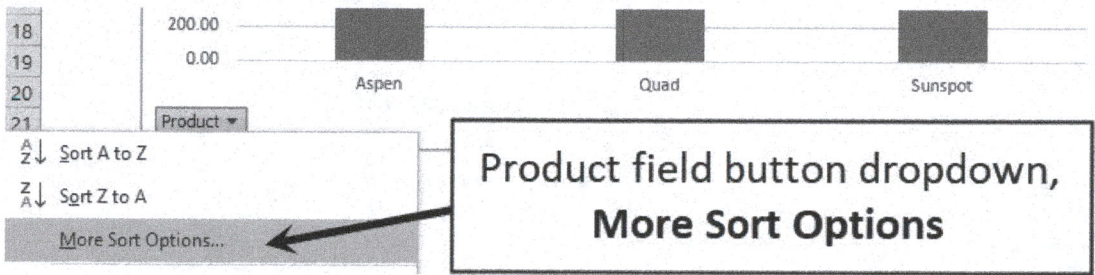

Figure 18.139 *The field buttons in a PivotChart can help you sort the columns.*

6. In the Sort (Product) dialog box that appears, as shown in Figure 18.140, select the Descending (Z to A) By option button and select Total Sales ($) from the dropdown.

7. Click OK in the Sort (Product) dialog box.

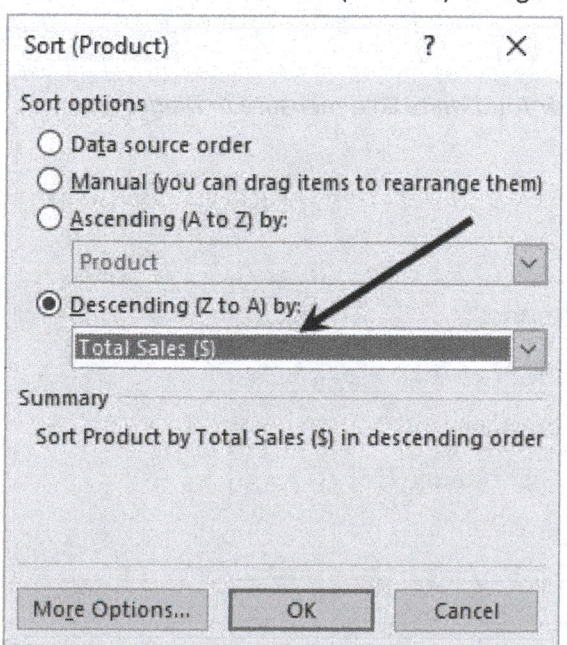

Figure 18.140 *Sort the product total sales amounts from largest to smallest.*

8. To remove the gray field buttons, right-click one of them and select Hide All Field Buttons on Chart.

9. To edit the chart title, click inside the chart title and when you see the dashed outline surrounding the chart title, highlight the existing text and type **Total Sales ($) by Product** (see Figure 18.141). Then click outside the chart title to enter the new name.

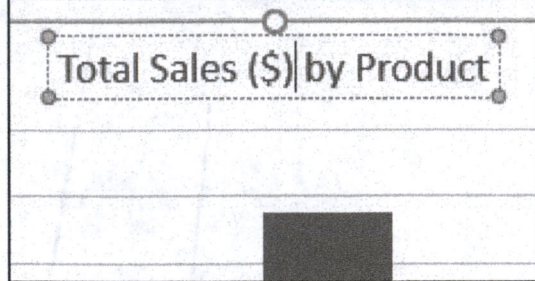

Figure 18.141 *Edit the chart title to make it more helpful.*

Note: In Example 1, when you made the product sales chart, you added data labels to the tops of the columns to show exact values in the visualization. For the chart in this example, you will not add such data labels. However, you will leave the numbers in the vertical axis to emphasize the axis amounts and the comparative gridlines.

The completed PivotChart and PivotTable are shown in Figure 18.142.

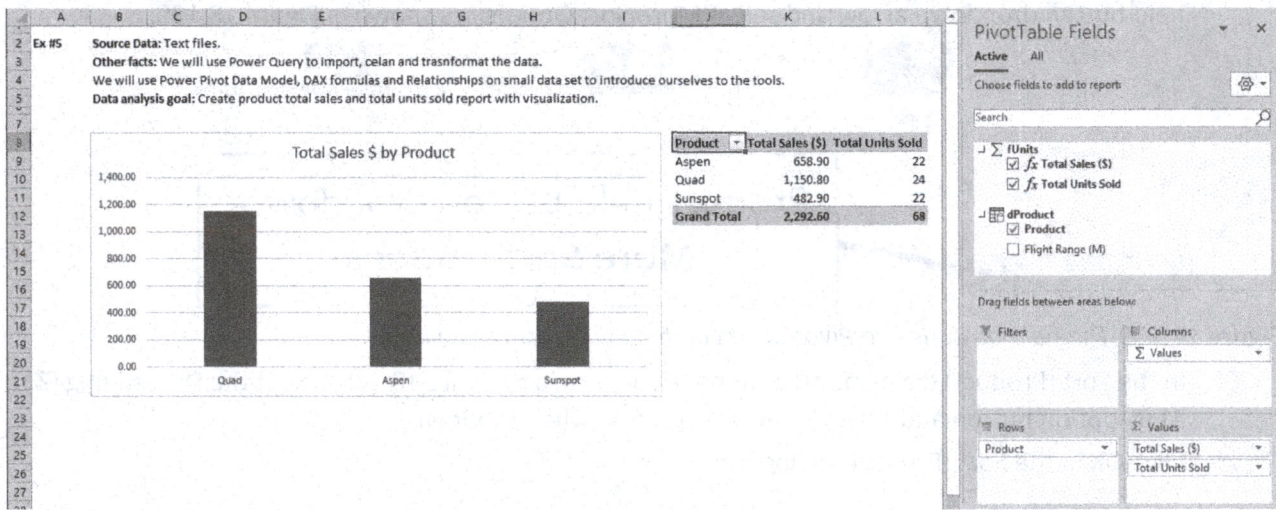

Figure 18.142 *Completed PivotChart and PivotTable.*

Figure 18.143 shows the star schema data model with the new Total Units Sold measure in Diagram view.

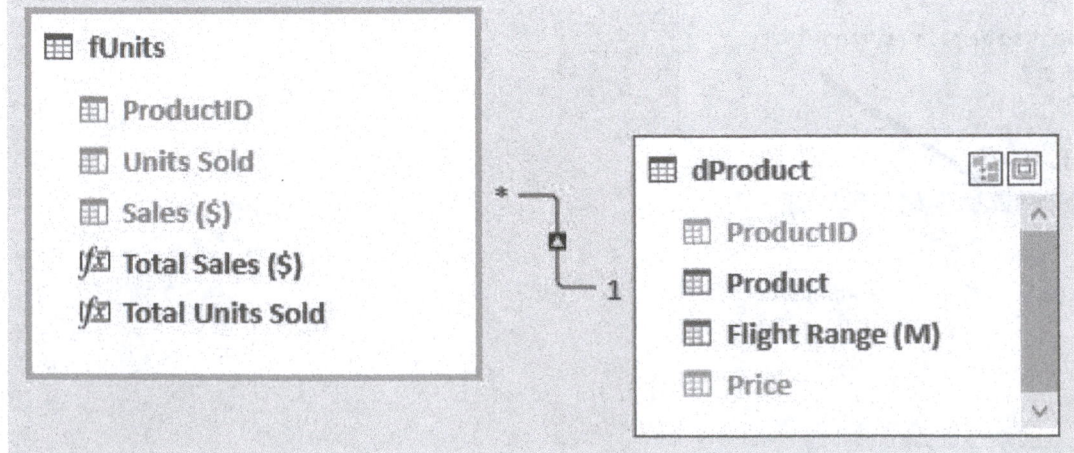

Figure 18.143 *The star schema data model in Diagram view.*

Filter Context: How DAX Measures Make Calculations

In Figure 18.144, you can see that the same measure calculates a different total product sales answer depending on where it is in the PivotTable. In the Aspen cell, the answer is 658.90; in the Quad cell, it is 1,150.80; in the Sunspot cell, it is 482.90; and in the Grand Total cell, it is 2,292.60. If you were using worksheet formulas, you would use two different formulas to get this information: the SUMIFS function for the product sales and the SUM function for the grand total. But with a DAX formula, you just use the SUM function, and it gets the right answer in every cell, thanks to the Data Model mechanism called *filter context*.

Product ▾	Total Sales ($)	
Aspen	658.90	← Total Sales ($):=SUM(fUnits[Sales ($)])
Quad	1,150.80	Total Sales ($):=SUM(fUnits[Sales ($)])
Sunspot	482.90	Total Sales ($):=SUM(fUnits[Sales ($)])
Grand Total	**2,292.60**	Total Sales ($):=SUM(fUnits[Sales ($)])

Figure 18.144 *The same measure in every row yields a different answer in each row because of filter context.*

Filter context allows DAX measures that are used in a PivotTable, PivotChart, or Power BI visualization to automatically use the conditions and criteria in the Rows, Columns, or Filters areas to make conditional calculations. This is the *context* part, where the DAX measure can see the surrounding situation and pick out all the conditions in the context of the report or visualization. In addition, when the behind-the-scenes Data Model engine evaluates the DAX context, it does not use the full fact table but instead uses only rows that match the conditions. This is the *filter* part, as the underlying tables are filtered down to a smaller size so that the formula has less work to perform and can make the calculation more quickly.

To illustrate how filter context works, let's consider the Aspen cell shown in Figure 18.144. When the context first hits the Aspen cell, Figure 18.145 shows that both tables in the underlying Data Model are not filtered: All rows are showing.

Fact Table = fUnits

ProductID	UnitsSold	Sales($)
1043	6	287.7
1069	3	89.85
1069	8	239.6
2005	3	65.85
1069	11	329.45
1043	8	383.6
2005	6	131.7
2005	13	285.35
1043	5	239.75
1043	5	239.75

Dimension Table = dProducts

ProductID	Product	FlightRange(M)	Price
1043	Quad	20	47.95
1069	Aspen	25	29.95
2005	Sunspot	15	21.95

Figure 18.145 *Before the measure in the Aspen cell makes the calculation, there is no filter context.*

However, as soon as the measure sees the Aspen condition, the dProduct table is filtered down to just the Aspen row, as shown in Figure 18.146.

Fact Table = fUnits

ProductID	UnitsSold	Sales($)
1043	6	287.7
1069	3	89.85
1069	8	239.6
2005	3	65.85
1069	11	329.45
1043	8	383.6
2005	6	131.7
2005	13	285.35
1043	5	239.75
1043	5	239.75

Dimension Table = dProducts

ProductID	Product	FlightRange(M)	Price
1069	Aspen	25	29.95

Figure 18.146 *In the Aspen row in the PivotTable, the dProduct table is filtered down to one row.*

Then, as the relationship arrow in Figure 18.143 shows, this Aspen filter is transferred across the one-to-many relationship from the dimension table to the fact table. As shown in Figure 18.147, the fact table becomes filtered down to just the matching records for the Aspen product. It is at this point that the DAX measure works with the three numbers to make the calculation: =SUM(89.85,239.6,329.45) = 658.9.

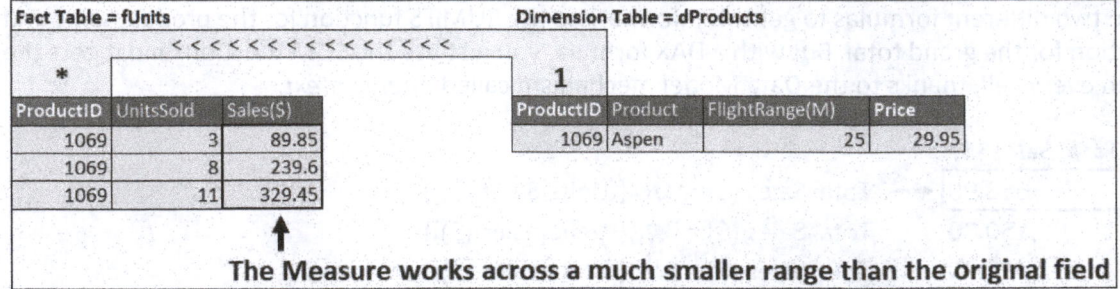

Figure 18.147 *The Aspen filter is transferred through the relationship from the dimension table to the fact table.*

The same filter context process is used in the Quad cell and the Sunspot cell to make the conditional calculation. For each of the cells, there is a different filter context. The term *current filter context* is used to describe the changing filter context as a measure moves from cell to cell. In this example, in the first cell, the current filter context is an Aspen filter. In the last cell, the current filter context is a Sunspot filter. In the Grand Total cell, there are no conditions flowing into the measure, and so no filtering is done on the underlying tables, and the measure delivers the grand total amount. This ability of the Data Model engine to filter a table down to a smaller size before making the final calculation is one of the main mechanisms that allows DAX measures to work with big data.

Putting it all together, *filter context* for DAX measures works as follows:

1. When a DAX measure is dropped into a PivotTable, PivotChart, or Power BI visualization, the measure automatically detects all the external row, column, and filter conditions. For any given cell, the row, column, and any filters determine the measure's current filter context.

2. The dimension table is filtered down to a smaller size, based on the conditions.

3. The relationship transfers the filter to the fact table.

4. The fact table is filtered down to a smaller size, based on the conditions.

5. The DAX measure works with the filtered fact table so that the formula has less work to perform and can make the calculation more quickly.

> **Note:** In Chapter 19, you will learn about another way to influence the filter context and the final filtered fact table: using the DAX CALCULATE function.

Here are a few additional notes about filter context:

- Figures 18.145 through 18.147 illustrate how filter context creates a smaller range of values for DAX measures. Technically, this is not how the Data Model engine with the columnar database does it. But the idea that the dimension table creates a filter and passes it through the relationship to create a smaller fact table is useful as a metaphor for understanding what is going on: The Data Model engine reconstructs the smaller fact table from the individual columns that are stored in the columnar database rather than filtering a full fact table.

- In a star schema data model, the filters always flow from the one-side to the many-side, but there are DAX functions, such as CROSSFILTER, and a Power BI bidirectional filter that can cause a filter to move in the other direction.

- Filter context helps quickly make calculations on big data, and, as you will see later, it makes complex calculations easier by skipping the many intermediate steps that worksheet or standard PivotTable calculations normally require.

Using DAX X Iterator Functions to Replace Two Formulas with One

When you created the Total Sales ($) measure in the previous section, you used a two-step process by building two formulas:

- **DAX calculated column:** Sales ($) =RELATED(dProduct[Price])*fUnits[Units Sold]

- **DAX measure:** Total Sales ($) :=SUM(fUnits[Sales ($)])

The goal was to calculate the transactional sales amounts for each row in the fact table and then aggregate those numbers into a total. But with the DAX formula language, you can skip over this two-step process and create a single DAX measure that combines the calculated column and the aggregating measure into one DAX measure. You can do this by using one of the amazing *DAX X iterator functions*: SUMX, AVERAGEX, COUNTX, COUNTAX, MINX, MAXX, CONCATENATEX, PRODUCTX, or RANKX. (There are other types of DAX iterator functions, but in this section, we consider only the X iterator functions.)

To make a calculation in each row of a fact table and then sum those results, you can use the *SUMX iterator function*, which has the following syntax:

```
=SUMX(table, expression)
```

This function simulates a calculated column inside a measure, iterating over each row in the specified table to create the values and then using the values generated to make the aggregate calculation.

You can often simply take the formula you would have used in a calculated column and place it into an X iterator function to create a one-step solution. You will do that in this example by turning the RELATED(dProduct[Price])*fUnits[Units Sold] calculated column into the following SUMX formula:

```
=SUMX(fUnits, RELATED(dProduct[Price])*fUnits[Units Sold])
```

In the first argument (the *table* argument), you place the table where you want to make a row-by-row calculation—in this case, fUnits. In the second argument (the *expression* argument), you place the formula that you want to iterate down the table to make a calculation in each row—in this case, (RELATED(dProduct[Price])*fUnits[Units Sold]). Figure 18.148 shows this SUMX formula in the measure grid below the fUnits table.

> **Note:** To create this figure, I deleted the original calculated column to prove to you that it is not needed to get the correct result; however, you do not need to delete your calculated column in your data model.

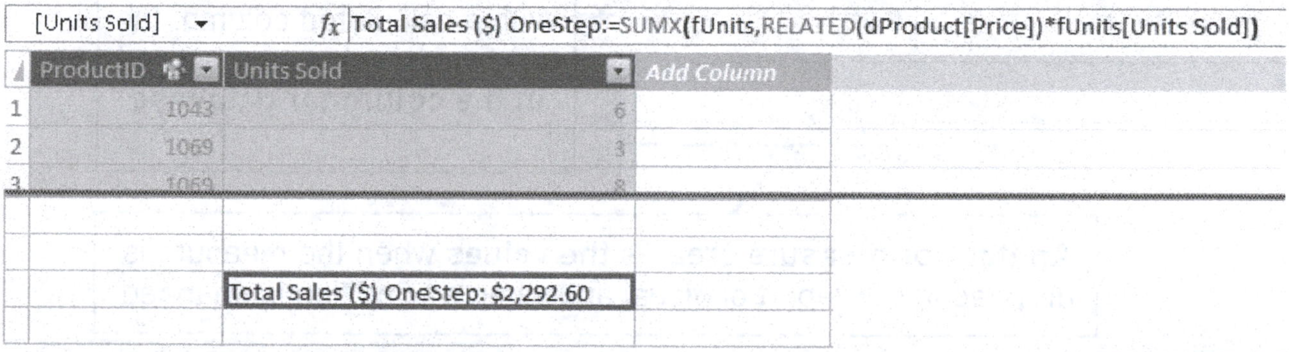

Figure 18.148 *Avoid using a calculated column by using the SUMX function to calculate Total Sales ($).*

The amazing thing about SUMX and the other X iterator functions is that they automatically create row context so that the formula can use the values from each row in the first argument table and so the RELATED function can look up the price for each row in the table. This single SUMX formula is a more compact solution than the Data Model two-step process with a calculated column and a measure, and it is more efficient than the worksheet formula and standard PivotTable method, where you have to create the Excel Table calculated column using the XLOOKUP function and then do a standard PivotTable calculation.

To create the SUMX measure, follow these steps:

1. In the Power Pivot for Excel window, click in the measure grid below the fUnits table.

2. As shown in Figure 18.148, create this new Measure: **Total Sales OneStep:=SUMX(fUnits,RELATED(dProduct[Price])*fUnits[Units Sold])**.

3. Press Enter to enter the formula.

4. Add number formatting to show a thousands separator.

Knowing When to Use a Two-Step Method (DAX Calculated Column) or a One-Step Method (DAX X Iterator Function)

What is the difference between using the two-step method with a calculated column and a measure and using the one-step method using a SUMX measure?

- **Two-step method:** With the two-step method, the values generated by the calculated column are stored in the columnar database and become part of what is stored in RAM. This increases file size. When you refresh the table, either in the Power Pivot for Excel window or in Power Query, the calculated column values are recalculated.

- **One-step method:** With the one-step method, the values that are generated inside the SUMX function are not stored in RAM. The values in the SUMX function are recalculated each time you drop the measure into the report/visual or when a condition is changed in the Rows, Columns, or Filters area of the report/visual.

The convention in building DAX measures in the Data Model is to use the one-step method because the measure can be created more quickly, and the in-RAM database does not have to store as much data. As the great DAX formula masters Marco Russo and Alberto Ferrari say, for most models under 100 million rows of data with simple calculations, either method will work fine, and so it becomes a matter of preference whether to use the two-step method or the one-step method. However, my rule of thumb is that if an X iterator measure calculates slowly every time you drop it into a report/visual, it might be better to move the calculation back to a calculated column. Figure 18.149 shows both the one-step method and the two-step method. Figure 18.150 shows that if you drag the one-step method measure into the report, both methods yield the same result.

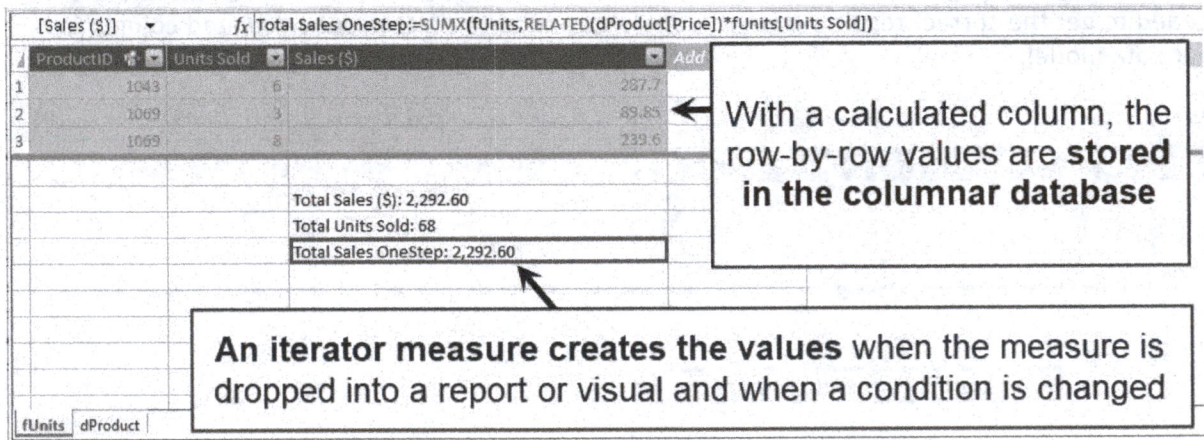

Figure 18.149 *Rule of thumb: If an X iterator measure calculates too slowly in the reporting area, use the two-step method.*

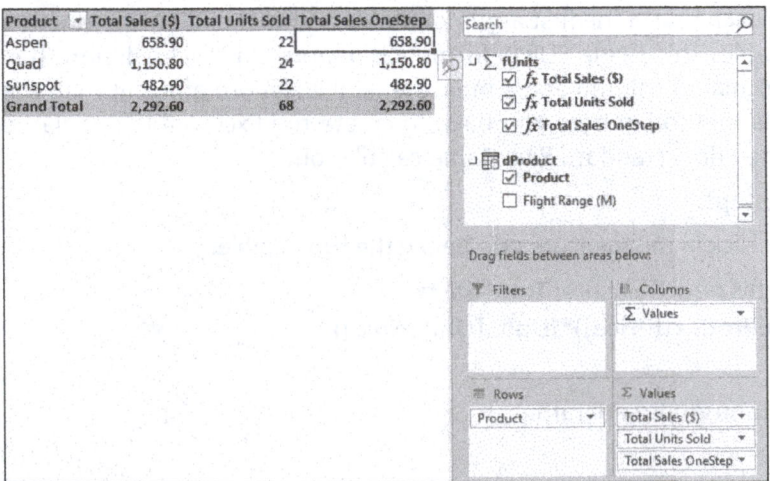

Figure 18.150 *The two-step measure and the one-step measure both yield the same result.*

Understanding How Filter Context and Row Context Work Together

When you use an X iterator function such as SUMX in a measure and then drop it into a report or a visual, filter context and row context work together to make the final calculation. As shown in Figure 18.151, when the SUMX measure is in the Aspen cell, the Aspen filter context filters the fUnits table in the first argument of the SUMX function down to three rows. Then, as shown in Figure 18.152, the SUMX function's row context allows the formula in the second argument to make the calculation row by row, pulling out the correct units sold, looking up the correct product price, and finally multiplying the amounts to get the transition sales amount for each row.

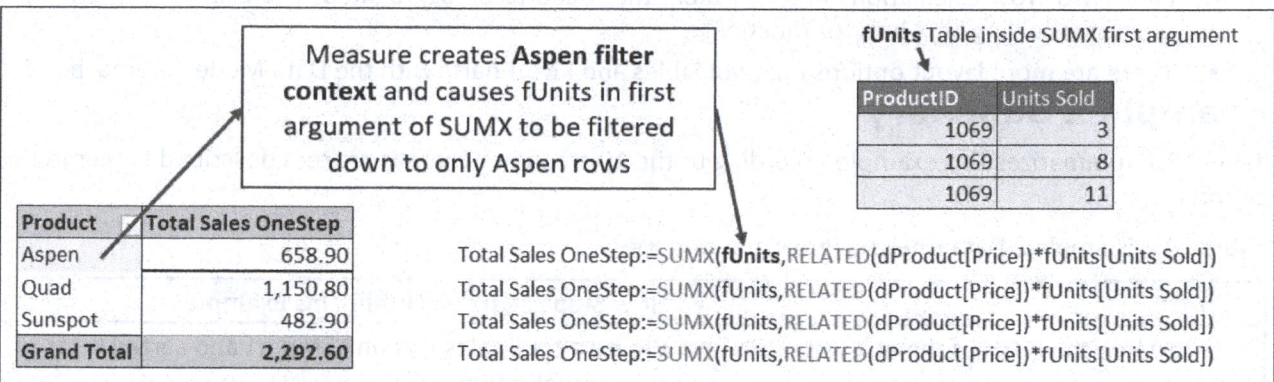

Figure 18.151 *Filter context filters the table in the first argument of SUMX.*

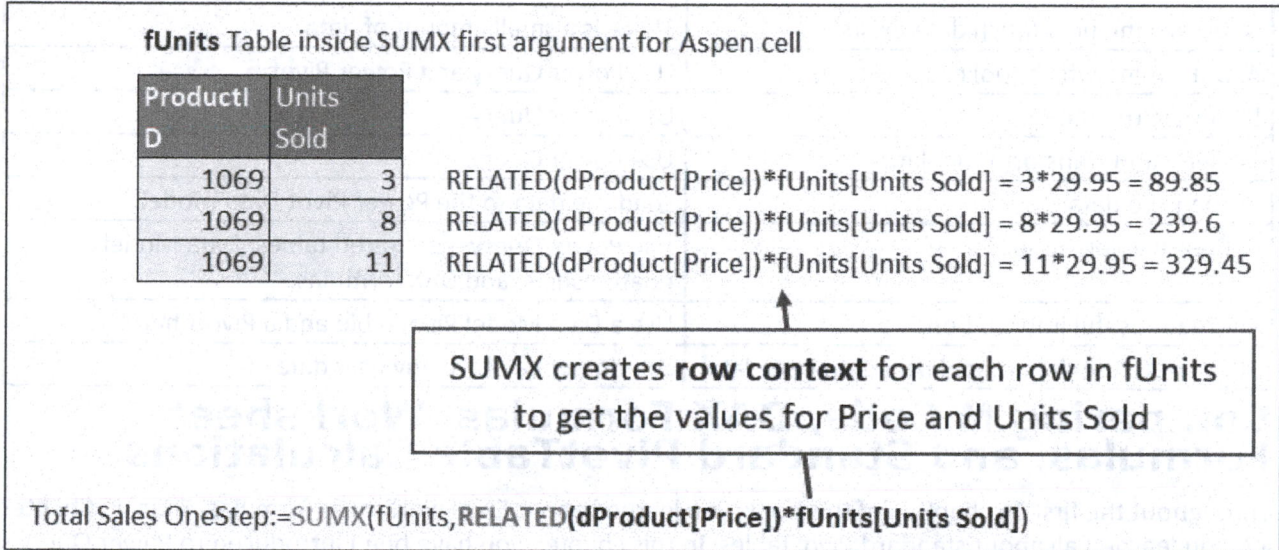

Figure 18.152 *SUMX generates row context so the formula can make a calculation in each row of the first argument table.*

As shown in Figure 18.153, once the three transaction sales amounts are calculated, the numbers are summed, and the result—658.90—is delivered to the cell. A similar process is used to calculate the total sales for the Quad and Sunspot products. In the grand total cell, there are no external conditions, and so SUMX uses the row context over the full fact table to calculate the transactional sales amount for all rows and then adds to get the grand total amount.

Total Sales OneStep:= 89.85 + 239.6 + 329.45 = **658.9**

Figure 18.153 *SUMX adds the values that are generated by the row context calculations.*

The good news is that when you need to make a row-by-row calculation in a fact table and then aggregate the results, you can choose between the two-step process, with a calculated column and an aggregate function, and the one-step process involving an X iterator function.

Even though this simple data analysis project does not involve big data or complex calculations, there are a number of benefits to using the Data Model PivotTable approach as compared to using the flat table standard PivotTable approach used in Example 1:

- You can directly drag the Product field from the dProduct table into the report rather than having to create an XLOOKUP formula in the fact table.
- You can drag premade formulas that already contain number formatting to the report.
- You can hide unnecessary fields.
- For row-by-row calculations in a fact table that need to be aggregated, you can use the one-step process involving an X iterator function.
- There are more layout options for PivotTables and PivotCharts with the Data Model approach.

Example 2 Summary

Table 18.2 summarizes this example according to the 10-step data analysis process described earlier in this chapter.

Table 18.2 Example 2 Data Analysis Process Summary

Step	How Step Is Carried Out in This Example
1. Determine the goals of the analysis	Create a total sales and units report and sorted total sales visualization.
2. Determine where the data is	The data is in two text files.
3. Determine how much data exists	There is a small amount of data.
4. Determine which tool or tools to use	Use Power Query and Power Pivot.
5. Import the data	Use Power Query.
6. Clean and transform the data	Use Power Query.
7. Load the data	Load the data to the Power Pivot Data Model.
8. Create a data model	Use Power Query–generated tables, Data Model relationships, and DAX formulas.
9. Create useful information	Use a Data Model PivotTable and a PivotChart.
10. Update the data model based on new data	You do not yet have any new data.

Comparing M Code, DAX Formulas, Worksheet Formulas, and Standard PivotTable Calculations

Throughout the first 16 chapters of this book, you learned about Excel worksheet formulas. Then, in Chapter 17, you learned all about standard PivotTables. In this chapter, you have been introduced to Power Query's M code function-based formula language and the Data Model's DAX function-based formula language. With the addition of M code and DAX, you now have four distinct tools in your Excel toolbox to accomplish any calculation or data analysis task you encounter. Table 18.3 compares these four tools.

Table 18.3 A Comparison of the Four Calculation-Based Tools in Excel

Characteristic	Worksheet Formulas	Standard PivotTables	M Code	DAX Formulas
Number of functions	More than 450 functions	11 aggregate functions and 14 Show Values As calculations	About 700 functions	About 250 functions
What it works with	Tables, fields, ranges, and individual cell references	Fields	Lists, fields, tables, files, databases, and much more	Fields and tables

Benefits	Can use a cell reference in any formula from anywhere in any workbook Can make almost any type of calculation and achieve many data analysis goals	Can create summary reports with conditional calculations Can use simple-to-use features like Group By and Show Values As	Can connect to almost any data source Can do almost any data analysis task, such as importing data, cleaning data, transforming data, and combining tables	Works easily with big data Can reduce intermediate steps in the calculation process Works easily with tables with different grains
Easiest aspect	Can just type a formula in any cell in a worksheet	Can easily and quickly drag and drop fields	Can rely on the user interface to write most of the code for you	Convenient reusable, preformatted formulas

In the next example, you will use the same small dataset that you used in Examples 1 and 2 to learn about using yet another tool: the Power BI Desktop app.

Example 3: Using the Power BI Desktop App to Create a Product Sales Report and Power BI Online for Sharing and Collaboration

Note: For this example, you will use the following files: Ch18UnitsTableExample03.xlsx and Ch18ProductTableExample03.accdb.

Power BI Desktop is a free tool that you can download from the Microsoft store. This app is a perfect complement to the Excel app because it contains the same Power Query and Data Model tools as in Excel, but it provides a larger variety of visualizations, and these visualizations are interactive and enable you to share results to the Power BI Online website. Power BI Online gives you a number of powerful sharing and collaboration tools.

Downloading the Free Power BI Desktop App and Getting Ready for This Example

You need to download and install the Power BI Desktop app in order to work through this example and many others in this book. There are two ways to download the free Power BI Desktop app:

- **Microsoft Windows Store:** Go to https://powerbi.microsoft.com/en-us/desktop/ to get the app. With this method, the app will automatically update each month.
- **Microsoft download page:** Go to https://aka.ms/pbiSingleInstaller. When you want to update the app, you have to re-download and reinstall the app.

Note: The first option—the Windows Store link—is the preferred method because the app will automatically update each month.

As shown in Figure 18.154, this example uses the same data as the previous two example, except that the fact table is in an Excel file, and the dimension table is in a Microsoft Access database file. When performing data analysis tasks like this, it is common to get data from different types of files, such as Excel files, database file, or text files (as you saw in Example 2).

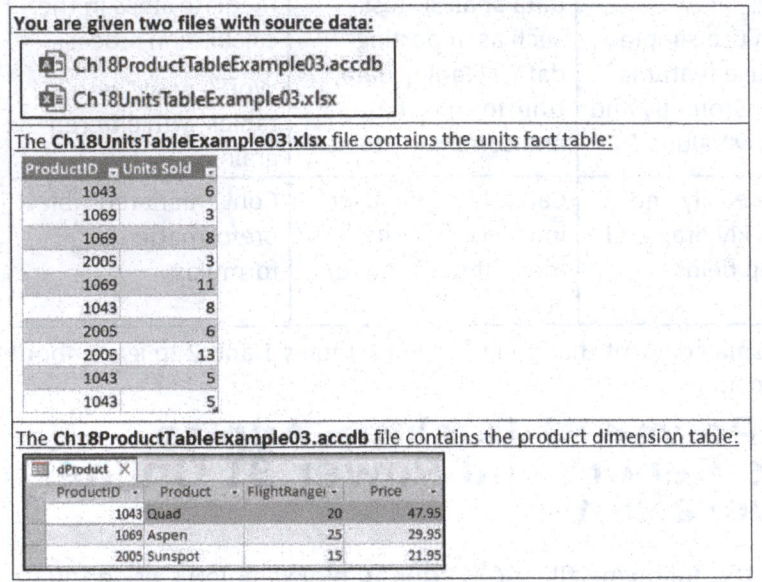

Figure 18.154 *The Excel file contains the fact table, and the Access file contains the dimension table.*

The data analysis goal for this project is the same as in Examples 1 and 2: Create a report that shows total sales and total units sold by product and create a visualization that shows total sales by product. To start this example, you will open a new Power BI Desktop file, save the file, use the Power Query tool inside Power BI Desktop to connect to the tables of data in the two different files, and then import them into the Power BI Desktop Data Model. After you create the relationships and DAX formulas, you will end up with the finished report and visual shown in Figure 18.155.

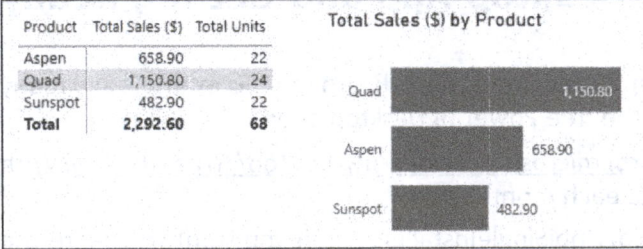

Figure 18.155 *Finished Power BI Desktop report and visual.*

Before you begin this project, you need to learn a bit about Power BI Desktop.

The Power BI Desktop and Power BI Online Tools

In 2013, Microsoft combined Excel Power Pivot Data Model tools, such as relationships and DAX formulas, with Excel's Power View and Power Query tools into a free download called Power BI Desktop. Microsoft introduced *Power BI Desktop* (where BI stands for *business intelligence*) as a tool for performing business analytics and creating interactive visualizations to build reports and dashboards.

Power BI Desktop contains these tools, among others:

- **Power Query and M code:** These tools allow you to clean, transform, and import data.
- **The Data Model:** This tool includes the in-RAM columnar database to efficiently store tables of data.

- **Relationships:** Relationships enable data modeling and reporting to occur between related tables.
- **DAX formulas:** You can use DAX to build analytics formulas that work efficiently on big data.

Microsoft introduced the Power BI Online website in 2015. To use Power BI Online, you must buy a Power BI Pro license or higher, and you need to use an e-mail address from an entity that has purchased a bulk license from Microsoft for a product such as Office. You can use Power BI Online to share reports, dashboards, and datasets.

> **Note:** Power Query does not exist in Power BI Online. Power BI Online includes a pared-down version of Power Query called Dataflows, but it does not have the full set of tools. For the full set of Power Query tools, you must use Power BI Desktop when building data models. In this book, you will learn about Power Query in the Power BI Desktop app. You will not learn about Dataflows.

These are the key reasons that you would switch from using Excel to using Excel's Power Query and Power Pivot to using Power BI Desktop and Power BI Online:

- Power BI Desktop is a free tool.
- Power BI offers a larger variety of visualizations than you can get in Excel.
- Visualizations tend to be easier to create and have a cleaner look in Power BI than in Excel. In addition, Power BI visualizations are interactive: Click on one element in a visual, and it filters the other visuals.
- The Data Model in Power BI Desktop and Power BI Online can work with multiple processors to deal with big data more efficiently than can the Power Pivot Data Model.
- You can use DAX table functions to build a table that you can use in the Data Model with the other tables that you import using Power Query. You cannot do this in PowerPivot's Data Model.
- There are more M code and DAX functions in Power BI Desktop and Power BI Online than there are in Excel PowerPivot.
- If you buy a Power BI Pro license or higher, you can publish your Power BI Desktop files and Excel workbook files to Power BI Online and share your results so that they can be viewed on any device. You can easily share data analysis results to help others make smarter, data-driven decisions.
- If you buy a Power BI Pro license or higher, you can publish tables of data and complete data models to Power BI Online to give others access to the data. This makes it possible for multiple people to work with the same data to perform their own specific analyses from a "single source of truth."

At this point, you know enough about Power BI to get started using it!

Opening Power BI Desktop and Saving As to Create a New File

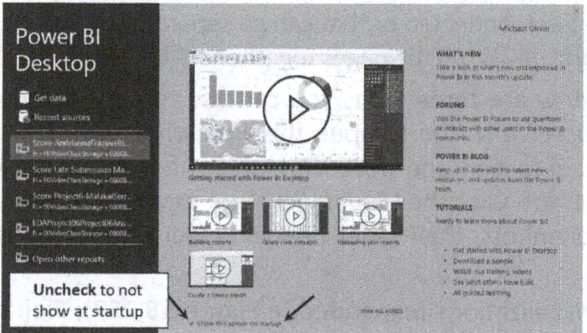

Figure 18.156 *There is an option to not show this startup screen in the bottom part of this window.*

To begin this example, follow these steps:

1. Open a blank Power BI Desktop file.
2. As shown in Figure 18.156, when you open a new Power BI Desktop file, an introduction startup widow pops up. Click the x button in the upper-right corner to close this window.
3. Press **F12** to open the Save As dialog box.
4. In the Save as dialog box, name the new file **Ch18-Example3-PowerBIDesktopReport** and then save the file.

Understanding the Power BI Desktop Window and User Interface

As shown in Figure 18.157, the Power BI Desktop app has a number of important features:

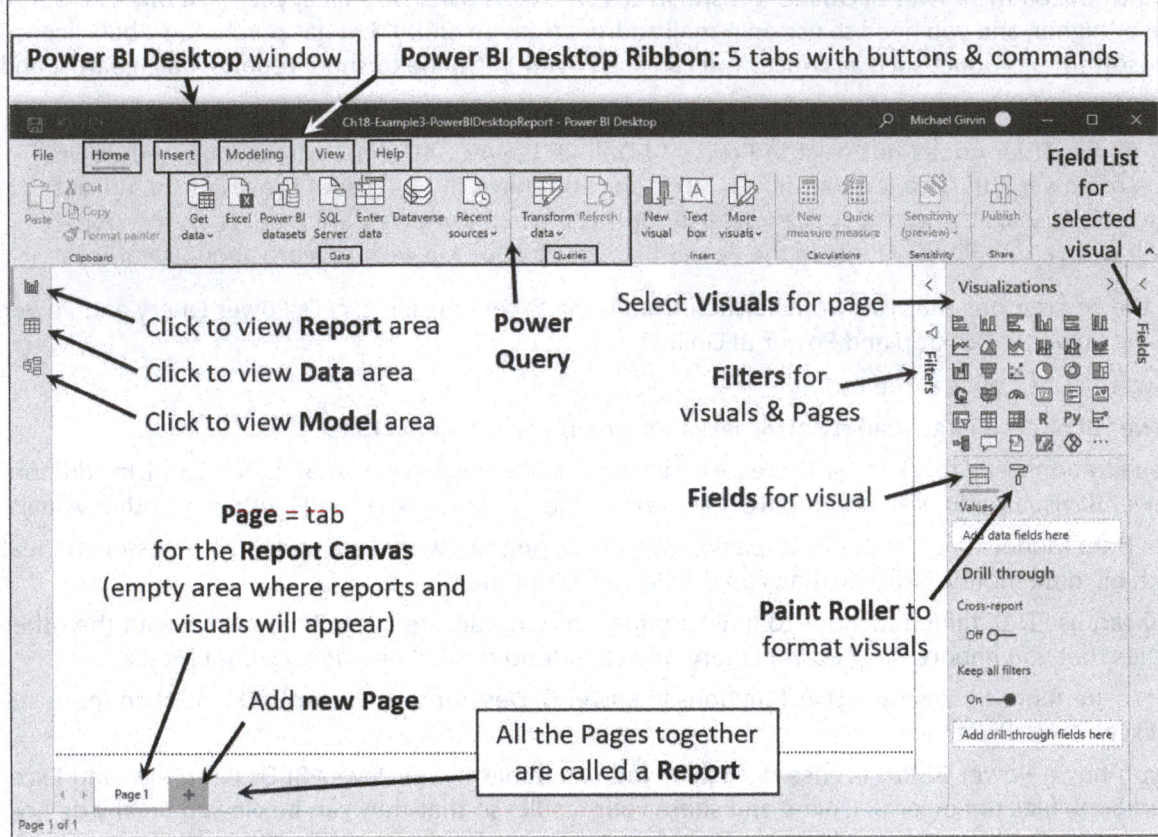

Figure 18.157 *The Power BI Desktop window, Ribbon, and user interface.*

- **Power BI Desktop Ribbon:** The Ribbon consists of five tabs: Home, Insert, Modeling, View, and Help. Most of your time is spent in the Home and Modeling tabs.
- **Power Query inside the Power BI Desktop:** A number of Power Query buttons and commands are available in the Data and Queries groups in the Home tab of the Ribbon.
- **Pages:** The tabs at the bottom of the Desktop are called *pages*. You use pages to build related reports and visuals. You can have multiple pages that can be interconnected or that can be separate standalone pages. The white area inside a page is called the *report canvas*. All the pages together are called a *report*.
- **Navigation icons:** On the far-left side of the window are three icons you can use to jump to the different areas in Power BI Desktop. Click the *Report View icon* to open the area where you build reports and visuals on pages. Click the *Data View icon* to view and work with tables of data; the Data view in Power BI Desktop is like Data view in Powe Pivot. Click the *Model View icon* to view and work with tables, relationships, and other data model elements; the Model view in Power BI Desktop is like Design view in Power Pivot.
- **Task panes:** On the right are three task panes: Visualizations (expanded in Figure 18.157), Fields (collapsed in the figure), and Filters (collapsed in the figure). The Visualizations pane allows you to create and format new visuals and reports. The Fields pane allows to you drag and drop fields and measures into your reports and visuals. The Filters pane allows you to filter reports, visuals, and pages.

Using Power Query to Import the Fact Table from an On-premises Excel File

To use Power Query to import the fact table from within the Excel file, follow these steps:

1. As shown in Figure 18.158, in the Home tab of the Ribbon, go to the Data group and click the Excel button.

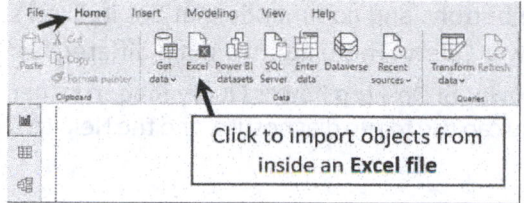

Click to import objects from inside an **Excel file**

Figure 18.158 *You are in the report area, but you can use Power Query to import data from any of the three areas.*

2. In the Open dialog box that appears, as shown in Figure 18.159, navigate to the Excel file named Ch18UnitsTableExample03.xlsx, select it, and click Open to bring the file into the Navigator dialog box.

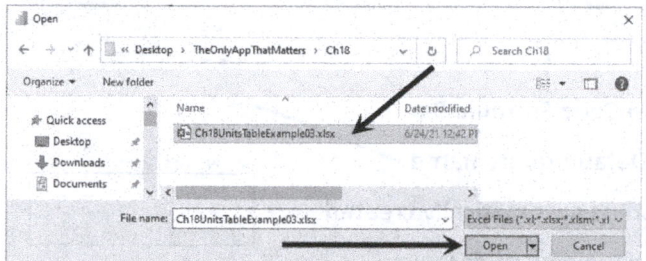

Figure 18.159 *The Open dialog box allows you to select files that contains data that you want to import.*

> **Note:** As shown in Figure 18.160, Power Query memorizes the on-premises file address. If you move the file later, you can edit the address in the Source step of the query or in Data Source Settings.

Figure 18.160 *Power Query memorizes this on-premises file address.*

3. In the Navigator dialog box, as shown in Figure 18.161, check the checkbox for the fUnits Excel Table object and then click the Transform Data button to bring the table of data into the Power Query Editor.

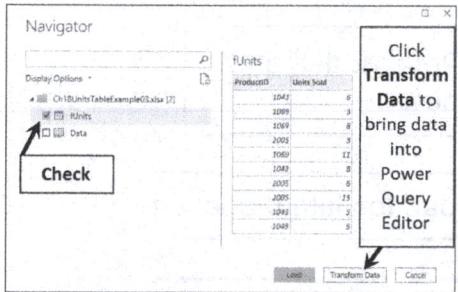

Figure 18.161 *The Navigator dialog box opens because the file can contain more than one object.*

> **Note:** The Power Query Navigator dialog box opens any time a data source can contain more than one data source object. In this example, you are looking into an on-premises Excel file that has a worksheet object named Data and an Excel Table named fUnits. Later in this example, you will see the same dialog box when you need to select a table from within an on-premises Microsoft Access database file. Later in the book, you will see the Navigator dialog box when you import data from an in-the-cloud SQL database location. For all these examples, the Navigator dialog box allows you to use checkboxes to select data source objects that you want to bring into the Power Query Editor. In almost all cases, it is best to click the Transform Data button rather than the Load button so that you can verify that the data is correctly structured before loading it to the Data Model.

As shown in Figure 18.162, after you click the Transform Data button in the Navigator dialog box, the Power Query Editor window opens. This window is similar to the Power Query Editor window in the

Excel app (refer to Figure 18.71). Almost all of the same buttons and commands that are in Excel's Power Query are also available in Power BI Desktop's Power Query. There are two main differences:

- As shown in Figure 18.162, there are six tabs in the Power BI Desktop Power Query Ribbon rather than four. The two new tabs are the Tools tab, which you can use to run diagnostics, and the Help tab.

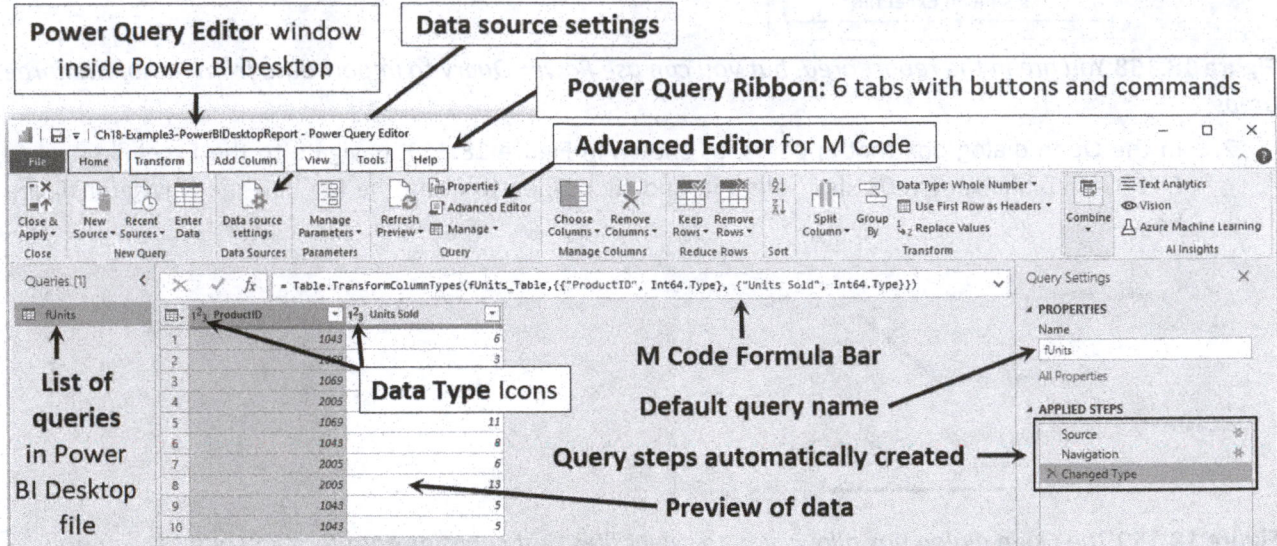

Figure 18.162 *Power Query Editor window in Power BI Desktop.*

- As shown in Figure 18.163, to load data to Power BI Desktop's Data Model, you use the Close & Apply button rather than the Close & Load button. This loading process is significantly different than the process in an Excel workbook. Whereas in Excel you must choose to load to the worksheet, a PivotTable cache, or the Data Model (with Connection Only selected), in Power BI Desktop, you can only load data to the Data Model. If you want to create a query that is a connection only, in the Power Query window, in the Queries pane on the left, you must right-click the query and uncheck the Enable Load option, as shown in Figure 18.164. In addition, two other differences with this load process are that you can close the Power Query Editor without loading the query (via the Close option), and you can load the data to the Data Model without closing the Power Query window (via the Apply option). You cannot perform either of those processes in Excel's Power Query.

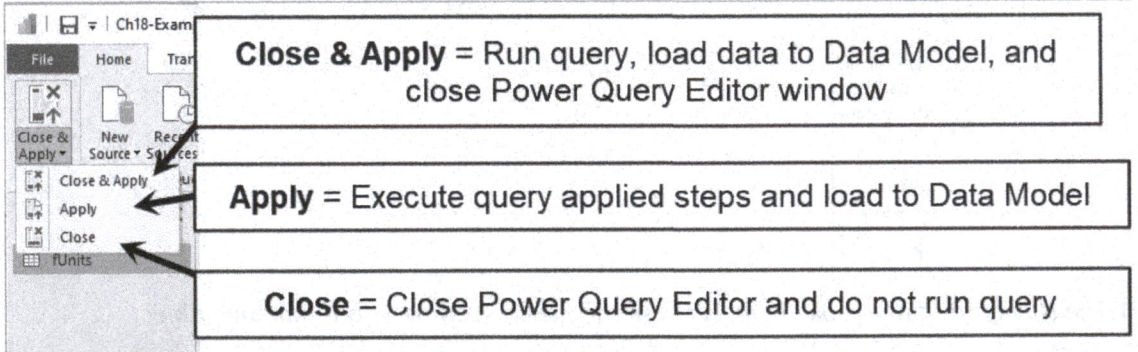

Figure 18.163 *There is only one location to load data in Power BI Desktop: the Data Model.*

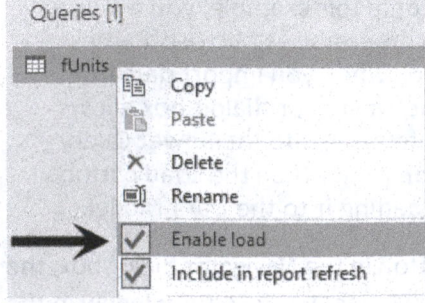

Figure 18.164 *Loading a query as a connection only is done differently in Power BI Desktop than in Excel.*

4. When the Power Query Editor, shown in Figure 18.162, opens, check the Applied Steps that were automatically created. In this case, they look correct, and the default query name, fUnits, is an informative name for the query, so you can load the fact table to the Data Model. As shown in Figure 18.163, in the Home tab of the Ribbon, in the Close group, click the Close & Apply dropdown arrow and then click Close & Apply.

5. After you click the Close & Apply button, click the Data View icon to see a preview of the data that was loaded to the Data Model (see Figure 18.165).

Note: With the 10 rows of data in this example, you can see all the records in this table, but in large datasets, you see only a preview of some of the data.

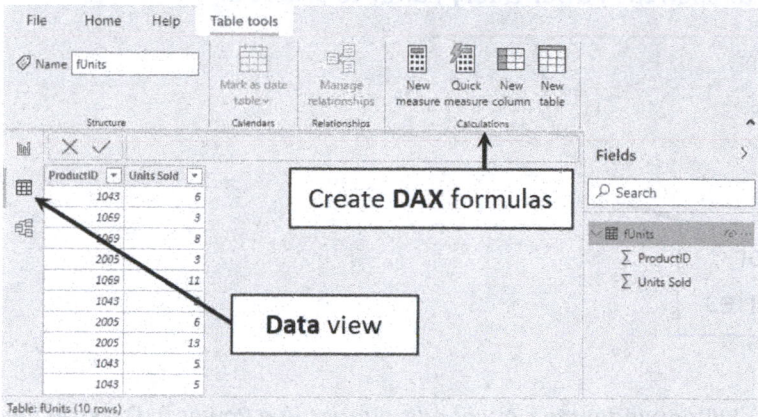

Figure 18.165 *In Data view, the Table Tools tab of the Ribbon offers various buttons for creating DAX formulas.*

6. Click the Model View button, as shown in Figure 18.166, to see a preview of the data that was loaded to the Data Model. In the Properties pane in the middle of the screen, click in the Description field and type **Fact Table with Product ID and Units**.

Note: In Model view, you can create relationships and perform other modeling tasks.

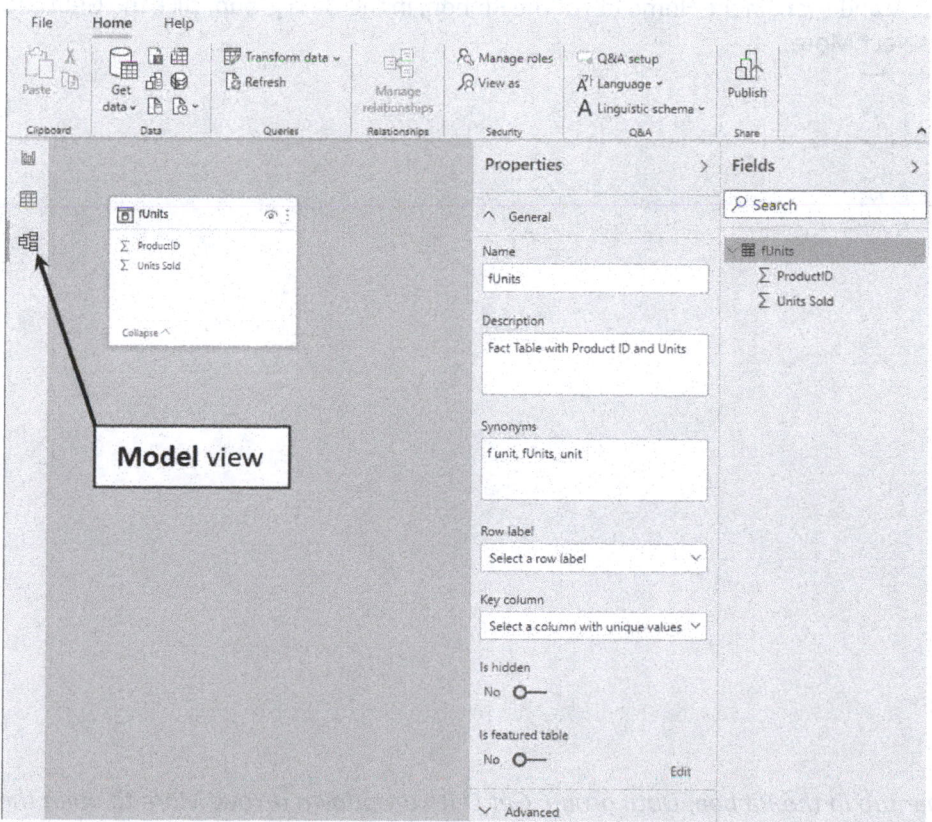

Figure 18.166 *In Model view, you can create relationships, set properties, hide fields, and more.*

Where Is the Queries Pane with All the Queries in Power BI Desktop?

When you create a query in Excel, the Queries & Connections pane opens automatically to show you all the queries in the Excel file. From that pane, you can double-click any query to open the Power Query Editor. But in Power BI Desktop, it is not as obvious how to open the Power Query Editor to view and edit queries. As shown in Figure 18.167, when you need to view or edit an existing query or when you just want to open the Power Query Editor in Power BI Desktop, in the Home tab of the Ribbon, in the Queries group, click the Transform Data dropdown arrow and select Transform Data.

> **Note:** Notice that a Data Source Settings option is available in the Transform Data menu also. This is convenient when you need to edit data source settings because it is listed in the Power BI Desktop Ribbon, and you do not have to open the Power Query Editor to access it.

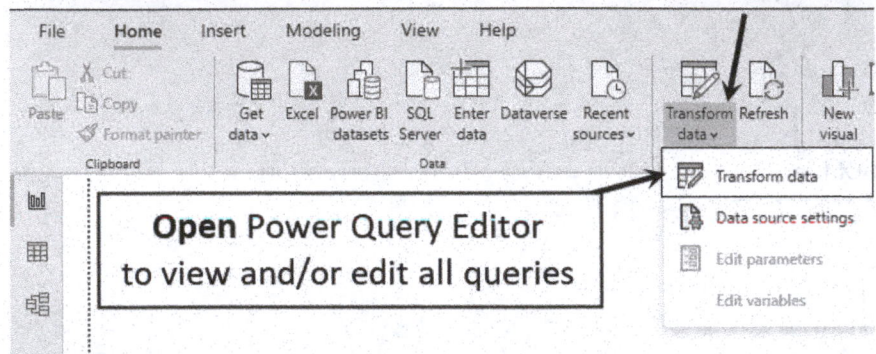

Figure 18.167 *How to open the Power Query Editor window to view or edit queries in a Power BI Desktop file.*

Using Power Query to Import the Dimension Table from an On-premises Access File

Now that you have imported the fact table from an Excel file, you need to import the dimension table from a Microsoft Access database file. Follow these steps:

1. To import the dimension table from inside the Access file, as shown in Figure 18.168, click the Data View icon to jump to Data view and then, in the Home tab of the Ribbon, in the Data group, click the Get Data dropdown arrow and select More.

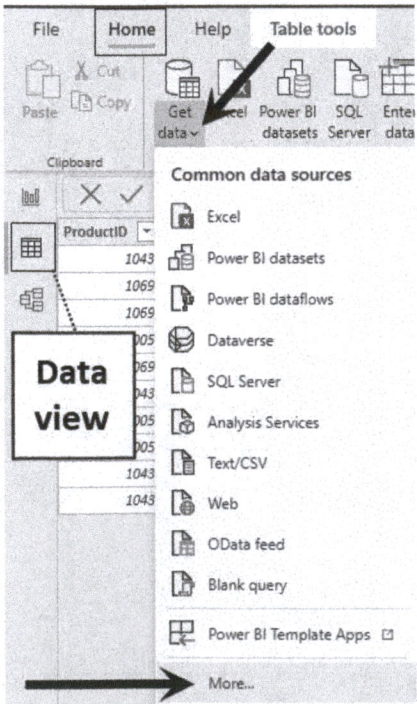

Figure 18.168 *Select the Home tab in the Ribbon, Data group, Get Data dropdown arrow, More to open the Get Data dialog box.*

2. In the Get Data dialog box that appears, as shown in Figure 18.169, click the Access Database option and then click the Connect button.

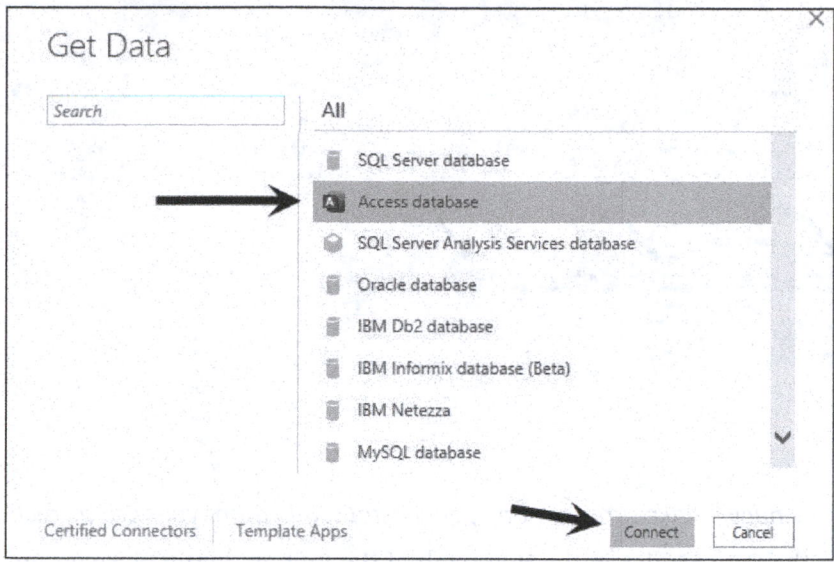

Figure 18.169 *Select Access Database and then click Connect.*

3. In the Open dialog box that appears, as shown in Figure 18.170, navigate to the file named Ch18ProductTableExample03.accdb, select the file, and click the Open button.

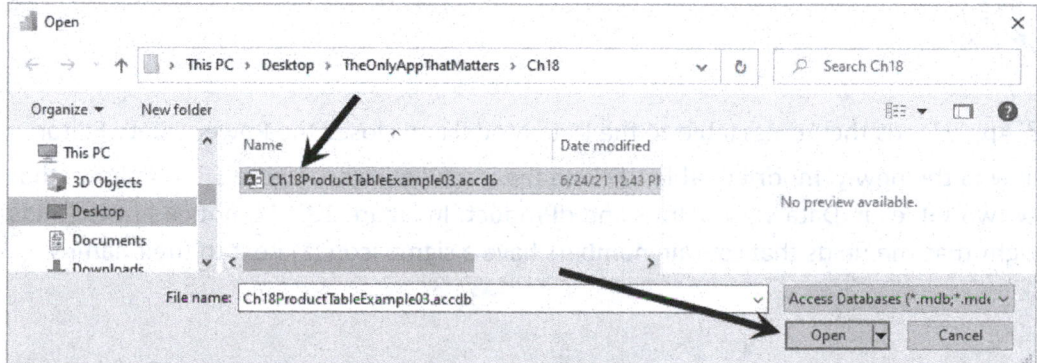

Figure 18.170 *Select the Access file and click Open.*

4. In the Navigator dialog box that appears, as shown in Figure 18.171, check the checkbox for the dProduct table and click the Transform Data button to open the Power Query Editor.

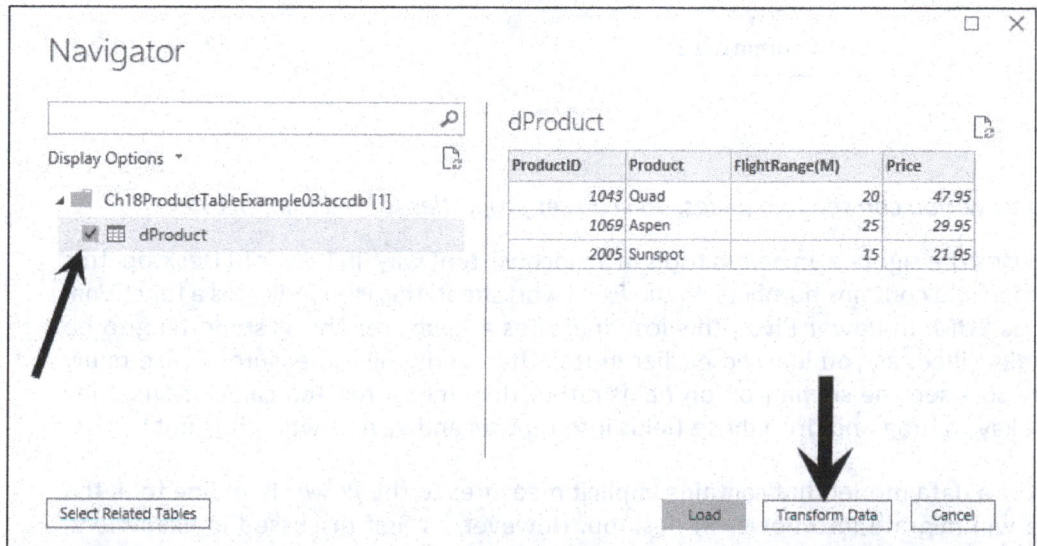

Figure 18.171 *In the Navigator dialog box, select the dProduct table and click Transform Data.*

5. As shown in Figure 18.172, in the Power Query Editor window, verify that the Applied Steps list and the data types are accurate. Note that the default name of the query is sufficient in this case, and you do not need to change it.

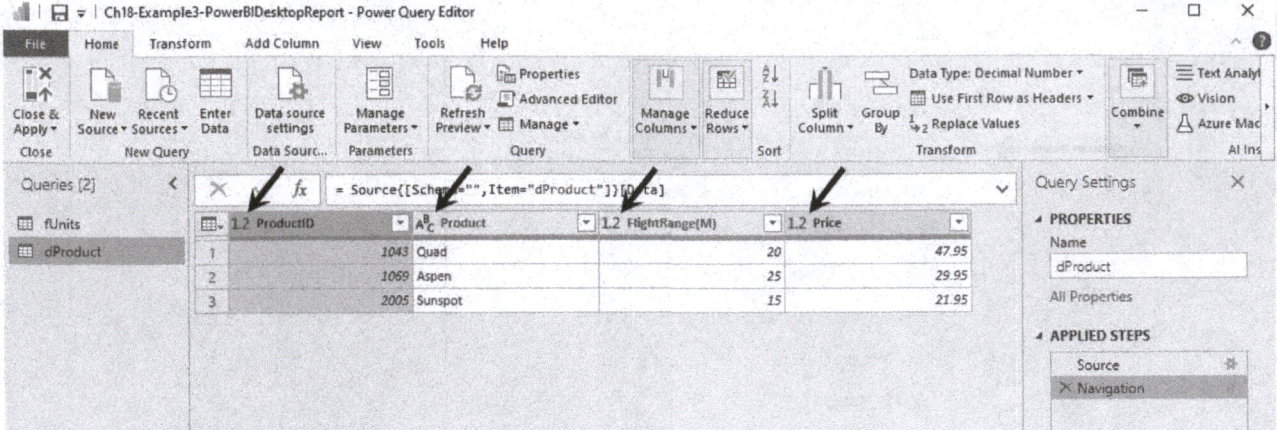

Figure 18.172 *In the Power Query Editor window, make sure the name, query steps, and data types are correct.*

6. To load the dimension table to the Data Model, in the Home tab of the Ribbon, in the Close group, click the Close & Apply button (see Figure 18.173).

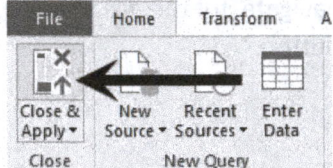

Figure 18.173 Close & Apply loads the Access table to the Data Model and closes the Power Query Editor.

7. To see a preview of the newly imported table, click on the Data View icon. Figure 18.174 shows that there are now two tables in Data view: fUnits and dProduct. In Figure 18.174, notice in the Fields pane on the right that the fields that contain numbers have a sigma icon (Σ) next to their names.

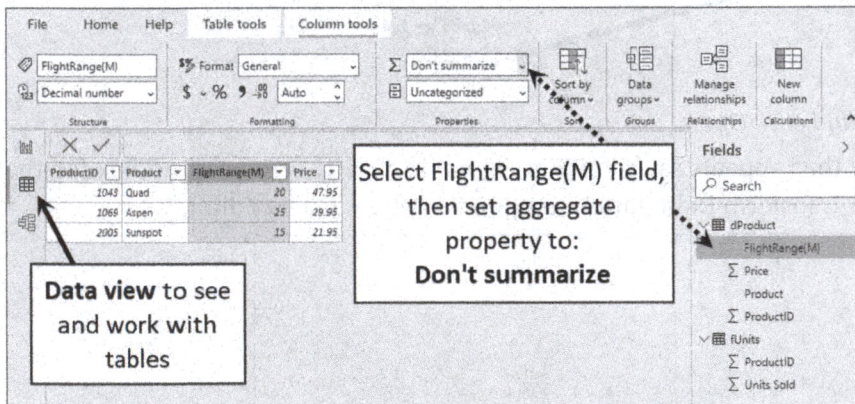

Figure 18.174 *In Data view, you can see two tables. You can set properties for fields in this view.*

Note: Microsoft uses the sigma icon across tools in an inconsistent way. In Power BI Desktop, this icon indicates that a field contains numbers. In the Excel worksheet, this icon indicates a functional calculation such as SUM. In Power Pivot, this icon indicates a measure. This is something to be aware of, especially since, as you learned earlier in this chapter, implicit measures cause many problems; when users see the sigma icon on fields rather than measures and calculations, they might think it is okay to drag and drop these fields into reports and visuals when it is not.

Note: If you export a data model that contains implicit measures to the Power BI online tool, the implicit measure will migrate into Power BI desktop. However, as first discussed in Example 2, using implicit measures is not a good habit to get into because if you create an implicit measure in Power BI Desktop and bring the model back to Excel, the implicit measure does not migrate.

8. To prevent reports and visuals from defaulting to a sum calculation when you drag and drop the FlightRange(M) field in Report view, as shown in Figure 18.174, select the field and then, in the Column Tools tab of the Ribbon, in the Properties group, use the Aggregate Calculation dropdown arrow to select Don't Summarize.

Completing the Data Model by Adding Relationships and Measures and Hiding Fields

Now that you have imported the tables, you need to create the rest of the data model. Follow these steps:

1. To create a one-to-many relationship between the two tables, as shown in Figure 18.175, click on the Model View icon and then click and drag the ProductID field in the dProduct table over and on top of the ProductID field in the fUnits table. Then let go of the ProductID field and, as shown in Figure 18.176, the one-to-many relationship is created. The relationship line indicates the one-side (the primary key) with the number 1 and the many-side (the foreign key) with an asterisk (*).

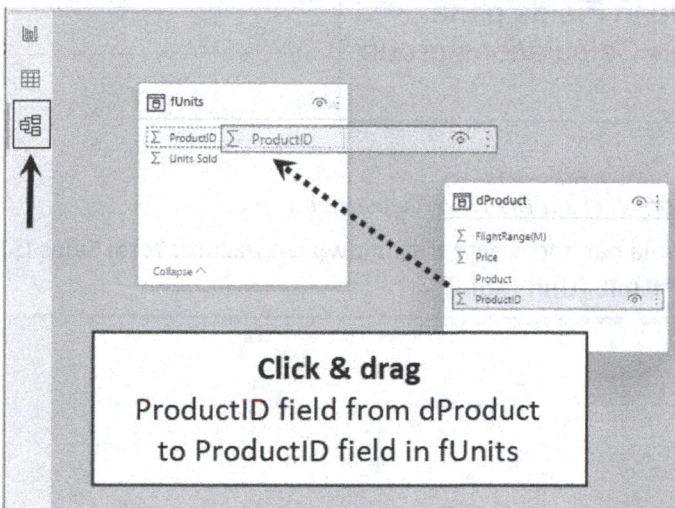

Figure 18.175 *In Model view, you can drag the ProductID field to create the relationship.*

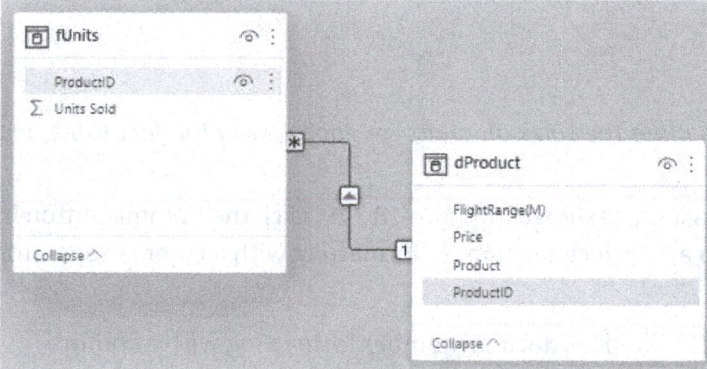

Figure 18.176 *A one-to-many relationship from ProductID in dProduct to ProductID in fUnits.*

2. To create a measure for total sales, as shown in Figure 18.177, on the far left on the Power BI window, click the Data View icon and then, on the right side of the Power BI window, in the Fields pane, select the fact table fUnits (which brings up the context-sensitive Table Tools tab). Then, in the Calculations group, click the New Measure button, and the Measure Tools context-sensitive tab appears.

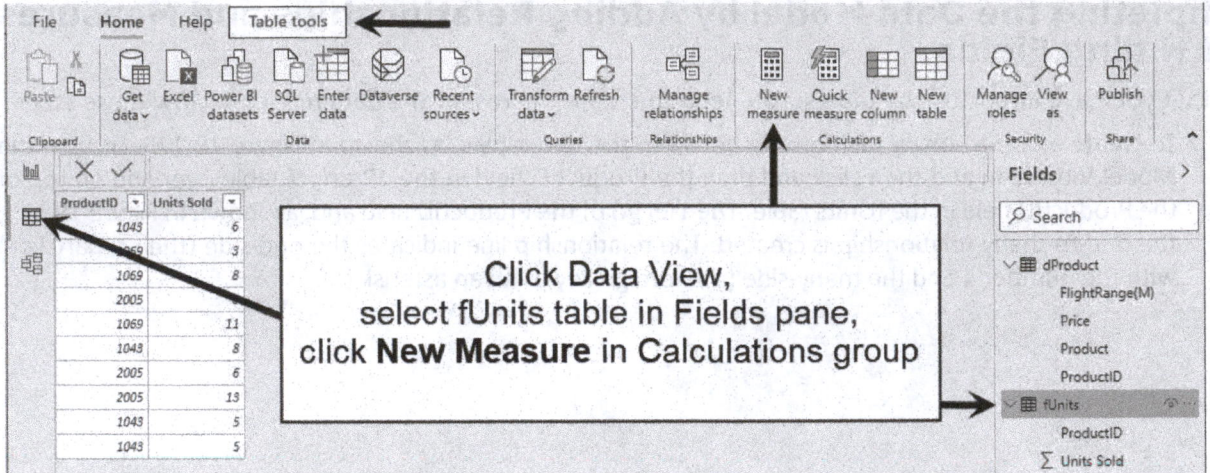

Figure 18.177 *Be sure to select the fUnits table before clicking the New Measure button.*

3. As shown in Figure 18.178, click in the formula bar and create the following measure: **Total Sales ($) = SUMX(fUnits,RELATED(dProduct[Price])*fUnits[Units Sold])**.

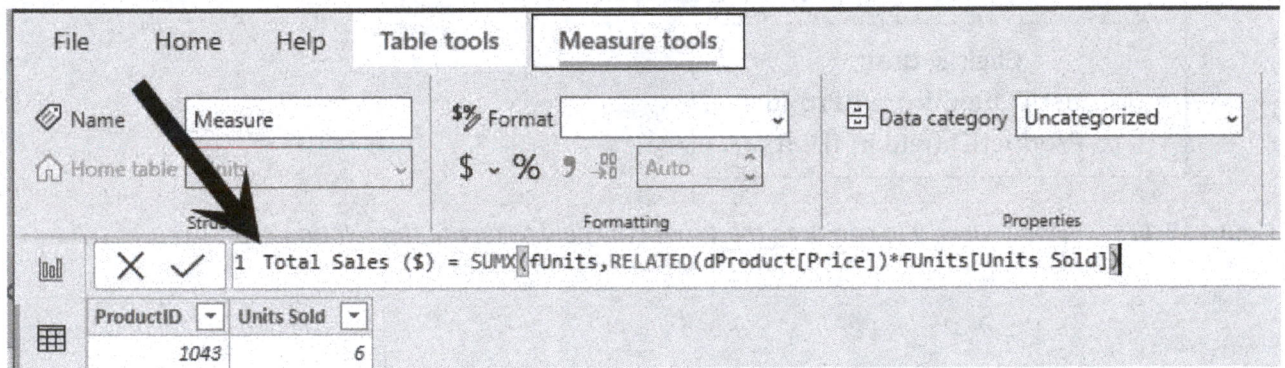

Figure 18.178 *Create a one-step measure to calculate the sales amounts for each row in the fact table and then add those amounts.*

4. Before you press Enter to create the measure, as shown in Figure 18.179, click the Comma button in the Formatting group. By doing this, you apply decimal number formatting with a comma separator to the measure.

Note: Whereas in Power BI the Comma button applies decimal number formatting with a comma separator, in Excel, the Comma button applies comma-separated number formatting.

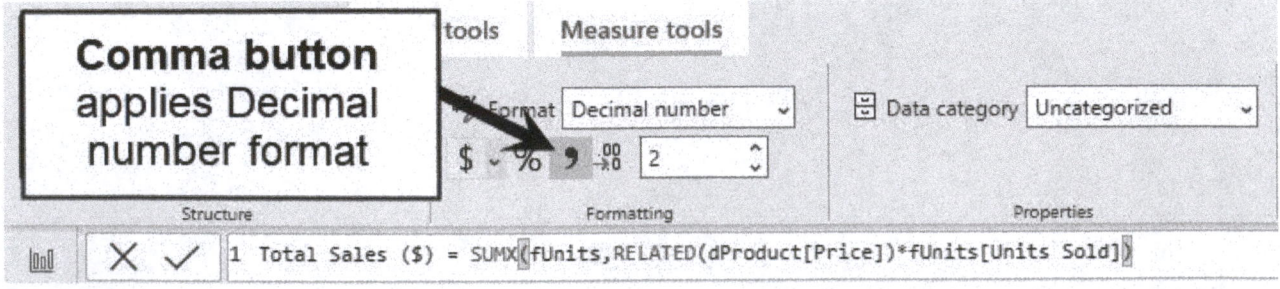

Figure 18.179 *With the Measure Tools tab still selected, add decimal number formatting to the measure.*

5. As shown in Figure 18.180, create a measure that calculates total units and then format it.

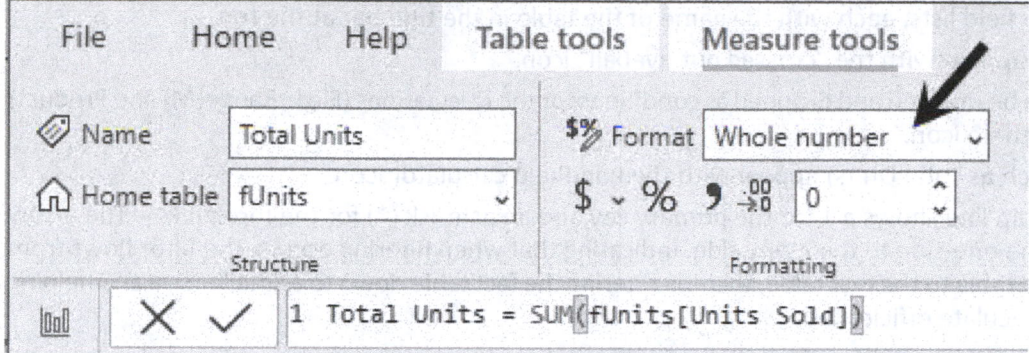

Figure 18.180 *Create a second measure for total units.*

6. To hide fields that are not necessary in the reporting area, on the left side of the Power BI window, click on the Model View icon, select the Price and ProductID fields in the dProduct table (by holding down the Shift key to select both), right-click one of the fields, and then click Hide in Report View (see Figure 18.181). Then, using the same technique, hide the ProductID and Units Sold fields in the fUnits table.

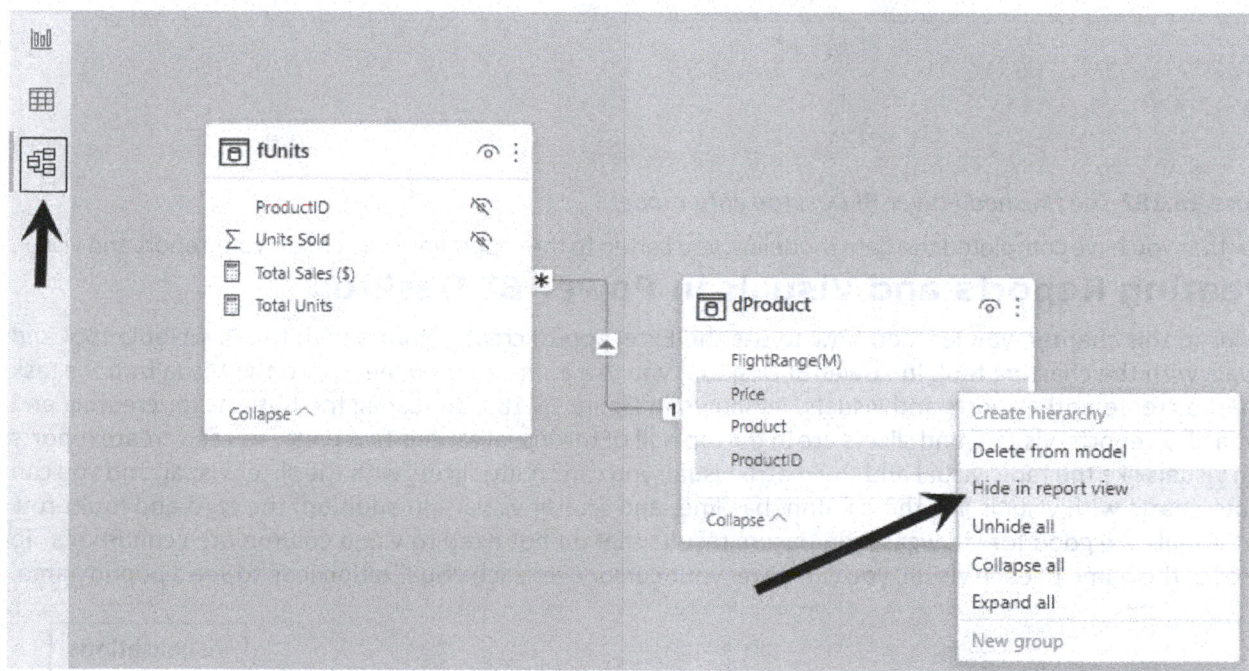

Figure 18.181 *In Model view, you can hide fields that are not necessary in Report view.*

Figure 18.182 shows the finished data model. In it, you can see that the data model has these important elements:

- There are two field lists, each with the name of the table in the title bar at the top.
- Hidden fields appear with the "crossed out eyeball" icon.
- Fields that can be dragged and dropped as conditions for the calculations (FlightRange(M) and Product) are shown with no icon.
- Measures (such as Total Units) appear with the handheld calculator icon.
- The relationship line shows a 1 for the primary key and an asterisk (*) for the foreign key. The arrow points from the one-side to the many-side, indicating that when filtering occurs, the filter flows from the dimension table to the fact table, thereby filtering the fact table down to a smaller size and helping formulas to calculate efficiently.

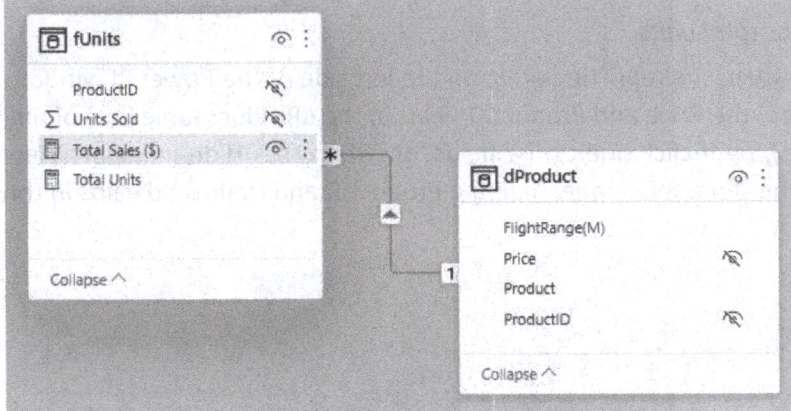

Figure 18.182 *The finished Power BI Desktop data model.*

Now that you have completed the data modeling, you can go to the report area and create your report and visual.

Creating Reports and Visuals in Power BI Desktop

Earlier in this chapter, you learned how to use the Excel app to create reports with the PivotTable tool and visuals with the charting tool. In Power BI Desktop, you use a single task pane, called the Visualizations task pane, to create both reports and visuals. As shown in Figure 18.183, almost all the buttons for creating and formatting reports, visuals, and slicers are in the top half of the Visualizations task pane. You can create reports with visuals like the table visual and the matrix visual, you can create slicers with the slicer visual, and you can create charts with visuals like the column, bar, line, and scatter visuals. In addition, the card and multi-row card visuals are good for showcasing measure results that do not need row and column area conditions. To discover the name of each visual, you can hover your cursor over each visualization icon to see a popup name.

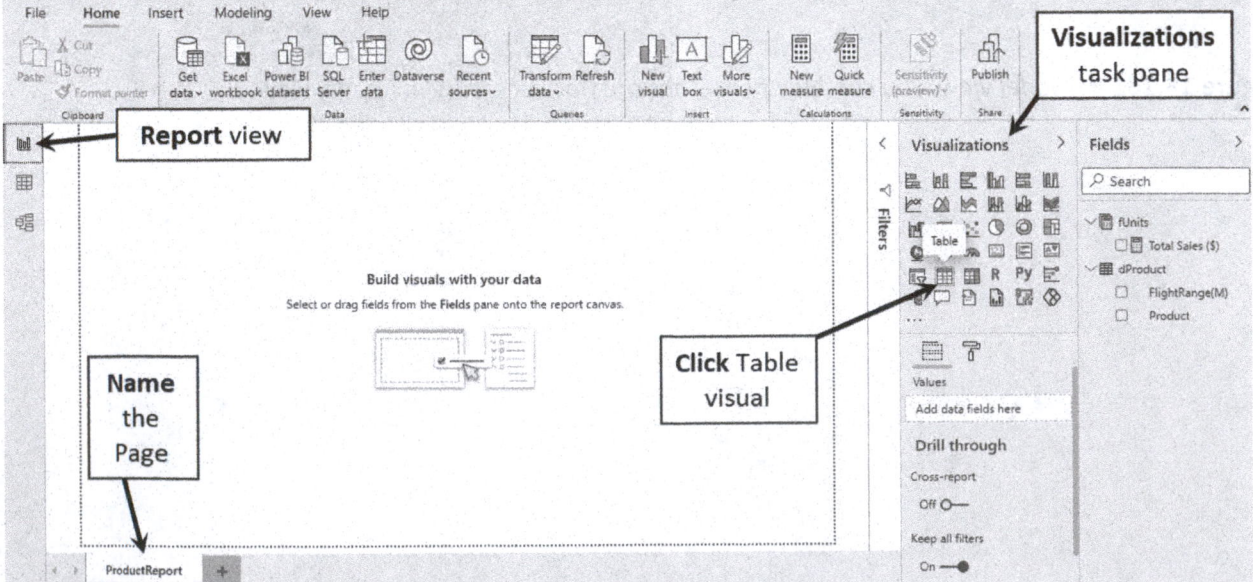

Figure 18.183 *After naming a page in Report view, click on the Table visual in the Visualizations pane.*

To create a table visual, follow these steps:

1. On the left side of Power BI Desktop, click the Report View icon to expose the page and empty report canvas. Double-click the page tab and replace the default name Page1 with **ProductReport**. To insert a visual into the empty report canvas, click somewhere in the report canvas and then, in the Visualizations task pane, click the Table visual icon (see Figure 18.183).

2. When the table visual appears in the report canvas, in the Fields pane on the far right, check the checkbox for the Product field in the dProduct table to insert a unique list of product names into the first column of the table visual (see Figure 18.184).

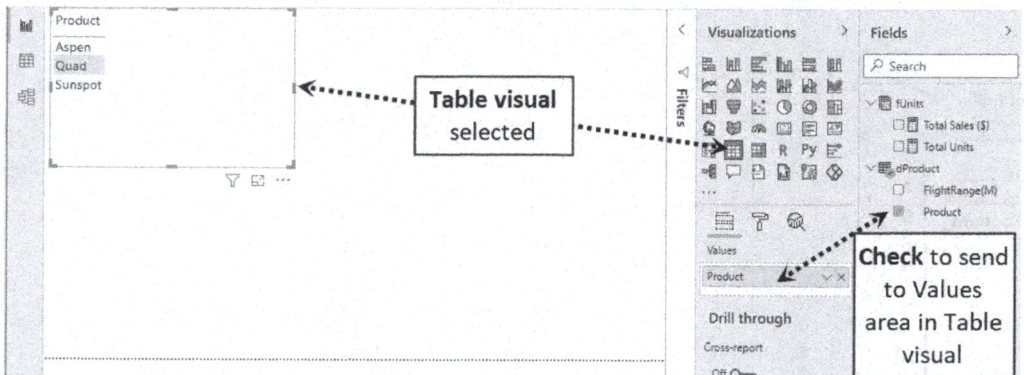

Figure 18.184 *With the table visual selected, check the Product field to add it to the report.*

3. To add the two measures to the visual, check the checkbox for the Total Sales ($) measure in the fUnits table and then check the checkbox for the Total Units measure. The finished report is shown in Figure 18.185.

> **Note:** In Figure 18.185, notice that in the bottom half of the Visualizations task pane, the Values area of the Fields tab lists the Product field and two measures. A table visual is a good visual to use when you have a list of conditions as the first field and then various measures listed one after the other on the right of the conditions. A table visual is different from a PivotTable report because it only has the Values area for dragging and dropping fields and measures. If you want to create a report similar to a PivotTable, with Rows and Columns area conditions and measures in the Values area, you can use a matrix visual, as described later in this chapter.

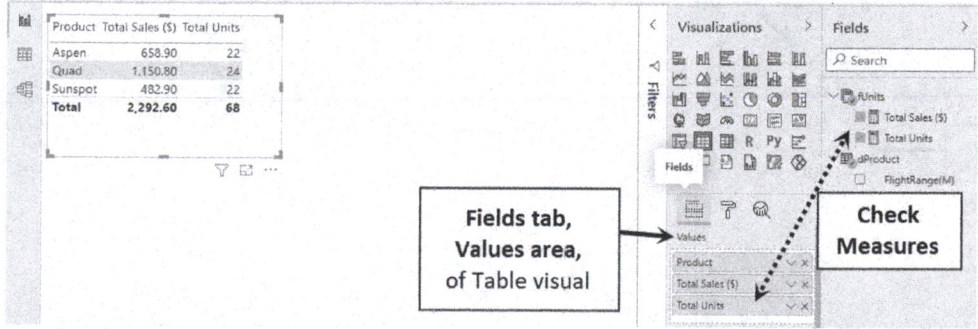

Figure 18.185 *With the table visual selected, check the Total Sales ($) and Total Units measures.*

Formatting Power BI Visuals

Next, you need to format the visual you just added. In Excel, when you want to format a PivotTable report or an Excel chart, you must select the individual element to which you want to apply formatting and then apply the formatting by using either a task pane or a dialog box. You must do this for each element, always selecting the element first and then clicking the command to add the formatting. In Excel, just by clicking an element, you can add formatting.

In Power BI Desktop, you only have to select a visual one time and then, in the Paint Roller Format tab in the middle part of the Visualizations task pane (see Figure 18.186), you choose the element to format from the list of visual elements and then click the command to add the format. In Power BI, you do not have to pre-select the element of the visual before adding formatting. You use the list of visual elements to select which item you want to format. Figure 18.186 shows a list of multiple formatting options that are available for the table visual in this case.

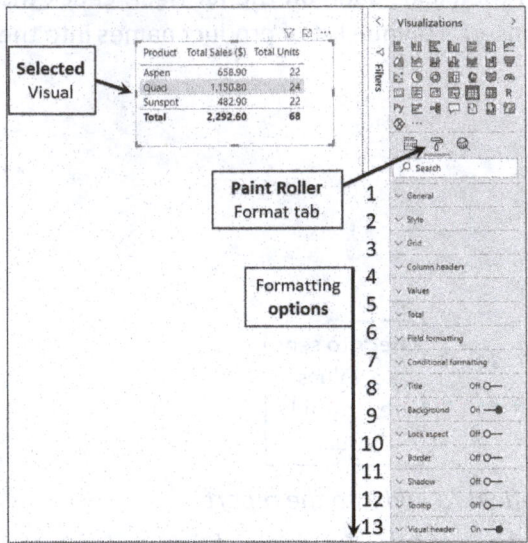

Figure 18.186 *Formatting visuals: Select a visual and then, in the Paint Roller Format tab, select visual element to format.*

Follow these steps to begin formatting Power BI visuals:

1. With the table visual selected, click the Paint Roller Format tab in the Visualizations task pane. Then, as shown in Figure 18.187, click the Grid dropdown arrow. In the list of elements to format, change the Text Size setting to 12 pt.

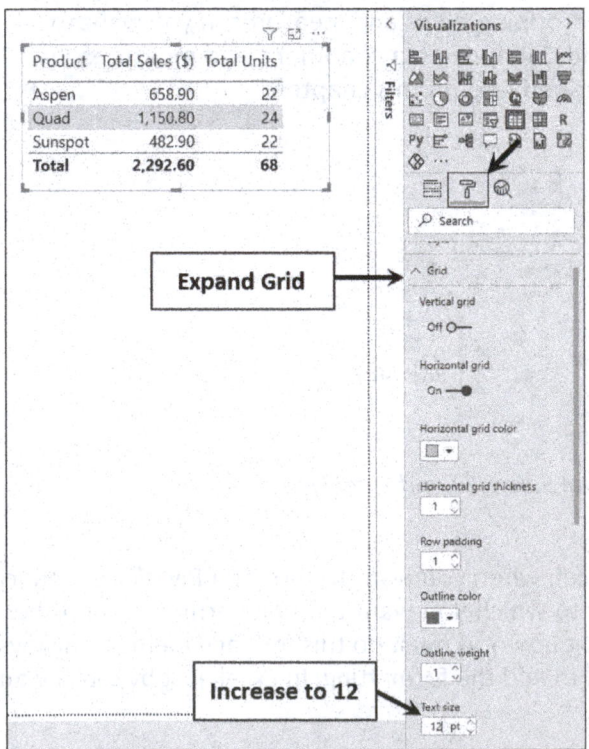

Figure 18.187 *Format the table visual grid so that it has a text size of 12 points.*

2. After you change the text size, you need to resize the visual so that all the information is visible. Figure 18.188 shows the cursors you use in Power BI Desktop for moving and resizing visuals.

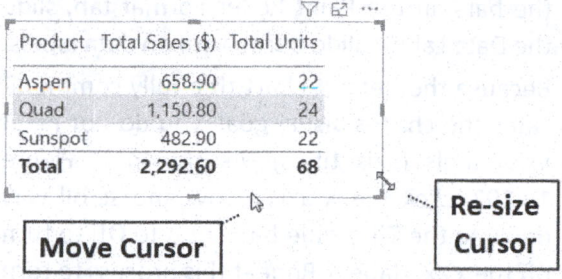

Figure 18.188 *The move cursor is a diagonal outlined white arrow. The resize cursor is a thin double-headed arrow.*

Creating a Clustered Bar Chart Visual in Power BI

To create a clustered bar chart visual, follow these steps:

1. Click in the empty white area in the report canvas and then click the button for a clustered bar chart, as shown in Figure 18.189. Power BI adds a clustered bar chart to your report canvas.

> **Note:** Be sure to click in the white area first before clicking the button for the new visual. If you accidentally leave the table visual selected and then click the clustered bar chart button, your table will be converted to a clustered bar chart.

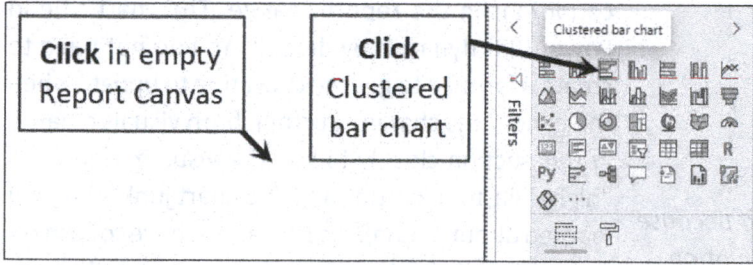

Figure 18.189 *To add a new visual, you must click in the empty report canvas before selecting the visual.*

2. With the bar chart selected, in the Fields task pane, check the checkboxes for the Product field and the Total Sales ($) measure, as shown in Figure 18.190.

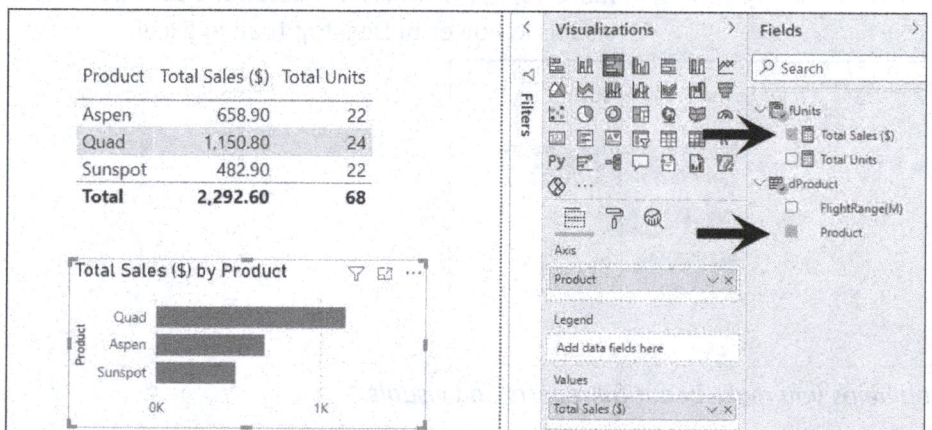

Figure 18.190 *Select the Product field and the Total Sales ($) measure.*

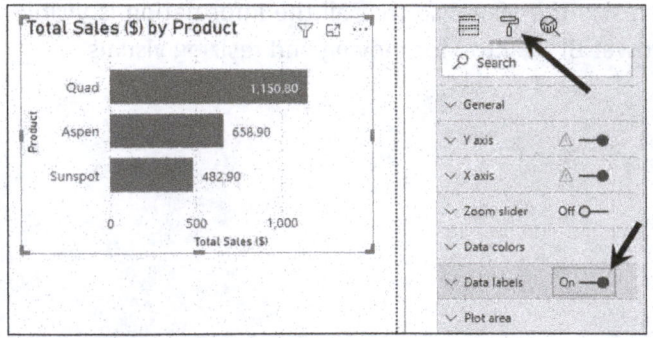

Figure 18.191 *Turn on bar chart data labels.*

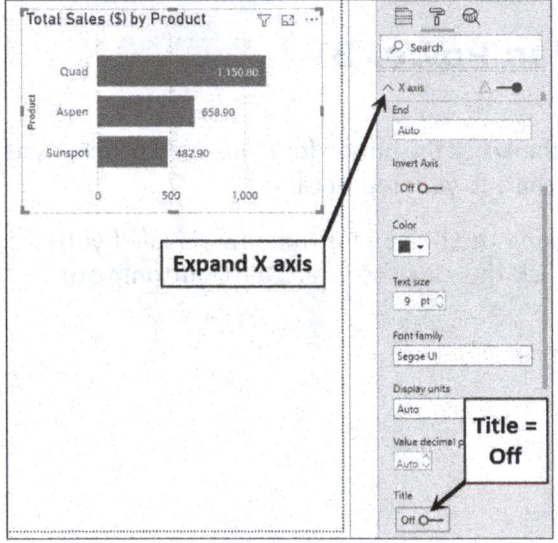

Figure 18.192 *The axis titles are not needed because the chart title already provides enough information.*

3. As shown in Figure 18.191, to add data labels to show the exact sales amounts at the ends of the bars, in the Paint Roller Format tab, slide the Data Labels slide bar to turn on data labels.

4. Because the default chart title fully communicates the chart's visual goal, you do not need axis labels (axis titles). As shown in Figure 18.192, click the X axis arrow and scroll way down to the Title slide bar; set it to Off to turn off the x axis labels. Repeat this process to turn off the titles in the y axis.

The finished Power BI Desktop table and chart are shown in Figure 18.193. These visuals are usually cleaner and more refined in Power BI Desktop than in Excel. For example, in this example, Power BI Desktop gave you the title for the chart by default. As you learned in Chapter 17, in Excel, when you need a chart title like this, you have to perform a lot of steps, including creating a text formula in the worksheet cell to make the chart title updatable if conditions in the report change. The chart title in Power BI is dynamic by default: You do not need to create a formula to get the chart title to update when the conditions change. Further, both visuals created in this section closely follow the visualization rules "high data-to-ink ratio" and "no chart junk" that you learned about in Chapter 17. You did have to turn off the axis labels for the chart, so you do need to pay close attention to make sure your visuals and reports communicate efficiently. But in general you need to make far fewer manual alterations to reports and visuals in Power BI Desktop than in Excel.

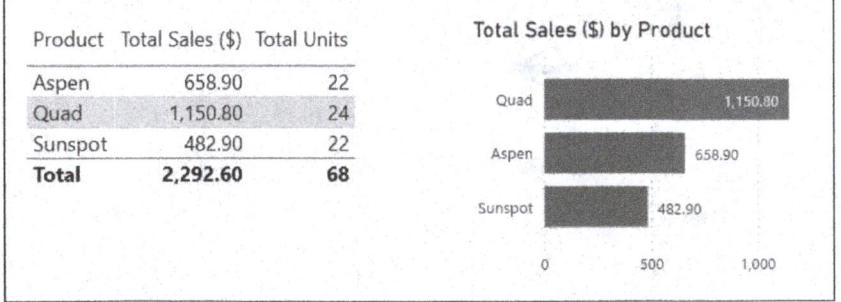

Figure 18.193 *Power BI Desktop helps you make beautiful reports and visuals.*

5. To set the parameters for how you would like the visuals to interact with each other when you select an item in visual, begin by selecting the table visual. Then, as shown in Figure 18.194, click the Format tab in the Ribbon and, in the Interactions group, toggle on the Edit Interactions button. Once you do this, when you hover your cursor over the clustered bar chart visual, interaction option buttons appear in the top-right corner of the clustered bar chart. The Highlight interaction option is on by default, but if it is not on, click to turn it on.

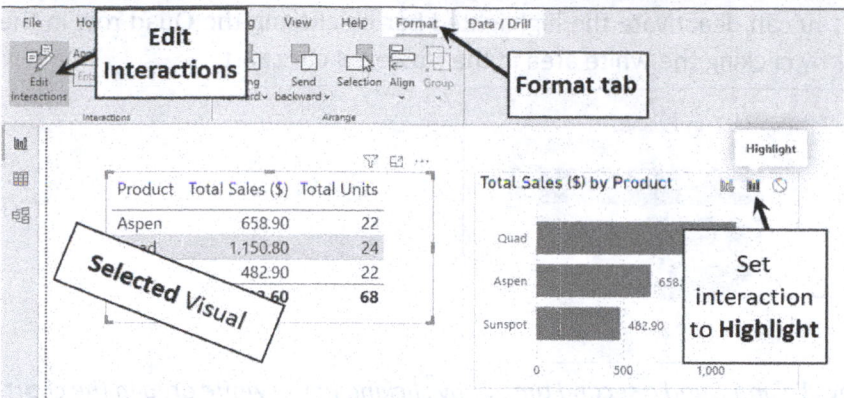

Figure 18.194 The Edit Interactions button toggles on the interaction buttons on visuals.

6. Select the clustered bar chart visual to show the interaction option buttons in the top-right corner of the table visual. Then, as shown in Figure 18.195, click the None option to turn off filtering for the table visual. When you turn off all interactions for a visual, the selected visual no longer affects it.

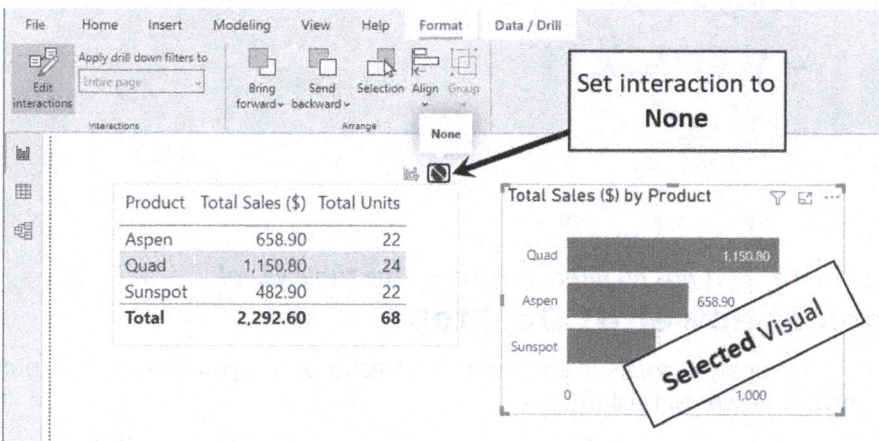

Figure 18.195 *You can set interactions to None so that clicks on other visuals will have no filtering effect.*

7. When you are done setting the interactions between visuals, toggle off the Edit Interactions button, as shown in Figure 18.196.

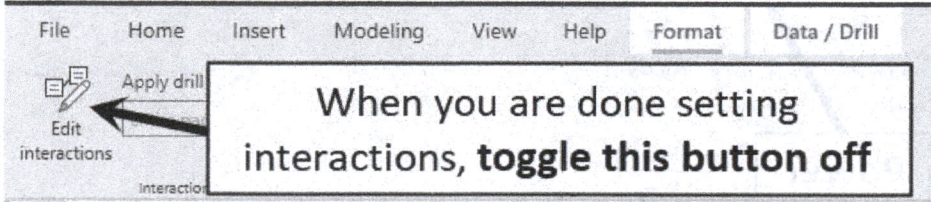

Figure 18.196 *Be sure to toggle off the Edit Interaction button when you are done.*

8. As shown in Figure 18.197, to test the interactions, click the Quad row in the table visual and ensure that the Quad bar is highlighted in the clustered bar chart.

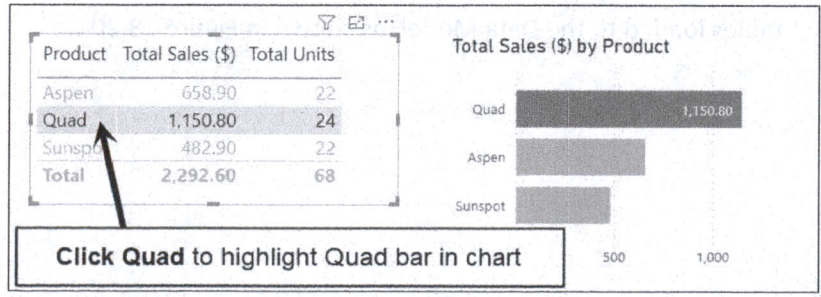

Figure 18.197 *Click on Quad in the table visual to highlight the Quad bar in the chart.*

As shown in Figure 18.198, you can deactivate the highlighted bar by clicking the Quad row in the table visual a second time or by clicking the white area in the clustered car chart.

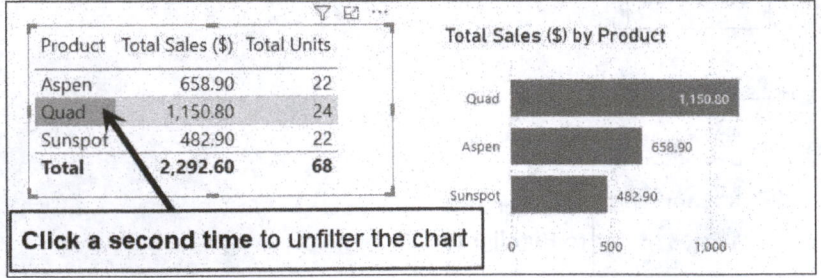

Figure 18.198 *Turn off the highlight by clicking Quad a second time or by clicking in the white area in the chart.*

9. As shown in Figure 18.199, to ensure that no filtering will occur in the table visual as a result of a click in the bar chart, click the Quad bar in the clustered bar chart. You should not see any filtering occur in the table visual.

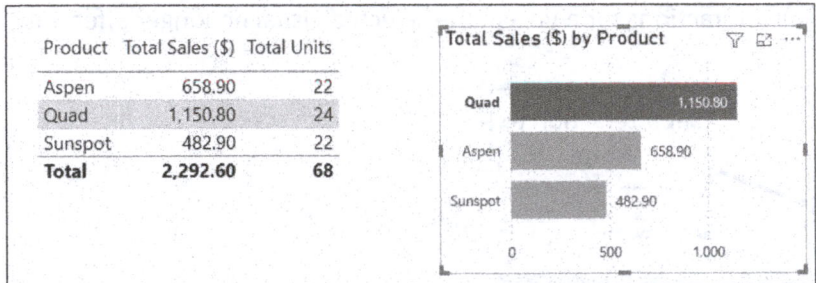

Figure 18.199 *Clicking the Quad bar in the chart has no filtering effect on the table visual.*

The Four Main Sections of Power BI Desktop

Now that you have completed your data analysis goals in the Power BI Desktop file, you have these four sections, or areas, of components in your Power BI Desktop file:

- You have fUnits and dProduct queries created with Power Query, as shown in Figure 18.200.

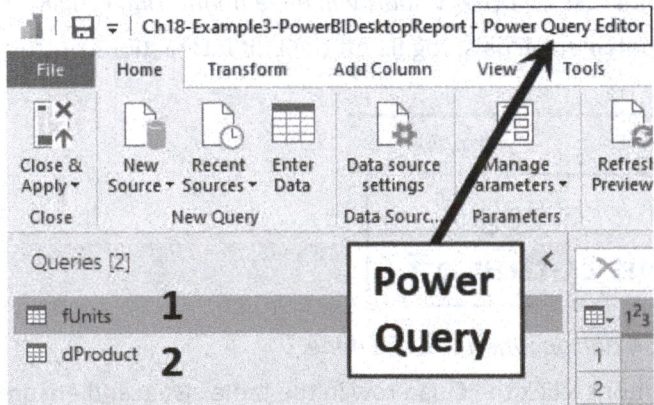

Figure 18.200 *Two queries created using Power Query inside Power BI Desktop.*

- You have the fUnits and dProduct tables loaded to the Data Model, as shown in Figure 18.201.

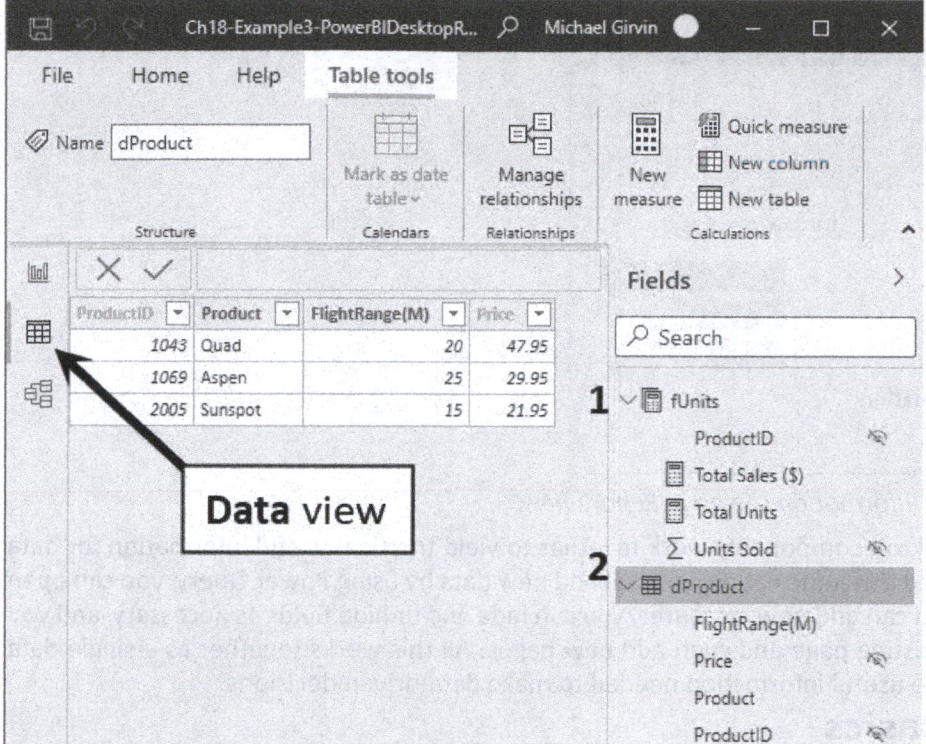

Figure 18.201 *Preview of two tables and DAX measures in Data view.*

- You have a completed star schema data model with tables, relationships, DAX formulas, and hidden fields, as shown in Figure 18.202.

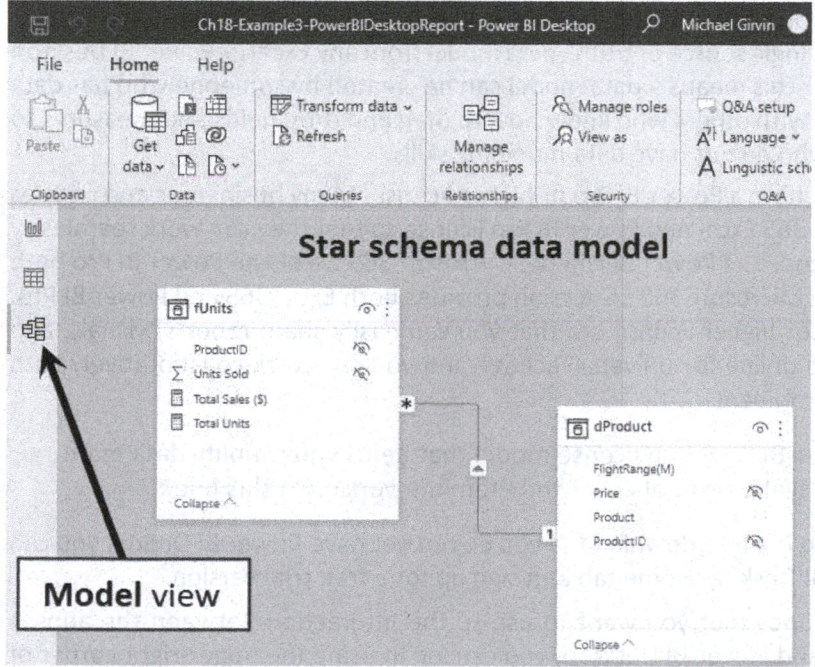

Figure 18.202 *Star schema data model is shown in Model view.*

- You have a page with visuals that constitutes the final useful information, as shown in Figure 18.203.

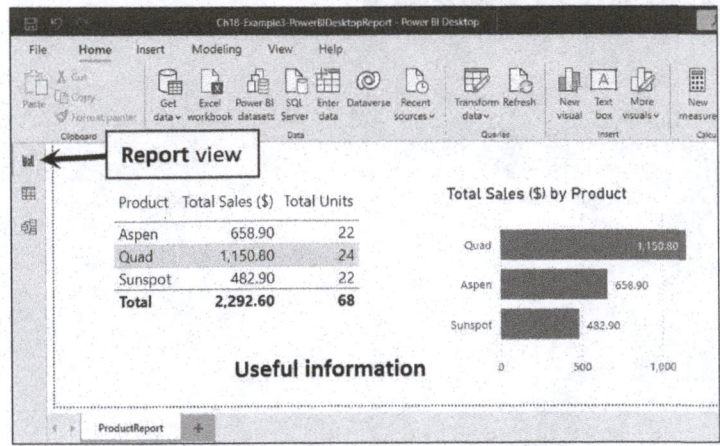

Figure 18.203 *The final useful information shown in Report view.*

All the different Power BI Desktop components work together to yield the final useful information for data analysis. After you have created this information, you can add new data by using Power Query, you can open the queries and edit them, you can add new measures, you can hide and unhide fields as necessary, and you can add new visuals to the existing page and even add new pages. All this works together as a single data analysis system to produce the useful information needed to make data-driven decisions.

Power BI Online Basics

When you publish a Power BI Desktop file to Power BI Online, you get these benefits:

- You can easily share your data analysis results so they can be viewed on any supported device.
- You can create new reports in the Power BI Online environment.
- You can easily share the in-the-cloud data model from the published Power BI Desktop file so that users can access the published "single source of truth" data model from any Excel or Power BI Desktop file that is open and logged into. This means a data model can be created by someone who has data modeling skills and then shared with others who know how to drag and drop fields and measures to create reports and visuals but who do not have data modeling skills.

To publish to Power BI Online, you must have a Power BI Pro or higher license. Many businesses and entities provide employees with both Microsoft 365 Excel and Power BI Pro license so that they can work seamlessly between Microsoft 365, Power BI Desktop, and Power BI Online. Microsoft 365 Excel and Power BI Pro both must be purchased from Microsoft. The Microsoft 365 E5 version provides both Excel 365 and Power BI Pro. The main benefits of the Power BI Pro or higher license are that you can easily share reports, visuals, and dashboards; you can store data models online for universal access; and you can work collaboratively with teammates in the Power BI Online environment.

> **Note:** Microsoft also offers a Power BI Premium license model that helps you simplify data management and access at enterprise scale. I do not cover the Premium version in this book.

As you learned earlier, Power BI Desktop is a free download. If you do not yet have Power BI Online, you can click the Publish button on the Power BI Desktop Home tab and sign up for a free trial version.

You need to properly log in to all the apps that you want to use so the interaction between the apps is seamless. In both Microsoft 365 Excel and Power BI Desktop, you can log in using the upper-right corner of the title bar. You know you are logged in if your name appears in the title bar. Once you are logged in to both apps, when you publish a Power BI Desktop or Excel file, Power BI Online asks you to log in to the Power BI Online site. You can also log in directly to Power BI Online at the website powerbi.com. Furthermore, if you use the Outlook or Excel Online apps, when you are logged in to them, the app icon in the upper-left corner allows you to jump over to the Power BI Online website, where you will already be logged in. When you log in to any of the Microsoft 365 Online tools, you are automatically logged in to Power BI Online also.

Before you can publish a Power BI Desktop file, you need to log in to Power BI Online and create a workspace. A Power BI *workspace* is a location in the Power BI Online website where you can load Power BI Desktop files and Excel workbook files and create shareable dashboards so that authorized Power BI Pro users can access the content and collaborate as a team. You can create a workspace with just a few clicks, and then you can add e-mail addresses for the people you want to be able to access the workspace.

> **Note:** There is a location called My Workspace that is for personal use only. When you want to share and collaborate, you use the Workspace option, not the My Workspace option.

Logging In to Power BI Online and Creating a Workspace

To log in to Power BI Online and create a workspace, follow these steps:

1. In a browser, go to the website powerbi.com. Figure 18.204 shows the login screen, where you can sign in to your account or try Power BI for free.

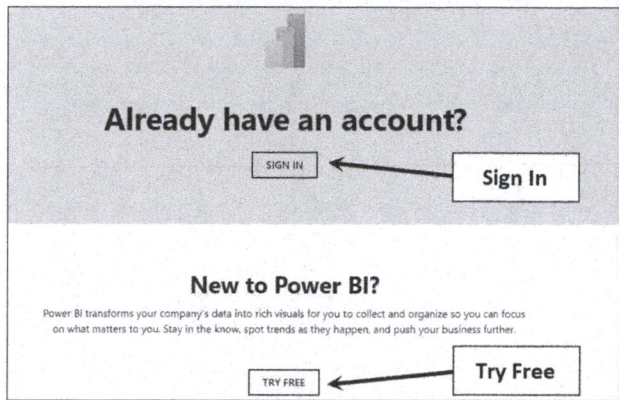

Figure 18.204 *powerbi.com login window.*

> **Note:** In order to try Power BI Pro for free, you need to use an e-mail address from an entity that has purchased a bulk license from Microsoft for a product such as Office. For hacks to get around this requirement, watch this Guy in a Cube YouTube video: https://www.youtube.com/watch?v=uZyy_qqRPiU.

2. When you log in, you see the Power BI Online home page, as shown in Figure 18.205. At the bottom of the navigation pane on the left side of the Power BI home page, expand the Workspaces option and then click the Create a Workspace Button, as shown in Figure 18.206.

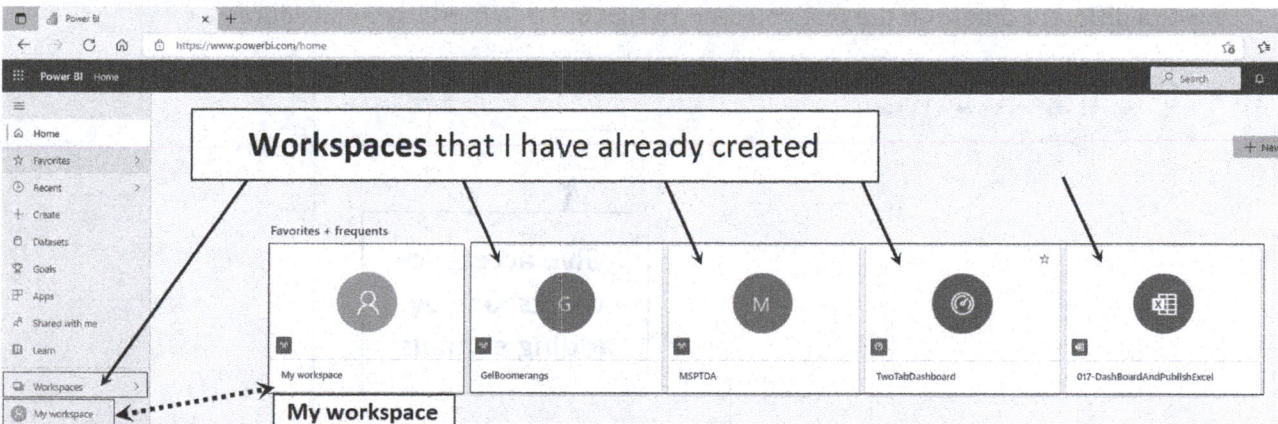

Figure 18.205 *The home page of Power BI Online offers established workspaces.*

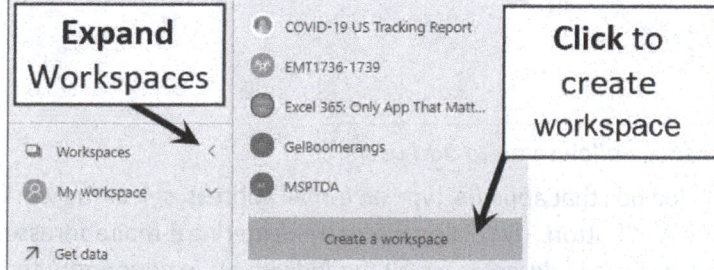

Figure 18.206 *Click the Create a Workspace button.*

3. In the Create a Workspace dialog box that appears, enter the name **The Only App The Matters** into the Workspace Name textbox (see Figure 18.207). Then, in the Description box, type **This is a workspace for examples from the book The Only App The Matters**. To create this workspace, click the Save button.

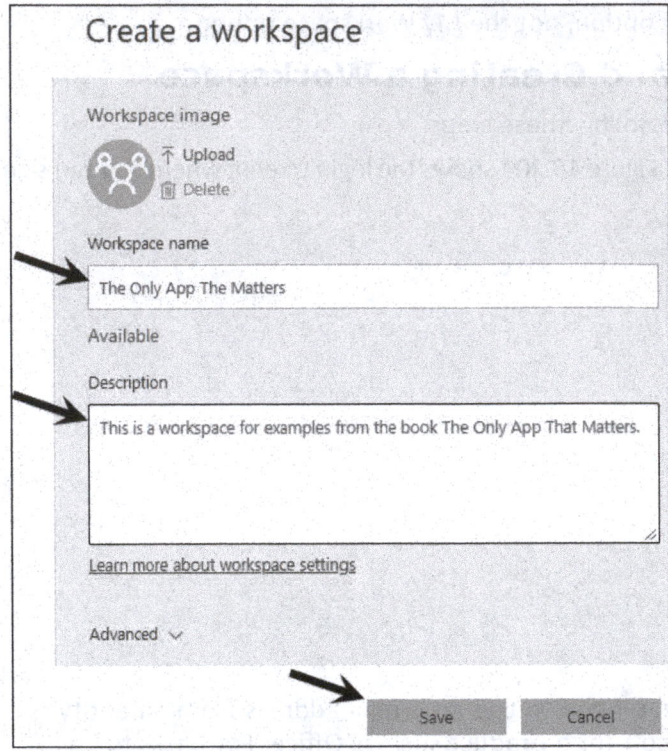

Figure 18.207 *Enter a workspace name and description and then click the Save button.*

4. As shown in Figure 18.208, in the workspace area, click the Access button to add e-mail addresses of people who should have access to the workspace.

Note: You do not have to add any e-mail addresses for this example, but if you want to see the e-mail notification that shows up when you publish content, you can add an e-mail address of your own (a different one from the one you used to sign up) or a friend's e-mail address.

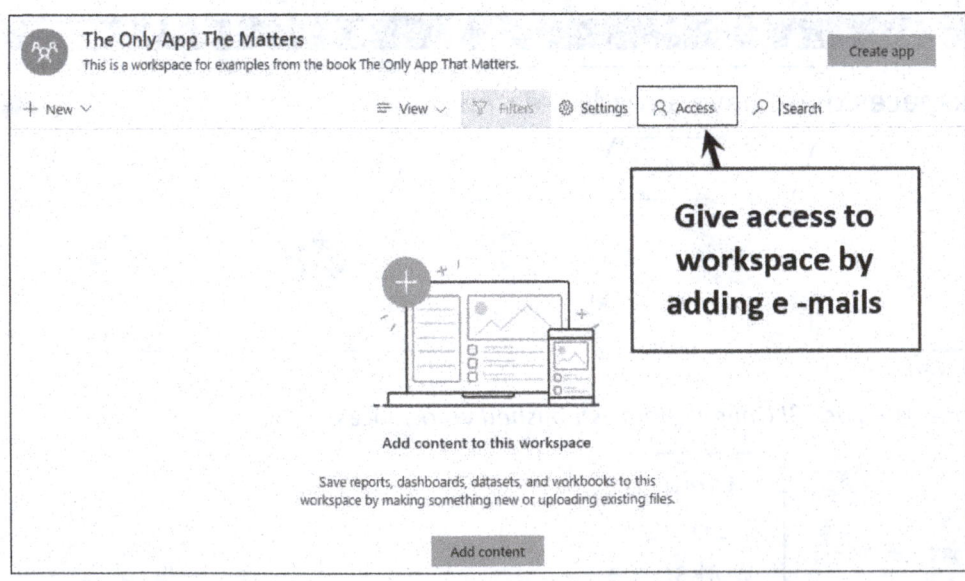

Figure 18.208 *The Access button in the new workspace allows you to add users.*

5. As shown in Figure 18.209, in the Access dialog box that appears, type an e-mail address, select the workspace role for that person, and then click the Add button. This dialog box makes entering e-mail addresses easy because as soon as you start typing, the e-mail addresses for all the individuals in your entity that

are similar to what you have typed appear in a dropdown list that you can select from. In addition, if you have a list of e-mails separated by semicolons, you can copy and paste them into the e-mail address textbox in the Access dialog box to give all those e-mail addresses access to the workspace.

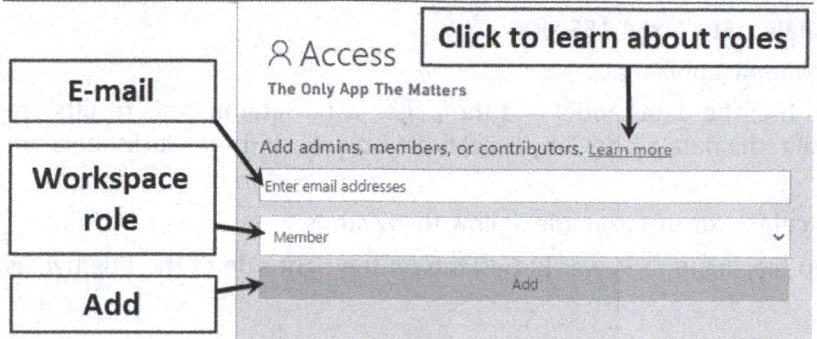

Figure 18.209 *Type an e-mail address, select the role, and then click the Add button for each person who should have access to this workspace.*

> **Note:** Four different workspace roles are available, each with different capabilities. Table 18.4 lists the roles and the capabilities each one grants. Often, I use the Contributor role because it allows teammates to load and edit content and collaborate to a great degree.

Table 18.4 Admin, Member, Contributor, and Viewer Workspace Roles

Capability	Admin	Member	Contributor	Viewer
Update and delete the workspace	X			
Add/remove people, including other admins	X			
Allow contributors to update the app for the workspace	X			
Add members or others with lower permissions	X	X		
Publish, unpublish, and change permissions for an app	X	X		
Update an app	X	X		
Share an item or an app	X	X		
Allow others to reshare items	X	X		
Feature apps on colleagues' home pages	X	X		
Manage dataset permissions	X	X		
Feature dashboards and reports on colleagues' home pages	X	X	X	
Create, edit, and delete content in the workspace	X	X	X	
Publish reports to the workspace and delete content	X	X	X	
Create a report in another workspace, based on a dataset in this workspace	X	X	X	
Copy a report	X	X	X	
Create goals based on a dataset in this workspace	X	X	X	
Schedule data refreshes via on the on-premises gateway	X	X	X	
Modify gateway connection settings	X	X	X	
View and interact with an item	X	X	X	X
Read data stored in workspace data flows	X	X	X	X

Publishing Power BI Desktop and Excel Files to Power BI Online

Once you have created a workspace, you can publish the Power BI Desktop file and the Excel workbook file that you created earlier in this chapter. These are the two files you will publish in this example:

- Ch18-Excel365-AdvancedDataAnalysisStartEx64-155.xlsx
- Ch18-Example3-PowerBIDesktopReport.pbix

When you publish a Power BI Desktop file, the data model and the pages with data analysis results are published. When you publish an Excel file, the data model, any Excel table objects, and the worksheets are published.

To publish the Power BI Desktop and Excel file for this example, follow these steps:

1. To publish the Power BI Desktop file, log in to Power BI Desktop on the right side of the title bar, as shown in Figure 18.210.

2. Make sure your Power BI Desktop file is saved.

3. In the Home tab of the Ribbon, in the Share group, click the Publish button (see Figure 18.210).

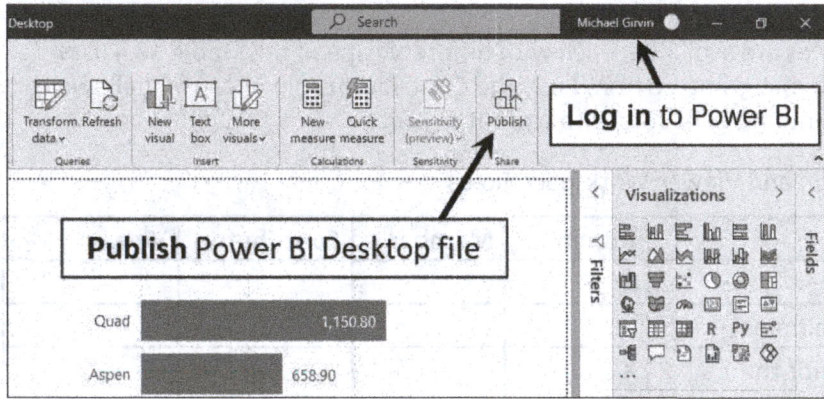

Figure 18.210 *Before you publish a file, you must log in.*

4. As shown in Figure 18.211, when the Publish to Power BI dialog box pops up, select the workspace where you want to publish—in this case, The Only App The Matters—and then click the Select button.

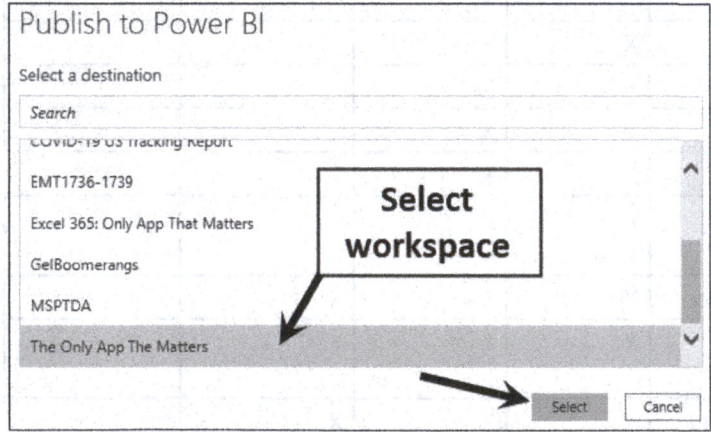

Figure 18.211 *You need to select a workspace to publish the file to and then click the Select button.*

5. When the Publishing to Power BI dialog box reads Success!, click the Got It button (see Figure 18.212).

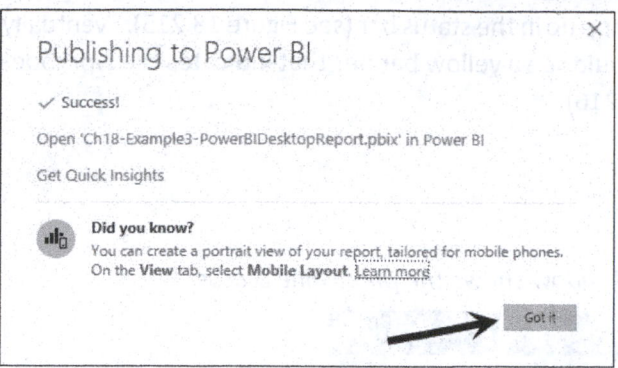

Figure 18.212 *Click the Got It button to close the Success! information box.*

6.   To publish the Excel file, open the Excel workbook file named Ch18-Excel365-AdvancedDataAnalysisStartEx63-153.xlsx.

7.   In the Excel file, click File and then click Publish, as shown in Figure 18.213.

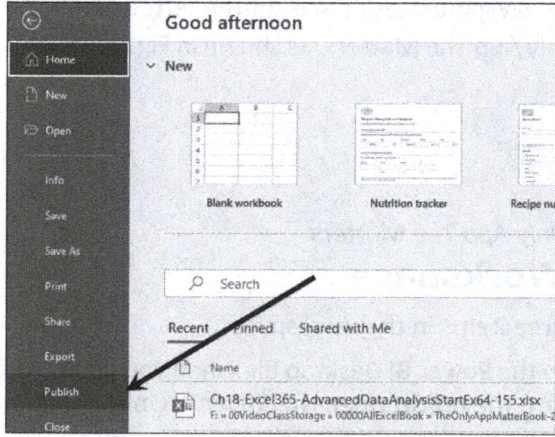

Figure 18.213 *To publish an Excel file to Power BI Online, go to the Excel File menu and click Publish.*

8.   In the Publish dialog box that appears, as shown in Figure 18.214, select the workspace The Only App The Matters from the Select Where You'd Like to Publish in Power BI dropdown. Then click the Upload button to publish the workbook file and the Power Pivot data model.

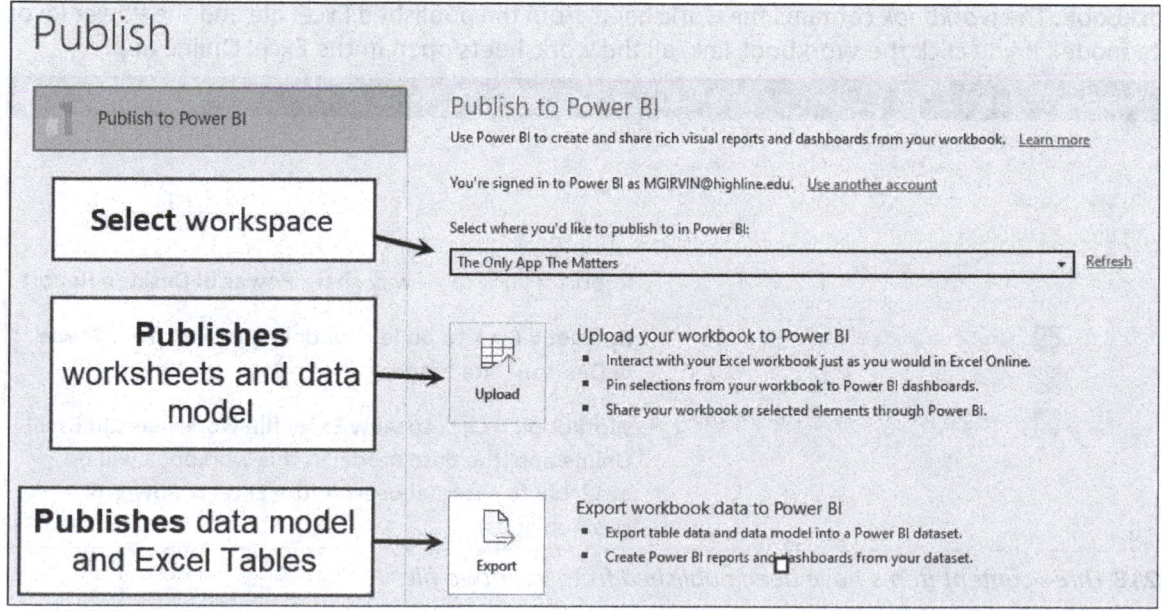

Figure 18.214 *Select a workspace to publish to and then select what you want to publish.*

You should now see the publishing progress bar pop up in the status bar (see Figure 18.215). Eventually, the workbook should be published, and you should see a yellow banner that indicates the workbook has been uploaded successfully (see Figure 18.216).

Figure 18.215 *The status bar at the bottom of the Excel widow shows the publishing status.*

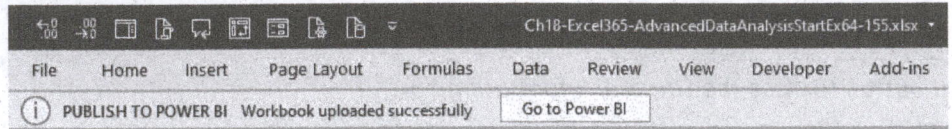

Figure 18.216 *When the workbook is successfully published, a yellow banner appears below the Excel Ribbon.*

9. Do not click the Go to Power BI button in the yellow banner shown in Figure 18.216. Instead, navigate to the Power BI Online site and then, from the navigation task pane on the left, expand the Workspaces option and click on the workspace The Only App The Matters, as shown in Figure 18.217.

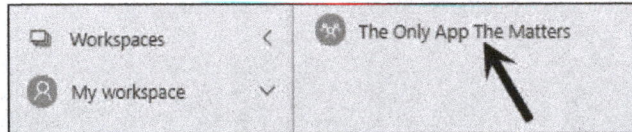

Figure 18.217 *In Power BI Online, select the workspace The Only App The Matters.*

Exploring What Is Possible Within a Workspace

As shown in Figure 18.218, the workspace home page lists three items in the workspace:

*   **Report:** The *report* consists of all the pages that were in the Power BI Desktop file when you published it. In your file, you had only one page. If you click Report, the report opens in Power BI Online so that you can interact with it and share it.

*   **Dataset:** The *dataset* is the published data model. The term Dataset on this screen is somewhat misleading because it is not just a single table or group of tables; rather, it is the full data model, with tables, relationships, DAX measures, and hidden fields. If you click the Dataset link, you get options to create a new report online or to connect to the data model with a new blank Excel workbook file.

*   **Workbook:** The *workbook* contains the worksheets from the published Excel file and the Power Pivot data model. If you click the Workbook link, all the worksheets open in the Excel Online app.

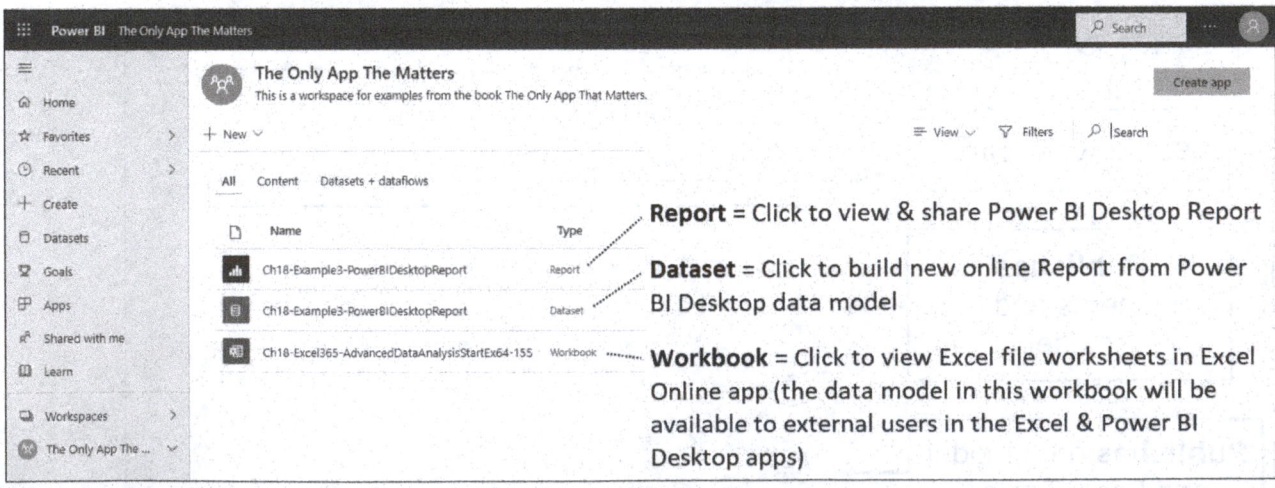

Figure 18.218 *Three content items have been published from your two files.*

The Excel Online app does not have the full capabilities of Excel 365, but it does allow you to view and interact with the worksheet content.

Note: The Power Pivot data model is not listed as a separate dataset, but if you open any Excel file or Power BI Desktop file, you can access the published Excel file's data model.

To open a published report and explore what is possible within the workspace, follow these steps:

1. To open the report in Power BI Online, in the workspace's Name column, click on the report link. Figure 18.219 shows your report in Power BI Online. You can click the Quad row in the table visual to see that the Quad bar is highlighted here in the online version of Power BI.

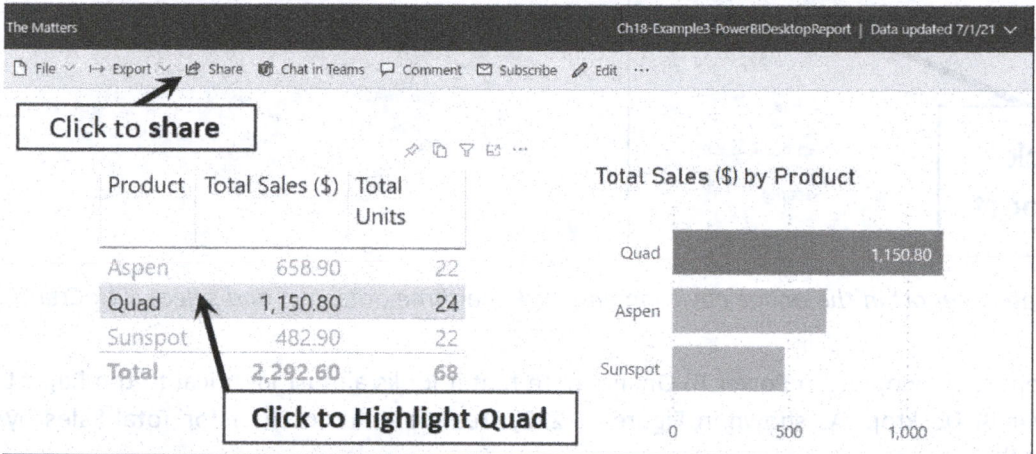

Figure 18.219 *When you open the report in Power BI Online, you see that it is interactive and can be shared.*

2. Click the Share button above the report canvas, as shown in Figure 18.219, and the dialog box shown in Figure 18.220 pops up. In this dialog box, the Copy Link button copies the report link to the Clipboard. The Outlook button opens the Outlook Online app and prepares an e-mail with a link to the report. The Teams button opens the report in the Teams app. You will not share the report in this case, so click the X button in the upper right to close the dialog box.

Note: Remember that the recipient of a report cannot view the report without a Power BI Pro or higher license.

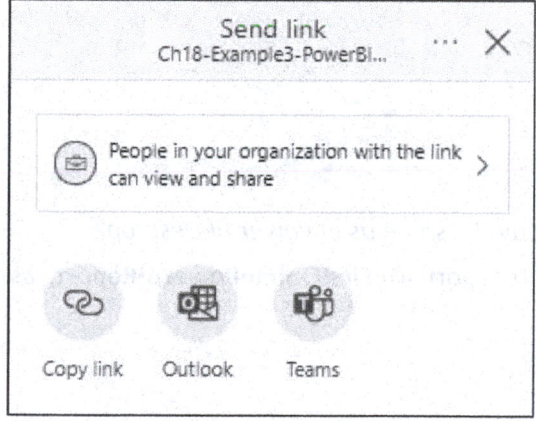

Figure 18.220 *In this dialog box, you can copy a link to the report, open Outlook online to share, or share in Teams.*

3. To navigate from the online report view back to the workspace home page, click the back arrow in your browser.

4. To use your data model to create a new online report, click the three vertical dots to open a menu of options and, as shown in Figure 18.221, click Create Report. (Note that this menu also offers other useful options, like Delete and Rename.)

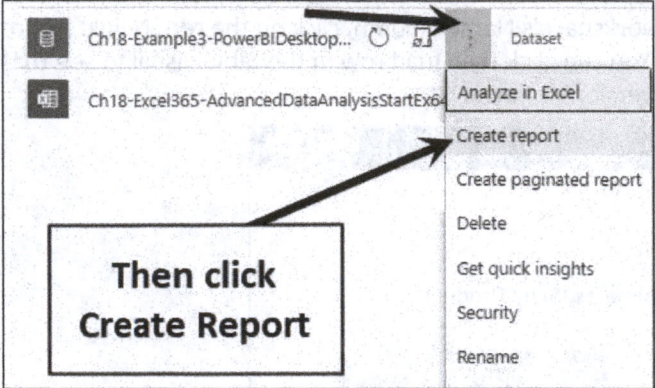

Figure 18.221 *To create a report in the online environment, click the three dots icon and select click Create Report.*

5. When the Report view opens in Power BI Online, note that it looks almost identical to the Report view in Power BI Desktop. As shown in Figure 18.222, create a column chart for Total Sales by FlightRange(M).

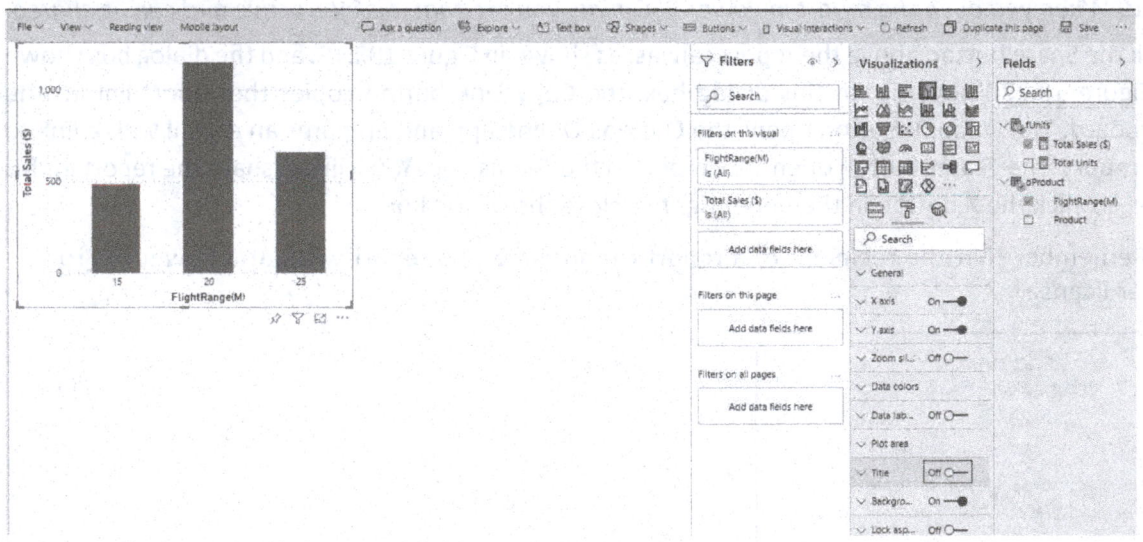

Figure 18.222 *The Report view in Power BI Online is almost exactly the same as in Power PI Desktop.*

6. Save the new report by pressing Ctrl+S and name the report **MyFirstOnlinePowerBIReport**, as shown in Figure 18.223. Then click the Save button.

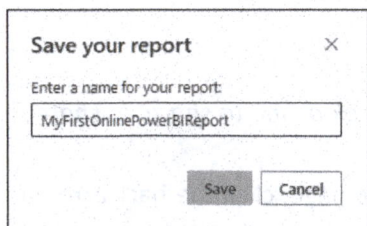

Figure 18.223 *Press Ctrl+S to save the report you created in Power BI Online to the workspace.*

7. To see where the new report is saved, in the navigation pane on the left, expand the Workspaces option and click on the workspace The Only App The Matters. Figure 18.224 shows that there are now four items listed in the workspace, and the new report is the bottom item. You can view and share this new report just as you would any other report.

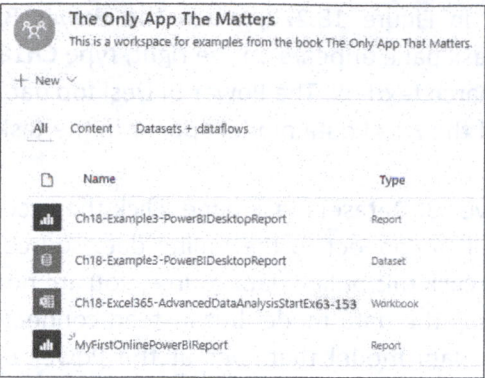

Figure 18.224 *The new report is shown in the list of items in the workspace.*

8. To view the published Excel file, navigate back to the list of items in the workspace home page and click the Excel workbook link. As shown in Figure 18.225, when you click on a Workbook link, Power BI opens the Excel Online app inside the Power BI Desktop app and allows you to click on worksheet tabs to view content. This content is interactive, but it does not give you all the capabilities you would have in the Excel 365 app.

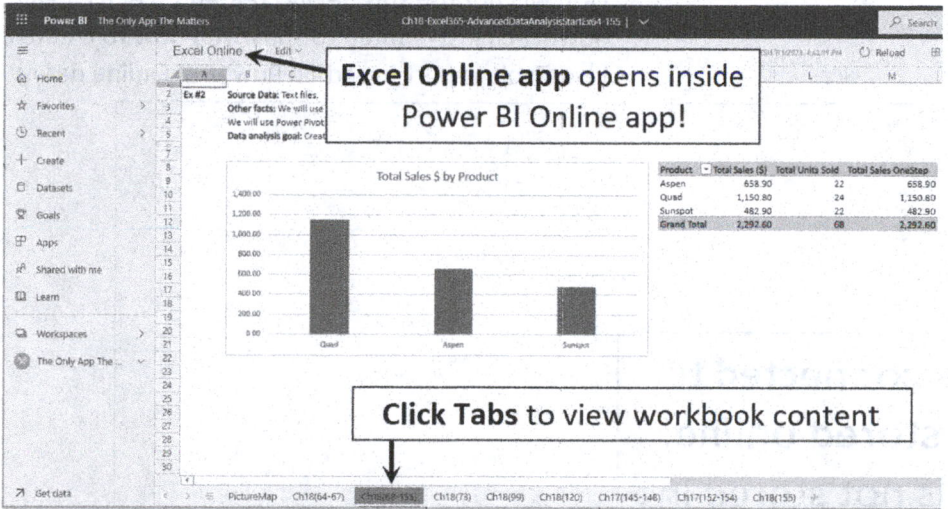

Figure 18.225 *When you click to view the Excel file, the Excel Online app opens inside Power BI Online.*

9. To connect to a Power BI Online dataset in an Excel 365 workbook and make a PivotTable report, open a blank Excel workbook file and log in to Microsoft 365 using the login option on the right side of the title bar. Then click on the Insert tab in the Excel Ribbon and, in the Tables group, click the PivotTable dropdown arrow and select From Power BI, as shown in Figure 18.226.

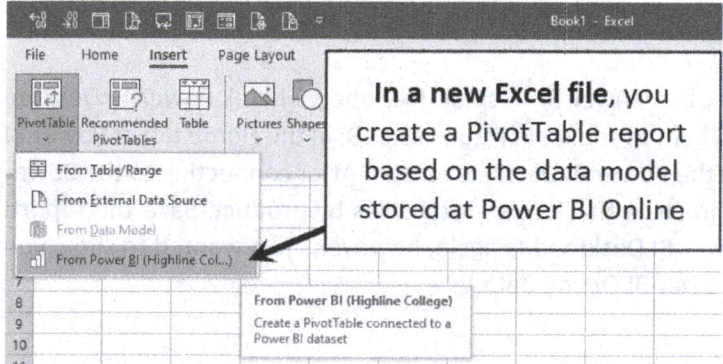

Figure 18.226 *If you are logged in to Excel 365 and have access to a workspace, you can build a PivotTable based on online data from that workspace.*

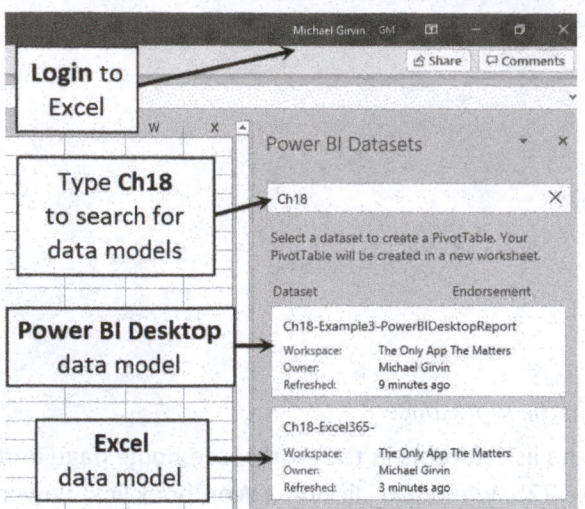

Figure 18.227 *In the Power BI Datasets task pane, you can search for Power BI Online data models.*

10. As shown in Figure 18.227, when the Power BI Datasets task pane appears on the right, type **Ch18** into the search textbox. The Power BI Desktop data model and the Excel data model appear in the task pane.

11. In the Power BI Datasets task pane, click the Excel data model to connect to the online data source. When you click this online data source, you are not downloading the data model but instead connecting to the data model that lives at the Power BI Online server.

12. As shown in Figure 18.228, from the PivotTable Fields task pane, drag and drop the fields and measures necessary to make a product report that shows total sales and total units. When you are done, you can save the Excel file to your computer. (You will not use this newly created Excel file again, however. I just wanted to show you how to create a PivotTable report based on Power BI Online data.)

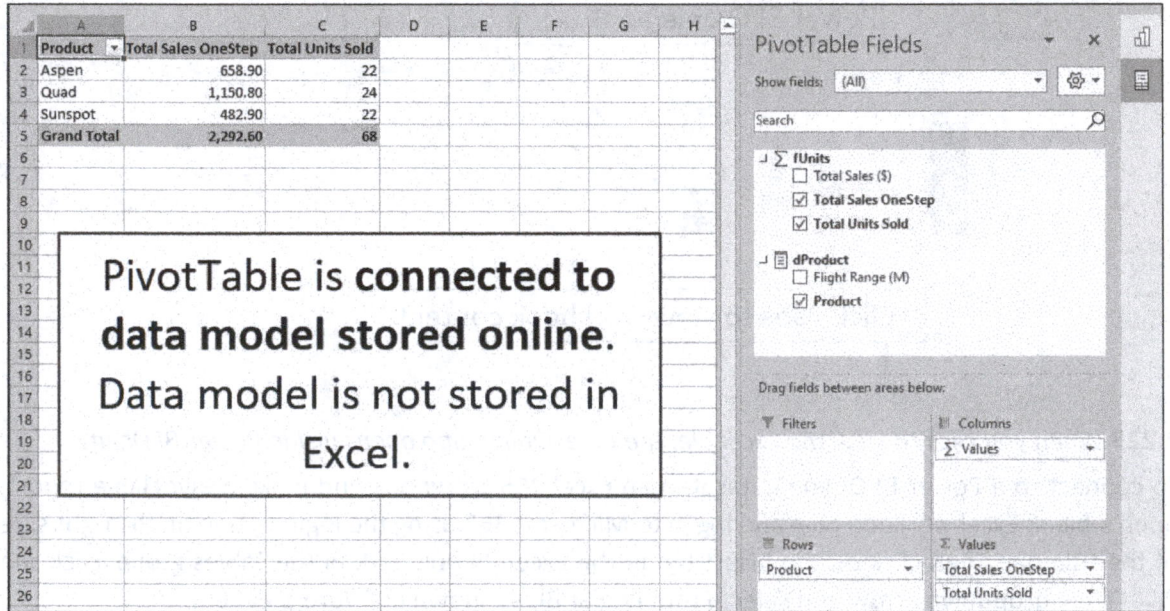

Figure 18.228 *When you connect to a data model from Power BI Online, you use the PivotTable user interface to build reports.*

13. To connect to a Power BI Online dataset in a Power BI Desktop file, open a blank Power BI Desktop file and save the file to your computer. Then, as shown in Figure 18.229, in the Home tab of Power BI Desktop, go to the Data group and click the Power BI Datasets button. After connecting to the Power BI Desktop data model, create a column chart that shows total sales by product. Save the report. (You will not use this newly created Power BI Desktop file again, however. I just wanted to show you how to create a new report based on Power BI Online data.)

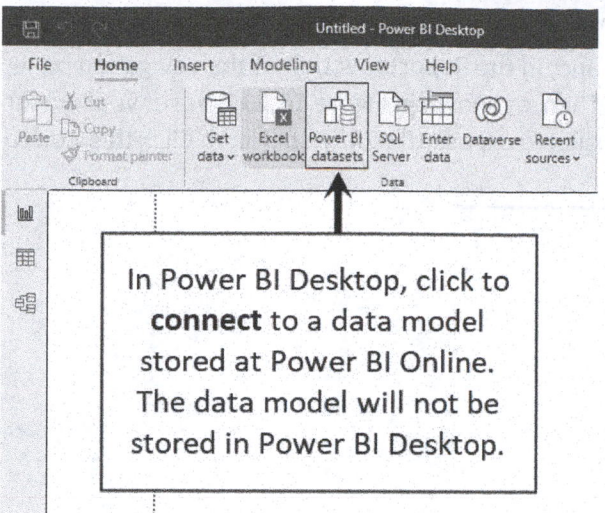

Figure 18.229 *If you are logged in to Power BI Desktop, you can connect directly to online data models.*

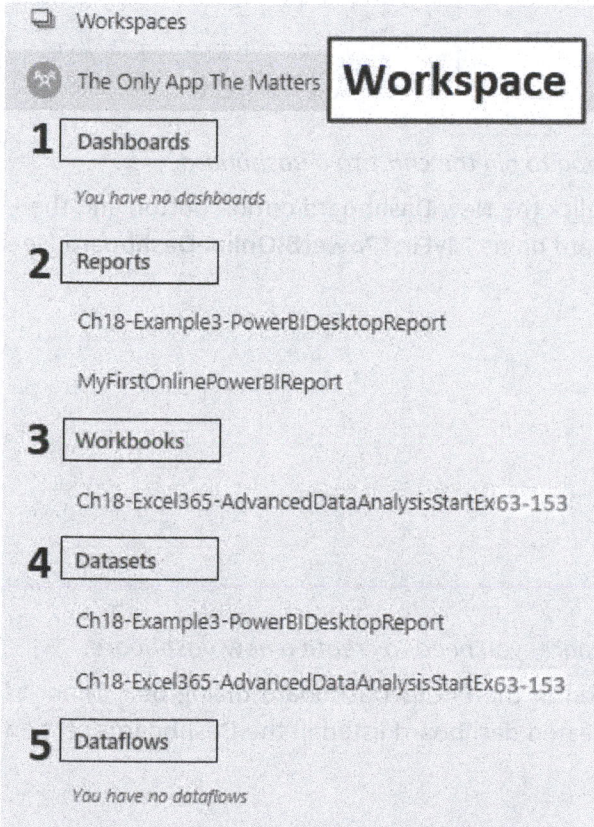

Figure 18.230 *Five sections in this workspace.*

14. Navigate back to Power BI Online and, to see the full list of items that are stored in the workspace The Only App The Matters, in the navigation pane, expand the Workspaces option and click on the workspace The Only App The Matters. Figure 18.230 shows the different sections of the workspace and the items stored in each section:

- **Dashboards:** This section lists the dashboards in the workspace, where each dashboard is a collection of pinned Power BI visuals, Power BI pages, or ranges selected from an Excel Online worksheet from within the workspace. Figure 18.230 shows that you do not have any dashboards yet, but you will create one next.

- **Reports:** This section lists the reports in the workspace that have been published from Power BI Desktop or that have been created with the Power BI Online website. Figure 18.230 shows that there are two reports: the one you published from Power BI Desktop and the one you created in Power BI Online.

- **Workbooks:** This section lists all published Excel workbooks for the workspace. Figure 18.230 shows that there is one published Excel workbook.

- **Datasets:** This section lists all published datasets (that is, data models or Excel Tables) for the workspace. Figure 18.230 shows that there are two datasets: the data model you published from Power BI Desktop and the data model you published from inside the Excel Power Pivot tool in the Excel file.

- **Dataflows:** This section lists the dataflows for the workspace. *Dataflows* are data sources created using the Dataflows online tool. Figure 18.230 shows that you have no dataflows. You will not learn how to use Dataflows in this book.

Creating a Dashboard in Power BI Online

As described earlier in this chapter, a dashboard can contain reports, charts, visualizations, and other useful information in one location so that decision makers can view and interact with the information to gauge performance, see patterns and trends, and gain insights. The general term *dashboard* can refer to a dashboard created on an Excel worksheet or on a page in Power BI Desktop. However, in the Power BI Online environment, the term *dashboard* refers to a dashboard created and saved in the Power BI workspace.

A Power BI Online dashboard has an important advantage over a dashboard on an Excel worksheet or a Power BI page: It allows you to pick and choose dashboard elements from any published Power BI report or Excel file in a workspace and pin them all in the dashboard location so that the dashboard can be easily shared. Within a given workspace, you have the freedom to pin an entire page from a Power BI report, just an element of a Power BI page, or a section from a published Excel worksheet to your dashboard.

To create a Power BI Online dashboard, follow these steps:

15. Go to your The Only App The Matters workspace and, in the Reports section of the navigation pane, click on the MyFirstOnlinePowerBIReport report. Then, as shown in Figure 18.231, hover your cursor over the lower-right corner of the column chart visual to expose the Pin Visual icon. Click this icon to pin the visual to a new dashboard.

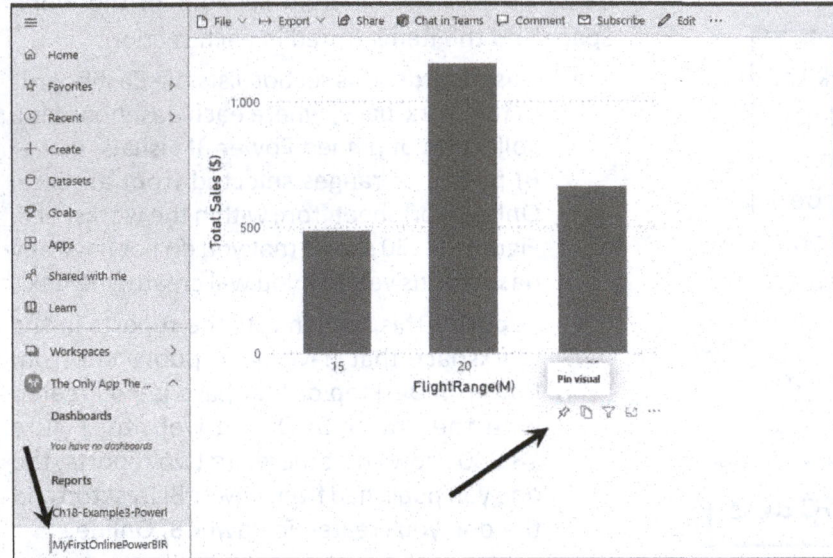

Figure 18.231 *The Pin Visual icon on column chart allows you to pin the chart to a dashboard.*

16. In the Pin to Dashboard dialog box that appears, click the New Dashboard option button and then, in the Dashboard Name textbox, type the dashboard name **MyFirstPowerBIOnlineDashboard** (see Figure 18.232).

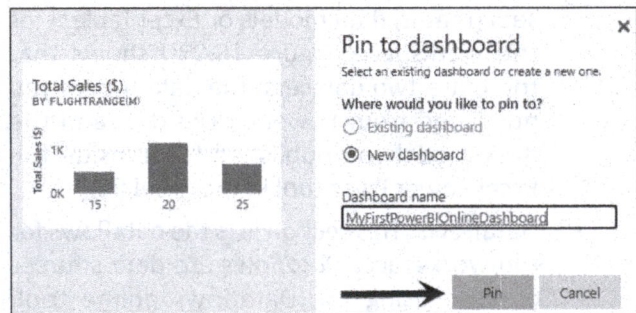

Figure 18.232 *Since there are no dashboards in this workspace, you need to create a new dashboard.*

17. To create the new dashboard, click the Pin button in the Pin to Dashboard dialog box. Then, as shown in Figure 18.233, you can see the newly created dashboard listed in the Dashboards section of the workspace.

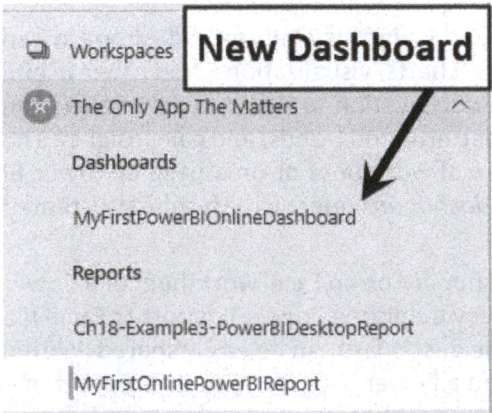

Figure 18.233 *The new dashboard appears in the Dashboards section of the workspace.*

18. In the Reports area of the navigation pane, click on the Ch18-Example3-PowerBIDesktopReport report. Then, as shown in Figure 18.234, in the upper-right corner, click the three dots icon and select the Pin to a Dashboard option.

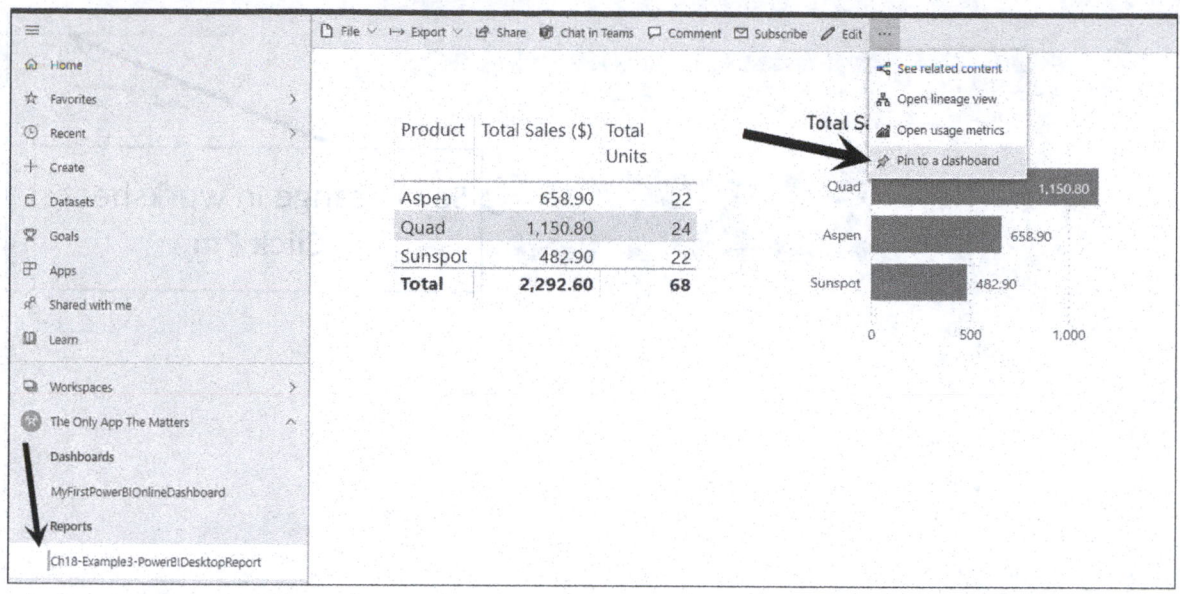

Figure 18.234 *Pin the page from the Ch18-Example3-PowerBIDesktopReport report.*

19. In the Pin to Dashboard dialog box that appears again, click the existing dashboard option button and then, from the Select Existing Dashboard dropdown, select the dashboard named MyFirstPowerBIOnlineDashboard (see Figure 18.235). To pin to an existing dashboard, click the Pin Live button.

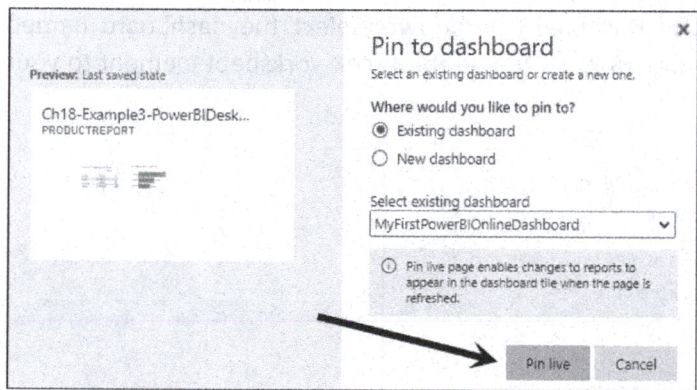

Figure 18.235 *Link the page to the existing dashboard.*

20. In the Workbooks area of the navigation pane, click on the Ch18-Excel365-AdvancedDataAnalysisStartEx63-153 workbook. Then, as shown in Figure 18.236, select the range J8:M12 on the worksheet named Ch18(67-153) and click the Pin button in the upper-right corner of the Excel Online window.

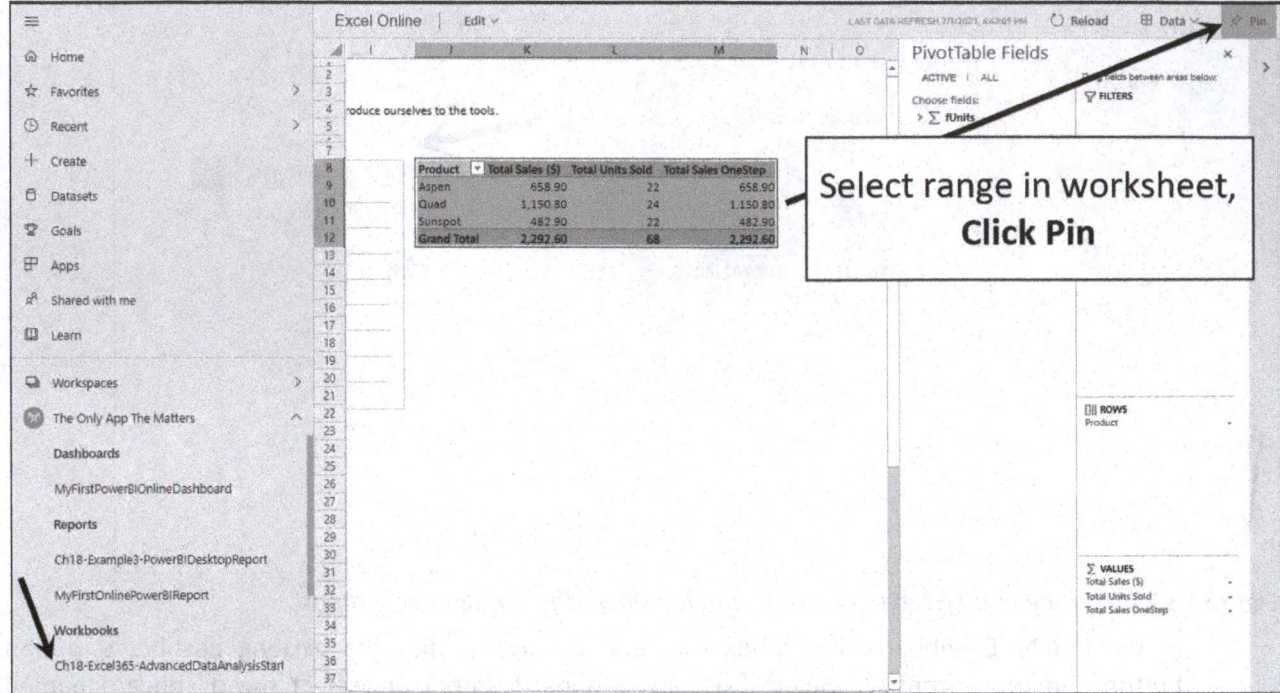

Figure 18.236 *Select the range J8:M12 on the worksheet named Ch18(67-153) and click the Pin button.*

21. In the Pin to Dashboard dialog box that appears again, click the Existing Dashboard option button and then, from the Select Existing Dashboard dropdown, select the dashboard named MyFirstPowerBIOnlineDashboard (see Figure 18.237). To add the Excel worksheet element to your dashboard, click the Pin button.

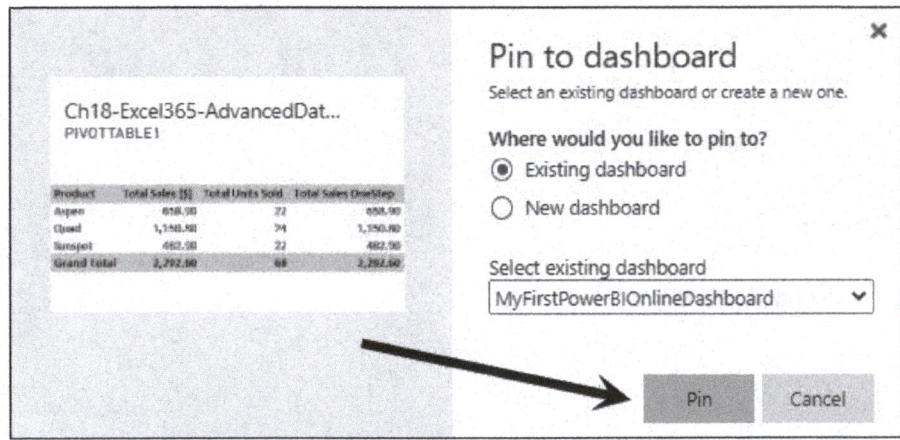

Figure 18.237 *Click Pin to pin the selected worksheet range to the dashboard.*

22. In the Dashboards area of the navigation pane, click on the MyFirstPowerBIOnlineDashboard dashboard link to view the finished dashboard. Figure 18.238 shows the finished dashboard with the three pinned elements. The Share button at the top of the online dashboard makes it easy to share the dashboard. In addition, the dashboard will update when the data changes. To see that the dashboard will update when the source visuals are changed, you can change the pinned Excel worksheet element in the original Excel 365 file.

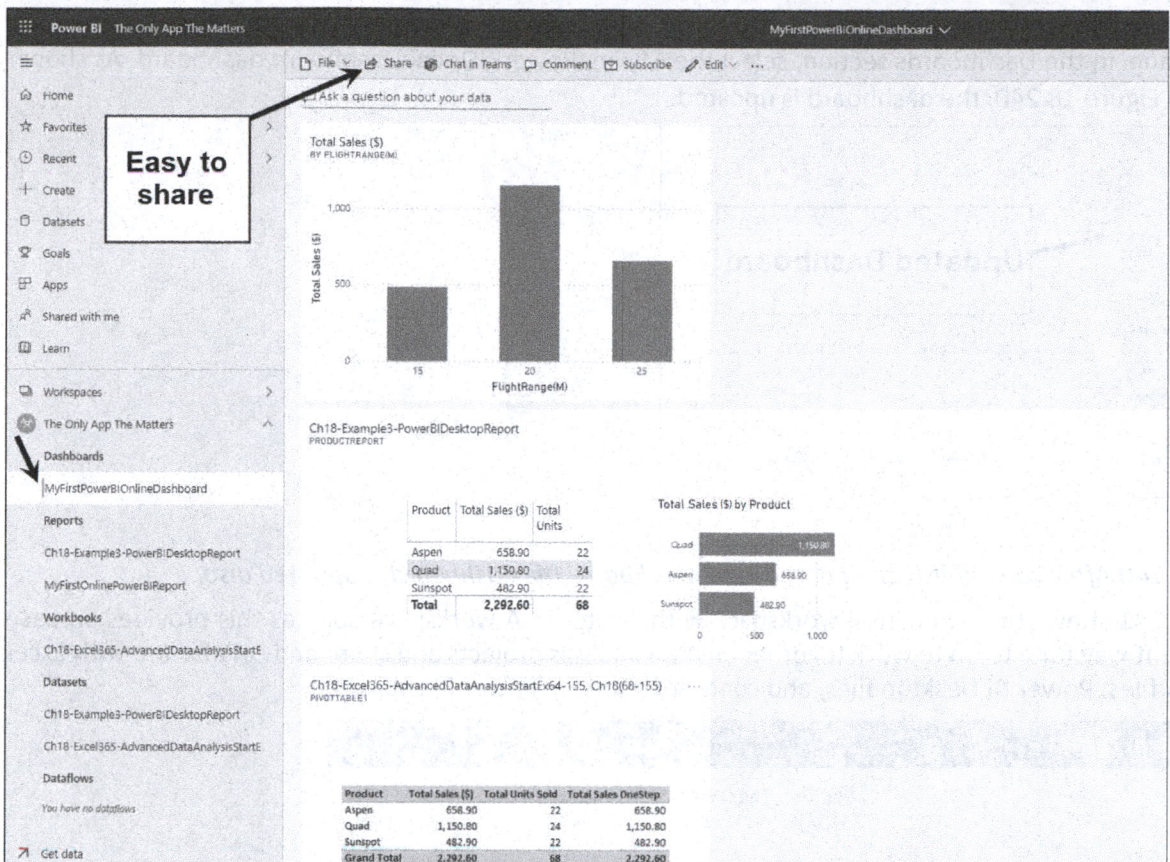

Figure 18.238 *All three pinned elements are now in the easy-to-share MyFirstPowerBIOnlineDashboard dashboard.*

23. To change the pinned Excel worksheet element in the original Excel 365 file, open the workbook named Ch18-Excel365-AdvancedDataAnalysisStartEx63-153. Then, as shown in Figure 18.239, remove the Total Sales OneStep measure from the PivotTable on the worksheet named Ch18(67-153). Save the file and then click the File menu and select Publish to publish the workbook to the workspace The Only App The Matters.

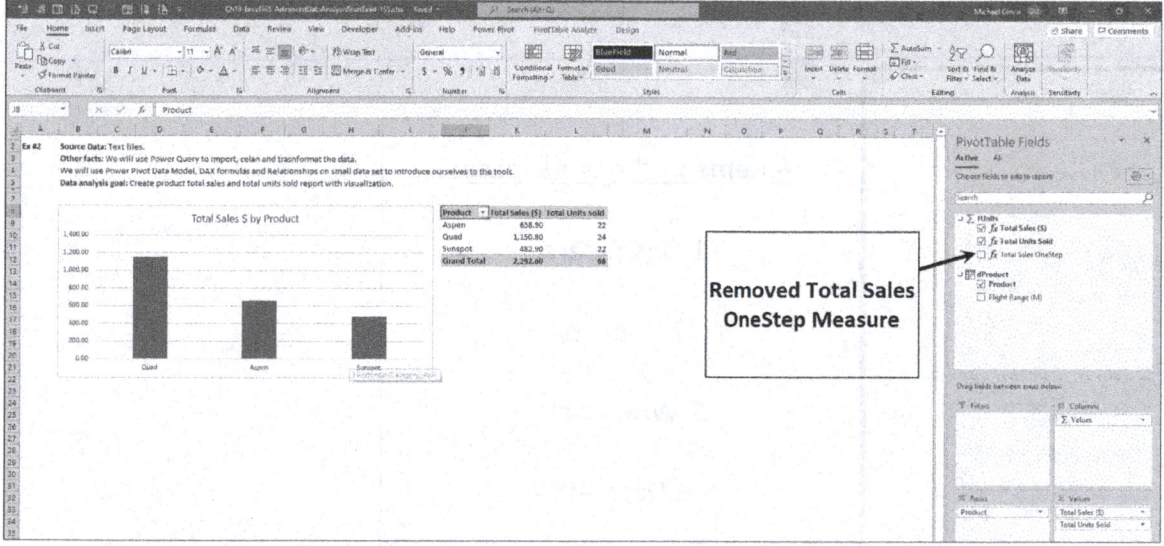

Figure 18.239 *Using Excel 365, edit the original Excel file, save it, and then publish it.*

24. Go back to the Power BI Online website and, in the workspace The Only App The Matters navigation pane, in the Dashboards section, select the MyFirstPowerBIOnlineDashboard dashboard. As shown in Figure 18.240, the dashboard is updated.

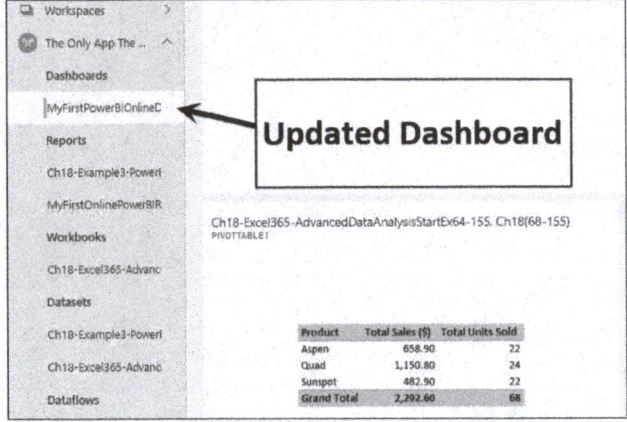

Figure 18.240 *After you publish an updated Excel workbook, the dashboard is updated also.*

Figure 18.241 shows the completed workspace with six items. A workspace such as this provides an easy and efficient way for a team to work together on data analysis projects and share and collaborate with Excel workbook files, Power BI Desktop files, and content created in Power BI Online.

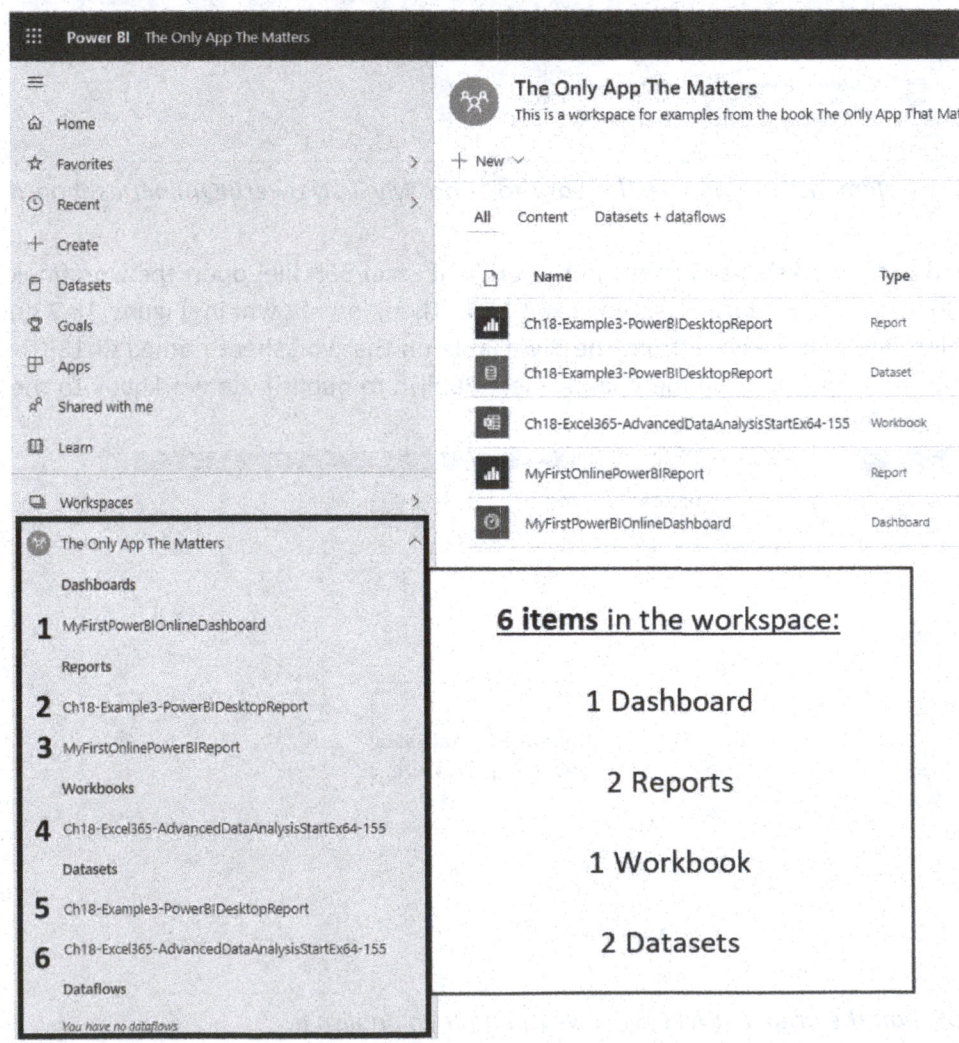

Figure 18.241 *Completed workspace with six items.*

Example 3 Summary

Table 18.5 summarizes this example according to the 10-step data analysis process described earlier in this chapter.

Table 18.5 Example 3 Data Analysis Process Summary

Step	How Step Is Carried Out in This Example
1. Determine the goals of the analysis	Create a data model and interactive reports and visuals that enable easy collaboration and sharing.
2. Determine where the data is	The data is in an Excel file and an Access file.
3. Determine how much data exists	There is a small amount of data.
4. Determine which tool or tools to use	Use Power BI Desktop and Power BI Online.
5. Import the data	Use Power BI Desktop Power Query.
6. Clean and transform the data	Use Power BI Desktop Power Query.
7. Load the data	Load the data to the Power BI Desktop Data Model.
8. Create a data model	Use Power Query–generated tables, Data Model relationships, and DAX formulas.
9. Create useful information	Use Power BI visuals, pages, and dashboards. Publish to Power BI Online.
10. Update the data model based on new data	Change the content in the Excel file and republish it.

Key Concepts in Chapter 18

- A **variable** is a value that can change. Examples include qualitative variables (non-numeric), quantitative variables (numeric), Booleans, lists, fields, tables, and files.

- **Raw data**, or just **data**, consists of qualitative, quantitative, Boolean, or other values collected for one or more variables and kept together for reference or analysis.

- A **field** is a column used to collect data for a variable that always has a descriptive name called a **field name**, at the top of the column.

- Data that is stored properly—usually in table format—is called a **proper dataset**. In a proper dataset, field names are always in the first row, and records of related data are in subsequent rows.

- You can convert a table to an **Excel Table** object to create a dynamic table object that will automatically expand when new rows or columns are added. You must convert tables to Excel Tables before you can import them into tools such as Power Query and Power Pivot and work with them.

- A **record** is a row of related data within a table, such as the date, product ID, units sold, or sales amount for a sales transaction within a sales transaction table.

- A **fact table** contains data that you want to summarize or measure (such as sales amounts or units sold).

- A **dimension table** contains a field with a unique list of entities (such as product IDs) with attributes in subsequent fields for conditional calculations (such as a product name) or lookup items (such as a product price). A field with the unique list of entities is called a **primary key** and is used to ensure that there are no duplicate records in the dimension table. When a primary key from a dimension table is used in a fact table, it is called a **foreign key**.

- **Relationships** are used to allow data modeling and reporting to occur primarily between a fact table with a foreign key and a dimension table with a primary key. Relationships can be created between other related tables as well. There are three common types of relationships: e one-to-many, many-to-many, and one-to-one relationships.

- A **data type** is a specific type of data that is allowed in a field, such as a decimal number, a whole number, a date, a text value, a list value, or a binary value. Once you define a single data type for a field, only that specified data type is allowed to be entered into the field. A data type is a safeguard you create for a field that helps to ensure data consistency and accuracy for your reports, visualizations, and other useful information that you create. Power Query is the best tool to use to set data types on fields in tables.

- **Text files** are a common vehicle to transfer tables of data from one system to another system. A **delimiter** is a character used to separate the field names and the cells of data in a text file and in other data analysis situations. A delimiter signals to a computer system where the data should be split into sperate fields, or columns.

- **Databases** are programs specifically designed to store raw data. Databases use tables to store raw data.

- A **query** is a command you create that does something to data, such as "combine the two tables into one table," "change the data type from text to date," or "access the database and load the fact table to the Data Model." Basically, a query is a question that you ask of raw data. There are many tools you can use to create queries in the Excel and Power BI Desktop apps, but Power Query is usually the most comprehensive and efficient tool for building queries.

- **Importing data** involves accessing external data and then loading it into either Excel or Power BI Desktop.

- **Cleaning data** involves fixing unusable raw data before loading it to the final location. For example, you might split data from a single field into two fields. You clean data so that it can be used to perform data analysis.

- **Transforming data** involves changing the structure of data so that it can more easily be used for data analysis. For example, you might convert a text file to a proper dataset that can then be used in the data analysis process.

- The **grain**, or **granularity**, of a table is the size of the aggregation for each number in each row, such as a sales amount that can be calculated with a grain at the transaction, day, month, or year level. As you move from a transaction grain to a year grain, the grain gets larger. DAX formulas are particularly good at making calculations at different grains.

- A **summary report** is an account of a particular subject or topic that has been carefully prepared and presented and contains detailed numbers with labels. The numbers are almost always metrics that help gauge performance or help make some decision.

- With a **Power BI Online dashboard**, within a given workspace you have the freedom to pin an entire page from a Power BI report, just an element of a Power BI page, or a section from a published Excel worksheet. A dashboard enables you to collect the most relevant components for the information that you want to deliver and present them all in one place.

- **Data modeling** involves all the steps necessary to get and transform data from an **original source** (such as a database, a text file, or data in a worksheet) into a source data structure (such as a single table, two or more tables, or a more complex structure) that can be used to create the useful information. Data modeling can be performed with Excel worksheet formulas, the Power Query tool, DAX formulas and relationships in the Data Model, and other tools. The **final source data** used to create useful information is called the **data model**. The term that Microsoft uses in Excel Power Pivot and Power BI Desktop to describe the location where you store the created data models is the **Data Model**. A wide variety of data models can be created, such as flat table data models, star schema data models, and snowflake data models. A **good data model** contains the data needed for the end solution, is easy for a decision maker to use, allows formulas to calculate quickly, has reports and visualizations that are easy to update when new data is available, and is easy to update when the situation changes.

- **Power Query** is a tool that helps users get and transform data. It exists in the Excel app and the Power BI Desktop app and is used to connect to data sources and prepare data so that it can be used with data analysis tools. It is the tool to use when you need to connect to an original data source, bring the data into the Power Query Editor window, clean and transform the data, and load the data. When you create a query in the Power Query Editor, the steps are saved so that you can easily edit the steps later and rerun them when you get new data.

- The language Power Query uses to write a query is called **M code**. It is a case-sensitive, function-based formula language that has more than 700 functions. Power Query allows a query creator to use a user interface, and it transforms the query into M code; you can also manually write code. An **expression** is M code that results in a value, such as a number, a list, or a query step. The **let expression** is designed to combine all query steps to deliver a final value.

- The **Power Pivot** tool helps you deal with big datasets and complex calculations involving multiple tables. Power Pivot is especially useful when you have a dataset with 50,000 rows of data or more and you want to create summary PivotTable reports with conditional calculations; it is also useful when you want to create reports and visualizations based on multiple tables. The Power Pivot tool consists of three components and together are considered the Data Model: the **in-RAM columnar database**, relationships, and the DAX modeling language.

- **Power BI Desktop** is a tool that helps you perform business analytics and create interactive visualizations to build reports and dashboards.

- **Power BI Online** is used to share reports, dashboards, and datasets. To use it, you must have a Power BI Pro or higher license.

Practice Problems for Chapter 18

Practice Problem 1

In your Excel file for this chapter (Ch18-Excel365-AdvancedDataAnalysisPracticeProblemsStart.xlsx), go to the worksheet named PPCh18(1) and create the solution for this practice problem. Figure 18.242 shows the goals that are listed on that worksheet.

In this practice problem, because you are given a small dataset and have simple summary calculations to make, an efficient solution can be constructed using worksheet formulas, a standard PivotTable, and an Excel chart. (In this practice problem, because there are multiple tables, you might also choose to use the Power Pivot Data Model. Practice Problem 2 will give you an opportunity to do that.)

	A	B	C	D	E F G H	I	J	K	L
2	Goals:	Source Data: Excel Tables on this worksheet.							
3		Data analysis goal:	Create a total sales by customer and product cross tabulated report						
4			and a visualization that emphasizes the differences between customer totals.						
5		Tools to use: Worksheet formulas, Standard PivotTable, Excel Chart.							
6	Hints:	Create data analysis results on this sheet.							
8		**Fact Table = fUnits**				**Dimension Table = dProducts**			
10		ProductID	CustomerID	UnitsSold		ProductID	Product	FlightRange(M)	RetailPrice
11		1503-YI	2185	94		1503-YI	Yanaki	35	27.95
12		6816-BN	2255	22		6816-BN	Bellen	25	26.95
13		6816-BN	2045	67		9720-CA	Carlota	20	31.95
14		3414-AN	2010	21		3414-AN	Aspen	40	37.95
15		1503-YI	2080	13					
16		6816-BN	2150	16					
17		3414-AN	2220	123		**Dimension Table = dCustomer**			
18		6816-BN	2185	64					
19		6816-BN	2080	71		CustomerID	CustomerName	Email	Contact
20		6816-BN	2220	120		2010	Kite Flight	han@kiteflight.com	Han
21		6816-BN	2255	12		2045	Fred Myer	tim@fredmyer.com	Tim
22		3414-AN	2080	69		2080	Great Winds	sonia@greatwinds.com	Sonia
23		9720-CA	2220	25		2115	Flying Toys	chantel@flyingtoys.com	Chantel
24		6816-BN	2220	24		2150	Boomerang Man	rich@boomerangman.com	Rich
25		6816-BN	2045	49		2185	Bailey Boomerangs	sioux@baileyboomerangs.com	Sioux
26		9720-CA	2220	32		2220	Top Ten Toys	miki@toptentoys.com	Miki
27		3414-AN	2010	52		2255	Flying High	gigi@flyinghigh.com	Gigi
28		1503-YI	2220	53					
29		1503-YI	2045	53					
136		9720-CA	2010	28					
137									
138									

| PPCh18(1) | PPCh18(2) | PPCh18(3) | PPCh18(4) | PPCh18(5) | + |

Figure 18.242 *On the worksheet named PPCh18(1), use worksheet formulas and a standard PivotTable to solve this problem.*

When you are done with this problem, you can check your work against the answer in the Excel workbook Ch18-Excel365-AdvancedDataAnalysisPracticeProblemsFinished.xlsx. In addition, Figure 18.243 shows one possible solution to this problem.

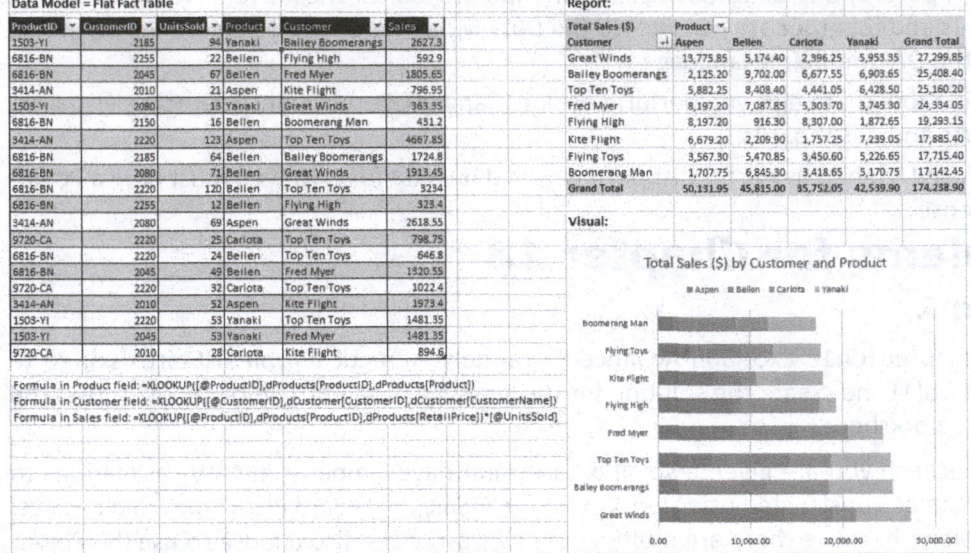

Figure 18.243 *Here is a possible solution for Practice Problem 1.*

Practice Problem 2

In your Excel file for this chapter (Ch18-Excel365-AdvancedDataAnalysisPracticeProblemsStart.xlsx), go to the worksheet named PPCh18(2) and create the solution for this practice problem. Figure 18.244 shows the goals that are listed on that worksheet.

In this project, because you are given multiple related tables that you need to use to create your solution, an efficient solution could be constructed using Power Query, the Power Pivot Data Model, and an Excel chart. (In this practice problem, because there are multiple tables, you might also choose to use the Data Model and visualizations in Power BI Desktop. Practice Problem 3 will give you an opportunity to do that.)

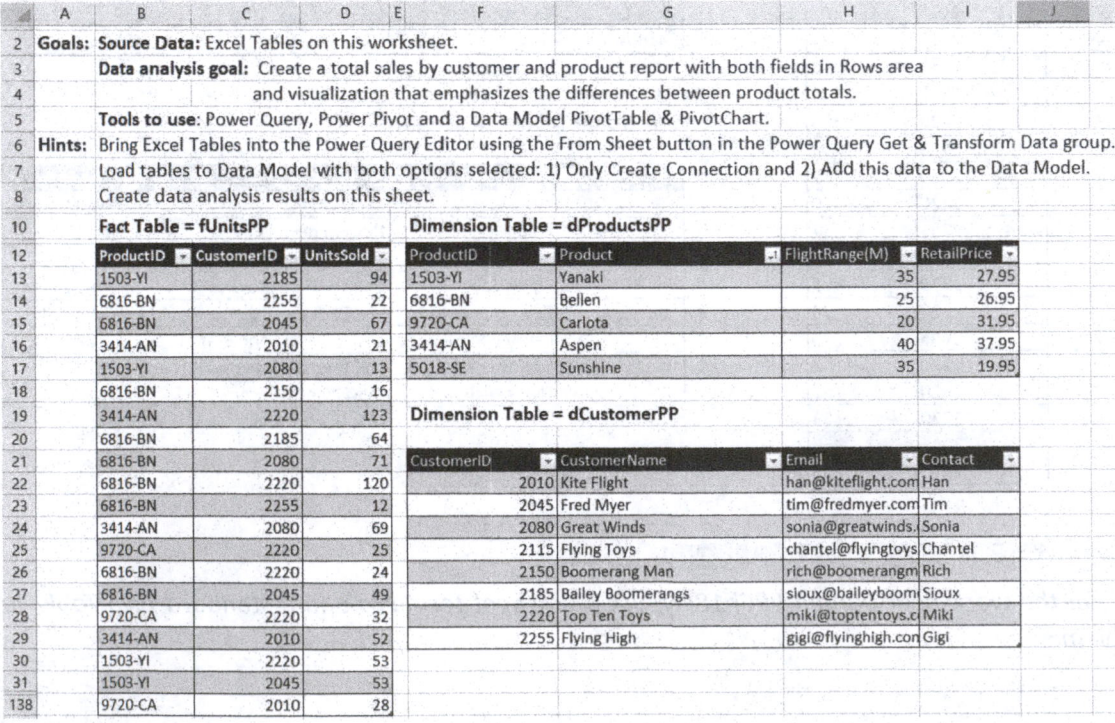

Figure 18.244 On the worksheet named PPCh18(2), use Power Query and Power Pivot to solve this problem.

Figure 18.245 shows the button that you should use to import the Excel Tables from the worksheet into the Power Query Editor.

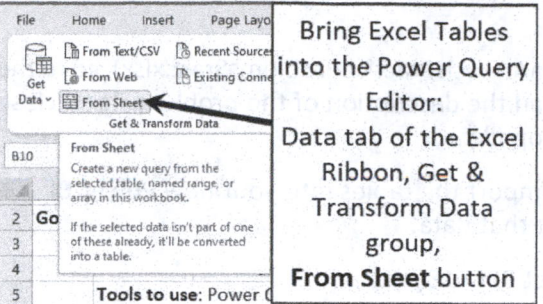

Figure 18.245 *The From Sheet button allows you to bring Excel Table data into the Power Query Editor.*

Figure 18.246 reminds you about the correct settings in the Import Data dialog box when you are loading data to the Power Pivot Data Model.

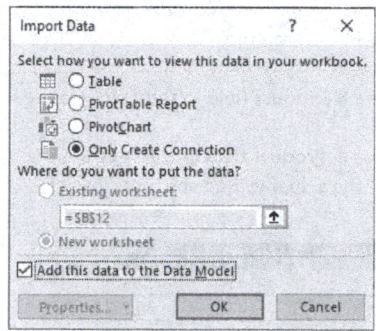

Figure 18.246 *Select the Only Create Connection option button and the Add This Data to the Data Model checkbox.*

Figure 18.247 shows what the finished data model could look like.

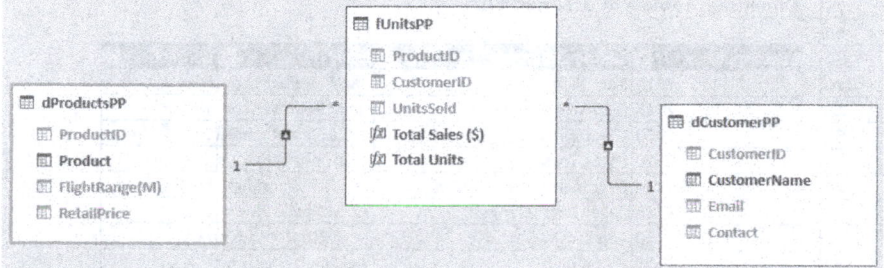

Figure 18.247 *The Power Pivot data model might look like this.*

When you are done with this problem, you can check your work against the answer in the Excel workbook Ch18-Excel365-AdvancedDataAnalysisPracticeProblemsFinished.xlsx. In addition, Figure 18.248 shows one possible solution to this problem.

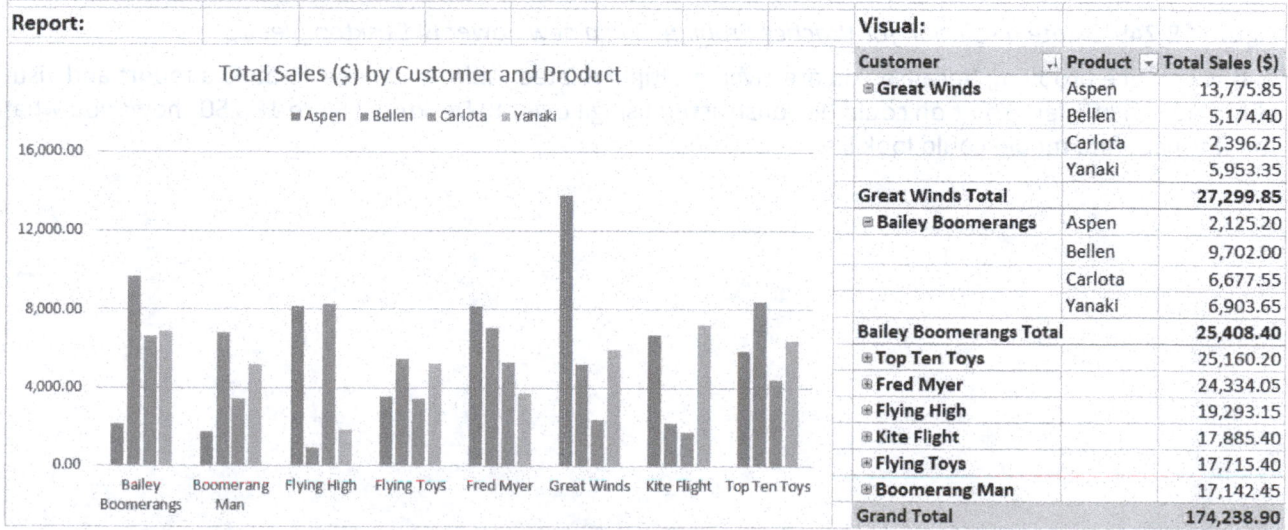

Customer	Product	Total Sales ($)
⊟ Great Winds	Aspen	13,775.85
	Bellen	5,174.40
	Carlota	2,396.25
	Yanaki	5,953.35
Great Winds Total		**27,299.85**
⊟ Bailey Boomerangs	Aspen	2,125.20
	Bellen	9,702.00
	Carlota	6,677.55
	Yanaki	6,903.65
Bailey Boomerangs Total		**25,408.40**
⊞ Top Ten Toys		25,160.20
⊞ Fred Myer		24,334.05
⊞ Flying High		19,293.15
⊞ Kite Flight		17,885.40
⊞ Flying Toys		17,715.40
⊞ Boomerang Man		17,142.45
Grand Total		**174,238.90**

Figure 18.248 *Here is a possible solution for Practice Problem 2.*

Practice Problem 3

In your Excel file for this chapter (Ch18-Excel365-AdvancedDataAnalysisPracticeProblemsStart.xlsx), go to the worksheet named PPCh18(3) and look at the datasets and read the description of the problem. Then close the Excel file and create the solution in a new Power BI Desktop file.

> **Note:** If you do not close the Excel file before trying to import the tables into your new Power BI Desktop file, you may not be able to successfully import that data.

Figure 18.249 shows the goals that are listed on the worksheet PPCh18(3).

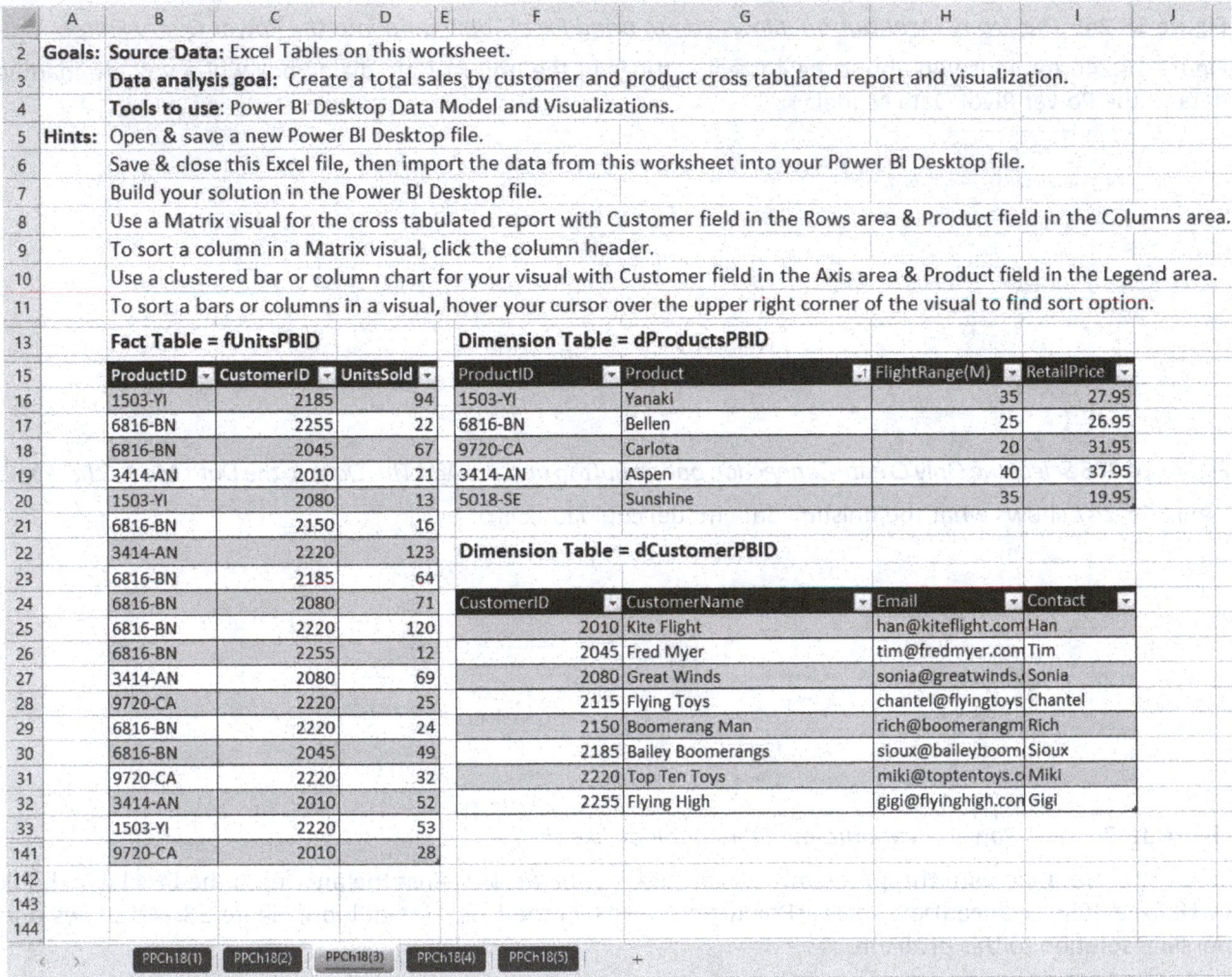

Figure 18.249 *Create a solution for Practice Problem 3 in a new Power BI Desktop file.*

In this practice problem, because you are given multiple related tables and need to build a report and visualizations, an efficient solution could be constructed using Power BI Desktop. Figure 18.250 shows you what the finished data model could look like.

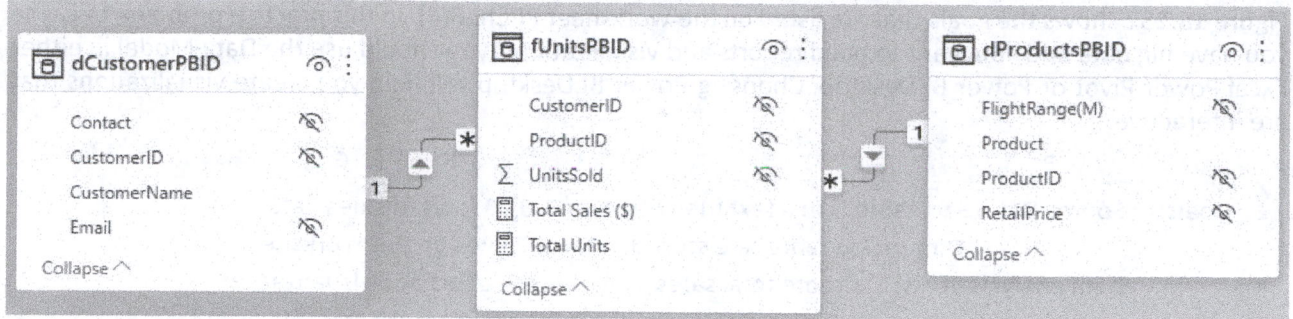

Figure 18.250 *The Power BI Desktop data model might look like this.*

When you are done with this problem, you can check your work against the answer in the Power BI Desktop file Ch18-PP03-Solution.pbix. In addition, Figure 18.251 shows one possible solution to this problem.

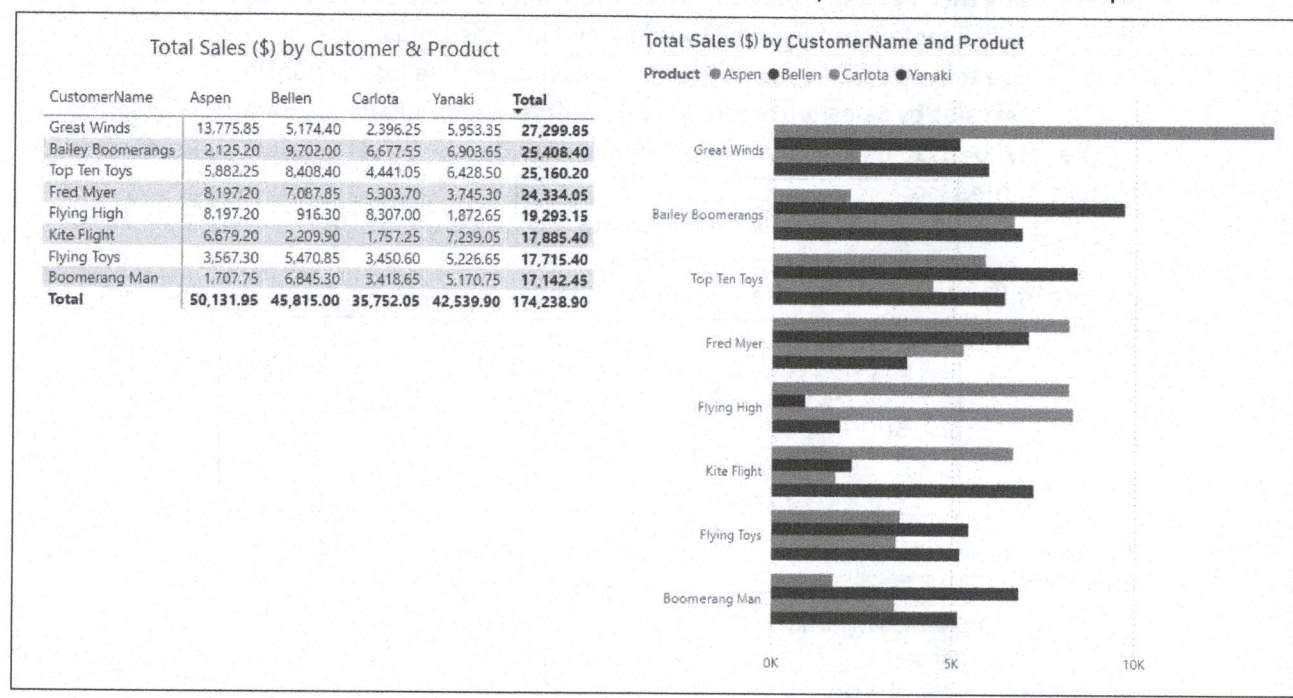

Figure 18.251 *Here is a possible solution for Practice Problem 3.*

Practice Problem 4

In your Excel file for this chapter (Ch18-Excel365-AdvancedDataAnalysisPracticeProblemsStart.xlsx), go to the worksheet named PPCh18(4) and look at the datasets and read the description of the problem. Then close the Excel file and create the solution in a new Power BI Desktop file.

> **Note:** If you do not close the Excel file before trying to import the tables into your new Power BI Desktop file, you may not be able to successfully import the data.

Figure 18.252 shows the goals that are listed on the worksheet PPCh18(4). In this practice problem, because you have big data and you want to build reports and visualizations, you should use the Data Model in either Excel Power Pivot or Power BI Desktop. Choosing Power BI Desktop will help you create visualizations that are interactive.

	A	B	C	D	E	F	G	H	I	J
2	Goals:	Source Data: Fact table is in a text file with over 700,00 rows of sales data.								
3		Dimension tables are stored in Excel Tables on this worksheet.								
4		Data analysis goals: 1) Create total sales by SalesRep report and visualization.								
5		2) Create total UnitsSold by Product report and visualization.								
6		Tools to use: Power BI Desktop Power Query, Data Model and Visualizations.								
7	Hints:	Open & save a new Power BI Desktop file.								
8		After closing this file, import the two dimension tables from this sheet into the Data Model.								
9		Import the fact table text file (as pictured below) into the Data Model.								
10		For the Page that you create inside Power BI Desktop, set the Interactions to:								
11		The total sales by SalesRep report should not filter the total sales by SalesRep visual.								
12		The total UnitsSold by Product report should not filter the total UnitsSold by Product visual.								
13		Picture of file:								
14				Ch18-PP04TextSalesData.txt						
15										
16		Picture of first few rows in table with a Tab Delimiter:								
17										
18			ProductID → SalesRepID→UnitsSold → Sales¶							
19			1400→ 9000→8 → 211.3¶							
20			500 → 9000→7 → 138.58¶							
21			1400→18000→47 → 788.19¶							
22			300 → 18000→5 → 127.34¶							
23										
24		Dimension Table = dSalesRepPP04				Dimension Table = dProductsPP04				
26		SalesRepID	SalesRep			ProductID	Product			
27		1500	Brandon Menendez			100	Aspen			
28		3000	Calista Li			200	Beaut			
29		4500	Chantel Awiti			300	Bellen			
30		6000	Christeen Bourgeois			400	Carlota			
31		7500	Elyse Sotelo			500	Eagle			
32		9000	Ewa Gamble			600	Elevate			
33		10500	Florentina Nugent			700	FastFly			
34		12000	Gigi Gabazi			800	Flattop			
35		13500	Huong Triplett			900	Kangaroo			
36		15000	Janita Romano			1000	Quad			
37		16500	Joey Stanfield			1100	Sunset			
38		18000	Karina Sterling			1200	Sunshine			
39		19500	Kris Turpin			1300	Vrang			
40		21000	Necole Cisneros			1400	Yanaki			
41		22500	Olene Toliver							
42		24000	Raina Lentz							
43		25500	Raymonde Painter							
44		27000	Sherrill Herron							
45		28500	Shizue Sorensen							
46		30000	Sioux Radcoolinator							
47		31500	Tyrone Smithe							
48		33000	Wilfredo Valadez							

Figure 18.252 *Create the solution for Practice Problem 4 in a new Power BI Desktop file.*

Figure 18.253 shows what the finished data model could look like.

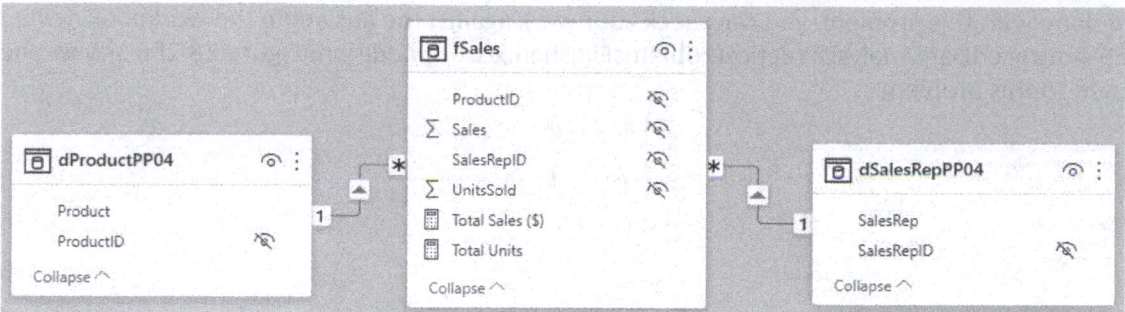

Figure 18.253 *The Power BI Desktop data model might look like this.*

When you are done, you can check your work against the answer in the Power BI Desktop file Ch18-PP04-Solution.pbix. In addition, Figure 18.254 shows one possible solution to this problem.

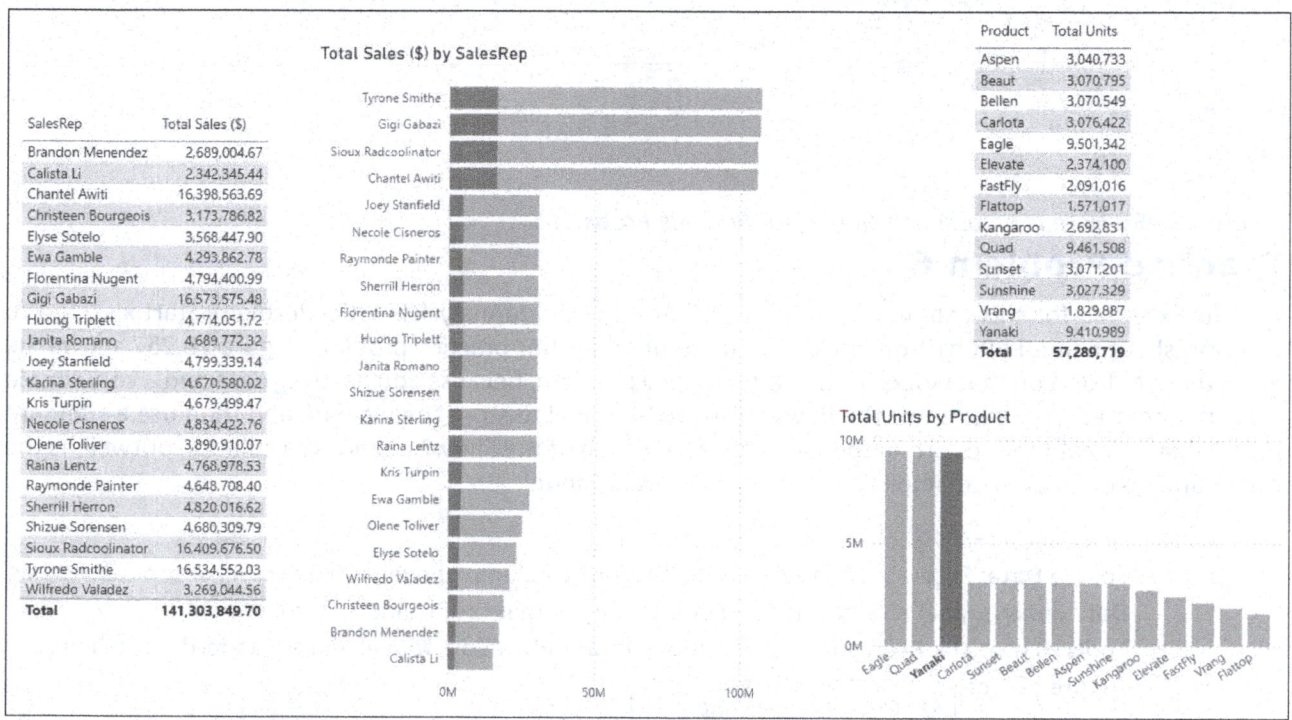

Figure 18.254 *Here is a possible solution for Practice Problem 4.*

Practice Problem 5

In your Excel file for this chapter (Ch18-Excel365-AdvancedDataAnalysisPracticeProblemsStart.xlsx), go to the worksheet named PPCh18(5) and complete Practice Problem 4 again, but this time use Power Query, Power Pivot, and Excel charts in the Excel app. It is good practice to create data analysis solutions using different tools. After using both Excel and Power BI Desktop, you can better decide which you prefer. You can place the reports and visuals on the worksheet named PPCh18(5).

Figure 18.255 shows what the finished data model could look like. Notice that because you already created one star schema data model, there are two start schema data models in the same Design View section on the Power Pivot window.

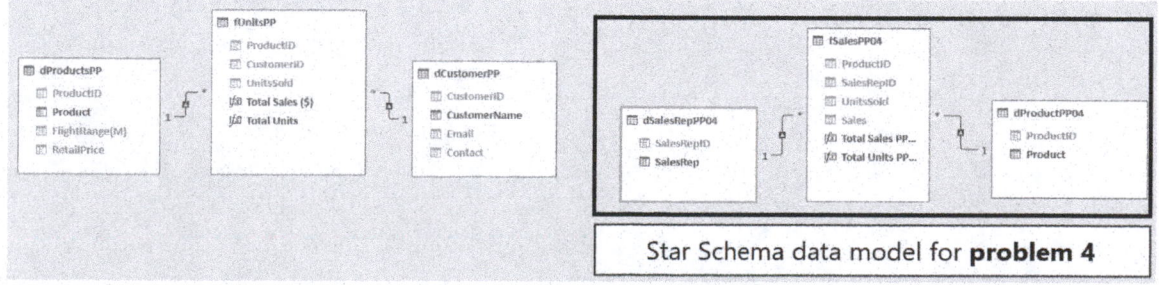

Figure 18.255 *The Power Pivot data model might look like this.*

When you are done with this problem, you can check your work against the answer in the workbook named Ch18-Excel365-AdvancedDataAnalysisPracticeProblemsFinished.xlsx. In addition, Figure 18.256 shows one possible solution to this problem.

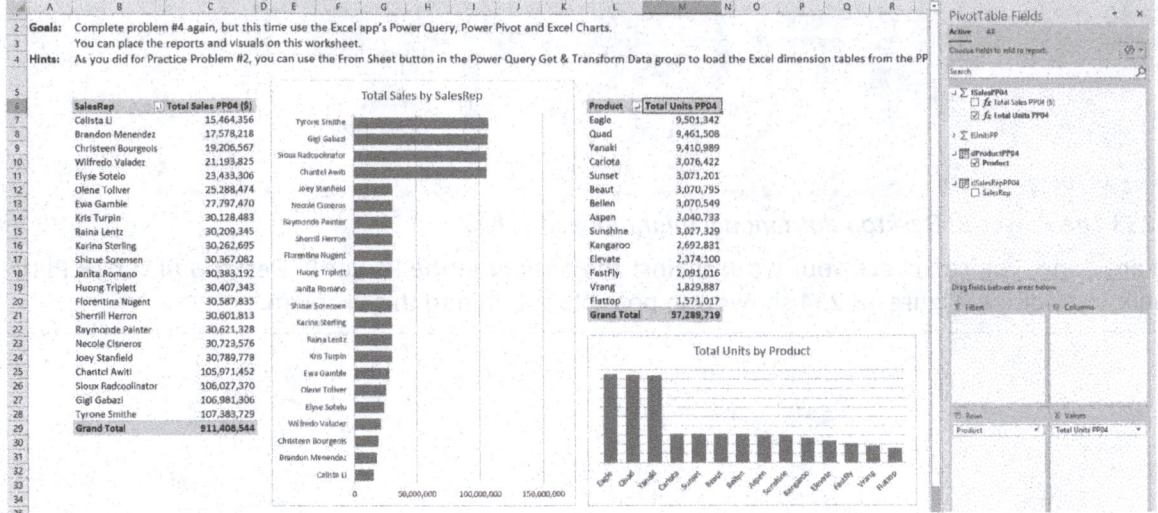

Figure 18.256 *Here is a possible solution for Practice Problem 5.*

Practice Problem 6

In your Excel file for this chapter (Ch18-Excel365-AdvancedDataAnalysisPracticeProblemsStart.xlsx), go to the worksheet named PPCh18(6) and create the solution for this practice problem. Figure 18.257 shows the goals that are listed on that worksheet. In this practice problem, because you have big data and a very simple report to create, it is okay to use the Power Pivot Data Model to store the big data and then use a standard PivotTable to create the report. In this case, the ease of use of the Show Values As calculation outweighs the disadvantage of creating an implicit measure in the Data Model.

	A	B	C	D	E	F	G	H	I	J	K	L
2	**Goals:**	**Source Data:** Fact table is in a text file with a single column of over 600,000 rows of product names.										
3		**Data analysis goal:** Create a frequency distribution that counts and % of total.										
4		**Tools to use**: The Excel app's Power Query, Power Pivot Data Model and a Standard PivotTable.										
5		Picture of file:										
6		Ch18-PP05TextProductData.csv										
7	**Hints:**	Create data analysis results on this sheet.										
8		You can load data to Data Model (because you have a lot of data), then:										
9		create a Data Model PivotTable based on that loaded data, and										
10		use Implicit Measures to calculate Count and % of Grand Total.										

Figure 18.257 *On the worksheet named PPCh18(6), create a solution by mixing standard and power data analysis tools.*

When you are done with this problem, you can check your work against the answer in the Excel workbook Ch18-Excel365-AdvancedDataAnalysisPracticeProblemsFinished.xlsx. In addition, Figure 18.258 shows one possible solution to this problem.

Product	Frequency	% Frequency
Aspen	40,116	5.81%
Beaut	35,494	5.14%
Bellen	40,351	5.84%
Carlota	40,304	5.84%
Eagle	116,290	16.84%
Elevate	27,395	3.97%
Flattop	23,848	3.45%
Kangaroo	31,117	4.51%
LongRang	20,774	3.01%
Quad	116,660	16.90%
Sunset	40,409	5.85%
Sunshine	40,552	5.87%
Yanaki	117,129	16.96%
Grand Total	**690,439**	**100.00%**

Figure 18.258 *Here is a possible solution for Practice Problem 6.*

Practice Problem 7

In your Excel file for this chapter (Ch18-Excel365-AdvancedDataAnalysisPracticeProblemsStart.xlsx), go to the worksheet named PPCh18(7) and answer the conceptual questions listed below.

In your own words, see if you can answer these conceptual questions:

1. Define *data analysis* and *business intelligence*.
2. When should you use worksheet formulas to create a data analysis solution?
3. When should you use a standard PivotTable to create a data analysis solution?
4. When should you use Power Pivot to create a data analysis solution?
5. When should you use Power BI Desktop to create a data analysis solution?
6. What does Power Query do?
7. What are the advantages of having a Power BI Pro license?
8. Which tool uses the M code functional language, and which tools use the DAX functional language?
9. How do relationships help in a data model?
10. What is the difference between an explicit measure and an implicit measure?
11. What is a dashboard?

When you are done, you can check your work against the answer in the Excel workbook Ch18-Excel365-AdvancedDataAnalysisPracticeProblemsFinished.xlsx.

Chapter 19: Data Analysis Examples: Big Data and Complex Data Analysis

In Chapters 17 and 18, you learned about the fundamentals of data analysis and how to use a number of Microsoft tools—some of them truly amazing—for data analysis. In this chapter, you will see examples of how to use Power Query, M code, Power Pivot, Power BI Desktop, and DAX to work with larger datasets and to solve more complex data analysis problems.

This chapter presents five data analysis projects:

Project 1: Converting 12 CSV Files with 35,000 Rows of Data into a Report with Four Key Metrics

- **Main skill you will learn:** How to use Power Query to prepare data for a standard PivotTable report
- **Other key skills you will learn:**
  - How to use the Power Query From Folder feature to import multiple text files from a folder
  - How to use the Combine Files option to combine all text file tables into a single proper dataset
  - How to use the Locale feature to set date data types to match regional settings
  - How to create custom columns in the Power Query Editor to avoid worksheet formulas
  - How to load data directly to the PivotTable cache to remove redundant tables and help reduce file size and the number of refresh clicks

Project 2: Importing SQL Big Data, Building DAX Formulas, and Creating an Interactive Power BI Desktop Report

- **Main skill you will learn:** How to work with big data and use DAX formulas
- **Other key skills you will learn:**
  - How to use Power Query to import 7 million rows of data from an online SQL Server database into the Data Model columnar database
  - How to use many DAX functions, such as CALENDAR, FORMAT, GENERATE, COUNTROWS, CAULCULATE, AVERAGEX, DISTINCTCOUNT, DIVIDE, VALUES, ALL, ALLSELECTED, DATESINPERIOD, and SAMEPERIODLASTYEAR
  - How to build a DAX date dimension table to help make date-related calculations at the correct grain and to allow the use of DAX time intelligence functions
  - How to build multiple DAX calculated columns and DAX measures
  - How to use the CALCULATE function to change the filter context and invoke context transition
  - How to create DAX formulas for various averages, such as average monthly sales and moving average
  - How to use context transition and pre-aggregate at different grains
  - How to use Power BI visualizations to build interactive reports and visualizations that can be filtered

Project 3: Combining Data from Multiple Excel Files and Creating a Summary Report—All with Power Query!

- **Main skill you will learn:** How to use the Excel.Workbook M code function to extract data from Excel files
- **Other key skills you will learn:**
  - How to use the From Folder feature to import multiple Excel files
  - How to use various Power Query features to clean and transform data
  - How to use Excel.Workbook to extract all objects from within Excel files
  - How to use the Table Expand feature to combine tables
  - How to use the Group By feature to make a summary report

Project 4: Combining All Excel Table Data in the Current Workbook File into a Standard PivotTable Report

- **Main skill you will learn:** How to use the Excel.CurrentWorkbook M code function to extract Excel Tables from within the current Excel file

- **Other key skills you will learn:**
  - How to use Excel Power Query's M code function Excel.CurrentWorkbook to import all Excel Tables from within the current workbook into the Power Query Editor
  - How to expand columns to combine tables
  - How to use the Power Query Merge feature to look up values
  - How to use the Load To option to load data directly to the PivotTable cache and avoid duplicate tables in the worksheet as well as the recursion problem

Project 5: Using Power Query M Code to Fix Inconsistent Datasets from Multiple Excel Files So They Can Be Combined

- **Main skill you will learn:** How to write advanced M code to convert multiple inconsistent datasets into a single proper dataset and perform various types of lookups
- **Other key skills you will learn:**
  - How to import Excel files by using the From SharePoint Folder option and the Excel.Workbook function
  - How to create an M code custom column formula to remove blank columns and fix inconsistent field names so that tables can be combined
  - How to create an M code custom column approximate match lookup formula by using the Table. Buffer function and a custom function with defined variables
  - How to convert text ISO dates to serial number dates with the date data type
  - How an M code two-way lookup formula works

Project 1: Converting 12 CSV Files with 35,000 Rows of Data into a Report with Four Key Metrics

For this project, you need to use 12 CSV files—that is, comma-separated values files, which use a comma delimiter—each containing a table of sales data for a different month. Each table has three fields: Date, Units, and Price. There are about 35,000 rows of data total. You need to create a monthly sales report that shows four metrics: monthly totals, monthly change, monthly percentage change, and percentage of total. The catch is that you start with only 8 CSV files, and you need to build a solution that is updatable. Each month, when you get a new CSV files, you need to be able to simply click a refresh button to update the project.

The 10-Step Data Analysis Process for Project 1

Before you begin creating this project, you need to consider the 10 steps in the data analysis process as they relate to this project. Table 19.1 provides a summary of these 10 steps and how you will carry them out for this project.

Table 19.1 Project 1 Data Analysis Process Summary

Step	How Step Is Carried Out in This Example
1. Determine the goals of the analysis	The goal is to use the CSV file data to create an updatable report with the four metrics: monthly totals, monthly change, monthly percentage change, and percentage of total.
2. Determine where the data is	The data is in the 12 monthly CSV text files.
3. Determine how much data exists	There are about 35,000 rows of data. This is small data.

4. Determine which tool or tools to use	Excel Power Query will be the perfect tool to use to combine the CSV files into a single table because:
	The From Folder feature will make it easy to add new files to the project as they are available each month. You will be able to simply click a refresh button to update the data analysis results.
	There is not a lot of data, so a standard PivotTable will be easy to use. To group monthly data together, you will use the Group By feature, and to make the other three calculations, you will use the Show Values As feature.
	Using Power Query, you can load the data directly to the PivotTable cache rather than to the worksheet. This way, you do not need to store the data in both the worksheet and the PivotTable cache.
	Since you will load the data directly to the PivotTable cache, you will need to multiply price by units in the Power Query Editor. The Add Column Multiply feature makes this task easy.
5. Import the data	You will use Power Query.
6. Clean and transform the data	You will use Power Query.
7. Load the data	You will use Power Query to load the data to the PivotTable cache.
8. Create a data model	You will use the Power Query Editor to create the single flat table data model.
9. Create useful information	You will use a standard PivotTable to create a four-column report.
10. Update the data model based on new data	You will get new data. The From Folder feature allows you to easily update your report.

You may at some point need to go back and change something in your report, and the Power Query process makes it easy to change and update your report.

Importing the Data for Project 1

You need to import a number of data files for this project. Figure 19.1 shows the Start folder for this project. This folder contains many different files, but you need to import only the CSV files. Power Query makes it easy to import all the files from the folder and then filter by the file extension CSV to import only the CSV files. However, because Power Query is case-sensitive, you have to make sure that the CSV extensions are all in lowercase letters. Power Query makes this step easy, too, giving you a one-click option to make everything in a column lowercase.

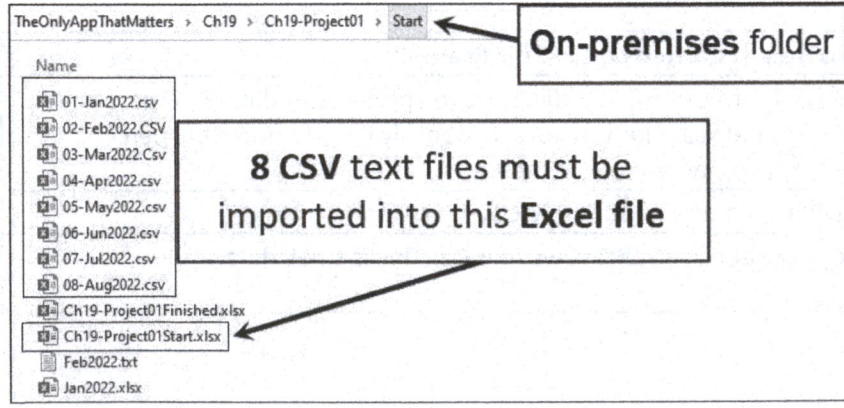

Figure 19.1 *You must import eight CSV files into the Excel file for this project.*

As shown in Figure 19.2, when you open the first CSV file in Notepad, you can see that the three field names (Date, Units, and Price) and the data in each record are separated by comma delimiters. All the monthly sales data CSV files that you use for this project have this same file structure and contain consistent field names.

This is important because, although you can import multiple files with different structures into the Power Query Editor, if you try to combine files that do not have the same structure and naming, it will not work. For example, if the field names in one of the CSV files are not the same as in all the other files, then that table will not be combined correctly, and you will end up with null records or extra columns.

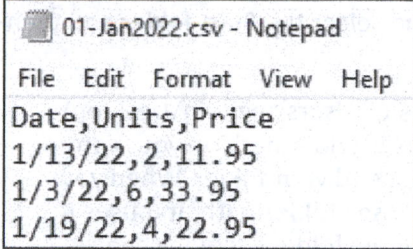

Figure 19.2 *Comma delimiter.*

Figure 19.3 shows a diagram of how the importing and combination process for this project works.

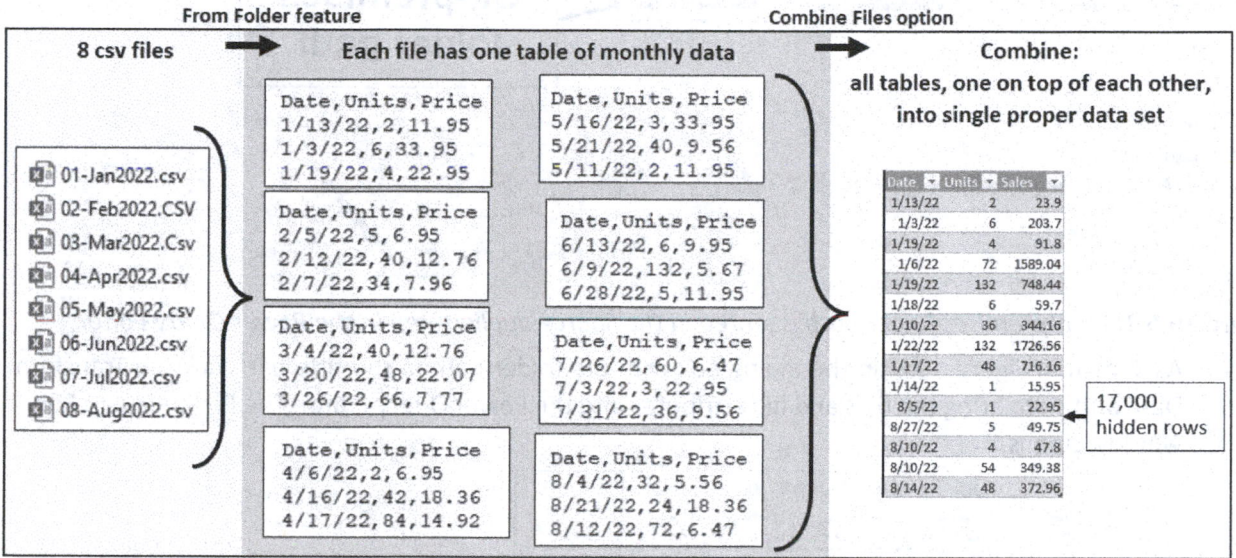

Figure 19.3 *Convert all CSV files into a single proper dataset.*

To complete this project, follow these steps:

1. Open the Excel file Ch19-Project01Start.xlsx.

2. As shown in Figure 19.4, in the Data tab of the Ribbon, in the Get & Transform group, click the Get Data dropdown arrow, select From File, and click on From Folder.

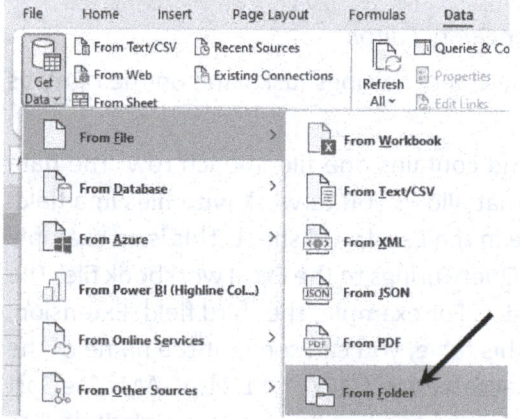

Figure 19.4 *The From Folder option imports all files from a folder as well as attribute data for each file.*

The From Folder feature allows you to point Power Query to a folder path so that you can easily import all the files from inside that folder into the Power Query Editor. This feature imports all the files into a single column and creates additional columns that contain file attributes (such as file extension, filename, and folder location). The From Folder feature is often used to get table data from different files and combine the tables into a single proper dataset, but it can also be used to get file attribute data such as a list of filenames from a folder.

3. As shown in Figure 19.5, in the Browse dialog box, navigate to and select the Start folder and then click the Open button.

> **Note:** In Figure 19.5, notice that the folder path on my computer is C:\Users\mgirvin\Desktop\ TheOnlyAppThatMatters\Ch19\Ch19-Project01\Start. The on-premises folder path on your computer will be different as it will match the location where you downloaded your folder. When you import from your Start folder, Power Query memorizes the on-premises folder path and uses it during the refresh process when you add new files to the folder later. If the folder location changes, you can use the Data Source Settings option to change the folder path.

Figure 19.5 *The on-premises folder path is stored in the Source applied step in the Power Query Editor.*

4. As shown in Figure 19.6, in the dialog box with the folder path in the title bar, click the Transform Data button to bring the files and file attributes into the Power Query Editor. The Power Query Editor window opens.

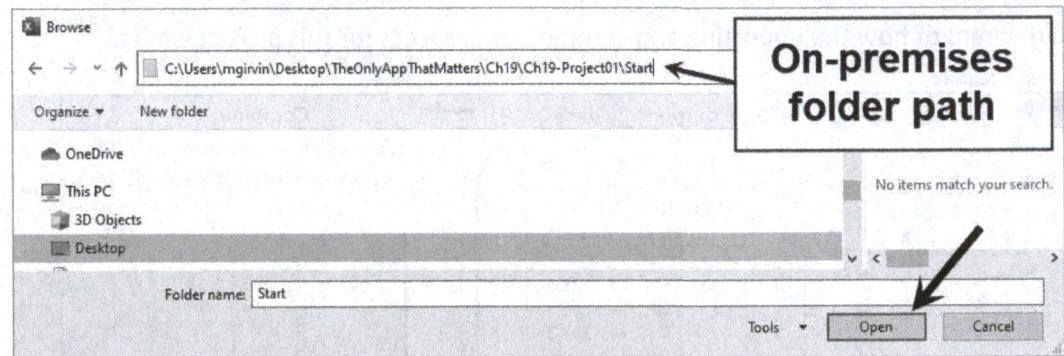

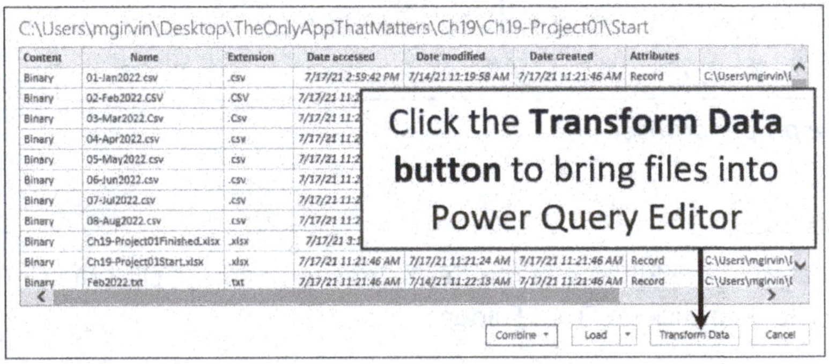

Figure 19.6 *The Transform Data button brings files into the Power Query Editor.*

5. In the Power Query Editor, rename the query **fSales** in the Query Settings task pane on the right, as shown in Figure 19.7.

    The first field shown in Figure 19.7 is named Content and contains one file in each row. The data type binary is applied to this field; this is the data type that allows you to work with files in a field. Working with files in each row of a column is not possible in the Excel worksheet. This is an example of the revolutionary data analysis capabilities that Power Query brings to the Excel workbook file. The remaining fields in this figure contain attributes for the files. For example, the third field, Extension, shows the file extension for each file. In the first row in this table, you can see that the name of the file is 01-Jan2021.csv, the extension is .csv, and the date accessed is 7/17/21 11:21:46 AM. The Sort & Filter dropdown arrows at the top of each field can be used to filter by any of the attributes to exclude or include files as needed. In the Content and Attributes fields, you can click on the right side of a cell to see more detail. In the next steps, you'll try this on two of the files in the Content field.

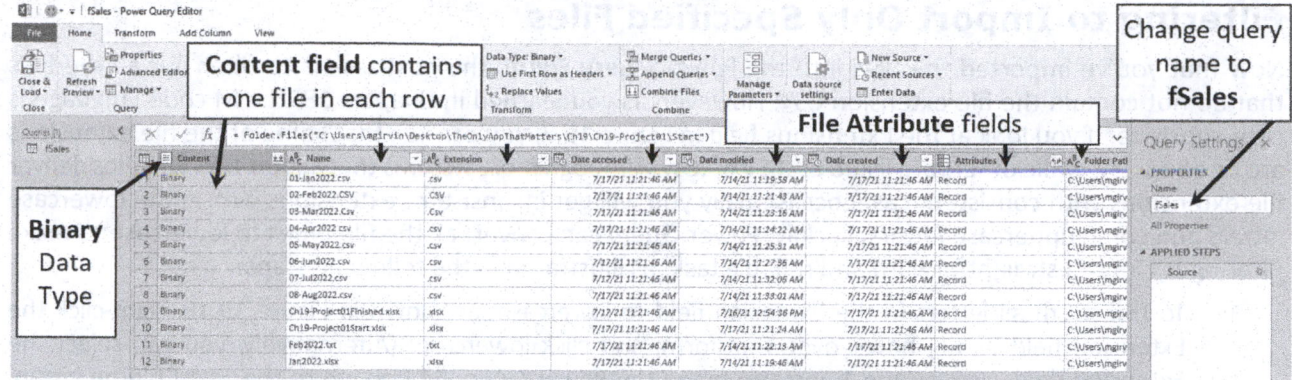

Figure 19.7 *The Content field has a binary data type, which allows files in each row of the column.*

6.   As shown in Figure 19.8, to see a preview of the file in the first row, in the first cell in the Content field, click to the right of the word Binary. You now see an icon and the name of the file below the table.

> **Note:** If you accidentally click on the word Binary instead of clicking to the right of it, you will extract the contents of the text file. If that happens, you need to delete the query step for it in the Applied Steps list in the Query Settings task pane.

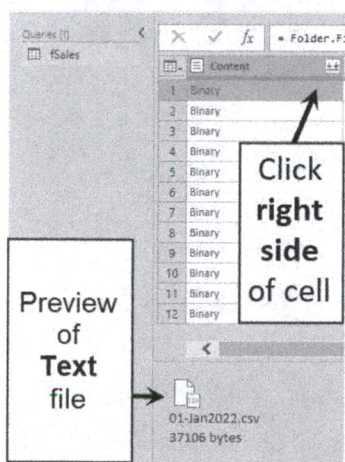

Figure 19.8 *The first row contains a CSV file.*

7.   As shown in Figure 19.9, to see a preview of the file in the ninth row, in the ninth cell in the Content field, click to the right of the word Binary. You can then see an icon and the name of the Excel file below the table.

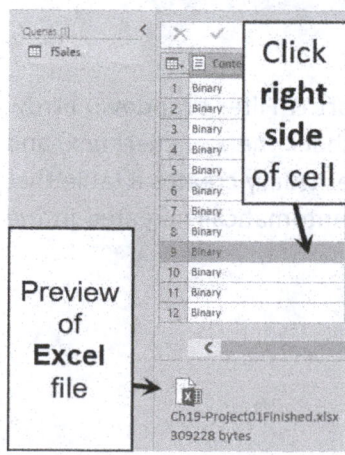

Figure 19.9 *The ninth row contains an Excel file.*

Filtering to Import Only Specified Files

Now that you've imported the files into the Power Query Editor, the next task is to filter out all the files that do not contain the file extension CSV. However, as you learned in Chapter 18, the M code language is case-sensitive. If you look at the Extensions field in Figure 19.7, you can see that some of the file extensions are listed as .csv, while others are listed as .CSV or .Csv. Although most systems that export text CSV files deliver file extensions with consistent case, occasionally you will get inconsistent extensions with some lowercase letters and some uppercase letters. Luckily, Power Query can convert all the file types to lowercase to make filtering by "csv" a straightforward and reliable task, as illustrated in the following steps:

1. To transform all letters in the Extension field to lowercase, as shown in Figure 19.10, right-click the Extension field name, hover over Transform, and click lowercase. (Alternatively, you can select the Extension field, click on the Transform tab in the Power Query Ribbon, go to the Text Column group, click the Format dropdown, and then click on lowercase.) As shown in Figure 19.11, all the extensions in the Extension field are converted to lowercase letters. In the formula bar, you can see the M code that was automatically created for you.

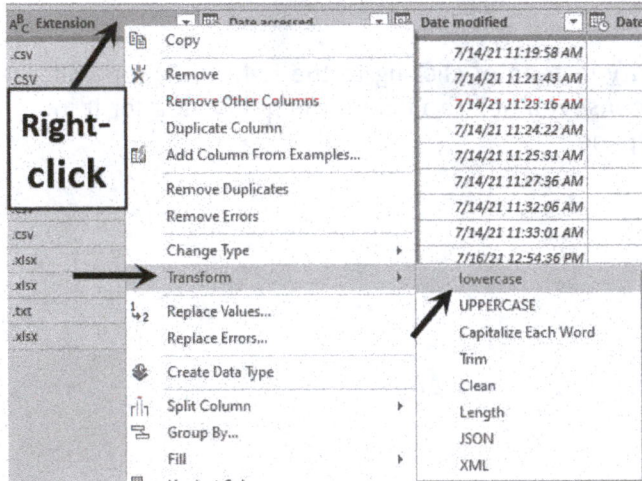

Figure 19.10 *Transform all letters in the Extension field to lowercase.*

`= Table.TransformColumns(Source,{{"Extension", Text.Lower, type text}})`

	Content	A^B_C Name	A^B_C Extension	Date accessed
1	Binary	01-Jan2022.csv	.csv	7/17/21 2:59:42 PM
2	Binary	02-Feb2022.CSV	.csv	7/17/21 11:21:46 AM
3	Binary	03-Mar2022.Csv	.csv	7/17/21 11:21:46 AM
4	Binary	04-Apr2022.csv	.csv	7/17/21 11:21:46 AM
5	Binary	05-May2022.csv	.csv	7/17/21 11:21:46 AM
6	Binary	06-Jun2022.csv	.csv	7/17/21 11:21:46 AM
7	Binary	07-Jul2022.csv	.csv	7/17/21 11:21:46 AM
8	Binary	08-Aug2022.csv	.csv	7/17/21 11:21:46 AM

Query Settings

PROPERTIES
Name
fSales

All Properties

APPLIED STEPS
Source
Lowercased Text

Figure 19.11 *M code for transforming a field containing text to lowercase.*

2. To filter the table to show only records that are CSV files, click the Sort & Filter dropdown arrow at the top of the Extensions field, uncheck the (Select All) checkbox, check the .csv checkbox, and click the OK button (see Figure 19.12). As shown in Figure 19.13, Power Query creates a table that contains the eight desired CSV files and shows the M code that was automatically created in the formula bar.

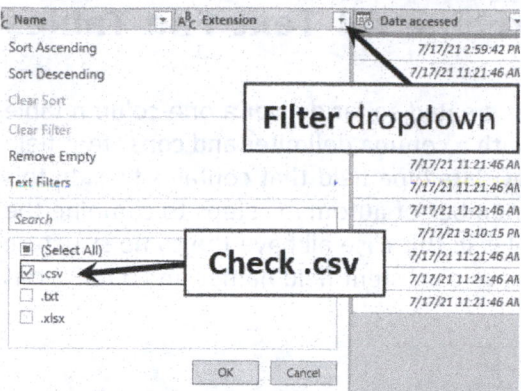

Figure 19.12 *Filter the Extension field to include only records where the extension is equal to .csv.*

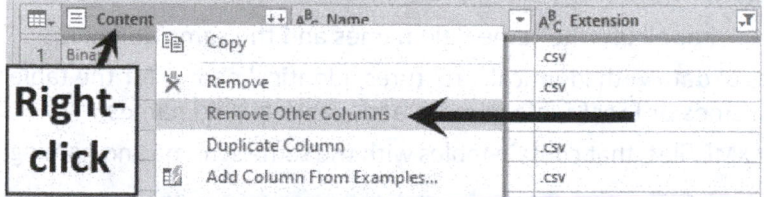

Figure 19.13 *M code to select rows where the extension is equal to .csv.*

3. Now that you have used the Extension field to filter the table, you no longer need that field—or any of the other attribute fields. To remove all fields except the Content field, as shown in Figure 19.14, right-click the Content field and then click on Remove Other Columns. As shown in Figure 19.15, Power Query removes all fields except for the Content field and shows the M code that was automatically created in the formula bar.

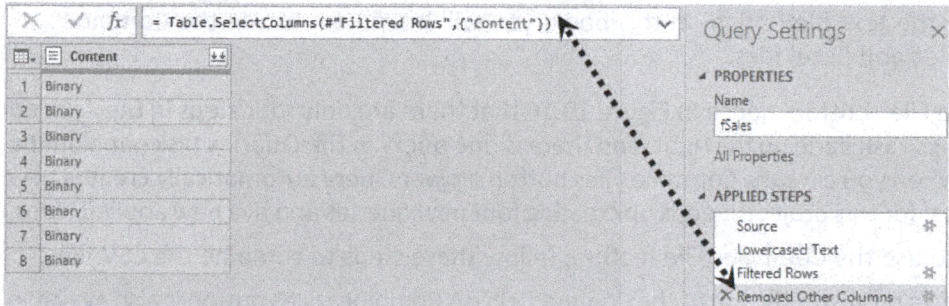

Figure 19.14 *To remove all fields except the Content field, use the Remove Other Columns option.*

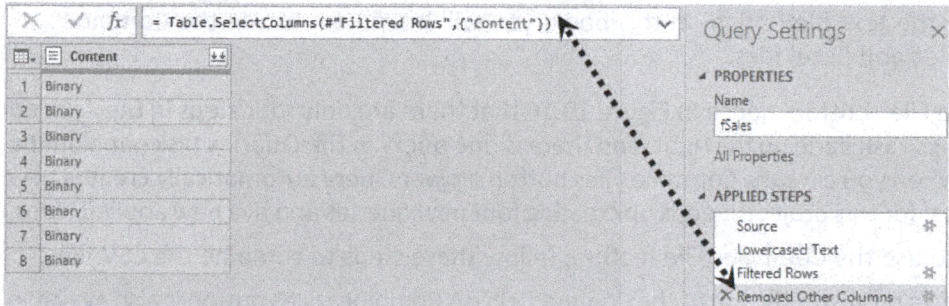

Figure 19.15 *M code to remove all fields except for the Content field.*

Using the Combine Files Option to Combine All Text File Tables into a Single Proper Dataset

As shown in Figure 19.16, the four query steps Power Query has created so far deliver a one-column table with eight rows, each with a CSV file that contains a text table with a comma delimiter and consistent field names. The Combine Files button appears at the top of a binary data type field that contains files. In this example, when you click this button, Power Query performs a number of automatic steps to combine the tables into a single proper dataset. It can do this because the files in this case all have the same structure or schema—that is, the file types are the same, and the tables have consistent field names and data. If this were not the case, the combination process would not work.

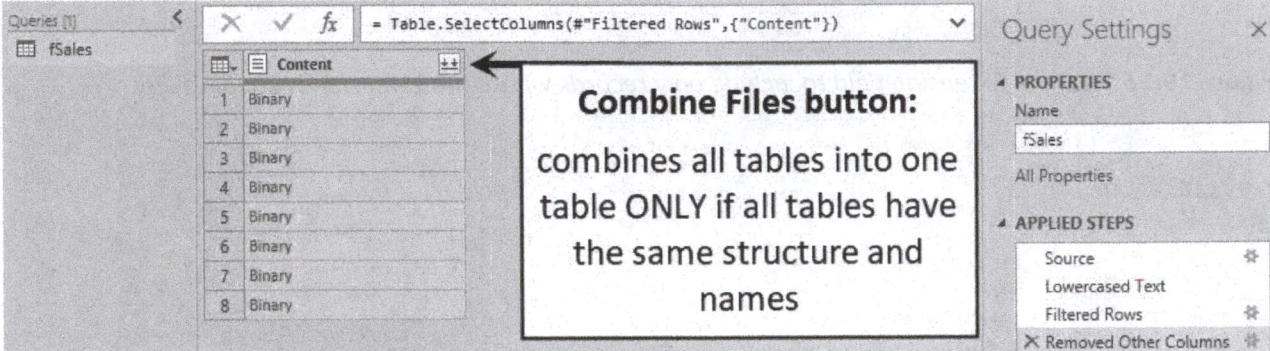

Figure 19.16 *The Combine Files button combines all equivalently structured tables into a single proper dataset.*

The problem with the Combine Files button is that it sometimes shows up on fields that contain files where the table objects do not have the same structure or schema. This is particularly true with binary data type fields that contain Excel files. An Excel file can contain many different types of objects with many different object names. You will encounter this issue in Project 3, later in this chapter. In that project, you will not use the Combine Files button but will instead use the M code function Excel.Workbook to extract all the objects from each Excel file so you can select the objects you want.

Microsoft says to use the Combine Files option "to combine multiple files with the same schema stored in a single folder into one table." Examples of situations when you can use the Combine Files button are:

- With text files, such as .csv or .txt files, that all use the same field names and the same delimiter
- With Excel files that all contain tables of data with identical structures, identical names for the table objects (that is, identical worksheet names or Excel Table names), and identical field names
- With other file types, such as JSON or XML files, that contain tables with the same schema and naming

Note: Without a doubt, the Combine Files feature works most effortlessly with text files. So, if you are given a choice of how tables of data are structured—as is the case with many government data websites—choose the text file option. In this book, you will learn how to use the Combine Files option with text files and Excel files.

Before you click the Combine Files button, notice in Figure 19.16 that there are only four steps in the Applied Steps box in the Query Settings task pane on the right, and there is one query in the Queries task pane on the left. As you will see shortly, when you click the Combine Files button, Power Query automatically creates new queries and new applied steps; for this project, it ends up creating four new queries and five new applied steps.

Now that you've seen how to use the Combines File feature, follow these steps to combine the CSV files:

1. Click the Combines Files button at the top of the Content field. (A Combines Files button is also available in the Combine group in the Home tab of the Power Query Ribbon.)

2. Complete the Combine Files dialog box that appears as shown in Figure 19.17. By filling in the following fields as shown in the figure, you provide details that will help Power Query automatically write the M code for the combination process:

    - **Sample File:** Select the file that Power Query should use as an example to write the code for combining the files. Given that all the files in the folder in this example have the same structure, you can use the first file to write the M code.

    - **File Origin:** Select the character set that is used by the file. This setting is almost always autofilled correctly based on the file chosen. If it is not correct, you can go to the Microsoft help link https://docs.microsoft.com/en-us/windows/win32/intl/code-page-identifiers to determine what character set to use.

    - **Delimiter:** Enter the delimiter type that is used in your files so that Power Query can break apart the data into the correct sets of table fields. Power Query does not always auto-populate this textbox correctly, so you need to ensure that it matches the delimiter used in your file.

    - **Data Type Detection:** Specify the number of rows of data (in this case, 200) that Power Query should use to try to guess the correct data type. This setting is not very important because it is easy to change field data types later by using the Power Query Editor.

    Power Query almost always correctly prepopulates these four textboxes with the correct details.

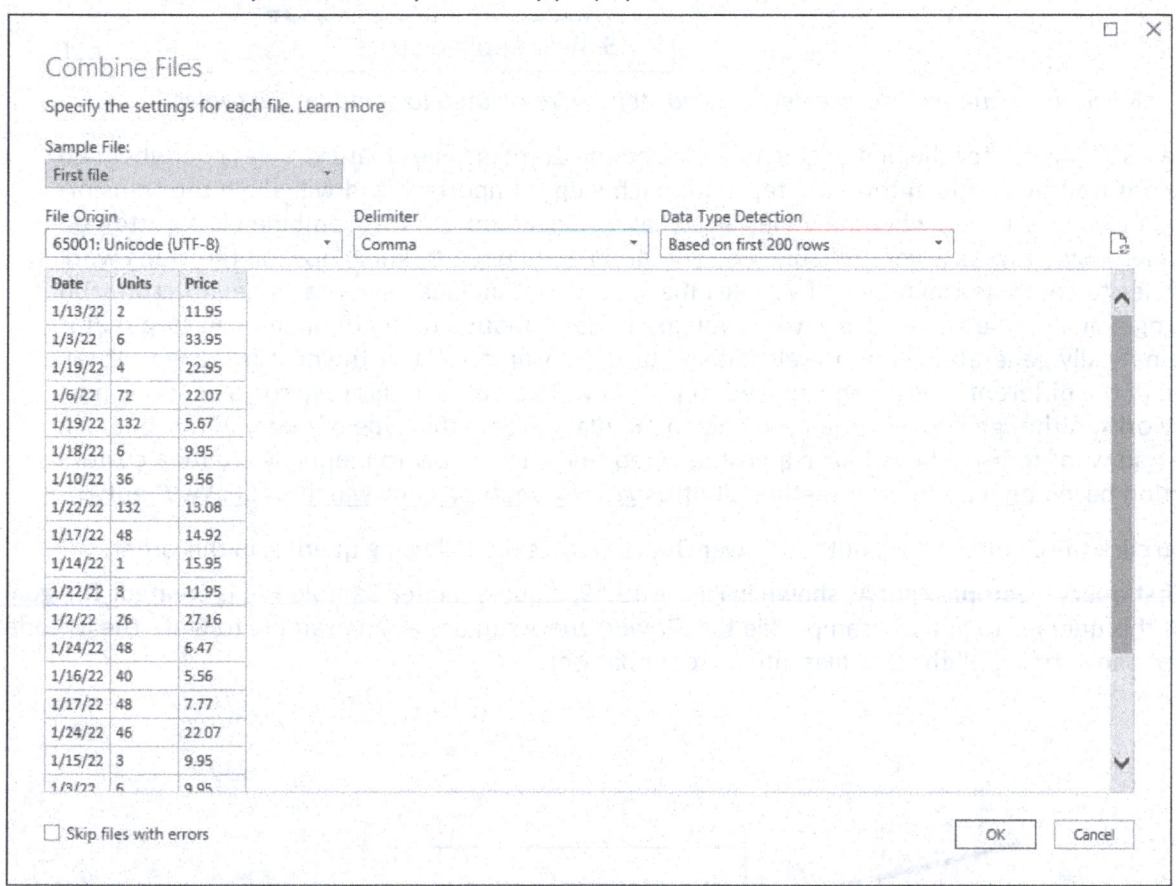

Figure 19.17 *Use the Combine Files dialog box to provide the details Power Query needs to write the M code for combining the files.*

3. Click the OK button. Power Query begins writing the M code to combine the text file tables.

Taking a First Look at Parameters and Power Query Custom Functions

Figure 19.18 shows the result of clicking the OK button in the Combine Files dialog box: Power Query creates four new queries in the Queries task pane on the left, five new steps in the Applied Steps box in the Queries Settings task pane on the right, and the single proper dataset with all the combined tables in the middle. In addition, you can see that the fourth query that was created—a custom function named Transform File—is used in the Invoke Custom Function1 query step to transform each CSV file into a proper dataset.

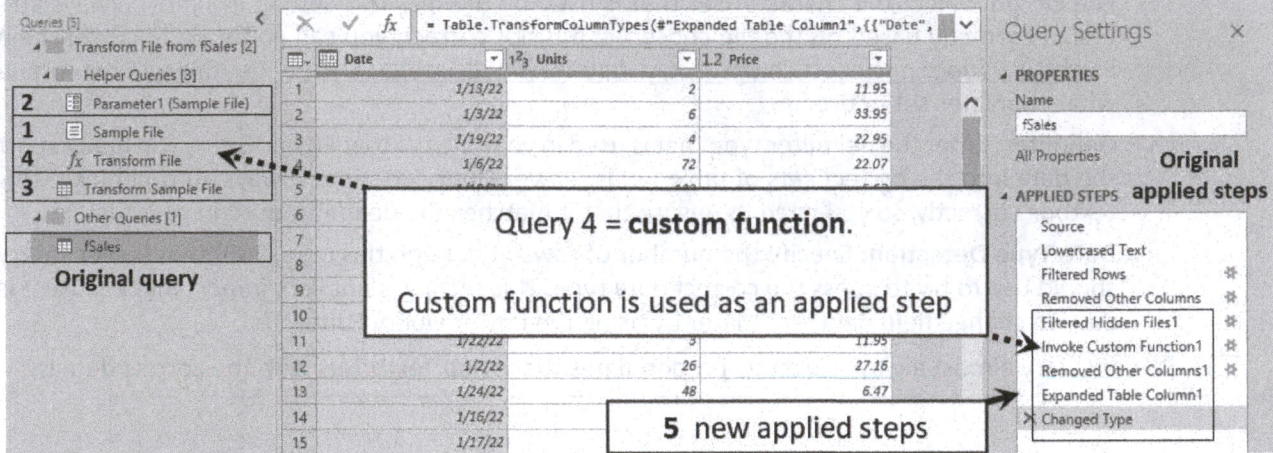

Figure 19.18 *Four new queries and five new applied steps were created to combine the tables.*

> **Note:** I still remember the first couple times I used the Combine Files feature: I was overwhelmed and confused by all the automatic steps. But each step is important and will allow the transformation to be refreshed when new files arrive later. When you use the Combine Files button on text files, this process is very reliable, and you don't even need to know how all the steps work together to combine the tables. If you just make sure that all files have the same structure and naming, you are good to go. However, if you are curious about a query or an applied step that is automatically generated, you can select it and take a closer look. Over the next few pages, I step through the different queries and applied steps that were created in this case so you can see how this works. Although you will not learn how to manually create this type of query in this book, in case you want to learn how, I have a posted video that shows how to manually create a custom function based on a parameter method at https://www.youtube.com/watch?v=SFgYwVVeqPA.

When you click the Combine Files button, Power Query creates the following queries, in this order:

- **First query—Sample File:** As shown in Figure 19.19, a query named Sample File is created. The goal of this query is to get one sample file that Power Query can use as an example to write the M code for transforming all the CSV files into a proper dataset.

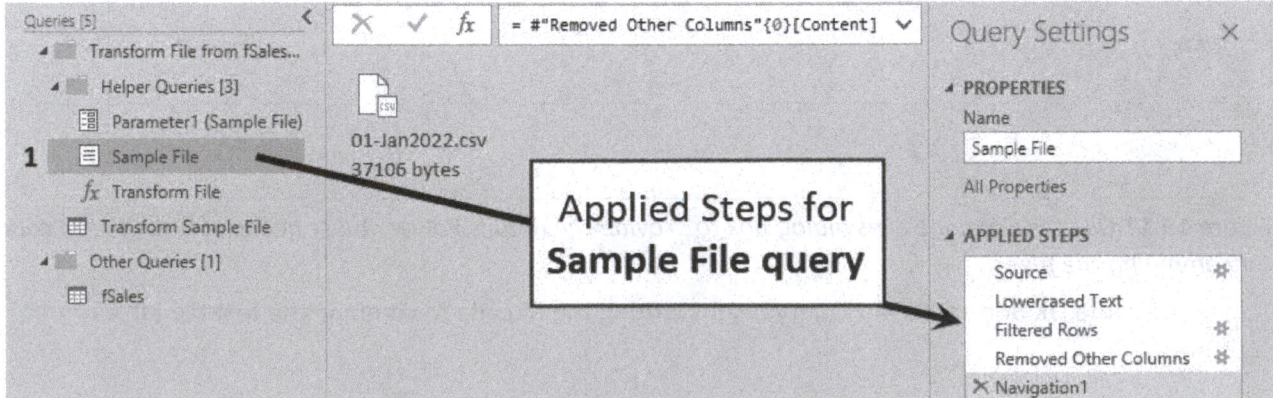

Figure 19.19 *The goal of the first query is to get a sample file that Power Query can use to build the M code.*

- **Second query—Parameter1:** As shown in Figure 19.20, a parameter named Parameter1 is created. A *parameter* is a stored variable value that can be used as a query input. When you change the parameter, the query will update to reflect the new value. The Parameter1 parameter created in this step will be used again by the other queries. Without this parameter, the third and fourth queries would not be dynamic and updatable.

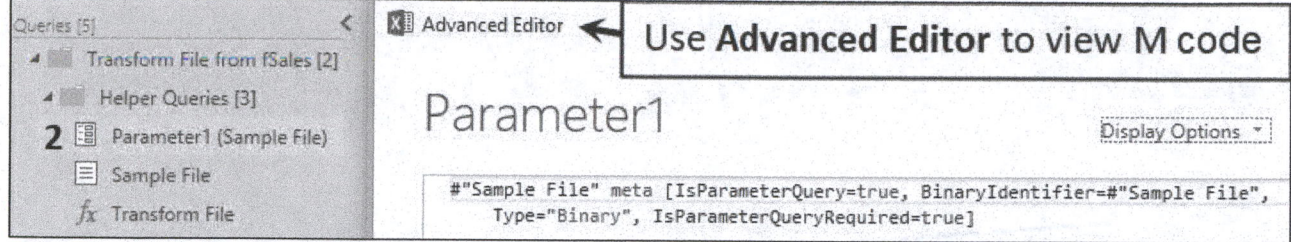

Figure 19.20 *The goal of the second query is to create a parameter for a CSV file input that can be used in the remaining steps.*

> **Note:** A *parameter* is a stored value that serves as a variable query input and can be used anywhere in the Power Query environment.

- **Third query—Transform Sample File:** As shown in Figure 19.21, a query named Transform Sample File is created. The source data input for this query is the parameter created in the second query. The goal of this query is to convert one CSV file to a proper dataset. Because the source data is a parameter, this query can be referenced by the fourth query to create a reusable custom function, where any changes made in this third query are automatically reflected in the fourth query.

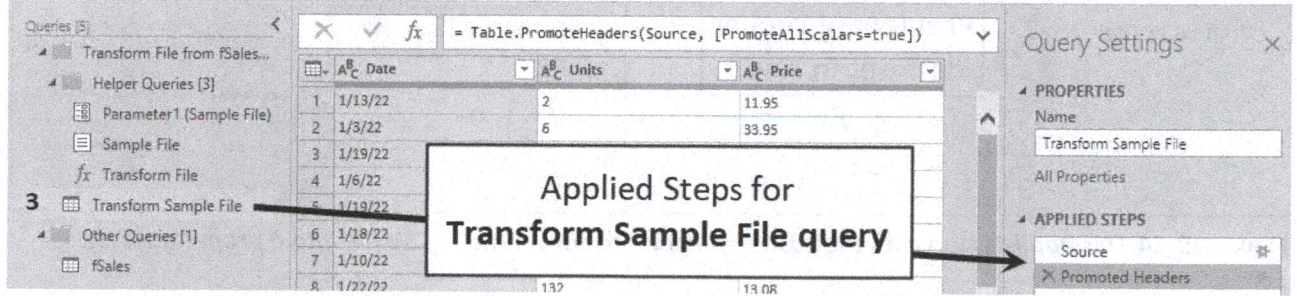

Figure 19.21 *The goal of the third query is to write the M code to convert one CSV file to a proper dataset.*

- **Fourth query—Transform File:** As shown in Figure 19.22, the fourth query defines a custom function named Transform File. Figure 19.22 shows the Parameter1 input as a variable in a custom function, where the purpose of the function is to transform a CSV file into a proper dataset.

> **Note:** A *custom function query* is a query that delivers a reusable function that can be used anywhere in the Power Query environment. A *custom function* defines variables (that is, query inputs or parameters) and then defines the mapping for those variables to deliver a final value. (You'll learn how to create your own custom function in Project 5, later in this chapter.)

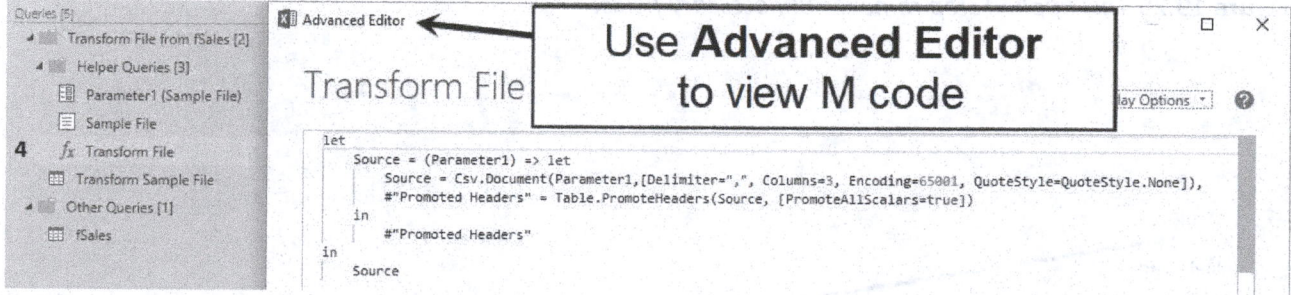

Figure 19.22 The goal of the fourth query is to create a reusable custom function that can be used on all the other CSV files.

Figures 19.23 through 19.27 show the five new applied steps that are created, as well as the custom function that transforms each file. Figure 19.27 shows the final single proper dataset, which contains records of data from all eight CSV files.

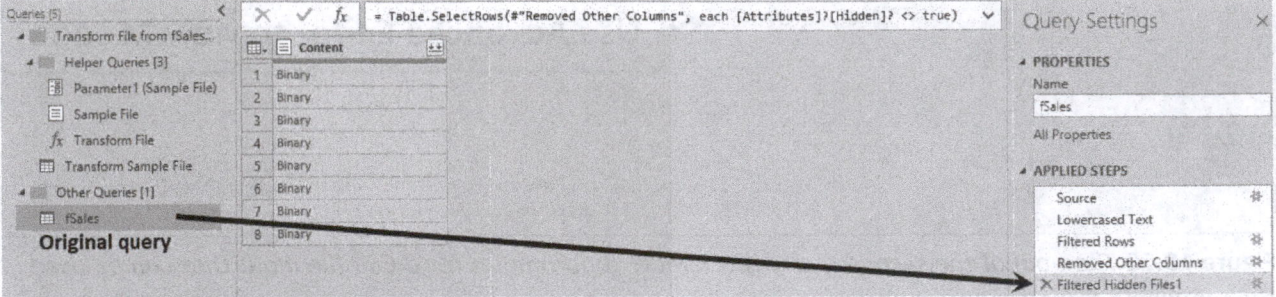

Figure 19.23 *This applied step is supposed to remove hidden files (though there are no hidden files in this case).*

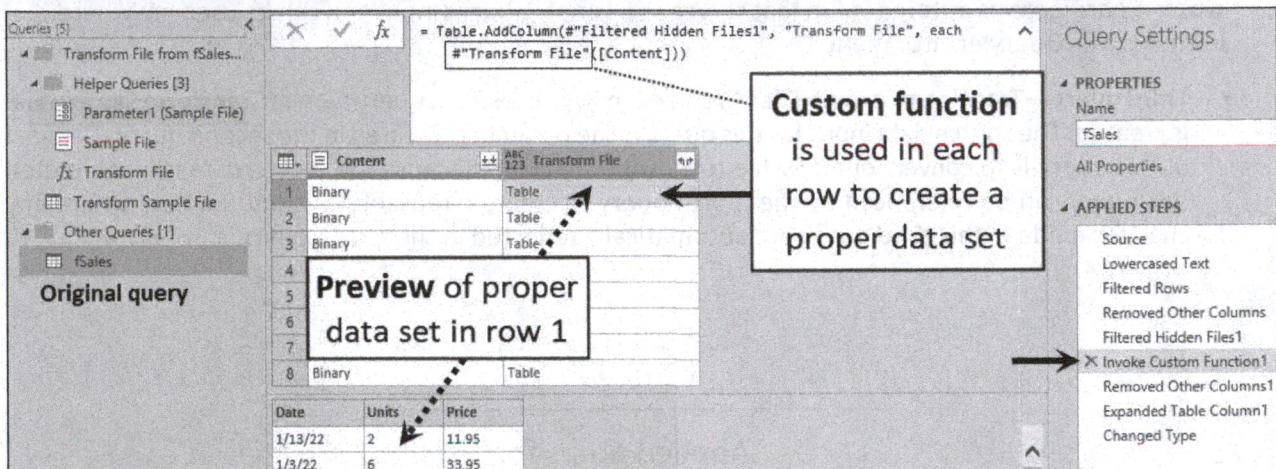

Figure 19.24 *This applied step uses the custom function to convert each CSV file into a proper dataset.*

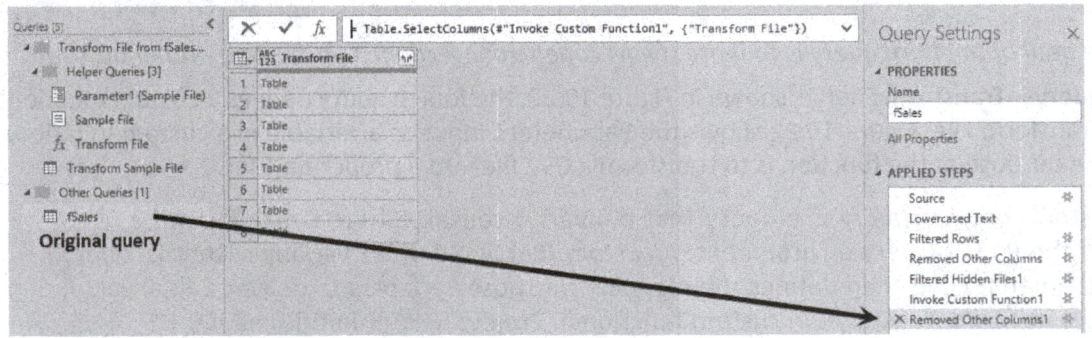

Figure 19.25 *This applied step removes unnecessary fields.*

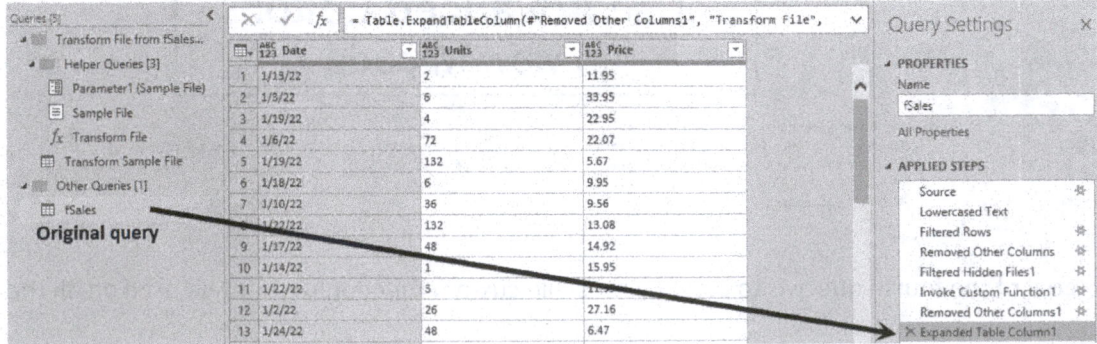

Figure 19.26 *This applied step combines the tables from all eight rows into a single proper dataset.*

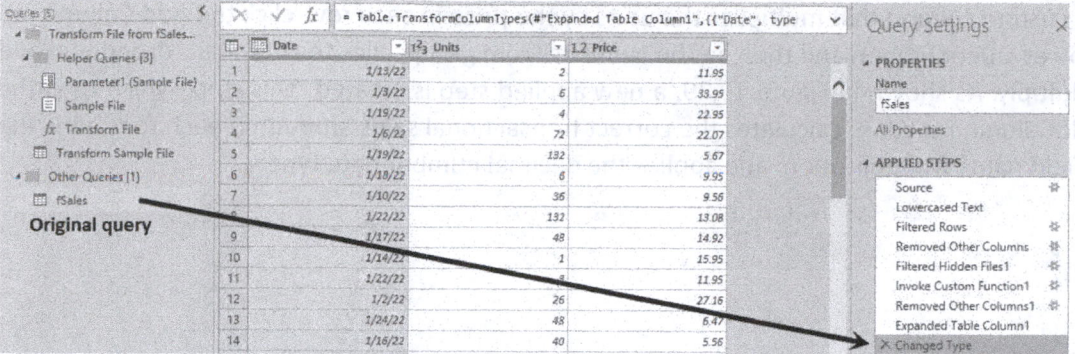

Figure 19.27 *This applied step adds the correct data type to each field and delivers the completed table.*

Using the Locale Feature to Set Date Data Types to Match Regional Settings

Figure 19.27 shows a table in which the dates in the Date field had the date data type automatically applied. This worked because the dates in the text file had the format m/d/yy, which matched the regional settings for dates in the Control Panel of my computer. If the files you receive have a different format than the format in your regional settings, you must use the Using Locale option to convert the format of the dates in the file to the format for dates that is defined in your regional settings. For example, if you are in France, and your computer interprets dates as d/m/yy, then you can use the Using Locale option to convert the text dates for this project to d/m/yy format. To do this, follow these steps:

1. Click the Date Type icon at the top of the Date field and then click Using Locale.
2. From the Data Type dropdown, select Date.
3. From the Locale dropdown, select your region—for example, French (for France).
4. Click the OK button.

Creating a Power Query Custom Column

Now that you have converted the eight CSV files into a proper dataset, you must perform the remaining data modeling step in the Power Query Editor so that you can load the single proper dataset directly to the standard PivotTable cache. The last step requires that you multiply, for each row, the Units field by the Price field to calculate the transactional sales amount for each row in the table. You need to create a custom column to do this—by following these steps:

> **Note:** *Custom column* is the term in Power Query for a new field added to a table that contains an M code formula.

1. As shown in Figure 19.28, in the Queries task pane on the left, select the fSales query.
2. in the Query Settings task pane on the right, select the last applied step, Changed Type.
3. Select the Units and Price fields.

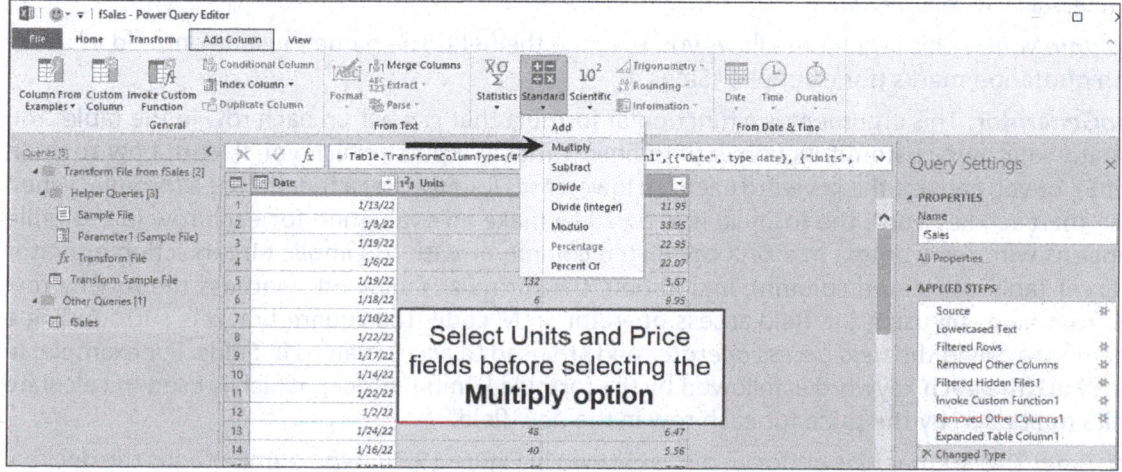

Figure 19.28 *Creating a new field to multiply values from different columns is easy with Power Query.*

4. To add a custom column that multiplies the units by the price in each row, click the Add Column tab in the Power Query Ribbon and then, in the Number From group, click the Standard dropdown and select Multiply. As shown in Figure 19.29, a new applied step is created. This step, which uses the Table.AddColumn function, calculates the correct transactional sales amount in each row, adds the default field name Multiplication, and applies the decimal number data type.

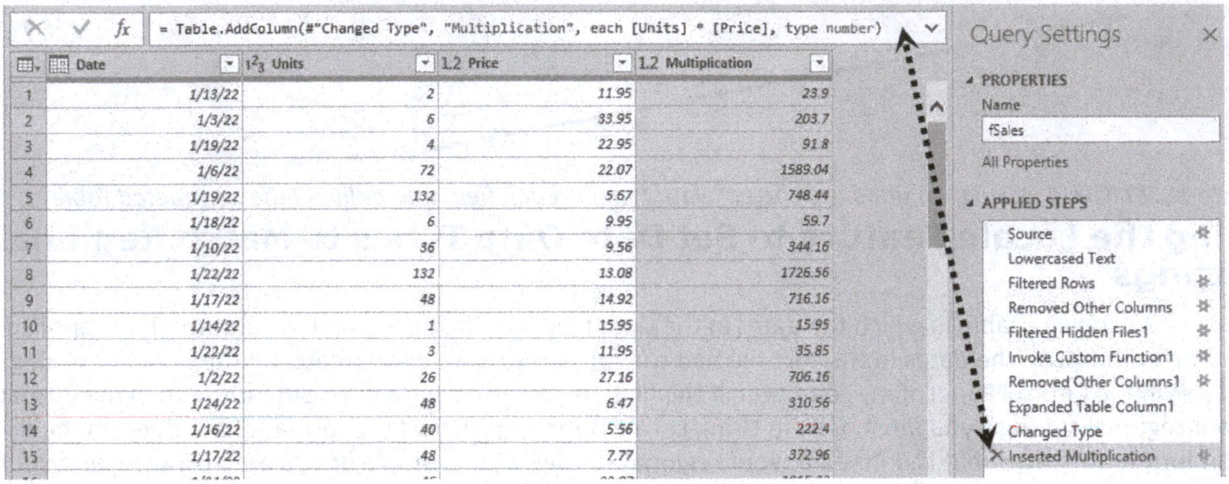

Figure 19.29 *The Table.AddColumn function uses the default field name Multiplication.*

5. To change the default field name, as shown in Figure 19.30, click in the formula bar to change the field name in the second argument of the Table.AddColumn function to **"Sales"**.

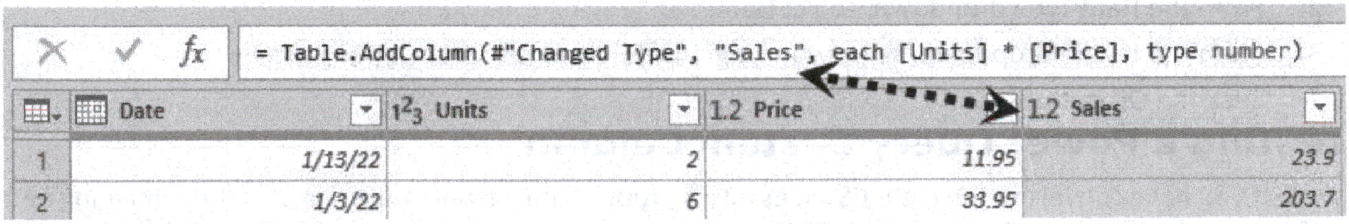

Figure 19.30 *You can edit the M code in the formula bar to change the field name for the new field.*

Using the Table.AddColumn M Code Function

Figures 19.24 and 19.30 show examples of how the M code function Table.AddColumn can add a new custom column to a table. Figure 19.31 shows the four arguments in the Table.AddColumn function side-by-side with the formulas used in Figures 19.24 and 19.30. These are the four arguments:

- **table:** This argument is often the table value that was created in the previous applied query step, but it can contain other table values. The Table.AddColumn function adds a new field to the table value and delivers a new table. For example, in Figure 19.24, the previous step name is #"Filtered Hidden Files1", and because it is a table value, it can be used by the Table.AddColumn function to create a new table value with a new field.

- **newColumnName:** This argument allows you to name the field. The name must be entered as a text value in quotation marks (for example, "Sales").

- **columnGenerator:** This argument is a function or formula that can act on each row in the table. You can create your own custom function with defined variable inputs (which you'll learn how to do in Project 5), or you can use the keyword each (all lowercase) followed by a function or a formula. When you use the each keyword, the formula is allowed to make an evaluation for each row in the table (as happens with row context in a DAX calculated column or with the implicit intersection operator in an Excel Table calculated column); in addition, the formula is allowed to access the row-by-row values from fields by using the field access operator. In M code, the square brackets surrounding a field name are called the *field access operator* and are used to access values in fields. For example, in Figure 19.30, the each keyword is followed by the formula [Units]*[Price], which is used to calculate the units multiplied by the price for each row in the new field.

- **columnType:** This argument is optional, but, as shown in Figure 19.30, **type number** adds the decimal data type to the new field.

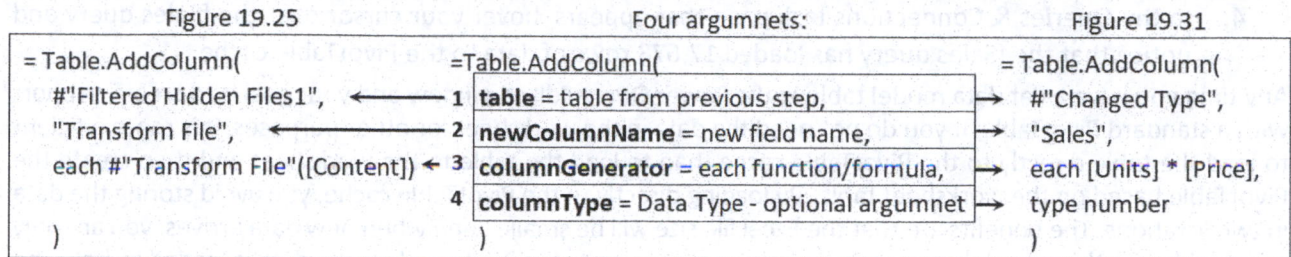

Figure 19.25	Four argumnets:	Figure 19.31
= Table.AddColumn(	=Table.AddColumn(	= Table.AddColumn(
#"Filtered Hidden Files1", ← **1**	**table** = table from previous step,	#"Changed Type",
"Transform File", ← **2**	**newColumnName** = new field name,	"Sales",
each #"Transform File"([Content]) ← **3**	**columnGenerator** = each function/formula,	each [Units] * [Price],
4	**columnType** = Data Type - optional argumnet →	type number
)	)	)

Figure 19.31 *The Table.AddColumn M code function has four arguments.*

Loading Directly to the PivotTable Cache

Now that you have imported the files, transformed the data, and modeled the Sales column data, you can load the final flat data model table to the PivotTable cache. To do this, follow these steps:

1. Click the Home tab in the Power Query Ribbon and, in the Close group, click the Close & Load dropdown and then click on Close & Load To.

2. In the Import Data dialog box that appears, as shown in Figure 19.32, select the PivotTable Report option button, select the Existing Worksheet option button, select cell A1 on the worksheet Proj(1), and click the OK button.

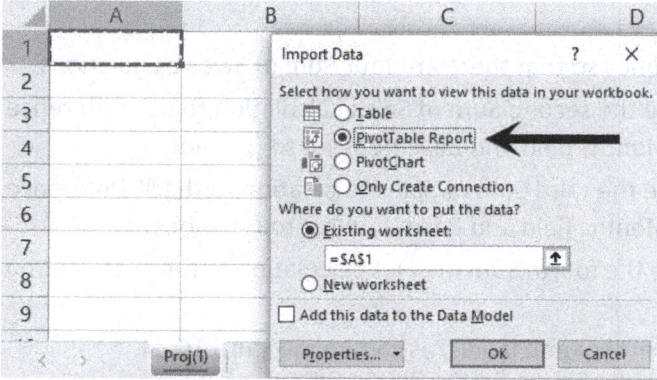

Figure 19.32 *You are loading directly to the PivotTable cache.*

3. On the far right of the Excel window and to the right of the PivotTable Fields task pane that automatically pops up, click the Queries & Connections button, as shown in Figure 19.33.

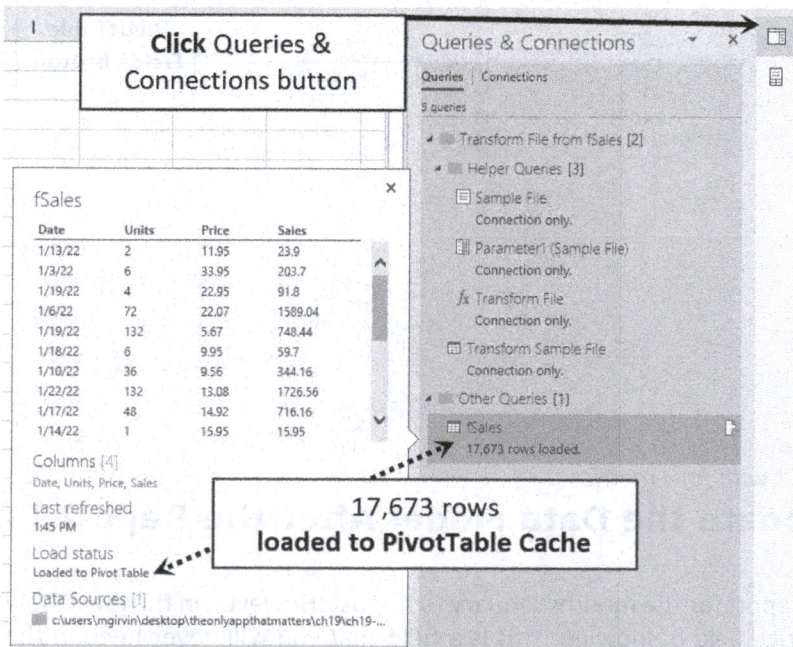

Figure 19.33 *The Queries & Connections task pane shows that the data is loaded to the PivotTable cache.*

4.   In the Queries & Connections task pane that appears, hover your cursor over the fSales query and notice that the fSales query has loaded 17,673 rows of data to the PivotTable cache.

Any time you have a flat data model table in the Power Query Editor window and your goal is to create a report with a standard PivotTable, if you do not need the data in the worksheet for other purposes, it is more efficient to load the table directly to the PivotTable cache than to load the table to the worksheet and then create the PivotTable based on the worksheet table. By loading directly to the PivotTable cache, you avoid storing the data in two locations. The benefits are that the Excel file size will be smaller, and when new data arrives, you are only required to use the refresh button one time rather than two times (that is, when the data is loaded to both the worksheet and the PivotTable cache). When you are required to refresh two times, if you forget the second refresh and use the unrefreshed report for analysis, you end up using a report that is not based on the latest data.

Creating the Final Standard PivotTable Report

Using your skills from Chapter 17, create the final standard PivotTable report by following these steps:

1.   On the far right of the Excel window and to the right of the Queries & Connections task pane, click the PivotTable Fields button.

2.   In the PivotTable Fields task pane that appears, drag the Date field to the Rows area. The PivotTable feature automatically groups the dates into months and lists the two fields, Months and Date, in the Rows area.

3.   Remove the Date field from the Rows area.

4.   Drag the Sales field to the Values area four times so that there are four Sum of Sales calculations.

5.   Using the Show Values As calculation, change the second Sum of Sales calculation to the Difference From calculation with Base Field set to the Months field and Base Item set to (previous).

6.   Using the Show Values As calculation, change the third Sum of Sales calculation to the % Difference From calculation with Base Field set to the Months field and Base Item set to (previous).

7.   Using the Show Values As calculation, change the fourth Sum of Sales calculation to the % of Column Total calculation.

8.   Add appropriate number formatting and report column labels, as shown in Figure 19.34.

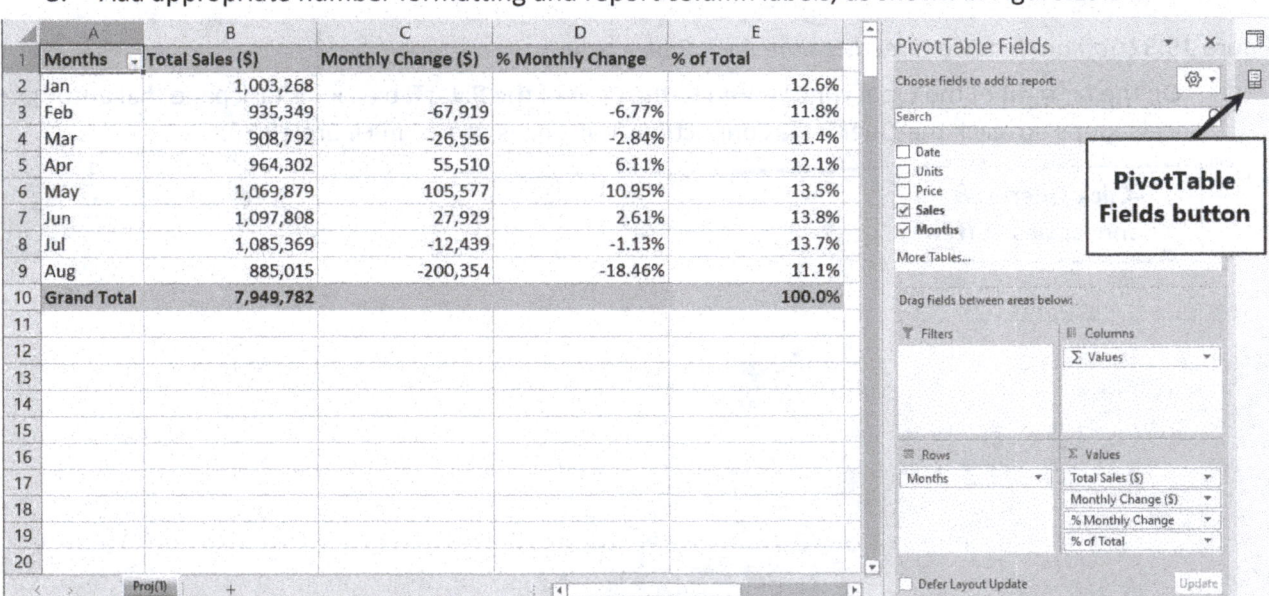

Figure 19.34 *The January to August report with four metrics.*

Using Power Query to Update the Data Model After the Report Is Finished

In Figure 19.34, you can see the finished report for the months January to August. However, in the PivotTable Fields task pane, you can see that the Price field is showing. This is a field that you will never need in the reporting area—and because you do not need it in the reporting area, you should remove it. To accomplish this, you can use the Power Query Editor.

As you work through the following steps, you will learn two amazing things about Power Query: First, even though you have completed the report, you are allowed to go back and edit the query and then reload the flat data model to the PivotTable cache without disrupting the report; and second, when you delete the Price field and therefore create a new last step in the Applied Steps list, that step will not interfere with the calculation for transactional sales amount that was completed in the previous applied step.

To edit the query, follow these steps:

1. On the far right of the Excel window and to the right of the PivotTable Fields task pane, click the Queries & Connections button.

2. To open the Power Query Editor and edit the fSales query, right-click the query in the Queries & Connections task pane and click on the Edit option. As an alternative, you can simply double-click the fSales query in the Queries & Connections task pane to open the query in the Power Query Editor.

3. As shown in Figure 19.35, right-click the Price field name and click the Remove option. Power Query removes the Price field and creates a new last step in the Applied Steps list to reflect the change.

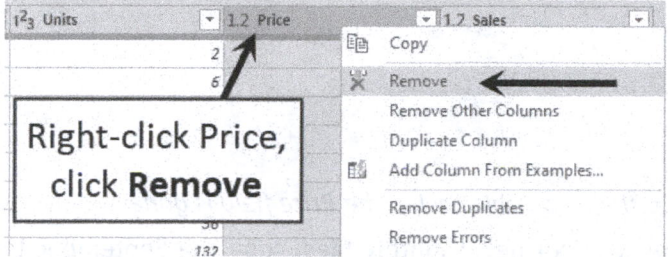

Figure 19.35 *In the Power Query Editor, remove the Price field.*

> **Note:** As shown in Figure 19.36, when you use the Price field in the Inserted Multiplication step to create the Sales field and then remove the Price field in the following step, the sales field still calculates correctly. Deleting a field used in a previous step is possible with a query in the Power Query Editor but is not possible with worksheet formulas. With worksheet formulas, say that you use a Units field and a Price field in a formula to create a new field named Sales. If you then delete the Price field, the entire Sales field is filled with #REF! errors (indicating that a reference no longer exists). With worksheet formulas, if you delete a precedent reference used in a formula, you destroy any dependent formulas. In contrast, in Power Query, if you delete a field that is used in a previous applied step, you will not get an error value, and your calculations and transformation will remain intact. This is a pretty amazing feature of Power Query queries!

	Date	1²₃ Units	1.2 Sales	
1	1/13/22	2	23.9	
2	1/3/22	6	203.7	
3	1/19/22	4	91.8	
4	1/6/22	72	1589.04	
5	1/19/22	132	748.44	
6	1/18/22	6	59.7	
7	1/10/22	36	344.16	
8	1/22/22	132	1726.56	
9	1/17/22	48	716.16	
10	1/14/22	1	15.95	
11	1/22/22	3	35.85	
12	1/2/22	26	706.16	
13	1/24/22	48	310.56	
14	1/16/22	40	222.4	
15	1/17/22	48	372.96	
16	1/24/22	46	1015.22	
17	1/15/22	3	29.85	
18	1/3/22	6	59.7	

fx = Table.RemoveColumns(#"Inserted Multiplication",{"Price"})

Query Settings

PROPERTIES
Name
fSales

All Properties

Step uses the **Price field**

Price field removed

Sales field still **works!**

APPLIED STEPS
Source
Lowercased Text
Filtered Rows
Removed Other Columns
Filtered Hidden Files1
Invoke Custom Function1
Removed Other Columns1
Expanded Table Column1
Changed Type
Inserted Multiplication
X Removed Columns

Figure 19.36 *In Power Query, if you delete a field used in a previous step, things still work!*

4. As shown in Figure 19.37, to close the Power Query Editor and reload the table to the PivotTable cache, click the Home tab in the Power Query Ribbon and, in the Close group, click the Close & Load button. (Because you have already loaded the table to the PivotTable cache, you cannot use the Close & Load To option in this case.)

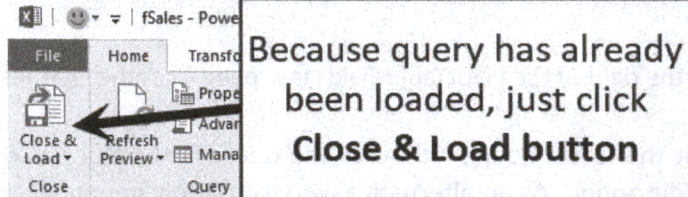

Figure 19.37 *Click the Close & Load button to load to the previous location.*

Figure 19.38 shows that the Price field is no longer listed in the PivotTable Fields task pane.

Months	Total Sales ($)	Monthly Change ($)	% Monthly Change	% of Total
Jan	1,003,268			12.6%
Feb	935,349	-67,919	-6.77%	11.8%
Mar	908,792	-26,556	-2.84%	11.4%
Apr	964,302	55,510	6.11%	12.1%
May	1,069,879	105,577	10.95%	13.5%
Jun	1,097,808	27,929	2.61%	13.8%
Jul	1,085,369	-12,439	-1.13%	13.7%
Aug	885,015	-200,354	-18.46%	11.1%
Grand Total	7,949,782			100.0%

Figure 19.38 *When you load the edited query beck to the PivotTable cache, the Price field is gone.*

5. To see if your full project will update when you get new monthly files, copy the September to December files from the folder Ch19-Project01, as shown in Figure 19.39.

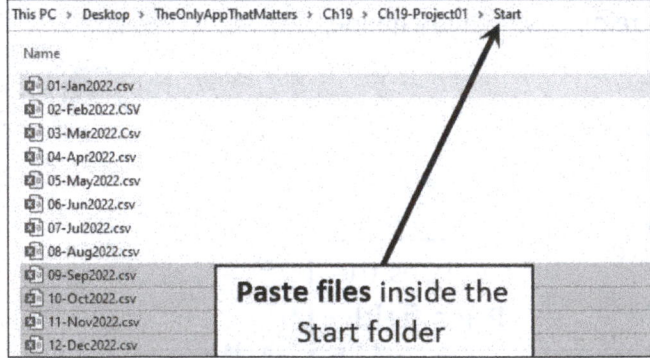

Figure 19.39 *Copy the new CSV files.*

6. Paste the September to December files into the folder Start, as shown in Figure 19.40.

This PC > Desktop > TheOnlyAppThatMatters > Ch19 > Ch19-Project01 > Start

Name

01-Jan2022.csv
02-Feb2022.CSV
03-Mar2022.Csv
04-Apr2022.csv
05-May2022.csv
06-Jun2022.csv
07-Jul2022.csv
08-Aug2022.csv
09-Sep2022.csv
10-Oct2022.csv
11-Nov2022.csv
12-Dec2022.csv

Paste files inside the Start folder

Figure 19.40 *Paste the new CSV files into the folder that Power Query is pointing to.*

7. As shown in Figure 19.41, in the Queries & Connections task pane, select the fSales query and then click the Refresh button on the right of the selected query. Because you loaded the data directly to the PivotTable cache, this one refresh updates both the query output and the report.

Months	Total Sales ($)	Monthly Change ($)	% Monthly Change	% of Total
Jan	1,003,268			6.7%
Feb	935,349	-67,919	-6.77%	6.3%
Mar	908,792	-26,556	-2.84%	6.1%
Apr	964,302	55,510	6.11%	6.5%
May	1,069,879	105,577	10.95%	7.2%
Jun	1,097,808	27,929	2.61%	7.4%
Jul	1,085,369	-12,439	-1.13%	7.3%
Aug	885,015	-200,354	-18.46%	5.9%
Sep	885,901	886	0.10%	5.9%
Oct	1,440,527	554,626	62.61%	9.7%
Nov	2,240,605	800,078	55.54%	15.0%
Dec	2,393,729	153,125	6.83%	16.1%
Grand Total	14,910,544			100.0%

Refresh button updates both the query and the report

Figure 19.41 *When you refresh the query, the query loads 33,096 rows of data, and the report updates!*

8. To determine whether all 12 files made it into the Power Query Editor and see if all the transformations you created work correctly with the new data added, open the fSales query in the Power Query Editor and then click the Refresh Preview button in the Query group in the Home tab of the Power Query Ribbon. You can select the various queries and applied steps to verify that things work correctly. Figure 19.42 shows, for example, that the transformation made on the December CSV file in the Invoke Custom Function1 step works correctly.

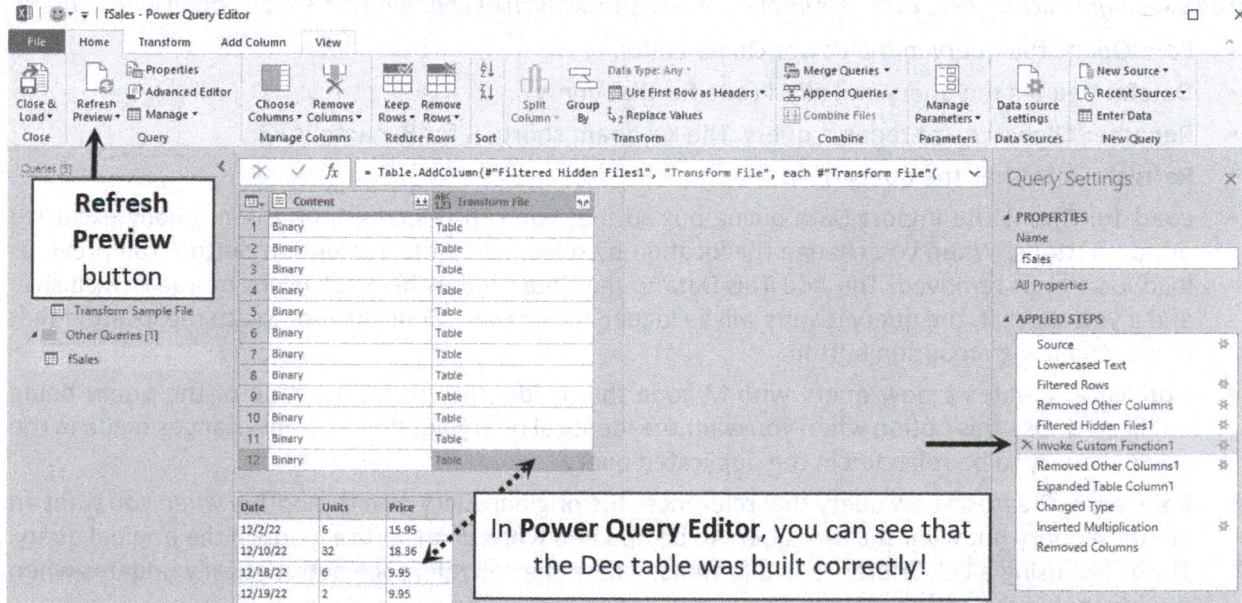

Refresh Preview button

In **Power Query Editor**, you can see that the Dec table was built correctly!

Figure 19.42 *In the Power Query Editor, you must click the Refresh Preview button to see all the new data.*

9. When you are done looking around in the updated fSales query, you can use the X close button in the Power Query Editor title bar to close the window.

Using Load To Location, Duplicate, Reference, Export, and Other Query Tasks

Occasionally you may need to change the load location for a query, duplicate a query, reference a query, or export a query. If you right-click a query that is listed in the Queries & Connections task pane, you get the following options (see Figure 19.43):

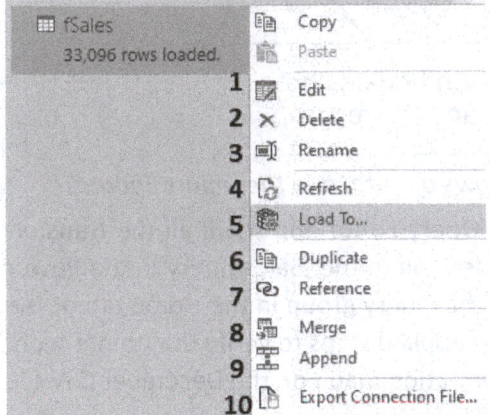

Figure 19.43 *Right-click a query to access important query tasks such as changing the load location with Load To.*

- **Edit:** Opens the query in the Power Query Editor.
- **Delete:** Deletes the query and all M code for that query.
- **Rename:** Allows you to rename query. The keyboard shortcut for Rename is F2.
- **Refresh:** Refreshes the query output.
- **Load To:** Opens the Import Data dialog box so that you can select among the mutually exclusive option buttons. When you change the location by selecting a different option button, the previous load location is removed. The Add This Data to the Data Model checkbox is not mutually exclusive, and if you check it, the query results will be loaded to the Data Model in addition to the location that is selected using an option button.
- **Duplicate:** Creates a new query with M code that is identical to the M code of the query being duplicated. Use this option when you want the identical query but do not want changes made in the original query to be reflected in the duplicated query.
- **Reference:** Creates a new query that references the original query. Use this option when you want an identical query but want the new query to be updated when changes are made in the original query. This is like using a cell reference in a formula, where the cell reference automatically updates when the content in the cell changes.
- **Merge:** Allows you to do an exact match lookup or to perform a database join.
- **Append:** Allows you to add a table to the bottom of the existing table when the structure and naming of the table that is being appended are the same as those of the original query.
- **Export Connection File:** Allows you to export a query as an .odc (Office Data Connection) file that, when opened, will create the same query in a new Excel workbook file.

Project 1 Summary

The key data analysis and power tool takeaways from this project are as follows:

- If you have multiple files that contain tables with the same structure and naming, and you need to combine them into one tale, use the From Folder and Combine Files options in Power Query.
- Be careful with the Combine Files button. Use it only when a binary data type column contains tables with the same structure and naming. Text files work great with this feature. Excel files can sometimes cause problems.
- You can use the Using Locale feature to set date data types to match your regional settings.
- Using the Power Query user interface, you can easily create useful queries and alter steps that appear in the Applied Steps list—and Power Query creates M code behind the scenes. However, it is always a

good idea to try to understand how the automatically created M code is working. Looking at each new query that is created and reading each new applied step in the formula bar or the Advanced Editor helps you understand the full process and gives you more control in getting accurate data analysis results. In addition, as you watch and learn from the automatically created code, you will eventually learn how to write your own M code, which brings even more control and better outcomes. You are journeying toward this end and will be able to write some M code by the end of this book.

- Data modeling can be done with worksheet formulas and in the Power Pivot and Power BI Data Model, but as you saw in this project, powerful and effective data modeling is possible with Power Query as well. In this project, you saw three important data modeling tasks: how to combine multiple tables into one table, how to create custom columns to make row-by-row calculations, and how to remove fields that are not required in the final data model. You also learned that you can go back and make changes in the Power Query Editor after a report has been completed.

- When you are importing data with Power Query and using the standard PivotTable tool, if you do not need the data in the worksheet, you can load directly to the PivotTable cache to avoid redundant tables and reduce the file size and the number of refresh clicks.

- In this project, you got a first look at Power Query parameters and custom functions. A *parameter* is a stored value that serves as a variable query input and can be used anywhere in the Power Query environment. A *custom function query* is a query that delivers a reusable function that can be used anywhere in Power Query environment. A *custom function* defines variables (query inputs or parameters) and the mapping for those variables to deliver a final value.

Project 2: Importing SQL Big Data, Building DAX Formulas, and Creating an Interactive Power BI Desktop Report

In this project, you are going to connect to an online SQL Server database and import 7 million rows of data to create an interactive Power BI Desktop report to help analyze product sales and gross profit by product, product category, and website. To complete this project, you will use Power Query to import data and then build more than 20 DAX formulas to create the data model.

Figure 19.44 shows the product metrics page you will create to allow a user to filter by product category and sales website.

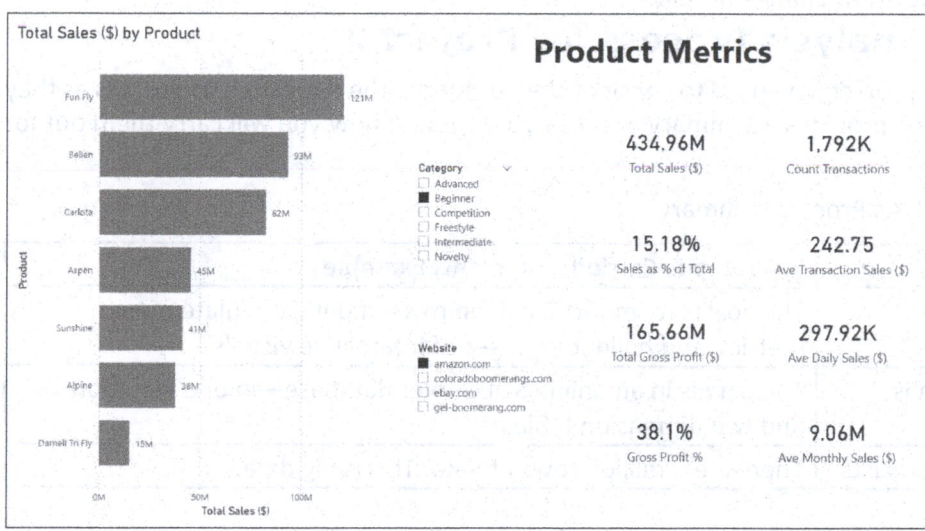

Figure 19.44 *Power BI page with eight metrics for product by category and website.*

In this project, you will also create a page with two line charts to show the trends in metrics over months (see Figure 19.45). The first line chart you create will show gross profit amount and gross profit percentage. Gross profit is a metric that assesses how well the company can manage the production and labor costs that go into producing a product or service. The second line chart you create will show total sales and the 12-month moving average, which is a metric that can smooth out the sales number and show the general trend when there are volatile or seasonal changes in sales.

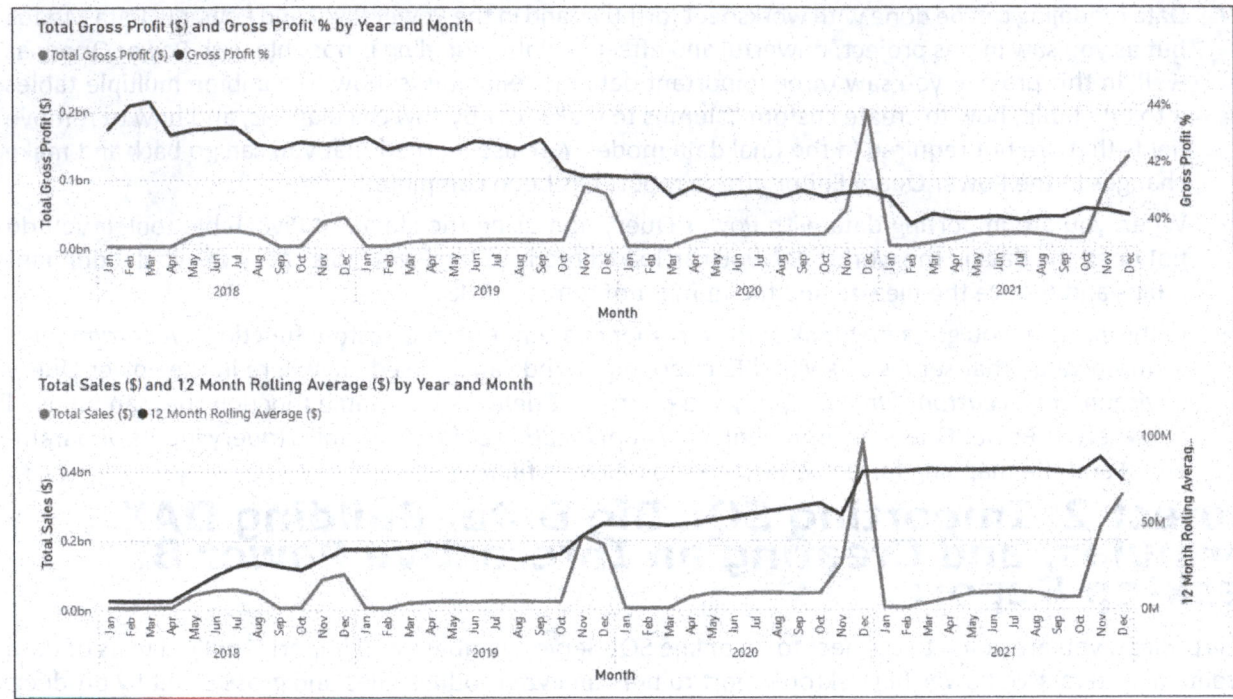

Figure 19.45 *The top chart shows trends in gross profit by month, and the bottom chart shows trends in sales by month.*

You will also create two other pages in a Power BI Desktop report: one with a table that lists all metrics and the other to show the year-over-year changes in sales.

The 10-Step Data Analysis Process for Project 2

Before you begin creating this project, you need to consider the 10 steps in the data analysis process as they relate to this project. Table 19.2 provides a summary of these 10 steps and how you will carry them out for this project.

Table 19.2 Project 2 Data Analysis Process Summary

Step	How Step Is Carried Out in This Example
1. Determine the goals of the analysis	The goal is to import 7 million rows of data, calculate many metrics, and build four pages of interactive visuals.
2. Determine where the data is	The data is in an online SQL Server database—in one fact table and two dimension tables.
3. Determine how much data exists	There are 7 million rows of data. This is big data.

4. Determine which tool or tools to use	Power BI Desktop will be the best tool because:
	
	• The Data Model columnar database can store and work with big data efficiently.
	• Power Query makes it easy to import data from an online SQL Server database.
	• Relationships can help create an efficient star schema data model.
	• DAX table functions and calculated columns can be used to create a date dimension table.
	• DAX calculated columns and measures can be used to create the following 12 metrics:
	  • Count Transactions
	  • Total Sales
	  • Total COGS
	  • Gross Profit
	  • % Gross Profit
	  • % of Grand Total Sales
	  • % of Filtered Grand Total Sales
	  • Average Transactional Sales
	  • Average Daily Sales
	  • Average Monthly Sales
	  • 12-Month Moving Sales Average
	  • % Year-Over-Year Sales Change
	• Power BI visualizations can accomplish the interactive visualization goals.

5. Import the data	You will use Power Query.
6. Clean and transform the data	You will use Power Query.
7. Load the data	You will use Power Query to load the data to the Data Model columnar database.
8. Create a data model	You will use relationships, DAX formulas, and hidden fields to create a star schema data model. Figure 19.46 shows a picture of the finished data model for this project.
9. Create useful information	You will use Power BI Desktop to create interactive pages. You can use Power BI Online if you want to share the results easily and if consumers of the useful information have a Power BI Pro or higher license.
10. Update the data model based on new data	You will not get new data. However, the data model you build will be able to accommodate new data.

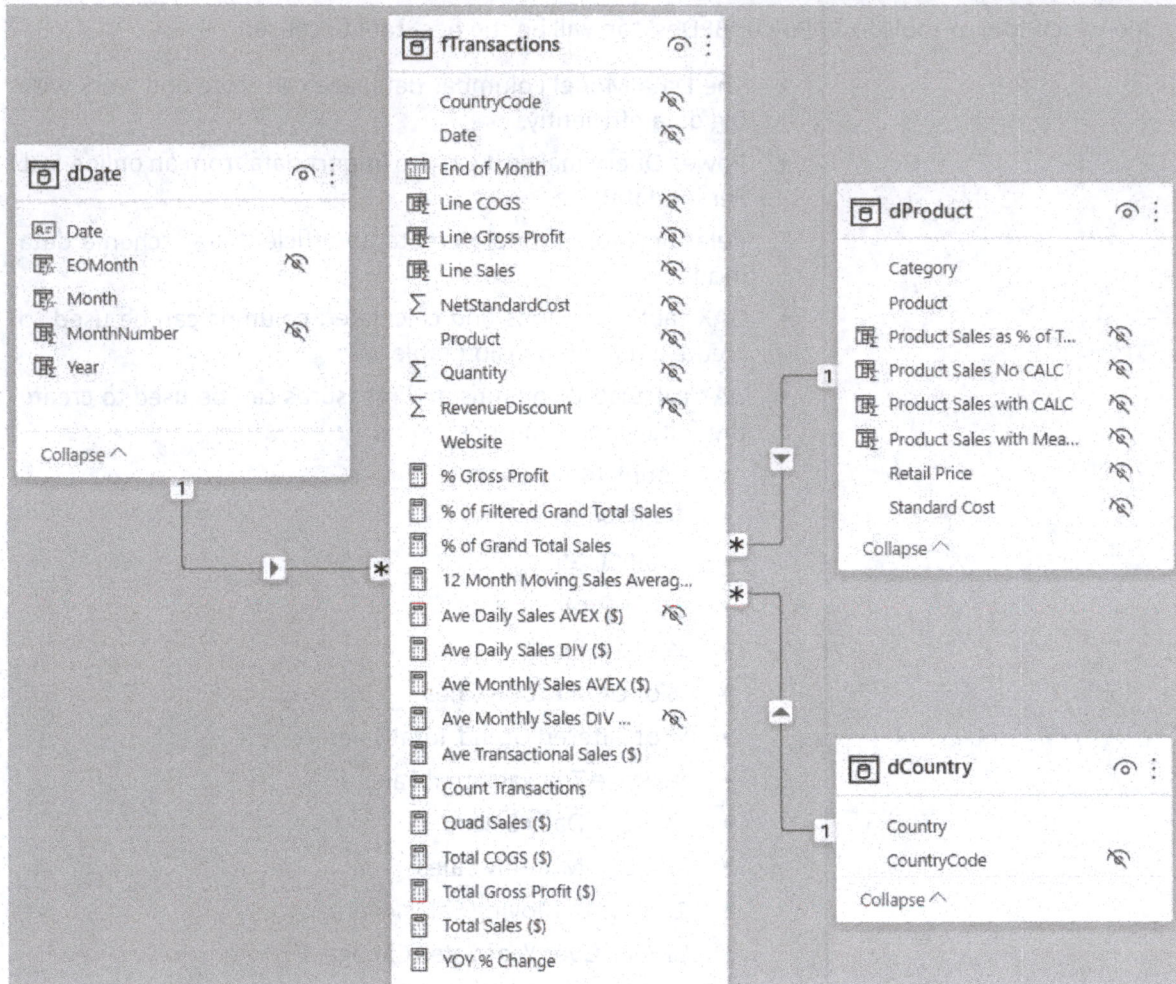

Figure 19.46 *Finished star schema data model for Project 2.*

You may at some point need to go back and change something in your report, and the Power Query process makes it easy to change and update your report.

SQL Server Databases, the SQL Computer Language, and Power Query

For this project, you need to know just a little bit about SQL and SQL Server databases. This section provides the very basics you need to know before you begin working through the project.

SQL Server is a relational database management system that can hold one or more databases and that can be located on-premises or in the cloud. The main goal of the SQL Server software product is to make it possible to store and retrieve data requested by other software applications, such as Power Query. When you send a request for data to an SQL Server database, you must have the correct credentials to connect.

SQL, which stands for *Structured Query Language*, is a computer language that allows you to build and query databases. It is an effective and efficient computer language for dealing with related tables of data. In addition, SQL Server can typically automatically determine the fastest way to execute a query against a database by using SQL code; that is, SQL Server can *optimize* a query request sent to a database.

When you use Power Query to connect to an SQL Server database, bring the data into the Power Query Editor, and make transformations, Power Query writes the M code to do all that. In addition, because the data source is an SQL Server database, Power Query also writes SQL code, when possible, to try to execute the query more efficiently back in SQL Server. This is called *query folding*. Query folding is particularly helpful with big data because SQL Server can often execute a query more quickly than can M code. The process happens automatically, and you do not even need to be aware of it. However, if you know SQL and you want to see the code, you can right-click any step in the Applied Steps list in the Power Query Editor and click on View Native Query to see the SQL code that was sent back.

When a step in the Applied Steps list has the View Native Query option grayed out, this indicates that it was not possible to send the step back to SQL Server for execution. In addition, when an applied step is grayed out, all applied steps after that step are also grayed out and are not sent back to SQL Server.

A number of query actions can be sent back in query folding, including removing columns, renaming columns, filtering rows with static values, grouping, appending or merging queries based on the same source, and adding custom columns with simple formulas, such as multiplication. Some query actions cannot be sent back in query folding, including changing a data type for a field, appending or merging queries based on different sources, adding custom columns with complex formulas, and adding index columns. The rule of thumb for how to order the steps when connecting to an SQL Server database is that you should put the steps that can be sent back to the database at the top of the Applied Steps list. When you do so, more of the query can be sent back to SQL Server for efficient processing. Any steps that you create that cannot be sent back are executed with M code in Power Query.

The SQL Server database that you will be connected to in this project is stored in the cloud; that is, it is stored online and not on-premises. The benefit of connecting to a data source that is stored in the cloud is that as long as you are connected to the internet, you can move the file that you load the data into to any location, and the data source connection remains valid. In contrast, when an on-premises file is moved, the connection to the data source is lost.

In order to connect to the online SQL Server database in this project, you will need to use these credentials:

- **Server:** pond.highline.edu
- **Database:** boomdata
- **User:** excelisfun
- **Password:** ExcelIsFun!

> **Note:** Note that this password has an uppercase **E** in the first position, and uppercase **I** in the sixth position, and an uppercase **F** in the eighth position. It has a **!** (exclamation point) in the last position. All the other letters in the password are lowercase.

Importing the Data for Project 2

You need to import data from three tables that are stored in an SQL Server database:

- **fTransactions:** The fTransactions fact table, shown in Figure 19.47, contains 7,742,561 rows of transactional boomerang product sales data for the years 2018 to 2021. There are three foreign keys in this fact table that you will use to create relationships with the dimension tables: Date, Product, and CountryCode. The RevenueDiscount field contains the quantity discount for each transaction, and the NetStandardCost field contains the net COGS equivalent that is multiplied by the standard cost to get the COGS amount for each transaction. You will have to use both fields in the calculations for sales and COGS.

fTransactions = 7,742,561 transactional sales

Date of transaction	Product sold	Web site were sale made	Country where sale made	# products sold	Discount given on transaction sale	Net COGS equivalent
Foreign Key	Foreign Key		Foreign Key			
Date	Product	Website	CountryCode	Quantity	RevenueDiscount	NetStandardCost
5/12/18	Carlota	ebay.com	FRA	58	0	0.99
11/22/19	Fun Fly	amazon.com	USA	71	0.373	1.02
3/23/18	Crested Beaut	coloradoboomerangs.com	JPN	38	0.15	0.98
11/25/21	Phoenix	ebay.com	GBR	3	0	1.04

Figure 19.47 *The fTransactions fact table in the SQL Server database.*

- **dCountry:** The dCountry dimension table, shown in Figure 19.48, contains country data, such as the name of the country where the sale was made.

- **dProduct:** The dProduct dimension table, also shown in Figure 19.48, contains product data such as retail price and standard cost.

dCountry = 126 country codes and names

County code Primary Key	Country name
CountryCode	**Country**
AFG	Afghanistan
ALB	Albania
APR	Aprine
ARE	United Arab Emirates

dProduct = 22 rows of product data

Product name Primary Key	Retail price for 1 unit	COGS for 1 unit	Product category
Product	**Retail Price**	**Standard Cost**	**Category**
Alpine	23.95	10.09	Beginner
Aspen	23.95	9.48	Beginner
Bellen	26.99	10.75	Beginner
Bower Aussie Round	45	18.45	Competition

Figure 19.48 *The dCountry and dProduct dimension tables in the SQL Server database.*

To import the data for this project, follow these steps:

1. Open a new Power BI Desktop file and save it with the name Ch19-Project02-SQL-DataReport.pbix.

2. To connect to the online SQL Server database, in the Home tab of the Power Query Ribbon, in the Data group, click the SQL Server button, as shown in Figure 19.49.

Figure 19.49 *The button to connect to SQL Server is located in the Data group of the Home tab in the Power Query Ribbon.*

3. In the SQL Server Database dialog box that appears, as shown in Figure 19.50, in the Server textbox enter the server name **pond.highline.edu**. In the Database textbox, enter the database name **boom-data**. In the Data Connectivity Mode area, select the Import option button to import the data into the Data Model columnar database. Then click the OK button.

> **Note:** If you want to write your own SQL code to retrieve and transform data rather than use the Power Query features, you can click the Advanced Options arrow at the bottom of the SQL Server Database dialog box and write the SQL code that will be sent to the SQL Server database.

SQL Server database

Server ⓘ

> pond.highline.edu

Database (optional)

> boomdata

Data Connectivity mode ⓘ

◉ Import

○ DirectQuery

▷ Advanced options

OK   Cancel

Figure 19.50 *In the SQL Server Database dialog box, enter the server name and the database name.*

Note: In the SQL Server Database dialog box, you might have noticed the DirectQuery option in the Data Connectivity Mode area. You can use this option if you have very large data, if you need near-real-time reporting, or if you have data sovereignty restrictions (which means data can't leave the organization's premises). There are significant limitations to this option. For example, not all transformations and calculations are possible. This book does not cover the DirectQuery option, but you can find good information about it at https://docs.microsoft.com/en-us/power-bi/connect-data/desktop-directquery-about.

4. In the second SQL Server Database dialog box that appears, select Database on the left side, as shown in Figure 19.51. Do not leave the Windows option (which is the default) selected and do not click the Microsoft Account option. In the User Name textbox, enter **excelisfun**. In the Password textbox, enter **ExcelIsFun!**. In the Select Which Level to Apply These Settings To dropdown, select **pond.highline.edu;boomdata**. Then click the Connect button.

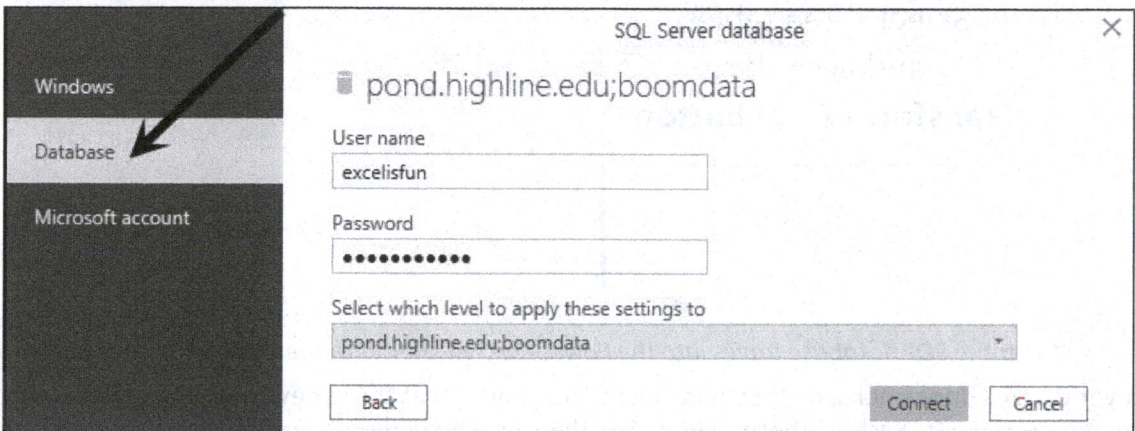

Figure 19.51 *In the second SQL Server Database dialog box, select Database on the left and then enter the remaining credentials.*

5. In the Encryption Support dialog box that appears (see Figure 19.52), click OK.

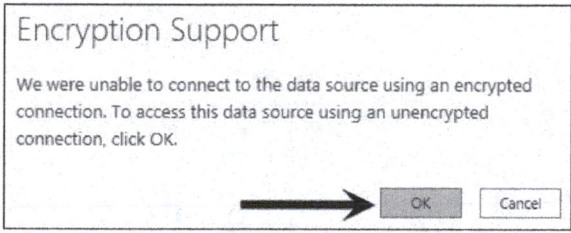

Figure 19.52 *This publicly available data is not encrypted and does not need to be.*

6.   In the Navigator dialog box that appears, as shown in Figure 19.53, check the checkboxes for the tables fTransactions, dCountry, and dProduct. Then, to bring the SQL database tables into the Power Query Editor, click the Transform Data button.

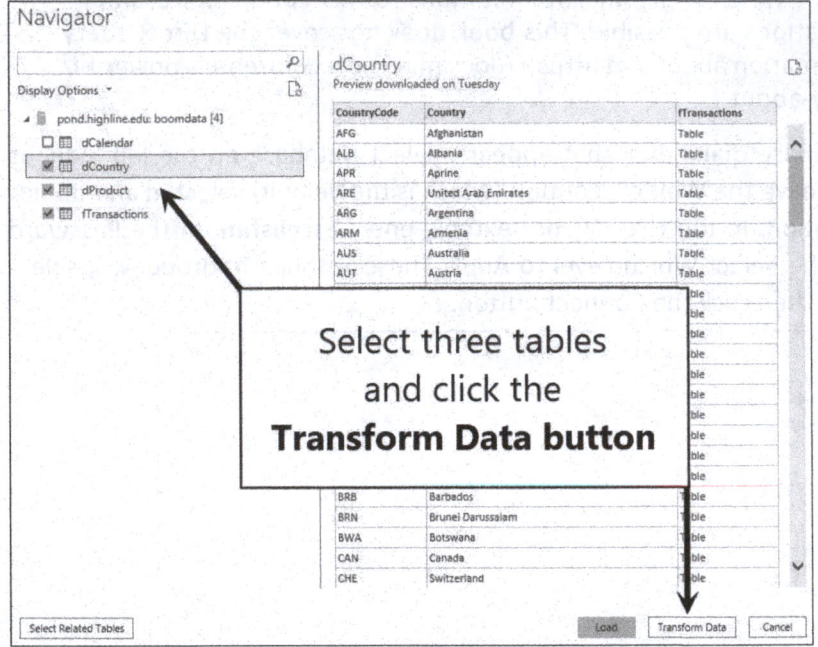

Figure 19.53 *Bring the three SQL database tables into the Power Query Editor with the Transform Data button.*

When the Power Query Editor opens, as shown in Figure 19.54, note that three new queries appear in the Queries task pane on the left. Each of these queries has the same two query steps shown in the Applied Steps list in the Query Settings task pane on the right. For all three queries, the M code for the Source step is identical, as shown in Figure 19.55. This Source step connects to the SQL Server database and displays a table where the Data field contains the tables, and the remaining fields contain attributes of the table.

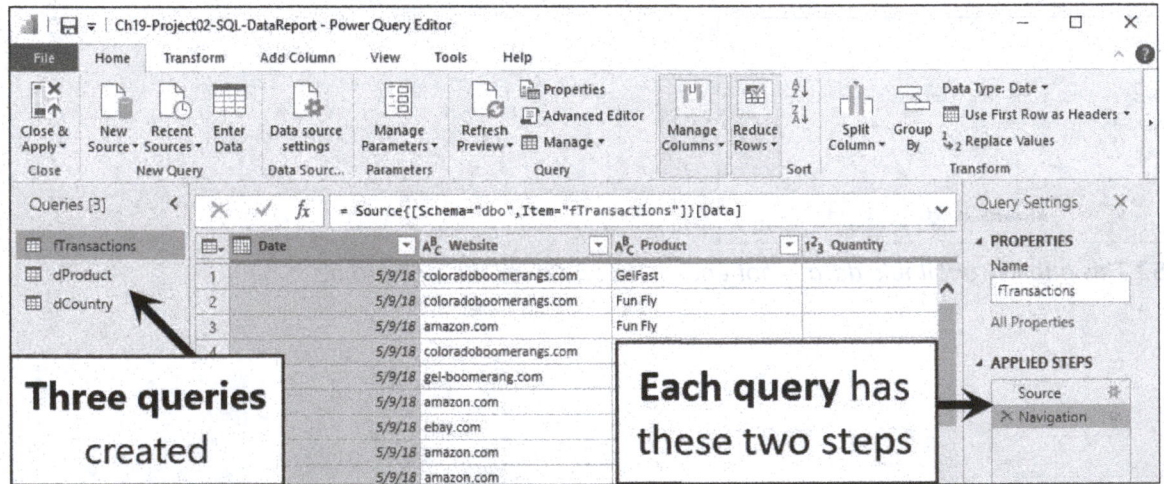

Figure 19.54 *Importing three tables from a data source creates three separate queries.*

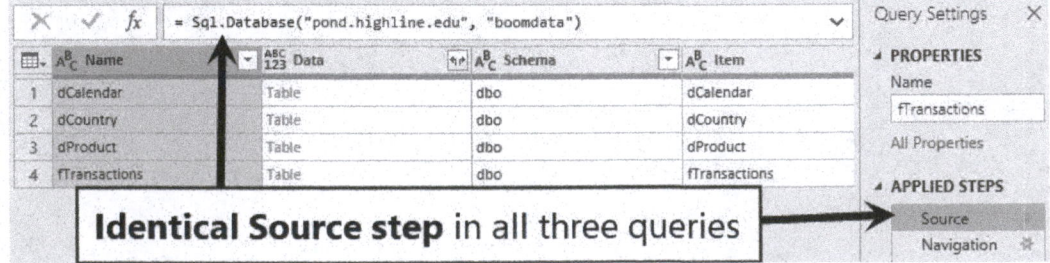

Figure 19.55 *The Source step in all three queries uses the same M code to connect to the database and display all the tables.*

The Navigation step of each query pulls the specified table from the Data field. Figures 19.56 through 19.58 show the M code that Power Query creates for the Navigation step for each query. In each case, the M code uses a two-way lookup, with the fTransactions table row and the Data columns as inputs. (You will learn how to manually perform this type of M code two-way lookup in Chapter 20.)

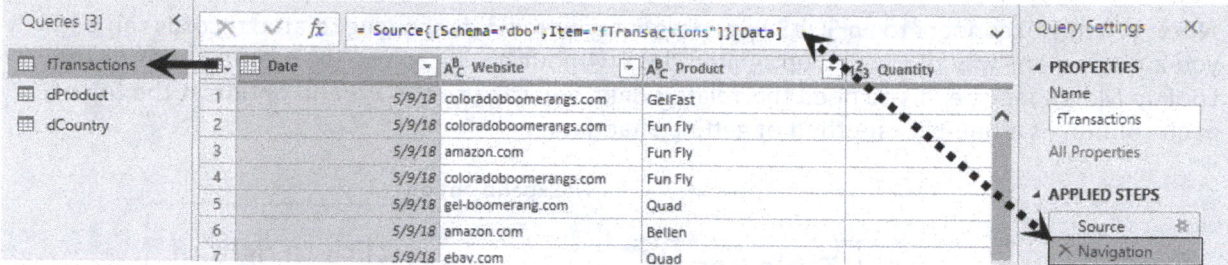

Figure 19.56 *The Navigation step in the fTransactions query selects the fTransactions table from the list of database tables.*

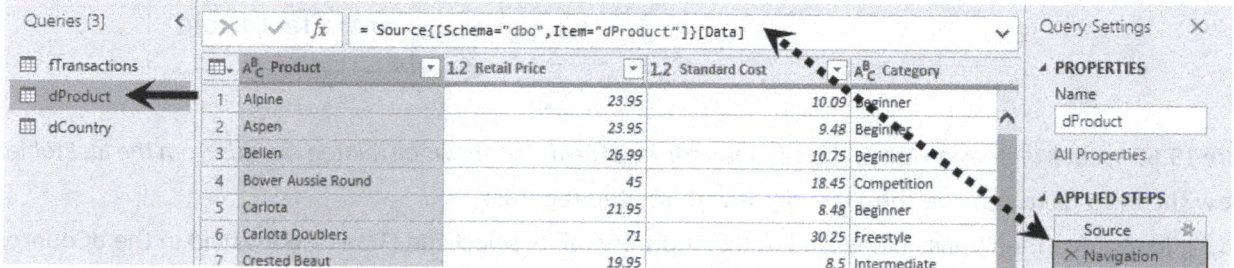

Figure 19.57 *The Navigation step in the dProduct query selects the dProduct table from the list of database tables.*

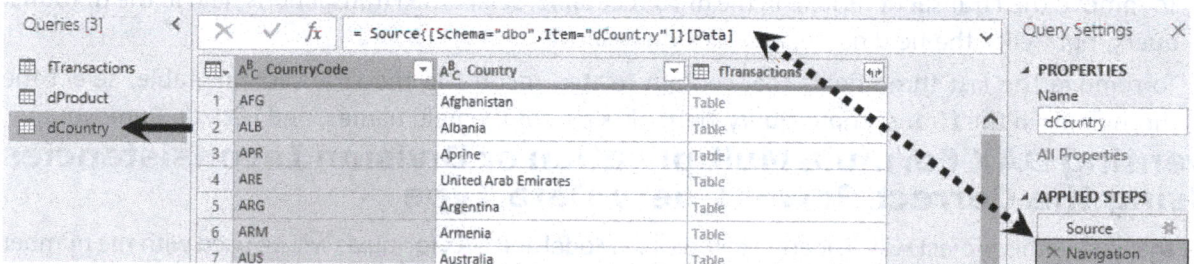

Figure 19.58 *The Navigation step in the dCountry query selects the dCountry table from the list of database tables.*

Removing Extra Fields from the Tables

When you connect to an SQL Server database that contains related tables (that is, tables with relationships between the tables) and then import the tables, you get the data from the tables themselves plus extra fields that contain data from the related tables. For example, as shown in Figure 19.59, the last three fields in the fTransactions fact table are extra fields added to the existing fields—one for each related dimension table: dCalendar, dCountry, and dProduct. Because each of the dimension tables is on the one-side of the one-to-many relationship, for each row in these additional columns, the related record from the dimension table is listed. As shown in Figure 19.59, for the first record in the fTransactions table, where a GelFast product was sold, the dProduct field shows the record for the GelFast product.

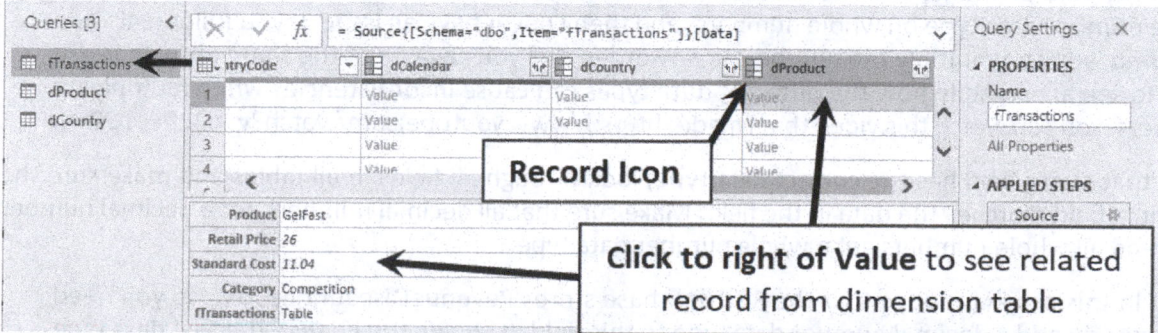

Figure 19.59 *In the fact table, there are three additional fields that show the related records from the dimension tables.*

As shown in Figure 19.60, the last field in the dCountry dimension table is a new field named fTransactions, where each row shows all the related records from the fact table. For example, the fourth row in the dCountry table shows all the transactions from the fact table for products sold in the United Arab Emirates. You are not going to use these extra fields with related records in this project, so you can remove them.

Note: When you connect to an SQL Server database, extra fields showing related records can give you a convenient way of looking up related data without having to use lookup functions or the Lookup Merge feature. If you need this related data, you can use the Expand option at the top of each column as a one-click method of getting that data.

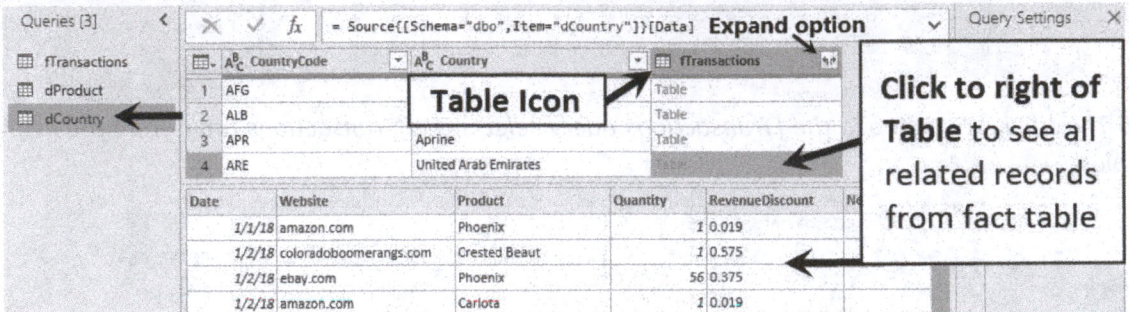

Figure 19.60 *In each dimension table, there is one additional field that shows all related records from the fact table.*

Follow these steps to remove the extra fields with related records:

1. To remove the fTransactions field in the dCountry table, select the fTransactions field in the dCountry query, right-click the field name, and click on Remove.

2. To remove the fTransactions field in the dProduct table, select the fTransactions field in the dProduct query, right-click the field name, and click on Remove.

3. To remove the last three fields that contain related records in the fTransactions table, select the three fields in the fTransactions query, right-click one of the field names, and click on Remove.

Preventing DAX Formula Multiplication or Division Inconsistencies by Using the Correct Power Query Data Type

Because the data in this project will be loaded to the Data Model and DAX formulas will be used with the number data to perform multiplication and division, you need to make sure to use the decimal number data type (which allows up to 15 digits) on all decimal number fields and the whole number data type (with 0 decimal places) on all whole number fields. If you use the decimal number data type on some decimal number fields and the fixed decimal number data type (which allows up to 4 decimal places) on other decimal number fields, if the order changes, you may get inconsistent results. This is because of how the DAX calculation engine treats the decimal number data type and the fixed decimal number data type during multiplication. The commutative property of multiplication does not hold when you use the decimal number data type on some numbers and the fixed decimal number data type on other numbers, so by simply changing the order of the numbers in a multiplication operation, you can get different results. This does not happen with Excel worksheet formulas. In Excel, you can multiply a set of numbers in any order, and you will always get the same answer.

Note: My rule of thumb is to use the decimal number data type on decimal numbers and the whole number data type on whole numbers, and then I never have an issue. If you follow this rule of thumb, you can multiply the numbers in any order, and you always get the same answer. If you want to see an example how the different data types can cause inconsistencies when multiplying numbers, you can watch this video that I made: https://www.youtube.com/watch?v=6420PcTGBv8.

To ensure that every field has the correct data type, look through all fields in all tables and make sure the data type in a field matches the data in the field. Make sure that all decimal numbers get a decimal number data type and all whole numbers get a whole number data type.

Note: In this project, notice that the SQL database stores RevenueDiscount as text, so you need to be sure to add a decimal number data type to this field. If you do not change the text data type on this field, you will get calculation errors when you try to use the values in this field as numbers.

Cleaning the Country Data

In the second field in the dCountry table, in a couple cases, a country name contains quotation marks and has two parts, separated by a comma (see Figure 19.61). For reporting, you do not want country names to contain quotation marks and multiple parts. You therefore need to clean this data by removing the quotation marks and everything after the comma. The cleaning task will involve replacing the quotation marks with nothing and extracting everything before the comma delimiter. This pattern will accomplish the cleaning goal and will not adversely affect any of the 126 names in this field because there are not any country names in this data that actually need the quotation marks or anything after the comma.

> **Note:** If there were even one case where you needed the quotation marks or the text after the comma for a country name, you would have to use a different pattern for the cleaning task. You would need to closely examine the data to detect the correct pattern.

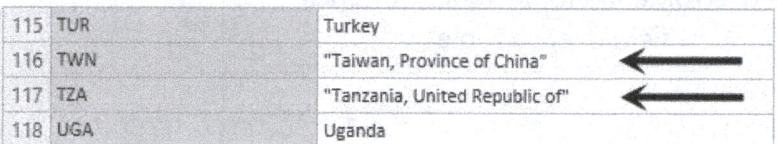

115	TUR	Turkey
116	TWN	"Taiwan, Province of China"
117	TZA	"Tanzania, United Republic of"
118	UGA	Uganda

Figure 19.61 *The quotation marks in this data are not needed, and everything after the comma is not needed.*

To accomplish this cleaning task, you can use the Transform tab in the Power Query Ribbon. The Transform tab allows you to take actions on a field to clean or transform it in some way.

To clean the country data to create data that is more suitable for reporting, follow these steps:

1. As shown in Figure 19.62, in the dCountry query, select the last step in Applied Steps list, select the Country field, click the Transform tab of the Ribbon, and in the Any Column group, click Replace Values.

2. In the Replace Values dialog box that appears, type a quotation mark (") into the Value To Find textbox, leave the Replace With textbox empty, and click the OK button.

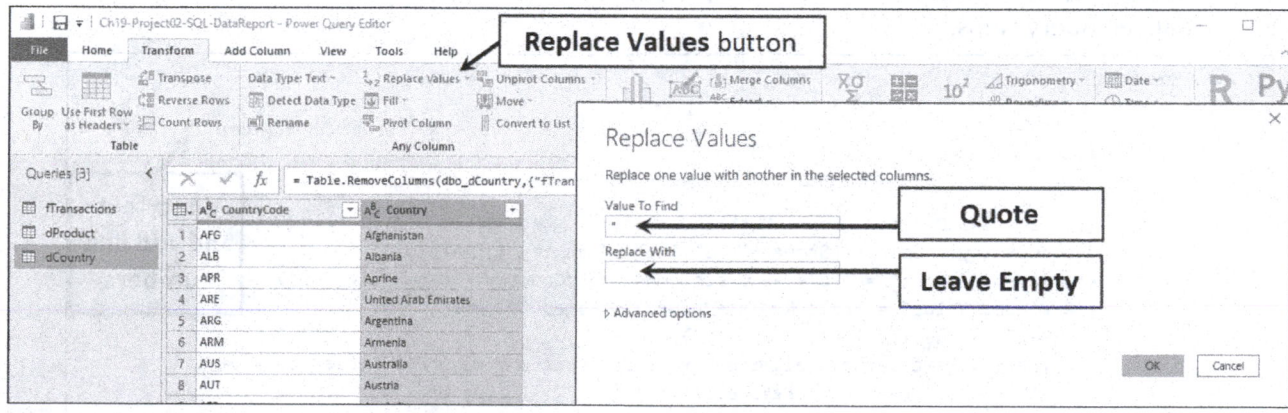

Figure 19.62 *Replace a quotation mark (") with nothing.*

3. As shown in Figure 19.63, with the Country field still selected, in the Transform tab of the Ribbon, go to the Text Column group, click the Extract dropdown arrow, and select Text Before Delimiter.

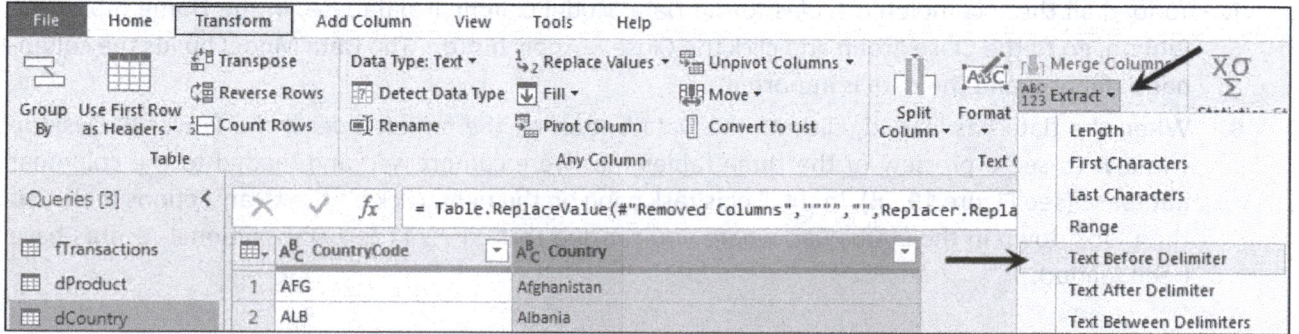

Figure 19.63 *Extract the text before the comma delimiter.*

4.   In the Text Before Delimiter dialog box that appears, enter a comma as the delimiter and then click the OK button.

5.   To automatically check the quality of the data in each field, click the View tab of the Ribbon and then, in the Data Preview group, check the Column Quality checkbox. Figure 19.64 shows the result for the first several fields in the fTransactions table. As you look through the other tables, you should find that each field shows that 100% of the values are valid and that there are no errors or empty cells.

Note: The Column Quality feature can sometimes help you find problems before you make reports.

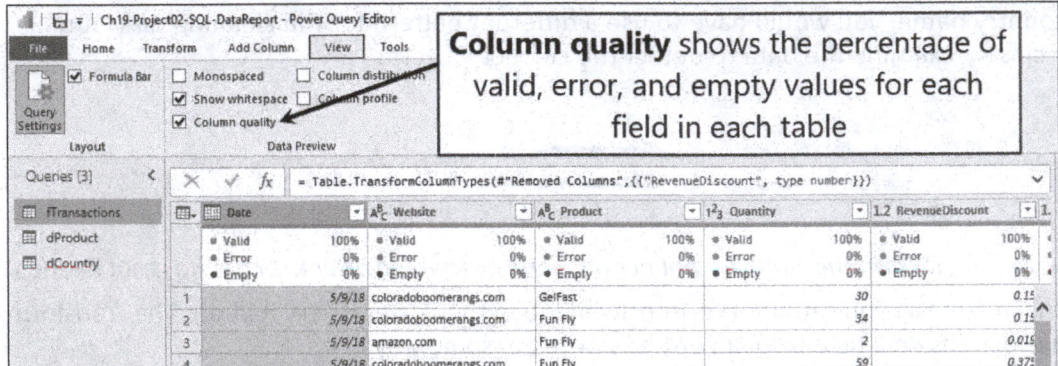

Figure 19.64 *Column Quality helps you find bad data.*

6.   To look at the final M code and let expression for each query, select the query and then, in the Home tab of the Ribbon, go to the Query group and click the Advanced Editor button. You can do this for each query to check the M code for each step in the query before loading the data to the Data Model. Figure 19.65 shows the dCountry query let expression with the M code for each of the five applied query steps.

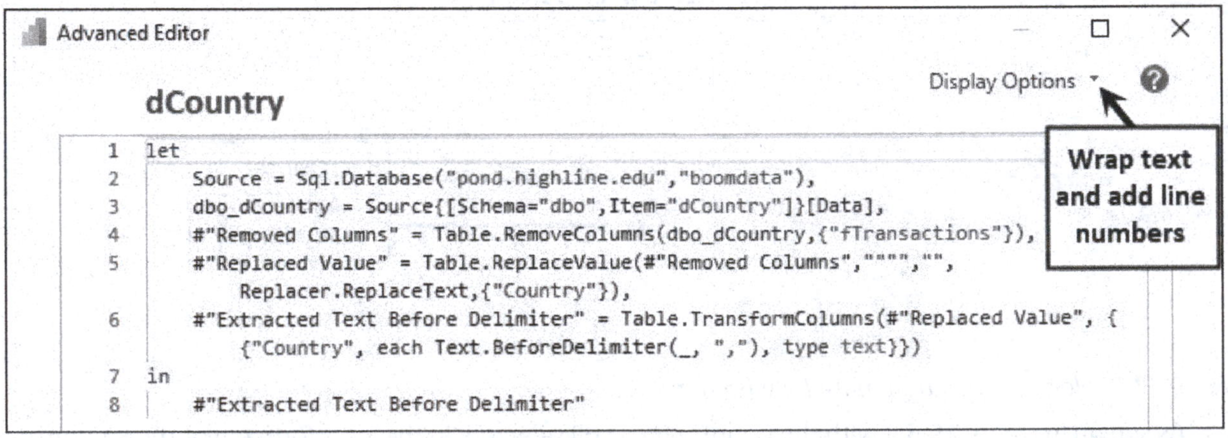

```
dCountry

1   let
2       Source = Sql.Database("pond.highline.edu","boomdata"),
3       dbo_dCountry = Source{[Schema="dbo",Item="dCountry"]}[Data],
4       #"Removed Columns" = Table.RemoveColumns(dbo_dCountry,{"fTransactions"}),
5       #"Replaced Value" = Table.ReplaceValue(#"Removed Columns","""","",
            Replacer.ReplaceText,{"Country"}),
6       #"Extracted Text Before Delimiter" = Table.TransformColumns(#"Replaced Value", {
            {"Country", each Text.BeforeDelimiter(_, ","), type text}})
7   in
8       #"Extracted Text Before Delimiter"
```

Figure 19.65 *A let expression with five applied steps to deliver the final transformed and cleaned dCountry table.*

7.   To load all three completed tables to the Data Model columnar database, in the Home tab of the Ribbon, go to the Close group and click the Close & Apply button. The Data Model builds the columnar database, and the data is imported.

8.   When the data has loaded, click on the Data button on the far-left side of the Power BI Desktop window to see a preview of the three tables that were compressed and loaded to the columnar database (see Figure 19.66). In the Fields task pane on the right, click on the fTransactions table and then look down in the status bar, where you can see that all 7,742,561 transactional records have been loaded.

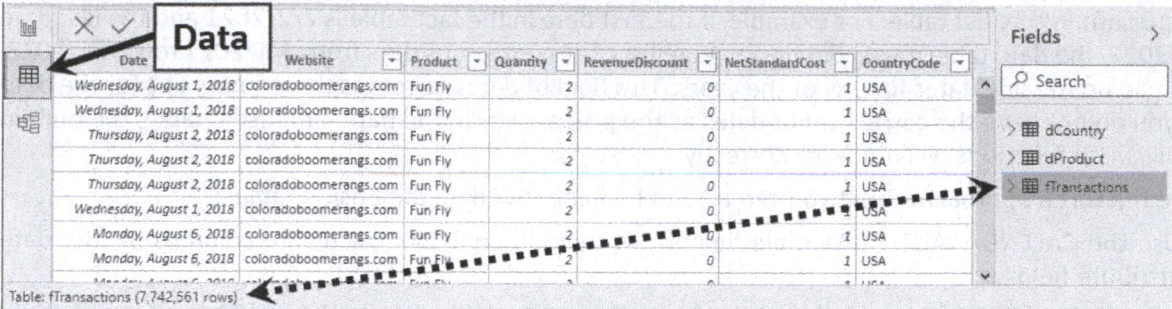

Figure 19.66 *In the data area of Power BI Desktop, the status bar shows that 7,742,561 rows of data have been loaded.*

9. Click on the Model button on the far-left side of the Power BI Desktop window to see the tables and the automatically created relationships (see Figure 19.67). You can move a table by clicking on its title bar and dragging it. You should see the one-to-many relationships in a star schema data model, with the dimension tables on the one-side and the fact table on the many-side.

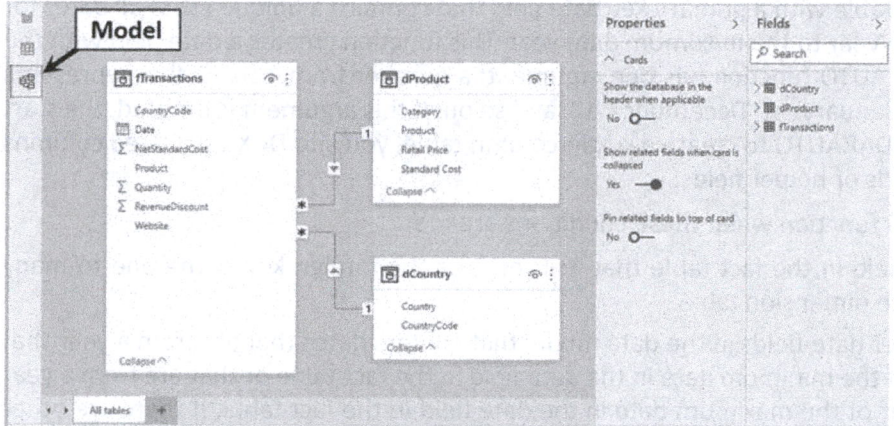

Figure 19.67 *In the Model area of Power BI Desktop, you can see the automatically created one-to-many relationships.*

Date Dimension Tables (Calendar Tables) in the Data Model

In Figure 19.67, you can see two dimension tables in the star schema data model. However, for the calculations and reports that you need to create in this project, you need a date dimension table as well. Although there was a date dimension table named Calendar in the SQL Server database, it had the wrong dates, and so you did not import it.

A date dimension table, also referred to as a *calendar table*, is often the most important dimension table in a star schema data model because it provides date attribute fields such as day, week, month, quarter, year, fiscal quarter, and fiscal year to help create any particular date summary report that may be required. In addition, there can be helper columns in date tables that help with sorting and making calculations at the correct grain. Furthermore, if you have a correctly structured date dimension table, the full set of DAX time intelligence functions, including DATESINPERIOD, SAMEPERIODLASTYEAR, and TOTALYTD, are available for your DAX formulas. Because of these benefits, it is usually worthwhile to add a date dimension table to a star schema data model if your transactional data contains dates.

When you are building a date dimension table in Power Pivot, you can use a single-click method to create a date table if the correct conditions are met; otherwise, you create the date table in the worksheet and import it (as you will see in Practice Problem 3 at the end of this chapter). When you are building a date dimension table in Power BI Desktop, you can build the table using DAX formulas (or Power Query). In this project, you will learn three different ways to build a DAX date dimension table, each with a specific advantage. You will also see that when you create a DAX table using the New Table button, the table is automatically loaded to the Data Model columnar database.

When you build a date dimension table, you must be careful to structure it correctly. For the DAX time intelligence functions to correctly work, the date dimension table must have a unique list of all dates for all years that are present in the fact table. For example, if the first date in the fact table is 2/2/2021 and the last date is 11/15/2022, the date table must contain a unique list of all contiguous days from 1/1/2021 to 12/31/2022. There can be no missing dates for any of the years. This field of dates becomes the primary key for the date table. If you do not have the correct set of dates as the primary key in the date dimension table, the built-in time intelligence functions will not work correctly.

These are the three approaches that you can take to building DAX date dimension tables:

- Use the CALENDARAUTO DAX table function with additional DAX calculated columns for the date attribute fields.
- Use the CALENDAR DAX table function with additional DAX calculated columns for the date attribute fields.
- Use the GENERATE and ROW DAX table functions to build a single DAX formula that creates the correct primary key date field and all the date attribute fields with a single formula.

Figures 19.68 through 19.83 in the following sections provide examples of using the CALENDARAUTO DAX table function with additional DAX calculated columns for the date attribute fields. The CALENDARAUTO DAX table function automatically searches all tables in the data model, finds the minimum date and maximum date, and then builds a single-column table with a primary key date field that contains a unique list of all dates for all years from the minimum date year to the maximum date year. This function creates a date field with the field name Date. The CALENDARAUTO function has one argument: a number from 1 to 12 that represents the starting fiscal month, where January = 1, December = 12, and so on. If this argument is omitted, the start month is 1. After you use CALENDARAUTO to create a single-column table, you add DAX calculated columns to create your date attribute fields or helper fields.

You can use the CALENDARAUTO function when these conditions are met:

- You have a single date field in the fact table that will serve as the foreign key in the one-to-many relationship with the date dimension table.
- You do not have any other date fields in the data model that contain dates that are from a year that is earlier than the year of the minimum date in the date field in the fact table or that are from a year that is later than the year of the maximum date in the date field in the fact table. If there are other date fields in the data model, the CALEDARAUTO function may create a date table that is too big.
- You do not have time fields in any of the tables in the data model. Time fields can cause the CALENDARAUTO function to create date dimension tables that are much too big.

In the steps in the next section, you will see an example of how to use the CALENDARAUTO function when the start date for the year is January 1 (see Figure 19.69).

The advantage of the CALENDARAUTO function is that it is fast and easy to use. The disadvantage of the CALENDARAUTO function is that it searches the entire data model for minimum and maximum dates and may create a data table that is too big.

The second approach is to use the CALENDAR DAX table function with additional DAX calculated columns for the date attribute fields. The CALENDAR DAX table function builds a single-column table with a primary key date field containing a unique list of all dates for all years from a specified start date to a specified end date. This function creates a date field with the field name Date, based on its two arguments: *start_date* and *end_date*. After you use CALENDAR to create the single-column table, you add DAX calculated columns to create your date attribute fields or helper fields.

In the steps in the next section, you will see an example of how to use the CALENDAR function with dynamic start and end dates, based on the dates in the fact table (see Figure 19.70). The DAX formula element DATE(YEAR(MIN(fTransactions[Date])),1,1) defines the start date and the formula element, and DATE(YEAR(MAX(fTransactions[Date])),12,31) defines the end date. When dates change in the fact table, these formula elements create the correct start and end dates for the primary key date field.

An advantage of the CALENDAR function is that it always gives the correct set of dates, based on your fact table. In addition, the CALENDAR function is not subject to any of the potential difficulties that CALENDARAUTO encounters. The disadvantage of the CALENDAR function is that it takes longer to use than the CALENDARAUTO function.

The third approach is to use the GENERATE and ROW DAX table functions to build a single DAX formula that creates the correct primary key date field and all the date attribute fields with a single formula. (You will see an example of this in Figures 19.84 to 19.86.) This is an advanced approach, but the beauty of it is that you create a solution with a single formula, and the formula can be copied and pasted into other Power BI Desktop data models.

Basically, the GENERATE DAX table function takes the primary key date field and does a cross-join with the ROW DAX table function, which holds a one-row table with each of the desired data attribute calculated columns, to create the full date dimension table with a single formula.

Using the CALENDAR Function or the CALENDARAUTO Function to Create a DAX Data Dimension Table

To create a DAX data dimension table, follow these steps:

1. On the far-left side of the Power BI window, click the Data button (see Figure 19.68). Power BI opens the section of the file where you can preview and create tables and the context-sensitive Table Tools tab of the Power BI Desktop Ribbon.

2. To create a new DAX table, in the Calculations group on the Table Tools tab, click the New Table button.

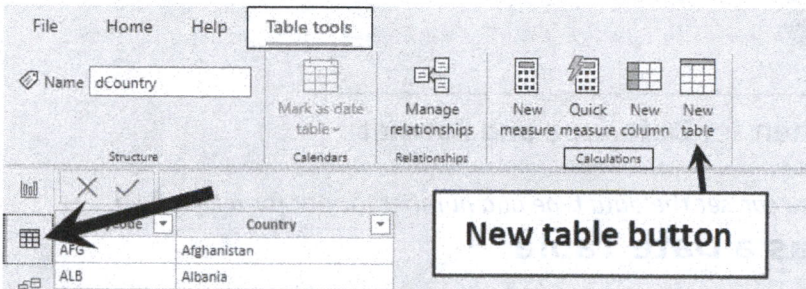

Figure 19.68 *The New Table button allows you to create DAX tables that are automatically loaded to the Data Model.*

3. Because your data model matches the conditions required for using the CALENDARAUTO function, click in the formula bar and type the table name, the assignment operator, and the formula, as shown in Figure 19.69. When you press the Enter key, a one-column table with the field name Date appears on the left, and the new dDate table appears in the Fields task pane on the right, as you can see in the figure.

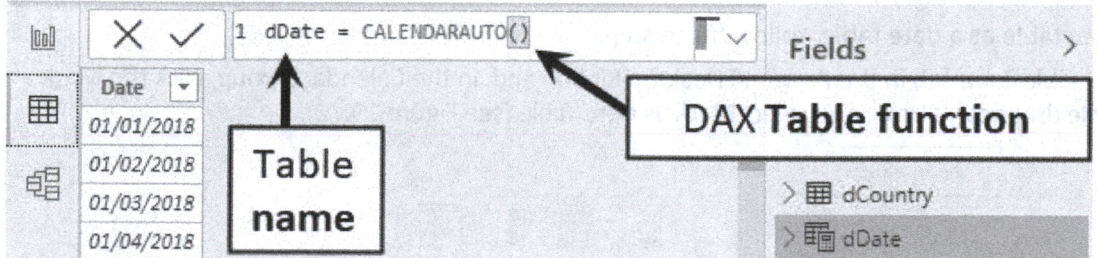

Figure 19.69 *The CALENDARAUTO function works if the fact table date field is the only date or time field in the model.*

If the conditions required for using the CALENDARAUTO function are not met, you need to instead use the formula shown in Figure 19.70.

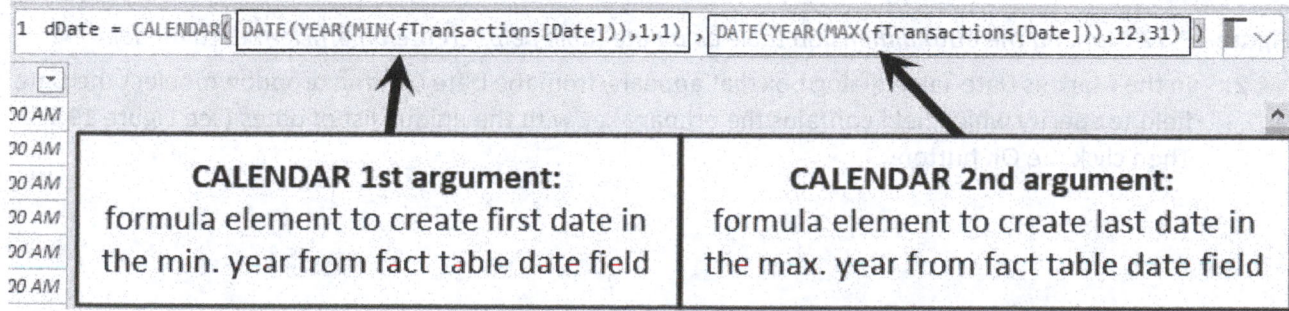

Figure 19.70 *This DAX table formula works no matter how many date or time fields there are in the data model.*

Note: When you create a DAX table and DAX calculated columns, Power BI Desktop and Power Pivot enable you to add data types to the fields. As discussed in Chapter 18, data types are important because they help formulas calculate accurate results.

4. To add a date data type to the Date field, as shown in Figure 19.71, select the Date field. When you select the Date field, the context-sensitive Column Tools tab appears in the Power BI Desktop Ribbon. In the Structure group of this tab, click the Data Type dropdown arrow and select Date.

5. To add number formatting to the field, go to the Formatting group, and select the formatting that you would like from the Format dropdown. You can see here that I selected the number format mm/dd/yyyy.

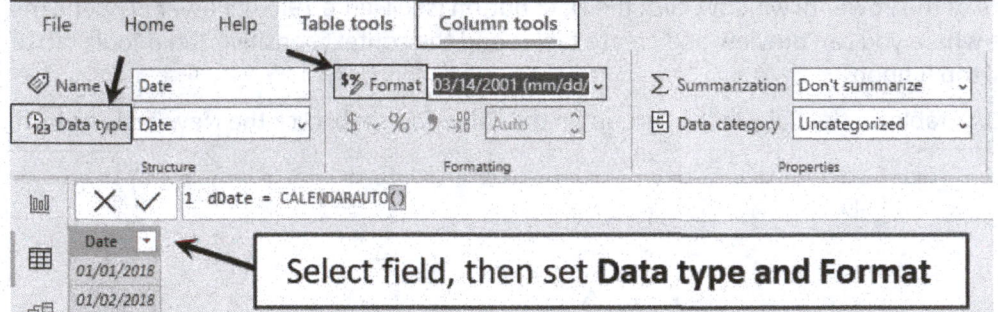

Figure 19.71 *In the Column Tools tab, you can set the data type and number format for a DAX field.*

Marking the Date Table as a Date Table

When you create a date dimension table, you must mark the date table as a date table so that the Data Model can work efficiently. If you do not mark the data table as a date table (or change the universal settings in the options area), unnecessary automatic date tables can be created when you drag and drop date fields. This is the case in both Power BI Desktop and Excel Power Pivot. These automatic date tables are a feature that Microsoft added to help beginners who do not know how to build data models. (Microsoft advertises this as a feature that everyone can use, but don't believe it.) In Power Pivot, this feature adds DAX calculated columns to the fact table. In Power BI Desktop, the feature adds hidden date tables. In both cases, the feature does not provide you with as much control over reporting as you get when you build your own date table, and the feature adds a lot of unnecessary data to the columnar database.

To mark your data table as a date table, follow these steps:

1. Click the Table Tools tab in the Power BI Desktop Ribbon and, in the Calendars group, click the Mark as Data Table dropdown arrow and select Mark as Date Table (see Figure 19.72).

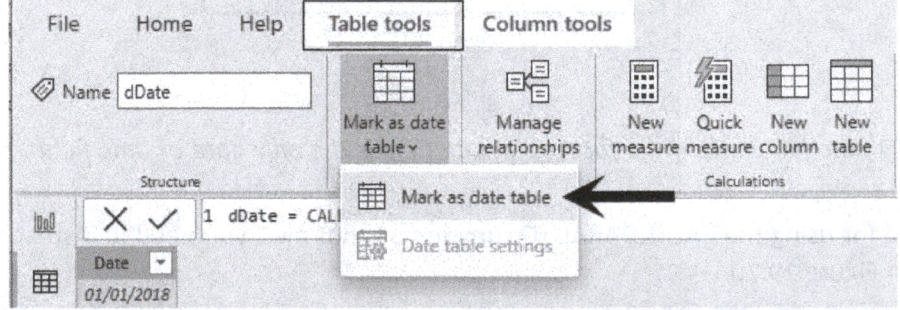

Figure 19.72 *Marking the data dimension table as a date table helps create an efficient data model.*

2. In the Mark as Date Table dialog box that appears, from the Date Column dropdown, select the Date field to specify which field contains the primary key with the unique list of dates (see Figure 19.73). Then click the OK button.

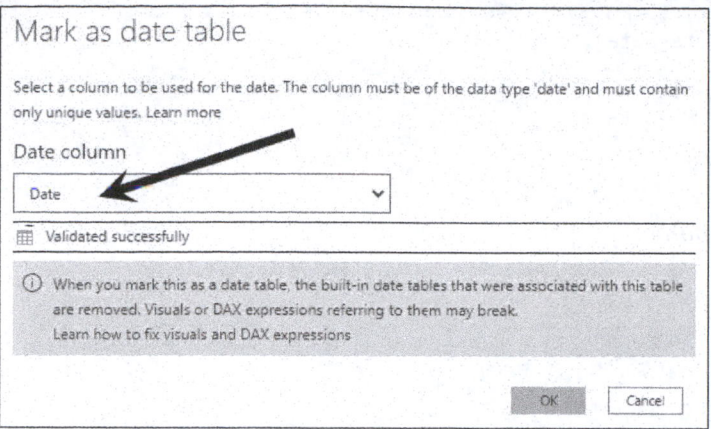

Figure 19.73 *You must specify which field in the date table is the primary key.*

Using DAX Calculated Columns to Create Date Attribute Fields Using the FORMAT function

After you create the primary key for the date dimension table with either the CALENDARAUTO or CALENDAR function, you must create each of the date attribute fields, one by one, with DAX calculated columns. All the Excel worksheet formula date attribute fields shown in Figure 17.172 in Chapter 17 can be used to create the DAX calculated column date attribute fields, except for the formulas that use the TEXT worksheet function. DAX functions like MONTH, YEAR, DAY, EOMONTH, ROUNDUP, and IF all work the same as the worksheet function equivalents.

In DAX, when you want to format a serial number date as a day name, month name, or in some other way using custom number formatting, rather than use the TEXT function, you use the FORMAT function. The FORMAT DAX function works the same as the TEXT function. For example, the worksheet formula TEXT(fSales[@ Date]),"*mmm*") and the DAX formula FORMAT(fSales[Date],"*mmm*") both take a serial number and display it as a text three-letter month abbreviation. Your reporting goals in this project require four date attributes: month number, month name, year, and end of the month. To create date attribute fields, as shown in Figure 19.74, you can use the New Column button in the Calculations group in the Table Tools tab of the Power BI Desktop Ribbon.

To create the DAX calculated columns, with the dDate table selected, go to the Table Tools tab of the Power Query Ribbon, and in the Calculations group, click the New Column button, as shown in Figure 19.74, and create the four DAX calculated columns that are shown in Figures 19.75 through 19.78. The default data types and number formatting for each of the fields will be fine, except in the case of the EOMonth field, but you will change that later on. Figure 19.79 shows the finished data table.

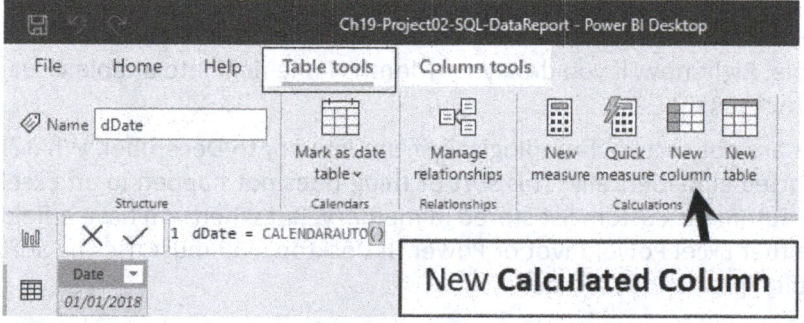

Figure 19.74 *Use the New Column button to create your date attribute fields.*

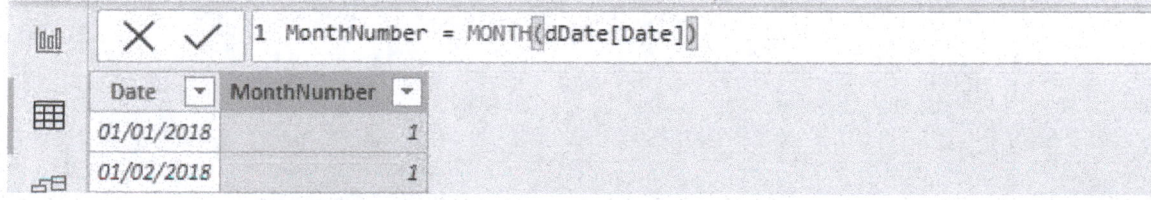

Figure 19.75 *DAX calculated column for month number.*

1 Month Name = FORMAT(dDate[Date],"mmm")
Date
MonthNumber
Month Name
01/01/2018
1
Jan
01/02/2018
1
Jan

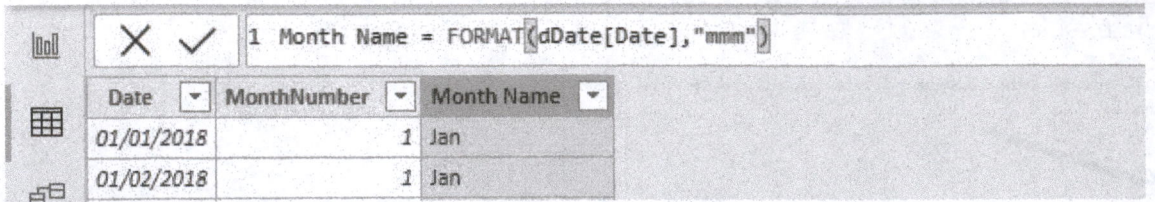

Figure 19.76 *DAX calculated column for month name.*

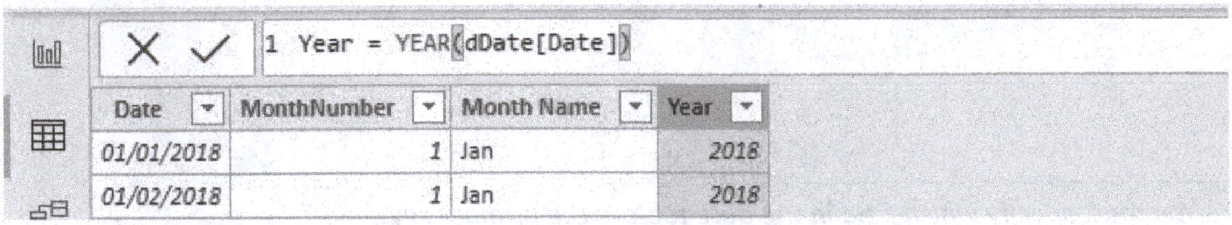

1 Year = YEAR(dDate[Date])
Date
MonthNumber
Month Name
Year
01/01/2018
1
Jan
2018
01/02/2018
1
Jan
2018

Figure 19.77 *DAX calculated column for year.*

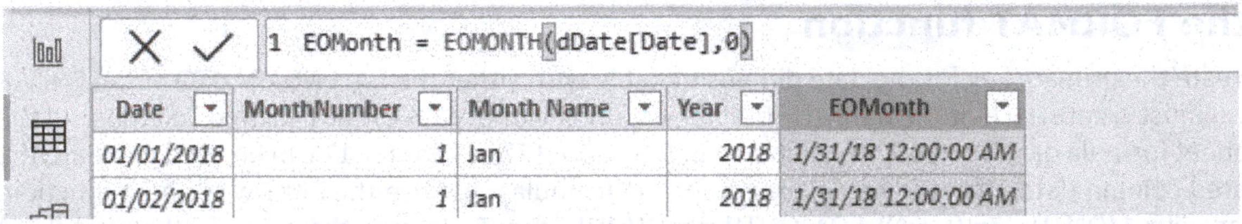

1 EOMonth = EOMONTH(dDate[Date],0)
Date
MonthNumber
Month Name
Year
EOMonth
01/01/2018
1
Jan
2018
1/31/18 12:00:00 AM
01/02/2018
1
Jan
2018
1/31/18 12:00:00 AM

Figure 19.78 *DAX calculated column for end of month.*

1 EOMonth = EOMONTH(dDate[Date],0)
Fields
Search
Icon for DAX Table
Icon for primary key
Icons for Calculated Columns
dCountry
dDate
Date
EOMonth
Month Name
MonthNumber
Year

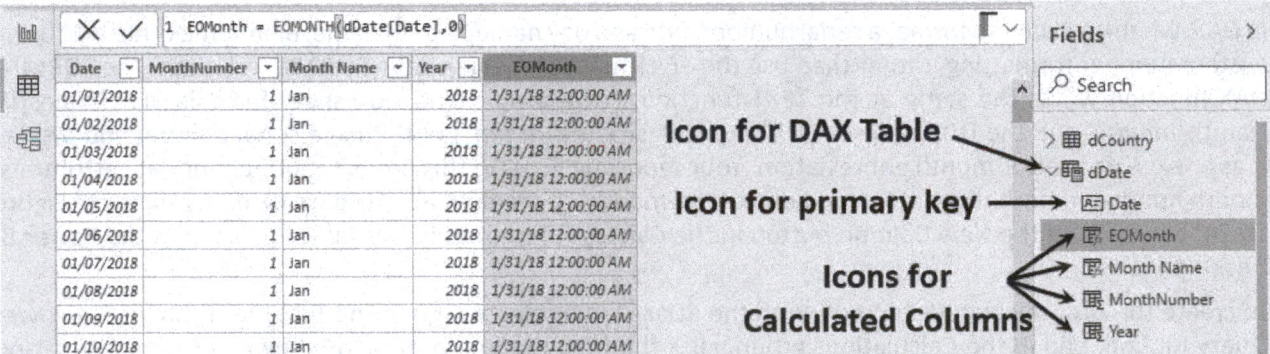

Figure 19.79 *When you create a DAX table, the icons in the Fields pane look different from the icons for imported tables.*

Using the Sort By Column Feature to Sort Month Names Correctly

After you create a date dimension table and mark the table as a date table, you have to do a few additional data modeling tasks to complete the table. Right now, if you drag your Month Name field into a table visual in the reporting area, you will not like the results.

As shown in Figure 19.80, month names are not sorted chronologically from January to December. What?! In the Data Model, month names are sorted alphabetically. This sort of thing does not happen in an Excel standard PivotTable because there is an automatic custom list stored in memory. But when you have a field of month names in the Data Model, in either Excel Power Pivot or Power BI Desktop, you must use the Sort By Column feature to override the default alphabetic sort order.

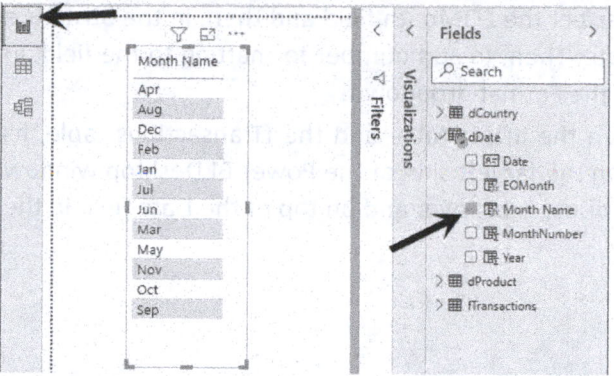

Figure 19.80 *By default, month names sort alphabetically.*

By using the Sort By Column feature, you can instruct the Data Model to sort the Month Name field by the MonthNumber field. Because the MonthNumber field uses the numbers 1 to 12, where 1 = January, 2 = February, and so on to 12 = December, when the Month Name field is sorted by MonthNumber, you get the correct chronological sort. In this way, the MonthNumber field is a helper column that only exists in the Data Model to help sort the Month Name field correctly.

There are also other situations when you will need to override the default alphabetic sort order, and in each case, you will have to invent a helper column and use the Sort By feature. For example, a concatenated Month Name-Year does not sort correctly unless you use the Sort By Column feature with a helper column like EOMonth.

To use the Sort By Column feature to sort month names correctly, follow these steps:

1. Select the Month Name field in the dDate table and, as shown in Figure 19.81, in the Column Tools tab of the Power BI Desktop Ribbon, in the Sort group, click the Sort By Column dropdown arrow and select MonthNumber. This causes the month names to sort in chronological order in all reports and visuals.

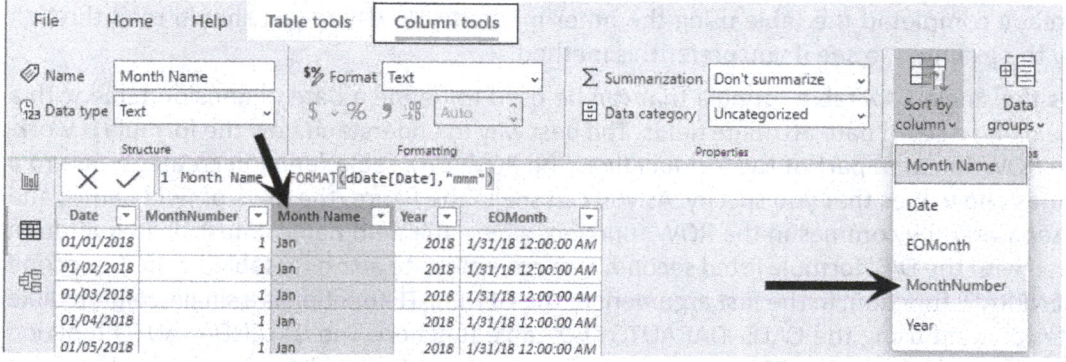

Figure 19.81 *Always sort the Month Name field by MonthNumber.*

2. To prevent the Year field from being used as a number for aggregate calculations in the reporting area, select the Year field and then, in the Column Tools tab of the Power BI Desktop Ribbon, in the Properties group, click the Summarization dropdown and select Don't Summarize (see Figure 19.82).

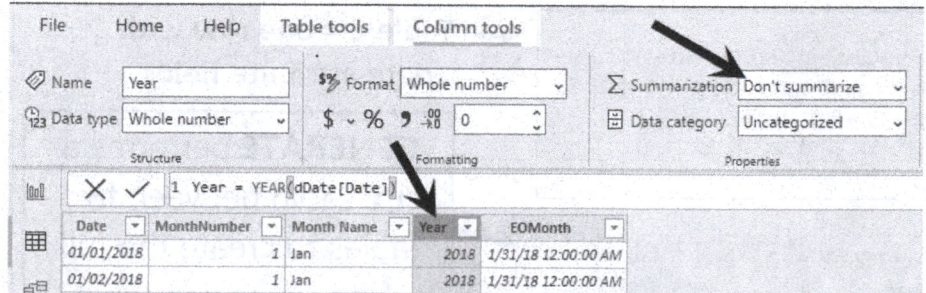

Figure 19.82 *Select the Year field and then set the Summarization property to Don't Summarize.*

3. To add a date data type to the EOMonth field, select the EOMonth field and then, in the Structure group, from the Data Type dropdown, select Date. Then, to add number formatting to the field, in the Formatting group, select mm/dd/yyyy from the Format dropdown.

4. To create the one-to-many relationship between the dDate table and the fTransactions table, as shown in Figure 19.83, click the Model button on the far-left side of the Power BI Desktop window and then drag and drop the Date field from the dDate table over and on top of the Date field in the fTransactions table.

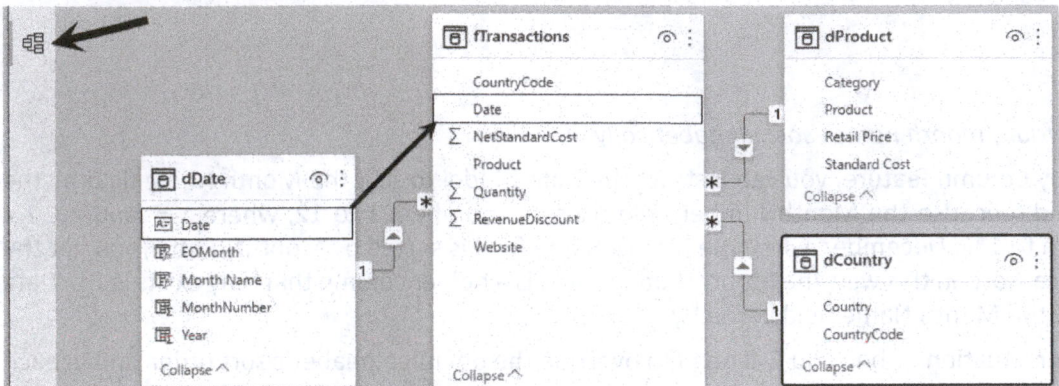

Figure 19.83 *Drag the Date field in dDate over and on top of the Date field in fTransactions.*

The date dimension table that you will use for this project is now complete.

Using the GENERATE and ROW Functions to Create a DAX Date Dimension Table

I mentioned earlier in this chapter that there is a third method for creating a date dimension table: using the GENERATE and ROW DAX table functions. You do not have to create the date table using this third method because you've already completed the table using the other methods. However, you should read through this section and try the example to see if you prefer this method.

Figure 19.84 shows the single DAX table formula that can be used to define a date dimension table with a primary key date field and a set of date attribute fields. The best way to understand how the formula is working is to look at the ROW function part of the formula first. The ROW DAX table function creates a one-row table with field names and values that you specify. As you can see in the figure, the pairs of field names and DAX formulas are separated by commas in the ROW function, where the field names must be in quotation marks and listed first, with the DAX formula listed second. This one-row date attribute table sits in the second argument of the GENERATE function. In the first argument of the GENERATE function is a single-column table of primary key dates created using the CALENDARAUTO DAX table function. The CALENDARAUTO function automatically names the field Date. The ROW function can access the date field by using the field name in square brackets (for example, [Date]).

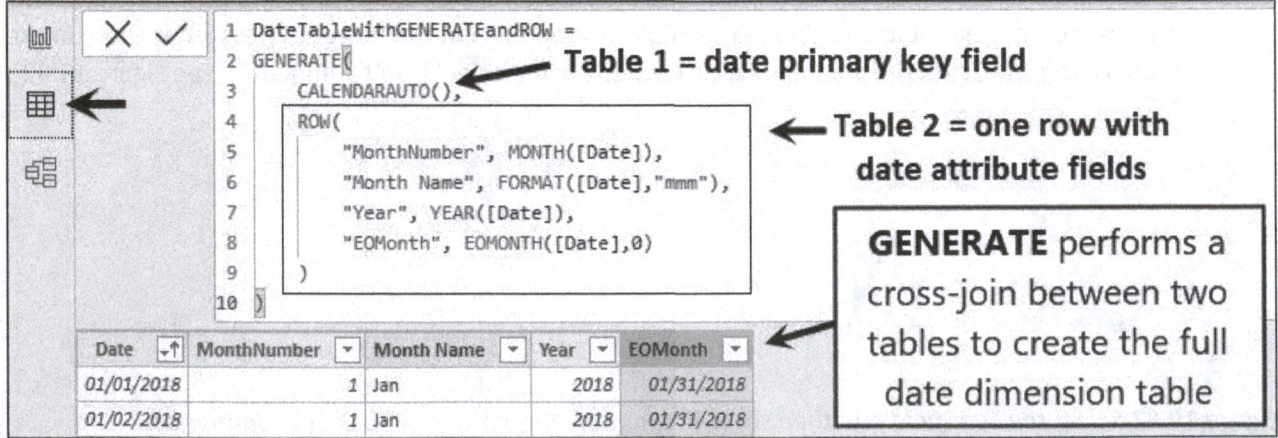

Figure 19.84 *You can use the GENERATE and ROW DAX table functions to create a single-formula date dimension table.*

Referring to a field without prefacing it with the table name violates the convention for referencing DAX columns. However, in a formula like this, you are not allowed to use the table name as a preface to the column because the table itself has not been defined yet. This just means that you must be acutely aware that the square brackets are not referencing a measure but instead are referencing the Date field generated by CALENDARAUTO.

> **Note:** To make a long DAX formula easier to read, as shown in Figure 19.84, you can add line breaks (by pressing Shift+Enter) and spaces or tabs. When you press Shift+Enter to add a line break, line numbers are shown on the left in the DAX formula bar.

The GENERATE DAX table function takes two or more tables and performs a cross-join (which is a Cartesian product in set theory) between the two table functions to generate a new third table. A cross-join simply matches up each row from the first table with a row from the second table. Because the first table is a single column of dates, and the second table is a single row with date attribute DAX formulas, each date in the first table will have a single row of data attributes added to it to create a full date dimension table.

The amazing thing about this formula is that you can copy and paste it into any Power BI Desktop file where the CALENDARAUTO function will work, and the formula will create a date table with the five fields Date, MonthNumber, Month Name, Year, and EOMonth. Figure 19.85 provides a pictorial description of how this amazing formula creates the full date dimension table.

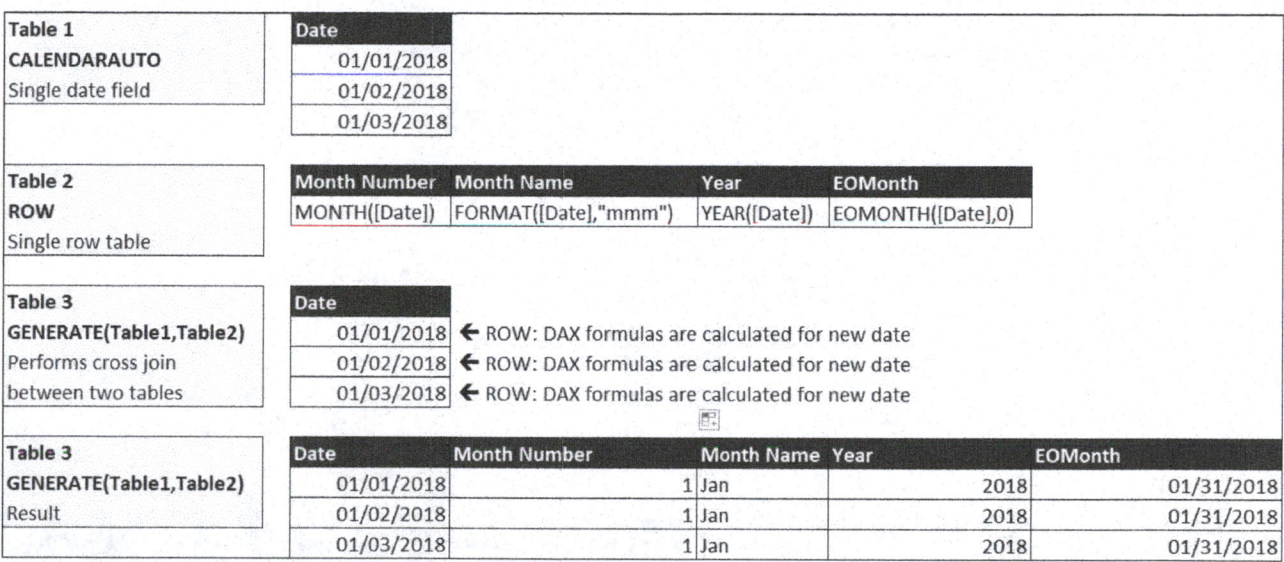

Figure 19.85 *How GENERATE creates the full date dimension table with one formula.*

> **Note:** The guidelines for formatting DAX formulas come mostly from the DAX formula masters Marco Russo and Alberto Ferrari. The general rule is to add a new line for and indent each new function and then list each function argument on a new line. When you close off a function, you put the closing parenthesis on a new line directly below the function name. You can also copy any DAX formula to Marco Russo and Alberto Ferrari's DAX Formatter website (daxformatter.com), which will format the formula for you.

Using DAX VAR Variables with the GENERATE and ROW Functions to Create a DAX Date Dimension Table

Figure 19.86 shows an advanced version of a formula that includes GENERATE and ROW to create a date dimension table. This formula uses the keyword VAR to define variables and the keyword RETURN to return a value using the variables. In addition, line 15 uses a double backslash to add a note to the DAX formula.

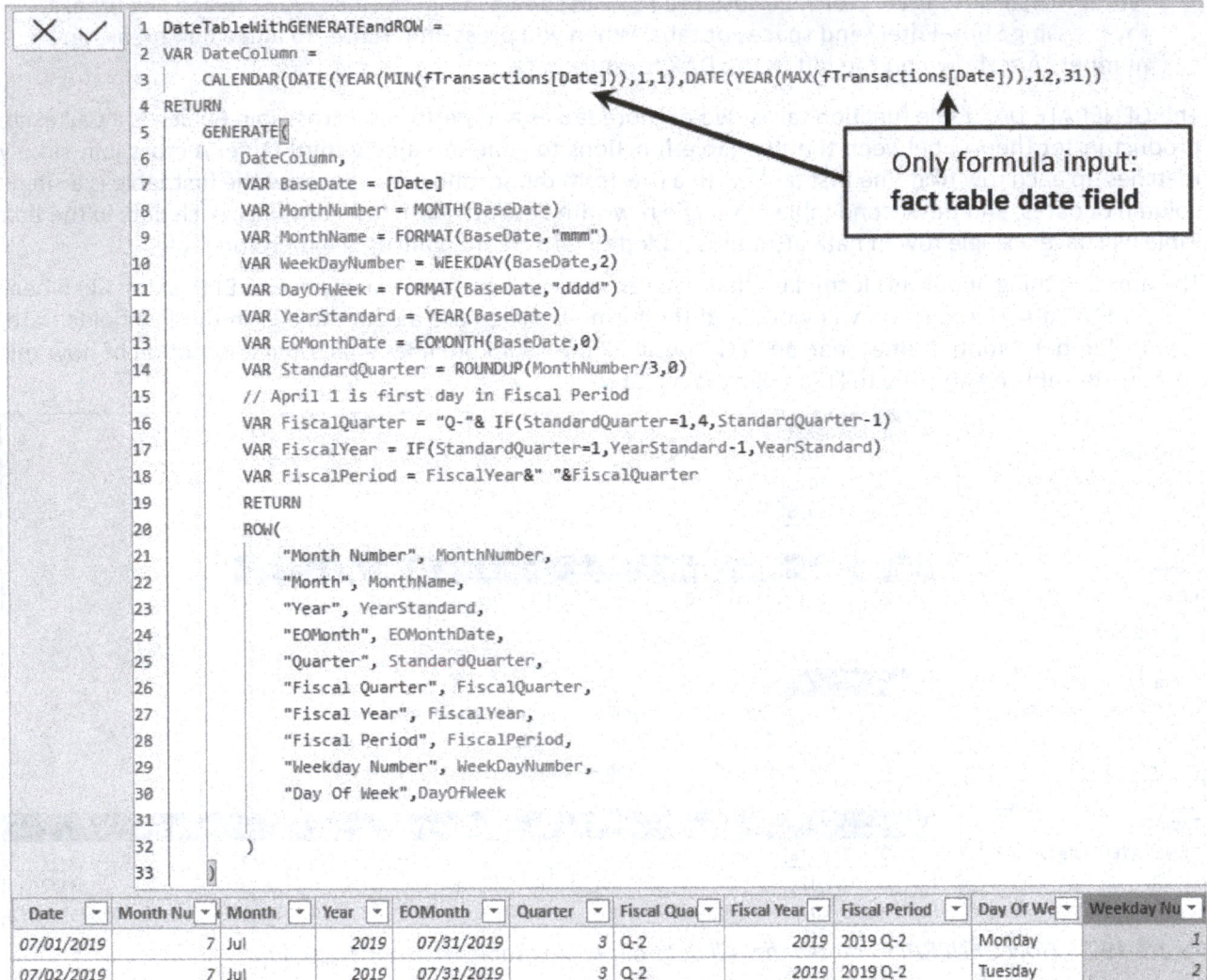

```
1  DateTableWithGENERATEandROW =
2  VAR DateColumn =
3      CALENDAR(DATE(YEAR(MIN(fTransactions[Date])),1,1),DATE(YEAR(MAX(fTransactions[Date])),12,31))
4  RETURN
5      GENERATE(
6          DateColumn,
7          VAR BaseDate = [Date]
8          VAR MonthNumber = MONTH(BaseDate)
9          VAR MonthName = FORMAT(BaseDate,"mmm")
10         VAR WeekDayNumber = WEEKDAY(BaseDate,2)
11         VAR DayOfWeek = FORMAT(BaseDate,"dddd")
12         VAR YearStandard = YEAR(BaseDate)
13         VAR EOMonthDate = EOMONTH(BaseDate,0)
14         VAR StandardQuarter = ROUNDUP(MonthNumber/3,0)
15         // April 1 is first day in Fiscal Period
16         VAR FiscalQuarter = "Q-"& IF(StandardQuarter=1,4,StandardQuarter-1)
17         VAR FiscalYear = IF(StandardQuarter=1,YearStandard-1,YearStandard)
18         VAR FiscalPeriod = FiscalYear&" "&FiscalQuarter
19         RETURN
20         ROW(
21             "Month Number", MonthNumber,
22             "Month", MonthName,
23             "Year", YearStandard,
24             "EOMonth", EOMonthDate,
25             "Quarter", StandardQuarter,
26             "Fiscal Quarter", FiscalQuarter,
27             "Fiscal Year", FiscalYear,
28             "Fiscal Period", FiscalPeriod,
29             "Weekday Number", WeekDayNumber,
30             "Day Of Week",DayOfWeek
31         )
32     )
33 )
```

Only formula input: **fact table date field**

Date	Month Nu	Month	Year	EOMonth	Quarter	Fiscal Qua	Fiscal Year	Fiscal Period	Day Of We	Weekday Nu
07/01/2019	7	Jul	2019	07/31/2019	3	Q-2	2019	2019 Q-2	Monday	1
07/02/2019	7	Jul	2019	07/31/2019	3	Q-2	2019	2019 Q-2	Tuesday	2

Figure 19.86 *When you copy and paste this formula into the Data Model, be sure to change the date field input.*

Note: Want to see a single-formula solution for either the GENERATE function (refer to Figure 19.84) or the ROW function (refer to Figure 19.86)? You can find them in the solution file for this project: Ch19-Project02-SQL-DataReport-Finished.pbix.

Adding a View of Your Data Model and Hiding Tables

If you want to practice creating date dimension tables for this project, you can create a data model that looks as shown in Figure 19.87. In this project, you need only one date table, and you already created the relationship, so in this case, it would be good to create a different view of the data model that does not include the extra date tables. In other situations, you might have extra tables that you do not want to see, or you might have two distinct fact table data models in one Power BI Desktop file. All the tables that you have in your file will show up in the model area on the All Tables tab.

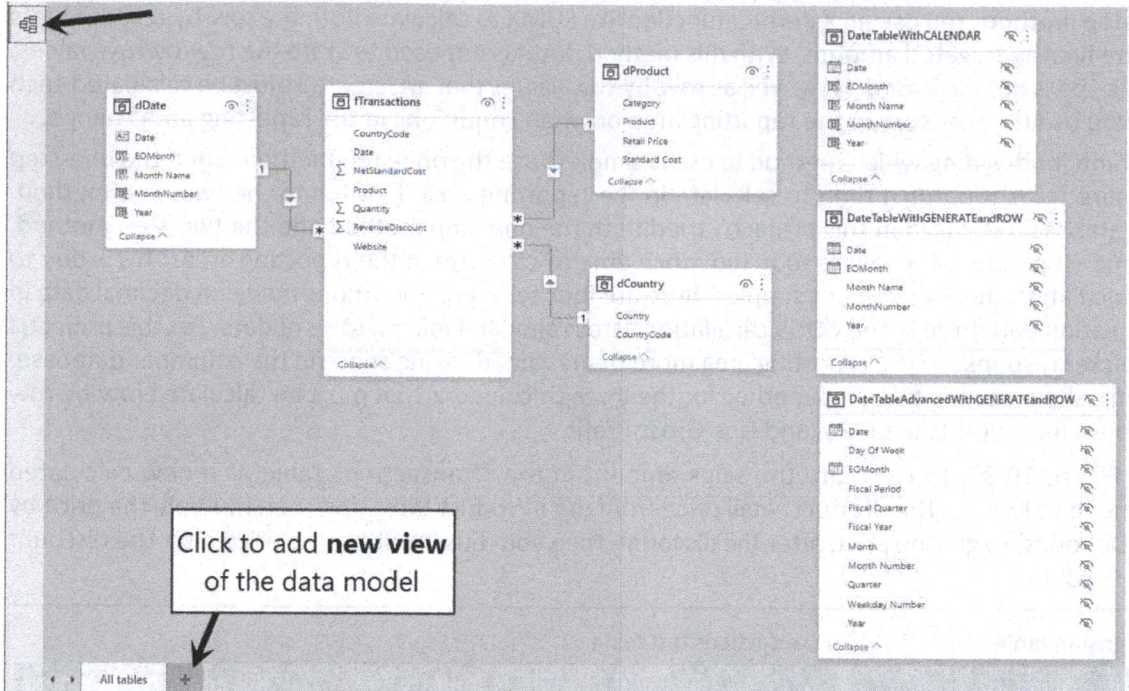

Figure 19.87 *You can click the plus icon in the model area to create a new view of the data model.*

If you want to create different view with just a specified number of tables, you can click the plus icon at the bottom of the model view area, as shown in Figure 19.87, to create a new tab. You can name this tab and then drag and drop tables from the Fields task pane into the model area to create your new view. Figure 19.88 shows an example for the Project 2 data model.

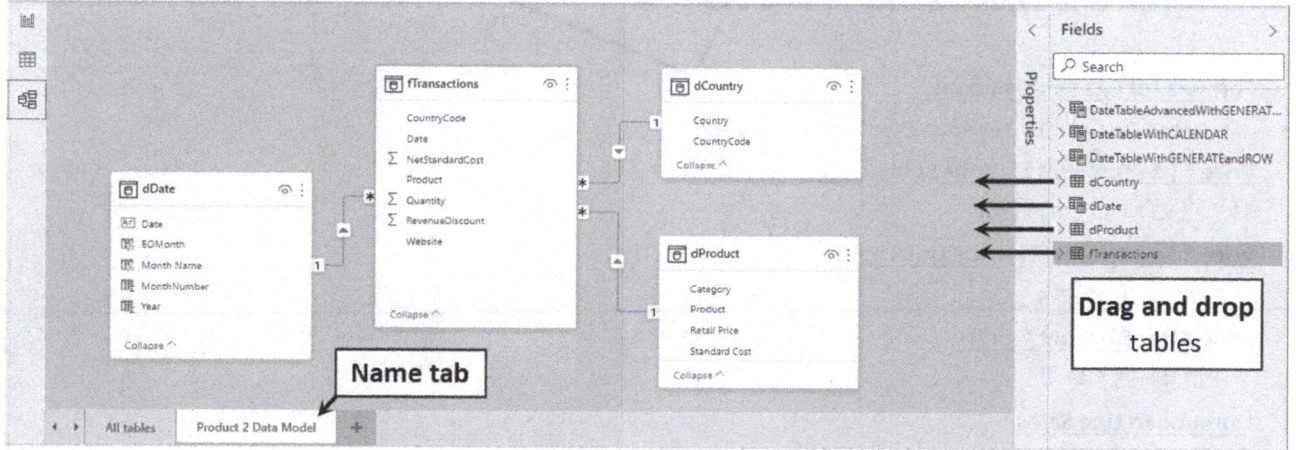

Figure 19.88 *To create a new view, click the plus icon and then drag and drop tables from the Fields task pane.*

Finally, if a table will not be used in the reporting area, you can hide it by right-clicking the table title bar and then clicking Hide in Report View.

Using DAX Calculated Columns and Measures for Total Sales, Total COGS, and Total Gross Profit

Now that the tables have been imported from the SQL database, the date table has been created, and the relationships have been established, you can move on to the next phase of the data modeling process: creating the DAX measures. In Chapter 18, you learned about two methods to create DAX measures:

- **Two-step method:** First, you use a calculated column in the fact table to calculate the row-by-row amount; second, you use an aggregate function to summarize the values from the calculated column to create the measure. With this method, the calculated column values are stored in the columnar database, increasing the use of RAM and increasing the file size. However, measures can sometimes calculate more quickly when they are used in the reporting area or when conditions in the reporting area change.

- **One-step method:** You use an X iterator function like SUMX to calculate both the row-by-row amounts and the final aggregated amount. With this method, RAM is not used to store the row-by-row values, and file size is not increased. However, all row-by-row values that are created must be calculated each time you use the measure in the reporting area or when conditions in the reporting area change.

My rule of thumb for deciding which method to use is simple: I use the one-step method, but if the one-step method measure takes too much time to calculate in the reporting area, I switch to the two-step method. For the SQL database data used in this project, I tried both the one-step method and the two-step method. For me, the one-step method measure took too much time to calculate in the reporting area. This is due to the fact the calculations needed are not simple: There are four separate operations made on decimal data in the sales calculation and three in the COGS calculation across almost 8 million rows of data. For this project, I valued the quicker response in the reporting area more than I valued saving space in the columnar database. For this reason, I show you the two-step method for the three calculations that must be calculated row-by-row in the fact table: Line Sales, Line COGS, and Line Gross Profit.

As shown in Figure 19.89, to calculate the sales amount in the fTransactions table as a new calculated column, you need to look up the product retail price from the dProduct table and then multiply the price by (1 – RevenueDiscount) to get the price after the discount; then you must multiply the price after the discount by the quantity sold.

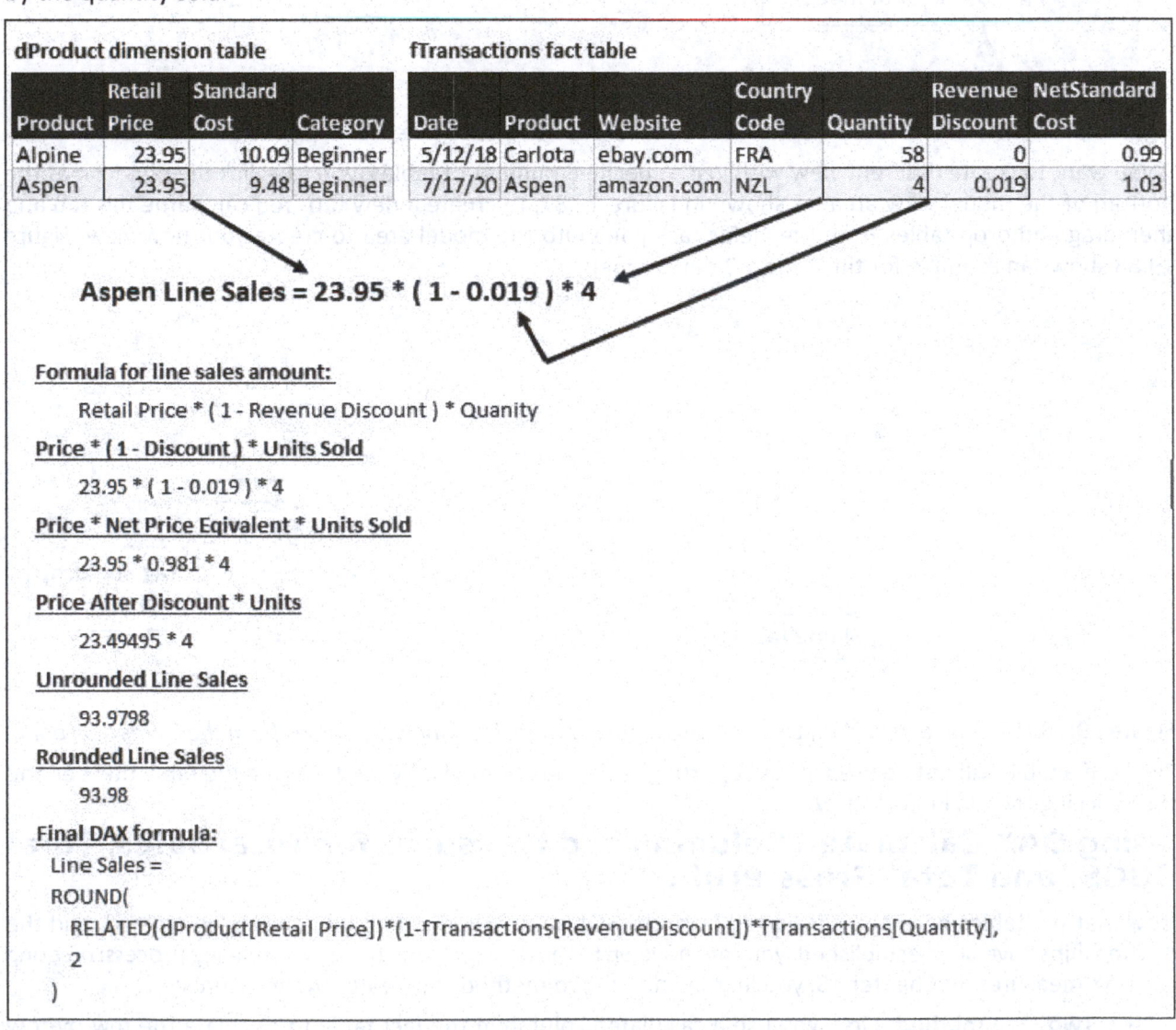

dProduct dimension table

Product	Retail Price	Standard Cost	Category
Alpine	23.95	10.09	Beginner
Aspen	23.95	9.48	Beginner

fTransactions fact table

Date	Product	Website	Country Code	Quantity	Revenue Discount	NetStandard Cost
5/12/18	Carlota	ebay.com	FRA	58	0	0.99
7/17/20	Aspen	amazon.com	NZL	4	0.019	1.03

Aspen Line Sales = 23.95 * (1 - 0.019) * 4

Formula for line sales amount:

Retail Price * (1 - Revenue Discount) * Quanity

Price * (1 - Discount) * Units Sold

23.95 * (1 - 0.019) * 4

Price * Net Price Eqivalent * Units Sold

23.95 * 0.981 * 4

Price After Discount * Units

23.49495 * 4

Unrounded Line Sales

93.9798

Rounded Line Sales

93.98

Final DAX formula:

```
Line Sales =
ROUND(
   RELATED(dProduct[Retail Price])*(1-fTransactions[RevenueDiscount])*fTransactions[Quantity],
   2
)
```

Figure 19.89 *Calculating line sales with number inputs from two tables.*

Why do you have to multiply the price by (1 – Discount)? The reason is because a discount given is an amount that must be subtracted from the price, so rather than use the formula element (Price – Price * Discount), which would involve two lookups to get the price (or a VAR variable), you can use the equivalent formula element Price * (1 – Discount), which allows you to create a shorter and more efficient formula. In addition, whereas a discount tells you how many pennies for every one dollar of price are given as a reduction, (1 – Discount) tells you how many pennies for every one dollar of price must be paid.

When you use (1 – Discount) on a price, the result is called a *net price equivalent*. When you use (1 – Discount) on a cost, the result is called a *net cost equivalent*, and it tells you how many pennies for every one dollar of cost must be incurred. The formula element (1 – Discount) is a common way to express a discount in formulas in accounting, finance, statistics, and other professions. In fact, the similar but more universal formula that can be used for percentage decreases or percentage increases in amounts is (1 + Percentage Change). If the percentage change reflects the direction of the change by using a negative value for a percentage decrease and a positive value for a percentage increase, then the formula (1 + Percentage Change) can be used any time there is a change in an amount.

To understand both a percentage change decrease and a percentage change increase, you can consider the NetStandardCost field in the fact table, as shown in Figure 19.89. Whereas with the RevenueDiscount field, the discount is given, and you must calculate the net price equivalent, with the NetStandardCost field, the net cost equivalent is already given, and you can directly multiply it by the standard cost from the dProduct table to get the COGS amount for each transaction. But notice that for the first record, NetStandardCost is 0.99, and for the second record, it is 1.03. You can infer from this that for the 0.99 net cost equivalent, the percentage change is –1%, and the formula that was used to calculate the 0.99 was (1+-0.01), and for the 1.03 net cost equivalent, the percentage change is 3%, and the formula that was used to calculate the 1.03 was (1+0.03). With the 0.99 net cost equivalent, there was a one-penny discount on each one dollar of cost, and with the 1.03 net cost equivalent, there was a three-penny increase on each one dollar of cost.

As shown in Figure 19.89, the final DAX formula uses the DAX functions RELATED and ROUND. In Chapter 18, you learned that the RELATED function performs an exact match lookup through the one-to-many relationship, using the product name on the many-side, to retrieve the product price from the one-side. In this chapter, you will use the DAX ROUND function to round the row-by-row amounts to the penny. (The DAX ROUND functions works exactly the same as the worksheet ROUND function that you learned about in Chapter 10.)

With an understanding of how the RevenueDiscount and NetStandardCost fields will be used in the formulas, you can now create the DAX calculated columns for Line Sales, Line COGS, and Line Gross Profit and then the DAX measures for Total Sales, Total COGS, and Total Gross Profit.

To create the calculated columns, DAX measures, and measure report needed in this project, follow these steps:

1. As shown in Figure 19.90, click the Data button on the far-left side of the Power BI Desktop window, right-click the fTransactions table in the Fields task pane, and select New Column.

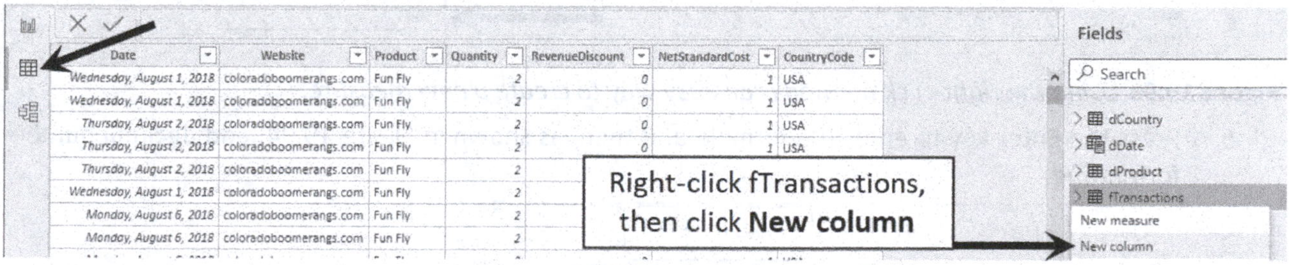

Figure 19.90 *Create a new DAX calculated column in the fact table.*

2. As shown in Figure 19.91, in the formula bar, type the column name, the assignment operator, and the following formula: **Line Sales = ROUND (RELATED (dProduct[Retail Price]) * (1 - fTransactions[RevenueDiscount]) * fTransactions[Quantity], 2)**.You can create this formula with or without the line breaks, depending on your preference.

```
1  Line Sales =
2  ROUND (
3      RELATED ( dProduct[Retail Price] ) * ( 1 - fTransactions[RevenueDiscount] ) * fTransactions[Quantity],
4      2
5  )
```

Figure 19.91 *Formatting your DAX formula with line breaks (Shift+Enter) and spaces can make it easier to read.*

3. Press the Enter key to enter the formula. The formula is copied down the column automatically and uses row context to access the values in each row, make the row-by-row calculation, and then deliver the result in each row. Then, as shown in Figure 19.92, add a decimal number data type and number formatting. (Using the Comma button in the Formatting group is a fast way to add decimal number formatting.) If the formula bar is not expanded and you cannot see your full formula with all the line breaks, you can expand the formula bar by clicking the expand arrow, as shown in Figure 19.92.

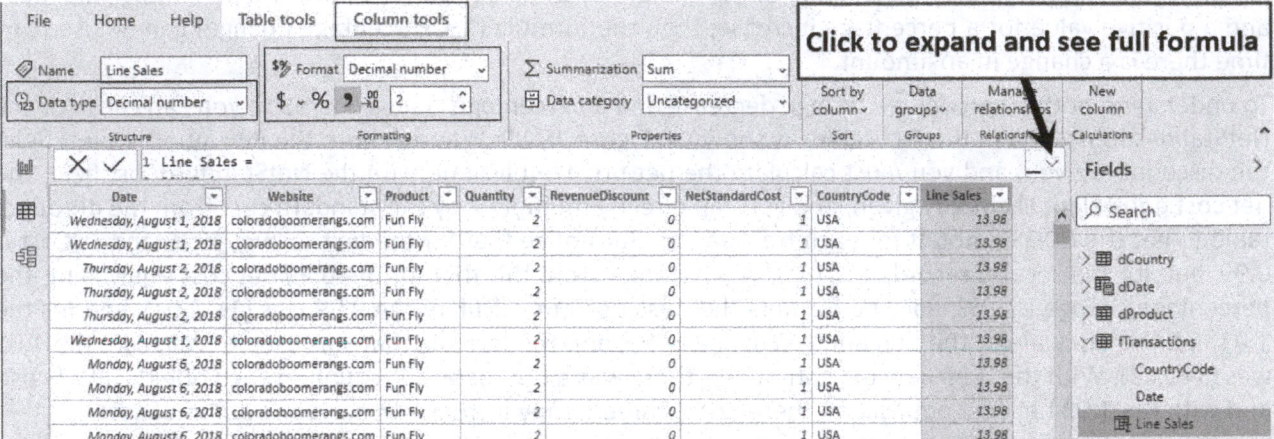

Figure 19.92 *Add a data type and formatting to your formula.*

4. As shown in Figure 19.93, to create the measure to add the line sales amounts, right-click the fTransactions table and click on New Measure. Then, in the formula bar, type the formula **=SUM(fTransactions[Line Sales])**.

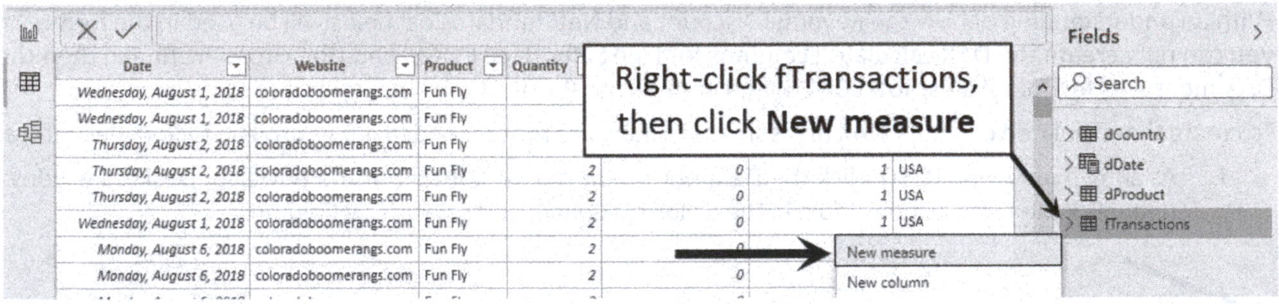

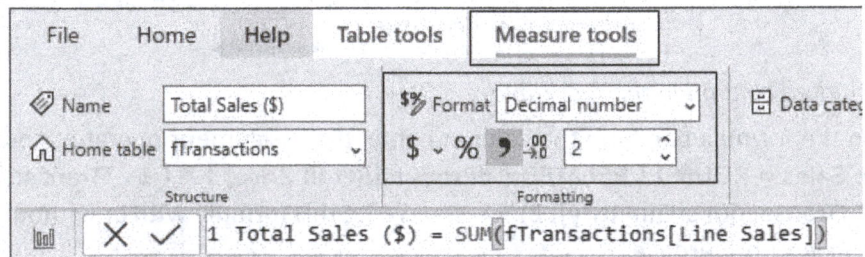

Figure 19.93 *Using the right-click method is an easy way to create a new measure.*

5. Press the Enter key to enter the formula and then, as shown in Figure 19.94, add decimal number formatting.

File	Home	Help	Table tools	Measure tools

Name   Total Sales ($)   Format   Decimal number   Data categ
Home table fTransactions $ ~ % 9 .00 2

        Structure   Formatting

1 Total Sales ($) = SUM(fTransactions[Line Sales])

Figure 19.94 *The Total Sales ($) measure with decimal number formatting.*

6. To create the calculated column for line COGS, right-click the fTransactions table in the Fields task pane and click on New Column. In the formula bar, create the formula **Line COGS = ROUND (RELATED (dProduct[Standard Cost]) * fTransactions[NetStandardCost] * fTransactions[Quantity], 2)**. Add the decimal number data type and number formatting. Figure 19.95 shows the result.

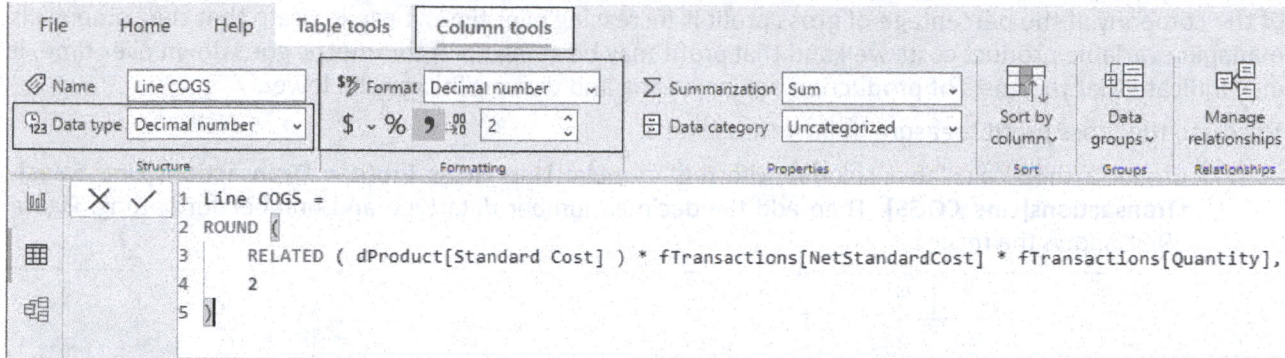

Figure 19.95 *The Line COGS formula with a decimal data type and number formatting.*

7. To create the measure for total COGS, right-click the fTransactions table in the Fields task pane and then click on New Column. As shown in Figure 19.96, create the measure for total COGS by using the formula **Total COGS ($) = SUM(fTransactions[Line COGS])**. Then add decimal number formatting.

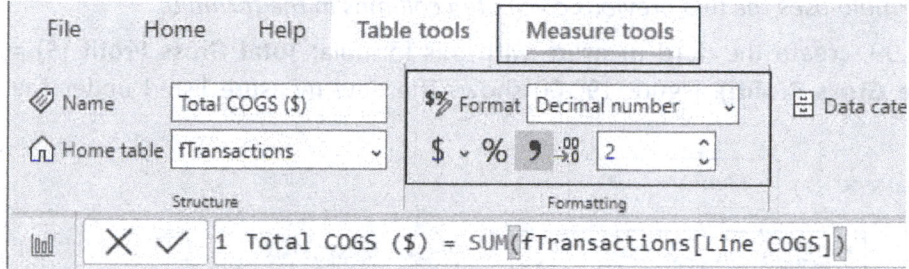

Figure 19.96 *The Total COGS ($) measure with decimal number formatting.*

Figure 19.97 shows the fTransactions table with two new calculated columns and two new measures. The next measure that you need to create is the gross profit measure.

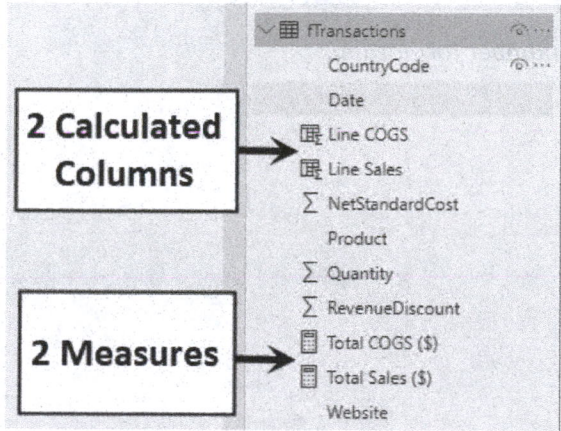

Figure 19.97 *Two new calculated columns and two new measures.*

Gross profit is a metric that assesses how well a company can manage the variable production and labor costs that go into producing a product or service. The formula for the gross profit calculation is:

```
Gross Profit = Total Sales - Total COGS
```

Gross profit tells you how much of the total sales is left over after subtracting all the variable production costs, which can then be used to cover fixed costs (such as rent, utilities, and administrative costs) and profit for the company. For a boomerang manufacturing company, total sales would be the revenue brought in from selling the finished boomerang products, and COGS (cost of goods sold) would be the variable costs incurred from producing the boomerangs, such as wood, paint, labor to make the boomerangs, packaging, and other costs that went into producing the boomerangs. The formula for the percentage of gross profit calculation is:

```
% Gross Profit = Total Gross Profit/Total Sales
```

The percentage of gross profit expresses the number of pennies for every one dollar of sales that can be used to cover fixed costs and profit. For a manufacturer, this is an important metric that indicates the health of the company. If the percentage of gross profit is increasing over time, it can indicate that the company is managing variable product costs well and that profit may be going up. If this metric goes down over time, it may indicate that the costs of production are increasing and that profits may be lower.

To create the gross profit measure, follow these steps:

1.   Create a third calculated column with this formula: **Line Gross Profit = fTransactions[Line Sales]-fTransactions[Line COGS]**. Then add the decimal number data type and number formatting. Figure 19.98 shows the result.

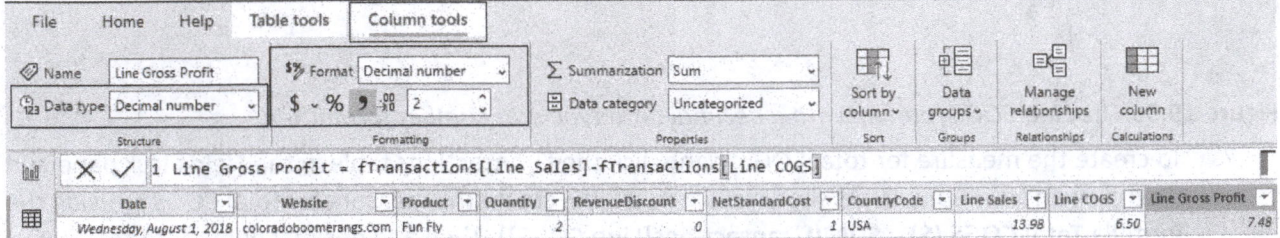

Figure 19.98 *The row-by-row formula uses the two previous calculated columns in the formula.*

2.   As shown in Figure 19.99, create the third measure with this formula: **Total Gross Profit ($) = SUM(fTransactions[Line Gross Profit])**. Figure 19.100 shows the new measure listed under the fTransactions table.

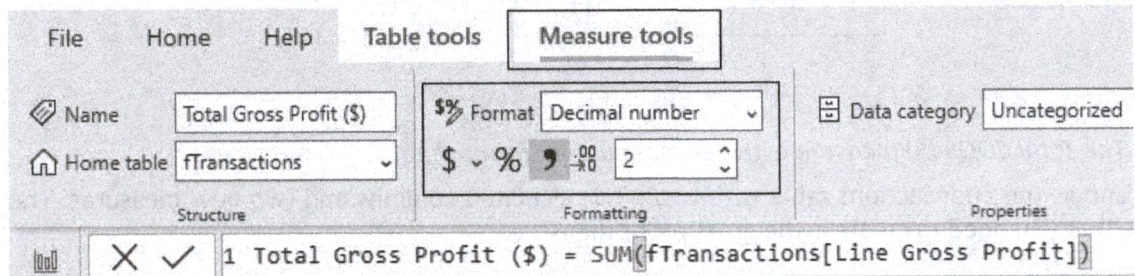

Figure 19.99 *The Total Gross Profit ($) measure with decimal number formatting.*

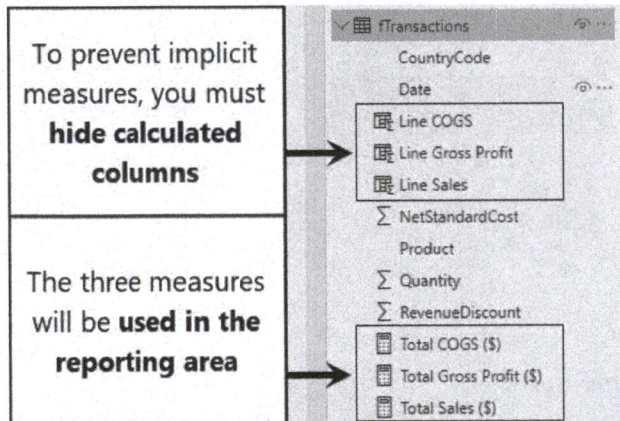

Figure 19.100 *Hiding the fact table calculated columns will prevent users from using them in the reporting area.*

Now that you have created three calculated columns and three measures, you must hide the calculated columns to prevent users from accidentally dragging and dropping them in the reporting area, thereby creating inefficient implicit measures. In addition, you should hide other fields that will not be used in the reporting area.

To hide fields in your project, follow these steps:

1.   On the far-left side of the Power BI Window, click the Model button.

2.   As shown in Figure 19.101, multi-select the fields to hide, right-click, and then click on Hide in Report View. Some of the important fields to hide are the foreign keys, the number fields and calculated columns in the fact table, and the helper columns in the date dimension table. In Figure 19.101 you can see all the fields that I hid; they are marked with the crossed-out eyeball icon.

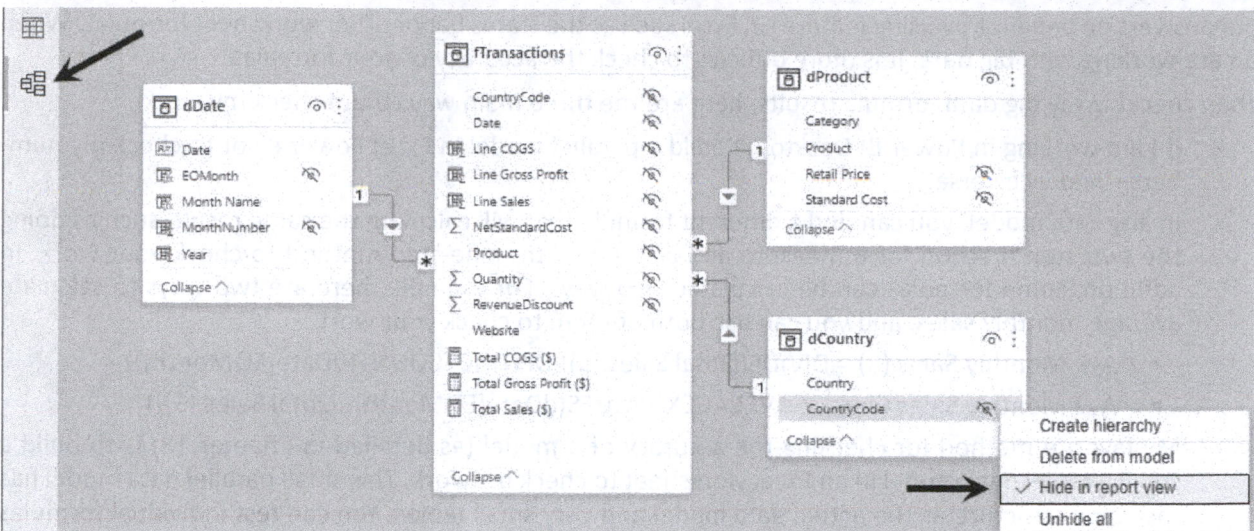

Figure 19.101 *In Model view, hide all fields that are not required in the reporting area.*

Next, you need to jump over to Report view and build a table visual to list the measures that you have created so far. To do this, follow these steps:

1. As shown in Figure 19.102, on the far-left side of the Power BI Window, click the Model button. Then name the page **All Metrics**.

2. To create a table visual with the measures, in the Visualizations task pane, click the Table visual. Then, in the Fields task pane, check the Product field from the dProduct table and check the three measures from the fTransactions table, in this order: Total Sales ($), Total COGS ($), and Total Gross Profit ($). Figure 19.102 shows the result.

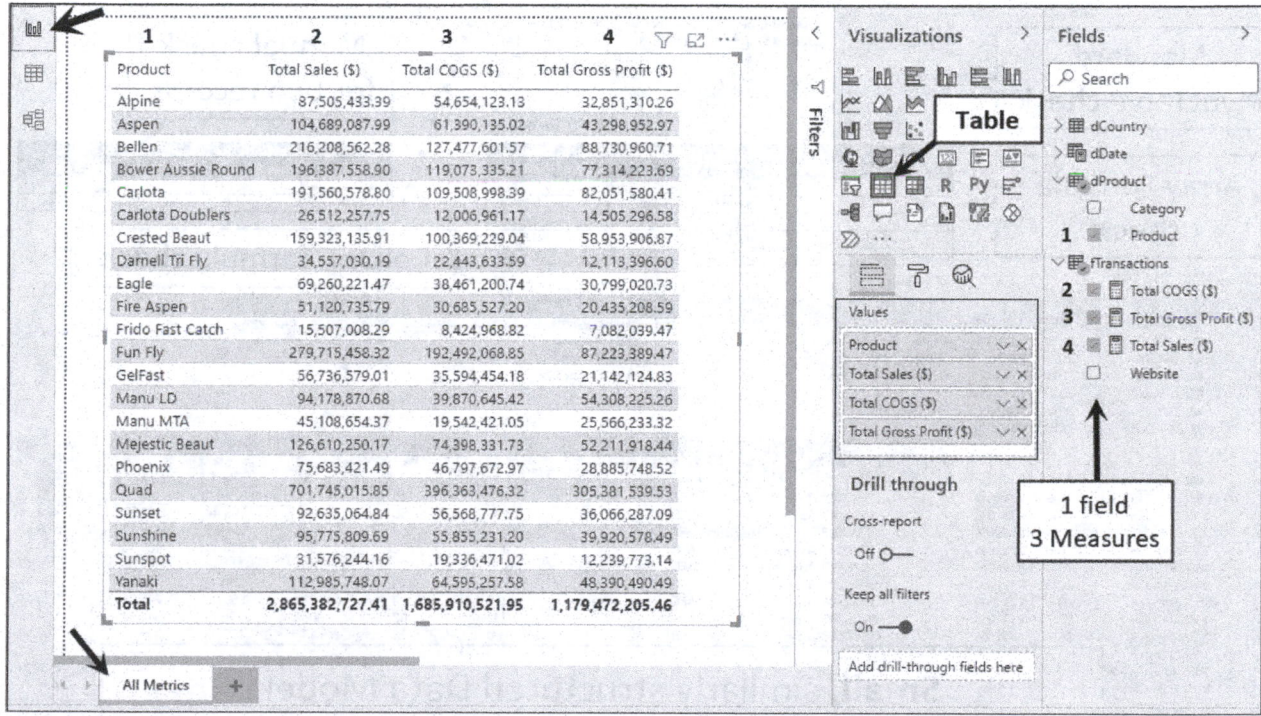

Figure 19.102 *Create a table visual with the Product field and your three measures.*

Using Techniques to Check Formula Results, Including Building a Small Parallel Data Model

In Figure 19.102, it looks like measures are yielding the correct results. But how do you really know with big data? With big data, it can be hard to find a way to double-check your numbers. If you are using the Excel worksheet to create summary reports and visuals, you can double-check a standard PivotTable report by using worksheet formulas—and vice versa. In addition, with small datasets, sometimes you can manually check your answers on paper or by using features in Excel such as the status bar or other worksheet formulas. When you are working with big data, it is more difficult to check the accuracy of your formulas.

When checking my big data formula results, here are the three main ways that I check my work:

- If I am working in Power BI Desktop, I build a parallel model in Excel Power Pivot to check my numbers—and vice versa.

- In any data model, you can find a different formula that will calculate the same result, such as doing the two-step method for a measure and also doing the one-step method to check your work. In addition, some formulas can be calculated two ways. For example, here are two ways to calculate average monthly sales, and you can use both of them to check your work:

    - Ave Monthly Sales ($) = DIVIDE([Total Sales ($)],DISTINCTCOUNT(dDate[EOMonth]))
    - Ave Monthly Sales Check = AVERAGEX(VALUES(dDate[EOMonth]),[Total Sales ($)])

- My favorite method for checking the accuracy of a model (as detailed in Chapter 18) is to build a small parallel data model in an Excel worksheet to check my work. This small parallel data model has the same structure as the actual data model and very small tables. You can test individual formulas and summary reports to see if you can get them to work. You can verify the results by using several different methods, such as a standard PivotTable, array formulas, and manual checks. (Figure 19.103 shows an example that I created for this project.) You can even use this approach at the outset of a project to design a data model.

> **Note:** Often, when I am hired to build a data analysis solution, I build a small data model solution in the Excel worksheet, and then I try to translate the small worksheet methods into Power Pivot; finally, I try to translate the small worksheet methods into Power BI Desktop. It is only after these three small dataset successes that I scale the data model up into a big data solution

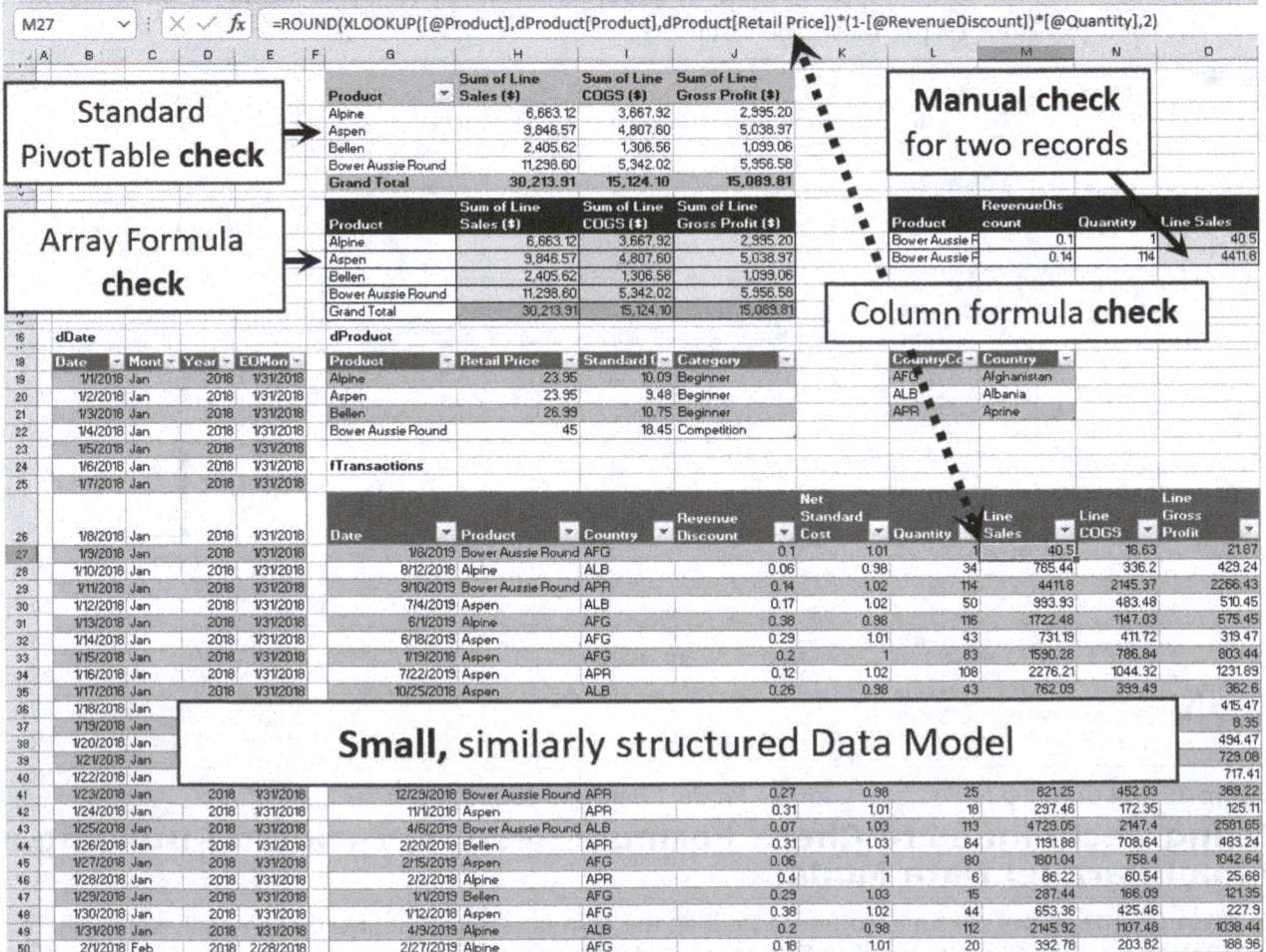

Figure 19.103 *When dealing with big data, building a small parallel data model to check the accuracy of your larger model is very helpful.*

Note: You can view the solution shown in Figure 19.103 in the Excel file named Ch19-Project02-PicturesSmallModel.xlsx.

Creating the % Gross Profit Measure

Now you need to create the % Gross Profit measure in Report view. Before you can get down to that business, though, you need to understand that some calculations, including the calculation to find the percentage gross profit, cannot be done row-by-row in the fact table.

Earlier, when you multiplied numbers in each row of the fact table to calculate the line gross profit amount, you could then aggregate the column of numbers to get the total gross profit. If you want a measure that you can use in the reporting area for percentage gross profit, however, you cannot divide values in each row of the fact table to calculate line percentage gross profit and then aggregate the column values to create the measure. As shown in Figure 19.104, you must aggregate the numerator amount and denominator amount *before* performing the division.

If you divide a row value by another row value, you can calculate the correct result for that one row, yielding the correct transactional % gross profit, but you cannot aggregate the column values to attain a measure that will accurately perform the same calculation at an aggregate level. To accurately perform the same calculation at an aggregate level, you must add the values for the numerator and denominator and then perform the division.

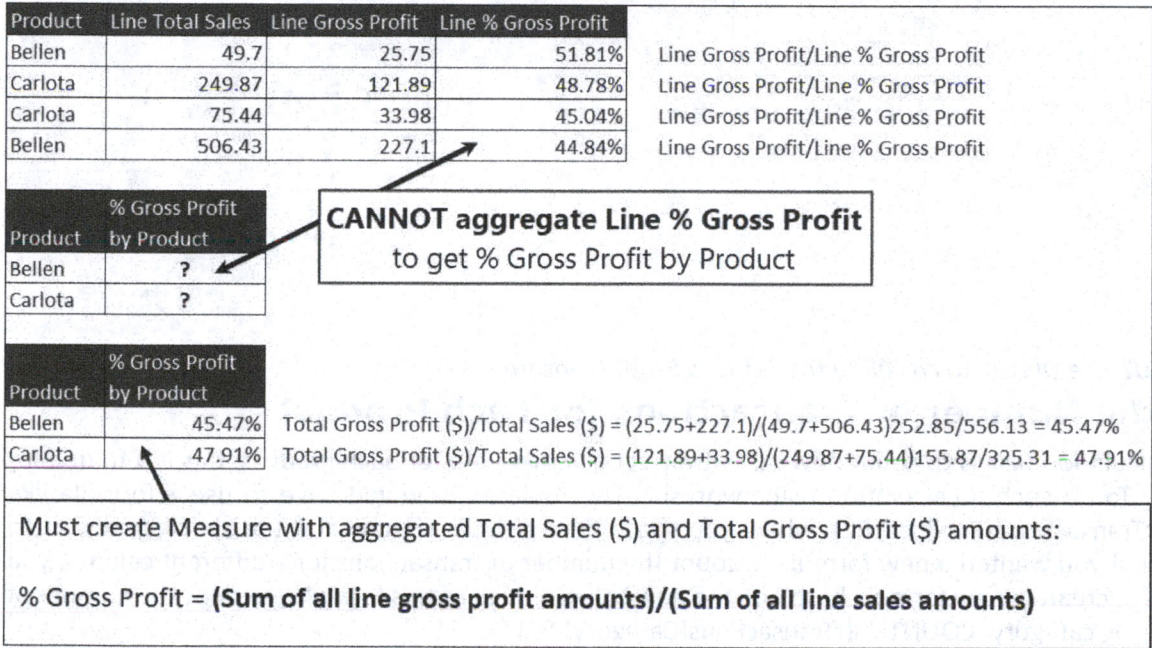

Figure 19.104 *Some calculations, like percentage gross profit by product, must be created with a one-step-method measure.*

In order to create the % Gross Profit measure, you have to perform division. In the DAX formula language, there is a built-in function to do this: DIVIDE. The DIVIDE function, which delivers the quotient of two numbers and allows you to specify an alternative value when the denominator is zero, has the following syntax:

```
DIVIDE(Numerator, Denominator, [AlternativeResult])
```

If you omit the third argument, [*AlternativeResult*], you get a DAX blank value, which is neither an empty cell, as you might get in the Excel worksheet, nor a null value, as you might get in Power Query. Figure 19.105 shows an example of the results you get if you make the math calculation 2/0 using the division operator—which happens when you use the DIVIDE function with the third argument omitted and the DIVIDE function with a 0 in the third argument. Notice that in the Data Model, the error value that shows for a divide-by-zero error is the infinity symbol, whereas in an Excel worksheet, you see the error value #DIV/0.

Numerator	Denominator	DivisionOperator	DIVIDE-3rdArgumentOmitted	DIVIDE-3rdArgumentEnteredAs0
1	2	0.5	0.5	0.5
2	0	∞		0

Figure 19.105 *Three DAX formulas that perform division with a zero in the denominator.*

To create the % Gross Profit measure, follow these steps:

1. As shown in Figure 19.106, while still in Report view, in the Fields task pane, right-click the fTransactions table and select New Measure. In the formula bar, create this formula: **% Gross Profit = DIVIDE([Total Gross Profit ($)],[Total Sales ($)])**.

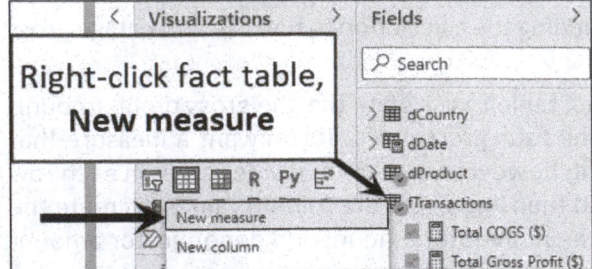

Figure 19.106 *You can create measures in Report view.*

1. As shown in Figure 19.107, add percentage number formatting with one decimal place showing.

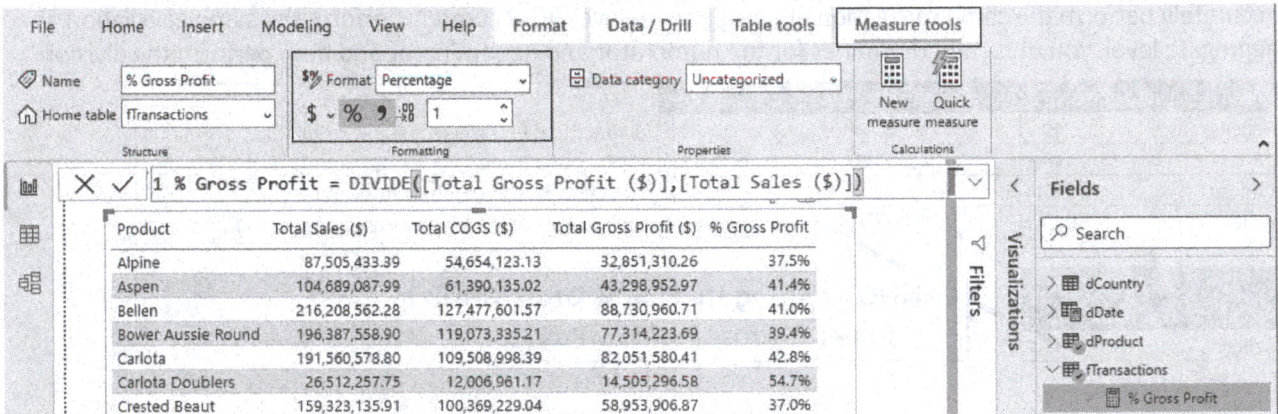

Product	Total Sales ($)	Total COGS ($)	Total Gross Profit ($)	% Gross Profit
Alpine	87,505,433.39	54,654,123.13	32,851,310.26	37.5%
Aspen	104,689,087.99	61,390,135.02	43,298,952.97	41.4%
Bellen	216,208,562.28	127,477,601.57	88,730,960.71	41.0%
Bower Aussie Round	196,387,558.90	119,073,335.21	77,314,223.69	39.4%
Carlota	191,560,578.80	109,508,998.39	82,051,580.41	42.8%
Carlota Doublers	26,512,257.75	12,006,961.17	14,505,296.58	54.7%
Crested Beaut	159,323,135.91	100,369,229.04	58,953,906.87	37.0%

Figure 19.107 *Use DIVIDE to calculate the % Gross Profit Measure.*

Count the Number of Transactions for Each Product

The next calculation task is to count how many transactions there are for each product; this is a frequency calculation. To do such a calculation using worksheet formulas, you would have to use a formula like COUNTIFS(fTransactions[Product],B2), where you specify the product column and the specific product to count. Then, if you wanted a new formula to count the number of transactions for a different column, you would have to create a new formula based on the new column, such as this formula to count the number of transactions by category: COUNTIFS(fTransactions[Category],B2).

With DAX formulas, you can build a single frequency formula that will work on any set of conditions. To do so, you use the COUNTROWS DAX function, which counts the number of rows in a table based on the current filter context. In a star schema data model, if you use the fact table inside COUNTROWS, the formula will count records in the fact table based on any condition. This makes a formula like COUNTROWS(*FactTable*) a one-stop-shopping frequency formula that can be used to count based on any set of conditions. This is an example of a DAX formula that is much easier to create and use than formulas created with worksheet formulas, Power Query M code, or the standard PivotTable feature.

For the calculation task at hand, the formula COUNTROWS(fTransactions) will work to count how many transactions there are for each product if the Rows area of your table lists the product names. For each row in the table, the specific row condition will flow in and filter the fact table, and COUNTROWS will count the number of rows. If a new condition is added to the table or to a slicer or filter, the fact table will be filtered to reflect the new conditions, and the formula will yield the correct count! This is a simple formula that can do a lot!

To create the Count Transactions measure, follow these steps:

1. While still in Report view, in the Fields task pane, right-click the fTransactions table and select New Measure. In the formula bar, create this formula: **Count Transactions = COUNTROWS(fTransactions)** (see Figure 19.108).

2. Add whole number formatting with zero decimal places showing.

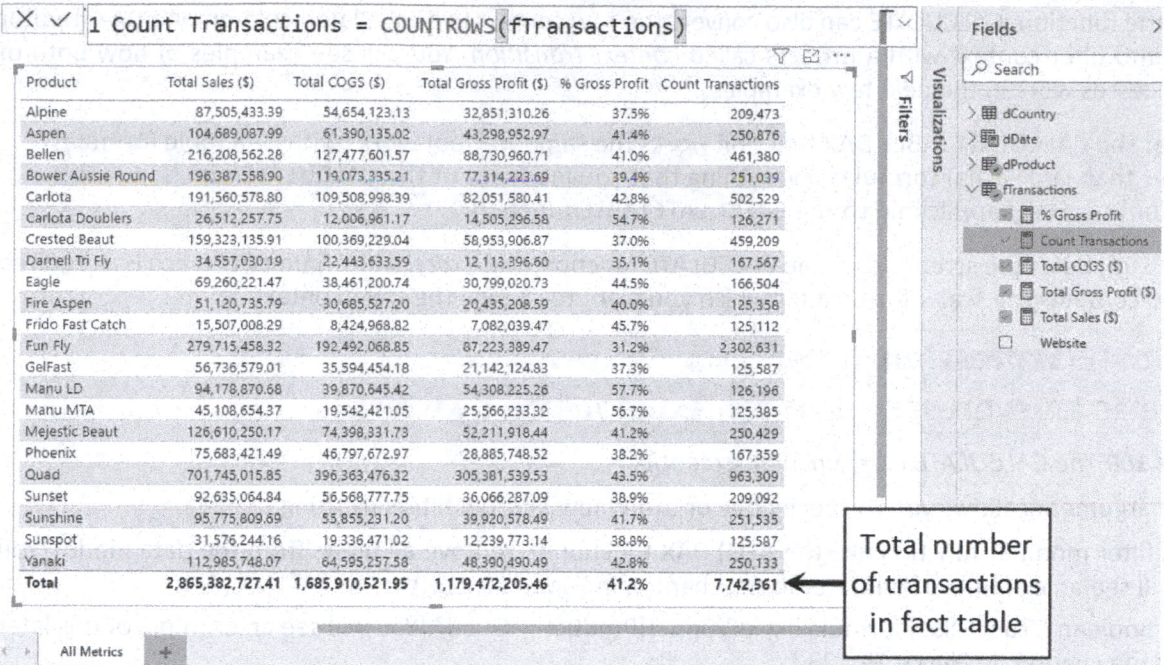

Figure 19.108 *COUNTROWS is the universal one-stop-shopping frequency formula.*

Creating the % of Grand Overall Total Sales DAX Measure

The next measure that you need to create is a measure that will calculate sales as a percentage of total sales. The goal is to divide the total sales for any given set of conditions by the grand overall total sales and show the result as a percentage. For example, you might use the Alpine product total sales amount 87,505,433.39 in the numerator and the grand overall of 2,865,382,727.41 in the denominator to calculate the quotient like this: 87,505,433.39/2,865,382,727.41 = 0.035, or 3.05%. This tells you that 3.05% of all sales came from the that Alpine product.

If you change the numerator to the sales amount for the beginner product category, the calculation is 1,010,011,960.66/2,865,382,727.41 = 0.3525, or 35.25%. The metric would then communicate that 35.25% of all sales come from the beginner product category.

In both examples, the denominator is the same number. But with a DAX formula, how do you get the same number in each cell of a report?

If it is true that filter context always filters the underlying tables in the Data Model so that the result for a measure changes in each cell, how do you get a measure like [Total Sales ($)] to not change in each cell and to always show the grand overall total of 2,865,382,727.41? Of course, if you were using worksheet formulas, the denominator would just be a cell reference that points to the grand overall total at the bottom of the column.

As shown in Figure 19.108, in the Total row for the Total Sales ($) column, you can see the correct grand overall total of 2,865,382,727.41, but in the DAX formula language, there is no way to reference that number. In DAX, rather than point to the grand overall total cell to get the amount, you need to build a DAX measure that calculates the grand overall total amount in every cell, no matter what conditions or criteria are in the report. In order to do this, the measure needs to change the filter context by removing all external conditions coming from the Rows area, the Columns area, and slicers so that all rows in all tables in the underlying Data Model are showing and the measure can calculate the line sales for every row in the fact table before aggregating those numbers to get 2,865,382,727.41.

The way that you change the filter context for a measure is to use the CALCULATE DAX function, and the way that you remove all external criteria and conditions from the reporting area—and thereby remove all filters from the fact table in the underlying Data Model—is to use the ALL DAX function.

The CALCULATE DAX function is the most supercharged, powerful function in the DAX formula language because it can change the filter or row context for any measure or scalar formula. The CALCULATE DAX function allows you to change the external filter context (conditions from the Rows area, Columns area, Filters area, and slicers) for a measure by specifying one or more new internal filters (logical tests and conditions) inside in the function. CALCULATE can also convert the row context in a calculated column or a DAX iterator function into filter context with a process called *context transition*. You will see examples of how both of these processes work in the next few examples.

> **Note:** The CALCULATETABLE DAX function works the same way but works with DAX table formulas rather than DAX scalar formulas. Everything that you learn about the CALCULATE function in this section is equally applicable to the CALCULATETABLE function.

Figure 19.109 shows the screentip for the CALCULATE function. The *Expression* argument, which is a required argument, contains the scalar formula for which you want to change the filter context.

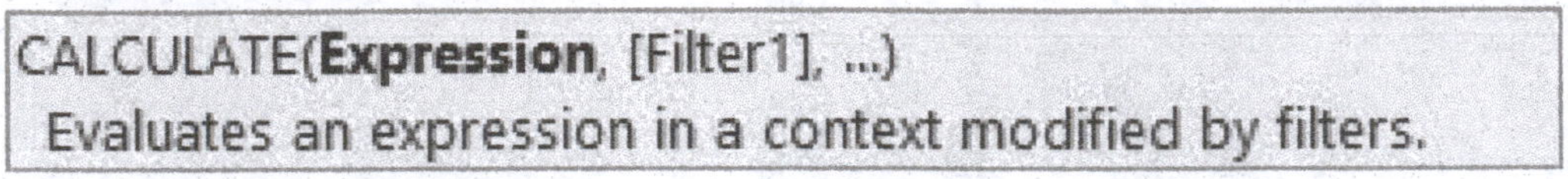

> CALCULATE(**Expression**, [Filter1], ...)
>
> Evaluates an expression in a context modified by filters.

Figure 19.109 *The CALCULATE DAX function screentip.*

The *Filter* arguments allows you to specify one or more new internal filters by using:

- A filter modifier function like the ALL() DAX function to remove all filters from the data model (You will see an example of this later in the chapter, in Figure 19.112.).
- A Boolean (True/False) formula like dProduct[Product]="Quad" (You will see an example of this later in the chapter, in Figure 19.123.)
- A DAX table function that defines a valid list of values as a filter like the DATESINPERIOD DAX function to define a new set of dates (You will see an example of this later in the chapter, in Figure 19.163.)

When you enter two or more internal filters into the *Filter* arguments, the filters are run as an AND logical test. If a field is used in both the external and internal filters, the external filter is removed and replaced with the internal filter. For example, if a measure is in the Aspen product row in a report, and the filter inside CALCULATE is dProduct[Product]="Quad", the internal filter dProduct[Product]="Quad" would replace the external filter dProduct[Product]="Aspen", and the measure would calculate an amount for the Quad product.

The *Filter* arguments are not required. If you omit these arguments, CALCULATE will perform context transition without an internal filter. If you use the *Filter* arguments and row context is available, external filters, internal filters, and the transitioned row filters are all merged in an AND logical test.

You can use the ALL DAX table function as a filter inside CALCULATE to remove all filters from a specific table, column, or multiple columns and return a valid table of values that serves as a filter. In Power BI Desktop, if you use the ALL function with no tables or columns as arguments inside a *Filter* argument of CALCULATE, it serves as a filter modifier that removes all filters in the external filter context and that can be used to calculate the grand overall total for a measure. If you are in Power Pivot and want to remove all filters from the external filter context, you can use the ALL function with the fact table in its argument. As a filter in the CALCULATE function, the ALL function can be thought of as a remove operator because it can remove filters from the underlying data model.

When all external and internal filters are evaluated by the CALCULATE function, CALCULATE creates the final filter context by running an AND logical test with all remaining external and internal filters. The final filter context is used to filter the underlying data model tables so the measure can calculate the formula result. You will see multiple examples of how to use the CALCULATE function throughout this chapter.

To see how the CALCULATE and ALL DAX functions can work together to calculate the sales grand overall total that can be used as the denominator in the % of Grand Total Sales DAX measure, you will build the formula step-by-step and view each intermediate step in the table visual. This will help you better understand how this clever DAX formula is working. Follow these steps:

1. In Report view, in the Fields task pane, right-click the fTransactions table and select New Measure. In the formula bar, create this formula: **% of Grand Total Sales = [Total Sales ($)]**. When you are done with the formula, press Enter.

   As shown in Figure 19.110, the result is not the final formula. The sales amount in each row is the same sales answer as in each row in the Total Sales ($) column. The result is a measure where filter context has been allowed to work in each row of the report to filter the underlying fact table down to just the rows for the specified product.

Note: When you use a measure in a formula, the convention is to place the measure name in square brackets without the table name as a preface (for example, [*Measure Name*]). This alerts users that it is a measure and not a column reference, which requires a table name followed by a field name in square backets (for example, *TableName*[*FieldName*]).

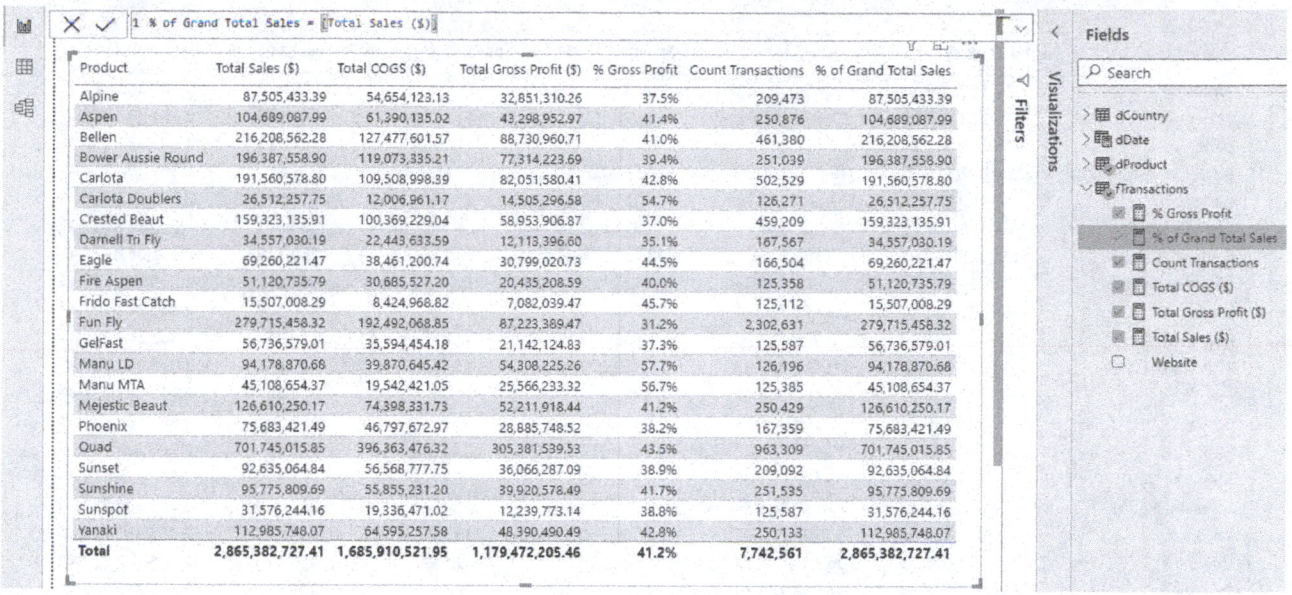

Figure 19.110 *The Rows area product condition flows into the measure as an external filter and filters the fact table.*

2. To change the filter context so that the Rows area condition will *not* filter the underlying fact table, click back in the formula bar and, as shown in Figure 19.111, edit the formula so it is **% of Grand Total Sales = CALCULATE([Total Sales ($)]**.

Note: The scalar formula in the *Expression* argument will have the filter context changed by CALCULATE.

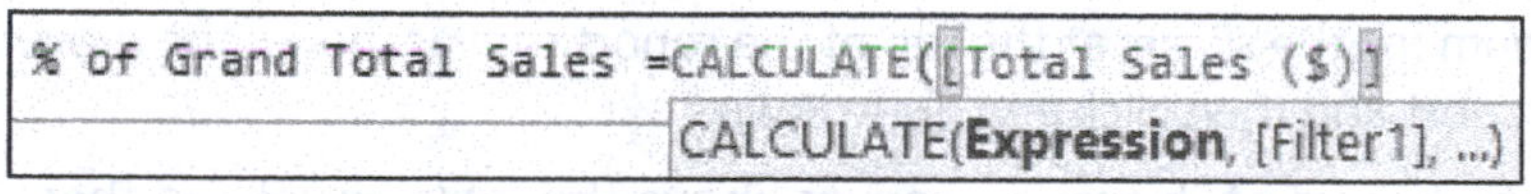

```
% of Grand Total Sales =CALCULATE([Total Sales ($)]
                         CALCULATE(Expression, [Filter1], ...)
```

Figure 19.111 *The CALCULATE function's Expression argument holds the scalar formula for which you want to change context.*

3. Complete the formula as shown in Figure 19.112, so it is **% of Grand Total Sales = CALCULATE([Total Sales ($)],ALL())**. With ALL() in the *Filter1* argument, the CALCULATE function now has the filter modifier it needs to remove all filters in the external filter context. In this example, it will only remove the Product column filter from the dProduct table—and, therefore, from the fact table—because that is the only condition applied in the reporting area. Press the Enter key to complete the formula.

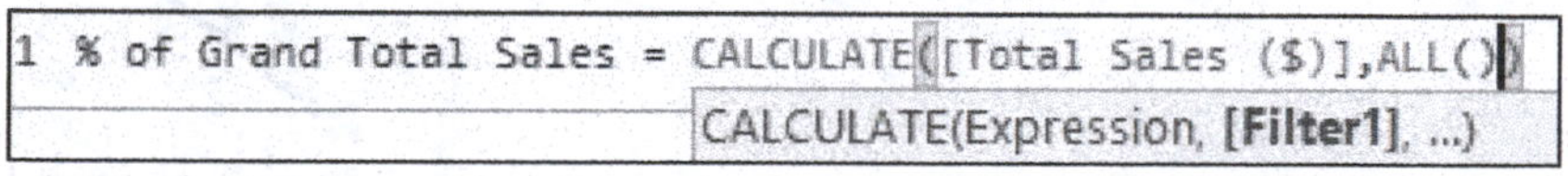

```
1 % of Grand Total Sales = CALCULATE([Total Sales ($)],ALL())
                           CALCULATE(Expression, [Filter1], ...)
```

Figure 19.112 *The Filter1 argument holds the internal filter. The ALL() filter modifier will remove all external filters.*

As shown in Figure 19.113, the measure now delivers the sales grand overall total of 2,865,382,727.41 in every row. The ALL() and CALCULATE combination achieved the goal of removing the filter context in every cell in the % of Grand Total Sales report column.

```
1 % of Grand Total Sales = CALCULATE([Total Sales ($)],ALL())
```

Product	Total Sales ($)	Total COGS ($)	Total Gross Profit ($)	% Gross Profit	Count Transactions	% of Grand Total Sales
Alpine	87,505,433.39	54,654,123.13	32,851,310.26	37.5%	209,473	2,865,382,727.41
Aspen	104,689,087.99	61,390,135.02	43,298,952.97	41.4%	250,876	2,865,382,727.41
Bellen	216,208,562.28	127,477,601.57	88,730,960.71	41.0%	461,380	2,865,382,727.41
Bower Aussie Round	196,387,558.90	119,073,335.21	77,314,223.69	39.4%	251,039	2,865,382,727.41
Carlota	191,560,578.80	109,508,998.39	82,051,580.41	42.8%	502,529	2,865,382,727.41
Carlota Doublers	26,512,257.75	12,006,961.17	14,505,296.58	54.7%	126,271	2,865,382,727.41
Crested Beaut	159,323,135.91	100,369,229.04	58,953,906.87	37.0%	459,209	2,865,382,727.41
Darnell Tri Fly	34,557,030.19	22,443,633.59	12,113,396.60	35.1%	167,567	2,865,382,727.41
Eagle	69,260,221.47	38,461,200.74	30,799,020.73	44.5%	166,504	2,865,382,727.41
Fire Aspen	51,120,735.79	30,685,527.20	20,435,208.59	40.0%	125,358	2,865,382,727.41
Frido Fast Catch	15,507,008.29	8,424,968.82	7,082,039.47	45.7%	125,112	2,865,382,727.41
Fun Fly	279,715,458.32	192,492,068.85	87,223,389.47	31.2%	2,302,631	2,865,382,727.41
GelFast	56,736,579.01	35,594,454.18	21,142,124.83	37.3%	125,587	2,865,382,727.41
Manu LD	94,178,870.68	39,870,645.42	54,308,225.26	57.7%	126,196	2,865,382,727.41
Manu MTA	45,108,654.37	19,542,421.05	25,566,233.32	56.7%	125,385	2,865,382,727.41
Mejestic Beaut	126,610,250.17	74,398,331.73	52,211,918.44	41.2%	250,429	2,865,382,727.41
Phoenix	75,683,421.49	46,797,672.97	28,885,748.52	38.2%	167,359	2,865,382,727.41
Quad	701,745,015.85	396,363,476.32	305,381,539.53	43.5%	963,309	2,865,382,727.41
Sunset	92,635,064.84	56,568,777.75	36,066,287.09	38.9%	209,092	2,865,382,727.41
Sunshine	95,775,809.69	55,855,231.20	39,920,578.49	41.7%	251,535	2,865,382,727.41
Sunspot	31,576,244.16	19,336,471.02	12,239,773.14	38.8%	125,587	2,865,382,727.41
Yanaki	112,985,748.07	64,595,257.58	48,390,490.49	42.8%	250,133	2,865,382,727.41
Total	**2,865,382,727.41**	**1,685,910,521.95**	**1,179,472,205.46**	**41.2%**	**7,742,561**	**2,865,382,727.41**

Figure 19.113 *The sales grand overall total of 2,865,382,727.41 appears in every cell in the % of Grand Total Sales report column.*

To test this new measure, you can add two slicers to the reporting area to add conditions to the external filter context. To add the slicers, follow these steps:

1. To move the table visual and make room for the slicers at the top of the report canvas, hover the move cursor over the bottom edge of the report and then click and drag down.

2. To insert the first slicer, click in an empty part of the report canvas above the table visual and then, in the Visualizations task pane, click the Slicer option, as shown in Figure 19.114. With the first slicer selected, in the Fields task pane, click the checkbox for the Category field in the dProduct table.

3. Add a second slicer for the Website field from the fTransactions table. Figure 19.114 shows the two completed slicers above the table visual.

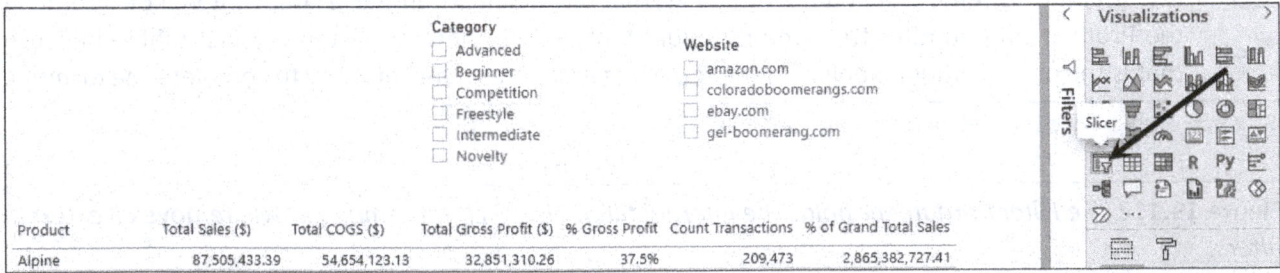

Figure 19.114 *Add two slicers above the table visual.*

4. As shown in Figure 19.115, select the category Beginner and the website amazon.com. Notice that the grand overall total in every cell is still 2,865,382,727.41. This tells you that the CALCULATE and ALL() combo is working, no matter what the external filter context is. You have used the CALCULATE function to change the filter context in every cell in the % of Grand Total Sales report column so that no filters are applied to the underlying data model.

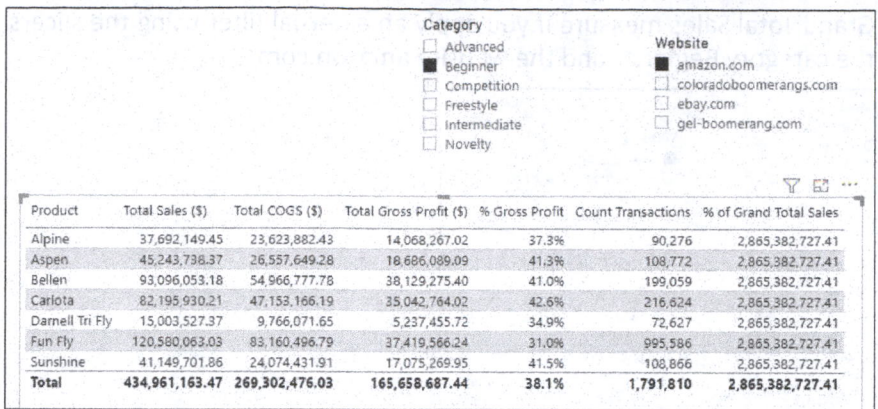

Product	Total Sales ($)	Total COGS ($)	Total Gross Profit ($)	% Gross Profit	Count Transactions	% of Grand Total Sales
Alpine	37,692,149.45	23,623,882.43	14,068,267.02	37.3%	90,276	2,865,382,727.41
Aspen	45,243,738.37	26,557,649.28	18,686,089.09	41.3%	108,772	2,865,382,727.41
Bellen	93,096,053.18	54,966,777.78	38,129,275.40	41.0%	199,059	2,865,382,727.41
Carlota	82,195,930.21	47,153,166.19	35,042,764.02	42.6%	216,624	2,865,382,727.41
Darnell Tri Fly	15,003,527.37	9,766,071.65	5,237,455.72	34.9%	72,627	2,865,382,727.41
Fun Fly	120,580,063.03	83,160,496.79	37,419,566.24	31.0%	995,586	2,865,382,727.41
Sunshine	41,149,701.86	24,074,431.91	17,075,269.95	41.5%	108,866	2,865,382,727.41
Total	**434,961,163.47**	**269,302,476.03**	**165,658,687.44**	**38.1%**	**1,791,810**	**2,865,382,727.41**

Figure 19.115 *No matter what the external filter context is, the overall total 2,865,382,727.41 appears in every cell.*

5. Now that you are done testing the external filters, remove the two slicer filters by deselecting the boxes for the Beginner category and the amazon.com website.

6. To use the grand overall total DAX formula element in the denominator of the percentage of grand total sales calculation, as shown in Figure 19.116, complete the formula so it is **% of Grand Total Sales = DIVIDE([Total Sales ($)], CALCULATE([Total Sales ($)],ALL()))**. Press the Enter key to complete the formula.

```
1  % of Grand Total Sales = DIVIDE([Total Sales ($)], CALCULATE([Total Sales ($)],ALL()))
          DIVIDE(Numerator, Denominator, [AlternateResult])
```

Figure 19.116 *The numerator uses the external filter context; the denominator does not.*

7. Add percentage number formatting with one decimal place showing. Figure 19.117 shows the formula results in the report.

```
X ✓  1  % of Grand Total Sales = DIVIDE([Total Sales ($)], CALCULATE([Total Sales ($)],ALL()))
```

Product	Total Sales ($)	Total COGS ($)	Total Gross Profit ($)	% Gross Profit	Count Transactions	% of Grand Total Sales
Alpine	87,505,433.39	54,654,123.13	32,851,310.26	37.5%	209,473	3.1%
Aspen	104,689,087.99	61,390,135.02	43,298,952.97	41.4%	250,876	3.7%
Bellen	216,208,562.28	127,477,601.57	88,730,960.71	41.0%	461,380	7.5%
Bower Aussie Round	196,387,558.90	119,073,335.21	77,314,223.69	39.4%	251,039	6.9%
Carlota	191,560,578.80	109,508,998.39	82,051,580.41	42.8%	502,529	6.7%
Carlota Doublers	26,512,257.75	12,006,961.17	14,505,296.58	54.7%	126,271	0.9%
Crested Beaut	159,323,135.91	100,369,229.04	58,953,906.87	37.0%	459,209	5.6%
Darnell Tri Fly	34,557,050.19	22,443,633.59	12,113,396.60	35.1%	167,567	1.2%
Eagle	69,260,221.47	38,461,200.74	30,799,020.73	44.5%	166,504	2.4%
Fire Aspen	51,120,735.79	30,685,527.20	20,435,208.59	40.0%	125,358	1.8%
Frido Fast Catch	15,507,008.29	8,424,968.82	7,082,039.47	45.7%	125,112	0.5%
Fun Fly	279,715,458.32	192,492,068.85	87,223,389.47	31.2%	2,302,631	9.8%
GelFast	56,736,579.01	35,594,454.18	21,142,124.83	37.3%	125,587	2.0%
Manu LD	94,178,870.68	39,870,645.42	54,308,225.26	57.7%	126,196	3.3%
Manu MTA	45,108,654.37	19,542,421.05	25,566,233.32	56.7%	125,385	1.6%
Mejestic Beaut	126,610,250.17	74,398,331.73	52,211,918.44	41.2%	250,429	4.4%
Phoenix	75,683,421.49	46,797,672.97	28,885,748.52	38.2%	167,359	2.6%
Quad	701,745,015.65	396,363,476.32	305,381,539.53	43.5%	963,309	24.5%
Sunset	92,635,064.84	56,568,777.75	36,066,287.09	38.9%	209,092	3.2%
Sunshine	95,775,809.69	55,855,231.20	39,920,578.49	41.7%	251,535	3.3%
Sunspot	31,576,244.16	19,336,471.02	12,239,773.14	38.8%	125,587	1.1%
Yanaki	112,985,748.07	64,595,257.58	48,390,490.49	42.8%	250,133	3.9%
Total	**2,865,382,727.41**	**1,685,910,521.95**	**1,179,472,205.46**	**41.2%**	**7,742,561**	**100.0%**

Fields
- Search
- > dCountry
- > dDate
- > dProduct
- ∨ fTransactions
  - % Gross Profit
  - % of Grand Total Sales
  - Count Transactions
  - Total COGS ($)
  - Total Gross Profit ($)
  - Total Sales ($)
  - Website

Figure 19.117 *The finished % of Grand Total Sales measure.*

The beautiful thing about this formula is that the [Total Sales ($)] measure in the numerator is allowed to use the external filter context, but the [Total Sales ($)] measure in the denominator is not allowed to use the external filter context because the CALCULATE function changes the filter context.

> **Note:** As shown in Figure 19.118, although the REMOVEFILTERS DAX function can be used in CALCULATE as a substitute for the ALL function to remove all external filters, it is only available in the Power BI Data Model and is not available in the Power Pivot Data Model. I mention it here only because the name of the function is easier to remember than ALL.

```
1  % of Grand Total Sales = DIVIDE([Total Sales ($)], CALCULATE([Total Sales ($)],REMOVEFILTERS()))
```

Figure 19.118 *Inside of the Filter1 argument of CALCULATE, REMOVEFILTERS() does the same thing as ALL().*

To see what happens to the % of Grand Total Sales measure if you apply an external filter using the slicers, as shown in Figure 19.119, select the category Beginner and the website amazon.com.

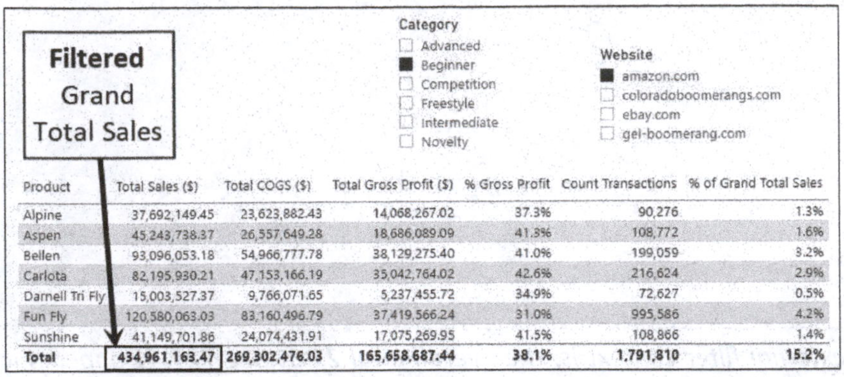

Figure 19.119 *When the slicer is used, the Total row for the % of Grand Total Sales measure correctly shows 15.2%.*

As shown in Figure 19.119, the Total row for the % of Grand Total Sales Measure correctly shows 15.2%. The percentage is calculated by using the total sales for the Beginner product category at the Amazon website in the numerator and the grand overall sales total in the denominator, like this: 434,961,163.47/2,865,382,727.41 = 0.152, or 15.2%.

Using ALLSELECTED() to Remove Row and Column Filters to Calculate a Filtered Grand Total

What if you want to see each product sales total as a percentage of the filtered grand total (that is, the 434,961,163.47 amount shown at the bottom of the Total Sales ($) column)? For example, in the first row of the report, for the Alpine product, say that you want to see the calculation 37,692,149.45/434,961,163.47 = 0.087, or 8.7%.

To calculate the filtered grand total amount in the denominator, you can use the ALLSELECTED() DAX function in the *Filter1* argument of the CALCULATE function rather than the ALL() function. Inside the *Filter1* argument of the CALCULATE function, the ALLSELECTED() DAX function, with no tables or columns added as arguments, serves as a filter modifier that will remove the row and column filters from the report or visual and leave the filters that are external to the report or visual intact. In this way, for the current table visual, the measure will remove the product row filter and keep the slicer filters, and it will therefore always get the correct filtered grand total amount.

To see that the ALLSELECTED() function can help get the filtered grand total in each cell in the report, follow these steps:

1. Create the following measure in the fTransactions table: **% of Filtered Grand Total Sales = CALCULATE([Total Sales ($)],ALLSELECTED())**. Figure 19.120 shows that the ALLSELECTED() function in the *Filter1* argument of CALCULATE removes the row product filter but not the slicer filters and returns the filtered grand total sales amount in each cell.

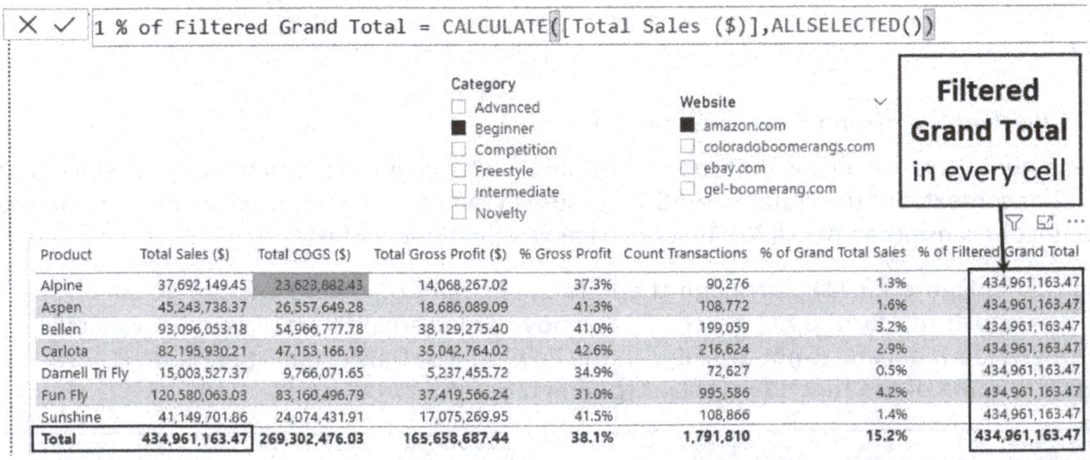

Figure 19.120 *ALLSELECTED() removes the table row filter but not the slicer filters.*

2. To use the filtered grand total sales amount as the denominator and the [Total Sales ($)] measure as the numerator, click in the formula bar and edit the measure so that it is **% of Filtered Grand Total Sales = DIVIDE([Total Sales ($)],CALCULATE([Total Sales ($)],ALLSELECTED()))**.

3. Add percentage number formatting with one decimal place showing for the measure. Figure 19.121 shows the formula results in the report.

| X ✓ | 1 % of Filtered Grand Total = DIVIDE([Total Sales ($)],CALCULATE([Total Sales ($)],ALLSELECTED())) |

Category
- ☐ Advanced
- ☑ Beginner
- ☐ Competition
- ☐ Freestyle
- ☐ Intermediate
- ☐ Novelty

Website
- ☑ amazon.com
- ☐ coloradoboomerangs.com
- ☐ ebay.com
- ☐ gel-boomerang.com

Product	Total Sales ($)	Total COGS ($)	Total Gross Profit ($)	% Gross Profit	Count Transactions	% of Grand Total Sales	% of Filtered Grand Total
Alpine	37,692,149.45	23,623,882.43	14,068,267.02	37.3%	90,276	1.3%	8.7%
Aspen	45,243,738.37	26,557,649.28	18,686,089.09	41.3%	108,772	1.6%	10.4%
Bellen	93,096,053.18	54,966,777.78	38,129,275.40	41.0%	199,059	3.2%	21.4%
Carlota	82,195,930.21	47,153,166.19	35,042,764.02	42.6%	216,624	2.9%	18.9%
Darnell Tri Fly	15,003,527.37	9,766,071.65	5,237,455.72	34.9%	72,627	0.5%	3.4%
Fun Fly	120,580,063.03	83,160,496.79	37,419,566.24	31.0%	995,586	4.2%	27.7%
Sunshine	41,149,701.86	24,074,431.91	17,075,269.95	41.5%	108,866	1.4%	9.5%
Total	**434,961,163.47**	**269,302,476.03**	**165,658,687.44**	**38.1%**	**1,791,810**	**15.2%**	**100.0%**

Figure 19.121 *The two different measures, together, can help to provide more insight.*

Both the % of Grand Total Sales and % of Filtered Grand Total Sales measures are valid and useful. In fact, when they sit side-by-side in a report, as they do in the table visual in Figure 19.121, together they can bring more insight than just one or the other alone can bring. This illustrates an advantage that the DAX formula language has over the standard PivotTable show values as a percentage of the grand total calculation. With the show values as a percentage of the grand total calculation, the denominator always contains the filtered sales amount, and it cannot make the same calculation as the % of Grand Total Sales measure, where the denominator is always the full grand overall sales total.

If you want both measures in a report, then using a Power Pivot PivotTable or a Power BI visual with DAX measures is the way to go. Finally, if you remove all the filters from the slicers, as shown in Figure 19.122, both measures deliver the same results.

Product	Total Sales ($)	Total COGS ($)	Total Gross Profit ($)	% Gross Profit	Count Transactions	% of Grand Total Sales	% of Filtered Grand Total
Alpine	87,505,433.39	54,654,123.13	32,851,310.26	37.5%	209,473	3.1%	3.1%
Aspen	104,689,087.99	61,390,135.02	43,298,952.97	41.4%	250,876	3.7%	3.7%
Bellen	216,208,562.28	127,477,601.57	88,730,960.71	41.0%	461,380	7.5%	7.5%
Bower Aussie Round	196,387,558.90	119,073,335.21	77,314,223.69	39.4%	251,039	6.9%	6.9%
Carlota	191,560,578.80	109,508,998.39	82,051,580.41	42.8%	502,529	6.7%	6.7%
Carlota Doublers	[Hidden rows] 12,006,961.17		14,505,296.58	54.7%	126,271	0.9%	0.9%
Phoenix		46,797,672.97	28,885,748.52	38.2%	167,359	2.6%	2.6%
Quad	701,745,015.85	396,363,476.32	305,381,539.53	43.5%	963,309	24.5%	24.5%
Sunset	92,635,064.84	56,568,777.75	36,066,287.09	38.9%	209,092	3.2%	3.2%
Sunshine	95,775,809.69	55,855,231.20	39,920,578.49	41.7%	251,535	3.3%	3.3%
Sunspot	31,576,244.16	19,336,471.02	12,239,773.14	38.8%	125,587	1.1%	1.1%
Yanaki	112,985,748.07	64,595,257.58	48,390,490.49	42.8%	250,133	3.9%	3.9%
Total	**2,865,382,727.41**	**1,685,910,521.95**	**1,179,472,205.46**	**41.2%**	**7,742,561**	**100.0%**	**100.0%**

Figure 19.122 *When there are no items selected in the slicer, the two measures yield the same answer.*

When you create a measure that uses the ALLSELECTED() function in the *Filter1* argument of CALCULATE to get report or visual filtered grand total amounts, you must be careful to use the measure in the report or visual where you have row or column filters that you want to remove. For example, say that you create a measure that is used in the table visual, where you have a row condition that you want to remove. In this case, the measure works as expected, and you get the correct answer. However, if you use the measure in other measures, such as in iterator functions, your formula will remove the row condition from the table being iterated—rather than removing any row or column conditions—from a given report or visual.

The Microsoft help website defines ALLSELECTED as follows:

```
The ALLSELECTED function gets the context that represents all rows and col-
umns in the query, while keeping explicit filters and contexts other than
row and column filters. This function can be used to obtain visual totals in
queries.
```

Microsoft uses the word *query* in this definition rather than the phrase *report or visual*, as I did. When Microsoft says *query* here, it is referring to whatever the object is that has rows and columns, whether it is a report or visual in the report canvas, a PivotTable report in a worksheet, or a table that is being iterated by an iterator function.

Using a Boolean Filter

Both ALL() and ALLSELECTED() can be used as filter modifiers in the *Filter1* argument of the CALCULATE function. You can also write a Boolean filter in the *Filter1* argument of the CALCULATE function. For example, if you want to see the sales amount for the Quad product in every cell in the % of Grand Total Sales report column, as shown in Figure 19.123, you can use a Boolean filter like dProduct[Product]="Quad". This filter uses a field name, a comparison operator, and the condition. Because the product name is a text value, you must place the product name in quotation marks.

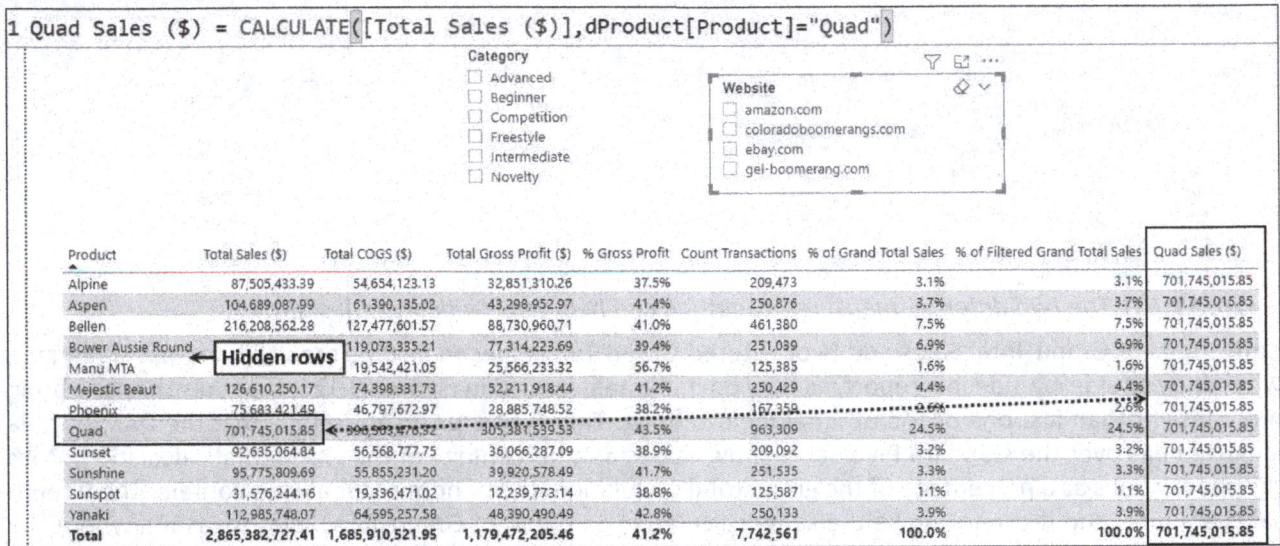

Figure 19.123 *With no slicer conditions, the Quad total is 701,745,015.85.*

A Boolean filter can use only one field from a table and cannot use aggregate functions for conditions. To accomplish those tasks, you must use the DAX FILTER function, as demonstrated in Project 5, later in this chapter. When you use a Boolean filter, if the field is used in both the external and internal filters, the external filter is removed and replaced with the internal filter. In this case, because the Product field is used in the Rows area of the report and it is used in the internal filter, for each cell in the % of Grand Total Sales report column, the Product row condition is removed and replaced with the Quad condition.

A formula like this might be useful if you needed to compare each of the other product total sales amounts against the Quad sales total. This is not a calculation that you need in your data model for this project, but I showed it here as another example of what the CALCULATE function can do.

Figure 19.124 shows the measure result when the report is sliced by the Freestyle category and amazon.com website. You can try to create this formula on your own as a challenge.

```
1 Quad Sales ($) = CALCULATE([Total Sales ($)],dProduct[Product]="Quad")
```

Product	Total Sales ($)	Total COGS ($)	Total Gross Profit ($)	% Gross Profit	Count Transactions	% of Grand Total Sales	% of Filtered Grand Total Sales	Quad Sales ($)
Carlota Doublers	11,345,279.60	5,192,500.27	6,152,779.33	54.2%	54,604	0.4%	3.6%	302,801,194.38
Quad	302,801,194.38	171,693,948.16	131,107,246.22	43.3%	416,261	10.6%	96.4%	302,801,194.38
Total	314,146,473.98	176,886,448.43	137,260,025.55	43.7%	470,865	11.0%	100.0%	302,801,194.38

Figure 19.124 *CALCULATE changes the filter context so that every cell calculates the Quad product sales.*

Understanding Context Transition

Think about the DAX task of adding a calculated column to the dProduct dimension table to calculate the product total sales in each row. As shown in Figure 19.125, if you try to use the SUM function to add the line sales from the fTransactions table, the formula does not work to get the product total sales. Instead, the formula calculates the grand overall total sales amount in every row in the fact table. There is no filter context in a calculated column or DAX iterator function, and aggregate functions like SUM will always provide the grand total result.

In each cell in the column, the SUM function is adding the full unfiltered column of line sales amounts from the fact table. You don't want that. What you want is for the fact table to "see" the product condition in each row and then use it as a filter to filter the fact table down to just the rows for that product. Then the SUM function can add the filtered product line sales.

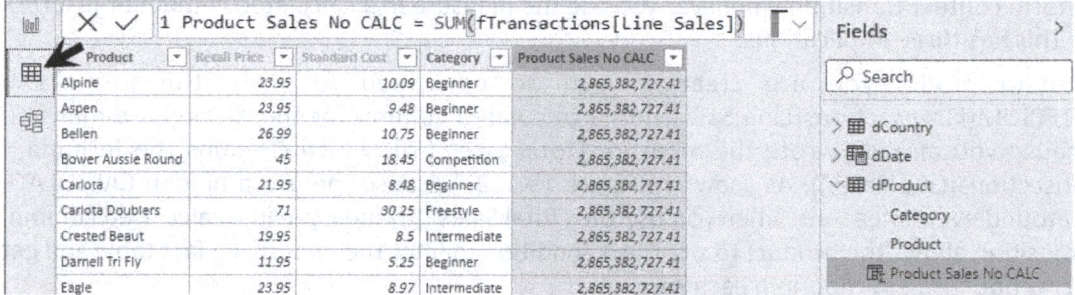

Figure 19.125 *An aggregate function in a calculated column returns the unfiltered grand total amount.*

You want the product row context to be converted to a product filter context. The CALCULATE function can do exactly that. The CALCULATE function can convert the available row context into filter context, in a process known as *context transition*. As shown in Figure 19.126, as soon as you wrap the CALCULATE function around the SUM function, the product row condition in each row is used to filter the fTransactions Line Sales field down to just the rows for that product, and the formula calculates the correct product total sales in each row.

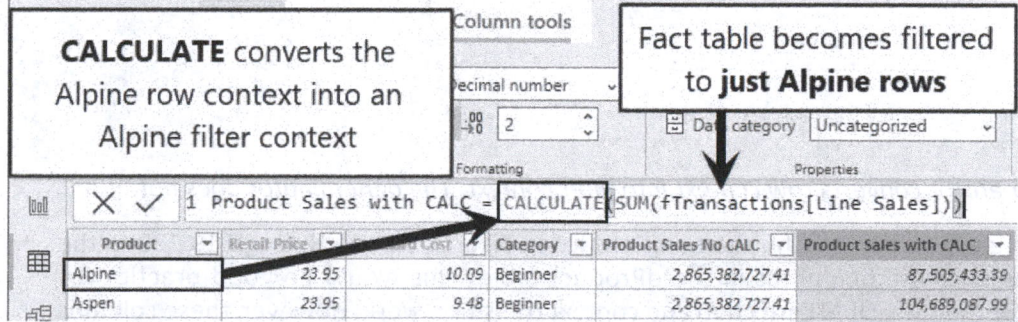

Figure 19.126 *The CALCULATE function performs context transition, converting the row context to filter context.*

As shown in Figure 19.127, for the first row in the dProduct table, the CALCULATE function converts the Alpine row context condition into an Alpine filter context condition so that the underlying fact table is filtered down to just the rows for the Alpine product. Then the SUM function adds to get the correct Alpine sales total. This same process happens in every row in the dProduct table.

CALCULATE converts the Alpine row context into an Alpine filter context

Fact table becomes filtered to **just Alpine rows**

Column tools

Decimal number

.00 → 2

Da category   Uncategorized

Formatting   Properties

1 Product Sales with CALC = CALCULATE(SUM(fTransactions[Line Sales]))

Product	Retail Price	Cost	Category	Product Sales No CALC	Product Sales with CALC
Alpine	23.95	10.09	Beginner	2,865,382,727.41	87,505,433.39
Aspen	23.95	9.48	Beginner	2,865,382,727.41	104,689,087.99

Figure 19.127 *CALCULATE helps the Alpine row condition to filter the fact table.*

If you use the CALCULATE function in a calculated column or in an iterator function, it will convert all available row contexts into filter contexts. This process, which CALCULATE performs, is called *context transition* because it transitions the row contexts into filter contexts.

Note: I am using the plural *row contexts* here because you can have back-to-back row context situations, like using two iterator functions or using an iterator function in a calculated column.

When you invoke context transition, you want to do it in a table with a primary key, such as a dimension table. If you invoke context transition in a fact table with duplicate records and no primary key, you will get incorrect results. (You will see an example of this later in this chapter, in Figures 19.153 through 19.159.)

Now for the big DAX measure hidden surprise: All measures have a *hidden CALCULATE function wrapped around them to facilitate automatic context transition.* What?! Yes, it is true. There is a hidden CALCULATE for every measure that you create. You can't go and look at the hidden CALCULATE, but it is there! And it will automatically perform context transition whenever you use the measure in a calculated column or in a DAX iterator function. This has three implications:

- For the data model you are creating, you do not need to write the formula = CALCULATE(SUM(fTransactions[Line Sales])) in a calculated column for the dProduct dimension table because you already wrote the measure [Total Sales ($)], which contains the formula = SUM(fTransactions[Line Sales]). As shown in Figure 19.128, because there is a hidden CALCULATE wrapped around every measure, when you use the [Total Sales ($)] measure in a calculated column, context transition allows the product row context condition to filter the underlying fact table and get the correct product sales amount in each row.

- The number of ways that you can use a given measure is dramatically increased. Not only is a measure a reusable formula for reports and visuals, it is also a reusable formula that can be used in calculated columns and DAX iterators (such as the AVERAGEX function).

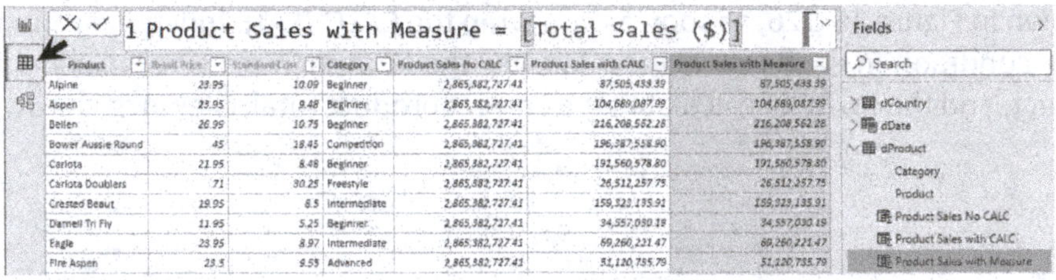

Figure 19.128 *Every measure has a hidden CALCULATE function that performs context transition.*

- You must be careful when using measures where context transition might not be what you want. For example, if you wanted to calculate the product sales as a percentage of grand overall total sales in a calculated column, you would need the grand overall total sales in the denominator. In this case, you would want to use the formula element SUM(fTransactions[Line Sales]) in the denominator rather than [Total Sales ($)]. Figure 19.129 shows an example of the product sales as a percentage of grand overall total sales calculated column formula.

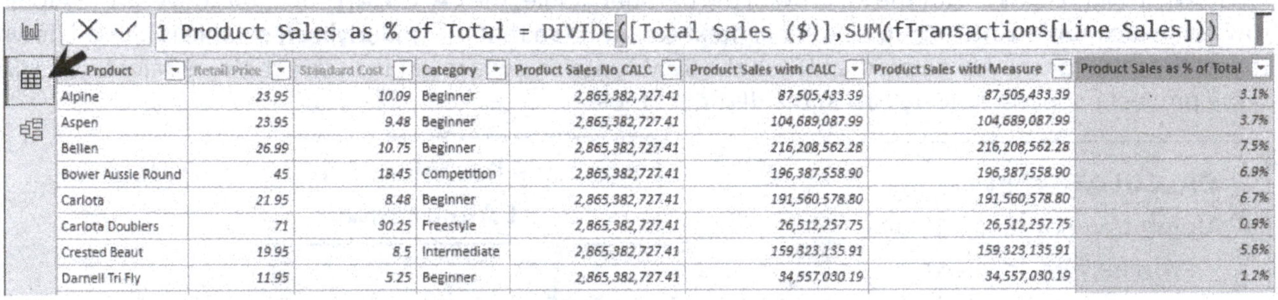

1 Product Sales as % of Total = DIVIDE([Total Sales ($)],SUM(fTransactions[Line Sales]))

Product	Retail Price	Standard Cost	Category	Product Sales No CALC	Product Sales with CALC	Product Sales with Measure	Product Sales as % of Total
Alpine	23.95	10.09	Beginner	2,865,382,727.41	87,505,433.39	87,505,433.39	3.1%
Aspen	23.95	9.48	Beginner	2,865,382,727.41	104,689,087.99	104,689,087.99	3.7%
Bellen	26.99	10.75	Beginner	2,865,382,727.41	216,208,562.28	216,208,562.28	7.5%
Bower Aussie Round	45	18.45	Competition	2,865,382,727.41	196,387,558.90	196,387,558.90	6.9%
Carlota	21.95	8.48	Beginner	2,865,382,727.41	191,560,578.80	191,560,578.80	6.7%
Carlota Doublers	71	30.25	Freestyle	2,865,382,727.41	26,512,257.75	26,512,257.75	0.9%
Crested Beaut	19.95	8.5	Intermediate	2,865,382,727.41	159,323,135.91	159,323,135.91	5.6%
Darnell Tri Fly	11.95	5.25	Beginner	2,865,382,727.41	34,557,030.19	34,557,030.19	1.2%

Figure 19.129 *The numerator converts row context into filter context. The denominator does not.*

Note: As a challenge, you can try the examples shown in Figures 19.125 through 19.129 in the data area as new calculated columns in the dProduct table. This would be good practice for understanding how the CALCULATE function and context transition work. However, these columns will not be needed in the reporting area, so you should hide them from Report view after you complete them.

So, as you have just seen, the CALCULATE function is powerful in two ways:

- It can change the external filter context for a measure by applying internal filters to help change the filter context.

- It can perform context transition, converting any available row contexts into filter contexts.

Calculating Averages at Different Grains and with Different Formulas

There are many different types of averages, such as mean, median, mode, and geometric mean. The most common average is the *arithmetic mean*, also called just the *mean*. This metric is commonly known as an *average*, and I will refer to it as such. The average calculation involves adding up a set of numbers and dividing by the count of that set of numbers. This metric is helpful because it gives you a single number that represents all the data points and can be used to gauge the typical performance for a given set of numbers.

In analytics, you are usually given a fact table with a certain *grain* (which refers to the size of the number in each row). The fact table in this project has a transactional grain, where each row in the table represents a sale of a product, at a specified website, in a specified country, on a specified date. If you average the sales amounts in all the rows of the fact table, because the grain of each number is at the transactional level, you are calculating the *average transaction sales*. If you add the transactional sales amounts to get the daily sales total amounts and then use those numbers to calculate an average, because the grain of each number is now at the day level, you are calculating the *average daily sales*. If you add the transactional sales amounts to get the monthly sales total amounts and then use those numbers to calculate an average, because the grain of each number is now at the month level, you are calculating the *average monthly sales*. Each of these metrics communicates the typical sales amount at the given grain.

You need to make three average calculations at this point in the project:

- Average transactional sales by product
- Average daily sales by product
- Average monthly sales by product

If the goal is to calculate the average transactional sales, you can just use the Line Sales field from the fact table inside the AVERAGE DAX function, which works the same as the Excel worksheet AVERAGE function. That formula uses the fact table row line sales numbers as a set of numbers; it adds them up and divides by the count.

However, you often need to make aggregate calculations, such as averages, with a grain that is larger than the grain in the fact table. For example, to calculate the average daily sales, the grain of the numbers needed in the formula is larger than the grain of the numbers in the fact table. Luckily, DAX formulas can deal with such grain disparities easily; in fact, this ability is one of the main benefits of DAX formulas.

For the average daily sales calculation, there are two useful approaches to building the DAX formula:

- The first approach is to pre-aggregate the daily sales amounts and then, once you have the daily sales totals, average those numbers. The pre-aggregation is necessary because there are many records in the fact table for any given day. You must add up the sales for each day and then, once you have that set of daily sales numbers at the correct grain, you can average them. For this approach, you can use the AVERAGEX DAX function.

Note: If you needed to calculate the average daily sales with only the standard PivotTable tool and worksheet formulas, because there is no way to pre-aggregate numbers with a standard PivotTable calculation, you would be forced to create an intermediate table in the worksheet with the total sales for each date and then make a standard PivotTable from that intermediate table. This approach was common before the Data Model and DAX, but it was time-consuming, did not work well with large datasets, and could become very complex.

- The second approach to calculating average daily sales is to just add up all sales and then divide by the unique count of dates in the Date field in the fact table. This approach is more straightforward than the first approach, but it is possible only because there is a field in the fact table that allows you to create a unique list of dates. For some calculations, such as average monthly sales, there is usually not a field in the fact table that allows you to get a unique count of months for the denominator, and therefore you cannot use this second approach (though the first approach will work). When you have an attribute field in the fact table, you can use the DIVIDE and DISTINCTCOUNT DAX functions.

Note: If you needed to calculate the average daily sales with only the standard PivotTable tool and worksheet formulas, because there is no unique count calculation in the standard PivotTable, you would once again be stuck with a more inefficient worksheet solution if you wanted to use this second approach.

To create the average transactional sales measure for this project, follow these steps:

1. In Report view, create the following formula in the fact table: **Ave Transactional Sales ($) = AVERAGE(fTransactions[Line Sales])**.

2. Add decimal number formatting with two decimal places showing. Figure 19.130 shows the result.

```
1 Ave Transactional Sales ($) = AVERAGE(fTransactions[Line Sales])
```

Product	Total Sales ($)	Count Transactions	Ave Transactional Sales ($)	
Alpine	87,505,433.39	209,473	417.74	
Aspen	104,689,087.99	250,876	417.29	← **Hidden rows**
Phoenix	75,683,421.49	167,359	452.22	
Quad	701,745,015.85	963,309	728.47	
Sunset	92,635,064.84	209,092	443.03	
Sunshine	95,775,809.69	251,535	380.77	
Sunspot	31,576,244.16	125,587	251.43	
Yanaki	112,985,748.07	250,133	451.70	
Total	**2,865,382,727.41**	**7,742,561**	**370.08**	

Figure 19.130 *Average transactional sales measure.*

As shown in Figure 19.130, the average transactional sale for the Alpine product was $417.74, and for the Quad it was $728.47. These numbers tell you that these are numbers you can expect for any given typical sale over the four-year period. The calculation process for each cell in the report column is simple: The product external filter context flows into the measure, the fact table is filtered down to just the row-specific product, and the AVERAGE function uses the numbers to calculate the average transactional sales for the filtered product. The average in the total row is the average of all transactions in the fact table.

Using AVERAGEX to Calculate Average Daily Sales

In Chapter 18, you learned about the DAX X iterator functions, which allow you to iterate a formula down a table row by row, calculate a column of intermediate values, and then aggregate those intermediate values. As you saw in Chapter 18, the SUMX DAX iterator function is used for sum calculations. The AVERAGEX DAX iterator function is another iterator X function that is used for average calculations. It has the following syntax:

```
=AVERAGEX(Table, Expression)
```

where the *Table* argument holds the table to be iterated, and the *Expression* argument holds the formula that will iterate down the table.

Importantly for the average calculation, when there are no records in the fact table for a particular row in the table being iterated, a DAX blank is returned so that row position is not counted in the denominator of the average calculation.

Using DAX X Iterator Functions to Get the Correct Grain

A DAX iterator function allows you to decide what the grain of the table is in the first argument of the function. The grain of the table will determine the grain of each value in the intermediate column of numbers. For a calculation like average daily sales, the grain of the table would have to be at the day level, whereas for a calculation like average monthly sales, the grain of the table would have to be at the month level. For the average daily sales calculation, this means you need a table with a unique list of dates, and for the average monthly sales calculation, this means you need a table with a unique list of months.

Luckily, for the average daily sales calculation in this project, the date dimension table has a unique list of all days from the fact table and has a day-level grain. This means you can use the formula:

```
=AVERAGEX(dDate,[Total Sales ($)])
```

This formula will take the [Total Sales ($)] measure, iterate down each row in the date table, calculate an intermediate column of daily sales totals, and then, from that set of total sales numbers at the day grain, average them to get the average daily sales.

Next, you will create this measure and add it to your table visual, and then you will take a look at the clever and amazing process that the DAX engine uses to make this calculation. To create the average daily sales measure, follow these steps:

1. Create the following average daily sales formula in the fact table: **Ave Daily Sales AVEX ($) = AVERAGEX(dDate,[Total Sales ($)])**.

2. Add decimal number formatting with two decimal places showing. Figure 19.131 shows the result.

X ✓ | 1 Ave Daily Sales AVEX ($) = AVERAGEX(dDate,[Total Sales ($)])

Product	Total Sales ($)	Count Transactions	Ave Transactional Sales ($)	Ave Daily Sales AVEX ($)
Alpine	87,505,433.39	209,473	417.74	59,935.23
Aspen	104,689,087.99	250,876	417.29	71,704.85
Phoenix	75,683,421.49	167,359	452.22	51,837.96
Quad	701,745,015.85	963,309	728.47	480,647.27
Sunset	92,635,064.84	209,092	443.03	63,448.67
Sunshine	95,775,809.69	251,535	380.77	65,599.87
Sunspot	31,576,244.16	125,587	251.43	21,627.56
Yanaki	112,985,748.07	250,133	451.70	77,387.50
Total	**2,865,382,727.41**	**7,742,561**	**370.08**	**1,962,590.91**

← **Hidden rows**

Figure 19.131 *Average daily sales measure using an iterator function.*

As shown in Figure 19.131, the average daily sales amount for the Alpine product was $59,935.23, and for the Quad product, it was $480,647.27. These averages communicate the typical product daily sales numbers over the four-year period. In the total row at the bottom, the result $1,962,590,91 represents the average daily sales for all products over the four-year period. The calculation for each cell in the column uses several processes simultaneously, including filter context, iteration, and context transition. To better understand how this formula works, let's take a closer look at the full calculation process.

In the first row of the table visual in Figure 19.131, the [Ave Daily Sales AVEX ($)] measure takes seven steps to calculate the Alpine product average daily sales of $59,935.23:

1. As shown in Figure 19.132, the first step in the calculation process is not really a step as much as it is an important concept to understand about how the formula works. At the beginning of the calculations process, the fact table in the formula contains all 7,742,561 rows.

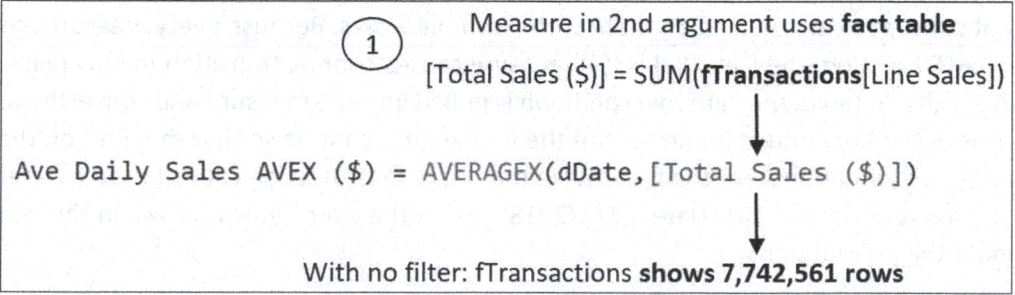

Figure 19.132 *With no external filter context, the fact table shows all rows.*

2. As shown in Figure 19.133, in the first row of the table visual, the Alpine external filter context flows into the measure. If it were just this filter, the fact table would become filtered down to only the records for the Alpine product, and the fact table would show 209,473 rows.

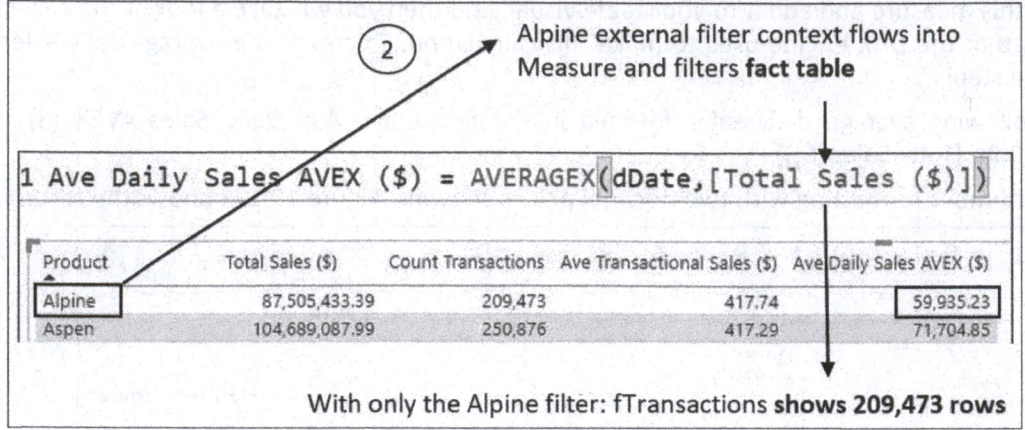

Figure 19.133 *For the first row in the table visual, the Alpine condition filters the fTransactions table.*

3. As shown in Figure 19.134, the [Total Sales ($)] measure iterates down all 1,461 rows in the dDate table and makes the daily sales total calculation in each row. When there are no records in the fact table for a particular date, a DAX blank is returned so that the date is not counted in the denominator of the average calculation. For the Alpine product, this happens one time because it was sold on 1,460 of the 1,461 possible days.

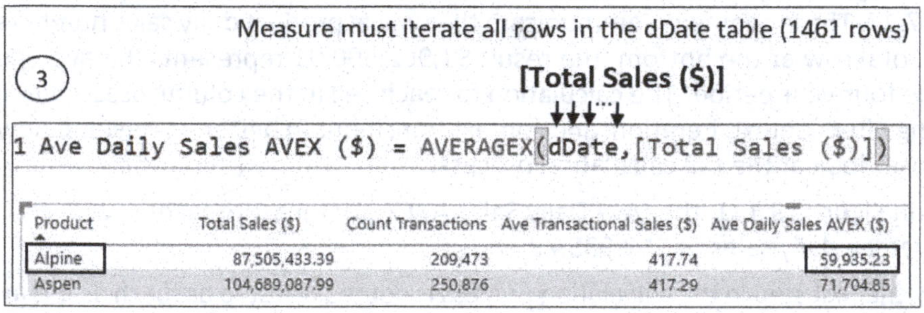

Measure must iterate all rows in the dDate table (1461 rows)

[Total Sales ($)]

1 `Ave Daily Sales AVEX ($) = AVERAGEX(dDate,[Total Sales ($)])`

Product	Total Sales ($)	Count Transactions	Ave Transactional Sales ($)	Ave Daily Sales AVEX ($)
Alpine	87,505,433.39	209,473	417.74	59,935.23
Aspen	104,689,087.99	250,876	417.29	71,704.85

Figure 19.134 *The measure must iterate down every row in the date table.*

4. As shown in Figure 19.135, the fourth step in the calculation process is not really a step as much as it is an important concept to understand about how the formula works. Because every measure has a hidden CALCULATE function, the [Total Sales ($)] measure causes context transition to take place: For each row in the dDate table, the date row condition is pulled into the measure and converted to filter context. This date filter context is joined with the Alpine filter context so that the filter on the fact table now has two conditions! For the first row in the dDate table, the logical test used to filter the fact table is Product = Alpine AND Date = 1/1/2018. Out of the over 7 million rows in the fact table, 9 rows meet these conditions.

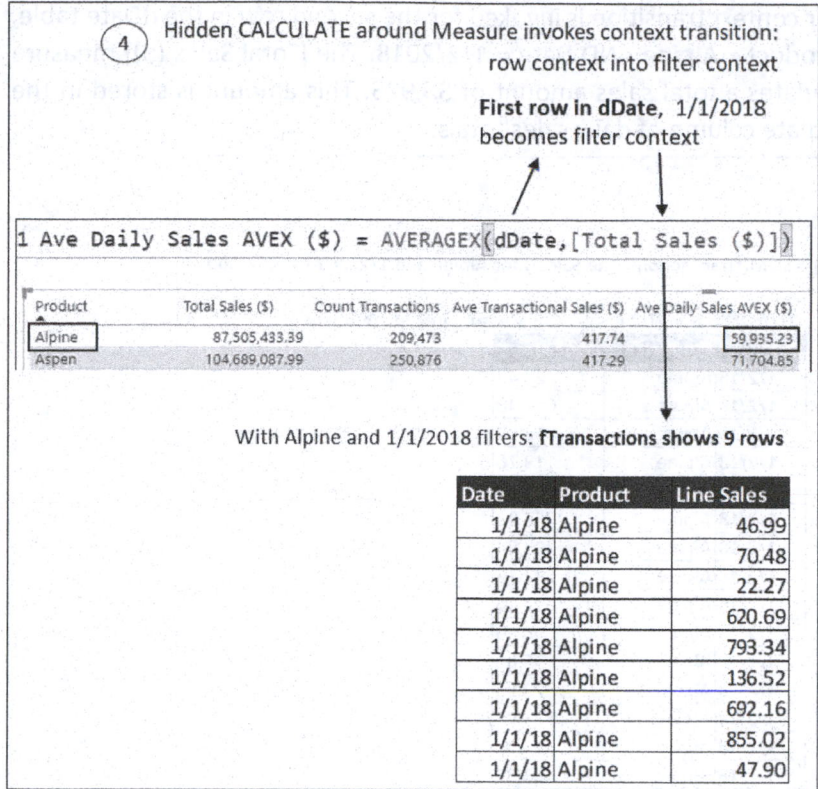

Figure 19.135 *For the first row in the dDate table, the fact table is filtered down to just 9 rows!*

5. As shown in Figure 19.136, the SUM function in the [Total Sales ($)] measure adds the 9 rows of line sales to get total sales for the Alpine product on 1/1/2018 of $3,285.37. This amount is stored in the first position in the intermediate column of daily sales totals.

dDate in 1st argument of AVERAGEX

Date	Total Sales
1/1/18	3285.37
1/2/18	
1/3/18	
1/4/18	
1/5/18	
1/6/18	
1/7/18	
1/8/18	
1/9/18	
1/10/18	
1/11/18	
1/12/18	
1/13/18	
1/14/18	
12/30/21	
12/31/21	

← [Total Sales ($)] = SUM(fTransactions[Line Sales]) for Alpine and 1/1/2018 = 3,285.37

5

fTransactions in [Total Sales ($)] Measure in 2nd argument of AVERAGEX

Date	Product	Line Sales
1/1/18	Alpine	46.99
1/1/18	Alpine	70.48
1/1/18	Alpine	22.27
1/1/18	Alpine	620.69
1/1/18	Alpine	793.34
1/1/18	Alpine	136.52
1/1/18	Alpine	692.16
1/1/18	Alpine	855.02
1/1/18	Alpine	47.90
	Total	3,285.37

Hidden rows →

Figure 19.136 *For the first row in the dDate table, the SUM function works across 9 rows to deliver the answer.*

6. As shown in Figure 19.137, after context transition is invoked for the second row in the dDate table, the filter on the fact table is Product = Alpine AND Date = 1/2/2018. The [Total Sales ($)] measure works across 17 rows and calculates a total sales amount of $5,925. This amount is stored in the second position in the intermediate column of daily sales totals.

dDate in 1st argument of AVERAGEX

Date	Total Sales
1/1/18	3,285.37
1/2/18	5,925.00
1/3/18	
1/4/18	
1/5/18	
1/6/18	
1/7/18	
1/8/18	
1/9/18	
1/10/18	
1/11/18	
1/12/18	
1/13/18	
1/14/18	
1/15/18	
1/16/18	
1/17/18	
1/18/18	
1/19/18	
1/20/18	
1/21/18	
1/22/18	
1/23/18	
12/30/21	
12/31/21	

Hidden rows →

← [Total Sales ($)] = SUM(fTransactions[Line Sales]) for Alpine and 1/2/2018 = 5,925.00

⑥

fTransactions in [Total Sales ($)] Measure in 2nd argument of AVERAGEX

Date	Product	Line Sales
1/2/18	Alpine	23.49
1/2/18	Alpine	641.48
1/2/18	Alpine	853.22
1/2/18	Alpine	113.76
1/2/18	Alpine	978.36
1/2/18	Alpine	753.23
1/2/18	Alpine	793.94
1/2/18	Alpine	692.16
1/2/18	Alpine	692.16
1/2/18	Alpine	95.80
1/2/18	Alpine	95.80
1/2/18	Alpine	23.95
1/2/18	Alpine	23.95
1/2/18	Alpine	23.95
1/2/18	Alpine	23.95
1/2/18	Alpine	47.90
1/2/18	Alpine	47.90
	Total	5,925.00

Figure 19.137 *In the second row of the dDate table, the SUM function works across 17 rows to deliver the answer.*

dDate with all Alpine daily sales total

Row	Date	Total Sales ($)
1	1/1/18	3,285.37
2	1/2/18	5,925.00
1072	12/8/20	957,787.28
1073	12/9/20	1,024,288.34
1074	12/10/20	1,065,297.90
1075	12/11/20	1,067,465.54
1453	12/24/21	232,561.74
1454	12/25/21	217,980.91
1455	12/26/21	7,822.85
1456	12/27/21	6,249.10
1457	12/28/21	9,953.27
1461	12/31/21	9,447.31

Hidden rows →

⑦ Intermediate column used to calculate average

↓

Ave Daily Sales AVEX ($) = AVERAGEX(↓) = 59,935.23

Figure 19.138 *After every Alpine daily sales total number has been calculated, AVERAGEX calculates the average.*

7. As shown in Figure 19.138, after the [Total Sales ($)] measure has iterated over all rows in the dDate table, the intermediate column of Alpine daily sales totals is used as a set of numbers to calculate the final average daily sales for the Alpine product: $59,935.23. This amount is delivered to the first row in the table visual. This process occurs in each cell in the table visual to calculate average daily sales for each product. In the total row cell, there is no external filter context, and the result represents the average daily sales for all products.

You can see that that DAX formula performs a lot of behind-the-scenes steps before it calculates the final answer. The fact that there are so many unseen steps and processes can make DAX formulas seem mysterious and difficult to understand. At the same time, however, it is also what makes them so powerful. This formula was able to use multiple tables as part of the process, take both external filter context from the report and row context from the rows in the date table, filter the fact table down to a much smaller size before it made each of the iterating calculations, store each iterated result in an intermediate column, and then use that completed intermediate column to calculate the average.

A formula like AVERAGEX(dDate,[Total Sales ($)]) is simple, beautiful, and elegant at making complex calculation over big data. Worksheet formulas and Power Query M code have a much harder time with calculations like this. If you are working with big data, DAX is the only way to go!

Calculating Average Daily Sales in a Cross-Tabulated Month and Year Report

As an example of the versatility of DAX formulas, Figure 19.139 shows the very same [Ave Daily Sales AVEX ($)] measure used in a matrix visual with the dDate table Month Name field in the Rows area and the dDate table Year field in the Columns area. The interior part of the report calculates the average daily sales for a given month, the total row at the bottom calculates the average daily sales for given year, the total column on the right calculates the average daily sales for the given month across all four years (2018 to 2021), and the grand total cell shows the average daily sales across all days in the dataset. For example, the average daily sales number for January 2018 was $163,202.91, the average daily sales number for the year 2018 was $1,145,221.89, the average daily sales number across the four Januarys from 2018 to 2021 was $180,989.54, and in the grand total cell, the average daily sales number across all days in the dataset was $1,962,590.91. You can try creating this matrix visual on a new page in your Power BI Desktop file if you like.

1 Ave Daily Sales AVEX ($) = AVERAGEX(dDate,[Total Sales ($)])

Month Name	2018	2019	2020	2021	Total
Jan	163,202.91	165,541.92	161,743.10	233,470.24	**180,989.54**
Feb	160,714.67	158,796.60	160,619.52	224,723.56	**176,213.59**
Mar	160,080.33	608,117.28	160,065.71	593,449.58	**380,428.22**
Apr	164,513.34	782,115.08	1,199,808.70	1,036,120.30	**795,639.35**
May	1,367,716.78	777,894.82	1,541,540.52	1,506,839.43	**1,298,497.89**
Jun	1,852,128.49	785,927.34	1,544,514.81	1,646,243.21	**1,457,203.46**
Jul	1,859,304.96	786,958.65	1,536,675.29	1,646,110.31	**1,457,262.31**
Aug	1,424,045.52	789,208.28	1,551,860.75	1,514,078.75	**1,319,798.32**
Sep	163,437.26	785,589.85	1,532,611.97	1,153,506.47	**908,786.39**
Oct	164,689.03	781,951.54	1,537,774.21	1,128,573.68	**903,247.12**
Nov	2,894,603.56	7,074,285.04	4,429,604.39	7,903,053.21	**5,575,386.55**
Dec	3,288,879.75	6,095,449.14	15,780,621.54	10,648,508.09	**8,953,364.63**
Total	**1,145,221.89**	**1,636,829.03**	**2,619,376.05**	**2,448,936.68**	**1,962,590.91**

Figure 19.139 *External date table month and year conditions flow in and filter the measure.*

To understand how this [Ave Daily Sales AVEX ($)] measure is working, consider the January 2018 cell in the report ($163,202.91) and the steps in the calculation process:

1. As shown in Figure 19.140, the external filter context January 2018 flows into the measure and filters the dDate table in the first argument of the AVERAGEX function down to the 31 days in January 2018.

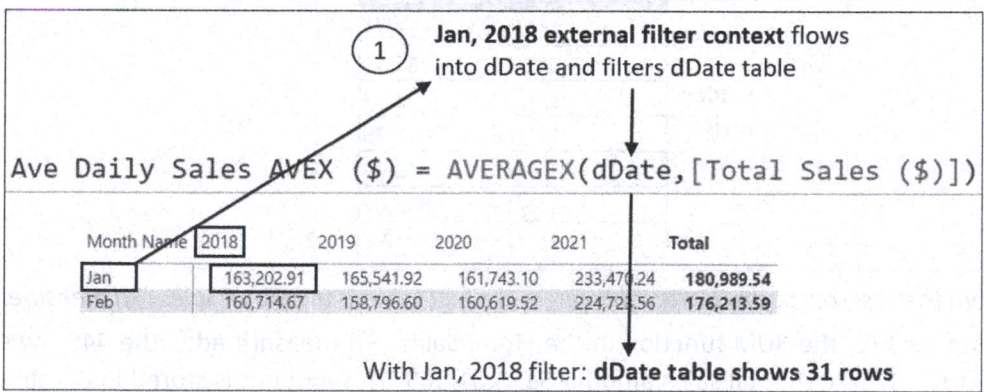

Figure 19.140 *The external filter context filters the dDate table.*

2. As shown in Figure 19.141, because the external filter context filters the dDate table down to 31 rows, the [Total Sales ($)] measure only has to iterate down 31 rows in the dDate table. (This is different from the last example, where the measure always had to traverse all 1,461 rows in the dDate table.)

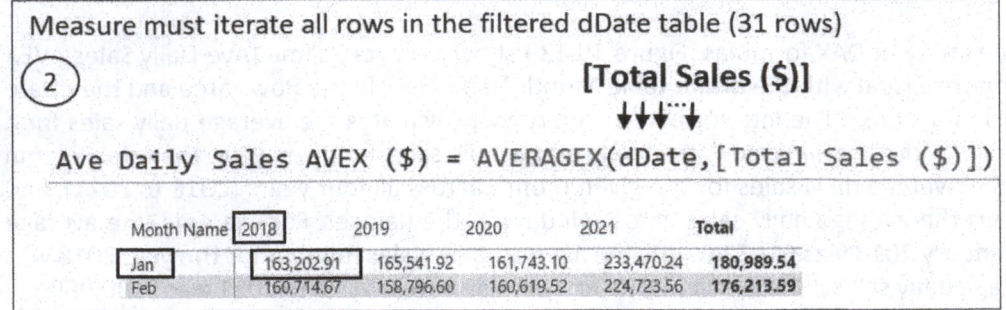

Figure 19.141 *The [Total Sales ($)] measure makes a calculation for each day in January 2018.*

3. As shown in Figure 19.142, the hidden CALCULATE function around the [Total Sales ($)] measure invokes context transition for the first day in the dDate table and pulls the row context day condition 1/1/2018 into the measure, converts it to filter context, and uses it to filter the fTransactions table down to the 448 sales transactions for the date 1/1/2018.

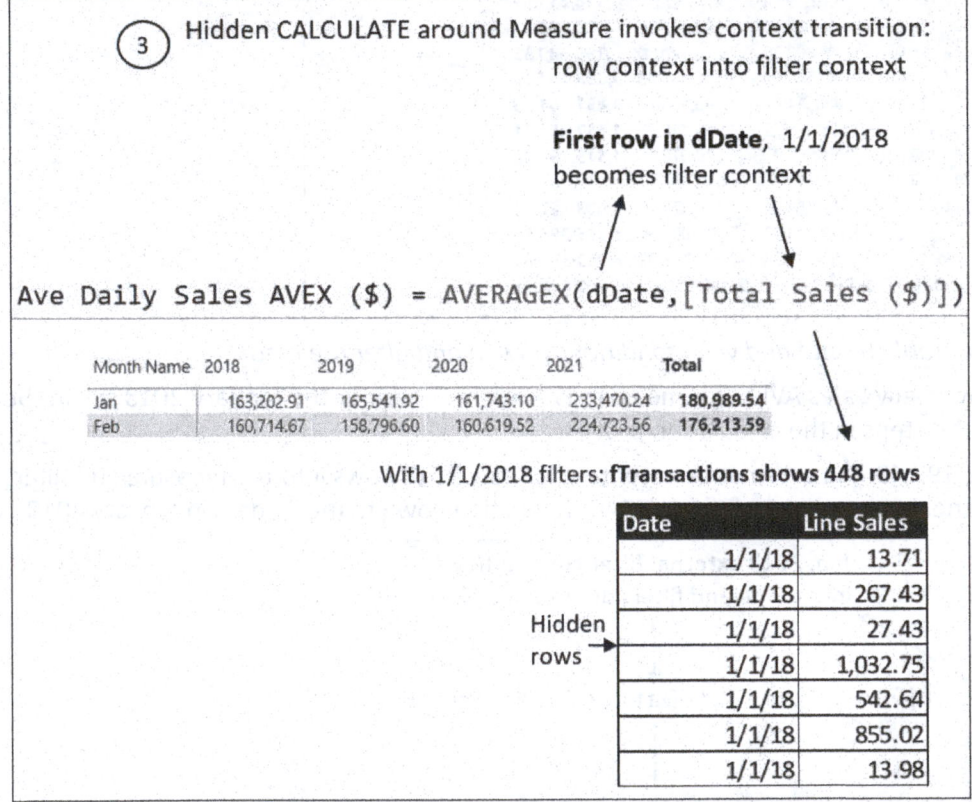

Figure 19.142 *The date from the first row of the dDate table filters the fact table in the [Total Sales ($)] measure.*

4. As shown in Figure 19.143, the SUM function in the [Total Sales ($)] measure adds the 448 rows of line sales to get the 1/1/2018 total sales amount $175,011.65. This amount is stored in the first position in the intermediate column of daily sales totals.

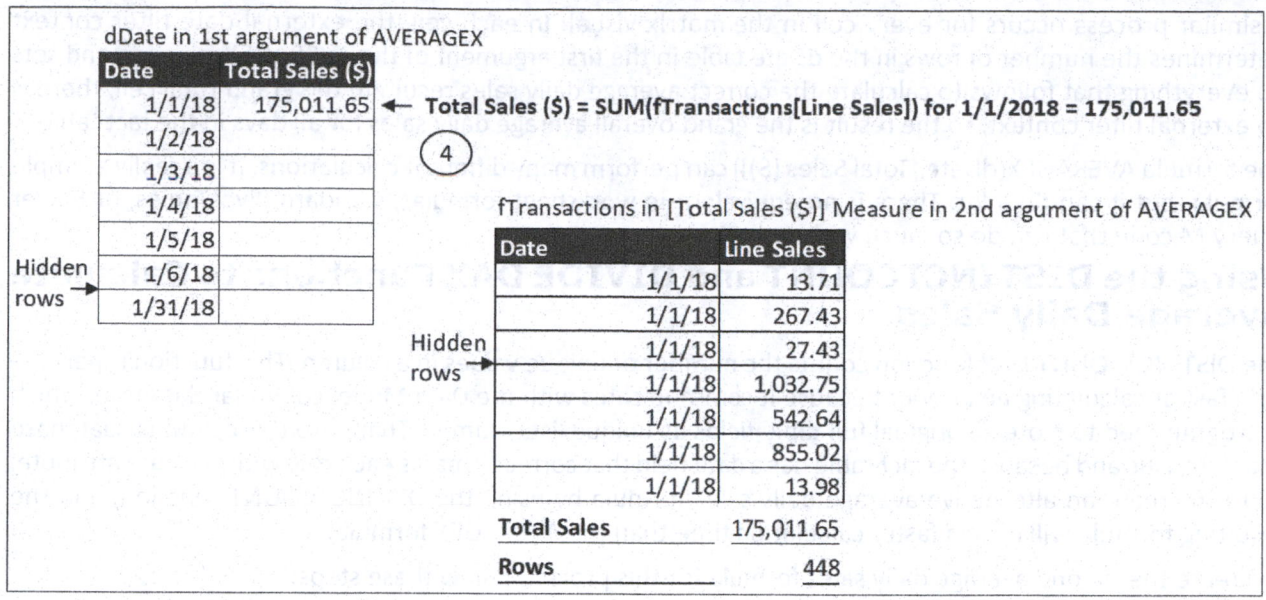

Figure 19.143 *The [Total Sales ($)] measure delivers the 1/1/2018 sales total to the first row in the dDate table.*

5. As shown in Figure 19.144, after context transition is invoked for the second row in the dDate table, the filter on the fact table is Date = 1/2/2018. The [Total Sales ($)] measure works across 420 rows and calculates the total sales amount $164,500.29. This amount is stored in the second position in the intermediate column of daily sales totals.

dDate in 1st argument of AVERAGEX

Date	Total Sales ($)
1/1/18	175,011.65
1/2/18	164,500.29
1/3/18	
1/4/18	
1/5/18	
1/6/18	
1/31/18	

5

← Total Sales ($) = SUM(fTransactions[Line Sales]) for 1/2/2018 = 164,500.29

* For the 1/2/2018 row, Measure calculates daily sales using a 420 row fact table

Hidden rows

Figure 19.144 *The [Total Sales ($)] measure delivers the 1/2/2018 sales total to the second row in the dDate table.*

6. As shown in Figure 19.145, after the measure has iterated over all 31 rows in the dDate table, the intermediate column of daily sales totals for the month of January 2018 is used as a set of numbers to calculate the final average daily sales amount $163,202.91. This amount is delivered to the January 2018 cell in the matrix visual.

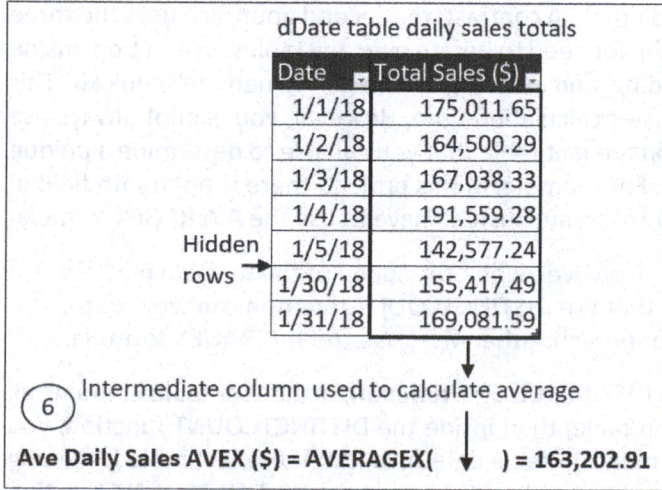

dDate table daily sales totals

Date	Total Sales ($)
1/1/18	175,011.65
1/2/18	164,500.29
1/3/18	167,038.33
1/4/18	191,559.28
1/5/18	142,577.24
1/30/18	155,417.49
1/31/18	169,081.59

Hidden rows

Intermediate column used to calculate average

6

Ave Daily Sales AVEX ($) = AVERAGEX(↓ **) = 163,202.91**

Figure 19.145 *An average is calculated from the 31 daily sales totals.*

A similar process occurs for every cell in the matrix visual: In each cell, the external date filter context determines the number of rows in the dDate table in the first argument of the AVERAGEX function and sets up everything that follows to calculate the correct average daily sales result. In the grand total cell, there is no external filter context, so the result is the grand overall average daily sales for all days in the fact table.

The formula AVERAGEX(dDate,[Total Sales ($)]) can perform many different calculations. It is a really a simple formula, but it can do a lot. There is no equivalent in worksheet formulas, standard PivotTables, or Power Query M code that can do so much with so little.

Using the DISTINCTCOUNT and DIVIDE DAX Functions to Calculate Average Daily Sales

The DISTINCTCOUNT DAX function counts the number of unique values in a column. This function is particularly fast at calculating an answer because it communicates with the Data Model columnar database, which is programmed to store all original full table fields as unique list columns. Thanks to this columnar database characteristic and because the fact table has a date field that correctly marks each row with the date attribute, you can create an alternative average daily sales formula by using the DISTINCTCOUNT function, and the resulting formula will have a faster calculation time than the AVERAGEX formula.

To create the second average daily sales formula for this project, follow these steps:

1. In the fact table, enter the following formula: **Ave Daily Sales DIV ($) = DIVIDE([Total Sales ($)],DISTINCTCOUNT(fTransactions[Date]))**.

2. Add decimal number formatting with two decimal places showing. Figure 19.146 shows the result.

```
1 Ave Daily Sales DIV ($) = DIVIDE([Total Sales ($)],DISTINCTCOUNT(fTransactions[Date]))
```

Product	Total Sales ($)	Count Transactions	Ave Transactional Sales ($)	Ave Daily Sales AVEX ($)	Ave Daily Sales DIV ($)
Alpine	87,505,433.39	209,473	417.74	59,935.23	59,935.23
Aspen	104,689,087.99	250,876	417.29	71,704.85	71,704.85
Bellen	216,208,562.28	461,380	468.61	148,088.06	148,088.06

Figure 19.146 *Average daily sales measure using the DISTINCTCOUNT function on the fact table Date field.*

As shown in Figure 19.146, the results for the two different average daily sales measures are the same for every product. For example, both measures calculated the same Alpine product average daily sales amount: $59,935.23. You can also use this new measures in other reports, such as the cross-tabulated year and month report, and the results will be the same as with the AVERAGEX version of the formula.

For the DISTINCTCOUNT formula, the calculation process for each cell in the report column is simple: The product external filter context flows into the measure, and for both the SUM function (in the [Total Sales ($)] measure) and the DISTINCTCOUNT function, the fact table is filtered down to just the specified product, the sum in the numerator is determined, the count in the denominator is determined, and the division is performed to get the average daily sales by product.

So which measure should you use? If you need a formula to calculate quickly, the DISTINCTCOUNT and DIVIDE formula is the way to go. For the first approach, the AVERAGEX function must internally materialize the date table so the formula can iterate over it (and that takes time). In contrast, the second approach uses the three functions SUM, DIVIDE, and DISTINCTCOUNT, which do not need to iterate over any tables; in addition, inside the DAX engine, math calculations like summing, dividing, and counting can be performed really quickly. This second approach results in a formula with a much faster calculation time. However, you cannot always use the second approach because there is often no field in the fact table that you can use to determine a unique count in the denominator of the average calculation. For example, in this project, there is no month field in the fact table, so you can't use the DISTINCTCOUNT formula and instead have to use the AVERAGEX formula.

> **Note:** For small datasets, either approach is fine. However, when the speed of the formula matters and you have an attribute field in the fact table that the DISTINCTCOUNT function can work with, using the DISTINCTCOUNT formula is the best approach; otherwise, use the AVERAGEX formula.

For the average daily sales calculation that uses the DISTINCTCOUNT function, if the fact table contains all possible dates that are present in the date dimension table, then inside the DISTINCTCOUNT function, you can use either the fact table date field or the date dimension table date field. But if the fact table is missing some dates that are in the date dimension table, the average calculation using the DISTINCTCOUNT function on the date dimension field will yield an incorrect result. In the dataset for this project, there is one date in the date table that is not in the fact table, and so you cannot use the date dimension table date field inside the DISTINCTCOUNT function to make the average daily sales calculation.

Note: Even if the fact table has no missing dates, I always feel safer using the fact table attribute field inside DISTINCTCOUNT for these types of calculations.

Using the AVERAGEX and VALUES DAX Table Functions to Calculate Average Monthly Sales

Since there is no month field in the fact table for this project, you can just use the AVERAGEX function with a table in the first argument that contains a unique list of all the possible year/month combinations. This will create the correct month grain that the [Total Sales ($)] measure can iterate across before calculating the average monthly sales. If you look through the data model, however, you'll see that there is no table with a month grain. The dDate tables does have the fields Year, Month Name, and EOMonth, but those fields have many duplicates and are located in the dDate table, which has a day grain. The designers of the DAX formula language anticipated this problem and provided several useful DAX table functions that can create unique lists from a field and deliver them as tables. For example, the VALUES DAX table function can accept a column or a table as its argument and then create a unique list of records based on the current filter context and deliver it as a table.

You can use the VALUES function in the first argument of AVERAGEX. But which column from the dDate table should you use inside the VALUES function to create a unique list of months? Say that you use the Month Name field in a formula, like this:

```
=AVERAGEX(VALUES(dDate[Month Name]),[Total Sales ($)])
```

The VALUES function would deliver a unique list of the 12 months (January to December) as a table, but the average result would be much too big. A formula like this would work only if the fact table contained just one year of dates. What you really need inside the first argument of AVERAGEX is a unique list of all the year/month combinations that are possible. This formula, which uses the Year and Month Name fields, could accomplish that:

```
= AVERAGEX(CROSSJOIN(VALUES(dDate[Year]),VALUES(dDate[Month Name])),[Total Sales ($)])
```

In this formula, the two VALUES functions deliver a unique list of years and months, and then CROSSJOIN performs a cross-join to get all the possible combinations of years and months.

The downside of the CROSSJOIN(VALUES,VALUES) formula is that it can lead to errors if the same Year and Month Name fields are used as external filters and the user of the report filters the report with a complex filter that uses a combination of OR logical tests and AND logical tests across both fields. Marco Russo and Alberto Ferrari (the ultimate DAX formula masters) call this problem a *complex filter reduction error*. The solution to this issue is to create an even more complex formula in which the KEEPFILTERS DAX function forces the external filters and internal filters to run as an AND logical test and avoids CALCULATE's replacement mechanism when fields exist in both the external and internal filters. The formula to safely calculate the average monthly sales would therefore be:

```
=AVERAGEX(KEEPFILTERS(CROSSJOIN(VALUES(dDate[Year]),VALUES(dDate[Month Name]))),[Total Sales ($)])
```

That is complicated.

Note: I wanted to show you both of these formulas because these are common approaches that people take. If you want to learn more about the complex filter reduction error and the KEEPFILTERS DAX function, see my video with all the details: https://youtu.be/wQT3vbNpETc.

Data Modeling to Simplify DAX Formula Complexities

There is a much easier way to average monthly sales than by using CROSSFILTER and KEEPFILTERS. It involves smart data modeling. If there were a field in the dDate table that marked each year/month combination with a unique marker, you could use that field inside the VALUES function. One way to accomplish this is to create a helper column that joins the Year and Month Name fields. The other way to do this is to use the end-of-the-month date, where the underlying serial number is the unique marker for each year/month combination. The good news is that, in the initial data modeling stage of this project, you already added an end-of-the-month field to the dDate table. That field can serve as a helper column that you can use in your formula to make an accurate and less complicated average monthly sales calculation.

To create the DAX formula for average monthly sales, follow these steps:

1. Create the average monthly sales formula in the fact table as follows: **Ave Monthly Sales AVEX ($) = AVERAGEX(VALUES(dDate[EOMonth]),[Total Sales ($)])**.
2. Add decimal number formatting with two decimal places showing. Figure 19.147 shows the result.

```
1 Ave Monthly Sales AVEX ($) = AVERAGEX(VALUES(dDate[EOMonth]),[Total Sales ($)])
```

Hidden rows

Product	Total Sales ($)	Count Transactions	Ave Transactional Sales ($)	Ave Daily Sales AVEX ($)	Ave Daily Sales DIV ($)	Ave Monthly Sales AVEX ($)
Alpine	87,505,433.39	209,473	417.74	59,935.23	59,935.23	1,823,029.86
Quad	701,745,015.85	963,309	728.47	480,647.27	480,647.27	14,619,687.83
Sunset	92,635,064.84	209,092	443.03	63,448.67	63,448.67	1,929,897.18
Sunshine	95,775,809.69	251,535	380.77	65,599.87	65,599.87	1,995,329.37
Sunspot	31,576,244.16	125,587	251.43	21,627.56	21,627.56	657,838.42
Yanaki	112,985,748.07	250,133	451.70	77,387.50	77,387.50	2,353,869.75
Total	**2,865,382,727.41**	**7,742,561**	**370.08**	**1,962,590.91**	**1,962,590.91**	**59,695,473.49**

Figure 19.147 *Average monthly sales measure using an iterator function.*

As shown in Figure 19.147, the average monthly sales amount for the Alpine product was $1,823,029.86, for the Quad it was $14,619,687.83, and in the total row at the bottom, because there is no external filter context, the average monthly sales amount for all products was $59,695,473.49. These averages communicate what a typical monthly sales number was over the four-year period. The calculation process for each cell in the column uses the same steps as with the average daily sales formula except that the iteration of the [Total Sales ($)] measure is performed over end-of-the-month dates rather than over daily dates. The abbreviated calculation steps for this formula are as follows:

1. Because there is no date table field in the external filter context, the VALUES function uses the full set of unique end-of-the-month dates in every calculation.
2. The [Total Sales ($)] measure iterates over each unique end-of-the-month date in the VALUES-generated table.
3. For each row in the VALUES-generated table:
   - The external filter context, product condition, and context transition–invoked end-of-the-month condition are run in an AND logical test to filter the fTransactions table.
   - The line sales from the filtered fTransactions table are added, and the result is stored in the corresponding position in the intermediate column of product monthly sales totals.
4. The completed intermediate column of product monthly totals is created.
5. Those product monthly totals are used to calculate the average.

Just as with the [Ave Daily Sales AVEX ($)] measure, this [Ave Monthly Sales AVEX ($)] measure is versatile and can be used with many types of criteria in your reports and visuals. As shown in Figure 19.148, if you use the [Ave Monthly Sales AVEX ($)] measure in a visual that has the Year field in the Rows area, you can calculate the average monthly sales for each year. Notice that the total row average month sales amount $59,695,473.49 is the same as in Figure 19.147. This is because, in both cases, there is no external filter context in that cell, and therefore the overall average monthly sales amount shows for all records in the fact table. This formula calculates the same as the previous one, except that the end-of-the-month field in the VALUES function is filtered by the external filter context. For example, in Figure 19.148, in the 2018 cell ($34,833,832.34), the 2018 year external filter flows into the VALUES function and filters the end-of-the-month field down to just the dates for 2018. The VALUES function then delivers a unique list of 12 end-of-the-month dates for the year 2018. After the [Total Sales ($)] measure iterates over the 12 months to determine the 12 monthly sales totals, those values are used to calculate the average. You can try creating this table visual on a new page in your Power BI Desktop file, if you like.

```
1 Ave Monthly Sales AVEX ($) = AVERAGEX(VALUES(dDate[EOMonth]),[Total Sales ($)])
```

Year	Ave Monthly Sales AVEX ($)
2018	34,833,832.34
2019	49,786,882.87
2020	79,672,688.08
2021	74,488,490.65
Total	**59,695,473.49**

Figure 19.148 *Average monthly sales by year.*

In addition to the VALUES function, there are other important DAX table functions that can deliver unique lists. A summary of these functions is provided in Table 19.3.

Table 19.3 DAX Table Functions That Can Be Used to Create Unique Lists

Function	Description
ALL(*Column or columns from same table*)	Removes all filters and returns a unique list of records as a table, with an additional single blank row if there are unmatched items in the relationship. ALL does not "see" the current filter context. ALL removes filters from the current filter context.
ALL(*Table*)	Removes all filters and returns a full table. ALL does not "see" the current filter context.
VALUES(*Column*)	Returns a unique list of records in the current filter context, with an additional single blank row if there are unmatched items in the relationship. VALUES can "see" the filter context.
VALUES(*Table*)	Returns a full table, filtered in the current filter context.
ALLEXCEPT(*Table,Column*)	Removes all filters from a table except for the specified column from that table and returns a unique list of records.
ALLNOBLANKROW(*Table or column or columns*)	Gives the same results as ALL but without an additional single blank row if there are unmatched items in the relationship.
DISTINCT(*Column or Table*)	Gives the same results as VALUES but without an additional single blank row if there are unmatched items in the relationship.
CROSSJOIN(*Table,Table*)	Returns the Cartesian product of two or more tables as a table. This function can be used to create a unique list of records from two or more fields in the current filter context with a formula construction like this: CROSSJOIN(VALUES(*Column1*),VALUES(*Column2*)).

However, most of the time not all of these functions are really necessary. For example, ALLNOBLANKROW and DISTINCT are usually not needed if you practice smart data modeling and make sure the unique list of items in the primary key of each dimension table represents all possible items in the fact table. You do not have to use CROSSJOIN either if you create dimension table helper columns that can uniquely mark each record when two or more other fields make up a key (as you did when you created the EOMonth field to uniquely mark each combination of the Year and Month Name fields).

The two most commonly used DAX table function that can deliver unique lists from a column are the VALUES and ALL functions. Figure 19.149 shows two formulas that I created to illustrate the fact that the VALUES function can "see" the current filter context, but the ALL function cannot. These formulas use the CONCATENATEX DAX iterator function, which can iterate over a table and join the items in a column with a delimiter. For the CONCATENATEX formula that uses the VALUES function, the VALUES-generated unique list contains only the products in the current filter context. These products represent the products sold by the sales rep. In contrast, for the CONCATENATEX formula that uses the ALL function, the ALL-generated unique list contains all the products in every cell, no matter what the current filter context. Notice that in the grand total cell at the bottom of each report, VALUES and ALL return the same result. This is always the case when there is no filter context.

> **Note:** You can go and look at the solution that is shown in Figure 19.149 in the Power BI Desktop file Ch19-Project02-VALUES-ALL-Unmatched.pbix.

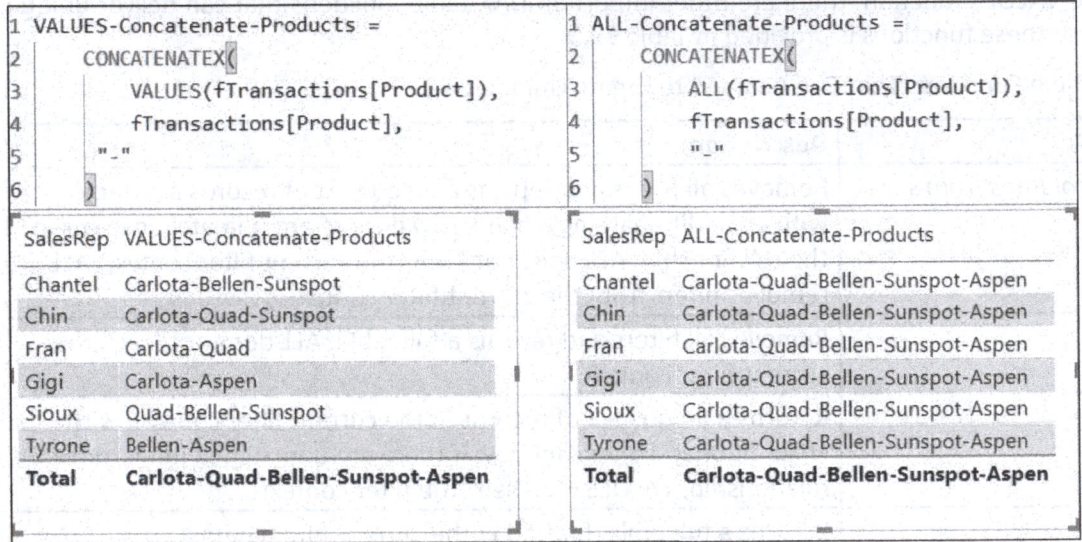

Figure 19.149 *The table report on the left shows a list of all the products that a sales rep sold.*

Understanding Unmatched Items in a Relationship and Empty Cells

In the previous section, I mentioned "unmatched items in the relationship." This refers to the situation in which a fact table has a foreign key attribute field that has more unique items than the primary key in the related dimension table. For example, the fact table may have a product name in the Product field that is not listed in the product dimension table. If you do not catch unmatched items in the data modeling phase of a project, you might see an empty cell in the Rows or Columns area of a visual after you drag a dimension table field into the visual as a filter.

Product	Total Sales ($)	Product	Total Sales ($)
	24,540.00	Aspen	24,540.00
Bellen	14,418.25	Bellen	14,418.25
Carlota	14,785.55	Carlota	14,785.55
Quad	20,709.06	Quad	20,709.06
Sunspot	12,650.00	Sunspot	12,650.00
Total	**87,102.86**	**Total**	**87,102.86**

Figure 19.150 *The table on the left uses the dimension table Product field. The table on the right uses the fact table Product field.*

The table visual on the left in Figure 19.150 shows an empty cell in the Product column with a calculated result for total sales next to it. This means that the fact table Product field has at least one item (product name or an empty cell) in that field that is not in the primary key product field in the product dimension table. The DAX engine purposely adds an empty row so it can catch all sales amounts from unmatched items. It does this so the totals at the bottom are correct. When this happens, you need to fix the dimension table so that it includes all the product names that are present in the fact table. The table visual on the right in Figure 19.150 shows the result you would see if you were to drag the fact table Product field into the report. In this case, the missing Aspen product name shows up.

Figure 19.151 shows what happens if you use the fact table Product field and it contains an actual empty cell and an unmatched product name.

Product	TotalSales($)
	25,957.45
Bellen	14,418.25
Carlota	14,785.55
Quad	20,709.06
Sunspot	12,650.00
Total	**88,520.31**

Product	TotalSales($)
	1,417.45
Aspen	24,540.00
Bellen	14,418.25
Carlota	14,785.55
Quad	20,709.06
Sunspot	12,650.00
Total	**88,520.31**

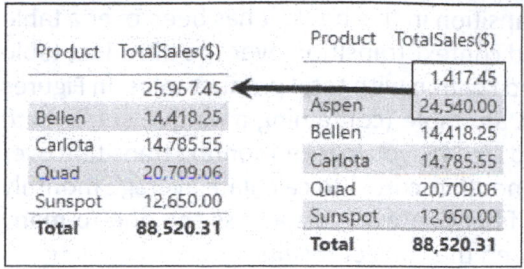

Figure 19.151 *An unmatched empty cell and product amounts are consolidated into one cell in the dimension table report.*

Note: You can go and look at the solution that is shown in Figures 19.150 and 19.151 in the Power BI Desktop file Ch19-Project02-VALUES-ALL-Unmatched.pbix.

Using Power Query and DAX Formulas to Calculate Average Monthly Sales

In the fact table for this project, there was no month field that you could use inside the DISTINCTCOUNT function to help create the average monthly sales measure. The approach you took to creating the average monthly sales measure was to add an end-of-the-month helper column to the dDate dimension table and then use that new field inside the VALUES and AVERAGEX functions. When you created the end-of-the-month DAX calculated column in the dDate table, there were 1,461 rows in that table, but there were only 48 unique values stored in the columnar database. If you were to instead add an end-of-the-month helper column to the fact table that contains more than 7 million rows, exactly the same number of unique values—48—would be stored in the columnar database! In addition, in Power Query, it is simple to add an end-of-the-month field. The only potential downside is that when the data source is refreshed, it may take a bit longer to load to the Data Model. The upside to the Power Query approach, as shown in Figure 19.152, is that you can use the DISTINCTCOUNT function on the fact table end-of-the-month field, and the formula will calculate more quickly than the AVERAGEX version you created earlier.

```
1 Ave Monthly Sales DIV ($) = DIVIDE([Total Sales ($)],DISTINCTCOUNT(fTransactions[End of Month]))
```

Product	Total Sales ($)	Count Transactions	Ave Transactional Sales ($)	Ave Daily Sales AVEX ($)	Ave Daily Sales DIV ($)	Ave Monthly Sales AVEX ($)	Ave Monthly Sales DIV ($)
Alpine	87,505,433.39	209,473	417.74	59,935.23	59,935.23	1,823,029.86	1,823,029.86
Aspen	Hidden rows	250,876	417.29	71,704.85	71,704.85	2,181,022.67	2,181,022.67
Phoenix		167,359	452.22	51,837.96	51,837.96	1,576,737.95	1,576,737.95
Quad	701,745,015.85	963,309	728.47	480,647.27	480,647.27	14,619,687.83	14,619,687.83
Sunset	92,635,064.84	209,092	443.03	63,448.67	63,448.67	1,929,897.18	1,929,897.18
Sunshine	95,775,809.69	251,535	380.77	65,599.87	65,599.87	1,995,329.37	1,995,329.37
Sunspot	31,576,244.16	125,587	251.43	21,627.56	21,627.56	657,838.42	657,838.42
Yanaki	112,985,748.07	250,133	451.70	77,387.50	77,387.50	2,353,869.75	2,353,869.75
Total	**2,865,382,727.41**	**7,742,561**	**370.08**	**1,962,590.91**	**1,962,590.91**	**59,695,473.49**	**59,695,473.49**

Figure 19.152 *Average monthly sales measure with the help of Power Query and DISTINCTCOUNT.*

I do not provide step-by-step instructions for using Power Query and DAX formulas to calculate average monthly sales, but you can look at an example in the solution file for this project, Ch19-Project02-SQL-DataReport-Finished.pbix. I will tell you that these are the steps for adding the end-of-the-month field in the fTransactions table by using Power Query:

1. Open Power Query (Home tab in the Power BI Desktop Ribbon, Queries group, Transform Data button).
2. Select the Date field in the fTransactions table.
3. Click the Add Column tab in the Power Query Ribbon and, in the From Date & Time group, click the Date dropdown, hover over the Month option, and click the End of Month option.

Note: In this project, there are no missing months in the fact table, and so you could use the date dimension table EOMonth field inside DISTINCTCOUNT. However, as mentioned earlier, it is safer to use a fact table attribute field in the DISTINCTCOUNT function for calculations like this.

Invoking Context Transition in a Fact Table with Duplicate Records

When you invoke context transition, you need to do it in a table with a primary key, such as a dimension table. If you invoke context transition in a fact table with duplicate records and no primary key, you will get incorrect results. Luckily, each time you have invoked context transition in this book, it has been over a table containing a unique set of records. In Figure 19.126, you invoked context transition over the dProduct table (containing a unique set of product records) to create a calculated column with total product sales; in Figures 19.131 and 19.145, you invoked context transition over the dDate table (containing a unique set of date records) to calculate average daily sales; and in Figures 19.147 and 19.148, you invoked context transition over the VALUES-generated table (containing a unique set of end-of-month records) to calculate average monthly sales. In each case, the single row condition was converted to filter context, sent across the one-to-many relationship, and filtered the fact table—and the formula delivered the correct results.

However, if you invoke context transition over a fact table with duplicate records, you will not get correct results. For example, Figure 19.153 shows a simple fact table with three records. Rows 1 and 3 are duplicate records. This is not a mistake. In this case, a duplicate record just means that the same type of sale happened on the same day. This type of situation occurs in business all the time. Figure 19.153 shows what the correct results would be if you were to create a calculated column to calculate line sales.

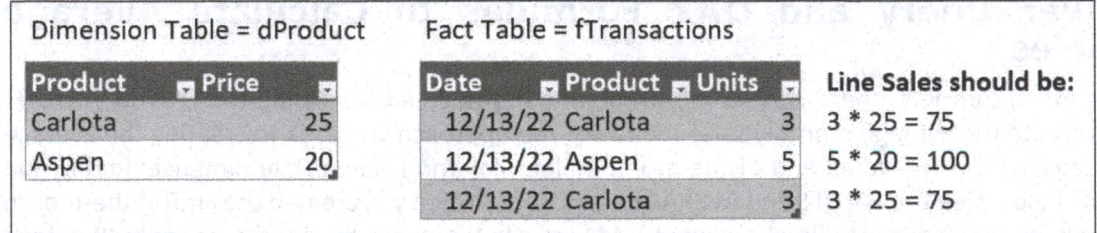

Dimension Table = dProduct				Fact Table = fTransactions				
Product		**Price**		**Date**		**Product**	**Units**	**Line Sales should be:**
Carlota		25		12/13/22		Carlota	3	3 * 25 = 75
Aspen		20		12/13/22		Aspen	5	5 * 20 = 100
				12/13/22		Carlota	3	3 * 25 = 75

Figure 19.153 *There are duplicate records in the fact table.*

Figure 19.154 shows a smart measure that can calculate total sales. However, this measure can only be smartly used in a report, a visual, a calculated column in a dimension table, or an iterator function that uses a table with a unique set of records. Figure 19.155 shows that if you use this [Total Sales SUMX] measure in a calculated column in the fact table from Figure 19.153, you will get the incorrect results in rows 1 and 3. In both rows, the hidden CALCULATE function invokes context transition, which leads to the double counting of the line sales amount.

Total Sales SUMX:=
SUMX(fTransactions,RELATED(dProduct[Price])*fTransactions[Units])

Figure 19.154 *You can use this measure in a report, visual, or dimension table iteration.*

[LineSalesMe... ▼	f_x =[Total Sales SUMX]			
Date	**Product**	**Units**	**LineSalesMeasure**	
1	12/13/2022	Carlota	3	150
2	12/13/2022	Aspen	5	100
3	12/13/2022	Carlota	3	150

Figure 19.155 *You should not use this measure in a fact table calculated column because sales might be double counted.*

Figure 19.156 illustrates how the double counting error for row 1 occurs. When the measure lands in row 1, context transition is invoked, and the row context is converted to filter context. Because the row is not a unique record, when the row context is invoked, the fact table is filtered down to the two matching rows. The measure then uses both rows to calculate total sales. Rather than deliver the correct sales result $75, it delivers a double count amount $150. If there were four duplicate records, the incorrect amount would be $300.

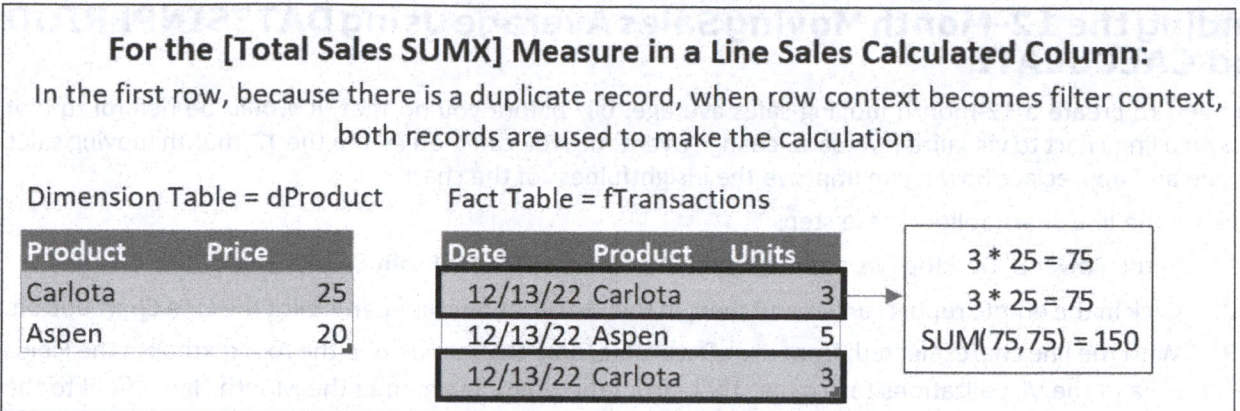

For the [Total Sales SUMX] Measure in a Line Sales Calculated Column:

In the first row, because there is a duplicate record, when row context becomes filter context, both records are used to make the calculation

Dimension Table = dProduct   Fact Table = fTransactions

Product	Price
Carlota	25
Aspen	20

Date	Product	Units
12/13/22	Carlota	3
12/13/22	Aspen	5
12/13/22	Carlota	3

3 * 25 = 75
3 * 25 = 75
SUM(75,75) = 150

Figure 19.156 *Row context is converted into filter context and yields two rows for the calculation rather than one.*

The solution to the double counting problem is simple: Just use the formula for line sales. Figure 19.157 shows this simple formula. Using a measure overcomplicates things and leads to the wrong results. Most of us would never think to use a measure this way in a fact table. Most people just use a formula that does not contain a measure. I used this example to illustrate because it helps you see what is going on.

[LineSalesFor... ▼   *fx* =RELATED(dProduct[Price])*fTransactions[Units]

	Date	Product	Units	LineSalesMeasure	LineSalesFormula
1	12/13/2022	Carlota	3	150	75
2	12/13/2022	Aspen	5	100	100
3	12/13/2022	Carlota	3	150	75

Figure 19.157 *The correct method for a fact table calculated column is to just make a formula with no measure.*

Where the problem arises is when people start creating formulas like the average transaction sales measure shown in Figure 19.158. It seems simple enough, especially if you already created the [Total Sales SUMX] measure. However, because the measure is iterating over a fact table with duplicate records, the amounts in rows 1 and 3 will be incorrect, and the resulting average will be incorrect as well. The solution is to just use the formula, rather than a measure, in the second argument of AVERAGEX, as shown in Figure 19.159.

Ave Transactional Sales AVEX with Measure:=
AVERAGEX(fTransactions,[Total Sales SUMX])

Figure 19.158 *This seems like a good formula, but it is a trap that yields incorrect results.*

Ave Transactional Sales AVEX:=
AVERAGEX(fTransactions,RELATED(dProduct[Price])*fTransactions[Units])

Figure 19.159 *This measure yields the correct results.*

Another potential solution is to use a fact table with a primary key. Then all tables in the star schema data model would be tables with unique sets of records. However, a primary key in a fact table would increase the size of the columnar database because the stored unique list for the primary key would be the same size as the fact table.

The moral of the story is to be careful any time you iterate over a fact table and invoke context transition. Invoking context transition while iterating over tables like the dDate table or a VALUES-generated table is fine because each of those tables contains a unique set of records.

Note: You can look at the measures I created for this section in the Excel file Ch19-Project02-DoubleCount.xlsx.

Finding the 12-Month Moving Sales Average Using DATESINPERIOD and CALCULATE

You need to create a 12-month moving sales average, but before you do that, it would be helpful to plot sales on a line chart to visualize how sales change over time. You can then create the 12-month moving sales average and appreciate how it can improve the insightfulness of the chart.

To create the line chart, follow these steps:

1. In the Power BI Desktop file, add a new sheet and name it **Gross Profit & Total Sales**.

2. Click in the empty report canvas and then, in the Visualizations task pane, click the Line Chart button.

3. With the line chart selected, from the dDate table, drag the Year field to the Axis textbox in the Fields area in the Visualizations task pane. Then, from the dDate table, drag the Month Name field to the Axis textbox below the Year field. You should have the two fields Year and Month Name in the Axis textbox, with Year on top of Month Name.

4. Drag the [Total Sales ($)] measure to the Values textbox in the Fields area in the Visualizations task pane.

5. To simultaneously show Year and Month Name in the horizontal axis, as shown in Figure 19.160, in the upper-right corner of the line chart, click the Expand All Down One Level in the Hierarchy button.

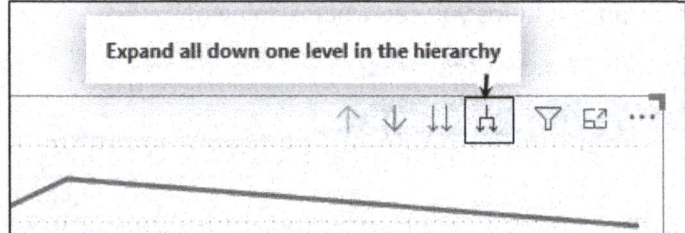

Figure 19.160 *Expand All Down One Level in the Hierarchy allows you to see months and years on a chart together.*

6. As shown in Figure 19.161, in the Visualizations task pane, click the Paint Roller Format tab and then, under X Axis, set Concatenate Labels to Off. Figure 19.162 shows the result.

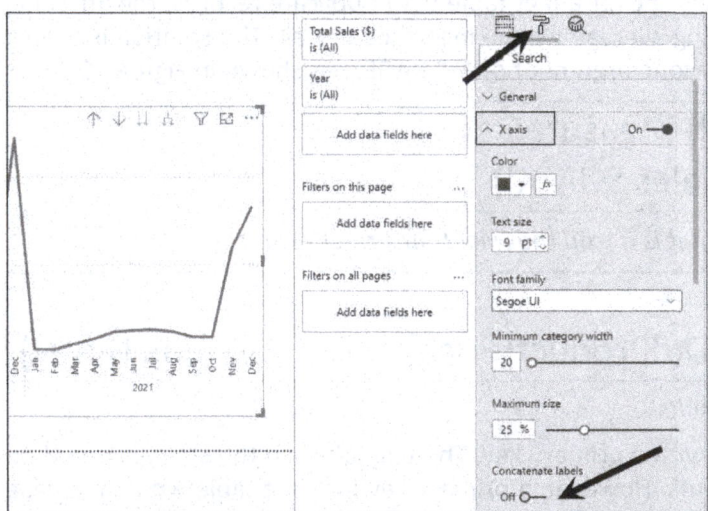

Figure 19.161 *In the X Axis area of the Paint Roller Format tab, turn off Concatenate Labels.*

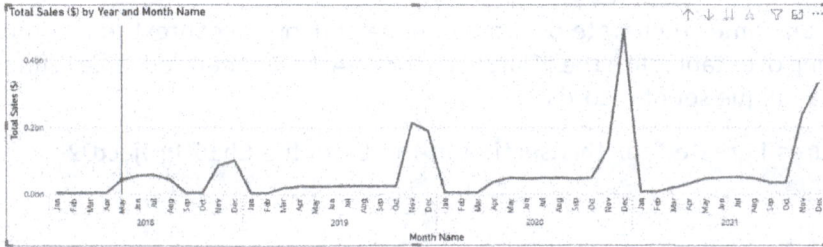

Figure 19.162 *The seasonal pattern reveals that winter always has the highest sales.*

The line chart in Figure 19.162 reveals a seasonal pattern, where sales for the year are always highest in the winter months. But what if you want to know the trend in sales over the four-year period? That trend can be hard to detect in a line chart plotting monthly sales when there is a seasonal pattern. A 12-month moving sales average metric is designed to overcome this problem when plotting the value on a line chart. This metric can smooth out the sales number and show the general trend when there are volatile or seasonal changes in the sales.

If you want to create a 12-month moving metric using a DAX measure, for each point on the chart, the measure will have to "see" the single-month current filter context and then change it to a filter context that extends 11 months back, for a total of 12 months. For example, in the month September 2020, the average calculation will need to average the monthly sales totals for the months October 2019 to September 2020. To change the filter context, you use the CALCULATE function, and to provide a valid list of dates to the CALCULATE function as a filter that extends 12 months back, you use the DATESINPERIOD function. The DATESINPERIOD DAX table function takes a start date and creates a table of dates based on the size of the period (Day, Month, Quarter, or Year) and the number of periods to move backward or forward.

Using DAX Time Intelligence Functions

DAX includes more than 35 different time intelligence functions that enable you to manipulate data using time periods—including days, months, quarters, and years—and build and compare calculations over those periods. Table 19.4 lists and briefly describes many of these amazing functions. A good way to create a 12-month moving average is to use one of these functions.

Table 19.4 Some of the Amazing DAX Time Intelligence Functions That Work with the Date Table

Function	Description
DATEADD	Returns a table that contains a column of dates, shifted either forward or backward in time by the specified number of intervals from the dates in the current context.
DATESBETWEEN	Returns a table that contains a column of dates that begins with a specified start date and continues until a specified end date.
DATESINPERIOD	Returns a table that contains a column of dates that begins with a specified start date and continues for the specified number and type of date intervals.
DATESMTD	Returns a table that contains a column of the dates for the month to date, in the current context.
DATESQTD	Returns a table that contains a column of the dates for the quarter to date, in the current context.
DATESYTD	Returns a table that contains a column of the dates for the year to date, in the current context.
ENDOFMONTH	Returns the last date of the month in the current context for the specified column of dates.
ENDOFQUARTER	Returns the last date of the quarter in the current context for the specified column of dates.
ENDOFYEAR	Returns the last date of the year in the current context for the specified column of dates.
FIRSTDATE	Returns the first date in the current context for the specified column of dates.
FIRSTNONBLANK	Returns the first value in the column, filtered by the current context, where the expression is not blank.
LASTDATE	Returns the last date in the current context for the specified column of dates.
LASTNONBLANK	Returns the last value in the column, filtered by the current context, where the expression is not blank.
NEXTDAY	Returns a table that contains a column of all dates from the next day, based on the first date specified in the dates column in the current context.

NEXTMONTH	Returns a table that contains a column of all dates from the next month, based on the first date in the dates column in the current context.
NEXTQUARTER	Returns a table that contains a column of all dates in the next quarter, based on the first date specified in the dates column, in the current context.
NEXTYEAR	Returns a table that contains a column of all dates in the next year, based on the first date in the dates column, in the current context.
PARALLELPERIOD	Returns a table that contains a column of dates that represents a period parallel to the dates in the specified dates column, in the current context, with the dates shifted a number of intervals either forward in time or back in time.
PREVIOUSDAY	Returns a table that contains a column of all dates representing the day previous to the first date in the dates column, in the current context.
PREVIOUSMONTH	Returns a table that contains a column of all dates from the previous month, based on the first date in the dates column, in the current context.
PREVIOUSQUARTER	Returns a table that contains a column of all dates from the previous quarter, based on the first date in the dates column, in the current context.
PREVIOUSYEAR	Returns a table that contains a column of all dates from the previous year, given the last date in the dates column, in the current context.
SAMEPERIODLASTYEAR	Returns a table that contains a column of dates shifted one year back in time from the dates in the specified dates column, in the current context.
STARTOFMONTH	Returns the first date of the month in the current context for the specified column of dates.
STARTOFQUARTER	Returns the first date of the quarter in the current context for the specified column of dates.
STARTOFYEAR	Returns the first date of the year in the current context for the specified column of dates.
TOTALMTD	Evaluates the value of the expression for the month to date, in the current context.
TOTALQTD	Evaluates the value of the expression for the dates in the quarter to date, in the current context.
TOTALYTD	Evaluates the year-to-date value of the expression in the current context.

DATESINPERIOD is a DAX time intelligence function that specifically works with the date dimension table to help make date-related DAX calculations. The syntax for the DATESINPERIOD function is:

```
=DATESINPERIOD(dates, start_date, number_of_intervals, interval)
```

The arguments of the DATESINPERIOD function are as follows:

- **dates**: This argument specifies a column of dates in the table where you want to define a new set of dates—usually the Date field in the date dimension table. The resulting table of dates includes only dates that exist in this Date column.
- **start_date**: This argument specifies the start date for the table of dates to be created.
- **number_of_intervals**: This argument specifies an integer that indicates how many periods to move backward or forward.
- **intervals**: This argument specifies a type of date interval: DAY, MONTH, QUARTER, or YEAR.

To create the 12-month moving sales average measure using a DAX time intelligence function, follow these steps:

1. As shown in Figure 19.163, create the average monthly sales formula in the fact table as follows: **12 Month Moving Sales Average ($) = CALCULATE([Ave Monthly Sales ($)], DATESINPERIOD(dDate[Date], MAX(dDate[Date]), -12,MONTH))**.
2. Add decimal number formatting with two decimal places showing.

3. Drag the [12 Month Moving Sales Average ($)] measure to the Secondary Values textbox under Fields in the Visualizations task pane.

```
1 12 Month Moving Sales Average ($) =
2 CALCULATE (
3     [Ave Monthly Sales AVEX ($)],
4     DATESINPERIOD ( dDate[Date], MAX ( dDate[Date] ), -12, MONTH )
5 )
```

Figure 19.163 *CALCULATE and DATESINPERIOD create a new filter context that extends 12 months back.*

1. To filter the Power BI visual you have just created, with the visual selected, open the Filters task pane. As shown in Figure 19.164, in the Year area, from the Show Items When the Value dropdown, select Is Greater Than. Then, in the textbox below that, type the year **2018** and click Apply Filter at the bottom of the Year area of the Filters task pane. By doing this, you filter the chart to show only the years 2019 to 2021; this is necessary because the 12-month moving sales average measure cannot go backward a full 12 months for any of the first 11 months in the year 2018.

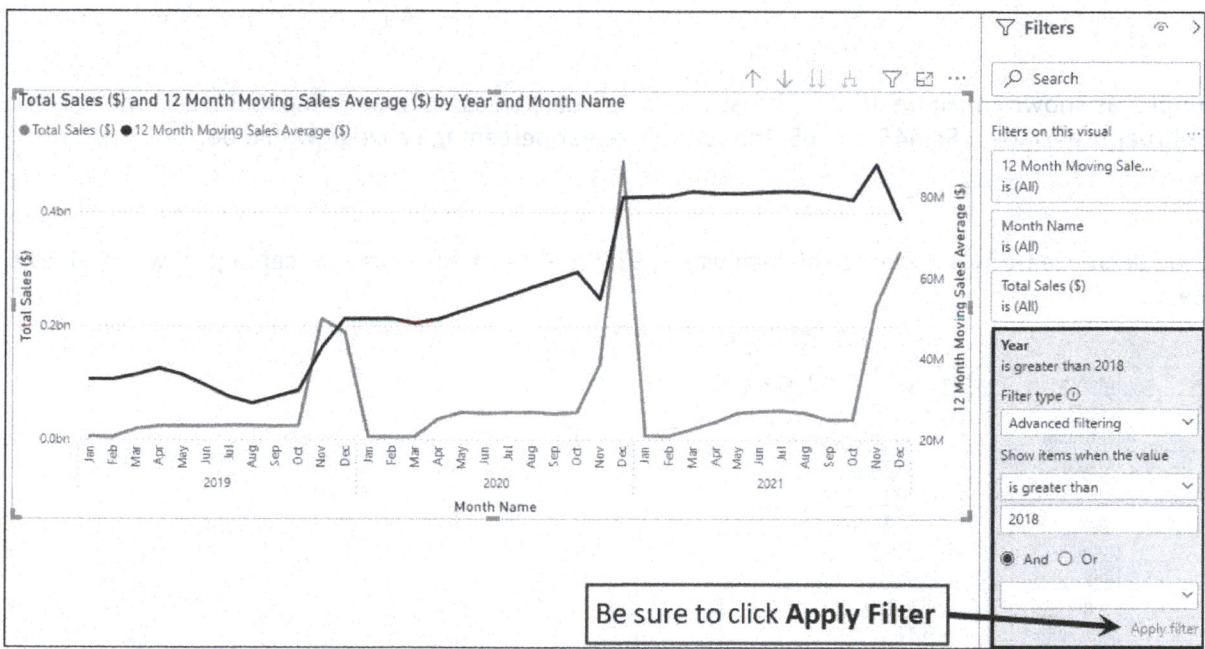

Figure 19.164 *The 12-month moving sales average calculation plotted on a line chart reveals an upward trend.*

As shown in Figure 19.164, this new metric shows that there is an upward trend from 2018 to 2021. Together, both lines help provide insight. Whereas the plotted total sales line reveals the seasonal pattern of largest sales in the winter, the moving average line reveals that sales are trending upward over the three-year period. But how does the DAX 12-month moving sales average measure work to calculate a result at each point in the chart?

You put the Date field from the date dimension table the first argument of the DATESINPERIOD function so that the table will accept the new date filter that the function creates. In the second argument, you used the MAX function to pick out the maximum date from the date dimension table Date field in the current filter context. This maximum date will select the last date in the current filter context (the end of the month), which is then used as the start date when working backward for the prior 12 months. In the third argument, you specified -12, and in the last argument, you specified the period size MONTH so that the function will jump back 12 months from the start date.

As a filter inside the CALCULATE function, the DATESINPERIOD function provides a new date filter with the dates extending 12 months back. The CALCULATE function uses this new filter to filter the fact table, and then the [Ave Monthly Sales ($)] measure calculates the average monthly sales based on the new fact table. For example, in the chart in Figure 19.164, for the month September 2020, DATESINPERIOD uses the start date September 30, 2020, and when it jumps back 12 months, it lands on the date October 1, 2019. The DATESINPERIOD function provides a table of dates from October 1, 2019 to September 30, 2020 to the

CALCULATE function. The CALCULATE function changes the filter context from September 1, 2020 to September 30, 2020 into a new filter context from October 1, 2019 to September 30, 2020. This filter is passed through the relationship from the dDate table to the fTransactions table. The fTransactions table becomes filtered, and the [Ave Monthly Sales ($)] measure calculates the 12 monthly sales totals, averages those 12 numbers, and delivers the average monthly sales figure $80,119,929.70.

In the next DAX measure you need to create, you will use the DAX time intelligence function SAMEPERIODLASTYEAR. You will use this function inside the CALCULATE function to provide a valid list of dates so you can get the sales from the same period last year. This will help you calculate a year-over-year percentage change formula.

A year-over-year percentage change formula is a common and useful metric that communicates the percentage change from one year to the next and helps gauge performance by showing the increases or decreases in percentage terms. The generic formula that works in all situations is:

```
(End - Start)/Start = Change/Start = Percentage Change
```

The specific formula is this case is:

```
(This Year's Sales - Last Year's Sales)/Last Year's Sales = Change in Sales/
Last Year's Sales = YOY % Change
```

For example, as shown in Figure 19.165, if last year's February sales were $4,500,010.81, and the current year's February sales were $4,446,304.65, the year-over-year percentage change would be:

```
(4,446,304.88 - 4,500,010.81)/4,500,010.81 = -53,705.93/4,500,010.81 =
-0.0119 = -1.19%
```

That is, the decrease from last year to this year was –$53,705.93. Expressed as a percentage, it was a –1.19% decrease.

	A	B	C	D	E	F	G
2		Year	Month	Total Sales ($)	YOY % Change		
3		2018	January	5,059,290.23			
4			February	4,500,010.81			
5			March	4,962,490.25			
6			April	4,935,400.11			
7			May	42,399,220.10			
8			June	55,563,854.71			
9			July	57,638,453.80			
10			August	44,145,411.12			
11			September	4,903,117.73			
12			October	5,105,360.03			
13			November	86,838,106.83			
14			December	101,955,272.38			
15		2018 Total		418,005,988.10			
16		2019	January	5,131,799.65	=(D16-D3)/D3		
17			February	4,446,304.88	-1.19%		Feb YOY % change = (4,446,304.88-4,500,010.81)/4,500,010.81 = -53,705.93/4,500,010.81 = -0.0119 => -1.19%
18			March	18,851,635.57	279.88%		
19			April	23,463,452.27	375.41%		

Figure 19.165 *Referencing a previous cell in a column is easy with worksheet formulas.*

How do you make this calculation using a DAX formula?

Back in Figures 19.114 through 19.117, when you created the DAX measure % of Grand Total Sales, it was not possible to reference the overall total in the grand total row of the table visual as part of the formula. You had to create a formula element to calculate the grand overall total in each cell of the report. You will run into a similar problem when you try to create a DAX formula to calculate the year-over-year percentage change formula because you cannot reference the previous year's sales amount as you would if you were using worksheet formulas.

As shown in Figure 19.165, with worksheet formulas, you are allowed to build formulas using cell references that can refer to previous cells in the column. You cannot do that with DAX. For the % of Grand Total Sales measure, you used the CALCULATE and the ALL functions to calculate the grand overall total in each cell. For the year-over-year percentage change formula, you need to use the CALCULATE and SAMEPERIODLASTYEAR functions to calculate the previous year's total in each cell. The SAMEPERIODLASTYEAR DAX table function is a time intelligence function that takes the dates in the current filter context and shifts them one year back and delivers the dates as a table. What is amazing about this function is that it works for a date interval of any size, whether a day, month, year, or other. In addition, the function only needs a single date field input to work, such as the Date field in the date dimension table. The SAMEPERIODLASTYEAR function delivers a valid table of dates to the CALCULATE function, changes the filter context, and calculates the previous year's sales based on the current filter context in the report or visual.

To create the first part of the YOY % Change measure, for the previous year's sales, follow these steps:

1. In the Power BI Desktop file, add a new sheet and name it **Year-Over-Year Sales Change**.

2. Click in the empty report canvas and then, in the Visualizations task pane, click the Matrix visual button.

3. With the matrix selected, drag the Year and Month Name fields from the dDate table to under Rows area in the Fields area in the Visualizations task pane so that Year is on top of Month Name.

4. Drag the [Total Sales ($)] measure under Values in the Fields area in the Visualizations task pane.

5. As shown in Figure 19.166, create the measure in the fact table as follows: **YOY % Change = CALCULATE([Total Sales ($)],SAMEPERIODLASTYEAR(dDate[Date]))**.

6. Add decimal number formatting with two decimal places showing.

7. Drag the [YOY % Change] measure under Values in the Fields area in the Visualizations task pane.

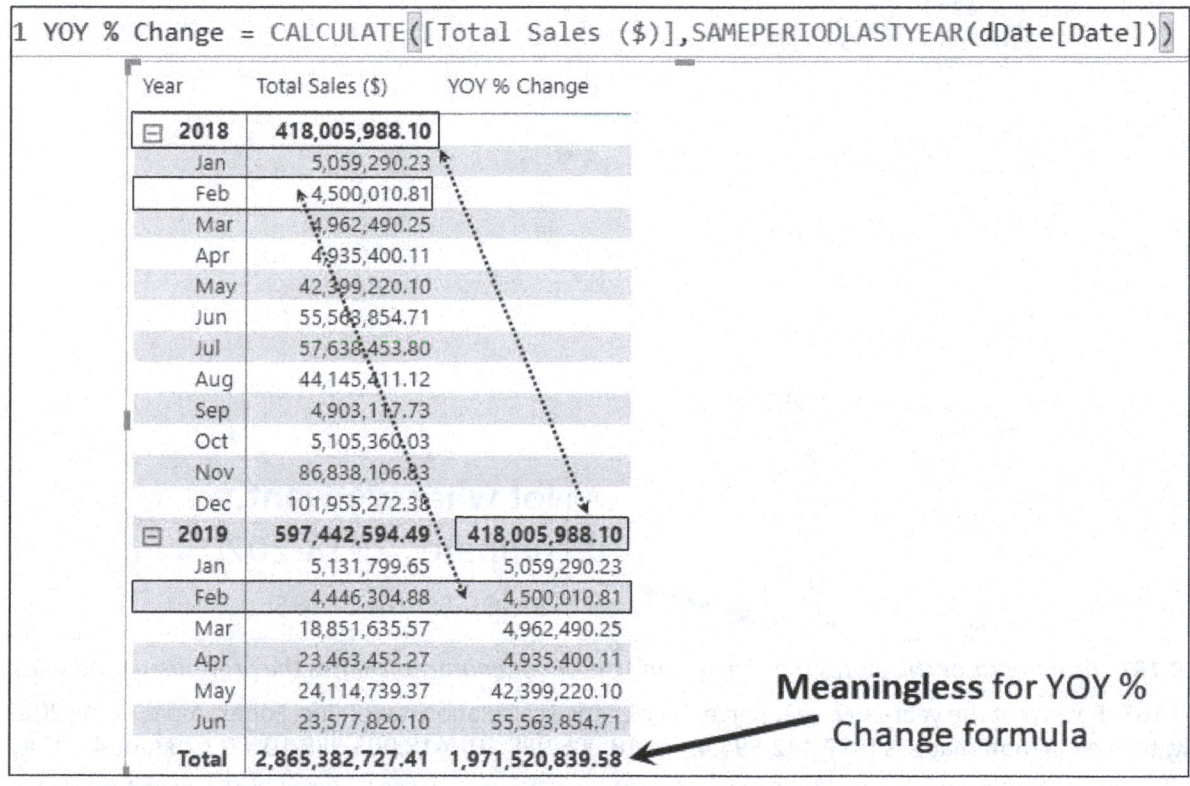

Figure 19.166 *The measure calculates the previous year's sales.*

In Figure 19.166, you can see that in the 2019 total row, the new measure calculates the previous year's 2018 sales amount as $418,005,988.10. In the February 2019 row, the measure correctly calculates the February 2018 sales amount $4,500,010.81. The measure correctly returns a DAX blank for all months in 2018 because there are no sales records that are one year back for those months. This means that any of the cells in this YOY % Change column except for the grand total cell will work as the denominator in the year-over-year percentage change calculation.

In the grand total cell, the SAMEPERIODLASTYEAR function returns a table of dates from January 1, 2018 to December 31, 2020, and the measure returns the sales amount $1,971,520,839.58 for the years 2018 to 2020. That is not a number you can use in the year-over-year percentage change formula. You will remove the calculation from that cell later. But for the rest of the column, the amount can be used to make the calculation. For example, in the 2019 total row, both the 2019 sales and 2018 sales are present, so the percentage change can be calculated as:

```
(597,442,594.49 - 418,005,988.10)/418,005,988.10
```

Now you can edit your measure to calculate this quotient:

```
(This Year's Sales - Last Year's Sales)/Last Year's Sales.
```

To do so, follow these steps:

1. As shown in Figure 19.167, click in the formula bar and edit the measure so it becomes **YOY % Change =DIVIDE([Total Sales ($)]-CALCULATE([Total Sales ($)], SAMEPERIODLASTYEAR(dDate[Date])), CALCULATE([Total Sales ($)],SAMEPERIODLASTYEAR(dDate[Date]))).**

2. Add percentage number formatting with two decimal places showing.

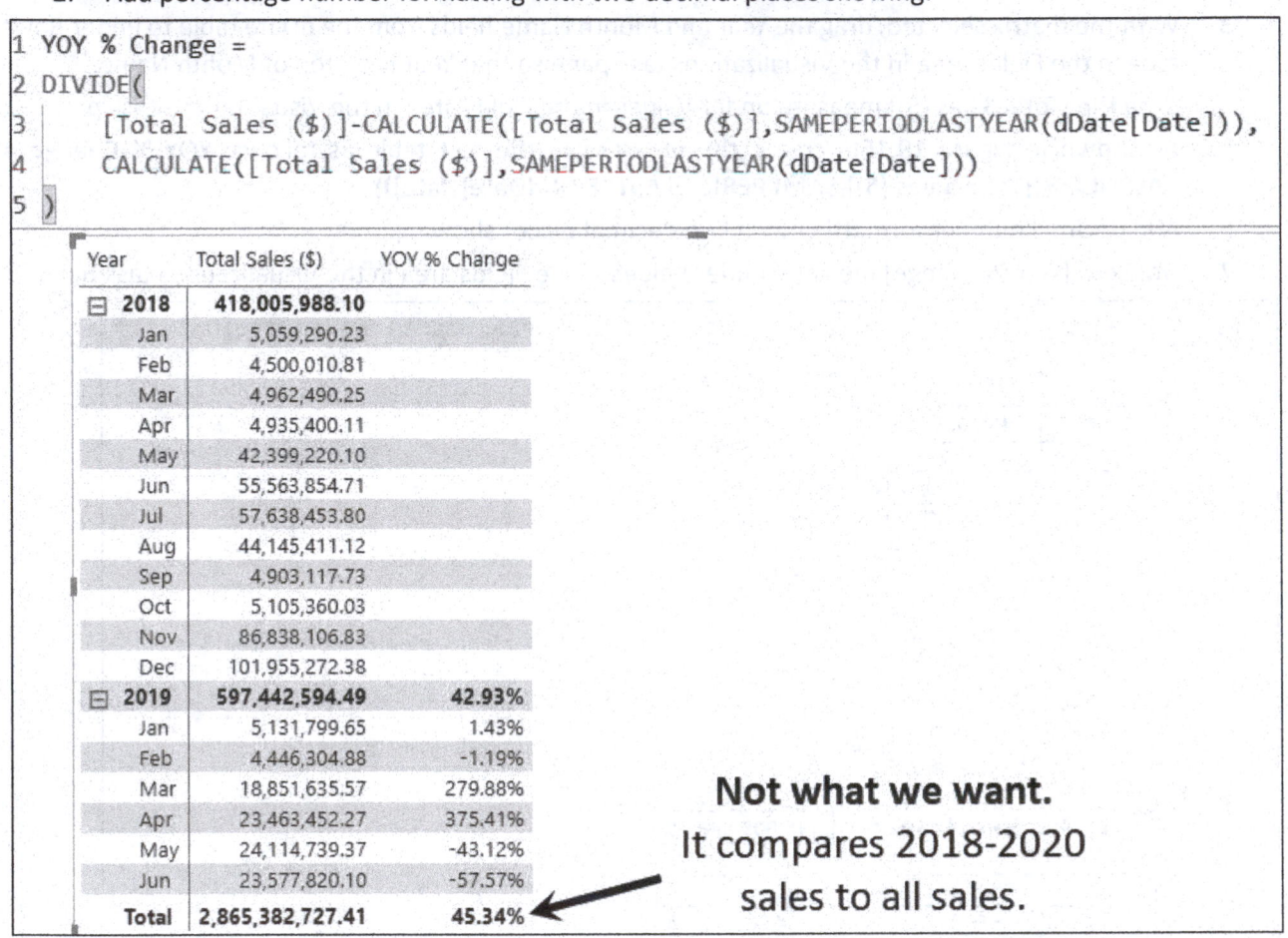

```
1 YOY % Change =
2 DIVIDE(
3    [Total Sales ($)]-CALCULATE([Total Sales ($)],SAMEPERIODLASTYEAR(dDate[Date])),
4    CALCULATE([Total Sales ($)],SAMEPERIODLASTYEAR(dDate[Date]))
5 )
```

Year	Total Sales ($)	YOY % Change
2018	**418,005,988.10**	
Jan	5,059,290.23	
Feb	4,500,010.81	
Mar	4,962,490.25	
Apr	4,935,400.11	
May	42,399,220.10	
Jun	55,563,854.71	
Jul	57,638,453.80	
Aug	44,145,411.12	
Sep	4,903,117.73	
Oct	5,105,360.03	
Nov	86,838,106.83	
Dec	101,955,272.38	
2019	**597,442,594.49**	**42.93%**
Jan	5,131,799.65	1.43%
Feb	4,446,304.88	-1.19%
Mar	18,851,635.57	279.88%
Apr	23,463,452.27	375.41%
May	24,114,739.37	-43.12%
Jun	23,577,820.10	-57.57%
Total	**2,865,382,727.41**	**45.34%**

Not what we want. It compares 2018-2020 sales to all sales.

Figure 19.167 *The numerator calculates the change, and the denominator calculates the previous-period sales.*

Figure 19.167 shows that the year-over-year percentage change calculation is working. For example, in the 2019 total row, the calculation made is (597,442,594.49 – 418,005,988.10)/418,005,988.10 = 0.4293, or 42.93%.

However, you still need to amend the formula so that the quotient is not calculated in the grand total row. The function you can use to prevent a formula from executing in the grand total row is the HASONEVALUE DAX function. HASONEVALUE is a Boolean DAX function that returns TRUE when a field in the current filter context contains only one value and FALSE when it contains more than one value. If you run the HASONEVALUE function on the Year field, it will return TRUE in every cell except the grand total row. For example, in the January 2018 row, the Year field contains only the 2018 value; in the January 2019 row, the Year field contains only the 2019 value; and in the 2019 total row, the Year field contains only the 2019 value. It is only in the grand total cell where the field contains more than one year value: It contains all four years.

To fix the formula by using the IF and HASONEVALUE functions, click in the formula bar and edit the measure so it becomes **YOY % Change = IF(HASONEVALUE(dDate[Year]),DIVIDE([Total Sales ($)]-CALCULATE([Total Sales ($)], SAMEPERIODLASTYEAR(dDate[Date])),CALCULATE([Total Sales ($)],SAMEPERIODLASTYEAR(dDate[Date]))))** (see Figure 19.168). The IF function uses the HASONEVALUE DAX function to check whether the Year field in the date table has one value, and if it does, it runs the division; otherwise, it delivers a DAX blank. The grand total cell gets a DAX blank, and a result is not shown in the report.

Look at the formula in Figure 19.168 and notice that there is the repeated formula element: CALCULATE([Total Sales ($)],SAMEPERIODLASTYEAR(dDate[Date]). Any time you see a formula element repeated like this, you can make the measure more efficient by using DAX variables.

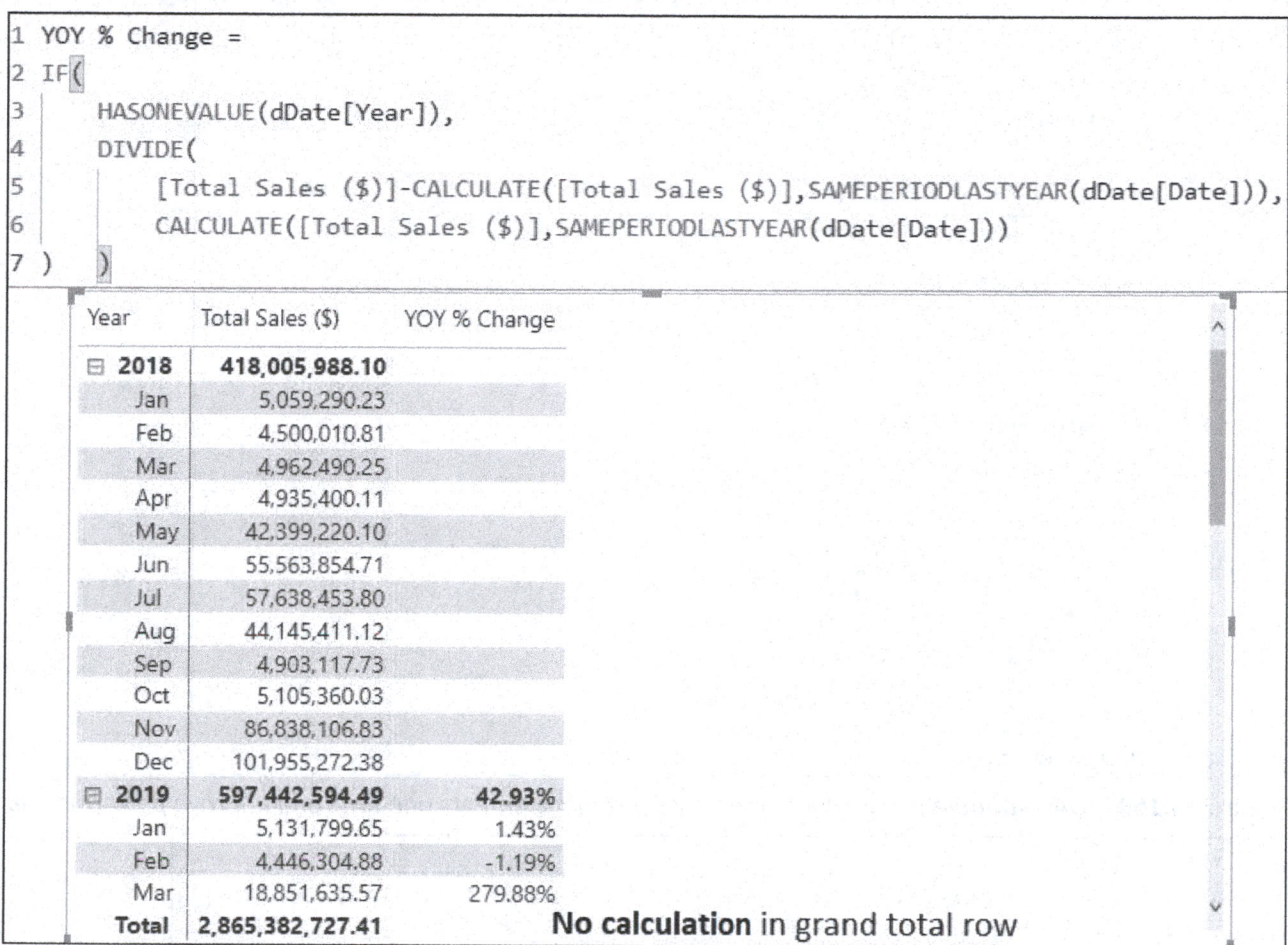

```
1 YOY % Change =
2 IF(
3       HASONEVALUE(dDate[Year]),
4       DIVIDE(
5           [Total Sales ($)]-CALCULATE([Total Sales ($)],SAMEPERIODLASTYEAR(dDate[Date])),
6           CALCULATE([Total Sales ($)],SAMEPERIODLASTYEAR(dDate[Date]))
7 )    )
```

Year	Total Sales ($)	YOY % Change
⊟ 2018	418,005,988.10	
Jan	5,059,290.23	
Feb	4,500,010.81	
Mar	4,962,490.25	
Apr	4,935,400.11	
May	42,399,220.10	
Jun	55,563,854.71	
Jul	57,638,453.80	
Aug	44,145,411.12	
Sep	4,903,117.73	
Oct	5,105,360.03	
Nov	86,838,106.83	
Dec	101,955,272.38	
⊟ 2019	597,442,594.49	42.93%
Jan	5,131,799.65	1.43%
Feb	4,446,304.88	-1.19%
Mar	18,851,635.57	279.88%
Total	2,865,382,727.41	**No calculation** in grand total row

Figure 19.168 *This YOY % Change measure has duplicate formula elements.*

Back in Figure 19.86, you saw DAX variables used in a date dimension table. In addition, in Chapter 16, you learned about the worksheet formula LET, which allows you to define variables in a formula to gain efficiencies. Variables provide a number of benefits:

- A variable is evaluated a single time, and the result is stored in memory so that it can be used throughout the formula. For formulas with repeating formula elements, this can reduce overall calculation time by preventing duplicate evaluation procedures.

- Variables make it easier to edit formulas with repeating elements because there is only one location to edit.

- Complex formulas can be visually easier to read because each element is given a name. In addition, you can use the keyboard shortcut for a line feed, Shift+Enter, to place an element on a new line.

To remove the formula repetition from the [YOY % Change] measure, you have a couple options. As shown in Figure 19.169, when you define a DAX variable, you use the VAR keyword, followed by the name of the variable, an equal sign, and then the variable calculation. You can use the keyword RETURN to return a value using the variables and other formula elements. However, unlike the worksheet LET function or Power Query's let expression, which both allow you to define variables, with DAX variables, you do not need a comma after defining the variable. Figure 19.170 shows the formula, and it has all four distinct parts of the formula defined as variables and then uses the RETURN keyword to build the final calculation. Whereas the formula in Figure 19.169 uses the variable to avoid duplicate calculation processes, the formula in Figure 19.170 uses the variable to avoid duplicate calculation processes and creates a formula that is easier to read. You can experiment and choose which of these DAX variable styles you prefer.

```
1 YOY % Change =
2 VAR LastYear = CALCULATE([Total Sales ($)],SAMEPERIODLASTYEAR(dDate[Date]))
3 RETURN
4 IF(HASONEVALUE(dDate[Year]),DIVIDE([Total Sales ($)]-LastYear,LastYear))
```

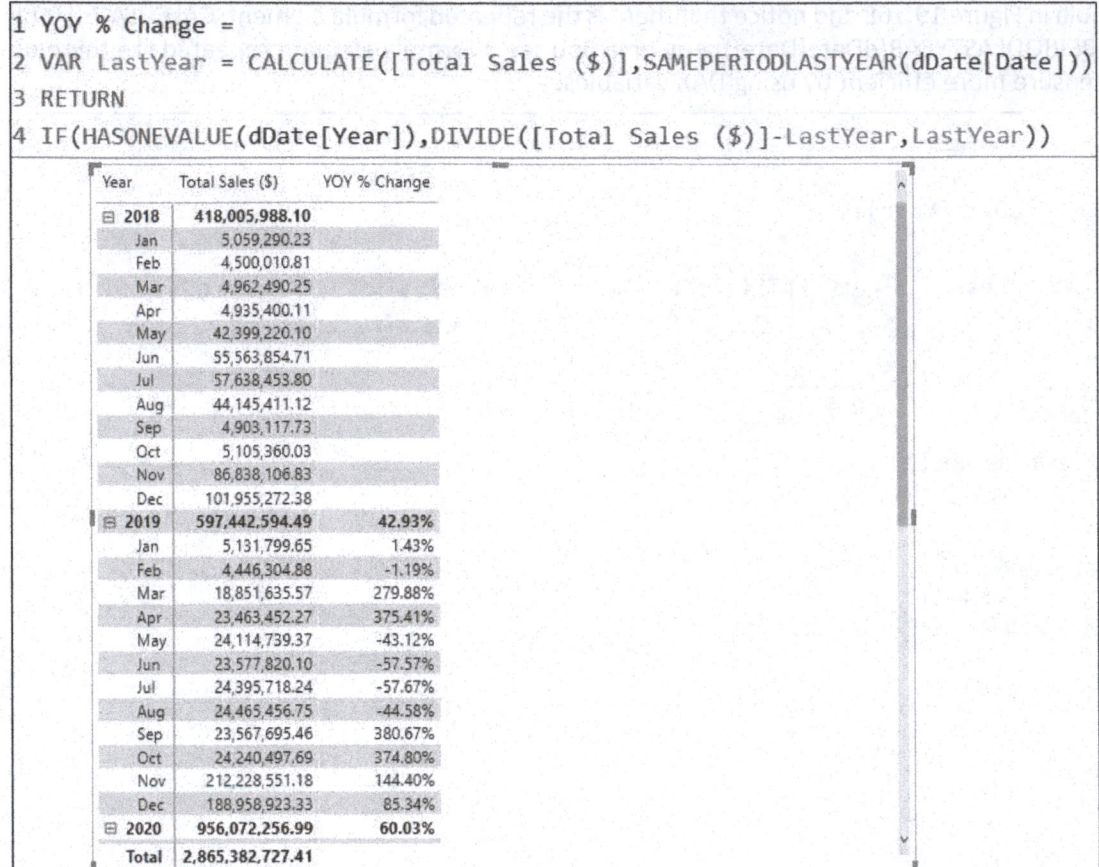

Figure 19.169 *A DAX variable can evaluate repeating formula elements one time and improve performance.*

```
1 YOY % Change =
2 VAR LastYear = CALCULATE([Total Sales ($)],SAMEPERIODLASTYEAR(dDate[Date]))
3 VAR ThisYear = [Total Sales ($)]
4 VAR Change = ThisYear-LastYear
5 VAR NotGrandTotalCell = HASONEVALUE(dDate[Year])
6 RETURN
7 IF(NotGrandTotalCell,DIVIDE(Change,LastYear))
```

Figure 19.170 *The four distinct parts of the formula are defined as variables to create a cleaner formula.*

The [YOY % Change] measure will work in all cells in your reports and visuals because you have sales data for completed years. But what if you want to create a report that compares the current year's incomplete data to last year's data?

To illustrate a DAX year-over-year percentage change measure that will work when there is incomplete data for the current year, I created a small dataset in the Excel file Ch19-Project02-YOY%ChangeIncompleteYear. xlsx. Figure 19.171 shows the fact table, three PivotTables, the measure in each PivotTable, and the helper column in the dDate table for the third PivotTable measure. This fact table has 1,155 rows of sales data; the first date in the Date field is 1/1/2020, and the last date for the current year in the Date field is 4/23/2021.

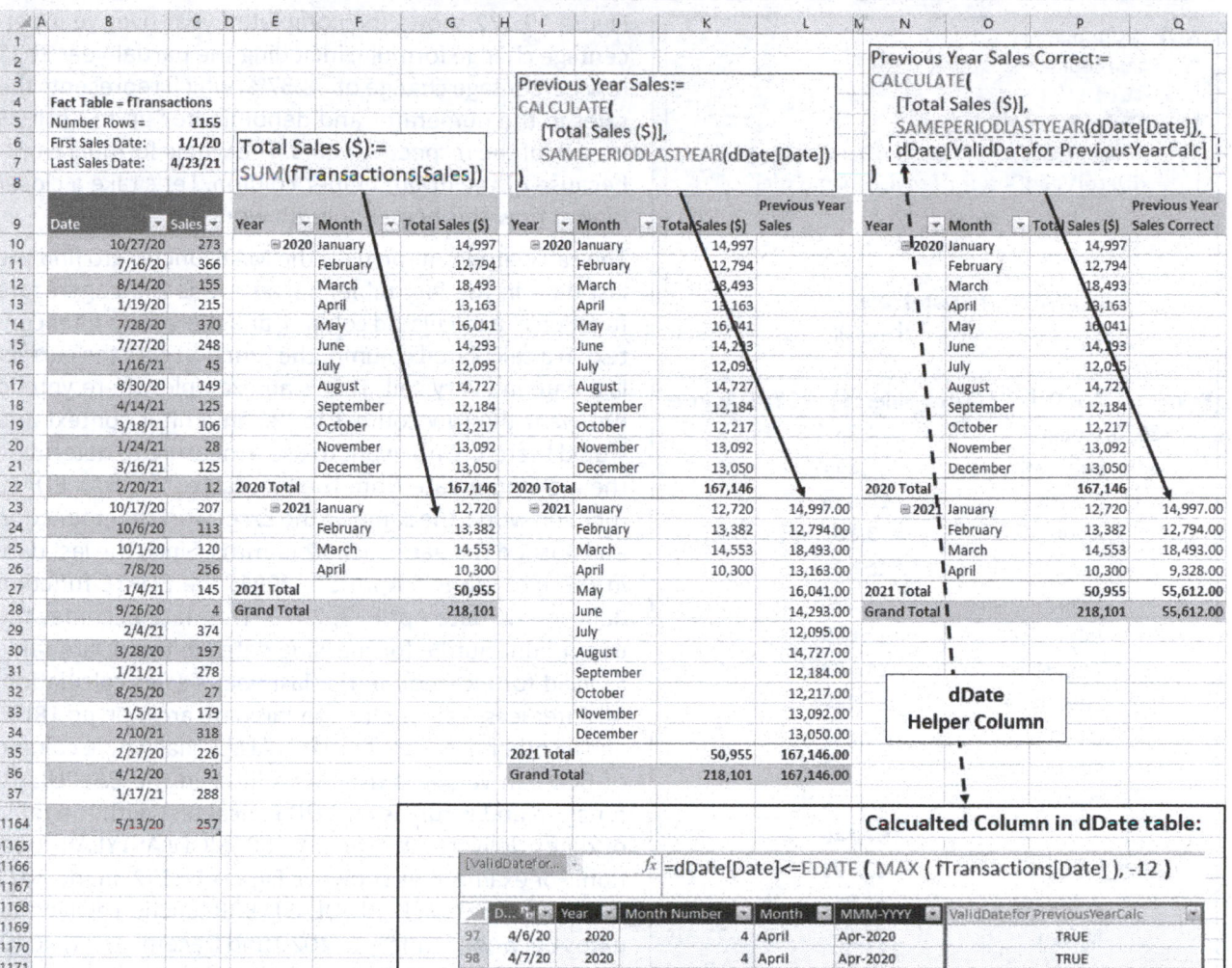

Figure 19.171 *The dDate table helper column used as a filter in CALCULATE prevents unwanted rows in the report.*

In the first PivotTable on the left, because there are no sales after April 23, 2021, the [Total Sales ($)] measure correctly shows no results for the months May to December 2021. But as soon as you add a measure that calculates the previous year's sales, as shown in the second PivotTable, because there are sales in every month for the year 2020, the [Previous Year Sales] measure shows results for all 12 months in the year 2021, even though there are no current sales in the months May to December 2021. If you completed the formula for year-over-year percentage change using the measure from the second PivotTable as the denominator, the months May to December would all show a 100% decrease. This is not what you want. The third PivotTable shows a dDate helper column to determine valid dates for the previous year's sales calculation added as a second filter in the CALCULATE function. This formula correctly shows the previous sales amounts for only the months in the current year, 2021, that have sales.

```
YOY % Change :=
VAR LastYear =
    CALCULATE (
        [Total Sales ($)],
        SAMEPERIODLASTYEAR ( dDate[Date] ),
        dDate[ValidDatefor PreviousYearCalc]
    )
RETURN
    IF (
        HASONEVALUE ( dDate[Year] ),
        DIVIDE ( [Total Sales ($)] - LastYear, LastYear )
    )
```

Year	Month	Total Sales ($)	YOY % Change
2020	January	14,997	
	February	12,794	
	March	18,493	
	April	13,163	
	May	16,041	
	June	14,293	
	July	12,095	
	August	14,727	
	September	12,184	
	October	12,217	
	November	13,092	
	December	13,050	
2020 Total		**167,146**	
2021	January	12,720	-15.18%
	February	13,382	4.60%
	March	14,553	-21.31%
	April	10,300	10.42%
2021 Total		**50,955**	**-8.37%**
Grand Total		**218,101**	

Figure 19.172 *This year-over-year percentage change formula will dynamically update to get correct results as new data is added.*

Figure 19.172 shows the completed year-over-year percentage change formula, including the partial-year 2021 row percentage change of –8.37%, which represents the sales in the numerator and denominator up to April 23 in each of the respective years. The whole formula works because of the dDate helper column. Let's take a closer look at how this helper column works.

The calculated column uses the MAX function to find the last date in the fact table. Because this is an aggregate function in a calculated column, and there is no filter context in a calculated column, the function gets the correct last date in every cell. This is an example where you do not want the row context to become filter context and would therefore not want to use a measure to determine the maximum date from the fact table. The DAX EDATE function works the same as the Excel worksheet function and pushed the date back 12 months. Since the last date in the fact table is April 23, 2021, the EDATE function delivers the date April 23, 2020. This date becomes the upper limit hurdle for marking dates in the dDate table as valid for inclusion in the last year's sales calculation. All dates less than or equal to this date are marked TRUE, and all other dates are marked FALSE. That whole column of Boolean values is used as a filter in the CALCULATE function and is run as an AND logical test with the table of dates delivered by the SAMEPERIODLASTYEAR function. For example, as shown in Figure 19.172, in the 2021 total row, the SAMEPERIODLASTYEAR function delivers all dates between January 1, 2020 and December 31, 2020, and the dDate table Boolean helper column delivers the valid dates between January 1, 2020 and April 23, 2020; therefore, the only overlap is the dates between January 1, 2020 and April 23, 2020. The CALCULATE function uses these valid dates to filter the fact table and calculate the correct total sales for the previous year. The correct total sales for the previous year and the correct sales for the current year are then used to calculate the correct year-over-year percentage change: –8.37%.

Adding a Tooltip to a Visual

Now you are ready to jump back to your Power BI Desktop file and complete the Year-Over-Year Sales Change page with the visual for the year-over-year percentage change. You also need to add a tooltip that will pop up whenever someone hovers over the visual on the worksheet. With Power BI, you can drag a measure into a visual to create a tooltip. A tooltip adds useful information to a visual without cluttering up the visual.

To create a line chart with a total sales line and a tooltip for year-over-year percentage change, follow these steps:

1. In the Power BI Desktop file, select the page Year-Over-Year Sales Change, click in the empty report canvas, and then, in the Visualizations task pane, click the Line Chart visual button.

2. With the line chart selected, from the dDate table drag the Year and Month Name fields under Axis in the Fields area in the Visualizations task pane so that Year is on top of Month Name. Drag the [Total Sales ($)] measure under Values. Drag the [YOY % Change] measure under Tooltips. Figure 19.173 shows the fields in the correct places.

3. To simultaneously show Year and Month Name in the horizontal axis, in the upper-right corner of the line chart, click the Expand All Down One Level in the Hierarchy button.

4. In the Visualizations task pane, click the Paint Roller Format tab and then, under X Axis, set Concatenate Labels to Off.

5. As shown in Figure 19.173, hover your cursor over the November 2020 point in the chart. The tooltip that pops up shows the total sales amount and year-over-year percentage change for November 2020.

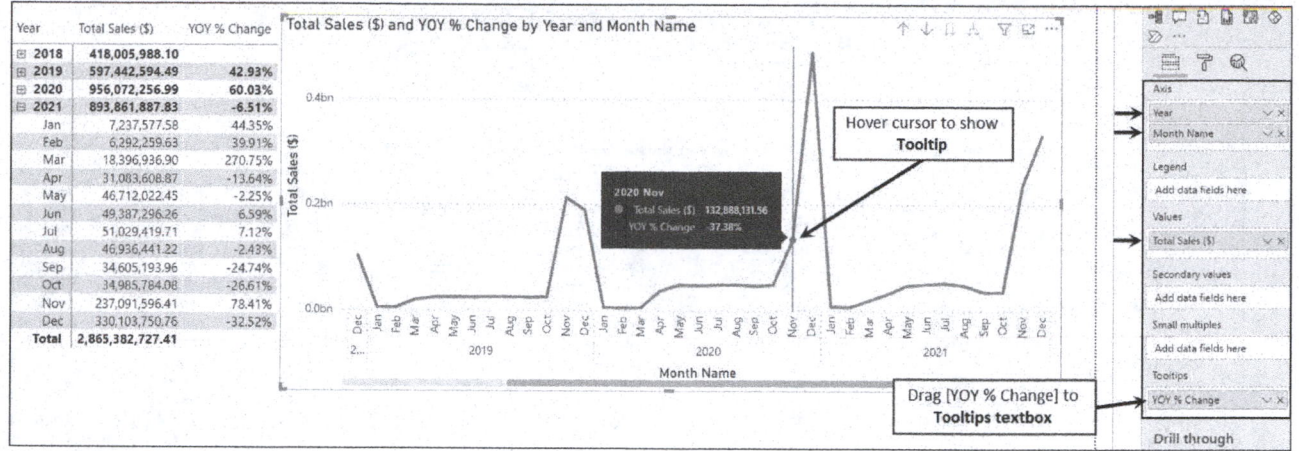

Figure 19.173 *Create a line chart with a total sales line and a year-over-year percentage change tooltip.*

Now you have finished creating measures for this project and can move on to finishing the visuals in the Power BI Report.

Finishing the Power BI Report

In Figure 19.173, notice that Month Name is used to describe the month. That seems a bit clunky for the final report. For all the visuals in the Power BI report file, it would be better to use the term Month rather than Month Name. To change the dDate table field name from Month Name to Month, follow these steps:

1. Click the Data button on the far-left side of the Power BI Desktop window and, in the Fields task pane, select the dDate table.

2. Double-click the Month Name field name in the dDate table, type **Month**, and press Enter. After you press Enter, all tables, visuals, DAX formulas, and other references to this field in the Power BI file reflect this new field name.

3. As shown in Figure 19.174, click the Report button on the far-left side of the Power BI Desktop window, click on the page Gross Profit & Total Sales, and then create a second line chart that shows the [Total Gross Profit ($)] and [% Gross Profit] measures by Year and Month.

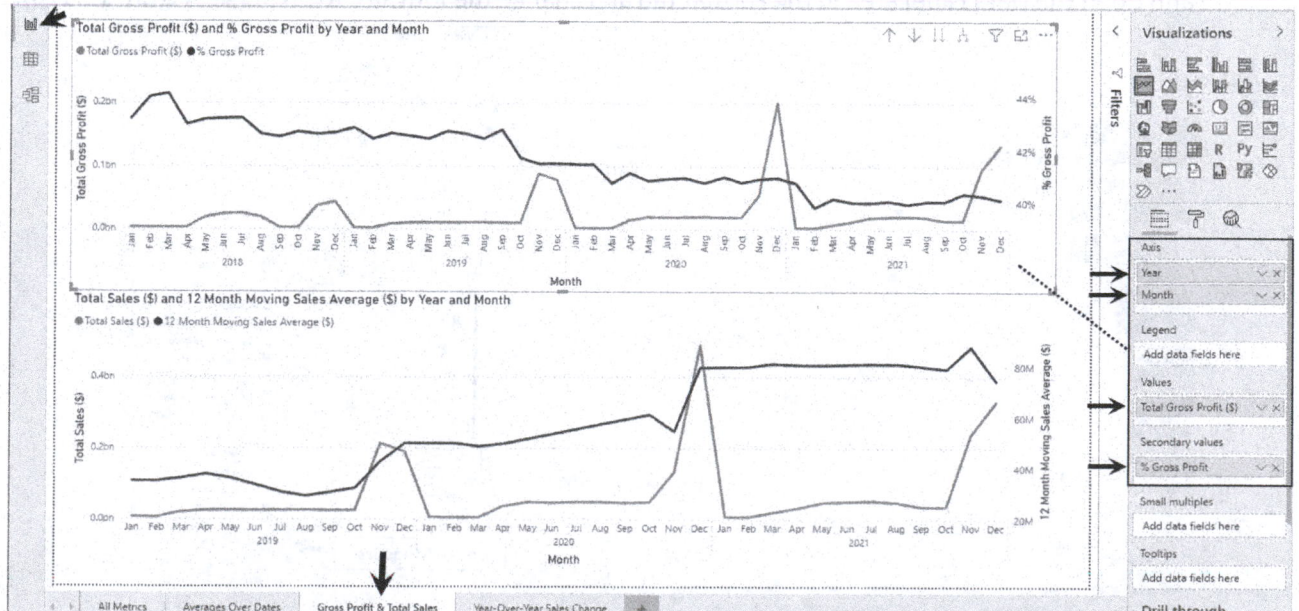

Figure 19.174 *Add a second line chart that shows gross profit and percentage gross profit by Year and Month.*

4. Click on the page All Metrics, select the table visual, and then add, remove, and reorder the nine measures as shown in Figure 19.175.

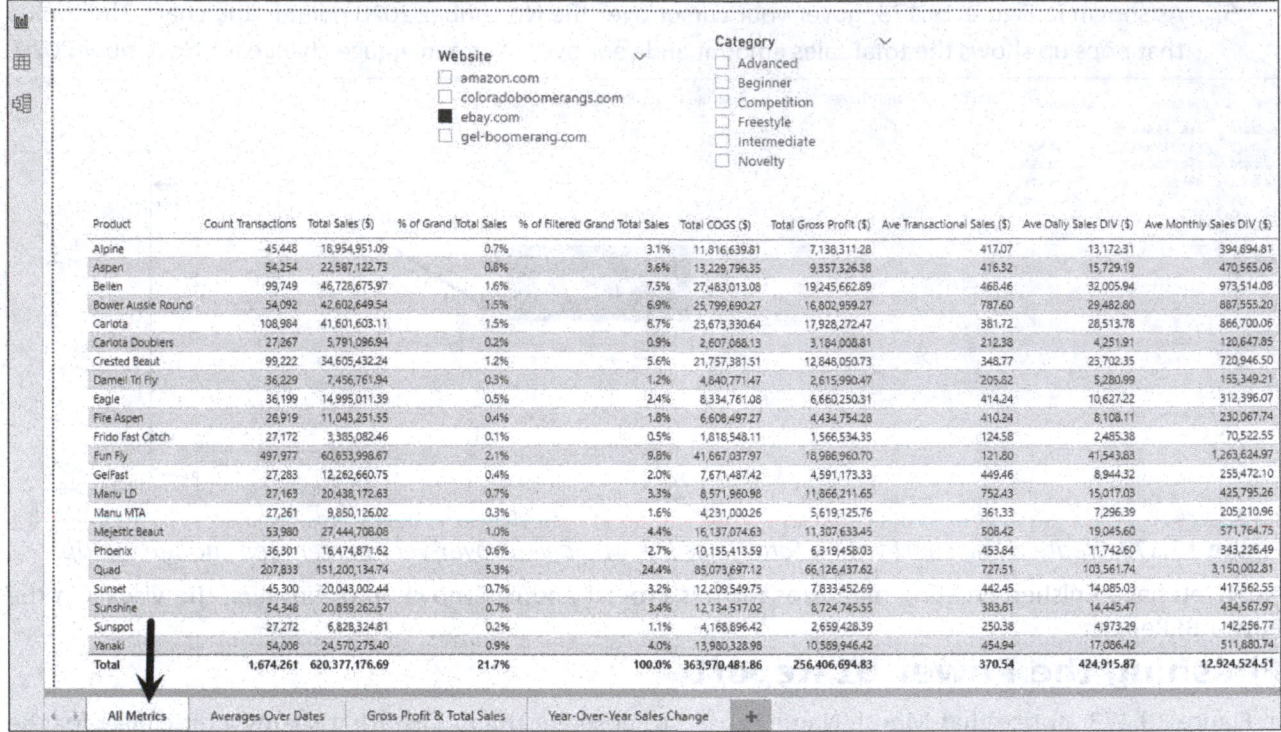

Figure 19.175 *The finished table visual with nine metrics.*

5. Create a new page and name it **Product Metrics**.

6. Add a clustered bar chart visual that shows [Total Sales ($)] by Product.

7. With the clustered bar chart visual selected, click the Paint Roller Format tab in the Visualizations task pane, set Data Label to On, and select Millions from the Display Units dropdown.

8. Add slicers for the Category field from the dProduct table and the Website field from the fTransactions table.

9. To create a card visual, click in an empty area of the report canvas, click the Card Visual button in the Visualization task pane, check the checkbox for the [Total Sales ($)] measure in the Fields task pane, and open the Data Label area in the Format tab and change the font size to 30 pt (see Figure 19.176).

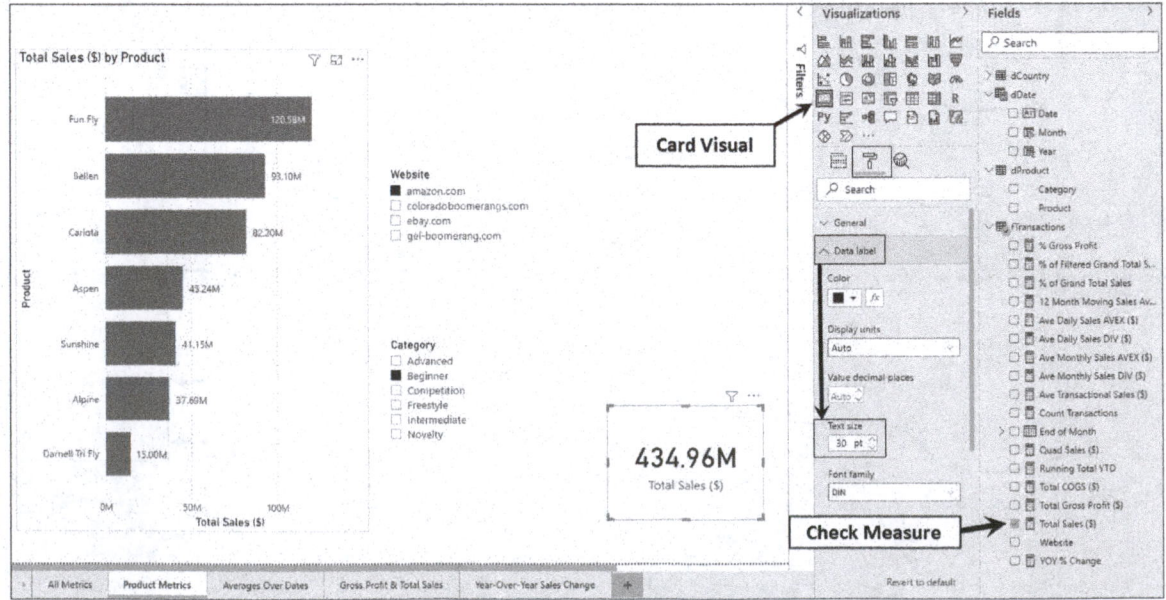

Figure 19.176 *The card visual can show a measure name and result based on filters from the page.*

10. Copy the card visual, paste the visual, and move it to the side. Repeat this process six more times so there are seven duplicate card visuals. Using the Format tab in the Visualizations task pane and the Fields task pane, change each of the measures so that the measures in your card visuals look the same as in Figure 19.177. For the Count Transactions card visual, change the Display Units setting from Auto to Thousands.

11. Edit the names of the measures to create shorter, more user-friendly names. For example, for the Ave Daily Sales DIV ($) measure, you need to remove DIV from the measure name. (However, I have left it in the figures for educational purposes.)

Figure 19.177 *Copy and paste the first card and change the measure for each copy.*

12. To add a header to the page, click in the empty report canvas and then, in the Power BI Desktop Home tab, in the Insert group, click the Textbox button. Type the text **Product Metrics**. Format and adjust the textbox so it looks neat. Figure 19.178 shows the final page in the Power BI Desktop report file.

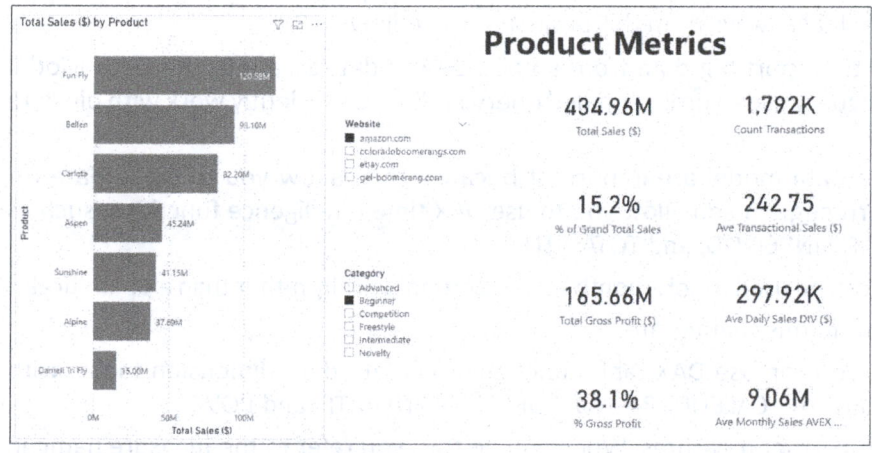

Figure 19.178 *Product Metrics page.*

The finished data model is shown in Figure 19.179.

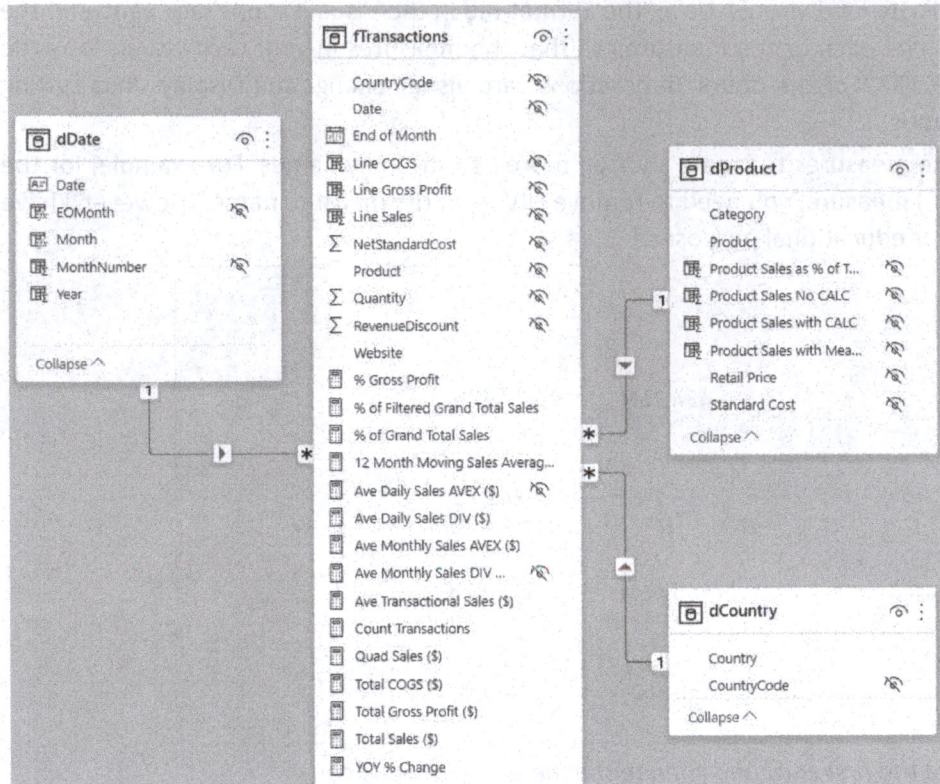

Figure 19.179 *The finished data model.*

Project 2 Summary

Wow! This project gave you a lot of experience with data analysis on big data. In it, you used Power Query to import SQL data, DAX formulas to create the data model, and Power BI Desktop to create reports and visuals. The key data analysis and power tool takeaways from this project are as follows:

- You can use Power Query to import big data from an SQL Server database into the Data Model columnar database. Power Query uses a process called query folding to efficiently work with big data from SQL Server databases.

- Date dimension tables in a data model are important because they allow you to make date-related calculations at the correct grain and allow you to use DAX time intelligence functions, such as SAMEPERIODLASTYEAR, DATESINPERIOD, and TOTALYTD.

- The Sort By Column feature can be used to sort month names chronologically rather than alphabetically.

- The key DAX formula lessons in this chapter are:

  - In Power BI Desktop, you can use DAX table functions to create date dimension tables with functions such as CALENDAR, CALENDARAUTO, FORMAT, GENERATE, and ROW.

  - You can use measures in other measures. When you do this, you refer to the measure name in square brackets without a table preface, like this: [*Measure Name*].

  - When it is necessary to make row-by-row calculations in a fact table with a lot of data and then aggregate the values in a measure, if your one-step X iterator measure calculates too slowly in the report area, try the two-step measure process by moving the calculation to a calculated column and using an aggregate function for the measure. Often this can improve response time in the report area.

  - Not all measure calculations allow you to choose between the one-step and two-step methods for creating measures. Some calculations, such as percentage gross profit, cannot be done row-by-row in the fact table and then aggregated in a measure. For a calculation like this, you must use a measure that aggregates the numerator amount and denominator amount *before* performing the division.

- When you use the COUNTROWS function on a fact table in a star schema data model, it counts the number of records in the fact table with any set of filter conditions.

- The CALCULATE function can change the external filter context for a measure. It can also perform context transition, converting any available row contexts into filter context. In calculated columns and in DAX iterator functions, when you wrap the CALCULATE function around a formula, context transition occurs, and all available row contexts are converted into filter contexts. When you invoke context transition, you need to do it in a table with a primary key, such as a dimension table. If you invoke context transition in a fact table with duplicate records and no primary key, you get incorrect results. As filter modifiers in CALCULATE, you can use ALL() to help create grand totals and ALLSELECTED() to create filtered grand totals.

- X iterator functions like AVERAGEX, MAXX, and MINX can be used to iterate over a table and then make an aggregate calculation. The power of these functions is that you get to decide what the grain of the table is in the first argument of the function. The grain of the table determines the grain of each value in the intermediate column of numbers before you make the final calculation. This allows you to make aggregate calculations at the day, month, year, or other levels more easily than with worksheet formulas or standard PivotTables.

- DAX table functions such as VALUES and ALL can be used to create unique lists of values. The VALUES function "sees" the current filter context. The ALL function removes all filters and does not "see" the current filter context. These functions can be used in the first argument of AVERAGEX to create the correct grain for pre-aggregating values.

- DAX variables can be used to remove repeated formula element, improve calculation time, and make formulas easier to read.

- When working with big data, it can be difficult to double-check your work. One way to check whether formulas yield reasonable and accurate results is to build a small parallel model in an Excel worksheet. Another way is to use alternative formulas to calculate a given metric.

- In Power BI Desktop, you can drag a measure into a visual to create a tooltip that pops up whenever a user hovers over the visual. In addition, the Filter task pane allows you to filter a visual, a whole page, or all the pages in a Power BI report file.

Project 3: Combining Data from Multiple Excel Files and Creating a Summary Report—All with Power Query!

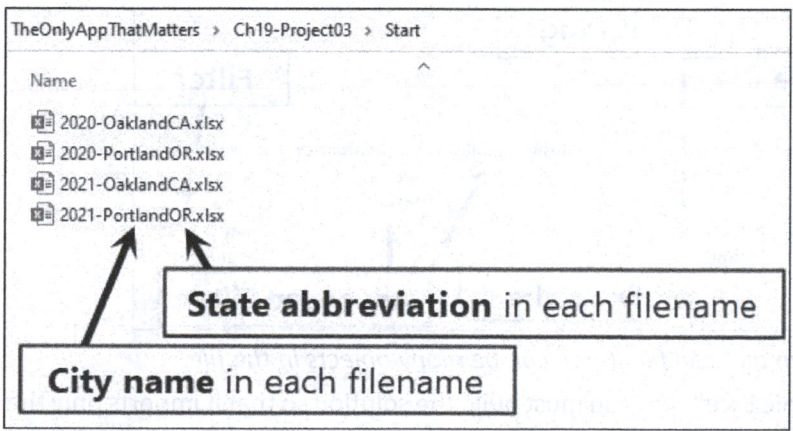

Figure 19.180 Each Excel filename contains the city and state abbreviation that you will need in the final dataset.

Sometimes in data analysis, you get "messy" data, where the data is not given to you in a single proper dataset. In Project 1, you combined multiple text files into a single proper dataset by using Power Query. In that project, each text file had a proper dataset with all the necessary fields in each table, and so it was relatively easy to combine the data into a single table. In this project, you will be given multiple Excel files, each with many incomplete tables that you need to carefully transform into a single proper dataset. In addition, each table has about 100,000 rows of data, for a total of over 2 million rows of data across all tables.

Figure 19.180 shows the first messy data problem you need to solve: You are given Excel files with the city and state abbreviation in the filename, and you must extract the names into the two new fields City and State.

Figure 19.181 *The solution you build will have to accommodate new data and new city and state names.*

Figure 19.181 shows the second problem you need to solve: You will get new Excel files in the future, and your solution must accommodate the new data and the new city and state names.

The third problem you will have to solve, as shown in Figure 19.182, is that in each Excel file, there are multiple sales rep worksheets, each with a single proper dataset with consistent field names that you must combine into a single table. But the added complication is that you must add a fourth field to each table that lists the sales rep name from each sheet tab.

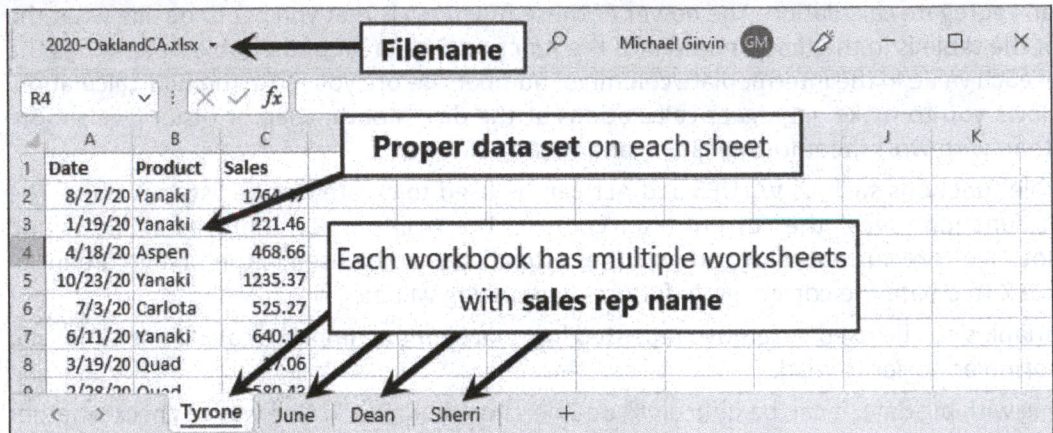

Figure 19.182 *Multiple worksheets will need to be combined, with sales rep as a new field.*

The fourth problem is that when you import multiple Excel files, there can be many different objects in the file, such as worksheets, Excel Tables, and defined names. In contrast, a text file almost always includes a single table object.

As shown in Figure 19.183, the 2020-PortlandOR.xlsx file includes objects that you want to import, such as the sales rep worksheets, as well as objects that you do not want to import, such an unnamed worksheet (Sheet1), an Excel Table, and a defined name.

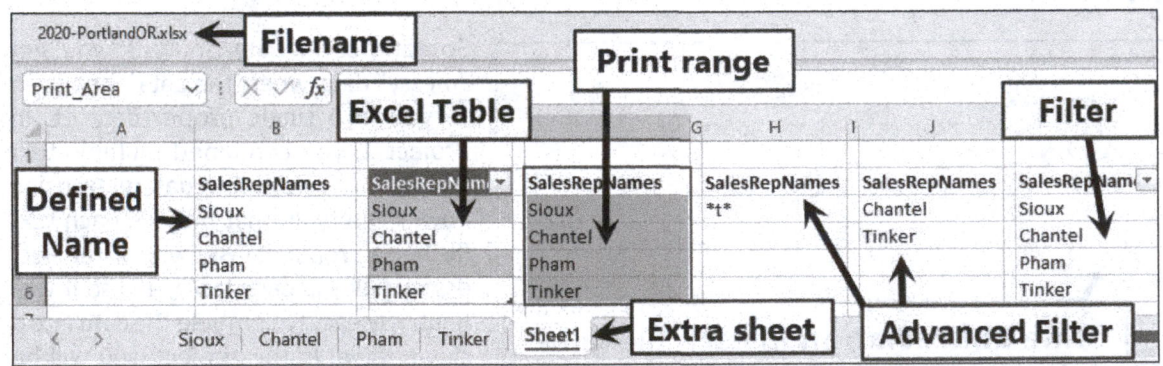

Figure 19.183 *When you import data from an Excel file, there can be many objects in the file.*

Any time that you import data from multiple Excel files, you must build the solution so that it imports only the objects that you want. Before Power Query existed, this common task of importing data from multiple Excel files was very difficult to accomplish and either required a long manual process or careful VBA code writing. But with Power Query, the From Folder feature, and the Excel.Workbook function, you can quickly build a solution that will import the desired objects, clean and transform the data, and update when new data arrives.

In addition, because the reporting goal in this project is a simple 17-row summarized table report, as shown in Figure 19.184, you do not need to load the 2 million rows of data to the Data Model. Instead, you can make a table report by using Power Query and then load it to the worksheet. This project demonstrates that when your goal is a simple table report, you can use one tool, Power Query, to complete a number of steps: import, clean, transform, and report!

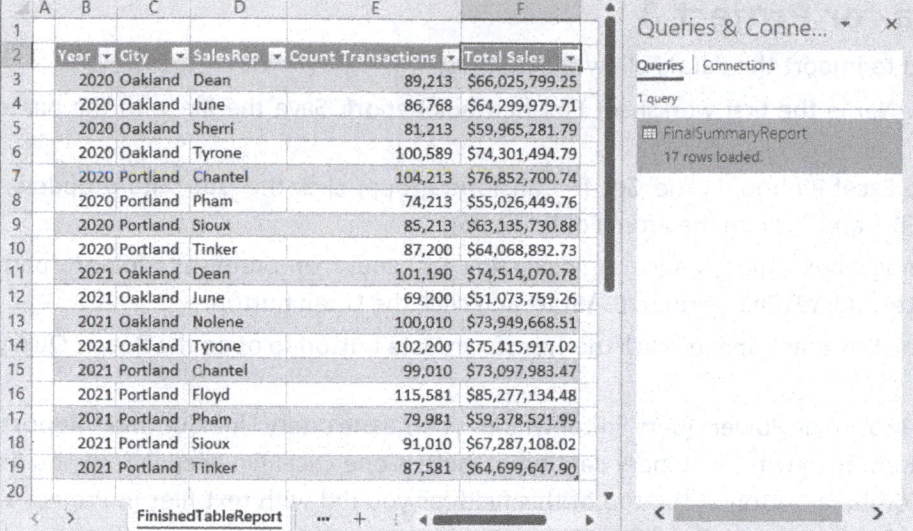

Figure 19.184 *Each row in this Power Query summary report represents one worksheet of data.*

The 10-Step Data Analysis Process for Project 3

Before you begin creating this project, you need to consider the 10 steps in the data analysis process as they relate to this project. Table 19.5 provides a summary of these 10 steps and how you will carry them out for this project .

Table 19.5 Project 3 Data Analysis Process Summary

Step	How Step Is Carried Out in This Example
1. Determine the goals of the analysis	The goal is to combine data from multiple Excel files and create a summary table report.
2. Determine where the data is	The data is in multiple Excel files.
3. Determine how much data exists	There are about 2 million rows of data.
4. Determine which tool or tools to use	You can use Power Query for all steps: import, clean, transform, and report.
	You will learn about these Power Query tools:
	From Folder to import multiple Excel files from an on-premises location
	Various features for cleaning data
	Excel.Workbook to extract all objects from within the Excel files
	The Table Expand feature to combine all tables
	The Group By feature to make a summary report
5. Import the data	You will use Power Query.
6. Clean and transform the data	You will use Power Query.
7. Load the data	You will not load the full dataset but only the final report to the worksheet.
8. Create a data model	All Power Query import and transform steps lead to the final report.
9. Create useful information	You will use Power Query to create the final report.
10. Update the data model based on new data	Yes, you will get new data, and the solution will require a refresh when new data arrives.

You may at some point need to go back and change something in your report, and the Power Query process makes it easy to change and update your report.

Importing the Data for Project 3

To begin this project, you need to import the data. Follow these steps:

1. Open a new Excel file. Name the first worksheet **FinishedTableReport**. Save the file with the name **Ch19-Project03.xlsx**.

2. In the Data tab in the Excel Ribbon, in the Get & Transform group, click the Get Data dropdown arrow, point to From File, and click on the From Folder option.

3. In the Browse dialog box that appears, navigate to your on-premises folder path **TheOnlyAppThatMatters\Ch19\Ch19-Project03\Start** and click the Open button.

4. In the folder path dialog box that appears, click the Transform Data button to open the Power Query Editor.

5. As shown in Figure 19.185, in the Power Query Editor window, name the query **FinalSummaryReport**. Notice that in the Content field with the binary data type, there is one Excel file in each row. You do not want to use the Combine button at the top of this field (as you did with text files in Project 1) because doing so would not work with Excel files that contain many objects. Also notice that in each row of the Name field, the full filename for each Excel file is listed.

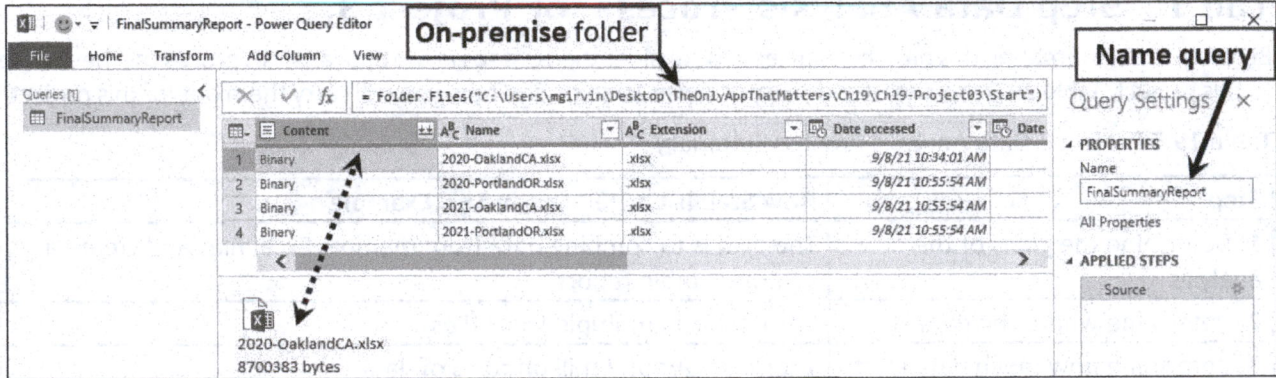

Figure 19.185 *The From Folder feature pulls in four Excel files, one in each row.*

Understanding Patterns for Cleaning and Transforming Data

Before you can extract the city name and state abbreviation from the filename in the Name field, you must identify a consistent pattern that you can use to build a query solution. In this case, you can see that the text you want is between a dash delimiter and a period delimiter. Using this pattern will allow to you extract the text. In addition, you can see that the state abbreviation is always listed as the last two characters on the right. Using this pattern will allow to you split the city and state names into two columns at the second character position from the right. To use these two patterns to clean and transform the data, follow these steps:

1. To extract the city name and state abbreviation from the filename, as shown in Figure 19.186, select the Name field, click on the Transform tab in the Power Query Ribbon, and then, in the Text Column group, click the Extract dropdown arrow and select Text Between Delimiters.

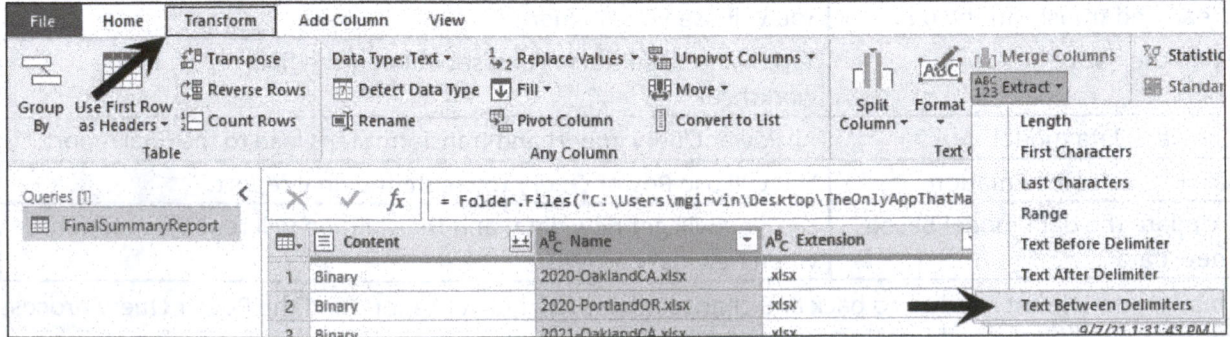

Figure 19.186 *Text Between Delimiters allows you to extract the city name and state abbreviation.*

2. In the Text Between Delimiters dialog box that appears, as shown in Figure 19.187, type a dash in the Start Delimiter textbox and a period in the End Delimiter textbox. Then click the OK button. This leaves the Name field with just the city name and state abbreviation.

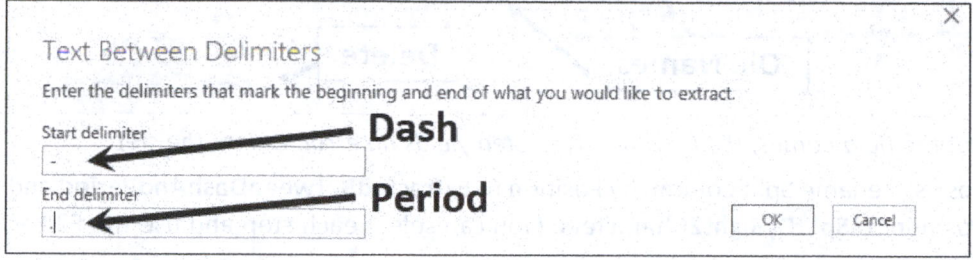

Figure 19.187 *Type the start and end delimiters and then click OK to extract text between the delimiters.*

3. To split the field into two, as shown in Figure 19.188, in the Transform tab, in the Text Column group, click the Split Column dropdown arrow and select By Number of Characters.

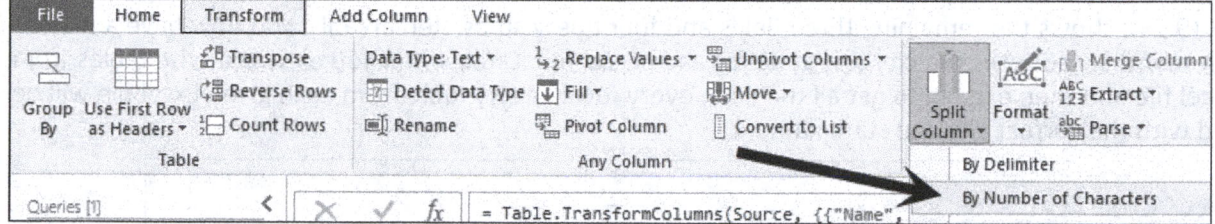

Figure 19.188 *By Number of Characters allows you to split based on a fixed number of characters.*

4. As shown in Figure 19.189, in the Split Column by Number of Characters dialog box, type **2** in the Number of Characters textbox and then, in the Split area, select the Once, as Far Right As Possible option button. Then click OK.

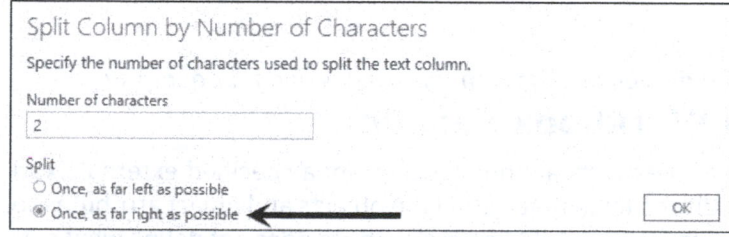

Figure 19.189 *Split by 2 characters from the right.*

As shown in Figure 19.190, two steps are added to the Applied Steps list: Split Column by Position and Changed Type (though you may not see the Changed Type step on your screen, depending on your settings).

5. In the Applied Steps list, select the Split Column by Position step and click in the formula bar and edit the last argument in the Table.SplitColumn function so that the list {"Name.1","Name.2"} becomes **{"City","State"}**. Press Enter when the formula is complete. Now you have split the single column into two columns, each with the correct field name.

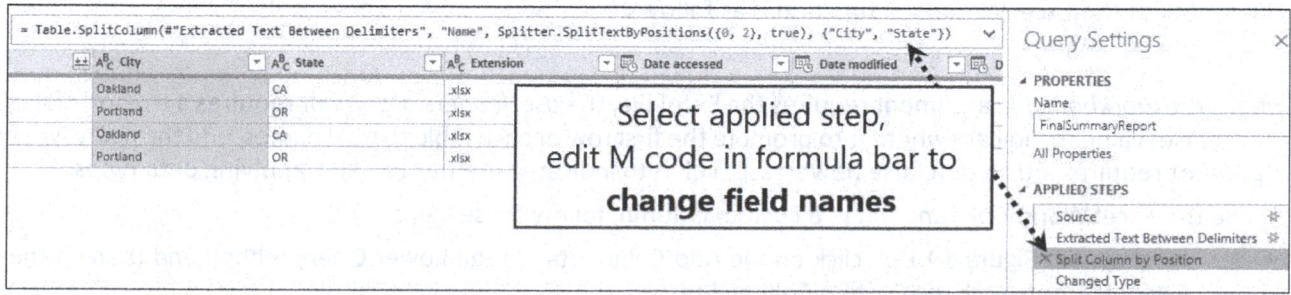

Figure 19.190 *Edit the M code so that the field names become City and State.*

6. Because the Changed Type step now yields an error, as shown in Figure 19.191, select this step from the Applied Steps list and press the Delete key.

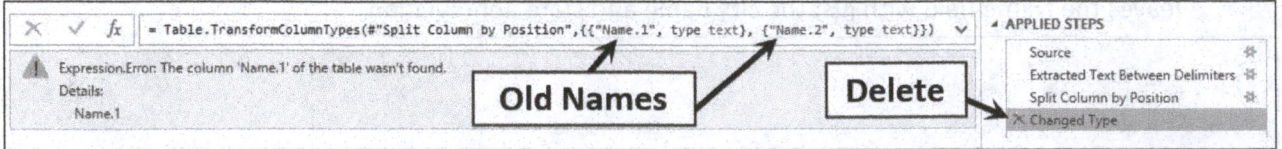

Figure 19.191 *After you edit the field names, the Changed Type step yields an error. Delete the step.*

7. In the Applied Steps list, rename Split Column by Position to **ExtractedBetweenDashAndPeriod** and Split Column by Position to **SplitByRight2Characters**. (You can select each step and use the F2 key to rename it.)

8. To keep only the Content, City, and State fields, select these three fields, right-click any one of the field names, and click on Remove Other Columns. When Power Query adds a new applied step for this, rename it **RemoveUnnecessaryFileAttributeFields**.

Figure 19.192 shows the remaining three fields and four query steps. Remarkably, you now have a marker in each row that indicates the city and state for each Excel file. Later, when you extract all the tables from the Excel file and then expand to get all the data, every row in every table from each given Excel file will be marked with the correct city and state name.

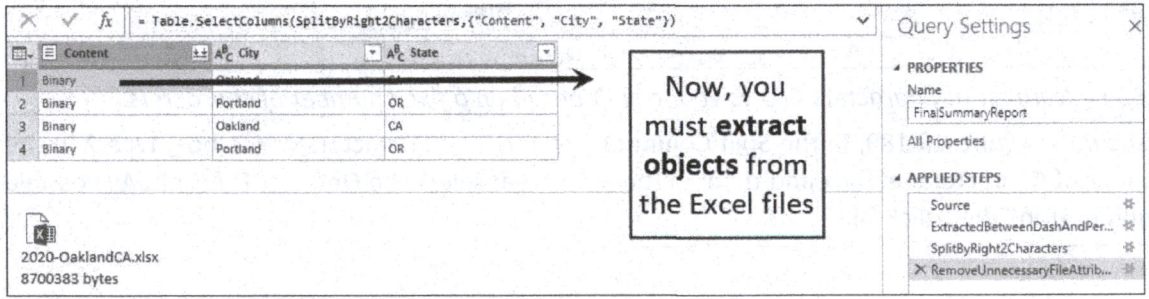

Figure 19.192 *After you remove the unwanted fields, you are left with three fields and four query steps.*

Using the Power Query Excel.Workbook Function

The Power Query M code Excel.Workbook function extracts all the objects from a specified external Excel workbook file and delivers to the Power Query Editor a table that lists all the objects and object attributes so that you can chose which objects to import. Although the official Microsoft website does not define what sort of objects this function will extract, I have found that these are some of the objects the function can extract:

*   Excel worksheets with all content on the sheet
*   Excel Tables
*   Defined names that are manually created
*   Defined names that are automatically created when you define print ranges
*   Defined names that are automatically created when you use the Auto Filter feature
*   The defined names, Criteria and Extract, that are created when you use the Advanced Filter feature

The syntax of the Excel.Workbook function is as follows:

```
=Excel.Workbook(workbook file, useHeaders, delayTypes)
```

where the *workbook file* argument requires the Excel file, the *useHeaders argument* requires a true or a false (lowercase) value to indicate whether to promote the first row of each table to field names, and the *delayTypes* argument requires a true or a false (lowercase) value to indicate whether to delay applying data types.

To use the Excel.Workbook function in a custom column, follow these steps:

1. As shown in Figure 19.193, click on the Add Column tab in the Power Query Ribbon and then, in the General group, click the Custom Column button.

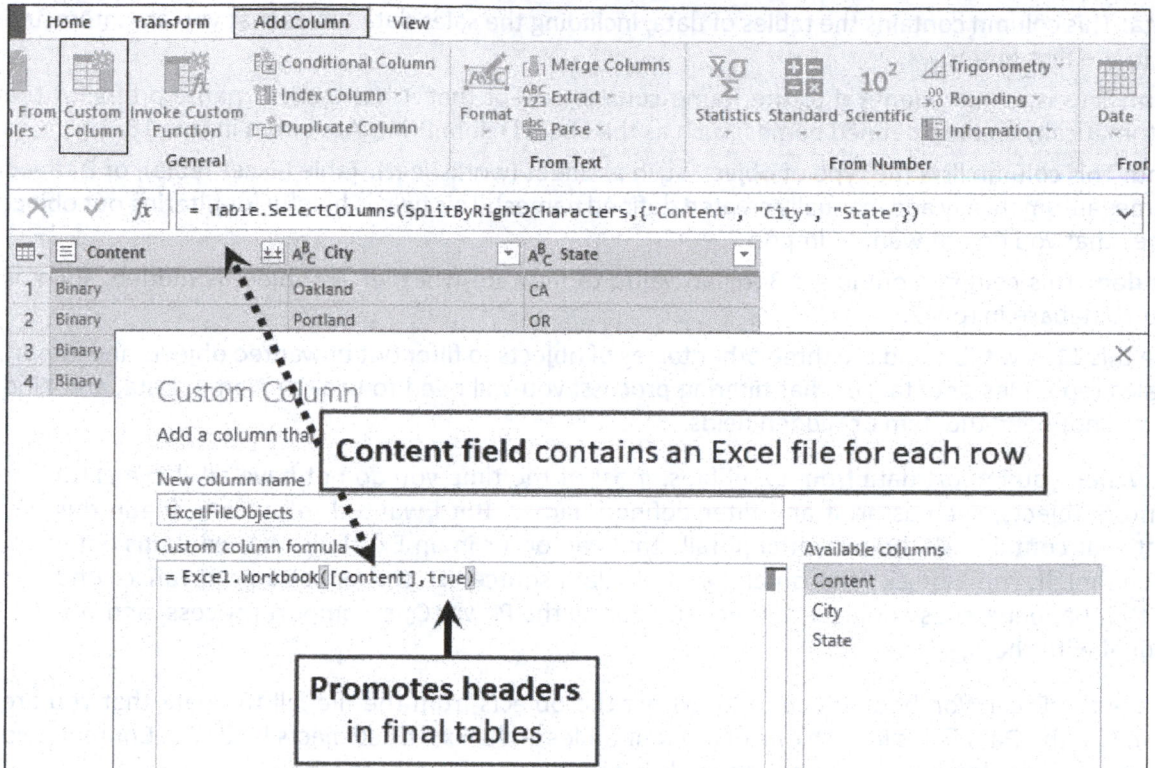

Figure 19.193 *The Excel.Workbook M code function extracts all the objects from each Excel file.*

2. In the Custom Column dialog box that appears, in the New Column Name textbox, type **ExcelFileObjects**, and in the Custom Column Formula textbox, type the formula **=Excel.Workbook([Content],true)**.

3. Click OK in the Custom Column dialog box to create a new field with a table of Excel objects for each Excel file. Rename the query step **GetExcelObjects**. Figure 19.194 shows the result.

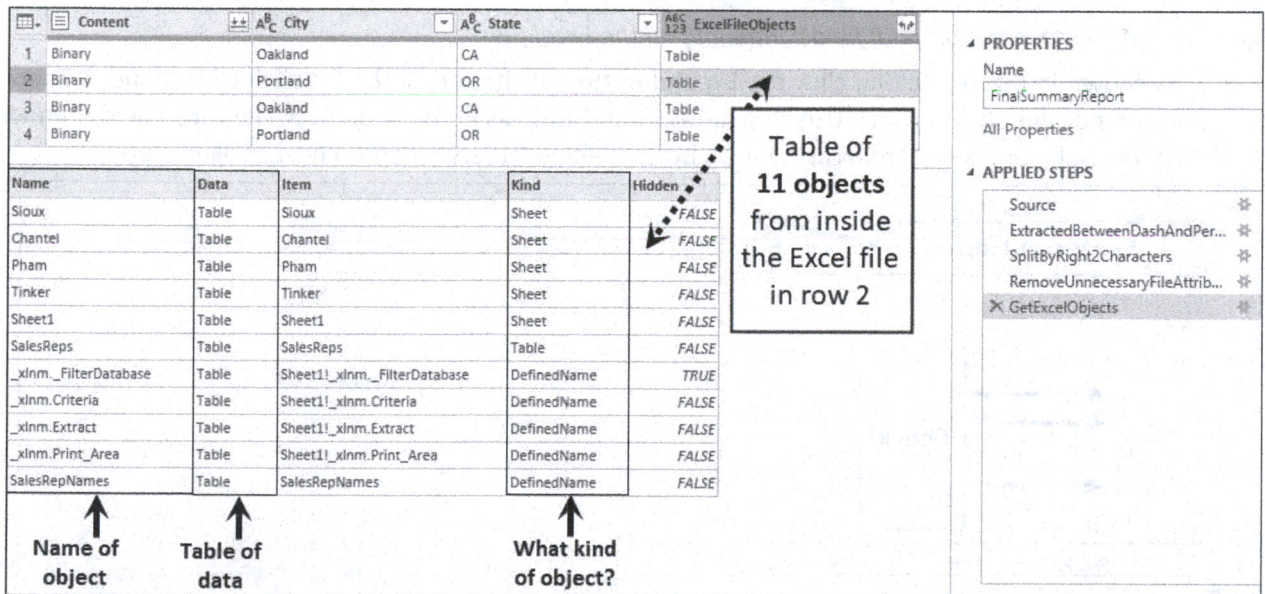

Figure 19.194 *The table of Excel objects in each row allows you to filter to remove unwanted objects.*

Figure 19.194 shows the new field ExcelFileObjects. In each row of this column, the Excel.Workbook function created a table that lists all of the objects that it extracted from the row's Excel file. For example, in the second row, Figure 19.194 shows the 11-row table that the function created. This table has these five fields:

*   **Name:** This column contains the name of the object, including the worksheet name, Sioux, in row 1; the generic sheet name Sheet1 in row 5; the automatic print area name, xlnm.Print_Area, in row 10; and the manually created defined name SalesRepNames in row 11. The Name field is helpful for filtering out objects such as worksheets that begin with the generic text *Sheet*.

- **Data:** This column contains the tables of data, including the sales data tables that you are interested in, in the first four rows.
- **Item:** This is almost identical to the Name column except that it has a sheet name prefix for the automatically created defined names, such as the Sheet1!xlnm.Print_Area item in row 10.
- **Kind:** This column lists the type of object, such as Sheet (worksheet), Table (Excel Table), or Defined Name (automatically and manually created defined names). This field is helpful for filtering out object types that you do not want to import.
- **Hidden:** This column contains a Boolean value to indicate whether an object is hidden, such as FilterDatabase in row 7.

You will use this 11-row table and the three other tables of objects to filter out unwanted objects and import only the sales rep tables of data. For that filtering process, you will need to use the Name, Data, and Kind fields. You will not need the Item or Hidden fields.

> **Note:** When you import data from Excel files, most of the time you do not have all these extra unwanted objects, such as print and filter defined names. But I wanted to put one file in this project that contains all the potential pitfalls that can occur in an Excel file that contains data. Someone might run a quick filter on an Excel file data source like this or set a print range. And when that happens, these objects will show up during the Power Query import process, and you must deal with them.

Once you use the Excel.Workbook function to extract the objects from the file, all the data that you are interested in is in the Data fields in each one of the four tables in the ExcelFileObjects field. The Content field with the original Excel files is therefore not needed. To remove it, follow these steps:

1. As shown in Figure 19.195, right-click the Content field and then click on Remove. Rename the query step **RemovedContentField**.

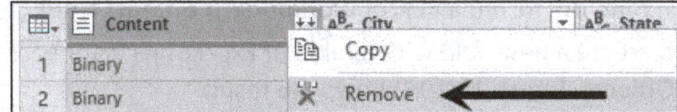

Figure 19.195 *Remove the original field containing all the Excel files.*

2. As shown in Figure 19.196, click the Expand button at the top of the ExcelFileObjects field. Then, in the pop-up box, uncheck Use Original Column Name as Prefix and check the three field names: Name, Data, and Kind. Then click the OK button. Power Query creates a new applied step.

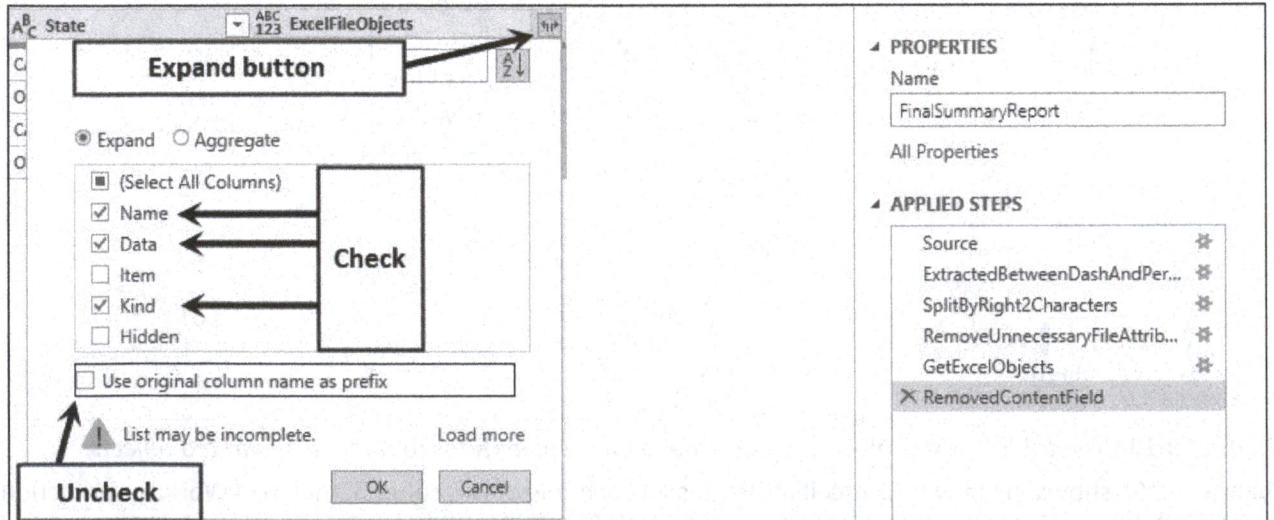

Figure 19.196 *Expand the field that contains the tables that the Excel.Workbook function created.*

3. Rename the new applied step **ExpandedExcelFileObjects**.

4. To change the Name column field name to SalesRep, in the formula bar, click in the last argument of the Table.ExpandTableColumn function and, as shown in Figure 19.197, change the list {"Name", "Data", "Kind"} to **{"SalesRep", "Data", "Kind"}**.

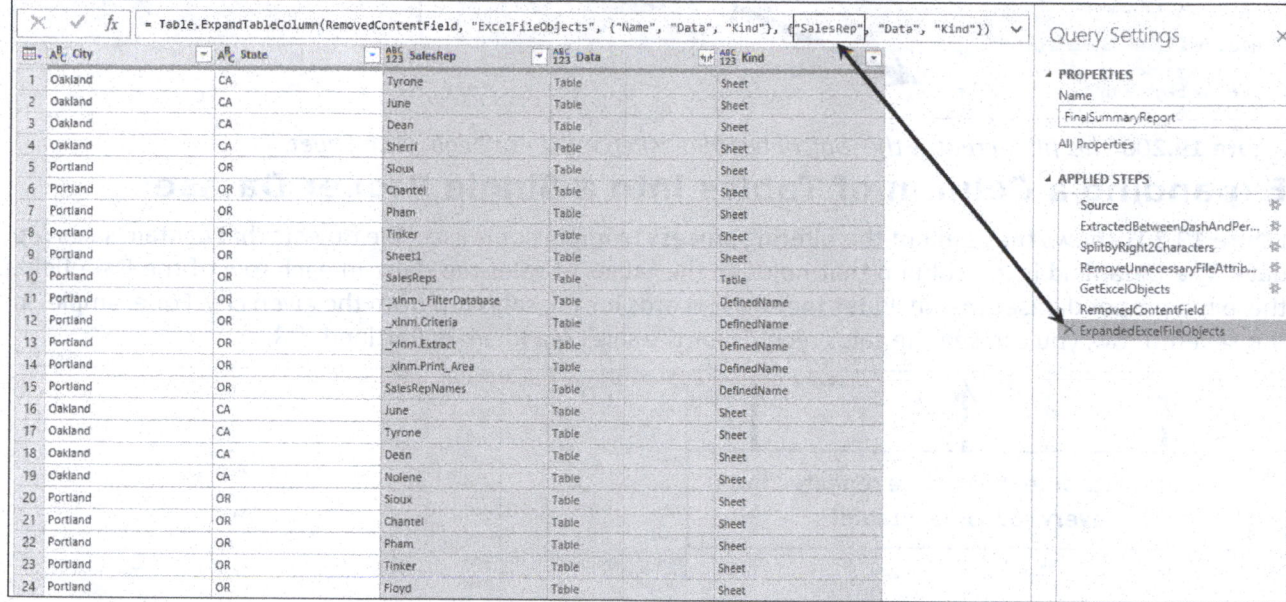

Figure 19.197 *All of the Excel objects are marked with the correct city and state names.*

Filtering to Exclude Excel Objects That You Don't Want

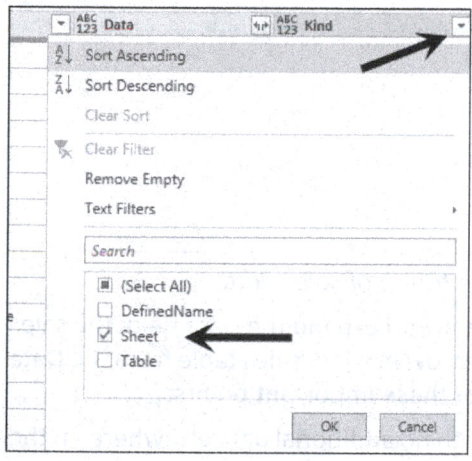

Once you have the table with all the Excel objects, as shown in Figure 19.197, you must create the logical tests that will allow you to exclude objects that you do not want and import objects that you do want. To do so, follow these steps:

1. As shown in Figure 19.198, to filter to include only worksheet objects, click the Sort & Filter dropdown arrow at the top of the Kind field and uncheck everything except Sheet. Click the OK button and rename the query step **KeepSheetKind**.

2. To remove worksheet objects that have a name that begins with the default worksheet name *Sheet*, as shown in Figure 19.199, click the Sort & Filter dropdown arrow at the top of the SalesRep field, hover your cursor over the Text Filters option, and click on Does Not Begin With.

Figure 19.198 *This filter creates the logical test "Kind must equal Sheet."*

3. As shown in Figure 19.200, in the Filter Rows dialog box that appears, type **Sheet** in the Does Not Begin With textbox. Click the OK button and rename the query step **RemoveDefaultSheets**.

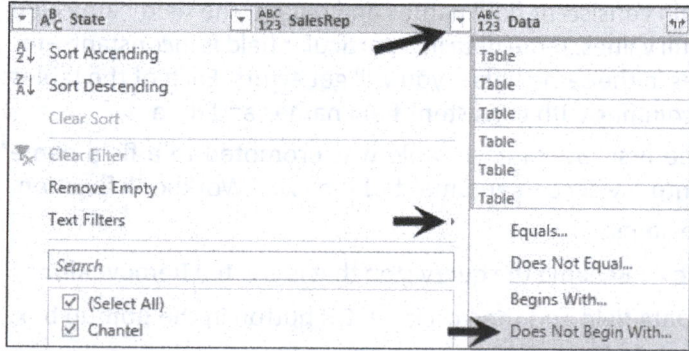
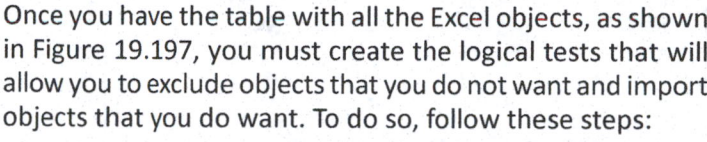

Figure 19.199 *Add a text filter that runs a "does not begin with" logical test.*

Filter Rows

Apply one or more filter conditions to the rows in this table.

◉ Basic   ○ Advanced

Keep rows where 'SalesRep'

| does not begin with ▾ | Sheet ▾ |

[Default worksheets begin with Sheet]

[OK]   [Cancel]

Figure 19.200 This filter creates the logical test "SalesRep must not begin with Sheet."

Expanding a Column of Tables into a Single Proper Dataset

Figure 19.201 shows the result of the filtering process to import only Excel file objects that contain sales rep data. The Data field is the column that holds all the tables of sales rep data. In each row of the Data field, there is a proper dataset that includes the sales records for the sales rep from the given city. For example, in the seventh row, you can see the sales records for the sales rep Pham in Portland, OR.

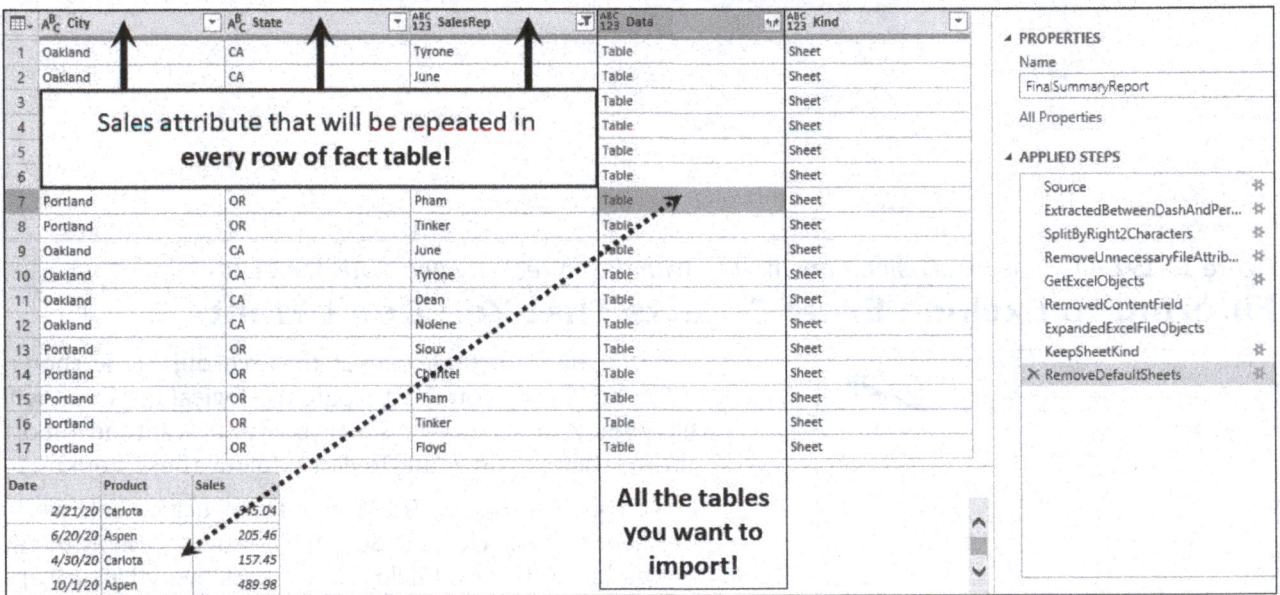

Figure 19.201 The filtering process resulted in a Data field with all the tables of sales data.

An amazing thing about the full FinalSummaryReport table is that when you expand the Data field, the sales record attributes for city, state, and sales rep will be repeated for every row in every sales table from the Data field. Before you combine all the table into a single table, take note of these important points:

- Each worksheet object must contain a single proper dataset with no additional data elsewhere on the sheet; otherwise, the process will not work, and the resulting table will have extra fields containing many null values. Each of the worksheets in this project contains a single proper dataset.

- As you learned in Project 1, in order to be combined into a single table, the tables in the Data field must all have the same structure and must contain consistent field names and data. If the field names are inconsistent, you will get extra fields with null values. If the data in a particular field is inconstant—for example, serial number dates and text dates in the same field—you will get errors. Each of the tables in the Data field for this project has three columns with consistent field names and data.

- For each of the tables in the Data field, the first row of each table was promoted to a field name because of the true value that you placed into the second argument of the Excel.Workbook function.

To create the final sales records table, follow these steps:

1. Right-click the Kind field and then click Remove. Rename the query step that is created **RemoveKind**.

2. Click the Expand button at the top of the Data field and then click the OK button in the pop-up box. Rename the query step that is created **ExpandedSalesTables**.

3. To change the data types for all six resulting fields, select the six fields, click on the Transform tab of the Ribbon, and in the Any Column group, click the Detect Data Type button. Make sure this automatic feature adds the correct data types to the fields. (It usually does.) Rename the query step **AddedDataTypes**.

Figure 19.202 shows the final proper dataset created from the individual sales rep proper datasets from across many worksheets in multiple workbooks.

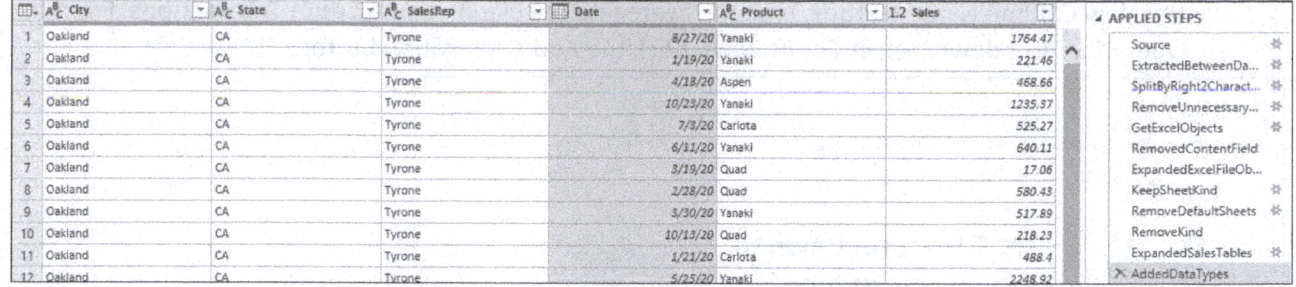

Figure 19.202 *Final single proper dataset with over 1.5 million rows of data.*

Determining Whether to Load to the Data Model or Finish Reporting in Power Query

Figure 19.202 shows the top part of the final sales table, which contains over 1.5 million rows of data. This table has the original three fields from the sales tables—Date, Product, and Sales—and three sales attribute fields created from the file and sheet tab names—City, State, and SalesRep. At this point, you could load the table to the Data Model and create various reports and visualizations. You could also run exactly the same query steps in Power BI Desktop and use the visualizations from that tool. However, because the goal of this project is to create a simple summary table report, in this case you should use Power Query to complete the reporting steps.

To create the table report in Power Query, follow these steps:

1. To convert the Date field to a Year field, select the Date field, click on the Transform tab of the Ribbon, go to the Data & Time Column group, click the Date dropdown arrow, hover over Year, and click on Year. Rename the query step that is created **DateToYear**.

2. To rename the Date field, double-click the Date field name at the top of the column, type **Year**, and press Enter. Rename the query step that is created **NameYearField**.

Using Power Query Group By to Simulate a PivotTable

In a standard PivotTable, you drag one or more fields to the Rows area to create a unique list of criteria for each row in the PivotTable, and then you drag a field to the Values area to make an aggregate calculation based on the row criteria. In Power Query, you can simulate this process by using the Group By feature, which is based on a command that is common in the SQL computer language. The Power Query Group By feature creates a unique list of row header conditions based on one or more fields and then makes aggregate calculations based on the row header conditions. This feature is called Group By because it groups together all the records from the source table based on the row conditions and then uses that smaller subset of grouped records to make an aggregate calculation.

For this project, you need to create a table report that contains a unique list of row conditions from the Year, City, and SalesRep fields. Then you will count the number of transactions and sum the sales based on those conditions. To create the report, follow these steps:

1. Select the Year, City, and SalesRep fields, right-click any one of these fields, and select Group By.

2. In the Group By dialog box that appears, as shown in Figure 19.203, use the dropdown arrows to select fields in the order in which you want the row criteria to appear: Year, City, and SalesRep. In the New Column Name textbox, type the aggregate calculation name **Count Transactions**. From the Operation dropdown, select Count Rows. Click the Add Aggregation button.

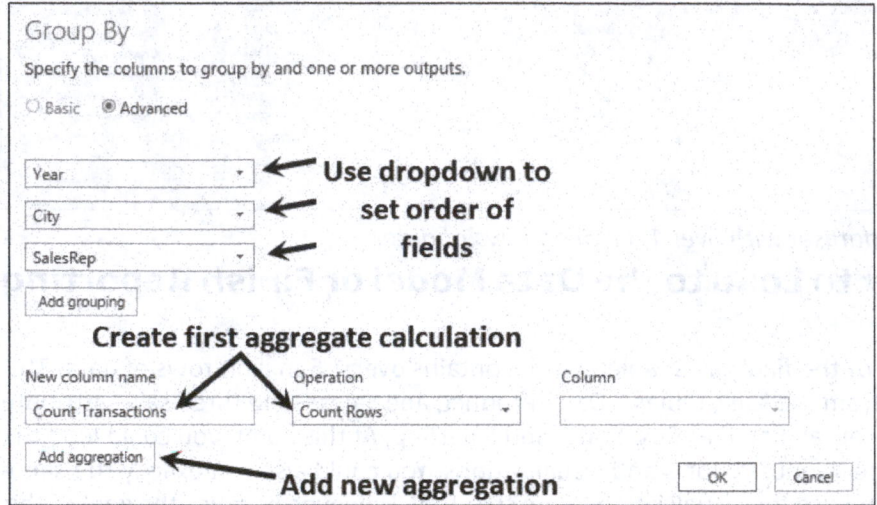

Figure 19.203 *The Group By feature with three row conditions and the Count Transactions aggregate calculation.*

3. As shown in Figure 19.204, for the second aggregation line, in the New Column Name textbox, type **Total Sales**, select Sum from the Operation dropdown, and select Sales from the Column dropdown. Click the OK button. Power Query takes about 20 second to create the report, which is shown in Figure 19.205. Rename the newly added query step **GroupByReport**.

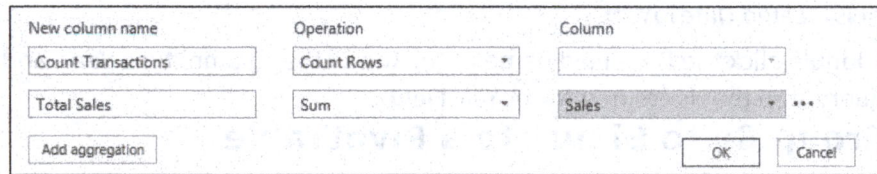

Figure 19.204 *Add the second aggregation in the Group By dialog box.*

	Year	City	SalesRep	Count Transactions	Total Sales
1	2020	Oakland	Tyrone	100589	74301494.79
2	2020	Oakland	June	86768	64299979.71
3	2020	Oakland	Dean	89213	66025799.25
4	2020	Oakland	Sherri	81213	59965281.79
5	2020	Portland	Sioux	85213	63135730.88
6	2020	Portland	Chantel	104213	76852700.74
7	2020	Portland	Pham	74213	55026449.76
8	2020	Portland	Tinker	87200	64068892.73
9	2021	Oakland	June	69200	51073759.26
10	2021	Oakland	Tyrone	102200	75415917.02
11	2021	Oakland	Dean	101190	74514070.78
12	2021	Oakland	Nolene	100010	73949668.51
13	2021	Portland	Sioux	91010	67287108.02
14	2021	Portland	Chantel	99010	73097983.47
15	2021	Portland	Pham	79981	59378521.99
16	2021	Portland	Tinker	87581	64699647.9
17	2021	Portland	Floyd	115581	85277134.48

Figure 19.205 *1.5 million rows grouped to show the number of transactions and total sales.*

Sorting in Power Query

In Chapter 17, when you learned how to sort in the Excel worksheet, you learned how to sort using the Sort dialog box (which does a major sort first) and using the Sort dropdown arrows (which does a major sort last). You saw that it is a bit confusing to use both of those features in a worksheet because they work in opposite ways. In Power Query, sorting is not so confusing because when you have multiple fields to sort, you do it in the most logical way: major sort first (as in the Sort dialog box in Excel). For example, if you want to sort the

Year field and then the City field, you first sort Year and then sort City. In addition, Power Query shows little numbers next to the field names to remind you of the order in which the sort was done.

For your report, you want to sort by the three fields Year, City, SalesRep—in that order. To sort the report by Year, then by City, then by SalesRep and then finalize this report, follow these steps:

1. Use the Sort & Filter dropdown at the top of the Year field to select A to Z.

2. Use the Sort & Filter dropdown at the top of the City field to select A to Z.

3. Use the Sort & Filter dropdown at the top of the SalesRep field to select A to Z.

4. Rename the sorting query step **SortedReport**. Figure 19.206 shows the result of this sorting. Notice the numbers in the field names, which indicate the order in which the sort was performed. The number 1 indicates the major sort.

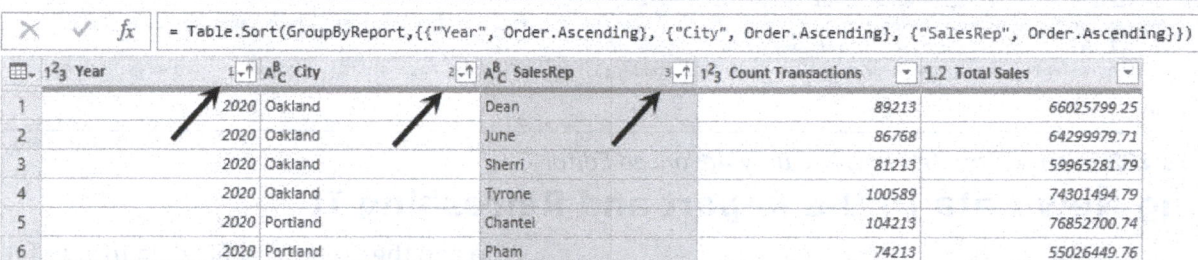

Figure 19.206 *When you sort in Power Query, numbers indicating the sort order appear in the field names.*

5. To load the finished report to the worksheet, use the Close & Load To feature to load the report to cell B2 on the worksheet FinishedTableReport. It will take about 20 seconds to load the table report.

6. After the report is loaded to the worksheet, add Excel worksheet number formatting to the Count Transactions column and the Total Sales column so they look as shown in Figure 19.207.

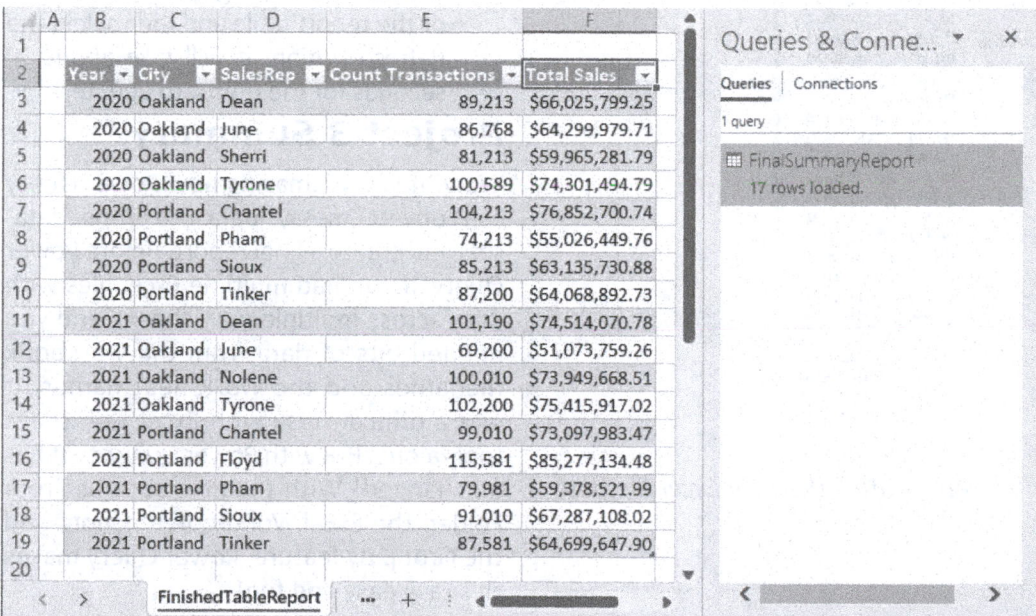

Figure 19.207 *Finished Power Query–generated report with worksheet number formatting added.*

Note: When you create a query with Power Query, you can copy the M code for the query into Power BI Desktop, and the query automatically creates a let expression. You might do this, for example, to repeat the same steps you just performed to create a table report from data that comes from multiple worksheets in multiple Excel files. Figure 19.208 shows the final M code let expression for this project's report in the Advanced Editor. This code will be executed every time you refresh the query. In addition, you can copy and paste this code into the Power Query Advanced Editor in Power BI Desktop to create the same results. Further, if you want the full 1.5 million rows in the Power BI Data Model, you can copy the code, remove the steps after the AddedDataTypes step, remove the comma after AddedDataTypes, place the step name AddedDataTypes after the in keyword, and then click Close & Apply.

```
let
    Source = Folder.Files("C:\Users\mgirvin\Desktop\TheOnlyAppThatMatters\Ch19-Project03\Start"),
    ExtractedBetweenDashAndPeriod = Table.TransformColumns(Source, {{"Name", each Text.BetweenDelimiters(_, "-", "."), type text}}),
    SplitByRight2Characters = Table.SplitColumn(ExtractedBetweenDashAndPeriod, "Name", Splitter.SplitTextByPositions({0, 2}, true),
        {"City", "State"}),
    RemoveUnnecessaryFileAttributeFields = Table.SelectColumns(SplitByRight2Characters,{"Content", "City", "State"}),
    GetExcelObjects = Table.AddColumn(RemoveUnnecessaryFileAttributeFields, "ExcelFileObjects", each Excel.Workbook([Content],true)),
    RemovedContentField = Table.RemoveColumns(GetExcelObjects,{"Content"}),
    ExpandedExcelFileObjects = Table.ExpandTableColumn(RemovedContentField, "ExcelFileObjects", {"Name", "Data", "Kind"},
        {"SalesRep", "Data", "Kind"}),
    KeepSheetKind = Table.SelectRows(ExpandedExcelFileObjects, each ([Kind] = "Sheet")),
    RemoveDefaultSheets = Table.SelectRows(KeepSheetKind, each not Text.StartsWith([SalesRep], "Sheet")),
    RemoveKind = Table.RemoveColumns(RemoveDefaultSheets,{"Kind"}),
    ExpandedSalesTables = Table.ExpandTableColumn(RemoveKind, "Data", {"Date", "Product", "Sales"}, {"Date", "Product", "Sales"}),
    AddedDataTypes = Table.TransformColumnTypes(ExpandedSalesTables,{{"City", type text}, {"State", type text}, {"SalesRep", type
        text}, {"Date", type date}, {"Product", type text}, {"Sales", type number}}),
    DateToYear = Table.TransformColumns(AddedDataTypes,{{"Date", Date.Year, Int64.Type}}),
    NameYearField = Table.RenameColumns(DateToYear,{{"Date", "Year"}}),
    GroupByReport = Table.Group(NameYearField, {"Year", "City", "SalesRep"}, {{"Count Transactions", each Table.RowCount(_),
        Int64.Type}, {"Total Sales", each List.Sum([Sales]), type nullable number}}),
    SortedReport = Table.Sort(GroupByReport,{{"Year", Order.Ascending}, {"City", Order.Ascending}, {"SalesRep", Order.Ascending}})
in
    SortedReport
```

Figure 19.208 *M code from the Power Query Advanced Editor.*

Adding New Data to the Report and Refreshing It

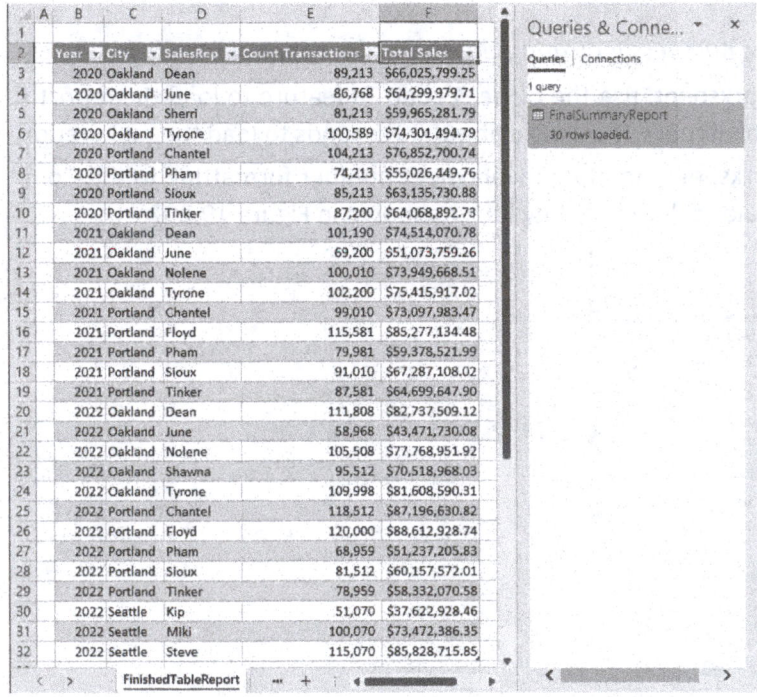

Figure 19.209 *The table report after the new Excel file data is added.*

To add the 2022 Excel file data to your finished report, follow these steps:

1. Copy the three Excel files containing the 2022 data and paste them into the Start folder. In the Queries & Connections task pane, click the Refresh icon or right-click the query or the report table and then select the Refresh option. It will take about 30 seconds for the report to update.

Project 3 Summary

Wow! It is just amazing how Power Query can convert "messy" data into proper datasets and create a final report. Before Power Query, if you had multiple Excel files with data across multiple worksheets, and you needed bits of data from the workbook filenames and the worksheet names, it was a difficult task with Excel worksheet tools alone. But with Power Query, that has all changed! With features such as From Folder, the Excel.Workbook function, and the Group By feature, Power Query makes this task easy and fun!

The key data analysis and power tool takeaways from this project are as follows:

- You can use the From Folder feature to import multiple Excel files and file attributes into the Power Query Editor. This feature allows you to build a solution based on the data in the Excel files, and when you get new files later, you just paste them into the on-premises folder and click Refresh, and the data analysis output updates to reflect the new data.

- You can use Power Query data cleaning and transforming features such as Text Between Delimiter and Split Column By Number of Characters to extract data from imported files.

- The Power Query M code Excel.Workbook function extracts all the objects from a specified external Excel workbook file and delivers to the Power Query Editor a table that lists all the objects and object attributes so that you can choose which objects to import. The table of Excel objects includes these file object attribute fields: Name, Data, Item, Kind, and Hidden. The Data field contains the tables of data from the Excel objects. This is the field that you can expand to combine all tables into a single proper dataset. The Kind field allows you to filter by object type, such as sheet for a worksheet, table for an Excel Table, or defined name for both manually and automatically created defined names. The Name field provides the Excel object names. When the Data field is expanded, these object names are repeated for each row in the table. When you use the From Folder feature to import multiple Excel files, you can extract the objects from each file by using the Excel.Workbook function in a custom column.

- When a field contains table objects that all have the same structure and naming conventions, you can use the Expand button at the top of the field to combine all the tables into a single proper dataset.

- The Power Query Group By feature is similar to a PivotTable in that it can create a unique list of row header conditions based on one or more fields and then make aggregate calculations based on the row header conditions. The Power Query Group By feature can be used to create finished table reports.

- In Power Query, you can sort by using the Sort & Filter dropdown at the top of each field. When you have multiple fields to sort, you perform the major sort first, followed by the minor sorts. For example, if you want to sort the Year field and then the City field, you first sort Year and then sort City. In addition, Power Query shows little numbers next to the field names to remind you of the order in which the sort was done.

Project 4: Combining All Excel Table Data in the Current Workbook File into a Standard PivotTable Report

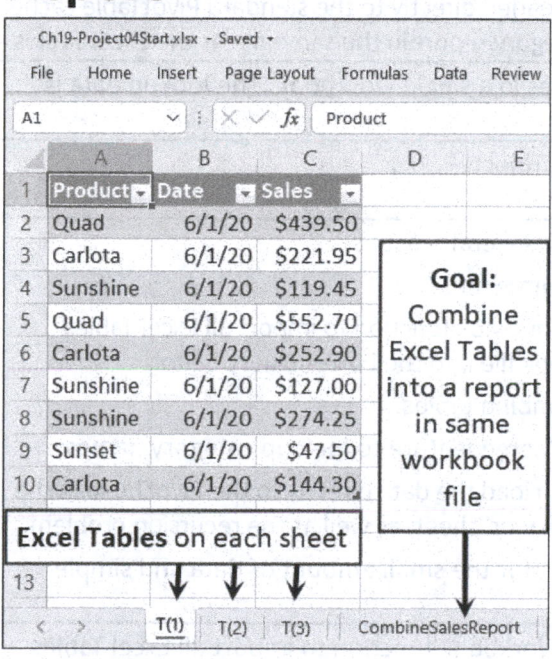

Figure 19.210 *The goal is to dynamically grab all Excel Tables in the current workbook and create a report.*

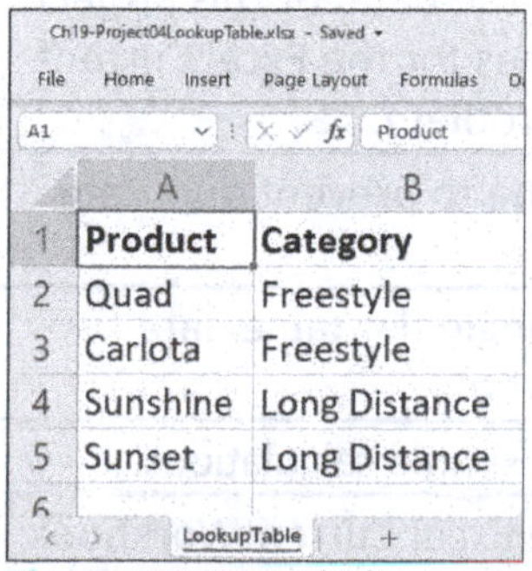

In this project, the goal is to complete the example first shown in Chapter 1 in Figures 1.15 to 1.19. In that example, the goal was to use the M code Excel. CurrentWorkbook function to help combine all Excel Tables in a workbook file into a single proper dataset and then make a PivotTable report. The Excel. CurrentWorkbook function is different from the Excel.Workbook function because whereas the Excel.Workbook function imports all Excel objects from a specified external Excel file, the Excel. CurrentWorkbook function imports only Excel Tables and defined names from within the current Excel workbook file.

Figure 19.210 shows the workbook file you start with in this project. It contains the daily sales data stored in Excel Tables on different worksheets, and your goal is to combine all the Excel Table data into a single table and then make a report on a different worksheet in that same Excel file. The Excel file contains Excel Table objects but no defined name objects.

Figure 19.211 shows a lookup table in a sperate workbook file that you will use in creating the final report.

For this project, there is not much data, and the report calculations are simple. Therefore, you can use Power Query to import the various tables, make the transformations, and then load the final table directly to the PivotTable cache to make your report,

Figure 19.211 *This is a product lookup table in a different workbook file.*

which will look like the one in Figure 19.212. In this project, you will also learn two efficient ways to deal with the infamous Excel.CurrentWorkbook recursion problem.

Category	Product	Sum of Sales ($)
⊟ **Freestyle**	Carlota	1,316.10
	Quad	1,879.65
Freestyle Total		**3,195.75**
⊟ **Long Distance**	Sunset	1,618.95
	Sunshine	1,962.20
Long Distance Total		**3,581.15**
Grand Total		**6,776.90**

Figure 19.212 *A finished report based on all the Excel Table data and the lookup table.*

The 10-Step Data Analysis Process for Project 4

Before you begin creating this project, you need to consider the 10 steps in the data analysis process as they relate to this project. Table 19.6 provides a summary of these 10 steps and how you will carry them out for this project.

Table 19.6 Project 4 Data Analysis Process Summary

Step	How Step Is Carried Out in This Example
1. Determine the goals of the analysis	The goal is to combine all Excel Tables from within the current workbook into a single table and then add a product category field to the table to create a single flat table. The flat table can be loaded directly to the standard PivotTable cache so you can create a product category report in the same file as the Excel Tables.
2. Determine where the data is	The data is stored in Excel Tables in a single workbook. The lookup data is stored in a separate Excel file.
3. Determine how much data exists	There is very little data in this project.
4. Determine which tool or tools to use	Power Query will be perfect for several reasons:
	There is very little data in this project.
	You can use the Excel.CurrentWorkbook function to import all Excel Tables from within the current workbook file into the Power Query Editor.
	You can expand columns to combine tables.
	You can use the Power Query Merge feature to look up category names.
	The Load To option allows you to load the data directly to the PivotTable cache and avoid duplicate tables in the worksheet, as well as the recursion problem.
	A standard PivotTable is perfect for the small amount of data and simple calculations in this project.
5. Import the data	You will use the Excel.CurrentWorkbook function to import all Excel Tables in the current workbook file into the Power Query Editor. You will import the lookup table into the reporting Excel file.
6. Clean and transform the data	Power Query is great for cleaning and transforming the data for this project. You need to make sure to filter out query table names for the Excel.Current-Workbook function import to avoid the recursion problem.
7. Load the data	You will load the data directly to the PivotTable cache to prevent duplicate data and the recursion problem.
8. Create a data model	You will use the Power Query Editor to create the single flat table data model that can be used in the standard PivotTable tool.
9. Create useful information	You can use a standard PivotTable for small data with simple calculations.
10. Update the data model based on new data	You will get a new Excel Table of data each day. The Excel.CurrentWorkbook function is fully dynamic and will automatically detect any new Excel Tables in the current workbook when the query is refreshed.

You may at some point need to go back and change something in your report, and the Power Query process makes it easy to change and update your report.

Importing the Data for Project 4

In this project, you will use the Power Query M code Excel.CurrentWorkbook function to import all the Excel Table and defined name objects (manually and automatically created) from within the current Excel workbook file and deliver to the Power Query Editor a table that lists all the objects and object attributes so that you can chose which objects to import. The Excel.CurrentWorkbook function does not import worksheet objects. It is an argument-less function, which requires that you create a blank query and then type the formula **=Excel. CurrentWorkbook()**.

> **Note:** The *current Excel Workbook file* is the file where a function is being used.

Before the Excel.CurrentWorkbook function was invented, if you had to combine all the data from within the current workbook file, it was a messy manual process, or you had to use VBA code, and it was hard to update the solution when new data arrived. When you store your data in Excel Tables and use the Excel. CurrentWorkbook function, when new data arrives, you simply click Refresh, and your solution updates to reflect the new data.

Consider these important details related to the Excel.CurrentWorkbook function:

- If you are using this function to combine tables of data, the data must be stored in Excel Tables, and those tables must all have the same number of fields and consistent field names and data.

- The Excel Tables can be on different worksheets or on the same worksheet.

- When you use the Excel.CurrentWorkbook function to combine Excel Tables, if you load the query to the worksheet, because the data is loaded as an Excel Table, when you refresh the query, the Excel. CurrentWorkbook function will incorrectly import the query output (an Excel Table) and thereby double the number of records. This is referred to as the *recursion problem*. There are two simple solutions to the recursion problem:

  - Do not load the data to the Excel worksheet. If you are doing your reporting with a standard PivotTable, load the data to the PivotTable cache. If you are doing your reporting with a Data Model PivotTable, load the data to the Data Model.

  - If you want to load the data to the worksheet, add to the Name field a filter that filters out the query name. For example, if the query is named AllfSalesExcelTables, filter the Name field with the "does not equal" logical test for the query name AllfSalesExcelTables.

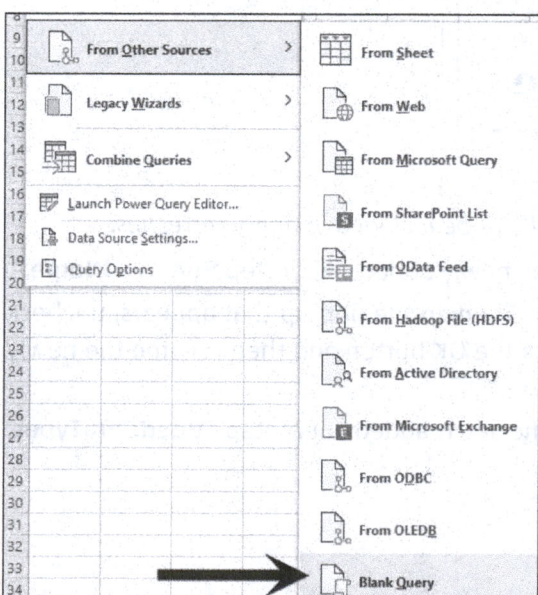

Figure 19.213 *Blank Query in the very last option. If you use this option a lot, it is best to add a button for it to the QAT.*

Now you can begin the project. To start, import the data by following these steps:

1. Open the Excel workbook file Ch19-Project04Start. Look around in the file to become familiar with the data. You should see three Excel Tables with the table names fSales1, fSales2, and fSales3.

   Note: There is also a fourth table that has not been converted to an Excel Table yet. You will do this conversion later on, so you can see how the Excel. CurrentWorkbook function update process works. There are no defined names in the file.

2. In the CombineSalesReport worksheet, select cell B2.

3. To begin a blank query, click on the Data tab in the Excel Ribbon and, in the Get & Transform group, click the Get Data dropdown arrow, hover over the From Other Sources option, and then, at the very bottom of the sub-menu, click on Blank Query (see Figure 19.213).

Note: Figure 5.10 in Chapter 5 shows how to add the Blank Query option to the QAT.

4. In the Power Query Editor window, name the query **AllfSalesExcelTables**, as shown in Figure 19.214.

5. In the formula bar, type the formula **=Excel.CurrentWorkbook()**. Press Enter. A table with the fields Content (listing the Excel Tables) and Name (listing the Excel Table names) appears. Figure 19.214 shows the result. Notice that in this workbook, there are only Excel Table objects. There are no defined names or other objects.

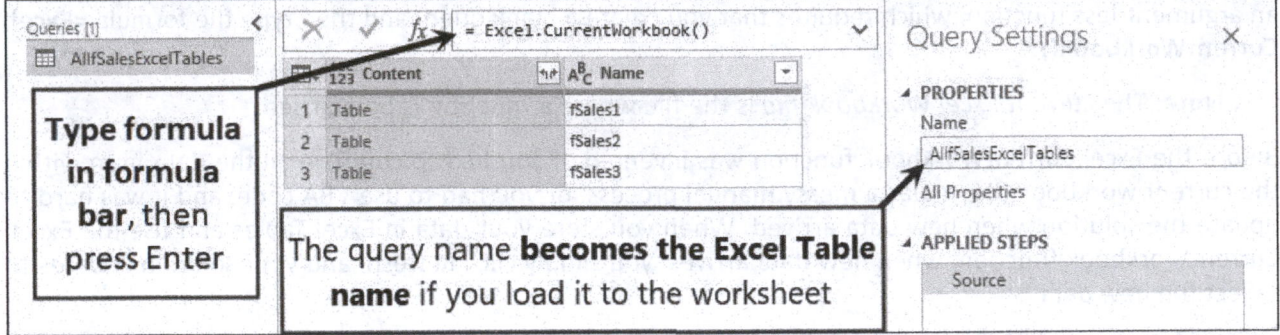

Figure 19.214 *The =Excel.CurrentWorkbook() formula retrieves all Excel Tables from within the current workbook file.*

Filtering Out a Query Name to Prevent the Excel.CurrentWorkbook Recursion Problem

You will avoid the recursion problem in this project by loading the data to the standard PivotTable cache. However, as a safeguard to prevent doubling the records if you later decide to load to the worksheet, follow these steps:

1. Click on the Sort & Filter dropdown at the top of the Name field, hover over Text Fields, and select Does Not Equal.

2. As shown in Figure 19.215, in the Filter Rows dialog box that appears, type the query name **AllfSalesExcelTables** to the right of Does Not Equal. Click the OK button. Name the newly added query step **FilterOutQueryTable**.

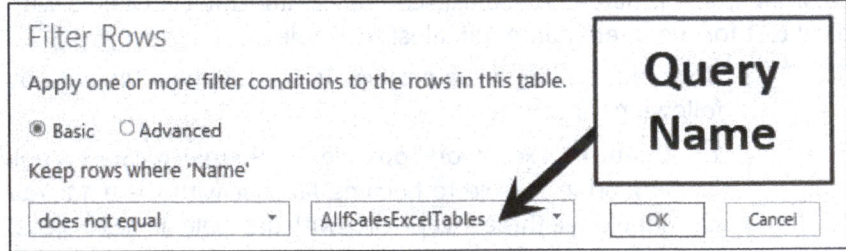

Figure 19.215 *Filter the Name field so that the query output will not be included in query refreshes.*

3. Right-click the Name field and select Remove. Name the newly added query step **RemovedName**.

4. Click the Expand button at the top of the Content field. Then, in the pop-up that appears, uncheck the Use Original Column Name as Prefix checkbox. Click the OK button and then rename the newly added query step **ExpandedExcelTables**.

5. Add the correct data types to the fields and then name the newly added query step **AddedDataTypes**. Figure 19.216 shows the combined Excel Table data.

▦▾	A^Bc Product	▾	▦ Date	▾	1.2 Sales	▾
1	Quad		6/1/20		439.5	
2	Carlota		6/1/20		221.95	
3	Sunshine		6/1/20		119.45	
4	Quad		6/1/20		552.7	
5	Carlota		6/1/20		252.9	
6	Sunshine		6/1/20		127	
7	Sunshine		6/1/20		274.25	
8	Sunset		6/1/20		47.5	
9	Carlota		6/1/20		144.3	
10	Quad		6/2/20		200.5	
11	Carlota		6/2/20		121.95	

PROPERTIES
Name
AllfSalesExcelTables

All Properties

APPLIED STEPS
Source
FilterOutQueryTable   ⚙
RemovedName
ExpandedExcelTables   ⚙
✕ AddedDataTypes

Figure 19.216 *Three Excel Tables combined into one table.*

The Power Query Merge Feature

When you need to perform various types of lookups with a worksheet function, you can use the XLOOKUP function. When you need to perform an exact match lookup in the Data Model, you can use relationships and the RELATED function. In Power Query, when you need to perform an exact match lookup based on one or more fields, you can use the Merge feature. By choosing one or more fields in a left table and one or more related fields in a right table, you can join the tables, pulling data from both tables, from just the left table, or from just the right table.

> **Note:** The terms *merge* (from Power Query) and *join* (from the SQL computer language) are synonyms.

Six types of merges can be done in Power Query, as shown in Figures 19.217 and 19.218.

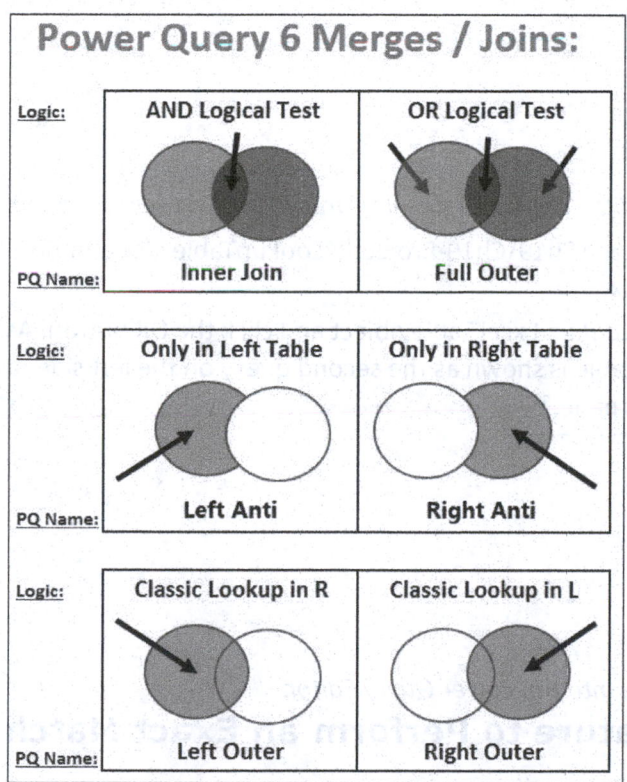

Figure 19.217 *Six types of exact match lookups are possible with Power Query merges/joins.*

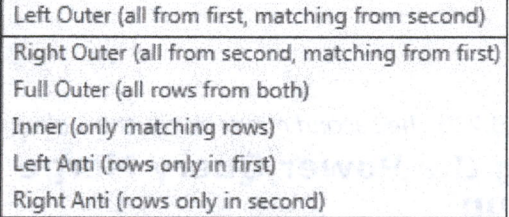

| Left Outer (all from first, matching from second) |
| Right Outer (all from second, matching from first) |
| Full Outer (all rows from both) |
| Inner (only matching rows) |
| Left Anti (rows only in first) |
| Right Anti (rows only in second) |

Figure 19.218 *Dropdown menu of join kinds when you perform a Power Query merge.*

The left outer join merge performs a classic exact match lookup between two fields in two tables. In Figure 19.217, the Venn diagram for the left outer join illustrates that all records will remain on the left, but only matching records will be returned on the right. For example, in the Product field in a fact table, if you use the product name as a lookup value to try to retrieve a product category, all records in the fact table will remain; this is the left side. But when the product lookup value is used to find a match in the Product primary key field of the lookup table, only matching records are returned to the fact table—and categories for products not listed in the fact table are not returned; this is the right side.

Although you will only use the left outer join merge to perform an exact match lookup in this project, some common uses for the other Power Query merge types are listed here:

- **Inner join:** This type of join is used to check whether an item is in both fields. Use this type when you want to compare two lists and keep only items that are in both lists.
- **Full outer join:** This type of join is used to merge all items from both fields. When you use this type of join on tables and some items are not in both fields, you get all records from both tables with null values where a match was not made.
- **Left anti and right anti:** A left anti join is used to check whether an item is only on the left. Use this type of join when you want to compare two lists and keep only items from the left that are not on the right. A right anti join does the same thing but checks whether an item is only on the right.
- **Left outer and right outer:** A left outer join is used to perform a classic worksheet formula exact match lookup from the left side to return one or more fields of data from the right side. A right outer join does the same thing but with the lookup value on the right.

Starting a New Query to Import an Excel Lookup Table

To start a new query from the Power Query Editor window to import an Excel lookup table, follow these steps:

1. To import the lookup table, in the Power Query Editor window, right-click the gray area in the Queries task pane on the left, hover over the new query, hover over the file, and click on Excel Workbook (see Figure 19.219).

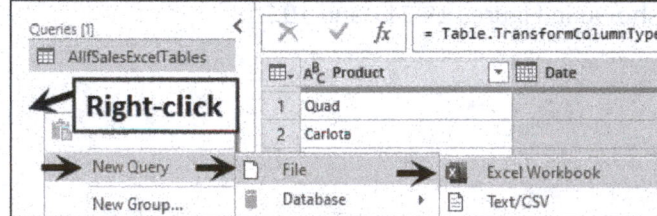

Figure 19.219 *To start a new query in the Power Query Editor, right-click the gray area in the Queries task pane.*

2. Navigate to the file path TheOnlyAppThatMatters\Ch19\Ch19-Project04LookupTable.xlsx and double-click the file to open the Navigate dialog box.

3. In the Navigate dialog box, select the dProductLookup Excel Table object and click the OK button. As shown in Figure 19.220, a two-column lookup table is shown as the second query on the left side of the Power Query Editor window in the Queries pane.

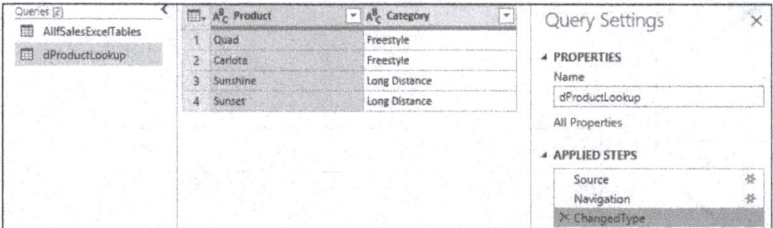

Figure 19.220 *The second query brings the lookup table into the Power Query Editor.*

Using the Power Query Merge Feature to Perform an Exact Match Lookup

To perform an exact match lookup, follow these steps:

1. To add to the fact table a new field for the product category, as shown in Figure 19.221, select the AllfSalesExcelTables query in the Queries task pane and then, in the Home tab of the Ribbon, go to the Combine group and click the Merge Queries button.

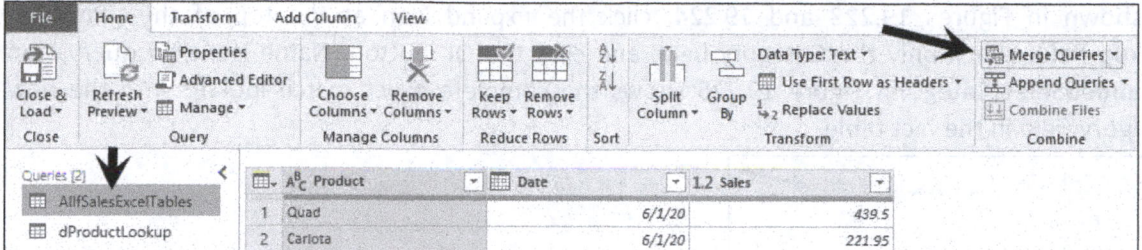

Figure 19.221 *To look up the product category, select the fact table and click the Merge Queries button.*

2. In the Merge dialog box that appears, complete these five steps, as shown in Figure 19.222:

- a. In the top of the dialog box, select the Product field in the AllfSalesExcelTables query. This table is the top table, or left table. This Product field contains the lookup value.

- b. From the dropdown in the middle of the dialog box, select the lookup table dProductLookup. This table is the bottom table, or right table.

- c. Select the Product field in the dProductLookup table. This Product field is the primary key where the lookup value is matched.

- d. Under Join Kind, from the dropdown select Left Outer (All from First, Matching from Second).

- e. Click the OK button.

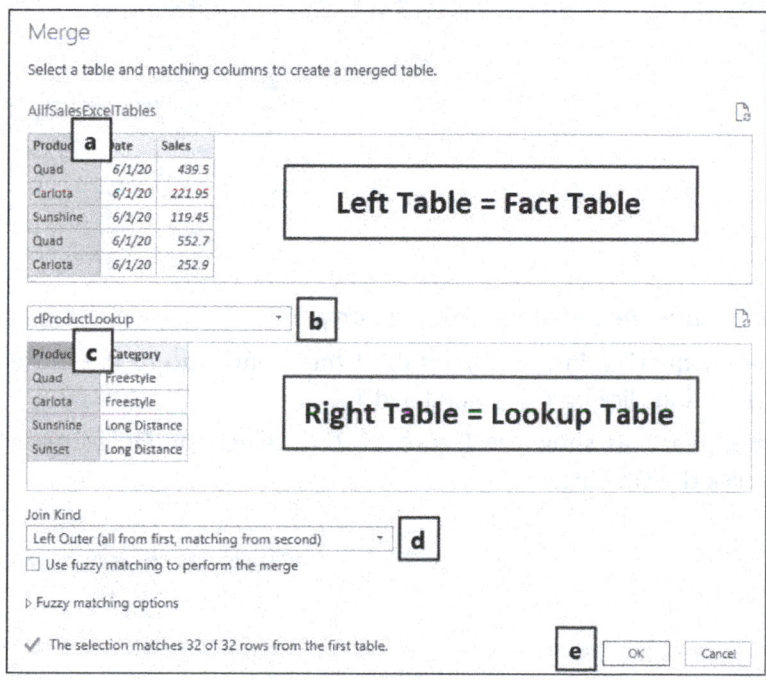

Figure 19.222 *Five steps to perform a left outer join with the Merge feature.*

3. Name the new query step **MergeLookupCategory**. Figure 19.223 shows the result of the merge.

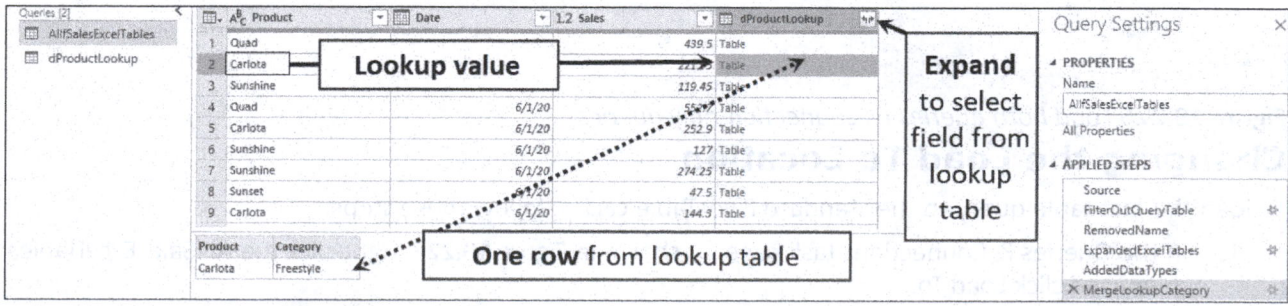

Figure 19.223 *The lookup value helps return a one-row table. The Expand button allows you to select retrieved values.*

4. As shown in Figures 19.223 and 19.224, click the Expand icon at the top of the dProduct-Lookup field, check only the Category field, and click the OK button. Name the new query step **ExpandedSelectCategory**. Figure 19.225 shows the complete exact match lookup with the new Category field in the fact table.

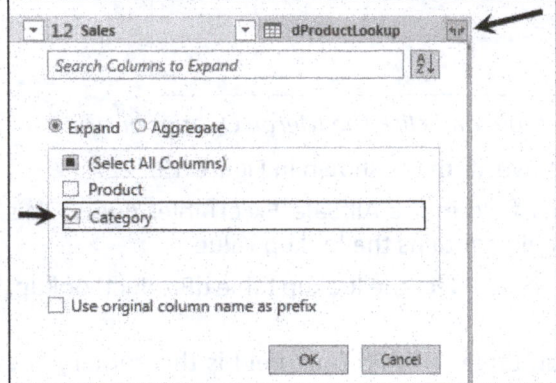

Figure 19.224 *Select the field that contains the values you want to retrieve.*

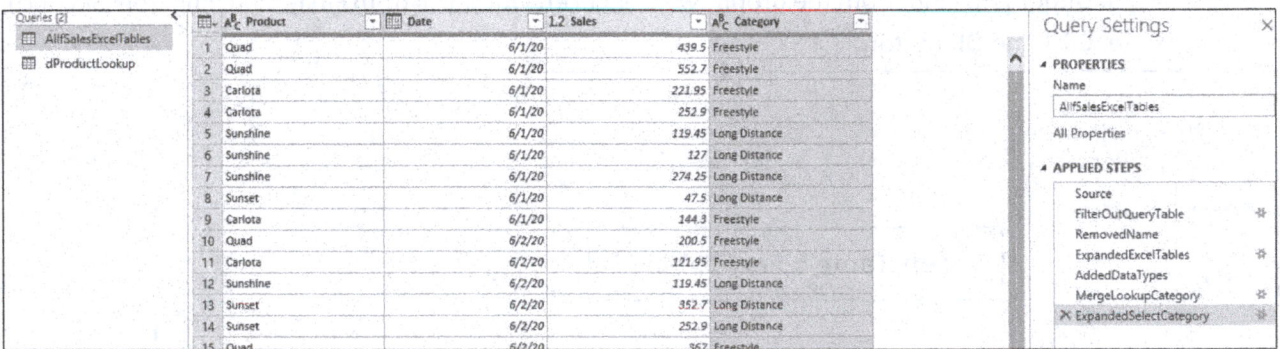

Figure 19.225 *Using the Power Query Merge feature, the Category lookup is complete.*

5. To load both queries as connection-only queries, in the Home tab of the Ribbon, go to the Close group, click the Close & Load dropdown, and click on Close and Load To.

6. In the Import Data dialog box that appears, as shown in Figure 19.226, select the Only Create Connection option button and then click the OK button.

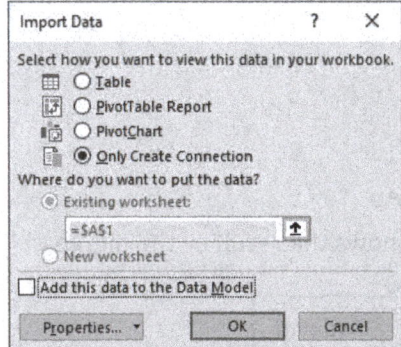

Figure 19.226 *Load both queries as connection-only queries.*

Changing the Load To Location

To load the fact table query to the standard PivotTable cache, follow these steps:

1. In the Queries & Connections task pane, as shown in Figure 19.227, right-click the AllfSalesExcelTables query and click Load To.

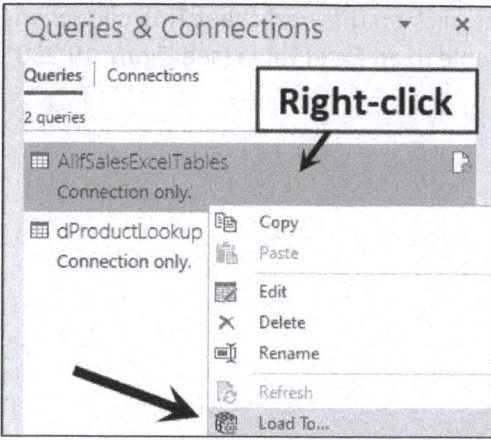

Figure 19.227 *Right-click the fact table query and then click Load To.*

2. In the Import Data dialog box that appears, as shown in Figure 19.228, select the PivotTable Report option button and the Existing Worksheet option button. Then click in cell B2 on the worksheet CombineSalesReport. Click OK in the Import Data dialog box.

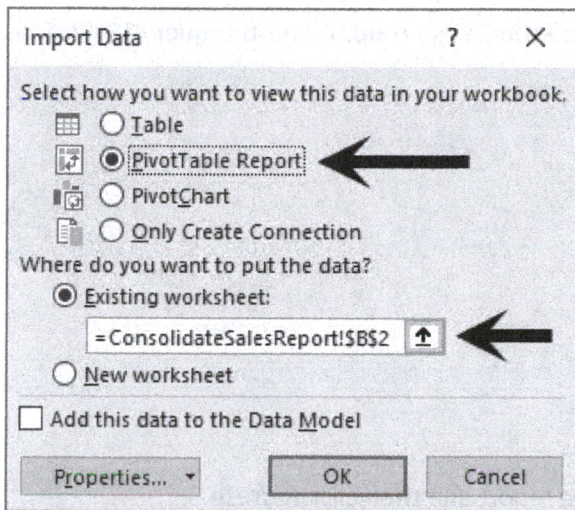

Figure 19.228 *Load the fact table data to the PivotTable cache.*

3. Create a category and product sales report like the one shown in Figure 19.229 by using the PivotTable Fields task pane. Notice that the flat data model table that was loaded to the PivotTable cache has 32 rows of data.

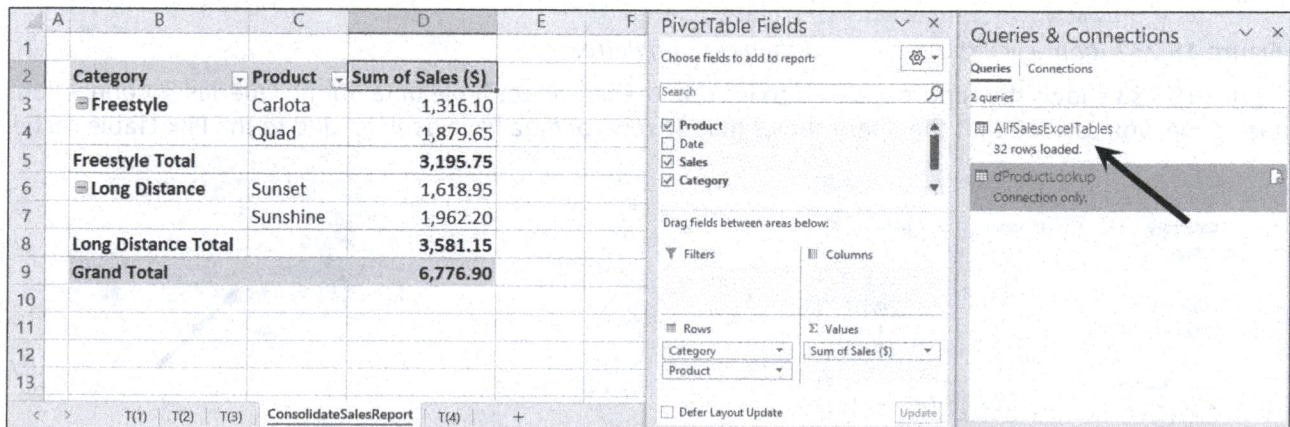

Figure 19.229 *Create the category and product sales report based on the combined 32-row table.*

4. To add a new Excel Table of daily sales records to the report, click on the worksheet T(4), click in one cell in the proper dataset, and press Ctrl+T to convert the table to an Excel Table (see Figure 19.230). Click the OK button in the Create Table dialog box.

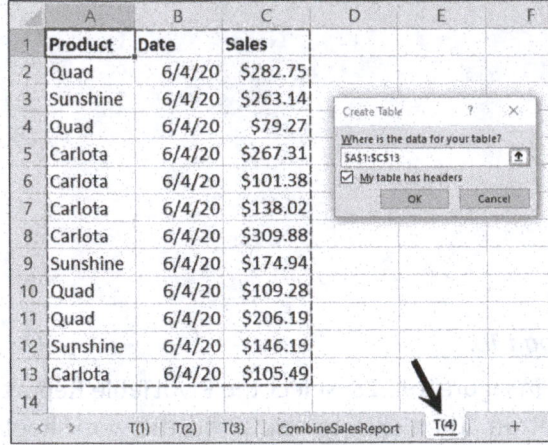

Figure 19.230 *Convert the proper dataset on the worksheet T(4) to an Excel Table.*

5. In the Table Design tab of the Excel Ribbon, in the Properties group, name the query **fSales4**. as shown in Figure 19.231.

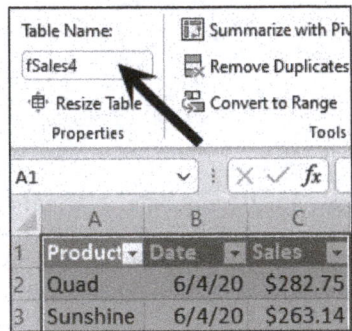

Figure 19.231 *Name the new Excel Table.*

6. As shown in Figure 19.232, right-click the PivotTable report and then click Refresh.

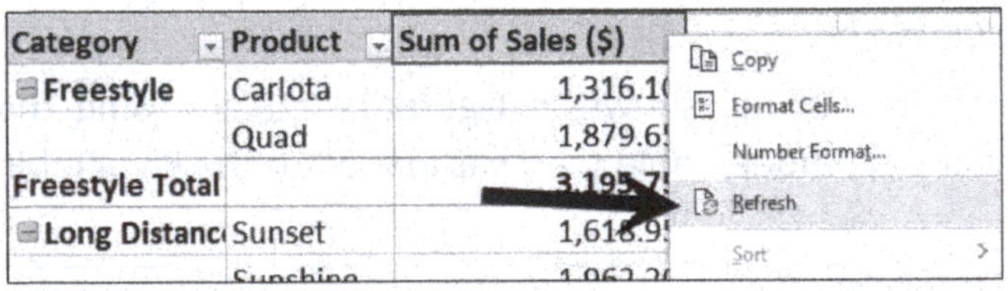

Category	Product	Sum of Sales ($)	
⊟Freestyle	Carlota	1,316.1(	▢ Copy
	Quad	1,879.6!	▣ Format Cells...
Freestyle Total		**3,195.7!**	Number Format...
⊟Long Distanc	Sunset	1,618.9!	▣ Refresh
	Sunshine	1,962.2(	Sort >

Figure 19.232 *Right-click the report and then click on Refresh.*

Figure 19.233 shows the report updated to include the new Excel Table data. In the Queries & Connections task pane, you can see that the query shows that 44 rows of data have been loaded to the PivotTable cache.

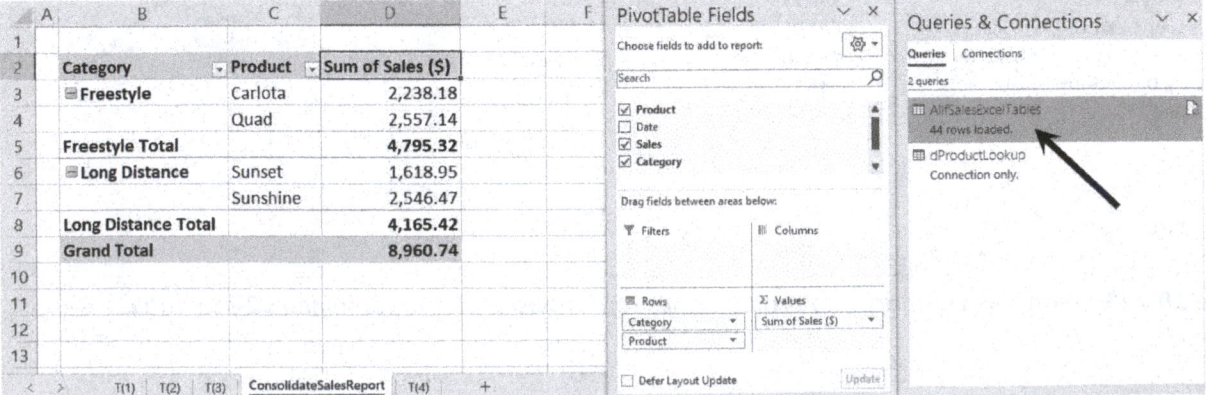

Figure 19.233 *The Excel.CurrentWorkbook function adds the new data to the report.*

Figure 19.234 shows that if you open the AllfSalesExcelTables query, the first step of the query shows all four tables. You can refresh this reporting system each day when you add a new Excel Table to the workbook. It's an amazing solution!

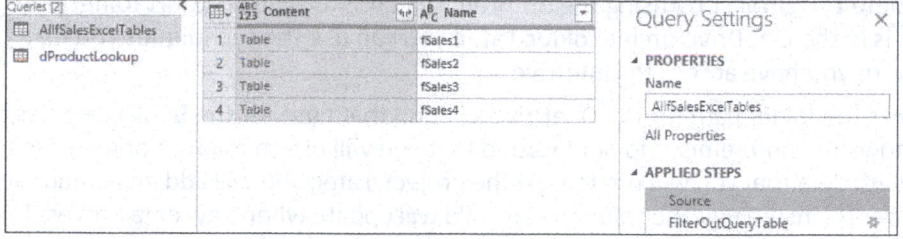

Figure 19.234 *After you refresh, the first step in the query shows that there are now four Excel Tables.*

Project 4 Summary

The key data analysis and power tool takeaways from this project are as follows:

- The Power Query M code Excel.CurrentWorkbook function imports all the Excel Table and defined name objects (manually and automatically created) from within the current Excel workbook file and delivers to the Power Query Editor a table that lists all the objects and object attributes so that you can chose which objects to import. The *current Excel Workbook file* is the file where a function is being used. This function does not import worksheet objects. If you want to import all your data into the Power Query Editor, your data must be stored in Excel Tables. Excel.CurrentWorkbook is an argument-less function, which requires that you create a blank query and then type the formula =**Excel. CurrentWorkbook()**. If you need to load the resulting query to the worksheet, to prevent recursion, you must filter the Name field to exclude the query name. When you load the query directly to the PivotTable cache or the Data Model, you avoid the recursion problem.

- You can start a blank query in Power Query by clicking the Data tab in the Excel Ribbon, going to the Get & Transform group and clicking Get Data, hovering over the From Other Sources option, and clicking on Blank Query. If you use this option often, it would be a good idea to add a Blank Query button to the QAT, as demonstrated in Chapter 5.

- In Power Query, when you need to perform an exact match lookup based on one or more fields, you can use the Merge feature. By choosing one or more fields in a left table and one or more related fields in a right table, you can join the tables, pulling data from both tables, from just the left table, or from just the right table. In this project, you learned how to create a left outer join merge to perform a classic exact match lookup to retrieve a category name based on a product name.

Project 5: Using Power Query M Code to Fix Inconsistent Datasets from Multiple Excel Files So They Can Be Combined

Sometimes when you are collaborating on projects and datasets are coming from multiple people, the datasets you get cannot be combined into a single fact table due to inconsistencies. If the inconsistent data involves things like blank columns in the datasets or inconsistent field names, both of which prevent you from combining tables into a single proper dataset, in order to clean and transform the data with Power Query, you probably need to write M code.

> **Note:** Because you will be writing M code in this project, it might be helpful to review Chapter 18, which has several sections that cover the basics of M code.

In this project, you will learn how to write M code for complex data transformation tasks, and you will learn about many M code functions, concepts, and techniques, including how to get the Power Query user interface to write most of the code for you. You will be given a sales discount lookup table that you will have to use to calculate a net sales amount from the sales amounts given. This will involve performing an approximate match lookup in Power Query. To perform approximate match lookups using worksheet formulas, you use the XLOOKUP function. However, Power Query has no approximate match lookup functions, and you have to use M code formulas to do approximate match lookups.

Also in this project, you will learn how to use Power Query to import data files from OneDrive, Microsoft's online file-sharing service. For organizations that have Microsoft 365 Enterprise edition, OneDrive is a great way to share files and do collaborative work. Since you will not have access to the OneDrive location that I show in the book, you can complete this project by using the on-premises Ch19-Project05\Start folder path that contains the same data that is in the OneDrive online folder. Later, you can use the techniques you learn about OneDrive in situations where you have access to OneDrive.

The left side of Figure 19.235 shows the folder path for the OneDrive location that I use for the book examples, and the right side of the figure shows the on-premises folder location that you will use to follow along. In each folder, there are three Excel files with data that you will use to start the project. Later, you will add an additional file, named Seattle.xlsx, to this folder to ensure that the solution you build will update when new data arrives. To make the complexities of this project easier to deal with, you will use small datasets for this project.

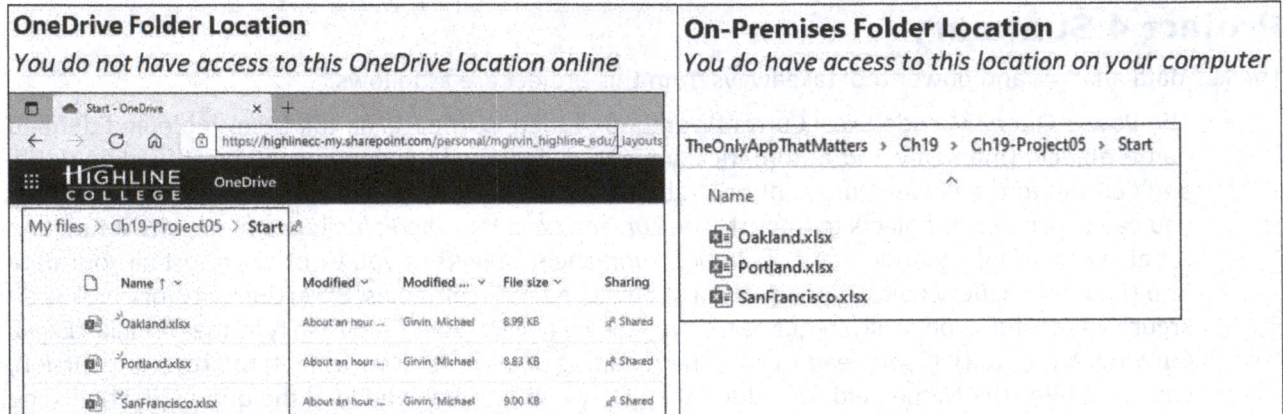

Figure 19.235 *Excel files that must be imported using Power Query.*

Figure 19.236 shows the four datasets that you will use in this project and lists the problems with each dataset. Each of the datasets is stored in a separate Excel file, on a worksheet with no other data besides the three columns of data, with a sheet tab city name; none of the datasets are stored in Excel Table objects. Further, although the field names may be spelled incorrectly, you will always get the three fields Date, Product, and Sales—in that order.

Oakland Data Set in Oakland.xlsx			Portland Data Set in Portland.xlsx			San Francisco Data Set in SanFrancisco.xlsx			Seattle Data Set in Seattle.xlsx		
Date	Product	Units	Date	Prodct	Sales	Date	Produtc	Sales	Date	Product	Sales
20210915	Quad	994.42	20210915	Aspen	149.32	20210915	Yanaki	851.42	20210915	Carlota	15.3
20210916	Quad	989.2	20210916	Aspen	963.25	20210916	Yanaki	411.05	20210916	Carlota	1176.36
20210917	Quad	283.18	20210917	Aspen	11.28	20210917	Yanaki	348.75	20210917	Carlota	816.42
20210918	Quad	1008.84	20210918	Aspen	611.16	20210918	Yanaki	315.87	20210918	Carlota	285.07
20210919	Quad	42.85	20210919	Aspen	165.57	20210919	Yanaki	1065.35	20210919	Carlota	561.73
20210920	Quad	1124.49	20210920	Aspen	219.25	20210920	Yanaki	79.91	20210920	Carlota	730.35
20210921	Quad	858.89	20210921	Aspen	504.32	20210921	Yanaki	1114.04	20210921	Carlota	507.23
Problems:			**Problems:**			**Problems:**			**Problems:**		
Blank Columns			Misspell field names			Blank Columns			Spaces at end of field names		
Wrong field names			ISO Dates are Text			Misspell field names			ISO Dates are Text		
ISO Dates are Text						ISO Dates are Text					

Figure 19.236 *Tables in the Excel files are not proper datasets and cannot be combined unless you fix them.*

In this project, you will have to use M code to solve the following problems:

- Remove blank columns.
- Create consistent field names.
- Use the city name from each worksheet in a new field named City.
- Combine all proper datasets into one table.
- Create serial number dates from ISO dates (YYYYMMDD).
- Create a Net Sales field based on a discount lookup table and the original Sales field.

Figure 19.237 shows what the final single proper dataset should look like.

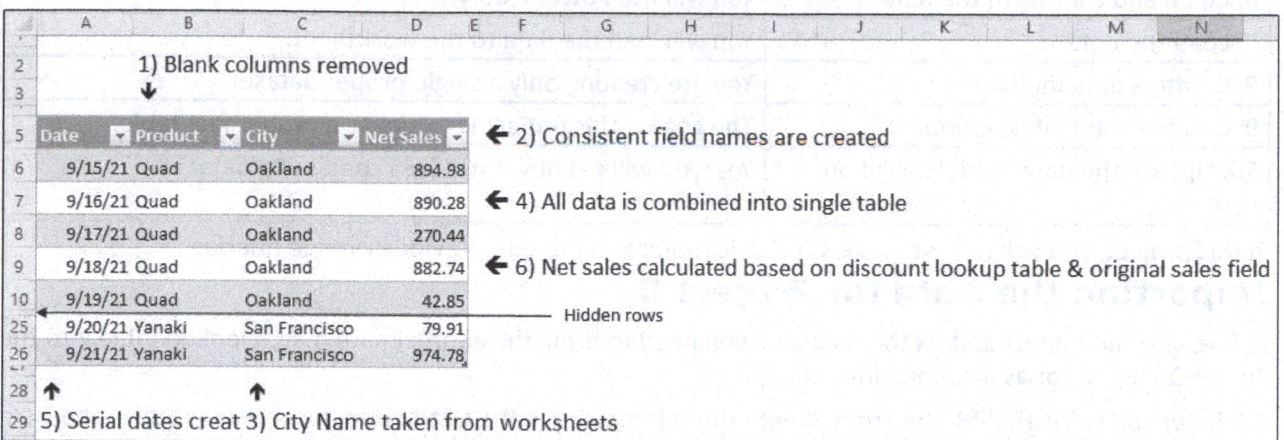

Figure 19.237 *The goal is to create this single proper dataset (the fact table) from multiple improper datasets.*

In this project, you will learn these important M code formula techniques:

- How to do an exact match two-way lookup
- How to buffer a table that is used in another query to reduce calculation time
- How to use the Power Query user interface to write M code that you can use in custom column formulas
- How to create custom function with defined variables
- How to do an approximate match lookup

The 10-Step Data Analysis Process for Project 5

Before you begin creating this project, you need to consider the 10 steps in the data analysis process as they relate to this project. Table 19.7 provides a summary of these 10 steps and how you will carry them out for this project.

Table 19.7 Project 5 Data Analysis Process Summary

Step	How Step Is Carried Out in This Example
1. Determine the goals of the analysis	You will import worksheet datasets from individual Excel files, convert each improper dataset into a proper dataset, add a new field for the city name, combine the tables into a single fact table, convert ISO text dates to serial number dates, and create a net sales field using approximate match lookup.
2. Determine where the data is	The data is in a shared folder on OneDrive and is also available in an on-premises folder.
3. Determine how much data exists	There is a very small amount of data.
4. Determine which tool or tools to use	Power Query is a good tool for this project for several reasons:
	You can import Excel file data using the From SharePoint Folder option and the Excel.Workbook function.
	You can create an M code custom column formula to remove blank columns and fix inconsistent field names so that tables can be combined.
	You can create an M code custom column approximate match lookup formula by using the Table.Buffer function and a custom function with defined variables.
	You can convert ISO dates to serial number dates by using the date data type.
5. Import the data	You will use Power Query.

6. Clean and transform the data	You will use Power Query.
7. Load the data	You will load the data to the worksheet.
8. Create a data model	You are creating only a single proper dataset.
9. Create useful information	The goal of this project is to create a proper fact table.
10. Update the data model based on new data	Yes, you will get new Excel files containing data.

In this project, you will run into issues that will require you to edit previously made queries.

Importing the Data for Project 5

Before you can import and fix the datasets, you need to bring the approximate match lookup table into the Power Query Editor as a connection-only query.

As shown in Figure 19.238, the From Sheet button is located in the Get & Transform Data group in the Data tab of the Excel Ribbon. This button allows you to bring Excel Tables, defined names, or dynamic spilled arrays from a worksheet in the current workbook into the Power Query Editor. This button cannot, however, bring a worksheet object into the Power Query Editor. The keyboard shortcut for the From Sheet button is Right-click key, G. This is a succession keyboard shortcut, which means you must tap the Right-click key, then tap the G key. If you want to use this keyboard shortcut to bring a defined name from a worksheet in the current workbook into the Power Query Editor, you must have the cells in the worksheet that are part of the defined name highlighted. For Excel Tables or dynamic spilled arrays, this keyboard shortcut works if you have the full object selected or just a single cell within the object.

> **Note:** For a reminder of what the Right-click key is and where you can find it, see Figure 6.1 in Chapter 6.

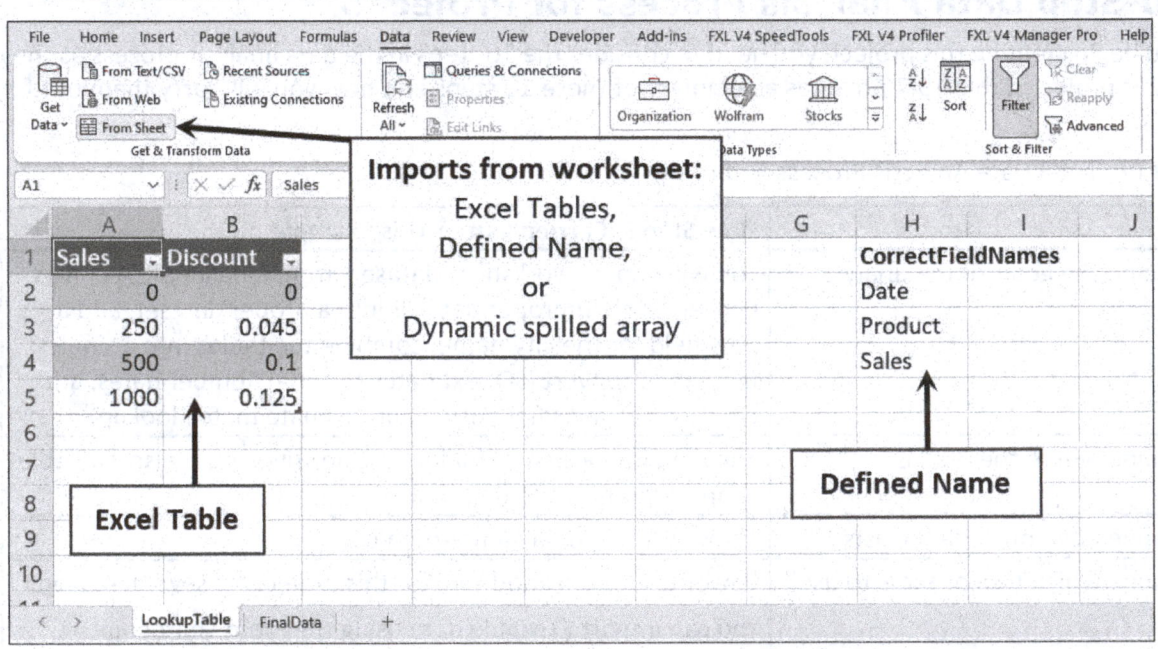

Figure 19.238 *The From Sheet button brings data from a worksheet into the Power Query Editor.*

> **Note:** For this project, you will use the file Ch19-Project05Start.xlsx to import the OneDrive data. This file includes the lookup table shown in Figure 19.238.

To complete this project, follow these steps:

1. Open the Excel file Ch19-Project05Start.xlsx.

2. As part of the proper due diligence you should always do when working with a new data file, look around and see what is in the file. Notice that on the worksheet LookupTable, there is a lookup table that is an Excel Table object named dSalesDiscount. There is also a defined name object named CorrectFieldNames that contains the correct field names in the range H2:H5.

3. To bring the approximate match lookup table into the Power Query Editor, click in one cell in the lookup table and then, in the Data tab of the Excel Ribbon, in the Get & Transform group, click the From Sheet button. (Or you can use the keyboard shortcut Right-click key, G.)

4. When the Power Query Editor window opens, notice that the From Sheet button has accomplished the goal of bringing the lookup table into the Power Query Editor. Click on the Source applied step to reveal the M code that Power Query created for this step in the formula bar (see Figure 19.239).

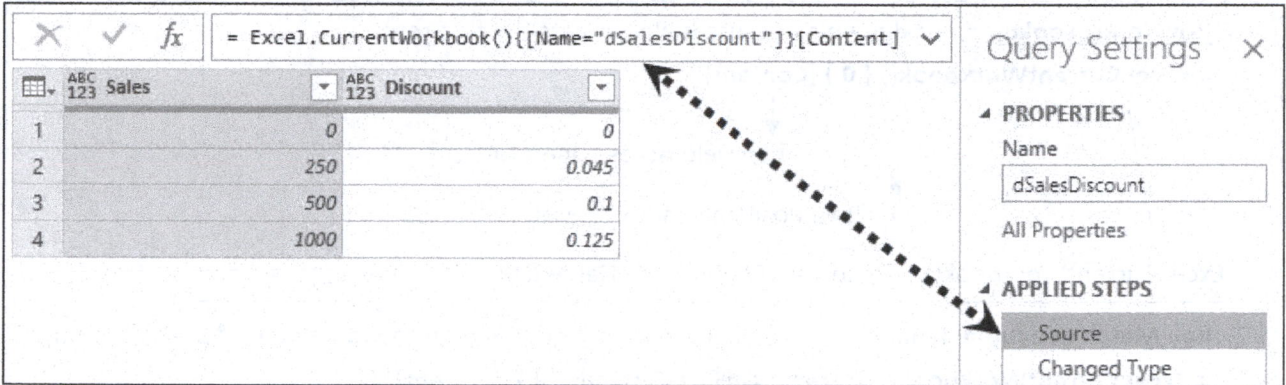

Figure 19.239 *This is the M code formula that brought the Excel Table dSalesDiscount into the Power Query Editor.*

The name of the query created here, dSalesDiscount, is perfect because you will load this as a connection-only query. But how did Power Query bring the table into the Power Query Editor? By clicking on the Source step, you can see in the formula bar that Power Query used the Excel.CurrentWorkbook() function. The full formula to bring the table into the Power Query Editor is:

```
= Excel.CurrentWorkbook(){[Name="dSalesDiscount"]}[Content]
```

Using a Power Query M Code Exact Match Two-Way Lookup

What does the M code listed after the Excel.CurrentWorkbook() function in the formula above mean? Think about what the Excel.CurrentWorkbook() function delivers. As you learned in Project 4, the Excel.CurrentWorkbook() function is programed to deliver a table that contains all the Excel Tables and defined names in the current workbook. Figure 19.239 shows what the Source step formula would deliver if you removed all the M code after the Excel.CurrentWorkbook() function. As you can see, a table is delivered with the two Excel file objects from your workbook. If the goal is to retrieve just one of the table objects from this table, then the formula must perform an *M code exact match two-way lookup*, where the row position and the column position are determined to retrieve the value from the intersecting cell.

Back in Example 9 in Chapter 14, you learned how to use the worksheet function XLOOKUP to do a two-way lookup. In that example, you had to select a row position and a column position to look up the intersecting tax amount. In this Power Query example, you must perform an exact match two-way lookup by selecting a row position and a column position so that you can retrieve the table object. As you will see shortly, these formula elements were used after the Excel.CurrentWorkbook function to get the row and column positions:

- **Row position:** {[Name="dSalesDiscount"]}
- **Column position:** [Content]

Figure 19.240 shows the Power Query M code syntax that is used in this exact match two-way lookup formula.

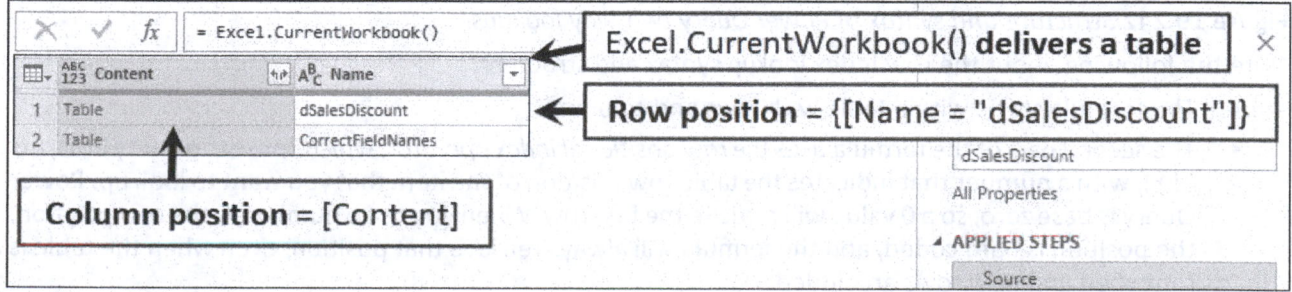

Figure 19.240 *The Excel.CurrentWorkbook() function returns a table of Excel objects.*

As shown in Figure 19.241, there are two types of M code exact match two-way lookups:

- **Row index lookup:** This type of lookup is used when you want to hard code the row position into the formula.
- **Key match lookup:** This type of lookup is used when you want a dynamic row position based on a lookup value that will be matched against a primary key field that contains a unique list. The key match lookup formula is the one used by the Excel.CurrentWorkbook function.

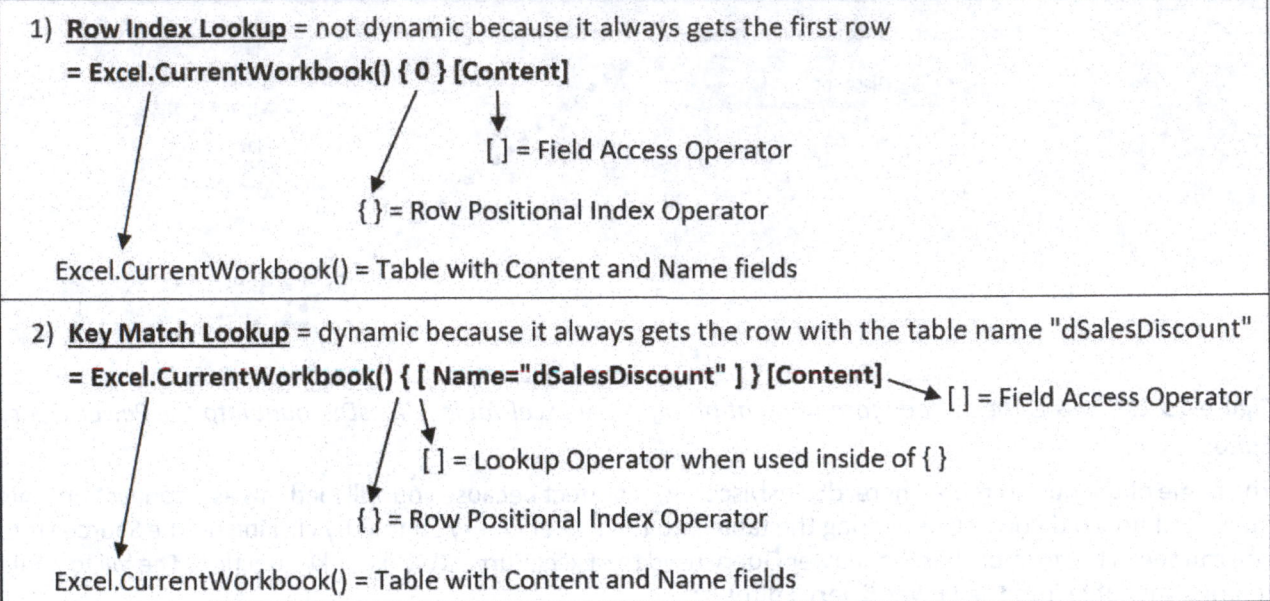

Figure 19.241 *Syntax for the two types of M code exact match two-way lookups.*

Figure 19.242 shows the syntactical structure for the two types of exact match two-way lookup formulas.

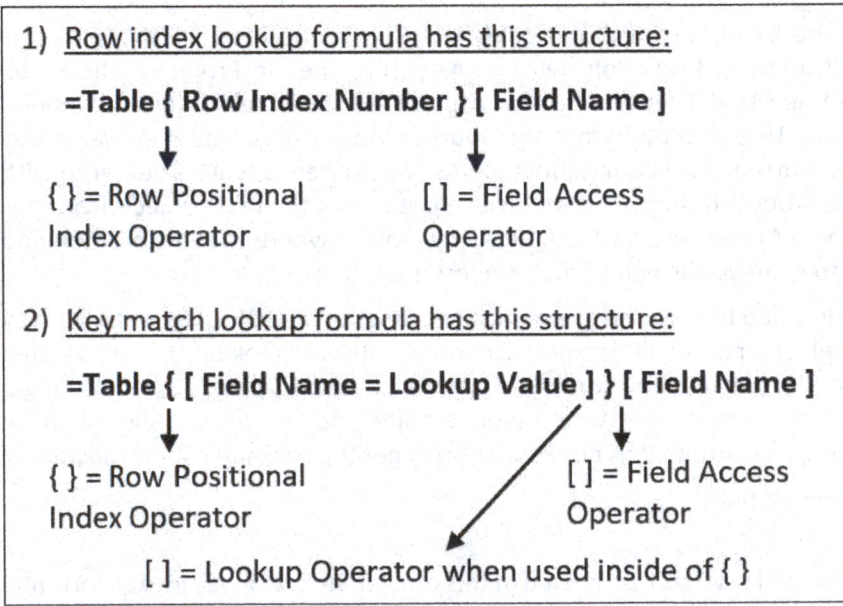

Figure 19.242 *Structure and syntax of Power Query two-way lookups.*

Note the following about the row index lookup syntax and structure:

- The formula starts with a table with rows and columns.
- The second part of the formula uses the *row positional index operator*, which consists of curly brackets ({ }), with a number that indicates the table row position of the item that you want to look up. Power Query is base zero, so a 0 value will retrieve the first row. When you use a number as the row position, the position is hard coded, and the formula will always retrieve that position, even when the table is refreshed and new rows are added.

- The third part of the formula uses the *field access operator*, square brackets ([ ]), around the field name to indicate the table column position of the item that you want to look up.
- When you use the drilldown feature to extract a value from a table on a field that is not a primary key, a row index lookup is automatically applied. You will see how this works later in this chapter.

Note the following about the key match lookup syntax and structure:

- The formula starts with a table consisting of rows and columns.
- The second part of the formula uses the row positional index operator, but inside that operator is the *lookup operator*, which is a pair of square brackets ([ ]) and is used to define the lookup value. This operator can be confusing for people learning M code because both the lookup operator and the field access operator are square brackets. However, because they are inside the row positional index operator, they work in different ways. You can use the lookup operator to define a lookup value that can be matched against a primary key field to determine the table row position. Inside the lookup operator, the primary key field name is used without square brackets (and is called a *generalized identifier*), followed by an equal sign and then the lookup value. The lookup value must have the same data type as the primary key field. For example, if the name of the table that you are looking up is a text value, you must place the table name in quotation marks, as the formula in Figure 19.239 does with "dSalesDiscount".
- The third part of the formula uses the field access operator around the field name to indicate the table column position of the item that you want to look up.
- When you use the drilldown feature to extract a value from a table on a field that is a primary key, a key match lookup is automatically applied. The formula in Figure 19.239 is an example of this.

Note: You might be wondering why I am asking you to spend so much time learning about the M code exact match two-way lookup. It is used many places throughout Power Query. As you use Power Query more frequently and learn more about M code, you will notice how often it is used and how helpful it is. Basically, any time you extract a single value from a table, this M code exact match two-way lookup formula is used. Further, the same mechanics of this two-way lookup can be used to look up a row or column in a table.

Looking Up a Record or Converting a Field in a Table to a List

It is common to need to look up a record from a table or extract a column from a table and convert it to a list. (You will see an example of converting a column to a list later in this chapter.) The syntactical structures for both actions are closely related to a two-way lookup formula, and their structures are shown in Figure 19.243. The action of extracting a column from a table and converting it to a list is of particular importance because all Power Query aggregate functions, like List.Sum and List.Last, require that the field in the table you are analyzing be converted to a list before the aggregate function can be used. (You will see an example of this later in this project.)

---

1) Look up record in table (lookup row):

   =Table { Row Index Number }

   =Table { [Field Name = Lookup Value] }

2) Extract field from table and convert to a list:

   =Table [Field Name]

Figure 19.243 *M code structure and syntax for looking up a row or column in a table.*

Using the Table.Buffer Function to Cache a Lookup Table and Reduce Query Runtime

Now that you have learned about two-way lookups in Power Query, the next step in the project is to buffer the lookup table to help speed up query runtime.

In this project, you will use a lookup table in every row of the fact table. Because the lookup table is a query, for every row in the fact table, the query will have to be rerun so that the formula can go back to the lookup query to get the values. This can dramatically increase formula calculation time the first time you create the formula and each time you refresh the query—and that slows everything down. It would be much better if the column that uses the lookup table could retrieve the lookup table one time, store it in cached memory, and then use the stored values in every row of the fact table. The Table.Buffer M code function can help you to do exactly that!

The Table.Buffer function can store a table in a cache and allow the destination query to pull the values from the source query one time and then reuse the stored values in each row of the destination query. Using the Table.Buffer function can decrease the query runtime for the destination query. Microsoft says that Table. Buffer "buffers a table in memory, isolating it from external changes during evaluation." This is true. But this function also helps you with query runtime when you use a lookup table.

> **Note:** If you ever need to buffer a list, you can use the List.Buffer function, which works on lists rather than on tables.

To add the Table.Buffer function to your query, follow these steps:

1. Rename the Changed Type query step in the Applied Steps list to **AddedDataTypes**.

2. With the AddedDataTypes step selected, click the fx button in the formula bar, as shown in Figure 19.244.

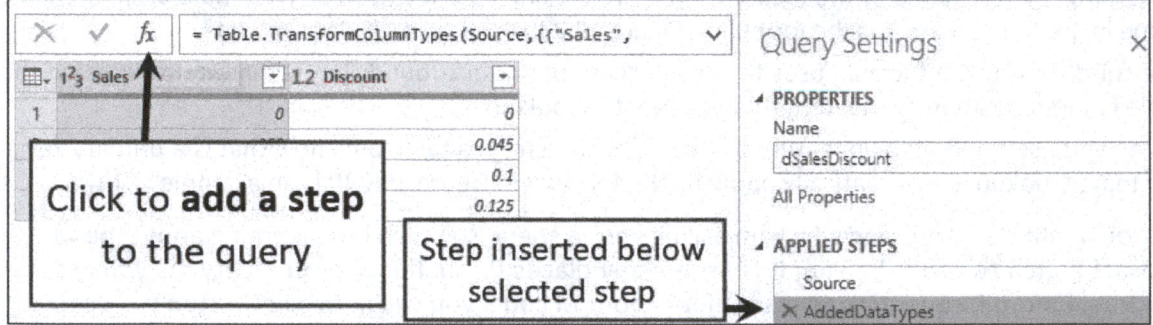

Figure 19.244 *The fx button adds a new query step.*

> **Note:** The fx button in Power Query allows you to add a new step to a query. This button adds a step below the selected step in the Applied Steps list and inserts the name of the previous query step into the formula bar. It auto fills the formula bar with the name of the previous step because it assumes that you will build the formula based on the previous step.

3. In the formula bar, as shown in Figure 19.245, carefully type the formula **=Table. Buffer(AddedDataTypes)** and press the Enter key.

> **Note:** In this step, I say to type the M code formula "carefully." I say this because the Power Query formula auto complete feature does not work correctly. Sometimes when you use the Tab key to try to accept an item from the dropdown list, Power Query deletes the parts of the formula that you have already completed. Microsoft has known for years that this feature does not work but has still not fixed it. This feature has remained broken for many years and has caused a lot of people a lot of trouble. So, until Microsoft fixes this, it is best practice to type all the characters needed for your M code and avoid the auto complete feature. Although the auto complete feature for worksheet formulas and DAX formulas works great, the same feature in M code formulas does not.

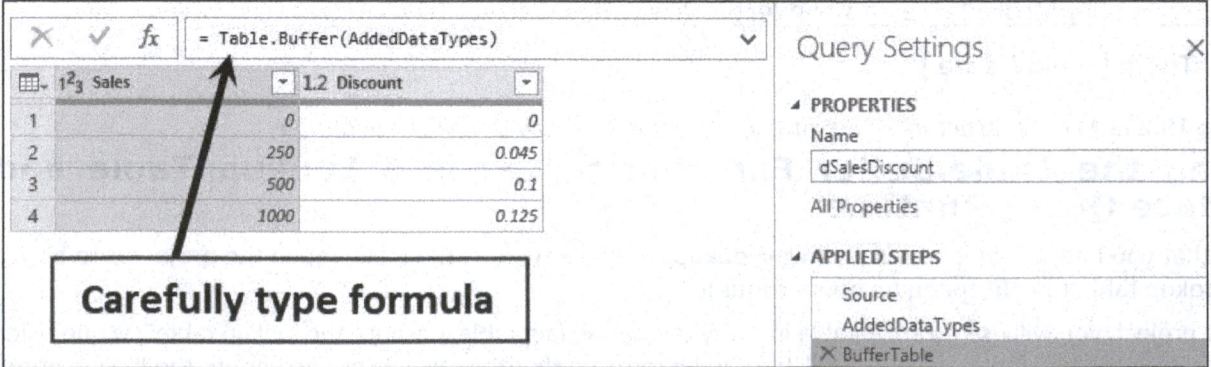

Figure 19.245 *Add the Table.Buffer function as the last step in creating the lookup table query.*

4. Load the query as a connection-only query. Figure 19.246 shows the loaded query.

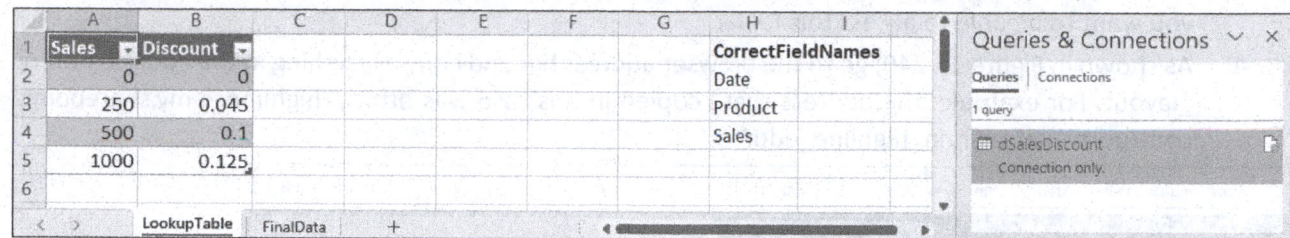

Figure 19.246 *To avoid duplicate data, load the lookup query as a connection-only query.*

You need to load this query as a connection-only query because the data is already loaded on the LookupTable worksheet in the workbook where you will create the completed fact table. If you loaded it back to the worksheet, it would unnecessarily duplicate the data. In addition, if you need to change a value in the lookup table or add a new lookup category, you can simply change it in the lookup table on the worksheet, and when you refresh the query, everything will update.

Using the From Sheet Button to Import a Defined Name

The next task is to import the defined name that contains the correctly spelled field names and then convert the field of correctly spelled names to a list. This list will have to be used later in the formula to create the correct field names for the fact table. To accomplish this, follow these steps:

1. To verify that the defined name exists, select the range H2:H4 and look at the name box on the far-left side of the Excel formula bar and ensure that you see the name CorrectFieldNames. Then click the From Sheet button to bring the defined name into the Power Query Editor. Notice that the field name for this defined name is Column1. Defined names are always imported with generic field names that begin with Column.

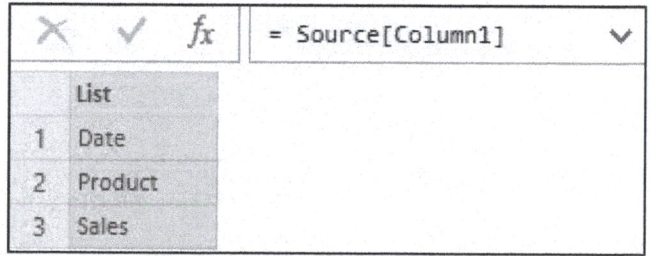

Figure 19.247 *Formula to convert the correctly spelled field names to a list.*

2. When your defined name appears in the Power Query Editor, if a Changed Type step was automatically added as the second step in the Applied Steps list, click the X next to the step to delete it.

3. Click the fx button in the formula bar to add a new step and then, as shown in Figure 19.247, type this formula in the formula bar: **=Source[Column1]**. By doing this, you look up a column and deliver a list of column values with the generic formula *Table[Field Name]*.

4. Load the query as a connection-only query.

Importing Excel Files from OneDrive by Using the Power Query From SharePoint Folder Option

At this point in the project, you will use the Power Query From Folder skills you learned in Project 3 to import the three Excel files from the on-premises Ch19-Project05\Start folder path that contains the same data that is in the OneDrive online folder. For the next few steps (Figures 19.248 to 19.253), I show how to use the Power Query From SharePoint Folder option to import files from OneDrive. This option allows you to import multiple files from a OneDrive or SharePoint folder and is available in Excel and Power BI Desktop if your organization has Microsoft 365 Enterprise edition.

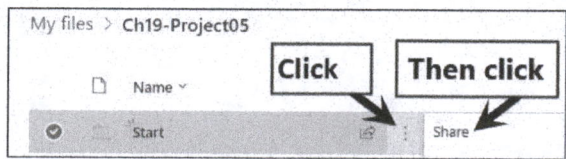

Figure 19.248 *You can give other people in your organization access to a folder by using the Share option.*

To see how to import Excel files from OneDrive by using the Power Query From SharePoint Folder option, read these steps (and follow them, if you can):

1. Log in to OneDrive and make sure you have the files in the folder that you want.

2. To share the folder with others in your organization, as shown in Figure 19.248, click the three vertical dots icon on the right side of the folder and then click Share.

3.   In the Share dialog box that appears, enter the e-mail addresses of the people in your organization you want to be able to access this folder.

4.   As shown in Figure 19.249, go to the browser address bar and copy everything in the address before _layout. For example, the address that I copied in this case was https://highlinecc-my.sharepoint. com/personal/mgirvin_highline_edu/.

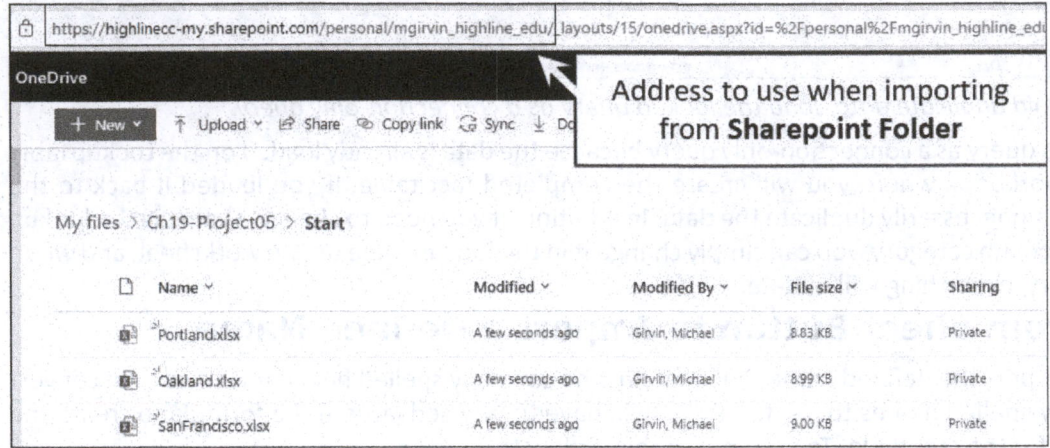

Figure 19.249 *Copy all of the OneDrive web address up to _layout.*

5.   As shown in Figure 19.250, in the Excel file for this project, in the Data tab in the Excel Ribbon, in the Get & Transform group, click the Get Data dropdown arrow, point to From File, and click on the From SharePoint Folder option.

6.   In the SharePoint Folder dialog box that appears, paste the address into the Site URL textbox and then click the OK button.

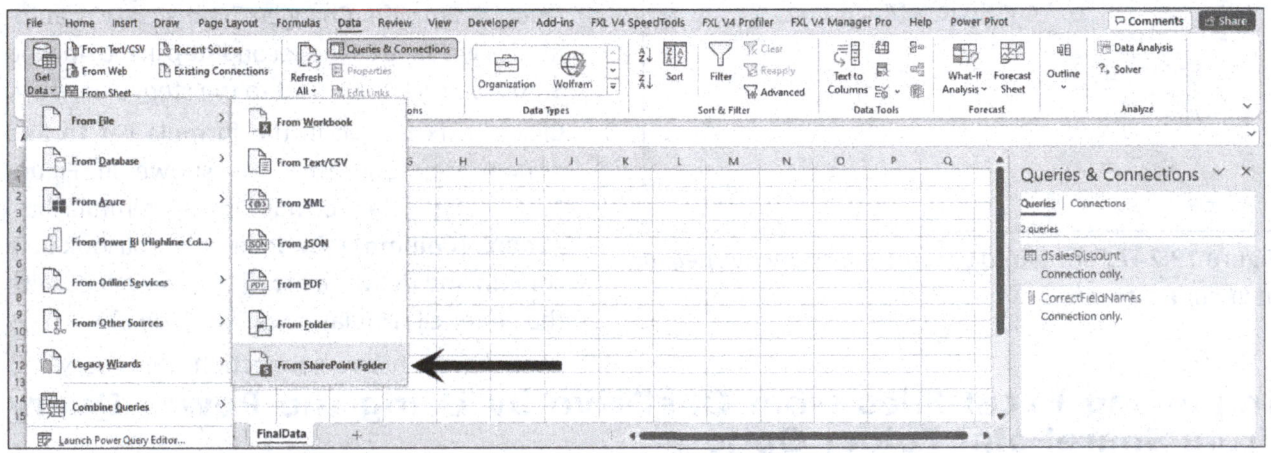

Figure 19.250 *Use the Power Query From SharePoint Folder option.*

7.   As shown in Figure 19.251, on the left side of the SharePoint dialog box that appears, click the Microsoft Account option. Then click the Sign In button, sign in, and click the Connect button.

8.   In the SharePoint Address dialog box that appears, click the Transform Data button to open the Power Query Editor.

9.   In the Power Query Editor, name the query **fNetSales**.

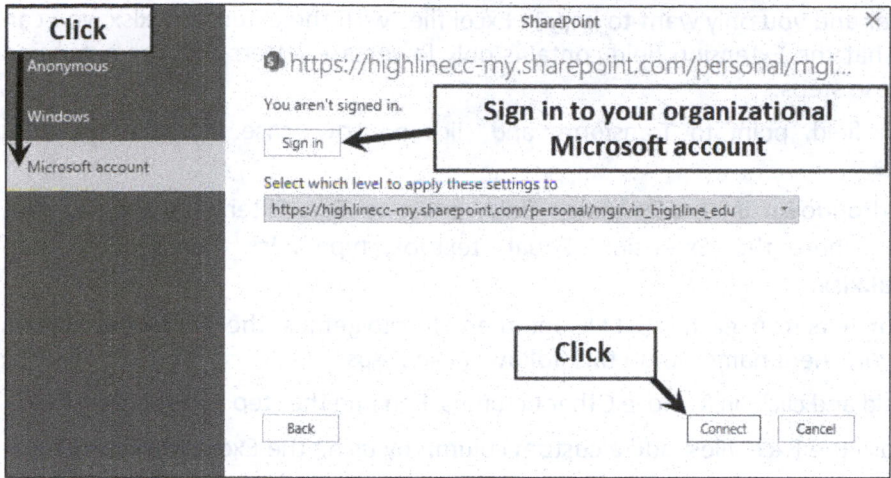

Figure 19.251 *Sign in to your organizational Microsoft account.*

10. To filter to show only files in the Start folder, as shown in Figure 19.252, click the Sort & Filter button at the top of the Folder Path field and then, in the Search box, type **Project05**. In the dropdown filter checkbox list, check the folder https://highlinecc-my.sharepoint.com/personal/mgirvin_highline_edu/Documents/Ch19-Project05/Start/. Click the OK button.

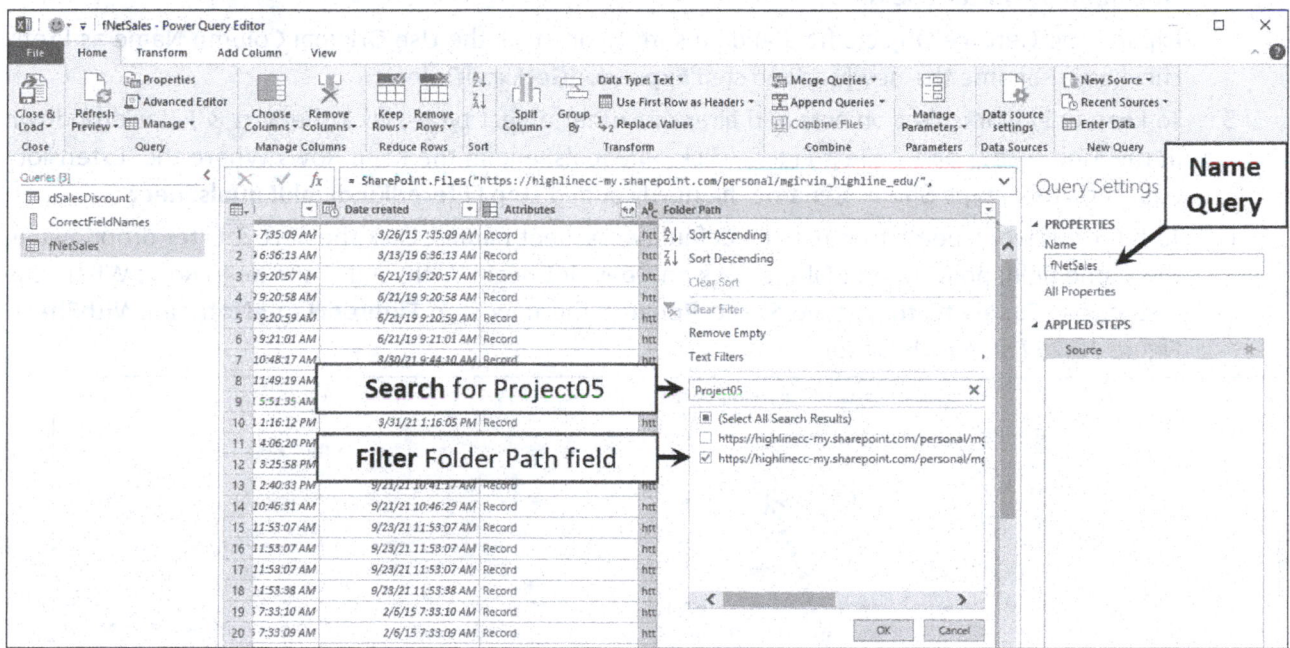

Figure 19.252 *Use the folder path field to filter down to just the files in the desired folder.*

11. Rename the query step **FilterFolderPathFieldToProject05**. Figure 19.253 shows the result.

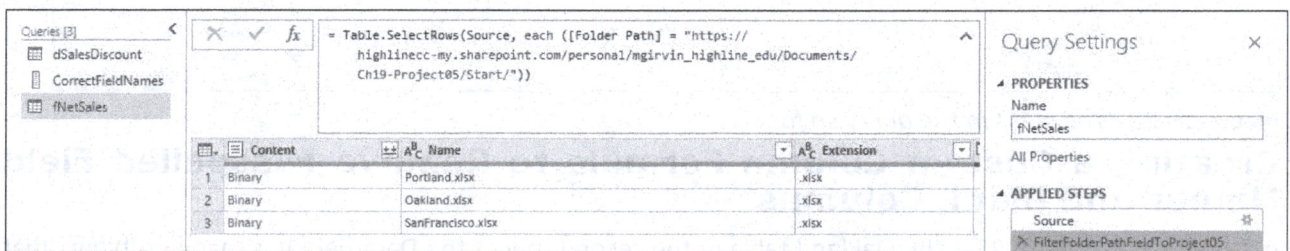

Figure 19.253 *The query now shows just the three Excel files in the Start folder.*

Now that we are done looking at how to access files in a OneDrive folder, if you used the From Folder option rather than the From SharePoint Folder option, you can follow the remaining steps in this project, and they will work the same for either From Folder method.

Because this is a SharePoint folder and you only want to import Excel files with the extension .xlsx, you can add two query steps to ensure that the Extension field contains only lowercase letters and the extension equals .xlsx. To do this, follow these steps:

1. Right-click the Extension field, point to Transform, and click on Lowercase. Rename the step **ExtensionsFieldLowercase**.

2. Click the Sort & Filter dropdown in the Extension field, point to Text Filters, click on Equals, and in the Keep Rows Where the 'Extension' Equals textbox, type **.xlsx**. Rename the step **FilterExtensionFieldEqual.xlsx**.

Next you must extract the Excel objects from each Excel file and then filter to get just the worksheet objects for which there is not a default worksheet name. To do this, follow these steps:

1. Right-click the Content field and click on Remove Other Columns. Rename the step **KeepContentField**.

2. To extract the objects from the Excel files, add a custom column by using the Excel.Workbook function. However, unlike in Project 4, do not put a true value in the second argument to promote headers. In this case, you want to intentionally leave the misspelled field names as the first record of the table so that you can remove them later. The formula should be **=Excel.Workbook([Content])**. Name the custom column **GetExcelObjects**. Rename the new query step **ExcelWorkbookCC**.

3. Right-click the GetExcelObjects field and click on Remove Other Columns. Rename the newly added step **RemoveContentField**.

4. Expand the GetExcelObjects field and be sure to uncheck the Use Original Column Name as Prefix checkbox. Rename the newly added step **ExpandedGetExcelObjects**.

5. To keep only worksheet objects and filter out other object types, click the Sort & Filter dropdown in the Kind field, point to Text Filters, click on Equals, and in the Keep Rows Where the 'Extension' Equals textbox, type **Sheet**. Rename the newly added step **FilteredKindFieldEqualsSheet**.

6. To filter out worksheets that use the default worksheet names, click the Sort & Filter dropdown in the Name field, point to Text Filters, click on Does Not Begin With, and in the Keep Rows Where the 'Extension' Equals textbox, type **Sheet**. Rename the new step **FilteredNameNotBeginWithSheet**. Figure 19.254 shows the result.

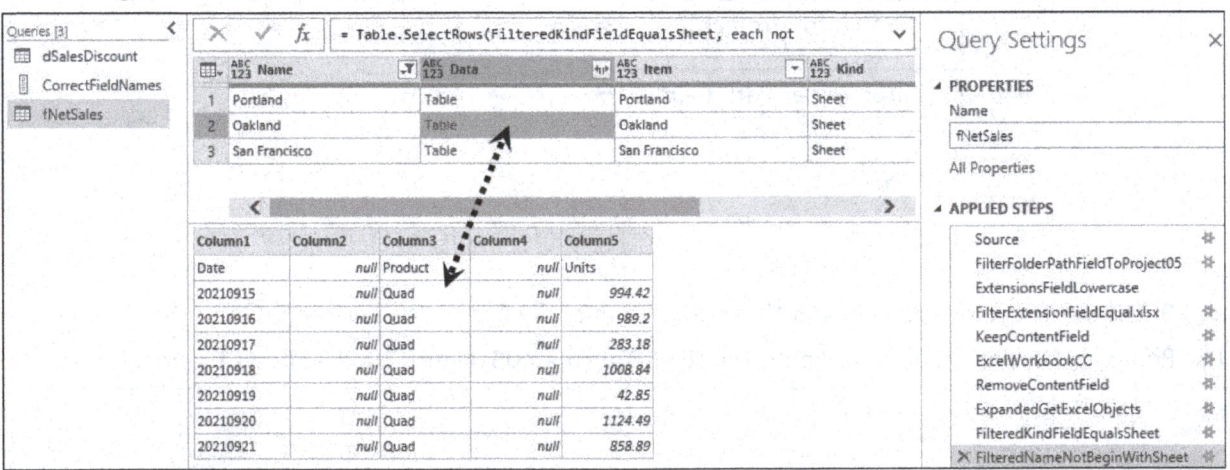

Figure 19.254 *The steps in the query so far.*

Creating a Custom Column Formula to Remove Misspelled Field Names and Blank Columns

As shown in Figure 19.254, the Oakland table in the second row of the Data field has many problems that prevent you from combining it with the other tables. The other tables in this column also have problems. To fix all the improper datasets in this field, you can build a custom column formula that will convert each table in each row to a proper dataset. The custom column must remove the first row of misspelled field names and remove blank columns. Then you can use the consistent default column names (Column1, Column2, Column3) that Power Query added to each table to combine the tables. At that point, you can complete the remaining tasks, such as adding the correct field names and creating ISO dates and a net sales field.

The custom column that you need in this situation involves a lot of M code functions, and you must type it out very carefully. However, there are a number of useful tricks that you can use to get Power Query to write the code for you.

One crazy trick you can use to get Power Query to write the code for you is to extract one table and then use the Power Query user interface to write the code necessary to remove the misspelled field names and blank columns. Then you can open the Advanced Editor, and with some copying and pasting, you can create the custom column formula that you need without writing any M code. Then, once you have the custom column, you can delete the steps that you used to create the formula. To do this, follow these steps:

1. To extract the Oakland table as a new query step, right-click the second cell in the Data field and click on Drill Down. Figure 19.255 shows the result. Notice the two-way lookup formula that was automatically created by the Drill Down command.

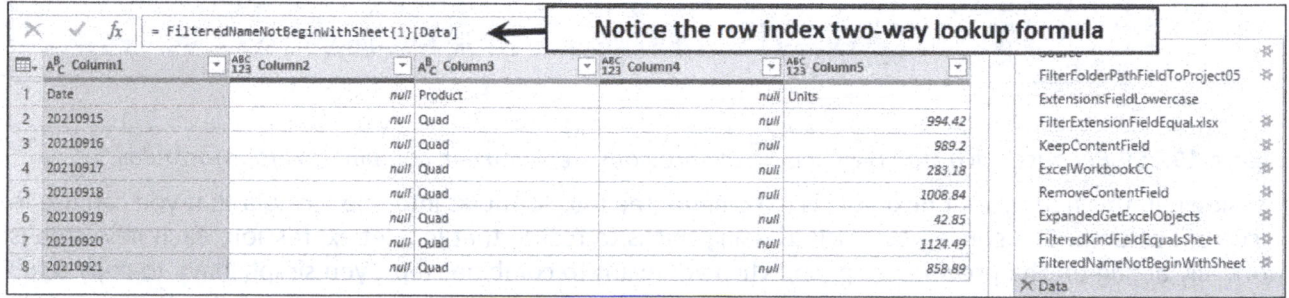

Figure 19.255 *Use Drill Down to extract the Oakland table.*

2. To remove the first row in the Oakland table, as shown in Figure 19.256, in the Home tab of the Power Query Ribbon, go to the Reduce group, click the Remove Rows dropdown arrow, and click Remove Top Rows.

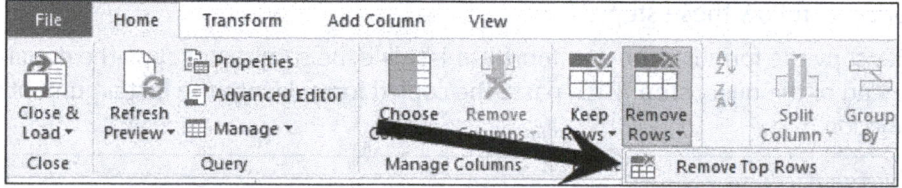

Figure 19.256 *Remove the first row in the Oakland table.*

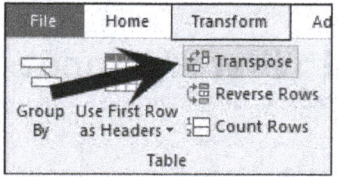

Figure 19.257 *Transpose the Oakland table.*

3. In the Remove Top Rows dialog box that appears, type **1** into the Number of Rows textbox. Then click the OK button.

4. As shown in Figure 19.257, to transform the table so that the blank columns become blank rows, in the Transform tab of the Ribbon, in the Table group, click the Transpose button.

5. To remove the blank rows in the Oakland table, in the Home tab of the Power Query Ribbon, go to the Reduce group, click the Remove Rows dropdown arrow, and click Remove Blank Rows.

6. To flip the table back after removing the blank rows, in the Transform tab of the Ribbon, go to the Table group and click the Transpose button. Figure 19.258 shows the five steps Power Query created to fix the one table.

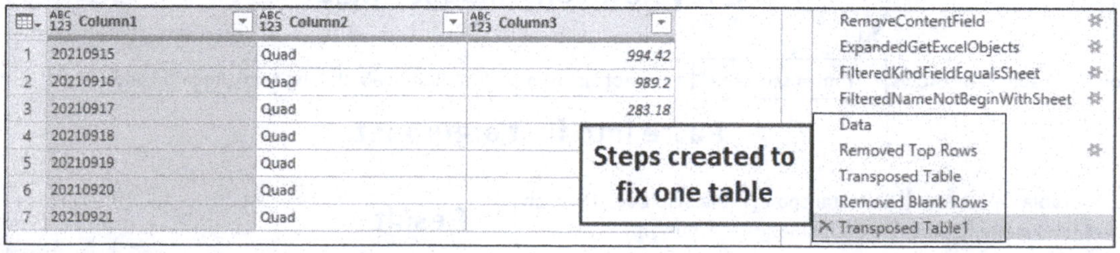

Figure 19.258 *These are the temporary steps that Power Query created to help you write the M code.*

7. To copy and paste the steps into a single formula in the Advanced Editor, in the Home tab of the Ribbon, go to the Query group and click the Advanced Editor button. Figure 19.259 shows the Advanced Editor.

```
fNetSales

let
    Source = SharePoint.Files("https://highlinecc-my.sharepoint.com/personal/mgirvin_highline_edu/", [ApiVersion = 15]),
    FilterFolderPathFieldToProject05 = Table.SelectRows(Source, each ([Folder Path] = "https://highlinecc-my.sharepoint.com/personal/mgirvin_highline_
    ExtensionsFieldLowercase = Table                                                ject05,{{"Extension", Text.Lower, type text}}),
    FilterExtensionFieldEqual.xlsx =                                    each [Extension] = ".xlsx"),
    KeepContentField = Table.Select      Combine the four formulas       ent"}),
    ExcelWorkbookCC = Table.AddColum                                    Excel.Workbook([Content])),
    RemoveContentField = Table.Selec        into one formula            ),
    ExpandedGetExcelObjects = Table.                                    celObjects", {"Name", "Data", "Item", "Kind", "Hidden"}, {"Name", "Data
    FilteredKindFieldEqualsSheet = Table.SelectRows(ExpandedGetExcelObjects, each [Kind] = "Sheet"),
    FilteredNameNotBeginWithSheet = Table.SelectRows(FilteredKindFieldEqualsSheet, each not Text.StartsWith([Name], "Sheet")),
    Data = FilteredNameNotBeginWithSheet{1}[Data],
    #"Removed Top Rows" = Table.Skip(Data,1),
    #"Transposed Table" = Table.Transpose(#"Removed Top Rows"),
    #"Removed Blank Rows" = Table.SelectRows(#"Transposed Table", each not List.IsEmpty(List.RemoveMatchingItems(Record.FieldValues(_), {"", null}))),
    #"Transposed Table1" = Table.Transpose(#"Removed Blank Rows")
in
    #"Transposed Table1"
```

Figure 19.259 *Because each step is acting on the previous step, you can combine the four formulas.*

As shown in this figure, your next goal is to combine the four formulas into one formula that you can use in a custom column. The conceptual trick to doing this is to realize that in a let expression, each new step is normally acting on the previous step. So, when you want to combine steps, you simply have to copy a full formula (without the query step name or equal sign) from a given line and then paste it into the first argument of the function in the subsequent query step. If you do this three times for the last three steps, the last step will have the formula you need for your custom column with a slight adjustment necessary when you get to the custom column.

Figures 19.260 through 19.262 show the process of combining the last four lines in the let expression. To create this "hacked-together" formula, follow these steps:

1. As shown in Figure 19.260, copy the formula from the fourth-to-last line. Be sure to not copy the equal sign or the comma at the end of the query step. Then paste the copied formula into the first argument of the Table.Transpose function.

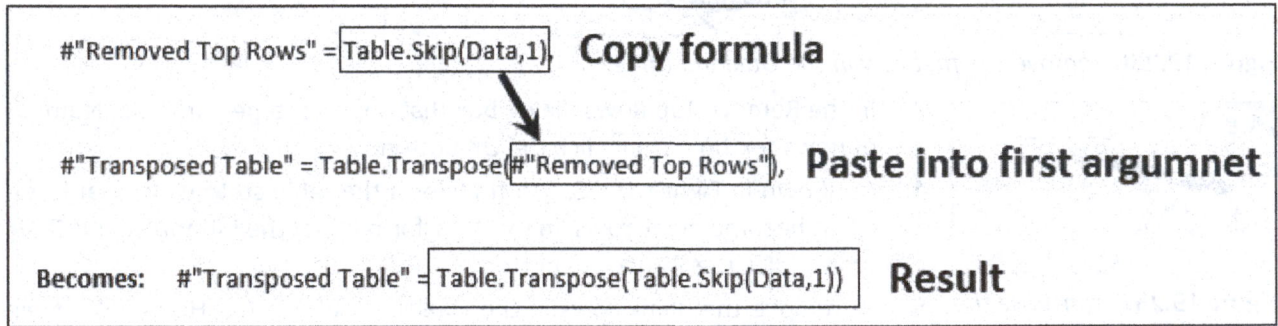

Figure 19.260 *Copy the first formula and paste it into the first argument of the Table.Transpose function.*

2. As shown in Figure 19.261, copy the newly combined formula from the third-to-last line. Paste it into the first argument of the Table.SelectRows function.

```
#"Transposed Table" = Table.Transpose(Table.Skip(Data,1))   Copy new combined formula

#"Removed Blank Rows" = Table.SelectRows(#"Transposed Table", each not List.IsEmpty(List.RemoveMatchingItems(Record.FieldValues(_),
{"", null}))),
                                        Paste into first argumnet

#"Removed Blank Rows" = Table.SelectRows(Table.Transpose(Table.Skip(Data,1)), each not
List.IsEmpty(List.RemoveMatchingItems(Record.FieldValues(_), {"", null}))),   Result
```

Figure 19.261 *Copy and paste the new combined formula into the first argument of the Table.SelectRows function.*

3. As shown in Figure 19.262, copy the newly combined formula from the third-to-last line. Paste it into the first argument of the Table.Transpose function. This formula is the final formula that you can use in the custom column.

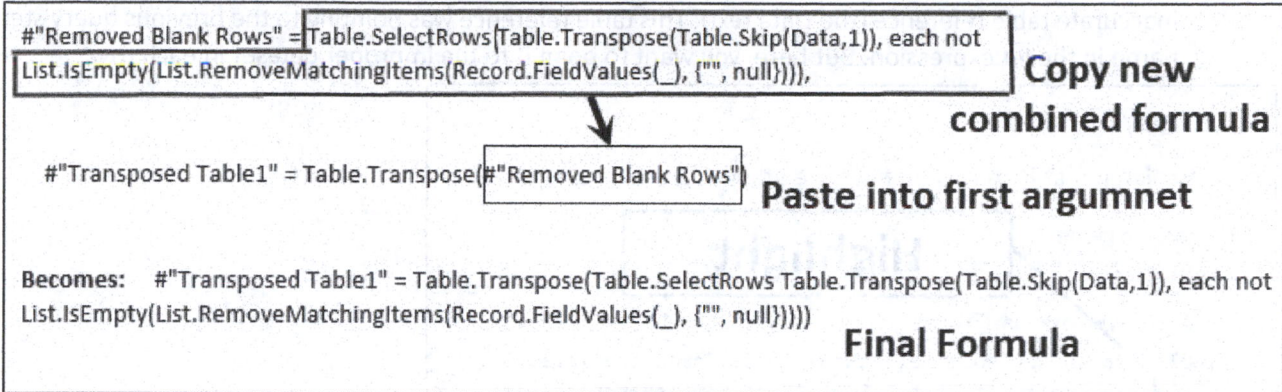

Figure 19.262 *Copy and paste the new combined formula into the first argument of the Table.Transpose function.*

The completed formula should look like this:

```
#"Transposed Table1" = Table.Transpose(Table.SelectRows(Table.
Transpose(Table.Skip(Data,1)), each not List.IsEmpty(List.RemoveMatching-
Items(Record.FieldValues(_), {"", null}))))
```

However, in the next step, you are going to copy only this part:

```
Table.Transpose(Table.SelectRows(Table.Transpose(Table.Skip(Data,1)), each
not List.IsEmpty(List.RemoveMatchingItems(Record.FieldValues(_), {"",
null}))))
```

4. As shown in Figure 19.263, copy the formula from the last line without the query step name or the equal sign. Then click the Cancel button to close the Advanced Editor so that the changes are not saved.

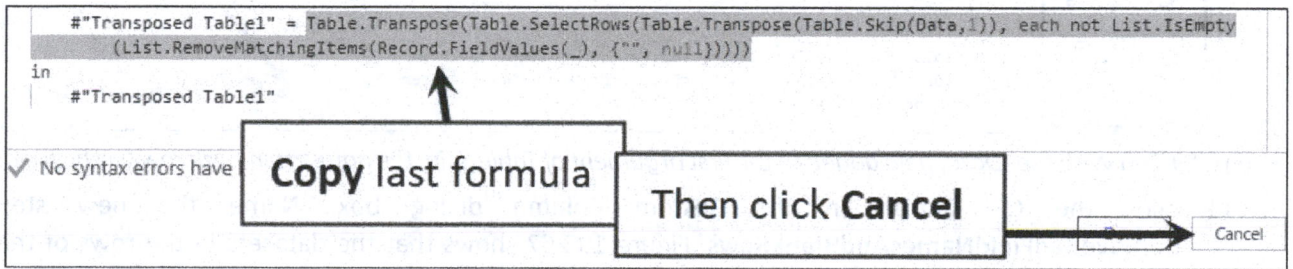

Figure 19.263 *The last formula is the one that you will use in the custom column.*

5. When the Discard Query Changes dialog box pops up, as shown in Figure 19.264, click the Discard button.

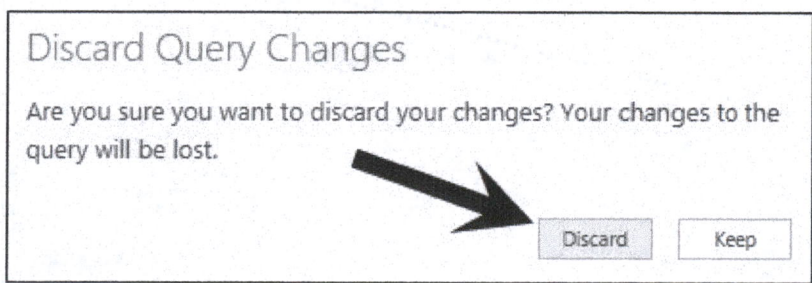

Figure 19.264 *In the Discard Query Changes dialog box, click the Discard button.*

6. In the Applied Steps list, select the FilteredNameNotBeginWithSheet step. This is the step directly above the Data step (and it is the first temporary step).

7. In the Add Column tab of the Power Query Ribbon, go to the General group and click the Custom Column button.

8. In the Insert Step dialog box that appears, click the Insert button.

9. As shown in Figure 19.265, name the new field FixedTables and paste the formula you copied earlier into the Custom Column Formula area. In the first argument of the Table.Skip argument, highlight the inaccurate table reference (the Data text). This table reference was pointing to the previous query step name in the let expression. But here, you want to point it to the improper dataset in each row.

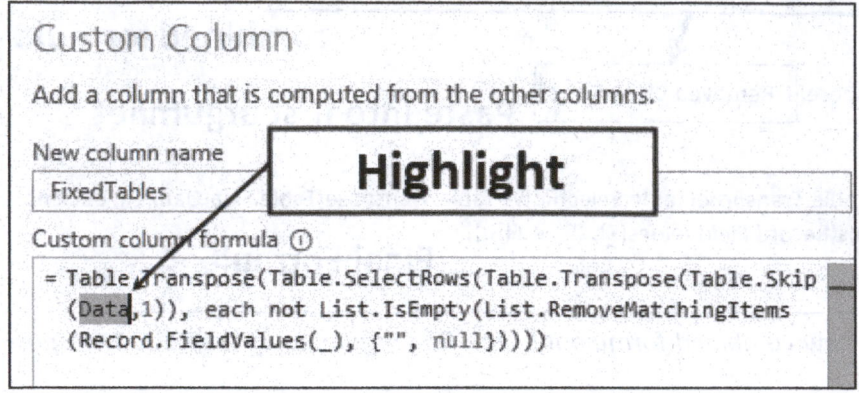

Figure 19.265 *Name the new field, paste the copied formula, and then highlight the first argument of Table.Skip.*

10. As shown in Figure 19.266, to provide the correct table to the first argument of the Table.Skip function, on the far-right side of the Custom Column dialog box, double-click the Data field in the Available Columns list. You should see the field inside the field access operator as [Data]. Because the Data field contains the improper datasets in each row, now the formula you pasted can fix the datasets in each row.

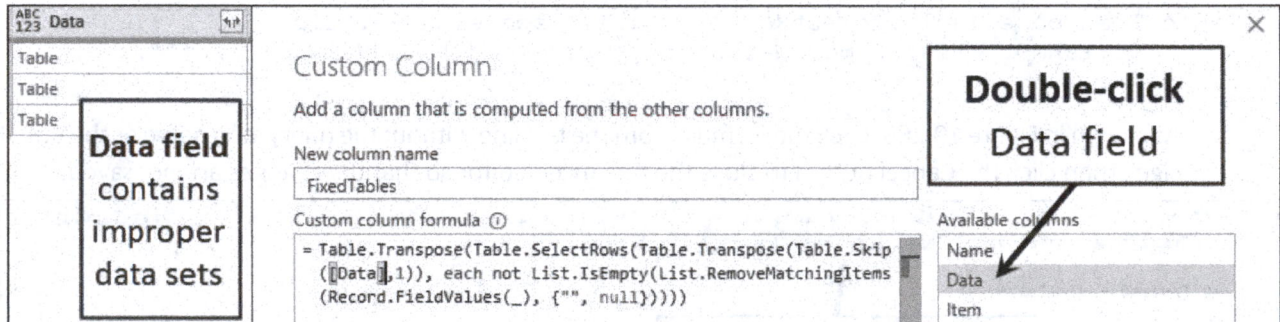

Figure 19.266 *With the [Data] field added to the first argument of Table.Skip, the datasets in each row will be fixed.*

11. Click the OK button in the Custom Column dialog box. Name the new step **RemoveBadFieldNamesAndBlankRows**. Figure 19.267 shows that the datasets in the rows of the Data field are now fixed and are proper datasets.

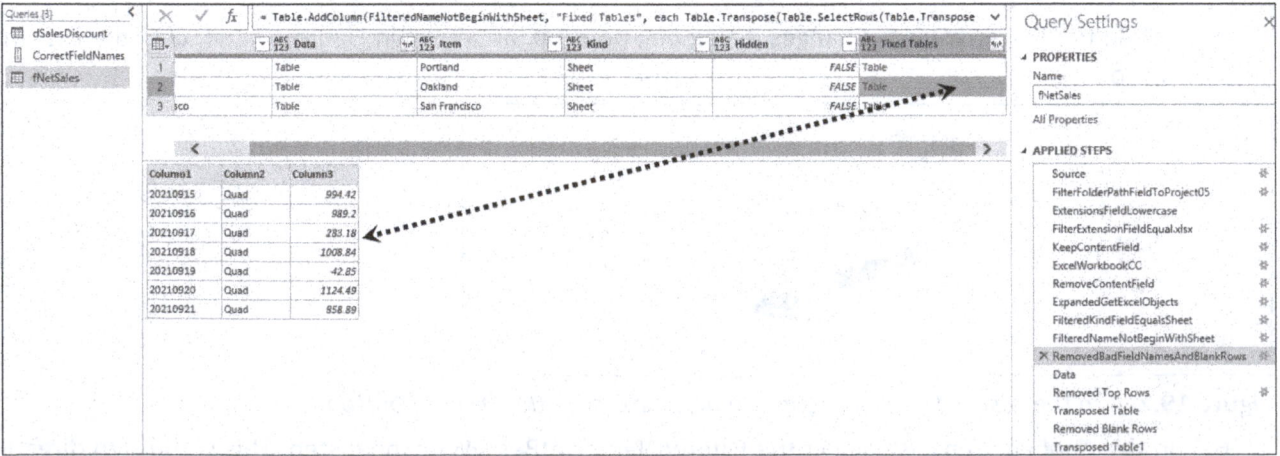

Figure 19.267 *Each improper dataset is now a proper table with the field names Column1, Column2, and Column3.*

12. To remove the temporary query steps, right-click the Data step and click on Delete Until End (see Figure 19.268).

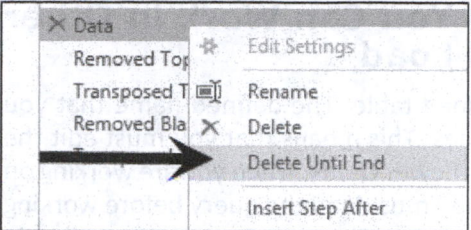

Figure 19.268 *Delete Until End deletes all steps from Data to Transposed Table 1.*

13. In the Delete Step dialog box that appears, click the Delete button. Figure 19.269 shows the result.

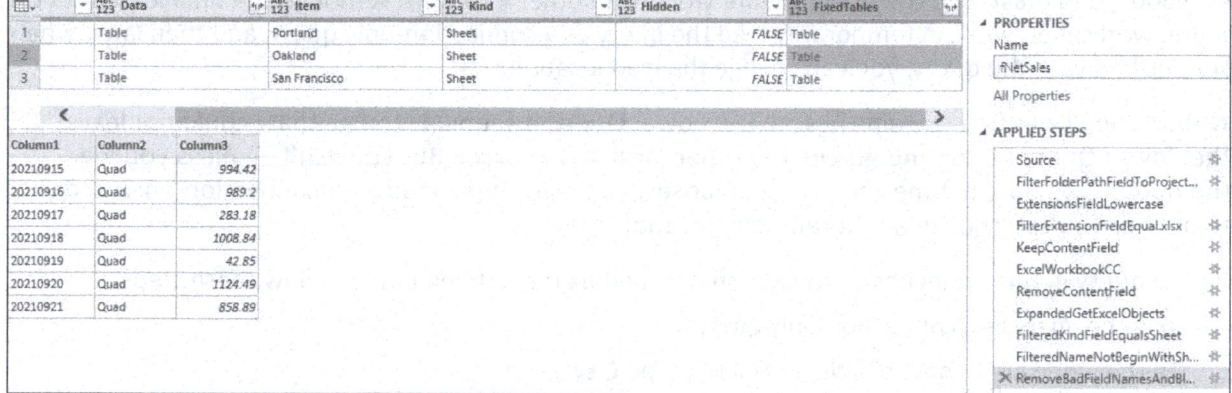

Figure 19.269 *After you delete the temporary steps, the newly hacked-together custom column is the last step.*

What you just did to create a custom column was some crazy copy-and-paste hacking! There are other ways to create custom columns like this, such as by typing the full formula manually or creating a custom function based on a parameter. The advantage of the method that you just learned is that it is fast and easy, and it allows you to write most of the code using the user interface. The disadvantage is that editing the M code formula would be tricky since you did not leave an audit trail with your steps; you would have to manually edit the code in the Custom Column dialog box or in the Advanced Editor.

> **Note:** If you use a custom function based on a parameter, then an audit trail that is easily updatable will be created, and you will not have to do any manual code writing. You will not learn this method in this book, but I have a video posted at YouTube that shows the custom function based on a parameter method here: https://www.youtube.com/watch?v=SFgYwVVeqPA.

Expanding Fixed Tables

The next task is to combine the fixed tables by using the Expand button. To accomplish this, follow these steps:

1. While holding down the Ctrl key, select the FixedTables field and then the Name field. (You must select the fields in this order because the order in which the fields are selected will determine the left-to-right order of the fields in the resulting table.) Right-click any of the selected field names and click on Remove Other Columns. Name the new step **KeepFixedTablesAndNameFields**.

2. Expand the FixedTables field and make sure the Use Original Column Name as Prefix checkbox is not checked. Rename the new step **ExpandedFixedTables**. Figure 19.270 shows the result.

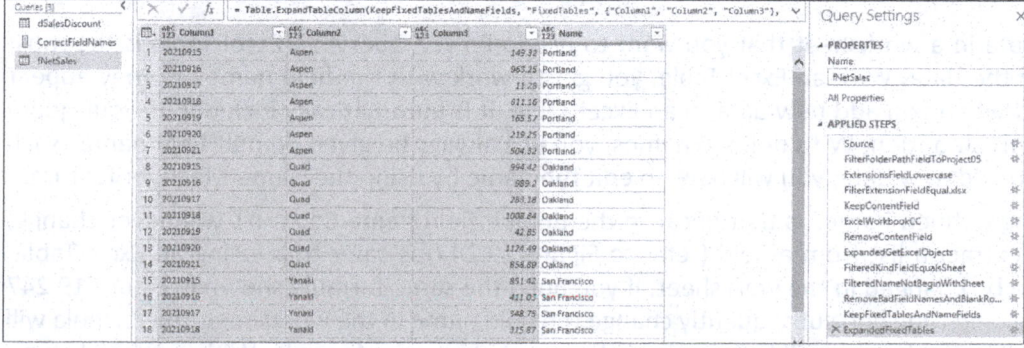

Figure 19.270 *Combined tables using the Expand Table Column feature.*

Loading a Query as a Connection Only So You Can Work in Other Locations in an Excel File Before the Final Load

As you can see in Figure 19.270, there are four fields in the combined table. The defined name that you imported with the correct field names contains only three field names. This means that you must edit the defined name in the worksheet and add the fourth field name. In Excel Power Query, when you are working on a query and you need to go back to the worksheet to make an edit, you must load the query before working in the worksheet. This is different from in Power BI Desktop. In Example 3 in Chapter 18, you learned that in Power BI Desktop Power Query, you can close a query without loading (that is, applying) it. But here in an Excel workbook file, if you are working in the Power Query Editor and you want to work in other locations in the workbook, you must load the query before working in other locations. Although the final load location will be the worksheet, you can temporarily load the query as a connection-only query, and then later, when you are finished with the query, you can change the load location.

> **Note:** When I was first learning how to use Power Query, it seemed strange that I could not leave the Power Query Editor and go work in other locations in Excel. But you can't—unless you load the query first. So any time this situation arises, you can simply load as a connection only, and then later you can choose a different load location.

To load the query in this project as a connection only and fix the defined name, follow these steps:

1. Load the query as a connection-only query.

2. On the worksheet LookupTable, in cell H5, type **City**.

3. Although Excel Tables automatically include new rows when data is added, defined names do not automatically adjust when new data is added. To edit a defined name, click on the Formulas tab in the Excel Ribbon and, in the Defined Names group, click the Name Manager button. (Or you can use the keyboard shortcut Ctrl+F3 to open the Name Manager directly.)

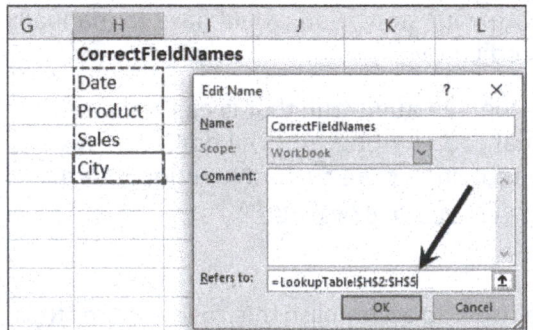

4. In the Name Manager dialog box that appears, select the defined name CorrectFieldNames and click Edit.

5. In the Edit Name dialog box that appears, edit the reference in the Refers To textbox so that cell H4 becomes H5, as shown in Figure 19.271. When you are done, click the OK button in the Edit Name dialog box and then click the Close button in the Name Manager dialog box.

6. To open the Power Query Editor and verify that the new City field name has been added to the CorrectFieldNames query, in the Queries & Connections task pane, double-click the CorrectFieldNames query.

7. In the Home tab of the Power Query Editor, in the Query group, click the Refresh Preview button. You should now see all four field names.

Figure 19.271 *Using a defined name to store data in the worksheet requires a manual edit if source data changes.*

Determining Whether to Use a Defined Name or an Excel Table as Source Data

Usually, if you have data in a worksheet that you want to use in Power Query, an Excel Table is the most efficient container for the data. With an Excel Table, you get to work with the field names as they appear in the Excel Table, and when you add new data to an Excel Table, it is automatically included in your query when you click the Refresh option. With defined names, you will always be given default field names such as Column1, and if you add new data, you will have to edit the name by using the Name Manager feature.

The advantage to using defined names is that because the default field name Column1 will never change, using the formula to extract a list from a field (refer to Figure 19.247) is safer than using an Excel Table, where field names can be changed in the worksheet. If you build the same formula shown in Figure 19.247 by using an Excel Table, and then you subsequently change the field name in the worksheet, the formula will yield an error because the field name will be incorrectly hard coded into the formula. With a defined name formula, you will not get this error. The majority of the time, however, the Excel Table feature is a better tool for storing data in a worksheet.

Adding Field Names to a Table

There are several different ways that you can add new field names to a table. The first method is to simply type the new field names directly into the query. This method is the easiest method by far, but it will hard code the field names into the query. This manual method is fine if you are sure that the field names that you will type in will not change or if you do not mind manually coming back to edit the M code when names change later. You will use this method first, and then I will show you a second, more dynamic, method that will add the new field names based on the defined name values in the worksheet.

To create the new field names manually, follow these steps:

1. In the Power Query Editor, select the fNetSales query.

2. Double-click the Column1 field name, type **Date**, and press Enter. Using the same process, rename Column2 to **Product**, Column3 to **Sales**, and Name to **City**. Name the new query step **CreateFieldNames**.

As shown in Figure 19.272, the M code formula that is written for you uses the Table.RenameColumns function, which allows you to rename the fields in a table and requires a table with the field names that you want to change in the first argument and a *list of lists* with the original field names and the new field names in the second argument. As you learned back in Chapter 18, a list value in Power Query is a one-dimensional list of values that requires curly brackets ({ }) and commas to separate the values in the list. If the values that you want to list are actual lists, then you must create a list of lists, where each list is separated by a comma and housed in a pair of curly brackets. Because the renaming field names task in this project involves pairs of original and new field names, the formula handles the list of lists like this:

```
{{"Column1", "Date"}, {"Column2", "Product"}, {"Column3", "Sales"}, {"Name",
"City"}}
```

Figure 19.272 *The Table.RenameColumns function uses a list of lists to rename fields.*

The hard-coded values in this list of lists are efficient M code if you do not mind coming back to this line of code when you need to edit field names later. This method is pretty safe in this case because all the original field names were created by the Power Query user interface, and they will not change. If you are okay with coming back and editing M code later, then you are done with this formula!

However, if you want a more dynamic solution that will work regardless of what the original field names were and that will reflect any name changes from the defined name in the worksheet, then you can use the following formula:

```
Table.RenameColumns(
        ExpandedFixedTables,
        List.Zip({Table.ColumnNames(ExpandedFixedTables),CorrectField-
Names})
        )
```

This formula uses the Table.ColumnNames function, which can extract the field names from a table, and the List.Zip function, which can create a list of lists from two different lists. The List.Zip function will take the current field name list created by the Table.ColumnNames function and the new field names in the CorrectFieldNames list, both housed in list syntax, and convert them into the necessary list of lists with the four paired original and new field names.

To create this formula with some more Power Query user interface "hacking," follow these steps:

1. Select the ExpandedFixedTables step in the Applied Steps list.

2. Click the fx button in the formula bar.

Figure 19.273 *Table.ColumnNames will dynamically list the field names.*

3. In the Insert Step dialog box that appears, click the Insert button. In the formula bar, carefully type the formula **=Table.ColumnNames(ExpandedFixedTables)** and press the Enter key. Figure 19.273 shows the list of field names that is created. Click back in the formula bar, highlight the formula without the equal sign, and copy the formula. When you are done copying the formula, because the step you just created is a temporary step, delete the query step named Custom1.

4. Select the CreateFieldNames query step and click the fx button in the formula bar to insert a new step. In the formula, bar create this formula: **=List.Zip({Table.ColumnNames(ExpandedFixedTables),CorrectFieldNames})**.

5. Press the Enter key to enter the formula.

6. In the warning popup that appears because you are combining queries from OneDrive and an Excel workbook (see Figure 19.274), click the Continue button.

Note: If you are using the files from an on-premises folder, you will not see this warning popup.

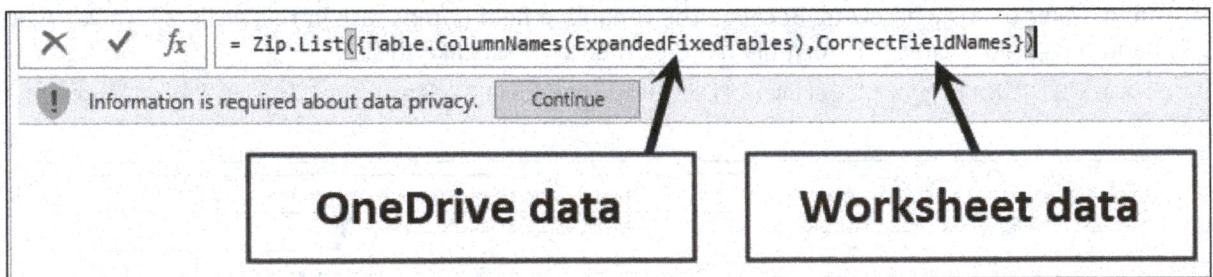

Figure 19.274 *The two lists are from different data sources.*

7. In the Privacy Levels dialog box that appears, warning you that sensitive or confidential data might be improperly shared or combined (see Figure 19.275), check the checkbox Ignore Privacy Levels or set the privacy level to Organizational. Then click Save. (In general, you must consult the IT department in your organization to decide what privacy level to use.)

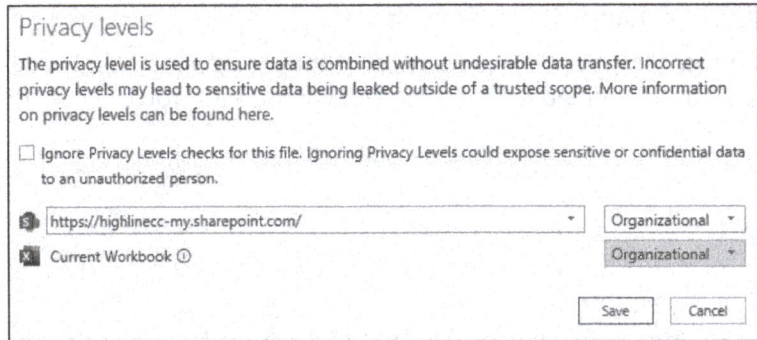

Figure 19.275 *You must ask your organizational IT department what the privacy level should be.*

Figure 19.276 shows the list of lists created by the List.Zip function. The List.Zip function took the four-element list of table field names created by the Table.ColumnNames function and matched it up with the corresponding four-element list of correctly spelled field names from the defined names and then created the four correct lists of paired original and new paired names in a list. This formula is fully dynamic. Whatever the table field names may be or whatever names you type into the defined name, this formula will correctly create the list of lists for the correct paired field names.

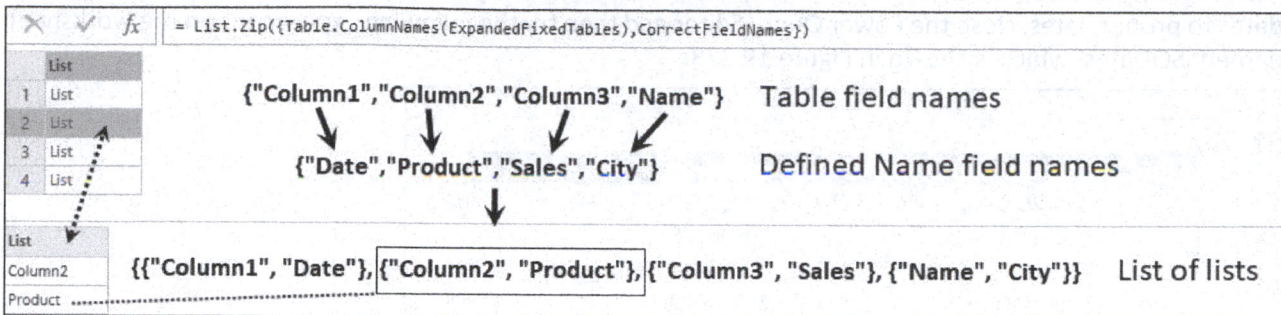

Figure 19.276 *List.Zip creates the correct list of paired original and new field names.*

8. Click back in the formula bar, highlight the formula without the equal sign, and copy the formula **List.Zip({Table.ColumnNames(ExpandedFixedTables),CorrectFieldNames})**. When you are done copying the formula, because the step you just created is a temporary step, delete the query step named Custom1.

9. Select the CreateFieldNames step. Carefully highlight everything in the second argument of the Table.RenameColumns function and paste your copied formula element into the second argument (see Figure 19.277). There is currently no difference between the output of this formula and the output of the previous formula, but with this formula, if you change the field names in the work-sheet, everything will update.

    Note: You can use Shift+Enter to add line breaks and the spacebar to add some spaces if you want to format the M code formula using DAX formula formatting. Doing so isn't necessary, but as you can see in Figure 19.277, it makes the formula easier to read .

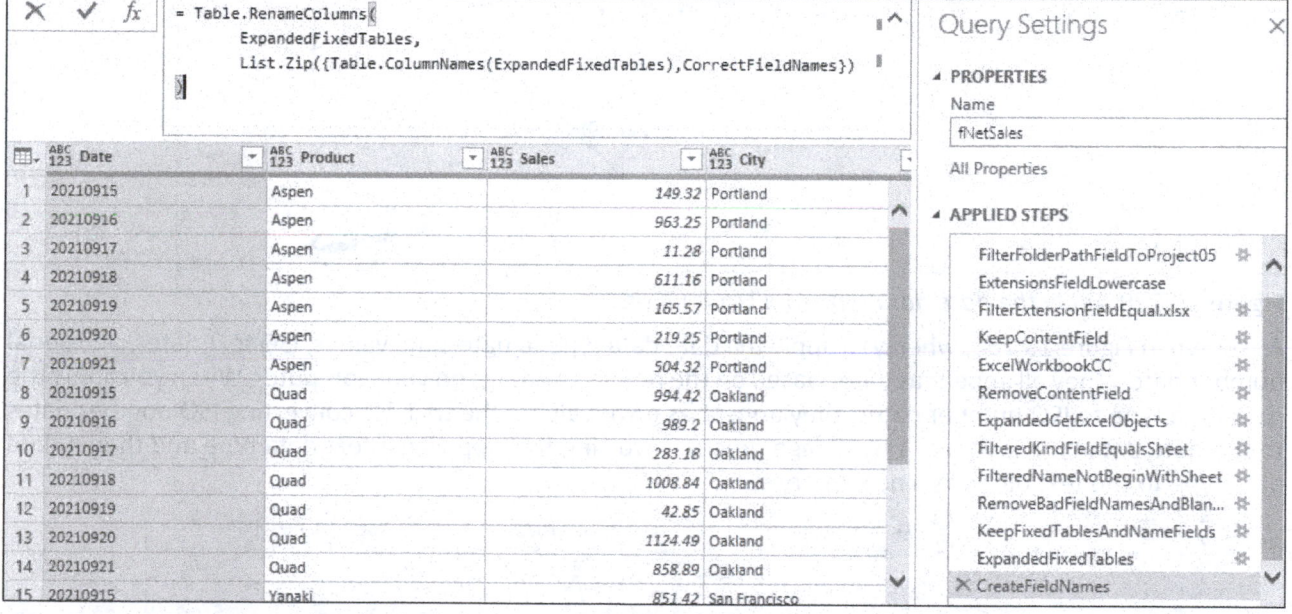

Figure 19.277 *This formula will dynamically rename the field names based on the names in the defined name.*

Converting ISO Dates to Serial Number Dates

ISO (International Organization for Standardization) dates provide a universal way to store and share dates. When you get ISO dates with the format YYYYMMDD, it is easy to use Power Query to convert them to proper serial number dates. When you convert ISO dates to serial number dates, the dates will match the regional settings in your Control Panel. For example, if you get the ISO date 20210929 and use Power Query to convert it to a serial number date, on a computer with an English (United States) setting, the date will appear as 9/29/2021, and on a computer with a French (France) setting, the date will appear as 29/9/2021.

When you convert ISO dates to proper serial number dates, the method you use depends on whether the ISO date values are stored as text values or as number values. To learn about the two methods of converting ISO dates to proper dates, close the Power Query Editor and then try the following experiment on the worksheet named ISODates, which is shown in Figure 19.278:

	A	B	C	D	E
1					
2		Dates	ISOTextDates	ISONumberDates	SerialNumberDates
3		9/29/21	20210929	20210929	44468
4		5/25/99	19990525	19990525	36305
5		8/14/12	20120814	20120814	41135
6		9/29/21	20210929	20210929	44468
7					

< >   ISODates   LookupTable   FinalData   +

Figure 19.278 *Four fields of dates. Each row has the same date with a different format and structure.*

1. Since you have already loaded all three queries as connection-only queries, in the Home tab of the Ribbon, go to the Close group and click the Close & Load button.

2. From the ISODates worksheet, bring the Excel Table into the Power Query Editor. Name the query **TestForISODates**.

3. If an applied step called Data Types was added, delete that step.

4. To simultaneously apply the date data type to all four fields, as shown in Figure 19.279, select all four fields, right-click any one of the selected fields, hover over Change Type, and click on Date. Name this new step **AddedFirstDataTypes**.

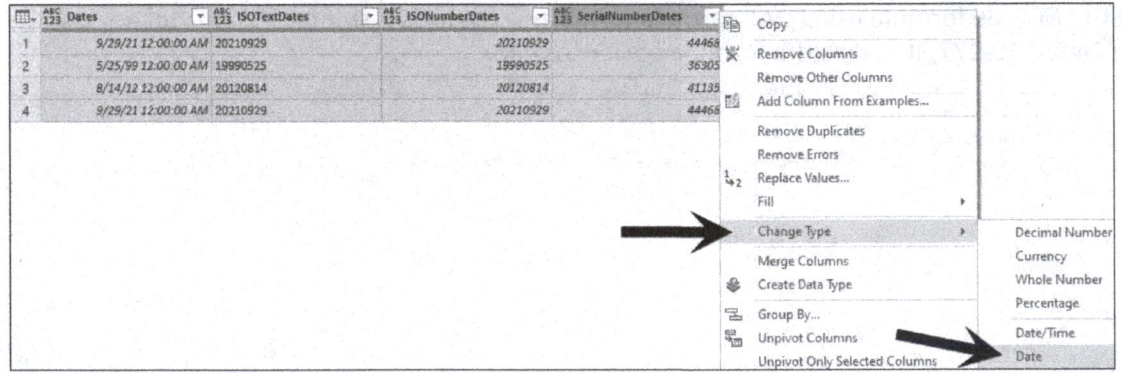

Figure 19.279 *Apply the date data type to all four fields.*

As shown in Figure 19.280, when you apply the date data type to date-time values, ISO text dates, and serial number dates, they all appear as dates based on the regional settings on your computer. When you apply the date data type to ISO number dates, they appear as error values. The trick for converting ISO number dates to the date data type is to use a two-stage process involving first applying a text data type and then a date data type to the text dates as a new query step.

	Dates	ISOTextDates	ISONumberDates	SerialNumberDates
1	9/29/21	9/29/21	Error	9/29/21
2	5/25/99	5/25/99	Error	5/25/99
3	8/14/12	8/14/12	Error	8/14/12
4	9/29/21	9/29/21	Error	9/29/21

Figure 19.280 *ISO text dates and serial number dates show the correct dates. ISO number dates yield errors.*

To convert ISO number dates to the date data type, follow these steps:

1. Click the Data Type icon at the top of the ISONumberDates field and click Text.

2. In the Change Column Type dialog box that appears (see Figure 19.281), click the Replace Current button.

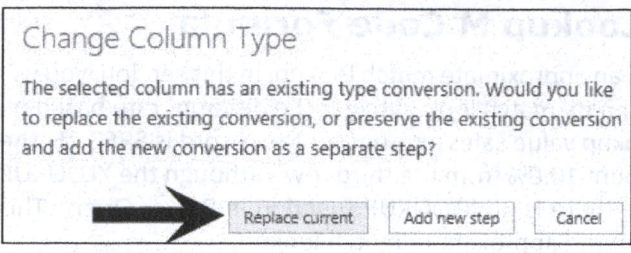

Figure 19.281 *Click Replace Current.*

3. Click the Data Type icon at the top of the ISONumberDates field a second time and click Date. The Change Column Type dialog box appears again.
4. In the Change Column Type dialog box, as shown in Figure 19.282, click the Add New Step button.

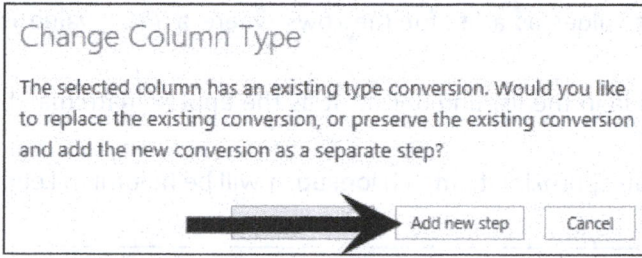

Figure 19.282 *The second time you see this dialog box, click Add New Step.*

5. Name the new step **AddedSecondDateDataTypesForISODates**. Figure 19.283 shows the result.
6. Load the query as a connection-only query.

	Dates	ISOTextDates	ISONumberDates	SerialNumberDates
1	9/29/21	9/29/21	9/29/21	9/29/21
2	5/25/99	5/25/99	5/25/99	5/25/99
3	8/14/12	8/14/12	8/14/12	8/14/12
4	9/29/21	9/29/21	9/29/21	9/29/21

Figure 19.283 *All rows have the same dates.*

Here is a summary of how to convert ISO dates to serial number dates:

1. If the ISO dates are text values, use the date data type to convert them to serial number dates.
2. If the ISO dates are number values, first apply a text data type and then apply a second change data type action to apply the date data type. During the second action, make sure to click the Add New Step button in the Change Column Type dialog box.

To continue with the project, follow these steps:

1. Open the fNetSales query.
2. Because the ISO dates in the fNetSales query are text, convert them to serial number dates by adding the date data type to the Date field.
3. Add the text data type to the Product and City fields and the decimal data type to the Sales field.
4. Name the new step **AddDataTypes**. Figure 19.284 shows the result.

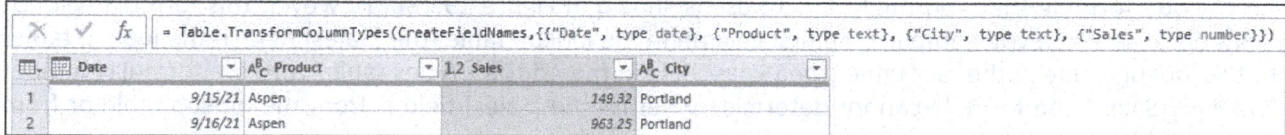

```
= Table.TransformColumnTypes(CreateFieldNames,{{"Date", type date}, {"Product", type text}, {"City", type text}, {"Sales", type number}})
```

	Date	Product	Sales	City
1	9/15/21	Aspen	149.32	Portland
2	9/16/21	Aspen	963.25	Portland

Figure 19.284 *The Table.TransformColumnTypes function applies the data types to the fields in the table.*

In Figure 19.284, notice that the Table.TransformColumnTypes function uses a list of lists in the second argument to list the pairs of field names and data types. The Power Query list of lists syntax is common when there are paired values like field name and data type or original field name and new field name.

Creating an Approximate Match Lookup M Code Formula

The next task is to create an M code formula to perform an approximate match lookup. In this section, you will create a custom column formula to perform an approximate match lookup to get the discount rate based on the sales amount. As shown in Figure 19.285, if the lookup value sales amount for the record is $963.25, the formula must use the lookup table to retrieve the discount 10.0% from the third row. Although the XLOOKUP function can do approximate matches in a worksheet, there is no XLOOKUP function in Power Query. This means you have to build an M code formula to perform the approximate match lookup.

Figure 19.285 shows the three-step logic for the formula you will build:

1. First, the formula must determine which values in the first column of the lookup table are less than or equal to the lookup value 963.25. For the lookup value 963.25, the first three rows in the sorted lookup table get a TRUE value for this logical test.

2. Next, the formula must extract the discount values as a list for the rows where a TRUE value is present.

3. Finally, the formula must look up the last value in the list and deliver it as the approximate match lookup discount value.

As you move on to the advanced M code formula for an approximate match lookup, it will be helpful to keep this visualization of the formula's mechanics in mind.

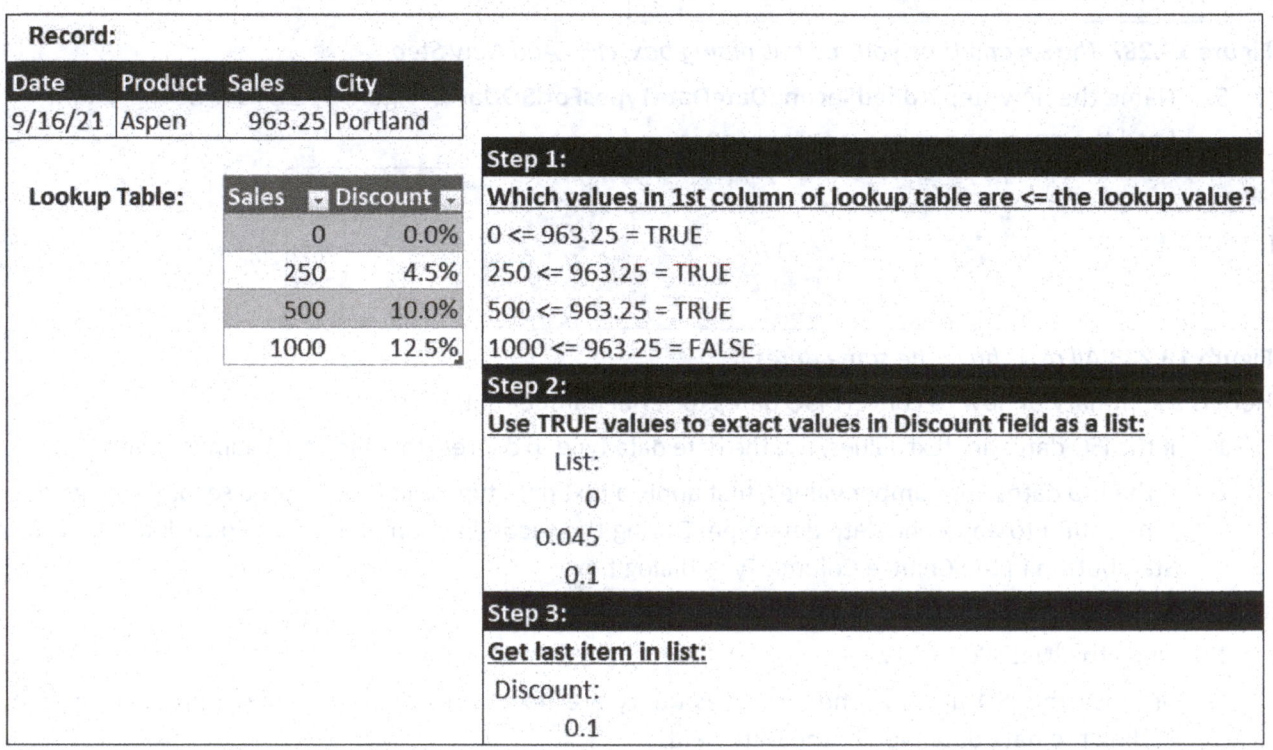

Figure 19.285 *Three-step logic for the M code approximate match lookup formula to get the discount for $963.25.*

An M code formula that you might like to use is shown in Figure 19.286. However, this formula will not work because when you compare the first column in the lookup table (the [Sales] field in the lookup table) to the lookup value in the fact table (the [Sales] field in the AddDataTypes table) with the formula element [Sales]<=[Sales], the formula cannot determine whether the [Sales] field is from the lookup table or from the fact table.

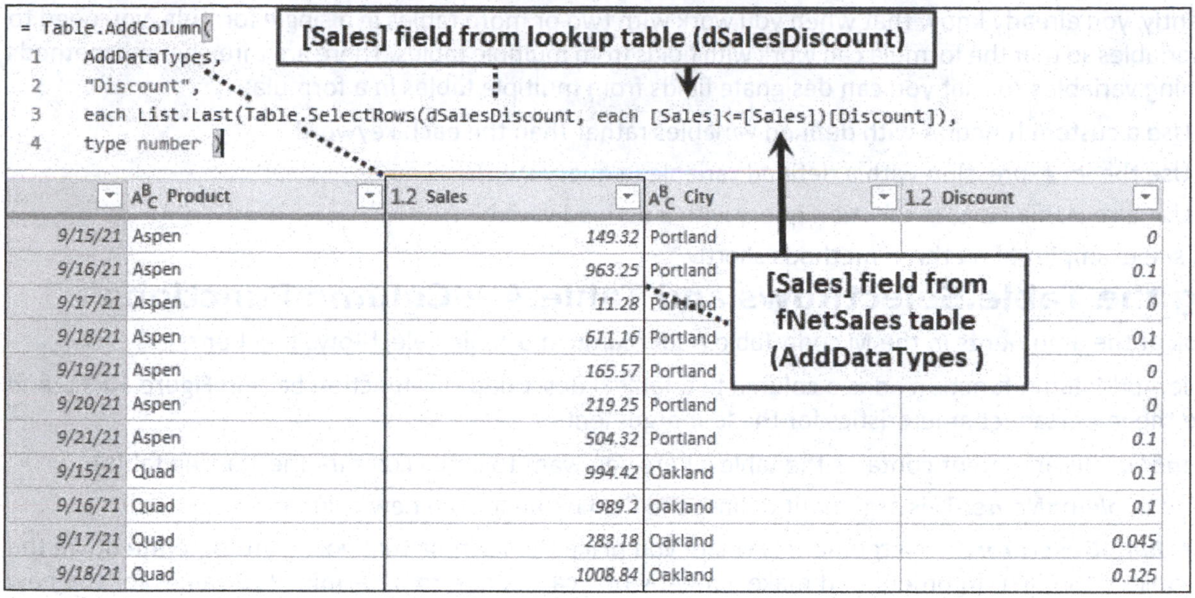

```
= Table.AddColumn(
1    AddDataTypes,
2    "Discount",
3    each List.Last(Table.SelectRows(dSalesDiscount, each [Sales]<=[Sales])[Discount]),
4    type number )
```

[Sales] field from lookup table (dSalesDiscount)

[Sales] field from fNetSales table (AddDataTypes)

A^B_C Product		1.2 Sales	A^B_C City	1.2 Discount
9/15/21	Aspen	149.32	Portland	0
9/16/21	Aspen	963.25	Portland	0.1
9/17/21	Aspen	11.28	Portland	0
9/18/21	Aspen	611.16	Portland	0.1
9/19/21	Aspen	165.57	Portland	0
9/20/21	Aspen	219.25	Portland	0
9/21/21	Aspen	504.32	Portland	0.1
9/15/21	Quad	994.42	Oakland	0.1
9/16/21	Quad	989.2	Oakland	0.1
9/17/21	Quad	283.18	Oakland	0.045
9/18/21	Quad	1008.84	Oakland	0.125

Figure 19.286 *This is the function you might like to use, but the two each keywords in a single formula will not work.*

If you were building a worksheet formula solution, you could easily solve this problem by using cell references to refer to the lookup column and the lookup value. But in M code, you do not have cell references. One good solution to this problem is to remove the each keywords from the Table.AddColumn and Table.SelectRows functions and instead define two custom functions that use defined variables and allow the formula to determine which table the [Sales] field is coming from. Figure 19.287 shows how using variables, rather than the each keywords, can allow the logical test IT[Sales]<=OT[Sales] to correctly designate that the IT[Sales] field is coming from the dSalesDiscount lookup table and the OT[Sales] field is coming from the AddDataTypes fact table.

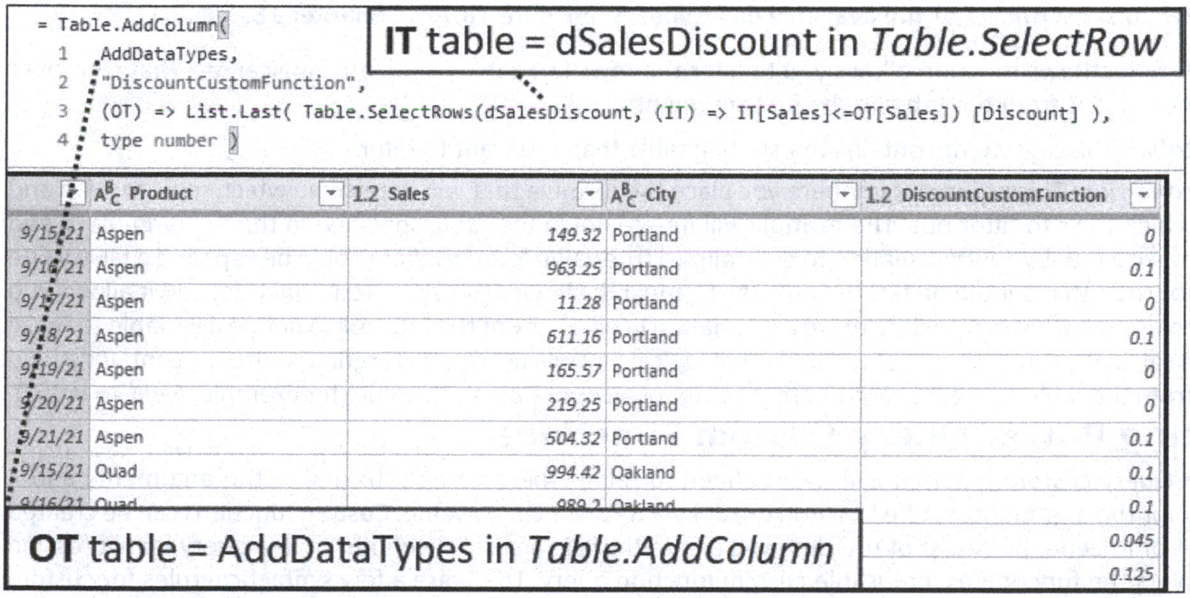

```
= Table.AddColumn(
1    AddDataTypes,
2    "DiscountCustomFunction",
3    (OT) => List.Last( Table.SelectRows(dSalesDiscount, (IT) => IT[Sales]<=OT[Sales]) [Discount] ),
4    type number )
```

IT table = dSalesDiscount in *Table.SelectRow*

A^B_C Product		1.2 Sales	A^B_C City	1.2 DiscountCustomFunction
9/15/21	Aspen	149.32	Portland	0
9/16/21	Aspen	963.25	Portland	0.1
9/17/21	Aspen	11.28	Portland	0
9/18/21	Aspen	611.16	Portland	0.1
9/19/21	Aspen	165.57	Portland	0
9/20/21	Aspen	219.25	Portland	0
9/21/21	Aspen	504.32	Portland	0.1
9/15/21	Quad	994.42	Oakland	0.1
9/16/21	Quad	989.2	Oakland	0.1
				0.045
				0.125

OT table = AddDataTypes in *Table.AddColumn*

Figure 19.287 *With two custom functions to define the variables OT and IT, this approximate match lookup will work.*

But this all sounds complicated. I mean, I have not even given you a definition of a custom function or shown the details of the Table.AddColumn and Table.SelectRows functions! Don't worry: I will show you these things shortly.

Importantly, you already know that when you work with two or more tables in a single formula, you need to define variables so that the formula can work with fields from multiple tables. There are three helpful methods for defining variables so that you can designate fields from multiple tables in a formula:

- Use a custom function with defined variables rather than the each keyword.
- Use the let expression with a defined variable (a query step).
- Use a reusable custom function query with a defined variable.

You will see examples of all three methods shortly.

Using the Table.SelectRows and Table.AddColumn Functions

Let's look at the arguments in the M code Table.AddColumn and Table.SelectRows functions.

The Table.AddColumn function adds a column to a table. I described this function back in Figure 19.31, and here are the important characteristics for the four arguments:

- *table*: This argument contains the table where you want to add a column (the starting table).
- *newColumnName*: This argument defines the field name for the new column.
- *columnGenerator*: This argument is where you place the formula that you want to iterate down the table in the first argument and make a row-by-row calculation to determine the values for the new field. The formula is called a Power Query custom function, and it allows you to use the keyword each to make a calculation in each row of the table or to define a variable to make a calculation in each row of the table.
- *columnType*: This argument allows you to define the data type for the newly created field with M code, such as:
  - **type number:** For a decimal data type
  - **type text:** For a text data type
  - **Int64.Type:** For a whole number data type
  - **type date:** For a date data type

Note: To see a full list of the available data types, see Figure 18.72 in Chapter 18.

The Table.SelectRows function allows you to filter the rows in a table based on a logical test that runs over one or more fields from the table in the first argument:

- *table*: This argument contains the starting table that you want to filter.
- *condition*: This argument is where you place the formula that will determine which rows to keep and which rows to filter out. The formula will iterate down the table specified in the first argument and make a row-by-row calculation to determine a true value for rows that should be kept and a false value for rows that should be filtered out. The formula is a Power Query custom function, and it allows you to use the keyword each to make a calculation in each row of the table or to define a variable to make a calculation in each row of the table. The logical formula used in this argument usually contains a field from the table in the first argument, a comparison operator, and a value (for example, *Field <= Value*).

Creating Power Query Custom Functions

A *Power Query custom function* is a user-defined formula where you get to define the arguments and a mapping for the arguments so the function can deliver a Power Query value. Custom functions can be created in any bit of M code, but most of the time you create them in a custom column or in a query let expression that delivers the function as a reusable custom function query. There are a few syntactical rules for custom functions that you need to be aware of:

- You type one or more variables separated by commas and enclosed in parentheses. You get to invent your own variable names. However, if you use spaces, you must use the #"*Variable Name*" identifier naming convention.
- After the variable or variables, you type the go to operator (an equal sign and a greater-than sign with no space, like this: =>). The go to operator informs the custom function that everything that comes next is the formula.
- Finally, you type a formula that uses the variable or variables (though a formula is not required to use variables).

The general syntax for a custom function is:

```
(variable1,variable2) => formula that uses zero or more variables
```

Here is an example of a custom function used in a custom column that calculates the monthly rate from an annual mortgage rate in a field named Rate:

```
(APR) => APR[Rate]/12
```

The variable for the annual mortgage rate is APR. The formula is APR[Rate]/12, which divides the APR by 12 to yield the monthly rate.

You can define a data type for each variable in parentheses. You can also define a data type for the function's resulting value directly after the defined variable's close parenthesis.

Defining data types in custom functions is optional. The general syntax for a custom function that defines data types is:

```
(variable1 as type,variable2 as type) as type => formula that uses zero or
more variables
```

Here is an example of a custom function in a custom column that calculates the monthly rate from an annual mortgage rate in a field named Rate with defined data types for the variable and custom function result:

```
(APR as number) as number => APR[Rate]/12
```

The variable APR is defined as a decimal data type. The function returns a value with the decimal data type.

In these first two examples, the custom function is working with only a single table. When this is the case, you do not need to explicitly define a variable and can use the go to operator. When you have a single table or are working in a single scope (like a single table), you can use the each keyword (all lowercase) as a substitute for defining an explicit variable. The each keyword is shorthand for a custom function. So the formula:

```
(APR) => APR[Rate]/12
```

Can be more easily written as:

```
each [Rate]/12
```

So far in this book, you have seen the each keyword used in many of the automatically created M code formulas where custom functions were required. For example, any time you used the user interface to filter an Extension field to include only rows where the file has the extension .xlsx, this formula was automatically created:

```
= Table.SelectRows(ExtensionsFieldLowercase, each [Extension] = ".xlsx")
```

Here, the each keyword allows the custom function [Extension] = ".xlsx" to act on each row in the table. The each keyword is a substitute for defining an explicit variable with a formula like this:

```
= Table.SelectRows(ExtensionsFieldLowercase, (x) => x[Extension] = ".xlsx")
```

The each keyword is easier to use when there is a single value that you are working with, such as a table or a list. However, when you need to work across multiple tables or lists, it is useful to define variables so that within the scope of a single table or list, you can pull values from inside or outside that scope (for example, from another table).

In the examples above, I showed you custom functions in custom columns. If you instead define a custom function in a new query as part of a let expression in the Advanced Editor, you can create a reusable custom function query, where the name of the query becomes the name of the reusable function. Here is an example:

```
(APR) =>
let
MonthlyRate = APR/12
in
MonthlyRate
```

In this case, the variable is APR. After the go to operator is a let expression that defines a *Power Query function value* that can be used throughout the file (Excel or Power BI Desktop).

> **Note:** You will see how to create a custom function query later in this chapter.

Power Query custom functions are also useful when there is no built-in function to perform a task. For example, there is no built-in M code function to calculate an effective interest rate, but here is a custom function to calculate an effective interest rate:

(APR, NumOfPeriods) => Number.Power(1+APR/ NumOfPeriods, NumOfPeriods) - 1

The last important detail I want to mention about custom functions is that you can use the *underscore character* with the each keyword to get the full row from a table or list. If your goal is to extract the full record from each row in a table or the item from each row in a list, then this simple formula will do it:

```
each _
```

This is important because you have now learned how to:

- Extract a value from a table using a two-way lookup by using *Table{RowIndex or KeyMatchLookup}[FieldName]*
- Extract a list from a field in a table by using *Table[FieldName]*
- Extract a record from a table or an item from a list when making a row-by-row calculation by using each _

Now that you have learned about the Table.SelectRows and Table.AddColumn functions and custom functions, you can build the approximate match formula with custom functions and variables. As shown in Figure 19.288, you have to define variables for the formula element [Sales]<=[Sales] because the formula element must access the full [Sales] field from the dSalesDiscount table from within the scope of the Table.SelectRows function and the row-by-row values in the [Sales] field from the AddDataTypes table from outside the scope of the Table.SelectRows function. Further, whereas the Table.AddColumn function iterates down each row in the AddDataTypes table and pulls out a sales value for each row from the [Sales] field to use as a conditional hurdle, the Table.SelectRows function uses the full [Sales] field, iterates down that field to compare each sales value to the hurdle, and then delivers a column of true and false values to help filter the table. (In this case, both of the field names just happen to have the same Sales name. This is not the reason that you are defining variables. You are defining variables so that your formula can work within the scope of the Table. SelectRows function and reference fields outside that scope.)

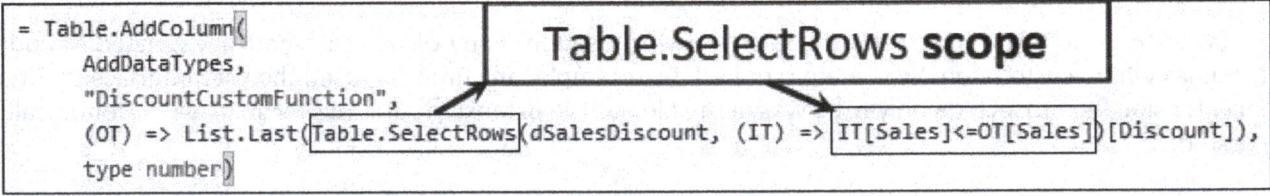

Figure 19.288 The formula element is working within the scope of the Table.SelectRows function.

Creating a Custom Function with Two Variables for an Approximate Match Lookup Formula

The variable names I chose for this project are IT (for *inside table*) and OT (for *outside table*). Because the dSalesDiscount table sits inside the first argument of the Table.SelectRows function and is literally a tiny table inside each cell in the Discount field, I call it the inside table. Because the AddDataTypes table is the larger table that the Table.AddColumn iterates down and is the table that contains each of the tiny IT tables, I call it the outside table. In addition, from the point of view of the Table.SelectRows function, the dSalesDiscount table is inside the scope of that function, and the AddDataTypes table is outside the scope of that function.

To create the approximate match lookup formula, follow these steps:

1. As shown in Figure 19.289, create a custom column that shows the lookup table in every row. Name the query step **AproxMatchLookupDiscountCC**.

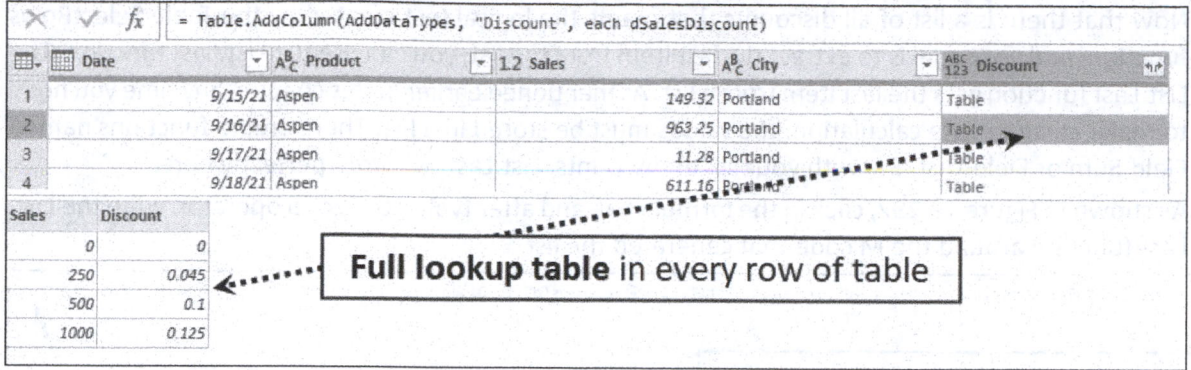

Figure 19.289 *You can use the each keyword because the scope is for the single function Table.AddColumn.*

2. As shown in Figure 19.290, click in the formula bar and edit the second argument of the Table. AddColumn function so that the custom function is **(OT) => Table.SelectRows(dSalesDiscount, (IT) => IT[Sales]<=OT[Sales]**. Press the Enter key. Now the table in each row of the Discount field is filtered based on the sales value from the fact table.

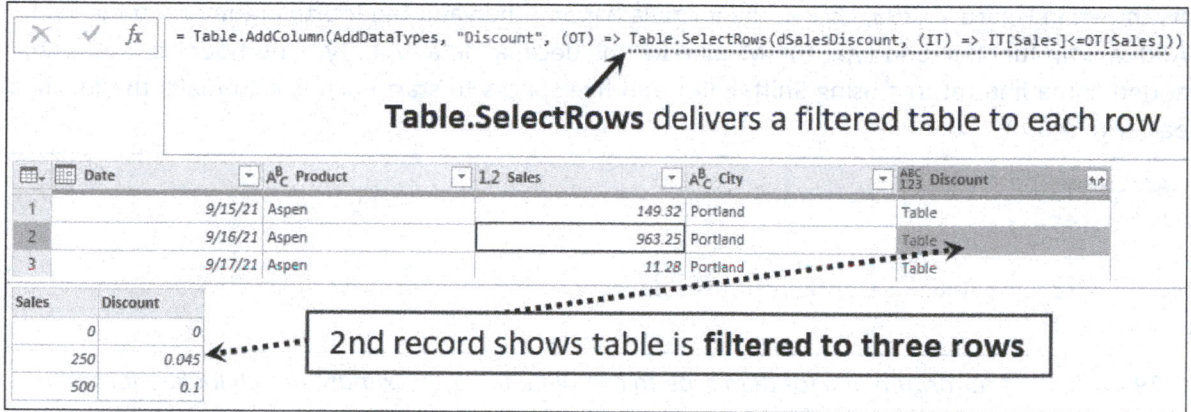

Figure 19.290 *Defining variables allows the Table.SelectRows and Table.AddColumn functions to work together.*

The next task is to extract the filtered Discount field as a list so that you can make an aggregate calculation. To extract a list from a field in a table, you use the field access operator and the name of the field. Because Table.SelectRows delivers a table, you can place [Discount] after this table, and it will extract the field as a list.

3. As shown in Figure 19.291, click in the formula bar and carefully place your cursor after the close parenthesis of the Table.SelectRows function and type **[Discount]**. Then, before you press the Enter key, carefully place your cursor after the close parenthesis of the Table.AddColumn function and press Enter to evaluate the formula.

Note: Remember that Power Query's IntelliSense is not great, so it's very important to carefully place your cursor in this step.

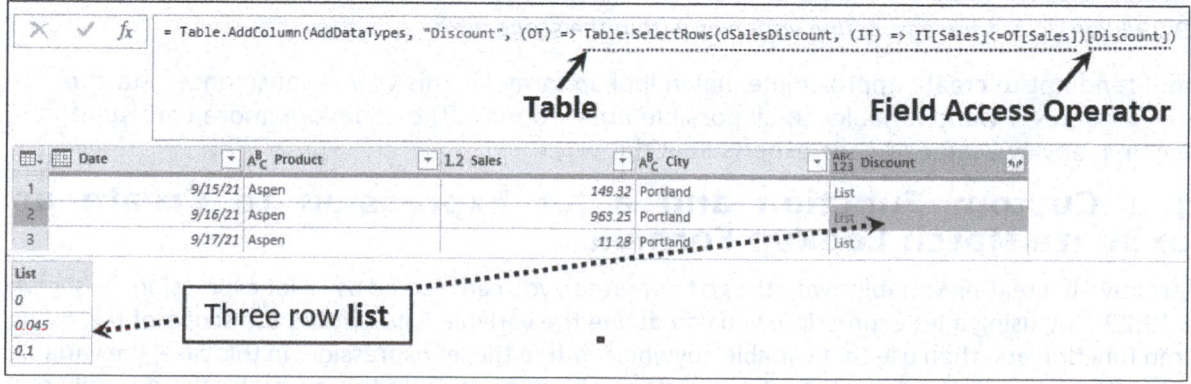

Figure 19.291 *Extract a list from a field in a table by using the field access operator.*

Now that there is a list of all discounts that meets the logical test created by the Table.SelectRows function, and your goal is to extract the last item from the list, you can use the List.Last function. The List.Last function gets the last item from a list. As mentioned earlier in this chapter, any time you need to make an aggregate calculation, the values must be stored in a list. There are no functions named Field.Sum or Field.Last. So, with your list of discounts, List.Last will work perfectly here.

4. As shown in Figure 19.292, click in the formula bar, and after typing the go to operator, wrap the List. Last function around the M code that generated the list.

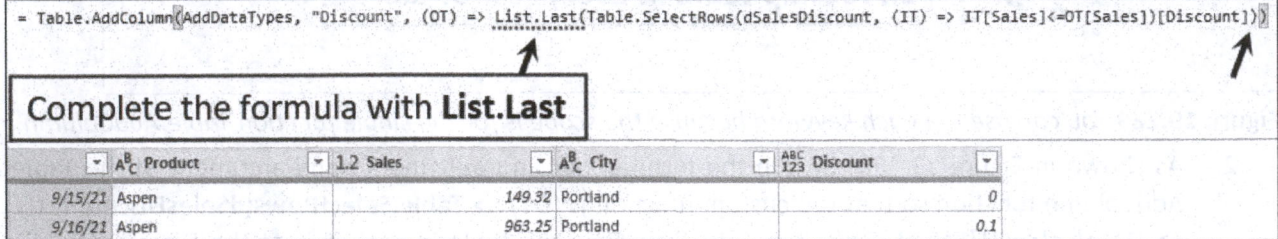

= Table.AddColumn(AddDataTypes, "Discount", (OT) => List.Last(Table.SelectRows(dSalesDiscount, (IT) => IT[Sales]<=OT[Sales])[Discount]))

Complete the formula with List.Last

▼	A^B_C Product	▼	1.2 Sales	▼	A^B_C City	▼	ABC 123 Discount	▼
9/15/21	Aspen		149.32	Portland			0	
9/16/21	Aspen		963.25	Portland			0.1	

Figure 19.292 *Wrap List.Last around the M code that generated the list.*

5. As shown in Figure 19.293, click in the formula bar and then add the fourth argument to the Table. AddColumn function and type the M code for the decimal data type: **type number**. (In this case, I added some line returns using Shift+Enter and five spaces to start each line to make the formula easier to read.)

```
= Table.AddColumn(
     AddDataTypes,
     "Discount",
     (OT) => List.Last(Table.SelectRows(dSalesDiscount, (IT) => IT[Sales]<=OT[Sales])[Discount]),
     type number)
```

Figure 19.293 *Add the four arguments for data type to complete the approximate match lookup formula.*

Using a Custom Function with One Variable and the each Keyword to Create an Approximate Match Lookup Formula

As an alternative to creating two variables in two different back-to-back table functions, you can create just a single variable for the variable that is outside the scope of the function where the formula is located, as shown in Figure 19.294. In the second argument of Table.SelectRows, you can use the each keyword and no variable prefix for the Sales field that is referencing the dSalesDiscount table in the first argument of the Table.SelectRows function.

```
= Table.AddColumn(
     AddDataTypes,
     "Discount",
     (OT) => List.Last(Table.SelectRows(dSalesDiscount, each [Sales]<=OT[Sales])[Discount]),
     type number)
```

each works inside function's scope

Figure 19.294 *You do not have to define variables within the scope area.*

Note: I tend not to create approximate match lookup formulas this way because once I start to define variables, I want variables in all possible areas to make the code look more consistent. However, many awesome M code experts do it this way.

Using a Custom Function and a let Expression to Create an Approximate Match Lookup Formula

As an alternative to creating variables with the go to operator, you can instead use a let expression. As shown in Figure 19.295, by using a let expression, you can define the variable Sales within the scope of the Table. AddColumn function and then use that variable anywhere within the let expression; in this case, the variable is used after the in keyword, where the let expression delivers a result. In this example, there is only one query step, but if the formula required more than one variable from this scope, you could add more query steps to the let expression.

```
= Table.AddColumn(
    AddDataTypes,                    let expression to define a variable
    "Discount",
    each  let Sales = [Sales] in  List.Last(Table.SelectRows(dSalesDiscount, each [Sales]<=Sales)[Discount]),
    type number)
```

Figure 19.295 *The let expression can be used to define variables within a given scope area.*

Using a Custom Function Query to Create an Approximate Match Lookup Formula

As a last example of creating an approximate match lookup formula, you will see how to create a reusable custom function query. This method is particularly useful if you are going to look up discounts in multiple queries because you can create the function one time and use it over and over. As shown in Figure 19.296, in a blank query, you type a custom function with the variable and go to operator at the top, followed by a let expression that delivers a function value. This function value can be used anywhere in the Power Query Editor.

```
Advanced Editor

FxAproxDiscountLookup

(Sales) =>
let
    AMLFunction = List.Last(Table.SelectRows(dSalesDiscount, each [Sales]<=Sales)[Discount])
in
    AMLFunction
```

Figure 19.296 *The let expression delivers a Power Query function value that can be reused.*

Figure 19.297 shows the Invoke Custom Function button in the Add Colum tab of the Power Query Editor. If you create the function and add a column to the fNetSales table, you can click the Invoke Custom Function button to open the Invoke Custom Function dialog box (shown in Figure 19.298), where you can create the field name, select the reusable function, and decide which field in the table should be used for the variable.

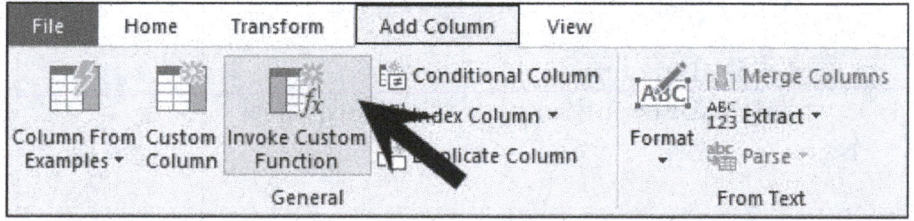

Figure 19.297 *The Add Column tab in the Power Query Ribbon has an Invoke Custom Function button.*

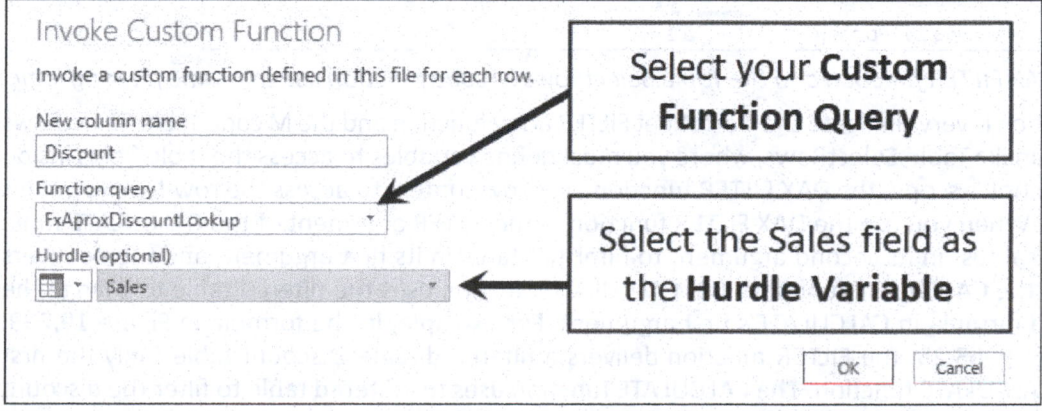

Figure 19.298 *Name the field, select the function, and select the field in the table that represents the variable.*

Note: You can try these alternative methods if you would like. I do not provide detailed steps for these formulas. However, the finished file for this project, Ch19-Project05-FinishedOnPremise. xlsx, includes examples of all these formulas, so you can look at them before trying it yourself.

Using a DAX Calculated Column to Perform an Approximate Match Lookup on a Large Dataset

I tend to use a custom function with the go to operator and defined variables because this method seems cleanest and most easily understood. When I use a particular formula more than one time, I tend to create a reusable custom function query. However, all of these methods are fine to use. There is one HUGE caveat, though: *M code approximate match lookup formulas calculate slowly*. If you have large datasets, you should not use Power Query to perform an approximate match lookup. If you try to use the M code formulas shown here, it will take a very long time to make the calculations. If you have big data, you should load the data to the Data Model and use a DAX calculated column. The good news is that the DAX and M code formulas for this are logically very similar.

Even though this project is all about creating Power Query transformations, I want to briefly show you how to use a DAX calculated column to perform an approximate match lookup. If you want to go and look at this formula and try it for yourself, you can use the Excel file named Ch19-Project05-DAX-AproxMatchLookup.xlsx. The data model in this Excel workbook has the same two tables that you have been using in the project. The fact table is named fNetSales, and the lookup table is named disSalesDiscount. There is no relationship between these two tables.

In the Data Model, a relationship requires a primary key and a foreign key with an exact match between the two fields. There is no such thing as an exact match when you are doing an approximate match lookup. The dis prefix in the lookup table name disSalesDiscount stands for *disconnected* because when two tables do not have a relationship in the Data Model, the two tables are disconnected. These disconnected tables will work perfectly for performing an approximate match look up because you can use the CALCULATE function to pick out the maximum discount rate from the discount column based on a filtered discount table.

Figure 19.299 shows that in the first argument of the CALCULATE function, the MAX function is looking at the full discount field. Then, in the second argument of the CALCULATE function, you can use the FILTER function. The DAX FILTER function is an iterator function that delivers a table. Earlier, you learned that an iterating function like SUMX delivers an aggregate value; however, the FILTER function is an iterating function that delivers a table. The FILTER function contains the starting table to be filtered in the first argument and a field from that table in the second argument that it uses to iterate across to determine which rows to filter out.

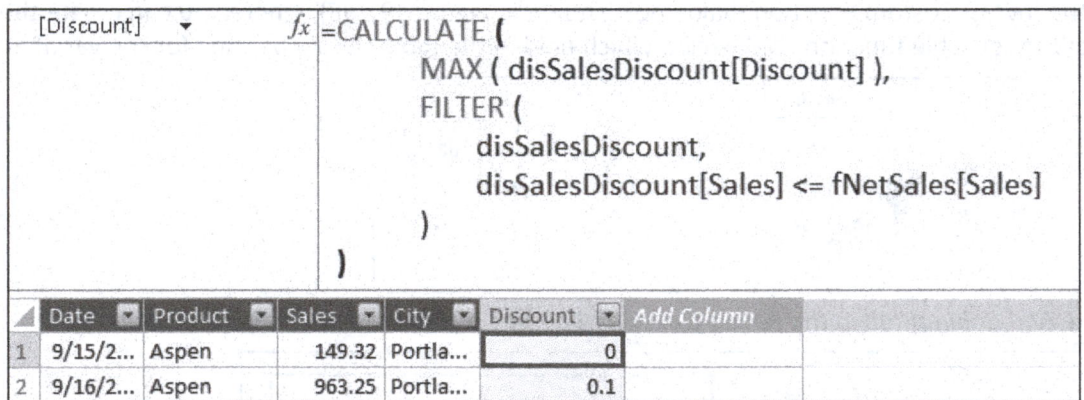

Figure 19.299 *The DAX FILTER function and the Table.SelectRows M code function use the same filtering logic.*

The DAX FILTER function is very similar to the worksheet FILTER array function and the M code Table.SelectRows function. However, unlike Table.SelectRows, where you must define variables to access the table fields inside and outside the function's scope, the DAX FILTER function uses row context to access the row-by-row values from the Sales field. When you use the DAX FILTER function in the FILTER argument of the CALCULATE function, it uses the logical test in its second argument to filter the table in its first argument and then delivers the filtered table to the CALCULATE function. The CALCULATE function uses the filtered table to change the filter context for the formula in CALCULATE's first argument. For example, in the formula in Figure 19.299, for the sales amount $963.25, the FILTER function delivers a filtered disSalesDiscount table (only the first three rows) to the CALCULATE function. The CALCULATE function uses the filtered table to filter the discount column in the MAX function down to three rows, and the MAX function calculates the maximum value of 0.1 and delivers it as the discount.

Using the Number.Round and Number.RoundAwayFromZero M Code Functions

When you want to round a number with worksheet formulas or DAX formulas, you use the ROUND function. The ROUND function, as you learned in Chapter 10, performs standard rounding. In Power Query, when you want to round a number, you can use the Number.RoundAwayFromZero function to perform standard rounding or the Number.Round function to perform banker's rounding. In the first argument of each function, you place the number to be rounded, and in the second argument, you place the digit to be rounded to.

> **Note:** *Banker's rounding*, also called *Gaussian rounding* or *half-way even rounding*, works the same way as standard rounding except when it has to deal with the digit 5. At 5, it rounds to the nearest even number. This means that with the digit 5, the function will sometimes round up and sometimes round down, thereby eliminating some of the upward bias associated with standard rounding, which always rounds up. When you have large sets of numbers, banker's rounding is more accurate, and some industries (such as banking) require banker's rounding. In this project, you will use the Number.Round function to perform banker's rounding.

To calculate net sales based on the Sales and Discount fields, follow these steps:

1. As shown in Figure 19.300, add a custom column to calculate net sales based on the formula Sales*(1-Discount). Round the result of the formula by using the Power Query rounding function Number.Round. Press Enter to evaluate the formula. Name the query step **NetSalesCC**. In the formula bar, add the fourth argument to the Table.AddColumn function to add a decimal data type.

```
= Table.AddColumn(AproxMatchLookupDiscountCC, "Net Sales", each Number.Round([Sales]*(1-[Discount]),2),type number)
```

A^BC Product	1.2 Sales	A^BC City	1.2 Discount	1.2 Net Sales
9/15/21 Aspen	149.32	Portland	0	149.32
9/16/21 Aspen	963.25	Portland	0.1	866.92
9/17/21 Aspen	11.28	Portland	0	11.28
9/18/21 Aspen	611.16	Portland	0.1	550.04
9/19/21 Aspen	165.57	Portland	0	165.57

Figure 19.300 *Add a custom column to calculate net sales.*

2. To remove the fields that are not needed when you load the table to the worksheet, select the fields in this order: Date, Product, City, and Net Sales. Right-click any one of these fields and click on Remove Other Columns. Name the step **KeepDateProductCityNetSalesFields**.

The completed transformations for the fNetSales query are shown in Figure 19.301.

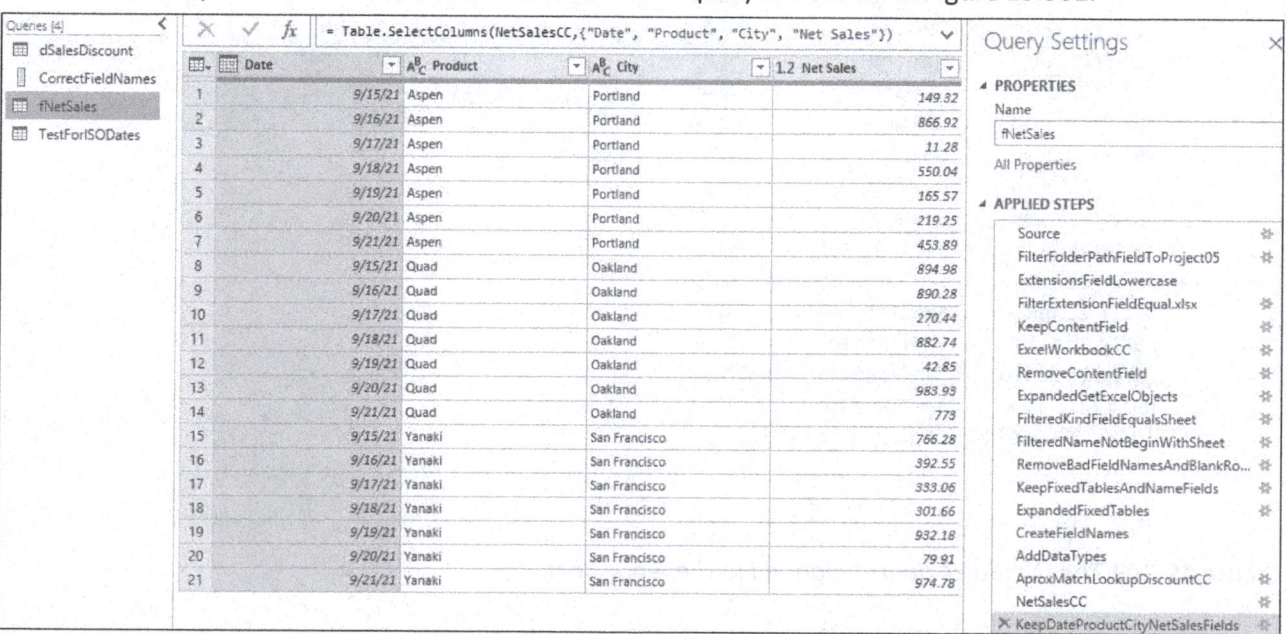

Figure 19.301 *Done! 18 query steps that will be rerun each time new data arrives.*

3. Now that the query is finished, in the Home tab, go to the Close group and click the Close & Load button.

4. To change the load location and load the query to the worksheet, right-click the fNetSales query in the Queries & Connections task pane and click Load To.

5. As shown in Figure 19.302, in the Import Data dialog box that appears, click the Table option button, click the Existing Worksheet option button, navigate to cell B2 on the worksheet FinalData, and click OK. The loaded query is shown in Figure 19.303.

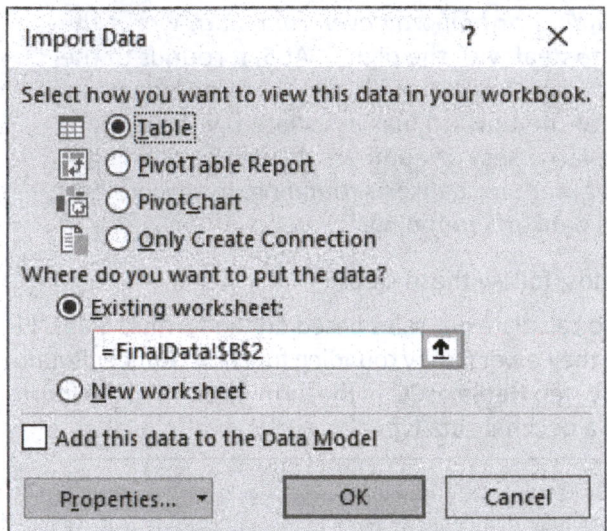

Figure 19.302 *Change the load location to cell B2 in the worksheet FinalData.*

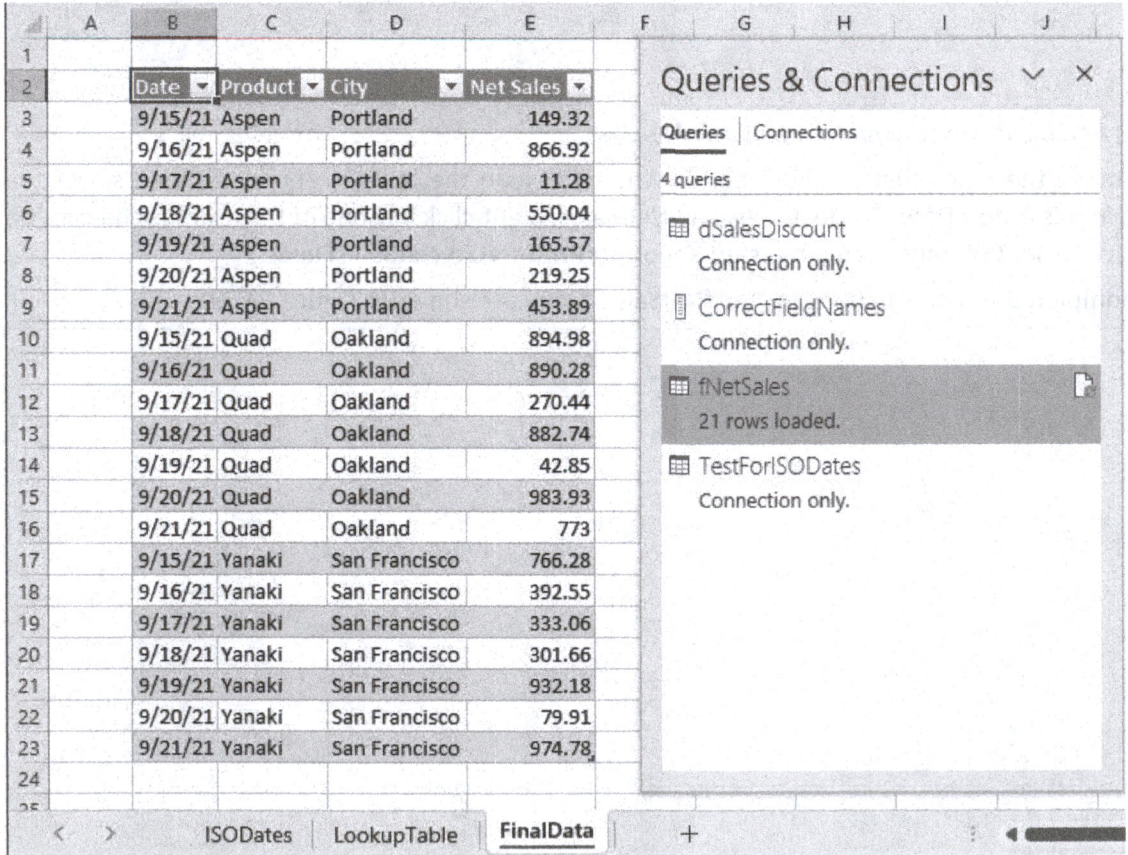

Figure 19.303 *The fNetSales query is loaded to the worksheet.*

Adding a Sort Command to an Approximate Match Lookup Table as a Safeguard

What often happens after you finish a long data analysis project like this is that you realize that you forgot to perform an important step in the process. Well, in this project, I forgot to sort the first column of the lookup table! When you do an approximate match lookup, the first column of the table is required to be sorted from smallest to largest. The table you used was sorted. But if someone accidentally sorted the table in the worksheet in a different way, the approximate match lookup formula could yield the wrong answer. The solution to this is simple: You just add a sort step to the lookup table query, and then it does not matter what the sort order is in the worksheet.

To change the sort order in the dSalesDiscount query, follow these steps:

1. In the Queries & Connections task pane, double-click the dSalesDiscount query. The dSalesDiscount query opens.

2. In the Applied Steps list, select the AddedDataTypes step.

3. At the top of the Sales field, click the Sort & Filter dropdown and then click on Sort A to Z.

4. In the Insert Step dialog box that appears, click the Insert button.

5. Name the step **SortFirstField**.

6. Close and load the query.

Adding New Data to the Table and Refreshing It

To determine whether the query can accommodate new data, add the Seattle.xlsx file to the Start folder and then refresh the query. Figure 19.304 shows the results with the new Seattle data added.

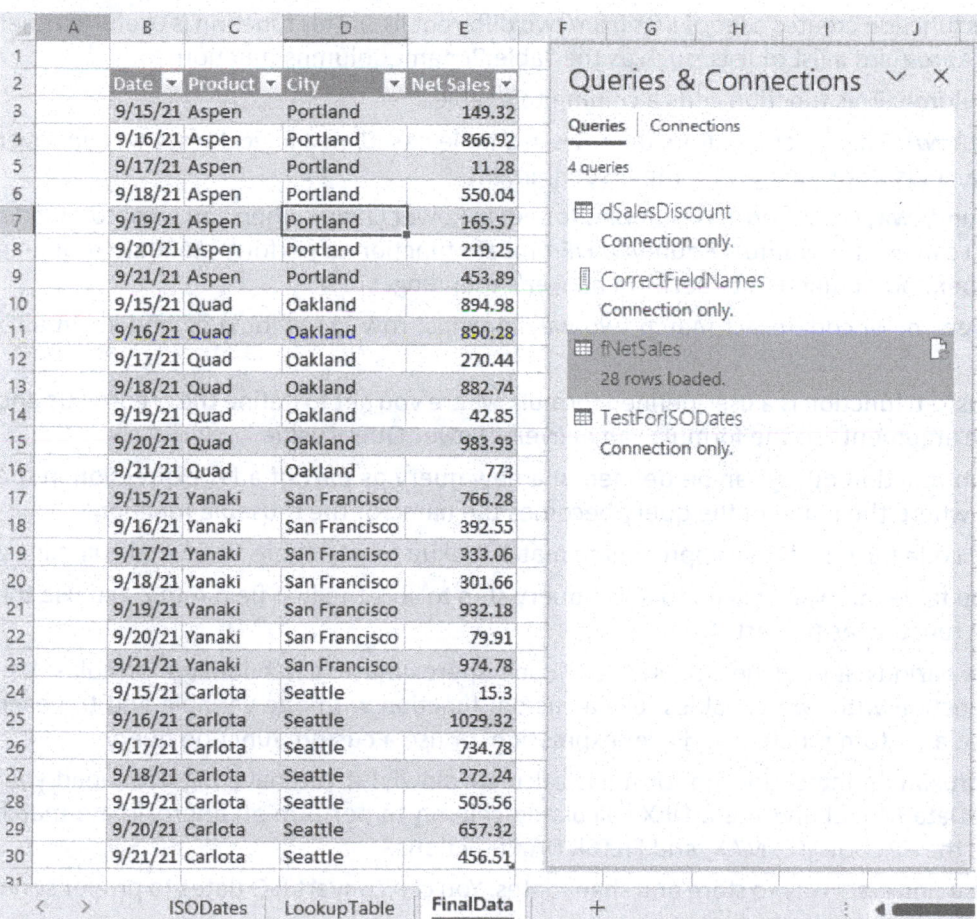

Figure 19.304 *After the new data is added and the query is refreshed, the new data is in the table.*

Project 5 Summary

Wow! You have just learned a lot about advanced M code! The key data analysis and power tool takeaways from this project are as follows:

- OneDrive is a Microsoft online file sharing service that comes with Microsoft 365. To import files from OneDrive by using the From SharePoint Folder Power Query feature, an organization must have Microsoft 365 Enterprise edition.
- The Power Query From Sheet button allows you to bring Excel Tables, defined names, or dynamic spilled arrays from a worksheet in the current workbook into the Power Query Editor.
- When you use Power Query to write M code formulas for you, you need to understand that in a let expression, each new step is usually acting on the previous step. So, when you want to combine steps, you can copy a full formula (without the query step name or equal sign) from a given line and paste it into the first argument of the function in the subsequent query step. By doing this for multiple steps in a query, you can combine many lines of code into a single line of code that you can use in other locations, such as a custom column formula.
- You learned about a number of Power Query M code functions, including:
    - **Table.Buffer:** This function stores a table in a cache and allows the destination query to reuse the stored values rather than call the query multiple times.
    - **Table.RenameColumns:** This function renames the fields in a table and requires a table with the field names that you want to change in the first argument and a list of lists with the original field names and the new field names in the second argument.
    - **Table.ColumnNames:** This function extracts the field names from a table
    - **List.Zip:** This function creates a list of lists from two different lists. This function is useful in other functions that require a list of lists, such as the Table.RenameColumns function.
    - **Table.AddColumn:** This function adds a column to a table.
    - **Table.SelectRows:** This function filters the rows in a table based on a logical test that runs over one or more fields from the table in the first argument.
    - **Number.RoundAwayFromZero and Number.Round:** In Power Query, when you want to round a number, you can use the Number.RoundAwayFromZero function to perform standard rounding or the Number.Round function to perform banker's rounding.
- There are two types of M code exact match two-way lookups: row index lookups and key match lookups.
- A Power Query custom function is a user-defined formula where you get to define the arguments and a mapping for the arguments so the formula can deliver a Power Query value.
- A reusable custom function query can be defined in a new query as part of a let expression in the Advanced Editor, where the name of the query becomes the name of the reusable function.
- A Power Query M code formula for an approximate match lookup must adhere to several guidelines:
    - In the lookup table query, you need to add a query step to sort the first field A to Z and use the Table.Buffer function as the last step.
    - You can take various approaches to writing M code approximate match lookup formulas: Use a custom function with two variables, use a custom function with one variable and the each keyword, use a custom function and a let expression, or use a custom function query.
    - M code approximate match lookup formulas calculate slowly! If you have big data, load your data to the Data Model and use a DAX calculated column to perform an approximate match lookup with the CALCULATE, MAX, and FILTER DAX functions.
- ISO dates provide a universal way to store and share dates. You can convert ISO dates to proper serial number dates in Power Query in two ways:
    - If the ISO dates are text values, use the date data type to convert them to proper serial number dates.
    - If the ISO dates are number values, first apply a text data type and then apply a second new change data type action to apply the date data type.

Key Concepts in Chapter 19

This long chapter presents advanced data analysis with big data, Microsoft's power tools, and a lot of important technical facts about the DAX and M code formula languages. At the end of each of the five projects in this chapter is a summary of the key data analysis concepts covered in that project.

Now you have advanced skills to complete almost any data analysis project that comes your way. Be sure to complete the practice problems in this chapter, including Practice Problem 6, where you will get try to use Power BI Desktop mapping capabilities on 911 call data and Practice Problem 7, where you will build dashboards in both Excel and Power BI Desktop.

Keyboard Shortcuts Learned in Chapter 19

Keyboard Shortcut	Description
F2	Renames the selected query or applied query step
Shift+Enter	Adds a line break in the DAX formula bar
Right-click key, G =	With the cursor inside an Excel Table, a defined name, or a dynamic spilled array, brings the Excel Table into the Power Query Editor

Practice Problems for Chapter 19

Practice Problem 1

Open the Excel file named Ch19-PP01Start.xlsx, which is in the following folder: TheOnlyAppThatMatters\ Ch19\Ch19-PP01. In addition, you will need to access the .txt files from the following folder path: TheOnlyAppThatMatters\Ch19\Ch19-PP01\TextFiles.

Go to the worksheet PPCh19(1). Figure 19.305 shows the goals that are listed on the worksheet.

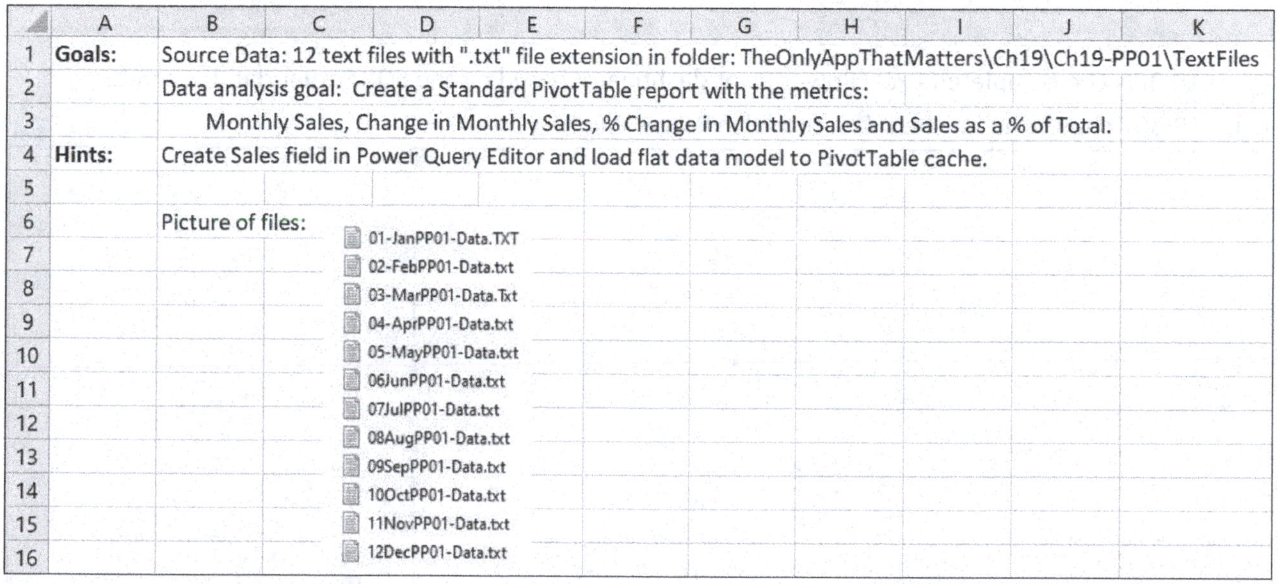

Figure 19.305 On the worksheet PPCh19(1), use Power Query and a standard PivotTable to solve this problem.

When you are done with this problem, you can check your work against the answer in the Excel workbook Ch19-PP01Finished.xlsx.

Practice Problem 2

For this problem, you are going to apply all the Power Query and DAX formula skills you learned using Power BI Desktop in Project 2, but for this practice problem, you will use Excel Power Pivot. You will use the Excel file Ch19-PP-02-Start.xlsx to complete this project. Your goal is to create the Boom Incorporated sales dashboard shown in Figure 19.306, using the same SQL Server database data that you used in Project 2.

To connect to the SQL Server database, use these credentials:

- **Server:** pond.highline.edu
- **Database:** boomdata

- **User:** excelisfun
- **Password:** ExcellsFun!

Figure 19.306 shows the finished dashboard that you are required to create.

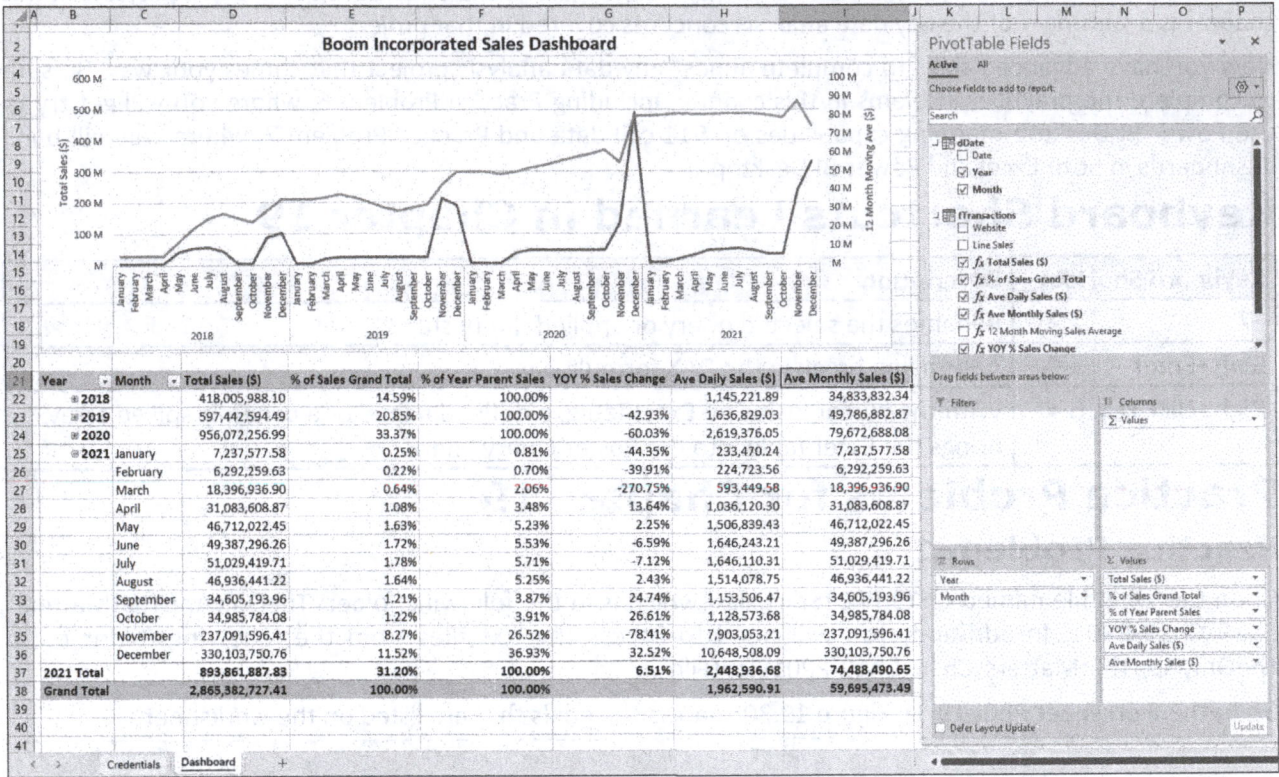

Figure 19.306 The completed Excel Power Pivot dashboard, based on the SQL Server database data.

Figure 19.307 shows the finished data model in Power Pivot.

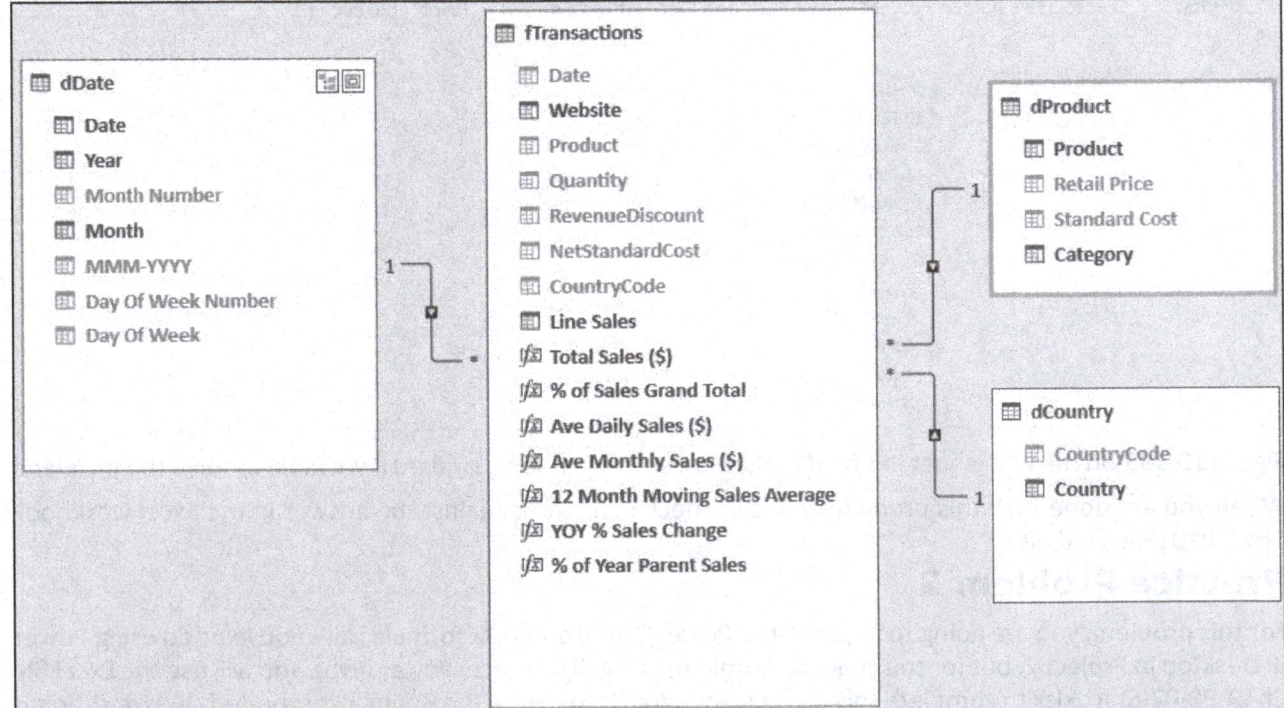

Figure 19.307 The finished data model in Power Pivot.

Figure 19.308 shows how you connect to an SQL Server database with Excel Power Query.

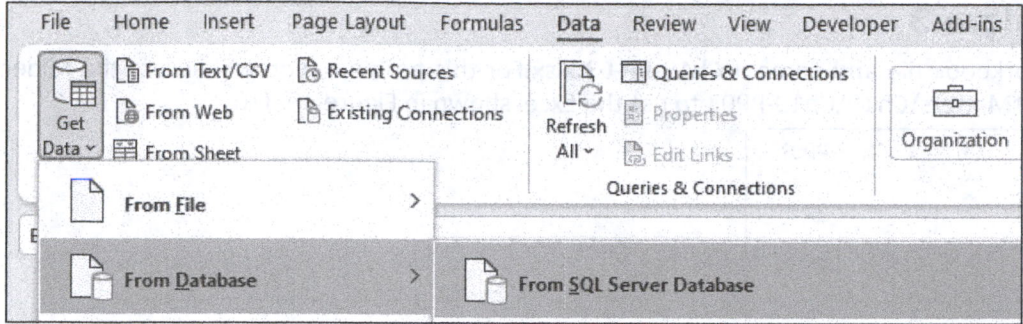

Figure 19.308 This is how you connect to an SQL Server database with Excel Power Query.

Figure 19.309 shows how to create a date dimension table in the Power Pivot data model with a single click. This is different from in Power BI Desktop, where you must manually create the date dimension table with DAX formulas. This automatic date table even creates a calculated column with a MMM-YYYY field that you can use as a helper column in the average monthly sales calculation. The table also automatically sorts the Month Name column by the Month Number column. This single-click method is subject to the same constraint as the DAX CALENDARAUTO DAX function that you learned about in Project 2: The unique date column created for the primary key is based on all dates in the data model, so if you have other date fields besides a single date field in the fact table, be careful. For the SQL data, this feature works perfectly.

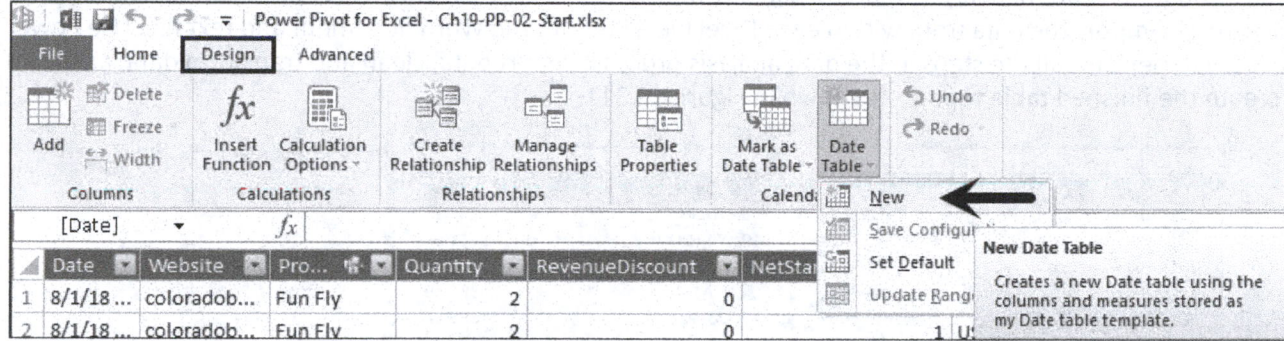

Figure 19.309 In Power Pivot, there is a button that automatically creates a date dimension table for you.

After you create the automatic date dimension table, rename the sheet tab and change the table name from Calendar to **dDate**. Then you need to create a DAX calculated column for the line sales.

When you create the measure for percentage of sales total, use ALL(fTransactions) as a filter in CALCULATE to remove all filters from the external filter context.

You need to create the following measures:

- Total Sales ($)
- % of Sales Grand Total
- % of Year Parent Sales

> **Note:** For the % of Year Parent Sales measure, the formula is =DIVIDE([Total Sales ($)],CALCULATE([Total Sales ($)],ALL(fTransactions), VALUES(dDate[Year]))). I am showing you the formula on this one because I did not teach this in the project. In order to have CALCULATE remove all filters except the year, you use the ALL function to remove all filters and then you use the VALUES function to add the year field back.

- Ave Daily Sales ($)
- Ave Monthly Sales ($)
- 12 Month Moving Sales Average
- YOY % Sales Change

When you are done with this problem, you can check your work against the Excel file Ch19-PP-02-Finished.xlsx.

Practice Problem 3

Open a new Excel workbook file and name it **Ch19-PP-03.xlsx**.For this problem, you will access the folder path TheOnlyAppThatMatters\Ch19\Ch19-PP03 to get the Excel shown in Figure 19.310.

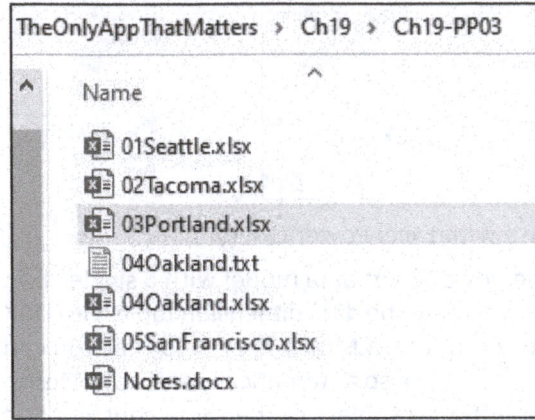

Figure 19.310 Five Excel files with data that you must import.

You need to import the data from the Excel files. Open each file and look around so that you can see what sort of data you are dealing with and what sort of Excel objects are in each Excel file. Use the From Folder feature to import the data from within each Excel file. Filter out the Word document and text file. Use Power Query to perform all the steps in the data analysis process: import data, clean and transform data, and then create the finished table report, as shown in Figure 19.311.

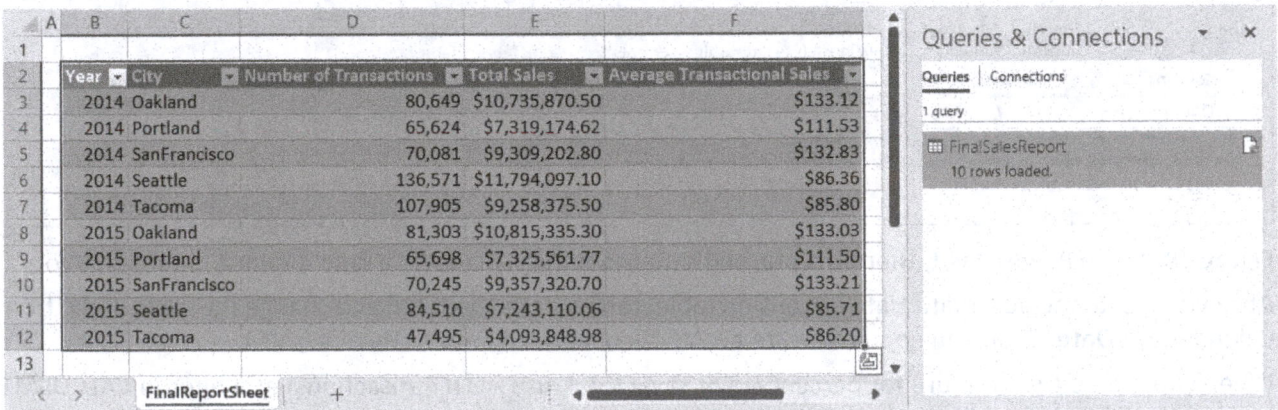

Figure 19.311 Finished table report created by Power Query.

You can check your work against the file Ch19-PP-03-Finished.xlsx.

Here is one hint: You will need to get the city name from the filename. I used the Replace Values option in the Any Column group in the Transform tab in the Power Query Ribbon to replace .xlsx with nothing. Then I used the Split by Position feature in the Text Column group in the Transform tab in the Power Query Ribbon to split by position 2. Those two steps enabled me to get the city name.

Practice Problem 4

Open the Excel workbook file Ch19-PP-04-Start.xlsx. As shown in Figure 19.312, create a solution that will combine all seven Excel Tables into a single Excel Table on the worksheet named AllStudents.

There is no summary report to create. The only goal is to combine the many student tables into a single table containing all student data. Make sure the query can be refreshed when new Excel Tables are added.

You can check your work against the file Ch19-PP-04-Finished.xlsx.

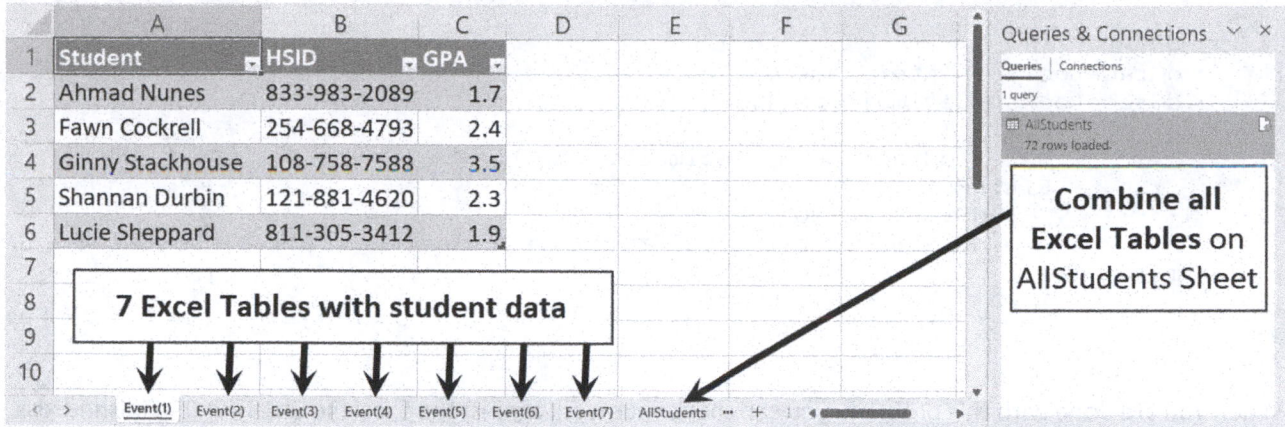

Figure 19.312 Combine all the Excel Tables into a single proper dataset.

Practice Problem 5

Open the Excel workbook file Ch19-PP-05-Start.xlsx. As shown in Figure 19.313, create a solution that will combine all four class Excel Tables into a single Excel Table on the worksheet named AllGrades, containing letter grades for all students from the grade lookup table on the worksheet LookupTable.

In addition, the field names for the tables are inconsistent. Use Power Query M code to assign the correct field names: StudentID and DecimalGrade. There is no list of correct field names, so you will have to create that.

In addition, for M code writing practice, complete the approximate match lookup formula in at least four different ways. This means that the final result with have four fields with the repeated letter grades. When you are done, convert the table on the worksheet Class(5) to an Excel Table and click the Refresh button. When you load the lookup table, in the Import Data dialog box, load it as a connection only and load it to the Data Model (because you will use the table in the Data Model later). When you load the fact table, in the Import Data dialog box, select the Table option button.

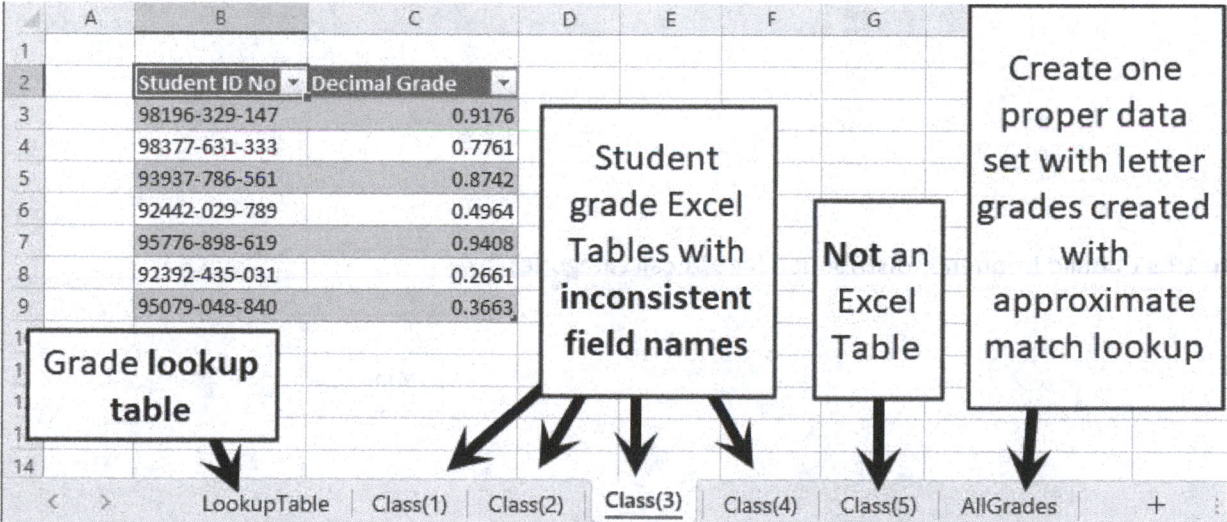

Figure 19.313 Combine all Excel Tables, fix inconsistent field names, and perform an approximate match lookup.

For the second part to this project, you need to try creating a DAX approximate match formula to look up the letter grade for each student. To load the fact table to the Data Model, in the Power Query Editor, right-click the combined student data query (the fact table with four approximate match formulas) and then, from the submenu, click on Duplicate to duplicate the query and copy all the M code in the Advanced Editor. Because you do not need the four approximate match formulas in this duplicated query, remove the four fields. Once the four lookup fields are removed, load the duplicated query to the Data Model. In the Data Model, create an approximate match lookup calculated column in the fact table. Here is an example of a DAX calculated column that you could use:

```
=
LOOKUPVALUE (
    dGradeLookup[LetterGrade],
    dGradeLookup[DecimalGrade],
        CALCULATE (
            MAX ( dGradeLookup[DecimalGrade] ),
            FILTER (
                dGradeLookup,
                dGradeLookup[DecimalGrade] <= AllGradesInOneTableDataModel[-
DecimalGrade]
            )
        )
)
```

When you are done with this problem, you can check your work against the Excel file Ch19-PP-05-Finished.xlsx.

Practice Problem 6

The goal for this project is to create a Power BI Desktop report with three pages to help visualize the different types of 911 call data from the city of Seattle. The three pages are shown in Figures 19.314 through 19.316. You will have to import a large CSV text file named Ch19-PP01-Code_Complaints_and_Violations.csv into a new Power BI Desktop file. The visualization goal of the three pages is to show the frequency and map locations of the different types of city of Seattle 911 calls.

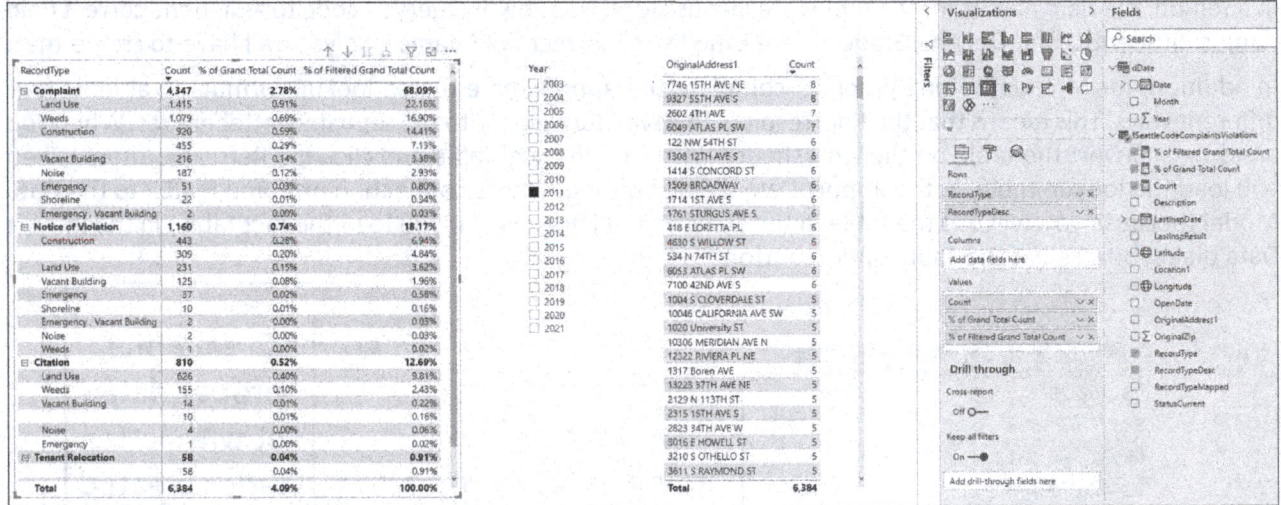

Figure 19.314 Build frequency distribution for 911 call categories.

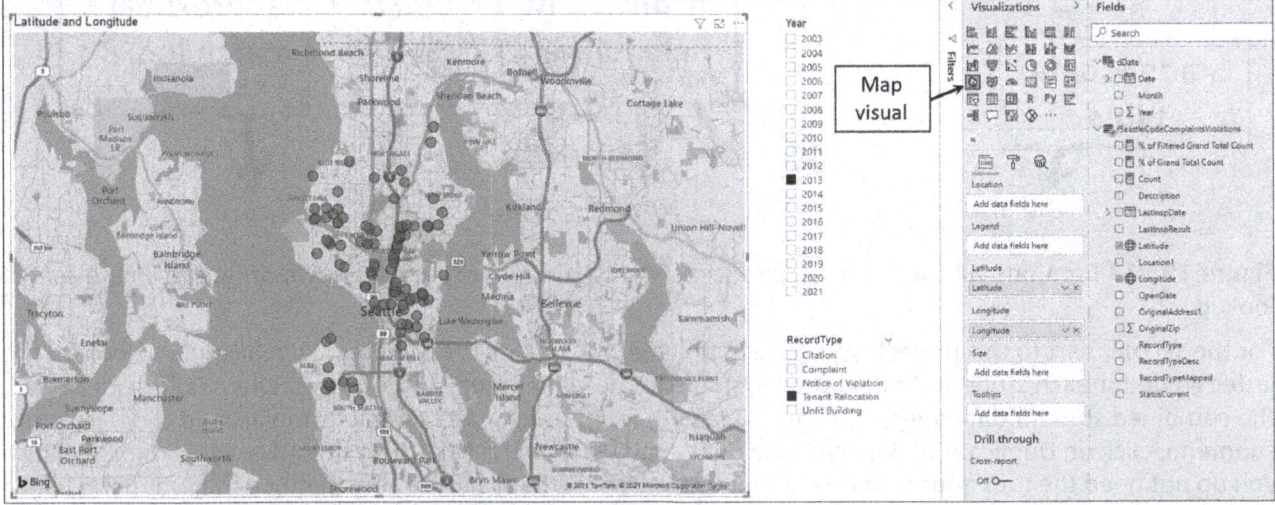

Figure 19.315 Map 911 calls using the map Power BI Visual.

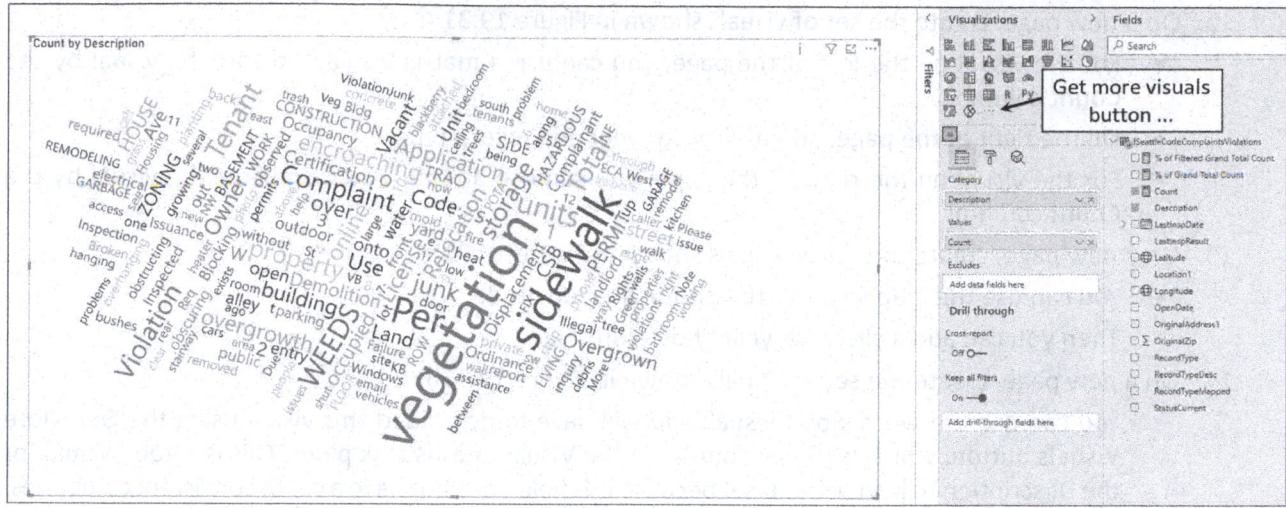

Figure 19.316 Download the word cloud Power BI visual with the Get More Visuals button.

Here are the general steps you can take to complete this problem:

1. Open a new Power BI Desktop file and press the F12 key to use the Save As feature and name your file **Project06-Visualizing911CallData.pbix**.

2. Using Power Query, import the CSV file named Ch19-PP06-Code_Complaints_and_Violations.csv.

3. Give the query a name that conveys the meaning of the data. Do not leave the default filename as the name of the query.

4. Remove all fields in the table except for these:
   - RecordType
   - RecordTypeDesc
   - Description
   - OriginalAddress1
   - OpenDate
   - Latitude
   - Longitude

5. Filter out null values in the Latitude field.

6. Make sure each field has the correct data type.

7. Use Apply & Close to send the table to the Data Model.

8. Create a date table in the Data Model and name the table dDate. The date table must have at least fields for date, month, and year.

9. Create a relationship between the dDate table Date field and the Open Date field in the fact table.

10. In the fact table, use the Column Tools tab in Power BI Desktop, in the Properties group, to select the following fields in the fact table and set their properties as shown here:
    - Latitude:
      - Data Category: Latitude
      - Summarization: Don't summarize
    - Longitude:
      - Data Category: Longitude
      - Summarization: Don't summarize

11. Create these three measures:
    - Count (to count the rows in the fact table)
    - % of Grand Total Count
    - % of Filtered Grand Total Count

12. On a new page, create the set of visuals shown in Figure 19.314:

- For the visual on the left of the page, you can use a matrix visual and sort the visual by the Count column.
- On the right of the page, add a slicer for year and record type.
- For the visual on the right of the page, you can use a table visual and sort the visual by the Count column.

13. On a new page, create the set of visuals shown in Figure 19.315:

- You can use the map visual with latitude and longitude.
- Then you can add a slicer for year and record type.

14. On a new page, create the set of visuals shown in Figure 19.316:

- You can use the word cloud visual. You will have to download this visual using the Get More Visuals button, which is the last button in the Visualizations task pane. This is a good visual for the Description field in the dataset because this field does not have a set of consistent categories. This visual shows that in Seattle, most of the complaints and violations in the city are related to vegetation, sidewalks, and weeds.
- In the Paint Roller Format tab, you can turn on Default Stop Words to avoid showing words like "the" and "and" in the visual, as shown in Figure 19.317.

Figure 19.317 Remove words like "the" and "and" from the word cloud.

When you are done with this problem, you can check your work against the file Ch19-PP06-Finished.pbix.

Practice Problem 7

Open the Excel workbook file Ch19-PP-07-Start.xlsx. Figure 19.318 shows the dataset for Chantel Washington, who is a manager at a large hardware and lumber store with many customer accounts. Customer service is not part of her main duties, and Chantel wants to document the excessive customer service duties she is performing. To this end, she keeps this Excel Table with a record of each customer service encounter.

Chantel has asked you to build a dashboard for her. Chantel wants to be able to get a quick visual impression of the frequency of customer contact by hour and a second visual of frequency of customer contact by day. She also wants to see specific counts for topics of meetings, counts of meeting types (as a percentage), and the average meeting duration. She wants to have the dashboard update easily when she adds new records and wants to be able to print out the dashboard about once a week. Your goal is to create two dashboards: one in an Excel workbook and one in Power BI Desktop. For the Excel dashboard, you can use a standard PivotTable because there is a small amount of data, and the calculations are simple.

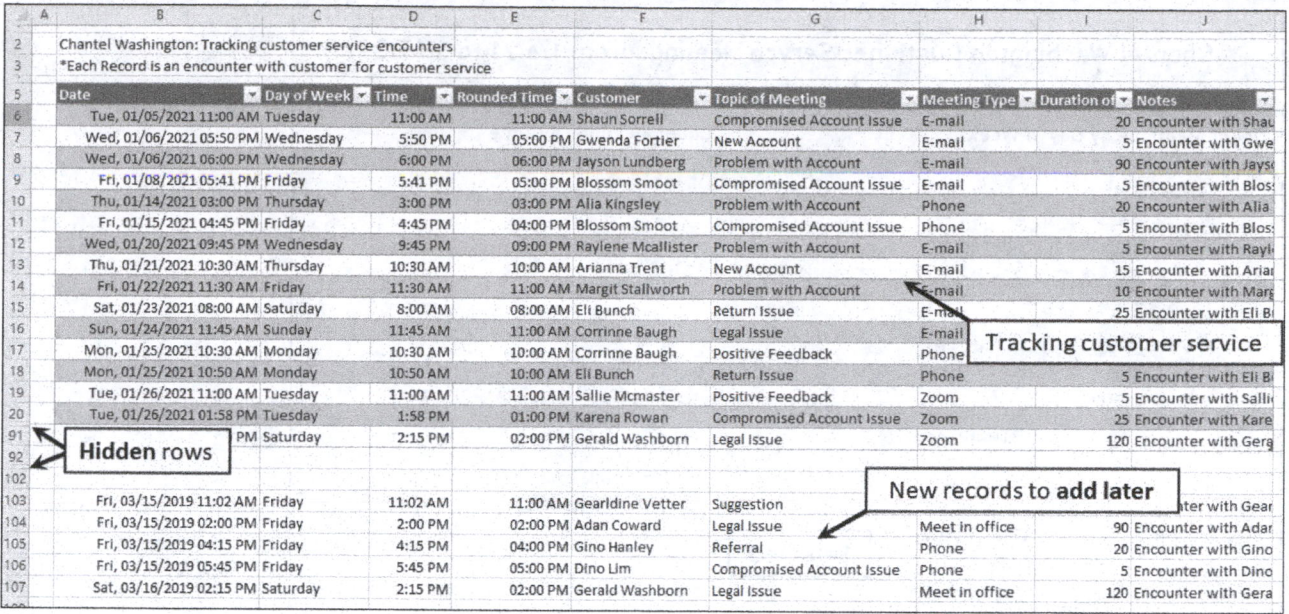

Figure 19.318 This Excel Table tracks Chantel Washington's customer service contacts.

Figure 19.319 shows an example of the Excel dashboard you should create, and Figure 19.320 shows an example of the Power BI Desktop dashboard. For the Power BI Desktop dashboard, you can import the Excel Table from the Excel file Ch19-PP-07-Start.xlsx to use as the source data.

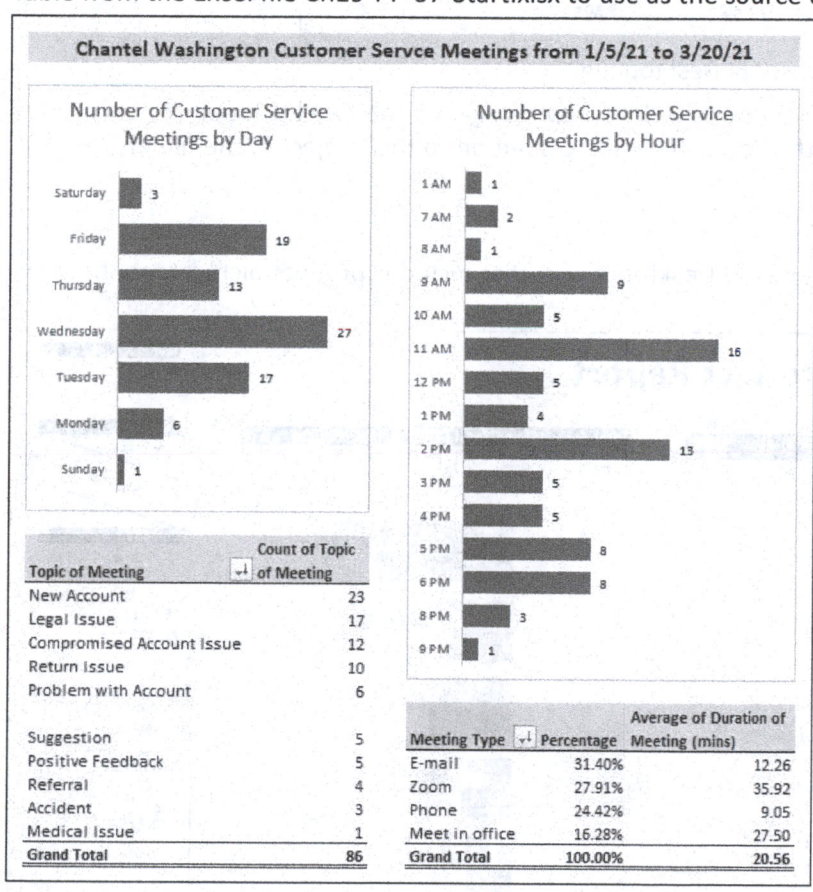

Figure 19.319 Dashboard created in an Excel workbook file.

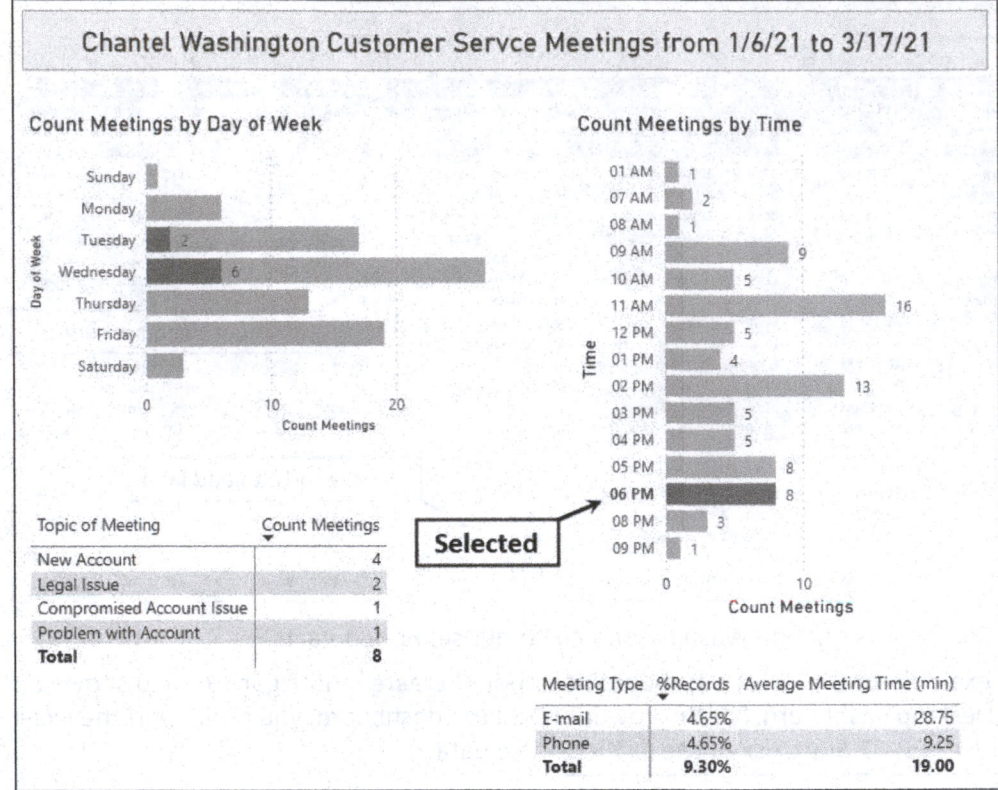

Figure 19.320 Dashboard created in a Power BI Desktop file.

When you are done with this problem, you can check your work against the Excel solution to this project in the file Ch19-PP07-Finished.xlsx and the Power BI Desktop solution to this project in the file Ch19-PP07-Finished.pbix.

Practice Problem 8

The goal for this project is to create a Power BI Desktop report that includes product pictures, as shown in Figure 19.321.

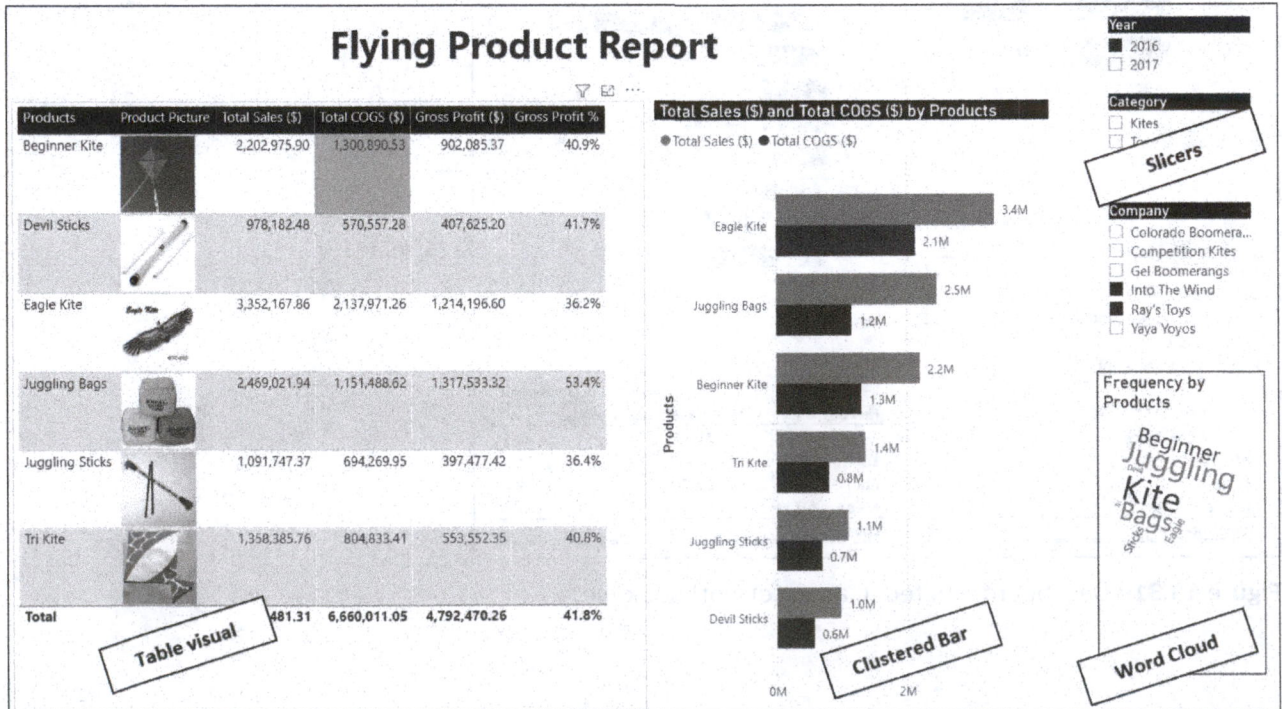

Figure 19.321 Power BI Desktop report page created using the table, clustered bar chart, slicer, and word cloud visuals.

You will have to import two fact table text files from a folder and three tables from an Access database file, as shown in Figure 19.322. The files that you need for this project are in the zipped folder Ch19-PP08.zip.

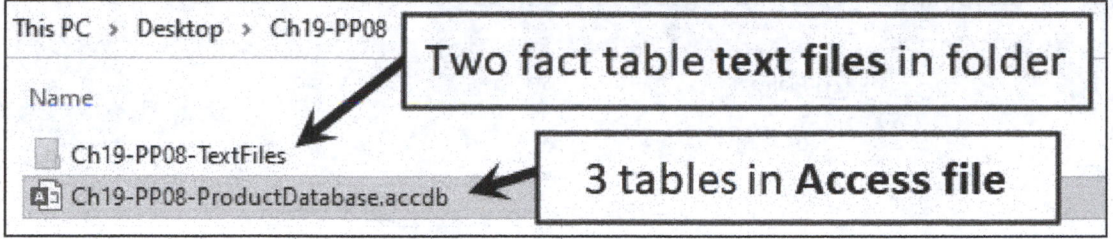

Figure 19.322 Data sources for this project.

Here are the general steps you can take to complete this problem:

1. Open a blank Power BI Desktop file.

2. Use Save As to save the file with the name **Ch19-PP08-ProductReports**.

3. Use Power Query to import the three tables in the Access file named Ch19-PP08-ProductDatabase. accdb. Figure 19.323 shows the relationships between the three tables that exist in the Access file.

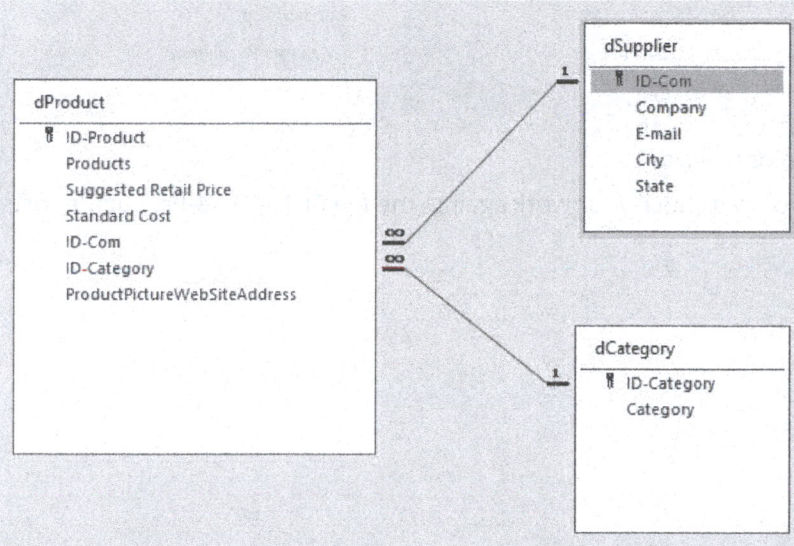

Figure 19.323 Related tables in an Access database file.

4. Import the three tables into the Power Query Editor and convert the snowflake relationships between the dProduct, dSupplier, and dCategory tables into a single product dimension table name dProduct. Rename the ProductPictureWebSiteAddress field in the dProduct table to **Product Picture**. Use only the Category field from the dCategory table and only the Company field from the dSupplier table. Before you load the dProduct table, be sure to right-click the other two tables and uncheck Enable Load so that these two tables are not loaded to the Data Model. Then load the dProduct table to the Data Model.

5. In Data view, select the Product Picture field in the dProduct table, click the Column Tools tab in the Power BI Desktop Ribbon, go to the Properties group and, from the Data Category dropdown, select Image URL. This step allows your reports to display the product images.

6. Import the two fact table text files from your on-premises folder and combine them into a single fact table names fSales.

7. Create a dDate table in the Power BI Desktop file.

8.   Create the measures shown in Figure 19.324.

Note: If you need a reminder about how to get the word cloud visual, refer to Practice Problem 6.

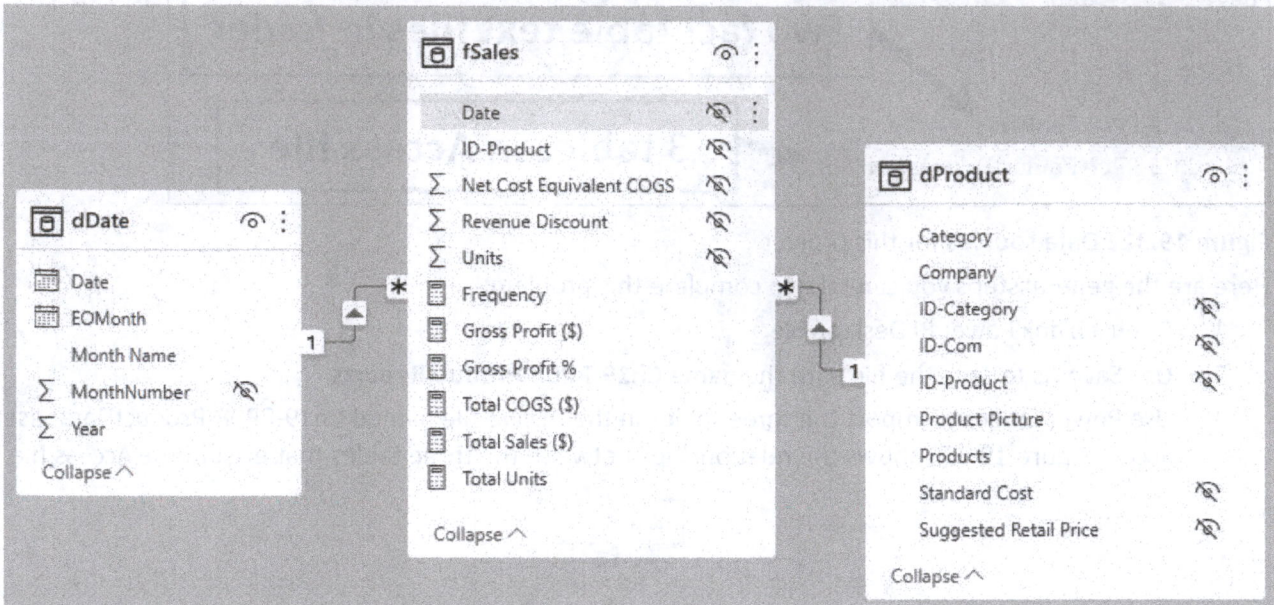

Figure 19.324 *Finished Power BI Desktop data model.*

When you are done with this problem, you can check your work against the file Ch19-PP08-ProductReports-Finished.pbix.

Chapter 20: The Macro Recorder and the VBA Editor

Imagine that at the end of each month, you get a report, like the one shown in Figure 20.1, and every time you get this report, you must add the same formatting and formulas to make the report look as shown in Figure 20.2. Performing the same repetitive steps each month is a drag. Wouldn't it be nice if there were a way to record the steps that you perform the first time you create the report and then, in subsequent months, simply click a button to play those steps back and instantly complete the report? With Excel's Macro Recorder feature, you can do exactly that!

	A	B	C
1	Client	Begin Asset	End Asset
2	Audrey Davis	336811	343547
3	Kay Stokes	973876	1149174
4	Irene Greene	112982	115242
5	Tim Gordon	53374	51773
6	Darnell Porter	322859	339002
7	Irma Boone	987206	957590
8	Bertha Montg	886223	1001432
9	Jeanne Gray	19057	21916
10	Lorene Mason	770301	878143
11	Marcos Lee	313418	294613

Figure 20.1 *Each month you get the same report that needs two formulas and formatting.*

	A	B	C	D	E
1	Client	Begin Asset	End Asset	Change ($)	% Change
2	Audrey Davis	336,811.00	343,547.00	6,736.00	2.00%
3	Kay Stokes	973,876.00	1,149,174.00	175,298.00	18.00%
4	Irene Greene	112,982.00	115,242.00	2,260.00	2.00%
5	Tim Gordon	53,374.00	51,773.00	(1,601.00)	-3.00%
6	Darnell Porter	322,859.00	339,002.00	16,143.00	5.00%
7	Irma Boone	987,206.00	957,590.00	(29,616.00)	-3.00%
8	Bertha Montg	886,223.00	1,001,432.00	115,209.00	13.00%
9	Jeanne Gray	19,057.00	21,916.00	2,859.00	15.00%
10	Lorene Mason	770,301.00	878,143.00	107,842.00	14.00%
11	Marcos Lee	313,418.00	294,613.00	(18,805.00)	-6.00%

Figure 20.2 *After you apply the formulas and formatting, the report looks like this.*

When you turn on the Macro Recorder, it saves all of the steps you perform into a macro so that you can later play them back again. The steps are recorded using VBA code, which is a coding language that has been available in Excel since 1993. (VBA stands for Visual Basic for Applications.) A *VBA macro*, also called just a *macro*, is a set of commands created with VBA code that you can reuse. You can create VBA macros with the Macro Recorder or by writing the code out by hand in the VBA Editor window.

> **Note:** Much of what VBA code used to be used for in the past has been replaced with features like Power Query, dynamic spilled array formulas, the LET worksheet function, and the LAMBDA worksheet function.

This chapter looks at how to use the Macro Recorder and how to copy and paste VBA code from the internet into the VBA Editor window. This chapter covers the skills you need to accomplish most of what you need from the VBA coding language.

> **Note:** This chapter does not show how to write VBA code. A lot of prewritten code is available on the internet.

Using the Excel Workbook .xlsm File Extension to Allow VBA Code in an Excel File

When you want to use macros in an Excel file, you must use the file extension .xlsm, which indicates an Excel macro-enabled workbook. (The *m* at the end of .xlsm stands for *macro*.) If you record a VBA macro in a workbook file that has the default .xlsx file extension, you will have to use the Save As command to change the extension on the file to .xlsm.

> **Note:** If you try to save a VBA macro in an .xlsx workbook file, you will get a warning telling you to save in an Excel macro-enabled workbook with a .xlsm file extension. If you click through this warning, the macro is deleted.

Showing the Developer Tab in the Excel Ribbon

The Developer tab in the Excel Ribbon contains the commands you need to create and work with macros. By default, the Developer tab does not appear in the Excel Ribbon. To show the Developer tab in the Excel Ribbon, follow these steps:

1. Click File and select Options.

2. On the left side of the Excel Options dialog box that appears, click Customize Ribbon and then click the checkbox for the Developer tab. Then click OK.

Figure 20.3 shows the Developer tab in the Excel Ribbon. In the Code group, notice the Record Macro button. You click this button to start a macro.

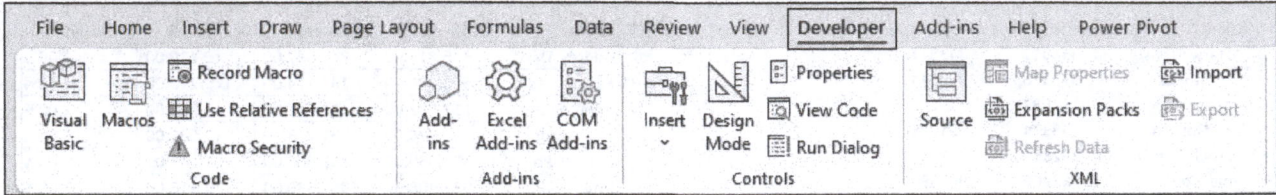

Figure 20.3 *The Developer tab in the Excel Ribbon.*

You can use the Macro Security button in the Code group to set your security level to Disable VBA Macros with Notification so that you get a warning any time an Excel file includes a macro; when you get this yellow warning message, you must click to enable macro content.

You can use the Use Relative References button in the Code group to determine how the Macro Recorder records a selected cell. There are two options for recording selected cells in a macro:

- If the Use Relative References button is selected, a macro records selected cells with the Offset command so that a selected cell moves relative to the starting location—either up or down and left or right.

- If the Use Relative References button is not selected, your macro records selected cells with the Range command so that the selected cell's actual reference is recorded, such as cell A1 when you select cell A1. With this option, all cell addresses selected during the recording are hard coded into the VBA code.

Using the Macro Recorder and a Form Control Button to Help a User Refresh a Query

When you build solutions and send them to other people, the goal is to make it easy for those users to accomplish the tasks in the Excel workbook. For example, say that you have built the query shown in Figure 20.4. It would be nice to add to the worksheet a button a user can click to refresh a query instead of hunting through the Ribbon tabs for the Refresh button or remembering to use the right-click method. To add this button, you just need to record a macro and assign it to a button.

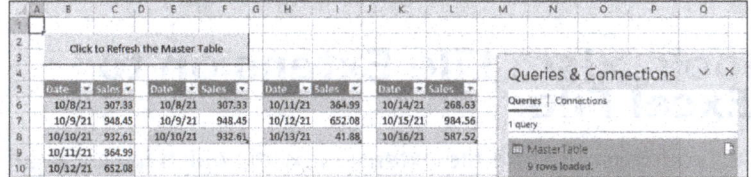

Figure 20.4 Recording a macro and assigning it to a button makes the task of refreshing a query much easier.

To create a VBA macro to refresh a query and assign it to a form control button, open the Ch20-Excel365-MacroRecorderStart.xlsx file and follow these steps:

1. Because the Excel Start file for this example uses the file extension .xlsx, use the Save As feature to change the file extension to .xlsm.

2. Select the worksheet M1(1) and click cell A1, which is outside the query area.

> **Note:** It is important to have a cell outside the query area selected before you record this macro so that the first step in the recorded macro selects a cell inside the query table. In addition, it is important not to select the Use Relative References button because you want the macro to record the actual reference.

3.   As shown in Figure 20.5, in the Developer tab, go to the Code group and click the Record Macro button.

Figure 20.5 *The Record Macro button in the Code group in the Developer tab of the Excel Ribbon.*

4.   As shown in Figure 20.6, in the Record Macro dialog box that appears, name the macro **RefreshMasterTableQuery**.

> **Note:** Like defined names, macro names cannot include spaces or special characters.

Record Macro	?	✕

Macro name:

    RefreshMasterTableQuery

Shortcut key:

        Ctrl+ ☐

Store macro in:

    This Workbook ▾

Description:

    Query to refesh MasterTable Query on the worksheet M1(1).
    This will be assigned to a Control Button.

            [OK]   [Cancel]

Figure 20.6 *Complete the Record Macro dialog box carefully.*

5.   From the Store Macro In dropdown, select the This Workbook option.

> **Note:** This option stores the macro in the current workbook file so that it is only available in this workbook file. This is a good option because you would never need this macro in any other workbook except the one with the query.

6.   In the Description area, type a description that indicates the purpose of the macro to help others understand what the macro does.

7.   Click the OK button.

After you click the OK button in the Record Macro dialog box, everything you do is recorded—even mistakes. Every time you click on a cell, select a range, or choose a command, it is recorded. The recording is not stopped until you click the Stop Recording button (see Figure 20.7). This button appears only after you click the Record Macro button; when you click Stop Recording, it once again becomes the Record Macro button.

> **Note:** If you make a mistake while recording a macro, it is best to click the Stop Recording button, delete the macro, and start over. It is also good practice to rehearse what you are going to do before clicking the Record Macro button. Rehearsing can help you avoid making mistakes.

Figure 20.7 *After you click the OK button, the Record Macro button converts to a Stop Recording button.*

8. Select cell B5 in the query Excel Table. This is the first step that is recorded by the macro.

9. Right-click cell B5 and select Refresh (see Figure 20.8). This is the second step that is recorded by the macro.

10. To stop the recording of the macro, click the Stop Recording button.

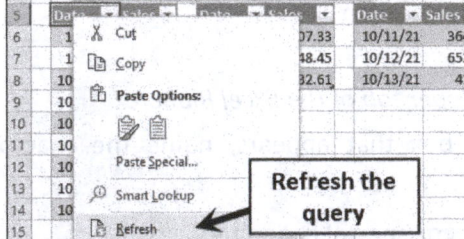

Figure 20.8 *Refresh the query from cell B5.*

11. To add a button to the worksheet, in the Developer tab, go to the Controls group and click the Insert dropdown and select the Button (Form Control) option (see Figure 20.9). When you click this option, your cursor converts to a thin crosshairs curser that allows you to draw a button in the worksheet area.

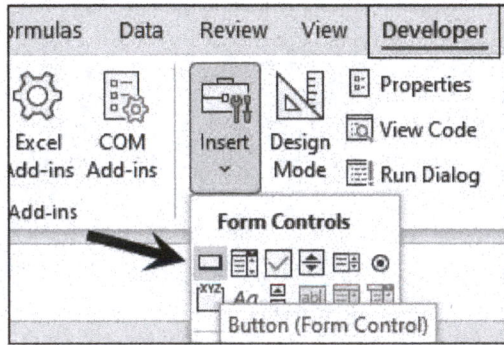

Figure 20.9 *Click the Button (Form Control) option in the Controls group in the Developer tab.*

12. To draw the shape of a button in the worksheet above the query, click, hold the click, and drag your mouse about two rows down and five columns to the right. Then let go of the click.

13. In the Assign Macro dialog box that appears, shown in Figure 20.10, select the macro that you created and then click the OK button.

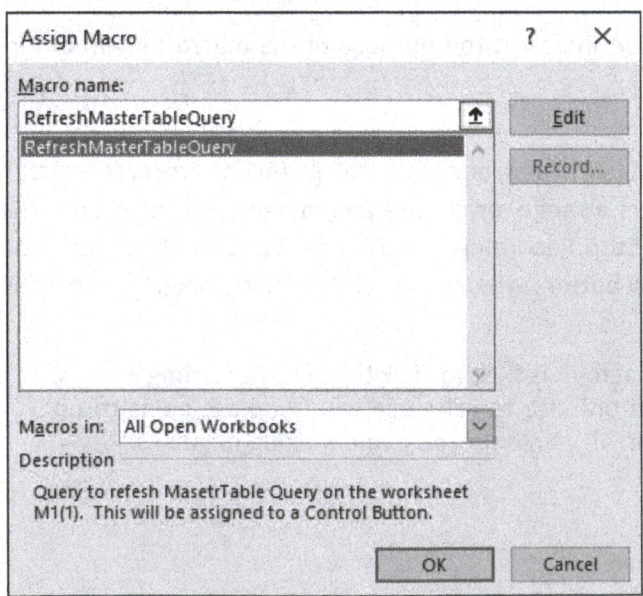

Figure 20.10 *Assign the macro you created to your button.*

14. To add a name to the button, click inside the button and type the name **Click to Refresh the Master Table** (see Figure 20.11). Notice that the button has little white circles along the outside edge. This indicates that the button is in edit mode, and you can rename, resize, and move it.

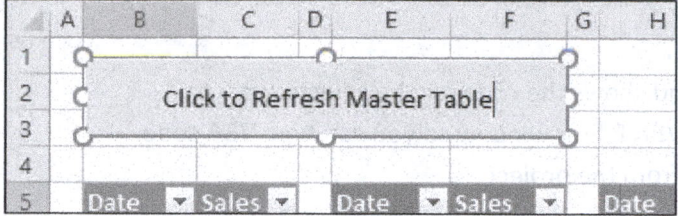

Figure 20.11 *Type a name that helps the user understand what the button does.*

15. With the button in edit mode, right-click the button and drag it to a location where it does not cover up the Excel Tables or the query. If you want, you can also resize the button; to resize the button and have it snap to the grid, hold down the Alt key while you are resizing.

16. To deselect the button and activate it so that it can be used, click in a cell somewhere in the worksheet.

17. To test the button, add a new record to the third Excel Table and click the VBA macro button. As shown in Figure 20.12, the query shows the new record at the bottom of the table.

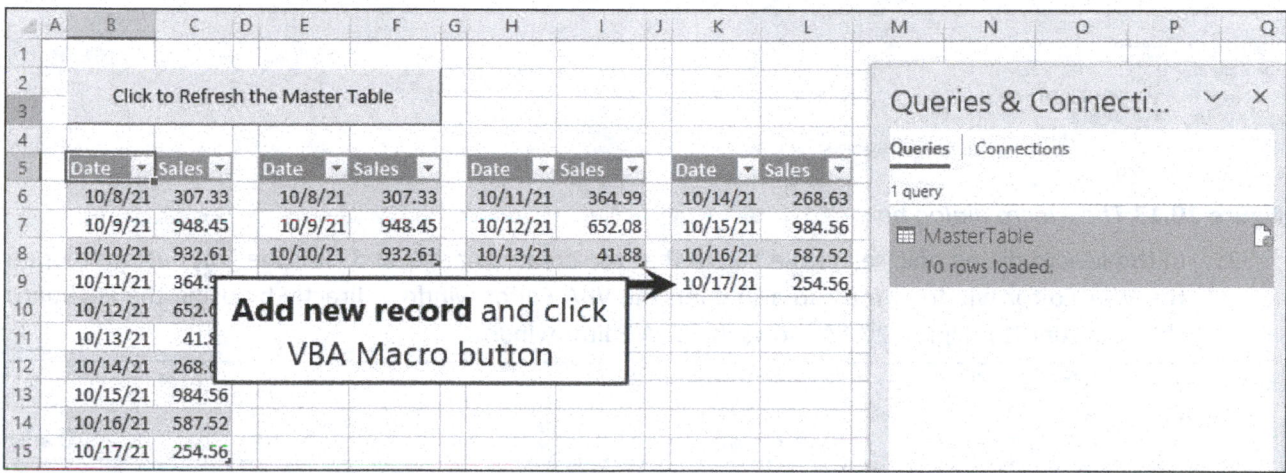

Figure 20.12 *Test the VBA macro button.*

Using the Macro Dialog Box and the VBA Editor Window to View VBA Code

After you create macros, you can view them in the Macro dialog box and in the VBA Editor window. The VBA Editor window allows you to view the code that is automatically written for a macro. It also allows you to paste code that you get from the internet (which you will do later in this chapter). To open the Macro dialog box and VBA Editor window, follow these steps:

1. To view your list of macros, in the Developer tab, go to the Code group and click the Macros button (or use the keyboard shortcut Alt+F8). The Macro dialog box appears. As shown in Figure 20.13, the Macro dialog box offers these buttons:

    *   **Run:** Runs the selected macro.
    *   **Step Into:** Debugs a macro line by line.
    *   **Edit:** Opens the VBA Editor window and shows the code for the selected macro.
    *   **Create:** Creates a new module in the VBA Editor window so you can type VBA code.
    *   **Delete:** Removes the selected macro from the project.

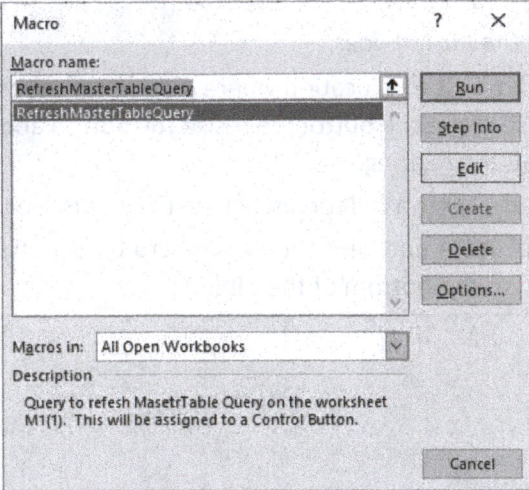

Figure 20.13 *The Macro dialog box.*

2. In the Macro dialog box, select the macro that you created earlier and click the Edit button to open the VBA Editor window. You can also open the VBA Editor window directly by using the keyboard shortcut Alt+F11. Figure 20.14 shows the VBA Editor window.

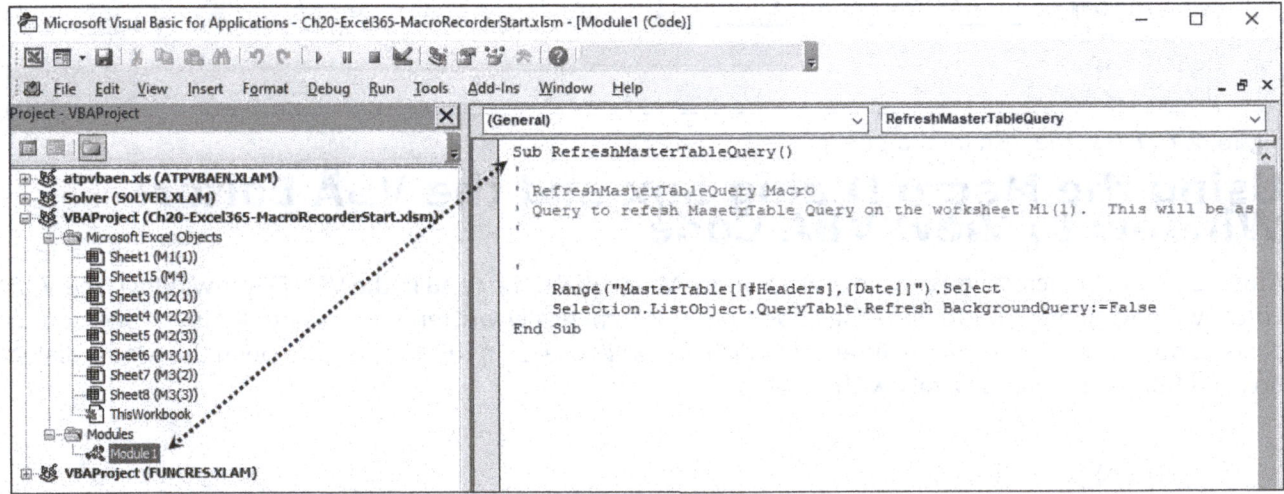

Figure 20.14 *The VBA Editor window.*

3. When you are done viewing the VBA Editor window, close it by clicking the X in the title bar.

If you need to delete a macro, open the Macro dialog box (by pressing Alt+F8), select the macro to delete, and click the Delete button.

Figure 20.14 shows the VBA Editor window with Module1 selected in the Projects Explorer area on the left. A *module* is a new area where you can create VBA code. The VBA code appears in the *code area* on the right. Notice that Module1 is in a folder called Modules. As you create more modules, they will appear in this folder. The Module1 module is located in a VBA project named VBA Project (Ch20-Excel365-MacroRecorderStart. xlsm). In the code area on the right, the code starts with a Sub statement (that is, a subroutine statement), followed by notes (each of which starts with a single quotation mark), two lines of code, and finally an End Sub statement.

Later, when you see how to copy VBA code from the internet, you will use the VBA Editor window to insert your own module and then paste the copied code into the code area on the right.

Using the Macro Recorder and the Use Relative References Button to Write VBA Code That You Can Use for Repetitive Tasks

If you are given a report each month, as shown in Figure 20.15, and you need to add formatting and formulas, as shown in Figure 20.16, you can save a lot of time if you use the Macro Recorder the first time, save the macro, and then reuse the macro each subsequent month. However, as you know well by now, you must know your data before building a solution. For this report, you will always be given three fields of data with no empty cells. There will be a variable number of rows in each report, and the proper dataset will always start in cell A1.

Month 1:

	A	B	C
1	Client	Begin Asset	End Asset
2	Audrey Davis	336811	343547
3	Kay Stokes	973876	1149174
4	Irene Greene	112982	115242
5	Tim Gordon	53374	51773
6	Darnell Porter	322859	339002
7	Irma Boone	987206	957590
8	Bertha Montg	886223	1001432
9	Jeanne Gray	19057	21916
10	Lorene Mason	770301	878143
11	Marcos Lee	313418	294613

Month 2:

	A	B	C
1	Client	Begin Asset	End Asset
2	Audrey Davis	343547	342056
3	Kay Stokes	1149174	1148700
4	Irene Greene	115242	113847
5	Tim Gordon	51773	57962
6	Chantel Mims	258154	260892

Figure 20.15 *You get monthly reports with different numbers of rows.*

	A	B	C	D	E
1	Client	Begin Asset	End Asset	Change ($)	% Change
2	Audrey Davis	336,811.00	343,547.00	6,736.00	2.00%
3	Kay Stokes	973,876.00	1,149,174.00	175,298.00	18.00%
4	Irene Greene	112,982.00	115,242.00	2,260.00	2.00%
5	Tim Gordon	53,374.00	51,773.00	(1,601.00)	-3.00%
6	Darnell Porter	322,859.00	339,002.00	16,143.00	5.00%
7	Irma Boone	987,206.00	957,590.00	(29,616.00)	-3.00%
8	Bertha Montgo	886,223.00	1,001,432.00	115,209.00	13.00%
9	Jeanne Gray	19,057.00	21,916.00	2,859.00	15.00%
10	Lorene Mason	770,301.00	878,143.00	107,842.00	14.00%
11	Marcos Lee	313,418.00	294,613.00	(18,805.00)	-6.00%

Figure 20.16 *This is what the report looks like for Month 1.*

If the number of rows in each report were the same each month, you would record the macro without selecting the Use Relative References button (refer to Figure 20.3), and the cell addresses that you select would be hard coded into the macro's VBA code. For example, in Figure 20.15, if you selected the range A1:C11 for the Month 1 report, that range would be hard coded into the VBA code. This would cause problems if you then tried to use the macro for the second month because the Month 2 report is located in the range A1:C6—and the macro would add formatting and formulas to an area where there is no data. However, if you click the Use Relative References button at the right moment in the recording and you use keyboard shortcuts for selecting ranges, you can get your macro to work on reports with variable numbers of rows.

To record a macro that applies formatting and formulas to a report, follow these steps:

> **Note:** Before you click the Record Macro button to start the macro, rehearse these steps to avoid making mistakes when you actually record the macro.

1. Select the worksheet M2(1) and click in a cell outside the report area, such as cell I1. (Remember that you need to select this cell before beginning the recording so that the first action of the macro can be to select a cell within the query area.)

2. Make sure the Use Relative References button is not selected. In this case, you want the first action of the macro to be selecting cell D1 as a hard-coded reference.

3. Click the Record Macro button, enter the macro details in the Record Macro dialog box, and click OK.

4. Begin the macro by selecting cell D1.

5. Type **Change ($)** and press Tab to enter the text into cell D1 and select cell E1.

6. In cell E1, type **% Change** and press Enter to enter the text in cell E1 and select cell D2.

7. In cell D2, create the formula **=C2-B2** and press Tab to enter the formula in cell D2 and select cell E2.

8. In cell E2, create the formula **=D2/B2** and press Ctrl+Enter to enter the text in cell E2.

9. Select cell C2 and then, to jump to the last value in column C, no matter how many rows there are, press Ctrl+DownArrow.

> **Note:** If you were to click in cell C11 instead of pressing Ctrl+DownArrow, that value would be hard coded into the macro, and you do not want that.

10. To turn on the Use Relative References button, go to the Developer tab in the Excel Ribbon, and in the Code group, click Use Relative References.

> **Note:** You need to click the Use Relative References button here because you will have a variable number of rows in the datasets, and when you select the two cells to the right, you want this action to happen relative to the last value in column C.

11. Select the range D11:E11. Because the Use Relative References button is turned on, the macro does not hard code the range D11:E11 into the macro but just selects whatever two cells are to the right of the last value in column C.

12. Click the Use Relative References button again to turn it off.

> **Note:** This is the only time that you have to use this button in this macro. The rest of the macro will use either the hard-coded cell addresses or keyboard shortcuts to dynamically select ranges.

13. To dynamically select the range all the way up to the cells with the formulas, press Ctrl+Shift+Enter.

14. With the two formulas and the range below selected, press Ctrl+D to copy the formulas down. The Ctrl+D keyboard invokes the Fill Down command, which dynamically fills down through the selected range.

15. To dynamically select all cells in the report, press Ctrl+* (on the number pad) or Ctrl+Shift+8 (on the regular keyboard). Both of these shortcuts select all cells in the report, no matter how many rows there are.

16. To add borders to the report, in the Home tab of the Excel Ribbon, go to the Font group, click the Border button, and select All Borders.

17. To add bold to the hard-coded range A1:E1, select the range A1:E1 and press Ctrl+B.

18. To add the Accounting number format to all the dollar values, select the range B2:D2 (as a hard-coded range) and press Ctrl+Shift+DownArrow. Then, in the Home tab of the Excel Ribbon, go to the Number group and click the Comma button.

> **Note:** Ctrl+Shift+DownArrow dynamically selects all cells below the selected range that have values. It always selects to the bottom of the report, regardless of how many rows are in the report.

19. To add the Percentage number format to all values in the % Change column, select cell E2 (hard coded) and press Ctrl+Shift+DownArrow to dynamically select all cells below the selected cell that have values. Then press Ctrl+1 to open the Format Cells dialog box, click the Number tab, and add percentage number formatting with two decimal places showing.

20. Click in cell F1 to ensure that a cell is selected outside the report each time you run the macro later.

21. To stop the macro recording, in the Developer tab, go to the Code group and click the Stop Recording button.

You should rehearse this sequence of steps a few times before you try it with the Macro Recorder on. While you are learning how to record macros, you will make a lot of mistakes—at least that is how it went for me. In fact, I still mess up my macro recording sessions if I do not practice enough.

> **Note:** It is easy to forget to turn off the Macro Recorder and end up with a real mess . I've done it many times. So remember: If you make a mistake and need to delete a macro, press Alt+F8 to open the Macro dialog box, select the macro, and click the Delete button.

Using the Personal Macro Workbook to Create Universal VBA Macros

When you record a VBA macro, the Record Macro dialog box gives you three options for where to store the macro:

- **New Workbook:** Choose this option to store the macro in a new workbook and allow the macro to run only in the new workbook file.

- **This Workbook:** Choose this option to store the macro in the current workbook and allow the macro to run only in the current workbook file.

- **Personal Macro Workbook:** Choose this option to store the macro in a hidden workbook file so that the macro will be available for use in other .xlsm Excel workbook files located on your computer.

The Personal Macro Workbook file is a hidden file that exists on all computers that have Excel installed. For example, on my computer, the Personal Macro Workbook file is stored in this location: C:\Users\mgirvin\ AppData\Roaming\Microsoft\Excel\XLSTART\PERSONAL.XLSB. If you ever need to access this hidden workbook file, in the View tab in the Excel Ribbon, go to the Window group and click the Unhide button. It is important to know how to unhide this file because you might want to open it and delete a macro that you do not want. When you are done making a change like that, you must save the Personal Macro Workbook file and then hide it (by selecting the View tab, going to the Window group, and clicking the Hide button).

Because the macro you just created will be used to format reports in many different workbook files on your computer, you should not save it in the current workbook file. You should instead store it in the Personal Macro Workbook so that the macro is available anywhere on your computer.

> **Note:** If you store a macro in a particular file and want to use it again, you can copy the code from the VBA Editor window, open a new workbook, press Alt+F11 to open the VBA Editor window, click the Insert menu, click on Module, and paste the code into the code area. The keyboard shortcut to insert a new module in the VBA Editor window is Alt, I, M.

After rehearsing the steps in the preceding section, try to create the macro and save it in your Personal Macro Workbook file. Figure 20.17 shows what my Record Macro dialog box looked like when I recorded this macro.

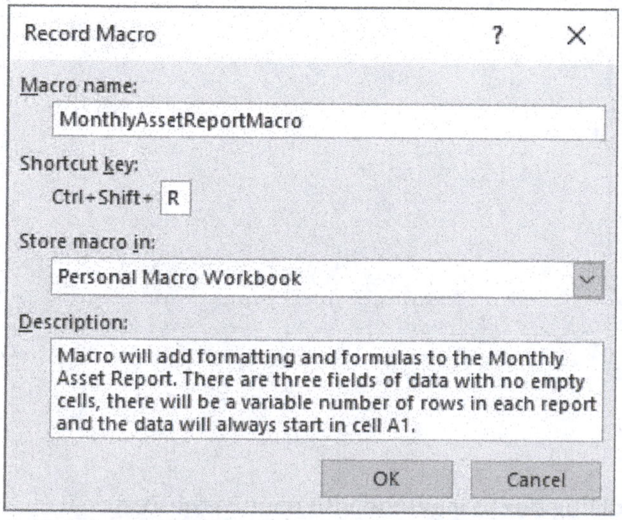

Figure 20.17 *The Record Macro dialog box for the asset report macro.*

For a macro like this that will be used often, it is a good idea to add a keyboard shortcut that you can use to invoke the macro. When you add a keyboard shortcut, choose a combination that is not already in use. (For example, you would not want to select Ctrl+C because then you could no longer use that shortcut for a copy action.) To specify a keyboard shortcut for a macro, in the Macro dialog box, you click in the Shortcut Key textbox and type the key or keys you want to use in addition to Ctrl. For example, if you want to use the shortcut Ctrl+Shift+R, you click in the Shortcut Key textbox and press Shift+R, and if you want Ctrl+Q, then you only have to click in the Shortcut Key textbox and press Q.

Once you create the macro, you can try it on the reports on the worksheets M2(2) to M2(8). I added many worksheets for practice in case you need it. (I know I did when I was learning.)

Figure 20.18 shows what the report and selected cell looked like when I clicked the Stop Recording button. Figure 20.19 shows what the report looked like on worksheet M2(2) after I ran the macro. Figure 20.20 shows what the Macro dialog box looked like after I created one macro in the Personal Macro Workbook file and another one in the current file.

	A	B	C	D	E	F
1	Client	Begin Asset	End Asset	Change ($)	% Change	
2	Audrey Davis	336,811.00	343,547.00	6,736.00	2.00%	
3	Kay Stokes	973,876.00	1,149,174.00	175,298.00	18.00%	
4	Irene Greene	112,982.00	115,242.00	2,260.00	2.00%	
5	Tim Gordon	53,374.00	51,773.00	(1,601.00)	-3.00%	
6	Darnell Porter	322,859.00	339,002.00	16,143.00	5.00%	
7	Irma Boone	987,206.00	957,590.00	(29,616.00)	-3.00%	
8	Bertha Montgo	886,223.00	1,001,432.00	115,209.00	13.00%	
9	Jeanne Gray	19,057.00	21,916.00	2,859.00	15.00%	
10	Lorene Mason	770,301.00	878,143.00	107,842.00	14.00%	
11	Marcos Lee	313,418.00	294,613.00	(18,805.00)	-6.00%	

Figure 20.18 *Worksheet M2(1) after I clicked the Stop Recording button.*

	A	B	C	D	E	F
1	Client	Begin Asset	End Asset	Change ($)	% Change	
2	Audrey Davis	343,547.00	342,056.00	(1,491.00)	-0.43%	
3	Kay Stokes	1,149,174.00	1,148,700.00	(474.00)	-0.04%	
4	Irene Greene	115,242.00	113,847.00	(1,395.00)	-1.21%	
5	Tim Gordon	51,773.00	57,962.00	6,189.00	11.95%	
6	Chantel Mims	258,154.00	260,892.00	2,738.00	1.06%	

Figure 20.19 *Worksheet M2(2) after I pressed Ctrl+R to invoke the macro.*

> **Note:** If you need to change a macro's keyboard shortcut or change the description for a macro, you can click the Options button in the Macro dialog box.

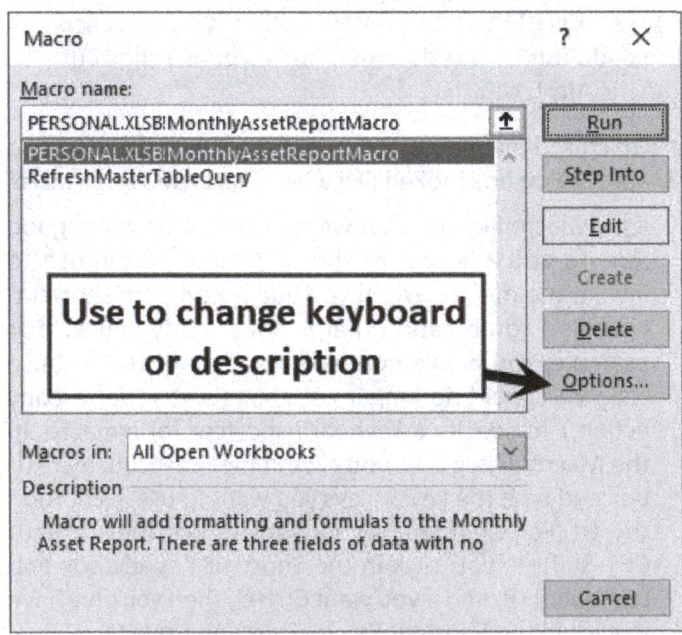

Figure 20.20 *The Macro dialog box with two macros.*

> **Note:** You cannot use the Edit button in the Macro dialog box to view the VBA code in the Personal Macro Workbook file unless you unhide the workbook (by selecting the View tab in the Excel Ribbon, going to the Window group, and clicking the Unhide button).

Copying VBA Code from the Internet and Pasting It into a VBA Module

In an Excel worksheet, there is no built-in function that can take a number and spell it out in words. But if you search online for "Excel VBA spell out numbers as words," you will find a bunch of VBA code that does this. In addition, if you ask for help with a complex task in an online forum such as the MrExcel Message Board at mrexcel.com/board, someone might provide you with VBA macro code. In either case, you can copy and paste the VBA code into a module so that you can use it in the worksheet.

To get VBA code from the internet and use it in Excel, follow these steps:

1. In the workbook Ch20-Excel365-MacroRecorderStart.xlsm, select the worksheet M3.

2. Go to https://www.ablebits.com/office-addins-blog/2013/08/29/convert-numbers-words-excel/, scroll down to step 5, and copy the VBA code you see there. This code will define a VBA user-defined function named SpellNumber that you can use in the worksheet.

3. In your workbook, open the VBA Editor by pressing Alt+F11.

4. Click on the Insert menu and click Module (or press Alt, I, M), and paste the copied code into the code area.

5. Use Ctrl+S to save the macro and the Excel workbook. Figure 20.21 shows what the worksheet should look like at this point.

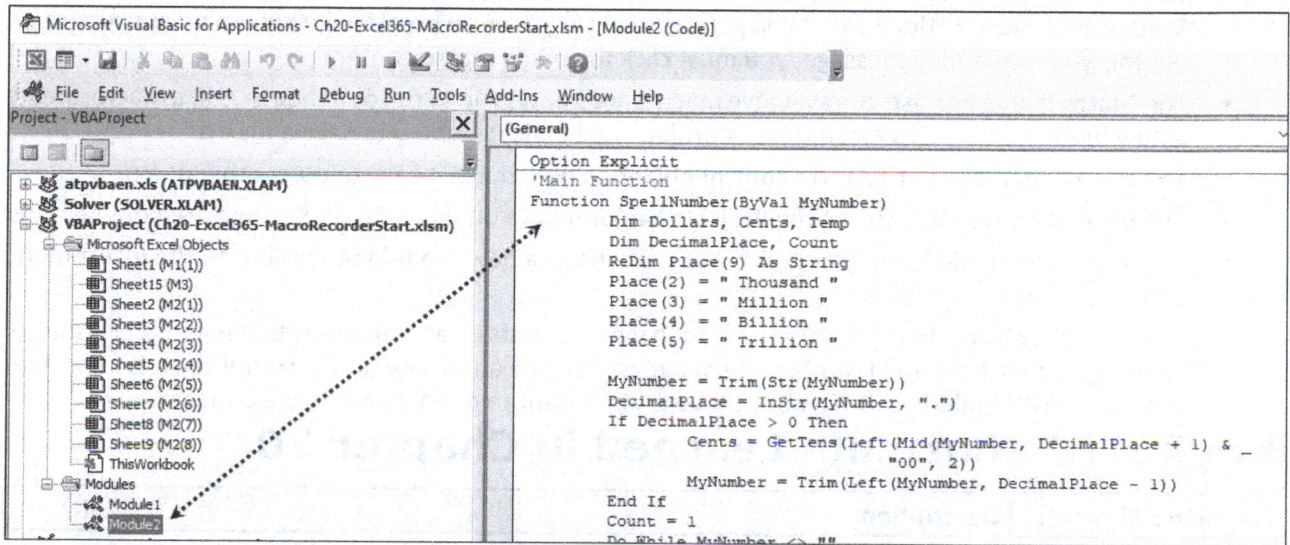

Figure 20.21 *The SpellNumber VBA user-defined function pasted into a module in the VBA Editor Window.*

6. As shown in Figure 20.22, in cell B2, type the formula **=SpellNumber(A2)**. Enter the formula and then copy it down the column.

	A	B
1	Numbers	Words
2	12.23	Twelve Dollars and Twenty Three Cents
3	64537.2	Sixty Four Thousand Five Hundred Thirty Seven Dollars and Twenty Three Cents
4	857564	Eight Hundred Fifty Seven Thousand Five Hundred Sixty Four Dollars and No Cents
5	1	One Dollar and No Cents

Figure 20.22 *The user-defined function SpellNumber used in a worksheet.*

In this chapter, I showed you two recorded macro examples and an example of using VBA code to create a user-defined function. The best way to learn how to use the Macro Recorder, though, is to just play around with it. When I was learning how to create recorded macros, I tried it many times, and each time I just created something small, stopped the recorder, and then played it back. For example, you might try to make a small income statement or an inventory tracker and then play back the macro on a new sheet. Your experimentation can be a great learning tool.

Chapter 20 Key Concepts

- When you turn on the **Macro Recorder**, it saves all of the steps you perform into a macro so that you can later play them back again. The steps are recorded using **VBA code**, which is a coding language that has been available in Excel since 1993. (VBA stands for **Visual Basic for Applications**.) A *VBA macro*, also called just a **macro**, is a set of commands created with VBA code that you can reuse. You can create VBA macros with the Macro Recorder or by writing the code by hand in the VBA Editor window. The Macro Recorder is useful when you need to do repetitive tasks such as refreshing a query or formatting a monthly report.

- When you want to use macros in an Excel file, you must use the **Excel macro-enabled workbook** file extension .xlsm. The *m* at the end of .xlsm stands for *macro*.

- The **Developer tab of the Excel Ribbon** contains the commands you need to create and work with macros. By default, the Developer tab does not appear in the Excel Ribbon, and you need to add it if you want to use it.

- You use the **Use Relative Reference button** to determine how the Macro Recorder records a selected cell: as an actual reference or as a relative reference.

- You can use the **Macro Security** button in the Code group to set your security level to **Disable VBA Macros with Notification** so that you get a warning any time an Excel file includes a macro; when you get this yellow warning message, you must click to enable macro content.

- The **Macro dialog box** lists the available macros and allows you to run or debug or edit a macro, create a new module, remove a macro from a project, and indicate where to save a macro.

- You can assign a macro to a **form control button** to help make it easy to access the macro.

- The **VBA Editor window** shows the **Projects Explorer area** on the left and the **code area** on the right.

- When you copy code from the internet, you can insert a new **module** by clicking on the Insert menu and then clicking on Module.

- The **Personal Macro Workbook** file is a hidden file that exists on all computers that have Excel installed. When you store a macro in this file, the macro is available anywhere on the computer. It is important to know how to unhide this file because you might want to open it and delete a macro.

Keyboard Shortcuts Learned in Chapter 20

Keyboard Shortcut	Description
F8	Opens the Macro dialog box
Alt+F11	Opens the VBA Editor window
Alt, I, M	Creates a new module in the VBA Editor window
Ctrl+D	Invokes the Fill Down command to fill values in the top cells to selected cells below

Practice Problems for Chapter 20

Practice Problem 1

Open the Excel file Ch20-PP-01and02-Start.xlsm. Each month, you receive a three-column report like the one shown in Figure 20.23. Your goal is to build a macro that will add a new column that contains a formula that subtracts the Store Expense values from the Store Totals values and formats the report as shown in Figure 20.24.

The report always starts in cell A1 and has three columns. There will be a varying number of rows for each new report.

Once you build the macro, you can try it on each of the worksheets from M1(2) to M(12).

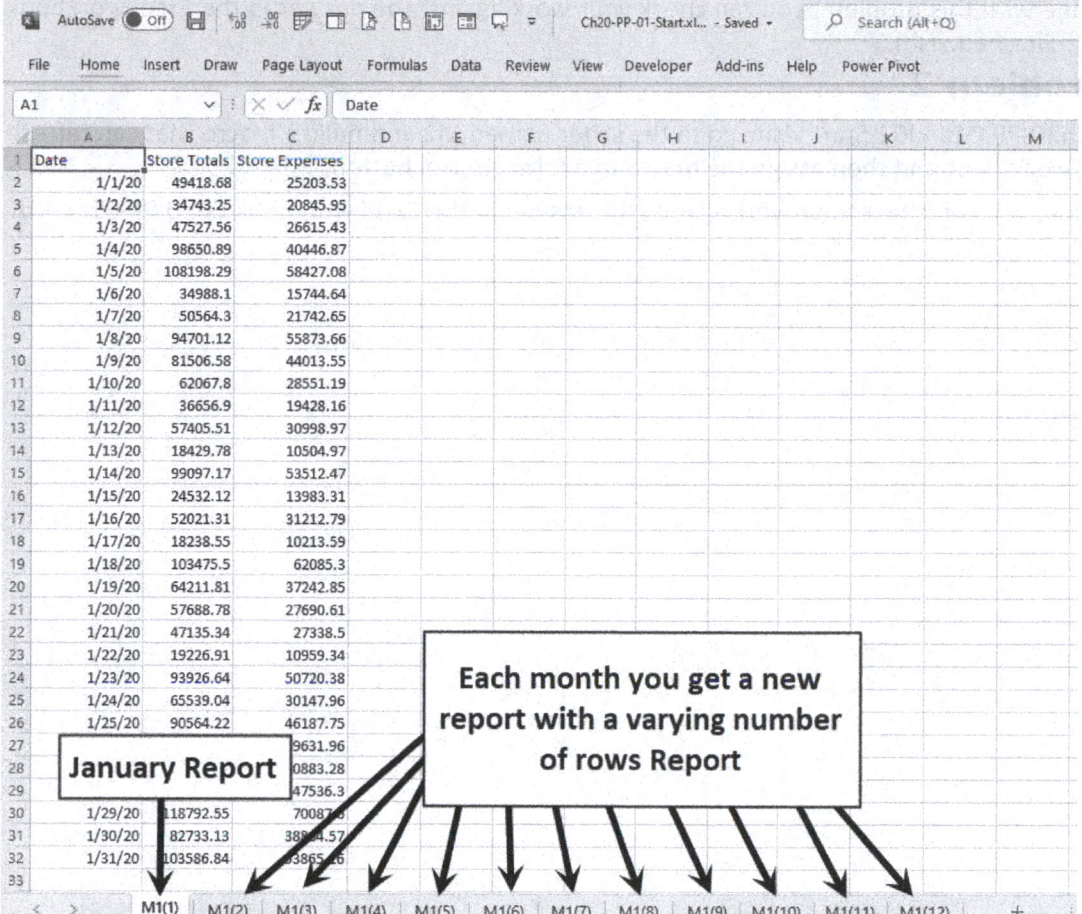

Figure 20.23 *You want to build a macro that will prepare the report you get each month.*

	Date	Store Totals	Store Expenses	Store Profit ($)	
1	Date	Store Totals	Store Expenses	Store Profit ($)	
2	1/1/20	49,418.68	25,203.53	24,215.15	
3	1/2/20	34,743.25	20,845.95	13,897.30	
4	1/3/20	47,527.56	26,615.43	20,912.13	
5	1/4/20	98,650.89	40,446.87	58,204.02	
6	1/5/20	108,198.29	58,427.08	49,771.21	
7	1/6/20	34,988.10	15,744.64	19,243.46	
8	1/7/20	50,564.30	21,742.65	28,821.65	
9	1/8/20	94,701.12	55,873.66	38,827.46	
10	1/9/20	81,506.58	44,013.55	37,493.03	
11	1/10/20	62,067.80	28,551.19	33,516.61	
12	1/11/20	36,656.90	19,428.16	17,228.74	
13	1/12/20	57,405.51	30,998.97	26,406.54	
14	1/13/20	18,429.78	10,504.97	7,924.81	
15	1/14/20	99,097.17	53,512.47	45,584.70	
16	1/15/20	24,532.12	13,983.31	10,548.81	
17	1/16/20	52,021.31	31,212.79	20,808.52	
18	1/17/20	18,238.55	10,213.59	8,024.96	
19	1/18/20	103,475.50	62,085.30	41,390.20	
20	1/19/20	64,211.81	37,242.85	26,968.96	
21	1/20/20	57,688.78	27,690.61	29,998.17	
22	1/21/20	47,135.34	27,338.50	19,796.84	
23	1/22/20	19,226.91	10,959.34	8,267.57	
24	1/23/20	93,926.64	50,720.38	43,206.26	
25	1/24/20	65,539.04	30,147.96	35,391.08	
26	1/25/20	90,564.22	46,187.75	44,376.47	
27	1/26/20	82,719.94	49,631.96	33,087.98	
28	1/27/20	48,565.78	20,883.28	27,682.50	
29	1/28/20	103,339.79	47,536.30	55,803.49	
30	1/29/20	118,792.55	70,087.60	48,704.95	
31	1/30/20	82,733.13	38,884.57	43,848.56	
32	1/31/20	103,586.84	53,865.16	49,721.68	

Figure 20.24 *The macro should add the new column and the formatting for each new report.*

When you are done with this problem, you can check your work against the answer in the Excel workbook Ch20-PP-01and02-Finished.xlsm.

Practice Problem 2

In the Excel file Ch20-PP-01and02-Start.xlsm, go to the sheet named M2 and build a macro that can refresh the query on the worksheet and then assign the macro to a form control button.

When you are done, you can check your work against the answer in the Excel workbook Ch20-PP-01and02-Finished.xlsm.

Chapter 21: Financial Worksheet Functions

The financial industry was the first industry to adopt spreadsheets as the go-to tool for making financial calculations and building financial models. The spreadsheet's ability to allow users to create models with variable formula inputs was perfect for many types of financial models—and especially for cash flow analysis models. In fact, back in 1979, in the first version of the original spreadsheet, VisiCalc, the NPV financial function (NPV = net present value) was 1 of the 21 original built-in functions, and it was the only financial function.

Now, in Microsoft 365, there are more than 50 financial functions—and more than 450 other functions— available in a worksheet. The DAX formula language includes the same set of financial functions as the Excel worksheet. Power Query M code, on the other hand, does not contain any financial functions; Power Query is built to work with data rather than make financial calculations.

In finance, cash flow analysis is helpful for tasks such as determining the value of an asset (for example, a business) or the amount of a periodic payment for a debt instrument (for example, a home mortgage). Cash flow analysis can get complicated when you have to determine all the net cash flows at a particular point in time, including tax implications and non-cash expenses, and then determine an appropriate rate that reflects the risks in the situation. You will not get into that in this book, but you will learn how to use a few of the important built-in worksheet financial functions with a given set of predetermined cash flows and rates so that you can answer questions like "How much will I earn from a savings plan?" and "How much will my home mortgage loan payment be?" and "What is the worth of an asset, given a set of assumed future cash flows?"

Most financial formulas are based on the *time value of money principle*, which says that a dollar received today is worth more than a dollar received later. Money in hand today can be invested and can earn interest so that it grows to a larger amount later. Time value of money financial formulas have been around for hundreds of years. Financial archeologists believe that Leonardo of Pisa, commonly known as Fibonacci, first published time value of money formulas in 1202—over 800 years ago! Fibonacci and other financiers in the past did not have spreadsheets to help them with their calculations—and, as shown in Figure 21.1, the math that is required to calculate the payment on a loan is not easy. This PMT math formula has been around for hundreds of years and is commonly taught in finance classes to this day. First it was used by hand, and then it was typed into handheld calculators. Today, we can use Excel.

Financial math formula to calculate a loan payment:

An = Annuity = Periodic Payments (PMT) Made at End of Each Equal Time Period
LS = Lump Sum Payment = Payment Made Once
FV=Future Value (Lump Sum Value in the Future)
PV=Present Value (Lump Sum Value in the Present)
PMT = Regular Payment Made at Regular Time Intervals
i = Annual Interest Rate
n = Number of Compounding Periods per Year
x = Years

$$PMT_{PV_{An}} = \frac{PV_{An}}{\left(\dfrac{1 - \left(1 + \dfrac{i}{n}\right)^{-(n*x)}}{\left(\dfrac{i}{n}\right)} \right)}$$

Figure 21.1 *Financial math formulas like this have been used for hundreds of years.*

As shown in Figure 21.2, the Excel financial function PMT makes constructing a loan payment model simple. In addition, with Excel, you can change the formula imports, and the results change.

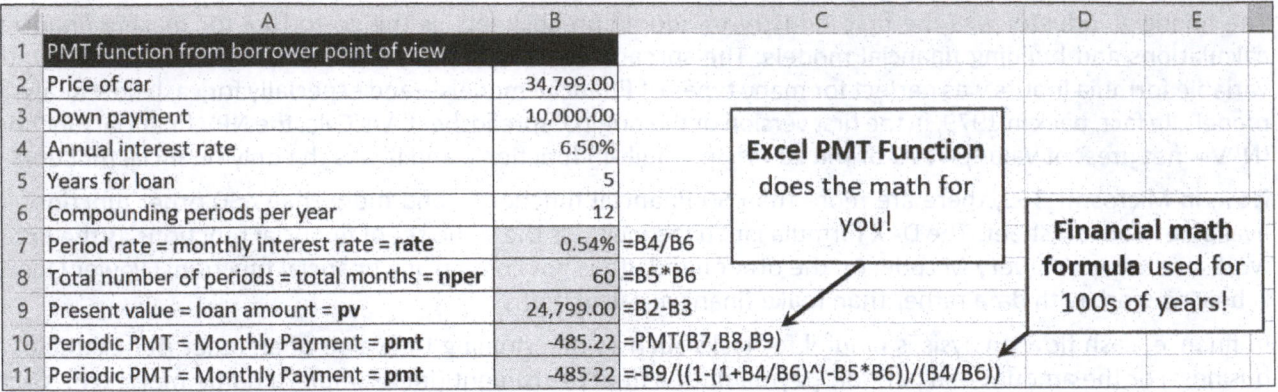

	A	B	C	D	E
1	PMT function from borrower point of view				
2	Price of car	34,799.00			
3	Down payment	10,000.00			
4	Annual interest rate	6.50%			
5	Years for loan	5			
6	Compounding periods per year	12			
7	Period rate = monthly interest rate = **rate**	0.54% =B4/B6			
8	Total number of periods = total months = **nper**	60 =B5*B6			
9	Present value = loan amount = **pv**	24,799.00 =B2-B3			
10	Periodic PMT = Monthly Payment = **pmt**	-485.22 =PMT(B7,B8,B9)			
11	Periodic PMT = Monthly Payment = **pmt**	-485.22 =-B9/((1-(1+B4/B6)^(-B5*B6))/(B4/B6))			

Excel PMT Function does the math for you!

Financial math formula used for 100s of years!

Figure 21.2 *The Excel PMT function makes calculating a monthly loan payment easy!*

Financial Terms and Variables Used in Financial Cash Flow Analysis

Excel's built-in financial functions significantly reduce the difficulty of financial math in financial models. Before you can fully appreciate these powerful functions, you need to understand a number of important financial terms and variables used in financial cash flow analysis:

- **Annual interest rate:** The yearly rate of return on an investment or the yearly interest rate paid on a loan. This rate is often given as *APR* (for *annual percentage rate*). This rate is either an assumed rate for an investment, a stated contractual rate for a loan, or an assumed discount rate for the net present value calculation. In each case, the rate is assumed to be constant over the given time period.

- **Number of compounding periods per year:** The number of equal time periods per year that interest is paid or return is earned. For example, you would use the number 12 if a loan payment were made monthly or use the number 365 if a savings account paid interest daily.

- **Equal time period:** The same time between compounding periods. The equal time period could be a day, month, quarter, year, or other lengths. Examples of equal time periods are a month for a loan with a monthly payment and a day for a savings account that pays interest daily.

- **Period rate:** The rate per one compounding period per year. The formula for the period rate is: Annual Interest Rate / Number of Compounding Periods per Year. For example, if a car loan requires monthly payments with a 12% APR, period rate = 12%/12 = 1%. That 1% period rate means that for every $1 of loan amount owed, $0.01 (one penny) would be paid in interest. In Excel's financial functions, the period rate variable is given in the *rate* argument.

- **Years:** The duration of an investment or a loan, in years. For example, you might put $10,000 in a bank account for 10 years or take out a home mortgage loan for 30 years.

- **Total number of periods:** The total number of equal time periods for an investment or a loan. The formula for the total number of periods is Number of Compounding Periods per Year * Number of Years. For example, a 30-year loan that requires monthly payments would require a total number of payment periods of 12 * 30 = 360. In Excel's financial functions, the total number of periods variable is given in the *nper* argument.

- **Consistent time period formula inputs:** The ability to enter variables that reflect a consistent time period. For example, if you are calculating a monthly loan payment, you need a monthly interest rate (period rate) and the total number of months (total number of periods) to make your calculation—not the annual rate and number of years. For example, here are two formula inputs that demonstrate a consistent month time period:

  - **Period rate:** If the annual rate is 12% and the number of compounding periods per year is 12, then the period rate = 12%/12 = 1%.

  - **Total number of periods:** If a loan must be paid back in 5 years based on monthly payments, then the total number of periods = 5 * 12 = 60.

- **Return:** The amount that is earned on an investment. For example, if you put $1 in the bank and you earn interest paid by the bank of $0.10, your balance is $1.10, and the return that you earned is $0.10. As another example, if you send a $1,200 loan payment to the bank, and $603 of the loan payment goes toward the period interest payment and $597 of the loan payment goes toward the period principal payment, the return on your loan to the bank for that month is $603.

- **Compound interest:** The result of reinvesting interest (or return), rather than paying it out, so that in the next period you can earn interest on the original amount plus the reinvesting interest. This is also known as earning interest on interest. For example, if you invest $100 with an APR of 10% compounded one time a year, you earn a $10 return at the end of year 1, and the balance is $110. For the second year, that $110 is used to calculate the interest for the second year. The new balance is then $110 + $110 * 10% = $110 + $11 = $121. After the first year, the compound interest provides you a return on the original amount and on the return that is reinvested.

- **Cash flow:** The net monetary transfer (cash flow) amount at a particular point in time. For example, you might pay $1,200 in month 10 for a home mortgage loan, receive quarterly interest of $10 in quarter 2 for a bank account, or estimate that a machine will generate $50,000 of cash flow in year 1.

- **Periodic cash flow:** A cash flow amount that is the same amount for each equal time period. For example, your monthly loan payment might be $1,200 at the end of each month, or the amount you withdraw from your retirement account at the beginning of each month might be $3,500. In Excel's financial functions, the periodic cash flow variable is given in the *pmt* argument.

- **Irregular cash flow:** A cash flow amount that is not the same for each equal time period. For example, you might estimate that a new machine will help generate a cash flow of $50,000 in the first 3 years but only $25,000 in the last 2 years.

- **Direction of cash flow:** Either negative or positive cash flow:

    - **Negative:** Cash going out of your wallet or purse is negative. For example, if you pay the bank $1,200 each month for your loan payment, that cash flow is coming out of your wallet or purse and is therefore recorded as a negative amount: –$1,200.

    - **Positive:** Cash coming into your wallet or purse is positive. For example, if the bank receives your $1,200 loan payment each month, that cash flow is coming into the bank's wallet or purse and is therefore recorded as a positive amount: $1,200.

    All cash flows have two parties involved. There is the side that receives the cash as a positive value and the side that pays the cash as a negative value. Recording the correct sign for the cash flow depends on which side you are on. For example, for a loan payment, the person paying the loan amount would record it as a negative, but the bank would record it as a positive. As another example, for a savings plan, the person making the deposit would record it as a negative, but the bank would record it as a positive. Notice that with a savings plan, even though the depositor has the right to the cash and deposits it into their account, it must be recorded as a negative cash flow when the deposit is made. For the depositor, a cash flow can only be recorded as a positive when a withdrawal is made. The analogy of the wallet or purse is helpful because it gives you the correct point of view to determine the direction of the cash flow.

- **Future value:** The value of an investment or a loan in the future, after the total number of periods has elapsed. For example, the future value calculation can tell you what a savings plan is worth after 10 years, or it may be an input for a calculation that represents a balloon payment at the end of the loan. In Excel's financial functions, the future value variable is given in the *fv* argument.

- **Present value:** The current value of future cash flows that have been discounted back to time zero at an assumed discount rate. You can think of it as: "How much is something worth today—right now?" The present value concept is usually the single most difficult financial concept to understand. If you have some future cash flows and you want to know what they are worth today, at time zero, how do you do that? The simple answer is that you remove all the assumed interest or return from those future cash flows to see what the value is today. In finance, if you have future cash flows and you want to know the present value of those cash flows, you use an assumed rate, called a *discount rate*, and you discount the cash flows back to time zero. Discounting future cash flows is the process of removing all the assumed interest or return that you expect to get in order to determine the value at time zero.

You can think of the present value as "interest in reverse." For example, as shown in Figure 21.3, if you invest $1 in a bank for one year and earn a 10% interest rate at the end of the year, the value in the account will be $1.10. The $1 invested at time zero is the present value, and the $1.10 at the end of one year is the future value. Because you can now see both sides, present value and future value, you can ask a question from either side. From the present value side, you already know that you have $1, so you can ask: "What will the future value be in one year?" Once you complete the future value math calculation, your answer is that the future value will be $1.10. From the future value side, if you know that you want to have $1.10 in the bank in one year, you can ask: "How much do I have to invest today, right now at time zero, to get that $1.10 in the future?" After you complete the present value math calculation, you get a present value answer of $1. I created this simple $1 example to make it easy to understand that when you calculate the future value, you are adding interest or return, and when you calculate the present value, you are subtracting interest or return.

A useful real-world example for the present value calculation is when a parent asks a bank: "If I need $50,000 in 18 years to help my newborn daughter with her college education, how much should I deposit in the bank today?" If the parents could earn 5% APR, compounded daily, then, after doing the present value math to remove all the interest that will be earned, they would have to invest $20,330 today to have $50,000 in 18 years. As another example, the present value calculation can also be used to determine the maximum amount that should be paid for a machine, where, in this case, the present value math calculation would remove all the assumed return from the estimated future cash flows to get a value for the machine today. Finally, the present value amount can be an input value at time zero, like the amount of a loan before any payments are made. We will see a number of examples later in this chapter. In Excel's financial functions, the present value variable is given in the *pv* argument.

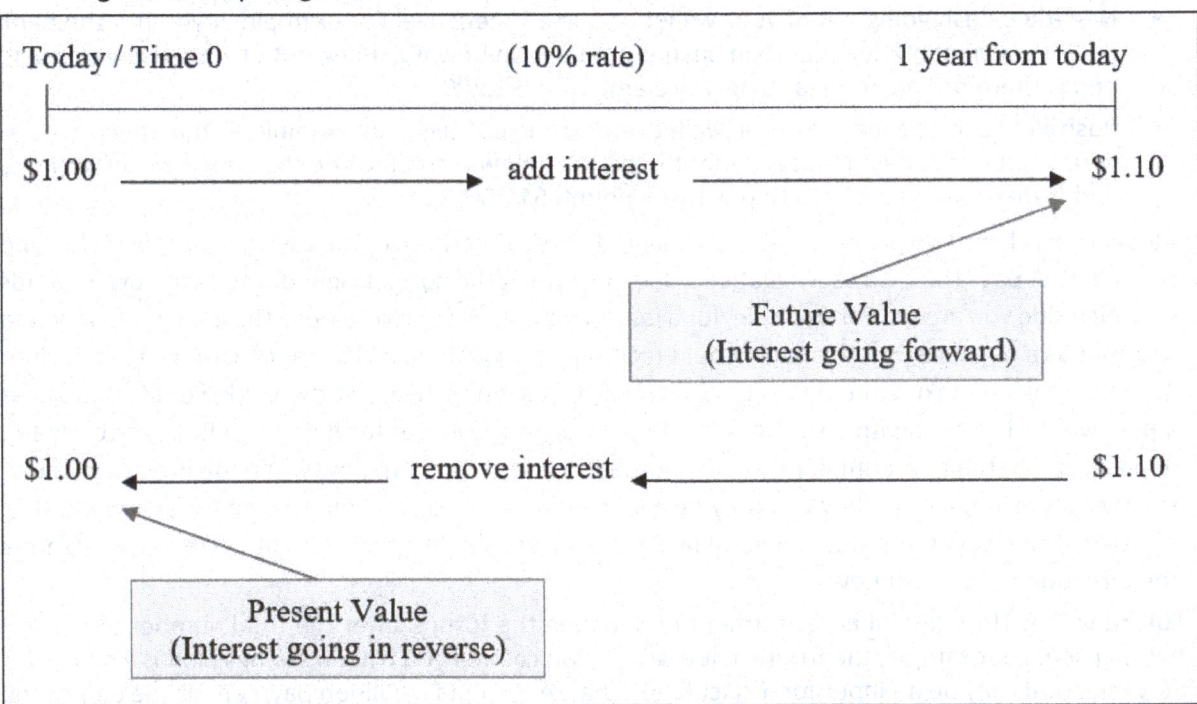

Figure 21.3 *Future value involves adding interest or return. Present value involves removing interest or return.*

- **Annuity:** A pattern of continuous periodic cash flows for a defined amount of time with a constant annual rate. For example, a home mortgage loan that requires that you pay $1,200 at the end of each month for the next 20 years and has a fixed APR of 3.5% is an annuity. A retirement plan that allows you to withdraw $3,500 at the beginning of each month for the next 25 years and has a fixed APR of 2.5% is also an annuity.

  There are two types of annuities:

  - **End annuity:** Cash flow occurs at the end of a period.
  - **Begin annuity:** Cash flow occurs at the beginning of a period.

In Excel's financial functions, the type of annuity variable is listed in the *type* argument.

- **Net present value:** The value of all future cash flows over the entire life of an investment, discounted to the present (time zero) and compared to the cost at time zero. The discount rate is the assumed required rate of return of the investment. A net present value amount that is zero or greater indicates that the investment should be considered, and a value that is less than zero should not be considered. For the net present value calculation, in Excel's financial functions, the cash flow variable is listed as the *value* argument.

Now that you have read the definitions of the important terms and variables, you're ready to see how to use 7 financial worksheet functions to answer 12 financial questions (see Table 21.1).

Table 21.1 Using Financial Functions to Answer Financial Questions

Function	Question(s) It Will Help You Answer
FV	How much will $10,000 invested today be worth in 10 years?
	If you invest $50 at the end of each month, how much will you have in 40 years?
PV	How much do you need to deposit today to have $50,000 in 18 years?
	How much do you need on the day you retire in order to withdraw $3,500 each month for the next 25 years?
PMT	How much do you need to invest at the end of each month if you want to have $781,801.35 on the day you retire?
	What is the monthly payment for a 20-year home mortgage loan?
	How much does the bank take as interest for each mortgage payment?
	What is the monthly payment for a 3-year car loan with a $5,000 balloon payment at the end?
NPER	How long will it take to pay off a credit card bill if you make only the minimum payment?
RATE	What is the adjusted APR when there are points and fees for a loan?
NPV	What is the most you should you pay for a machine when you have irregular cash flows and equal time periods?
XNPV	What is the most you should you pay for a machine when you have irregular cash flows and unequal time periods?

Note: For all of the following examples, you can open and work with the file Ch21-Excel365-FinancialFunctions.xlsx.

The FV Function

The FV function calculates the future value of an investment or loan, based on a constant interest rate. You can use the FV function with either an annuity cash flow pattern or a single present value lump sum payment at time zero. The arguments in the FV function are as follows:

- *rate:* Period rate (month, quarter, yearly, etc.).
- *nper:* Total number of periods.
- *pmt:* Equal periodic cash flow. If *pmt* is skipped, it is assumed to be 0, and you must include the *pv* argument.
- *[pv]:* Present value—the amount invested at time zero, or the amount of the loan on the day it is issued. If *pv* is omitted, it is assumed to be 0, and you must include the *pmt* argument.
- *[type]:* The type of annuity. This argument can have one of two values:
  - End = 0 or omitted: Payment at end of period.
  - Begin = 1: Payment at beginning of period.

Question 1: How Much Will $10,000 Invested Today Be Worth in 10 Years?

As shown in Figure 21.4, you can use the FV function to determine how much $10,000 invested today will be worth in 10 years at an APR of 5.00%, compounded monthly. The FV function uses a lump sum present value amount of $10,000 to calculate all the interest that should be added to get the future value amount of $16,470.09.

You can try this example on the worksheet named Ch21(4).

	A	B	C	D
2	Q #1	How much will $10,000 invested today be worth in 10 years at an APR of 5.00%, compounded monthly?		
4		Variables and function arguments:	Inputs & formulas:	Formulas:
5		Amount to invest today = **pv**	$10,000.00	
6		Annual interest rate = APR	0.05	
7		Years	10	
8		Compounding periods per year	12	
9		Period rate = **rate**	0.004166667	=C6/C8
10		Total number of periods = **nper**	120	=C7*C8
11		Future value = fv	$16,470.09	=FV(C9,C10,,-C5)
12				
13		FV(rate , nper , pmt , [pv] , [type])		
14		Future value is positive	Period rate	No annuity so type is omitted
15		because money is		
16		coming into wallet /		Present value must be negative because
17		purse. This is a	Total number of periods	$ coming out of wallet / purse
18		withdrawal.	No pmt, so argument skipped	
19				
20		Math formula fv:	$16,470.09	=C5*(1+C9)^C10

Figure 21.4 *The FV function can calculate how much a lump sum amount invested today will be worth in the future.*

Question 2: If You Invest $50 at the End of Each Month, How Much Will You Have in 40 Years?

As shown in Figure 21.5, if at the end of each month you invest $50 into a stock index fund with an estimated APR of 13.00%, and your stock account had $250 in it at the beginning of the first month, you can use the FV function to calculate how much will be in your stock account in 40 years. The FV function uses a lump sum present value amount of $250 and a periodic payment amount of $50 to calculate all the interest that should be added to get the future value amount of $853,021.58.

For a problem like this, there is no contractual APR, as you would have with a savings plan or loan. But stock market history suggests that over a 40-year period, 13% is a reasonable estimate of what you could earn. The real knowledge power gained from this example comes from calculating the total amount that you invested, $24,250, in cell C14, and subtracting it from the future value amount, $853,021.58, in cell C13, to determine the total return gained amount, $828,771.58, in cell C15. The total return is over $800,000. This illustrates that the most powerful variable when it comes to investing is time. Even if you invest only a small amount, if you start early in life and continue for a long time, a lot can be gained.

You can try this example on the worksheet named Ch21(5).

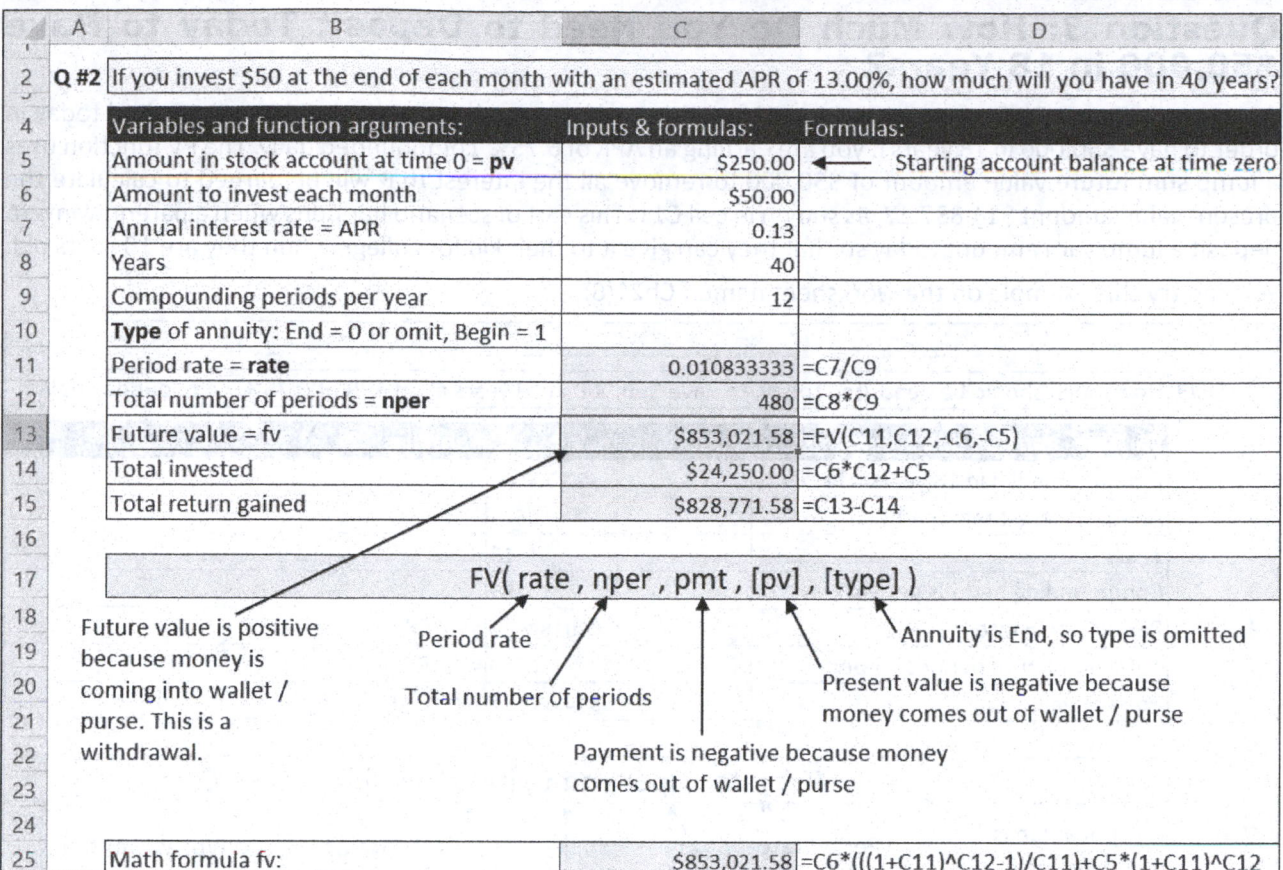

Figure 21.5 *The FV function can calculate how much your investment plan will be worth in 40 years.*

PV Function

The PV function calculates the present value of a loan or an investment, based on a constant interest rate. You can use the PV function with either an annuity cash flow pattern or a single future value lump sum payment at the end of the last time period. The arguments in the PV function are as follows:

- **rate**: Period rate (month, quarter, yearly, etc.).
- **nper**: Total number of periods.
- **pmt**: Equal periodic cash flow. If *pmt* is skipped, it is assumed to be 0, and you must include the *fv* argument.
- **[fv]**: Future value—an investment or loan cash balance you want to attain after the last payment is made. If *fv* is omitted, it is assumed to be 0, and you must include the *pmt* argument.
- **[type]**: The type of annuity. This argument can have one of two values:
  - End = 0 or omitted: Payment at end of period.
  - Begin = 1: Payment at beginning of period.

Question 3: How Much Do You Need to Deposit Today to Have $50,000 in 18 Years?

As shown in Figure 21.6, you can use the PV function to determine how much should be deposited today in order to have $50,000 in 18 years if you are earning an APR of 6.75%, compounded daily. The PV function uses a lump sum future value amount of $50,000 to remove all the interest that will be earned to calculate the present value amount $14,837.17, as shown in cell C11. This sort of scenario happens when a parent wants to deposit a lump sum amount today so that they can give it to their kid for college when they are 18 years old.

You can try this example on the worksheet named Ch21(6).

	A	B	C	D
2	Q #3	How much should be deposited today, to have $50,000 in 18 years at an APR of 6.75%, compounded daily?		
4		Variables and function arguments:	Inputs & formulas:	Formulas:
5		Amount needed in 18 years = **fv**	$50,000.00	
6		Annual interest rate = APR	0.0675	
7		Years	18	
8		Compounding periods per year	365	
9		Period rate = **rate**	0.000184932	=C6/C8
10		Total number of periods = **nper**	6570	=C7*C8
11		Present value = pv	-$14,837.17	=PV(C9,C10,,C5)
13		PV(rate , nper , pmt , [fv] , [type])		
14		Present value is	Period rate	No annuity so type is omitted
15		negative because		
16		money is coming out		Future value must be positive because
17		of wallet / purse.	Total number of periods	money is coming into wallet / purse
18		This is a deposit.	No pmt, so argument skipped	
20		Math formula pv:	-$14,837.17	=-C5/(1+C9)^C10

Figure 21.6 *The PV function can calculate how much should be deposited today to get a lump sum amount in future.*

Question 4: How Much Do You Need on the Day You Retire in Order to Withdraw $3,500 Each Month for the Next 25 Years?

Figure 21.7 shows the PV function being used to figure out how much money you need on the day you retire if you want to withdraw $3,500 at the beginning of each month for the next 25 years. The PV function uses the annuity future periodic cash flows of $3,500 to remove all the interest and deliver a present value amount of $781,801.35, which represents the amount you would need to put into the bank on the day that you retire. This present value amount would then sit in the bank and continue to earn interest as you make the $3,500 withdrawals at the beginning of each month. The question is, though, how do you get the $781,801.35 on the day you retire? The answer to that is coming up next, when you learn how to use the PMT function.

You can try this example on the worksheet named Ch21(7).

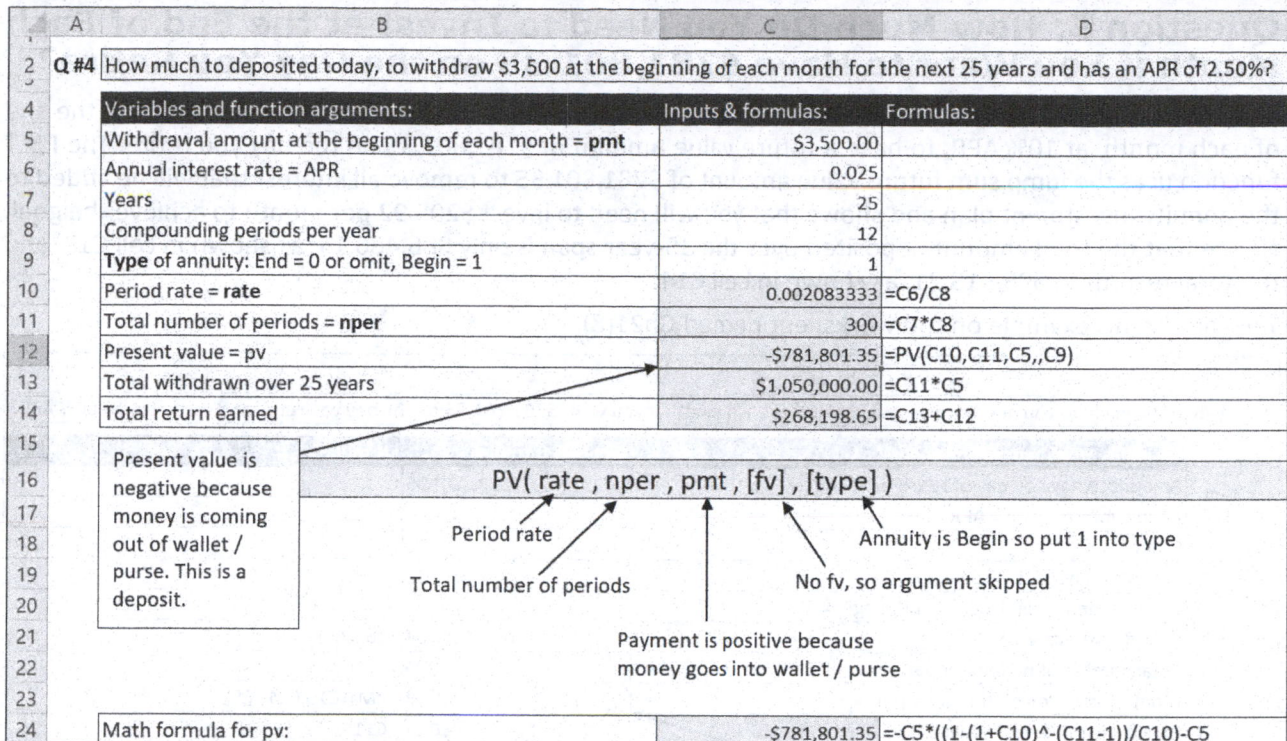

Figure 21.7 *The PV function can tell you how much money you need on the day you retire if you want to achieve a specified withdrawal plan.*

PMT Function

The PMT function returns the periodic payment for an annuity. The arguments in the PMT function are as follows:

- **rate**: Period rate (month, quarter, yearly, etc.).

- **nper**: Total number of periods.

- **pv**: Present value—an amount invested at time zero, or the amount of a loan on the day it is issued. If *pv* is skipped, it is assumed to be 0, and you must include the *fv* argument.

- **[fv]**: Future value—an investment or loan cash balance you want to attain after the last payment is made. If *fv* is omitted, it is assumed to be 0, and you must include the *pv* argument.

- **[type]**: The type of annuity. This argument can have one of two values:
    - End = 0 or omitted: Payment at end of period.
    - Begin = 1: Payment at beginning of period.

Question 5: How Much Do You Need to Invest at the End of Each Month if You Want to Have $781,801.35 on the Day You Retire?

As shown in Figure 21.8, you can use the PMT function to determine how much you need to invest at the end of each month, at 10% APR, to have a future value amount of $781,801.35 on the day you retire. The PMT function uses the lump sum future value amount of $781,801.35 to remove all interest that will be added to the annuity investment plan and shows that you will need to invest $205.92 per month to achieve the goal. Notice that the total amount deposited over the 35-year span is only $86,486.14, as shown in cell C13, and the total return is $695,315.21, as shown in cell C14.

You can try this example on the worksheet named Ch21(8).

	A	B	C	D
2	Q #5	How much do you need to invest at the end of each month if you want $781,801.35 on the day you retire and assume a 10.00% APR?		
4		Variables and function arguments:	Inputs & formulas:	Formulas:
5		Amount to have on day of retirement = **fv**	$781,801.35	
6		Annual interest rate = APR	0.1	
7		Years	35	
8		Compounding periods per year	12	
9		**Type** of annuity: End = 0 or omit, Begin = 1		
10		Period rate = **rate**	0.008333333	=C6/C8
11		Total number of periods = **nper**	420	=C7*C8
12		Monthly investment amount = **pmt**	-$205.92	=PMT(C10,C11,,C5)
13		Total invested over 35 years	$86,486.14	=C11*-C12
14		Total return earned	$695,315.21	=C5-C13
15				
16		Payment is negative because money is coming out of wallet / purse. This is a monthly payment.	PMT(rate , nper , pv , [fv] , [type])	
17				
18			Period rate	Annuity is End, so type is omitted
19			Total number of periods	Future value is positive because money is coming into wallet / purse
20			No pv, so	
21			argument skipped	
22				
23		Math formula for pmt:	-$205.92	=-C5/(((1+C10)^C11-1)/C10)

Figure 21.8 *The PMT function can show you how much to invest each month to have $781,801.35 on the day you retire.*

Question 6: What Is the Monthly Payment for a 20-Year Home Mortgage Loan?

As shown in Figure 21.9, you can use the PMT function to determine the monthly payment for a 20-year, 3.5% APR, $206,910.92 home mortgage loan. The PMT function uses a lump sum present value amount of $206,910.92 to add all the interest and deliver the monthly payment $1,200, as shown in cell C13, which will be paid at the end of each of the 240 future months.

Question 7: How Much Does the Bank Take as Interest for Each Mortgage Payment?

An *amortization table* is a set of calculations that shows the interest paid and principal reduction for every scheduled loan payment. In Figure 21.9, the amortization table repeats the $1,200 mortgage payment 240 times, with each row showing the amount that the bank takes as interest and the amount that it uses to reduce the balance. The most important calculation in the amortization table is the formula that calculates the row-by-row monthly interest amount. For example, for Month 1, the interest is calculated by multiplying the previous month's loan balance of $206,910.92 by the monthly rate of 0.2917% to get $206,910.92 * 0.2917% = $603.49. This means that the homeowner sent in $1,200, and the bank got more than half of it as interest. This is because at the beginning of the loan, the balance is very large. In the last row of the amortization table, month 240, the interest is calculated as follows: Previous Month Balance * Period Rate = $1,196.51 * 0.2917% = $3.49. The interest here is very small because the loan balance is very small.

You can try this example of the worksheet named Ch21(9).

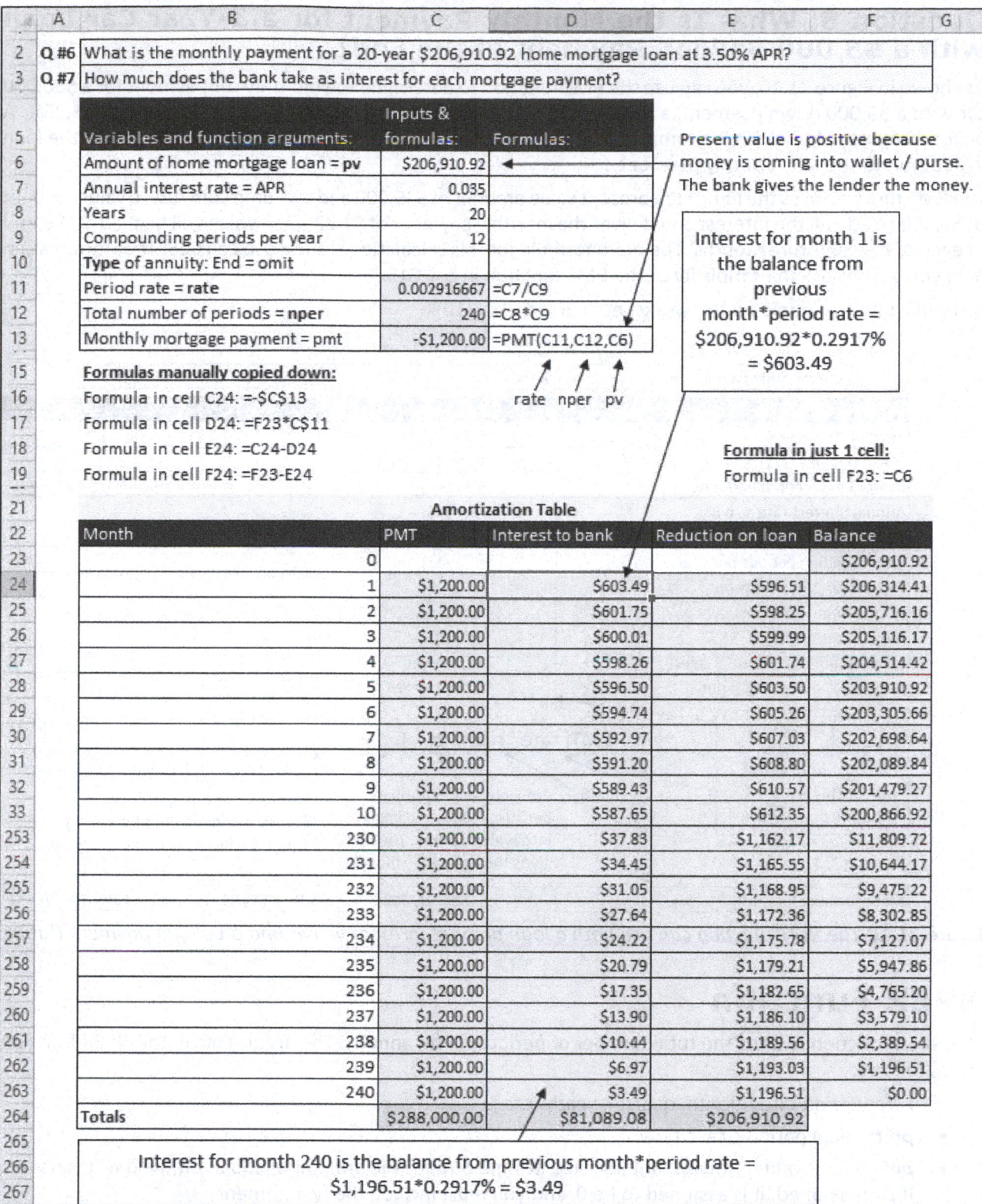

	A	B	C	D	E	F	G
2	Q #6	What is the monthly payment for a 20-year $206,910.92 home mortgage loan at 3.50% APR?					
3	Q #7	How much does the bank take as interest for each mortgage payment?					
5		Variables and function arguments:	Inputs & formulas:	Formulas:	Present value is positive because		
6		Amount of home mortgage loan = **pv**	$206,910.92	←	money is coming into wallet / purse.		
7		Annual interest rate = APR	0.035		The bank gives the lender the money.		
8		Years	20				
9		Compounding periods per year	12		Interest for month 1 is		
10		**Type** of annuity: End = omit			the balance from		
11		Period rate = **rate**	0.002916667	=C7/C9	previous		
12		Total number of periods = **nper**	240	=C8*C9	month*period rate =		
13		Monthly mortgage payment = pmt	-$1,200.00	=PMT(C11,C12,C6)	$206,910.92*0.2917%		
15		**Formulas manually copied down:**			= $603.49		
16		Formula in cell C24: =$C$13		rate nper pv			
17		Formula in cell D24: =F23*C$11					
18		Formula in cell E24: =C24-D24			**Formula in just 1 cell:**		
19		Formula in cell F24: =F23-E24			Formula in cell F23: =C6		
21				**Amortization Table**			
22		Month	PMT	Interest to bank	Reduction on loan	Balance	
23		0				$206,910.92	
24		1	$1,200.00	$603.49	$596.51	$206,314.41	
25		2	$1,200.00	$601.75	$598.25	$205,716.16	
26		3	$1,200.00	$600.01	$599.99	$205,116.17	
27		4	$1,200.00	$598.26	$601.74	$204,514.42	
28		5	$1,200.00	$596.50	$603.50	$203,910.92	
29		6	$1,200.00	$594.74	$605.26	$203,305.66	
30		7	$1,200.00	$592.97	$607.03	$202,698.64	
31		8	$1,200.00	$591.20	$608.80	$202,089.84	
32		9	$1,200.00	$589.43	$610.57	$201,479.27	
33		10	$1,200.00	$587.65	$612.35	$200,866.92	
253		230	$1,200.00	$37.83	$1,162.17	$11,809.72	
254		231	$1,200.00	$34.45	$1,165.55	$10,644.17	
255		232	$1,200.00	$31.05	$1,168.95	$9,475.22	
256		233	$1,200.00	$27.64	$1,172.36	$8,302.85	
257		234	$1,200.00	$24.22	$1,175.78	$7,127.07	
258		235	$1,200.00	$20.79	$1,179.21	$5,947.86	
259		236	$1,200.00	$17.35	$1,182.65	$4,765.20	
260		237	$1,200.00	$13.90	$1,186.10	$3,579.10	
261		238	$1,200.00	$10.44	$1,189.56	$2,389.54	
262		239	$1,200.00	$6.97	$1,193.03	$1,196.51	
263		240	$1,200.00	$3.49	$1,196.51	$0.00	
264		Totals	$288,000.00	$81,089.08	$206,910.92		
266		Interest for month 240 is the balance from previous month*period rate =					
267		$1,196.51*0.2917% = $3.49					

Figure 21.9 *PMT and amortization table showing mortgage payments and interest paid to the bank each month.*

Question 8: What Is the Monthly Payment for a 3-Year Car Loan with a $5,000 Balloon Payment at the End?

As shown in Figure 21.10, you can use the PMT function to determine the monthly car payment for a $50,000 car with a $5,000 down payment, a $5,000 balloon payment at the end of the loan, and an APR of 5.25%. A *balloon payment* for a loan is a lump sum cash payment that you must pay back on the last day of the loan in addition to the last monthly payment.

The PMT function uses the lump sum present value amount of $45,000 and the lump sum future value amount of $5,000 to add all the interest and deliver the monthly payment of $1,225.21, which will be paid at the end of each of the 36 future months. The math formula for this calculation is shown in cell C25. That formula can help you appreciate the simplicity of the PMT function in cell C15.

You can try this example on the worksheet named Ch21(10).

	A	B	C	D
2	Q #8	What is the monthly payment for a 3-year, $45,000 car loan with a $5,000 balloon payment and a 5.25% APR?		
4		Variables and function arguments:	Inputs & formulas	Formulas:
5		Price of car	$50,000.00	
6		Down payment on car	$5,000.00	
7		Balloon payment at end = **fv**	$5,000.00	
8		Annual interest rate = APR	0.0525	
9		Years	3	
10		Compounding periods per year	12	
11		**Type** of annuity: End = omit		
12		Loan amount = price - down payment = **pv**	$45,000.00	=C5-C6
13		Period rate = **rate**	0.004375	=C8/C10
14		Total number of periods = **nper**	36	=C10*C9
15		Monthly car payment = pmt	-$1,225.21	=PMT(C13,C14,C12,-C7)

PMT(rate , nper , pv , [fv] , [type])

Payment is negative because money is coming out of wallet / purse. This is a monthly payment.

Period rate

Total number of periods

Present value is positive because money is coming into wallet / purse. The bank gives the lender the money.

Annuity is End, so type is omitted

Future value is negative because money is coming out of wallet / purse. This is a balloon payment at the end.

| 24 | | Math formula for pmt: | $1,225.21 | =C12/((1-(1+C13)^-C14)/C13)-C7/(((1+C13)^C14-1)/C13) |

Figure 21.10 *The PMT function can use both a loan amount (present value) and a balloon payment (future value).*

NPER Function

The NPER function returns the total number of periods for an annuity. The arguments in the NPER function are as follows:

- *rate*: Period rate (month, quarter, yearly, etc.).
- *pmt*: Equal periodic cash flow.
- *pv*: Present value—an amount invested at time zero, or the amount of a loan on the day it is issued. If *pv* is skipped, it is assumed to be 0, and you must include the *fv* argument.
- *[fv]*: Future value—an investment or loan cash balance you want to attain after the last payment is made. If *fv* is omitted, it is assumed to be 0, and you must include the *pv* argument.
- *[type]*: The type of annuity. This argument can have one of two values:
  - End = 0 or omitted: Payment at end of period.
  - Begin = 1: Payment at beginning of period.

Question 9: How Long Will It Take to Pay Off a Credit Card Bill if You Make Only the Minimum Payment?

As shown in Figure 21.11, you can use the NPER function to determine the total number of months it takes to pay off a credit balance of $7,500 with an APR of 18% and a minimum payment at the end of each month of $125. The NPER function uses the lump sum present value amount $7,000, the monthly payment amount $125, and the monthly interest rate (period rate) 1.5% to solve for the total number of periods variable—in this case, the total number of months to pay off the credit card. As shown in cell C12, if you want to know how many years it takes to pay off the credit card, you divide the total number of months by 12.

You can try this example on the worksheet named Ch21(11).

	A	B	C	D
2	Q #9	How long to pay off a credit card bill making only the minimum payment?		
4		Variables and function arguments:	Inputs & formulas Formulas:	
5		Balance on credit card = **pv**	$7,500.00	
6		Annual interest rate = APR	0.18	
7		Compounding periods per year	12	
8		Minimum monthly payment = **pmt**	125	
9		**Type** of annuity: End = omit		
10		Period rate = **rate**	0.015 =C6/C7	
11		Total number of periods = **nper**	154.6541086 =NPER(C10,-C8,C5)	
12		Years	12.88784238 =C11/C7	
13				
14	Total number of periods uses the unit of time "months". So this is: total months to pay off loan.	NPER(rate , pmt , pv , [fv] , [type])		
15		Period rate	Annuity is End, so type is omitted	
16				
17		Payment is negative because money is coming out of wallet / purse. This is the monthly payment.	No fv, so argument omitted	
18			Present value is positive because money is coming into wallet / purse. The bank gives the lender the money.	
19				
20				
21				
22				
23		Math formula for nper:	154.6541086 =LOG(-(1/(C5/C8*C10-1)),1+C10)	

Figure 21.11 *The NPER function can solve for the total number of periods variable.*

RATE Function

The RATE function returns the period rate for an annuity. RATE is calculated through iteration and can have zero or more solutions. If the successive results of RATE do not converge to within 0.0000001 after 20 iterations, RATE returns the #NUM! error value. The arguments in the RATE function are as follows:

- **nper**: Total number of periods.
- **pmt**: Equal periodic cash flow.
- **pv**: Present value—an amount invested at time zero, or the amount of a loan on the day it is issued. If *pv* is skipped, it is assumed to be 0, and you must include the *fv* argument.
- **[fv]**: Future value. An investment or loan cash balance you want to attain after the last payment is made. If *fv* is omitted, it is assumed to be 0, and you must include the *pv* argument.
- **[type]**: The type of annuity. This argument can have one of two values:
  - End = 0 or omitted: Payment at end of period.
  - Begin = 1: Payment at beginning of period.
- **[guess]**: A rate you think the answer is near. If you omit *guess*, it is assumed to be 10%. If RATE does not converge, try different values for *guess*. RATE usually converges if *guess* is between 0 and 1.

Question 10: What Is the Adjusted APR When There Are Points and Fees for a Loan?

As shown in Figure 21.12, you can use the RATE function to determine the adjusted APR when a bank quotes an APR but takes points and fees from the original loan amount. *Points* and *fees* are both costs to the borrower for a loan transaction, but whereas points are expressed as a percentage of the original loan amount, fees are explicitly stated monetary amounts. When these borrower costs are not paid separately from the original loan amount, they must be subtracted from the loan amount and therefore increase the quoted APR. When these fees are subtracted from the loan amount, two things happen:

- The original full loan amount is still owed, and it is used to determine the monthly payment that the borrower must make, using the original quoted APR.

- The reduced cash amount that is received becomes the present value cash flow that is used to determine the true rate, or *adjusted APR*. This adjusted APR is always higher than the quoted rate. This adjusted APR is useful because it gives the borrower a clear picture of the annual rate charged based on the actual cash flows.

In Figure 21.12, the RATE function uses the lump sum present value amount $197,250, the monthly payment amount $1,073.65, and the original monthly interest rate to solve for the new adjusted period rate, as shown in cell C16. When the new adjusted period rate is multiplied by 12, the result is the adjusted APR, shown in C17.

> **Note:** To manually calculate a period rate for more than five periods, you must use an iterative process. Luckily, in Excel, the RATE function can crunch those iterations for you and make the calculations simple.

You can try this example on the worksheet named Ch21(12).

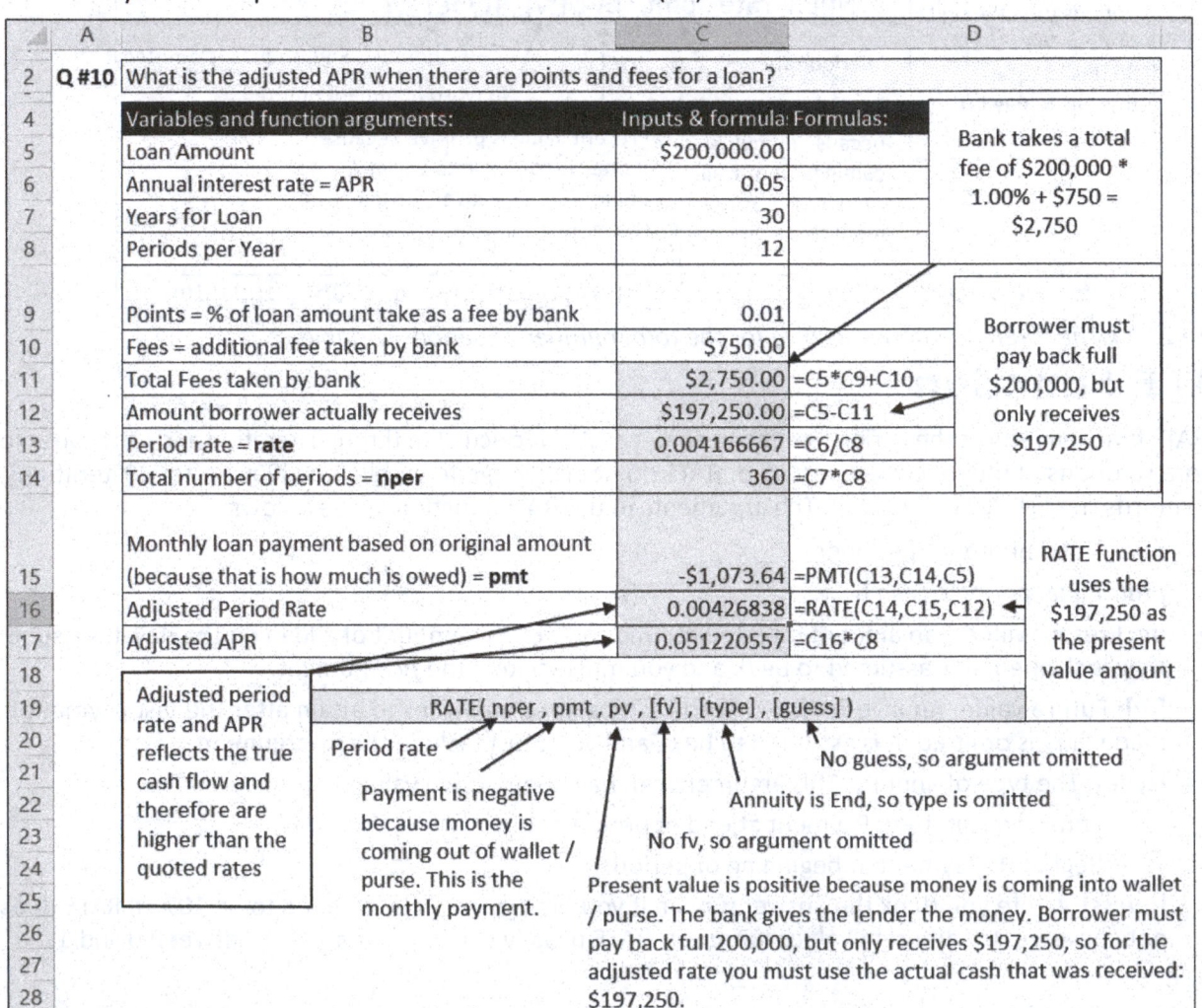

Figure 21.12 *The RATE function can solve for the period rate variable.*

NPV Function

The NPV function calculates the current value of all future cash flows at time zero for an investment by using a discount rate and a series of future cash flows (either periodic cash flows or irregular cash flows) that occur at the end of equal time periods. The arguments in the NPV function are as follows:

- **rate:** Period rate (month, quarter, yearly, etc.). Also known as the period discount rate or the period required rate of return.
- **value1, value2,…:** Periodic or irregular cash flows that occur at the ends of equal time periods.
  - A *value* argument accepts 1 to 254 entries representing the cash flows. The order of the values is used to interpret the order of cash flows.
  - The NPV calculation is based on future cash flows. If your first cash flow occurs at the beginning of the first period, the first value must be added to the NPV result and not included in the *value* arguments.

Question 11: What Is the Most You Should You Pay for a Machine When You Have Irregular Cash Flows and Equal Time Periods?

As shown in Figure 21.13, you can use the NPV function to determine the maximum amount to pay for a C & C router machine when you have irregular cash flows and equal time periods for those cash flows. When a company considers buying an asset such as a C & C router machine in a production wood shop, or when one company buys another company, the company does not want to buy an asset unless it is going to add value to the business.

Capital budgeting is the process of determining whether buying as asset is profitable. In capital budgeting, the net present value metric is often used to make decisions. The company must estimate the cash flows that the asset will generate in the future and then determine the required rate of return (the discount rate). The *required rate of return*, or *RRR*, is the return or profit that the company hopes to make from the asset. Once the company has the required rate of return, it can use it in the net present value calculation to remove all future profit or return from the cash flows to determine the cash flow value at time zero. The company compares the discounted cash flow value at time zero to the cost at time zero to decide whether the asset purchase should be considered. The rule is as follows:

- Discounted cash flow value at time zero > cost: Asset adds value.
- Discounted cash flow value at time zero = cost: Asset earns exactly the required rate of return.
- Discounted cash flow value at time zero < cost: Asset does not add value.

Another way to make this capital budget decision is to first subtract the cost from the discounted cash flow value at time zero to calculate the net present value. When you make this calculation, a positive number adds value, zero earns exactly the estimated required rate of return, and a negative number indicates that value would be lost. The net present value rule is as follows:

- Net present value is positive: Asset adds value.
- Net present value is zero: Asset earns exactly the required rate of return.
- Net present value is negative: Asset does not add value.

In Figure 21.13, the cost of the C & C router machine is $200,000, the required rate of return is estimated to be 15%, and the estimated cash flows for the 5 years are listed. The NPV function will use the RRR of 15% and the cash flows from the range C10:C14 to make the calculation and remove all the expected return and then deliver a discounted cash flow at time zero of $288,582.20. Because the value at time zero is bigger than the cost, the machine is estimated to be profitable. When you subtract the cost from the value, you get a net present value of $288,582.20 – $200,000 = $3582.20, as shown in cell C16.

You can try this example on the worksheet named Ch21(11).

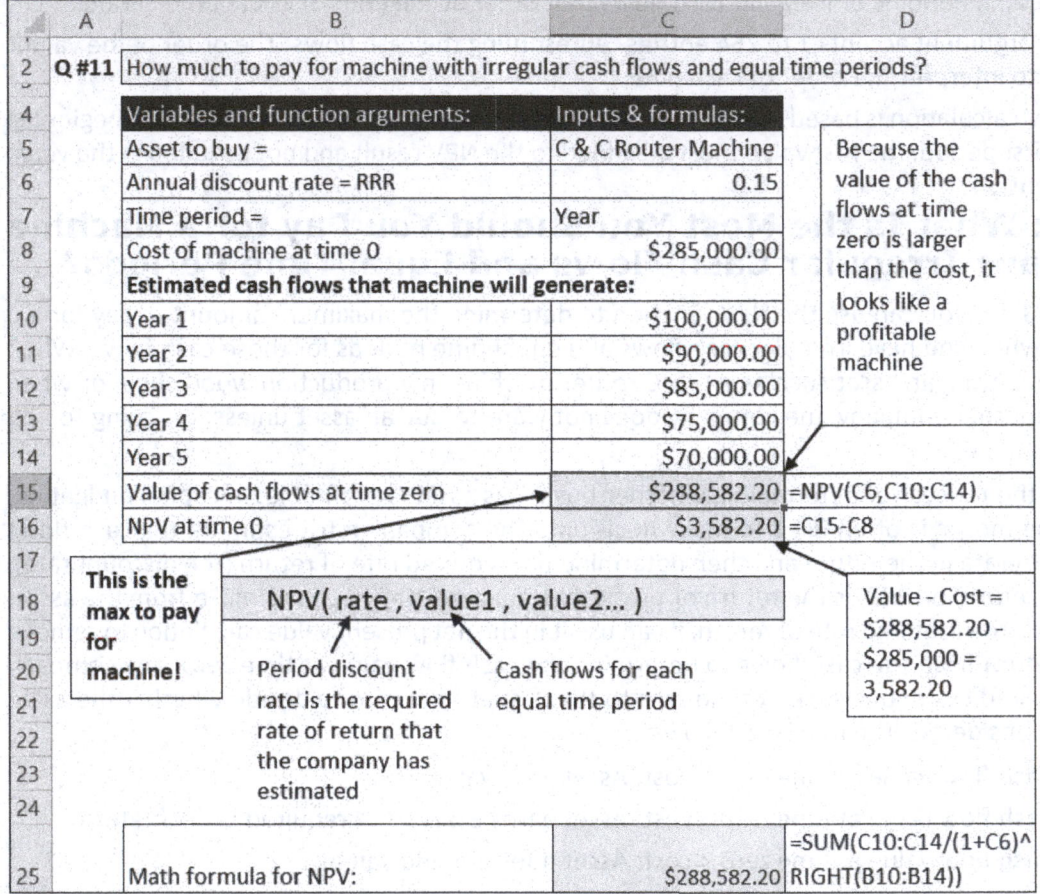

Figure 21.13 *The NPV function can use irregular cash flows in equal time periods to calculate the present value.*

XNPV Function

The XNPV function returns the net present value for a schedule of cash flows (periodic or irregular cash flows) and an associated schedule of dates. This function is different from the NPV function because it includes the cash flow at time zero and can accommodate irregular time periods. The arguments in the XNPV function are as follows:

- *rate*: Period rate (month, quarter, yearly, etc.). Also knows as the period discount rate.
- *values*: A series of cash flows that corresponds to the series of dates in the *dates* argument.
  - The first cash flow is optional and corresponds to a cost or payment that occurs at the beginning of the investment. If the first value is a cost or payment, it must be a negative value. All succeeding payments are discounted based on a 365-day year.
  - The series of values must contain at least one positive value and one negative value.
- *dates*: A series of dates that corresponds to the series of cash flows in the *values* argument.
  - The first date indicates the beginning of the series of cash flows. All other dates must be later than this date, but they may occur in any order.

Question 12: What Is the Most You Should You Pay for a Machine When You Have Irregular Cash Flows and Unequal Time Periods?

As shown in Figure 21.14, you can use the XNPV function to discount any set of cash flows with any set of time periods to calculate the net present value. If you have dates and cash flows, and you want to calculate the net present value directly, the XNPV function is easier to use than the NPV function.

In Figure 21.14, the XNPV function uses the rate 15% from cell C6, the cash flows from the range C9:C14, and the dates from the range B9:B14 to calculate a positive net present value of $4,344.87. The benefits of this function as compared to the NPV function are that you can include the cost at time zero in the range of cash flows, and the calculation is not dependent of having cash flows occur at the end of each equal-size time period.

You can try this example on the worksheet named Ch21(14).

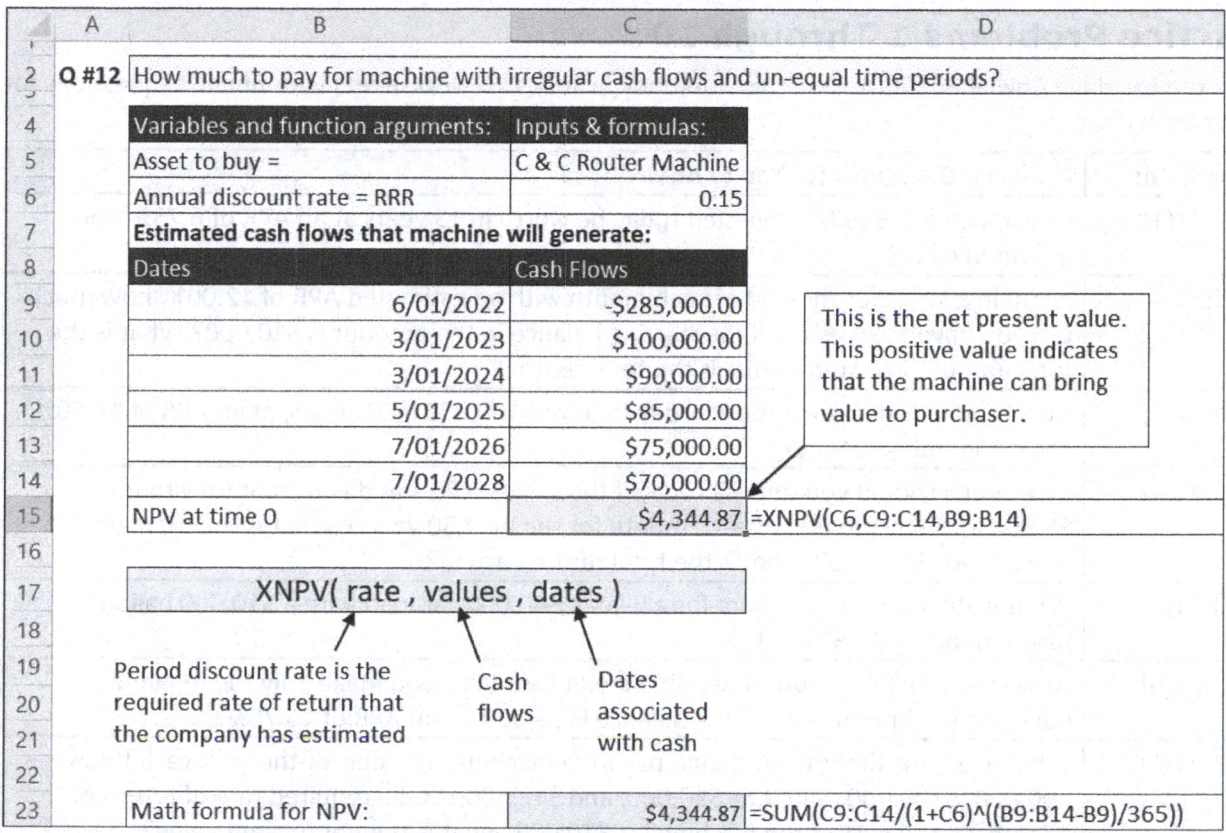

Figure 21.14 *The XNPV function can use irregular cash flows in unequal time periods to calculate the present value.*

Chapter 21 Key Concepts

- Most financial formulas are based on the **time value of money principal**, which says that a dollar received today is worth more than a dollar received later. Money in hand today can be invested and earn interest so that it grows to a larger amount later. Time value of money financial formulas are helpful for tasks such as determining the value of an asset (for example, a business) or the amount of a periodic payment for a debt instrument (for example, a home mortgage).

- Some of the key terms and variables in **financial cash flow analysis** are annual interest rate, period rate, return, compound interest, cash flow, balloon payment, future value, present value, and net present value.

- Seven **Excel worksheet functions** are presented in this chapter:

  - **FV:** Calculates the future value of an investment or a loan based on a constant interest rate. You can use the FV function with either an annuity cash flow pattern or a single present value lump sum payment at time zero.

  - **PV:** Calculates the present value of a loan or an investment, based on a constant interest rate. You can use the PV function with either an annuity cash flow pattern or a single future value lump sum payment at the end of the last time period.

- **PMT:** Returns the periodic payment for an annuity.
- **NPER:** Returns the total number of periods for an annuity.
- **RATE:** Returns the period rate for an annuity.
- **NPV:** Calculates the current value of all future cash flows at time zero for an investment by using a discount rate and a series of future cash flows (either periodic cash flows or irregular cash flows) that occur at the ends of equal time periods.
- **XNPV:** Returns the net present value for a schedule of cash flows (periodic or irregular cash flows) and an associated schedule of dates. This function is different from the NPV function because it includes the cash flow at time zero and can accommodate irregular time periods.

Practice Problems for Chapter 21

Practice Problems 1 Through 10

Open the Excel file Ch21-PP01Start.xlsx. This workbook includes 10 worksheets with financial questions for you to answer:

Worksheet	Financial Questions for You to Answer
PPCh21(1)	How much will $25,000 invested today be worth in 15 years at an APR of 6.75%, compounded daily?
PPCh21(2)	If you invest $25 at the end of each month with an estimated APR of 12.00%, how much will you have in 35 years, if the starting balance in the account is $10,000? What is the total amount invested? What is the total return?
PPCh21(3)	How much should you deposit today to have $100,000 in 15 years, at an APR of 12.50%, compounded quarterly?
PPCh21(4)	How much should you deposit today if the APR is 5,00% and you want to withdraw $5,000 at the beginning of each month for the next 30 years? What is the total withdrawn over 30 years? What is the total return earned?
PPCh21(5)	What is the monthly payment for a 5-year, $40,000 car loan with a $10,000 balloon payment and a 3.75% APR?
PPCh21(6)	How long will it take you to pay off a credit card bill if you make only the minimum payment ($75 per month) if the balance is $5,000, at an APR of 16.75%?
PPCh21(7)	What is the maximum you should pay for a machine with end-of-the-year cash flows $90,000, $100,000, $90,000, $80,000, and $125,000 and a required rate of return of 17.00%? If the cost of the machine is $310,000, what is the net present value?
PPCh21(8)	What is the maximum you should pay for a machine with scheduled cash flows of $90,000, $100,000, $90,000, $80,000, and $125,000 that occur on the following dates: 3/1/23, 3/1/24, 5/1/25, 7/1/26, and 7/1/28, with a required rate of return of 17.00% and a machine cost of $310,000 incurred on 6/1/22? What is the net present value?
PPCh21(9)	What is the interest that is taken out of your home mortgage payment each month? To answer this, create an amortization table for a 30-year $525,000 home mortgage loan at 4% APR.
PPCh21(10)	What is the net present value for the yearly cash flows $55,000, $10,000, $20,000, $30,000, and $30,000 at a discount rate of 15% and a cost at time zero of –$100,000? Answer this question is two ways: In cell F15, use the NPV function. In cell F16, use the XNPV function. Is there a difference between the results of these two methods?

On each worksheet, read the problem, list all the variables in the worksheet, and use Excel worksheet functions and formulas to answer the questions.

Chapter 22: Simple Linear Regression Worksheet Functions

If a business tracks the weekly amount it spends on advertising and the weekly amount it makes in sales, the logical question for the business to consider is: Does increasing the amount spent on advertising tend to increase the amount earned in sales? As you learned in Chapter 17, in Examples 16 through 18, this question can be answered visually with an X-Y scatter chart. Figure 22.1 shows a dataset with the weekly ad expense and sales records in the range B2:C182 and an X-Y scatter chart that shows that there is a direct, or positive, relationship between the x-variable, weekly ad expense, and the y-variable, weekly sales. Based on past data, this visualization provides the answer: As the business spends more on advertising, the amount earned in sales tends to increase.

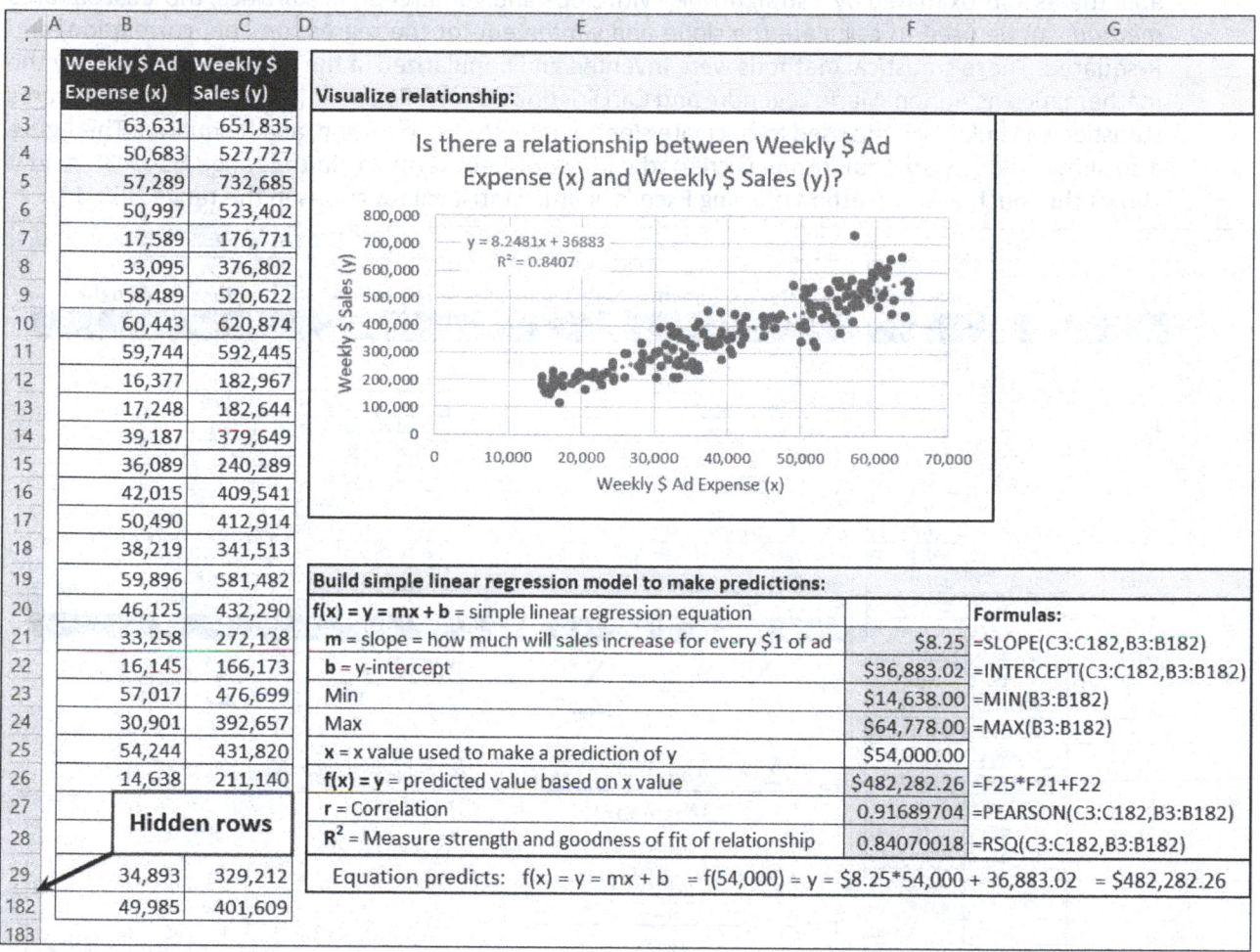

Figure 22.1 *If advertising expenditures are $54,000, the equation predicts that sales should be $482,282,26.*

However, what if the business wants more precise answers to these questions:

- What is a good estimate for how much sales will increase for every dollar spent on advertising?
- Is it possible to make a sales prediction based on a specified amount of advertising?

After building the X-Y scatter chart, the business can use simple linear regression statistical techniques to find the answers. Using the least squares statistical technique, it can answer the first question by calculating the slope of the regression line; it can answer the second question by determining the simple linear regression equation.

You have probably already learned about the famous simple linear regression equation:

```
y = m * x + b
```

The problem with the way that most of us learned this equation is that we learned it in a math class without being give a good real-world practice example of how to use it. That is where this book comes in. With a practical use for this equation and the Excel worksheet to make the calculations easy, this equation can provide great predictive power!

I will show you the statistical formulas as a reference point (in Figure 22.2), and then I will show you the Excel worksheet functions that will perform all the statistical math for you. The built-in functions described in this chapter are only available in an Excel worksheet; they do not exist in the DAX or M code formula languages. Before we get to all that, I want to define the important variables and concepts used in simple linear regression.

Simple Linear Regression Variables and Definitions

The following are some of the variables and concepts used in the least squares method for creating a *simple linear regression model*:

- **Simple linear regression:** A relationship between one independent variable and one dependent variable that is approximated by a straight line, with slope and y-intercept. In statistics, the *least squares method* can be used to calculate the slope and y-intercept for the regression line, correlation, and R-squared. These statistical methods were invented and popularized in the early 19th century by the mathematicians Adrien-Marie Legendre and Carl Friedrich Gauss. Figure 22.2 shows the least squares statistical formulas that are used to calculate slope, y-intercept, correlation, and R-squared. This figure also shows those statistical formulas created with worksheet formulas in the range H30:H38, and it shows the much easier method of using Excel's built-in statistical functions in the range H6:H13.

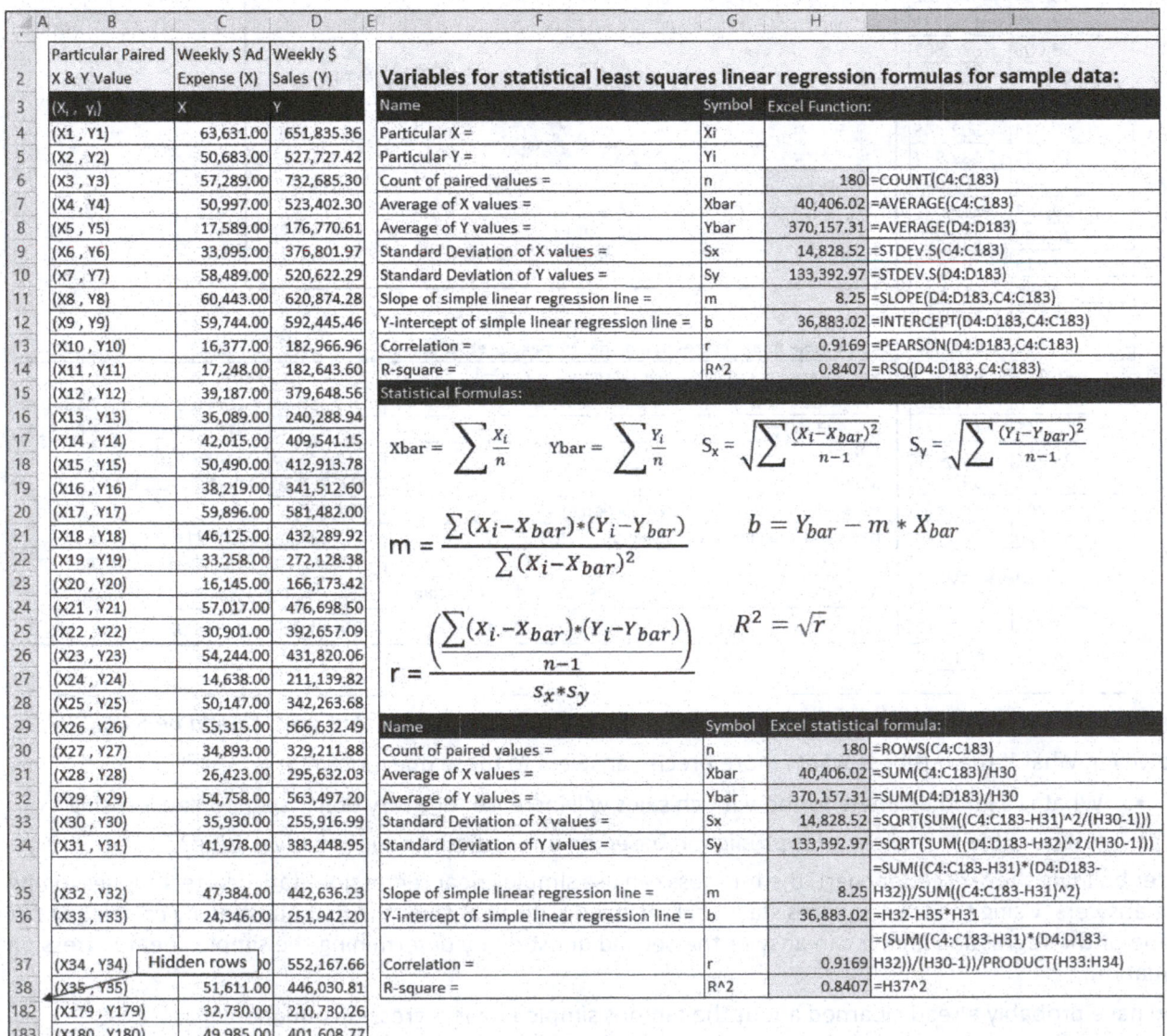

Figure 22.2 *Statistical least squares linear regression methods and built-in Excel functions.*

- **Independent variable (x):** The predictor variable. For example, the number of hours studied for a test can be the predictor variable for the score on the test.

- **Dependent variable (y = f(x)):** The variable that is predicted or estimated. For example, a score on a test can be the predicted variable based on the number of hours studied, which would be the predictor variable.

- **Experimental region:** The range of values from the minimum to maximum x-values from the original dataset. This is the range of values that can be used to make predictions based on the simple linear regression model. x-values used to make predictions outside this range are not reliable because the source data used to create the model does not support those values. However, if the pattern has persisted over time and it is reasonable to assume that the pattern will continue, you can use the model to forecast future trends.

- **Slope (m):** The amount of change in the y-variable for every one unit of change in the x-variable. The slope variable answers the question "For every one unit of x, how much does y change?" For example, as shown in Figure 22.1 in cell F21, for every $1 increase in weekly advertising, the equation predicts that weekly sales will increase by $8.25. If the slope is positive, the relationship is *direct*, or *positive*, indicating that as the x-value increases, the y-value increases. Figure 22.1 shows a regression line with a positive slope because as the amount spent on advertising increases, the sales amount increases. If the slope is negative, then the relationship is *indirect*, or *negative*, indicating that as the x-value increases, the y-value decreases. Later in this chapter, Figure 22.3 shows a regression line with a negative slope. In that example, the regression line predicts that for every 1-pound reduction in the weight of the BMX bike, the price should drop by $58.61.

- **Y-intercept (b):** The point on the y-axis where the regression line cross the y-axis. The y-intercept variable answers the question "When x = 0, what is the y value?" For example, as shown in Figure 22.1 in cell F22, when x = 0, the equation predicts that the weekly sales will be $36,883.02. Because 0 is not in the experimental region, extrapolating what the sales will be at x = 0 yields an unreliable estimate. But you still can use the intercept value in the equation to make predictions over the experimental region.

- **Simple linear regression line or equation (f(x) = y = m*x+b):** An equation that describes a straight line and that can be used to make predictions based on x-variable values from the experimental region.

- **Coefficient of correlation (r):** A measure of the strength and direction of a linear relationship for the x- and y-variables. This is a number between −1 and 1. *Positive* means that there is a direct, or positive, relationship. *Negative* means that there is an indirect, or negative, relationship. 0 means there is no relationship. The closer to 1, the stronger the positive relationship. The closer to −1, the stronger the negative relationship. If the measure is close to 0, then there is not much relationship. For example, as shown in cell F27 in Figure 22.1, a correlation of 91.7% indicates a strong positive relationship.

- **Coefficient of determination (R-squared = R^2 = R^2):** A measure of goodness of fit of the simple regression equation/line to the x/y sample data points. It can be interpreted as the proportion of the variance in y attributable to the variance in x. This is a number between 0 and 1. The closer to 1, the better the fit of the simple regression equation/line to the x/y sample data points. For example, as shown in Figure 22.1 in cell F28, 84.1% indicates a strong fit of the simple regression equation/line to the x/y sample data points.

Excel Worksheet Functions for Simple Linear Regression

You can use four Excel worksheet functions to build a simple linear regression model:

- **SLOPE:** Calculates the slope.
- **INTERCEPT:** Calculates the y-intercept.
- **PEARSON:** Calculates the correlation.
- **RSQ:** Calculates R-squared.

All four of these functions require the same two arguments: The first argument is the y-values, and the second argument is the x-values.

An important caveat for using an X-Y scatter chart or Excel's worksheet functions to build a simple linear regression model: Simple linear regression analysis does not prove a cause-and-effect relationship, but it can show a relationship or correlation that allows you to create a model that can make predictions or estimations based on past data.

As a second example of using past data to build a simple linear regression model, Figure 22.3 shows a dataset with the independent variable BMX racing bike weight and the dependent variable BMX racing bike price in the range B2:D22; it uses an X-Y scatter chart and a predictive model. In this example, you can see an indirect, or negative, relationship between bike weight and bike price. As the BMX racing bike weight increases, the price of the BMX racing bike decreases. Said a different way: As the bike gets lighter, the price is higher. For racing bikes, this makes sense because lighter bikes tend to help you race faster, and the materials used to make the bikes are more expensive. As shown in cell G21, the slope for the model predicts that for every 1-pound increase in bike weight, the price should decrease by $58.61. In cell G26, the formula m*x+b predicts that if the bike weighs 22 pounds, the price should be about $443.10.

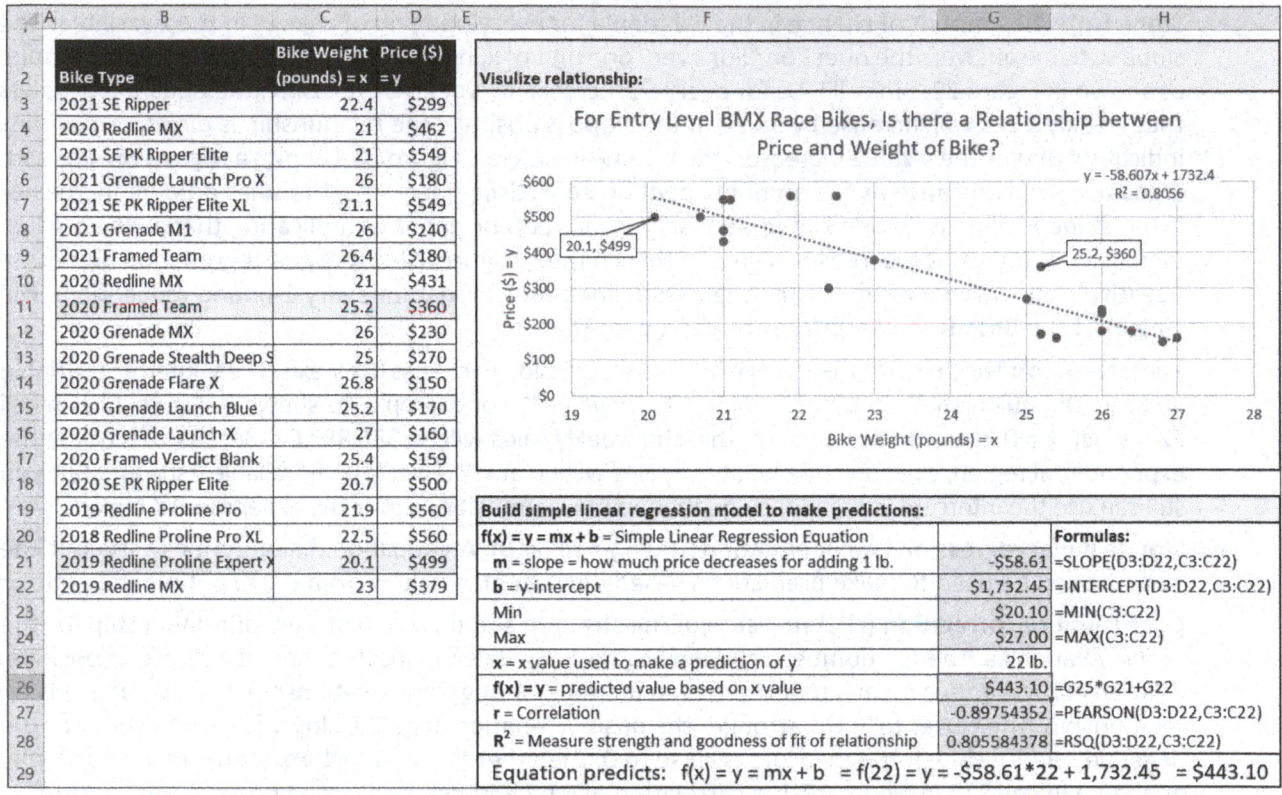

Figure 22.3 *If the BMX bike weighs 22 pounds, the equation predicts that the bike price should be $433.10.*

Note: In the workbook file Ch22-Excel365-SimpleLinearRegression.xlsx, you can try the example shown in Figure 22.1 on the worksheet named Ch22(1), and you can try the example shown in Figure 22.3 on the worksheet named Ch22(3). Be sure to review Example 18 in Chapter 17, where I showed you the one-click Analyze Data option in the Analysis group in the Home tab of the Excel Ribbon to create an X-Y scatter chart.

Chapter 22 Key Concepts

- **Simple linear regression** is the relationship between one independent variable and one dependent variable that is approximated by a straight line, with a slope and a y-intercept.

- The **independent variable (x)** is the predictor variable. For example, the number of hours studied for a test is the predictor variable for the score on the test.

- The **dependent variable (y = f(x))** is the variable that is predicted or estimated. For example, a score on a test is the predicted variable based on the number of hours studied, which is the predictor variable.

- The **experimental region** is the range of values from the minimum to maximum x-values from the original dataset. This is the range of values that can be used to make predictions based on the simple linear regression model.

- **Slope (m)** is the amount of change in the y-variable for every one unit of change in the x-variable.

- The **y-intercept (b)** is the point on the y-axis where the regression line cross the y-axis.

- The **simple linear regression line or equation (f(x) = y = m*x+b)** is a straight line that can be used to make predictions based on x-variable values from the experimental region.
- The **coefficient of correlation (r)** is a measure of the strength and direction of a linear relationship for the x- and y-variables. It is a number between –1 and 1.
- The **coefficient of determination (R-squared = R^2 = R²)** is a measure of goodness of fit of the simple regression equation/line to the x/y sample data points..
- You can use four Excel worksheet functions to build a simple linear regression model:
  - **SLOPE:** Calculates the slope.
  - **INTERCEPT:** Calculates the y-intercept.
  - **PEARSON:** Calculates the correlation.
  - **RSQ:** Calculates R-squared.
- Simple linear regression analysis does not prove a cause-and-effect relationship but can show a relationship or correlation that allows you to create a model that can make predictions or estimations based on past data.

Practice Problems for Chapter 22

Practice Problem 1

In your Excel file for this chapter (Ch22-SimpleLinearRegression.xlsx), go to the worksheet named PPCh22(1) and create the solution for this practice problem. Figure 22.4 shows the goals that are listed on that worksheet.

	A	B	C	D	E	F
2		Goal:	Create an X-Y Scatter Chart to show the relationship between hours studied for a test and score on the test.			
3			Create a simple linear regression model based on the independent variable, hours studied for a test,			
4			and the dependent variable, score on the test.			
6		Sample Data:				
8		No.	Hours Studied = x	Test Score = y		
9		S 1	7	58		
10		S 2	20	98		
11		S 3	13	79		
35		S 27	Hidden rows 8	29		
36						

Figure 22.4 *On the worksheet PPCh22(1), create an X-Y scatter chart and a predictive model.*

When you are done with this problem, you can check your work against the answer sheet named PPCh22(1an).

Practice Problem 2

In your Excel file for this chapter (Ch22-SimpleLinearRegression.xlsx), go to the worksheet named PPCh22(2) and create the solution for this practice problem. Figure 22.5 shows the goals that are listed on that worksheet.

	A	B	C	D	E	F	G	H
2		Goal:		Is there a relationship between Batting Average x and Runs Scored y?				
3				Is there a relationship between At Bats x and Homeruns y?				
4				Build a model that can predict the number of runs scored based on batting average.				
5		Big Hint: when creating X-Y Scatter chart, if you want to use the Analyze Data tool in the Analysis group in the Home Ribbon,						
6				use Ctrl key to select the two fields before using the feature.				
8		Team Name		Batting Average	At Bats	Runs Scored	Homeruns	
9		Arizona Diamondbacks		0.236	5,489	679	144	
10		Atlanta Braves	Hidden	0.244	5,363	790	239	
37		Toronto Blue Jays	rows	0.266	5,476	846	262	
38		Washington Nationals		0.258	5,385	724	182	
39								

Figure 22.5 *On the worksheet PPCh22(2), create an X-Y scatter chart and a predictive model.*

When you are done with this problem, you can check your work against the answer sheet named PPCh22(2an).

The End

You made it to the end of the book! Now you are a true master of Excel, Power Query, Power BI, Power Pivot, DAX formulas, M code formulas, worksheet formulas, PivotTables, data analysis, and model building! Thanks for buying the book and making it to the end. I will see you in the next book and at my Excel channel on YouTube: https://www.youtube.com/user/excelisfun. Go, Team!

Index

No other version in history has as much power, as many features, or more possibilities than Excel 365

This is a book about Microsoft 365 Excel, or Excel 365. With a new formula calculations engine and many new built-in functions, creating formula solutions and business models in Excel 365 is dramatically easier than at any time in the history of spreadsheets. In addition, with the new data tools like Power Query, Power Pivot, and Power BI, performing data analysis to make data driven decisions can be easily done on data with different structures, with different sources, and on small and big data alike. With this exciting new Excel 365 version, we will learn three types of formulas: Worksheet, M Code, and DAX, and we will learn three types of Reporting/ Dashboarding tools: Standard PivotTables, Data Model PivotTables, and Power BI Visualizations. This means that the New Excel 365 is the only app that matters in our age of analytics and data driven decisions. Who is this book/class for? Everyone. The book starts at the beginning and moves to an advanced level by telling a logical story about how to use Excel and Power BI to build models, make calculations and perform data analysis. With this book and The Only App That Matters, you will have the power to efficiently build any solution that you can imagine!

About the Author:

Mike Girvin has been a Microsoft Excel MVP since 2013, a Highline College business instructor since 2002, and the creator and mastermind of the excelisfun YouTube channel since 2008 with more than 3,500 Excel videos and 100 playlists of Excel video topics, including 10 free Excel YouTube courses covering topics such as Excel basics, advanced Excel, data analysis, analytics, statistics, math, and much more. Mike has also authored a number of Excel books and DVDs and has won numerous awards for teaching Excel. Before joining academia in 2002, Mike (nicknamed "Gel") ran the boomerang manufacturing company Gel Boomerangs, in Oakland, California, from 1984 to 2002 and won numerous boomerang design and competition awards. Currently, when Mike is not creating Excel solutions, you can find him racing and parking BMX bikes with fellow rad old guys.

ISBN 978-1-61547-070-9

US$49.99

Holy Macro! Books
PO Box 541731
Merritt Island, FL 32953